PRENTICE HALL NEWSLETTERS

A DIVISION OF BBP

24 ROPE FERRY ROAD

WATERFORD, CT 06385-9985

BUSINESS REPLY MAIL

FIRST CLASS MAIL   PERMIT NO. 18   WATERFORD, CT

POSTAGE WILL BE PAID BY ADDRESSEE

PRENTICE HALL NEWSLETTERS

A DIVISION OF BBP
24 ROPE FERRY ROAD
WATERFORD, CT 06385-9985

1993
Prentice Hall
Federal Tax Adviser

SUMMARY TABLE OF CONTENTS

(Detailed Table of Contents appear on the first pages of each Chapter. Complete Alphabetical Index begins at page 4001.)

Important Tax Facts & Strategies

Figuring the Individual Tax — Taxable & Tax-Free Income — Employee Benefits

Maximizing Deductions & Credits — Travel & Entertainment — Depreciation

Withholding — Minimum Tax — Tax Accounting

Corporate Tax — S Corporations — Partnerships — Estates & Trusts

Returns & Payments — Foreign Income & Taxpayers

Publisher's Note: Every care has been taken in the preparation of the *1993 Federal Tax Adviser* to provide accurate and helpful information regarding the nation's tax laws. However, this publication is sold with the clear understanding that the publisher is not engaged in rendering legal, accounting or other professional service. If legal advice or other expert assistance is required, the services of a competent professional person should be sought.

¶ 1   NEW TAX LAW CHANGES FOR 1993

Important new tax changes for 1993 are part of a major tax bill that may be enacted into law in the fall of 1992. The contents of a number of paragraphs throughout the **1993 Federal Tax Adviser** would be affected by the new law.

Help on the way. Prentice Hall will publish the *CONCISE EXPLANATION OF THE NEW 1992 TAX LAW* if the bill is enacted. The booklet will explain the tax law's important new changes–pointing out the tax-saving opportunities it presents (especially on your 1992 return) and steering you clear of the tax crackdowns you can avoid. You will be mailed a free copy of the *CONCISE EXPLANATION* if you send in the postcard that is inside the front cover of the **1993 Federal Tax Adviser**.

Important: The *CONCISE EXPLANATION* includes **1993 Federal Tax Adviser** paragraph references that alert you to how the tax law changes affect specific tax rules explained throughout the **Adviser**.

KEY TAX FACTS

¶ 101   PERSONAL INCOME TAX

Following are key tax numbers you need to know when filling out the 1992 personal tax return (or reviewing returns for open years):

Type of Deduction	1992	1991	1990	1989
Personal Exemption*				
Single person	$2,300	$2,150	$2,050	$2,000
Married filing jointly	4,600	4,300	4,100	4,000
Dependency Deduction				
For each dependent	2,300	2,150	2,050	2,000
Standard Deduction**				
Married filing jointly	6,000	5,700	5,450	5,200
Qualified surviving spouse	6,000	5,700	5,450	5,200
Single person	3,600	3,400	3,250	3,100
Married filing separately	3,000	2,850	2,725	2,600
Head of household	5,250	5,000	4,750	4,550
Additional Standard Deduction for Those Age 65 or Over or Blind [+]				
Married persons	700	650	650	600
Single persons	900	850	800	750

* Since 1991 the personal exemption has been reduced for those who have incomes greater than a threshold amount. The 1992 threshold amounts are as follows:

Married, filing joint return	$157,900
Head of Household	$131,550
Unmarried Persons	$105,250
Married filing separately	$78,950

The personal exemption is reduced by 2% for each $2,500 or fraction thereof ($1,250 for married filing separately) that your income exceeds the threshold amount. Thus the entire personal exemption is lost if you are married filing a joint return and have 1992 income greater than $280,400.

** As a general rule, you do not owe tax and do not have to file a return if your gross income is less than or equal to your personal exemption deduction plus your standard deduction.

+ An additional standard deduction is available for both blindness and age 65 or over. Thus, if you are both age 65 or greater and blind you are entitled to *two* additional standard deductions (a total of $1,400 for married persons in 1992).

"Kiddie tax": Tax on net unearned income of children under age 14 is computed at the parent's marginal tax rate, rather than at the child's—usually lower—marginal rate. To arrive at net unearned income for purposes of computing the 1992 kiddie tax, you subtract from unearned income the greater of $1,200 (up from $1,100 in 1991, $1,000 in 1989 and 1990) or $600 (up from $550 in 1991, $500 in 1989 and 1990) plus certain itemized deductions.

1992 TAX RATE TABLES

Married Filing Jointly

If Taxable Income Is:	The Tax is:
Not more than $35,800	15% of the taxable income
More than $35,800 but not more than $86,500	$5,370 plus 28% of the excess over $35,800
More than $86,500	$19,566 plus 31% of the excess over $86,500

Heads of Households

If Taxable Income Is:	The Tax is:
Not more than $28,750	15% of the taxable income
More than $28,750 but not more than $74,150	$4,312.50 plus 28% of the excess over $28,750
More than $74,150	$17,024.50 plus 31% of the excess over $74,150

Unmarried Individuals

If Taxable Income Is:	The Tax is:
Not more than $21,450	15% of the taxable income
More than $21,450 but not more than $51,900	$3,217.50 plus 28% of the excess over $21,450
More than $51,900	$11,743.50 plus 31% of the excess over $51,900

Married Filing Separately

If Taxable Income Is:	The Tax is:
More than $17,900	15% of the taxable income
More than $17,900 but not more than $43,250	$2,685 plus 28% of the excess over $17,900
More than $43,250	$9,783 plus 31% of the excess over $43,250

1991 TAX RATE TABLES

Married Filing Jointly

If Taxable Income Is:	The Tax is:
Not more than $34,000	15% of the taxable income
More than $34,000 but not more than $82,150	$5,100 plus 28% of the excess over $34,000
More than $82,150	$18,582 plus 31% of the excess over $82,150

Heads of Households

If Taxable Income Is:	The Tax is:
Not more than $27,300	15% of the taxable income
More than $27,300 but not more than $70,450	$4,095 plus 28% of the excess over $27,300
More than $70,450	$16,177 plus 31% of the excess over $70,450

Unmarried Individuals

If Taxable Income Is:	The Tax is:
Not more than $20,350	15% of the taxable income
More than $20,350 but not more than $49,300	$3,052.50 plus 28% of the excess over $20,350
More than $49,300	$11,158.50 plus 31% of the excess over $49,300

Married Filing Separately

If Taxable Income Is:	The Tax is:
Not more than $17,000	15% of the taxable income
More than $17,000 but not more than $41,075	$2,550 plus 28% of the excess over $17,000
More than $41,075	$9,291 plus 31% of the excess over $4,1075

1990 TAX RATE TABLES

Married Filing Jointly

If Taxable Income Is:	The Tax is:
Not more than $32,450	15% of the taxable income
More than $32,450 but not more than $78,400	$4,867.50 plus 28% of the excess over $32,450
More than $78,400 but not more than $162,770	$17,733.50 plus 33% of the excess over $78,400
More than $162,770	$45,575.60 plus 28% of the excess over $162,770, plus the lesser of (a) 5% of the taxable income in excess of $162,770, or (b) the number of personal and dependency deductions claimed multiplied by $574.

Heads of Households

If Taxable Income Is:	The Tax is:
Not more than $26,050	15% of the taxable income
More than $26,050 but not more than $67,200	$3,907.50 plus 28% of the excess over $26,050
More than $67,200 but not more than $134,930	$15,429.50 plus 33% of the excess over $67,200
More than $134,930	$37,780.40 plus 28% of the excess over $134,930 plus the lesser, of (a) 5% of taxable income in excess of $134,930 or (b) the number of personal and dependency deductions claimed multiplied by $574.

Unmarried Individuals

If Taxable Income Is:	The Tax is:
Not more than $19,450	15% of the taxable income
More than $19,450 but not more than $47,050	$2,917.50 plus 28% of the excess over $19,450
More than $47,050 but not more than $97,620	$10,645.50 plus 33% of the excess over $47,050
More than $97,620	$27,333.60 plus 28% of the excess over $97,620 plus the lesser of (a) 5% of taxable income in excess of $97,620, and dependency deductions claimed multiplied by $574.

Married Filing Separately

If Taxable Income Is:	The Tax is:
Not more than $16,225	15% of the taxable income
More than $16,225 but not more than $39,200	$2,433.75 plus 28% of the excess over $16,225
More than $39,200 but not more than $123,570	$8,866.75 plus 33% of the excess over $39,200
More than $123,570	$36,708.85 plus 28% of the excess over $123,570 plus the lesser of (a) 5% of taxable income in excess of $123,570 or (b) the number of personal and dependency deductions claimed multiplied by $574.

1989 TAX RATE TABLES

Married Filing Jointly

If Taxable Income Is:	The Tax is:
Not more than $30,950	15% of the taxable income
More than $30,950 but not more than $74,850	$4,642.50 plus 28% of the excess over $30,950

| More than $74,850 but not more than $155,320 | $16,934.50 plus 33% of the excess over $74,850 |
| More than $155,320 | $43,489.60 plus 28% of the excess over $155,320 plus the lesser of (a) 5% of taxable income in excess of $155,320, or (b) the number of personal and dependency deductions claimed multiplied by $560. |

Heads of Households

If Taxable Income Is:	The Tax is:
Not more than $24,850	15% of the taxable income
More than $24,850 but not more than $64,200	$3,727.50 plus 28% of the excess over $24,850
More than $64,200 but not more than $128,810	$14,745.50 plus 33% of the excess over $64,200
More than $128,810	$36,066.80 plus 28% of the excess over $128,810 plus the lesser of (a) 5% of taxable income in excess of $128,810, or (b) the number of personal and dependency deductions claimed multiplied by $560.

Unmarried Individuals

If Taxable Income Is:	The Tax is:
Not more than $18,550	15% of the taxable income
More than $18,550 but not more than $44,900	$2,782.50 plus 28% of the excess over $18,550
More than $44,900 but not more than $93,130	$10,160.50 plus 33% of the excess over $44,900
More than $93,130	$26,076.40 plus 28% of the excess over $93,130 plus the lesser of (a) 5% of taxable income in excess of $93,130, or (b) the number of personal and dependency deductions claimed multiplied by $560.

Married Filing Separately

If Taxable Income Is:	The Tax is:
Not more than $15,475	15% of the taxable income
More than $15,475 but not more than $37,425	$2,321.25 plus 28% of the excess over $15,475
More than $37,425 but not more than $117,895	$8,467.25 plus 33% of the excess over $37,425

More than $117,895 $33,010.60 plus 28% of the
                                          excess over $117,895 plus the
                                          lesser of (a) 5% of taxable income
                                          in excess of $117,895, or
                                          (b) the number of personal
                                          and dependency deductions
                                          claimed multiplied by $560.

¶ 102   CORPORATE INCOME TAX

Corporate taxable income is subject to tax under the following graduated rate system:

If taxable income is: Over	The tax is: but not over--	
$ 0	$ 50,000	15% of taxable income
$ 50,000	$ 75,000	$7,500 + 25% of excess over $50,000
$ 75,000	$ 100,000	$13,750 + 34% of excess over $75,000
$ 100,000	$ 335,000	$22,250 + 39% of excess over $100,000
$ 335,000	---	$113,900 + 34% of excess over $335,000

The 39% bracket is the result of a 5% surtax imposed on a corporation's taxable income between $100,000 and $335,000. This surtax phases out the benefit of graduated rates for high income corporations. Corporations with taxable income in excess of $335,000, in effect, pay a flat tax at a 34% rate.

Personal service corporations are taxed at a flat 34% rate.

¶103   SOCIAL SECURITY TAX

Social security tax is paid by earnings of both employees and self-employeds. In the case of employees, the tax is called FICA (Federal Insurance Contributions Act); for self-employeds, it's called SECA (Self-Employment Contributions Act). FICA is paid by both the employer and employee. The SECA tax rate is double that of FICA to take into account the fact that only one party is paying this tax on the earnings.

Both FICA and SECA taxes are paid on only wages or earnings not in excess of certain levels that rise with the cost of living annually. Prior to 1991, there was a single wage base. Since 1991, different wage bases have been used for two components—Old Age, Survivors and Disability Insurance (OASDI) and Hospital Insurance (HI or Medicare)—of the tax.

Here's a rundown of the tax rates and wage/earnings bases since 1989:

1989: $48,000 base; 7.51% FICA tax and 13.02% (net of a 2% credit) SECA tax
1990: $51,300 base; 7.65% FICA tax and 15.3% SECA tax
1991:   OASDI: $53,400 base; 6.2% FICA tax and 12.4% SECA tax
        HI: $125,000 base; 1.45% FICA tax and 2.9% SECA tax
1992:   OASDI: $55,500 base; 6.2% FICA tax and 12.4% SECA tax
        HI: $130,200 base; 1.45% FICA tax and 2.9% SECA tax
1993:   OASDI: 1992 base of $55,500 with cost of living increase;
        6.2% FICA tax and 12.4% SECA tax
        HI: 1992 base of $130,200 with cost of living increase;
        6.2% FICA tax and 12.4% SECA tax

> ▶ **IMPORTANT** (1) If you have two or more employers and your total wages exceed the base, you can get a refund of the excess FICA taken out of your pay when you file your tax return. (There is no similar refund for your employers.) (2) If you have both wages and self-employment income, you pay SECA on no more than the amount by which your wages are below the base amounts.

SECA tax deduction: Since 1990, self-employeds get an income tax deduction for one-half of the SECA tax they pay. This parallels the fact that employers can deduct their share of FICA tax paid on employees' wages.

¶ 104   FEDERAL UNEMPLOYMENT TAX

The Federal Unemployment Tax Act (FUTA) imposes a tax on persons who employ one or more individuals for some portion of a day in each of 20 weeks in the current or preceding year, or who pay $1,500 or more of wages in a calendar quarter of a current of preceding calendar year. Employees do not pay FUTA tax on their wages.

> ▶ **TAX RATE** The tax is currently 6.2% on the first $7,000 of wages paid to each employee. After 1996, the rate will be 6.0%.

Employers can reduce their FUTA tax bills by taking a credit for their contributions under state unemployment insurance laws. The maximum credit for state contributions made on or before the due date for filing the federal unemployment tax return (January 31 of the following year) is 5.4%. So these contribution can cut the net FUTA tax rate to as low as 0.08%. The maximum credit for state contributions made after return due date is 4.86%, which can reduce the net FUTA tax rate to 1.34%.

State laws provide some form of merit rating under which a reduction in the state contribution rate is allowed to employers who, as shown by their benefit and contribution experience, have given steady employment. In order not penalize employers who have earned a reduction in the contribution rate under state law, the tax law allow employers to take an "additional credit" equal to the difference between the employer's actual state contributions and the amount that would have been contributed without any reduction or 5.4%, whichever is lower.

ROUNDUP OF NEW TAX DEVELOPMENTS

Among the new tax developments are a tax law enacted in the early summer of 1992 and some new tax rulings and court cases that were favorable to taxpayers.

¶201   NEW UNEMPLOYMENT BENEFITS LAW CONTAINS KEY TAX CHANGES

A 1992 law extended jobless benefits for the long-term unemployed. The new law made several important income tax law changes to pay for the benefits extension.

- A phaseout of your personal and dependency exemptions begins once your adjusted gross income exceeds certain levels. In 1992, the phaseout begins at: $157,900 for marrieds filing jointly; $131,550 for heads of households; $105,250 for single taxpayers; $78,950 for married persons filing separately. (These levels are indexed for inflation.) The phaseout had been scheduled to expire after 1995. The new unemployment benefits law has extended the phaseout one year—through tax years starting before 1997 [¶1112].

- Many corporations are subject to underpayment penalties unless they prepay at least a certain percentage of their tax for the current year. The rate had been scheduled to be 93% for 1992, but the new unemployment benefits law increased that rate. Under the new law, the rate is 97% for tax years beginning after June 30, 1992 and before 1997. In 1997 and beyond, the rate is scheduled to drop to 91%. Note: A small corporation—one with a taxable income of $1 million or less for each of the three preceding tax years—can base its estimated tax payments on 100% of last year's tax [¶3726].

- The new unemployment benefits law made two important changes in the retirement plan distribution rules, effective January 1, 1993. To begin with, you no longer have to withdraw at least 50% of the balance of your retirement plan account to get tax-free rollover treatment (i.e., no current tax when funds are rolled into an IRA or another tax-qualified retirement plan). Any nonperiodic distribution can qualify as a tax-free rollover [¶1334].

> **TAX TRAP** While your rollover distribution may not be subject to tax, it may nonetheless be subject to 20% income tax withholding under the new law. Reason: Employers must withhold a 20% tax on retirement plan payouts unless there is a direct rollover (e.g., the rollover is made between plan trustees and you are not involved) [¶2516].

Contradictory result: Under the new law, a taxpayer may not owe any additional tax on an indirect rollover. But the withholding requirement could place the taxpayer in a situation where he or she ends up owing more tax.

Example: Mr. Martin Brown is retiring in 1993. His entire profit-sharing plan balance payout is $200,000. Brown hasn't decided how to invest it. So he gets the payout, puts it in his bank account and then moves the money into an IRA. The rollover is tax-free as long as he put the distribution into the IRA within 60 days. However, under the new law, his company must withhold 20% of the distribution since it isn't paid directly into an IRA. Unless he has $40,000 from another source, Brown has only $160,000 to roll over into the IRA.

Tax result: Brown owes tax on the $40,000 that he has not rolled over. True, he gets a refund for some of that $40,000 when he files his return in 1994 (the tax on the $40,000 subject to tax is less than the 20% withheld on the full $200,000 payout). But by that time, it will be too late to meet the 60-day tax-free rollover period.

¶202 IRS CHANGES MIND ON WRITEOFFS FOR COST OF TAX HELP

The IRS has changed its mind about how self-employed taxpayers and real estate investors should handle the cost of tax advice.

> **FAVORABLE RULING** The IRS ruled that the cost of tax return preparation and tax litigation connected with an unincorporated business or rental income can be written off directly [Rev. Rul. 92-29]. In the past, the IRS had taken the position that these costs could be deducted only as a miscellaneous itemized deduction--and, as such, subject to the 2%-of-adjusted gross income (AGI) floor.

New and improved result. This means that the portion of tax return fees allocable to the preparation of Schedule C (for a sole proprietorship) and Schedule E (for rental income) are fully deductible on those schedules.

The ruling doesn't help incorporated professionals because the cost of having their Forms 1040 prepared is not a business expense to these individuals. However, it appears that the rationale of the ruling would make it applicable to partners. In fact, these individuals should get a full deduction to the extent a return preparer is paid to report partnership income and expenses on a partnership return and a partner's own return.

> **TAX REFUNDS** This change is retroactive. So taxpayers who are affected by this IRS change-of-heart can take advantage of this break retroactively by filing Forms 1040 for 1991, 1990 and 1989.

For more information on this subject, see ¶1943.

¶203 IRS SHOWS HOW TO NAIL DOWN A CURRENT DEDUCTION FOR MORTGAGE POINTS

The IRS outlined the ground rules for claiming a current deduction for points paid to a mortgage lender [Rev. Proc. 92-12]. Under the guidelines, points are deductible in the year paid if: (1) They are paid as part of a mortgage financing for the purchase of a principal residence; (2) they are clearly shown or labelled on the title settlement statement; (3) They are shown not only as a dollar amount but as a percentage of the total amount borrowed; (4) the amount paid conforms to the business practices in the area.

As in the past, the points must be paid directly by the borrower. This used to mean that net proceeds loans—where the points are "paid" by having the lender reduce the loan proceeds by the amount of the points—disqualified borrowers from up-front deductions. But now that's not necessarily so.

> ➤ **IMPORTANT CHANGE**   Points will now be considered directly paid as long as the borrower pays over at the closing an amount equal to or greater than the points. This requirement may be satisfied by amounts paid for down payments, escrow deposits and any other funds that actually come from the buyer at the closing.

For more information on this subject, see ¶1903.

¶204   IRS EXTENDS TAX-FREE BENEFITS FOR SATURDAY-NIGHT STAYOVERS

An employee who pays his own business travel expenses can write off the cost of coming home for the weekend in the middle of the trip—if he can show that it's less expensive to come home than to stay at the business location [Rev. Rul. 54-497].

> ➤ **FLIP SIDE**   Now the IRS has ruled favorably on the flip side of this issue: The expense of staying longer at a business location can qualify for tax-favored treatment if staying would be less expensive than coming home as soon as the business is concluded.

The issue came up in the context of air fares. Many airlines charge substantially lower fares for travelers who stay at their destinations over a Saturday night. If the ticket discount is greater than the additional hotel and meal expenses, a business traveler who finishes doing business on Friday would be able to spend Saturday sightseeing and still write off the additional expenses on his or her return.

For more information on this subject, see ¶2000.

¶205   NEW RULING SHOWS HOW TO REPORT DISTRIBUTIONS FROM INHERITED IRAs

When an IRA owner dies, the assets of the IRA are included in the owner's taxable estate, and the IRA is turned over to the heirs or named beneficiaries. Under a new IRS ruling, the IRA assets can be taxed to the heir or beneficiary in one of three categories [Rev. Rul. 92-47].

First, the assets are treated as a tax-free return of capital to the extent the original owner made nondeductible contributions to the IRA. Second, the value of any additional assets—up to the value of the IRA at the time the original owner died—is treated as "income in respect of a decedent" (discussed below). Third, any appreciation in value after the owner's death is treated as regular taxable income.

In this context, "income in respect of a decedent" means IRA assets that would have been taxed to the original owner if they had been distributed during his or her lifetime. Income in respect of a decedent is taxed like other income, except the beneficiary can claim a deduction to offset the estate tax paid on the value of these assets.

¶206   NEW RULING MAKES HOME OFFICE DEDUCTION EASIER FOR DAY CARE PROVIDERS

Taxpayers generally cannot claim a deduction for business use of a home unless some part of the home is used regularly and exclusively for business. However, day care providers may claim the deduction even if the portion of the home used for day care is also used for family living. Expenses are allocated in proportion to the number of hours that a portion of the home is used for day care.

▶ **TAKE A BREAK** An IRS ruling provides a simplified method of allocating expenses between day care and family living use of the home [Rev. Rul. 92-3].

How it works. Day care providers don't have to keep detailed records of the number of hours a given room is used for day care (e.g., the amount of time spent in the kitchen serving meals and snacks to the children). Instead, a room that is available for day care use throughout the business day and is regularly used as part of the day care routine can be treated as used for day care during all hours of business operation.

For more information on this subject, see ¶2227.

¶207   FICA SAVINGS FOR SPOUSES WHO WORK TOGETHER

A district court has put its stamp of approval on a Social Security (FICA) tax cutting strategy for husband and wife employee teams.

Facts of the case. Richard and Jean Hoerl were each 50% owners of a professional corporation. They entered into separate two-year employment agreements with the corporation. Each spouse would get paid a set salary for two years of services every other year. Thus, each year one spouse would get two years' salary and the other spouse would get no pay. On a joint tax return, it's the same as if each received one year's salary [Hoerl & Associates, US Dist. Ct. (Colo.; 3/10/92].

▶ **FICA SAVINGS** For FICA taxes, though, there's a big difference. That tax (paid by both the corporation and employees) is 7.65% of the first $55,500 of earnings and 1.45% for earnings from $55,501 to $130,200 in 1992. By doubling up, the corporation and the couple can cut their FICA tax bill by as much as one-half.

¶208   NEW REGULATIONS MAKE IT EASIER TO DEDUCT ACCRUED EXPENSES

Accrual-basis companies generally cannot deduct expenses until, among other requirements, "economic performance" occurs (e.g., payment is made or goods are delivered). Key exception: Deductions are allowed before economic performance occurs for regularly recurring expenses, provided performance takes place within 8-½ months after the tax year in which the deduction is claimed.

▶ **GOOD NEWS** The IRS released final regulations clarifying the economic performance rules that contain milder administrative requirements than were set forth in earlier proposed regulations.

Important change: The final regulations give companies more time to elect the recurring-expense rule without IRS approval. What's more, gone is the requirement that companies identify each trade or business and type of item for which the tax break is to be used. All that's required is to simply implement the change on the 1992 return.

For more information on this subject, see ¶2840.

¶209   OWNER GETS LOSS WRITE-OFFS FOR LEASE TO HIS OWN COMPANY

Taxpayers generally can't write off a business loss unless they entered into the business with the intention of making a profit. This rule was aimed at taxpayers who run up losses on "businesses" that are really personal hobbies. But the IRS recently tried to expand this no-writeoff rule far beyond the hobby area.

New Case: Mr. Kuhn bought two properties with the intention of developing a trailer park. The deal fell through so, instead, Kuhn leased the properties to his closely held construction company. The company used the properties to house employees and store equipment. The company leased the land for less than the fair market rent and, over several years, Kuhn reported tax losses on the lease ranging from $8,000 to $28,000.

The IRS disallowed the writeoffs on the ground that Kuhn had no intention of making a profit on the lease; he merely wanted to benefit his company. But the Tax Court ruled in Kuhn's favor.

➤ **TAXPAYER WINNER** The Court said that Kuhn did not have to profit directly from the property rental. He is entitled to the loss writeoffs because he intended to profit indirectly by increasing his company's earnings [Kuhn, T.C. Memo 1992-460].

For more information on this subject, see ¶2325.

TAX-SAVING STRATEGIES

Tax-saving strategies can be used throughout 1993 to slash both your personal and business tax bills. Some of the most effective help put tax-free investment income in your pocket, nail down top-dollar deductions for your business travel and entertainment, and show you how your employer can pay you in tax-sheltered dollars.

HOW TO BUILD TAX-FREE INCOME

¶301 HOW ONE TYPE OF TAX-FREE MUNICIPAL PROTECTS YOU AGAINST A RISE IN INTEREST RATES

A long-term municipal bond locks in tax-free interest income over the long haul. The problem is, however, that with interest rates at a 30-year low, buying a new bond now could put you at risk. Interest rates will inevitably rise and investors won't pay face value for a bond that pays lower interest than the prevailing rate. So if you want to sell such a bond to get into a higher-yielding investment, you have to sell at a loss. That means having less to reinvest.

How can you protect yourself? What can you do to avoid a loss if you want to reinvest your funds at a better rate of return?

➤ **"PUT" BONDS** You might want to consider tender-option bonds or "put" bonds. They have maturities that range up to 30 years and pay tax-free interest, just like other bonds issued by state or local governments. However, "put" bonds have one feature that sets them apart: You have the option of "putting" the bond to the issuer at least once a year, beginning at a specified date after the bond is issued. That means you can make the issuer redeem the bond at full face value, even if the bond is selling at a discount at that time.

Result: "Put" bonds virtually eliminate the risk of losing your original investment dollars due to interest rate fluctuations. You know you can get the par value of the bond from the issuer at least once a year.

➤ **IDEA IN ACTION** If interest rates rise, you can get your full investment back from the issuer and buy another bond that pays higher interest. And if interest rates fall, you may be able to collect the higher interest rate for the life of the bond.

In effect, a "put" bond is comparable to a series of short-term municipal bonds that mature on the dates the bond can be redeemed. The interest rate on a newly issued "put" bond is usually higher than the rate for short-term bonds. That's another reason put bonds are popular with investors.

Are there any disadvantages to "put" bonds? The interest paid on these bonds is a bit lower than on long-term bonds of equal quality. And the issuer of "put" bonds often has the right to call the bonds—to redeem them before maturity. The issuer may even be required to do so on a regular schedule. This may prevent "put" bonds from rising above par value, the way other bonds do when interest rates fall. So although these bonds won't decline in value if interest rates rise, they generally won't increase in value if interest rates fall.

➤ **WHAT TO DO** You may want some "put" bonds in your portfolio as a hedge against a possible rise in interest rates. If you're interested, check with your investment adviser. He or she will be able to point out which bonds offer the "put" feature, and whether they fit into your overall investment strategy.

¶302   HOW TO BUY MUNICIPAL BONDS THAT ARE SURE TO PAY

Many investors want extra assurance that a municipal bond issuer will (1) make interest payments on schedule during the life of the bond, and (2) redeem the bond at maturity. That's why there's a growing market in insured municipal bonds. There are two popular ways to purchase municipals that have an extra layer of protection.

Individually insured municipal bond. Here, an insurance company backs a specific bond issue of a state or municipality. In the event of the issuer's default, the insurance company will step into the shoes of the municipality: It will (1) make interest payments during the remaining life of the bond, and (2) redeem the bonds at par from their holders upon the stated redemption date.

Generally, these privately insured issues are given the highest ratings, but carry slightly lower yields because of the cost of the insurance. In addition, they give the purchaser—

➤ **THREE BIG BENEFITS** You get (1) peace of mind, plus (2) tax-free yields, and (3) thanks to the extra protection, an extremely marketable investment.

A portfolio of insured municipals. When you put your money into an insured municipal bond fund, you buy triple protection:

- Instead of owning one or two bonds, you own a fractional interest in many bonds. So you aren't putting all of your eggs in one basket.
- The bonds the fund buys have good ratings.

- You get more than just a promise that bond interest and principal will be paid. You also get a guarantee from an insurance company that it will take over payments in case of default by an issuer.

➤ **TAX-FREE PASS-THROUGH** Municipal bond interest received by the fund is tax-free, and it retains this tax-free status when distributed to you. So the interest you get is free of federal income tax—just as if you bought the bonds directly.

Added benefit: Some insured funds invest only in bonds of a particular state. If you live in that state, the bond interest is also exempt from state and local tax.

For more information on this subject, see ¶1503.

¶ 303 ONE KIND OF MUNICIPAL ESCAPES ALL INCOME TAXES NO MATTER WHERE YOU LIVE

The interest from a municipal bond is free of federal income tax, but not necessarily free of state and local taxes. You pay state and local taxes if the bond is issued by a state other than your own (and a few states even tax their own bonds).

➤ **TAX-SAVING EXCEPTION** Bonds issued by some U.S. holdings are tax-free across the board—no matter where you live. They are specifically exempted by law from federal tax and state and local tax. Owning one of these bonds is just like owning a bond issued by your state or municipality (assuming it doesn't tax its own issues). Prime example: Commonwealth of Puerto Rico bonds. Other bonds that receive full tax-free treatment include bonds issued by the U.S. Virgin Islands and Guam.

With states and localities taking an ever-increasing share of your income, this total tax-free break can be a big plus.

¶304 HOMESELLERS GET TWO CRACKS AT TAX-FREE PROFITS

Your home may be the best tax-sheltered investment you own. You get not one but two chances to pull down—

➤ **TAX-FREE PROFITS** There are two ways to avoid tax on the sale of a home: (1) by electing to exclude up to $125,000 of profit, and (2) by buying a more expensive home and automatically postponing the tax on the profit (the so-called rollover).

Both breaks apply only to the sale of a principal residence and both can save you thousands of tax dollars. But that's about all they have in common.

Who is eligible: A homeseller is more likely to qualify for the tax deferral than for the tax exclusion (although, as we'll see in a moment, some homesellers qualify for both).

- You can take advantage of the exclusion only if you (or your spouse, if you own the home jointly) are at least 55 years of age on the date of the sale. The rollover is available regardless of your age.
- To qualify for the exclusion, you must have resided in your home for three out of the five years prior to the sale. There's no minimum residency requirement with the rollover.
- You can only use the exclusion once: It's literally a once-in-a-lifetime break. There's no limit on the number of times you can use the rollover (exception: you can't use it more than once in a two-year period unless the second sale is job-related).

How these breaks work: The exclusion is a more valuable tax break than the rollover.

- The exclusion allows you to permanently avoid the tax on the first $125,000 of your home sale profit. The rollover is a tax deferral—the taxable gain potential is simply transferred to your new home (without any dollar limit).

• With the exclusion, you avoid all the tax on your profit (up to $125,000), whether you buy a replacement home or not. With the rollover, you avoid the entire tax only if you buy a replacement home that costs at least as much as the sales price of your old home. You must make the purchase within certain time limits (generally, two years before or after the sale). If the replacement home costs less than the sales price, you pay tax on the profit to the extent of the difference. For example, if you sell your home for $80,000 at a $20,000 profit and then buy another place for $75,000, you pay tax on $5,000 ($80,000 less $75,000).

Tax-free parlay for homesellers. The exclusion can be combined with the rollover in a really impressive tax-free parlay.

> ➤ **WELCOME NEWS** This parlay is a big break for the homeseller who's "buying down"—for example, a retiree who's selling his big home and buying a condominium. By combining the exclusion and the rollover, you can take down more than $125,000 in profit, buy a much less expensive home, and pay not one dime in taxes.

Example: Mr. Parker, age 56, has bought and sold several homes over the years. Each successive home was more expensive than the one that preceded it, so he used the rollover break on each of the sales to postpone the tax on his profit. He wants to sell his present home—he expects to get $190,000 for it—and move into a smaller home that costs $95,000. He will have a potential taxable profit of $165,000 on the sale (most of it built up from profits on prior home sales).

Result: (1) By using the exclusion, Parker is treated as if he had sold his old home for $65,000 ($190,000 less $125,000), rather than $190,000. (2) Since his new home costs more than the "sales price" of his old home ($65,000), he can take full advantage of the rollover break. Payoff: Parker owes no tax on the sale—he avoids tax on $125,000 of his profit forever and postpones tax on the other $40,000 until (and if) he sells his new home and does not buy another one.

For more information on this subject, see ¶1702, 1708.

¶305 BUILT-IN REAL ESTATE TAX-SHELTER ADVANTAGE—THE TAX-FREE SWAP

Real estate investors can take advantage of one tax-saving move almost no other kind of investor can make. It's called the tax-free swap.

If you want another investor's property and he or she is willing to swap it for one you own—and these are *"like kind" properties*—then chances are good you can each get what you want without paying any tax.

> ➤ **STILL ANOTHER TAX BREAK** Tax-free swaps are an important exception to the tough recapture of depreciation rules. These rules can cause part or all of your profit to be treated as ordinary income (taxed at a maximum rate of 31%) instead of capital gain (taxed at only 28%). However, there's no recapture on a tax-free swap unless you received cash or other "boot" in the exchange.

The definition of "like kind"—property held for productive use in trade or business, or for investment—leaves you plenty of latitude, too.

You can exchange trade or business property for investment property, or the reverse. "Like kind" refers to the nature or character of the property, not its grade or quality: improved real estate can be swapped for unimproved real estate; city real estate for a ranch or farm; a leasehold interest of 30 years or more in real estate for other real estate. In addition, courts have held that the following constitute nontaxable exchanges: lots held for investment for land and building held for investment; exchange of multifamily rental buildings held for investment for a ranch held for investment.

But note that the government has said that raw land and a building to be newly constructed (as opposed to a building plus land) do not constitute "like kind" property.

> ➤ **WATCH THIS** You can't work a tax-free exchange with stock in trade, or real estate held for sale to customers in the ordinary course of business. This applies to both properties in the exchange. In other words, both the old property, and the new one acquired in the exchange, must be held for investment, or for use in a trade or business. And a taxpayer who swaps property with a related party must hold on to the property for two years to benefit from tax-free treatment.

How tax-free swaps work. In an even-up exchange, there's no tax at all. In general, you carry over your basis for an old property to the new property. For example, let's say your $100,000 apartment building is now worth $250,000. Your gain of $150,000 goes untaxed, and your basis for the office building you get in exchange is $100,000.

Exchanges where you give cash boot. When you give cash boot as part of a tax-free swap, there's ordinarily no gain or loss recognized. Basis for the new property you receive in the swap is the total basis of the old property transferred, increased by any cash boot given.

> **Example:** Your basis in a raw-land parcel is $40,000 and it's now worth $50,000. You give up the raw land, plus $10,000 cash, for a building lot worth $60,000. No gain or loss is recognized on the swap. Your basis for the building lot is $50,000 ($40,000 basis plus $10,000 cash given).

Exchanges where you get boot: When you receive boot as part of a tax-free exchange, gain is recognized to the extent of the cash boot. Your basis for the new property is your basis for the old property given up less the cash boot received, plus the amount of gain recognized in the exchange.

> **Example:** Your basis for an apartment building, which you own free and clear, is $200,000. It's now worth $500,000, and you swap it for a $400,000 commercial property, plus $100,000 cash. Only $100,000 of your gain is recognized. Your basis for the commercial building you receive in the exchange is $200,000 ($200,000 basis for apartment building less $100,000 cash boot received, plus $100,000 gain recognized on the exchange).

Swaps involving mortgaged property: Say you give up mortgaged property in a tax-free swap, and the other party to the exchange assumes the mortgage, or takes the property subject to the mortgage. In this case, the mortgage debt at the time of the swap is treated as cash received by you for purposes of figuring recognized gain. This mortgage debt treated as cash is reduced by any cash boot you give up on the exchange. It's also reduced by any mortgage debt on the property you receive on the exchange, if you assume the mortgage, or take the property subject to the mortgage.

For more information on this subject, see ¶1614-1619.

TAX-WISE T&E STRATEGIES

¶306   HOW TO GET A DOUBLE TAX BREAK FROM YOUR BUSINESS MEALS

You can make your business meals with customers or clients do double duty: A business discussion at a meal not only can make the meal deductible, but can also help you write off other business entertainment.

The key here is the tax rule that an expense for any entertainment associated with your business is deductible as long as it either precedes or follows a substantial and bona fide business discussion.

Typical situation.   Mark Graham, a salesman, wants to entertain Bill Blaine, a buyer. On Monday, Graham takes Blaine to a restaurant for lunch. They play a leisurely round of golf in the afternoon. No business is discussed during the day. On the following Friday, Graham and Blaine meet again for lunch and discuss Graham's new line of products.

Result: Graham gets a deduction for the Friday lunch—and that's all. (Actually, only 80% of the cost of business meals is deductible.) He gets no writeoff for the Monday lunch or for the greens fees he pays in the afternoon. Reason: There is no business discussion before, during or after the lunch. And the same applies to the round of golf—no discussion, no deduction.

> ➤ **WHAT TO DO**   If you have a mix of deductible and nondeductible meals, schedule other entertainment before or after the deductible meals. Reason: That way, the business discussion during the deductible meals will also count as a discussion for the purpose of writing off the other entertainment.

For example, let's say that Graham postpones the golf match. Instead of taking Blaine to the links on Monday, they go on Friday after their business lunch.

New result: The golf match now follows a business discussion (the discussion during the Friday lunch). So the greens fees are deductible.

For more information on this subject, see ¶2009.

¶307   HOW TO GET TOP DEDUCTIONS WHEN YOU TREAT A CUSTOMER TO A BALL GAME

Whether your favorite sport is football, baseball or basketball—or all three—taking a customer to a game is a top way to build business goodwill.

The deductibility of the tickets you buy depends on how they are used. For example, suppose you merely give a customer tickets to a game. That may be treated differently than if you go along.

> ➤ **KEY DISTINCTION**   Treated as a gift, your deduction is limited to $25 per recipient per year. As goodwill entertainment, there is no dollar limit on the deduction—but the game must precede or follow a "substantial business discussion." And your entertainment deduction is limited to 80% of your cost.

If you and the customer go to the park, you can deduct the ticket only as entertainment (i.e., the game must precede or follow a substantial business discussion). But if you don't go, you have a tax choice: (1) You can deduct the customer's ticket as a gift subject to the $25 limit, or (2) you can deduct it as business entertainment subject to the 80% limit (as long as you meet the business discussion test).

> **Example:** You and a customer discuss business at your office. After the discussion, you give the customer two tickets to a sporting event, but don't go along. If the tickets cost $15 a piece, you can deduct $25 as a gift or $24 (80% of $30) as entertainment. If they cost $20 a piece, you're better off treating them as entertainment—$25 deduction versus $32 (80% of $40).

Q.   Many of my customers will be attending a convention in my area. Can I claim an entertainment deduction if I take them to night games while the convention is in town—even if we don't discuss business?

A. Yes. The tax rules say a business convention can pinch hit for a "substantial business discussion."

Q.   I have some good customers. Can I give them tickets more than once?

A. Sure. You can give each one up to $25 worth of tickets a year and deduct the cost. Anything over that, and you generally bear the extra cost unless you are able to treat them as entertainment.

Q. How about this—suppose I give one of my customers $25 worth of tickets and also give his wife tickets. Will that avoid the $25 limit?

A. No. A gift to the spouse is considered part of the customer's gift. Result: Your deduction would still be limited to $25.

Q. Does the $25 limit on deductible gifts apply if the tickets are given to my employees?

A. No. The tickets are fully deductible as long as they are not given only to key employees.

> ➤ **RECORDKEEPING IS A MUST** First of all, you'll have to designate whether it's a business gift or business entertainment. If it's entertainment, you must show the cost of the tickets, date of the game, whom you entertained and the business relationship, time, duration, place and nature of the business discussion; plus identification of those who were at the business discussion. For business gifts, you'll have to record cost, date, who received the gift and business relationship, and the expected business benefit.

For more information on this subject, see ¶2008-2011.

¶ 308 HOW TO NAIL DOWN MAXIMUM WRITEOFFS WHEN YOU ATTEND A BUSINESS CONVENTION

You probably receive flyers for trade shows, business conventions, seminars and the like. If you plan to attend one of these out-of-town sessions in the near future, do not forget about taxes. You can deduct all registration charges provided they qualify as an "ordinary and necessary" business expense. But what about the cost of getting to and from the convention (including meals and lodging en route if you take a multi-day trip)?

The tax rules for the cost of traveling to and from the convention site vary depending on where the convention is held—within the United States, outside the U.S. but within the "North American area," or elsewhere on the globe. Furthermore, there are special restrictions that apply to conventions held on cruise ships.

1. Domestic. The simplest rules apply to conventions held in the United States. If you attend primarily for business reasons, the full transportation cost (and 80% of the cost of meals while traveling) is deductible.

2. North American area. Transportation expenses relating to conventions held within the North American area, but outside the U.S. are deductible only if they meet two tests: Your primary purpose for attending the convention must be business *and* you must not spend too much time during the trip on pleasure. If you fail the business vs. pleasure test, you have to allocate your transportation cost to and from the convention. Only the business portion is deductible.

> ➤ **TAX-SAVING EXCEPTION** You can deduct the full cost—without having to make an allocation for the nonbusiness portion of the trip—if (1) you are outside of the U.S. for no more than one week and (2) at least 75% of your trip is devoted to business-related activities.

For these purposes, the North American area includes U.S. possessions, the Pacific Trust Territory, Canada, Mexico, Jamaica and certain Caribbean basin countries that have agreements to swap tax information with the U.S.

3. Other foreign. To qualify for a deduction for foreign conventions held outside the North American area, you must pass an additional test: You must be able to show that it is as reasonable for the convention to be held outside the North American area as within it. In other words, there's no deduction if there's more reason to have the convention held within, rather than outside, North America.

In making the determination of what is reasonable, the IRS looks at these three factors: (1) The purpose of the convention and the activities taking place at the convention; (2) The purpose and activities of the sponsoring organization or groups; and (3) The residences of the active members of the sponsoring organization and the places at which other meetings of the sponsoring organization or groups have been held or will be held.

Once you pass the "reasonableness" test, then the size of your deduction is governed by the allocation rules for foreign business travel.

4. Cruises.   Conventions held aboard cruise ships are subject to the toughest rules of all. First off, there is no deduction unless the convention is (a) held on a U.S. flagship and (b) all ports of call are within the U.S. or its possessions. In addition, unlike other conventions, there's an absolute dollar cap on your convention deductions. You can write off no more than $2,000 annually for the cost of attending cruise ship conventions.

➤ **DOUBLE DOLLAR CAP**   The deductible limit is applied on a per-taxpayer-basis. So, for example, if you and your spouse both work in a family-owned business and both attend a deductible cruise ship convention, up to $4,000 is deductible on a joint return. Of course, if there's no business reason for your spouse to attend, you can't deduct any of his or her other costs.

Recordkeeping rules: To substantiate the purpose of your trip to your company, be sure to hold on to a program, cataloging sessions related to your business. As a further precaution, check off the sessions you attended and take notes. If each session has a sign-in book, make sure you sign in. Then, if the sponsoring organization keeps this book after the sessions are concluded, you can request certified abstracts, photostats or even the books themselves, should the need arise.

Special rules apply to cruise ship conventions. You must attach two written statements to your tax return. One is a statement signed by you that contains the number of days of the cruise, the number of hours of each day devoted to business activities and a program of the activities. The other is a statement signed by a representative of the sponsoring organization which includes a schedule of the business activities of each day and the number of hours you attended.

For more information on this subject, see ¶2001.

¶ 309   HOW A CHANGE IN DRIVING HABITS MAY GET YOU A CASUALTY LOSS DEDUCTION

Gary Green owns two cars. He uses one primarily for business and the other purely for personal use. Early in January of this year, Green is involved in a minor fender-bender in his personal car. He suffers uninsured damages of $400. Green's adjusted gross income (gross income less business expenses) is expected to be $50,000.

Green cannot deduct the damage as a casualty loss. Reason: Casualty losses are deductible only to the extent they exceed a fixed dollar floor and a 10% of adjusted gross income. In Green's case, 10% of adjusted gross income is $5,000.

➤ **TAX STRATEGY**   After the accident, Green may want to use his personal car as his business car. Result: Business cars are not subject to the deduction limitations. If Green puts 10,000 business miles on the car during the year and 5,000 personal or commuting miles, he can claim a business expense deduction for ⅔ of his uninsured loss.

For more information on this subject, see ¶2304.

¶ 310   HOW A TWO-CAR FAMILY CAN RACK UP BONUS AUTO DEDUCTIONS

Under the latest auto deduction rules, sometimes even a small change in the way you handle things can produce—

▶ **BIGGER DEDUCTIONS**   For example, if you own two cars, a little switch in your driving habits can help you boost your auto deduction substantially.

To see how, let's take a look at this—

Typical situation.   You're a two-car family that doesn't do much driving. You deduct your actual auto expenses. One car is for business; the other is a family car. You drive 10,000 business miles a year. Additionally, you and your spouse travel about 5,000 personal miles a year. You buy a new business car and a new family car this year at a cost of $13,000 each.

Let's compare the results of doing things the usual way with the results of doing things the better way.

- The usual way. You use one car solely for business all year. Your depreciable cost is $13,000, and your depreciation deduction this year comes to $2,600.
- The better way. You split your business-connected driving between the two cars. Result: You drive each car 7,500 miles, 5,000 of which are business miles. As a result, you can depreciate EACH car on a ⅔ business-use basis.

▶ **DOLLARS-AND-CENTS COMPARISON**   Doing things the "better way," each car has a depreciable cost of $8,667.

Result: Your total depreciation deduction for this year jumps to $3,467—a boost of nearly $900. Over the six-year writeoff period for cars, you'll deduct $17,334. That adds up to more than $4,000 of extra depreciation deductions.

And there's more. Since you're itemizing all your costs, doing things the "better way" will enable you to deduct ⅔ of the cost of oil, lube, repairs, tires, insurance and gasoline for each car.

¶311 SHOULD YOU SELL YOUR OLD BUSINESS CAR OR TRADE IT IN?

Are you better off, from a tax perspective, selling your present car or trading it in? Answer: It depends on whether you have a profit or a loss on the transaction.

▶ **TAX-SAVING CHOICE**   If you have a profit, you don't pay any tax if you trade in your present car. You do if you sell. On the other hand, you may have a loss. You can deduct that loss *in full* if you sell—but not if you trade in.

"Wait," you say, "I certainly can't have a profit from my present car. It's worth much less than what I paid for it." That may be true. But keep in mind that the depreciation deductions you claim reduce your "cost" of the car for tax purposes. If your selling price exceeds your depreciated cost, you have a profit—even though the selling price is less than your original cost.

For example, if you purchased a car for $13,000 and wrote off $8,000 worth of depreciation, your tax cost is $5,000. If the car is worth $7,000, you have a profit of $2,000. But if the car is worth only $3,000, you have a loss of $2,000.

For more information on this subject, see ¶1600.

TAX IDEAS FOR EXECUTIVE COMPENSATION

¶312   'RABBI TRUST'—A DEFERRED COMPENSATION FAVORITE

Tough tax law rules make many employee benefit plans prohibitively expensive for small companies. For key employees to get tax-favored benefits, your company must also provide benefits to a large portion of its workforce—not just the top people. But this is not always the case.

> ➤ **EXECS ONLY**   The deferred compensation arrangement called a "rabbi trust" is a long-time favorite plan for "execs only." It is called a rabbi trust because the first ruling approving the arrangement involved a rabbi.

Best of both worlds.   With a rabbi trust, your company irrevocably sets aside compensation for you and other key execs for future payment. Yet you still postpone tax on the funds until payment is actually made. Other types of deferred compensation plans typically offer one benefit but not both.

Why rabbi trusts have an edge: Deferred compensation arrangements are either funded or unfunded. With an unfunded plan, the company simply promises to pay compensation at a future date (e.g., retirement). The employee owes no tax (and the company gets no deduction) until the compensation is paid.

Two different tax rules come into play with funded plans (i.e., the funds are actually set aside and earmarked for an employee). One rule says the employee is in "constructive receipt" of compensation if it's available to him, even though he doesn't actually receive it. The other rule—the so-called economic benefit doctrine—says that even where there is no constructive receipt, an employee is currently taxed on a funded plan if he has an absolute right to future payment.

To overcome these obstacles, most funded plans use a forfeiture provision to defer taxes. For example, the exec and the company agree that the exec will lose his rights to the funds if he leaves the company before payments commence.

Tax alternative.   With a rabbi trust there's no need for a forfeiture provision. Instead, the company deposits the funds in a trust with no conditions imposed on the employee.

The rabbi trust qualifies for tax deferral because, by the terms of the plan, the trust assets are available to the company's general creditors as well as the employee. As long as the employee has no greater right to the funds than other creditors, the IRS says there is sufficient restriction to get tax deferral.

For more information on this subject, see ¶1365.

¶313   HOW A DEFERRED PAY PLAN CAN ESCAPE HIGHER-THAN-EVER SOCIAL SECURITY TAX

Social Security and Medicare taxes are taking an increasingly large bite out of employees' paychecks—and company profits as well.

> ➤ **TAX-SAVING MOVE**   If your company has a deferred compensation plan for you and other top employees, ask to have things set up so that the benefit payouts are effectively free of employment taxes.

In a typical deferred compensation plan, your company agrees to pay you a certain amount at retirement.

But the promised compensation comes with strings attached—for example, an agreement that you work for the company until retirement.

Although this restriction makes good business sense, it has one unpleasant tax consequence. You and the company may end up having to pay Social Security and Medicare taxes on the deferred comp.

Reason: Deferred compensation is subject to employment taxes as it is earned or when you have an unqualified right to receive it, whichever is later. Since you don't have an unqualified right to the benefits until retirement, the benefits will be subject to employment taxes in the year of retirement.

If you have little or no salary in that year, employment taxes will have to be paid on part or all of the deferred comp. The taxable amount will be the difference between the Social Security and Medicare wage bases for that year and any other salary the exec gets.

➤ **A BETTER WAY**   Set up the pay plan so that your right to the benefits "vest" (i.e., become nonforfeitable) in the year *before* retirement.

Result: The benefits become taxable in that year. But since you will be drawing a full salary that year, you will most likely be paying the maximum employment taxes already. So there will be no extra employment tax bite on the deferred compensation.

Note: Even though you may not know precisely when you will retire, the plan should set a specific year for the pre-retirement payout. You can always modify the payout date as retirement approaches.

¶314 HOW INTEREST-FREE COMPANY LOANS CAN PUT THOUSANDS OF TAX-FREE DOLLARS IN YOUR POCKET

An interest-free loan has to be one of the best bargains around. Instead of borrowing from a financial institution and paying high interest, you borrow from a friendlier lender—your company—at zero interest.

Example: Suppose you want to move into a new home in the $200,000 price range. After selling your old home and paying off the mortgage, you'll still need about $85,000. By getting an interest-free 30-year loan from your company—instead of taking out, say a 8-1/2% 30-year mortgage from the bank—you wind up saving a total of $150,289 in interest. The interest savings amount to an average "cash bonus" from the corporation of about $5,010 a year—every year for 30 years.

Tax story.   When you take an interest-free loan from your company, you are treated as receiving phantom taxable compensation equal to the value of the benefit (i.e., what the company could have charged on the loan). This amount is calculated using rates set by law.

➤ **HASSLE-FREE ROUTE**   The tax law provides a special break for interest-free company loans of $10,000 or less. As long as tax avoidance is not a principal purpose of the loan, you have no taxable compensation.

Even if you do have taxable compensation, you still may not actually have to pay any tax. Reason: You are treated as using the phantom compensation to "pay" the interest on the loan. And you may be entitled to a deduction for this phantom interest payment. If you do get a deduction, it offsets the phantom compensation—in other words, the loan is tax-free.

- *Home loans:* You can claim a full deduction for home mortgage interest on (1) loans totaling up to $1 million that are taken out to buy or substantially improve one or two homes plus (2) loans totaling up to $100,000 that are used for any purpose (but either way, the loans must be secured by the homes).
- *Investment loans:* If you pay investment interest, you can deduct it up to your taxable investment income. The phantom income from the loan is additional compensation, not investment income. But that doesn't mean you get no deduction.

When you use an interest-free loan to make an investment, you may get an interest deduction even if the investment you buy throws off no current income (for example, if you buy growth stock). Reason: You can deduct the phantom interest expense on the loan against your taxable investment income from other sources.

Company angle. Your company also comes out okay when it makes an interest-free loan to you. The company receives phantom interest income from you, but it gets an offsetting compensation deduction.

For more information on this subject, see ¶1216.

¶315 HOW TO GET TAX-FREE REIMBURSEMENTS FROM YOUR BUSINESS

Tough rules on company reimbursements or allowances can actually increase your tax bill if you don't handle things right—even when the reimbursements simply offset business expenses incurred on behalf of your company. Fortunately, there's an IRS-approved way to sidestep this tough tax crackdown.

> ➤ **TAX-FREE SETUP** A reimbursement or allowance will remain 100% tax-free to you if your company has a policy that requires you to (1) substantiate your expenses to the company within a reasonable time after incurring them and (2) return any amount the company gives you that you don't spend on business.

Employees who satisfy these requirements don't report the amounts they get from the company as income and don't deduct the business expenses incurred on behalf of the company. In short, the reimbursements and expenses cancel each other out as a wash for tax purposes. But an employee who doesn't substantiate expenses doesn't get this beneficial tax treatment. Instead, reimbursements or allowances are taxed to the owner as compensation.

Q. What's the big deal? If a reimbursement is added to my income, can't I just subtract the expenses as an offsetting deduction?

A. Yes, but there's a catch. You can write off your offsetting expenses only as a "miscellaneous itemized deduction." And expenses that fall into this "miscellaneous" category are deductible to the extent they total more than 2% of your adjusted gross income. Bottom line: If the expenses don't reach the 2% mark, you end up with a fully taxable reimbursement.

What's more, there's another new limitation on your itemized deductions. Your overall itemized deductions—except for medical expenses, investment interest and casualty and theft losses—are reduced by 3% of your adjusted gross income above $105,250 in 1992 ($52,625 for marrieds filing separately).

> ➤ **GOOD NEWS** If you get a reimbursement or allowance for your business expenses, and you satisfy the substantiation rules, you avoid both the 2% and 3% rules. The amount you get from your company is both tax-free to you and deductible by the company.

Now that you know what's at stake, you may wonder how you substantiate expenses.

As an employee of your closely held corporation, you must submit adequate records to the company of the amount, time, place and purpose of each business expense. For travel expenses, you must also submit a record of the number of business miles traveled. And for entertainment expenses, you must submit a record of the business relationship of those entertained.

Q. What are adequate records?

A. Adequate records are an account book, diary, log, statement of expense, trip sheets or similar written statement. Records must be made at or near the time you incur an expense so that you can accurately distinguish between business and personal expenses. You must also submit receipts of (1) any lodging expense or (2) any other expense of $25 or more.

For more information on this subject, see ¶2003.

ESTATE AND GIFT TAX OVERVIEW

¶ 401   LIFETIME GIFTS CAN BE THE KEY TO ESTATE PLANNING

You can reduce your estate subject to tax with a series of well-designed lifetime gifts. Let's look at some of the ways lifetime gifts can cut the tax bite on your estate.

1. You can give away up to $10,000 per year per recipient without eating into your unified credit and without owing any gift tax. Over a period of twenty years, this can shelter as much as $200,000 per recipient.

2. Your spouse also can give away up to $10,000 per year per recipient without any gift tax consequences. What's more, you and your spouse can elect to "split" your gifts.

That means you can give away twice as much—$20,000 per year per recipient. The two of you will each be treated as making half the gift, so neither will exceed the $10,000 maximum.

3. Another way to lower your taxable estate is by making lifetime gifts of the right kind of property. If you have a choice, you want to give property that will appreciate in value. Reason: The amount of your taxable gift is the *current* value of the property. On the other hand, if the property remains in your estate, it will be subject to estate taxes at its higher future value.

¶ 402   HOW TO MAKE THE MOST OF THE UNLIMITED MARITAL DEDUCTION

The marital deduction allows one spouse to transfer an unlimited amount of property to the other without owing any gift or estate taxes. This important tax break can be combined with the $192,800 unified estate and gift tax credit, which shelters up to $600,000 of property left to others.

> **Example:** Mr. Johnson leaves his entire $1 million estate to his spouse. Due to the unlimited marital deduction, his estate pays no estate taxes on the transfer. Mrs. Johnson then passes on the $1 million to her children when she eventually dies. Of the $1 million, $400,000 is subject to estate tax when Mrs. Johnson dies. Estate tax bill: $153,000. Mr. Johnson's mistake was to waste his own $600,000 exemption. Combining two unified credits with the unlimited marital deduction can shelter estates worth as much as $1.2 million. But knowing how to combine the tax breaks is the trick.

Estates Up to $1.2 Million

Strategy #1. One strategy for Mr. Johnson is to leave $600,000 to his wife and $400,000 to his children. His estate pays no tax (what passes to his spouse is exempt because of the unlimited marital deduction, and what passes to his children is sheltered by his credit). And his spouse's estate pays no tax when her property goes to the children (it is sheltered by her credit).

Strategy #2. The problem with the obvious strategy is that Mrs. Johnson loses the economic benefit of $400,000 after Mr. Johnson dies. Better approach: Mr. Johnson puts the $400,000 in a non-marital-deduction trust for his children with Mrs. Johnson receiving income from the trust during her lifetime.

> **Example:** Mr. Johnson leaves $600,000 outright to Mrs. Johnson and puts the other $400,000 in trust. Mrs. Johnson has the right to all trust income and the right to trust principal for her health, education, support and maintenance. The children get anything remaining in the trust at Mrs. Johnson' death.

The $600,000 Mr. Johnson leaves to his wife is sheltered by the marital deduction. And, when Mrs. Johnson dies, that same $600,000 will be sheltered by her unified credit. The $400,000 left to the trust is sheltered by Mr. Johnson's unified credit. Bottom line: No estate tax at the death of either spouse.

Q.   Why shouldn't Mr. Johnson leave $400,000 to Mrs. Johnson outright and $600,000 to the trust? Won't that allow Mrs. Johnson's estate to appreciate by $200,000 without gift or estate tax consequences?

A. Yes. And that can be a good strategy. The only problem is that Mrs. Johnson many not feel comfortable with only $400,000 of wealth that she can control. If Mrs. Johnson doesn't have a problem with this, the strategy definitely should be considered.

Q.   What if Mrs. Johnson dies first?

A. Mr. Johnson's estate will pay estate taxes (unless he remarries). His estate consists of $1 million, $600,000 of which passes tax-free to his children. The remaining $400,000 is subject to tax since the marital deduction expires with his spouse. This possibility can be a problem for spouses who are close in age. One way to mitigate this problem is—

Strategy #3. Take advantage of the unlimited gift tax marital deduction. Where feasible, a couple splits ownership of the property down the middle during their lifetimes. Each spouse then leaves his estate in trust to the children with an income interest to the other spouse. Result: No estate tax.

> **Example:** Mr. Johnson owns property worth $1 million, and Mrs. Johnson owns none. Mr. Johnson gives $500,000 worth of property to his wife. He then leaves the remaining $500,000 to a non-marital-deduction trust. His wife has the right to income from the trust for life and a limited right to principal. The children have a right to the trust remainder after Mrs. Johnson's death. Mrs. Johnson makes the same arrangement with Mr. Johnson as income beneficiary and the children as principal beneficiaries of her trust.

Assuming Mr. Johnson dies first, the $500,000 he leaves to the trust is sheltered by his unified credit. Although the money in this trust is available to Mrs. Johnson during her life, it bypasses her estate. When Mrs. Johnson eventually dies, the children get $500,000 from Mr. Johnson's trust plus $500,000 from Mrs. Johnson's estate. The trust money is not subject to gift or estate tax at this time, and the estate money is sheltered by Mrs. Johnson's unified credit.

What if Mrs. Johnson dies first? The bottom line results are exactly the same. The children ultimately get everything, and no estate tax is paid.

Estates Over $1.2 Million

Strategy #4. Estate tax will fall due at the death of the second spouse if the combined value of both estates tops $1.2 million. Reason: The sum of the two $600,000 exemptions is $1.2 million. Anything over that amount is subject to estate tax—unless the spouses cash in on another tax break.

> ➤ **LIFETIME GIVING**   Each spouse can give the children up to $10,000 per year without paying gift tax or dipping into the unified credit. The $600,000 exemption stays intact to shelter the estate from tax. Result: If enough gifts are made, the taxable estate will be at $1.2 million or below.

If the second spouse joins in the gift-giving, the exclusion is double—20,000 tax-free dollars can be given to each child every year.

> **Example:** Mr. and Mrs. Brown have an estate of $1,520,000. They give $20,000 per year to each of their two children for eight years, a total of $320,000. Mr. Brown leaves $600,000 directly to his wife and $600,000 in trust for the children (Strategy #2). The children get $1.2 million when Mrs. Brown dies.

Result: The entire $1.52 million ends up in the children's hands without any gift or estate taxes owed. The gift tax annual exclusions shelter the $320,000 of lifetime gifts. And the Browns' two unified credits shelters the remaining $1.2 million.

Strategy #5. Suppose an estate exceeds $1.2 million by so much that lifetime transfers can't bring the taxable estate down to the magic figure of $1.2 million. Or maybe the spouses prefer not to make lifetime gifts to their children. In either case, an estate tax will be paid. Nevertheless, there is a way to minimize the amount of the tax: They can forgo the maximum marital deduction and—

> ▶ **BALANCE THE ESTATES** Because of the graduated estate tax rates, by transferring enough assets (either by gift or by will) to make both estates equal, the minimum possible overall estate tax will be paid. The sum of the taxes on both estates will be less than the tax would be if the total amount were taxed in only one estate.

> **Example:** Mr. Allen has an estate of $2.5 million. Mrs. Allen has a negligible estate. If Mr. Allen leaves his entire estate to his wife, the estate pays no tax. But when Mrs. Allen eventually dies, her estate pays tax of $833,000.

If, on the other hand, Mr. Allen leaves $1.25 million to his wife and the rest to a non-marital-deduction trust, Mr. Allen's estate pays tax of $255,500. On her death, Mrs. Allen's estate pays tax of the same amount. Total estate tax bill for both estates: $511,000—a savings of $322,000.

¶ 403   HOW TO CLAIM THE MAXIMUM MARITAL DEDUCTION AND PROVIDE FOR YOUR CHILDREN

The marital deduction permits unlimited transfers of property to a spouse free of gift and estate tax. In general, however, the marital deduction is not available for transfers of less than a full ownership interest.

For example, if one spouse gives or leaves the other spouse income from a trust for life and then gives or leaves the trust principal to someone else, the transfer in trust generally does not qualify for the marital deduction.

> ▶ **KEY EXCEPTION** The estate can make a so-called QTIP election to qualify a bequest for a marital deduction. To be eligible, the bequest must give the surviving spouse the right to all income from the trust or property for life, payable at least once a year. In addition, no one can have the power to give any portion of the property or trust interest to a person other than the surviving spouse during that spouse's lifetime.

Once the QTIP election is made, the trust property is taxed in the surviving spouse's estate when that spouse eventually dies. This amount can be sheltered by the surviving spouse's unified credit.

How to elect: An executor must make the QTIP election on the estate tax return.

¶404   HOW TO ESTIMATE THE ESTATE TAX

You can get an idea of what someone's estate will be by adding up the anticipated wealth that will be owned at death. You also add in taxable gifts made after 1976 because property given away and property held at death are subject to a single unified tax (the taxpayer later claims an offsetting credit for gift taxes paid).

The resulting figure is an approximation of the gross estate. Then subtract out any portion of that wealth left to a surviving spouse, bequests the estate makes to charity, debts the taxpayer owes at death and an estimate of the funeral expenses and other expenses of winding up the estate. These are the key estate tax deductions, and they reduce the amount of wealth subject to the tax.

This net figure is the amount of the taxable estate. This figure is applied against the unified estate and gift tax rates [¶405] to compute the tentative estate tax. Then subtract out the unified credit of $192,800 (to the extent not used to shelter lifetime transfers from gift tax) as well as a credit for gift taxes paid after 1976. The remaining amount is an estimate of the taxpayer's eventual estate tax liability.

What's included in the gross estate?   The gross estate is the total value of all property—real or personal, tangible or intangible—that the decedent had beneficial ownership of at the time of death. Except for the joint interests of spouses, the full value of jointly held property is included in the gross estate of the deceased joint tenant, except to the extent the survivor can prove that he paid part of the property's cost. For spouses, half the value of jointly held property is included in the estate of the first spouse to die. But the property included in the spouse's estate is eligible for the marital deduction.

Life insurance. Life insurance proceeds are included in the decedent's estate if the policy proceeds are payable to the estate or the decedent owned the policy at death or had the power to name or change the beneficiary.

Transfers reserving right to use, enjoyment, or income. Property transferred by a decedent before death can be included in the gross estate if the decedent retained a life interest in the possession or enjoyment of the property or its income. Transferred property also is included when the decedent had the right (either alone or in conjunction with another person) to name the persons to possess or enjoy the property or its income.

Transfers taking effect at death. Property interests transferred by a decedent during life (except a bona fide sale for adequate consideration) generally must be included in the decedent's gross estate if: (1) the decedent has a reversionary interest in the transferred property which, immediately before death, was worth more than 5% of the value of the property; and (2) possession or enjoyment of the transferred interest could be obtained only by the transferee surviving the decedent. A *reversionary interest* includes the possibility that the transferred property may return to the decedent or his estate or may be subject to his power of disposition. A transfer that takes effect at death is not taxable unless the transferee's possession or enjoyment of the property is dependent on surviving the decedent.

Transfers reserving power to alter, amend, revoke or terminate. The value of any property transferred by the decedent during life is included in the decedent's estate if, at the time of death, the decedent had the power to make a substantial change in the beneficial enjoyment of the property transferred.

Transfers within three years of death. The value of the following types of property is pulled back and taxed in the decedent's estate if the decedent gave away the property within three years of death: transfers of life insurance, transfers with retained life estates, transfers taking effect at death or revocable transfers.

Under a so-called "gross-up" rule, any gift tax paid by the decedent or his estate on gifts made by the decedent or his spouse within three years of death is also pulled back into the gross estate. The "gross-up" rule does not apply to the gift tax paid by a consenting spouse on a gift made by a decedent within three years of death which is treated as made one-half by the spouse.

¶ 405   UNIFIED ESTATE AND GIFT TAX RATES

Taxable transfer more than—	But not more than—	Tax on amount in Col.	Rate of tax on excess of amount in Col.
(1)	(2)	(1)	(1)
$ 0	$ 10,000	$ 0	18%
10,000	20,000	1,800	20%
20,000	40,000	3,800	22%
40,000	60,000	8,200	24%
60,000	80,000	13,000	26%
80,000	100,000	18,200	28%
100,000	150,000	23,800	30%
150,000	250,000	38,800	32%
250,000	500,000	70,800	34%
500,000	750,000	155,800	37%
750,000	1,000,000	248,300	39%
1,000,000	1,250,000	345,800	41%
1,250,000	1,500,000	448,300	43%
1,500,000	2,000,000	555,800	45%
2,000,000	2,500,000	780,800	49%
2,500,000	3,000,000	1,025,800	53%*
3,000,000	and over	1,290,800	55%*

* For estates of decedents dying or gifts made in 1993 or later, the maximum rate is 50% for transfers over $2,500,000.

Note: A surtax on very large gifts and estates phases out the benefit of the unified credit and graduated nature of the rate schedule. The surtax is equal to 5% of the regular tax due on asset transfers between $10,000,000 and $21,040,000 ($18,340,000 after 1992).

FIGURING THE INDIVIDUAL INCOME TAX

Chapter 1—INDIVIDUALS—FILING STATUS, PERSONAL EXEMPTIONS, STANDARD DEDUCTION AND RATES
(Detailed Table of Contents below)

Chapter 2—GROSS INCOME—INCLUSIONS
(Detailed Table of Contents at page 1201)

Chapter 3—RETIREMENT PLANS
(Detailed Table of Contents at page 1301)

Chapter 4—EMPLOYEE FRINGE BENEFITS
(Detailed Table of Contents at page 1401)

Chapter 5—GROSS INCOME—EXCLUSIONS
(Detailed Table of Contents at page 1501)

Chapter 6—GAIN OR LOSS—BASIS—RECOGNITION
(Detailed Table of Contents at page 1601)

Chapter 7—GAIN OR LOSS—SALE OF RESIDENCE— CASUALTY—THEFT—CONDEMNATION
(Detailed Table of Contents at page 1701)

Chapter 8—CAPITAL GAINS AND LOSSES OF INDIVIDUALS
(Detailed Table of Contents at page 1801)

CHAPTER

INDIVIDUALS—FILING STATUS, PERSONAL EXEMPTIONS, STANDARD DEDUCTION AND RATES

1

TABLE OF CONTENTS

INDIVIDUAL INCOME TAX RETURNS

In general, if your income exceeds the total of your personal exemption and standard deduction, you must file a tax return. However, there are lower income thresholds for those who can be claimed as a dependent on someone else's return and for self-employeds. Some people who owe no tax must nevertheless file a return. Individuals who have earned less than the filing threshold, but have had tax withheld from their pay, should file to get a refund of what was withheld.

¶1100   WHO MUST FILE

To determine if you must file an income tax return, you need to know your gross income [IRC Sec. 61], standard deduction [IRC Sec. 63(a)] and exemption amount [IRC Sec. 151, 6012(a)], unless you are self-employed [(c) below]. Gross income is all your income subject to tax [¶1200]. It includes salary, fees, profits from business, interest, rents, dividends gains and social security benefits subject to tax. The standard deduction is an audit-proof amount you can write off in lieu of listing your actual expenses that constitute itemized deductions. The size of the standard deduction varies with your filing status [¶1107]. The exemption amount is a fixed allowance in place of a deduction for personal, family and living expenses [¶1111].

(a) Income Levels. The income levels that necessitate filing a 1992 return are [IRC Sec. 6012(a)(1)]:

Single (not a dependent)	$ 5,900
Single—65 or over	6,800
Married—filing jointly	10,600
Married—filing jointly (one spouse 65 or over)	11,300
Married—filing jointly (both 65 or over)	12,000
Surviving spouse	8,300
Surviving spouse—65 or over	9,000
Head of household	7,550
Head of household—65 or over	8,450

NOTE: Although blind taxpayers are entitled to an additional standard deduction amount [¶1107], regardless of whether or not they can be claimed by another as a dependent, that extra deduction does not raise their income filing requirements.

Suppose an individual can be claimed by another as a dependent. Under the latest tax rules, he or she must file a 1992 return if (1) unearned income exceeds $600 ; or (2) total gross income exceeds the greater of (a) $600 plus the additional standard deduction for blind or elderly taxpayers [¶1107(a)], or (b) earned income up to the basic standard deduction plus the additional standard deduction amount for blind or elderly taxpayers [¶1107(a)]; or (3) the individual cannot claim a standard deduction [¶1107(c)].

NOTE: No return needs to be filed by an under-age-14 child whose income is reported on his or her parents' return (¶1240) [IRC Sec. 1(1)(7)(A)].

Example 1: Mr. Black is single and 60 years old. He received $1,500 in wages and $3,000 in unearned investment income during 1992. He cannot be claimed as a dependent on anyone else's tax return. Black is not required to file a return since his income does not exceed $5,900.

Example 2: Ms. Green is 16 years old and can be claimed as a dependent on her parents' tax return. Her only 1992 income is $650 from interest on a bank account. Green must file a return since her unearned income exceeds $600.

Example 3: Ms. White, age 68 and single, has $2,800 of earned income and no unearned income in 1992. She can be claimed as a dependent on her son's tax return. As a single person, her standard deduction is $4,500 ($3,600 + $900). Since her earned income does not exceed $4,500, she is not required to file a return.

Example 4: Ms. Blue, age 72, is a widow. She can be claimed as a dependent on her sister's tax return. She has $1,000 in unearned income and no earned income. Since her unearned income does not exceed $1,500 ($600 + $900), Blue is not required to file a return.

Excluded income from the sale of a residence [¶1702 et seq.] and excluded foreign earned income [¶3825] must be counted in the gross income amounts that require filing a return [IRC Sec. 6012(c); Reg. Sec. 1.6012-1(a)(3)].

(b) If No Tax Is Due. Suppose you are entitled to claim sufficient tax deductions and credits to avoid owing any tax. Nonetheless, if your gross income equals or exceeds the filing limit, you must still file a return.

➤ **TAX IDEA** An employee who will owe no tax may be able to have his wages exempted from income tax withholding by filing Form W-4.

(c) Self-Employeds. If you run your own business or professional practice, you must file a return if your net earnings from the activity are $400 or more [IRC Sec. 6017]. Special rules apply for self-employment income.

(d) Aliens. Individuals who are resident aliens for the entire year are subject to the same filing requirements as U.S. citizens. Nonresident aliens who are engaged in a trade or business in the U.S. or who have income subject to U.S. tax must file a return regardless of their income level, unless sufficient tax was withheld at the source of the income [Reg. Sec. 1.6012-1(a)].

Residents of Puerto Rico are subject to the general filing requirement income thresholds. However, the gross income of a full-year resident of Puerto Rico does not include income from sources within Puerto Rico, except income received as an employee of the U.S. or any U.S. agency [¶3827].

¶1101   RETURN FORMS

Individual taxpayers file their income tax returns on Form 1040 or, if eligible, a short form (Form 1040A or Form 1040EZ). If you cannot use either of the short forms, you must use the regular Form 1040 [Reg. Sec. 1.6012-1(a)(6), (7)]. The IRS mails forms to most taxpayers. However, you must file even if no form has been sent to you. You must attach to your return all the withholding statements (Form W-2) received from your employers for the year. The time and place of filing and other details about returns are discussed in Chapter 26.

(a) Filing Form 1040. This is the all-purpose form for individuals. Some taxpayers must use it; others can choose to use one of the more simplified versions as their tax return. You must use Form 1040 if you have taxable income of $50,000 or more, itemize your deductions, or pay self-employment or alternative minimum tax. You generally need to attach additional schedules and forms to your return.

(b) Who May Use Form 1040A. There are several restrictions on who can file this form. For example, your taxable income must be below $50,000 and you cannot itemize deductions. And all of your income must be from wages, salaries, tips, taxable scholarships and fellowships, interest, dividends, unemployment compensation, pensions and annuities, IRA distributions and social security benefits.

(c) Who May Use Form 1040EZ. The less detailed Form 1040EZ is available only to those who meet all of the following conditions: (1) file a single return and claim no dependents; (2) claim no additional standard deduction for being 65 or over or blind; (3) have taxable income of less than $50,000; (4) have only wages, tips and $400 or less of taxable interest; (5) have no dividend income; (6) do not itemize deductions or claim any adjustments to income (e.g., IRA deduction or alimony) or tax credits (e.g., dependent care or earned income credits).

NOTE: Nonresident aliens file Form 1040NR instead of any of the above three forms.

HOW TO FIGURE THE TAX

¶1102   WHAT IS INVOLVED IN THE COMPUTATION

To figure how much tax you owe for 1992, you must know your (a) gross income, (b) deductions for adjusted gross income, (c) adjusted gross income, (d) itemized deductions, (e) standard deduction, (f) personal exemptions and (g) taxable income.

(a) Gross Income. Gross income includes all types of income not expressly exempt from tax (Ch. 2 - 8) [IRC Sec. 61].

(b) Deductions for Adjusted Gross Income. You claim the following expenses as deductions for adjusted gross income [IRC Sec. 62(c)]:

1. Expenses directly incurred in carrying on a trade or business (not as an employee).

2. Reimbursed expenses connected with employment (including those of outside salespersons who are employees) for which the employee provides an adequate accounting to the employer.

3. Certain expenses of performing artists who are employees.

4. A deduction for losses from sales or exchanges of property.

5. Deductions attributable to rents and royalties.

6. Deductions for depreciation and depletion, for a life tenant or income beneficiary of property held in trust, or an heir, legatee or devisee of an estate.

7. Deductions for contributions to self-employment retirement plans.

8. Deductible contributions to individual retirement arrangements.

9. The total taxable amount of lump-sum distributions from retirement plans.

10. Deduction for penalties forfeited because of a premature withdrawal from time savings accounts or deposits.

11. Alimony deductions.

12. Deduction for certain reforestation expenses.

13. Deduction for repayment of supplemental unemployment compensation benefits.

14. Deduction for jury pay turned over to the employer.

(c) Adjusted Gross Income. Adjusted gross income is gross income less the deductions listed above [IRC Sec. 62(a)].

(d) Itemized Deductions. After your deductions for adjusted gross income and your deductions for personal exemptions, you can then claim all other allowable deductible expenses as itemized deductions [IRC Sec. 63(d)]. Itemized deductions include, for example, property taxes and mortgage interest on your home.

Unless you elect to itemize for the tax year, no itemized deductions are allowed [IRC Sec. 63(e)]. You should make the election if you have itemized deductions in excess of the standard deduction.

High-income taxpayers. Some high-income taxpayers may not be able to deduct all their itemized deductions. Total itemized deductions are reduced if your adjusted gross income exceeds $105,250 ($52,625 for married persons filing separately) (¶1900) [IRC Sec. 68].

(e) Standard Deduction. The standard deduction is a flat dollar allowance that can be taken in place of itemized deductions. The allowance amounts are annually adjusted for inflation. The standard deduction for 1992 is as follows [IRC Sec. 63(c)]:

Single persons	$3,600
Heads of households	5,250
Married persons filing jointly	6,000
Surviving spouses	6,000
Married persons filing separately	3,000

An additional standard deduction is allowed if you are elderly and/or blind. In 1992, the additional standard deduction is $700 if you are married and either elderly or blind

($1,400 if you are both elderly and blind). If you are an unmarried individual and either elderly or blind, the additional amount is $900 ($1,800 if you are both). If you are married and file separately, additional amounts are available for your elderly or blind spouse, if your spouse has no gross income and is not another's dependent. Certain individuals cannot claim the standard deduction [IRC Sec. 63(c)(6)]. Included among these are married individuals filing separately whose spouses itemize their deductions, U.S. citizens with excludable income from U.S. possessions, and nonresident aliens.

The 1992 standard deduction of a person who can be claimed as a dependent on another's return (for example, a child) cannot exceed the greater of $600 or the dependent's earned income, plus the additional deduction amount for blind or elderly taxpayers [IRC Sec. 63(c)(5)].

(f) Personal Exemptions. There are two kinds of personal exemptions: (1) personal exemptions for you [¶1111] and your spouse [¶1113] and (2) exemptions for your dependents (¶1115) [IRC Sec. 151].

Exemption phaseout. The deduction for personal and dependency exemptions can be reduced or eliminated for high-income taxpayers (¶ 1112) [IRC Sec. 151(d)].

(g) Taxable Income. If you itemize your deductions, your taxable income is your gross income minus both your itemized deductions and your deduction for personal exemptions. If you do not itemize your deductions, taxable income means your adjusted gross income less both your standard deduction and your deduction for personal exemptions [IRC Sec. 63].

¶1103   STEPS IN FIGURING THE TAX

Here are nine steps to follow in computing a tax bill:

> **OBSERVATION** The income and deduction facts and figures needed for each step are entered on different lines and schedules on the tax return, and in a different order than that given here. The order of steps used here is designed to make it easier to understand the tax computation structure.

(a) Step by Step Procedures. STEP 1. Start with GROSS INCOME. This includes, for example, compensation for services [¶1201]; bonuses and prizes [¶1203]; pensions [Ch. 3]; rent and royalties [¶1232]; dividends [¶1218]; taxable interest [¶1211-1217]; gains from sales and exchanges of property [Ch. 7; 8]; and gross receipts from business [¶2701; 3406]. But it *excludes,* wholly or partially, such items as: interest on certain government obligations [¶1503-1504]; annuities [¶1522-1524]; insurance proceeds [¶1507-1510]; gifts and bequests [¶1518-1519]. You include the income of your spouse, if any, on a joint return.

STEP 2. Subtract DEDUCTIONS FOR ADJUSTED GROSS INCOME from your gross income [Step 1] to get ADJUSTED GROSS INCOME. These deductions include, among others: reimbursed trade or business deductions of an employee [¶2229]; deductions due to rent and royalty property [¶2221]; and losses from the sale or exchange of business or investment property [¶1810; 2400].

STEP 3. Determine ITEMIZED DEDUCTIONS and the STANDARD DEDUCTION.

> **DEDUCTION PHASEOUT** High-income taxpayers may have to reduce their itemized deductions. For a further discussion of this change and a worksheet for figuring the reduction, see ¶1900.

STEP 4. Select the greater of the total of ITEMIZED DEDUCTIONS or the STANDARD DEDUCTION [Step 3].

STEP 5. Determine how many PERSONAL EXEMPTIONS can be claimed. These include: one exemption each for (a) you [¶1111]; (b) each person for whom you can claim a dependency exemption [¶1115]; and (c) your spouse, if you file a joint return [¶1113]. If you are married and file separately, you get the exemption for your spouse only if your spouse had no gross income and could not be claimed as the dependent of another.

> **DEDUCTION PHASEOUT** High-income taxpayers may lose personal and dependency exemption deductions. For a further discussion of this change and a worksheet for figuring the phaseout, see ¶1112.

STEP 6. Multiply the number of personal exemptions by $2,300 for 1992 returns.

STEP 7. To determine TAXABLE INCOME, subtract both the deduction for Step 4 and the value of the personal exemptions [Step 6] from your adjusted gross income [Step 2].

STEP 8. Find the amount of TAX from either the tax table [¶1124] or the rate schedules [¶1123].

STEP 9. Subtract CREDITS, if any, from the tax found in Step 8 to figure the net tax payable or overpayment refundable. These include the credits for: prepaid estimated taxes or tax withheld on wages [¶2416; 2500]; earned income [¶2402]; the elderly or disabled [¶2403]; any social security tax overpayment; foreign taxes and taxes of U.S. possessions [¶3801]; child care [¶2401].

(b) Tax Figured by Revenue Service. The computation of tax may be left to the IRS in some instances. The instructions to Forms 1040, 1040A and 1040EZ explain the requirements [IRC Sec. 6014; Reg. Sec. 1.6014-2]. By making the election, you need only complete your return through the line for taxable income and fill in certain other lines, such as tax withholding and estimated tax payments. Some key requirements for making this election: Your income must be derived from only wages, tips, interest, dividends, pensions and annuities; you cannot itemize your deductions; and you cannot be claimed as a dependent on another person's return.[1] In addition, the return must be filed by its due date (without extensions) [Reg. Sec. 1.6014-2(b)].

The IRS will calculate any credit for the elderly or disabled and earned income credit to which you are entitled, provided you supply sufficient information.

Once the Revenue Service figures the tax, it sends you a refund or a bill for additional tax due. There is no interest charge or late payment penalty so long as the bill is paid within 30 days from the notice mailing date (or the tax return due date, if later). A balance of less than $1 need not be paid, and an overpayment of less than $1 is refunded only on application.[2]

Husband and wife who file jointly may have the IRS compute their tax. The tax is the lesser of the tax for a joint return, or (if sufficient information is given) the tax figured as if the spouses filed separately [Reg. Sec. 1.6014-2(d)].

WHAT IS YOUR FILING STATUS?

¶1104   **MARRIED COUPLES**

If you file a joint return, you get the "split-income benefit" reflected in the tax rates. The tax table and tax rate schedules for married persons filing jointly split your total income, and reflect the tax at a lower rate than would apply if you were a single person with the same taxable income who filed individually.

(a) Who May File a Joint Return. The rules for filing as a married couple apply regardless of how much gross income each spouse has during the tax year. You and your spouse may file jointly if, on the last day of the tax year, any one of the following apply [IRC Sec. 6013; Reg. Sec. 1.6013–4(a)(1)]:

- You are married and living as husband and wife. You are considered living together at the end of the tax year even though you or your spouse may be away temporarily due to business, vacation, military service or other special circumstances [Reg. Sec. 1.6012-1(a)(2)(iv)].
- You are living together in a common-law marriage recognized by the state where the marriage began.[1]
- You are married and living apart, but not legally separated under a decree of divorce or separate maintenance.
- You are separated under an interlocutory decree of divorce.[2]

You are not considered single unless the decree is final on or before the last day of the tax year. However, if you filed a joint return and your marriage is later annulled, you must file amended returns as singles. You would still be considered married for tax purposes if you divorced at year-end to avoid tax and then remarried to each other early the next year.[3]

> ➤ **IMPORTANT** If your spouse dies, you may file a joint return for the year of death [IRC Sec. 6013(a)(2)]. You are considered married for the whole year. You may also be entitled to continue to file as if you were still married for the next two years [¶1105]. Beyond that, you may be treated as a head of household with a special tax-favored filing status [¶1106].

If you remarry before the end of the year your spouse dies, you file a joint return with your new spouse. Your deceased spouse's filing status is married filing separately.

U.S. citizens married to nonresident aliens. Generally, if you are married to a nonresident alien at any time during the tax year, you cannot file a joint return [IRC Sec. 6013(a)]. You must file as a married person filing separately[4] unless qualified to file as a head of household [¶1106]. However, if you (a U.S. citizen or resident) are married to a nonresident alien at the end of the tax year, you may file jointly if you elect to be taxed on your world-wide income. An election applies to the tax year for which made and to all subsequent years until terminated. If the election is terminated for any individuals, neither of them can make a new election [IRC Sec. 6013(g),(h)]. If the election is made, certain specific allocations of community property income, as provided in the Code, will not apply [IRC Sec. 879].

Regardless of any foreign community property laws, a couple, both of whom are nonresident aliens, must treat one spouse's earnings or business income as that spouse's income without income allocation [IRC Sec. 879(a)].

(b) Married Persons Filing Separate Returns. You and your spouse may file separate returns, whether or not you both had income. If you file separately, you should each report only your own income, and claim only your own exemptions and deductions on your individual returns.

> ➤ **OBSERVATION** There are a number of situations where you and your spouse may come out tax dollars ahead by filing separate returns rather than a joint return. For example, let's take a look at a high-income couple that is above the $105,250 AGI cap for the itemized deduction limitation ($52,625

for married persons filing separately)[¶1102(d); 1900], where one spouse has substantial miscellaneous itemized deductions.

Example: Mr. Parker has $65,000 of adjusted gross income and $10,000 of itemized deductions, none of which are miscellaneous expenses. Mrs. Parker has $45,000 of adjusted gross income, $4,600 of miscellaneous expenses and $4,000 of other itemized deductions.

If the Parkers file a joint return, only $2,400 ($4,600 less 2% of $110,000 combined AGI) of their miscellaneous itemized deductions can be included with their other itemized deductions. In addition, since their combined AGI exceeds $105,250, the Parkers must reduce their itemized deductions by $142.50 [3% of $4,750 ($110,000 less $105,250 threshold].

Suppose, however, the Parkers file separate returns. *Result:* Mr. Parker's deductions are cut by $371.25 (3% of $65,000 less the $52,625 threshold for married persons filing separately). As for Mrs. Parker, her miscellaneous expenses are only reduced by $900 (2% of $45,000 AGI). Since her AGI falls below the $52,625 threshold, her total deductions are not further reduced.

Payoff: The Parkers save $85 in taxes by filing separately in 1992—even after taking into account the higher tax rates for separate returns.

Community income.
Generally, income that is community property under state law is taxed equally to you and your spouse, and your deductions are similarly divided. However, the tax law disregards community property laws if you and your spouse file separate returns, live apart for the entire year, and don't transfer earned income between one another either directly or indirectly. To qualify, at least one of you must have earned income (such as wages). If the requirements are met, earned income is the income of the spouse who rendered the personal services, while business income is treated as the husband's, unless the wife exercised substantially all management and control. The benefits of community property laws may be disallowed if you acted as if solely entitled to the income and failed to notify your spouse of the nature and amount of the income before the due date of the return. The IRS may also issue regulations to relieve you from liability if you failed to include in income an item of community income, provided that you file a separate return and had no knowledge, nor reason to know, of the unreported community income. As a result, including the community income in your income would be inequitable [IRC Sec. 66].

(c) Married Persons Living Apart.
Both you and your spouse must consent to file a joint return. When one fails to consent, each of you generally must complete a return using the higher, married filing separately rates. However, if you and your spouse are living apart and meet certain tests, you are eligible for some tax relief. You are treated as if you were not married. As such, you can use the more favorable tax rates available to single taxpayers.

> ➤ **TAX SUGGESTION** If you qualify, you most likely also qualify as a head of household [¶1106]. In that case, you should use the lower head-of-household rates, rather than the rates for singles or marrieds filing separately.

To qualify for the special filing status for tax purposes, you must meet all of the following conditions [IRC Sec. 2(c)]:

- You file a separate return.
- You paid more than half the cost to keep up your home.
- Your spouse lived apart from you for the last 6 months of the tax year.
- Your home is the principal residence *for more than half the year* of the child for whom you can claim a dependency deduction. However, a custodial spouse can still qualify as a "married person living apart," even though the noncustodial spouse can claim the exemption for the child.

The requirements of maintaining a household for a dependent relative are substantially the same as described in ¶1106(b),(c).

¶1105   SURVIVING SPOUSE

You can file a joint return for the year your spouse dies [¶1104(a)]. Additional split-income benefits may be available in later years. You get the same split-income benefits as on a joint return for the first two years after the year in which your spouse died, if [IRC Sec. 2(a); Reg. Sec. 1.2-2]:

- You are eligible to file a joint return the year your spouse died; and
- You live with your child, stepchild or foster child for the entire tax year (except for temporary absences), and may claim a dependency exemption for such child [IRC Sec. 152(a)]; and
- You pay over half the household costs (here the same tests apply as found in ¶1106(c) for heads of household); and
- You did not remarry by the end of the tax year.

¶1106   HEAD OF HOUSEHOLD

If you qualify as a head of household, you can compute the tax by using the special rate in the tax table or tax rate schedules. This special rate is available for a tax year only you meet *all* of the following conditions [IRC Sec. 2(b); Reg. Sec. 1.2-2(b)]:

- You must be unmarried on the last day of the tax year [(a) below];
- Your household must be the principal residence for at least one relative for more than half of the tax year [(b) below];
- You must (1) maintain a household and (2) contribute over half the cost of maintaining the home [(c) below];
- You must not be a nonresident alien at any time during the year.

NOTE: If you satisfy these conditions, you do not have to add the income of relatives living in the household to your own, and you can take all your exemptions for dependents.

Background and purpose. An unmarried person required to maintain a home for another person's benefit is likely to have income that is shared with that other person in much the same way a married couple share their income [¶1104]. This, it is believed, justifies the extension of some of the income-splitting benefits to a head of household, and is the reason for a special rate for a head of household.

(a) Marital Status. You are considered unmarried for head of household purposes if [Reg. Sec. 1.2-2(b)(5)]:

- You have never been married; or
- You are a widow or widower whose spouse died before the tax year; or
- You are separated from your spouse under a final decree of divorce or separate maintenance; or
- Your spouse is a nonresident alien; or

- Your spouse did not live in your house during the last 6 months of the tax year, and your child lived in your home for more than half the year.[1]

NOTE: Since you are considered married for the tax year in which your spouse dies, you cannot use the special head of household tax rate. However, you may qualify as a "surviving spouse" [¶1105].

(b) Maintenance of Household for Relative. Generally, you must maintain as your home for more than six months of the year a household in which your children (natural or adopted), their descendants, or your stepchildren (but not their descendants) live; or in which any other relative lives who qualifies you for a dependency exemption (¶1117) [Reg. Sec. 1.2-2(b)(3)]. However, a second alternative eligibility test (explained below) is available when the relative is your parent.

> ➤ **OBSERVATION** In general, the relative must be your dependent. However, a more lenient rule applies when the relative qualifying you for head of household status is your unmarried child (or your child's descendant) or stepchild. The head of household rules do not require that these relatives be your dependent. Thus, an adult unmarried child who lives with a parent can make the parent eligible for head of household status, as long as the parent pays more than half of the household bills.

NOTE: The IRS maintains that the household must be your principal place of abode (i.e., the home you live in most of the time).[2] However, the 4th Circuit has held that a taxpayer need only live in the household with his or her relative "for a substantial part of the time in question."[3] And the 9th Circuit has held that occupancy by a taxpayer need not be actual or physical; a token or implied occupancy may be sufficient.[4] Temporary absences for vacation, sickness or school are disregarded in determining if a related person actually lived in your household [Reg. Sec. 1.2-2(c)].

Parents. To qualify for the head of household status, you need not live in the same household as your parent whom you can claim as a dependent. It is sufficient if your parent lives in a separate household that you maintain by paying over half the maintenance cost for the entire year. A rest home or home for the aged qualifies as a household for this purpose.[5]

Cousins or unrelated persons living in your household do not qualify you as a head of household even if they are your dependents.

Alien spouse. If you are a U.S. citizen or resident alien and married to and living with a nonresident alien, you can use the head of household rates provided a dependent child lives with you (but see ¶1104(a)).[6]

Multiple support agreements. If the relative must qualify as your dependent, that status may not arise from a multiple support agreement [¶1116(d)].

(c) Furnishing Costs of Maintaining Home. You must contribute over half the cost of maintaining the home. These costs include rent, mortgage interest, taxes, property insurance, upkeep and repairs, utility charges, and food consumed in the home. They do not include the cost of clothing, education, medical treatment, vacations, life insurance, transportation, the rental value of the home,[7] or the value of services rendered by you or by a member of the household [Reg. Sec. 1.2-2(d)].

Example 1: Mr. Baker is single. His mother lived with his brother in an apartment, not Baker's home, until her death in September. Of the $7,000 it cost to maintain that home for the year, Baker paid $5,000 and his brother paid $2,000. His brother made no other contribution toward the mother's support. Baker's mother had no income and contributed nothing to the household. Since Baker paid more than half the cost of maintaining the home for his mother until her death, and since she qualifies as his dependent, Baker is entitled to the head of household benefit.

Example 2: Mr. Cain's wife died 5 years ago and he has not remarried. His unmarried son lives with him but does not qualify as his dependent. Since Cain furnishes more than half the cost of maintaining a home for his unmarried son, Cain qualifies as a head of household, even though he may not claim his son as a dependent.

STANDARD DEDUCTION

¶1107   AMOUNT OF STANDARD DEDUCTION

The standard deduction is a flat allowance you can take in place of itemizing your personal deductions. The increase in the standard deduction, coupled with changes to the itemized deduction rules, has reduced the number of individuals who itemize.

The basic standard deduction is determined by the individual's filing status [IRC Sec. 63(c)].

Single persons	$3,600
Heads of households	5,250
Married persons filing jointly	6,000
Surviving spouses	6,000
Married persons filing separately	3,000

➤ **INFLATION ADJUSTMENT** The standard deductions—the basic, the additional and the deduction for dependents—increase annually with the cost of living [IRC Sec. 63(c)(4)].

(a) Additional Standard Deduction. In 1992, an additional standard deduction of $700 is allowed if you are married and either age 65 or over or blind ($1,400 if you are both elderly and blind; $1,400 for joint filers who are both at least age 65). If you are unmarried and either elderly or blind, the 1992 additional amount is $900 ($1,800 if both) [IRC Sec. 63(c)(3),(f)].

For purposes of getting an additional standard deduction, you are considered to be blind if one of the following is met:

- Visual acuity does not exceed 20/200 in the better eye with corrective lenses; or
- The widest diameter of the visual field subtends an angle no greater than 20 degrees [IRC Sec. 63(f)(4)].

In general, you cannot claim an additional standard deduction for a dependent (e.g., a blind child). However, there is an exception for a spouse who files a separate (rather than joint) return. If your elderly/blind spouse can be claimed as a dependent on your return, you can claim the additional standard deduction as well. For this to occur, your elderly or blind spouse must have no gross income and not be a dependent of anyone else [IRC Sec. 63(f)(1)(B),(2)(B)].

(b) Dependent's Standard Deduction. Individuals who can be claimed as a dependent on another taxpayer's return (such as children) must claim a reduced standard deduction. The limitation applies even if that taxpayer does not actually claim the exemption deduction or get any tax benefit on account of it. A dependent's 1992 standard deduction is the greater of $600 or the individual's earned income (to the extent of the individual's basic standard deduction), plus any additional standard deduction amount available if the dependent is blind or elderly [IRC Sec. 63(c)(5)].

Example 1: Bill Smith, a college student, has unearned income (interest and dividends) of $4,000 in 1992. He has no earned income. His parents can claim Bill for a dependency exemption on their return. Bill's standard deduction is limited to $600.

Example 2: Assume the same facts as in Example 1 except that Bill also has $1,000 in wages from a summer job. His standard deduction is limited to his $1,000 earned income.

Example 3: Assume the same facts as in Example 1 except that Bill also has $4,000 in wages. His standard deduction is $3,600, the basic standard deduction for single individuals.

Example 4: Mrs. Brown is age 70. She has $1,600 of interest income and is claimed as a dependent on her son's tax return. Brown's standard deduction shelters $1,500 ($600 plus her $900 additional standard deduction) of the interest income.

(c) Individuals Not Eligible for Standard Deduction.

Certain individuals are not eligible to use the standard deduction. These include [IRC Sec. 63(c)(6)]:

- Married taxpayers filing separately if either spouse itemizes deductions.
- Nonresident aliens.
- U.S. citizens with excludable income from U.S. possessions.
- Individuals who file returns for periods of less than 12 months because of accounting period changes.
- Estates or trusts, common trust funds, or partnerships.

Married taxpayers who file separate returns must either both itemize or both take the standard deduction [IRC Sec. 63(c)(6)(A)].

PERSONAL EXEMPTIONS

¶1111   AMOUNT OF YOUR PERSONAL EXEMPTIONS

The personal exemption amount is $2,300 in 1992. This amount is adjusted for inflation each year [IRC Sec. 151(d)(3)]. However, the tax benefit of the personal exemption is phased out for taxpayers with adjusted gross income exceeding specified levels [¶1112].

The number of exemptions you can claim. You can claim an exemption for yourself, your spouse and each person who is your dependent [IRC Sec. 151(b),(c)]. For example, in 1992, if you are married and have two dependent children and a dependent parent, you are entitled to five exemptions equal to $11,500 (five times $2,300), unless your adjusted gross income exceeds certain levels [¶1112].

There is a special rule for dependent taxpayers. No personal exemption amount is allowable on the return of an individual who is eligible to be claimed as a dependent on another taxpayer's return. For example, no exemption can be claimed on the return of your child who is eligible to be claimed for a dependency exemption on your return [IRC Sec. 151(b)(2)]. Note that it doesn't matter whether you actually claim the exemption; your dependent child still loses it.

> ➤ **TAX STRATEGY** If you have been claiming exemptions for your dependents, you should consider whether you wish to have your dependents get the tax savings of the exemptions for themselves instead. To make the shift, you must disqualify yourself from being eligible to claim the dependency exemption. This can be done by giving your former dependent income-producing assets that bring his or her income above $2,300 (except for minor children and students under age 24) or failing to provide more than one-half support.

Short tax year. The personal exemption amount is not ordinarily affected if the return covers less than 12 months. Thus, the deduction on the return for a taxpayer who dies on June 30, 1992, would be $2,300 even though the return covered only half of 1992. The exemption deduction must be prorated, however, in returns for short periods made necessary by a change in accounting period (¶2819) [IRC Sec. 443(c)].

¶1112   PHASEOUT OF PERSONAL EXEMPTIONS

[New tax legislation may affect this subject; see ¶1.]

You get *no* deduction for personal and dependency exemptions if your adjusted gross income exceeds the following level in 1992:

- $280,400 for married persons filing jointly and surviving spouses.
- $254,050 for heads of household.
- $227,750 for single taxpayers.
- $140,200 for married persons filing separately.

If your adjusted gross income falls into one of the following ranges, you are entitled to a *partial* deduction for your personal and dependency exemptions [IRC Sec. 151(d)]:

- $157,900–$280,400 for marrieds filing jointly and surviving spouses.
- $131,550–$254,050 for heads of household.
- $105,250–$227,750 for single taxpayers.
- $78,950–$140,200 for married persons filing separately.

NOTE: These amounts are indexed for inflation.

Partial deduction: The personal and dependency exemptions are phased out gradually over the course of the ranges; the higher your income position in a range, the smaller your deduction. For each $2,500 increment (or fraction thereof) you move along the range, you lose 2% of your total exemptions (married filing separately lose 2% for each $1,250). For 1992, this works out to a deduction loss of $46 per exemption for every $2,500 of extra income in the range.

If your adjusted gross income falls below the ranges, you are entitled to a full deduction for your personal and dependency exemptions.

Exemption Phaseout Worksheet

Line 1. Enter your AGI . . . .   _____

Line 2. Enter: $105,250 if single

$157,900 if married filing jointly or qualifying widow(er)

$78,950 if married filing separately

$131,550 if head of household . . . .   _____

Line 3. Subtract line 2 from line 1 . . . .   _____

Line 4. Divide the amount on line 3 by $2,500

($1,250 if married filing separately).

If the result is not a whole number, increase it

to the next whole number . . . .   _____

Line 5. Multiply the number on line 4 by .02.

Enter the result as a decimal, but not more than 1 . . . .   _____

Line 6. Multiply $2,300 by the number of exemptions you plan to claim . . . .   _____

Line 7. Multiply the amount on line 6 by the decimal on line 5

to get your exemption amount that is phased out and not deductible . . . .   _____

Line 8. Subtract line 7 from line 6. The result is your total

remaining exemption deduction . . . .   _____

Example 1: Mr. and Mrs. Blake have an adjusted gross income on their 1992 joint return of $188,000. They are eligible to take five personal and dependency exemptions for the year, or $11,500 (5 × $2,300). However, since their AGI exceeds the $157,900 threshold for joint return filers, their deduction phaseout for personal exemptions is $2,760 and their deduction for the 5 exemptions is $8,740.

Line 1. AGI $188,000

Line 2. $157,900 threshold since married filing jointly   157,900

Line 3. Subtract line 2 from line 1 . . . . $ 30,100

Line 4.Divide the amount on line 3 by $2,500   12
Line 5.Line 4 × .02 24
Line 6.$2,300 × 5 exemptions   11,500
Line 7.Phaseout amount (line 6 × line 5)   2,760
Line 8.Remaining exemption (subtract line 7 from line 6) . . . . $ 8,740

Example 2: Same facts as in Example 1, except the Blakes have a 1992 adjusted gross income of $223,000. Result: Their deduction phaseout is $5,980 and their deduction for the 5 exemptions is $5,520 ($11,500 less $5,980).

Line 1. AGI $223,000
Line 2. $157,900 threshold since married filing jointly   157,900
Line 3. Subtract line 2 from line 1   65,100
Line 4. Divide the amount on line 3 by $2,500   26
Line 5. Line 4 × .02 52
Line 6. $2,300 × 5 exemptions.   11,500
Line 7. Phaseout amount (line 6 × line 5)   5,980
Line 8. Remaining exemption (subtract line 7 from line 6) . . . . $ 5,520

Example 3: Same facts again, except the Blakes have a 1992 adjusted gross income of $283,000. Result: Their deduction is completely phased out.

Line 1. AGI $283,000
Line 2. $157,900 threshold since married filing jointly   157,900
Line 3. Subtract line 2 from line 1.   125,100
Line 4. Divide the amount on line 3 by $2,500   50
Line 5. Line 4 × .02   1
Line 6. $2,300 × 5 exemptions   11,500
Line 7. Phaseout amount (line 6 × line 5)   11,500
Line 8. Remaining exemption (subtract line 7 from line 6) . . . . $ 0

NOTE: This phaseout rule had been due to expire after 1995. But a new tax law has extended the phaseout one year— through tax years starting before 1997.

➤ **TAX-SAVING IDEA** If you are hit by the exemption phaseout, you may want to lower your adjusted gross income below the threshold amounts. One way, of course, is by investing in tax-free municipals. But your AGI can also be cut, for example, by contributing to your employer's salary reduction plan (such as a 401(k)) and by making deductible contributions to IRAs and Keogh plans.

¶1113   EXEMPTIONS OF MARRIED PERSONS

You and your spouse need not live together for the rules below to apply. You must, however, be married at the close of the tax year or, if one dies, on the date of death. If you are legally divorced or separated under a decree, you are considered single, not married [IRC Sec. 7703]. If you are separated under an interlocutory decree of divorce, you are considered married until the decree becomes final.[1]

(a) If a Joint Return Is Filed. If you and your spouse file a joint return, you get two exemption deductions for 1992 of $2,300 each, or a total of $4,600, subject to the phaseout [¶1112]. But in that case, neither you nor your spouse may be claimed as a dependent by any other person [IRC Sec. 151(b); Reg. Sec. 1.151-1(b)]. If one spouse dies, the other may file a joint return for the year of death [¶1104(a)] and claim an exemption deduction for the deceased spouse, unless the surviving spouse remarries during the year of the spouse's death.

(b) If Only One Spouse Files a Return. If you do not file a joint return and one of you files a separate return, that person may claim two exemptions (one for himself and one for his spouse), but only if the spouse, for the calendar year in which the tax year began, has no gross income and is not a dependent of another [IRC Sec. 151(b); Reg. Sec. 1.151-1(b)].

(c) If Husband and Wife File Separate Returns. If you and your spouse each file a separate return, you are entitled to one exemption for yourself on your return, and your spouse is entitled to one exemption for herself on her return [IRC Sec. 151(b); Reg. Sec. 1.151-1(b)]. Neither of you may use the other's deduction.

Most married couples file joint returns to take advantage of the split-income benefit. If you file separate returns, you may change to a joint return even after the due date of the return, if you pay the tax in full when you file the joint return [¶3602]. Also, if you filed separate returns in one year, you may file a joint return the next year, provided that you are eligible to file jointly for the year in question [¶1104(a)].

If one spouse dies. If your spouse dies during tax year 1992, you can claim one exemption for yourself and one exemption for your spouse on your separate return, if your spouse had no gross income and was not a dependent of another taxpayer. But if you remarry during the same year, you cannot claim an exemption for your deceased spouse.[2] You can, however, claim an exemption for your present spouse, if she has no gross income and is not a dependent of another person.

If your spouse dies during the tax year, and you (the surviving spouse) have no gross income and are not a dependent of another for the year, you may claim two exemptions (one for each of you) on the final separate return filed for your deceased spouse. If, however, each of you has gross income, neither of you is entitled to an exemption for the other, unless you file a joint return [¶3602].

> **Example 1:** George and Amelia are married. Amelia received $1 in interest before she died on September 30, 1992. George gets one $2,300 exemption for himself, but no exemption for Amelia on a separate return. If the conditions for filing a joint return are met, one may be filed, and the exemptions for both George and Amelia may be taken.

Although a widow who remarries in the same calendar year her husband dies cannot claim both husbands on her separate return, she can be claimed twice; once on her deceased husband's separate return and again on her new husband's separate calendar year return, but only if she has no gross income and is not a dependent of another.[3]

> **Example 2:** Laura's husband Charles died on January 31, 1992. Six months later, Laura married Arthur. She had no income or deductions on her own. A $2,300 exemption for Laura is allowed on the separate returns of both Charles and Arthur.

EXEMPTIONS FOR DEPENDENTS

¶1115   DEPENDENCY EXEMPTIONS

The following five tests must be met for a person to qualify you for a dependency exemption:

- Support [¶1116].
- Relationship or member of household [¶1117].
- Gross income [¶1118].
- Joint return [¶1119].
- Citizenship or residency [¶1120].

▶ **DEPENDENT'S NUMBER** As a general rule, when you claim a dependency exemption for someone you must report the dependent's social security number on your return [IRC Sec. 6109(e)]. The penalty for not including the correct number or for listing an incorrect number is $50 per number per return [IRC Sec. 6724(d)(3)]. You apply for a social security number by filing Form SS-5 with the Social Security Administration.

▶ **NUMBERS NEEDED FOR YOUNG DEPENDENTS** A social security number is necessary for dependents who are at least one year old.

Birth or death during the year. If the five tests or conditions are satisfied, the fact that a person was born or died during the year will not affect your right to claim the full exemption. No proration is required. But no exemption is allowed for an unborn or stillborn child.[1]

¶1116   SUPPORT

You must furnish over one-half the total support of the person for the calendar year in which your tax year begins [IRC Sec. 152(a); Reg. Sec. 1.152-1]. There are, however, exceptions covering children of divorced parents [(b) below], students [(c) below], and multiple support agreements [(d) below]. If you and your spouse file separate returns and both contribute to your child's support, the exemption is taken by the one furnishing more than half the support.

Even though you have not actually paid for the support, you may still qualify for the deduction if you (1) take affirmative steps to provide the support, and (2) incur an unconditional obligation to pay for the items of support. But a promise to pay for the support "if and when it is possible to do so" is not enough.[1]

(a) What Is Support. Support includes amounts spent for food, shelter, clothing, medical and dental care, education, church contributions,[2] child care expenses,[3] wedding apparel and receptions,[4] capital items such as a car or T.V. set,[5] and the like, but not the value of services performed for a dependent,[6] nor scholarships received by the dependent student [see (c) below]. Items furnished in the form of property or lodging[7] are measured by their fair market value [Reg. Sec. 1.152-1(a)(2)]. Thus, if you own the house in which the dependent lives, you count the fair rental value of the lodging furnished (which includes the cost of upkeep[8]). If you live rent-free in the dependent's home, you must offset the fair rental value of the lodging furnished against the amounts you spent in support of the dependent.[8] If the dependent lives in his or her own home, its fair rental value is considered support the dependent provides for himself or herself.[8] Premiums for medical care insurance count toward support but not: (1) the benefits themselves; (2) payments for civil damages; (3) services in government medical facilities.[9] Neither Medicare (basic or supplemental) nor Medicaid payments are support items.[10] However, social security benefits paid to a disabled parent's child are contributions to the child's own support.[11]

▶ **SOCIAL SECURITY BENEFITS** Social security retirement benefits count as support to the extent they are used to pay for food, clothing, shelter, medical care and other items of support. On the other hand, Medicare benefits that provide health care do not count as support. By covering expenses that would otherwise count as support, Medicare makes it easier for you to pass the more-than-half support test for an elderly relative.

If the dependent is alive the entire year, the fact that you do not support him or her for the entire year does not affect your right to the exemption.[12]

Example 1: Mr. Malone supports his father for 7 months of the year, at a cost of $5,800, and Malone's sister supports the father for the remaining 5 months at a cost of $5,400. Malone can claim the entire $2,300 exemption for his father's support in 1992. If his sister supported her father for 5 months at a cost of $6,000, she would get the exemption.

If a serviceman is supporting another, the entire amount of support furnished, including any nontaxable allowances for dependents, is counted for this test.[13]

Dependent's income. If dependents have funds of their own from any source, only the amounts they actually spend on their support are matched against the support you furnished to determine if you furnished over one-half the support. For example, social security benefits[14] and state benefit payments based solely on need[15] are treated as contributions to the dependent's own support to the extent the benefits are so used.

Example 2: Mr. Gary's father gets social security of $5,400 a year. This year, the father put $1,000 into a savings account and spent the remaining $4,400 on clothing, entertainment, and the like. Gary contributed $5,000 to the support of his father who had no other income. Gary meets the support test.

Parents treated as a unit. The total support of your parents is presumed to be spent on both equally, unless you prove otherwise.[16]

Example 3: During the year, Mr. Brown's parents received $14,000 total support: $8,000 from his father's social security benefits and $6,000 from Brown. Brown is not considered to have provided more than half the support of either parent, even though he may have actually provided more than half his mother's support. The parents are treated as a unit; the benefits are allocated evenly between the two.

Group support. If you contribute a lump sum for the support of two or more dependents, it is allocated among the dependents on a pro rata basis. If a member of a household contributes more to the support of the household than his or her pro rata share, the difference counts toward the support of the other members of the household in equal amounts.[17]

Community property states. If separate returns are filed in community property states, and the dependent is supported by community funds, either the husband or wife must take the entire exemption.[18]

(b) Children of Divorced or Separated Parents. If you are divorced or separated, special support test rules may apply to your child. But the special rules apply only if: (1) you and your ex-spouse together furnish more than half the child's support; (2) the child is in your or your ex-spouse's custody for more than half the year; and (3) you are divorced, separated under a decree of divorce or separate maintenance, or separated under a written separation agreement, or lived apart at all times during the last six months of the year. These rules do not apply if you file a joint return or the child is the subject of a multiple support agreement [IRC Sec. 152(e); Reg. Sec. 1.152-4]. If you remarry, you can treat support furnished by your new spouse as furnished by you.[19]

Parent with custody. Generally, if you have custody of the child for the greater part of the year (the custodial parent), you are entitled to the exemption [IRC Sec. 152(e)(1)]. It does not matter whether you actually provided more than half the support.

Example 4: Fred and Sally Jones were divorced in 1987. Under the terms of their divorce, Sally has custody of their child for 10 months of the year. Fred has custody for the other 2 months. Fred and Sally provide the child's total support. Sally is considered to have provided more than half the child's support.

If you do not have custody or have it for a lesser period (noncustodial parent), you can claim the exemption in a few circumstances. You can claim the exemption by attaching a declaration that your ex-spouse (the custodial parent) will not claim the exemption, provided your ex-spouse has signed a written declaration to this effect [IRC Sec. 152(e)(2)]. You can also claim the exemption if a multiple support agreement [(d) below] gives it to you [IRC Sec. 152(e)(3)]. The same is true if the exemption is given to you in a divorce decree or agreement executed before 1985 and not modified after 1984, provided you provide at least $600 of support during the year. For this purpose, you count child support payments as a contribution to support, whether or not you actually spent the amounts spent for child support [IRC Sec. 152(e)(4); Reg. Sec. 1.152-4(d)(4)].

(c) Scholarships as Support. If a child, stepchild, adopted child or foster child is a student, a scholarship at an educational institution is not counted in determining if you furnished more than half the support [IRC Sec. 152(d); Reg. Sec. 1.152-1(c)], unless the grant was given in return for the student's promise of future services.[20]

> **Example 5:** Mr. Ben Davis gets $8,000 support from his father and $9,000 in scholarship granted by his university. The terms of the grant require only that he be a third-year medical student in good standing. Ben has no other income. His father can claim Ben as a dependent.

> ► **LIBERAL SUPPORT RULE** Scholarships are nontaxable to the extent they are used for tuition, books, and related expenses. Amounts received for room and board or other purposes are taxable. For purposes of the support test, though, there is no distinction. Neither taxable nor nontaxable scholarships count as support.

Who is a student. Your child is a "student" if, during each of any five calendar months of the calendar year in which your tax year begins, the child (1) is in full-time attendance at an "educational institution," or (2) is taking a full-time course of institutional on-farm training [IRC Sec. 151(c)(4); Reg. Sec. 1.151-3(b)].

An educational institution is one that maintains a regular faculty and curriculum, and normally has a regularly organized body of students in attendance where the educational activities are carried out [IRC Sec. 151(c)(4); Reg. Sec. 1.151-3(c)]. Thus, primary, secondary, preparatory and normal schools, colleges, universities, technical and mechanical schools are covered, but not correspondence schools and on-the-job training.

On-farm training, to qualify, must be supervised by an accredited agent of an educational institution or a state or a political subdivision of a state [IRC Sec. 151(c)(4)(B)].

Night school attendance only is generally not considered full-time attendance. But full-time attendance may include some night attendance related to a full-time course of study [Reg. Sec. 1.151-3(b)].

(d) Multiple Support Agreements. When two or more persons furnish over half the support of an individual, one of the contributing group is entitled to take the dependency exemption if [IRC Sec. 152(c); Reg. Sec. 1.152-3]:

- No one person contributed more than half the dependent's support, and
- Each member of the group, were it not for the support test, would have been entitled to claim the individual as a dependent, and
- The one claiming the deduction gave more than 10% of the dependent's support, and
- Every person (other than the one claiming the exemption) who gave more than 10% of the dependent's support files a written statement on Form 2120 that he or she will not claim the exemption in the same calendar year (or any tax year starting in the calendar year).

(e) High-income Taxpayers. High-income taxpayers can lose the tax savings from dependency exemptions [¶1112].

> ► **TAX-SAVING STRATEGY** If you are affected by the phaseout, you may want to ensure that your dependents claim personal exemption deductions for themselves. For example, you can have your dependents pay at least half of their own expenses. By scaling back on the support you provide,

you can allow your child, elderly parent or some other relative to claim the exemption's full benefit. You can also take the maximum advantage of multiple support agreements. Only individuals eligible to claim a dependency deduction under the multiple support agreement [¶1116(d)] who are not subject to the phaseout (or who are subject to the smallest amount of the phaseout) should claim the dependency deduction.

¶1117   RELATIONSHIP OF DEPENDENT

The person you support must be (a) your relative, or (b) a member of your household.

(a) A Taxpayer's Relatives. The following relations qualify as "relatives" for purposes of the relationship test [IRC Sec. 152(a)]:

- Son, daughter, grandchild, or great-grandchild,
- Stepchild,
- Brother, sister, half brother, half sister, stepbrother or stepsister,
- Parent, grandparent, or great-grandparent,
- Stepmother or stepfather,
- Brother's or sister's son or daughter,
- Father's or mother's brother or sister, and
- Son-in-law, daughter-in-law, father-in-law, mother-in-law, brother-in-law, or sister-in-law.

Adopted children. A legally adopted child, or one placed with you for adoption, is considered a child by blood. (If you claim an exemption for a child placed with you for adoption, you must file a statement with the return giving the child's name, the agency's name and address, and the date you filed the application with the agency.) [IRC Sec. 152(b)(2); Reg. Sec. 1.152-2(c)].

Foster children qualify if they meet the tests in (b) below [IRC Sec. 152(b)(2); Reg. Sec. 1.152-3; 1.152-2].

Cousins do not qualify unless they are members of the household [(b) below].

Spouse's in-laws. The wife of your wife's brother is not your sister-in-law.[1]

Your spouse is never your dependent [IRC Sec. 152(a)(9); Reg. Sec. 1.152-1(b)].[2]

Joint returns. On a joint return, the relationship test is satisfied if the qualifying relationship exists between the person you claim as dependent and *either* you or your spouse [Reg. Sec. 1.152-2(d)].

> **Example:** Taxpayer supported his wife's niece (the daughter of his wife's sister). The niece had her own home. Neither taxpayer nor his wife had legally adopted the wife's niece. If taxpayer and his wife file a joint return, an exemption for support of the wife's niece will be allowed. But if the taxpayer files a separate return he cannot claim an exemption for his support of his wife's niece.[3]

Relationships created by marriage do not end by divorce or the death of a spouse. So, for example, you may continue to claim an exemption for a dependent mother-in-law even after your spouse dies [Reg. Sec. 1.152-2(d)].

(b) Member of Taxpayer's Household. For purposes of the relationship test, a member of your household is someone who, during your entire tax year (or the part of it during which the household member lived), used your home as his principal place of abode [IRC Sec. 152(a)(9)].

Illegal relationships. A person is not a member of your household if the relationship with you is against the law [IRC Sec. 152(b)(5); Reg. Sec. 1.152-1(b)].

¶1118   DEPENDENT'S GROSS INCOME

You cannot generally claim someone as your dependent unless their gross income for the year in which your tax year begins is less than the exemption amount ($2,300 in 1992) [IRC Sec. 151(c)(1)(A)]. This does not apply to your children who are under 19 or students under 24 [(a) below].

Excludable income. In figuring your dependent's gross income, you exclude any type of exempt income. However, tax-exempt income is generally included in determining whether the support test is met [¶1116], if your claimed dependent has used that income for his or her support [Reg. Sec. 1.152-1(a)(2)]. Thus, state aid benefits based solely on your dependent's needs are considered in determining support, to the extent that they are used for the dependent's support.[1] On the other hand, the gross income of a permanently and totally disabled person does not include income attributable to services performed at a sheltered workshop [IRC Sec. 151(c)(5)].

> **Example 1:** John's father earned $950 at odd jobs. He also received $5,200 during the year in social security benefits. He put $300 in the bank, but used the rest for his own support. John paid $6,000 toward his father's support and claims him as a dependent. Since the social security payments are not considered income, the $2,300 gross income test is met. And while the father received a total of $6,150, only $5,850 was used for his support. Therefore, John furnished more than half his father's support.

If the dependent has rental income, the gross rents are included, without deduction for taxes, repairs, etc.[2]

(a) Children Under 19 or Students Under 24. The gross income limitation does not apply if the dependent is your child and (1) is a student who has not reached the age of 24 [¶ 1116(c)], or (2) has not reached age 19 by the end of the calendar year in which your tax year begins [IRC Sec. 151(c)(1); Reg. Sec. 1.151-2(a)].

Your children include a stepson, stepdaughter, adopted son or daughter, or a foster child who is a member of your household [IRC Sec. 152(b)(2); Reg. Sec. 1.151-3; 1.152-2].

> **Example 2:** Phil Smith is a 21-year-old college student. He earned $2,500 from a job and has $400 of investment income. Thus, Phil's gross income exceeds the exemption amount. However, as long as Phil's parents furnished more than half of his support, they are eligible to claim him as a dependent on their tax return.

(b) If the Dependent Files a Return. No exemption is allowed on the return of an individual who is eligible to be claimed for a dependency exemption on another taxpayer's return [IRC Sec. 151(d)(2)]. This applies, for example, to your child who could be claimed on your return. This rule eliminates the "double benefit" allowed under prior law when a dependent child could claim his or her own personal exemption.

> ▶ **OBSERVATION** It doesn't matter whether you actually claim the dependency exemption for your child, or whether you get real tax savings from the exemption [¶1112; 1123]. The key factor is that you had the right to claim your child as a dependent.

> **Example 3:** Mr. and Mrs. Jackson's taxable income is $300,000. They furnish full financial support for their 18-year-old daughter, Joan. The phaseout of personal and dependency exemptions applying to high-income individuals totally eliminates the Jacksons' tax benefit from claiming Joan as a dependent. However, since the Jacksons are eligible to claim Joan as a dependent, she cannot use a personal exemption to shelter her own income from tax.

(c) Medical Dependent. If you cannot claim a dependency exemption for an individual solely on account of the gross income test, you may still be in line for some tax savings on account of the person they help to support. Medical expenses you pay for an individual who passes the dependency exemption support, relationship and citizenship or residency tests can be added to your own for purposes of computing the medical expense deduction. What's more, if a group of taxpayers collectively provides more than half of an individual's support, it can designate one of its members who supplied more than 10% support as being eligible for this tax break [IRC Sec. 213(a); Reg. Sec. 1.213-1(a)(3)(i)].

¶1119   MARRIED DEPENDENTS

You cannot claim an exemption for a married dependent who files a joint return[1] [IRC Sec. 151(c)(2); Reg. Sec. 1.151-2(a)].

> **TAX STRATEGIES** Students and recent graduates who are choosing between a December and January wedding date may be able to give their parents a tax advantage by tying the knot in January. Let's assume your child was a full-time student during at least five months of the year or had gross income of less than the exemption amount, and received more than half support from you and your spouse. You can claim a dependency deduction if the child marries after the end of the year. (Of course, if your income level is high enough to subject them to the phaseout of the dependency exemption [¶1112; 1123], the family can be better off reversing this strategy.) Alternatively, the young married couple can file separate returns. That way, they preserve your dependency exemption even though they have married. Before doing this, however, your family should make sure that filing separate returns will not cost the couple more in taxes than you save.

¶1120   CITIZENS OF FOREIGN COUNTRIES AS DEPENDENTS

To qualify for the exemption, your dependent generally must be a U.S. citizen, or a resident of the U.S., Canada or Mexico at some time during the calendar year in which your tax year begins [IRC Sec. 152(b)(3)]. Children are usually citizens or residents of the same country as their parents.[1] Puerto Rican residents do not qualify unless they are U.S. citizens.

Adopted alien child living abroad. If you are a U.S. citizen living abroad and legally adopt a child who is neither a U.S. citizen nor a resident of the places named above, you may claim the child as a dependent, providing that during the entire tax year your home is the child's principal residence and he or she is a member of your household [IRC Sec. 152(b)(3); Reg. Sec. 1.152-2(a)(2)].

METHODS OF FIGURING THE TAX

¶1123   TAX RATE SCHEDULES

There are three tax rates for individuals: 15%, 28% and 31% [IRC Sec. 1]. However, many high-income taxpayers will pay a top rate of over 31% in 1992.

If you file jointly and have an adjusted gross income of between $157,900 and $280,400 ($105,250 and $227,750 if you are single), you face a phaseout of your personal and dependency exemptions. You lose 2% of your exemptions for every $2,500 your income rises [¶1112]. This is equivalent to an effective increase in the marginal tax rate of 0.5% for each exemption. So if you are within the ranges, you pay a top rate that is 0.5% per exemption higher than those taxpayers above the ranges.

If you are above the exemption phaseout range, you do not necessarily pay a top rate of 31% in 1992. That's because you lose part of your itemized deductions if your adjusted gross income is above $105,250 ($52,625 if you are married filing separately). You must reduce your deductions by an amount equal to 3% of the difference between your adjusted gross income and $105,250 [¶1900]. This, in effect, increases your marginal tax rate by 0.93%. So many high-income taxpayers pay a true top rate of 31.93%—or possibly higher.

Example 1: Mr. and Mrs. Smith have two children. The Smiths' 1992 adjusted gross income is $120,000, and their itemized deductions are 20% of their AGI. The Smiths' marginal rate is 31.93%. Reason: The Smiths are in the 31% tax bracket. But since their AGI exceeds $105,250, they are subject to the itemized deduction reduction, which adds another 0.93% to their marginal rate.

Example 2: Same facts as in Example 1, except the Smiths' 1992 AGI is $200,000. The Smiths' marginal rate is 33.93%. Reason: The Smiths are in the 31% bracket and subject to the 0.93% increase for the itemized deduction reduction. But now since the Smiths' AGI also exceeds $157,900, they are subject to the exemption phaseout. That adds another 2% to their marginal rate—0.5% × 4 exemptions.

Example 3: Same facts as in Example 1, except the Smiths' 1992 AGI is $285,000. The Smiths' marginal rate is 31.93%. Reason: Their marginal rate drops because their exemption phaseout is complete once their AGI exceeds $280,400.

The tax rate schedules for 1992 follow:

Married Taxpayers Filing Joint Returns and Surviving Spouses

If taxable income is:		The tax is:
Over—	but not over—	
$ 0	$35,800	15% of taxable income
$35,800	86,500	$ 5,370 + 28% of excess over $35,800
$86,500	——	$19,566 + 31% of excess over $86,500

Heads of Households

If taxable income is:		The tax is:
Over—	but not over—	
$ 0	$28,750	15% of taxable income
$28,750	74,150	$ 4,312.50 + 28% of excess over $28,750
$74,150	——	$17,024.50 + 31% of excess over $74,150

Single Taxpayers

If taxable income is:		The tax is:
Over—	but not over—	
$ 0	$21,450	15% of taxable income
$21,450	51,900	$ 3,217.50 + 28% of excess over $21,450
$51,900	——	$11,743.50 + 31% of excess over $51,900

Married Individuals Filing Separate Returns

If taxable income is:		The tax is:
Over—	but not over—	
$ 0	$17,900	15% of taxable income
$17,900	43,250	$2,685 + 28% of excess over $17,900
$43,250	——	$9,783 + 31% of excess over $43,250

Here's a look at how taxpayers figure their 1992 tax liability, applying the rules and tax rate schedules.

Example 4: Mr. and Mrs. Green's joint return for 1992 shows a taxable income of $88,000. Their tax liability is $20,031—$19,566 + $465 [31% of $1,500 ($88,000 less $86,500)].

Example 5: In 1992, Mr. and Mrs. Drake have an adjusted gross income of $120,000. Their itemized deductions for mortgage interest and taxes total $9,000. They are entitled to 2 exemptions. The Drakes compute their tax liability as follows:

Adjusted gross income			$120,000
Less: Itemized deductions	$9,000		
Reduction [3% of $14,100 ($120,000 less $105,900)]	423	$8,577	
Personal exemptions (2 × $2,300)		4,600	13,177
Taxable income			$106,823
Tax liability (Rate schedule—Joint return)			$ 25,866

Example 6: Bob Enfield has an adjusted gross income of $157,000. He fully supports his mother for whom he claims a dependency exemption. He uses the standard deduction to compute his tax liability as follows:

Adjusted gross income		$157,000
Less: Standard deduction	$5,250	
Personal exemption ($4,600 less $920)	3,680	8,930
Taxable income		$148,070
Tax liability (Rate schedule—Head of household)		$ 39,940

Since Enfield's adjusted gross income exceeds the $131,550 threshold amount for a head of household filer, he must reduce his personal and dependency exemption deduction by $920, figured as follows:

$$\$157,000 \text{ less } \$131,550/\$2,500 \times 2\% \times \$4,600 = \$920$$

¶1124   USING THE TAX TABLE

The Revenue Service will prepare tax tables that reflect the tax liability of an individual based on taxable income of up to $100,000. Higher-income taxpayers must use the rate schedules.

How to use the tax table. The following illustrates how to find your tax by using the 1992 tax table.

Sample Tax Table for 1992

At least	But less than	Single	Married filing jointly	Married filing separately	Head of a household
47,000	47,050	10,379	8,513	10,953	9,430
47,050	47,100	10,393	8,527	10,969	9,444
47,100	47,150	10,407	8,541	10,984	9,458
47,150	47,200	10,421	8,555	11,000	9,472

Example: Mr. and Mrs. Henry file jointly. Their taxable income is $47,132. To determine their tax from the table: (1) Find the $47,100—$47,150 income line; (2) find the column for married filing jointly; (3) read down the column. Note that the amount shown where the income line and filing status columns meet is $8,541. This is the Henrys' tax.

¶1125   INFLATION ADJUSTMENTS

The rate structure is adjusted annually. The inflation adjustment applies to the breakpoint between the 15%, 28% and 31% brackets. Generally, inflation adjustments that are not a multiple of $50 are rounded down to the nearest lowest multiple of $50. For married taxpayers filing separately, inflation adjustments (to the rate structure and personal exemption) that are not a multiple of $25 are rounded down to the next lowest multiple of $25 [IRC Sec. 1(f)].

Footnotes to Chapter 1

(For your added convenience, in brackets [] with the footnotes below, you will find citations to related paragraphs in the "RIA United States Tax Reporter"(USTR), "CCH Federal Tax Reporter"(CCH) and "RIA Federal Tax Coordinator 2d"(FTC) multi-volume services.)

FOOTNOTE ¶ 1100 [USTR ¶ 60,124; CCH ¶ 36,450; FTC ¶ S-1700].

FOOTNOTE ¶ 1101 [USTR ¶ 60,124; CCH ¶ 36,450; FTC ¶ A-1714].

FOOTNOTE ¶ 1102 [USTR ¶ 634; CCH ¶ 5504; 6005; 6023; 8005; FTC ¶ A-1000].

FOOTNOTE ¶ 1103 [USTR ¶ 634; CCH ¶ 5504; 6005; 6023; 8005; FTC ¶ A-1000].

(1) Treas. Dept. booklet "Your Federal Income Tax" (1991 Ed.), p. 180.

(2) Treas. Dept. booklet "Your Federal Income Tax" (1991 Ed.), p. 12.

FOOTNOTE ¶ 1104 [USTR ¶ 14.03; 24; CCH ¶ 36,450; 36,471; FTC-A-1500].

(1) Rev. Rul. 58-66, 1958-1 CB 60.

(2) Comm. v. Eccles, 208 F2d 796, 45 AFTR 34; W. G. Oster, 237 F2d 501, 50 AFTR 314; Rev. Rul. 57-368, 1957-2 CB 896.

(3) Rev. Rul. 76-255 (IR-1632), 1976-2 CB 40.

(4) Hoyle, ¶ 70,172 PH Memo TC; Schinasi, 53 TC 382; Rev. Rul. 74-370, 1974-2 CB 7.

FOOTNOTE ¶ 1105 [USTR ¶ 24.02; CCH ¶ 3230; FTC ¶ A-1700].

FOOTNOTE ¶ 1106 [USTR ¶ 14.04; CCH ¶ 3240; FTC ¶ A-1400].

(1) Treas. Dept. booklet "Your Federal Income Tax" (1991 Ed.), p. 17.

(2) Rev. Rul. 72-43, 1972-1 CB 4.

(3) Muse v. U.S., 26 AFTR 2d 70-5771, 434 F2d 349.

(4) Smith v. Comm., 13 AFTR 2d 1633, 332 F2d 671.

(5) Rev. Rul. 70-279, 1970-1 CB 1; Robinson, 25 AFTR 2d 70-807.

(6) Rev. Rul. 55-711, 1955-2 CB 13; Rev. Rul. 74-370, 1974-2 CB 7.

(7) Treas. Dept. booklet "Your Federal Income Tax" (1991 Ed.), p. 18.

FOOTNOTE ¶ 1107 [USTR ¶ 634; CCH ¶ 6023; FTC ¶ A-2800].

FOOTNOTE ¶ 1111 [USTR ¶ 1514; CCH ¶ 8005; FTC ¶ A-3500].

FOOTNOTE ¶ 1112 [USTR ¶ 1514; CCH ¶ 8005; FTC ¶ A-3500].

FOOTNOTE ¶ 1113 [USTR ¶ 1514; CCH ¶ 8005; FTC ¶A-1600].

(1) Rev. Rul. 57-368, 1957-1 CB 896.

(2) Rev. Rul. 71-158, 1971-1 CB 50.

(3) Rev. Rul. 71-159, 1971-1 CB 50.

FOOTNOTE ¶ 1115 [USTR ¶ 1524; CCH ¶ 8006; FTC ¶ A-3600].

(1) Treas. Dept. booklet "Your Federal Income Tax" (1991 Ed.), p. 19.

FOOTNOTE ¶ 1116 [USTR ¶ 1524; CCH ¶ 8006; FTC ¶ A-3700].

(1) Rev. Rul. 58-404, 1958-2 CB 56; Rev. Rul. 67-61, 1967-1 CB 27.

(2) Rev. Rul. 58-67, 1958-1 CB 62.

(3) Lustig v. Comm., 5 AFTR 2d 657, 274 F2d 448.

(4) Rev. Rul. 76-184, 1976-1 CB 44.

(5) Rev. Rul. 77-282, 1977-2 CB 52.

(6) Markarian v. Comm., 16 AFTR 2d 5785, 352 F2d 870.

(7) Rev. Rul. 58-302, 1958-1 CB 62.

(8) Treas. Dept. booklet "Your Federal Income Tax" (1991 Ed.), p. 22.

(9) Rev. Rul. 64-223, 1964-2 CB 50.

(10) Rev. Rul. 79-173, 1979-1 CB 86; Alfred Turecamo, 554 F2d 564, 39 AFTR 2d 77-1487; Mary E. Archer, 73 TC 963.

(11) Rev. Rul. 74-543, 1974-2 CB 39.

(12) Scott, ¶ 50, 248 PH Memo TC.

(13) Rev. Rul. 70-87, 1970-1 CB 29.

(14) Rev. Rul. 57-344, 1957-2 CB 112; Rev. Rul. 58-419, 1958-2 CB 57.

(15) Rev. Rul. 71-468, 1971-2 CB 115.

(16) Abel, ¶ 62,192 PH Memo TC; Rev. Rul. 72-591, 1972-2 CB 84.

(17) Rev. Rul. 64-222, 1964-2 CB 47.

(18) Treas. Dept. booklet "Federal Tax Information on Community Property" (1991 Ed.), p. 3.

(19) Rev. Rul. 73-175, 1973-1 CB 58.

(20) Rev. Rul. 58-403, 1958-2 CB 49.

FOOTNOTE ¶ 1117 [USTR ¶ 1524; CCH ¶ 8006; FTC ¶ A-3606].

(1) Rev. Rul. 71-72, 1971-1 CB 49.

(2) See also Dewsbury v. U.S., 146 F. Supp. 467, 50 AFTR 955.

(3) McCann, 12 TC 239.

FOOTNOTE ¶ 1118 [USTR ¶ 1524; CCH ¶ 8006; FTC ¶ A-3616].

(1) Rev. Rul. 71-468, 1971-2 CB 115.

(2) Treas. Dept. booklet "Your Federal Income Tax" (1991 Ed.), p. 20.

FOOTNOTE ¶ 1119 [USTR ¶ 1524; CCH ¶ 8006; FTC ¶ A-3607].

(1) Rev. Rul. 54-567, 1954-2 CB 108; Rev. Rul. 65-34, 1965-1 CB 86.

FOOTNOTE ¶ 1120 [USTR ¶ 1524; CCH ¶ 8006; FTC ¶ A-3623].

(1) Treas. Dept. booklet "Your Federal Income Tax" (1991 Ed.), p. 20.

FOOTNOTE ¶ 1123 [USTR ¶ 14; CCH ¶ 3170; FTC ¶ A-1002].

FOOTNOTE ¶ 1124 [USTR ¶ 14; CCH ¶ 3170; FTC ¶ A-1100].

FOOTNOTE ¶ 1125 [USTR ¶ 14; CCH ¶ 3170; FTC ¶ A-1103].

CHAPTER 2

GROSS INCOME—INCLUSIONS

INCOME SUBJECT TO TAX

"Gross income" is what the tax law calls the total income subject to income tax. It includes all types of income not expressly exempt from tax. This chapter covers major categories of income: compensation for services, interest, dividends, rents and royalties. Gross income is the starting point to find the amount of income tax you owe.

¶1200   **WHAT IS GROSS INCOME**

(a) General Rule. Your "gross income" includes all items of income except those specifically excluded by statute, such as municipal bond interest, life insurance proceeds and gifts [See Ch. 5]. It includes pay for your personal and professional services, many fringe benefits, business income, profits from sales of and dealings in your property, interest, rent, dividends and gains, profits and income derived from any source whatever unless exempt from tax by law [IRC Sec. 61(a); Reg. Sec. 1.61-1]. Your income may be realized in the form of services, meals, accommodations, stock or other property, as well as in cash. You must report income other than cash at the fair market value of the goods or services you received. Fair market value is the price at which the property would change hands between a willing buyer and a willing seller, neither being required to buy or sell, and both having reasonable knowledge of the relevant facts.

> **Example:** Mr. Sloan owns an apartment building. He received janitorial services from Mr. Daley in return for allowing Daley to use his apartment rent-free. Sloan must include in income the janitorial services' fair market value, and Daley must include the fair rental value of the apartment.

(b) To Whom Income Is Taxable. Salaries and other forms of pay for services generally are income to the person who performs the services. Income from property and gain from the sale of property generally are income to the property's owner. However, as to a husband and wife, the income-splitting benefits on a joint return have the effect of taxing the income as if one-half belonged to each. There are other important exceptions that are subject to special rules, such as income from partnerships and from estates and trusts.

> ➤ **INCOME-SHIFTING STRATEGIES** You can cut your overall tax bills by moving income out of your high tax bracket and into the lower brackets of other family members. A popular method of doing this is by making gifts of income-producing property to your children or other relatives you help to support or intend to have inherit your assets. The gifts can be made outright or in trust or by giving out interests in a family partnership or corporation.

If you merely receive physical possession of income belonging to another, you are not taxed on it.[1] If you receive it as an agent, it is taxable to your principal when you receive it.[2] However, if you really own the income, you cannot escape being taxed on it by having it paid to another party.

(c) Title in Which Property Is Held. If you and your spouse file a joint return, the problem of who is entitled to the income from property held by you as tenants by the entirety (a form of joint ownership by a husband and wife) is of little importance, because of the split-income benefits available on the joint return. However, if you file separate returns, applicable state law controls who is taxed on the income. In most states, you can no longer claim an exclusive right to the income from property owned under a tenancy by the entirety.

When you and another person hold property as joint tenants or as tenants in common, state law determines who is taxed on the income from the property.[3] In most cases, the income is divided equally among you and the other tenants. If you sell the property, the sale price is allocated in equal amounts to the tenants. As a practical matter, though, banks and other such payors will use the social security number of only the first person listed on a joint return when reporting investment earnings to the Revenue Service on Form 1099.

Community property income. If you and your spouse live in a state that has the community property system of ownership for marital property (Arizona, California, Idaho, Louisiana, Nevada, New Mexico, Texas, Washington or Wisconsin, which is considered a community property state for federal income tax purposes), you may each report one-half the community property income on separate returns.[4] Each state has its own rules for determining whether income is community income or separate income. Generally, however, income earned by you and your spouse through your efforts or investments during your marriage is community income. Likewise, income from property acquired during marriage by either you, your spouse or both (except property acquired by gift, bequest, devise or inheritance) is generally community income. Property acquired by either of you before marriage is separate property.

For income tax purposes, the rules for community income are important only when *separate* returns are filed by you and your spouse in a community property state. If you file a joint return, you get the benefit of income splitting.

(d) Income From Illegal Activities. Income from an illegal business,[5] swindling operations[6] or extortion[7] is taxable. Proceeds of embezzlement are taxable.[8]

COMPENSATION, PRIZES AND AWARDS AND PENSIONS

¶1201   TAXABILITY OF COMPENSATION

All pay for your personal services must be included in your gross income [IRC Sec. 61(a); Reg. Sec. 1.61-2]. If you are an employee, the amount of compensation you include in your gross income is generally the total amount *before payroll deductions* by your employer for such items as withheld taxes, U.S. Savings Bond purchases and union dues. However, your gross income does not include payroll deductions that are excluded from tax, such as your pre-tax contributions to your Sec. 401(k) plan and reimbursements for business expenses where you have adequately accounted to your employers.

What your compensation is called, how it is figured and the form of payment are immaterial. The fact that your services are merely part-time, casual, seasonal or temporary is also immaterial.

Taxable

Wages, salaries, commissions on sales or on insurance premiums (including commissions on life insurance on the agent's own life[1] and on the lives of his children[2]); commissions on real estate bought for salesman's own account;[3] compensation received in form of property (stocks, bonds or notes).

Fees, such as marriage fees, baptismal offerings, sums received for saying masses for the dead, and other contributions received by a clergyman, evangelist or religious worker for services rendered [Reg. Sec. 1.61-2], directors' fees, fees for serving on a jury (but not mileage reimbursement payments).[4]

Tips. If taxpayers in certain occupations, such as taxicab operators or waiters, fail to report tips, the IRS can estimate the amount based on a percentage (usually 10 to 15%) of the gross fares or table receipts.[5] For withholding, see Ch. 15.

Financial counseling fees paid by corporations for the benefit of their executives.[6]

Employer-provided transportation. Employer-provided automobiles or air transportation are treated as fringe benefits and are generally taxable. Their taxable value is provided under the regulations [Temp. Reg. Sec. 1.61-2T]. Transit passes or tokens of no more than $21 per month, provided to employees, are excludable from income [Reg. Sec. 1.132-6(d)(1)].

Golden parachute payments. Taxable compensation includes payments made, under an agreement with the corporation, to officers, shareholders and other similar "disqualified individuals" contingent on a change in corporate control. If these payments exceed an amount considered to be reasonable, the excess over reasonable compensation is subject to a nondeductible 20% excise tax (as well as being nondeductible for the corporation). Reasonable compensation generally is limited to three times the average annualized compensation of the individual over the five-year period preceding the change in control (¶2217) [IRC Sec. 280G; 4999].

Nontaxable

Car pool receipts for transporting car pool members to and from work, to the extent they do not exceed the expenses (repairs, gasoline, etc.), are not taxable.

Donated services. Value of services donated to an exempt charitable organization is generally not taxable to the person performing them. However, if by agreement, Moore renders services for Gold and Gold pays the compensation to an exempt charity instead of to Moore, the amount paid is taxable to Moore [Reg. Sec. 1.61-2(c)].

Group-term life insurance. Premiums paid by an employer for group-term life insurance coverage up to $50,000 are generally not taxable to the employee [¶1407].

Reimbursement of job-related expenses. In general, you do not report reimbursements of job-related expenses on your tax return if they are provided under an accountable plan [¶1943]. If the reimbursements are not provided under an accountable plan, you must report the reimbursements on your return. Then you can claim a deduction for these expenses, but only to the extent they and your other miscellaneous itemized deductions exceed 2% of your adjusted gross income. Unreimbursed employee business expenses are deductible only to the extent they exceed 2% of your adjusted gross income.

¶1202   COMPENSATION DISTINGUISHED FROM GIFT

The tax law specifically excludes gifts from gross income. However, it also states that amounts transferred by your employer to or for your benefit cannot come under this exclusion [IRC Sec. 102(c)]. Such transfers may, though, qualify under the special, narrower exclusions for employee achievement awards or de minimis fringes [¶1418; 1423].

¶1203   PRIZES AND AWARDS

Generally, you must pay tax on your contest winnings, whether you participated in a TV quiz show or a sales contest [IRC Sec. 74]. However, there are three categories of prizes and awards that are excludable: qualified scholarships and awards given for certain kinds of recognition and employee achievement.

> ➤ **OBSERVATION** If you make arrangement before you receive an award or prize, it may be possible to split the proceeds among members of your family to reduce taxes.

Recognition awards. Recognition awards you receive primarily for your religious, charitable, scientific, educational, artistic, literary or civic achievement are not taxable, if [IRC Sec. 74(b); Reg. Sec. 1.74-1; Prop. Reg. Sec. 1.74-1]:

- You were selected without action on your part to enter the contest or to submit work in the proceeding; and
- You did not have to perform substantial future services as a condition to receiving the prize and awards; and
- You "designate," in writing, within 45 days of the date the item was granted, that the prize or award be transferred by the payor to a governmental unit or tax-exempt charitable organization. (For a cash award, the designation must occur before you spend, deposit or otherwise invest the funds.) Neither your employer nor you may claim a charitable contribution deduction.

Example: Dr. Dalton was awarded $10,000 for her medical research. She did not enter a contest for the award, and Dalton designates that the funds are to go to the American Heart Association. Result: The $10,000 is excluded from her income.

NOTE: Dalton may be better off qualifying for the exclusion instead of taking the $10,000 into income and then claiming an offsetting charitable contribution deduction. Here's why: (1) Some personal itemized deductions (e.g., medical and miscellaneous expenses) have a percentage-of-adjusted gross income floor [¶1931; 1942]. By excluding the $10,000, she increases her deduction for those items. (2) There are percentage-of-adjusted gross income ceilings on the charitable contribution deduction [¶1919]. The exclusion route helps her avoid running up against them.

For qualified scholarships, see ¶1525; for employee achievement awards, see ¶1418.

¶1204   PENSIONS AND EMPLOYEE DEATH PAYMENTS

[New tax legislation may affect this subject; see ¶1.]

Pensions and retirement allowances generally are taxable. Usually, if you did not contribute to the cost of the pension, and were not taxable on your employer's contributions, you must include the full amount of the pension in your gross income [IRC Sec. 61(a)(11); Reg. Sec. 1.61-11]. Amounts you receive under employee annuity, pension or profit-sharing plans may not be fully taxable [Chapter 3; ¶1524].

Payments to widow. Amounts paid by an employer to you as the survivor of a deceased employee are taxable as compensation for past services of the deceased employee if the employer was required to make the payments.[1] Voluntary payments for past services are taxable unless a gift was intended.[2]

(a) Employee Death Benefits. Payments of up to $5,000 made by or for an employer to you as a deceased employee's beneficiary (or the deceased employee's estate) on account of the employee's death can be excluded. It makes no difference whether the payments represent compensation or a gift, or whether the employer is legally obligated to make the payments [IRC Sec. 101(b)(1); Reg. Sec. 1.101-2]. The death benefit exclusion also applies to self-employeds, but only for distributions under qualified pensions, etc., and from tax-sheltered annuities [IRC Sec. 101(b)(3)].

If excludable death benefits are held by an insurer or the employer under an agreement to pay interest, the interest payments are taxable [IRC Sec. 101(c); Reg. Sec. 1.101-3].

If you are a surviving annuitant under a joint and survivor's annuity contract, you get no exclusion if the employee received, or was entitled to receive, any annuity before his or her death [IRC Sec. 101(b)(2)(C); Reg. Sec. 1.101-2(e)].

More than one beneficiary. If the payments exceed $5,000 and are made to more than one beneficiary of the employee, the nontaxable amount is allocated among the beneficiaries [Reg. Sec. 1.101-2(c)].

> **Example 1:** One beneficiary who receives $8,000 excludes $5,000 from his gross income and is taxed on $3,000. If there are 4 beneficiaries and each receives $2,000, $1,250 will be excluded from the return of each and $750 taxed to each.

More than one employer. The total exclusion cannot exceed $5,000, even if payments are made by more than one employer [IRC Sec. 101(b)(2)(A); Reg. Sec. 1.101-2(a)(3)]. There is a separate exclusion, however, for each employee.

> **Example 2:** A decedent had two jobs. Each employer provided a $4,000 death benefit. The beneficiary can exclude only $5,000. The $3,000 excess is taxable.

> **Example 3:** Assume a mother, as beneficiary of her two sons, received $4,000 under a death benefit contract for each son from one employer. She can exclude the entire $8,000 received.

Vested rights. There is no exclusion for amounts to be paid after death to which the employee had a vested right while living. Exception: The exclusion applies to both vested and unvested rights when a lump-sum distribution is paid to you as the beneficiary within one of your tax years by an exempt pension, profit-sharing or stock bonus trust, or under an annuity contract under a qualified annuity plan [IRC Sec. 101(b)(2)(B)].

> **Example 4:** At the time of his death, Mr. Martin was 90% vested in the qualified profit-sharing plan of the company where he worked. However, the plan provided for 100% vesting upon retirement or death. Martin's balance in the plan was $20,000. Thus, $18,000 of this amount was vested prior to his death, and the remaining $2,000 was unvested. If, for example, the amount was paid over five years, only the $2,000 that had not vested could qualify for the exclusion. However, if the $20,000 had been paid to Martin's widow in a lump sum, $5,000 could be excluded.

The death benefit exclusion also may apply to total distributions payable under annuity contracts purchased by certain tax-exempt employers, even though the employee had vested rights in the contract [IRC Sec. 101(b)(2)(B)(ii)]. The benefit is restricted to annuities purchased by schools and colleges, publicly supported charities and religious organizations. However, there is no exclusion if the public school, college or hospital is an integral part of a local government.[3] The death benefit exclusion applies to the portion of the distribution represented by the employer's contributions that was excluded from the employee's income during the employee's working years [¶1524(e)]. The following formula may be used:

$$\frac{\text{Amount excluded under 20\% rule}}{\text{Employer's total contributions}} \times \text{Total distribution} = \text{Exclusion}$$

The total distribution is the death benefit provided by the employer, less amounts contributed by the employee, and less employer's contributions taxable to the employee. The exclusion cannot exceed $5,000 [IRC Sec. 101(b)(2)(B)].

Death benefits received as an annuity. If a death benefit is received in the form of an annuity, the amount that can be excluded is the value of the annuity at the time the employee died, less the larger of the (1) employee's contribution, or (2) amount of his vested rights in the contract. However, the exclusion cannot be more than $5,000. The excludable amount is treated as consideration paid by the employee for the annuity, and is added to the employee's contributions for the purpose of computing the tax on the annuity payments [IRC Sec. 101(b)(2)(D); Reg. Sec. 1.101-2(e)].

The exclusion applies to an annuity paid under a retired serviceman's survivor benefit plan only if the serviceman dies before reaching normal retirement age [IRC Sec. 101(b)(2)(D)].

(b) Nontaxable Pensions. A retired clergyman is not taxed on payments from his congregation when they were not made under an enforceable agreement, established plan or past practice, but were based on his financial needs and the financial capacity of his congregation. These payments are considered gifts, rather than compensation.[4]

¶1205   COMPENSATION OF GOVERNMENT EMPLOYEES

The pay of all federal, state and municipal officers and employees is taxable [IRC Sec. 61].

¶1206   COMPENSATION OF MEMBERS OF ARMED FORCES

Generally, the pay for service in the armed forces of the United States is fully taxable to officers as well as enlisted personnel, including students at service academies.[1] Monthly allotments chargeable to the serviceman's pay must be included in gross income, but not monthly basic allowances for quarters to dependents.[2]

¶1207   COMPENSATION OTHER THAN CASH

If you are paid in a form other than money, the fair market value of the property or services on the date received is the amount you include in income [Reg. Sec. 1.61-2(d); Reg. Sec.

1.83-1].[1] If it has no fair market value, you report no income. However, you will be taxed on the full amount realized when you sell the property.[2]

Certain employer-paid compensatory benefits are tax-free [Chapter 4].

(a) Insurance Premiums paid by your employer under policies that protect you, your family or estate, are treated as follows:

Ordinary life insurance. Premiums paid by your employer on your life generally are taxable to you if the proceeds are payable to your beneficiaries [Reg. Sec. 1.61-2(d)]. However, when a corporation is the beneficiary and owner of an insurance policy on the life of an employee or stockholder, premiums paid by the corporation are not income to the insured employee.[3]

Group life insurance. Group-permanent life insurance premiums paid by your employer for its you are ordinary income to you and must be reported as wages.[4]

Group-term life insurance. Premiums paid by your employer for coverage up to $50,000 are not taxed to you [¶1407].

Split-dollar life insurance. Under split-dollar life insurance, your employer pays the premiums on your life insurance policy to the extent of the annual increase in the cash surrender value of the policy. You pay the balance. When you die, your employer receives the cash surrender value. The balance is paid to your beneficiaries.

For policies purchased after November 13, 1964, you are taxed on the total value of all the benefits received under the arrangement during the year, including cash dividends or additional life insurance, less any part of the premiums you pay. You may use either the insurance company's current published gross rate for one-year term insurance or the IRS rates (see table below) to figure the taxable value—whichever is lower. Neither your employer, nor your beneficiaries, are taxed on their share of the proceeds of the policy.[5]

1-Year Term Premiums Per $1,000

AGE	PREMIUM	AGE	PREMIUM	AGE	PREMIUM
24	$1.86	38	$3.87	52	$10.79
25	1.93	39	4.14	53	11.69
26	2.02	40	4.42	54	12.67
27	2.11	41	4.73	55	13.74
28	2.20	42	5.07	56	14.91
29	2.31	43	5.44	57	16.18
30	2.43	44	5.85	58	17.56
31	2.57	45	6.30	59	19.08
32	2.70	46	6.78	60	20.73
33	2.86	47	7.32	61	22.53
34	3.02	48	7.89	62	24.50
35	3.21	49	8.53	63	26.63
36	3.41	50	9.22	64	28.98
37	3.63	51	9.97	65	31.51

Example 1: XYZ Corp. buys a $100,000 whole-life policy for employee Smith, age 45. The premium is $2,105. In the first year, XYZ pays $1,900 (cash value) and Smith pays $205. Smith is really paying for $98,100 of coverage since XYZ would recoup the cash value upon his death. The insurer's published rate for $98,100 of one-year term insurance is $630. However, the IRS table indicates a cost of $618.03 (based on a one-year term premium of $6.30 per $1,000). Therefore, the IRS table figure is used to calculate the amount included in Smith's income. Since Smith paid only $205, the excess premium of $413.03 is income to Smith.

Example 2: Same facts as above. In the tenth year (when Smith is 54), the policy has a cash value of $24,000 and pays a dividend of $500. This more than covers the portion of the premium Smith would otherwise have had to pay. Thus, Smith pays nothing that year for his $76,000 of protection. Assuming the IRS table again produces a lower cost of coverage than the insurer's published rates, Smith must include $962.92 in gross income ($12.67 × 76—with no reduction for employee premium payments, since Smith made none).

(b) Salary Received in Tax-Exempt State or Local Bonds is not exempt.[6] The tax is not on the medium of payment, but on wages or salary received.

(c) Guaranteed Annual Wage Plans. Taxability of benefits under guaranteed annual wage plans depends on how the plan is set up and on the nature of your interest in it. It makes no difference whether the plan is union negotiated or is set up by your employer alone.[7] In general, supplemental unemployment benefit (SUB) payments made by your employer directly to former employees are includible in gross income.[8]

Example 3: When the employee had exclusive right of ownership of the account, and also had a nonforfeitable beneficial interest in the cash benefits payable under the plan, the employer's contributions to the plan were taxable to the employee.[9]

Example 4: When the employee's eligibility for benefits depended upon meeting prescribed conditions after termination of the employment relationship (auto industry), the employee was taxed on the benefits actually received, rather than the employer's contributions.[10]

¶1208   COMPENSATION PAID IN STOCK

An employee[1] or independent contractor who receives the employer's corporate stock as compensation must include in income the stock's fair market value at the time of the transfer.[2] Special rules apply to restricted property received as compensation as well as to restricted stock options and plans [Reg. Sec. 1.61-2(d)(4), (5)].

(a) Restricted Property as Compensation. You (particularly if you're an executive) may receive shares of your employer's stock or other property as compensation. Often, this form of compensation carries restrictions under which you may have to forfeit the property if some event occurs. When you (independent contractor as well as employee) receive property for services rendered, its fair market value must be included in income in the year the property is transferable or is not subject to a substantial risk of forfeiture. However, this general rule is limited by various exceptions [IRC Sec. 83].

Example 1: On December 1, 1992, Ace Corp. sells Mr. Eaton, an employee, 100 shares of its stock for $90 a share. The stock is trading at $150 a share at that time. Under the terms of the transfer, Eaton must sell the stock back to Ace for $90 a share if he leaves its employ before December 1, 2002. Eaton's rights in the stock are subject to a substantial risk of forfeiture. So, on December 1, 1992, he realizes no income from the transfer.

Property transferred to you as an employee that is subject to (a) the "insider profit" restriction of the Securities Exchange Act or (b) a restriction on transfer required to comply with the "Pooling of Interest Accounting" rules set forth in Accounting Series Releases Numbered 130 (10/5/72) and 135 (1/18/73), is considered subject to a "substantial risk of forfeiture." The transfer is not taxable to you until the restrictions are removed [IRC Sec. 83(c)(3)].

1. General rule. You are not required to pay taxes on restricted property until the restrictions lapse. The property's fair market value at the time is includible in gross income and is found without regard to any restrictions except one that, by its terms, will never lapse [see (3) below]. The effect of this rule is to tax as ordinary income any appreciation of the property between the time it is received as compensation and the time restrictions lapse. Appreciation in later years is treated as capital gain.

If you give restricted property received as compensation to another person, you remain liable for the taxes when the restrictions lapse. If you sell the restricted property in an arm's-length transaction, you realize income at that time [IRC Sec. 83(a),(c); Reg. Sec. 1.83-1, 1.83-3].

2. Election. You can elect to treat restricted property subject to a substantial risk of forfeiture or nontransferable as compensation when you receive the property. Your income is the excess of fair market value [ignoring restrictions except those that will never lapse; see (3) below] over any amount you paid for the property. Any later appreciation of the property would be treated as capital gain. However, if you make the election and the property is later forfeited, you get neither a refund nor a deduction [IRC Sec. 83(b); Reg. Sec. 1.83-2]. You could, however, claim a loss deduction for any excess of your cost for the property over any amount realized at the time of forfeiture or premature sale.

> **Example 2:** Same facts as in Example 1. If Eaton makes the election, he is treated as having received $6,000 of compensation ($150 value less $90 purchase price times 100 shares) on December 1, 1992. Eaton's basis for determining capital gain or loss when he later sells the stock is $150 per share.

> ➤ **TAX STRATEGY** If you paid the full fair market value for shares of your company's stock, you should make the election. Reason: You owe no current tax on account of the election. However, any appreciation after that date is taxed as capital gain,subject to a top tax rate of 28% [¶1809], compared to the regular top rate of 31%. On the other hand, if you pay less than full fair market value for the shares, your choice isn't that cut and dried. While you may enjoy the capital gains tax break down the road when you sell the shares, you owe tax on the bargain element of the property transfer right away; without the election, tax on this income is deferred.

3. Restrictions that never lapse. Special rules apply to those restrictions that will never lapse (for example, a requirement that you or your estate must sell your stock back to your employer at its then-existing book value). They are the only ones considered in determining the property's fair market value. If, under such a restriction, the restricted property can only be sold at a formula price, then the formula price is treated as the property's fair market value unless the IRS proves a higher value. If the restriction is later cancelled, you have compensation income when the cancellation occurs on the excess of the full value over the sum of the restricted value at that time and any consideration paid for cancellation. However, this does not apply if you can show that the cancellation was not compensatory and not treated as such by your employer [IRC Sec. 83(d); Reg. Sec. 1.83-5].

(b) Employee Stock Options. An employee stock option is essentially an offer by a corporation to sell stock to its employees at a bargain price. You do not become obligated to pay the purchase price until you elect to exercise the option. You have taxable income if you receive nonstatutory options to buy stock (or other property) that has a readily ascertainable fair market value [Reg. Sec. 1.83-7]. You do not pay tax when you receive options subject to a substantial risk of forfeiture or with no readily ascertainable value. However, if you receive statutory options, special rules generally postpone the tax until the employees sell their stock. Two kinds of statutory stock options are in current use: stock purchase plan options and incentive stock options [IRC Sec. 421, 422, 423].

Background and purpose. Employee stock options are frequently used as incentive devices by corporations who wish to attract new management, to convert their officers into "partners" by giving them a stake in the business, to retain the services of executives who might otherwise leave or to give their employees generally a more direct interest in the success of the corporation.

1. Stock purchase plan options. These are designed to you and other employees to buy stock of your employer corporation, usually at a discount. The plan must be nondiscriminatory and include all employees.

What plans qualify. Only employees owning less than 5% of the stock can participate. Stockholder approval of the plan is required. The plan must not discriminate in favor of officers or highly compensated personnel, but the amount of optioned stock may be proportionate to salary. All employees must be included under the plan, except highly compensated personnel, certain part-time workers and those employed less than two years. The price must be at least 85% of the value of the stock at the time of grant or exercise. If the price under the plan is 85% of the stock's value at the time of exercise, the option may run for five years; otherwise, 27 months. Finally, no more than $25,000 (valued at time of grant) of stock may accrue for purchase in any one year [IRC Sec. 423(b); Reg. Sec. 1.423-2].

The employee receiving the option must be an employee of the granting corporation, its parent or subsidiary continuously from the grant to three months before the option is exercised [IRC Sec. 423(a)(2)].

Tax treatment. You realize no income when you receive or exercise an option granted under a stock purchase plan. You must hold the stock acquired by exercise of the option for at least one year after it was acquired and at least two years after the option is granted, and the option must be at least equal to the stock's fair market value when the option was granted. If the shares are sold before then, any gain is taxed as compensation (ordinary income).

2. Incentive stock options (ISOs) defer tax until the shares of option stock are sold, and turn what would otherwise be compensation (ordinary income) into long-term capital gain, which may be eligible for favorable tax treatment [¶1809].

What options qualify. To qualify as an ISO, the terms of the option must satisfy the following conditions [IRC Sec. 422(b)]:

- The option must be granted under a plan that specifies the number of shares of stock to be issued and the employees or class of employees eligible to receive options. Also, the plan must be approved by the corporation's stockholders within 12 months before or after the plan is adopted.
- The option must be granted within ten years of the date the plan is adopted, or the date the plan is approved by the shareholders, whichever is earlier.
- The option must be exercisable only within ten years of the date it is granted.
- The option price must equal or exceed the fair market value of the stock when the option is granted. However, a good faith effort to accurately value the stock will excuse a failure to meet this requirement [IRC Sec. 422(c)(1)].
- The option must not be transferable other than on death and, during the employee's lifetime, must be exercisable only by the employee.
- The employee must not, immediately before the option is granted, own stock representing more than 10% of the voting power of all classes of stock of the employer corporation or its parent or subsidiary. However, this limitation is waived if the option price is at least 110% of the stock's fair market value when the option is granted and the option must be exercised within five years of the date it is granted [IRC Sec. 422(c)(5)]. To apply the 10% limit, certain attribution rules apply, as they did under prior law [IRC Sec. 424(d)].

- For options granted before 1987, the option must provide that it can't be exercised while any other incentive stock option granted to the employee earlier is still outstanding. An option which hasn't been fully exercised will, even if it's cancelled, be considered as outstanding for the period during which, under its initial terms, it could have been exercised. Incentive stock options granted after 1986 needn't be exercisable in chronological order [Temp. Reg. Sec. 14a.422A-1, Ans. 2(c)].

- An employee should not have more than $100,000 worth of ISOs that are first exercisable during any one calendar year. If the $100,000 ceiling is exceeded, enough of the more recently issued options will lose their ISO status so that the ceiling is met [IRC Sec. 422(d)].

Generally, for options granted after March 2, 1984, the stock's fair market value is determined without regard to any restrictions except those that will never lapse [IRC Sec. 422(c)(7)]. Also, a change in an option's terms to make it nontransferable so that it qualifies as an incentive stock option will be treated as the granting of a new option [IRC Sec. 424(h)].

Incentive stock options may be subject to any condition not inconsistent with the qualification requirements of the options [IRC Sec. 422(c)(4)].

When you exercise an option, you can pay for it with a stock of the corporation granting the option [IRC Sec. 422(c)(4)].

Tax treatment. You have no taxable income when the option is granted or when exercised. If you hold stock bought under the option for more than one year, and more than 2 years pass from the date the option was granted, the excess of the stock's sales price over the amount paid for it (option price) is capital gain, which may be eligible for favorable tax treatment [¶1809]. If both holding periods are not met, the difference between the option price and the stock's fair market value when the option is exercised is ordinary income—taxed in the year the stock is sold. However, this amount may not be more than your gain on the sale. If the sale results in a loss, it is a capital loss, whether or not the holding periods have been met.[1]

Note that at all times from the date the option was granted through a period ending on the day three months before the date of exercise, you must be an employee of the corporation granting the option, its parent or subsidiary, or a corporation, or its parent or subsidiary, that issues or assumes the stock option as a result of a corporate merger, reorganization, and the like. However, a disabled employee has 12 months after leaving employment to exercise the option [IRC Sec. 422(a),(c)(6)].

Example 3: Assume that Employee Jones is granted an incentive option to buy 100 shares of his employer's stock at its current $100 per share value on February 1, 1991. He exercises the option on March 31, 1992 when the stock's value is $110 a share and actually receives the stock on April 14, 1992. He sells the stock when its value is $130 a share.

If Jones sells the stock after April 14, 1993, his $3,000 gain will be capital gain and his employer will not get any deduction. However, if he sells the stock before April 14, 1993, $1,000 of his $3,000 gain will be ordinary income, resulting in a $1,000 deduction for his employer, and the remaining $2,000 will be capital gain.

The bargain element is considered an adjustment for purposes of calculating the alternative minimum tax (AMT) [¶2600 et seq.].

➤ **TAX CONSIDERATION** Corporations get no deduction for the issuance and exercise of ISOs. However, if the employee violates the holding period rule and disqualifies the ISO, the company can deduct the difference between the market price at the time of exercise and the exercise price. This deduction is allowed in the year of the disqualifying sale of the stock (i.e., when the employee is taxed).

NOTE: An employer can designate that an option granted after 1986 is not an ISO—even though the option otherwise meets all the requirements of being an ISO [IRC Sec. 422(b)(6)]. By doing this, the employer gets the deduction described above.

(c) Other Stock Options. When you receive a stock option as compensation, and it does not qualify as an employee stock option, the tax treatment of the option depends on whether it has a readily ascertainable fair market value [Reg. Sec. 1.61-15(a)].

Option without readily ascertainable value. There is no tax when the option is granted but you have taxable compensation on its exercise. This is measured by the difference between the stock's fair market value and the lesser amount you paid for it. However, the restricted property rules apply if the stock received under the option is subject to a restriction which substantially affects its value. Under these rules, tax may be postponed until the restriction lapses ((a) above) [Reg. Sec. 1.421-6(d)].

Option with readily ascertainable value. If an option has a readily ascertainable fair market value, the difference between the option's value and any lesser amount you paid for it is taxable compensation to you when the option is granted [Reg. Sec. 1.61-15, 1.421-6].

A stock option has a readily ascertainable fair market value if it is actively traded on an established market. If there is no market value, a value may be ascertainable by showing that the following conditions exist: (1) you can freely transfer the option; (2) the option is exercisable immediately and in full; (3) the option or property subject to it is not subject to restrictions significantly affecting its value; (4) its fair market value is readily ascertainable [Reg. Sec. 1.421-6(c)(3)(i)].

¶1209   COMPENSATION PAID IN NOTES

Notes you receive in payment for your services are income to the extent of their fair market value (usually the discount value) when received.[1] But a note you receive as additional security or to cover overdue interest, rather than in payment of a debt, does not result in income.[2] If you are paid with a note regarded as good for its face value at maturity, but not bearing interest, you report as income the discounted value of the note. As you receive payments on the note, you must include in income the portion of each payment that represents the proportionate part of the discount originally taken on the entire note [Reg. Sec. 1.61-2(d)(4)].

¶1210   BARGAIN PURCHASES BY EMPLOYEES

If you are an employee or independent contractor and buy property for less than its fair market value from a person for whom you perform services, the difference between the price and its fair market value is included in your gross income. Your basis for the property is increased by the amount of that taxable income [Reg. Sec. 1.61-2(d)(2), 1.83-1]. See also employee discounts and other tax-free fringe benefits, Ch. 4.

Example: R Co. sold to Mr. Conroy, an employee, shares of its stock with a fair market value of $2,000. He paid $1,700. Conroy reports $300 income. The stock's cost to him is $2,000.

INTEREST INCOME

¶1211   INTEREST IN GENERAL

All interest is taxable income unless it is specifically exempt from tax (for example, interest on municipal government bonds, ¶1503). In general, you owe tax when the interest is actually received or credited to your account. However, in some situations, the government imputes taxable interest income before payment is due—or even where the transaction calls for no stated interest payment.

(a) Taxable Interest. This includes interest on corporate bonds, mortgage bonds, notes and bank deposits and interest received from tax-exempt organizations, such as charitable, religious or educational institutions [IRC Sec. 61(a)(4); Reg. Sec. 1.61-7]. Interest is defined as compensation for the use, forbearance or detention of money.[1] When payment on a transaction is deferred, the tax law may deem the seller to have charged interest. Thus, a portion of a deferred payment sales price can be recharacterized as interest, even though the sales contract treats the entire price as payment for the underlying property or services.

Taxable interest includes: Interest on award paid for loss of life (but award itself is not income)[2]; interest on refund of federal tax; interest on legacies (not property received by gift, but income from such property)[3]; interest on life insurance policies paid by reason of the death of the insured; usurious interest[4] unless under state law it is a payment of principal [Reg. Sec. 1.61-7].

Bonds bought "flat." If you buy bonds "flat" (price covers unpaid interest as well as principal), the entire amount is a capital investment. Any accrued interest that is in arrears at the time of purchase is not income and is not taxable when paid later. These payments are returns of capital that reduce the remaining cost basis [Reg. Sec. 1.61-7(c)].

> **Example:** On June 15, Mr. Brown bought for $800 "flat" a bond of Apex Corp. with a face value of $1,000. The bond bore interest at 8%, payable each November 1. At the time of the purchase, $160 of unpaid interest had accrued. On November 1, Apex Corp. paid Brown $240 interest on the bond. The $160 accrued interest that was in arrears is considered to be a return of capital. Thus, Brown reports only $80 of interest on his tax return. The basis of the bond is $640 ($800 less $160).

When payments of the accrued interest exceed your basis in the bonds (as could happen when there is a high risk of the bond issuer defaulting), any further interest payments are capital gain.[5] Capital gains treatment applies, even if it appears certain that the bonds ultimately will be paid in full.[6] However, capital gains treatment does not apply to interest that accrues after the bonds are purchased.[7]

Bonds redeemed before maturity. If bonds are redeemed before the maturity date, future interest paid for the period between the date of redemption and the maturity date is treated not as interest, but as part of the redemption proceeds.[8]

Long-term savings accounts. You must include in income the entire amount of interest credited on your account, even if a forfeiture penalty was imposed on a premature withdrawal. You may, however, deduct the penalty [¶1947].

Tax return tip. If your taxable interest is more than $400 or you claim an interest exclusion under the Education Savings Bond Program [¶1217(b); 2828], you attach Schedule B (Form 1040) or Schedule 1 (Form 1040A) to your return.

(b) Exempt Income. Interest on state and municipal bonds and obligations of U.S. possessions is generally exempt. However, there are two notable exceptions. The interest on private activity bonds (i.e., bonds issued to provide conduit financing for activities other than general governmental operations or governmental owned-and-operated facilities) issued after August 15, 1986, is usually taxable unless the bond qualifies as an exempt facility, qualified mortgage, qualified veterans' mortgage, qualified small issue or qualified student loan bond [IRC Sec. 103(b)(1), 141(e)]. And even if the bond meets these special classifications, it may be subject to the alternative minimum tax (¶2603(b)) [IRC Sec. 57(a)(5)]. Important: The tax exemptions for qualified mortgage bonds and small-issue manufacturing bonds are scheduled to expire after June 30, 1992.

> ➤ **INVESTMENT OPPORTUNITY** If you are not hit by the alternative minimum tax, you can receive fully tax-exempt interest income by investing in so-called AMT bonds. These bonds tend to offer a higher yield than other municipals since they are not tax-free to investors who are subject to the alternative minimum tax.

> **NOTE:** Interest paid on indebtedness incurred to buy tax-exempt certificates is not deductible (¶1905) [IRC Sec. 265].

¶1212   INTEREST ACCRUED ON BONDS SOLD BETWEEN INTEREST DATES

If taxable bonds are sold between interest dates, the accrued interest *to* the date of sale is taxable to the seller; the accrued interest *from* the date of sale is taxable to the buyer.

¶1216   IMPUTED INTEREST INVOLVING INTEREST-FREE AND LOW-INTEREST LOANS

[New tax legislation may affect this subject; see ¶1.]
When you make a below-market loan (i.e., a loan where less than the prevailing federal rate or no interest is charged) to another, income may be imputed to you and the borrower. The amount imputed is what's needed to bring the interest charges up to the applicable federal rate [¶1217(f)]. The loan is recharacterized as a two-step transaction in which: (1) you transfer an amount equal to the foregone interest to the borrower and (2) the borrower retransfers the amount back to you as interest. The amount transferred to the borrower may be a gift, compensation, dividend or capital contribution, depending on the relationship of the parties [IRC Sec. 7872].

(a) Tax Consequences. The income tax consequences of interest-free and low-interest loans depend on the type of loan transaction.

Gifts loans involve gratuitous transfers of the type subject to gift taxes. For example, you probably do not charge interest when you loan money to your children. You are deemed to make a (nondeductible) gift to your child in the amount of the foregone interest and to receive an equivalent amount of interest income. Your child is treated as having received an (income tax-free) gift and used it to pay the phantom interest income to you. Thus, your child may be able to claim an interest deduction equal to the amount of your phantom income.

Compensation loans are made in connection with the performance of services between an employer and employee, independent contractor or contracting party or partnership and partner. For example, your company may loan you money to purchase a home. Your employer is deemed to pay deductible compensation equal to the foregone interest. It is also treated as having received an equal, offsetting amount of interest payments from you for the use of the funds. The phantom compensation is taxable to you. However, the phantom interest payments made by you may provide offsetting deductions.

Dividend loans. In this type of transaction, your corporation lends funds to you as a shareholder at below-market rates. The corporation is deemed to distribute dividends equal to the interest it did not charge and then get the funds back from you in the form of an interest payment. This phantom dividend is taxable to you under the same rules as actual dividend distributions. Corporations cannot deduct dividends they pay out. Therefore, your corporation gets no deduction to offset its interest income. You are taxed on the imputed dividends. However, you are deemed to have made the same amount of interest payments.

Capital contribution loans are made by a shareholder to the corporation. You (the shareholder) are deemed to receive phantom taxable interest payments from your corporation—and then contribute that amount of money to the corporation. Such contributions of capital are not deductible by you. However, your basis in the stock is increased by the amount of the imputed capital contribution. Your corporation gets deductions for the interest payments it's treated as having made. It's not taxed on the phantom contributions.

(b) Exempted Loans. The imputed interest rules do not apply to loans between two parties totaling $10,000 or less, unless (1) for gift loans between individuals, the loans are directly attributable to the acquisition or carrying of income-producing assets or (2) for compensation and shareholder loans, one of the principal purposes of the loans is tax avoidance [IRC Sec. 7872(c)(2), (3)].

There's a ceiling on the amount of interest that can be imputed to gift loans between individuals that do not exceed $100,000. The amount of interest that is deemed to have been transferred between you and the borrower is limited to the borrower's net investment income for the year. If the net investment income is $1,000 or less, then the net investment income is deemed to be zero. The $100,000 exception, though, does not apply if tax avoidance is one of the principal purposes of the loan [IRC Sec. 7872(c),(d); Reg. Sec. 1.7872-8,9].

Continuing care facilities. For loans to a "continuing care facility," generally, the below-market-loan rules do not apply to loan amounts up to $114,100 for 1992[1] made by a taxpayer (and spouse) age 65 or older. A qualified continuing care facility must provide a separate living unit for the taxpayer or his or her spouse for the rest of their lives. Also, the facility must undertake to provide later long-term nursing care without substantial additional cost and meet other requirements. [IRC Sec. 7872(c),(g)].

> **NOTE:** All loans to such facilities made on or before October 11, 1985 are excepted from the below-market loan rules.

(c) Timing of Interest Imputation. For demand loans and gift term loans, the imputed transfer is determined one year at a time [Reg. Sec. 1.7872-6(b)]. Thus, phantom funds are deemed to flow back and forth between the lender and the borrower in equal amounts.

In the case of term loans other than gift loans, the imputed amount for the entire term of the loan is deemed to have been transferred from the lender to the borrower at the time the loan began. The imputed interest is figured using the original issue discount rules [¶1217]. For example, suppose your company makes an interest-free loan to you. Repayment is due in the form of a lump-sum payment five years later. Under the OID rules, the true purchase price would be determined by discounting the balloon payment back five years to the time of sale. The difference between the discounted figure and the balloon payment would be the full imputed amount that is treated as having been transferred from the lender to the borrower. Thus, your company gets a big up-front deduction and you have an equally large amount on which to pay tax.

On the other side of the tax equation, though, the timing is different. The retransfer back from the borrower to the lender is deemed to occur annually. So your phantom interest payments—that can provide offsetting deductions—are spread out over five years. And your company's interest income that offsets its initial deduction is also (fortunately for it) spread out.

Loans that have a stated term, but are also contingent on your future performance of services, are treated as demand loans [IRC Sec. 7872(f)(5)]. Thus, you do not have a bunching of taxable compensation if the loan from your employer is conditioned on future employment with it.

¶1217   ORIGINAL ISSUE DISCOUNT BONDS AND OTHER DEBT INSTRUMENTS

[New tax legislation may affect this subject; see ¶1.]

Complex rules apply to debt instruments when insufficient interest is accrued or sufficient interest is accrued, but it is not paid currently. An amount known as the original issue discount (OID) is spread over the term of the instrument, and a portion of the OID is taxed to the holder as interest income each year (even though no payment is actually received). The OID also affects the amount of gain or loss if the bond is sold before maturity [IRC Sec. 1273].

The OID on a debt instrument is the excess of the stated redemption price at maturity over the issue price. The issue price is: (1) the initial offering price for a publicly offered debt instrument not issued for property, (2) the price paid by the first buyer for other debt instruments not issued for property, (3) the fair market value of publicly traded debt instruments issued for property or (4) in the case of non-traded instruments issued for property (e.g., seller financed sales of property), the stated principal amount, if adequate, or in any other case, the imputed principal amount—see (f) below [IRC Sec. 1273(b), 1274(a)].

> **Example 1:** XYZ Corp. issues bonds for $3,000 that pay no current interest, but have a redemption price of $10,000 in 15 years. The $7,000 difference is original issue discount. Bondholders are taxed on a portion of it during each of the 15 years of the bond's term.

(a) Corporate Bonds. The amount of OID that must be included in income each year (and the gain or loss on sale or redemption) depends on the type of bond and when it was issued:

Corporate bonds issued before July 2, 1982. If you hold a corporate debt instrument issued after May 27, 1969, and before July 2, 1982, you must include a portion of the OID in income on a ratable (i.e., straight-line) basis. This is done for each month (plus fraction of a month) you held the bonds during the year.

Example 2: Mr. King purchased a 15-year original issue discount bond for $2,800 when it was issued on July 1, 1981. The bond has a redemption price of $10,000. Thus, the discount is $7,200. King is taxed on $40 of interest income monthly or $480 for 1992 if he held the bond throughout the year.

You increase your basis in the bond each year by the discount included in gross income [IRC Sec. 1272(b)]. This affects your gain or loss upon sale or if the bond is called before maturity.

Example 3: Same facts as in Example 2, except that King sold the bond on March 31, 1992, for $4,700. Prior to 1992, he had included 126 months of interest—or $5,040—in income. King reports three months of interest—$120—on his 1992 return. That brings his adjusted basis up to $7,960 ($2,800 + $5,040 + $120). The $3,260 difference between the selling price and the adjusted basis is King's loss on the transaction.

➤ **OBSERVATION** There is more likely to be a loss than a gain on a sale using the straight-line method. Reason: You are deemed to receive the same amount of OID—and increases his basis accordingly—for each month you have held the bond. In true economic terms, however, the amount of OID should be smallest in the first month and increase in each succeeding month as the OID compounds. Since this compounding is taken into account in the marketplace (i.e., the value of the bond increases more slowly in the early part of the term than in the later part), the adjusted basis of the bond is likely to exceed the selling price.

If a bond issued after May 27, 1969, and before July 2, 1982, is sold during a month, the monthly portion of discounts is allocated on a daily basis between the seller and the buyer. The buyer continues to include the ratable portion of discounts in income, but reduces the inclusion by the ratable amount of any excess the buyer paid over the seller's basis for the bond [IRC Sec. 1272(b)].

Debt instruments issued after July 1, 1982. If you hold such a debt instrument with OID, you must include in income the sum of the "daily portions" of the OID for each day during the tax year you held the bond [IRC Sec. 1272(a)]. The daily portion is determined by allocating to each day in any "accrual period" its ratable portion of the increase in the "adjusted issue price" during that period (i.e., constant interest method). To find the increase: (1) multiply the bond's adjusted issue price at the start of the accrual period by the yield to maturity (determined on the basis of compounding at the close of each accrual period and adjusted for the length of the period) and (2) subtract the sum of the amounts payable as interest during that period. The adjusted issue price at the start of any accrual period is the sum of the bond's issue price plus the increases in the adjusted issue price for all prior accrual periods. Generally, the accrual period is each six-month period determined by reference to the maturity date and the date 6 months before maturity (or shorter period from the issue date).

Example 4: On January 1, 1992, Mr. Prince purchases a ten-year bond for $4,146 that pays no current interest, but has a $10,000 redemption price. The bond's maturity date is December 31, 2001. Assume the bond's yield to maturity is 9%, using semi-annual compounding (i.e., a six-month accrual period). Thus, Prince is deemed to receive $187 for the first six months ($4,146 × .09 × $^6/_{12}$). His adjusted basis then becomes $4,333, and his interest accrual for the second half of 1992 is $195. Prince's adjusted basis for determining interest accrued during the subsequent period is $4,528.

If the OID bond is sold before maturity at a price that exceeds the issue price plus the daily portions of the OID, the buyer gets an offset. Thus, the daily portion that he must include in income is reduced by the daily portion of such excess purchase price, computed by dividing it by the total number of days beginning with the purchase date through the day before the date of maturity [IRC Sec. 1272(a)]. As a result, the purchasing taxpayer has less interest income than the original holder.

Example 5: Same facts as above. Assume, though, that Prince sells the bond on December 31, 1999, for $8,500. His adjusted basis at that time would be $8,386. Result: Prince would have a $114 gain. And the buyer would reduce the amount of interest he is deemed to receive (using the 9% interest rate) by $57 in each of the two years remaining until maturity.

Exceptions to OID rules. The above OID inclusion rules do not apply to holders of: tax exempt obligations; U.S. savings bonds [(b) below]; short-term obligations (fixed maturity date not more than one year from date of issue); obligations issued by natural persons before March 2, 1984; and loans between natural persons which are not made in the course of the lender's trade or business, are not in excess of $10,000 when combined with prior loans, and do not have tax avoidance as one of its principal purposes [IRC Sec. 1272(a)(2)].

De minimis rule. You can disregard the discount if it is less than one-fourth of 1% (.0025) of the stated redemption price (i.e., $25 per $1,000 of redemption price) at maturity, multiplied by the number of complete years to maturity [IRC Sec. 1273(a)(3)].

> **Example 6:** Mr. Carter bought a ten-year bond with a stated redemption price at maturity of $1,000, issued at $980 and having OID of $20. One-fourth of 1% of $1,000 (the stated redemption price) times ten (number of full years from the date of original issue to maturity) equals $25. Since the $20 discount is less than $25, Carter can disregard the OID.

Tax-exempt OID bonds. The OID on obligations issued by a state or municipality are generally exempt from tax. But OID must still be computed to determine the bondholder's basis in the bond; each year's OID is an upward adjustment in basis for figuring gain or loss on a sale or redemption. OID is figured using the constant interest method (which reflects true economic accrual) for tax-exempt instruments issued after September 3, 1982, and acquired after March 1, 1984. For older tax-exempt bonds, OID is apportioned on a straight-line basis.

(b) U.S. Savings Bonds are not subject to the current inclusion of interest rules [IRC Sec. 1272(a)(2)(B)]. As a cash-basis taxpayer, you may defer tax on the interest until the certificates are redeemed, mature or are disposed of (whichever comes first), or you may elect to report the annual increase as taxable income [IRC Sec. 454; Reg. Sec. 1.454-1].

To switch from the postponed tax method to reporting the interest annually, you simply report the current interest accrual plus the prior untaxed accrual. However, once the current tax method is elected, it is binding for all subsequent tax years (and subsequent bond purchases). A switch back to the postponed tax method is considered a change in accounting and cannot be done without IRS approval [Reg. Sec. 1.454-1(a)]. However, you can get approval automatically by attaching a completed Form 3115 (Change in the Method of Accounting) with your tax return for the year. At the top of page one of Form 3115, print or type "FILED UNDER REV. PROC. 89-46." Also attach a statement that you agree to report all untaxed interest when the bonds are redeemed, mature or are disposed of, whichever is earlier.[1]

> **NOTE:** This expedited method for getting IRS approval can be used no more often than once every five years.

Exclusion for interest from education savings bonds. You may be able to avoid the tax on Series EE savings bonds if you spend an amount equal to or greater than the bond proceeds on higher education for yourself, your spouse or your dependents[IRC Sec. 135].

To be eligible to exclude the interest, *all* of the following conditions must apply: (1) you cashed in qualified U.S savings bonds (see below) during the year; (2) you paid higher education expenses during the year for yourself, your spouse or your dependent; (3) you are not filing as a married person filing separately; and (4) your modified adjusted gross income for 1992 is less than $59,150 ($96,200 if you are a married person filing jointly).

> **NOTE:** Generally, modified adjusted gross income means your adjusted gross income before the interest exclusion. However, certain exclusions for foreign income must be added back [¶ 3825(a), (d); 3827(a), (c)].

A bond is a qualified education savings bonds and therefore eligible for the exclusion if it is issued: (1) in 1990 or later; (2) to an individual who has reached age 24 [IRC Sec. 135(c)(1)]. Furthermore, the bond must be owned either solely by you or jointly with your spouse.

If the proceeds (principal plus interest) of the bonds redeemed during the tax year are more than the year's qualified higher education expenses (i.e., tuition and fees), only a proportionate part of the interest on the bonds is excludable.

> **Example 7:** John and Mary Simpson redeem qualified bonds in 1992 and receive $5,000 of principal and $5,000 of accrued interest. In the same year, they pay $8,000 in tuition and fees for their 18-year-old daughter's first year of college. John and Mary can exclude $4,000 of the accrued interest—$5,000 interest × ($8,000 qualified expenses ÷ $10,000 redemption amount).

Phaseout. The interest exclusion is phased out for taxpayers with modified adjusted gross income (AGI) above certain levels [IRC Sec. 135(b)(2)]. For 1992, for single taxpayers, heads of households and surviving spouses, the phaseout range is from $44,150 to $59,150. For joint filers, the phaseout range is from $66,200 to $96,200.[2] (These figures are adjusted annually for inflation [IRC Sec. 135(b)(2)(B)].)

After figuring the amount of the otherwise allowable interest exclusion, you determine your actual excludable savings bond interest as follows:

1. Enter your modified adjusted gross income.

2. Subtract the threshold amount based on your filing status ($44,150 if single, head of household or surviving spouse; $66,200 if married filing jointly).

3. Divide the amount determined in (2) above by $15,000 ($30,000 if married filing jointly).

4. Apply the percentage found in (3) above to the otherwise allowable interest exclusion.

5. Subtract the amount in (4) from the otherwise allowable interest exclusion. This is your excludable savings bond interest.

> **Example 8:** Same facts as Example 7 except that the Simpsons' modified AGI is $75,000. The Simpsons can exclude only $2,840 of the interest on the redeemed bonds figured as follows:
>
> 1. Otherwise allowable interest $4,000
> 2. Modified adjusted gross income $75,000
> 3. Less: Threshold amount 66,200
> 4. Balance   . . . . $ 8,800
> 5. Applicable percentage ($8,800/$30,000) 29
> 6. Multiply line 1 by line 5 1,160
> 7. Excludable savings bond interest $2,840

Reporting the exclusion. Taxpayers must file Form 8815 if they are excluding Series EE savings bond interest from their income.

(c) Stripped Bonds.   The interest and principal elements of a bond may be separated by a process known as "stripping" the bond. For instance, as the owner of a $10,000 coupon bond, you can strip and sell the coupons while keeping the right to receive the $10,000 face value at maturity. Or you can sell the right to principal and retain the coupons; or transfer ownership of both parts to separate parties.

➤ **OID RULES APPLY** For dispositions after July 1, 1982, the stripped bond and detached coupon are each treated as original issue discount instruments for tax purposes [IRC Sec. 1286].

Exception: Certain mortgage loans that are stripped bonds are to be treated as market discount bonds [(d) below] rather than OID instruments.[3] Suppose a taxpayer sells mortgages while, at the same time, enters into a contract to service them for an amount received from the initial mortgage payments. The mortgage is a "stripped bond" if, under the contract, the taxpayer can receive amounts that exceed reasonable compensation for the services performed. Since August 8, 1991, buyers of these bonds must account for any discount on the bond as market discount rather than original issue discount [Temp. Reg. Sec. 1.1286-1T].

Treatment of seller. If you are a seller of a stripped bond, you are taxed on any income that accrued between the last interest payment (or issue date, if no interest had yet been paid) and the date of disposition. This raises your basis in the bond. That basis must then be allocated between the principal element and the interest element in relation to their respective fair market values. You compute your capital gain or loss on the segment you sold using this allocated basis.

Stripped tax-exempt bonds. The OID on stripped tax-exempt bonds may be taxable. A portion of OID exceeding the "tax-exempt" portion is treated as taxable OID.

➤ **OBSERVATION** In effect, the holder of the stripped bond or coupon is being taxed on market discount. The taxable OID arises from the fact that the yield on the stripped bond when it is purchased is higher than the yield on the bond when it was originally purchased.

The tax-exempt portion of the OID is the amount by which the stated redemption price at maturity (or the amount payable on the due date of a coupon) exceeds an issue price that would produce a yield to maturity as of the purchase date of the stripped bond or coupon equal to the lower of: the coupon rate on the tax-exempt obligation from which the coupons were separated, or the yield to maturity based on the purchase price of the stripped bond or coupon. The taxpayer can elect to use the original yield to maturity instead of the coupon rate for these purposes.

Example 9: On January 1, 1990, Muni City issues tax-exempt obligations with a face amount of $100 due January 1, 1993, for $100. Assume they have a coupon rate of 10%, compounded semi-annually. One of these bonds is stripped on January 1, 1992. The right to receive the principal amount is sold on the same day for $79.21, reflecting a yield to maturity at the time of the strip of 12%, compounded semiannually. The tax-exempt portion of discount on the stripped bond is limited to the difference between the stated redemption price of $100 and the issue price that would produce a yield to maturity of 10% ($82.27). This portion of the discount ($17.73) is treated as OID on a tax-exempt obligation. The difference between the total discount of $20.79 and the tax-exempt portion of $17.73 is treated as OID with respect to an obligation that isn't tax-exempt. So $3.06 ($20.79 minus $17.73) is treated as OID with respect to an obligation that isn't tax-exempt. This $3.06 is reported as taxable income under the normal OID accrual rules.

(d) Market Discount. The price of bonds on the secondary or resale market varies with interest rate shifts and the creditworthiness of the issuer. When you acquire the debt instrument for less than its issue price (adjusted for any OID allocable for prior periods), the difference is known as "market discount." A market discount bond is any bond, debenture, note, certificate or evidence of indebtedness that has been traded at such a discount [IRC Sec. 1278(a)].

Unlike OID, you can hold off on paying tax on all of the market discount until you dispose of the bond. At that time, you are taxed on the difference between your basis for the bond and the redemption price.

De minimis rule. You can disregard the discount and treat it as zero if it is less than one-fourth of 1% (.0025) of the stated redemption price at maturity multiplied by the number of full years to maturity [IRC Sec. 1278(a)(2)(C)].

The market discount rules do not apply to obligations with a fixed maturity date not exceeding one year from the date of issue, tax-exempt obligations (see below), U.S. savings bonds and certain installment obligations.

Current income election. You can elect to pay tax on market discount as it accrues. In other words, you can choose to have market discount taxed as OID, and increase your basis in the bond by the amount included in gross income. The election is binding on all market discount bonds acquired on or after the beginning of the election year and also applies to all subsequent years. The election cannot be revoked without IRS approval [IRC Sec. 1278(b)].

Loss of corresponding interest deduction. If you incur debt to purchase or hold market discount bonds, you may lose a portion of your current deduction for interest payments. If the interest expense exceeds any current taxable income from the bond (including OID), you cannot deduct the excess to the extent of the current market discount accrual. In other words, you can deduct interest only up to the sum of (a) the taxable income from the bond and (b) the amount by which the remaining interest expense exceeds the current market discount accrual.

You carry forward the nondeductible portion of the interest payments and write it off to the extent the taxable income from the bond in a subsequent year exceeds the interest expense for that year. Any remaining interest is treated as having been paid or accrued in the year the bond is disposed of [IRC Sec. 1277].

> **NOTE:** Interest deductions are not deferred under the above rules if you elect to include market discount in income as it accrues [IRC Sec. 1278(b)(1)(A)].

> **Example 10:** Mr. Baron takes out a $45,000 loan to purchase a bond with a $50,000 redemption price. He pays $4,200 of interest to the lender this year. The bond pays him $3,000 of interest this year, and the accrued market discount for the portion of the year he owned the bond is $1,000. Result: Baron gets a $3,200 interest deduction (subject to the deduction limitations for investment-related interest expense—see ¶1904). The deduction is the sum of the taxable interest income he received on the bond plus the excess of the $1,200 additional interest he paid over the $1,000 accrued market discount. If Baron sells the bond next year, for instance, he can deduct the remaining $1,000.

Tax-exempt obligations with market discount. The difference between the purchase price and disposition price (i.e., the market discount) of a tax-exempt obligation is taxable capital gain at the time of disposition. Interest on indebtedness incurred to purchase or carry tax-exempt obligations, though, is not deductible—regardless of whether there is market discount [IRC Sec. 265(a)(2)].

(e) Discount on Short-Term Obligations. For short-term obligations (bonds, debentures, notes, certificates or other evidences of indebtedness with a fixed maturity not over a year), "acquisition discount" must be included in income on a daily basis, if the obligation is: (1) held by an accrual basis taxpayer, (2) held primarily for sale to customers in the ordinary course of business, (3) held by a bank, regulated investment company or common trust fund, (4) identified by the taxpayer as being part of a hedging transaction or (5) a stripped bond or coupon that the holder (or someone whose basis the holder carries over) stripped [IRC Sec. 1281(b)(1)]. The mandatory accrual rule also applies to certain partnerships, S corporations, trusts or other pass-through entities formed to avoid this rule [IRC Sec. 1281(b)(2)].

Other holders of short-term obligations can defer tax on their discount until they dispose of the bond. However, their deduction for interest incurred with respect to the bond is limited in the same manner as for long-term market discount instruments—unless they elect to include the market discount in income currently [IRC Sec. 1282(b)].

(f) Deferred Payment Transactions. The OID rules also apply to sales calling for deferred payments. If the debt instrument does not have sufficient stated interest paid currently over the term of the debt, the seller must include an OID amount in income each year—in addition to any interest actually received.

> **NOTE:** If a debt instrument calls for an excessively high rate of interest, the government can recharacterize part of the stated interest as a portion of the purchase price. That could cause the buyer to lose interest deductions [Prop. Reg. Sec. 1.1274-1(d)].

Transactions to which these rules apply. Debt instruments given for the sale or exchange of property are covered by these rules if some or all of the payments are due more than six months after the date of the sale or exchange, unless one of the following exceptions applies (but see non-OID imputed interest below) [IRC Sec. 1274(c)(3)]:

- Sales for $1,000,000 or less of farms by individuals or small businesses.
- Sales of principal residences.
- Sales involving total payments of $250,000 or less.
- Debt instruments which are publicly traded or are issued for publicly traded property [the original issue discount rules apply instead—see (a)].
- Certain sales of patents with payment contingent on the productivity, use or disposition of the property transferred.
- Certain land transfers between related persons.

Adequate stated interest. The first question to answer in analyzing a deferred payment transaction is whether there is adequate stated interest. There is adequate stated interest if the stated principal amount of the debt instrument is not more than its imputed principal amount. For this purpose, the stated principal amount is the principal payments actually called for in the instrument. The imputed principal amount is the total principal and interest payments discounted by the applicable rate (i.e., their present value) [IRC Sec. 1274(b)].

Discount rate. The discount rate is generally 100% of the applicable federal rate (AFR) based on semiannual compounding (or an equivalent rate based on another compounding period). However, for debt instruments not exceeding $3,234,900 in 1992[4] (the amount is adjusted annually for inflation), the test rate is the lower of 100% of the applicable federal rate or 9%, compounded semiannually. This lower rate applies only to instruments issued on account of a sale or exchange of assets other than tangible personal property used in a business [IRC Sec. 1274(b)(2)(B), 1274A(a)].

For a sale-leaseback, the discount rate is 110% of the AFR. This rate must be used even if the transaction involves less than $3,234,900 in 1992 [IRC Sec. 1274(e)].

Determining the applicable federal rate. The rate used bears a relationship to the term of the debt instrument. If the term is no longer than three years, the AFR is the federal short-term rate; for instruments with terms of over three years, but not over nine years, the AFR is the federal mid-term rate; for instruments with terms of over nine years, the AFR is the federal long-term rate. Taxpayers may use the lowest AFR in the three-month period ending with the month during which a binding written contract was made [IRC Sec. 1274(d)].

Transactions requiring interest imputation. Interest is imputed in the following two situations:

- The stated interest is inadequate. This occurs when the redemption price exceeds the imputed principal amount of the debt obligation.
- The stated interest rate is adequate, but the stated redemption price at maturity exceeds the principal amount stated in the debt instrument [IRC Sec. 1274(c)].

Example 11: An office building is sold for a $1 million, 11% note. The note calls for both principal and interest to be paid in one balloon payment at the end of five years. Assume the test rate is 10%. The stated interest rate is adequate, but the OID rules apply because the $1,550,000 amount due upon redemption exceeds the $1 million principal amount stated in the note.

How to impute interest. Once you determine that a deferred payment transaction requires interest imputation, you must determine how much interest needs to be imputed and when it is to be imputed. To determine the "how much," subtract the stated principal amount (if adequate stated interest) or the imputed principal amount (if inadequate stated interest) from the redemption price.

As for the timing of the interest imputation (i.e., how much is imputed each year) the constant interest method that applies to post-July 1982 OID bonds applies—see (a) above.

Potentially abusive situations. For a tax shelter whose principal purpose is tax evasion or some other potentially abusive situation, the imputed principal amount of a debt instrument received in exchange for property cannot exceed the property's fair market value [IRC Sec. 1274(b)(3), 1274A(c)(4)].

Variable or contingent interest. In general, if a debt instrument calls for a variable rate of interest based on an index, the adequacy of interest test is based on the rate of interest determined under the index as of the date the sale or exchange occurs. Contingent payments of interest usually are disregarded in determining whether a debt instrument calls for adequate stated interest [Prop. Reg. Sec. 1.1274-3(d)].

Cash basis election. In general, both parties to a seller-financed transaction have to account for the OID annually, as it accrues (i.e., seller has income and buyer has deductions). However, if both parties are cash basis taxpayers, they can elect jointly to account for the OID on a cash basis—as interest is paid and received. To qualify for this tax break, the total principal payments on the debt may not exceed $2,310,600 in 1992[4] (the amount is adjusted annually for inflation) [IRC Sec. 1274A(c)].

Non-OID imputed interest. There can be imputed interest even if a transaction meets one of the exceptions to the rules explained above (e.g., the sale of a principal residence). Since the OID rules do not apply, however, there is no change in the timing of the tax. In other words, cash basis taxpayers do not recognize income until payments are received. What does happen is that a portion of the sales price is recharacterized as interest charges.

These imputed interest rules apply if the contract calls for some or all the payments to be made more than *one year* after the date of the sale or exchange. If there is unstated interest, then interest is imputed to all payments that are due more than *six months* after the date of the sale or exchange [IRC Sec. 483(c)(1)].

Unstated interest. There is unstated interest if the principal payments due more than six months after the sale or exchange exceed the sum of the present values of the interest and principal payments due under the contract. That unstated interest is imputed to each of the payments using the "daily portions" method that applies to OID debt instruments issued after July 1, 1982 [(a) above] [IRC Sec. 483(a), (b)].

The present value is determined by discounting the payments by the lower of the applicable Federal rate or 9% compounded semiannually or an equivalent rate based on an appropriate compounding period—the same as under the OID rules explained above for deferred payment sales. However, special rates apply to certain types of sales [IRC Sec. 483(b),(d)].

- Sale or exchange of land between family members: The rate is 6% compounded semiannually or an equivalent rate based on an appropriate compounding period for up to $500,000 of such indebtedness (including prior such sales). Note that this special rate applies to land only, and not to houses on it [Prop. Reg. Sec. 1.483-4(b)(2)].
- New tangible depreciable business property: The rate is 100% of the AFR.
- Sale-leasebacks: For transactions occurring after June 30, 1985, the rate is 110% of the AFR.
- Certain sales of principal residences: The AFR for a debt with a stated principal amount of no more than $3,234,900 in 1992 [4] (the amount is adjusted annually for inflation).

Exceptions. The imputed interest rules do not apply to the following transactions:

- Sales prices of $3,000 or less.
- Sales of patents with contingent payments.
- Certain annuities dependent on life expectancy [IRC Sec. 483(d); Reg. Sec. 1.483-2(b)].

DIVIDENDS IN GENERAL

¶1218   **WHAT IS A DIVIDEND**

Generally speaking, a dividend is a distribution of a corporation's current or accumulated earnings and profits to the shareholders. Distributions in excess of earnings and profits are not ordinary dividends. Instead, they represent a return of capital. As such, they can be either tax-free or capital gain. Dividends can be made in the form of cash payments, shares of the payer's stock or property distributions. (Note: There are special tax rules for S corporations. For example, S corporations don't have current earnings and profits, and thus can pay dividends out of accumulated E&P. See Chapter 21 for details.)

The chart on page 1226 provides an overview of the general tax treatment of dividends:

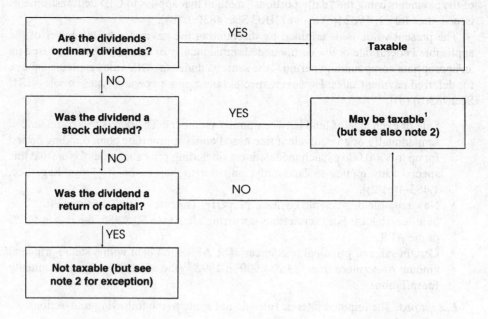

Notes: (1) A stock dividend is taxable if: (a) you have the option to receive cash or other property in place of stock; (b) a disproportionate share of stock is received by one class of shareholders; (c) stock you receive is not the same class of stock as you previously owned; (d) there is a disproportionate distribution of convertible preferred stock. See ¶1222.
(2) The dividend is taxable only when the payment (when added to past payments) exceeds your original investment. It is then taxed as a capital gain. See ¶1219.

(a) What Are Earnings and Profits. Your corporation's earnings and profits (E&P) are often not the same as its taxable income. Your corporation's earnings and profits (E&P) represent its retained profits from its operations. A number of items that are excludable in figuring taxable income serve to increase your corporation's retained earnings. For example, big up-front accelerated depreciation deductions cannot be used in figuring E&P; special straight-line depreciation rules apply instead. In addition, certain deductions, not allowed for tax purposes, affect the retained earnings.

The amount of your corporation's accumulated earnings and profits available for dividend payments is the annual earnings and profits less losses and prior dividends over your corporation's life. (In the case of long-established corporations, only E&P accumulated since March 1, 1913, is taken into account.)

(b) The Source of the Distribution. As we've said, the tax treatment of a distribution hinges on its source. Distributions are conclusively presumed to come from (1) current E&P and then (2) accumulated E&P to the extent there are any of each of these [IRC Sec. 316(a); Reg. Sec. 1.316-2(a)].

Example 1: At the beginning of the year, Bellar Corp. had $12,000 of accumulated earnings and profits. Its earnings for the year amounted to $30,000. Assume that it paid a single annual dividend as follows:

(a) Dividend of $20,000. The entire dividend would be taxable since it did not exceed the $30,000 earnings of the tax year.

(b) Dividend of $40,000. The entire dividend would be taxable since it did not exceed the $30,000 earnings of the tax year, plus the $12,000 accumulated earnings and profits ($30,000 plus $12,000, for a total of $42,000).

(c) Dividend of $60,000. The dividend would be taxable to the extent of $42,000 ($30,000 plus $12,000). The remaining $18,000 is not taxable.

Current earnings and profits are computed at the end of the tax year, without reduction for accumulated deficits from prior years. Thus, a distribution made when your corporation had no earnings and profits could turn out to be a dividend if your corporation ended the year with a profit.

Example 2: Astor Corp.'s E&P account showed a deficit balance in excess of $5,000 at the beginning of the year. However, it then turned a profit—ending up with $5,000 of E&P from the current year's operations. Assume that Astor made a $5,000 distribution that year. Result: The distribution is a taxable dividend since there was sufficient current E&P. Astor does not net its current and accumulated E&P accounts first to show a net deficit.

➤ **SUGGESTED MOVE** Astor should have considered holding off on declaring the distribution until the following year. If it had no current E&P that year, the distribution would be a return of capital—instead of a taxable ordinary dividend. Reason: The prior year's $5,000 E&P would have been netted with the larger accumulated deficit to determine the new year's accumulated E&P. Suppose Astor had another $5,000 profit that year. The $5,000 delayed dividend would sop up those E&P. Thus, any other distributions made that year would not be taxable dividends.

(c) Matching Cash Dividends and Distribution Source. Companies often make distributions more than once during the course of a year. Suppose the distributions exceed your corporation's current and accumulated E&P and occur both before and after the shares change hands. It can make a big tax difference to you and the other shareholders how the E&P is allocated with respect to each of the distributions. For example, if you receive distributions for which no E&P are allocated, you get a return of capital.

Current earnings. First, allocate the earnings of the tax year to each individual dividend. The proportion of each dividend which the total of the earnings or profits of the year bears to the total dividends paid during the year is regarded as out of the earnings of that year.

Example 3: Current earnings and profits are $30,000. Four dividends of $15,000 were paid, for a total of $60,000. The proportion which the current earnings and profits ($30,000) bears to the total dividends ($60,000) is 30,000/60,000 or 50%. Thus, 50%, or $7,500, of each dividend is regarded as out of current earnings and profits and taxable to that extent.

If current earnings and profits exceed the current year's distributions, the excess either reduces prior deficits, if any, or is added to accumulated earnings and profits at the beginning of the following year.

Accumulated earnings and profits. Allocate the earnings and profits accumulated since February 28, 1913, in sequence to the portion of each individual dividend not out of current earnings and profits. The allocation is made to the extent of such earnings and profits available on the date of each distribution.

Example 4: Assume the same facts in Example 3, except that earnings and profits accumulated since February 28, 1913, amount to $12,000. Four dividends of $15,000 each were paid on March 15, June 15, September 15, and December 15. On March 15 the entire $12,000 earnings and profits accumulated since February 28, 1913, were available. Thus, $7,500, the portion of the March 15 dividend not regarded as out of earnings or profits of the tax year, is entirely taxable, since it does not exceed

$12,000. As of June 15, the date of the second dividend, only $4,500 of the $12,000 is available ($12,000 less $7,500 allocated to the March 15 dividend). Thus, only $4,500 of the $7,500 portion of the second dividend not regarded as out of earnings of the year is taxable. After the second dividend is paid, there are no more accumulated earnings or profits available, since the entire $12,000 was allocated to the first two dividends. The portions of the third and fourth dividends not out of the earnings of the year ($7,500 each) are nontaxable.

Date	Dividends Amount	Portion out of earnings or profits of the tax year	Portion out of earnings accumulated since 2-28-13	Taxable amount of each dividend	Return of capital amount of each dividend
Mar. 15	$15,000	$7,500	$7,500	$15,000	$ . . . . .
June 15	15,000	7,500	4,500	12,000	3,000
Sept. 15	15,000	7,500	. . . . .	7,500	7,500
Dec. 15	15,000	7,500	. . . . .	7,500	7,500
Total	$60,000	$30,000	$12,000	$42,000	$18,000

Each shareholder should report as taxable income:

(a) 100% of his Mar. 15 dividend.
(b) 80% of his June 15 dividend.

(c) 50% of his Sept. 15 dividend.
(d) 50% of his Dec. 15 dividend.

➤ **TAX DIFFERENCE** Suppose a 40% shareholder sold his stock to another individual on July 1. Each would receive $12,000 of distributions in the year. However, the owner for the first half of the year would be taxed on $10,800, while the second shareholder would receive only $6,000 of taxable dividends.

(d) Reporting Dividends When Earnings Are Unknown. You may have to report the entire distribution as taxable if your corporation's earnings and profits are unknown when you file your return. A situation of this kind might occur, for example, if your corporation had a fiscal year ending June 30 and you used the calendar year.[1] If necessary, you can file a refund claim later.

➤ **OBSERVATION** Shareholders should receive a copy of Form 1099-DIV from the corporation showing the payments made to them.

¶1219   HOW DISTRIBUTIONS ARE TAXED

A dividend is taxed as ordinary income to you in the year you actually or constructively receive it.

A distribution that exceeds earnings and profits is treated first as a nontaxable reduction of your basis (in effect, you are recovering your investment). Any excess over your basis is usually a capital gain [IRC Sec. 301 (c); Reg. Sec. 1.301-1, 1.316-2].

Tax return tip. If your dividend income exceeds $400, you must fill out Schedule B (Form 1040) or Schedule 1 (Form 1040A) and attach it to your return. See also ¶1211(a).

(a) Property Distributions. The rules for property distributions are analogous to those for cash given by a corporation to its shareholders. The portion of a distribution that is taxed as a dividend cannot exceed the distributing corporation's E&P [Reg. Sec. 1.316-1(a)(2)].

You are deemed to have received a distribution equal to the fair market value of the property on the distribution date, reduced (but not below zero) by any liability assumed or to which the property remains subject [IRC Sec. 301(b); Reg. Sec. 1.301-1, 1.305-2(c)]. Similarly, your basis for the property is its fair market value on the date of distribution [IRC Sec. 301(d)(1); Reg. Sec. 1.301-1(h)].

Example: Adelphi Corp. has earnings and profits of $10,000. It distributes property worth $16,000 to its shareholders. The shareholders have taxable dividend income of $10,000 and reduce their basis in Adelphi stock by $6,000. Their basis in the property distributed is $16,000. Note that Adelphi's basis in the property it distributed is irrelevant in making this determination.

NOTE: Adelphi may owe tax on account of the property distribution. Tax is generally due when the property's fair market value exceeds its basis in the hands of the corporation [¶3027].

(b) Mutual and Money Market Funds. Distributions by mutual stock funds and money market funds are both classified as dividends, even though money market funds invest in interest-bearing investments. If you choose to have your dividends automatically reinvested by the fund, you are taxed on the dividends, the same as if you had received cash.

(c) Capital Gain Dividends. Mutual funds, regulated investment companies and real estate investment trusts may designate part of a distribution as a capital gain dividend. [¶1230].

> **TAX RETURN IMPACT** Capital gains are taxed at no higher than a 28% rate. This is a break if you are in the 31% tax bracket—for example, you are a joint filer with 1992 taxable income over $86,500. However, the phaseout of personal exemptions and the limit on itemized deductions can effectively increase that capital gains ceiling above 28% (as well as on other income) for high-income taxpayers [see ¶1809]. You report the capital gains on a different tax schedule from dividends and you can shelter the capital gains from tax by capital losses without regard to the annual $3,000 capital loss deduction ceiling.

(d) Consent Dividends. Corporations are hit with a special tax if they accumulate too much earnings. Personal holding companies also need to distribute their income in order to avoid owing another special tax. A consent dividend represents a phantom distribution to shareholders. The shareholders agree to treat corporate income as having been distributed to them in cash and then immediately reinvested in the corporation. They are taxed on the consent dividend, and it increases the basis of their stock as a capital contribution. See also ¶3304(b).

¶1220 CONSTRUCTIVE DIVIDENDS

Some transactions not in the form of dividends are taxed as such because their effect is the same. They are taxed even though a dividend was not formally declared[1] and payment was not made to all the shareholders in proportion to stock ownership.

For example, suppose your corporation pays an unreasonably high salary to you as a shareholder-employee. The Revenue Service could treat the excessive portion of your compensation as a dividend. Similarly, payment made in the following circumstances can be recharacterized as dividends:

- Excessive royalties[2] and rents.[3]
- "Interest" on notes held to be an equity investment (stock)[4] rather than evidence of a corporate debt.
- Bargain sales of securities and other property to shareholders [¶1208].
- Cancellation of shareholder's debt to corporation.
- Corporation's purchase of shareholder's property for more than its value.[5]
- Bargain sales of inventory items to shareholders.[6]
- Life insurance proceeds paid to a shareholder if the corporation paid the premiums and held incidents of ownership [¶1207(a)].

- Interest-free and below market rate loans made by a corporation to its shareholders. For interest-free and below market term loans made after June 6, 1984, and demand loans outstanding after that date, the corporation is treated as having made a dividend distribution to the shareholder in the amount of the foregone interest [IRC Sec. 7872]. For loans made earlier, there had been some dispute, particularly between the Tax Court and the Claims Court, whether such a loan would constitute an actual loan or a constructive dividend.[7]

¶1221   TAX-EXEMPT AND SPECIALLY TREATED DISTRIBUTIONS

Dividends paid to policyholders on unmatured life or endowment insurance policies are not dividends. They are a return of premium and therefore, tax-free (until they exceed the total premium payments). However, dividends paid to the shareholders of these insurance companies are taxable [IRC Sec. 316(b); Reg. Sec. 1.316-1].

"Dividends" from savings banks, savings and loan associations and credit unions are not dividends. They are payments of interest and are treated as such.

The fact that the earnings of your corporation are derived from tax-exempt sources does not make the dividend exempt to you. For example, a dividend received from your corporation is not exempt merely because part or all of the corporate earnings consisted of interest on municipal bonds.

Some stock dividends and rights, dividends paid in corporate liquidations and reorganizations, and dividends paid by certain personal holding companies [IRC Sec. 316 (b)] are tax-exempt or subject to special tax rules.

DISTRIBUTIONS IN KIND

¶1222   WHAT IS A STOCK DIVIDEND

A stock dividend is a distribution by a corporation to its shareholders in its *own* stock. These dividends can be used either to split a shareholder's existing interest in the company into more parts or to alter that interest. "Stock," as used in this area, includes stock rights.

How stock dividends are taxed. Stock dividends that merely divide your interest into more parts generally are nontaxable. Reason: Your rights in your corporation remain subject to the same risks; the receipt of a stock dividend is part of a continuing investment position, not a separate investment. Since the stock dividend presents no opportunity for severing your investment ties, there is no occasion for imposing tax.

Not all stock dividends, however, are tax-free. The exceptions, listed below, are designed to tax you if you choose to receive additional shares rather than cash. The rules treat you much the same as if you had received cash and reinvested it in the corporation. Thus, a stock dividend is taxable if:

1. You have a choice of receiving cash or other property in place of stock [IRC Sec. 305(b)(1); Reg. Sec. 1.305-2].

2. The distribution is disproportionate (some shareholders get cash or other property and the others have an increase in their proportionate interests) [IRC Sec. 305(b)(2); Reg. Sec. 1.305-3].

> **FRACTIONAL SHARE EXCEPTION** Stock dividend formulas often entitle some shareholders to fractional shares of stock. In these instances, the tax law permits the corporation to ease its recordkeeping and registration chores by paying cash in lieu of the fractional shares—without turning the stock dividend plan into a disproportionate distribution. The actual amount of cash distributed must not exceed 5% of the total stock distributed [Reg. Sec. 1.305-3 (c)].

Example 1: Y Corporation has two classes of common, A and B, having equal rights, except that A pays only cash dividends and B only equivalent stock dividends. Since the stock dividend increases the B shareholders' proportionate interest, it is taxable.

Example 2: X Corporation has outstanding class A common and class B nonconvertible preferred. If dividends are declared, payable in additional shares of class A on the common and cash on the preferred, the distribution of stock is nontaxable because there is no increase in the class A shareholders' proportionate interest. However, taxability results if the dividend on class A is payable in class B stock.

Example 3: PY Corporation has outstanding common stock and convertible debentures. It pays cash interest on the debentures and distributes a stock dividend on the common stock. On these facts, the debentures are treated as a second class of stock. Therefore, the stock dividend and interest payment are taxable since the shareholders' equity increases.

3. The distribution involves preferred stock to some common shareholders and common stock to other common shareholders [IRC Sec. 305(b)(3); Reg. Sec. 1.305-4].

4. The distribution is on preferred stock except when there is a change in the conversion ratio to reflect a stock dividend or split [IRC Sec. 305(b)(4); Reg. Sec. 1.305-5].

5. The distribution involves convertible preferred and only some shareholders are anticipated to exercise their conversion rights. The dividend rate, length of exercise period, conversion price, marketability of convertible shares and redemption provisions are considered in predicting whether conversion rights will be exercised [IRC Sec. 305(d)(5); Reg. Sec. 1.305-6].

Example 4: NT Corporation distributes convertible preferred on common, the only prior outstanding issue. The dividend rates are normal in light of existing market conditions, and the conversion period is four months only. Since those who wish to increase their investment will convert and those who wish cash will sell, it is likely that the result will be a disproportionate distribution. So the distribution is taxable. But suppose the conversion period is long, say 20 years. And it is likely that by the end of the conversion period substantially all the preferred would be converted. The distribution would not be disproportionate and is not taxable.

NOTE: Subject to transitional rules, the rule in (2) did not apply until 1991 as to distributions on stock outstanding on January 10, 1969, or issued later under a contract binding on that date. The rule in (4) did not apply until 1991 if the stock is issued under terms in effect on January 10, 1969 [Reg. Sec. 1.305-8].

In general, when a stock dividend is a taxable distribution, you are taxed on the fair market value of the stock on the distribution date. That also becomes your basis in the new shares. The basis in the old shares is unchanged [Reg. Sec. 1.305-1(b)(1), 1.301-1(h)(1)]. The holding period of the new stock begins on the date you receive the stock dividend.

Special rule. If a regulated investment company offers its shareholders a choice of cash or stock of equal value, the taxable dividend will be equal to the amount of cash the shareholder could have received—even if the stock is worth a different amount when actually distributed [Reg. Sec. 1.305-1(b)(2)].

Example 5: In 1990, Mr. Kenny, a calendar year taxpayer, bought 100 shares of Joyce Co. stock for $12,000. Joyce paid a taxable stock dividend on March 22, 1992, and Kennny received 50 shares having a fair market value of $5,000. He must include the $5,000 in income as a dividend in 1992. On July 20, 1992, Kenny sold the 100 old shares for $11,000, and on August 4, 1992, he sold the 50 new shares for $5,300. On his 1992 return, he will show a long-term capital loss of $1,000 and a short-term capital gain of $300.

Basis of 100 old shares	$12,000
Selling price of 100 old shares	11,000
Long-term capital loss (since the old shares had been held for more than one year)	$ 1,000
Selling price of 50 new shares	5,300
Basis of new shares (fair market value when received)	5,000
Short-term capital gain (since the new shares had been held for not more than one year)	$ 300

NOTE: Short-term capital gains can be taxed at up to 31%, but the maximum tax on long-term capital gains is 28% [¶1809]. They are reported separately on Schedule D of Form 1040.

Example 6: Mutual Growth Inc., a regulated investment company, declared a dividend of $1 a share on common stock on January 9, 1992, payable February 9, 1992, in cash or in Mutual Growth stock of equal value determined as of January 23, 1992. The election to take stock or cash had to be made by January 23, 1992. Mr. Gaines owns 100 shares and elected to take the dividend in stock. He received a taxable dividend of $100. The result is the same if he elected to take cash.

¶1223   EFFECT OF NONTAXABLE STOCK DISTRIBUTIONS

The receipt of a nontaxable stock distribution does not, of course, result in taxable income. However, the sale or exchange of those shares is a taxable event. To calculate your amount of gain or loss, you have to first determine your basis in the stock.

(a) Basis of Old and New Stock. The basis of the stock depends on whether the old and new stocks are identical.

When old and new stock identical. Examples include stock splits and dividends of common on common. To find the basis of each share (old and new), divide the basis of the old stock by the total number of old and new shares [IRC Sec. 307(a); Reg. Sec. 1.307-1].

Example 1: Mr. Harrison owned 100 shares of Haron Corporation common stock bought in 1988 for $12,000 ($120 a share). In 1992, Haron Corporation declared a 50% stock dividend and Harrison received 50 new common shares. After the stock dividend, the basis of each share is $80 ($12,000÷150).

If you bought the old stock at different times and prices, your basis is found by allocating to each lot of the old stock the proportionate amount of dividend stock attributable to it.[1] This could raise an identification problem [¶1622(d)].

Example 2: Mr. Cleveland owned 150 shares of Haron Corporation common stock. He paid $12,000 for 100 of those shares ($120 a share) and $7,500 for the other 50 shares ($150 a share). Cleveland received 75 new common shares as a result of the 50% stock dividend. Fifty of those shares are allocated to the first block of stock, and 25 allocated to the shares he purchased for $150 a share. His new basis in each share is then allocated in the same manner as in Example 1: $80 for 150 shares and $100 for the other 75 shares.

Old and new stocks not identical.

An example of this would be preferred on common. Your basis in the old stock is allocated to the old and new stocks in proportion to their relative market values on the distribution date.

Example 3: Ms. Jackson bought 100 shares of Redy Corp. common stock for $12,000. She received a nontaxable stock dividend of 50 shares of Redy preferred stock having a fair market value of $5,000. The value of the old stock when the dividend was received was $15,000. After the stock dividend, the bases of the old and new stock are determined as follows:

Basis of 100 shares of old stock		$12,000
Fair market value of old stock	$15,000	
Fair market value of new stock	5,000	
Total	$20,000	

Basis of 100 shares of old stock after dividend: $12,000 × 15,000/20,000 = $9,000
Basis of 50 shares of new stock after dividend: $12,000 × 5,000/20,000 = $3,000

(b) Holding Period of New Stock. The holding period of the new shares starts on the same date as the holding period of the old [IRC Sec. 1223(5); Reg. Sec. 1.1223-1].

Example 4: Assume the same facts as in Example 1, except that 4 months after receipt of the stock dividend, Harrison sold the 50 new shares for $4,800. Since the holding period of his old shares begins in 1988, his holding period is more than a year. He realizes a long-term capital gain of $800, figured as follows:

Selling price	$4,800
Basis (50 × $80)	4,000
Long-term capital gain	$ 800

NOTE: Short-term capital gains can be taxed at up to 31%, but the maximum tax on long-term capital gains is 28% [¶1809]. They are reported separately on Schedule D of Form 1040.

¶1224   STOCK RIGHTS

Shareholders may receive rights to subscribe to a new issue of stock. The rights are issued to you, usually at less than the stock's quoted price, by the corporation in which you hold stock. You can either sell your rights, exercise them, or let them expire. The rules for finding if a stock right is taxed to you are the same as those for stock dividends [IRC Sec. 305(d); Reg. Sec. 1.305-1].

Bond rights are discussed at ¶1227.

¶1225   EFFECT OF NONTAXABLE STOCK RIGHTS

As with the nontaxable stock distributions, the receipt of nontaxable stock rights has no effect on your income when received. It is necessary, however, to find the basis of the stock and rights and the holding period of the rights.

(a) Basis of Stock and Rights. If the rights have a market value of less than 15% of the stock's value at the time they are distributed, you have a choice. You can either treat the rights as having a zero basis or elect to allocate part of your stock basis to the rights. If the value is 15% or more, you must allocate basis to the rights [IRC Sec. 307(b)(1), (2); Reg. Sec. 1.307-1, 1.307-2].

How to allocate basis. Your stock basis is allocated between the stock and rights in proportion to their relative market values on the distribution date [Reg. Sec. 1.307-1].

Example 1: On June 1, 1992, Ms. Hanson, a calendar-year taxpayer, bought 100 shares of Carr Corp. stock at $100 per share. On July 2, 1992, she received 100 rights entitling her to subscribe to an additional 100 shares at $95 per share. On the day the rights were issued, the fair market value of the stock was $110 a share and that of the rights was $15 each. The bases of the rights and the common stock to determine the gain or loss on a later sale are computed as follows, if the election is made:

Original cost of stock (100 × $100)	$10,000
Value of old stock when rights issued (100 × $110)	$11,000
Value of rights when issued (100 × $15)	1,500
Value of both old stock and rights when rights issued	$12,500
Basis of old stock after rights issued ($11,000/$12,500 × $10,000)	$ 8,800
Basis of rights ($1,500/$12,500 × $10,000)	$ 1,200
Basis of one share of old stock after rights issued ($8,800÷100)	$ 88
Basis of one right ($1,200 ÷ 100)	$ 12

If the rights are sold, the basis for determining gain or loss will be $12 per right. If the rights are exercised, the basis of the new stock acquired will be $107—the subscription price paid for it ($95) plus the basis of the rights exercised ($12). In both cases, the basis of the old stock will be set at $88 per share.

NOTE: The rights in Example 1 are worth less than 15% of the stock's value at the time of distribution. Therefore, Hanson could either assign a zero basis to the rights or allocate the cost of the original stock between that stock and the new right. This choice leaves room for tax maneuvering. To illustrate, assume Hanson sold her rights for $15 each in 1992.

- If her other capital transactions for the year result in capital gain, she could keep her gain on the sale of the rights to a minimum by electing to allocate basis. Thus, her gain would be $3 per right ($15 – $12, basis of one right), instead of $15, and the basis of her old stock would change from $100 to $88 per share.

- If her other capital transactions for the year result in a net loss, she could elect a zero basis and use more of the loss to shelter a bigger gain. The gain would be $15 per right instead of $3, and the basis of her old stock would remain at $100 per share.

(b) How to Elect Allocation. The election in (a) above applies to all rights received in any one distribution on the same class of stock owned when the rights were distributed. You make the election, which is irrevocable, in a statement attached to your return for the year you receive the rights. You should keep a copy of the election and tax return to support the allocated basis when you sell the new stock [Reg. Sec. 1.307-2].

(c) Holding Period of Stock and Rights. If you sell the rights, your holding period runs from the date the stock was acquired. If you exercise the rights, the new stock's holding period starts on the date of exercise [IRC Sec. 1223(5),(6); Reg. Sec. 1.1223-1].

Example 2: On June 5, 1989, Mr. Rice bought 100 shares of Delphi Corporation stock. On July 1, 1992, he received 100 nontaxable rights entitling him to subscribe to 25 additional shares at $120 a share. Assume the basis of each right is $4. He sold 60 of the rights on July 12, 1992, for $6 each. Rice has a long-term capital gain of $120 ($360 sales price less $240 basis), since the rights were held for more than one year, June 5, 1989 to July 12, 1992.

Example 3: Assume that Mr. Rice of Example 2 exercised the remaining 40 rights on July 12, 1992. He turned in the 40 rights with $1,200 for 10 new shares. On November 3, 1992, he sold the new shares for $1,500. He has a short-term capital gain of $140, figured as follows:

Selling price	$1,500
Basis of 10 new shares ($160 + $1,200)	1,360
Short-term capital gain (since date basis is July 12, 1992)	$ 140

¶1226   TAXABLE STOCK RIGHTS

A distribution of taxable stock rights is considered a property distribution treated as explained at ¶1219. The amount of the taxable distribution, and the basis of the rights, is generally the fair market value of the rights on the distribution date, whether the shareholder is an individual or a corporation. If you exercise the rights, your basis in the new shares is your basis in the rights plus the subscription price. Your basis in the old stock remains the same [IRC Sec. 305(b),(d)(1); Reg. Sec. 1.305-1(b)].

Holding period of stock and rights. If taxable rights are exercised, the holding period for the new shares begins on the date the rights were exercised. The holding period for the old shares remains unchanged [IRC Sec. 1223(6); Reg. Sec. 1.1223-1].

¶1227   RIGHTS TO BONDS

(a) Nontaxable Bond Rights. Rights to subscribe to bonds are treated in a manner similar to nontaxable stock rights if (1) the bonds are convertible into stock that, if distributed, would not result in a taxable dividend, and (2) the value of the rights arises from the conversion privilege. Your basis in the original stock is allocated between the stock and the rights in proportion to their relative market values. The computation is similar to that used in ¶1225, Example 1. Your basis in the bonds is your basis in the rights plus the subscription price. If you convert the bonds into stock, your basis in such stock is your basis in the bonds plus any consideration you pay at the time of the conversion.[1]

(b) Taxable Bond Rights. If the bonds are not convertible into stock, the rights are property dividends.[2] Your basis in the shares remains unchanged, and your basis in the bonds is determined as if they were new stock [¶1219; 1226].

RETURN OF CAPITAL DIVIDENDS

¶1228   HOW A RETURN OF CAPITAL IS TAXED

A return of capital dividend reduces your basis or investment in the stock. So long as you have basis remaining, the distribution is tax-free. However, once your basis becomes zero, additional returns of capital are taxed to you as capital gain. The stock's holding period determines if the stock is a long-term or short-term capital gain [¶1803].

> **Example:** Mr. Ames bought stock in the Ace Corp. for $500 in 1987. In 1989, he received a return of capital of $480 (nontaxable). Ames reduced his basis in the stock by the amount received, to an adjusted basis of $20. If Ames received a return of capital of $30 in 1992, his basis would be reduced to zero, and he would report the $10 excess as a long-term capital gain for 1992.

¶1229　　　　　　WHAT IS A LIQUIDATING DIVIDEND

In general, a liquidating distribution made in complete redemption of the stock of a corporate or noncorporate shareholder is treated as the sale or exchange of the distribution for the stock. The same rule applies to the partial liquidation of stock held by a corporate taxpayer. However, a distribution in partial liquidation of a noncorporate shareholder's stock may be fully taxed to the shareholder as a dividend. Payment for the redeemed shares can take the form of cash or other corporate assets. The tax effect on the liquidating corporation is discussed at ¶3233-3235.

(a)　Partial Liquidations to Noncorporate Shareholders. A partial liquidation distribution to you qualifies for capital gain or loss tax treatment only if the following requirements are met:

- The distribution is not essentially equivalent to a dividend (e.g., the distribution represents a substantially disproportionate redemption of stock).
- The distribution is made pursuant to a plan which was adopted in either the same or the year immediately preceding the year the distribution is made.

> ➤ **SAFE HARBOR** The tax law says that a distribution automatically meets the above requirement if your corporation distributes assets attributable to a segment of its operations that it has ceased to run. To qualify under this safe harbor, your corporation must, after the partial liquidation distribution, continue to be actively engaged in any business which it had been pursuing for the prior five year period [IRC Sec. 302(b),(e)].

(b)　Complete Liquidations. The tax code does not define this term. However, it generally refers to a winding up of your corporation's affairs, payment of its debts and distribution of corporate assets to you and the other shareholders.

(c)　How Liquidating Dividends Are Treated. The amount received in a (1) complete liquidation, (2) a partial liquidation to a corporate shareholder or (3) a qualifying partial liquidation to a non-corporate shareholder is treated as the proceeds from the sale of the redeemed stock by the shareholder. In computing the amount received, any property received is taken into account at its fair market value [IRC Sec. 331(a); Reg. Sec. 1.331-1].

Amount and character of gain or loss. The amount of gain or loss is the difference between the cost or other basis of the redeemed stock and the amount received in liquidation.

Example 1: In 1987, Mr. Barnett bought 100 shares of Rocket Corp. stock for $10,000. In 1992, the Corp. dissolved and Barnett received a final liquidating dividend of $4,000. His recognized loss is $6,000.

Example 2: In 1987, Ms. Dickens bought 100 shares of Storm Corp. stock for $10,000. In 1992, the Corp. dissolved and Dickens received a final liquidating dividend of $12,000. Her recognized gain is $2,000.

Since the stock is usually a capital asset, you will have capital gain or loss, unless the special rules on distributions by a collapsible corporation [¶1820] or personal holding company [¶3300 et seq.] apply. If the shares were acquired at different times and prices, you compute the gain or loss separately on each block for a single distribution.[1] The distribution is allocated among the various blocks in the same proportion that the number of shares in each block bears to the total number of shares outstanding[2] [Reg. Sec. 1.331-1(e)].

> **Example 3:** In 1986, Mr. Able bought 40% of the 200 shares outstanding of the Black Corporation for $800. He acquired the remaining 60% of Black stock in 1987 for $3,600. In 1992, Able receives a final liquidating dividend of $10,000 from the Black Corporation. Able has $3,200 in capital gain on the stock bought in 1986 [(40% × $10,000) less $800] and $2,400 in gain on the stock acquired in 1986 [(60% × $10,000) less $3,600].

> **Example 4:** Assume the facts as in Example 3 except that $5,000 in liquidating dividends are distributed in December 1992 and $5,000 in January 1993. In 1992, Able has $1,200 in capital gain on the stock bought in 1986 [$2,000 ($5,000 × 40%) less $800 basis] but has no gain recognized on the second block because he has not recovered his adjusted basis [$3,000 ($5,000 × 60%) reduction to his $3,600 basis]. In 1993, Able has $2,000 in long-term capital gain on the first block since the entire basis of that stock has been recovered. Long-term gain of $2,400 is recognized on the second block since $600 of the $3,000 prorated distribution represents recovery of basis.

If you report capital gain on a liquidating dividend, you are sometimes called on as transferees to pay the corporation's tax deficiencies. These payments are treated as capital losses.[3]

(d) Reporting Gain or Loss. If liquidating dividends are distributed in installments, you need not report gain until the cost or other basis of the stock is recovered[4] (see Example 4). Ordinarily, you can deduct a loss through liquidation in the year the final distribution is made. However, if your corporation distributes all of its assets, except a small amount of cash reserved for expenses of dissolution, there is, in effect, a final distribution. You may take a loss to you in that year, instead of being postponed until later when the remaining cash is distributed.[5]

Information filed with return. If you transfer stock to the issuing corporation in exchange for property, you should report all the facts and circumstances on your return, unless the dividend is paid under a corporate resolution reciting that it is made in liquidation of the corporation, and the corporation is completely liquidated and dissolved within one year after the distribution. The distributing corporation must file Form 966 within 30 days after adopting the plan of liquidation, but liquidating distributions will be treated as such whether or not the corporation filed Form 966[6] (¶3234) [Reg. Sec. 1.331-1(d)].

¶1230   WHAT IS A CAPITAL GAIN DIVIDEND

A capital gain dividend is a distribution by an investment company (such as a mutual fund) of capital gains it realizes on the sale of its investments. It is designated as such by the investment company in a written notice to its shareholders. Capital gain dividends are reported as long-term capital gains regardless of how long you owned the stock in the investment company [IRC Sec. 852(b)(3)]. Any loss from the sale of regulated investment company or real estate investment trust stock (RIC or REIT stock) held for six months or less is long-term capital loss, to the extent of any long-term capital gain from a capital dividend [IRC Sec. 852(b)(4), 857(b)(7)]. An exception is made for dispositions under a periodic redemption plan.

¶1231   UNDISTRIBUTED CAPITAL GAIN DIVIDENDS

In addition to the amounts actually received, you must include as capital gains, amounts that the investment company allocated to you capital gain dividends—even though you did not actually receive them. However, you are entitled to a credit for the tax the investment company paid [¶3328(a)].

MISCELLANEOUS INCOME

¶1232   RENTS AND ROYALTIES

While rents and royalties you receive are includible in your income [IRC Sec. 61; Reg. Sec. 1.61-8], you may also be entitled to a variety of offsetting deductions that can shelter all or some of the income from tax. These deductions include depreciation, or depletion, taxes and other ordinary and necessary expenses of operating the property. They are discussed in later chapters.

(a) Rent includes more than just cash payments you receive from a tenant.

Payment to third parties. If, instead of straightforward rent, the tenant pays the interest on bonds you issued[1] or dividends on stock you issued,[2] the payments are rental income to you and rental payments by the tenant. Amounts received by the stockholders and bondholders are dividends and interest to them.

Taxes paid by a tenant to or for you for business property generally are additional rent taxable to you [Reg. Sec. 1.162-11].

Cancellation of lease. If a tenant pays you to cancel, amend or modify a lease, the payment is taxable to you as ordinary income.[3] However, an amount paid to a tenant to cancel a lease is treated as proceeds from the lease's sale or exchange [IRC Sec. 1241; Reg. Sec. 1.1241-1]. A capital gain results if the lease is of nondepreciable property (¶1801; 1802) [IRC Sec. 1221; Reg. Sec. 1.1221-1].

> **Example:** Mr. Jones rents an apartment to Mr. Keltner. If Jones gives Keltner $1,000 to cancel the lease, Keltner has a capital gain of $1,000. The gain will be short- or long-term depending on the length of time Keltner had the leasehold.

The sale of inventory results in ordinary income, not capital gain. Therefore, lease cancellation payments received by a tenant who is in the business of entering into and marketing leases results in ordinary gain.

(b) Royalties include payments to the owner of a mine for permitting another to extract minerals from it, payments to an owner of a patent or private formula[4] for the use of it or the right to act under it, and payments to an author of a book. For coal and iron ore royalties, see ¶1816. For details of the offsetting depletion deduction of mine owners who receive royalties, see Ch. 12.

¶1233   IMPROVEMENTS BY LESSEE

Improvements made by your tenant that increase the value of the leased property are not income to you [IRC Sec. 109; Reg. Sec. 1.109-1]. You recognize gain or loss only when you dispose of the property.

Example 1: On July 1, 1972, Mr. Evans leased a parcel of land to Mr. Dugal for a 20-year term, with an annual rental of $800. The land had cost Evans $5,000. In 1973, Dugal erected a building at a cost of $40,000. The lease expired and Evans repossessed the property on June 30, 1992. On the next day, Evans sold the land and building for $60,000. The annual rent was income. But Evans realized no income from the improvement when it was made in 1973. Nor did he realize income from the improvement when the lease expired on June 30, 1992 and he repossessed the land and improvement. But when he sold the land and building for $60,000, his gain on the sale was $55,000 ($60,000 - $5,000).

(a) Adjustments to Basis. No adjustment to your basis in the property is made for improvements by your lessee [IRC Sec. 1019].

(b) Improvements Instead of Rent. The fair market value of improvements that a tenant makes instead of paying you rent is income to you when they are placed on the property [IRC Sec. 109; Reg. Sec. 1.109-1].

Example 2: In January 1988, Mr. Evans leased another piece of land to Mr. Dugal for a period of five years. Under the lease terms, Dugal was not required to pay rent, but in lieu of rent he was to install an irrigation system before the end of the 5th year. Dugal installed the system in the fall of 1992, at which time it had a fair market value of $5,000. Evans realized $5,000 income in 1992.

¶1234   FORGIVENESS OF DEBT

[New tax legislation may affect this subject; see ¶1.]

If a debt you owe is cancelled or forgiven, other than as a gift to you, you generally must include the cancelled amount in income [Reg. Sec. 1.61-12]. A debt is any indebtedness for which you are liable or which attaches to property you hold. Special rules apply where the debtor is bankrupt or insolvent.

Example 1: Mr. Anderson, a carpenter, owes Mr. Billson $1,000. Anderson repairs Billson's house. In return, Billson forgives the debt. Anderson must include the $1,000 in his income, as compensation for services.

(a) Bankrupt or Insolvent Debtor. Despite the general rule, a cancelled debt is not included in income, if: (1) cancellation takes place in a bankruptcy case or (2) cancellation takes place when the debtor is insolvent and the amount excluded is not more than the amount by which the debtor is insolvent [IRC Sec. 108(a)].

The tax treatment of debt discharges for bankrupt and other financially troubled taxpayers reflects general bankruptcy policy. To preserve the debtor's "fresh start," no income is recognized on a debt discharged in bankruptcy. However, some of the tax treatment, such as a reduction of tax attributes and reduction in the basis of depreciable assets, minimizes rather than cancels any tax effect.

Reducing tax attributes. This income exclusion for discharged indebtedness is not necessarily cost-free. As a bankrupt and insolvent taxpayer, you must reduce the amount of certain potentially tax-saving attributes you possess. Reducing these tax attributes serves to postpone, rather than entirely eliminate, tax on the cancelled indebtedness. This prevents an excessive tax benefit (e.g., duplicative tax breaks for the same expense) from the debt cancellation. For example, if you have $10,000 of debt cancelled, you avoid owing tax on that $10,000. However, you must reduce your tax attributes by $10,000.

The debt discharge amount is applied to reduce your tax attributes in the following order: (1) net operating losses and carryovers; (2) carryovers that constitute the general business credit and (3) net capital losses and carryovers. If any debt discharge amount is left, it is used to reduce your basis in assets, but not below the amount of your remaining undischarged liabilities. Any debt discharge amount that remains after the basis will reduce foreign tax credit carryovers. After that, any remaining debt discharge amount is disregarded [Sec. 108(b)]. The credits are reduced 33⅓ for each dollar of debt discharge amount. The other tax attributes are reduced dollar for dollar.

Election to reduce basis. You can elect, on Form 982, to apply all or part of the debt discharge amount to reduce basis (but not below zero) in certain property instead of or before reducing other tax attributes. Property subject to this election is depreciable property or real property held primarily for sale to customers in the ordinary course of a trade or business [Temp. Reg. Sec. 7a.1].

> ➤ **TAX STRATEGY** If you are an insolvent taxpayer who expects to earn a profit in subsequent years, you can benefit from this election. You would be able to hold on to operating loss carryovers that could be fully applied to shelter income as soon as it is earned. In return, you would be giving up depreciation deductions of equal amount in total—but spread out over several years. On the other hand, if you expect that the net operating loss carryover will expire before it could be used, you should choose not to make the election.

The treatment of a debt discharged outside of bankruptcy depends on whether you are solvent or insolvent when the discharge is made.

Insolvent debtors. The amount of debt discharge is excluded from income up to the point of insolvency. The excluded amount reduces tax attributes the same way as if the debt had been discharged in bankruptcy. Any amount not excluded is treated under rules for solvent debtors.

> **Example 2:** Baker Corp. has $8,000 of its liabilities discharged outside bankruptcy. Just before this, its liabilities totaled $22,000, and its assets' fair market value was $15,000. Since its liabilities were more ($7,000 more) than its assets, it was insolvent. Baker can exclude $7,000 of the debt cancellation.

(b) Corporation Issuing Stock to Cancel Debt. If a corporation issues its own stock in cancelling its debt, it realizes income [IRC Sec. 108(e)(10)]. Thus, the debtor corporation has income equal to the excess of the debt's principal amount over the stock's fair market value.

> **NOTE:** At one time, this rule did not apply to corporations in a Title 11 bankruptcy and insolvent corporations involving transfers of "disqualified stock." However, this stock-for-debt exception was repealed, starting with debt instruments issued (or stock transferred) after October 9, 1990, in satisfaction of any indebtedness. Disqualified stock is any stock with a stated redemption price if: (1) it has a fixed redemption date, (2) the issuer has the right to redeem it, or (3) its holder has a put right that can require its redemption by the issuer.

(c) Cancellation as a Gift. A debt cancellation that constitutes a gift or bequest is not treated as income to you [IRC Sec. 102]. A debt discharge that is only a medium for another form of payment, such as a gift or salary, is not treated under the debt discharge rules.[1]

(d) Debt Acquired by Related Party. An outstanding debt acquired by someone related to you is treated as if acquired by you [IRC Sec. 108(e)(4)].

(e) Settlement of Mortgage for Less Than Face Value. If settlement of a mortgage for less than its face value is gratuitous, no income results to the mortgagor. Otherwise, the discount is generally considered a taxable discharge of indebtedness.

▶ **SELLER FINANCING EXCEPTION** If the seller of specific property reduces the buyer's debt that arose out of the purchase, and the reduction to the buyer does not occur in a bankruptcy case or when the buyer is insolvent, then the reduction to the buyer of the purchase-money is to be treated for both the seller and the buyer as a purchase price adjustment on the property [IRC Sec. 108(e) (5)]. Thus, the buyer reduces his basis in the property and the seller adjusts his gain or loss on the transaction.

Example 3: Mr. Able sells a house to Mr. Baker for $250,000. Able receives $50,000 in cash at the time of sale and takes back a $200,000 mortgage on the home. Assume the price of real estate in the area has declined, and Able agrees to reduce Baker's indebtedness by $10,000. Result: The sales price of the house is now deemed to be $240,000.

Another alternative: Instead of reducing the indebtedness, the borrower and lender can restructure the debt—by charging less interest—without discharge of indebtedness income.[2]

¶1235   ALIMONY AND SEPARATE MAINTENANCE

Alimony and separate maintenance payments you receive from your ex-spouse—unlike property settlements—are includible in your income and deductible by your ex-spouse. To qualify as alimony or separate maintenance, the payments must meet the following conditions [IRC Sec. 71; Temp. Reg. Sec. 1.71-1T]:

- The payment must be made in cash. For purposes of this rule, cash includes checks and money orders payable on demand. It does not include transfers of services, execution of debt instruments or use of your ex-spouse's property.
- The payment cannot be designated as a payment that is excludable from your gross income and nondeductible by your ex-spouse.
- Spouses who are legally separated under a decree of divorce or separate maintenance cannot be members of the same household at the time the payments are made.

▶ **EXCEPTIONS** If and your ex-spouse are living together, you are not considered members of the same household if one of you is preparing to move out and does, in fact, do so within one month after the payment is made. Also, the living-apart condition does not apply to payments made under a written separation agreement or decree between you if you are not legally separated under a divorce or separate maintenance decree.

- All payments terminate on your death (this need not be specifically stated in the decree, though). If the payments are made along two separate streams, and one stream does not specifically terminate on death, only the nonterminating portion does not qualify. Substitute payments that begin, increase or are accelerated at your death are also disqualified.
- The payments cannot be made for child support. To be considered child support, the payments must be fixed as such under the divorce or separation instrument.
- Payments can't violate the excess front-loading rules (below).

NOTE: For divorce or separation instruments executed before 1985, that have not been modified, the above requirements do not apply. To qualify as alimony under the rules prior to that time, the payments must: (1) be made under a final decree of divorce or separation or a separation agreement, (2) be based on the marital or family relationship, (3) be periodic and (4) not be for child support.

(a) Excess Front-Loading Recapture Rules. If the payments diminish from year to year, special rules may apply. Amounts that have previously been deemed alimony can be recharacterized retroactively. The exact rules depend on whether the divorce or separation instrument was executed after 1986. In either case, though, your ex-spouse (as the paying spouse) would have to include in income funds that were previously deducted as alimony. You (the recipient), on the other hand, pick up a corresponding deduction.

Under the rules for post-1986 divorce or separation instruments, recapture occurs (if at all) in the third year payments are made. That recapture relates to both the first and second year payments. If payments made in the second year exceed third year payments by more than $15,000, the excess must be recaptured. That recaptured amount is then subtracted from the second year's payment. If the first year payment exceeds that averaged sum by more than $15,000, the first year excess is recaptured as well [IRC Sec. 71(f)].

> **Example 1:** Under a 1992 divorce decree, Blake pays Crystal $50,000. He makes no payments in the next two years. Result: $35,000 is recaptured in the third year ($50,000 less $15,000) (assuming no exceptions discussed below apply).

> **Example 2:** Assume that Blake in Example 1 pays $50,000 in the first year, $20,000 in the second year and $0 in the third year. Result: The recapture amount is $5,000 from the second year ($20,000 less $15,000) and $27,500 for the first year [$50,000 less $22,500 ($15,000 + 7,500)]. ($7,500 is the average payments per year for years two and three after reducing the payments by the $5,000 recaptured from year two.).

Different recapture rules apply to payments made pursuant to 1985 or 1986 divorce or separation instruments. The payments must be made for at least six consecutive years. If payments made during any of those years were more than $10,000 less than payments made in any prior years during the six-year period, the excess was recaptured as income to the payor—and deducted by the payee. Recaptures reduced the amount deemed to have been paid for calculating recaptures in later years.

> **Example 3:** Mr. Adams paid alimony of $30,000 in 1990, $18,000 in 1991 and $5,000 in 1992. In 1991, he had a recapture of $2,000 ($30,000 reduced by the sum of $18,000 plus $10,000). For later years, he is deemed to have paid $28,000 in 1990. In 1992, his recapture is composed of two elements. Recapture attributable to the 1990 payment is $13,000 ($28,000 less the sum of $5,000 plus the $10,000 threshold amount). Another $3,000 of recapture is attributable to the 1991 payment ($18,000 less the sum of $5,000 plus $10,000). Total 1992 recapture is $16,000.

There is no recapture for alimony paid under pre-1985 divorce and separation instruments.

Exceptions. The recapture rules do not apply if: (1) the payments are made under a support order, (2) the payments stop because you remarry before the end of the third post-separation year, (3) the payments stop because either of you dies before the end of the third post-separation year or (4) the payments are made under a liability to pay a fixed portion of income from a business or property or from compensation for employment or self-employment [IRC Sec. 71(f)(5)].

(b) Property Transfers Incident to Divorce. The transfer of property between spouses incident to a divorce or separation is a nontaxable transaction. Your ex-spouse has no gain or loss on the property he or she transfers to you, and you carry over his or her basis in the property you receive. Thus, if the property has appreciated in value, the gain is not included in income until you dispose of the property. This nontaxable treatment extends to transfers of cash or other property, the assumption of liabilities in excess of basis, and to transfers of installment obligations. However, your ex-spouse must recognize gain under a transfer in trust, incident to divorce, to the extent that liabilities assumed by the trust exceed his or her basis [IRC Sec. 1041].

A property transfer is incident to divorce if it occurs within one year after the marriage terminates or is related to the divorce [IRC Sec. 1041(c)].

(c) Support Payments. The part of an alimony payment that is specifically designated as child support is not included in your income (and it is not deductible by your ex-spouse). If your ex-spouse makes a payment for less than the full amount called for under the agreement, the amounts are allocated first to child support and then to alimony [IRC Sec. 71(c)(3)].

> **Example 4:** Joe Brown's divorce decree requires that he pay $500 a month alimony to his wife and $500 in child support for their son, Billy. Because of strained finances, Joe pays a total of $9,000 to his wife in 1991. Of this amount, Joe can deduct only $3,000 because the first $6,000 is allocated to child support ($500 × 12 months).

¶1236   GAMBLING INCOME

You must include in income your total gambling winnings. This can include the proceeds from lotteries, raffles, sweepstakes and the like. You can deduct your gambling losses to the extent of your winnings, but only if you itemize your deductions [¶1942].

¶1237   INCOME IN RESPECT OF A DECEDENT

Amounts that the decedent had the right to receive, and could have received had death not occurred, are treated as "income in respect of a decedent." This includes income that a cash basis taxpayer had accrued at the time of death (i.e., accounts receivable or interest on a discount bond) and claims to income that were contingent at death. These items are taxed as income to the decedent's successor upon receipt [IRC Sec. 691(a), 1014(c); Reg. Sec. 1.691(a)-1,2].

> **Example:** Mr. Stone, a cash basis taxpayer, purchased a U.S. Savings Bond five years before his death. He paid no tax on the interest accruing on it during his lifetime. Mrs. Stone inherited the bond. When she cashes it in, Mrs. Stone will be taxed on all interest that accrued on the bond during Mr. Stone's lifetime—as well as earnings allocable to her period of ownership.

¶1238   S CORPORATION AND PARTNERSHIP
PASSTHROUGH INCOME

S corporations and partnerships are so-called passthrough entities. Generally, they pay no tax because their income is passed through to (and taxed to) their shareholders or partners.

S corporations. Each shareholder must report his or her pro rata share of the S corporation's income—regardless of whether any of that income is actually distributed to the shareholder. The shareholder's basis is increased by that share of income. If a distribution is made, it is generally tax-free to the extent of the shareholder's basis, with the excess being treated as capital gain. However, a distribution from accumulated earnings and profits (for example, E&P accumulated prior to the corporation switching from C to S status) is taxable as a dividend.

Example 1: S corporation distributes $50,000 cash to shareholder Smith. S corp has $10,000 accumulated E&P. Smith's stock basis is $25,000. Result: $10,000 of the distribution is taxable to Smith as a dividend. As for the remaining $40,000, $25,000 is a tax-free return of Smith's stock basis and $15,000 is taxable capital gain.

For more information on S corporation passthrough income, see Chapter 21.

Partnerships. A partner's income includes his or her distributive share of "separately stated items" and the partnership's taxable income, even if the partner does not actually receive any distribution. (A partner's distributive share is usually fixed by the partnership agreement.) A partner does not generally recognize gain on a distribution of partnership property (until the partner sells the property). But a partner does recognize gain to the extent a cash distribution exceeds the adjusted basis of his or her partnership interest.

Example 2: XYZ Partnership distributes $8,000 in cash and property worth $3,000 to Mr. Brady, who has a $10,000 basis in his partnership interest. Result: Brady recognizes no gain. However, if Brady had received $11,000 in cash, he would have recognized $1,000 of capital gain.

For more information on partnership passthrough income, see Chapter 24.

¶1240   CHILD'S INCOME

[New tax legislation may affect this subject; see ¶1.]

Pay for your child's services and other income your child gets is included in his or her gross income and not in your gross income [IRC Sec. 73; Reg. Sec. 1.73-1]. Payments for board and lodging received by you from your employed child are income to you only to the extent they exceed the cost of household expenses attributable to your child.[1]

How child's income is taxed. If your child is 14 years of age or older, all of his or her income (earned and unearned) is taxed at the child's rate. However, if your child is under 14 and has over $1,200 of unearned income in 1992, special tax rules apply. Your child's "net unearned income" is taxed at your rate (assuming it is higher than the child's tax rate). If your rate is not known when your child's return is filed, a reasonable estimate should be made and an amended return filed when the correct information is ascertained.[2] In 1992, net unearned income means unearned income less the sum of $600 plus the greater of (1) $600 (attributable to either your child's standard deduction or itemized deductions) or (2) allowable itemized deductions directly connected with the production of unearned income [IRC Sec. 1(g), Temp. Reg. Sec. 1.1(i)-1T]. Use Form 8615 when computing tax on children's 1992 investment income of more than $1,200.

NOTE: The figures for figuring the tax on an under-age-14 child's unearned income are indexed annually for inflation [IRC Sec. 1(f)(6)].

Filing shortcut. If you are a parent of a child under age 14 who must file a return, you may elect to include the unearned income of the child on your return if certain requirements are met. This allows you to avoid filing Form 8615 by electing to include the child's gross income over $1,200 on your 1992 return. The family should end up paying the same combined tax, but the filing process is simplified as a result of the break.

(Note: A quirk in the tax law actually makes using this filing shortcut slightly more tax-expensive than having your child file his or her own return.)

To be eligible to make the election, all the following requirements must be met:

1. Your child has gross income only from interest and dividends.
2. The gross income is between $500 and $5,000.
3. No estimated tax payments are made in your child's name for the year.
4. Your child is not subject to backup withholding.

Itemized deductions directly connected with the production of income include investment adviser fees and safety deposit rental costs incurred to store investment property. Such expenses are allowable deductions only to the extent that they, when combined with other miscellaneous itemized deductions, exceed 2% of the taxpayer's adjusted gross income.

In 1992, income of up to $600 or the amount of allowable itemized deductions directly connected with the production of unearned income is sheltered from tax (either by the child's standard deduction or itemized deductions). The next $600 of unearned 1992 income is taxed in the child's bracket. That's why unearned income of $1,200 or less is never taxed at the parent's tax rate in 1992.[3]

Example 1: Sally Johnson, 13 years old, has $4,100 of investment income, $1,500 of itemized deductions (net of the 2% floor) related to producing that income and no earned income. Thus, Sally has $2,000 of net unearned income taxed at her parents' top tax rate. She also has $600 of income taxed at her own rate.

Example 2: Joe Jones, age 13, has $2,500 of interest income. He has $600 of itemized deductions (e.g., state income tax and charitable contributions) and no earned income. These deductions are not related to the production of unearned income. Therefore, no more than $600 of them may be used to shelter that income. Thus, his net unearned income taxed at his parents' tax rate is $1,300. As in Example 1, $600 is also taxed in the child's own bracket.

Example 3: Same facts as in Example 2, except that Joe also has $300 of earned income. The tax result for his unearned income remains the same, and he can use the remaining $100 of itemized deductions to shelter some of his earned income. The remaining $200 of earned income is taxed in Joe's own tax bracket.

Example 4: Anne Richards, age 13, has $2,100 of investment income and $900 of earnings from delivering newspapers. She can claim a $900 standard deduction—the amount of her earned income. Anne can use $600 of this to reduce her unearned income. Another $600 of unearned income is taxed at Anne's own tax bracket. The $900 of net unearned income left from the $2,100 she received is taxed at her parents' top tax rate. The other $300 of Anne's standard deduction is applied against her earned income. That means Anne is also taxed on $600 of earned income at her own tax rate.

NOTE: Your child may be subject to the alternative minimum tax if he or she has certain items given preferential tax treatment or certain adjustments to taxable income. See ¶2600 et seq.

¶1241   PROPERTY BOUGHT BY STOCKHOLDERS FOR LESS THAN FAIR MARKET VALUE

If property is transferred in a sale or exchange by your corporation to you for an amount less than its fair market value, you are treated as having received a distribution from the corporation.[1] The distribution is taxable as a dividend to the extent it is dividend income as determined by rules explained in ¶1218 et seq. If you are an individual, the amount of the distribution is the difference between the amount paid for the property and its fair market value.

¶1242   PROFIT ON STATE AND MUNICIPAL CONTRACTS

The profit from a contract with a state, municipality or other political subdivision, such as a school district, must be included in gross income. If payment is in warrants, their fair market value should be reported as income. If the amount received when they are cashed is more than the amount previously reported, the excess is income; if less, the difference is deductible [Reg. Sec. 1.61-3].

¶1243 BUSINESS INSURANCE PROCEEDS

The tax treatment of business insurance proceeds depends on the nature of the loss. Insurance payments for business property destroyed by a casualty are treated much like proceeds from the sale of the property. Only the amount by which they exceed the property's basis is included in income—not the gross insurance payment. And it is possible to avoid having to report even that excess by rolling over the full proceeds into the purchase of similar property [¶1710 et seq.]. If the proceeds are less than the property's basis, they reduce the deductible loss. See ¶2304 et seq.

Ordinarily, proceeds of insurance against loss of profits because of a fire or other casualty are income—as the profits themselves would have been. Use and occupancy insurance and business interruption insurance proceeds are examples [¶1710(e)].[1]

¶1244 RECOVERY OF TAX BENEFIT ITEMS

When you recover an amount attributable to a prior year's deduction, the amount is included in your income only to the extent it reduced your tax liability in the earlier year [IRC Sec. 111]. Here are some of the more common items to which this rule applies:

(a) State and Local Income Tax Refunds. These refunds are taxable (1) if you claimed the refunded taxes as an itemized deduction and (2) only to the extent your itemized deductions exceeded your standard deduction for the year those taxes were previously deducted.

> **Example 1:** Mr. Benson had $500 of state income taxes withheld from his paychecks in 1991. He claimed the standard deduction on his tax return. During 1992, Benson received a $200 refund of those state tax payments. The refund is excluded from tax since it did not reduce Benson's taxable income in 1991.

> **Example 2:** Assume the same facts as in Example 1, except that Benson itemized his deductions and they totalled $150 more than the standard deduction. Now Benson must report $150 of the refund on his return since his taxable income was previsouly reduced by that amount on account of the recovered funds.

(b) Real Estate Tax Rebate. The same rules apply here as to state and local income tax refunds.

(c) Medical Insurance Reimbursements. There is often a time lag between when you pay a medical bill and when you receive a reimbursement from an insurance company or employer. If the lag straddles the end of a year, the cost is a deductible medical expense (subject to the 7½% of adjusted gross income deduction floor) in the year you pay it. When (and if) you later receive a reimbursement, that reimbursement is taxable to the extent of any prior deduction in excess of the standard deduction.

> **Example 3:** Ms. Carter paid $3,000 of unreimbursed medical expenses in 1991. Her adjusted gross income was $35,000 that year. Therefore, she claimed a medical expense deduction of $375 ($3,000 less $2,625, which is 7½% of $35,000). Carter's other itemized deductions exceeded her standard deduction amount. Therefore, Carter received a tax benefit for the full $375 medical expense deduction. In 1992, Carter got a $1,000 reimbursement for some of those medical expenses from her insurance company. Result: Carter must report $375 of the reimbursement as income. The other $625 is exempt from tax.

(d) Theft or Casualty Losses. These are subject to a 10% of adjusted gross income deduction floor. The mechanics for determining how much of a recovery is taxable involves the same process as for medical expense reimbursements.

(e) Multiple Recoveries. When you recover more than one item that was previously deducted as an itemized deduction, the income inclusion is calculated as follows: (1) If a recovery is attributable to an item that is subject to a percentage of gross income deduction floor, subtract the recovery from the total deductible expenses for which it was received. Then figure out how much less the deduction would have been. (2) Add together the amounts in (1) plus the amount of any recovery for items not subject to deduction floors. (3) Compare that sum to the excess of actual deductions over the standard deduction for the year to which the recoveries are attributable. (4) The smaller of the two is the taxable recovery to be included in income.

(f) Tax Credits. If an amount is recovered in a tax year and a credit was based on that amount in a prior tax year, your tax is increased by the amount of the credit attributable to the recovered amount to the extent the credit reduced the amount of tax. This rule does not apply to amounts for which a credit was allowed under the foreign tax credit [IRC Sec. 111(b)].

(g) Special Situations. When a deduction reduces taxable income, but does not reduce the tax (because, for example, you are subject to the alternative minimum tax), recovery of the amount giving rise to the deduction can be excluded from income [IRC Sec. 111(d)].

¶1250 GINNIE MAE (Government National Mortgage Association) CERTIFICATES

You can get a return on your investment that reflects the relatively high interest rates homebuyers are paying plus the safety of government guarantees by buying a Ginnie Mae certificate. These certificates are issued by private firms (typically a mortgage company or a bank), backed by a pool of government-insured mortgages (VA, FHA and FmHA home loans) and guaranteed by the Government National Mortgage Association. They usually mature in thirty years.

You receive a return that reflects the interest rates that individual homeowners in the mortgage pool are paying. Each month, you receive a check that is a passthrough of taxable interest and a tax-free return of principal on the pooled mortgages—just like the monthly payments made by the homeowners. Ginnie Mae guarantees these monthly payments, whether or not they are actually made by the homeowners.

> ➤ **INVESTOR WARNING** As mentioned above, Ginnie Maes pay back principal over the course of the certificate. When the certificate payments end, there is no lump-sum repayment of principal as there is with bonds or bank certificates of deposit. Thus, you should have the discipline to set aside the return of principal portion of each check you receive and re-invest it if you intend to maintain your nest egg.

Ginnie Mae's guarantee of full repayment of principal applies to certificates held to maturity. If a certificate is sold before maturity, it may be sold at a loss. That occurs when the underlying mortgages bear lower interest rates than new mortgages. On the other hand, if mortgage interest rates decline, outstanding Ginnie Mae certificates should sell at a premium. The difference between your basis and sales proceeds is a capital gain or loss. These fluctuations in value can be avoided, though, with a Ginnie Mae certificate backed by an adjustable rate mortgage pool. Since the interest rate on the certificate is adjustable, the certificate should trade at prices close to its original issue price (less the amount of principal already distributed).

Fluctuating monthly payments. As a buyer of a Ginnie Mae certificate, you cannot be sure of the size of the payment that will be made from month to month. In addition to the scheduled payments of principal and interest, the checks may include unscheduled prepayments of principal that reflect foreclosures and prepayments made by the homeowners in the mortgage pool.

Investment options. You can get in on Ginnie Maes by purchasing the certificates themselves (minimum denomination: $25,000, with $5,000 increments above that), units of a trust that invests in a pool of Ginnie Mae certificates (for as little as $1,000, with $100 increments above that) or mutual fund shares (also, for as little as $1,000, with $100 increments above that). A unit trust is locked in to the same Ginnie Mae certificates during the life of the trust. A mutual fund, on the other hand, is actively managed, and its Ginnie Mae holdings can change. However, you pay a price for buying a fund; the fund usually pays a lower rate than a unit trust or certificate. Also, if interest rates rise—and stay high—mutual fund shares will go down in value. Thus, you lose some of your principal. Certificate or unit trust holders can recoup their full principal by holding the investment until maturity. Neither funds nor trusts are guaranteed by the government; only the Ginnie Mae certificates are. Profit or loss on the sale or redemption of these investment vehicles is capital gain or loss.

¶1251   REIT (Real Estate Investment Trusts) SHARES

This investment vehicle permits even a small investor to buy into a large real estate property. In essence, a REIT is an investment company that invests in real estate. (For tax rules governing the trust, see ¶3329). When you buy shares of REIT stocks you also invest in professionally managed real estate—the underlying properties of the REIT.

A REIT operates much the same way as a mutual fund. It is publicly traded on the stock market. Thus, unlike a limited partnership interest, a REIT investment is completely liquid.

Dividends paid out to you are generally taxed as ordinary income although part of the dividend may be considered a tax deferred return of principal, reflecting the deductions claimed by REIT equity investments. However, REITs may pass through net capital gain to you—with those dividends being treated as capital gain by the recipients [IRC Sec. 857(b)(3)(B)].

Investment options. There are four basic types of REITs:

1. Mortgage REITs. These REITs basically make only mortgage loans. As a result, the shares in these REITs perform much like bonds and offer little or no growth potential. Their prices go up and down in response to swings in interest rates. Also, if the borrower defaults, you lose money, even though the underlying property may have appreciated.

➤ **LOWER RISK REIT** With a Participating Mortgage REIT, you participate in the property's growth, as well as getting a return based on the mortgage interest.

2. *Equity REITs.* If you want an ownership position in real estate, you may prefer an equity REIT. The REIT owns the property itself, so you can share in an increase in the property's value. An equity REIT does especially well when property values grow.

3. *Hybrid REITs.* These invest in both properties and mortgages. A hybrid offers you a sampling of both worlds—an annual return and a shot at future appreciation.

4. *Finite REITs (FREITs).* This investment arrangement attempts to have its shares better reflect the value of its underlying property by being self-liquidating. A FREIT promises to liquidate its assets and distribute proceeds to shareholders within a specified period of time (usually seven to 15 years). This promise of a large chunk of money in the near future is supposed to keep FREITs' stock prices up. However, a problem arises if the real estate market is in a slump when the liquidation deadline arrives.

You have capital gain or loss on the sale or redemption of a REIT investment.

¶1252　　REMICS (Real Estate Mortgage Investment Conduits)

A REMIC is an entity that holds a fixed pool of mortgages secured by interests in real property. You can purchase either a regular or residual interest [IRC Sec. 860A—860G].

(a) A Regular Interest is treated like a bond for tax purposes, even though it may be issued in the form of stock or an interest in a partnership or trust. You receive taxable interest payments and a tax-free return of principal. You must use the accrual method of accounting to determine the amount of interest to include in income each year. Interests purchased at a discount are subject to the original issue discount and market discount rules [¶1217].

If a regular interest in a REMIC is sold at a profit, some or all of the gain may be ordinary income, rather than capital gain. To calculate the ordinary income portion, you must first determine how much interest the instrument would have yielded during the period you held it using a rate equal to 110% of the applicable federal rate as of the beginning of the holding period. The excess of that figure over the amount you actually took into income is ordinary income.

> **Example:** Ms. Moore purchased a regular interest for $10,000. Two years later, she sold it for $10,700—a $700 profit. Moore received $1,800 of taxable income from the REMIC. However, she would have gotten $2,000 of interest if the REMIC had yielded 110% of the applicable federal rate. Thus, $200 ($2,000 less $1,800) of her profit is ordinary income and the other $500 is capital gain.

(b) A Residual Interest is, in essence, the right to what's left after the regular interest is paid. As a residual interest owner, you get the difference between the cash flow from the mortgage payments and the lesser amount paid out to regular interest owners. The return fluctuates, for instance, if mortgagors default on payments or pay off early. Your residual interests are taxed like partnership interests. You take into income an allocable portion of the REMIC's income or loss—regardless of whether the income has been distributed. Generally, the allocation is made quarterly, based on the number of days each investor held the residual interest. REMICs may also pass through to you certain costs that may be deducted (subject to the 2% floor for deducting miscellaneous itemized deductions).

In determining the REMIC's net income, interest-type payments to regular interest holders are deductible.

Your basis is increased by the amount of taxable income and reduced by deductible losses. However, you may deduct losses only to the extent of your basis. Excess losses are carried over and used only to offset income from the same REMIC.

Footnotes to Chapter 2

(For your added convenience, in brackets [] with the footnotes below, you will find citations to related paragraphs in the "RIA United States Tax Reporter"(USTR), "CCH Federal Tax Reporter"(CCH) and "RIA Federal Tax Coordinator 2d" (FTC) multivolume services.)

FOOTNOTE ¶ 1200 [USTR ¶ 614; CCH ¶ 5504; FTC ¶ A-2502].

(1) Comm. v. Turney, 82 F2d 661, 17 AFTR 679.

(2) Strauss, 2 BTA 598.

(3) Treas. Dept. booklet "Investment Income and Expenses" (1991 Ed.), p. 3.

(4) Poe v. Seaborn, 282 US 101, 51 SCt 58, 9 AFTR 576; U.S. v. Malcolm, 282 US 792, 51 SCt 184, 9 AFTR 1063.

(5) U.S. v. Sullivan, 274 US 259, 47 SCt 607, 6 AFTR 6753.

(6) Akers v. Scofield, 167 F2d 718, 36 AFTR 981.

(7) Rutkin v. U.S., 343 US 130, 72 SCt 571, 41 AFTR 596.

(8) James v. U.S., 7 AFTR 2d 1361, 81 SCt 1052, 366 US 313.

FOOTNOTE ¶ 1201 [USTR ¶ 614.007; CCH ¶ 5507; FTC ¶ H-1000 et seq.].

(1) Comm. v. Minzer, 5 AFTR 2d 1572, 279 F2d 338.

(2) Ostheimer v. U.S., 3 AFTR 2d 886, 264 F2d 789.

(3) Comm. v. Daehler, 6 AFTR 2d 5082, 281 F2d 823.

(4) Jernigan, ¶ 68,018 PH Memo TC.

(5) Roberts, 10 TC 581, affd 176 F2d 221; Foster, ¶ 48,024 PH Memo TC; Cesanelli, 8 TC 776; Wexler, ¶ 60,266 PH Memo TC.

(6) Rev. Rul. 73-13, 1973-1 CB 42.

FOOTNOTE ¶ 1202 [USTR ¶ 614.016; CCH ¶ 6553; FTC ¶ J-6001].

FOOTNOTE ¶ 1203 [USTR ¶ 744; CCH ¶ 6204; FTC ¶ J-1200 et seq.].

FOOTNOTE ¶ 1204 [USTR ¶ 614.021, 614.111; CCH ¶ 5800; FTC ¶ H-1001].

(1) Florsheim v. U.S., 156 F2d 105, 34 AFTR 1515.

(2) Rev. Rul. 62-102, 1962-2 CB 37.

(3) Rev. Rul. 68-294, 1968-1 CB 46.

(4) Rev. Rul. 55-422, 1955-1 CB 14.

FOOTNOTE ¶ 1205 [USTR ¶ 614.36; CCH ¶ 5507.2712; 5507.42; FTC ¶ J-1455].

FOOTNOTE ¶ 1206 [USTR ¶ 614.040; CCH ¶ 5507.02-5507.08; FTC H-1001].

(1) Treas. Dept. booklet "Your Federal Income Tax" (1991 Ed.), p. 48.

(2) Rev. Rul. 70-87, 1970-1 CB 29.

FOOTNOTE ¶ 1207 [USTR ¶ 614.012; CCH ¶ 5508.01-5508.161; FTC ¶ E-5125].

(1) Rev. Rul. 79-24, 1979-1 CB 60.

(2) Jacques, 5 BTA 56; Davidson, 94 F2d 1011, 20 AFTR 1033.

(3) Casale v. Comm. 247 F2d 440, 52 AFTR 122; Prunier v. Comm. 248 F2d 818, 52 AFTR 693.

(4) Treas. Dept. booklet "Your Federal Income Tax" (1991 Ed.), p. 44.

(5) Rev. Rul. 64-328, 1964-2 CB 11; Rev. Rul. 66-110 1966-1 CB 12; Rev. Rul. 67-154, 1967-1 CB 11; Rev. Rul. 78-420, 1978-2 CB 67; Rev. Rul. 79-50, 1979-1 CB 138.

(6) Hitner v. Lederer, 63 F2d 877, 12 AFTR 329.

(7) Rev. Rul. 58-128, 1958-1 CB 89.

(8) Rev. Rul. 60-330, 1960-2 CB 46.

(9) Rev. Rul. 57-37, 1957-1 CB 18.

(10) Rev. Rul. 56-249, 1956-1 CB 488.

FOOTNOTE ¶ 1208 [USTR ¶ 614.032; CCH ¶ 5508; FTC ¶ H-2805].

(1) Rev. Rul. 67-402, 1967-2 CB 135.

(2) Comm. v. Fender Sales, 14 AFTR 2d 6076, 338 F2d 924.

FOOTNOTE ¶ 1209 [USTR ¶ 614.034; CCH ¶ 5508.01; 5509.01-5509.075; FTC ¶ H-1508].

(1) Treas. Dept. booklet "Your Federal Income Tax" (1991 Ed.), p.42.

(2) Schlemmer v. U.S., 94 F2d 77, 20 AFTR 645.

FOOTNOTE ¶ 1210 [USTR ¶ 614.030; CCH ¶ 8587.2825; FTC ¶ H-2810].

FOOTNOTE ¶ 1211 [USTR ¶ 614.067; CCH ¶ 5704.342; FTC ¶ J-2975 et seq.].

(1) Fall River Electric Light Co., 23 BTA 168.

(2) Kieselbach v. Comm. 317 U.S. 399, 30 AFTR 371.

(3) Rev. Rul. 73-322, 1973-2 CB 44.

(4) Terrel, 7 BTA 773.

(5) W. Noll, 43 BTA 496; Campbell v. Sailer, 224 F2d 641, 47 AFTR 1490.

(6) Est. of Ricaby, 27 TC 886, Rev. Rul. 60-284, 1960-2 CB 464.

(7) Jaglom, 9 AFTR 2d 1686, 303 F2d 847.

(8) Treas. Dept. letter, 2/7/49.

FOOTNOTE ¶ 1212 [USTR ¶ 614.081; CCH ¶ 5704.3025-5704.3129; FTC ¶ J-3002].

FOOTNOTE ¶ 1216 [USTR ¶ 614.148; CCH ¶ 5704.02; FTC ¶ H-2000 et seq.].

(1) Rev. Rul. 92-7, IRB 1992-4, superseding Rev. Rul. 91-12, 1991-1 CB 282.

FOOTNOTE ¶ 1217 [USTR ¶ 12,714.01; CCH ¶32,760-32,762.07; FTC ¶ J-3601 et seq.].

(1) Rev. Rul. 89-46, 1989-1 CB 272.

(2) Rev. Proc. 91-65, IRB 1991-50.

(3) Rev. Proc. 91-46, IRB 1991-34.

(4) Rev. Rul. 92-6, IRB 1992-4.

FOOTNOTE ¶ 1218 [USTR ¶ 614.108; CCH ¶ 5504.13; 5507; FTC ¶ J-2610 et seq.].

(1) Young, 6 TC 357.

FOOTNOTE ¶ 1219 [USTR ¶ 3014.06; CCH ¶ 5504.13; 5707; 15,202; FTC ¶ J-2622].

FOOTNOTE ¶ 1220 [USTR ¶ 3014.08; CCH ¶ 15,604.01; FTC ¶ J-2620].

(1) Hadley v. Comm., 8 AFTR 9877, 36 F2d 543.

(2) Rev. Rul. 69-513, 1969-2 CB 29.

(3) Limericks, Inc. v. Comm., 165 F2d 483, 36 AFTR 649.

(4) Peco Company, ¶ 67,041 PH Memo TC.

(5) Comm. v. Pope, 50 AFTR 1240, 239 F2d 881.

(6) Dellinger, 32 TC 1178.

(7) Dean, 35 TC 1083, nonacq., 1973-2 CB 4; Hardee, 50 AFTR 2d 82-5252; Martin v. Comm., 48 AFTR 2d 81-5537.

FOOTNOTE ¶ 1221 [USTR¶ 3164.02; CCH ¶ 15,604; FTC ¶ J-2800 et seq.].

FOOTNOTE ¶ 1222 [USTR ¶ 3054; CCH ¶ 15,300-15,304.85; FTC ¶ J-2800 et seq.].

FOOTNOTE ¶ 1223 [USTR ¶ 3054, 3074; CCH ¶15,402; FTC ¶ P-5701].

(1) Rev. Rul. 71-350, 1971-2 CB 176.

FOOTNOTE ¶ 1224 [USTR ¶ 3054, 3074; CCH ¶15,300-15,304.85; FTC ¶ P-5400 et seq.].

FOOTNOTE ¶ 1225 [USTR ¶ 3054.03; CCH ¶ 15,402; FTC ¶ P-5401 et seq.].

FOOTNOTE ¶ 1226 [USTR ¶ 3054.03; CCH ¶ 15,302; FTC ¶ J-2800 et seq.].

FOOTNOTE ¶ 1227 [USTR ¶ 3054.03; CCH ¶ 15,302.146; FTC ¶ J-2822].

(1) GCM 13275, XIII-2 CB 121.

(2) GCM 13414, XIII-2 CB 124.

FOOTNOTE ¶ 1228 [USTR ¶ 3014.06; CCH ¶ 5504.63; FTC ¶ J-2804].

FOOTNOTE ¶ 1229 [USTR ¶ 3314; CCH ¶ 16,004.1165-16,004.126; FTC ¶ F-13118].

(1) Cooledge, 40 BTA 110.

(2) Rev. Rul. 68-348, 1968-2 CB 141.

(3) Arrowsmith v. Comm. 344 US 6, 73 SCt 71, 42 AFTR 649.

(4) Ludorff, 40 BTA 32.

(5) Comm. v. Winthrop, 98 F2d 74, 21 AFTR 657.

(6) Rev. Rul. 65-80, 1965-1 CB 154.

FOOTNOTE ¶ 1230 [USTR ¶ 3314; CCH ¶ 26,620-26,7126; FTC ¶ E-6000].

FOOTNOTE ¶ 1231 [USTR ¶ 8524; CCH ¶ 26,620-26,712; FTC ¶ J-2861].

FOOTNOTE ¶ 1232 [USTR ¶ 614.084; CCH ¶ 5705; 5706.01-5706.70; FTC ¶ J-2000; J-2600].

(1) Wentz v. Gentsch (DC Ohio) 27 AFTR 1128.

(2) U.S. v. Joliet & Chicago R.R. Co., 315 US 44, 28 AFTR 215.

(3) Hort v. Comm., 313 US 28, 61 SCt 757, 25 AFTR 1207.

(4) Hopkins v. U.S., 82 F. Supp. 1015, 37 AFTR 1108.

FOOTNOTE ¶ 1233 [USTR ¶ 1094; CCH ¶ 8703; FTC ¶ J-2500].

FOOTNOTE ¶ 1234 [USTR ¶ 614.114; CCH ¶ 5801-5802.622; FTC ¶ S-7000 et seq.]

(1) Senate Report No. 96-1035, p. 82, 96th Cong., 2d Sess.

(2) Rev. Rul. 91-31, 1991-1 CB 19.

FOOTNOTE ¶ 1235 [USTR ¶ 614.110; CCH ¶ 5708; 6090-6094.89; FTC ¶ J-1392].

FOOTNOTE ¶ 1236 [USTR ¶ 614.182; CCH ¶ 5504.22; FTC ¶ J-1650].

FOOTNOTE ¶ 1237 [USTR ¶ 6914.01; CCH ¶ 840.05; 25,300-25,306.90; FTC ¶ C-9501 et seg; H-1024].

FOOTNOTE ¶ 1238 [USTR ¶ 7024 et seq.; 13,664; CCH ¶ 25,362; 33,484.09; FTC ¶ B-1802; D-1700 et seq.].

FOOTNOTE ¶ 1240 [USTR ¶ 734; CCH ¶ 3175; 5101.01; 6151; FTC ¶ A-1301 et seq.].

(1) Marinaccio, ¶ 49,081 PH Memo TC.

(2) Treas. Dept. booklet "Tax Rules for Children and Dependents" (1991 Ed.), p.10.

(3) Rev. Proc. 91-65, IRB 1991-50.

FOOTNOTE ¶ 1241 [USTR ¶ 3014.11; CCH ¶ 5504.051; FTC ¶ J-2771].

(1) Timberlake v. Comm., 132 F2d 259, 30 AFTR 583, affg. 46 BTA 1082; Comm. v. Gordon, 391 US 83, 21 AFTR 2d 1329.

FOOTNOTE ¶ 1242 [USTR ¶ 614.036; CCH ¶ 5512; FTC ¶ J-1455].

FOOTNOTE ¶ 1243 [USTR ¶ 614.167; CCH ¶31,550.238-31,550.242; FTC ¶ J-5828, 5829].

(1) Oppenheim's Inc. v. Cavanagh, 90 F. Supp. 107, 39 AFTR 468; Rev. Rul. 55-264, 1955-1 CB 11.

FOOTNOTE ¶ 1244 [USTR ¶ 1114; CCH ¶ 7060-7062.55; FTC ¶ J-5500 et seq.].

FOOTNOTE ¶ 1250 [USTR ¶ 1494; CCH ¶ 7905; FTC ¶ M-3708].

FOOTNOTE ¶ 1251 [USTR ¶ 8574; CCH ¶ 26,700-26,742; FTC ¶ E-6600 et seq.].

FOOTNOTE ¶ 1252 [USTR ¶ 860A4; CCH ¶ 26,800-26,921.10; FTC ¶ E-6900 et seq.].

(1) Treas. Dept. booklet "Investment Income and Expenses" (1991 Ed.), pp. 18.

CHAPTER 3

RETIREMENT PLANS

PENSION AND PROFIT-SHARING PLANS

¶1300　　　　　　　　QUALIFIED PLANS IN GENERAL

Retirement plans that meet requirements for special tax-favored treatment are called "qualified plans." The tax benefits are a key reason for adopting such plans.

Qualified plans are "funded." That means the money is accumulated in trust. Some plans are also "contributory" plans. They either permit or require an employee to contribute to the plan and get larger benefits or reduce employer costs.

The tax benefits of a typical employer-funded qualified plan are as follows:

- The employer gets an immediate deduction for contributions made to the plan [IRC Sec. 404(a)].
- The employee owes no tax on his share of employer contributions and remains untaxed until he receives a distribution, usually upon retirement.
- The employee is allowed to contribute to the plan but generally cannot deduct what he contributes. (But see discussion of 401(k) plans [¶1345].
- Both employer and employee contributions are held in a tax-exempt trust and accumulate tax-free.
- When a distribution is made, the employee may be eligible to calculate the tax using a favorable income averaging formula.

¶1301　　　　　　　　TYPES OF QUALIFIED PLANS

Qualified retirement plans are set up in one of two ways: Defined benefit plans or defined contribution plans.

With a defined benefit plan, the amount of benefit payable upon retirement is fixed at the outset. The contribution needed to produce that benefit is determined actuarially. For example, a plan might provide that an employee who retires at age 65, with ten years of service, will receive a pension equal to 50% of his salary. Factors such as the employee's age, length of service, employee turnover and plan earnings will determine the size of the contribution needed to produce that benefit.

Under a defined contribution plan, the rate or method of contribution is fixed. For example, the employer might contribute 10% of compensation for each employee. The amount actually yielded at retirement would depend on plan earnings. With a defined contribution plan, a separate account is maintained for each participant. That account reflects that participant's share of contributions, expenses, investment return and forfeitures. Profit-sharing and stock bonus plans are defined contribution plans with special features.

(a) Pension Plans. Some qualified plans can also be categorized as pension plans. Pension plans are designed to provide "definitely determinable" benefits to employees over a period of years after retirement. All defined benefit plans are pension plans. However, some pension plans—those called money purchase pension plans—are defined contribution plans. What's common is that the contribution (in *a money purchase pension plan*) or benefits (in *a defined benefit pension plan*) are based on a stipulated formula and not subject to employer discretion [Reg. Sec. 1.401(a)-1(b)].

(b) Profit-Sharing Plans. A profit-sharing plan is a type of defined contribution plan that differs from a pension plan in several key respects. First, the employer is not locked into an annual contribution; contributions can be reduced or avoided entirely during lean years [Reg. Sec. 1.401-1(b)(2)]. There is greater flexibility since the employer can assess his situation on a year-by-year basis and adjust the level of contributions accordingly. By contrast, even with a money purchase pension plan, contributions must be fixed and not geared to profits [Reg. Sec. 1.401-1(b)(1)(i)]. Employers—including tax-exempt entities—can make contributions to a profit-sharing plan irrespective of profits [IRC Sec. 401(a)(27)].

Another key difference concerns the allocation of contributions. While the contribution limit for profit-sharing plans is 15% of compensation, it refers to the employer's aggregate payroll and not each participant's compensation. While the allocation cannot discriminate in favor of highly compensated employees, there is some latitude [IRC Sec. 404(a)(3)].

A third key difference concerns the type of benefits that can be paid and the events triggering distributions. While pension plans can pay incidental benefits, they are generally unable to provide benefits not usually associated with pensions [¶1306]. Profit-sharing plans, on the other hand, can provide for distributions on account of illness, disability or layoff [Reg. Sec. 1.401-1(b)(1)].

(c) Stock Bonus Plans. Stock bonus plans are like profit-sharing plans except that benefits are distributable in employer stock [Reg. Sec. 1.401-1(b)(1)(iii)]. As with profit-sharing plans, contributions can be contingent on profits, and the plan must provide a definite predetermined formula for allocating contributions among participants and for distributing funds after a fixed number of years and attaining a certain age.

The most popular form of stock bonus plan is an employee stock ownership plan (ESOP) [¶1355].

(d) Other Types of Qualified Plans. A *target benefit plan* is a hybrid of a defined benefit and defined contribution plan. The benefit at retirement is projected and the annual contributions necessary to meet the projection are then fixed. But the ultimate benefit depends on the actual investment performance of the contributions. In a target benefit plan, the contributions are allocated to separate accounts for each of the participants.

Thrift or savings plans. These plans can take a variety of forms but the common feature is that the participants' contributions generally are matched, either dollar for dollar or according to some set formula, by employer contributions. The distinct advantage these plans offer is that the employee contributions can easily be made through payroll deductions.

¶1306   QUALIFIED PLAN FEATURES

[New tax legislation may affect this subject; see ¶1.]

(a) Employee Contributions. An employer can cut his costs, or the employee can increase the level of benefits, under a qualified plan by making employee contributions. They are divided into two classes—mandatory or voluntary.

"Mandatory contributions" means amounts that an employee is required to contribute either as a condition of (1) employment, (2) plan participation or (3) obtaining benefits attributable to employer contributions. For example, a savings plan benefit formula that matched dollar-for-dollar up to 5% of an employee's compensation involves a mandatory employee contribution. In order to participate in the plan, the employee has to kick in his own funds [IRC Sec. 411(c)(2)(C)].

"Voluntary contributions," on the other hand, are any other contributions which an employee makes. For example, a money purchase pension plan might provide employees with the opportunity to contribute up to 5% of salary. While the contribution is made in after-tax dollars, it can accumulate in the plan tax-free.

(b) Cash or Deferred Arrangements. Profit-sharing, stock bonus and certain pre-1974 money purchase plans can give employees the choice of receiving cash or having a contribution made to the plan, and thus deferring tax on the amount contributed [IRC Sec. 401(k)]. If the employee elects to have funds contributed to the plan, he is not subject to current tax because he could have taken the cash instead [¶1345].

> ➤ **INCIDENTAL BENEFIT RULE**   Qualified plans can only provide incidental death or non-retirement benefits. Other benefits under a pension plan must be secondary to the primary purpose of providing retirement benefits. Pension plans can provide a death benefit and pensions in the event of disability but cannot provide benefits for sickness, accident or layoff. Profit-sharing and stock bonus plans are permitted to provide a broader range of incidental benefits including life, accident and health insurance for a participant and his family [Reg. Sec. 1.401-1(b)(1)(i), (ii)].

(c) Life Insurance in Qualified Plans. The life insurance benefits supplied by a qualified plan are subject to the incidental benefit rule. Whole life coverage is "incidental" only if it meets certain dollar limits:

• Profit-sharing plans. The investment in ordinary life insurance must be less than 50% of the aggregate of current company contributions to the employee's account.[1] For this purpose, "current contributions" means company contributions that have been in the plan for less than two years. There is no limit on the use of company contributions to pay life insurance premiums to the extent the contributions have been held by the plan for two or more years.

Important: For life insurance to be considered incidental, the profit-sharing plan must also require the plan trustee to either (1) convert the entire value of the policy at or before the employee's retirement into cash or to provide periodic income (so no portion of the policy may be used to continue life insurance protection beyond retirement), or (2) distribute the policy to the employee.[2]

- Pension plans. A pension plan can buy insurance on an employee's life and satisfy the incidental benefit rule if the plan meets one of the following tests: (1) The face amount of the policy on the employee's life is not more than 100 times the anticipated monthly benefit payable at retirement.[3] So if an employee is due to receive $2,000 a month upon retirement, the plan can buy $200,000 of life insurance. (2) The premium paid by company contributions is less than 50% of the annual cost of funding the retirement benefit.[4] (3) The face amount of the policy on the employee doesn't exceed the amount which could be purchased by two-thirds of the level annual contribution required to fund the employee's projected monthly benefit.

NOTE: A money purchase plan, which is a hybrid plan, can choose to be tested under either the profit-sharing or pension plan incidental benefit rules.[5]

Tax cost to the employee. Unlike other retirement plan investments, insurance on an employee's life generates some taxable income to the employee. The amount subject to tax each year is the "net cost of the insurance at risk." In other words, the employee pays tax on the premium needed to buy each year's pure insurance element. The insurance at risk is simply the face value of the policy minus that year's cash value.

At retirement, the plan can either convert the policy into cash or it can distribute the policy as part of the employee's payout. If the employee takes the policy as part of the payout, he has several options—he can continue paying the premium, cash the policy in, or exchange it for paid-up insurance.

The plan must offer the insurance option to all covered employees. Coverage cannot be restricted to key employees.

> **ADDED ADVANTAGES** As a general rule, life insurance premiums are a nondeductible expense. But contributions to retirement plans are deductible by the company, even if they are used to purchase insurance. Since the premium dollars are paid for with part of the company's normal retirement plan contribution, the company is supplying an extra benefit without incurring an added expense. Also, since retirement plan income accumulates tax-free, the cash-value buildup of plan-owned policies is sheltered from current tax. The employee does pay some tax if the plan buys insurance on his life. However, he is relieved of a major expense that would otherwise be paid for with nondeductible, after-tax dollars.

(d) Health Insurance Coverage. The use of plan funds to pay the cost of health insurance for an employee or family (including hospitalization, major medical, or similar types of insurance) is generally a "distribution." If the insurance is bought only with funds that have been accumulated for at least two years, there is no limit on the amount of health insurance that may be bought. If the plan permits the use of funds that have not been accumulated for at least 2 years, the cost of the accident or health insurance must not exceed 25% of the funds allocated to the employee's account.[6]

If both ordinary life and accident or health insurance contracts are purchased, the premiums for the accident or health insurance plus one-half of the amount paid for ordinary life insurance premiums may not, in the aggregate, exceed 25 percent of the funds allocated to an employee's account within the last two years.[6]

Example 1: Employer makes a first-year contribution of $20,000 to its profit-sharing plan. If the plan provides ordinary life insurance only, the aggregate insurance premiums must be less than $10,000. If only health and accident insurance is provided, no more than $5,000 can be used to pay health and accident premiums. If, say, $6,000 is spent on ordinary life insurance premiums, then no more than $2,000 [$5,000 - (50% of $6,000)] can be spent on health and accident protection.

(e) Retiree Health Benefits. Employers can set up special accounts as part of their defined benefit pension plans to pay for health care benefits for future retirees, their spouses and dependents. Separate accounts must be established for "key employees" (e.g., 5% owners and highly paid employees). Contributions to the accounts are generally deductible by the company and tax-free to the employee. Contributions to the retiree health account cannot exceed 25% of actual pension contributions for the year. Thus, if an employer cannot contribute to the pension plan because of overfunding, no retiree health contribution is permitted [IRC Sec. 401(h)].

Prior to the 1990 tax law, pension plan assets could not be transferred to a retiree medical account. If such a transfer took place, the pension plan was no longer considered a qualified plan entitled to special tax treatment, and the transferred amounts were subject to both income tax and the asset reversion excise tax [¶1322(d)].

> ➤ **TRANSFERS ALLOWED** Employers can now transfer surplus pension plan assets to fund retiree health benefits. If certain requirements and limits are satisfied, these transferred funds are not includible in the employer's gross income and are not subject to the asset reversion excise tax [IRC Sec. 420].

How it works. Employers set up accounts (so-called 401(h) accounts) to pay health care benefits for retirees, their spouses and dependents as part of their pension plans. Surplus funds from the pension portion of the plan are then transferred to the 401(h) accounts.

Bottom line: The employer gets no deduction for amounts transferred, since it already took a deduction when the amount was first contributed to the pension plan. But the good news is that the employer does not owe any income taxes or excise taxes when the funds are shifted into the 401(h) accounts.

There are a number of conditions that apply to this new tax break. Among these are the following:

- Each participant's accrued retirement benefit (under the regular pension plan) must become fully vested, as if the pension plan had terminated immediately before the transfer. So, an otherwise-non-vested employee would have to become vested when a transfer is made [IRC Sec. 420(c)(2)(A)].
- The employer has to make a reasonable estimate of the cost of its retiree health liability for each year, and transfer only enough excess pension assets to its 401(h) account to cover this estimated liability [IRC Sec. 420(b)(3)].

NOTE: The estimate should be as accurate as possible. Reason: Amounts transferred into the 401(h) account that are not used to pay for current retiree health benefits must be transferred back into the pension plan. In addition, they are subject to a 20% excise tax.

- Employers must spend at least a minimum amount on retiree health care for a five-year period (that is, the transfer year and the next four years). The minimum amount is the greater of the "applicable employer cost" for retiree health benefit care in either of the two years prior to the transfer [IRC Sec. 420(c)(3)].

Example 2: Rex Corp. maintains a qualified retirement plan that has a 401(h) account. In 1992, Rex makes a qualified transfer to the 401(h) account. In tax years 1990 and 1991, qualified current retiree health liabilities were $200,000 and $250,000 respectively. During these years, there were 200 plan participants entitled to receive retiree health benefits. The applicable employer cost is $1,000 ($200,000 divided by 200) for the 1990 tax year and $1,250 ($250,000 divided by 200) for 1991. Thus, the minimum employer cost of health benefits that must be provided to covered retirees is $1,250 for tax years 1992 through 1996 (if no further transfers occur).

▶ **KEY EMPLOYEES NOT COUNTED** Key employees [¶1313(a)] are not taken into account when computing the employer's current retiree health liabilities or in calculating the "applicable employer cost."

- Only "excess pension assets" (pension funds that exceed at least 125% of the plan's current liabilities) can be transferred to the 401(h) account [IRC Sec. 420(e)(2)].
- Employers must notify the Labor and Treasury Departments (as well as plan participants and beneficiaries) at least 60 days before the transfer [ERISA Sec. 101(e)]. Filing a single notice with the Department of Labor is treated as filing with both the DOL and the Treasury.[7] This is done by mailing a letter that gives: (1) the employer's name, address and employer ID number; (2) the plan's name, employer ID number and PIN number; (3) the amount to be transferred; (4) a detailed account of the plan's assets before and after the transfer; and (5) the plan's liabilities at the time of the transfer.[8] Once a year limit: Generally, transfers may be made only once a year, starting with tax years beginning after December 31, 1990, and before January 1, 1996 [IRC Sec. 420(b)].

¶1307   BASIC REQUIREMENTS FOR PLAN QUALIFICATION

[New tax legislation may affect this subject; see ¶1.]

Qualified plan assets are generally held in trust. The trust is exempt from tax if it meets special requirements. A qualified plan must be written, communicated to employees, and maintained for the exclusive benefit of employees and their beneficiaries. It must be impossible for trust assets to be diverted for any other purpose [IRC Sec. 401(a)(2); Reg. Sec. 1.401-1(a)].

The requirements for qualification are outlined in IRC Sec. 401(a). Virtually every aspect of a qualified plan's operation and administration is regulated by the Code and Treasury regulations. In addition, the Department of Labor has jurisdiction over certain matters under ERISA.[1] For example, the form and content of notices to employees regarding their benefits under the plan and ERISA rights are under the jurisdiction of the Department of Labor.[2]

If a plan fails to satisfy the requirements for qualification, the IRS can revoke its qualified status—even retroactively. The resulting tax consequences to both employers and employees are severe. Employer deductions can be disallowed. Employees may have additional taxable income in years contributions were made, to the extent the employees' interest in the plan was nonforfeitable. In addition, the trust can be taxed on its earnings over the years because of the loss of its tax-exempt status. These harsh results can apply with respect to tax years for which the applicable statute of limitations has not run [IRC Sec. 6501].

The major qualification requirements addressed here are rules that require the plan to:

1. Permit employees to participate in the plan in accordance with minimum eligibility and participation rules [IRC Sec. 401(a)(3)];

2. Benefit a broad class of employees and not discriminate in favor of highly compensated employees [IRC Sec. 401(a)(4)];

3. Provide that a participant's right to his benefits under the plan are nonforfeitable (vested) after specified periods of time [IRC Sec. 401(a)(7)];

4. Distribute a participant's interest upon retirement in accordance with rules regulating the time and manner of benefit commencement [IRC Sec. 401(a)(9), (11)];

5. Comply with the maximum benefit and contribution limits [IRC Sec. 415].

Special qualification requirements regarding minimum funding standards and actuarial assumptions affect defined benefit plans.

¶1308   QUALIFIED PLANS—KEY TERMS

[New tax legislation may affect this subject; see ¶1.]

Certain concepts are central to an understanding of the design and operation of qualified plans. Here are some important terms used in discussions of qualified plans:

Year of service. An employee's tenure with the employer, both as an employee and plan participant, is important to determine his eligibility to participate in the plan, his right to plan benefits and the amount of benefits. "Year of service" is the measuring rod for counting these periods of time. A year of service is a consecutive twelve-month period, designated by the plan, during which 1,000 or more hours of service are performed [IRC Sec. 411(a)(5)]. Unlike tax years, a plan year need not end on the last day of a month.[1]

Break in service. If a plan participant works fewer than 500 hours during a 12-month period, it is considered a one-year break in service [IRC Sec. 411(a)(6)]. Sometimes when a break in service occurs, an employee's years of service before the break can be disregarded when determining his rights to benefits. This concept is also important in calculating the effect of a leave of absence.

Accrued benefits. Once an employee becomes a plan participant, he begins to earn benefits in accordance with the plan's benefit formula. The employee's "accrued benefit" is the amount he has earned, including employer contributions and his share of earnings or forfeitures.

Vesting. Although an employee begins to accrue benefits when he becomes a plan participant, his absolute entitlement to the benefits depends on his vested interest. In other words, vesting determines what portion of accrued benefits an employee gets if he leaves service. A participant must always be fully vested in his own employee contributions. His nonforfeitable share of employer contributions and earnings depends on the plan's vesting schedule.

Highly compensated employees. Qualified plans are prohibited from favoring "highly compensated" employees. A plan cannot discriminate in favor of an employee who at any time during the present or immediately prior plan year (a) is a 5% owner of the employer, (b) earns more than $93,518 in 1992 (this amount is increased annually by cost of living adjustments),[2] (c) earns more than $62,345 in 1992 (increased annually by cost of living adjustments),[2] and is also in the top paid 20% of employees, or (d) is an officer of the employer being paid at least $56,111 in 1992 (increased annually by cost of living adjustments).[2] This definition of highly compensated employees is also used for discrimination testing of certain tax-free employee benefit plans [IRC Sec. 414(q); Temp. Reg. Sec. 1.414(q)-1T].

¶1309   COVERAGE

To qualify for tax benefits, the plan must provide broad coverage. It cannot pick and choose which employees will be covered.

For plan years beginning after 1988. A plan must satisfy one of the following tests:

- Percentage test. A plan must cover at least 70% of all employees who are not highly compensated.

Example 1: ABC Corp. employs 275 people, 25 of whom are highly compensated. No employee is excluded by reason of age, service, or by coverage in a collective bargaining unit. 200 of the non-highly compensated employees accrue benefits under the plan (80%). Accordingly, the plan meets the percentage test.

- Ratio test. The percentage of non-highly compensated employees who benefit by the plan is 70% or more of the percentage of highly compensated employees who benefit. In general, an employee "benefits" under a plan for testing purposes only if the employee accrues a benefit under the plan for that year. However, for cash or deferred plans [¶1345], employees who are eligible to make deferrals are treated as benefiting even if they do not make elective contributions for the year [Reg. Sec. 1.410(b)-3]. For years before 1989, it was sufficient that a plan cover a fair cross-section of employees, which was a more subjective test.

Example 2: Widget America employs 260 people in two divisions, sales and service. It maintains a separate plan for each division. Twenty people are excluded from coverage because they do not meet minimum age and service requirements. Of the remaining 240 employees, 40 are highly compensated.

In the Sales Division Plan, 32 out of 40 (80%) highly compensated employees participate. Of the non-highly compensated employees, 60% (120 of the 200) participate. The Sales Division Plan must benefit 56% of the non-highly compensated employees (.7 of 80% = 56%) to meet the ratio test. Since it benefits 60% of the non-highly compensated employees, the test is met.

In the Service Division Plan, the eight remaining highly compensated employees (8/40 = 20%) and 40 of the 80 non-highly compensated employees participate. The plan must benefit 14% (.7 x 20% = 14%) of the non-highly compensated employees to meet the ratio test. Since the plan covers 40 out of 200 (20%) of the non-highly compensated employees, the test is satisfied.

- Average benefits test. The plan benefits a class of employees that is not discriminatory, and the average benefit provided to non-highly compensated employees (as a percentage of compensation) is at least 70% of the average benefit provided to highly compensated employees (as a percentage of compensation) [IRC Sec. 410(b)(2)]. In general, all employer provided benefits, contributions and employee contributions under all employer plans are taken into account to determine if this test is satisfied.

Starting with plan years beginning after 1992, a classification of employees is not discriminatory if (1) it reflects a bona fide business classification rather than one designed to increase benefit disparities, and (2) (a) the percentage of non-highly compensated employees benefiting equals or exceeds a sliding scale safe harbor percentage (contained in IRS regulations) multiplied by the percentage of highly compensated employees who benefit, or (b) a lower percentage test is met and the IRS finds that the classification is nondiscriminatory based on relevant facts and circumstances [Reg. Sec. 1.410(b)-4]. For plan years beginning before 1993, companies can use any "reasonable, good faith interpretation" of the tax law's nondiscrimination rules.[1]

Beginning in the 1989 plan year, an additional minimum coverage rule applied. Basically, the rule was aimed at employers that set up more than one plan for different groups of employees. Each of the plans would pass the general coverage test when aggregated with other comparable plans. Now the current rule requires that each of the plans also benefits at least 50 employees or 40% of all employees, whichever is less. And plans cannot be aggregated to satisfy this requirement [IRC Sec. 401(a)(26); Prop. Reg. Sec. 1.401(a)(26)-1].

Whether a classification is deemed to be discriminatory depends on all of the facts. Essentially a comparison is made between employees who are within the prohibited group as compared with all other employees benefited by the plan [Reg. Sec. 1.410(b)-1(d)(2)].[2]

The IRS has simplified the process for substantiating compliance with the non-discrimination rules in four key areas: (1) Employers do not have to have precise data, but can use the best data available at a reasonable cost. (2) An employer can substantiate compliance based on testing a single typical day during the plan year. (3) For purposes of snap-shot testing, an employer can use a simplified test for identifying highly compensated employees. (4) Testing is required only every three years, if there are no significant changes (e.g., in compensation practices, workforce composition or plan provisions) during the three-year period.[3]

¶1310   MINIMUM PARTICIPATION STANDARDS

[New tax legislation may affect this subject; see ¶1.]

The plan may condition an employee's participation in a plan on his having completed one year of service or having attained age 21, whichever is later [IRC Sec. 410(a)(1)(A)].

➤ **EXCEPTIONS** Generally, a plan can defer participation until two years of service have been completed (three years for pre-1989 plan years) provided that the employee becomes fully vested at that time [IRC Sec. 410(a)(1)(B)(i)]. For plan years beginning before 1988, a defined benefit plan or target benefit plan could exclude employees who were hired within five years of the plan's normal retirement age [Former IRC Sec. 410(a)(2)].

The measuring rod for participation is completion of a year of service. For this purpose, a year of service means at least 1,000 hours of work during a 12-month period [IRC Sec. 410(a)(3)]. Thus, part-time employees who work fewer than 1,000 hours need not be included in the plan. In addition, there are some categories of employees, such as nonresident aliens or members of a collective bargaining unit, that likewise need not be covered [IRC Sec. 410(b)(3)].

Once an employee meets the participation requirements, he must be brought into the plan no later than the earlier of: (1) the first day of the plan year beginning after the date on which the employee first satisfied the requirements, or (2) the sixth month anniversary date of the day he first satisfied the requirements [IRC Sec. 410(a)(4)]. Plans frequently have two semiannual entry dates to accommodate this.

Example 1: A calendar year plan provides that an employee may enter the plan only on the first semiannual entry date, January 1 or July 1, after he has satisfied the applicable minimum age and service requirements. The plan satisfies the requirements because regardless of when an employee becomes eligible to participate, an entry date will be no longer than six months away. And the first day of the plan year is one of those entry dates.

Example 2: A plan provides that an employee is not eligible to participate until the first day of the first plan year beginning after he has satisfied the minimum age and service requirements. In this case, an employee who satisfies the "6-month" rule will not be eligible to participate in the plan. Therefore, the plan does not satisfy the requirements.

Special rules come into play where a break in service has occurred. If an employee incurs a break in service (works fewer than 500 hours) at a time when he is vested in the qualified plan, he must be admitted to the plan immediately on his return. There is an exception if the consecutive one-year breaks in service equal or exceed the greater of: (a) five years or (b) years of service before the break [IRC Sec. 410(a)(5)(D)]. Then he is not required to be admitted until the next entry date.

Example 3: A calendar year plan provides that an employee may enter the plan only on the first semiannual entry date, January 1 or July 1, after he has satisfied the applicable minimum age and service requirements. After ten years of service, Mr. Jones separated from service in 1988 with a vested benefit. On February 1, 1992, he returns to employment covered by the plan. Assuming he completes a year of service after his return, Jones must participate immediately on his return, February 1. His prior service cannot be disregarded, and the plan may not postpone his participation until July 1.

Example 4: If Jones had five years of service but no vested benefit when he incurred five consecutive one-year breaks, his prior service can be disregarded. His participation in the plan may be postponed.

¶1311   VESTING REQUIREMENTS

A qualified plan must provide that plan participants vest in their accrued benefits (i.e., have a nonforfeitable right to them) at least as rapidly as one of the following schedules:

- Five-year cliff vesting. The employee is completely vested after five years, but not at all vested until then.
- Seven-year graded vesting. An employee's right to accrued benefits is 20% vested after three years. An additional 20% vests after each of the next four years. Thus, after seven years an employee is 100% vested [IRC Sec. 411(a)(2); Temp. Reg. Sec. 1.411(a)-3T(b)].

➤ **COST-CUTTING IMPACT** The choice of vesting schedules has a direct impact on the cost of operating the plan. For example, forfeitures result when an employee terminates employment and he is not fully vested in his accrued benefits. With respect to a defined benefit plan, forfeitures reduce future employer contributions. They cannot increase the benefits any participant would otherwise receive under the plan [IRC Sec. 401(a), (b)]. In a defined contribution plan, forfeitures can reduce the employer contribution or be allocated to the accounts of remaining participants. Depending on the nature of the workforce and rate of turnover, the choice of a five-year schedule or seven-year graded schedule may be critical.

There are several other important vesting rules that must be considered.

1. For vesting purposes, all of an employee's years of service with the employer, after he has attained age 18, must be counted [IRC Sec. 411(a)(4)]. In other words, in determining a participant's vested interest in his accrued benefit, years of service before he became a plan participant are counted if he was at least 18.

Break in service rules permit certain years of service to be disregarded for vesting purposes. As is true for the minimum participation standards [¶1310], a nonvested participant's worktime preceding breaks in service of longer than the greater of (1) five years or (2) the aggregate years of service before the breaks may be disregarded for vesting purposes [IRC Sec. 411(a)(6)].

Example: Smith separates from service in year two after completing two years of service. Because of the plan's seven-year graded vesting schedule (an employee earns the first 20% after three years of service), Smith has no vested benefits. Smith is rehired in year five, after incurring three one-year breaks in service. Since the three consecutive service breaks don't equal or exceed the greater of five or the two pre-break years, the two years before the break must be counted.

Leaves of absence occasioned by maternity or paternity (including childbirth, adoption or childcare immediately after the events) are disregarded. The affected participant will be credited for the hours of service that he or she would have worked, but for the leave [IRC Sec. 411(a)(6)(E)]. This rule applies to determine if a break in service has occurred (i.e., the participant has fewer than 500 hours of service during the year).

2. An employee must at all times be fully vested in accrued benefits derived from his own contributions [IRC Sec. 411(a)(1)].

3. Employees must be 100% vested in their retirement benefits when they reach "normal retirement age" as defined by the plan (usually age 65) [IRC Sec. 411(a)].

4. In the event of a plan termination, participants must be fully vested in their accrued benefits. A company layoff of a large block of employees has been treated as a partial termination, and all laid-off employees become fully vested.[1] In the event of a plan merger, participants are required to receive at least what they would have received under the prior plan [IRC Sec. 401(a)(12)].

5. In addition, an "anti-cutback" rule prevents an employer from amending a plan in a manner that reduces previously accrued benefits. Each participant with at least three years of service (five years through 1988 plan years) must be given the right to elect to have his nonforfeitable percentage determined under the prior vesting schedule [IRC Sec. 411(d)(6); Temp. Reg. Sec. 1.411(a)-8T(b)].

6. For purposes of vesting and benefit accrual, an employee can be given credit for past service for another related employer. All similarly situated employees must be treated in a uniform manner.

¶ 1312   LIMITS ON BENEFITS AND CONTRIBUTIONS

[New tax legislation may affect this subject; see ¶1.]

Section 415 imposes limits on the benefits that defined benefit plans can provide and the annual additions that can be made to defined contribution plans. For the benefit and contribution limits, only the first $228,860 of an employee's 1992 salary[1] may be taken into account [IRC Sec. 401(a)(17)]. This amount is subject to future cost of living adjustments.

> **Example 1:** Ms. Burger, the president of Stellar Consulting Company, receives a salary of $300,000. Stellar makes annual contributions to its defined contribution plan equal to 10% of each employee's compensation. However, it can contribute no more than $22,886 for Burger since the 10% may be based on no more than $228,860 of her compensation.

(a) Defined Benefit Plan Maximum Benefits. The maximum benefit limitation for a defined benefit plan is expressed in terms of the benefit that will be paid out upon retirement. Generally, the plan cannot provide an annual retirement benefit, in the form of a single life annuity beginning at age 65, that for 1992 exceeds the lesser of (1) $112,221 (adjusted for future years by changes in the cost of living)[1], or (2) 100% of compensation for a participant's average compensation for his three highest consecutive years [IRC Sec. 415(b)(1)]. A special limit applies if the employer maintains both a defined benefit and defined contribution plan [IRC Sec. 415(e)].

Effect of social security age. If retirement benefits commence before the participant reaches the social security retirement age (now 65), the dollar limit (adjusted annually), but not the 100% of compensation limit, must be reduced; the 1992 retirement benefit provided must be the actuarial equivalent of an annual benefit of $112,221 beginning at age 65 [IRC Sec. 415(b)(2)(c)].

The social security retirement age is scheduled to increase over a period of 20 years to age 67 from age 65. Thus, for a plan participant who attains age 62 before January 1, 2000, the social security retirement age is age 65; (2) for a plan participant who attains age 62 after December 31, 1999, and before January 1, 2017, the social security retirement age is age 66; and (3) for a plan participant who attains age 62 after December 31, 2016, the social security retirement age is age 67.

For a participant who has attained age 62 but who has not attained the social security retirement age when benefits commence, the dollar limit is to be reduced by a set percentage for each month by which benefits commence before the social security retirement age. For months between 65 and the social security retirement age, the percentage reduction is $5/12$ of 1 percent per month. For months between age 62 and age 65, the percentage reduction is $5/9$ of 1% per month.

Under the provisions, for example, if a participant's benefit commences at age 62, and if the participant's social security retirement age is 67, then the limit on annual benefits is reduced by 30 percent [the sum of 20% ($5/9$ x 36 months for the months between age 62 and age 65), and 10% ($5/12$ x 24 for the months between age 65 and age 67)].

> **IMPORTANT** If an employee continues to work past the normal social security retirement age, he can receive benefits in excess of the dollar limit ($112,221 in 1992). For these participants, the annual benefit ceiling is increased to reflect the actuarial equivalent of a $112,221 (for 1992) benefit beginning at the normal retirement age.

Fewer than ten years of service or participation. A reduction in the dollar limit is also mandated where a participant retires with fewer than ten years of service or plan participation. The 100% of compensation limit is reduced. It becomes 10% of compensation times the number of years of service, and the dollar limit ($112,221 as adjusted in 1992) is cut to 10% of the dollar limit for each year of participation. However, the reductions may not reduce the ceilings to less than $1/10$ of the ceilings [IRC Sec. 415(b)(5)].[2]

> **Example 2:** Ms. Singer has completed three years of participation under a plan. In 1992, the maximum annual benefit that could be provided by the plan would be the lesser of 30% of compensation or $33,666 (3/10ths of $112,221).

A transitional rule preserves an individual's accrued benefit if he was a plan participant before January 1, 1987, in a plan in existence on May 6, 1986. The applicable dollar limit for such individuals is their accrued benefit at the close of the last year beginning before January 1, 1987, if it is more than $90,000.[3]

For plans maintained by governments and tax-exempt organizations, age 62 and not the social security retirement age (now 65) is used to calculate adjustments to the benefit dollar cap for early retirement. This results in more generous benefit ceilings for employees [IRC Sec. 415(b)(2)(F)].

> **SPECIAL ELECTION** Alternatively, state and local government plans were allowed to elect to have benefit reductions go no lower than the participant's accrued benefit, as determined without regard to post-October 14, 1987 plan amendments. The election had to have been made before the close of the 1990 plan year. It applies only to those who first become plan participants before 1991 [IRC Sec. 415(b)(10)].

Whether or not the election was made, special rules also prevent the reduction of the benefit ceiling below $62,345 in 1992 (annually adjusted for inflation[1])for police, pilots and firefighters, regardless of age at retirement [IRC Sec. 415(b)(2)(G)].

(b) Defined Contribution Plan Caps. The maximum benefit that can be provided by a defined contribution plan is expressed in terms of limits on the amount of "annual additions." Annual additions include employer and employee contributions, plus forfeitures, if any. For any year, the annual additions cannot exceed the lesser of $30,000 or 25% of compensation. As with the dollar limit for defined benefit plans, the $30,000 figure is adjusted for cost of living increases. However, no adjustment will occur until the dollar limit for defined benefit plans has been adjusted to more than $120,000 (for

1991, the dollar limit has been adjusted to $112,221[1]). Although money purchase pension plans and target benefit plans are pension plans, they are tested under the defined contribution plan limits [IRC Sec. 415(c)].

(c) Combined Plan Limits. If a participant is covered by both a defined benefit plan and a defined contribution plan maintained by the same employer, an increased annual limit applies. Essentially, the limit is 25%–40% higher than each plan can separately provide [IRC Sec. 415(e)].

Here's how it works. Two fractions are created: (1) a defined benefit plan fraction and (2) a defined contribution fraction. The defined benefit plan fraction is the participant's projected annual benefit divided by the lesser of (a) 125% of the applicable dollar limit (e.g., $112,221 in 1992), or (b) 140% of the participant's average compensation for his three highest years. The defined contribution fraction is the sum of total annual addition to a participant's account over the lesser of (a) 125% of the dollar limit (e.g., $30,000), or (b) 35% of the year's compensation covered by the plan. These two fractions are added, and if the sum exceeds 1.0 (or 100%), then the possibility of plan disqualification exists. Special reduced combined plan limits apply to top-heavy plans [¶1313]. Special rules also apply to cash and deferred arrangements [Reg. Sec. 1.401(k)-1(f)].

(d) Excess Additions. Excessive contributions do not automatically cause a plan to lose its qualified status if the plan provides corrective actions. Essentially, the excess amounts are not considered annual additions if the sums are either reallocated among participants, allocated to suspense accounts or employer contributions are returned [IRC Sec. 415(c)(2)(C)].

¶1313   TOP-HEAVY PLANS

Tougher eligibility and vesting rules apply to plans in which more than 60% of the benefits are for "key employees" [IRC Sec. 416].

> ► **BIG IMPACT ON SMALL EMPLOYER PLANS** The tough top-heavy rules are aimed at plans created and maintained to benefit the owners and top paid employees of small businesses. In the past, a combination of slow vesting schedules, integrated benefits [¶1317] and employee turnover worked to deprive low-paid employees of benefits. Instead, employees who stayed for the long term, typically owners and high-paid people, made out very well. The top-heavy rules were introduced to insure that all employees get a minimum benefit; this is accomplished primarily through more rapid vesting schedules and minimum benefit requirements.

Although the top-heavy rules are aimed at abusive situations, a situation need not be deliberately skewed against low-paid workers in order for the rules to apply. Consider, for example, a plan maintained by a professional corporation which covers three doctors, two nurses and one office manager. The odds are that more than 60% of the cumulative accrued plan benefits (or contributions) will be paid to the doctors. Thus, the plan will be top-heavy. The top-heavy rules apply irrespective of actual abuse or intent to deprive lower-paid workers of benefits.

(a) Who Are Key Employees. Participants are "key employees" if during the plan year, or any of the four prior plan years, they are:

- Earning more than 50% of the defined benefit dollar limit ($56,111 in 1992) and are considered officers. Under this rule no more than 50 employees, or if less, the greater of three employees or 10% of all employees are counted as officers. In addition, persons can be deemed to be officers on the basis of facts and circumstances; they still must meet the salary threshold.

- Earning more than $30,000 and are among the ten employees owning the largest interest in the employer.
- Owners of more than a 5% interest in the employer.
- Earning more than $150,000 and own more than a 1% interest in the employer.

The number of people caught within the key employee net can be expanded by including certain related parties such as spouse, children and parents [IRC Sec. 416(i)].

(b) Faster Vesting. Plans that are top-heavy are required to vest participants more rapidly. They must satisfy one of the following schedules: (1) Full vesting in employer derived accrued benefits after three years of service or (2) 20% vesting each year, after the first year, so that a participant is 100% vested at the end of six years [IRC Sec. 416(b)].

> **Example:** Dr. Able M.D.P.C. maintains a profit-sharing plan. An annual contribution of 15% is made for each employee. A nurse employed by the professional corporation has an accrued benefit of $12,000 after four years of plan participation. If the plan is top-heavy, her vested accrued benefit must be at least $7,200 (60%). Compare: Under the regular vesting rules, her vested accrued benefit could be less. Under the five-year vesting rule, she is not required to be fully vested until completion of five years. Accordingly, she would not be required to have any vested benefit after four years of plan participation. Under the three-to-seven-year graduated vesting schedule she must be 40% vested after four years, so her vested accrued benefit would be $4,800.

Top-heavy status is determined on a year-by-year basis. Accordingly, it would be possible to change to a slower vesting schedule during a year when the plan was not top-heavy. However, any employee with three or more years of service (five years prior to the 1989 plan year) could elect to retain the top-heavy vesting schedule. Accrued benefits could not be decreased by virtue of a change in the vesting schedule [Reg. Sec. 1.416-1, Q&A V-7].

(c) Minimum Benefits or Contributions. All non-key employees in a top-heavy plan must be provided with a minimum benefit. Certain so-called "integrated plans" are generally permitted to provide smaller benefits, taking into account the employee benefit derived by the employer payments of social security tax. However, if a plan is top-heavy, employees cannot be excluded from coverage because their compensation is less than the social security wage base. In addition, employees cannot be excluded because they refuse to make employee contributions [IRC Sec. 416(e)].

In a plan year in which a defined benefit plan is top-heavy, a non-key employee must accrue a benefit that is not less than the smaller of 20% of pay, or 2% of pay for each year of service. With respect to a top-heavy defined contribution plan, contributions for non-key employees cannot be less than 3% of compensation, unless the contribution for key employees is less than 3%. For purposes of computing this minimum benefit, reallocated forfeitures and salary reduction contributions are taken into account.

If a non-key employee is eligible to participate in both a defined benefit and defined contribution plan maintained by the same employer, the minimum benefit is only required to be provided in one plan [IRC Sec. 416(f)]. Also for a key employee who does participate in two top-heavy plans, the combined plan minimum benefit and contribution limit is reduced (¶1312(c)) [IRC Sec. 416(h)(1)].

(d) Testing for Top-Heavy Status. Top-heavy status is tested on an annual basis. For benefits accruing before the 1989 plan year, only the first $200,000 of compensation is taken into account in determining benefits and contributions [Former IRC Sec. 416(d)].

¶1314 COMMONLY CONTROLLED BUSINESS

Special rules apply to plans maintained by groups of businesses or corporations that are related through some form of common ownership. In short, for purposes of the qualification requirements including minimum participation and vesting, limits on benefits and contributions and the top-heavy rules, all employees of members of a controlled group of corporations or an "affiliated service group" [(b) below] are treated as employed by a single employer.

(a) Controlled Group of Corporations. Corporations are considered related for purposes of the qualification rules if (1) a parent corporation owns 80% of subsidiary stock; (2) 80% of the stock in brother-sister corporations is owned by the same five or fewer individuals (who also own over 50% of the stock of each corporation); or (3) a combined group of three or more corporations if at least one is a member of both classifications described above [IRC Sec. 1563(a)].

(b) Affiliated Service Groups. An affiliated service group consists of at least one organization that is created to provide services to a related organization [IRC Sec. 414(m)].

Background. Before the enactment of these rules, it was possible to avoid the nondiscrimination rules by creating multiple entities that were not related. For example, a group of service professionals such as doctors or lawyers would separately incorporate. They would then form a partnership of their professional corporations (P.C.s) that would hire the support staff employees and maintain qualified plans for the employees. The qualified plans for the employees would be separately tested from the P.C. plans maintained by the doctors themselves. By maintaining separate service organizations, the professionals could provide generous benefits for themselves and little or no plan coverage for rank and file employees.

Under the affiliated service group rules now, all organizations involved in such an arrangement are treated as one employer to test the plan coverage and nondiscrimination requirements. The rules are very technical and the subject of extensive regulations [Reg. Sec. 1.414(m)-1].

¶1315 DEFINED BENEFIT PLANS—BENEFIT ACCRUAL

Defined benefit plans must satisfy one of three benefit accrual rules. These rules insure that a vesting schedule is not undercut by the timing of benefit accrual. For example, the following practice (called backloading) is prevented by the accrual rules: A defined benefit plan provides that at normal retirement age, an employee retires on 30% of final pay. The plan provides that participants will accrue a benefit of 0.2% of compensation times years of service, for the first 25 years. Thereafter, the benefits will accrue at the rate of 5% of compensation times years of service. If the employee stays for 30 years, he receives the full benefit (0.2% x 25 = 5% plus 5% x 5 = 25%). However, if the employee left after 25 years of service, he would receive only a 5% (0.2% x 25 years) of service retirement benefit.

To avoid this result, defined benefit plans must satisfy one of the following benefit accrual tests [IRC Sec. 411(b)]:

- Three percent rule. As of the close of a plan year, the participant must be entitled to a benefit for each year of his participation equal to 3% of the normal retirement benefit that he would be entitled to, had he begun participation at the earliest possible age and continued until the earlier of age 65 or the plan's normal retirement age [IRC Sec. 411(b)(1)(A); Reg. Sec. 1.411(b)-1(b)(1)].
- 133⅓% rule. The rate of accrual for a subsequent plan year cannot be greater than 133⅓% of the rate for a prior year [IRC Sec. 411(b)(1)(B); Reg. Sec. 1.411(b)-1(b)(2)]. For example, if a defined benefit plan provides that a participant's benefits will accrue at 1.5% of compensation up to age 55, and at 2% thereafter, the plan qualifies under the 133⅓% test.
- Fractional rule. The accrued benefit must equal a fraction of the benefit that would accrue at normal retirement age, assuming continuing compensation at the rate the plan would use if the participant retired on the date he separated from service. The fraction is the participant's total number of years of participation, over the total years he would have participated if he separated from service at normal retirement age [IRC Sec. 411(b)(1)(C); Reg. Sec. 1.411(b)(3)].

Example: A defined benefit plan provides a benefit of 60% of career average earnings at the normal retirement age of 65. The allowable accrual rates for an employee who terminates with 15 years of participation if he entered the plan at age 25 would be as follows:

1. Under the 3% rule, the participant must be entitled to a benefit of at least 27% of career average earnings (60% x 15 x .03).

2. Under the 133⅓% rule, the plan could specify that the later accruals do not exceed earlier accruals by more than 133⅓%. Accordingly, if the 60% benefit is based on accruals of 1½% for the first 11 years, 1¾% for the next 10 years and 2% for the next 13 years, the plan would meet the 133⅓% rule—since 2% is not greater than 133⅓% of 1½%. In that event, the participant who terminates with 15 years of service is entitled to a benefit of 23.5% of career average earnings.

3. Under the fractional rule, the participant must be entitled to a benefit of at least 22.5% [15/40 (maximum years until retirement) x 60%].

A participant's rate of benefit accrual cannot be decreased, nor can his accrued benefit be reduced, because of the participant's attainment of any age.

¶1316　　　　　　EMPLOYER TAX CONSEQUENCES

[New tax legislation may affect this subject; see ¶1.]

(a) Deductions. Employers can deduct contributions to a qualified pension, annuity, stock bonus or profit-sharing plan even though the employees or beneficiaries are taxed only when they receive benefits [IRC Sec. 404].

Contributions can be made after the end of the tax year to which they relate. They may be made up until the employer's tax return due date (including extensions) [IRC Sec. 404(a)(6)]. Thus, a calendar year corporation has until September 15 to make its retirement plan contributions for the prior year, if it files an extension. However, to satisfy the minimum funding rules [(b) below], the contribution is deemed made on the last day of the preceding plan year if it is made "on account of" the prior year and is made no later than the filing of the employer's return for the prior year.

Despite the liberal contribution deadline, employers must prepay their contributions to defined benefit pension plans in quarterly installments much like estimated tax payments. Otherwise, an interest penalty is imposed. For calendar year plans, the first installment is due by April 15 [IRC Sec. 412(m)(3)(B)].

The amount of the quarterly payments is based on a percentage of the plan's required annual payment (RAP). The RAP amount is, generally, the lesser of 90% of the amount to be contributed to the plan for the current year or 100% of the previous year's contribution [IRC Sec. 412(m)(4)(B)]. Each quarterly payment has to be 25% of the RAP amount [IRC Sec. 412(m)(4)(C)].

The interest penalty for late payments is the greater of: (1) 175% of the applicable federal midterm rate (as in effect for the plan year's first month), or (2) the interest rate used by the plan to determine costs (including certain adjustments) [IRC Sec. 412(m)(1)]. Moreover, this increased rate is charged until the actual date the payment is made, not just to the last day of the plan year.

(b) Limitations on Amounts Deductible. Contributions or benefits allowable under a qualified plan must not exceed certain limits or the plan will lose its tax-qualified status [IRC Sec. 415]. The measuring rod for determining compliance with the limits is a consecutive 12-month period referred to as the "limitation year." It is generally the calendar year unless the employer elects a different 12-month period.

As discussed at ¶1312, the annual additions (i.e., employer contributions, certain employee contributions and forfeitures) to accounts of participants in defined contribution plans cannot exceed the lesser of $30,000 or 25% of the employee's compensation. The maximum annual benefit that can be funded under a defined benefit plan is the lesser of $112,221 (the dollar limit in 1992, which will be adjusted for inflation in the future) or 100% of compensation for the highest three consecutive years. But minimum funding rules also come into play with defined benefit plans. Minimum funding rules are imposed regarding the timing and amount of contributions needed to fund benefits for past as well as future service counted by a plan [IRC Sec. 412].

> **Example:** XYZ Corp. establishes a defined benefit plan and decides to give current employees credit for all years with the employer, for vesting and benefit accrual purposes. At the time the plan is put in, Mr. Smith has worked for XYZ for ten years, and will receive credit for these ten years of service. The benefit Mr. Smith will accrue as a result of these prior years of service will have to be funded in the years to come. The funding rules dictate the manner and timing of contributions to pay for these past service benefits as well as benefits attributable to future periods of service.

The minimum funding rules are tied into the benefit accrual requirements and dictate how contributions will be allocated between past and future benefits, and how quickly the plan must fund benefits. An employer can deduct the largest amount necessary to: (a) satisfy the minimum funding standard, (b) provide all employees with their remaining unfunded cost of past and current service credits, distributed as a level percentage of compensation, over the remaining life of each employee (at least five years if three individuals account for over 50% of the remaining unfunded cost), or (c) amortize past service liabilities and other supplementary pension or annuity credits over ten years plus the normal cost of the plan.

The maximum deduction cannot exceed the amount of the full funding limitation for the year [IRC Sec. 404(a)(1)]. In general, the full funding limitation is the amount necessary to bring the plan balance up to the amount of the present value of what the employees are projected to receive at retirement.

To determine how much an employer must contribute to a defined benefit plan, the plan's actuary must select a retirement age. Then the actuary works backward, using an assumed investment return, to figure out how much the employer must contribute to fund future benefits. The more conservative the assumptions (earlier retirement age, lower investment return), the more the employer can contribute. The IRS has tried to use assumptions of an 8% investment return and a retirement age of 65. But the Tax Court rejected those assumptions and allowed contributions based on assumptions of a 5% return and a retirement age of 62.[1]

If the excess of a plan's liabilities over its assets at the end of the plan year is less than the minimum funding requirement otherwise applicable, the employer can contribute a lesser amount. If a plan's assets equal or exceed its liabilities, the plan will be treated as fully funded. There is a limit on deductions for contributions made to overfunded plans [IRC Sec. 412(c)(6), (7)].

(c) Deduction Limitation on Combination of Plans. If a combination of plans, one defined benefit and one defined contribution plan, are maintained, a separate deduction limitation applies. The overall deduction limitation for all the plans is the greater of (1) 25% of covered employees' compensation, or (2) the contribution limit if the defined benefit plan were the only qualified plan [IRC Sec. 404(a)(7)].

(d) Affiliated Corporations. Corporations eligible to file a consolidated return may establish and maintain a joint profit-sharing or stock bonus plan. If one corporation makes insufficient profits, the participating corporations may share the total contributions in any proportion they choose. This option may be less significant than in the past, now that current or accumulated profits are no longer required to make contributions to a profit-sharing plan. If the affiliated group doesn't file a consolidated return, the group members must divide the contribution so that each contributes in the proportion that its profits bear to the total profits of the members that make profits. A contribution is deductible by the corporation making it.

(e) Contributions in Kind. During lean years, an employer may have difficulty coming up with cash to make the year's contributions. Contributions of employer securities may be considered as an option.

Generally, a plan may not acquire employer securities to satisfy its contribution obligations. However, a limited exception exists if immediately after the acquisition, the fair market value of the securities does not exceed 10% of the fair market value of plan assets [IRC Sec. 401(a)(22)].

Although there is a limited opportunity to make a contribution of "qualifying employer securities," this area of the law is complex. Special rules, discussed at ¶1327, prohibit self-dealing between a plan and "interested parties," which would include the employer.[2] In addition, different rules apply if the employer corporation is controlled by an owner-employee who owns 50% or more of the stock. An employer considering a contribution in kind should review the host of prohibited transaction rules prescribed by ERISA.

¶1317   INTEGRATION WITH SOCIAL SECURITY

The integration rules can be viewed as an exception to the nondiscrimination requirements covered at ¶1309. Integration of a qualified plan with social security means that a private retirement plan is treated as part of an overall retirement system that includes social security.

Retirement plan benefits or contributions are reduced on account of social security benefits the employee is entitled to receive or social security tax the employer has paid.

An integrated plan is not discriminatory just because benefits or contributions differ for earnings above and below the social security wage base ($55,500 in 1992) [IRC Sec. 401(a)(5)]. Each employee's total benefits under the plan and social security must be part of an integrated system that is not discriminatory. Lower-paid employees derive a greater share of retirement benefits, as a percent of compensation, from employer payments of social security tax than do the higher-paid.[1] Higher-paid employees have only part of their compensation covered by social security—because no social security taxes are paid, nor are benefits earned under the system, for salary in excess of the social security wage base. Integrated plans are permitted to take this disparity into account—by favoring the higher-paid to even things out.

Before 1989, plans were permitted to provide no benefits to the extent salary was covered by employer contributions to social security. For example, in 1981, an integrated plan could provide no benefits for employees earning up to $29,700, the social security wage base. It could properly provide benefits for only those earning above that amount.

Under current law, however, minimum benefits must be provided for employees in integrated plans. The result of this change is to limit the disparity between contributions or benefits allocable to income above and below the wage base. For defined contribution plans, the permitted disparity cannot exceed the lesser of (1) twice the percentage of earnings put aside for earnings below the integration level, or (2) the sum of (a) the percentage for lower earners, plus (b) the OASDI tax rate (6.2% in 1992). For defined benefit plans, the disparity rules are more complicated. Basically, benefits for earnings above the integration level cannot be greater than (1) twice the benefit rate for earnings below the integration level, or (2) 3/4 of 1%, multiplied by the participant's years of service (up to 35 years), more than the benefit attributable to lesser earnings [IRC Sec. 401(l); Prop. Reg. Sec. 1.401(l)-2, -3]. It should be noted that the "integration level"—or break point at which contribution levels change—can be lower than the social security wage base, but it cannot be greater.

> **Example:** A profit-sharing plan provides contributions for each participant equal to 9% of compensation in excess of the social security wage base, and 5% on compensation up to the wage base. Since the 4% disparity is not more than the 5% paid on compensation below the wage base and doesn't exceed 6.2%, the plan is properly integrated.

¶1318　　　　　　　TRUST MUST PROVE EXEMPTION

The employer who establishes or amends a pension, profit-sharing or stock bonus plan or trust will want to know in advance if the proposed plan or trust qualifies for exemption from tax. The IRS will issue a so-called "determination letter," which is essentially an advance letter ruling as to the plan's qualified status. Requests for such letters are filed with the district director on Form 5301 for a defined contribution plan, and Form 5300 for a defined benefit plan. Advance approval can also be obtained for master and prototype employee plans upon proper application on Form 4461 by the sponsoring employer group.

¶1319   DISTRIBUTIONS FROM QUALIFIED PLANS

While the main function of retirement plans is to pay benefits, the time and manner of payment varies. Most defined benefit plans provide benefits in the form of an annuity, beginning at age 65. Defined contribution plans usually provide a lump-sum payout of the participant's individual account.

(a) Types of Distributions. Aside from a straight life annuity, the most common forms of benefit distribution are as follows:

Qualified joint and survivor annuity. In general, a qualified plan must provide that the normal form of benefit for a married participant is a so-called "qualified joint and survivor annuity" [IRC Sec. 401(a)(11)]. It is an annuity for the life of the participant with payments continuing for the surviving spouse. Payments to the surviving spouse must equal at least 50% of the amount paid to the participant [IRC Sec. 417].

> ➤ **IMPORTANT** The qualified joint and survivor annuity can only be waived by written spousal consent within 90 days of the annuity starting date. Consent is not required if the present value of nonforfeitable benefits is not more than $3,500 [IRC Sec. 417(a); Reg. Sec. 1.417(e)-1(b)(2)].

Lump-sum distribution. The usual benefit from a defined contribution plan is the individual's account balance paid out all at once in a "lump-sum." Also, for plans that pay benefits in the form of an annuity, the annuity can sometimes be converted into a lump-sum. Many plans require this form of payout where a plan participant terminates employment for reasons other than retirement. However, if a participant's annuity benefit has a value above $3,500, he cannot be compelled to receive the benefit as a lump-sum until the later of age 62 or the plan's normal retirement age [Reg. Sec. 1.411(a)-11].

Life annuity with term certain. Under this form of benefit, the participant receives an annuity for a term certain. Usually the payout period is structured so that benefits (in the same amount) will continue to another beneficiary, for the balance of the guaranteed period, subsequent to the participant's death.

Joint and survivor annuity. A life annuity for the participant coupled with payments continuing to a beneficiary is a joint and survivor annuity. Payments are usually 50%, but may not exceed 100% of the amount paid to the participant. For a joint and survivor annuity, other than to a surviving spouse, the survivor annuity of 100% is permitted if the age difference between the participant and survivor is ten years or less. It declines to almost 50% where the age gap is more than 44 years [Prop. Reg. Sec. 1.401(a)(9)-2 Q&A-6].

(b) When Payments Must Start. If a participant terminates employment before age 70½, distribution must commence no later than 60 days after the close of the plan year in which the latest of the following occurs: (a) participant turns 65, or the plan's normal retirement age (if earlier); or (b) the tenth anniversary of the year in which the participant began participating in the plan; or (c) the termination of employment [IRC Sec. 401(a)(14)].

> **Example:** Jones has been in the Widget Corp. pension plan for 15 years. He terminates employment in 1993 at age 50. The plan is on the calendar year and the normal retirement age is 60. Under the rules described above, the plan would not be required to pay Jones his benefits until 60 days after the close of the plan year in which Jones turns 60. If Jones will turn 60 in 2003, the plan must commence benefits by March 1, 2004. That date is later than his tenth anniversary in the plan and his year of termination.

Benefits must begin by the April 1 following the calendar year in which the participant reaches age 70½.[1] The rule applies even if the participant is still working. A harsh 50% excise tax is imposed for failure to distribute [IRC Sec. 4974].

> ▶ **EXCEPTION**   Non-5% owners born before July 1, 1917, are permanently exempt from the age 70½ required beginning date rule.[2]

Death prior to retirement.   Defined benefit plans must provide a so-called "pre-retirement survivor annuity" to married vested participants who die before they begin to receive benefits under the plan [IRC Sec. 401(a)(11)]. The benefit must at least equal the benefit the spouse would have received had the participant begun to receive benefits before he died, in the form of a qualified joint and survivor annuity [IRC Sec. 417(c)].

If a participant dies prior to retirement, defined contribution plans usually pay over the participant's account balance to the surviving spouse or other beneficiary. The distribution must be completed within five years after the year of death. For example, if a participant dies on January 1, 1993, distributions must be complete by December 31, 1998.

The five-year rule does not apply if an individual beneficiary is designated to receive benefit installments over his life. Then the distribution must begin by the calendar year following the year of death.

> ▶ **BREAK FOR SURVIVING SPOUSE**   The five-year rule also is not binding on a surviving spouse. A spouse is permitted to defer receipt of benefits until what would have been the required commencement date had the participant survived [Prop. Reg. Sec. 1.401(a)(9)-1 Q&A C-5(b)].

(c) In-Service Withdrawals. In-service withdrawals are prohibited in a defined benefit plan prior to the plan's normal retirement age. The same rule applies to money purchase pension plans.[3] The rules are different for profit-sharing and stock bonus plans. If permitted by the plan document, such plans can permit in-service withdrawals. However, such withdrawals may be subject to a premature withdrawal penalty [¶1322]. Employer contributions that have been in the plan for more than two years can be made available for withdrawals.[4] All employer contributions (not limited by the two-year rule) can be made available to employees who have participated in the plan for more than five years.[5]

In a 401(k) plan, discussed at ¶1345, employee contributions made pursuant to a cash or deferred election cannot be withdrawn prior to age 59½ unless there is a hardship. Income earned on 401(k) contributions cannot be withdrawn on account of hardship [IRC Sec. 401(k)(2)(B); Reg. Sec. 1. 401(k)-1(d)(2)].

(d) Amount of Distribution. When a distribution is made in a lump-sum, or in installments, there are no legal constraints on the minimum amount to be distributed (before age 70½). However, complex rules govern minimum distributions in connection with all types of annuities [IRC Sec. 401(a)(9)]. The rules are aimed at limiting the tax deferral, and tax-free accumulation, of plan benefits.

The key year here is that in which the participant turns 70½. The required minimum distribution is based on the participant's balance as of December 31 of the prior year. The minimum distribution required is calculated by dividing the prior year's balance by the life expectancy of the participant and, as applicable, a designated beneficiary [Reg. Sec. 1.72-9]. The participant's life expectancy may be recalculated each year. For example, the life expectancy of a participant who is age 71 is 15.3, and at age 72, it is 14.6 years (not 14.3 as might be expected).

> **NOTE:** The IRS has announced that retirees who receive reduced payouts because of state delinquency proceedings against financially troubled insurance companies that hold plan assets will not be subject to the 50% penalty, as long as certain conditions and requirements are satisfied.[6]

With a joint and survivor annuity, the beneficiary's life expectancy cannot be recalculated unless the beneficiary is the participant's spouse. For a nonspouse beneficiary, the life expectancy is determined in year one, and declines by one year in each subsequent year. Plans may, but are not required to, provide for this recalculation of either the participant's or beneficiary's life expectancy [Prop. Reg. Sec. 1.401(a)(9)-1].

> ► **PLANNING POINTER** A participant who can designate his spouse or another beneficiary of similar age will be able to increase tax deferral by designating his spouse. The ability to annually recalculate the spouse's life expectancy will allow the participant to take distributions at a slower rate.

A larger distribution may be required if a designated beneficiary is more than ten years younger than the participant. Special rules override the minimum distribution rules in this case [Prop. Reg. Sec. 1.401(a)(9)-2].

Death after benefits commence. If participants die after they have begun to receive benefits, the balance in their accounts must be distributed at least as quickly as under the method in place on the date of death [IRC Sec. 401(a)(9)(B)]. For a joint and survivor annuity, clearly the survivor annuity kicks in. If the survivor annuity goes to the surviving spouse, the recalculation of spouse's life expectancy is permitted.

¶1320   TAXATION OF DISTRIBUTIONS

[New tax legislation may affect this subject; see ¶1.]

In general, an employee is taxed on amounts received from a qualified plan, unless the distribution qualifies for special tax treatment as a tax-free rollover [IRC Sec. 402(a)].

(a) Taxation of Annuities. Unless participants have a basis in the plan as a result of making after-tax employee contributions, the entire amount of each annuity distribution is taxed as ordinary income in the year of receipt. If participants make nondeductible, after-tax contributions to a plan, they have an investment or basis in the plan. Accordingly, a portion of each distribution is considered a return of capital and is nontaxable. For this purpose, amounts contributed to a cash or deferred plan that were made in pre-tax dollars (i.e., were not subject to income tax) are not treated as employee contributions. They are subject to tax upon distribution. The tax treatment of annuities is discussed at ¶1522 et seq.

> ► **GRANDFATHER RULE** Plans that on May 5, 1986, permitted in-service withdrawal of employee contributions can allow participants to recover their pre-1987 investment in the contract, tax-free, before any portion of the distribution is subject to tax [IRC Sec. 72(e)(8)(D)].

(b) Lump-Sum Distributions. Lump-sum distributions are eligible for special favorable rates, or tax deferral opportunities if the distribution is rolled over to an IRA or to another qualified plan.

Lump-sum defined. A "lump-sum distribution" is a distribution within one taxable year of the "balance to the credit" of an employee. It must become payable to the recipient: (a) on account of the employee's death, (b) after the employee attains age 59½, (c) on account of the employee's separation from service, or (d) after the employee becomes disabled [IRC Sec. 402(e)(4)(A)]. No distribution to employees can be a lump-sum unless they have been a plan participant for at least five of their tax years prior to the year of distribution [IRC Sec. 402(e)(4)(H)]. This requirement is waived as to a beneficiary electing lump-sum treatment after a participant's death [Reg. Sec. 1.402(e)-2(e)(3)].

Balance to the credit. This refers to the employee's aggregate balance in all plans of the same type [IRC Sec. 402(e)(4)(C)]. For example, a distribution from a profit-sharing plan may qualify for lump-sum treatment even though the employee still has an interest in a pension plan maintained by the employer.

Only the vested portion of a participant's accrued benefit is considered in determining the balance to his or her credit [IRC Sec. 402(e), (b)]. Amounts attributable to deductible IRA contributions for 1982 through 1987 are ignored for these purposes [IRC Sec. 402(e)(4)(A)]. Amounts paid out under a qualified domestic relations order [¶1323] are also ignored [IRC Sec. 402(e)(4)(M)]. Accordingly, a partially vested employee may be eligible for special tax breaks afforded lump-sum distributions.

> **POTENTIAL TAX TRAP** If a partially vested employee receives a lump-sum distribution and later returns to work with the same employer, problems may arise. If the employee earns an additional vested interest in his pre-separation accrued benefit, the tax benefits he received on the earlier distribution will be recaptured [IRC Sec. 402(e)(6)(B)].

Distribution events. The reason the distribution is made is important in qualifying for special lump-sum tax treatment.

- Separation from service. This refers to termination of employment by reason of death, retirement, resignation or discharge. It does not occur if the employee continues on the same job with a different employer because of liquidation, merger or consolidation.[1] However, an employee may be deemed to have separated from service if the employer-employee relationship is terminated, even though he or she continues with the company as a consultant.[2] It should be noted a self-employed person cannot get lump-sum treatment by virtue of separation from service [IRC Sec. 402(e)(4)(A)].

Payment of the distribution does not have to occur in the year of or year following the separation event in order for the distribution to qualify for lump-sum treatment.[3] A deferred payout can still qualify for lump-sum treatment.[4]

> **PLANNING POINTER** Deferring the payout can be particularly beneficial to plan participants who retire before age 59½. Rolling over the funds to an IRA avoids the penalty, but also precludes the use of income averaging. Leaving the funds in the company plan until age 59½ avoids the penalty and preserves the option to income average.

- After age 59½. A distribution to a participant after attaining age 59½ is permitted, even though the participant continues working. But if the participant continues accruing benefits, the amount distributed must be the entire plan benefit earned to date, and cannot have been the subject of another lump-sum election.[5]
- Death or disability. Only a distribution to a self-employed person can qualify for lump-sum treatment by reason of disability. Lump-sum treatment is permitted in the event of death of the participant, whether an employee or self-employed [IRC Sec. 72(m)(7), 402(e)(4)(A)].

Five-year participation requirement. A participant must complete five years of participation to be eligible for special five- or ten-year averaging [IRC Sec. 402(e)(4)(H)]. There is conflicting authority as to whether five full years are required [Prop. Reg. Sec. 1.402(e)-2(e)(3); Temp. Reg. Sec. 1.402(f)-1T(b)]. However, the Tax Court has said that any part of a year counts toward the five-year requirement.[6] Years of participation during which no allocations are made to the participant's account do not count for purposes of the five-year rule.[7]

Tax on lump-sum distributions—five-year averaging. Five-year averaging must be applied to all eligible lump-sum distributions received during the same tax year of the recipient [IRC Sec. 402(e)(4)(B)(ii)]. Accordingly, participants cannot roll over a lump-sum distribution from one plan into an IRA in the same year they elect five-year averaging on a lump-sum distribution from another plan. But if participants do not have five years of participation, the rollover will not affect the right to elect averaging on an eligible lump-sum from a different plan [IRC Sec. 402(e)(4)(H)].

> ➤ **PLANNING POINTER** A participant who expects to receive distributions from more than one qualified plan should take the distributions in two tax years if he or she intends to roll one over and use the averaging election on the other.

One-time shot. Five-year averaging, which applies to distributions after 1986, can be elected only for distributions received on or after age 59½, and the break may be applied to only one lump-sum distribution. Prior to 1992, participants could also treat a portion of the distribution that was allocable to pre-1974 participation as capital gain. But that capital gain break was phased out and is no longer available with five-year averaging.

> ➤ **IMPORTANT** A ten-year income-averaging election (see below) made on a lump-sum received before 1987 does not prevent an employee from making one additional post-1986 election.

In general, with five-year averaging, the tax on one-fifth of the payout, reduced by a minimum distribution allowance, is computed using the tax rates for single people. Then the result is multiplied by five. The minimum distribution allowance is the lesser of $10,000 or ½ of the total taxable amount of the distribution. However, it is phased out for taxable distributions above $20,000. The phaseout formula is 20% of amounts in excess of $20,000 [IRC Sec. 402(e)(1)]. Thus, the allowance is completely phased out for distributions of $70,000 or more. Five-year averaging usually produces a lower tax than would otherwise be due using the graduated tax structure. With the compressed tax rates, however, very large distributions receive no tax benefit from income averaging.

Ten-year averaging. Distributions received before 1987 were eligible for 10-year income averaging, calculated in a similar manner. Employees could also elect to treat the portion of their lump-sum distribution attributable to pre-1974 plan participation as long-term capital gain.

> ➤ **SPECIAL BREAK** Under a special "grandfather rule," employees who were at least age 50 on January 1, 1986, are entitled to special treatment. For post-1986 distributions, they can choose between 10-year averaging using 1986 tax rates, or five-year averaging using the current tax rates. Participants may also disregard the phaseout for capital gain treatment. The full capital gain portion is taxed at a flat 20%. If employees elect this special relief, they cannot elect lump-sum treatment again after reaching 59½ [IRC Sec. 402(e)(4)(B)].

NOTE: Both the five- and ten-year averaging taxes are reported on Form 4972.

Example: Jim Lee, age 58, retires from XYZ, Inc. on June 1, 1992. One month later he receives the entire balance to his account—$480,000—from his company's qualified profit-sharing plan. One-fourth of Lee's period of plan participation occurred prior to 1974 and three-fourths was after 1973. Lee does not roll over any of the payout. Lee elects to treat the pre-1974 portion of the payout as capital gain. In 1991, 25% of that one-quarter of the $480,000, or $120,000, represents capital gain. Under the special grandfather rule, a flat 20% tax is applied. The tax on the capital gain portion of the distribution is, therefore, $24,000.

Since Lee was at least 50 years old on January 1, 1986, he has the choice of using five-year averaging or ten-year averaging on the $360,000 ordinary income portion of the distribution. Under five-year averaging it is as if Lee received his payout in five equal installments of $72,000. Using the 1992 tax rate schedule for single taxpayers, the tax is $17,974.50. This amount is multiplied by five to produce a tax of $89,872.50. This amount is added to the $24,000 tax on the capital gain portion to yield a total tax of $113,872.50.

Ten-year averaging is computed similarly. The tax on $36,000 ($\frac{1}{10}$th of $360,000) is computed using the 1986 rates. The annual tax of $8,740.20 is multiplied by ten and results in a tax of $87,402. This is added to the $24,000 tax on the capital gain portion to produce a total tax of $111,402. As a result, Lee is somewhat better off using ten-year averaging.

Five-year "lookback" rule. If a taxpayer receives more than one distribution during the five years preceding the year of current distribution, the base for computing the tax will be increased by the value of any lump-sum distributions or annuity contracts distributed after December 31, 1973.

Distributions including employer securities. Special rules apply if employer securities are included as part of a lump-sum distribution. The gain attributable to the period the securities were held by the plan, so-called "unrealized appreciation," is not taxed until the securities are sold [IRC Sec. 402(a)(1)]. Then it is taxed as capital gain. The value of the securities at the time they were contributed to the plan (plan's basis) is ordinary income and eligible for five- or ten-year averaging if the distribution otherwise qualifies.

Deferral of tax on unrealized appreciation. The unrealized appreciation is not included in the value of a lump-sum distribution [IRC Sec. 402(e)(4)(J)]. However, a participant can elect to be taxed on the appreciation at the time the distribution is made [IRC Sec. 402(e)(4)(J)].

(c) Rollover of Distributions From Qualified Plans. Amounts withdrawn from qualified plans may be eligible to be rolled over into another qualified plan or an IRA within sixty days [¶1334]. In that event, current income tax is deferred and the 15% excess distribution tax may be avoided [¶1322(b)]. Under the general rule, the rollover break applies to a pre-1993 distribution only if the distribution represents at least 50% of the vested balance to the participant's credit under the plan. However, a tax law change that takes effect for distributions after 1992 removes this 50% requirement. Under the new rules, any distribution can be rolled over, except pensions and installment payouts over ten years or more [IRC Sec. 402(a)(5)(A), (D)(i)]. A qualifying distribution may be rolled over into more than one IRA.[8]

Rollover requirements. To qualify for rollover treatment the distribution must be a "lump-sum distribution," or a partial distribution that meets certain requirements. There is no age requirement; thus, a 30-year-old who receives a lump-sum upon changing jobs can make a tax-free rollover. Likewise, the 5-year participation rule need not be satisfied. The lump-sum must be paid within one tax year of receipt. Distributions on account of plan termination may also be rolled over [IRC Sec. 402(a)(5)(E)(i)]. However, that part of any distribution representing a return of employee after-tax contributions cannot be rolled over [IRC Sec. 402(a)(5)(B)]. To the extent that a portion of the distribution is not rolled over (and is not a return of employee contributions) it will be taxed as ordinary income without the benefit of five- or ten-year averaging.

Rollover of partial distributions. Under certain circumstances, a rollover of a partial distribution is permitted. For pre-1993 distributions the portion rolled over must represent at least 50% of an employee's vested balance under the plan. For distributions after 1992, the distribution can be less than 50% of the vested balance. If an employee chooses to make a partial rollover, he or she is not required to withdraw the entire balance standing to his or her credit in the plan.

► **CAUTION** A partially vested plan participant can roll over a payout of his or her total vested balance; it is a lump-sum rollover. However, if the participant returns to service and receives additional vesting in his or her pre-separation accrued benefit, it becomes a partial rollover. A partial rollover will preclude use of five- or ten-year averaging on a future distribution from that plan or any other plan required to be aggregated with it [IRC Sec. 402(a)(5)(D), (e)(4)(C)].

Employer securities. With respect to a distribution including employer securities, a partial rollover will cause the unrealized appreciation on employer securities, derived from employee contributions, to be subject to current tax [IRC Sec. 401(a)(5)(D)(iv)]. This is the result even if the securities are not the portion of the distribution that is rolled over.

(d) Retirement Insurance Contracts. The trust can purchase life insurance contracts or some type of contract that combines retirement benefits with life insurance protection. Contributions by the employer for the insurance portion of the contract constitute income taxable to the employees. If an employee dies before retirement, amounts paid to a beneficiary because of such insurance protection are exempt (¶1507) [Reg. Sec. 1.72-16].

(e) Accident or Health Benefits. The annuity rules do not apply to pension or profit-sharing payments received as accident or health benefits [Reg. Sec. 1.72-15(b)]. To the extent such benefits result from employee contributions, they are tax-free. Benefits attributable to employer-paid or pre-tax dollars are taxable [IRC Sec. 104(a)(3), 105(a)]. However, amounts treated as employee contributions for this purpose are not counted as employee contributions in figuring the annuity exclusion for pension or profit-sharing benefits [Reg. Sec. 1.72-15(c)(3)]. Thus, the employee cannot get a double exclusion for the same amount. Employer contributions for these benefits are limited to 25% of the total contributed for all benefits (¶1306(d)) [Reg. Sec. 1.401-14(c)(1)].

(f) Distributions Upon Death. In addition to the regular annuity or lump-sum distribution rules, other special rules come into play for distributions received on account of the plan participant's death. First, a beneficiary may exclude up to $5,000 of a lump-sum distribution from a qualified plan. Only one exclusion per employee is permitted, even if payments are made to several beneficiaries [IRC Sec. 101(b); Reg. Sec. 1.101-2].

Life insurance. Although life insurance is the subject of complex rules, generally if the policy has been purchased by a qualified plan, the proceeds are tax-free to the beneficiary to the extent the death benefit exceeds the cash surrender value immediately before death [Reg. Sec. 1.72-16(c)].

15% estate tax. A tax similar to the tax on excess distributions [¶1322(b)] applies to distributions included in a decedent's estate. The tax applies to the same type of distributions and the same threshold grandfather rules apply. A surviving spouse who rolls over the funds into a separate IRA, after the 15% tax has been paid by the estate, will not be subject to the 15% tax again when those funds are eventually withdrawn from the IRA [Temp. Reg. Sec. 54.4981A-1T Q&A d-10]. Alternatively, if the spouse is the sole beneficiary of the decedent's retirement benefits (including IRAs), he or she may elect to have the estate not pay the tax and instead apply the excess distribution rules as he or she receives distributions of the benefits [IRC Sec. 4980A(d)(5)]. Unless the will or a state law specifies that the estate tax be paid out of the assets to which it relates, the 15% excise tax is paid out of the general estate. Thus, the surviving spouse can roll over the entire distribution, undiminished by tax [Temp. Reg. Sec. 54.4981A-1T Q&A d-8A].

¶1322   DISTRIBUTION TAXES AND PENALTIES

[New tax legislation may affect this subject; see ¶1.]

(a) Premature Distributions. A participant will be hit with a 10% additional tax on distributions from a plan before age 59½. This is the rule even though the distribution is made on account of separation from service or retirement. The tax will not apply if the distribution is rolled over, or is made on account of death or disability. An exception also applies if the distribution is made over the life or joint lives (as applicable) of the participant and a beneficiary [IRC Sec. 72(t)(2)(A)(ii)-(iv)].

> ➤ **TAX POINTER** This rule has the effect of exempting all nonsingle sum distributions from defined benefit plans from the 10% tax, regardless of the recipient's age. Why? Generally, all defined benefit plans only make distributions in the form of a life annuity.

ESOP exception. Many employee stock ownership plan distributions are also exempt from the penalty. These include dividend distributions, which provide an employer deduction [IRC Sec. 72(t)(2)(A)(vi)].

Other exceptions. Distributions for deductible medical expenses, those above the 7½% of adjusted gross income threshold, are not subject to the premature withdrawal tax [IRC Sec. 72(t)(2)(B)]. Neither are distributions pursuant to a qualified domestic relations order [¶1323] or excess deferrals under 401(k) plans [IRC Sec. 72(t)(2)(D), 402(g)(2)].

(b) Excess Distributions. A 15% excise tax generally applies to distributions in excess of the greater of (1) $112,500, plus cost of living adjustments ($140,276 in 1992), or (2) $150,000 in any calendar year. Distributions attributable to after-tax contributions by the participant are not counted in [IRC Sec. 4981A]. There is a special threshold for lump-sum distributions that qualify for income averaging. It is five times the regular limit ($750,000 or $701,380). All distributions received from any qualified plan, IRA or tax-sheltered annuity are applied against this limit. Not covered by the rule are qualified domestic relations distributions, amounts rolled over, return of a participant's contributions and distributions of excess deferrals under 401(k) plans [IRC Sec. 4980A(a), (c)].

Special grandfather rule. If a participant's accrued benefits were in excess of $562,000 as of August 1, 1986, the entire August 1, 1986, benefit could be exempted from the tax [IRC Sec. 4980A(c)(5)]. The exemption must have been elected on a tax return filed for a year ending before 1989, even though actual distribution of the exempted accrual may occur later. Pre-August 1, 1986, benefits are nevertheless included to determine if the post-August 1 accruals exceed the limit. For example, if a participant's account balance is $900,000 as of August 1, 1986, and with plan earnings, $1,000,000 is paid in a lump-sum in April 1992, only the $900,000 is exempted by the election.

(c) Maximum Penalty for Early Withdrawal/Excess Distribution. If a taxpayer gets a distribution subject to the penalty tax for early distribution (generally before age 59½), he receives a break if the distribution is also subject to the 15% penalty. The 10% penalty is credited against the 15% penalty that the taxpayer would otherwise owe [IRC Sec. 4980A(b)]. Therefore, the total penalty tax is never higher than 15%.

Example: Mr. Norton, age 54, receives a $200,000 distribution from his company retirement plan in 1992. The entire $200,000 is subject to the 10% penalty on early distributions. Since Norton's distribution is $50,000 over the $150,000 threshold, he would normally owe a $7,500 excess distribution penalty. But since he is also paying a $5,000 early distribution penalty on this $50,000, the excess distribution penalty is only $2,500. So Norton's total penalty tax is $22,500—$20,000 on the $150,000 plus $2,500 on the $50,000.

(d) Excise Tax on Plan Asset Reversions. The excise tax that applies to pension plan assets reverting to an employer on the plan's termination is at least 20%, and may be as high as 50%. A company's excise tax depends, in part, on the employer's actions in connection with the plan termination [IRC Sec. 4980]. Note: The excise tax on reversions occurring on or before September 30, 1990, was 15%.

NOTE: The excise tax is in addition to any income tax the employer may owe on the reversion.

20% excise tax. The company is subject to the 20% excise tax if either:

1. The company sets up a qualified replacement retirement plan (either a defined contribution or defined benefit plan) that covers at least 95% of the terminated plan's active participants and transfers 25% of the excess cash to the replacement plan. If the limitation on annual additions to defined contribution plans (the lesser of $30,000 or 25% of a participant's compensation) prevents any amount from being allocated to a participant, that amount is then allocated to other participants. Or—

2. The company increases benefits to participants and beneficiaries of the terminated plan on a pro rata basis by using 20% of the excess cash.

> **DOUBLE TAX WINNER** Amounts that are transferred to a replacement plan or used to increase plan benefits not only escape the excise tax, they are also not included in the company's taxable income. On the other hand, these amounts are not deductible by the company.

50% excise tax. The company is hit with the new 50% excise tax if it does not set up a replacement plan or increase benefits.

Example: Phelps Corp. terminates its defined benefit pension plan. There was $100,000 remaining in the plan after all the pension plan liabilities were satisfied.
If Phelps transfers $25,000 into a replacement plan, the $25,000 is not includible in the corporation's income. Also, it is not subject to the 50% excise tax. However, Phelps is liable for an excise tax of $15,000 [20% of $75,000 ($100,000 less $25,000 transferred to the replacement plan)], and $75,000 is subject to the corporate income tax of up to 34%, or $25,500. Thus, it retains a balance of $34,500 [$75,000 less $40,500 ($15,000 excise tax + $25,500 income tax)]. Note that if Phelps did nothing with the surplus, it would owe $34,000 in income taxes and $50,000 in excise tax.

¶**1323**   **QUALIFIED DOMESTIC RELATIONS ORDERS**

Under a complex series of rules, qualified plans can be directed to make payments to a participant's spouse in the event of divorce. These payments must be executed pursuant to statutorily prescribed "qualified domestic relations order" [IRC Sec. 414(p)].

¶**1325**   **PLAN LOANS**

Plan participants can gain access to their retirement funds before actually retiring by obtaining a loan from the plan. The retirement plan must satisfy several strict requirements: First, loans must be available to all plan participants, including both active and inactive employees, on a reasonably equivalent basis. Second, loans can't be made to highly compensated employees in an amount greater than what is available to other employees. Third, the plan must specifically set forth the terms under which loans will be made. Fourth, the debt must be adequately secured. And last, but not least, the plan must charge a reasonable rate of interest.[1]

There are also restrictions on how much can be borrowed and how long the loan may remain outstanding. If they are not complied with, the excess loan is treated as a distribution from the plan. And that results in tax plus penalties.

In general, the tax law limits plan loans to the lesser of (1) an aggregate of $50,000 reduced by the participant's highest outstanding loan balance during the preceding 12-month period, or (2) one-half of the participant's nonforfeitable accrued benefit (but not less than $10,000) [IRC Sec. 72(p)(2)(A)].

However, Department of Labor Regulations require plan loans to be adequately secured. Specifically, they require that a plan must be able to foreclose on the collateral in the event of a default, and the value of the collateral must be sufficient so that the plan will not suffer any loss of principal or interest between the date of default and the date of the foreclosure on the collateral.

A plan can use a portion of a participant's vested plan benefits as security for the loan. However, no more than 50% of a participant's vested benefits can be used for this purpose. As a result, if a company were to permit participants to borrow up to the limits allowed by the tax law (the greater of $10,000 or 50% of the vested benefit), a participant with less than $20,000 in vested benefits would be able to borrow an amount in excess of 50% of vested benefits. The Labor Department regulations supersede those imposed by the tax law.[2]

> **Example 1:** Ms. Brown's nonforfeitable accrued balance in her company's profit-sharing plan is $150,000. In general, she is limited to $50,000 of loans. If Brown has a $10,000 loan outstanding, she cannot borrow more than an additional $40,000. If she has no loan outstanding at present, but paid off $50,000 of indebtedness to the plan, say, ten months ago (and she made no loan payments during the prior two months), Brown could not take out another plan loan for an additional two months (i.e., until 12 months had elapsed).

> **Example 2:** Mr. Green's nonforfeitable accrued balance is $90,000. Thus, his loan ceiling is $45,000—one-half of his benefits. Suppose, though, he paid off $30,000 of indebtedness eleven months ago (and made no repayments during the prior month). In that case, he would be subject to the limitation computed as follows: $50,000 less highest outstanding loan balance during the preceding year. Result: He could not borrow more than $20,000 at this time.

Repayment terms. In general, retirement plan loans must be paid back within five years. The terms of repayment must be level amortization with payments due at least quarterly. In other words, the loan cannot call for a balloon payment at the end of five years [IRC Sec. 72(p)(2)(B), (C)].

> ➤ **HOME LOAN EXCEPTION** The five-year repayment requirement does not apply to loans used to acquire the plan participant's principal residence. This exception does not apply to loans to improve an existing residence, buy a second home or acquire a house for the participant's family members.

Interest deduction. Interest paid on plan loans is generally subject to the same deduction rules as interest on other loans (¶1901 et seq.) [IRC Sec. 163]. However, there is a special restriction that applies to company owners and other top-level employees. "Key employees" [¶1313(a)] cannot claim deductions for interest paid on retirement plan loans, regardless of how the loan proceeds are used [IRC Sec. 72 (p)(3)]. Also interest on loans secured by an employee's IRC Section 401(k) or 403(b) contributions is also nondeductible.

¶1327   PROHIBITED TRANSACTIONS

Certain transactions between a qualified plan and persons with authority over the plan (so-called "disqualified persons") are generally prohibited. Disqualified persons include plan fiduciaries, persons providing services to the plan and owner-employees. The list is far-reaching because members of an owner-employee's family and related entities in which the owner-employee owns at least 50% (corporation, partnership, and trust) are also "disqualified persons" for purposes of these rules.

Prohibited transactions. The types of transactions which are prohibited and subject to tax are:

1. Transfers of plan income or assets to, or use of them by or for the benefit of, a disqualified person (e.g., loan of plan funds to employer's business clients);

2. A fiduciary's dealing with plan income or assets in his or her own interest. A "fiduciary" is a person who has discretionary control over the administration of the plan or management of plan assets;

3. A fiduciary's receiving consideration on his or her account from a party that is dealing with the plan in a transaction that involves plan income or assets; or

4. Any of the following acts between the plan and a disqualified person:

- Selling, exchanging, or leasing property;
- Extending credit, such as a loan; or
- Furnishing goods, services, or facilities.

Exemption. A prohibited transaction does not take place if you are a disqualified person and receive any benefit to which you are entitled as a plan participant or beneficiary, as long as it is figured and paid under the same terms as for all other participants and beneficiaries.

Tax on prohibited transactions. The yearly tax rate on a prohibited transaction is 5% of the amount involved and, if the transaction is not corrected within the taxable period, the law imposes an additional tax of 100% of the amount involved. If more than one person takes part in the transaction, each person may be liable for the entire amount of the tax.

The amount involved in a prohibited transaction is the greater of:

- The money and fair market value of any property you gave, or
- The money and fair market value of any property you received.

If services are performed, the amount involved is any excess compensation given or received.

The 5% tax is based on the amount involved as of transaction date [IRC Sec. 4975(a)]. It is charged for each year in the taxable period, which starts on the transaction date and ends on the earliest day when:

- IRS mails a notice of deficiency for the tax,
- The tax is assessed, or
- You finish correcting the transaction.

The 100% tax is charged if the transaction is not corrected during the taxable period [IRC Sec. 4975(b)]. It is based on the highest fair market value, during the taxable period, of the amount involved.

Correcting the transaction. If you are a disqualified person, you can minimize the tax by correcting any prohibited transaction as soon as possible. Correcting it means undoing it as much as you can without putting the plan in a worse financial position than if the highest fiduciary standards had been followed.

INDIVIDUAL RETIREMENT ACCOUNTS

¶1330   WHO IS ELIGIBLE TO CONTRIBUTE

[New tax legislation may affect this subject; see ¶1.]
There are only two basic requirements:

- You must earn compensation at some time during the year [IRC Sec. 219(b)(1)(B)]; and
- You must be under age 70½ at the end of the year [IRC Sec. 219(d)(1)].

You can contribute 100% of your compensation up to a maximum of $2,000 annually ($2,250 if you have a nonworking spouse [¶1331]). Compensation includes wages, professional fees, or other amounts you derive from or receive for personal services rendered and included in your gross income for the tax year. Special rules come into play if you are receiving social security benefits [(b) below].

Married individuals. If both you and your spouse earn income, you are each eligible to set up an IRA. Thus, if you each have wages of $2,000, each can contribute up to $2,000 to your own plan. This rule applies without regard to any community property laws. If both of you have compensation, one of you may elect to be treated as having no compensation [IRC Sec. 219(c)(1)]. This allows the other spouse to make a contribution that exceeds his or her compensation.

You can make contributions up to the date for filing your income tax return (not including extensions) for the previous calendar year. In other words, you can make contributions as late as April 15 and attribute them to the preceding calendar year [IRC Sec. 219(f)(3)].

(a) Deductibility of Contributions. You may establish an IRA whether or not you are covered by any other retirement plan. However, your IRA contribution is not deductible for any year in which you or your spouse were an active participant in an employer plan and have adjusted gross income above $50,000 (on a joint return) or $35,000 (single). Active participation by either spouse counts against both spouses even if they file separate returns, unless they live apart for the entire year [IRC Sec. 219(g)(4)]. The full $2,000 deduction (or $2,250 for a spousal account) is phased out with adjusted gross income between $40,000 and $50,000 (on a joint return) and $25,000 and $35,000 if single.

> **NOTE:** The IRS has adopted a liberal position as to when an employee is an active participant in a fiscal year cash-or-deferred plan [¶1345]. You are an active participant only if employer or employee contributions are made on your behalf for a plan year ending within your tax year. Thus, if you first participate in a cash or deferred plan during its July 1, 1992, to June 30, 1993, fiscal year, you are not considered an active participant of the plan for IRA deduction purposes in 1992.[1]

Figuring the reduction. If you are an active participant in an employer-maintained retirement plan, your allowable IRA deduction might be reduced or eliminated as follows:

If your filing status is:	*Your deductible IRA contribution phases out when AGI exceeds:*	*will be zero when AGI is:*
Single or unmarried head of household	$25,000	$35,000
Married filing joint return or surviving spouse	$40,000	$50,000
Married filing separate return	0	$10,000

If your adjusted gross income falls within the phaseout range, take the following steps to determine your maximum IRA deduction:

Step 1: *AGI excess amount.* Subtract from AGI the applicable dollar amount (2nd col. above) for your filing status to get your AGI excess amount. If that amount is $10,000 or more, no deduction is allowed for IRA contributions, and you need go no further. Otherwise, complete Step 2.

Step 2: *Amount of reduction.* To get amount by which you reduce the IRA deduction limit, multiply that limit by a fraction as follows:

$$\frac{\text{AGI excess amount (Step 1)}}{\$10,000} \times \text{IRA deduction limit} = \text{Amt. of reduction}$$

Step 3: *Reduced deduction limit.* Subtract from the deduction limit the amount of reduction (Step 2) to get your reduced maximum allowable IRA deduction (but see the $200 floor, discussed below).

Example 1: Mr. and Mrs. Smith have a combined adjusted gross income on their joint return of $43,000. They both work and have IRAs. Mrs. Smith is an active participant in her employer-maintained retirement plan. The Smiths each contributed the maximum allowable amount of $2,000 to an IRA. They each figure their allowable deduction as follows:

Step 1 $43,000   (combined AGI)
           - 40,000   (applicable dollar amount)
           $3,000   (AGI excess amount)

Step 2 $ 3,000 × $2,000 = $600 (amount of reduction)
           $10,000

Step 3 $2,000   (IRA deduction limit)
           - 600   (amount of reduction)
           $1,400   (reduced deduction limit and allowable IRA deduction for each spouse)

The Smiths can each deduct contributions of $1,400 to their IRAs, for a combined total of $2,800. If either one contributes more than $1,400, the excess must be treated as a nondeductible contribution.

No reduction below $200 until complete phaseout.   Your IRA deduction cannot go below $200 if your adjusted gross income has not reached the phaseout levels of $35,000 for an unmarried individual, $50,000 for a married couple filing jointly, and $10,000 for a married person filing separately. For example, if you are unmarried and have an adjusted gross income of $34,500, you can have an IRA deduction of $200, even though the phaseout would limit your IRA deduction to $100 [IRC Sec. 219(g)(2)(b)].

(b) Deduction Limit for Social Security Recipients. Some social security benefits may be included in your adjusted gross income, depending on your gross income, as adjusted by certain items *including* the IRA deduction. On the other hand, your maximum IRA deduction depends on your adjusted gross income—which includes the taxable portion of social security benefits. To get around this circular chain of calculations, the maximum deductible IRA contribution should be determined as follows: (1) Figure the amount of your social security benefits that would be taxable if no IRA contribution is made. (2) Use that amount in determining the maximum IRA deduction. (3) When figuring the amount of social security benefits that are actually subject to tax, use the modified adjusted gross income after subtracting out the applicable IRA deduction.[2]

> **Example 2:** Miss Keller's adjusted gross income before taking into account her IRA contribution or social security benefits is $24,000. She received $8,000 in social security benefits. In calculating the maximum IRA deduction, Keller's adjusted gross income is $25,500 ($1,500 of social security benefits are added in—one-half of: $24,000 plus $4,000 less $25,000, since that is less than one-half of benefits). Thus, the maximum IRA deduction is $1,900:
>
> $$\frac{\$35,000 - \$25,500}{\$10,000} \quad \times \quad \$2,000$$
>
> Assuming Keller claims a $1,900 IRA deduction, her modified AGI (for calculating the tax on social security benefits) is $22,100 ($24,000 less $1,900). As a result, only $550 of social security benefits are actually taxed (one-half of: $22,100 plus $4,000 less $25,000).

(c) Nondeductible IRA Contributions. Generally, you can make designated nondeductible contributions to an IRA to the extent that deductible contributions are not allowed (because of reduced IRA deduction limit).

Limit on nondeductible contributions. You can make nondeductible contributions to an IRA up to the excess of (1) $2,000 ($2,250 for an individual IRA and spousal IRA) or 100% of compensation, whichever is less, minus (2) the amount of your allowable IRA deduction. You are permitted to elect to treat deductible IRA contributions as nondeductible [IRC Sec. 408(o)].

> ➤ **OBSERVATION** An individual might make this election, for example, if the individual had no taxable income for the year after taking into account other deductions.

As with deductible contributions, designated nondeductible contributions can be made up to the due date of your tax return for the tax year (without extensions).

Reporting nondeductible contributions. Since nondeductible IRA contributions do not reduce your gross income in the year they are made, you do not report them on Form 1040. However, you are required to file Form 8606 with your tax return for each year you make a nondeductible contribution or receive an IRA distribution and have ever made a nondeductible contribution. This form is used to keep track of the total nondeductible contributions you have made over the years. It is also used to determine the taxable portion of distributions received from an IRA. You do not pay tax on the distribution of your nondeductible contributions.

There is a $50 penalty for failing to file Form 8606 [IRC Sec. 6693(b)(2)].

¶1331   SPOUSAL IRAs

You, a working spouse, may be eligible to make contributions to an IRA for your nonworking spouse, as well as to an IRA for yourself. This arrangement is called a spousal IRA. You can contribute up to a total of $2,250 per year. You have flexibility in dividing the contribution between you and your spouse so long as no more than $2,000 is contributed to the account of either of you [IRC Sec. 219(c)].

➤ **SPOUSAL IRA ADVANTAGE** The ability to divide a single $2,250 contribution as you see fit offers great flexibility. If longer tax deferral is sought, a greater contribution can be made to the younger spouse's account. If the money will be needed sooner, a greater portion can be deposited in the IRA of the older spouse.

To be eligible to set up an IRA for your nonworking spouse, (1) you must be married at the end of the tax year; (2) you have compensation included in your income for the year; (3) you file a joint return for the year in which the contribution is made; and (4) your spouse must either have no compensation or choose to have no compensation during the next year.

➤ **NO COMPENSATION ELECTION** This offers unique planning opportunities. The key is that the manner in which $2,250 is split is not restricted by one spouse's earning level. Accordingly, an electing spouse earning $1,000 could contribute $1,500 to a spousal IRA account, so long as the other contributed no more than $750 to a spousal IRA.

You can make contributions to your nonworking spouse's IRA until the year in which he or she reaches age 70½, even if you can no longer make contributions to your own account because you are age 70½ or older.[1]

¶1332   EXCESS CONTRIBUTIONS

Contributions that exceed either the deductible or nondeductible limit, whichever applies, are subject to an annual 6% excise tax on excess contributions. You must pay the 6% excise tax each year on the excess amounts that remain in your IRA [Reg. Sec. 1.408-1(c)(1)]. The excess is taxed for the year you make the excess contribution and each year after that until you correct it. You will not have to pay the excise tax if you withdraw the excess before your return is due. Any amount of the excess contribution that resulted in a deduction will create income that must be reported. You can carry over excess contributions to, and deduct them in, a year in which less than the maximum contribution has been made. The penalty tax is figured on Form 5329.

Example 1: Mr. Thomas, a calendar year taxpayer, earned $1,500 in compensation includible in gross income for 1992. On December 1, 1992, he establishes an IRA and contributes $2,000 to it. He does not withdraw any money from the account after the initial contribution. Since his maximum contribution is $1,500, Thomas has a $500 excess contribution for 1992. He will owe a 6% excise tax for 1992 and each year thereafter until it is corrected.

Example 2: Assume in Example 1 that in 1993 Thomas has gross income of $12,000. He makes a $1,000 contribution to his IRA for 1993. Thomas is treated as having made an additional contribution of $500 for 1993 and will be allowed to deduct $1,500 as his 1993 IRA contribution. Although the excise tax will be imposed for 1992, it will not be imposed for 1993 because it has been corrected.

¶1333   DISTRIBUTIONS

Distributions from an IRA must begin no later than April 1 of the calendar year after the year in which you reach 70½. They can be paid out over your life or the lives of you and a designated beneficiary (or over a period not extending beyond your life expectancy or the life expectancy of you and a designated beneficiary). Life expectancy may be recalculated each year [IRC Sec. 401(a)(9)]. A nondeductible 50% excise tax may be imposed on the difference between what was paid out and what should have been paid out.

The minimum distribution for each year depends both on the amount that you have in your IRAs and your life expectancy [Prop. Reg. Sec. 1.408-8]. The required minimum distribution is computed separately for each IRA, but you are not required to withdraw the minimum from each.

➤ **BIG BREAK** You can add up the minimums required to be withdrawn from each IRA and withdraw the total amount from the IRAs in any manner you choose.[1] No penalty tax will be assessed so long as the required minimum is withdrawn from the IRAs, in the aggregate.

Example: Mr. Smith has two IRAs, one with a bank and one with a mutual fund. Smith had his 70th birthday on February 1, 1992. His minimum distribution for his bank IRA in 1992 is $4,000; for his mutual fund IRA, it's $2,000. On March 30, 1993, he withdraws $6,000 from his bank IRA. Smith owes no penalty tax, because his withdrawal from the bank IRA equals the sum of his required distributions from both IRAs.

¶1334   ROLLOVER CONTRIBUTIONS

A rollover is a tax-free transfer of cash or other assets from one retirement program to another. There are two types. In one, you transfer amounts from one IRA to another. With the other, you transfer amounts from a company retirement plan to an IRA. A rollover is an allowable contribution that you do not deduct on your tax return. The rollover must be completed within 60 days of receipt. You are limited to one tax-free rollover within a one-year period, counting from the date of receipt of the last distribution [IRC Sec. 408(d)(3)(B)]. (However, a trustee-to-trustee transfer is not considered a rollover, and there is no limit on the number of these transfers that can take place in one year.)

➤ **PLANNING OPPORTUNITY** The ability to withdraw funds and redeposit them within 60 days turns your IRA into a good source for a short-term "loan." You can pull out your funds when you need extra cash. During the 60 days, you have tax-free use of the money. And the rollover can actually be a "rollback." The funds can be redeposited in the same—or a different—IRA with you enjoying the rollover break.[1] However, to the extent the monies are not returned to the IRA at the end of the 60 days, you will be taxed currently and, if you are under age 59½, hit with a 10% premature distribution penalty.

Similarly, to the extent a lump-sum distribution from a qualified plan is contributed to a retirement account, annuity or bond within 60 days after receipt, you are not currently taxed on the distribution. However, if you roll over only part of the distribution, any portion of the lump-sum not rolled over is taxed as ordinary income, without the benefit of five- or ten-year averaging or long-term capital gain treatment (¶1320(b)) [IRC Sec. 402(a)(5), (e)]. Also, the taxable portion of plan distributions you receive before age 59½ that is not rolled over may be subject to a 10% premature withdrawal penalty as well.

Example: Mr. Taylor retires at age 62, and receives a $500,000 lump-sum distribution in 1992. Under five-year averaging it would be subject to a $133,272 tax and under ten-year averaging, a tax of $143,682. If Taylor rolled over 50% ($250,000) of the distribution, his current tax on the balance would be $73,155, assuming he's in the 31% tax bracket. He would be taxed on IRA distributions as they are received.

A partial distribution from a company retirement plan is eligible for tax-free rollover treatment only if it is: (1) at least 50% of the balance to the participant's credit for distributions prior to 1993 (no 50% requirement for post-1992 distributions); (2) not one of a series of periodic payments; (3) distributed on account of the participant's death or separation from service, or after becoming disabled; and (4) the employee elects rollover treatment [IRC Sec. 402(a)(5)(D)(i)]. You can choose to make a tax-free rollover of part or all of a partial distribution that meets these rules.

¶1335   IRA REQUIREMENTS

You may set up either an individual retirement account or an individual retirement annuity plan. In any case, the interest is not transferable. Use Form 5305 to adopt an officially prescribed model individual retirement trust account; Form 5306 is used to apply for approval of a prototype individual retirement account; and Form 5306-SEP is used to get approval of a prototype simplified employee pension plan.

Individual retirement accounts. IRAs are domestic trusts organized for the exclusive benefit of an individual or his beneficiaries [IRC Sec. 408(a)]. Normally the trustee must be a bank. The plan must include these terms: (1) no contribution (which must be in cash) on behalf of any individual may exceed $2,000 a year, not including tax-free rollovers; (2) the trust assets must be kept separately from other property except a common or trust investment fund; (3) the account must be nonforfeitable.

Individual retirement annuities are annuity or endowment contracts issued by an insurance company to the individual participants [IRC Sec. 408(b)]. The contract must be nonforfeitable and must contain no life insurance element. The annual premium on behalf of an individual may not exceed $2,000. Also, payout provisions similar to those above apply here.

¶1336   TAX ON DISTRIBUTIONS

Generally, you are taxed on IRA payouts as ordinary income in the year you actually receive the cash payments [IRC Sec. 408(d)]. No tax is due on withdrawals to the extent they are allocable to your original nondeductible contributions [¶1330(c)]. The allocation is based on a ratio of your nondeductible contributions to the total balance in all of your IRAs.

> **Example 1:** An individual makes a $2,000 IRA contribution in 1991, of which $1,500 is deductible. He has not made any prior IRA contributions or withdrawals, and his 1990 year-end IRA balance is $2,200. In 1992, he makes a $2,000 nondeductible contribution to another IRA, makes no IRA withdrawals, and has a total 1992 year-end balance in his IRAs of $4,600. And, in 1993, he makes no IRA contributions, makes a $1,000 withdrawal from the IRA funded in 1991, and has a 1993 year-end balance of $4,000 in his IRAs. There are no outstanding rollovers.
> The $1,000 withdrawn from the IRA in 1993 is treated as partially a return of nondeductible contributions. The portion of the withdrawal treated this way is based on the ratio of the nondeductible contributions ($500 + $2,000) to the total value of the IRAs ($4,000) at the end of 1993 plus the amount distributed in 1993 ($1,000). Thus, $2,500/$5,000 or 50% of the $1,000 withdrawal is treated as a nontaxable return of nondeductible contributions. Nontaxable return is therefore $500.

You can withdraw nondeductible contributions completely tax-free (i.e., no allocation between deductible and nondeductible contributions) at any time up to the tax return deadline, including extensions, for the year the contribution was made. However, you must withdraw all earnings attributable to the contributions as well [IRC Sec. 408(d)(4)].

> **NOTE:** IRA distributions are not eligible for capital gains treatment, or the special 5- or 10-year averaging rule available to retirement plan participants. However, an IRA distribution is income eligible for the credit for the elderly and disabled [¶2402].

Premature distributions. Premature distributions are amounts you withdraw from your IRA before you are age 59½. These are subject to a 10% nondeductible excise tax (except for death, disability or certain corrective withdrawals). The tax applies to actual as well as "deemed" distributions. Thus, if you benefit from a prohibited transaction, the tax can apply to the amount of the benefit. An investment by an IRA or any other qualified plan in collectibles (art, gems, stamps, etc.) is treated as a distribution of the cost of the item. However, IRAs may invest in legal tender gold and silver coins minted by the United States or any coins issued under the laws of any state [IRC Sec. 408(m)].

No penalty applies to pre-age 59½ withdrawals if the withdrawal is a lifetime annuity [IRC Sec. 72(t)(2)(A)(iv)]. Note: The IRS has said that there must be a formal payout schedule for this break to apply.[1]

Example 2: Mr. Jones withdraws IRA funds at age 58. He owes regular income tax, but not the 10% penalty tax if he will receive a life annuity that pays equal annual installments over his life expectancy.

OTHER RETIREMENT ARRANGEMENTS

¶1340   SIMPLIFIED EMPLOYEE PENSIONS

[New tax legislation may affect this subject; see ¶1.]

Simplified employee pensions (SEPs) are easy-to-administer qualified retirement plans to which employers can make deductible contributions that are excludable from employee income. They must meet participation, nondiscrimination, and other special rules that apply to other qualified plans. Form 5306-SEP can be used to request approval for prototype plans.

(a) Contributions. Employer contributions to SEPs are deductible by the employer and excludable from employee income to the extent they don't exceed $30,000 or 15% of employee's compensation, whichever is less. No more than $228,860 of an employee's compensation may be taken into account in calculating contributions in 1992. This figure will continue to be adjusted for cost of living increases in future years. The $30,000 amount will be subject to cost of living adjustments when the defined benefit maximum is adjusted above $120,000. Certain SEPs are permitted to offer a special cash or deferred feature, similar to that offered under a 401(k) plan [¶1345]. With a SEP cash or deferred feature, employer contributions are excludable from employee income even if the employee had the option to receive the contributed amounts from the employer in cash [IRC Sec. 402(h); 408(j)].

FICA and FUTA taxes apply only to amounts that the employee had the option to receive in cash [IRC Sec. 3121(a)(5)(C); 3306(b)(5)(C)]. SEPs are treated as defined contribution plans for purposes of the limits on plan contributions [IRC Sec. 415(e)(5)]. Contributions received by SEPs should be reported on Form 5498.

Contribution deadline. SEP contributions can be made up until the tax return due date for the year, including extensions [IRC Sec. 404(h)(1)(B)].

(b) Participation, Nondiscrimination, and Other Requirements. Participation. Employer contributions must be made to the SEP of each employee age 21 or over who has worked for the employer for at least three of the last five years and received compensation of $300 or more (subject to inflationary adjustments; for 1992, it is $374).

For this purpose, contributions that an employee elects to receive in cash (under rules explained below) are treated as though paid to the employee's SEP [IRC Sec. 408(k)(2)].

Nondiscrimination. Contributions to SEPs must not discriminate in favor of highly compensated employees. Prior law permitted an employer to combine nonelective SEP contributions with employer social security contributions in testing the SEP for discrimination, provided the employer did not maintain another integrated plan. This permitted small employers to maintain plans that contributed greater amounts on behalf of highly compensated employees than such employees could contribute to a personal IRA. Under current law, nonelective SEP contributions are tested for nondiscrimination under the new rules for qualified defined contribution plans [¶1312]. These rules permit a limited disparity between the contribution percentages applicable to compensation below and above the social security taxable wage base.

Written contribution formula. Employer contributions must be determined under a definite written allocation formula that specifies requirements for sharing in an allocation and the manner in which the amount allocated will be computed [IRC Sec. 408(k)(5)].

Withdrawals must be allowed. The employer must not prohibit withdrawals from the SEP, and employer contributions cannot be conditioned on retention in the SEP of any portion of the amount contributed [IRC Sec. 408(k)(4)].

(c) Elective Salary Reductions Permitted. Employers who have no more than 25 employees who were eligible to participate (or would have been eligible had there been a plan) during the preceding year can allow employees participating in a SEP (other than a SEP maintained by a state or local government) to elect to have contributions made to the SEP or paid to them in cash. Contributions to the SEP pursuant to such election are not currently taxable to the employee, and are not treated as employee contributions. Elective deferrals under a SEP are treated like elective deferrals under a 401(k) plan and are subject to the same dollar cap ($8,728 for 1992). Also, like elective deferrals under a 401(k) plan, elective deferrals under a SEP are exclusions from income, but are includible in the definition of wages for employment tax (FICA and FUTA) purposes [IRC Sec. 408(k)(6)].

The elective deferral option is available under a SEP only if certain conditions are met. First, at least 50% of the employees of the employer must elect to have amounts contributed to the SEP. Second, the amount deferred each year by *each* highly compensated employee as a percentage of pay (the "deferral percentage") can be no more than 125% of the *average* deferral percentage of all other employees. Integration with social security contributions is no longer permitted, as described above, nor can any nonelective SEP contributions be combined with the elective deferrals. Employer matching contributions are conditioned on elective deferrals. Employer matching contributions conditioned on elective SEP deferrals are not allowed.

¶1345   CASH OR DEFERRED PLANS

[New tax legislation may affect this subject; see ¶1.]

Cash-or-deferred Sec. 401(k) salary reduction plans have soared in popularity in recent years. And despite crackdowns, they still provide an effective way to shelter compensation.

These arrangements often take the form of a salary reduction agreement whereby the employer contributions are conditioned on the employee's election to reduce compensation or forego a raise or bonus. While such plans are conveniently administered through payroll deduction, contributions by employees are granted an added benefit: They are not subject to income tax in the year the contribution is made [IRC Sec. 401(k); Reg. Sec. 1.401(k)-1(a)(3)(iv)].

In 1992, employees can elect to contribute up to the lesser of 25% of compensation or $8,728 [IRC Sec. 402(g)(1), (5)]. These contributions also count towards the overall 25%/$30,000 cap on retirement plan contributions.

> **IMPORTANT**   The tax law contains stiff nondiscrimination rules for cash-or-deferred plans. The percentage of compensation eligible "highly compensated" employees defer cannot exceed the greater of (1) 125% of the deferral percentage of other eligible employees, or (2) 200% of the deferral percentage of other employees but not more than 2 percentage points more than what other eligible employees defer [IRC Sec. 401(k)(3)].

Net effect: Unless rank-and-file employees elect to defer an adequate amount, your company's executives cannot put as much aside for themselves on a tax-deferred basis.

Excess deferrals.   In 1992, all amounts contributed by an employee in excess of the $8,728 cap are currently taxable to him. However, the taxable amount does not increase his basis in the funds (i.e., he pays tax a second time on those same dollars when they are withdrawn).

> **ESCAPE HATCH**   Employees have until March 1 of the following year to designate excess deferrals. If an employee participates in more than one plan, he should allocate the excess deferrals among the plans. Then the plan(s) can distribute the excess deferrals (plus earnings on them) by April 15. Result: The excess deferral is taxable in the year to which the deferral relates. On the other hand, income on excess deferrals is taxed in the year it is distributed. These distributions are not subject to the 10% penalty tax on early distributions nor the 15% penalty tax on large retirement plan distributions [IRC Sec. 402(g)(2), 4980A(a)].

Withdrawals.   Employees can withdraw deferrals they have made to a 401(k) plan upon separation from service, disability or hardship.

Hardship distributions   can be made if a participant meets a two-prong test:

*   He has an immediate and heavy financial need.
*   Other resources are not reasonably available to meet the need.

Certain expenses such as medical costs, the purchase of a principal residence, and tuition for the participant and family members automatically constitute an immediate and heavy financial need. Other resources will be deemed unavailable if the financial need cannot be met (1) through reimbursement or compensation from insurance, (2) by reasonable liquidation of other assets, (3) by no longer making elective or employee contributions under the plan, (4) by other distributions and nontaxable loans from employer plans, or (5) by borrowing from commercial sources on reasonable terms.

NOTE: An employee's resources include his spouse's and minor children's assets that are reasonably available to the employee. Thus, a vacation home owned jointly by spouses is deemed to be available to each spouse. On the other hand, property held for a child under the Uniform Gift to Minors Act is not treated as the parent's resource.

If a hardship withdrawal is made, the employee's elective contribution ceiling in the following year is reduced by the amount of deferral in the hardship withdrawal year [Reg. Sec. 1.401(k)-1(d)(2)].

Pre-age-59½ distributions (including hardship withdrawals) from a 401(k) plan are subject to a 10% penalty tax. However, the 10% premature withdrawal penalty does not apply to the extent an employee has medical expenses in excess of 7.5% of his adjusted gross income. Participants may receive distributions from a profit-sharing or stock bonus plan after attaining age 59½—even without establishing hardship [IRC Sec. 72(t)(2)(B), 401(k)(2)(B)(i)].

Amounts withdrawn on account of hardship are limited to elective deferrals—and not employer contributions or income on elective deferrals [IRC Sec. 401(k)(2)(B)].

Planning pointers. Lower-paid employees generally have less discretionary income to set aside and are less tax sophisticated. Yet their participation is needed to yield tax benefits for all employees. A special pitch may be needed to encourage their participation in the plan. Here are some points to consider.

- Thrift option. Many companies match voluntary employee deferrals fifty cents on a dollar, for example. A company making matching contributions should make employees understand how this helps their account balance grow. A fifty-cent matching contribution would represent an immediate 50% return on their investment.
- Small reduction in take-home pay. Take-home pay will go down by less than the amount being deferred. For example, an employee in the 15% bracket will see his paycheck go down by only $8.50 (even less if the contribution is deductible for state income tax purposes) for every $10 he puts away for the future. This can be contrasted with U.S. Savings Bond or other post-tax payroll deduction saving plans.
- Compare with IRAs. IRA contributions are not deductible by an employee who (1) is an active participant of a company-paid retirement plan (or whose spouse is), and (2) has an adjusted gross income of more than $50,000 if married or $35,000 if single (the deduction starts being phased out for incomes in excess of $40,000 and $25,000 respectively).

➤ **KEY POINT** Suppose a Sec. 401(k) plan with matching contributions is your company's only retirement plan. Employees will not be treated as members of a company-paid plan for purposes of the IRA restriction as long as they do not elect deferrals. But the employees can come out ahead by participating in the 401(k) plan.

Added tax savings. Employees who still qualify for the IRA deduction can make deductible Sec. 401(k) contributions as well—picking up additional tax savings. Suppose these employees can afford to contribute to only one of the two. They may be better off contributing to the Sec. 401(k) plan than to their IRA. Here's why:

(a) If the company makes matching contributions, the employees will pick up the matching dollars.

(b) The Sec. 401(k) contributions are automatically deducted from each paycheck so it takes less discipline to save.

(c) The contributions are invested and managed by the plan. Thus, employees do not have the chore of choosing investment vehicles. Of course, the plan can provide some investment flexibility (e.g., stock or bond funds).

¶1350   KEOGH PLANS

[New tax legislation may affect this subject; see ¶1.]

If you are self-employed, as a sole proprietor or a partner, you can set up qualified plans for yourself and your employees [IRC Sec. 401(c)]. These plans are sometimes referred to as Keogh or H.R. 10 plans. Keogh and corporate plan contribution and deduction limits are on a fairly equal footing. Keogh plans can be defined contribution or defined benefit plans and are subject to the same limits as corporate plans. For defined contribution plans, that is an annual addition of the lesser of 25% of net earnings from self-employment or $30,000. (The deduction cap on profit-sharing plan contributions is 15% of compensation.) For defined benefit plans, the 1992 limit is an annual retirement benefit of the lesser of 100% of compensation for your high three years or $112,221. Keogh and corporate plans are both generally subject to the same qualification requirements [¶1307]—and the top-heavy plan rules [¶1313]—but some special rules come into play [IRC Sec. 401(d)].

(a) Who Are Owner-Employees. Owner-employees are (1) sole proprietors, (2) partners who own over 10% ownership of either the capital or profits interest in a partnership [IRC Sec. 401(c)(3)]. Businesses owned by owner-employees must be aggregated to determine if the qualification requirements are satisfied.

(b) Earnings from Self-Employment. Compensation for purposes of computing your contribution is based on your "net earnings from self-employment." The net earnings, however, are computed with regard to the deduction allowed to you for one-half of the self-employment tax, and taking into account the deduction for employer contributions on your behalf if you're an owner-employee [IRC Sec. 401(c)(2)]. This adjustment presents a problem, however, because the amount of the deduction and the amount of the net earnings are dependent on each other.

You can provide for this adjustment to net earnings indirectly by reducing the rate of contributions on your behalf called for in the plan. Thus, the 25% and 15% of net earnings caps mentioned above are equivalent to 20% and 13.0435% of compensation before deducting Keogh contributions. The following worksheet can help you find this adjusted contribution rate and the deduction for contributions on your behalf. No adjustment is made to the rate for contributions on behalf of any common-law employees.

(1) Rate of contribution in plan . . . . _____%
(2) Rate in (1), shown as a decimal, plus 1 . . . . _____
(3) Adjusted rate (divide (1) by (2)) . . . . _____%
(4) Net earnings reduced by one-half of your self-employment tax . . . . $_____
(5) Maximum deduction (multiply (4) by (3)) . . . . $_____

Example: You are a sole proprietor and have employees. Your qualified profit-sharing plan provides that you contribute on your behalf 15% of your net earnings, and on behalf of your employees 15% of their pay. Your net earnings from your business (not taking into account any deduction for contributions on your behalf to the plan) are $200,000. This amount is figured after deducting your employees' pay of $60,000 and contributions on their behalf of $9,000 (15% of $60,000). Finally, you determine your net earnings reduced by the deduction for the self-employment tax (one-half of your self-employment tax) [$194,671 ($200,000 less $5,329)]. Using the worksheet you figure the deduction for contributions on your behalf as follows:

(1) Rate of contribution in plan 15%
(2) Rate in (1), shown as a decimal, plus 1 . . . .   1.15
(3) Adjusted rate (divide (1) by (2)) 13.0435%
(4) Net earnings reduced by one-half of your self-employment tax . . $194,671
(5) Maximum deduction (multiply (4) by (3)) $25,392

➤ **CONTRIBUTION DEADLINE** As long as your Keogh plan is set up by year-end, you have until you file your tax return, including extensions, to make the contribution.

(c) More than One Plan. For purposes of these deduction limits, all of your defined contribution plans are treated as a single plan, and all of your defined benefit plans are treated as a single plan.

(d) Limited Use of Forfeitures. Forfeitures cannot be used to increase your benefits. They may only be used to reduce future employer contributions [Reg. Sec. 1.401-7].

(e) Limit on Ancillary Benefits. Plan contributions on behalf of you that are allocable to life, accident or health insurance remain nondeductible even if they are within the overall Sec. 415 limits. It does not count as your contribution [IRC Sec. 404(e); Reg. Sec. 1.401-12(i)(2)(ii)].

(f) Plan Loan Restrictions. Plan participants are generally permitted to borrow money from qualified plans as described in ¶1325. You, as owner-employee, however, are subject to special rules because of the unusual nature of your status as both owner and employee. Loans to you are considered prohibited transactions and are subject to special rules [¶1327].

¶1355   EMPLOYEE STOCK OWNERSHIP PLANS

An employee stock ownership plan is a defined contribution plan designed to invest primarily in employer securities. It can take the form of a money purchase or stock bonus plan that also meets the special requirements imposed by IRC Section 409. Employer securities generally must be common stock readily tradable on an established market. If none exists, the highest class of common stock with voting power and dividend rights is acceptable. Securities of a related employer in the same "controlled group" are also okay [IRC Sec. 1563(a)].

(a) Voting Rights. Each participant or beneficiary must be able to direct the voting of the securities allocated to his account. They must be given the right to vote on important corporate matters, such as mergers, dissolution, liquidations or sale of substantially all the assets.

(b) Put Option. Participants must be given the right to receive distributions in employer securities. If the securities are not readily tradable, the employer must give participants a "put option;" that is, the right to require the employer to repurchase the securities under a fair valuation formula made by an independent appraiser [IRC Sec. 401(a)(28)(c), 409(h)].

(c) Employer Benefits. In addition to the tax benefits of qualified plans, an ESOP offers several unique opportunities for an employer. Its principal feature, as compared with other qualified plans, is the ability to generate capital through tax-deductible loans. In effect, the ESOP is a conduit. The employer's deductible cash contributions to the ESOP are used by the ESOP to repay loans whose proceeds were used to buy employer stock. The other advantages of ESOPs, from the employer perspective, are:

- Leveraged investment in employer stock. An ESOP can borrow funds to purchase stock contributed to the plan—even if the stock or securities are purchased from the employer corporation or its shareholders. Moreover, the loan can be used to purchase more stock than is actually needed for contributions to the plan. The balance can be used for annual expenses discussed below.
- Expense reimbursements. Assuming the employer borrows more than it needs to cover the securities contributed to the plan, it can use the excess funds to cover the amount paid or incurred to set up the plan, up to 10% of the first $100,000 transferred to the plan plus 5% of the excess. Administrative expenses for the year, up to 10% of the first $100,000 of dividends paid on the stock plus 5% of the excess up to $10,000, can also be withheld [IRC Sec. 409(i)].
- Low interest rate on loans. To encourage lenders to make ESOP loans, 50% of the interest the lender receives from certain ESOP loans is tax-free. This means

that lenders can make such loans at more favorable rates. Loans made after July 10, 1989, qualify for the deduction only if, right after the ESOP acquires the employer securities, the ESOP owns more than 50% of each class of the issuing corporation's outstanding stock or of the total value of the corporation's outstanding stock [IRC Sec. 133].

- Deduction for dividends paid. A deduction for dividends on employer securities is available if the dividends are used to make payments on loans used to acquire securities. The dividends-paid deduction is limited to dividends on employer stock acquired with an ESOP loan [IRC Sec. 404(k)].

(d) Employee Tax Benefits. There are several advantages to participants in ESOPs, as well. They are as follows:

- Diversification option. Employees who have attained age 55 and completed ten years of service are not forced to have all their funds in a single investment (i.e., employer stock). Within 90 days after the close of an election period (later of age 55 or completion of ten years of service) the participant must be given the option to diversify up to 25% of his account balance [IRC Sec. 401(a)(28)]. During the participant's last election year, up to 50% of the account can be diversified.
- Distribution rules. Distributions can be made in stock or cash and are taxed as described in ¶1320. The ESOP must permit distributions to employees who separate from service before the plan's normal retirement age. The distribution of the entire account balance must begin no later than the later of the plan year: (1) when the participant retires, becomes disabled or dies, or (2) which is the fifth plan year after separation from service [IRC Sec. 409(o)].

NOTE: These rules are intended to accelerate the usual payment rules. If the general rules provide an earlier payment date, the participant may elect that date [IRC Sec. 401 (a)(14)].

- Capital gain tax deferral. Tax on long-term capital gain from the sale of stock to the corporation's ESOP can be deferred if the seller reinvests the proceeds in other securities. To qualify for this tax break, the employer stock must have been held for three years before the sale to the ESOP, and the ESOP must own at least 30% of each class of the corporation's outstanding stock or of the total value of all outstanding stock [IRC Sec. 1042].

¶1360   TAX-SHELTERED ANNUITIES

Certain tax-exempt organizations are permitted to offer employees a unique tax-sheltered annuity [IRC Sec. 403(b)]. The main tax benefit of a tax-sheltered annuity, sometimes called a 403(b) annuity or 403(b) annuity plan, is that employees are not taxed on employer contributions to the plan until payments under the annuity are received. Many tax-sheltered annuity plans also offer participants the opportunity to make deductible contributions through salary reduction.

(a) Qualifying Employers. Tax-sheltered annuity programs may be established only by a qualified employer. These include state or local governments or their agencies or instrumentalities, public schools, libraries and certain tax-exempt organizations. Generally a qualified tax-exempt organization qualifies if it is formed and operated exclusively for religious, charitable, scientific or educational purposes [Reg. Sec. 1.403(b)-1(b)(1)(i)].

(b) Exclusion from Gross Income. Generally, if you participate in a tax-sheltered annuity plan you can exclude from your income the employer's contribution made on your behalf equal to the lesser of (a) the employer contribution limit, or (b) the exclusion allowance for your tax year. It should also be noted that regardless of whether the employer contribution is excludable under the rules discussed here, they would not be immediately subject to tax if they are subject to a substantial risk of forfeiture [IRC Sec. 403(b); Reg. Sec. 1.403(c)-1(a), 1.83-3(b)].

(c) Contribution Limit. Annual employer contributions generally may not exceed the lesser of (1) $30,000 or (2) 25% of the employee's compensation for the year [IRC Sec. 415(c)(1)]. Employee salary reduction contributions of up to $9,500 per year (this figure will not rise with the cost of living until the Sec. 401(k) contribution ceiling [¶1345] exceeds $9,500) are permitted [IRC Sec. 402(g)(4)].

(d) Exclusion Allowance. The exclusion allowance is computed by determining 20% of current compensation, multiplied by years of service, and then reducing the product by (1) amounts contributed tax free in prior years, and (2) tax-free contributions to state and local deferred compensation plans for the employee's years of service [IRC Sec. 403(b)(2)(A)].

Example: For three years, Mr. Smith has worked for a public school maintaining a tax-sheltered annuity program. Smith's salary for 1993 is $20,000, after being reduced by $2,400 under a salary reduction agreement. The employer's contribution for the year totalled $2,400. In previous years the employer's contribution to the regular retirement plan totalled $7,200, all of which was excluded from Smith's gross income. To determine the amount that can be excluded from Smith's gross income:

Step 1: Limit on employer-contribution (lesser of $30,000 or 25% of compensation)
25% x 20,000 = $5,000 . . . . <u>$5,000</u>

Step 2: Exclusion Allowance
(1)   20% × $20,000 × 3 years of service = ...$12,000
(2)   Less amounts previously excludable . . . . <u>(7,200)</u>
Balance 4,800
Exclusion allowance . . . . <u>$4,800</u>

Step 3: Amount excludable from gross income
(1)   Employer contribution $2,400
(2)   Limit on employer contribution (Step 1) 5,000
(3)   Exclusion allowance (Step 2) 4,800
Amount excludable (Smallest of (1), (2) or (3)) . . . . <u>$2,400</u>

Other rules. Contributions toward a tax-sheltered annuity under a salary reduction agreement are considered wages for purposes of the social security tax (FICA). This is the rule even though the contributions may be wholly or partially excluded for income tax purposes. To the extent employer contributions are excludable from gross income, they are not subject to income tax withholding. However, any part of the contribution that is in excess of the exclusion allowance, or is used to purchase current life insurance protection, is subject to withholding.[1]

Distributions. Distributions received from a tax-sheltered annuity may be rolled over into an IRA or another tax-sheltered annuity. The general rollover rules, including the 60-day requirement, would apply [¶1334]. In most cases, payments you receive or that are made available to you are taxable as ordinary income. However, if you have a basis on your contract, because amounts contributed by your employer were taxable to you, then these amounts would be recovered tax-free.

Minimum distributions. Rules similar to those that apply to IRA distributions [¶1333] also apply to distributions from 403(b) annuities, if the employee has reached age 70½. In short, a distribution in excess of the minimum on one 403(b) annuity can cover a shortfall on another 403(b) annuity. However, an excess withdrawal from a 403(b) annuity does not cover an IRA shortfall and vice versa.

While required distributions from an IRA are based on a taxpayer's entire balance in his IRA, there is a different rule for a 403(b) annuity. If the issuer of the 403(b) annuity has a record of the December 31, 1986, balance, the minimum distribution rules only apply to benefits accruing after 1986 (including post-1986 earnings on pre-1987 contributions).[2]

(e) Nondiscrimination Requirements. Two sets of nondiscrimination rules for 403(b) plans took effect in 1989. One applied to contributions made through salary reduction agreements. The other applied to matching contributions and all other contributions that are not made under a salary reduction agreement.

- Salary reduction. In general, the nondiscrimination requirement here mandates that all employees be permitted to make a salary reduction contribution of more than $200. Contributions pursuant to a one-time irrevocable election made at the time of initial plan eligibility are not treated as salary reduction contributions [IRC Sec. 403(b)(12)(A)(ii)].
- Other 403(b) plans. These rules are more complicated. Basically, they limit the permitted disparity between contributions for highly compensated and other employees [IRC Sec. 403(b)(12)(A)(i)]. The IRS provides safe harbor disparities. The greater the percentage of non-highly compensated employees who are accruing benefits under the program, the larger is the permissible disparity. For example, the percentage of compensation contributed for highly compensated employees may be as much as 180% of contributions for other employees if (1) at least 50% of the non-highly compensated employees are currently accruing benefits under the plan, and (2) at least 70% of the employees who are currently accruing benefits are not highly compensated.[3]

¶1365 NONQUALIFIED DEFERRED COMPENSATION

As benefits in qualified plans have been curtailed by recent tax law changes, nontax qualified deferred compensation plans have become increasingly important. There are several distinct advantages that nonqualified deferred compensation plans offer. First, they are a useful tool in helping an employer keep or recruit top talent. They may offer that extra incentive as part of an overall compensation package. Second, and perhaps more importantly, nonqualified deferred compensation plans enable an employer to pick and choose the employees it would like to benefit. Finally, such plans can supplement qualified plan benefits for high earners.

Types of nonqualified plans. Deferred compensation arrangements are often modeled after their tax qualified counterparts in terms of plan format. For example, the plans may be pension, profit-sharing or stock bonus plans and frequently contain provisions governing such things as vesting and required distributions. A key distinction, however, is that nonqualified plans need not be funded, while qualified plans are required to be funded. The nonqualified plans are essentially contractual arrangements between the employer and the employee, where the employer promises a benefit in return for the employee's services.

Employer tax consequences. Unlike a contribution to a qualified plan, contributions to nonqualified plans are not currently deductible, even if the employer in fact sets aside funds to pay the benefits promised under a deferred compensation plan. Instead, the employer is entitled to claim a deduction only when the deferred compensation is picked up in income by the employee [IRC Sec. 404(a)(5); Reg. Sec. 1.404(a)-12(b)]. To claim the deduction, the employer must maintain a separate account for each employee.

Employee tax consequences. Employees need not include deferred compensation in income until they actually or constructively receive it. When their rights are substantially vested, either transferable or not subject to a substantial risk of forfeiture,[1] then they must include the compensation in income [¶1208] [IRC Sec. 83]. Deferred compensation plans are generally designed to shift the employee's income, and accompanying tax burden, into future retirement years, when the employee's income tax bracket may be lower. This strategy may be less meaningful in light of the cutback in graduated rates; however, don't overlook the importance of supplementing qualified plan benefits.

Funded or unfunded? There is no requirement that nonqualified plans be funded. In fact, a single unfunded promise to pay the deferred compensation avoids the constructive receipt problem (i.e., employees are not taxed until the compensation is actually paid to them). Using an unfunded plan, however, would not prevent the employer from actually setting aside funds or segregating the plan's funds on the company's books. Compare this with the funds held in a qualified plan. They are generally segregated in trust and cannot be used by the employer for general business purposes.

Rabbi trusts. Frequently, employees want the security of knowing that the promised deferred compensation will actually be there upon their retirement. This can be especially important when they are concerned about the whims of changing management or changes in corporate structure, particularly in this era of corporate takeovers. One popular vehicle for greater security in deferred compensation is the "rabbi" trust, so named because the first IRS ruling that approved the arrangement involved a rabbi.[2]

Under a rabbi trust, funds for the employee's benefit can be placed in trust and the employee's control of the funds is subject to substantial limitations. The employee will not be in constructive receipt of the funds, just because the trust has been set up, provided: (1) the company remains the owner of the funds, and all deductions and income are reported on the company's tax return, and (2) the assets of the trust are available to the employer's general creditors, in the event of the employer's insolvency or bankruptcy.

Secular trusts. These trusts offer employees even more security than do rabbi trusts. However, secular trusts have probably lost their appeal as a deferred compensation setup in light of a private letter ruling that subjects these trusts to double taxation.

How secular trusts work: The company puts money in a trust for the benefit of the employee. The contribution, plus accumulated earnings, will be paid to the employee at a later date, say, age 65. Unlike a rabbi trust, a secular trust's benefits are not forfeitable and are not subject to the claims of the company's creditors.

The company gets an immediate deduction for what it puts in the trust. The employee is currently taxed on what's put in the trust for him or her. And the Revenue Service has taken the position that there is a double tax when the property in the trust increases in value through interest earned or otherwise. The IRS says that both the trust and the employee are to pay tax on these earnings.[3]

> ➤ **PLANNING OPPORTUNITY** An employee-grantor trust can avoid the double taxation problem without giving up the security of a secular trust. Under this setup, the employee is considered to actually make the contributions—with money from the employer. The employer can actually make the contributions to the trust, as long as the employee has the right to decide whether he or she wants to take the money outright or deposit it in the trust. Result: No double taxation. The employee pays tax on the contributions and the trust income, but the trust doesn't pay tax.

Footnotes to Chapter 3

(For your added convenience, in brackets [] with the footnotes below, you will find citations to related paragraphs in the "RIA United States Tax Reporter" (USTR), "CCH Federal Tax Reporter" (CCH), and "RIA Federal Tax Coordinator 2d" (FTC) multi-volume services.)

FOOTNOTE ¶ 1300 [USTR ¶ 4014; CCH ¶ 17,501 et seq.; FTC ¶ H-5100 et seq.; ¶ H-6100 et seq.].

FOOTNOTE ¶ 1301 [USTR ¶ 4014.02; 104; CCH ¶ 15,501 et seq.; FTC ¶ H-10100 et seq.].

FOOTNOTE ¶ 1306 [USTR ¶ 4014.18; CCH ¶ 17,501 et seq.; FTC ¶ H-10501 et seq.].

(1) Rev. Rul. 54-51, 1954-1 CB 147.

(2) Rev. Rul. 60-84, 1960-1 CB 159.

(3) Rev. Rul. 60-83, 1960-1 CB 157.

(4) Rev. Rul. 74-307, 1974-2 CB 126.

(5) Rev. Rul. 68-31, 1968-1 CB 151.

(6) Rev. Rul. 61-164, 1961-2 CB 99.

(7) Announc. 92-54, IRB 1992-13.

(8) ERISA Technical Release No. 91-1.

FOOTNOTE ¶ 1307 [USTR ¶ 4014.15; CCH ¶ 17,501 et seq.; FTC ¶ H-10101].

(1) P.L. 93-406.

(2) DOL Regs at 29 CFR 2510 et seq.

FOOTNOTE ¶1308 [USTR ¶ 4114.05; CCH ¶ 19,076; 19,173; FTC ¶ H-7469; 11133].

(1) Rev. Rul. 89-13, 1989-1 CB 112.

(2) IR-92-3.

FOOTNOTE ¶ 1309 [USTR ¶ 4104.12; CCH ¶ 18,997; FTC ¶ H-7430].

(1) Announc. 92-29, IRB 1992-9.

(2) Rev. Rul. 83-58, 1983-1 CB 95.

(3) Announc. 92-81, IRB 1992-22.

FOOTNOTE ¶ 1310 [USTR ¶ 4104.10; CCH ¶ 18,984; 18,997; FTC ¶ H-7430].

FOOTNOTE ¶ 1311 [USTR ¶ 4114.02; CCH ¶ 19,076; FTC ¶ H-7420].

(1) Weil, 933 F.2d 106.

FOOTNOTE ¶ 1312 [USTR ¶ 4014.18; CCH ¶ 19,218; FTC ¶ H-10105].

(1) IR-92-3.

(2) Notice 89-45, 1989-1 CB 633.

(3) P.L. 99-514, Sec. 1106 (i)(3).

FOOTNOTE ¶ 1313 [USTR ¶ 4164.02; CCH ¶ 19,253; FTC ¶ H-7443].

FOOTNOTE ¶ 1314 [USTR ¶ 4144.07; CCH ¶ 19,166A; FTC ¶ H-9701, 10,115].

FOOTNOTE ¶ 1315 [USTR ¶ 4114.20; CCH ¶ 17,507.09; FTC ¶ H-7300 et seq.].

FOOTNOTE ¶ 1316 [USTR ¶ 4044; CCH ¶ 18,347 et seq.; 19,125; FTC ¶ H-10010 et seq.].

(1) Vinson & Elkins, 99 T.C. No. 2.

(2) P.L. 93-406, Sec. 406(a).

FOOTNOTE ¶ 1317 [USTR ¶ 4014.23; CCH ¶ 18,119 et seq.; FTC ¶ H-10129; 10213].

FOOTNOTE ¶ 1318 [USTR ¶ 4014.05; CCH ¶ 17,507.20; FTC ¶ H-10020].

(1) Ltr. Rul. 9118001.

FOOTNOTE ¶ 1319 [USTR ¶ 4114.15; CCH ¶ 17,507 et seq.; 19,262; FTC ¶ H-11159].

(1) Notice 89-42, 1989-1 CB 683.

(2) P.L. 99-514, Sec. 1121(d)(3), (4).

(3) Rev. Rul. 74-417, 1974-2 CB 131.

(4) Rev. Rul. 71-295, 1971-2 CB 184.

(5) Rev. Rul. 68-24, 1968-1 CB 150.

(6) Rev. Proc. 92-10, IRB 1992-2..

FOOTNOTE ¶ 1320 [USTR ¶ 4024; CCH ¶ 18,207 et seq.; FTC ¶ H-10102].

(1) Rev. Rul. 79-336, 1979-2 CB 187.

(2) Ltr. Rul. 8931054.

(3) Ltr. Rul. 8224055.

(4) Ltr. Rul. 8820092.

(5) Ltr. Rul. 7845027.

(6) Boyer, PH TC Memo 1988-220.

(7) Ltr. Rul. 8110050; Ltr. Rul. 8005023.

(8) Rev. Rul. 79-265, 1979-2 CB 186.

FOOTNOTE ¶ 1322 [USTR ¶ 724.22; CCH ¶ 6116.04; 18,207.044; FTC ¶ H-11142 et seq.].

FOOTNOTE ¶ 1323 [USTR ¶ 4144.20; CCH ¶ 19,171E; FTC ¶ H-8207 et seq.].

FOOTNOTE ¶ 1325 [USTR ¶ 724.33; CCH ¶ 17,508.89; FTC ¶ H-11114; 11117].

(1) Rev. Rul. 89-14, 1989-1 CB 111.

(2) See DOL Regs at 29 CFR 2550.408b.

FOOTNOTE ¶ 1327 [USTR ¶ 49,754; CCH ¶ 35,800 et seq.; FTC ¶ H-14036; 14039].

FOOTNOTE ¶ 1330 [USTR ¶ 4084.01; CCH ¶ 12,662; 18,922; FTC ¶ H-12000 et seq.].

(1) Ltr. Rul. 8919064.

(2) Announc. 88-38, IRB 1988-10.

FOOTNOTE ¶ 1331 [USTR¶ 2194.01; CCH ¶ 12,662; 18,922; FTC ¶ H-12026 et seq.].

(1) Treas. Dept. booklet "Individual Retirement Arrangements" (1991 Ed.), p. 5.

FOOTNOTE ¶ 1332 [USTR ¶ 4084.01; CCH ¶ 18,922.065-.067;2 FTC ¶ H-12043].

FOOTNOTE ¶ 1333 [USTR ¶ 4084.04; CCH ¶ 18,922.068; FTC ¶ H-12039 et seq.].

(1) Notice 88-38, 1988-1 CB 524.

FOOTNOTE ¶ 1334 [USTR ¶ 4084.03; CCH ¶ 18,922.076 et seq.; FTC ¶ H-11335; 11336].

(1) Ltr. Rul. 901007

FOOTNOTE ¶ 1335 [USTR¶ 4084; CCH ¶ 18,922.10; FTC ¶ H-11300 et seq.].

FOOTNOTE ¶ 1336 [USTR ¶ 4084.05; CCH ¶ 18,922.0984;; FTC ¶ H-11346 et seq.].

(1) Ltr. Rul. 9115041.

FOOTNOTE ¶ 1340 [USTR ¶ 4044.08; CCH ¶ 18,922.056; FTC ¶ H-12502].

FOOTNOTE ¶ 1345 [USTR ¶ 4014.17; CCH ¶ 18,112; FTC ¶ H-12509].

FOOTNOTE ¶ 1350 [USTR ¶ 4014.17; CCH ¶ 17,933 et seq.; FTC ¶ H-9300 et seq.].

FOOTNOTE ¶ 1355 [USTR ¶ 15,634; CCH ¶ 18,951; FTC ¶ H-11700 et seq.].

FOOTNOTE ¶ 1360 [USTR ¶ 4034.04; CCH ¶ 18,270; FTC H-13000 et seq.].

(1) Rev. Rul. 70-453, 1970-2 CB 257.

(2) Treas. Dept. booklet ''Pension and Annuity Income'' (1991 Ed.), p. 28.

(3) Notice 89-23, 1989-1 CB 654.

FOOTNOTE ¶ 1365 [USTR ¶ 4044.03; CCH ¶ 18,347.02; FTC ¶ H-9900 et seq.].

(1) Rev. Rul. 60-31, 1960-1 CB 174, as modified.

(2) Ltr. Rul. 8113107.

(3) Ltr. Rul. 9206009.

CHAPTER 4

EMPLOYEE FRINGE BENEFITS

TABLE OF CONTENTS

Employee benefits have proliferated in terms of use, cost and complexity. They range from health and life insurance to a company-owned car and child care. As a result, fringe benefits now account for approximately 35% to 40% of a company's payroll. Some types of fringe benefits receive favorable tax treatment. This makes those fringe benefits even more valuable to employees. However, there are often special rules and restrictions that must be met in order to qualify for the tax breaks.

COMPANY CARS AND AIRPLANES

¶1400   COMPANY CARS IN GENERAL

Many employers provide their employees with company-owned cars. If your employer provides you with a car, the portion of the value of the car use attributable to business-related driving is excludable from your gross income. Only the value of the nonbusiness use is taxable compensation to you.

> **Example 1:** Mr. Blake is provided a company car by XYZ Inc., his employer. The percentage of business use of the car is 80%. His taxable compensation on his nonbusiness use is 20% of his total use. If the total value of the company-provided car is $4,000, then $3,200 (80% of $4,000) is excludable from Blake's gross income as a working condition fringe benefit. Only $800 (20%) is taxable and included in his gross income.

Records needed. In order for an allocation to be made between business and personal use of a car, you must keep a diary or similar record that has detailed entries for business use (e.g., time, place, mileage, and business purpose of the trip). Where your employer is determining the vehicle's nonbusiness use, you turn the records over to your employer. In other cases, you retain the records. You should enter the beginning and ending odometer readings for the period covered by the diary. The difference between total business miles and the sum of all mileage is your personal mileage, which is taxable to you. If you deduct actual car expenses, you must maintain records of out-of-pocket costs (i.e., gas, tolls, parking, etc.) in order to substantiate the deduction.[1]

There is an exception to the recordkeeping rule for certain vehicles that by their very design are not susceptible to personal use. The value of using so-called "qualified" non-personal use vehicles (e.g., ambulances, police or fire vehicles, tractors and other special purpose farm vehicles, flatbed trucks, or trucks customized to hold equipment) is excluded from income. Absent adequate records, farming vehicles available for personal use are presumed to be used 75% for business; only the remaining 25% is deemed as taxable personal use [Reg. Sec. 1.132-5(g),(h)].

100% personal use. Your employer can choose to treat the car as being used 100% for your personal use. Your employer does not have the chore of finding out the breakdown (and making an allocation) between your business and personal usage. As a result, you must report the entire value of the car as compensation [Temp. Reg. Sec. 1.274-6T(c)]. To avoid paying tax on the business use, you claim an offsetting deduction for the value of business mileage.

> **NOTE:** The value of that business use must be deducted as a miscellaneous itemized deduction subject to the 2% of adjusted gross income floor (¶1942) [Temp. Reg. Sec. 1.162-25T].

> **Example 2:** Mr. Shaul is provided a company car that he uses 75% for business. His employer uses the 100% personal use method and includes $8,000 in Shaul's gross income. This represents the full value of Shaul's car use. Shaul's adjusted gross income is $75,000. To avoid paying tax on the complete value of the car, Shaul reports a $6,000 expense (75% of $8,000) for the business use on Form 2106. However, he actually deducts only $4,500 of this because of the 2% floor (assuming Shaul has no other deductible miscellaneous expenses).

Chauffeur services. If your employer provides a car and driver for your personal use, the fair market value of the chauffeur services, as well as the value of the use of the car, are taxable benefits to you. The fair market value of the chauffeur services is the amount an individual would have to pay to obtain comparable chauffeur services in the same geographic area during the same period of time [Reg. Sec. 1.61-21(b)(5)].

¶1401   VALUATION OF PERSONAL USE

Personal use of a company car can be valued using one of the following methods:

- Fair market lease value.
- Value computed using special IRS tables.
- Cents-per-mile method.
- Commuting use method.

NOTE: You must value the car use on your tax return by using either (1) the same valuation method as your employer has used or (2) the fair market value approach (even if your employer has used a different method) [Reg. Sec. 1.61-21(c)(2)].

Adopting valuation method. In general, you and your employer are locked into the valuation method that is selected when the car was first made available to you for personal use (except that the commuting valuation rule [(d) below] may still be used) [Reg. Sec. 1.61-21(d)(7), (e)(5)].

Your employer must notify you of the special valuation method being used by the later of January 31 of the year the election applies or 30 days after the benefit is first provided to the employee. The notice must alert you to the method being used, the substantiation requirements with which you must comply (e.g., keeping records of business and personal use) and the effect of failing to comply with those requirements. In addition, the notice must state the date on which the notice was provided.

An employer that fails to provide this notice can still use a special valuation method if it gets a statement from the employee by January 31 of the following year. The statement must say that the employee knows of: (1) the employer's use of the special method, (2) the substantiation requirements involved and (3) the effect of failing to comply with the requirements [Reg. Sec. 1.61-21(c)(3)] .

(a) Fair Market Value Approach. This method must be used if your employer does not elect any of the three special methods discussed in (b), (c) or (d) below. The starting point with this method is the cost of leasing a similar car on comparable terms, in the same geographic area [Reg. Sec. 1.61-21(b)(4)]. Then that figure is allocated between business and personal use. The personal use portion is included in your gross income.

➤ **TAX STRATEGY** If your employer gets price quotes from several leasing companies, it can select the lowest rate to figure the value of the fringe benefit. This results in a smaller taxable fringe benefit to you and its other employees—without reducing its deduction. Reason: Your employer's writeoffs come from depreciation deductions—which are calculated on your employer's basis in the car.

Example 1: Ms. Taylor is provided a company car by her employer, ABC Corp., which values the personal use of the vehicle under the fair market value approach. ABC Corp. contacted various leasing companies and determined that it would cost $3,600 to lease a similar car on comparable terms. Taylor's business use of the car is 60% of her mileage. As a result, $1,440, which represents her 40% personal use of the car, is included in her gross income.

(b) IRS Tables. This method is, in essence, a safe-harbor shortcut of the fair market value approach. Instead of obtaining price quotes from leasing companies, your employer can consult a Revenue Service table—contained in Reg. Sec. 1.61-21(d)(2) (and reproduced below)—that lists annual lease values based on the fair market value of the car. This value includes all costs that would be incurred to buy the car in an arm's-length transaction, including sales tax and title fees. For leased cars, your employer may use the manufacturer's suggested retail price less 8%, or refer to a nationally recognized pricing source that regularly reports automobile retail values (i.e., a "Blue Book") [Reg. Sec. 1.61-21(d)(5)(ii)(C), (iii)].

> **NOTE:** For employer-leased vehicles provided after 1988, your employer may use the manufacturer's invoice price (including options) plus 4% as the fair market value.[1]

> ➤ **OBSERVATION** The fair market value being used in the IRS table method is the fair market value for purchasing the car. The fair market value in (a) above is what it would cost to lease the car.

When using the IRS tables, the car's fair market value is determined as of the first day the car was made available to any employee for personal use (or January 1, 1985, if later). That value is used for four years. After that, your employer revalues the car and uses the new value for the next four years [Reg. Sec. 1.61-21(d)(2)(iv)].

In calculating the car's fair market value, your employer may exclude the value of a telephone or other specialized equipment in the car that is attributable to the employer's business needs. However, the exclusion is not available if the equipment is used by the employee in a business other than that of his employment by the employer providing the car [Reg. Sec. 1.61-21(d)(5)(iv)].

Automobile fair market value (1)	Annual Lease value (2)		
$0 to 999	$600	20,000 to 20,999	5,600
1,000 to 1,999	850	21,000 to 21,999	5,850
2,000 to 2,999	1,100	22,000 to 22,999	6,100
3,000 to 3,999	1,350	23,000 to 23,999	6,350
4,000 to 4,999	1,600	24,000 to 24,999	6,600
5,000 to 5,999	1,850	25,000 to 25,999	6,850
6,000 to 6,999	2,100	26,000 to 27,999	7,250
7,000 to 7,999	2,350	28,000 to 29,999	7,750
8,000 to 8,999	2,600	30,000 to 31,999	8,250
9,000 to 9,999	2,850	32,000 to 33,999	8,750
10,000 to 10,999	3,100	34,000 to 35,999	9,250
11,000 to 11,999	3,350	36,000 to 37,999	9,750
12,000 to 12,999	3,600	38,000 to 39,999	10,250
13,000 to 13,999	3,850	40,000 to 41,999	10,750
14,000 to 14,999	4,100	42,000 to 43,999	11,250
15,000 to 15,999	4,350	44,000 to 45,999	11,750
16,000 to 16,999	4,600	46,000 to 47,999	12,250
17,000 to 17,999	4,850	48,000 to 49,999	12,750
18,000 to 18,999	5,100	50,000 to 51,999	13,250
19,000 to 19,999	5,350	52,000 to 53,999	13,750
		54,000 to 55,999	14,250
		56,000 to 57,999	14,750
		58,000 to 59,999	15,250

For vehicles having a fair market value in excess of $60,000, the Annual Lease Value is equal to (.25 × automobile fair market value) + $500.

To figure your taxable benefit, your employer multiplies your personal use percentage by the appropriate table figure. If the car has just been purchased, your employer can value the car at cost. If a car is being shifted from one employee to another, its fair market value may generally be recomputed as of January 1 of the year of transfer (assuming tax savings is not the primary reason for the transfer). At that time, your employer can use a "Blue Book" value.

> ➤ **TAX STRATEGY** Suppose XYZ Inc. is seeking to purchase a car that sells for $12,000. XYZ Inc. should try to bargain the dealer down to the next lower thousand dollar bracket (i.e., $11,999). Reason: The car values in the IRS table are organized in thousand dollar increments. And a drop of just a few dollars in the value of a car could reduce an employee's taxable income by several hundred dollars per year.

Example 2: Enterprise, Inc. purchased a company car for $12,000 that will be provided to a salesperson. The annual lease value is $3,600. If Enterprise had paid $11,999, the annual lease value would be only $3,350. Assuming 30% of the employee's car use is personal mileage, the employee would have $75 less taxable compensation per year if the company had paid $1 less for the car.

Special rule for part-year use. The IRS table provides values for a full year's car use. However, your employer may prorate these values for a car made available to any employee for less than a full year. There are two proration formulas, depending on whether the car is available for less than 30 days or a greater portion of the year.

- If the car was made available for 30 days or more, the prorated lease value is determined by multiplying the applicable annual lease value by the number of days the car was available divided by 365.
- If the car was made available for less than 30 days, the daily lease value is determined by multiplying the annual lease value by four times the number of days the car was available divided by 365. However, the car may be treated as having been made available for 30 days if doing so would result in a lower valuation [Reg. Sec. 1.61-21(d)(4)].

Example 3: A $12,000 car is provided to an employee for 30 days. The $3,600 annual lease value is prorated. Thus, the value of the car's availability to the employee is $296 ($3,600 × 30/365).

Example 4: Same facts as Example 3, except the car is made available for only 25 days. The lease value is $986 [$3,600 × (4 × 25)/365]. However, by electing to treat the car as having been made available to the employee for 30 days, the figure can be reduced to $296.

NOTE: The prorated annual lease value cannot be used if the unavailability of the car is solely due to personal reasons of the employee (e.g., the employee is away on vacation) or is designed to reduce taxes [Reg. Sec. 1.61-21(d)(4)(iv)].

Employer provided fuel. The car use values listed in the IRS table do not include fuel. If the fuel is provided by your employer—either at a company-owned gas pump or by means of a reimbursement—the fuel can be valued either at its fair market value or at 5.5 cents per mile for all miles driven by the employee within the United States (and its territories), Canada and Mexico. The value of the fuel must be added to the annual lease value of the car to determine the fair market value of the benefit provided [Reg. Sec. 1.61-21(d)(3)(ii)].

Simplified table value method for large car fleets. Employers that maintain large car fleets can use a simplified fleet-average valuation rule. The rule may be used as of January 1 of the year following the year in which an employer acquires a fleet of 20 or more cars [Reg. Sec. 1.61-21(d)(5)(v)(B)]. Thus, the fleet average rule is not available if the car fleet is leased. Valuation under the fleet-average rule is determined as follows:

- Find the fair market value of each car in the fleet as of January 1, 1985, or the date it was made available to employees for personal use, whichever is later.
- Divide total fair market value of all cars by the number of cars to find the average fair market value for each car in the fleet.
- Find the fleet average dollar figure in the IRS table of lease values. The table amount may be used to value personal use of each car that's worth not more than $16,500 (adjusted for inflation after 1988) on January 1, 1985, or the date it was made available to an employee, whichever is later [Reg. Sec. 1.61-21(d)(5)(v)(D)].

The fleet average valuation rule can be applied only to cars that are regularly used for company business. Infrequent use, such as trips to the airport or between the employer's multiple business premises, is not regular use [Reg. Sec. 1.61-21(d)(5)(v)(D); (e)(1)(iv)]. The fleet average must be recomputed every two years. When a new car is added, it is assigned the fleet average then in effect. However, if the new car's fair market value exceeds $16,500 (adjusted for inflation), the fleet average option can't be used for that car. And when a company's car fleet drops below 20 for more than 50% of the days in a year, the company must discontinue using the fleet average valuation rule as of January 1 of that year. In this case, the annual lease value must be determined separately for each remaining automobile in the fleet [Reg. Sec. 1.61-21(d)(5)(v)(B)].

> **NOTE:** Employers need not include all eligible cars in the fleet; instead, employers can use the fleet valuation method for only those qualifying cars they wish. Also, employers can divide their cars up into more than one fleet [Reg. Sec. 1.61-21(d)(5)(v)(C)].

Finally, a company that uses the fleet average valuation rule gets a special break when it comes to valuing gas used for personal driving. If the company reimburses gas costs, or supplies a company credit card, it can (1) establish its average gas cost per mile for the fleet and (2) multiply this average cost by the employee's personal mileage. Average gas cost per mile can be found by averaging per-gallon fuel costs and miles-per-gallon rates of a representative sample of the fleet for a representative period of time (for example, two months). A representative sample is the greater of 10% of the number of cars in the fleet, or 20 cars. Alternatively, companies may value the fuel at 5.5 cents per mile if determining the actual reimbursement or amount charged for fuel would impose unreasonable administrative burdens [Reg. Sec. 1.61-21(d)(3)(ii)(D)].

(c) Cents-Per-Mile Method. This method is the simplest to apply and may be the least costly to you and other employees. Your employer values car use at 28 cents per mile. And there is no limit on the number of miles for which this rate can be used. (Prior to 1990, there was a two-tiered rate; mileage in excess of 15,000 was valued at 11 cents per mile.) To qualify for using this method, your employer must reasonably expect that the car will be regularly used in business. This requirement is met if more than 50% of the business mileage during the year is business-connected or the car carries at least three employees a day in an employer-sponsored commuting pool. Alternatively, this method may be used if the vehicle is driven at least 10,000 miles for the year and that use is primarily by employees—even if it is mostly for their personal purposes. If your employer does not own or lease the car for the entire year, the 10,000 mile threshold is reduced proportionately.

However, this method cannot be used on cars costing more than $12,800, plus inflation adjustments for cars placed in service after 1988 ($13,100 in 1989-90; $13,400 in 1991; $13,700 in 1992) [Reg. Sec. 1.61-21(e)(1)].

> **Example 5:** Weststar Corp. provided Ms. North with a company car costing $11,500. Weststar elects to value her personal use using the cents-per-mile method. During the year she traveled 22,000 miles, of which 6,000 was business mileage and 16,000 was personal use. Using the cents-per-mile method, Weststar includes $4,480 (16,000 × .28) in her gross income as personal use of the car. The business use is properly excluded from her gross income.

If your employer does not supply gas for your personal driving, the mileage allowance is reduced by up to 5.5 cents per mile. Thus, when you pay for gas, the valuation can be 22.5 cents per mile [Reg. Sec. 1.61-21(e)(3)(ii)].

The cents-per-mile method is available only for valuing actual personal use. It cannot be used when an employer is treating 100% of the car use as personal mileage (¶1400) [Reg. Sec. 1.61-21(e)(4)].

(d) Commuting Use Method. The value of the commuting use of an employer-provided vehicle is $1.50 per one-way commute (i.e., from home to work and from work to home) for each employee who commutes in the vehicle. Thus, the amount includible for each round-trip commute is $3.00 per employee. You can use this method if your employer has a non-compensatory business reason that requires you to commute to and/or from work in the car. In addition, your employer must have a written policy prohibiting you from using the car for other personal use (except de minimis use, such as stopping on a personal errand on the way between business and home). This method may not be used by a "control employee." A control employee is defined as a director; an owner of more than 1% equity, capital, or profit interest in the employer; an employee receiving compensation of at least $100,000; or an officer receiving compensation of at least $50,000; for government employees, an elected official or those earning at least the compensation paid to federal government employees at the Executive Level V [Reg. Sec. 1.61-21(f)].[1]

> **Example 6:** Mr. Brown is provided a company-owned vehicle for business use only. A written policy exists forbidding any personal use of the vehicle by Brown. Brown is required to commute to and from work in the vehicle, since there is no secure place for overnight parking at the worksite. The employer uses the commuting method. If Brown makes 150 commuting round-trips in the vehicle during the year, he is deemed to have received a $450 (150 days × $3.00) taxable fringe benefit.

¶1402   AUTOMOBILE CAR SALESPERSONS

If you are a full-time automobile salesperson, special, more liberal exclusion rules apply to your use of a company car. You can exclude the value of your use of a demonstration car in the dealership's geographic sales area. This car must be in the inventory of the car dealership and available for test drives by prospective buyers. Your employer must prohibit the car's use outside of business hours. For example, the car cannot be driven by your family or used for vacation trips [IRC Sec. 132(h)(3); Reg. Sec. 1.132-5(o)].

To qualify for the exclusion, you must (1) be employed by a car dealer, (2) spend your business day on the sales floor selling cars, (3) work full-time (not less than 1,000 hours per year), and (4) derive 25% or more of your gross income from the dealership as a direct result of your sales activities [Reg. Sec. 1.132-5(o)(2)].

¶1403   COMPANY-OWNED AIRCRAFT

If you travel on a company-owned plane primarily for business purposes, you can exclude the value of the flight from your gross income as a working condition fringe benefit. The exclusion applies even if you combine business and pleasure on the trip—as long as your trip is primarily for business purposes [Reg. Sec. 1.61-21(g)(4)].

Example 1: Mr. Lee travels on the company plane from Chicago to Tampa for business reasons. After conducting the business, Lee vacations in Tampa for a couple of days. Result: The round trip flight is tax-free to Lee, despite the vacation, because the trip was made primarily for business purposes.

If, for example, Lee chose to fly on to Palm Beach in the company plane for a vacation before flying back to Chicago, the value of the round-trip between Tampa and Chicago remains a tax-free working condition fringe benefit. However, Lee is taxed on the difference between the (1) value of his total flights (Chicago-Tampa-Palm Beach-Chicago) and (2) the value of the flights he would have taken if the trip was for business only (Chicago-Tampa-Chicago) [Reg. Sec. 1.61-21(g)(4)].

Valuation. As a general rule, a flight's value for income taxes and withholding is the cost of chartering a similar plane for a similar flight. And if more than one employee is on board, the cost of chartering must be allocated among the employees.

▶ **SPECIAL VALUATION METHOD** The government provides a shortcut for determining the value of your personal use of a company plane for any flight—domestic or international. The use of this method is optional. Neither you nor your employer is bound by the valuation method selected by the other. But, if you or your employer chooses this formula, it must be used to value all flights for the calendar year [Reg. Sec. 1.61-21(g)(5)].

The formula is: Valuation = (Aircraft multiple × SIFL figure) + Terminal charge.

Here's how it works:

Step 1: The starting point is the Standard Industry Fare Level (SIFL) rates.[1] These are per-mile rates, which are revised twice during the year and apply retroactively. For the last six months of 1991 the SIFL rates are as follows: $0.1652 per mile for the first 500 miles, $0.1259 per mile for miles 501–1500 and $0.1211 per mile for miles above 1500. For the first six months of 1992 the rates are: $0.1703 per mile for the first 500 miles, $0.1298 per mile for miles 501–1500, and $0.1248 per mile for miles above 1500. (Note: The SIFL rates are revised semi-annually by the Department of Transportation.)

Step 2: The SIFL figure for the employee's flight is multiplied by an "aircraft multiple"—a percentage that varies depending on the maximum certified takeoff weight of the plane and the employee's position with the company. They are:

Maximum Certified Takeoff Weight Of the Aircraft	Aircraft multiple for a Control Employee	Aircraft multiple for a Non-Control Employee
6,000 lbs. or less	62.5 percent	15.6 percent
6,001–10,000 lbs.	125 percent	23.4 percent
10,001–25,000 lbs.	300 percent	31.3 percent
25,001 lbs. or more	400 percent	31.3 percent

For the purposes of this rule, a control employee of a company is a 5% or more shareholder, a director, an officer earning at least $62,345 per year or a highly compensated employee (among the top 1% most highly paid). An employee who is a spouse, descendant, ancestor or sibling of a control employee is deemed to be a control employee as well [Reg. Sec. 1.61-21(g)(8)].

Step 3: A terminal charge—$30.19 for the last six months of 1991 and $31.13 for the first half of 1992—is added to the result to arrive at the valuation. This value is determined by the department of transportation, and issued by the IRS.

Example 2: Mr. Smith is a middle management employee of XYZ, Inc. On April 1, 1992, Smith takes a 2,000 mile round trip flight on the company's eight-seat plane for personal reasons. The plane has a certified takeoff weight of 11,000 pounds. The taxable amount under the formula is $118.57. The calculation is as follows: $(0.313 \times [(500 \times 0.1703) + (1,000 \times 0.1298) + (500 \times 0.1248)] + $31.13.

> **TAX-FREE PERSONAL TRIP** In general, where 50% or more of the aircraft seats are occupied by employees flying primarily for business purposes, other employees (not company directors) may fill the remaining seats tax-free. Your spouse and dependent children may qualify for tax-free trips under this rule. Seats occupied by working crew members of the flight crew are not counted [Reg. Sec. 1.61.21(g)(12)].

Your friends or relatives may come along—but the value of their flights is taxable to you. If control employees take friends or relatives (other than their spouses and dependent children) along on flights where the 50% test is met, the value of the friends' or relatives' flight is taxable to the control employee at the lower valuation rates for non-control employees [Reg. Sec. 1.61.21(g)(12)(i)(B)(2)].

Example 3: Brown, President of XYZ, takes a 2,000 mile flight on the company plane (see Example 2) for personal reasons. Two other employees also take the flight for business purposes. Result: Brown owes tax on $869.18. The aircraft multiple is 300% because Brown is a key employee.

Example 4: Same facts as in Example 2, except four other employees take the trip for business reasons. Result: No tax is owed by Brown. Reason: 50% of the plane's seats were used by the employees traveling on business.

Example 5: Same facts as in Example 2, except Brown and four middle management employees make the trip solely for personal purposes. Result: Brown owes tax on $869.18—the same as in Example 3. The taxable benefit to the other employees is much lower because they are not key employees. Their tax is $118.57—the same as in Example 2.

INSURANCE BENEFITS

¶1406   EMPLOYER-PROVIDED ACCIDENT AND HEALTH PLANS

The value of employer-provided accident or health plan coverage (i.e., employer-paid insurance premiums for all health-related plans—including medical expense reimbursements and disability coverage) is excluded from an employee's gross income [IRC Sec. 106]. However, the tax treatment of any amounts received from the health insurance coverage depends on who paid for it, the purpose of the insurance payments and whether the insurance plans pass certain nondiscrimination rules [IRC Sec. 105(a); Reg. Sec. 1.105-1(a)].

(a) Nondiscrimination Rules: Under the rules currently in effect, whether benefits received under a company health plan are tax-free to all employees depends on how coverage is provided: through an employer-paid policy issued by an insurance company or through a self-insured medical reimbursement plan.

Fully insured plans (e.g., plans issued by insurance companies) are generally not subject to nondiscrimination rules. As a result, there is no prohibition against a company setting up an executives-only *insured* health plan (as opposed to a self-insured plan). Premiums paid by the company, as well as benefits received under the plan, are tax-free to covered employees (and their dependents if the company chooses) [Reg. Sec. 1.105-1].

On the other hand, *self-insured* health plans must pass two nondiscrimination tests [IRC Sec. 105(h); Reg. Sec. 1.105-11]:

1. Nondiscriminatory eligibility test. The plan must pass one of three requirements: (a) The plan benefits 70% or more of all employees; (b) 70% of all employees are eligible to be covered under the plan and 80% of eligible employees actually are covered under the plan; or (c) the classification of which employees benefit under the plan does not discriminate in favor of the highly compensated.

2. Nondiscriminatory benefits test. All benefits provided to highly compensated employees (and their dependents) must be provided to all other participants in the plan. In addition, a plan may not discriminate in favor of the highly compensated in terms of its operation as well as in terms of benefits offered.

Highly compensated employees. For purposes of these nondiscrimination tests, highly compensated employees are the five highest paid officers, 10% shareholders and the top 25% highest paid employees.

Effect of being discriminatory. The penalty for failing the nondiscrimination tests is that income is imputed to the highly compensated based on the amounts reimbursed by the health plan, to the extent the plan or benefit under the plan is discriminatory [Reg. Sec. 1.105-11(e)].

> **Example 1:** XYZ Inc. maintains a self-insured medical reimbursement plan that covers all employees. However, there's a reimbursement cap of $5,000 for Mr. Brown, the owner of XYZ, and $1,000 for each of the other employees. If Brown receives reimbursements for $2,500 of medical expenses during 1992, $1,500 ($2,500 minus $1,000) is taxable to him as a discriminatory benefit.

> **Example 2:** LMN Inc.'s self-insured plan provides equal medical coverage to each employee. It also provides dental coverage to its president, Ms. Green. Whatever dental reimbursement Green receives is taxable as a discriminatory benefit.

(b) Employer Pays for Coverage. You are taxed on disability benefits that are based on the duration of work you missed. However, you are entitled to exclude from gross income accident and health plan reimbursements for medical expenses incurred by you, your spouse, or dependents. The exclusion does not apply to amounts attributable to medical expenses deducted in any prior tax year [IRC Sec. 105(b), (c); Reg. Sec. 1.105-2, -3].

> **Example 3:** Northstar Corp. provides accident and health plan coverage for its employees on a nondiscriminatory basis. Mr. Black, an employee, incurs medical expenses for his dependent child and is reimbursed by the plan. The health care reimbursement is excluded from Black's gross income.

You are also entitled to exclude payments from employer-provided plans where they are received on account of permanent loss or loss of the use of a body part or function, or for permanent disfigurement. Loss of use or disfigurement is considered permanent if it is expected to continue throughout the injured person's lifetime. You, as well as your spouse and dependents, are entitled to the exclusion [IRC Sec. 105(c)(1); Reg. Sec. 1.105-3].

An employee also can exclude amounts received from an employer-provided plan which represent payments based on the nature of the injury (e.g., loss of a leg, or an eye), and without regard to the amount of time you are out of work [IRC Sec. 105(c)(2); Reg. Sec. 1.105-3].

> **Example 4:** Mr. Jones, an employee of ABC Corp., is injured in a car accident. As a result of the accident, Jones has lost the sight in one eye. He was absent from work for four months. Under the ABC Corp.'s accident and health plan, Jones received $20,000 for the loss of an eye. The $20,000 received is excluded from gross income. The amount was based on the nature of the injury, not based on the length of time Jones was absent from work.

(c) Employee Pays for Coverage. In some companies, the employer and the employees share the cost of premium payments. If that is your situation and the insurance provides reimbursements for medical bills, the payouts are tax-free to you, even if premium payments are shared. However, if the premiums are for disability income coverage, the portion attributable to your employer's premium payments is a taxable benefit to you. Payments made under a disability plan are allocated in proportion to the premium funding arrangement. Only the amount attributable to employee contributions is tax-free [IRC Sec. 105(a); Reg. Sec. 1.105-1(c)].

> **Example 5:** Weststar Corp. maintains a plan where the company and the employees split the premium costs on disability income insurance. The company pays two-thirds of the premiums. Employer contributions are not included in the employees gross income. The employee pays one-third of the cost, by means of a payroll deduction from the employee's wages. Colby, an employee, received a payment of $150 on account of a disability that caused him to miss work. Colby excludes $50 (⅓ of the payment) and includes $100 (⅔ of the payment) in gross income.

> **NOTE:** You are treated as having paid for coverage where your employer actually pays the premiums, but the cost is included in your gross income [IRC Sec. 105(a); Reg. Sec. 1.105-1(a)].

(d) Continuation Coverage. Employers must offer continuing group health and accident coverage to employees who leave the company and to their spouses and dependent children who would lose coverage in the case of divorce or the employee's death [IRC Sec. 4980B]. This benefit is often referred to as "COBRA coverage," since the tax rule was orginally enacted as part of the Consolidated Omnibus Budget Reconciliation Act of 1985. The cost of the continuing group coverage, plus an additional 2% to cover the employer's administration costs, is paid by you or your beneficiary. Continuing coverage rules do not apply to small employers who had fewer than 20 employees on a typical business day during the calendar year immediately preceding a qualifying event (see below), or government agencies and churches. For other employers, continuing coverage must be offered to employees in these situations:

- You voluntarily or involuntarily leave the company—unless termination is for gross misconduct. If you would lose coverage because of a reduction in hours, you must also be offered continuing coverage. If accepted, the coverage must last for at least 18 months.
- If you are "disabled" at the time of termination or reduction in hours, continuation must last for up to 29 months. Prior to 1990, coverage only had to last for 18 months. This extension is aimed at helping AIDS victims; the additional coverage period allows disabled employees time to qualify for Medicare. An employer can charge these disabled employees 150% of its premium costs (rather than the normal 102%) during the additional 11 months of coverage.
- On your death, continuing coverage must be offered to your surviving spouse and dependent children who are beneficiaries under the plan on the day before the death. Coverage must be for at least 36 months.
- If you are divorced or legally separated, continuing coverage must be offered to your spouse and dependent children for at least 36 months.
- If you become eligible for Medicare benefits, continuing coverage under your employer's plan must be offered to your spouse and dependent children for at least 36 months.
- If a dependent child becomes ineligible under the plan on reaching a certain age, continuing coverage must be offered for at least 36 months.

- Continuing coverage must be offered for 36 months if regular coverage is eliminated because your employer has a bankruptcy proceeding under Title 11.

Your employer must provide you with written notice of the continuing coverage option. If one of the above qualifying events occurs, you, your spouse and dependent children generally have 60 days to elect continuing coverage.

In general, the penalty for failing to satisfy the health care continuation rules is an excise tax on the employer of $100 per day of noncompliance per qualified beneficiary with respect to whom the plan is in noncompliance. The maximum excise tax for a year is the lesser of 10% of the total cost of the employer's group health plans for the preceding year or $500,000.

¶1407   GROUP-TERM LIFE INSURANCE

Premiums paid by your employer for group-term life insurance coverage of up to $50,000 are not taxable to you. To qualify for this tax break, the group-term insurance plan must meet nondiscrimination rules (see below). The cost of coverage over $50,000 provided by one or more employers is taxable to you in your tax year in which the premiums are paid, even though your rights under the policy are assigned. The cost is figured from uniform premium rates for five-year age brackets (see table below). Your contributions to the cost of insurance reduce the taxable amount [IRC Sec. 79; Reg. Sec. 1.79-1, 3; Temp. Reg. Sec. 1.79-3T]. Generally, the same rules that apply to active employees apply to retired employees.

> **NOTE:** Employer-provided coverage of up to $2,000 on your spouse or dependent is considered a tax-free incidental benefit (de minimis fringe benefit). Suppose this coverage has a high face amount. How do you determine if this is a de minimis fringe benefit? Only the excess (if any) of the insurance cost over the amount paid for the insurance by the employee on an after-tax basis is considered.[1]

Uniform 1–Month Group-Term Premiums for $1,000 of Life Insurance Protection

AGE	COST per $1,000	AGE	COST per $1,000
Under 30	$0.08	50-54	$0.48
30-34	$0.09	55-59	$0.75
35-39	$0.11	60-64	$1.17
40-44	$0.17	65-69	$2.10
45-49	$0.29	70 and above	$3.76

> **Example:** Mr. Martin, age 62, works for Fair Corporation. During the year, he is insured for $100,000 group-term life insurance. He pays $2 of the cost of each $1,000 of coverage, and Fair Corporation pays the balance. Cost of insurance over $50,000 in Martin's age bracket is $702 (50 × $1.17 × 12). Martin is taxed on $502 [$702 minus employee's payment (100 × $2)].

Employer-paid premiums for coverage over $50,000 are not taxable to you if your employer is the direct or indirect beneficiary of the policy, or the sole beneficiary is an organization for which a charitable deduction could be taken [IRC Sec. 79(b); Reg. Sec. 1.79-2].

Nondiscrimination rules. Group-term life insurance plans must meet two basic nondiscrimination tests [IRC Sec. 79(d); Temp. Reg. Sec. 1.79-4T]:

1. Nondiscriminatory eligibility test. A group term life plan passes this test by meeting any one of the following: (a) The plan covers at least 70% of a company's employees; (b) at least 85% of the plan's participants are not "key employees" (see below); (c) the plan covers a nondiscriminatory classification of employees; or (d) in case

of a plan that is part of a cafeteria plan [¶1426], the plan meets the nondiscrimination requirements of IRC Sec. 125.

2. Nondiscriminatory benefits test. Benefits that are available to key employees must be available to all plan participants. However, a plan that offers the same multiple of pay to key and non-key employees is considered to pass the benefits test—even though higher-paid employees get more valuable benefits.

Key employees are officers with compensation greater than 50% of the maximum annual benefit available under a defined benefit retirement plan (compensation above $56,111 for 1992), the top ten highest paid employees who own the largest interests in the employer, 5% owners and 1% owners with compensation of more than $150,000.

The penalty for failing the nondiscrimination tests is that all key employees have imputed income on the entire employer-provided portion of their group-life coverage. This imputed amount includes any nondiscriminatory coverage as well as the first $50,000 of coverage which would otherwise be excluded.

Pension trust. Premiums paid for term life insurance protection out of your employer's contributions under a pension trust plan are taxable to you (the insured employee) [Reg. Sec. 1.402(a)-1].

Group life insurance. Group-permanent life insurance premiums paid by your employer for you is ordinary income to you and must be reported as wages.[2]

¶1408   OTHER COMMON INSURANCE BENEFITS

[New tax legislation may affect this subject; see ¶1.]

Here are some other types of insurance protection that many employers provide:

(a) Split-Dollar Insurance. With this type of coverage, your employer pays premiums on your policy to the extent of the annual increase in the cash surrender value. You pay the balance. Upon your death, your employer gets the cash surrender value, and the rest of the policy proceeds are distributed as you directed. The tax treatment for split-dollar insurance arrangements is discussed at ¶1207(a).

(b) Death Benefits. Payments of up to $5,000 made by or for your employer on account of your death may qualify for an exclusion from tax [¶1204(a)].

MEALS AND LODGING

¶1410   BOARD AND LODGING

If certain requirements are met, you are not taxed on the value of meals or lodging you are furnished for the convenience of your employer. However, a cash allowance or reimbursement from your employer for meals or lodging must be included in your gross income to the extent it is compensation and the meals are not taken on a working day [IRC Sec. 119; Reg. Sec. 1.119-1].

(a) Meals. The exclusion is limited to meals furnished by your employer on its business premises for a substantial noncompensatory business reason. Generally, this means that (1) you must be on duty during the meal period, (2) you are restricted to a very short meal period so you cannot be expected to eat elsewhere or (3) there are not sufficient eating facilities in the vicinity of the work site.

Generally, the meal must be furnished during your working hours. However, if your job duties prevent you from consuming an excludable meal during business hours, the meal can be taken immediately after work with the same tax-free result.

Suppose an employer does not have eating facilities on the company's regular business premises?

> ➤ **TAX STRATEGY** The employer can satisfy the business premises requirement by renting space in a restaurant or hotel. The Tax Court has held employer-provided meals to be tax-free under such an arrangement. The company rented a hotel suite for daily luncheon conferences, which company officers were required to attend. The substantial business reason for the luncheon conferences was that meeting during regular business hours would interrupt the work of the company and consume too much time.[1]

If the nature of the job requires that you must reside on the premises, then the value of all meals taken there qualifies for the exclusion. This applies even if taking meals on the job is not a condition of employment and the meals are not taken on a working day [Reg. Sec. 1.119-1(a)(2)(i)].

(b) Lodging. The exclusion is allowed only if you must accept the lodging on your employer's business premises to properly perform your job duties. Lodging includes the value of utilities, unless you buy them directly from the supplier.[2] The fact that a state statute or employment contract fixing the terms of your employment indicates the meals or lodging are intended as compensation does not necessarily mean that they were furnished for your employer's convenience [IRC Sec. 119(b)(1); Reg. Sec. 1.119-1(b)].

> **Example:** An employee of an institution, who must be on duty from 8 a.m. until 4 p.m., is given the choice of residing at the institution free of charge, or residing elsewhere and receiving an allowance of $30 per month in addition to his regular salary. If he elects to reside at the institution, the value of meals and lodging to the employee is taxable, because residence there is not a condition of employment necessary to properly performing his duties.

Examples of Excludable Lodging

Hotel manager required to live at hotel so as to be constantly available.[3]

Hospital employees on constant call at state hospital.[4]

Building manager whose presence at site is required at a moment's call.[5]

Construction workers at remote job site.[6]

Funeral home employees needed to be available for work on 24-hour basis.[7]

Lodging furnished by educational institutions to employees.

You must pay tax on the value of qualified campus housing (i.e., housing located on or near the campus, which is provided to you and used as your residence) to the extent the rent paid is less than the lesser of 5% of the lodging's appraised value or the average of rentals paid (other than by employees or students) to the school for comparable housing [IRC Sec. 119(d)].

(c) Property Occupied Rent-Free by Stockholder. The exclusion has been allowed for the officer-shareholders of a ranching corporation who were required to perform caretaker-type duties in an isolated location.[8] In a situation where there was no evidence that the rental value was compensation, the Fifth Circuit has held that it was a nontaxable gift from the corporation to its stockholders.[9]

(d) Clergy. A member of the clergy does not include in gross income either a cash allowance to rent or provide a home, or a dwelling's rental value used for that purpose [IRC Sec. 107; Reg. Sec. 1.107-1]. Rental allowance includes amounts spent for rent, utilities and for buying a home and furnishings. It can also include payment for a home (mortgage payments, interest, taxes, repairs) owned by a member of the clergy.[10] Those employed only to teach, or as administrators by an agency that's not an integral part of a religious organization, do not get the exclusion. However, those employed to teach, or as administrators by an agency that is an integral part of a religious organization, are entitled to the exclusion.[11]

¶1411   EMPLOYER-SUBSIDIZED CAFETERIAS

Many employers subsidize dining room/cafeteria facilities for their employees. If certain conditions are met, the value of the subsidy can be tax-free to the employees.

To remain a tax-free fringe benefit to you and the other employees, the facility must be located on or near your employer's business premises. Your employer can either lease or own the facility. The tax-free status is retained even if others run the food operations for your employer. In addition, substantially all the use of the facility must be by the company employees. Meals must be furnished during, immediately before, or after the workday [IRC Sec. 132(e)(2); Reg. Sec. 1.132-7(a)]. Thus, the tax-free benefit is lost if night shift workers use the facility for their midday meal.

The revenue from the facility must equal or exceed its direct operating costs. The direct costs of the facility include food, beverage and labor costs of the operation. As long as employee-generated revenues equal or exceed these costs, no employees pay tax on the subsidy. Employers with multiple dining facilities may choose to aggregate them when applying the direct operating costs test [IRC Sec. 132(e)(2); Reg. Sec. 1.132-7(b)].

> **Example 1:** ABC Inc. operates a company subsidized cafeteria on its premises for the exclusive use of its employees. The full cost of operating the facility, including rental for the space, is $300,000; the direct cost of operation is $190,000. The employees spend $200,000 in the cafeteria. If the employees ate elsewhere, they would spend $400,000. Since revenues exceed direct costs, the employees do not have to pay tax on the subsidy.

Suppose you must pay tax on the company subsidy. The taxable amount is the difference between the fair market value of the meals and what you actually pay [Reg. Sec. 1.132-7(c)]. Companies may set that value at 150% of the eating facility's direct operating costs. The taxable excess may be allocated among employees in proportion to amounts actually spent in the cafeteria or in any other reasonable manner [Reg. Sec. 1.61-21(j)(2)].

> **Example 2:** Assume the same facts as in Example 1. However, the direct operating costs (i.e., food, beverage and labor) are $220,000. As a result, the ABC Inc. employees owe tax on meals because the cost exceeds the revenues.
> The taxable amount is the difference between the fair market value of the meals and what the employees actually pay. If ABC Inc. uses the 150%-of-cost measure, the fair market value is $330,000. The taxable fringe benefit is $130,000 ($330,000 - $200,000). If ABC Inc. uses the actual fair market value of $400,000, the taxable benefit is $200,000.

> ► **NONDISCRIMINATION REQUIREMENT** The cafeteria subsidy is tax-free to highly-compensated employees only if access to the cafeteria is available to rank and file employees as well [IRC Sec. 132(e)(2); Reg. Sec. 1.132-8]. Thus, this exclusion does not apply to executive dining rooms.

OTHER EMPLOYEE BENEFITS

¶1414   EDUCATION REIMBURSEMENT

[New tax legislation may affect this subject; see ¶1.]

You may exclude from gross income certain reimbursements made to you for job-related education costs. The same break applies to tuition payments made by your employer directly to the educational institution. To qualify for this income exclusion, you must adequately substantiate to your employer the job-related nature of the education. Courses that prepare you for a new job or enable you to meet the minimum standards of your current job are not "job-related" [Reg. Sec. 1.162-5].[1] Education reimbursements that do not qualify for this exclusion may instead be offset by a deduction for job-related tuition costs, subject to the rules for deducting employee business expenses [¶1943].

> NOTE: Educational assistance plans, which also apply to graduate level courses, are scheduled to expire after June 30, 1992. There is no requirement that the courses be job-related to qualify for tax-free EAP payments. Under qualified EAPs, employees are not taxed on up to $5,250 of tuition paid by an employer.

¶1415   DEPENDENT CARE ASSISTANCE PLANS

You can exclude from your gross income up to $5,000 ($2,500 for marrieds filing separately) of employer-provided dependent care assistance as a tax-free fringe benefit. Any excess benefit is taxable to you in the year the dependent care services were provided, even if payment for them is made in the following year. Also, the exclusion cannot exceed the employee's (or spouse's, if lower) earned income. Dependent care assistance covers the same type of expenses that qualify for the dependent care tax credit [¶2401]. In general, these are expenses for household and dependent care services which are necessary for your gainful employment [IRC Sec. 129(e)]. They include the costs of child care help or a caretaker.

> NOTE: The plan can provide cash to pay for the assistance, furnish the actual care or take the form of a spending account [¶1426].

To be considered a tax-free fringe benefit, the dependent care assistance plan must be in writing and be for the exclusive benefit of the employees. At year-end, your employer must provide, to those employees benefitting from this program, a written statement reflecting the expenses paid on the employee's behalf. The plan also must comply with special nondiscrimination tests [IRC Sec. 129(d)].

> ► **SPECIAL NONDISCRIMINATION TESTS** Dependent care assistance plans must satisfy the following nondiscrimination requirements: (1) The benefits provided during the year to 5%-or-more owners (or their spouses and dependents) must not exceed 25% of the employer's total payments under the plan and (2) the average benefits provided to non-highly compensated employees must be at least 55% of the average benefits provided to highly compensated employees. (Note: For salary reduction dependent care plans, employees with annual compensation of less than $25,000 may be excluded from the 55% average benefits test.)

Benefits received from a dependent care plan reduce the maximum amount of expenses eligible for the dependent care tax credit [¶2401].

¶1416   SERVICES PROVIDED AT NO ADDITIONAL COST

Some employers give the same services to employees that they sell to customers. You pay no tax on the value of the services if your employer does not incur substantial additional cost in providing the service. Your employer's costs include lost revenue as well as out-of-pocket expenditures. This exclusion applies to price discounts or cash rebates as well as no-charge services. Example of these types of services include hotel accommodations and transportation by air, train, bus, subway, or cruise line [IRC Sec. 132(b); Reg. Sec. 1.132-2].

A retiree, a former employee who is disabled, and a former employee's surviving spouse, are all eligible for the tax-free treatment of these benefits. And so are the employee's spouse and dependent children. In the case of air transportation, parents of active employees can qualify for the tax exclusion [IRC Sec. 132(f)].

Example 1: Ace Airlines provides free tickets to its employees, their parents and their immediate families on a stand-by basis (i.e., only if seats remain unsold at flight time). Its customers are not displaced, and the airline incurs no substantial extra cost in providing this benefit. The exclusion applies because the employees and their family members occupy seats that would otherwise remain unused by customers. On the other hand, suppose Ace Airlines offered reserved seating to its employees. The airline could have to turn away paying customers, thus losing revenue. As a result, the exclusion does not apply; the employees would owe tax on the value of the flight.

There is a special rule for employers engaged in more than one line of business. To be tax-free, the benefit must be derived from the business for which the employee performs substantial services. If you are directly involved in more than one line of your employer's business (e.g., central payroll department staff), you are entitled to exclude the value of the benefits received from any one of those lines of business [Reg. Sec. 1.132-4(a)].

Example 2: Mr. Addison works for Lilton Inc., which owns Lilton Hotels and Lilton Airlines. Addison is employed as a hotel manager for one of the Lilton's hotels. Addison, because he is employed by Lilton Hotels, can exclude the value of his hotel room from his gross income. However, because he does not perform services for Lilton Airlines, he must include the value of the air travel in his gross income.

Example 3: Same facts as Example 2, except Addison is an executive in Lilton Inc. working for all segments of the company. Because he is directly involved in both the air travel and hotel portions of the business, he is eligible to exclude the value of the hotel room and the air travel from his gross income.

Reciprocal agreements. In certain cases, if you perform services in the same line of business, you may exclude fringe benefits received from other employers in their industry. To be eligible to exclude these no-additional-cost fringe benefits, a reciprocal written agreement must exist among the various, similar employers. The employers must be engaged in the same line of business, where similar services are provided to customers and neither employer must incur any substantial additional costs in providing the services [IRC Sec. 132(g); Reg. Sec. 1.132-2(b)].

Example 4: Ace Airlines has a written reciprocal agreement with other airlines. As a result, all the employees who work for the airlines covered by the agreement are considered to be working in the same line of business for all the employers. Employees of Ace Airlines may exclude from their gross income the value of free stand-by seating which they received from these other airline companies.

▶ **NONDISCRIMINATION RULES** In order to qualify for the exclusion, the no-additional-cost fringe benefits must be provided to all employees—rank and file as well as the highly compensated—on substantially the same terms [IRC Sec. 132(h)(1); Reg. Sec. 1.132-8].

¶1417   **EMPLOYEE DISCOUNTS**

You (as well as retirees, former employees who are disabled, surviving spouses and dependent children) may exclude from gross income certain discounts on purchases of your employer's goods and services [IRC Sec. 132(c), (f); Reg. Sec. 1.132-3].

The maximum tax-free discount on services bought from your employer cannot exceed 20% of the price offered to the public. In the case of property, the discount cannot exceed the gross profit percentage of the price at which the property is being offered to the public. The gross profit percentage is: (1) the total sales price of the property sold to customers (including employees) less your employer's total cost of the property, (2) divided by the total sales price [IRC Sec. 132(c)(2); Reg. Sec. 1.132-3(c)].

Employee discounts available through third parties, such as a manufacturer's representative, are also entitled to the exclusion from gross income. If the actual discount is larger than the allowable exclusion (e.g., 20% maximum for services), the difference is taxable to you [Reg. Sec. 1.132-3(a)(5), (e)].

> ➤ **OBSERVATION** If your employer provides property at no charge to you, you will be taxed on the regular selling price less the gross profit percentage; for services, the taxable benefit is 80% of the regular price.

Example 1: Ms. Smith, an employee of Appliance Inc., receives a 10% employee discount on her employer's appliances purchased at Goody's, a retail store that offers the appliances for sale to customers. Smith may exclude from gross income the amount of her employee discount on the purchased appliance.

Example 2: In 1992, United Department Store has total merchandise sales of $1,000,000. United's cost for this property was $600,000. The gross profit percentage is 40% [($1,000,000 - $600,000) ÷ $1,000,000]. As a result, the employee discount as to property sold by United cannot exceed 40% of the selling price of the merchandise to nonemployee customers. If United offers its employees a 50% discount, the extra 10% is taxable.

The tax-free discount rule does not extend to real property of any kind or personal property held for investment. As a result, you must pay tax on a discount for the purchase of residential or commercial real estate, securities, commodities, or currency. In addition, in this area you cannot get tax-free treatment under reciprocal agreements [Reg. Sec. 1.132-3(a)(2)(ii), 3].

¶1418   **EMPLOYEE ACHIEVEMENT AWARDS**

Your gross income does not include the value of certain awards you receive for length of service or safety achievement [IRC Sec. 74(c)(1); Prop. Reg. Sec. 1.274-8(c)]. The award must be tangible personal property—not cash or a gift certificate. The exclusion is generally limited to awards that cost your employer $400 per employee per year. However, the ceiling is $1,600 per employee per year for a qualified plan award. A qualified plan award is one made under an established written plan that does not discriminate in favor of highly paid employees [IRC Sec. 274(j)(2), (3)].

Aggregation rule. The $1,600 ceiling is the overall limit when an employee is given both qualified plan awards and other awards during the year. As a result, the $400 and the $1,600 maximums cannot be added together in one year [Prop. Reg. Sec. 1.274-8(b)].

NOTE: Your employer's deduction for your achievement award is limited by these same dollar caps [IRC Sec. 274(j)].

An excludable employee achievement award must be received either on account of length of service or for safety achievement. It must also be awarded as part of a meaningful presentation, emphasizing your achievement. The award must not represent disguised compensation (e.g., given in the place of a prior cash bonus program) [Prop. Reg. Sec. 1.274-8(c)].

Example: Mr. Barnaby is awarded a gold watch under a qualified plan award at his employer's annual awards dinner, in recognition of 25 years of service with the company. The value of the gold watch ($1,600 or less) is excluded from Barnaby's gross income. If the watch was worth $2,000, the $400 in excess of the exclusion cap would be included in his gross income.

Limitation on awards. A length of service award does not qualify for the exclusion from gross income if received during your first five years of service with the company, or if awards are given to you more frequently than five years apart. No exclusion is permitted for safety achievement awards if your employer previously gave safety achievement awards (other than ones that qualify as de minimis fringe benefits [¶1423]) during the tax year to more than 10% of the employees, or if safety awards were given to a manager, administrator, clerical, or professional employee [IRC Sec. 274(j)(4)(C)].

¶1419   ATHLETIC FACILITIES

The value of athletic facilities provided by your employer to you and its other employees is excluded from your gross income. The facility must be located on premises leased or owned by your employer. It need not be your employer's regular business premises. It must be operated by your employer, although your employer can hire someone to manage the facility. And your employer can join together with other companies to cut costs by collectively operating the facility. In addition, substantially all of its use must be by you and the other employees, your spouses, and dependent children or retired employees, widows and widowers of employees and their dependent children.

The on-premise facility can be a gym, a pool, tennis courts, or a golf course. The exclusion does not apply to any athletic facility if access to the facility is made available to the general public through the sale of memberships or the rental of the facility.

The exclusion does not apply to any athletic facility that is put to residential use (e.g., a resort with a swimming pool).

Discrimination permitted. The nondiscrimination rules do not apply to the athletic facilities. As a result, an employer may use the facility as an executives-only tax-free perk [IRC Sec. 132(h)(5); Reg. Sec. 1.132-1(e)].

¶1420   GROUP LEGAL SERVICES PLANS

[New tax legislation may affect this subject; see ¶1.]
For amounts paid for legal services, you (whether as an employee or self-employed), your spouse and dependents are able to exclude from income group legal service plan coverage valued at no more than $70 per employee per year. More expensive coverage is fully taxable. Coverage must be funded through contributions to an insurance company, qualified trust or prepayments to providers of the legal services. Direct reimbursements by your employer to you are not eligible for the exclusion [IRC Sec. 120].

NOTE: The exclusion for employer-provided group legal services is scheduled to expire as of June 30, 1992.

Nondiscrimination rules. The plan must not discriminate in favor of highly compensated employees, nor may contributions and benefits discriminate in favor of highly compensated employees. In addition, no more than 25% of your employer's contributions under the plan can go to more-than-5% owners. If a plan does not meet the nondiscrimination requirements, all benefits provided under the plan are taxable to all participants.

¶1421   FINANCIAL COUNSELING

Employer-provided financial counseling has grown in popularity as a way for employers to help employees plan for a financially secure future. The increasingly complex tax rules governing retirement plan distributions, life insurance and Social Security benefits have increased the need for employees to obtain professional advice on tax and investment matters. However, there is no special tax exclusion for this fringe benefit. The value of the counseling is included in your gross income. The same amount, though, may be claimed as a miscellaneous itemized deduction [¶1942]. As such, it is deductible to the extent the total of such miscellaneous expenses exceed 2% of your adjusted gross income [Sec. 67(a), (b)].

¶1422   WORKING CONDITION FRINGE BENEFITS

An employer-provided service or property is tax-free to you if it would have been deductible by you (as business expenses or through depreciation deductions) had you paid for it out of your own pocket. An expense can qualify as a working condition fringe benefit even if you could not have actually claimed a deduction because of the 2% floor on deducting miscellaneous expenses [IRC Sec. 132(d); Reg. Sec. 132-5(a)(1)]. Business-related use of a company car or airplane [¶1400-1403; 2007(c)] and travel and entertainment [¶2002(d); 2003; 2007(d); 2011] fit this description. There is one very common benefit—parking—that may be excluded from tax as a working condition fringe benefit even though it would not be deductible if you paid for it directly.

Parking. If your employer provides employees with parking at or near its business location, the value of the parking is excluded from your gross income as a working condition fringe benefit—even if you could not deduct parking fees had you paid them on your own. This provision applies whether your employer owns or rents the parking space. In addition, if you are given a specific parking allowance, you can exclude the amount from gross income. However, if you are given a general transportation allowance, the entire allowance is taxable, even if you used it for parking. The parking exclusion is not subject to the nondiscrimination rules. In other words, your employer can select those employees to whom the employer wishes to extend the parking privilege [IRC Sec. 132(h)(4); Reg. Sec. 1.132-5(p), (q)].

Example: Weststar Corp. rents a garage space only for the company president in the building where it is headquartered. The value of the parking is excluded from the gross income of the president—regardless of the cost—because it is considered a working condition fringe benefit.

NOTE: The exclusion does not apply to a parking space located on property owned or leased by you for residential purposes.

¶1423 SMALL FRINGE BENEFITS

The value of so-called de minimis fringe benefits is tax-free to you. These are benefits that are of such small value that accounting for them would be administratively impracticable and unreasonable. In determining value, the frequency with which the benefit is furnished should be taken into account; the less frequent the benefit is given, the more likely it is to be tax-free [IRC Sec. 132(e)(1)]. The following are examples of tax-free de minimis fringe benefits:

- Occasional typing of personal letters by a company secretary;
- Occasional personal use of the company photostat machine (provided that personal use is restricted to ensure that at least 85% of the machine's use is for business purposes);
- Occasional cocktail parties or picnics for employees and their guests;
- Traditional holiday gifts of property (not cash) with a low fair market value (i.e., a Thanksgiving turkey);
- Occasional theater or sporting tickets;
- Coffee and donuts;
- Flowers, fruit, books or similar items provided under special circumstances (e.g., on account of illness or outstanding performance).

The following items are not excludable as de minimis fringes:

- Season tickets to sporting or theatrical events;
- Commuting use of an employer-owned car for more than one day a month;
- Membership in a private country club or athletic facility;
- Use of an employer-owned or leased facility (e.g., an apartment, hunting lodge or boat) for a weekend [Reg. Sec. 1.132-6(e)].

NOTE: Companies can choose to reward only their highly compensated employees with a de minimis fringe benefit. The nondiscrimination rules do not affect the tax-free status of these small benefits [IRC Sec. 132(h)(1); Reg. Sec. 1.132-6(f)].

(a) Public Transportation Allowance. Your employer may provide you and its other employees with free public transportation subsidies (including tokens or fare cards) as an excludable fringe benefit. To be tax-free to you, this benefit must take the form of a transit pass, token, or fare card and be worth no more than $21 per month. You must pay tax on any amounts received from your employer which help to defray transit expenses incurred for personal travel other than commuting. You must also pay tax on the value of the entire benefit if that value exceeds $21 per month [Reg. Sec. 1.132-6(d)(1)].

Example 1: In August 1992, Green's Department Store gives its employees a $26 monthly transit pass. They must pay tax on the entire $26. They cannot exclude the first $21 of value and pay tax only on the excess $5.

(b) Overtime Expenses. You do not have to pay tax on employer payments of meal money (or the value of employer-provided meals) or local transportation fare home when you work overtime. To qualify for the exclusion, the payments must be provided on an occasional basis. In addition, the amount of the payment must not be calculated with reference to the number of hours worked (e.g., $1.00 per hour for each hour of overtime).

A special rule applies to some employer-provided commuting. If there is a bona fide, noncompensatory reason for you to travel in an employer-provided vehicle, you are taxed on only $1.50 per trip [Reg. Sec. 1.61(f)]. This tax break is not available to "control" employees [¶1401(d)].

Example 2: Ms. Gordon normally works the daytime shift at a factory. Her employer requests that she work the night shift for a week and reimburses her for her $15 daily cab fare getting to and from the factory. Gordon is taxed only on $3 ($1.50 each way) of the reimbursement per day. The other $12 is a tax-free fringe benefit.

Safety first: A similar exception applies for certain employees who would otherwise walk or take mass transportation under unsafe (e.g., high crime) conditions. These employees would be taxed on just $1.50 for each qualified commute in an employer-provided car or bus, rather than the full fair market value of the ride [Prop. Reg. Sec. 1.61-21(k)]. The break is available only to employees paid on an hourly basis and eligible for overtime.

SPECIAL RULES

¶1426   CAFETERIA EMPLOYEE BENEFIT PLANS

"Cafeteria" plans, or flexible benefits plans as they are sometimes called, permit you (as a covered employee) to select the fringe benefits you want from an assortment of employer-provided fringes. Such plans generally include cash (or other taxable benefits) and a variety of nontaxable benefits [IRC Sec. 125; Prop. Reg. Sec. 1.125-2]. Nontaxable benefits include the following:

* Accident or health plan coverage that would be excludable under other provisions of the tax law (i.e., IRC Sec. 105,106) [¶1406].
* Group-term life insurance, whether or not in excess of the $50,000 coverage exclusion [¶1407]. Important: Starting in 1992, employer-provided dependent life insurance may not be offered.
* Dependent care assistance benefits of up to $5,000 [¶1415].
* A cash or deferred arrangement that meets the requirements of IRC Sec. 401(k) [¶1345].
* Option to elect either additional or fewer paid vacation days.

NOTE: Except for Sec. 401(k) arrangements, a cafeteria plan may not include a plan that enables you to defer compensation. Thus, unused contributions to the plan in one year may not be carried over to a subsequent year. However, plans may pay you in cash for unused elective vacation days as long as you receive the cash by the end of the plan year or your tax year.

(a) Revoking Election. In general, you cannot revoke your cafeteria plan elections once the plan year has begun. There are exceptions for certain changes in circumstances (e.g., third-party health insurer changes premiums or curtails coverage, change in family status, separation from service). Also, a cafeteria plan may allow you to modify your contribution level under a cash or deferred arrangement [Prop. Reg. Sec. 1.125-2 Q & A-6].

(b) Nondiscrimination Rules. Eligibility to participate in the cafeteria plan must not discriminate in favor of highly compensated employees as to eligibility, contributions and benefits. Plus, it must pass a so-called concentration test.

1. Eligibility test. A cafeteria plan cannot discriminate in favor of highly compensated employees in terms of eligibility to participate in the plan. A safe harbor for this test is met in the following circumstances:

- No employee is required to complete more than three years of employment as a condition of participation in the plan; and
- Once an employee has completed the years of employment requirement, he or she begins to participate in the plan no later than the first day of the next plan year, unless the employee has separated from service before that date [IRC Sec. 125(g)(3)].

NOTE: A plan can pass the eligibility test even if it does not meet the safe harbor requirements.

2. Benefits and contributions test. A plan meets the benefits and contributions test if it satisfies two requirements:

- Employer contributions (including pre-tax salary reductions) for health benefits for each participant include an amount that (a) equals 100% of the cost of the health benefit coverage for the majority of similarly situated highly compensated participants, or (b) equals or exceeds 75% of the cost of health coverage for the similarly situated highly compensated participant having the highest cost under the plan.
- Any contributions or benefits in excess of the above amounts bear a uniform relationship to compensation.

3. Concentration test. The concentration test requires that no more than 25% of the total benefits paid under the cafeteria plan may go to key employees (as defined in ¶1313(a)).

If any of the nondiscrimination requirements are not met, the highly compensated or key employees are taxed on their benefits [IRC Sec. 125(b)].

(c) Employee Reimbursement Accounts. Cafeteria plans may be funded through employee contributions. Such plans, for example, can permit you to pay your child care and medical bills with pre-tax dollars. You elect to have funds deducted from your pay and deposited in the plan. The funds are then paid out as reimbursements for qualifying expenses. However, any funds that remain unused at year-end are forfeited by you [Prop. Reg. Sec. 1.125-1 Q & A-16]. Health plans that are funded in this manner must provide the full level of their coverage for the year as of the start of the year. Coverage cannot be tied to the level of employee funding up to the date of the claim. Reimbursements made during the year, though, do reduce the coverage available for the remainder of the year [Prop. Reg. Sec. 1.125-2 Q & A-7] .

Example: Ms. Smith elects to contribute $240 to her company's medical reimbursement plan. The company deducts $10 from each of Smith's semi-monthly paychecks. If she submits $240 of medical bills in January, the plan must reimburse Smith in full, even though it will take until December for the plan to receive that much from the salary reductions [Prop. Reg. Sec. 1.125-2 Q & A-7].

Footnotes to Chapter 4

(For your added convenience, in brackets [] with the footnotes below, you will find citations to related paragraphs in the "RIA United States Tax Reporter "(USTR), "CCH Federal Tax Reporter" (CCH) and "RIA Federal Tax Coordinator 2d" (FTC) multivolume services.)

FOOTNOTE ¶ 1400 [USTR ¶ 614.027; 1244; 13204.05; 2744 et seq.; CCH ¶ 5906; 5907.03; 5907.80; FTC ¶ H-1665].

(1) Treas. Dept. booklet "Your Federal Income Tax" (1991 Ed.), p. 150.

FOOTNOTE ¶ 1401 [USTR ¶ 614.027; CCH ¶ 5906; FTC ¶ H-1657].

(1) Notice 89-110, 1989-2 CB 447.

FOOTNOTE ¶ 1402 [USTR ¶ 1324.05; CCH ¶ 7438; FTC ¶ H-1814].

FOOTNOTE ¶ 1403 [USTR ¶ 614.027; CCH ¶ 5906; FTC ¶ H-1710].

(1) Rev. Rul. 91-64, IRB 1991-51.

FOOTNOTE ¶ 1406 [USTR ¶ 1054 et seq.; 1064; 4980B4; CCH ¶ 6711; FTC ¶ H-1864].

FOOTNOTE ¶ 1407 [USTR ¶ 794 et seq.; 1324.06; 4024.01; CCH ¶ 5506; 5508.01; FTC ¶ H-1905].

(1) Notice 89-110, 1989-2 CB 447.

(2) Treas. Dept. booklet "Your Federal Income Tax" (1991 Ed.), p. 44.

FOOTNOTE ¶ 1408 [USTR ¶ 1014.02, 06; CCH ¶ 5508.049; 5508.057; FTC ¶ H-1900].

FOOTNOTE ¶ 1410 [USTR ¶ 1074; 1094; CCH ¶ 7220-7220.085; FTC ¶ H-2250].

(1) Mabley, ¶ 65,323 PH Memo TC.

(2) Rev. Rul. 68-579, 1968-2 CB 61.

(3) Moulder v. U.S. (DC Mo.; 1955), 51 AFTR 1226.

(4) Diamond v. Sturr (2 Cir.; 1955), 221 F2d 264, 47 AFTR 433, rev'd (DC NY), 116 F. Supp. 28, 44 AFTR 716; Shad, ¶ 42,576 PH Memo TC. aff'd (8 Cir.; 1944), 139 F2d 961, 31 AFTR 1249; Rev. Rul. 68-354, 1968-2 CB 60.

(5) Giesinger, 66 TC 6 (A. 1976-2 CB 2).

(6) Olkjer, 32 TC 464 (A. 1960-1 CB 5).

(7) Schwartz, ¶ 63,175 PH Memo TC.

(8) McDowell et al., ¶ 74,072 PH Memo TC.

(9) Richards v. Comm., 111 F2d 376, 24 AFTR 1931; Peacock v. Comm., 256 F2d 160, 1 AFTR 2d 1931.

(10) Rev. Rul. 59-350, 1959-2 CB 45.

(11) Rev. Rul. 62-171, 1962-2 CB 39; Rev. Rul. 63-90, 1963-1 CB 27.

FOOTNOTE ¶ 1411 [USTR ¶ 614.027; 1324.06; CCH ¶ 7427; 7437; 7438.083; FTC ¶ H-1791].

FOOTNOTE ¶ 1414 [USTR ¶ 1624.185; CCH ¶ 8582; FTC ¶ H-2050].

(1) Treas. Dept. booklet "Your Federal Income Tax" (1991 Ed.), pp. 168-171.

FOOTNOTE ¶ 1415 [USTR ¶ 1294 et seq.; CCH ¶ 7380-7381.30; FTC ¶ H-2100].

FOOTNOTE ¶ 1416 [USTR ¶ 1320; 1322 et seq.; CCH ¶ 7422; 7431; 7438.04-7438.043; FTC ¶ H-1755].

FOOTNOTE ¶ 1417 [USTR ¶ 1320; 1322 et seq.; CCH ¶ 7423; 7432; 7438.047-7438.048; FTC ¶ H-1770].

FOOTNOTE ¶ 1418 [USTR ¶ 740; 1320; 2740; 2743; CCH ¶ 6204; FTC ¶ H-1602].

FOOTNOTE ¶ 1419 [USTR ¶ 1320; 1322.01; CCH ¶ 7438; FTC ¶ H-1656].

FOOTNOTE ¶ 1420 [USTR ¶ 1200; CCH ¶ 7241-7244; FTC ¶ H-2150].

FOOTNOTE ¶ 1421 [USTR ¶ 670; CCH ¶ 5507.2927; FTC ¶ H-1650].

FOOTNOTE ¶ 1422 [USTR ¶ 1320; 1322.05; CCH ¶ 7425; 7434; 7438.07-7438.075; 7438.080; FTC ¶ H-1802].

FOOTNOTE ¶ 1423 [USTR ¶ 1320; 1322.06; CCH ¶ 7426; 7435; 7438.08-7438.083; 7438.15; 7438.20; FTC ¶ H-1741].

FOOTNOTE ¶ 1426 [USTR ¶ 1050; 1060; 1250; 1253 et seq.; CCH ¶ 7320-7324.70; FTC ¶ H2220].

CHAPTER

5

GROSS INCOME—EXCLUSIONS

TABLE OF CONTENTS

TAX-FREE INCOME IN GENERAL

¶1501 BASIC RULES

All items of income "from whatever source derived" are subject to income tax [IRC Sec. 61; Reg. Sec. 1.61-1]. However, despite what the tax code says, not all income is subject to tax. Some items are not considered to be income at all or the tax law specifically says they are tax-free.

For instance, loan proceeds are generally not considered taxable income. The return of invested capital is also tax-free. Example: The part of sale proceeds that equals your tax basis in the property sold or the part of an annuity payment that represents premiums you previously paid is not taxable. Thus, rules exist to separate the part that is tax-free (return of capital) from the taxable portion (appreciation).

Other items are tax-free because, by law, they are excluded from gross income subject to tax. Examples: Gifts, inherited property and life insurance proceeds you receive. The exclusion for life insurance proceeds is intended to achieve certain socially desirable goals. The original intent for excluding gifts and inheritances was that these would be subject to separate tax rates.

¶1502 THE VALUE OF TAX-FREE INCOME

The extent to which taxes deplete income depends on the recipient's tax bracket, as the following table illustrates:

TAXABLE INCOME (joint return)	TAX RATE	To equal this amount of tax-free income		
		$1,000	$2,500	$5,000
		You'd need to earn the following amount of income subject to tax:		
$25,000	15%	$1,176	$2,941	$5,882
$50,000	28%	$1,389	$3,472	$6,944
$87,000	31%	$1,449	$3,623	$7,246

This chapter covers the main kinds of tax-free income:

- Municipal bond interest
- Insurance proceeds
- Medical and disability benefits
- Gifts and inheritances
- Annuities

Other items of excludable income are covered elsewhere in the text. They are:

- Corporation stock distribution [¶1222; 1223]
- Employee fringe benefits [¶1400 et seq.]
- The tax-free profit from the sale of a residence by a homeowner 55 years or older [¶1708]

INCOME ON GOVERNMENT OBLIGATIONS

¶1503   INTEREST ON STATE AND MUNICIPAL OBLIGATIONS

Generally, interest on state and local bonds is tax exempt [IRC Sec. 103(a); Reg. Sec. 1.103-1(a)]. And it is usually free from state and local income taxes to bondholders who reside in the state issuing the bond.

> **NOTE:** (1) Social Security recipients may be indirectly subject to tax on interest from municipals. Tax-exempt interest income can increase the portion of your Social Security benefits subject to tax [¶1526]. (2) You must report tax-exempt interest on Form 1040, even though it is not actually taxed.

The following table illustrates how you can increase your actual investment return by switching to tax-exempt obligations:

TAXABLE INCOME (joint return)	TAX RATE	When tax-exempt bond yield is				
		5%	6%	7%	8%	9%
		Rates of taxable interest necessary to yield same amount after tax are:				
$25,000	15%	5.88	7.06	8.24	9.41	10.59
$50,000	28%	6.94	8.33	9.72	11.11	12.50
$87,000	31%	7.25	8.70	10.14	11.59	13.04

(a) Exceptions to Tax-Free Status. There are some important exceptions to the tax-exempt status of state and local obligations:

1. Certain state or municipal bonds used for nongovernmental purposes. These are known as private activity bonds. Interest from such state and local bonds is taxable if (1) more than 10% of the proceeds from the bond issue are (a) put to any private business use and (b) secured by property used for private business use, or (2) more than 5% of the proceeds from the bond issue or $5,000,000 (whichever is less) is used to finance loans to nongovernmental entities [IRC Sec. 103(b)(1), 141].

2. Arbitrage bonds. These are taxable bonds issued to raise funds that the issuer, in turn, uses to acquire higher yielding investments [IRC Sec. 148].

3. Bonds not in registered form. To be tax-exempt, bonds issued after December 31, 1982 must be in registered form [IRC Sec. 149, 163(f)(2)]. The U.S. Supreme Court has upheld this requirement.[1] In other words, tax-exempt unregistered bonds are no longer being issued. Such bonds issued prior to that date are still available on the resale market and pay tax-exempt interest.

There is an exemption from the registration requirements for obligations that are designed to be sold to foreigners (i.e., sales to non-U.S. persons). Obligations issued after September 7, 1990 must meet the following three requirements to qualify: (1) The issuer or distributor generally cannot offer or sell the obligation to a person within the U.S. or its possessions during the "restricted period" (generally 40 days after the closing of the offering); (2) neither the issuer nor the distributor may deliver the obligation in definitive form within the U.S. or its possessions; and (3) the owner of the obligation must provide the issuer with certification that (a) the obligation is owned by a non-U.S. person, (b) the obligation is owned by the foreign branch of a U.S. financial institution (or by a U.S. person who holds the obligation through that institution), or (c) the obligation is owned by a financial institution for purposes of resale but not to a U.S. person, or to a person within the U.S. or its possessions [IRC Sec. 163(f); Reg. Sec. 1.163-5(c)(2)].

4. Stripped tax-exempt bonds. With bonds whose interest-bearing coupons have been stripped, all that you own is the right to principal at maturity. Thus, they are sold at a deep discount on their face value [¶1217]. For bonds traded after June 10, 1987, in general, your income from the bond is taxed to the extent it exceeds the stated interest rate [IRC Sec. 1286(d)].

> **WORD TO THE WISE** Before investing in a particular state or municipal obligation, you should check with a broker to verify the tax status of the bond.

(b) Ways to Invest in Tax-Free Municipals. You have a choice of investment opportunities when it comes to municipals.

1. Municipal bond trust. A municipal bond trust pays a fixed rate of tax-free interest and you receive your entire investment back at maturity. A trust is well-suited to investors who seek a steady stream of tax-free income and plan on holding to maturity. Investors buy into a trust by purchasing units from a securities broker or bond dealer, who charges a one-time sales charge. The maturities of the bonds range from three to 30 years.

2. Municipal bond funds. These are more suitable for an investor who likes to take advantage of changing market conditions. Generally, the yield from a municipal bond fund will fluctuate with the interest rate. The fund is tailored to those investors who believe that interest rates will drop or who are unsure of the length of their investment. You can invest in these funds through fund sponsors, who charge sales fees and management fees. Unlike a trust investor, as a fund investor you have no assurance that your original investment will be returned.

> **INVESTOR TIP** It is critical to check the ratings of the bonds in which a trust or a fund is investing. The highest rating is AAA. If the fund or trust includes lower-rated bonds (e.g., lower than A rated bonds), you may wish to invest in an insured fund or trust.

3. Insured municipal bonds. By purchasing insured municipal bonds, you have an extra layer of protection against the issuer's default. Here an insurance company backs a specific bond issue of a state or a municipality. In the event of the issuer's default, the insurance company will step into the shoes of the state. It will continue to make interest payments during the remaining life of the bond and redeem the bonds at par (face value) on the stated redemption date.

Generally, these privately insured issues are given the highest ratings, but carry slightly lower yields because of the cost of the insurance.

> **INVESTOR TIP** The insurance protects only against default. It does not protect against declines in the value of the bond due to rising interest rates. Thus, if you invest in insured municipals you can have a loss on the sale of a bond before maturity.

4. Municipal leases. With this type of investment, your money, in effect, goes to purchase equipment that the municipality leases from you. Municipal leases pay tax-free interest at higher rates than bonds—since they are riskier investments.

Example: A town needs equipment (e.g., police cars, fire trucks, computers) but it does not want to lay out cash or float a bond issue. Instead, the government agrees to buy the equipment under a short-term installment sales contract. The installment contract is called a municipal lease. However, the government actually purchases the equipment and ends up with clear title at the end of the lease period.

➤ **TAX-FREE INCOME**   You receive tax-free interest paid on the municipal obligation—whether it is a bond or an installment contract.

A municipal lease arrangement, unlike a municipal bond, is not backed by the municipality's taxing authority. It is based on annual appropriations, which the state and local government must vote to approve. If the government chooses not to spend the money necessary to make the lease payments, then it defaults on the deal. As a result, you should choose a lease arrangement carefully. Remember, they are not rated nor are they privately insured.

5. Alternative minimum tax bonds. Private activity bonds [(a)1. above] issued after August 7, 1986, that are free of regular income tax are subject to alternative minimum tax [¶2603(b)].

They bear a higher rate of return than comparable bonds that produce interest free of both regular income tax and alternative minimum tax.

➤ **INVESTOR STRATEGY** If you are subject to the alternative minimum tax, you should investigate whether the bonds you are thinking of buying are still completely tax-free.

On the other hand, if you who do not have an alternative minimum tax problem, you can get a higher tax-free return by investing in private activity bonds that are subject to alternative minimum tax, but free of regular income tax.

¶1504   INTEREST ON OBLIGATIONS OF THE UNITED STATES

Interest on United States bills, notes, and bonds is includible in your gross income and subject to federal income taxation. However, these obligations are free of state and local income taxation [IRC Sec. 103(a); Reg. Sec. 1.103-1(a)].

➤ **INVESTMENT STRATEGY** Interest on obligations of U.S. possessions (e.g., Puerto Rico, U.S. Virgin Islands, and Guam) are free of federal, state, and local income tax.

NOTE: Interest on some U.S. Savings Bonds (Series EE) used for qualified higher education expenses is tax-free if certain requirements are met [¶1217(b)]. Otherwise, interest on U.S. Savings Bonds can be tax-deferred until disposed of or until maturity [¶2828]. Interest on short-term U.S. Treasury Bills is not taxed until the year they mature.

LIFE INSURANCE

¶1506   CASH VALUE BUILD-UP

Increases in the cash value buildup of a whole life insurance policy are tax-free. What's more dividends from participating whole life insurance policies are also tax-free (whether used to reduce premiums or purchase additional paid-up insurance).

To qualify for this special tax treatment (as well as the other tax breaks discussed later in this chapter), policies issued after 1984 must satisfy one of the following two tests:

1. Cash value accumulation test: This allows traditional whole life policies, with cash values that accumulate at reasonable interest rates, to continue to qualify as life insurance. Under this test, the cash surrender value provided under the contract at any time cannot exceed the net single premium needed at that time to fund the contract's future benefits [IRC Sec. 7702(a)(1)].

2. Guideline premium and cash value corridor test: This test limits the definition of life insurance to contracts that allow relatively modest investments and investment returns. The two prongs of this test are designed to curb two different potential abuses. The guideline premium portion pinpoints contracts where the policyholder makes greater than usual investments in the policy. The cash value corridor pinpoints contracts with excessive cash value buildup [IRC Sec. 7702(a)(2)].

¶1507   LIFE INSURANCE PROCEEDS

[New tax legislation may affect this subject; see ¶1.]

Life insurance policies come in a variety of forms—term, cash value and combinations of the two. However, they all call for the insurer to make payments upon the insured's death to his estate or to his beneficiaries. Those proceeds, whether paid in a lump sum or as a series of payments, are generally excluded from the beneficiary's gross income. Some other death benefit payments have the characteristics of life insurance proceeds. They are payable under the terms of a contract by reason of death, and likewise qualify for this exclusion. Examples: Workers' compensation insurance contracts, endowment contracts, and accidental death policies [IRC Sec. 101(a)(1); Reg. Sec. 1.101-1(a)(1)].

> **Example 1:** Mr. Washington takes out a life insurance policy for $100,000 with his wife as beneficiary. When Washington dies, the $100,000 received by his widow is not subject to income tax.

> ➤ **OBSERVATION** Life insurance proceeds may be subject to *estate tax*. You can, however, escape this tax by having someone other than the insured (e.g., the beneficiary) be the owner of the policy.

(a) Transfer for Valuable Consideration. Life insurance proceeds are partially taxable when the policy is purchased from a prior owner. The proceeds are excludable only to the extent of the purchase price plus any premiums or other payments made after acquiring the policy [IRC Sec. 101(a)(2); Reg. Sec. 1.101-1(b)(1)].

> **Example 2:** Weststar Corp. purchases an insurance policy in the face amount of $10,000 upon the life of Mrs. Lane, one of its employees. Weststar Corp. transfers the policy to Eaststar Corp. for $6,000. Eaststar Corp. receives the proceeds of the $10,000 upon the death of Mrs. Lane. The amount that Eaststar Corp. can exclude from its gross income is limited to $6,000 plus any premiums paid by Eaststar following the transfer of the policy.

However, the entire insurance proceeds are excludable in the following two cases:

1. The recipient's basis (for purposes of determining gain or loss) in the policy is determined by reference to the transferor's basis [IRC Sec. 101(a)(2)(A); Reg. Sec. 1.101-1(b)(1)].

> **Example 3:** ABC, Inc. purchases a $20,000 policy on the life of an employee for a single premium of $5,000. ABC is the beneficiary. ABC transfers the policy to XYZ Corp. in a tax-free reorganization (XYZ carries over ABC's basis). XYZ Corp receives the proceeds of $20,000 upon the death of the employee. The entire $20,000 is excludable from the gross income of XYZ Corp.

2. The policy is transferred to the insured, his or her partner, partnership or to a corporation in which the insured is a shareholder or officer [IRC Sec. 101(a)(2)(B); Reg. Sec. 1.101-1(b)(1)].

Gratuitous transfers. If you receive a gratuitous transfer of a life insurance policy (e.g., a gift), you may exclude from gross income (1) the amount which would have been excludable by your transferor had no transfer taken place, *plus* (2) any premiums you pay after receiving the policy. However, the full proceeds are excludable when the policy is transferred by or to the insured, his or her partner, partnership or a corporation in which the insured is a shareholder or officer [Reg. Sec. 1.101-1(b)(2)].

Example 4: Mr. Taylor purchased a single premium life insurance policy for $20,000 with a face value of $100,000. Taylor transferred the policy to his daughter, Amy, as a gift. Upon her father's death, Amy can exclude the entire $100,000 from her gross income. Reason: This is the amount her father's estate would have excluded for income tax purposes had no transfer occurred.

Example 5: Tyler owns a $50,000 insurance policy on his own life. Tyler sells the policy to Elizabeth in return for $6,000. Elizabeth then transfers the policy to her son, Russell, as a gift. Russell makes additional premium payments of $5,000 following the transfer. Upon the death of Tyler, Russell receives the proceeds of the life insurance policy—$50,000. The amount which is excludable from Russell's gross income is limited to $11,000 [$6,000 (the amount that Elizabeth would have been entitled to exclude if no transfer had been made) *plus* $5,000 (the premiums paid by Russell following the transfer)].

Example 6: Mr. Cart purchases a life insurance policy on the life of Mr. Alvin. Cart sells the policy to Bert who gratuitously transfers the policy to Mr. Alvin, the insured. Alvin's estate receives the proceeds upon the death of Alvin. The entire amount is excluded from the gross income of Alvin's estate, since the gratuitous transfer was made to the insured.

(b) Employee Death Benefits. As a general rule, amounts paid by an employer on account of an employee's death are excludable from the beneficiary's gross income [IRC Sec. 101(b)(1); Reg. Sec. 1.101-2].

➤ **LIMITATION ON EXCLUDABLE AMOUNT** The exclusion is limited to $5,000. Any amounts received in excess of $5,000 are included in the beneficiary's gross income [IRC Sec. 101(b)(2)(A); Reg. Sec. 1.101-2(a)(1)].

Certain exceptions to this rule prevent amounts that the employee was scheduled to receive as taxable benefits from being turned into income excluded from tax. These exceptions are:

- nonforfeitable rights;
- joint and survivor annuities; and
- certain other annuities [IRC Sec. 101(b)(1), (2); Reg. Sec. 1.101-2(a)(1),(2)].

A nonforfeitable right includes vested retirement benefits which the employee was entitled to receive before his death. It also refers to any amount to which an employee would have been entitled if he had made an appropriate election or terminated his employment. Any amounts received by reason of nonforfeitable rights are included in the beneficiary's gross income.

Example 7: Mr. Lee was a participant under XYZ, Inc.'s pension plan. Lee retired on December 31, 1988. Upon his retirement, he became eligible for monthly payments of $250 for 10 years. Lee died on January 1, 1992. After his death, the monthly payments became payable to his estate. These payments do not qualify for the exclusion since Lee's right to them was non-forfeitable at the date of his death.

The exclusion does not apply to amounts received under a *joint* and *survivor annuity* obligation, where (1) the employee was the primary annuitant and (2) the annuity starting date occurred before the death of the employee.

Example 8: Vance Corp. provides joint and survivor annuities to its employees under its benefit plan. Mr. Abel was an employee of Vance Corp. Mr. Abel, the primary annuitant, began receiving annuity payments upon his retirement. Upon his death, Mrs. Abel began receiving the annuity payments. Mrs. Abel must include in her income the amounts received under the joint and survivor annuity contract. She is not entitled to avail herself of the exclusion.

The $5,000 exclusion does not apply to certain other annuity payments. These are amounts payable at regular intervals over a period longer than one year from the date of the first payment. To determine whether the exclusion applies to these payments, the recipient must know the annuity's present value at the date of the decedent's death. The exclusion applies only to the extent that the present value exceeds the larger of either employee contributions or nonforfeitable amounts.

> **Example 9:** Mr. Abel died while still an employee of Vance Corp. Under the company's plan Abel's widow is entitled to an immediate annuity of $2,000 per year for her life. At the time of his death, Abel had a vested benefit of $18,000. The annuity's present value at the time of Abel's death is $20,000. Abel made no contributions to the annuity plan. The $2,000 difference between the present value of the annuity ($20,000) and the nonforfeitable amount ($18,000) is excluded. (The $2,000 exclusion is spread among all payments received during her life expectancy, the same as an annuitant's investment in an annuity contract [¶1522].)

Suppose the employer death benefits are payable by certain employer-provided benefit plans, or by an insurance company (assuming the payment is not considered "life insurance" as described above). Then the payments are considered to be made by or on behalf of the employer to the extent they exceed the deceased employee's contribution [Reg. Sec. 1.101-2(b)(1)]. These payments are treated as plan distributions and are excludable within the $5,000 limitation. However, any part of the plan death benefits considered life insurance is fully excludable.

(c) Life Insurance Proceeds Held Under Agreement to Pay Interest. If the proceeds are held by the insurer under an agreement to pay interest, the interest payments must be included in the beneficiary's gross income [IRC Sec. 101(c); Reg. Sec. 1.101-3].

> **Example 10:** A $100,000 life insurance policy calls for payment of proceeds five years after the insured's death. The insurer does, however, make payments of $8,000 during each of those five years and then pays the $100,000 in a lump sum. Result: The beneficiary receives $8,000 of taxable interest income each year. The $100,000 policy proceeds are tax-free.

(d) Payments of Proceeds Over a Period of Time. Suppose there is an agreement or option in a life insurance contract to pay the proceeds at a time later than death. In this case, the beneficiary may be taxed on the interest element of the proceeds held by the insurer. This interest element is found by prorating the present value of the life insurance proceeds as of the date of death over the period of the payments. The prorated amount is excluded from the beneficiary's income. Amounts over that are taxable as interest [IRC Sec. 101(d); Reg. Sec. 1.101-4(a)].

> **Example 11:** A life insurance policy is worth $100,000 at the insured's death, but the beneficiary elects under the policy to take $12,000 a year for 10 years instead of the lump sum. He gets $10,000 a year tax-free, but the remaining $2,000 a year is taxable interest.

(e) Proceeds Payable to Shareholders. Life insurance proceeds paid to a corporation's shareholders will be taxed as dividends if the corporation uses its earnings to pay the premiums and owns the policy. This applies even if the corporation is not the beneficiary and so does not receive the proceeds.[1] However, the Sixth Circuit (which includes Ohio, Kentucky, Tennessee and Michigan) held that the proceeds are not taxable as dividends if they were neither a corporation's assets nor distributed by the corporation.[2]

¶1508   SURRENDER OF LIFE INSURANCE POLICY

If you surrender a life insurance policy to the insurance company for a lump sum, you have taxable income to the extent the amount received exceeds the net premiums paid [IRC Sec. 72(e)(2); Reg. Sec. 1.72-11(d)]. However, if a life insurance policy is surrendered before maturity and premiums paid exceed cash surrender value, you cannot write off the loss.[1]

¶1509   LIFE INSURANCE ENDOWMENT CONTRACTS

An endowment policy is an insurance policy under which the insurer agrees to pay a stated sum of money at the end of a definite period. The sum can be paid all at once or in installments.

A portion of the proceeds is excluded from gross income. If you receive the proceeds in a lump sum (on maturity or surrender), the exclusion is equal to the premiums paid less any dividends or other amounts previously received under the contract. Proceeds in excess of the aggregate premiums are included in gross income [IRC Sec. 72(e)(2); Reg. Sec. 1.72-11(d)]. Suppose the proceeds are payable in installments for a fixed number of years. Each year's exclusion is found by dividing the total premiums paid by the number of years over which installments are to be paid [IRC Sec. 72(c)(3)(B)].

As a beneficiary of an endowment contract, you may have the option of electing to receive payments as an annuity, rather than a lump-sum payment. If you make a timely election, the tax rules for annuities will apply [¶1522]. In other words, the tax will be spread out along with the payments, and part of each payment will be tax-free.

➤ **ELECTION DEADLINE** Beneficiaries have only 60 days from the time a lump sum becomes payable to elect to receive an annuity and qualify for annuity tax treatment. If you wait longer than 60 days, you will be taxed as though you received a lump sum—even though the distribution is actually made in the form of an annuity [Reg. Sec. 1.72-12].

¶1510 DIVIDENDS ON LIFE INSURANCE AND ENDOWMENT POLICIES

Dividends on unmatured life or endowment insurance policies are a partial return of premiums paid. They are tax-free until they exceed the accumulated net premiums paid for the contract. However, interest paid or credited by the insurance company on dividends left with the company is taxable.

Veterans' insurance proceeds and dividends are not taxable to veterans or their beneficiaries. The proceeds of a veteran's endowment policy paid before his death are also exempt. And the Revenue Service has ruled that interest on dividends left on deposit with the Veterans' Administration is also exempt from tax.[1] The "Veterans' Benefit Act of 1957," currently in force, continues the tax exemption of benefits under previous veterans' laws.[2]

¶1511   GROUP-TERM LIFE INSURANCE PREMIUMS

Premiums paid for you by your employer to give group-term life insurance coverage of up to $50,000 are excludable from your gross income [IRC Sec. 79]. Any cost above the $50,000 coverage must be included in income [¶1407]. To qualify for the exclusion, the group-term life insurance plan must meet nondiscrimination tests. Group-permanent life insurance premiums paid by your employer are ordinary income to you and must be reported as wages [Reg. Sec. 1.79-1].

DISABILITY BENEFITS

¶1515   MEDICAL AND DISABILITY BENEFITS

You can exclude from gross income a variety of benefits received on account of injuries or sickness.

(a) Medical Expense Reimbursement. You can exclude accident and health insurance reimbursements of medical costs to the extent you have not claimed a medical expense deduction for the underlying costs. Likewise, accident and health insurance payments made without reference to medical bills are generally excludable as well [IRC Sec. 104(a)(3), 105; Reg. Sec. 1.104-1(a),(d)].

> **Example:** Ms. Richardson had $5,000 of medical expenses in 1991. However, her actual medical expense deduction was limited to $400 on account of the $7\frac{1}{2}$% of adjusted gross income deduction floor. In 1992, Richardson received a $2,000 reimbursement for some of those expenses. She must include $400 of the reimbusement in income; the other $1,600 is excludable.

> **NOTE:** For the tax treatment of employer-provided accident and health insurance policies, see ¶1516.

(b) Income Replacement Policies. An income replacement policy or a disability policy protects you (the insured) against loss of income due to physical incapability of working. If you purchase such policies, you are entitled to exclude amounts you receive [IRC Sec. 104(a)(3); Reg. Sec. 1.104-1(d)].

(c) Workers' Compensation. If you receive payments under workers' compensation acts for personal injury or sickness, you are permitted to exclude these amounts from gross income. In addition, this exclusion is extended to your survivor(s) who receive amounts under a workers' compensation act [IRC Sec. 104(a)(1); Reg. Sec. 1.104-1(b)].

(d) Lawsuit Damages Award. There is an exclusion from gross income for any damages received for personal injury or sickness of the taxpayer. This exclusion extends to both court awards and settlement agreements entered into instead of litigating a case [IRC Sec. 104(a)(2); Reg. Sec. 1.104-1(c)]. However, certain types of damages are includible in gross income [¶1520].

(e) Government Disability Payments. You may exclude amounts you receive from a pension, annuity, or similar allowance for personal injury or sickness attributable to active service in the armed forces of any country, or in the Coast Guard and Geodetic Survey, or Public Health Service, or as a disability annuity payable under the Foreign Service Act of 1980 [IRC Sec. 104(a)(4); Reg. Sec. 1.104-1(e)].

Similarly, there's an exclusion for disability income received by individuals, who, as employees of the United States engaged in the performance of official duties outside the United States, are injured as a direct result of a terrorist attack [IRC Sec. 104(a)(5); Reg. Sec. 1.104-1(c)].

However, amounts received by survivors of a deceased individual under the Foreign Service Act of 1980 and the Retired Serviceman's Family Protection Plan as a disability annuity are included in the survivor's gross income [Reg. Sec. 1.104-1(e)(2),(3)].

¶1516   EMPLOYER-PROVIDED ACCIDENT AND HEALTH PLANS

Your employer may contribute to an employer-provided accident and health plan for the employees' benefit. This plan may make benefit payments to you and the other employees. Under certain conditions, the contributions made and the benefits received will be tax-free to you.

(a) Amounts Received Under Accident and Health Plans. In general, the tax treatment of accident and health plan payments depends on why benefits are paid, who pays the premiums and how benefits are calculated. If your employer pays the premiums on a disability income policy as a tax-free fringe benefit, you must include payments received under the plan in your gross income, unless one of the exceptions explained below applies. On the other hand, if the premiums are paid with your after-tax dollars (or you are taxed on premium payments your employer makes on your employee's behalf), the benefits are excluded from income. In those instances where you and your employer split the premium costs, the benefits are partially excludable, in proportion to how the premium costs were shared [IRC Sec. 105(a); Reg. Sec. 1.105-1(a), (c)].

> **Example 1:** Eaststar Corp. maintains a plan that pays regular wages to employees who are absent from work due to sickness or personal injury. Employees contribute 25% of the premium cost through payroll deductions. Mr. Taylor, an employee, received $2,000 from the plan for the four weeks of work he missed due to personal injury. He must include 75% of that amount—or $1,500—in gross income. Taylor may exclude the other 25%—or $500—allocable to his own premium payments.

Medical expense reimbursement. Amounts you receive as reimbursements from an accident or health plan for the medical care of you, your spouse or dependents are excluded from income [IRC Sec. 105(b); Reg. Sec. 1.105-2]. If you, your spouse or dependents incur an injury which results in permanent disfigurement, loss or loss of the use of a body part (i.e., loss of a leg), or a function of the body (i.e., loss of hearing), any amounts you receive under an accident or health plan are excluded from gross income [IRC Sec. 105(c)(1); Reg. Sec. 1.105-3]. In addition, amounts you receive that are paid based on the nature of the injury are excluded from gross income. No exclusion is permitted if payments are based on the amount of time you are absent from work [IRC Sec. 105(c)(2); Reg. Sec. 1.105-3].

> **Example 2:** XYZ, Inc. provides its employees with health insurance. Ms. Clark, an XYZ employee, receives a $300 reimbursement for medical bills incurred by herself and her dependent daughter. The reimbursement is excludable even though XYZ paid the insurance premiums.

> **Example 3:** Construction Corp. maintains an accident plan which provides that in the event of loss of a limb (i.e., arm, hand, leg) by an employee, such employee is entitled to receive $10,000. Mr. Russell, an employee who lost an arm, receives payment from Construction Corp.'s plan. The $10,000 is excludable from his gross income.

> **Example 4:** Same facts as above, except the plan provides for payment of $250 for each week the employee misses work on account of an injury up to a maximum period of 32 weeks, regardless of the nature of the injury. In this case, the amounts received by Russell are included in his gross income.

(b) Employer's Contribution to Accident and Health Plans. Your gross income does not include premiums your employer pays for accident or health plan coverage (i.e., compensation for personal injury or sickness) for yourself, your spouse, and dependents. Contributions that continue after your death or retirement are also excluded from gross income [IRC Sec. 106; Reg. Sec. 1.106-1].

> **NOTE:** Employers must offer employees the option to purchase continuation health care coverage when their regular coverage lapses (e.g., due to termination of employment) [1406(c)]. Employers can, however, charge the employees for the cost of their coverage [IRC Sec. 4980B(f)(2)(C)].

(c) Nondiscrimination Rules. To qualify for the exclusion, a self-insured accident or health plan must meet nondiscrimination rules (¶1406(a)) [IRC Sec. 105(h)].

GIFTS, INHERITANCES AND DAMAGES

¶1518   GIFTS

A gift is a gratuitous transfer from a donor to a donee. Generally, to be considered a gift, the donor must be under no legal obligation to make the transfer. Gifts you receive are not included your gross income. However, once the gift takes place, future earnings attributable to assets are taxable to you. (Furthermore, when you sell the asset, you could have income attributable to appreciation in its value prior to the date the gift was made. The donor's basis in the asset is generally carried over to the donee [¶1610].)

> **Example:** Amy received stock as a gift in January. The value of the stock is $10,000. The yearly dividend received from the stock is $600. Although the $10,000 value of the stock is excluded from Amy's gross income, the $600 dividend is included.

> ➤ **ANOTHER TAX** Gratuitous transfers may be subject to gift tax. This tax is imposed on the donor. However, there is an exclusion that can shelter the first $10,000 of gifts given by a donor to a donee.

(a) Employee Gifts. Transfers from your employer to you and other employees are automatically deemed not to be gifts. As a result, the tax-free treatment does not apply to such transfers—even if your employer calls a transfer a "gift" [IRC Sec. 102(c)]. However, the item may be tax-free on account of some other tax rule, such as the exclusion for employee achievement awards [¶1418].

(b) Gifts to Minors. The Uniform Gifts to Minors Act has been adopted by most states as a means for minors to own property (e.g., bank accounts, stocks and bonds) without the formalities and expense of a special guardianship or a trust. The designated custodian of the property has the legal right to act on behalf of the minor. Income earned from the property generally is taxed to the minor. Income from the gift used to satisfy an individual's legal obligation to support a minor is taxable to the person whose support obligation is satisfied, no matter who made the gift.

> ➤ **TAX SAVINGS** Income earned on a gift you make to your child is taxed to your child rather than to you in your higher tax bracket. However, 1992 unearned income, to the extent it exceeds $1,200, is taxed to your child at your top rate. In regard to the first $1,200 of unearned income, the first $600 is tax-free and the second $600 is taxed at your child's rate [¶1240].

¶1519   INHERITANCES

The value of property you acquire by inheritance is tax-free to you. Income earned on the property after the transfer is taxable to you and included in your gross income.

> ➤ **STEPPED-UP BASIS** Your basis in property you inherit generally is its fair market value at the date of the decedent's death. Thus, appreciation in the property's value prior to that date goes untaxed.

In contrast, your basis in property you acquire as a gift generally is equal to the donor's basis in the property at the time the gift was made (¶1610) [IRC Sec. 1014(a), 1015(a)].

Example: Mr. Tyler purchased shares of stock for $5,000. When the shares are worth $8,000, he makes a gift of them to his son, Matthew. Matthew's basis in the stock for computing gain is $5,000—the same as Tyler's had been. If instead Matthew had inherited the shares from Tyler when they were worth $8,000, his basis would be $8,000.

¶1520   DAMAGES

Damage awards are a form of reimbursement, whether you receive them under a judgment or in compromise of a claim. To find whether damages are income and therefore includible in gross income, the nature of the item for which the damages are received generally must be considered.[1] Damages relating to personal or family rights can be excluded from gross income.[2] Damages for loss of or injury to capital also can be excluded, unless they exceed the basis of the capital.[1] However, damages for loss of profits[3] and most punitive damages, such as treble damages under antitrust laws and exemplary damages for fraud, must be included in gross income [Reg. Sec. 1.61-14].

Excluded

Personal or family rights. Compensatory or punitive damages received on account of personal injuries or sickness[4] (Note: For punitive damages to be excludable, they must relate to actual *physical* injury—i.e., punitive damages in connection with a defamation or employment discrimination case are *includible* in gross income)[IRC Sec. 104(a)]; damages for age discrimination[5]; award for loss of life.[6]

Return of capital. Damages for injury to goodwill of a business except to the extent they exceed its basis.[7]

Sex discrimination awards: The United States Supreme Court has held that payments received in a settlement of a sex discrimination suit had to be reported as taxable income.[8] Reason: The payments in the underlying lawsuit were taxable because the only legal remedies available at that time (under Title VII of the Civil Rights Act) provided compensation only for economic losses through the recovery of back pay. In other words, sex discrimination was considered an economic injury and not a personal injury.

However, the Civil Rights Act of 1991 gives victims of intentional discrimination the right to sue their employers for pain and suffering and emotional distress. And the Court indicated that damages received for those reasons should be tax-free.

ANNUITIES

¶1522   ANNUITIES IN GENERAL

An annuity ordinarily is insurance you buy that provides for regular payments to you to begin at a fixed date and continue through your life or for a term of years. Each regular payment consists of earnings on what you paid for the annuity plus enough of your cost to complete the guaranteed payment. This liquidation of principal is calculated to extend over your life expectancy or the term of the annuity. The part of each payment that represents a return of the annuity's cost is tax-free. The part representing investment earnings is taxable [IRC Sec. 72].

(a) Types of Annuities. Annuity payments are amounts received under a life insurance, endowment or annuity contract. Generally, the contract is bought from an insurance company. However, an annuity may be issued by an individual or other party as well. Most common types of annuities are:

- Fixed annuity (paying a fixed amount at regular intervals for a fixed term).
- Single-life annuity (paying a fixed amount at regular intervals for the life of one individual).
- Joint and survivor annuity (paying a fixed amount at regular intervals to one person for life and, on his or her death, paying the same or different amount at the same or different intervals to a second individual for life).
- Variable annuity (payments vary in amount depending on the insurer's investment experience, cost-of-living indices, or similar factors; payments may be made over a fixed term or for the life of one or more persons).

Amounts received as an annuity. Only amounts you receive as an annuity are eligible for tax-free treatment [(c) below]. Payments constitute annuity amounts only if (1) you receive them on or after the annuity starting date; (2) they're payable at regular intervals over a period of more than one year from the annuity starting date; and (3) the total amount you are to receive can be determined from the terms of the contract or by the use of mortality tables, compound interest tables, or both [IRC Sec. 72(c)(4); Reg. Sec. 1.72-4(b)]. All other payments are "amounts not received as annuities" and get special tax treatment [(g) below].

> ➤ **CASH VALUE BUILD-UP** Ordinarily, the cash value build-up of annuity contracts (much like the cash value build-up of life insurance policies) is not subject to current tax. However, an exception applies to corporate-owned annuity contracts. Corporations are taxed on the excess of (1) the net surrender value plus distributions, over (2) the net premiums paid on the annuity contract plus amounts previously includible in gross income [IRC Sec. 72(u)].

(b) Annuity Starting Date. The annuity starting date is the later of (1) the date obligations under the contract become fixed or (2) the first day of the annuity pay period (e.g., monthly, quarterly) which ends on the date of the first payment [IRC Sec. 72(c)(4); Reg. Sec. 1.72-4(b)].

(c) Exclusion Ratio. The part of each payment that is attributable to your investment in the annuity rests on 3 factors: (1) amount received as an annuity; (2) investment in contract; and (3) expected return [IRC Sec. 72(b); Reg. Sec. 1.72-4]. The figures are determined as of the annuity starting date. Expressed as a fraction, the exclusion ratio is:

$$\text{Investment in the contract} \div \text{Expected return}$$

This fraction is multiplied by the amount of each annuity payment to determine how much you can exclude from income. The purpose of the exclusion ratio is to spread the tax-free portion of the annuity over your lifetime or other term of the annuity.

> **Example 1:** Mr. Bruckner bought an annuity for $12,650 that would pay him $100 a month starting January 1, 1992. His expected return under the contract is $16,000. The exclusion ratio is: $12,650/$16,000, or 79.1% after rounding.
> Mr. Bruckner can exclude from gross income $79.10 (79.1% × $100) of each $100 monthly payment he receives. Thus, for the year 1992 he can exclude a total amount of $949.20 ($79.10 × 12) and must include $250.80 in gross income.

Exclusion limited to investment. The total exclusion is limited to the amount you contribute. If you die before you recover your entire basis, the unrecovered amount may be claimed as a deduction in your final taxable year. Under prior law, once the amount to be excluded from each payment was determined for a particular contract, it generally remained the same, even if you outlived your life expectancy and had already recovered your entire investment in the contract.[1] Under present law, once your investment is recovered, there can no longer be any annuity excluded [IRC Sec. 72(b)(2), (3)].

(d) Investment in the Contract. Your investment in the contract is total amount of premiums you pay less: (1) any premiums refunded to you, rebates, or dividends you receive on or before the annuity starting date; and (2) the value of any refund feature [IRC Sec. 72(c); Reg. Sec. 1.72-6, 1.72-7]. The refund feature reduces your investment in the contract. This comes into play if your expected return depends on your life expectancy, and the contract provides either for refunds of the consideration or payment of a guaranteed amount.

(e) Expected Return. To find the expected return under a contract involving life expectancy, actuarial tables from the IRS are used [IRC Sec. 72(c)(3)(A); Reg. Sec. 1.72-9]. They provide a multiple that takes life expectancy into account in terms of total annual payments. Multiplying the amount of the annual payment by the multiple gives the expected return under the contracts [Reg. Sec. 1.72-5]. For a fixed annuity, the expected return is easily calculated by figuring out how much will be paid after the annuity starting date. For example, the expected return on an annuity of $200 a month for 10 years is $24,000 ($200 x 120 months).

➤ **OBSERVATION** These actuarial tables no longer make any distinction between male and female life expectancies.

(f) Actuarial Tables. Actuarial tables have been published by the IRS [Reg. Sec. 1.72-9], a sample of which (Table V) is reproduced below.

TABLE V - ORDINARY LIFE ANNUITIES
ONE LIFE - EXPECTED RETURN MULTIPLES

AGE	MULTIPLE	AGE	MULTIPLE	AGE	MULTIPLE
5	76.6	42	40.6	79	10.0
6	75.6	43	39.6	80	9.5
7	74.7	44	38.7	81	8.9
8	73.7	45	37.7	82	8.4
9	72.7	46	36.8	83	7.9
10	71.7	47	35.9	84	7.4
11	70.7	48	34.9	85	6.9
12	69.7	49	34.0	86	6.5
13	68.8	50	33.1	87	6.1
14	67.8	51	32.2	88	5.7
15	66.8	52	31.3	89	5.3
16	65.8	53	30.4	90	5.0
17	64.8	54	29.5	91	4.7
18	63.9	55	28.6	92	4.4
19	62.9	56	27.7	93	4.1
20	61.9	57	26.8	94	3.9
21	60.9	58	25.9	95	3.7
22	59.9	59	25.0	96	3.4
23	59.0	60	24.2	97	3.2
24	58.0	61	23.3	98	3.0
25	57.0	62	22.5	99	2.8
26	56.0	63	21.6	100	2.7

27	55.1	64	20.8	101	2.5
28	54.1	65	20.0	102	2.3
29	53.1	66	19.2	103	2.1
30	52.2	67	18.4	104	1.9
31	51.2	68	17.6	105	1.8
32	50.2	69	16.8	106	1.6
33	49.3	70	16.0	107	1.4
34	48.3	71	15.3	108	1.3
35	47.3	72	14.6	109	1.1
36	46.4	73	13.9	110	1.0
37	45.4	74	13.2	111	.9
38	44.4	75	12.5	112	.8
39	43.5	76	11.9	113	.7
40	42.5	77	11.2	114	.6
41	41.5	78	10.6	115	.5

Example 2: Mrs. Haskins, age 65 on the annuity starting date, bought an annuity on January 1, 1992, for $12,000 that will pay her $80 a month for her lifetime. Her expected return is determined as follows:

Annual payment ($80 × 12) . . . . $ 960
Multiple shown in Table V, male or female, age 65 20
Expected return ($960 × 20) $19,200

Her annual exclusion ratio is $12,000/$19,200, or 62.5%. She would exclude annually from gross income $600 ($960 × 62.5%).

(g) Amounts Not Received as an Annuity.

Funds you obtain on account of an annuity contract, but not received as an annuity [see (a) above] are included in your gross income. This applies to withdrawals, loans, pledges and assignments, dividends and partial surrenders. Amounts you receive before the annuity starting date are also, by definition, not amounts received as an annuity. However, they are taxable only to the extent the contract's *cash surrender value* exceeds your investment in the contract [IRC Sec. 72(e)(2),(3)].

Example 3: Ms. Brown owns an annuity that is scheduled to start payments at age 65. She is now age 55 and will be borrowing on the policy this year. Brown has paid in $50,000, but the contract has a cash value of $70,000. If Brown borrows $30,000, she will owe tax on $20,000 of the loan proceeds ($70,000 less $50,000). The other $10,000 is a tax-free return of Brown's investment.

Prior to a 1982 tax law change, the tax treatment was more favorable. You were taxed only to the extent the *amount received* exceeded the investment in the contract. This tax treatment is still in effect for amounts you receive that are allocable to a pre-August 14, 1982 investment [IRC Sec. 72(e)(5)].

Example 4: Same facts as in Example 3. Assume that Brown invested the $50,000 before August 14, 1982. Result: The full $30,000 is not taxable since it does not exceed her investment.

Additional penalty tax.

The tax law imposes a penalty on premature distributions from annuity contracts—in addition to any regular income tax that is due. The penalty is equal to 10% of the amount includible in gross income. However, this penalty does not apply to distributions made once you attain age 59½, or on account of death or disability [IRC Sec. 72(q)].

▶ **LIBERAL EXCEPTION TO PENALTY** The penalty does not apply to payouts in the form of a lifetime annuity calling for payments at least annually. This is true regardless of your age [IRC Sec. 72(q)(2)(D)].

The tax law also exempts distributions (1) from single premium contracts that start making substantially equal payments no more than one year after the contract is purchased, provided that those payments are made at least annually during the annuity period [IRC Sec. 72(q)(2)(I)] or (2) made to an employee upon separation from service from an annuity purchased by an employer on account of a qualified retirement plan's having been terminated [IRC Sec. 72(q)(2)(J)].

> ➤ **MORE PENALTY-FREE INCOME** Distributions allocable to pre-August 14, 1982 investments in the contracts are also exempt [IRC Sec. 72(q)(2)(F)].

¶1523   JOINT AND SURVIVOR ANNUITIES

Under this arrangement, the first annuitant receives periodic payments for life, and after death a second annuitant receives periodic payment in the same or different amounts for life. Generally, in finding the annual exclusion for a uniform payment joint and survivor annuity the rules in ¶1522 apply. However, the combined life expectancy of the annuitants must be used in determining expected return [Reg. Sec. 1.72-5(b)]. The rule for determining the survivor's income depends on when the first annuitant died. The ratio at which amounts received under the contract will be taxed may be determined at the outset of the contract by using the appropriate actuarial table.

¶1524   EMPLOYEE ANNUITIES

In General, if your employer buys an annuity contract under a qualified annuity plan (commonly referred to as a pension), or pays for any part of it, you are not taxed on your employer's payments when they are made. Benefits are taxed when you receive them, using the annuity rules [IRC Sec. 403(a)]. In applying these rules, your contributions are considered your investment in the contract. This reduces the portion of each annuity payment that counts as gross income. Effective with 1987 annuity starting dates, the total exclusion, though, is limited to your actual investment. When you reach your life expectancy, the exclusion ratio lapses, and subsequent annuity payments are fully taxable [IRC Sec. 72(b)(2)].

> **NOTE:** Prior to 1986, employees were taxed on employer-bought Sec. 403(a) qualified annuity plans and tax-deferred Sec. 403(b) annuities when amounts were actually paid *or made available* (i.e., when the employee had a right to receive funds, even though no distribution actually occurred). Under current law, tax is imposed only when amounts are actually paid.

If payments from your employer-sponsored plan do not qualify as an annuity, then special lump-sum retirement plan payout tax rules may apply [¶1320].

(b) Simplified Way to Figure Tax on Employee Annuities. Effective for distributions under employee annuities with starting dates occurring after July 1, 1986, you may use a simplified method to figure the taxable portion of each annuity payment you receive. This method may be used instead of the more complicated general rules for annuities [¶1522].

How it works: The table below shows the total number of monthly annuity payments expected to be paid out based on the recipient's age at the annuity starting date. The portion of each annuity payment that is excluded from income is calculated by dividing the total investment in the contract by the number of payments indicated.

Recipient's Age	Number of Payments
55 and under	300
56-60	260
61-65	240
66-70	170
71 and over	120

Example 1: In January, 1992, Mr. Brown, age 65, retires from his company and begins receiving a $1,000 a month joint and survivor annuity with his wife, age 60. During his working years, Brown contributed $24,000 to the company plan. Upon Mr. Brown's death, Mrs. Brown will receive $500 a month. Under the table, the set number of payments for someone age 65 is 240. So $100 of Brown's monthly checks ($24,000 divided by 240) represents a return of his investment. And that is the amount that can be excluded from tax until Brown recovers his $24,000. If Brown dies in, say, 15 years (180 months), only $18,000 will have been recovered. So Mrs. Brown will be able to exclude $100 from her $500 survivor checks for another 5 years (60 months).

(c) Annuities Purchased by Certain Tax-Exempt Organizations.

Public schools, hospitals, churches and certain other exempt organizations may offer their employees special tax deferred annuities. Contributions in the annuity are tax-free to the employee to the extent of an "exclusion allowance" for the year. The exclusion allowance is (1) 20% of the employee's pay for the last 12-month period, multiplied by the number of years of past service, (2) reduced by any amounts of employer contributions that were excluded in prior tax years (¶1312) [IRC Sec. 403(b); Reg. Sec. 1.403(b)-1(b),(d)]. In determining years of service, full-time employment for a full year equals one year of service. Part-time employees are credited with fractional years [IRC Sec. 403(b)(4)].

Example 2: Ms. Black, a public school teacher, earns $30,000 per year. This is her fifth year on the job. Black contributed $20,000 to a qualified annuity in prior years. Therefore, she may contribute up to $10,000 this year [20% of $30,000 × 5 years = $30,000 less $20,000 = $10,000].

➤ **ALTERNATIVE EXCLUSION** An election is available to have the exclusion computed under other rules [IRC Sec. 415]. If the election is made, the amount excluded is the amount that can be contributed by the employer to a defined contribution plan (¶1312) [IRC Sec. 403(b)(2)(B)].

(d) Investment in the Contract Where Employer Contributes.

Your investment in the contract includes amounts contributed by your employer only if the amounts (1) were includible in your income when contributed, or (2) would have been includible when contributed if they had been directly paid to you at that time [IRC Sec. 72(f)]. Amounts constructively received by you are included under (1) above. Exempt income is included under (2).

(e) Amounts Received Before Annuity Starting Date.

In general, the same rules apply to employee annuities as to other annuities [IRC Sec. 72(e)(8)(A)]. In other words, you are taxed on early withdrawals or loans to the extent the cash value exceeds your investment in the contract.

➤ **TAX-SAVING EXCEPTION** A special tax break applies to a plan which on May 5, 1986, permitted withdrawals of any employee contributions before separation of service. Employees are taxed only to the extent that total amount received before the annuity starting date exceeds the investment in the contract as of December 31, 1986 [IRC Sec. 72(e)(8)(D)].

SPECIAL RULES

¶1525   SCHOLARSHIPS

In general, scholarships granted after August 15, 1986 are tax-free to recipients only if the scholarships are used by degree candidates for "qualified tuition and related expenses."

Qualified expenses are limited to (1) tuition and fees for enrollment or attendance by a student enrolled in a qualified school and (2) fees, books, supplies and equipment required for the course of study [IRC Sec. 117(b)(2)]. The amount of an otherwise qualified grant awarded to a degree candidate is excludable (after considering the amount of any other grant also eligible for exclusion) up to the combined amount incurred for tuition and course-related expenses during the period to which the grant applies. Any excess amount of the grant is includible in income. No amount of a grant is excludable if the grant's terms earmark its use for other than tuition or course-related expenses (like room and board or meal allowances) or specify that the grant cannot be used for tuition or course-related expenses, even if the amount of the grant is less than the amount payable by the student for tuition or course-related expenses.

> ▶ **LIBERAL TAX RULE** Even if part of a scholarship is taxable under the latest rules, the student is entitled to a tax break. The taxable portion of the student's scholarship is considered "earned income" for purposes of the standard deduction. Thus, assuming your child who attends school has no other earnings, the full standard deduction—$3,600 in 1992—can be used to shelter the taxable scholarship.

However, your child probably cannot claim a personal exemption. Reason: A taxpayer is not entitled to the exemption ($2,300 in 1992) if he or she can be claimed as a dependent on someone else's return. As a result, if your child is your tax dependent, your child doesn't get a personal exemption. On the other hand, you are in for good tax news.

> ▶ **TAX DEDUCTION REMAINS** Under a longstanding rule, a student's scholarship has no effect on the dependency exemption claimed by his or her parents. Neither the taxable nor tax-exempt portion of a scholarship counts as support under the dependency deduction rules [¶1116(c)]. Since the scholarship is excluded from the equation, you can claim the dependency exemption even though your child's scholarship actually pays for most of his or her expenses. (You must, of course, provide more support than comes from your child himself and other nonscholarship sources.)

¶1526 SOCIAL SECURITY, UNEMPLOYMENT INSURANCE BENEFITS AND SIMILAR PAYMENTS

(a) Social Security Benefits. There's an exclusion for social security benefits. However, the exclusion is phased out above certain income levels. In any case, at least one-half of the benefits are excluded from gross income.

The portion of your social security benefits that are included in gross income is equal to the lesser of (1) one-half of the benefits you receive during the tax year, or (2) one-half of the excess of the sum of (a) your adjusted modified gross income plus (b) one-half of the social security benefits you receive over the base amount [IRC Sec. 86 (a), (b)].

In general, your adjusted modified gross income is your adjusted gross income plus any tax-exempt interest you receive. The base amount is $32,000 for married persons filing jointly, zero for married persons filing separately, and $25,000 for all other individuals.

Example 1: Mr. and Mrs. Smith, both age 69, have an adjusted gross income of $32,000 and $10,500 of social security benefits. They also have $2,000 of municipal bond interest. The amount of benefits includable in income is $3,625—the lesser of (a) or (b)—figured as follows:

(a)   50% of $10,500 (soc. sec. benefits) $5,250

(b)   Adjusted gross income $32,000

       Tax-exempt interest income   2,000

       50% of social security benefits . . . .   <u>5,250</u>

       Total $39,250

       Less base amount . . . .   <u>32,000</u>

       Excess   7,250

   50% of excess . . . .   <u>$3,625</u>

Example 2: Mr. and Mrs. Brown, both age 70, have an adjusted gross of $14,000 and $9,000 of social security benefits. Since their total adjusted gross is less than $32,000, none of their benefits is includible in income.

(b) Unemployment Compensation. All payments received as unemployment compensation are fully includible in gross income [IRC Sec. 85].

(c) Medicare Benefits. Basic Medicare benefits you receive under the Social Security Act are excluded from your gross income. Supplementary benefits (covering costs of doctors' services and other items not covered under basic Medicare) are also excluded since they are in the nature of medical insurance payments.[1] Employer-paid Medicare premiums are not income to an employee since these are considered contributions to employer accident or health plans.[2]

(d) Public Assistance Payments. Benefit payments from a general welfare fund in the interest of the general public, such as payments because of blindness or payments to crime victims, are excluded from gross income.[3]

¶ 1527   COMBAT PAY FOR PERSIAN GULF ARMED FORCES

An Executive Order was signed by President Bush on January 21, 1991, designating the Persian Gulf as a combat zone as of January 17, 1991. As a result, members of the armed forces who served in the Gulf could exclude some or all of their service pay from their 1991 gross incomes.

Enlisted personnel did not have to pay tax on any of their military pay for months during which they served at least one day on active duty in the combat area. Commissioned officers could exclude from their 1991 gross income the first $500 of pay for any part of a month they served in the combat area [IRC Sec. 112].

Personnel who were hospitalized as a result of combat service can continue to qualify for the exclusions for up to two years after the termination of combat.

Footnotes to Chapter 5

(For your added convenience, in brackets [] with the footnotes below, you will find citations to related paragraphs in the "RIA United Staxes Tax Reporter"(USTR), "CCH Federal Tax Reporter"(CCH) and "RIA Federal Tax Coordinator 2d"(FTC) multi-volume services.)

FOOTNOTE ¶ 1501 [USTR ¶ 614; CCH ¶ 5504; FTC ¶ J-1000].

FOOTNOTE ¶ 1502 [USTR ¶ 614.164; CCH ¶ 5504; FTC ¶ J-1000 et seq.].

FOOTNOTE ¶ 1503 [USTR ¶ 1034; CCH ¶ 6602; FTC ¶ J-3064].
(1) South Carolina v. Baker, 108 S. Ct. 1355, 61, AFTR 2d ¶ 88-995.
FOOTNOTE ¶ 1504 [USTR ¶ 1034; CCH ¶ 6607; FTC ¶ J-3060 et seq.].
FOOTNOTE ¶ 1506 [USTR ¶ 77,024; CCH ¶ 43,955; FTC ¶ J-4057].
FOOTNOTE ¶ 1507 [USTR ¶ 1014; CCH ¶ 6511; FTC ¶ J-4000 et seq.].
(1) Rev. Rul. 61-134, 1961-2 CB 250.
(2) Ducros v. Comm., 4 AFTR 2d 5856, 272 F2d 49.
FOOTNOTE ¶ 1508 [USTR ¶ 1014; CCH ¶ 6116; FTC ¶ J-4900 et seq.].
(1) London Shoe Co. v. Comm., 16 AFTR 1398, 80 F2d 230, cert. den.
FOOTNOTE ¶ 1509 [USTR ¶ 724; CCH ¶ 6116; FTC ¶ H-10508].
FOOTNOTE ¶ 1510 [USTR ¶ 724; CCH ¶ 5504.70; 6111 et seq.; FTC ¶ J-4054 et seq.].
(1) Rev. Rul. 91-14, 1991-1 CB 18.
(2) PL 85-56, 71 Stat. 122.
FOOTNOTE ¶ 1511 [USTR ¶ 794; CCH ¶ 6367; FTC ¶ H-1909; 1951].
FOOTNOTE ¶ 1515 [USTR ¶ 1054; CCH ¶ 6662; FTC ¶ H-2301 et seq.].
FOOTNOTE ¶ 1516 [USTR ¶ 1054; CCH ¶ 6711; FTC ¶ H-2321 et seq.].
FOOTNOTE ¶ 1518 [USTR ¶ 1024; CCH ¶ 6553.02; 6553.10; FTC ¶ J-6000].
FOOTNOTE ¶ 1519 [USTR ¶ 10,144; CCH ¶ 29,729; 29,742; FTC ¶ P-4101].

FOOTNOTE ¶ 1520 [USTR ¶ 1040; CCH ¶ 5900; FTC ¶ J-1300 et seq.; 5800 et seq.].
(1) Farmers' & Merchants Bk. v. Comm., 59 F2d 912, 11 AFTR 619.
(2) Rev. Rul. 74-77, 1974-1 CB 33.
(3) Sternberg, 32 BTA 1039.
(4) Rev. Rul. 84-108, 1984-2 CB 32.
(5) Rickel, 65 AFTR2d 90-800.
(6) Rev. Rul. 54-19, 1954-1 CB 179; Rev. Rul. 69-8, 1969-1 CB 219.
(7) Raytheon Prod. Corp. v. Comm., 144 F2d 110, 32 AFTR 1155.
(8) Burke, US S.Ct. No. 91-42 (5/6/92).
FOOTNOTE ¶ 1522 [USTR ¶ 724; CCH ¶ 6111 et seq.; FTC ¶ J-4400 et seq.].
(1) Rev. Rul. 71-435, 1971-2 CB 84.
FOOTNOTE ¶ 1523 [USTR ¶ 724; CCH ¶ 6111 et seq.; FTC ¶ H-2415; 2416].
FOOTNOTE ¶ 1524 [USTR ¶ 724; CCH ¶ 6100 et seq.; FTC ¶ J-4500 et seq.].
FOOTNOTE ¶ 1525 [USTR ¶ 1174; CCH ¶ 7183; FTC ¶ J-1230 et seq.].
FOOTNOTE ¶ 1526 [USTR ¶ 864; CCH ¶ 5504.1734; 5504.1742; 6412; 6421; 6803.30; FTC ¶ J-1430 et seq.].
(1) Rev. Rul. 70-341, 1970-2 CB 31.
(2) Rev. Rul. 67-360, 1967-2 CB 71.
(3) Rev. Rul. 71-425, 1971-2 CB 76.
FOOTNOTE ¶ 1527 [USTR ¶ 1122; CCH ¶ 7082; FTC ¶ H-1308 et seq.].

CHAPTER 6

GAIN OR LOSS—BASIS—RECOGNITION

GAIN OR LOSS IN GENERAL

Gain or loss is the difference between what you receive from a sale or exchange and the adjusted basis of the property you give up. In general, the starting point for calculating basis is your purchase price. (In some acquisitions, though, it may be the property's fair market value or the basis of the person from whom you acquired the property.) That figure is then adjusted if subsequent improvements have been made or depreciation deductions claimed. The difference between the final adjusted basis and what you received for the property determines your gain or loss. The next step is to determine whether the gain is taxable or the loss is deductible. This chapter discusses the factors that determine your basis for various types of property and the conditions under which gain or loss does—or does not—have immediate tax consequences. Chapter 7 explains the special rules that apply to involuntary conversions and the sale of a personal residence.

¶1600   FACTORS IN FIGURING GAIN OR LOSS

The following equations are used in determining the amount of your gain or loss on a sale or exchange:

$$\text{ADJUSTED BASIS} = \text{BASIS} + \text{ADDITIONS} - \text{REDUCTIONS}$$
$$\text{REALIZED GAIN} = \text{AMOUNT REALIZED} - \text{ADJUSTED BASIS}$$
$$\text{REALIZED LOSS} = \text{ADJUSTED BASIS} - \text{AMOUNT REALIZED}$$

The amount of realized gain (or loss) that is taxed (or deductible) is referred to as the recognized gain (or loss).

(a) Basis. Ordinarily, your basis is the purchase price of the property [¶1604]. However, in certain cases, you use another amount, such as the property's value as of a particular date [¶1610 et seq.].

(b) Adjusted Basis. To figure your adjusted basis, your original cost or other basis is increased or decreased by expenditures or tax writeoffs attributable to the property. Thus, you—

* *Add* expenditures or items chargeable to the capital account. These include improvements, purchase commissions, sales tax, freight charges to obtain the property, installation charges, legal costs for defending or perfecting title (including title insurance), surveying expenses and recording fees.[1] On the other hand, expenses that are written off currently are not added to basis.
* *Subtract* returns of capital. These include depreciation, depletion, obsolescence, recognized losses on involuntary conversions, deductible casualty losses, insurance reimbursements[2] [IRC Sec. 1016; Reg. Sec. 1.1016-1—10]. Important: You are never permitted to reduce the basis below zero.[3]

Example 1: Ms. King bought rental real estate for $400,000. She paid title and legal fees of $8,000. King has claimed $100,000 of depreciation deductions since she owned the property. In December 1992, King had new walls installed to subdivide an office suite in the building at a cost of $12,000. The property's adjusted basis is $320,000 as of January 1, 1993 ($400,000 + $8,000 - $100,000 + $12,000).

(c) Amount Realized. In most transactions, this is simply the cash price you receive or the sum of the cash plus the face amount of a note you take back as seller financing.

If you take other property as payment, your amount realized is the fair market value of the property you receive. Where cash changes hands in addition to other property, your amount realized is the fair market value of the property you receive, increased by any money you receive and decreased by any money you give in the exchange.[4]

If your amount realized on the sale exceeds your adjusted basis, you have a gain; if it is less, you have a loss [Reg. Sec. 1.1001-1(a)].

Example 2: Lincoln had a tractor with an adjusted basis of $2,000 and a fair market value of $8,000. Clyde had a car with a fair market value of $10,000. They exchanged vehicles, and Lincoln gave Clyde $2,000 in cash. Lincoln's amount realized on the exchange is $8,000 (the $10,000 fair market value received less the $2,000 cash given up). His gain is $6,000 (the $8,000 amount realized less his adjusted basis of $2,000).

Your buyer may agree to pay your personal obligations or assume or satisfy any outstanding encumbrances against the property. This is treated like an exchange of cash. Thus, your amount realized is *decreased* by the amount of any liabilities on the property you receive and *increased* by the amount of any liabilities on the property you give up [Reg. Sec. 1.1001-2].[5]

Example 3: Same facts as Example 2 except that Clyde's car is subject to an outstanding auto loan of $1,000, and Lincoln assumes the loan and pays only $1,000 in cash. Lincoln's amount realized is again $8,000—$10,000 property received, less both the $1,000 cash given up and the $1,000 debt assumed. His gain is again $6,000, computed as in Example 2.

Real estate taxes you owe on the date of sale and assumed or satisfied by your buyer are included in your amount realized [Reg. Sec. 1.1001-1(b)]. Your cost of transferring your property, such as selling expenses, reduces your amount realized.[6]

An employer paying for services with property realizes a gain to the extent that the fair market value of the property exceeds its adjusted basis on the date of the transfer. The value of the services the employer receives (amount realized) is considered equal to the fair market value of the property transferred.

(d) Capital Gains and Losses. From 1988 through 1990, gain from the sale or exchange of a capital asset [¶1801] was treated like ordinary income. However, since 1991, long-term capital gain (gain from capital assets held for more than one year) has been entitled to special tax treatment. The maximum tax rate on long-term gain is 28%, not the 31% that applies to other types of income [¶ 1808].

On the other hand, there are special restrictions that apply to capital losses. No more than $3,000 of a capital loss in excess of capital gain may be written off in a single year.

¶1601   RECOGNITION OF GAIN OR LOSS

Recognition means that the transaction is a taxable event. If a realized gain is fully recognized, the entire gain is taxable. A recognized loss is deductible, but capital losses are subject to annual deduction caps [¶1810]. Gain or loss from a sale or exchange is recognized unless a provision of the tax law exempts the transaction. These nonrecognition transactions are covered in ¶1610 et seq. and Chap. 7.

Recognized gain—nondeductible loss. In some situations, a gain is taxable, but a loss is not deductible. This rule applies to sales of "personal property," such as the sale of a family car or residence; "wash sales" (where identical securities are bought within 30 days of the sale) [¶2321]; and sales between related taxpayers [¶2323].

COST BASIS

¶1604   PROPERTY ACQUIRED BY PURCHASE

Your original basis in property is generally the purchase price or cost. The property's cost is the amount you pay for it, either in cash or other property, plus commissions and other expenses connected with the purchase [IRC Sec. 1012; Reg. Sec. 1.1012-1(a)]. Your basis in mortgaged property is the amount you pay plus the amount of the indebtedness. The mortgage is part of the buyer's basis and the amount the seller realizes whether or not the buyer assumes it, and regardless of whether the mortgage is recourse or non-recourse debt. Thus, your basis is not adjusted as you pay off a mortgage.

Example 1: Smith bought a house worth $260,000. She took the house subject to a $120,000 mortgage and paid $140,000 in cash. Smith's basis is $260,000.

Example 2: Same facts as Example 1, except that Smith has paid $20,000 of the mortgage. She then sells the house subject to the remaining mortgage and receives $200,000 in cash. The amount Smith realizes is $300,000 ($200,000 cash plus $100,000 mortgage). So she realizes a gain of $40,000 ($300,000 amount realized less $260,000 basis).

If you purchase an option to buy property and exercise the option, your basis in the property is the sum of the option's exercise price and your cost (or other basis) of the option.

Capitalized expenditures in buying, building or developing an asset are included in the asset's cost basis. (See the uniform capitalization rules at ¶2714.) Real estate taxes are figured as part of the property's cost if you assume the seller's obligation to pay them [IRC Sec. 1012; Reg. Sec. 1.1012-1]. When the "price" paid for property includes payments made for reasons other than acquisition (such as giving a gift to a family member, making a capital contribution to a related business, or shifting deductions), the amount in excess of fair market value is not part of your cost.[1]

NOTE: If property is bought under a deferred payment contract with interest deferred, not stated or at a low rate, a part of the price may be treated as interest. This "imputed" interest is not included in the property's basis [¶1216].

¶1605   TAXABLE EXCHANGES

There are two methods for finding the basis of property received in exchange for other property:
   1. The property's fair market value when received;[1] or
   2. The fair market value of the property given up, increased by payments made or decreased by payments received.[2]

Example 1: Ames traded his $7,200 car for a boat with a fair market value of $7,200. If the car's adjusted basis was $7,000, Ames has realized a $200 taxable gain on the exchange. His basis in the boat is $7,200. If Ames later sold the boat for $7,500, he would have a $300 gain.

➤ **OBSERVATION** The result will generally be the same under both methods. However, the result may be different if there is a nontaxable aspect to the transaction. In a part gift, part exchange, the property plus cash received is not equal to the value of the property given up.

Fair market value. Fair market value is the price a willing buyer and a willing seller would probably reach after bargaining, when neither is acting under compulsion and both have reasonable knowledge of relevant facts.[3] Property may have a fair market value even though no buyers presently exist.[4] However, there must be some assurance that the value is what a market would establish;[5] the value must be based on something more concrete than speculative assumptions.[6] And fair market value is not the price that would result from a forced sale.[7]

Actual sales of similar property on the open market provide reliable evidence of value. Stock exchange quotations are a prime example of this. Adjustments in value, though, may be required for large blocks of stock. Thus, the trading price for small transactions would not be conclusive in valuing very large interests.[8] The value of a closely held corporation depends on such factors as the corporation's financial condition, earnings capacity and the stock prices of companies that are traded on an exchange and are engaged in the same line of business.[9] Expert appraisers are often used to arrive at an asset's value.

Property acquired in trade-in. A dealer who sells new property and accepts used property in part payment has the option to include the used property in inventory. If placed into inventory, the basis of the traded-in property is equal to its bona fide selling price less direct selling costs [Reg. Sec. 1.471-2(c)]. If the trade-in is not put into inventory, its basis is equal to the fair market value given to it in the exchange for the new property.[10]

Automobile dealers may value used cars received as trade-ins at valuations listed in an official used car guide as the average wholesale prices for comparable cars.[11]

¶1606   PROPERTY RECEIVED AS PAYMENT FOR SERVICES

Your basis in property obtained in exchange for rendering services is the property's fair market value at the time of the exchange. This amount is also included in your gross income, the same as if the payment had been in cash [Reg. Sec. 1.61-2(d)(1)]. Your basis in restricted property received as payment for services is the sum of any amount you paid for the property plus any amount included in your gross income when the property is no longer subject to a substantial risk of forfeiture (¶1208(a)) [Reg. Sec. 1.83-4(b)].

¶1607   PROPERTY ACQUIRED BEFORE MARCH 1, 1913

Appreciation in value before March 1, 1913, is not taxed. Thus, the basis for determining gain can be different from the basis for figuring loss. The basis for gain is the greater of the property's fair market value on March 1, 1913 (with appropriate adjustments attributable to subsequent years), or the basis determined under the general rules. The fair market value on March 1, 1913, is not used to determine the basis if doing so would result in a loss [IRC Sec. 1053; Reg. Sec. 1.1053-1].

> **Example:** Property bought for $2,000 in 1912 was valued at $1,200 on March 1, 1913. The basis for gain or loss is $2,000. If the value on March 1, 1913, was $2,500, the basis for gain would be $2,500, but the basis for calculating loss would be $2,000.

OTHER TAX BASIS

¶1610   PROPERTY ACQUIRED BY GIFT

The basis of property you received as a gift depends on whether you have a gain or loss when you sell the property. You have gain if the amount realized exceeds the donor's basis. You have a loss if the amount realized is less than both the donor's basis and the property's fair market value at the time of the gift. These rules also apply to property acquired by a transfer to a trust. For gifts between spouses, see ¶1611.

(a) Figuring Basis for Gain. Your basis is the same as the donor's (or the last previous person by whom the property was not acquired by gift) basis had been [IRC Sec. 1015(a); Reg. Sec. 1.1015-1(a)(1)]. However, your basis may be increased by the amount of gift tax paid by the donor [see (d) below].

> ➤ **IMPORTANT** In general, the donor's basis is also used for computing depreciation, amortization and depletion, regardless of the property's fair market value at the time of the gift [Reg. Sec. 1.167(g)-1; 1.612-1].

Example 1: Mason bought bonds for $1,000. He gave them to Doran when their fair market value was $800. No gift tax was payable. If Doran sells the bonds for $1,200, his basis for calculating gain is $1,000. So he has a $200 gain.

(b) Figuring Basis for Loss. Your basis is the lesser of (1) the donor's basis (or the basis of the last previous person by whom the property was not acquired by gift) or (2) the property's fair market value at the time the gift is made [IRC Sec. 1015(a); Reg. Sec. 1.1015-1(a)(1)]. However, the basis may be increased for gift tax paid by the donor [see (d) below].

Example 2: Same facts as in Example 1, except that Doran sells the bonds for $700. His basis is the property's fair market value at the time of the gift: $800. That results in a $100 loss.

> ➤ **OBSERVATION** If the loss in value occurred in the donor's hands, you will not be permitted to take advantage of that loss for *loss* purposes. Yet it does decrease any *gain* you would otherwise realize on the property's disposition.

(c) Neither Gain nor Loss. Suppose the property's value at the time of the gift is less than the donor's basis, and you sell for an amount between those two amounts. Using the basis for finding a gain results in a loss, and using the basis for loss results in a gain. In that case, you have neither a gain nor a loss [Reg. Sec. 1.1015-1(a)].

Example 3: Assume the same facts as in Example 1, except that Doran sells the bonds for $900. His basis for gain is $1,000, which results in a loss. His basis for loss is $800, which results in a gain. Thus, Doran has neither gain nor loss.

> ➤ **OBSERVATION** If the figures in Example 1 had been reversed ($800 donor's basis and $1,000 value at the time of the gift), Doran would have had a $100 gain. Reason: His basis would have been $800.

(d) Adjustment for Gift Tax. In most cases, the basis for gift property is increased for gift taxes paid by the donor. The amount of the increase depends on when the gift was made.

Gifts after 1976. Your basis is increased by the portion of the gift tax attributable to the net appreciation in the value of the gift. Net appreciation is the excess of the fair market over the donor's adjusted basis immediately before the gift [IRC Sec. 1015(d)(6)]. The formula for computing the increase is as follows:

$$\text{Gift tax paid} \quad \times \quad \frac{\text{Fair market value - Adjusted basis}}{\text{Fair market value}}$$

Gifts after September 1, 1958, and before 1977. The basis is increased by the amount of gift tax paid, but not above the fair market value of the property at the time of the gift [IRC Sec. 1015(d)(1)(A); Reg. Sec. 1.1015-5(a)].

Gifts before September 2, 1958. Your basis is increased by the amount of gift tax paid. However, the increase cannot be greater than the difference between the property's fair market value and the donor's basis at the time the gift was made [IRC Sec. 1015(d)(1)(B); Reg. Sec. 1.1015-5(a)].

¶1611   PROPERTY TRANSFERS BETWEEN SPOUSES OR INCIDENT TO DIVORCE

No gain or loss is recognized on a property transfer between spouses. The recipient carries over the transferor's basis. The same rule applies to a property transfer between spouses (or former spouses) that is incident to divorce. The transfer is treated as a gift. Gain or loss is not recognized to the transferor. The transferee receives the property at the transferor's basis (whether the property has appreciated or depreciated in value) [IRC Sec. 1041(a),(b); Temp. Reg. Sec. 1.1041-1T].

A transfer is incident to a divorce if the transfer: (1) occurs within one year after the date on which the marriage ceases or (2) is related to the divorce [IRC Sec. 1041(c); Temp. Reg. Sec. 1.1041-1T(b)].

This no-tax rule applies whether the transfer is for relinquishing marital rights, for cash or other property, for assuming liabilities in excess of basis, or for other consideration and is intended to apply to any indebtedness which is discharged.

> **Example:** Pursuant to their divorce, Mr. Brown transfers shares of stock with a market value of $200,000. His basis in the shares was $150,000. Mr. Brown would not have a taxable gain on the transfer. On the other hand, Mrs. Brown would carry over his basis. Thus, she would have a $50,000 taxable gain if she sold them right away.

A transfer to a nonresident alien spouse (or former spouse) is not covered by this rule [IRC Sec. 1041(d)].

The no-tax rule for transfers incident to divorce is effective for transfers after July 18, 1984. However, transfers made under an instrument in effect on or before that date are tax-free if both spouses or former spouses elect it. In addition, both spouses can jointly elect no-tax treatment for all transfers made after December 31, 1983 [Temp. Reg. Sec. 1.1041-1T(f)].

A transferor must recognize gain under a transfer in trust incident to divorce, to the extent that liabilities assumed by the trust, plus the liabilities to which the property is subject, exceed the transferor's basis. The transferee's basis, though, is increased when the transferor is taxed on gain [IRC Sec. 1041(e)].

¶1612   PROPERTY ACQUIRED FROM A DECEDENT

Generally, if you inherit property, your basis in the property is its fair market value on the date of the decedent's death. However, if the executor elects the alternate valuation date for estate tax purposes [see (a) below], your basis is the property's value as of that date [IRC Sec. 1014(a); Reg. Sec. 1.1014-1(a)].

Example 1: Mrs. Horton died on February 12, 1992, leaving certain stock to her son, Clifford. Mrs. Horton bought the stock in 1984 for $10,000. When she died, it was worth $8,000. The stock was not actually distributed to Clifford until April 16, 1992, when it was worth $8,500. Clifford's basis in the stock is $8,000.

A special rule applies to inherited property that you (or your spouse) gave to the decedent within one year of death. If the property had appreciated in value prior to being given, your (or your spouse's) basis is the same as the decedent's basis had been [IRC Sec. 1014(e)].

Example 2: Jay's basis in XYZ stock is $10,000. The stock is presently worth $120,000. Jay gives the stock to his terminally ill grandmother, Tessie—for whom Jay is the sole heir. Tessie's basis in the stock is $10,000, the same as Jay's. If Tessie dies within a year of the gift, Jay will reacquire the stock with the $10,000 basis. If she survives the year, the inherited stock gets a step-up in basis to its value at the time of Tessie's demise.

If you inherit mortgaged property and don't assume the mortgage, there is no reduction in the property's fair market value for the debt.[1] But if you sell the property, the amount of the outstanding mortgage assumed by the purchaser is included in calculating your amount realized.

In general, a property's fair market value is the valuation placed on it for the federal estate tax. Or if the estate is not subject to estate tax, the value for the state inheritance tax [Reg. Sec. 1.1014-3(a)]. However, a higher value may be used, if it can be proven.[2]

➤ **OBSERVATION** If you inherit property through an estate that did not need to file an estate or inheritance tax return, take steps to substantiate the property's date-of-death value right away. For example, if the property is publicly traded stock, record the market quotation for the day; if it's real estate, get a professional appraisal. That will make it easier to calculate your taxable gain when you sell the property years in the future— when it would otherwise be difficult to reconstruct what the value had been at the decedent's death.

The basis of property received in settlement of a cash legacy is its fair market value on the date of receipt instead of the date of decedent's death. Such property is not acquired from the decedent. It is received in a transaction treated as a sale or other disposition by the executor [Reg. Sec. 1.1014-4(a)(3)].

(a) Alternate Valuation Date. The alternate valuation date allows property to be valued at a date other than the date of death. If the alternate date is elected, it covers *all* the property in the estate. Generally, this election allows estate property to be valued six months after the date of death [IRC Sec. 2032].

➤ **IMPORTANT** The alternate valuation date can be elected only if both the value of the gross estate and the combined estate and generation-skipping transfer taxes (after subtracting the unified credit) are reduced due to the election [IRC Sec. 2032(c)]. Thus, you cannot use the alternate valuation date merely to get a greater step-up in basis—and thereby reduce your gain on a future sale of the inherited property. And you cannot use the alternate valuation date if the estate is exempt from estate tax.

The following special rules apply when the alternate valuation date has been elected:

- Any property distributed, sold, exchanged or otherwise disposed of within six months after the decedent's death is valued as of the date of disposition [IRC Sec. 2032(a)(1)].
- If the valuation of a property interest is affected by the mere lapse of time (i.e., patents, life estates, remainders, reversions), it is valued as of the date of the decedent's death, with an adjustment made for any difference in its value not due to the lapse of time [IRC Sec. 2032(a)(3)].

Example 3: Charlie owned a patent with an unexpired term of ten years (120 months) and a value of $100,000 when he died. The patent was sold three months after his death for only $65,000 (due to the lapse of time and other causes). The value of the patent is determined as follows:

Value of patent on date of death	$100,000
Difference between value on date of death and date of sale ($100,000 - $65,000)	$35,000
Portion of difference due to three-month lapse of time (3/120 x $100,000) . 2,500	
Portion of difference due to reasons other than mere lapse of time	32,500
Adjusted value of patent	$67,500

(b) Joint Ownership. When property is owned jointly, the surviving owner automatically gets ownership of the decedent's interest in it. In general, your basis in the part of the property that has been included in the decedent's estate is its fair market value at the date of the death (or alternate valuation date). Your basis in the part of the property you owned all along is unaffected by the decedent's death.

> ➤ **ESTATE TAX RULE** For joint tenancies, other than between spouses, the full value of the property is included in the decedent's estate, except to the extent that the survivor can show that he or she paid part of the property's cost [IRC Sec. 2040(a)]. If the decedent paid the entire cost, the entire value is included in the decedent's estate, and the survivor's entire basis in the property is based on the date of death value.

Example 4: Frank and George bought real estate as joint tenants with right of survivorship for $10,000. Each paid one-half of the cost. When Frank died, the property was worth $15,000. George's basis in the property after Frank's death is $12,500 (his $5,000 cost basis for one-half of the property plus the $7,500 value of the portion included in Frank's estate).

Example 5: Same facts as Example 4, except Frank paid the entire cost. Thus, the property's full value is included in his estate. George's basis is $15,000.

Property owned jointly by a married couple (with no other joint owners) is treated differently. One-half of the property is included in the decedent-spouse's estate—without any inquiry into who paid for it [IRC Sec. 2040(b)].

Example 6: Same facts as Example 5, except Frank bought the property with himself and his wife as the only joint owners. Upon Frank's death, his widow's basis would be $12,500—the same as in Example 4.

TAX-FREE EXCHANGES

¶1614   NONTAXABLE EXCHANGES IN GENERAL

In nontaxable exchanges, you defer paying tax on gain or getting a tax writeoff for loss. For example, an exchange of one piece of business or investment property for another similar one is not a taxable event—even if your basis in the old property was zero due to depreciation deductions. For tax purposes, the exchange is simply a change of form. And recognition of gain is deferred until you sell the property received in the exchange.

In an even tax-free exchange of properties, your basis in the new property is the same as your basis had been in the property given up for it, not the new property's fair market value. When cash or dissimilar property (referred to as "boot") changes hands as part of the exchange, you may have to recognize a gain or loss. In that case, an adjustment must be made to your basis (¶1615) [IRC Sec. 1031].

> ➤ **OBSERVATION** To qualify for nonrecognition treatment as an exchange, there must be a direct transfer of properties. Receiving cash in exchange for the old property and then using the funds to buy new property does not qualify. However, in two instances—involuntary conversions and sales of a residence—you can defer tax on cash by purchasing new property [Ch. 7].

(a) Like-Kind Property. An exchange of property held for investment or business use for other investment or business property can qualify for nonrecognition treatment. Even though you may realize a gain or loss on the exchange, it will not be taxed at that time. Instead, the property you receive is treated as a continuation of your old investment. To qualify for this tax break, the original and replacement properties must be *like-kind* in nature or character. The grade or quality of the properties need not be the same. Business property may be exchanged for property held for investment and vice versa [IRC Sec. 1031; Reg. Sec. 1.1031(a)-1(a)]. Property held for personal purposes does not qualify. However, if property is put to both business and personal use, the business part qualifies for tax-free treatment [¶1622(b)].

> **NOTE:** Property held primarily for sale does not qualify for the like-kind exchange tax break [IRC Sec. 1031(a)(2)(A)]. In determining whether property has been held for resale or as business or investment property, your purpose forf acquiring and holding the property is controlling. Thus, holding property for rental indicates that it is business or investment property.[1]

> **Example 1:** Lester has a car he uses solely for business driving. He trades it with OK Used Cars, Inc., for a different vehicle. Lester does not recognize gain or loss since his exchange is of business property. However, OK Used Cars does not qualify for nonrecognition since it exchanges inventory.

Tangible personal property. Depreciable tangible personal property (e.g., office furniture, equipment, etc.) can be exchanged tax-free if the exchanged assets are *either* like-kind or like-class. The IRS has issued final regulations in this area that generally apply to exchanges occurring on or after April 11, 1991 [Reg. Sec. 1.1031(a)-2].

Like-class. Under the final regulations, the first step in determining if the business or investment properties are like-class is to decide whether they fall in the same "General Asset Class." There are 13 classes for assets frequently used in business [Reg. Sec. 1.1031(a)-2(b)(2)]. The classes range from a general class for office furniture, fixtures and equipment to a specific class for railroad cars and locomotives. If both properties are in the same class, the properties are like-class. If one property is in one of the classes and the other is in a different class or is not included in any of the classes, the properties are not like-class.

If neither of the exchanged properties falls into a General Asset Class, you can look further to determine if they fall in the same Product Class. The Product Classes are derived from the Standard Industrial Classifications set up by the Office of Management and Budget; they are not listed in IRS regulations [Reg. Sec. 1.1031(a)-2(b)(3)].

If neither of the properties falls in an asset class or in a product class, the determination of whether they are like-class is based on all the facts or circumstances.

> **NOTE:** The goodwill of one business is never like-kind to that of another business [Reg Sec. 1.1031(a)-2(c)(2)].

Multiple property exchanges. The tax-free treatment of multiple property exchanges (e.g., business-for-business swaps) must be determined on a property-by-property basis. However, you can separate the properties transferred and the properties received into exchange groups that include all properties of like-kind or like-class. The like-kind exchange rules are then applied separately to each exchange group to determine if any gain is required to be recognized on the exchange [Reg. Sec. 1.1031(f)-1].

Money or other property that is not eligible for tax-free treatment is placed in a residual group. Gain or loss is recognized on these residual assets under the general rules for sale and exchanges.

If a multiple property exchange also involves an assumption of liabilities, all liabilities you assumed are offset against your liabilities that are assumed by the other party. All liabilities are netted, even if some liabilities are secured by specific property in an exchange group. If you assume more liabilities than you are relieved of, the excess liabilities increase your basis in your exchange group properties. If you are relieved of more liabilities than you assume, the excess decreases your basis inthe residual group properties.

Exchanges that qualify for nonrecognition include: apartment house for building lots; city real estate for ranch; leasehold of 30 years or more for real estate; improved for unimproved real estate [Reg. Sec. 1.1031(a)-1(c)].

Exchanges that do not qualify for nonrecognition include: exchanging livestock of different sexes; realty for personalty; conversion of U.S. currency into foreign currency and its reconversion;[2] exchange of gold bullion for silver bullion, each held for investment[3] [IRC Sec. 1031(e); Reg. Sec. 1.1031(e)-1].

With respect to exchanges made after July 10, 1989, real property located in the U.S. and real property located outside the U.S. are not like-kind property [IRC Sec. 1031(h)].

Shares of stock, bonds, notes and other securities, partnership interests, inventory and certificates of trust or beneficial interests are not eligible for nonrecognition tax treatment [IRC Sec. 1031(a)(2)].

(b) Deferred Exchanges. There may be a time lag between your giving up property and receiving the like-kind asset in exchange. However, to qualify for nonrecognition, the like-kind property that will be received must be *identified* within 45 days after the transferred property is relinquished. In addition, you must receive that property (i.e., complete the transaction) by the earlier of (1) 180 days after the date on which you gave up your old property or (2) the due date for your tax return, including extensions [IRC Sec. 1031(a)(3)].

(c) Three-Party Exchanges. The taxpayer who wants your property may not own property that is acceptable to you. Therefore, the taxpayer can acquire property you want from a third party and then enter into a tax-free swap with you. More simply, though, the third party can transfer the new property directly to you; the taxpayer who is acquiring your property does not have to first take title to the third party's property and then transfer it to you.[4]

> **Example 2:** John Fickleton holds Blackacre, real property used in his business. He enters into a contract with Roy Ripleton to transfer Blackacre for Whiteacre, which is owned by Sarah Davis. Roy purchases Whiteacre and directs Sarah to transfer it directly to John, who then holds it for productive use in his business. John pays no income tax on the exchange.

(d) Exchanges Between Related Persons. A like-kind exchange between related persons made after July 10, 1989, does not qualify for nonrecognition treatment if either party disposes of the like-kind property within two years of the date of the last exchange transfer. In that case, any gain or allowable loss not recognized at the time of the original exchange is recognized as when the subsequent disposition takes place.

This related-person rule does not apply if the disposition is due to the death of either party. Nor does it apply to an involuntary conversion, as long as the original exchange occurred before the threat or imminence of the conversion. The related-person rule can also be overcome by showing that neither the original exchange nor the subsequent disposition had federal income tax avoidance as one of its principal purposes [IRC Sec. 1031(f)].

Example 3: Robert owned a factory building worth $1 million in Newfield County, with a basis of $250,000. His brother, Gene, owned a factory in Greene County. Gene's factory was also worth $1 million, but its basis was $700,000. Robert and Gene exchanged factories in a tax-free exchange. Thirteen months later, Gene sold his factory for $1 million. Gene is taxed on his $300,00 gain. Robert also must pay tax on $750,000 gain. Robert's basis in the factory he owns becomes $1 million.

¶1615   EFFECT OF GIVING OR RECEIVING "BOOT"

Boot is money or unlike property that is transferred along with an exchange. Relief from a mortgage obligation on the property transferred can also be boot [¶1616]. The giving or receiving of boot can result in the recognition of gain (and tax to pay) in an otherwise nontaxable exchange [Reg. Sec. 1.1031(d)-1(e)]. Boot also affects the basis of the property you acquired. If you receive two or more properties, their combined basis is apportioned according to their relative fair market values on the date of the exchange [Reg. Sec. 1.1031(d)-1(d)].

(a) Exchange With Boot Given. If you give boot, your basis in the acquired property is the same as the basis of the property you give (adjusted to the exchange date), increased by (1) your basis in any boot given and (2) gain recognized. Your basis in the acquired property is decreased by any loss recognized on the exchange [Reg. Sec. 1.1031(d)-1].

Example 1: Henry exchanged a delivery truck with a $6,000 adjusted basis plus $8,000 cash for a newer truck worth $16,000. Henry has a realized gain of $2,000. However, none of it is recognized because the transaction qualifies as a like-kind exchange of business property. His basis in the new truck is $14,000 ($6,000 plus $8,000).

Suppose the boot you give is non-like-kind property, rather than cash. In that case, you recognize gain or loss to the extent the non-like-kind property's fair market value differs from its basis.

NOTE: Only loss attributable to the non-like-kind property is recognized. Loss on the like-kind property exchanged is not deductible.

Example 2: Same facts as Example 1, except Henry gives up stock worth $8,000 instead of cash. If his basis in the stock is $7,000, he recognizes a gain of $1,000. His basis in the new truck is still $14,000 ($6,000 + 7,000 + 1,000). Now assume Henry's basis in the stock is $9,000. He has a recognized loss of $1,000, but his basis in the new truck remains $14,000 ($6,000 + $9,000 - $1,000).

(b) Exchange With Boot Received. You recognize gain to the extent you receive boot. On the other hand, you don't recognize loss [IRC Sec. 351(b), 1031(b), (c); Reg. Sec. 1.351-2, 1.1031(b)-1(a), -1(c)].

Cash boot. If the boot you receive is entirely money, your basis in the property acquired is your basis in the property you transferred (adjusted to the exchange date) decreased by the money you received and increased by the amount of gain you recognized.

Example 3: Katherine exchanges investment real estate with an adjusted basis of $40,000 for similar property with a fair market value of $60,000 plus $10,000 cash. She recognizes $10,000 of the gain. Katherine's basis in the new property is $40,000 ($40,000 - $10,000 + $10,000).

Example 4: Same facts as Example 3, except Katherine's adjusted basis in the property she is giving up is $75,000. She realizes a nondeductible $5,000 loss. Her basis in the new property is $65,000 ($75,000 - $10,000).

Noncash boot. If you receive non-like-kind property as boot, your basis must be apportioned between the various properties you acquire. Each non-like-kind property's basis is equal to its fair market value.

> **Example 5:** Mary exchanges a machine she uses in her business with an adjusted basis of $8,000 for a similar machine having a fair market value of $9,000, $1,000 in cash and a television set for her home. The television has a fair market value of $500. Mary has a realized gain of $2,500. She recognizes $1,500 of it—the cash and value of the television. Her combined basis in the machine and television is $8,500 ($8,000 - 1,000 + $1,500). The television is assigned a basis of $500, its fair market value. That leaves $8,000 to be apportioned as the machine's basis.

¶1616   EXCHANGE OF MORTGAGED PROPERTY

If you transfer mortgaged property in a tax-free exchange, the mortgage debt you are relieved from paying is treated as cash received in figuring your recognized gain. This is true whether the transferee takes the property subject to a mortgage or assumes personal liability for it.

The amount of boot you give on the exchange, whether it be money, property or a receipt by you of property subject to liabilities or mortgages, reduces the amount of liabilities or mortgages that are treated as boot you receive on the exchange. However, if you assume or take subject to a mortgage that exceeds the mortgage the other party assumes or takes subject to, the excess does not reduce any other boot received by you [IRC Sec. 1031(d); Reg. Sec. 1.1031(d)-2].

> **Example 1:** Roe owns a ranch with an adjusted basis of $50,000 and subject to a $10,000 mortgage. He exchanges it for a farm worth $65,000, the transferee assuming the mortgage. Roe realizes a gain of $25,000, but only $10,000 of the gain is recognized (the mortgage is treated as cash):
>
> | | |
> |---|---:|
> | Value of property received . . . . | $65,000 |
> | Mortgage on property exchanged . . . . | 10,000 |
> | Total consideration received . . . . | $75,000 |
> | Less: Adjusted basis of property transferred . . . . | 50,000 |
> | Gain realized . . . . | $25,000 |

> **Example 2:** The facts are the same as in Example 1, except that the farm Roe received is subject to a mortgage of $6,000 which he assumed. Roe realized a gain of $19,000 on the exchange, but only $4,000 of that gain is recognized. The gain is computed as follows:
>
> | | | |
> |---|---:|---:|
> | Value of property received . . . . | | $65,000 |
> | Mortgage on property exchanged, assumed by transferee . . . . | | 10,000 |
> | Total consideration received . . . . | | $75,000 |
> | Less: Adjusted basis of property transferred . . . . | $50,000 | |
> | Mortgage on property received . . . . | 6,000 | 56,000 |
> | Gain realized . . . . | | $19,000 |

The gain is recognized to the extent of $4,000 ($10,000 mortgage assumed by transferee less $6,000 mortgage assumed by transferor Roe).

If the transfer is to a controlled corporation, the mortgage is not considered boot received by the transferor in determining his recognized gain, unless the transaction lacks a real business purpose or is merely to avoid tax [IRC Sec. 357; Reg. Sec. 1.357-1]. See also ¶1619.

¶1617   EXCHANGE OF INSURANCE POLICIES

You carry over your basis and recognize no gain nor loss on the exchange of—

- A life insurance contract for another life insurance contract or for endowment contract;
- An endowment insurance contract for another endowment insurance contract providing regular payments starting at a date not later than the starting date under the old contract, or for an annuity contract;
- One annuity contract for another, whether or not the issuer of the contract received in exchange is the same as the issuer of the original contract[1] [IRC Sec. 1035(a); Reg. Sec. 1035-1].

NOTE: If you receive cash or other property in addition to the new contract, the rules in ¶1615 apply.

You recognize gain or loss, and adjust your basis accordingly, on an exchange of (1) an endowment or annuity contract for a life insurance contract; and (2) an annuity contract for an endowment contract [Reg. Sec. 1.1035-1(c)].

¶1618   SECURITIES FOR SECURITIES OF SAME CORPORATION

You do not recognize gain nor loss on an exchange of common for common or preferred for preferred stock in the same corporation. It does not matter whether the stock is voting or nonvoting. The exchange is nontaxable whether it is between a stockholder and the corporation or between two individual stockholders [IRC Sec. 1036; Reg. Sec. 1.1036-1]. Certain exchanges between a shareholder and the corporation are treated as a reorganization [¶3200 et seq.].

Nontaxable Exchanges

Restricted stock for unrestricted stock in the same corporation.[1]

Exercising right found in corporate bond to convert it into shares of that corporation's stock.[2] However, exercising the right to convert into stock of another corporation is a taxable exchange.[3]

Voting trust certificates turned in for common stock.[4]

Converting joint tenancy in corporate stock to tenancy in common; severing joint tenancy in corporate stock under partition action.[5]

Taxable Exchanges

Stock exchanged for bonds.
Preferred stock exchanged for common.[6] Common

stock of one corporation exchanged for common stock in another.

¶1619   TRANSFER OF PROPERTY TO CORPORATION
CONTROLLED BY TRANSFEROR

The nonrecognition rule applies to property transfers made by a controlling shareholder (or group of shareholders who collectively own enough shares to be in control) to the company. No gain or loss is recognized if the property is transferred solely in exchange for stock of that corporation and immediately after the exchange, the transferor(s) is in control of the corporation. Before October 3, 1989, other securities received the same nonrecognition treatment as stock, but debt obligations which did not qualify as securities were treated as boot. For transfers made after October 2, 1989, all non-stock securities are treated as boot [IRC Sec. 351(a); Reg. Sec. 1.351-1].

Control. To be in control of a corporation, the group of investors must own, immediately after the exchange, at least 80% of the total combined voting power of all classes of stock entitled to vote and at least 80% of the outstanding shares of each class of nonvoting stock outstanding [IRC Sec. 368(c); Reg. Sec. 1.351-1(a)].

> **Example 1:** Hunter owned 2,000 of the 3,000 shares of voting common stock of Homer Corporation, and 85 of the 100 shares of nonvoting preferred stock. Hunter transfers property to the corporation, in return for which the corporation gives him 7,000 shares of newly issued common stock. No gain is recognized because Hunter is now in control of the corporation. He owns 90% of the voting stock (9,000 of 10,000) and 85% of the other class of stock (85 of 100).

> **Example 2:** When starting up a corporation, Whitman contributed a building worth $200,000 (his basis in it is $50,000) in exchange for 200 shares of stock, and Bloom contributed equipment worth $100,000 in exchange for 100 shares. The corporation issued no other stock at that time. No gain or loss is recognized on the transaction since Whitman and Bloom are controlling shareholders after the exchange.

The nonrecognition provision applies only to contributed "property."[1] This does not include services rendered to the corporation. Nor does it include unsecured debts and claims against the corporation for accrued but unpaid interest on a debt [IRC Sec. 351(d)].

> **Example 3:** Smythe contributed property worth $4,000 and services worth $6,000 in exchange for 10 shares of stock with a fair market value of $10,000. If she is a controlling shareholder, Smythe would owe tax on the $6,000 of stock received in exchange for services, but not on the stock she got for the property.

Disproportionate exchanges. When more than one person transfers property, the stock they receive need not be in the same proportion as the property they contribute. However, the transaction will be recharacterized, according to its true nature, as though (1) the exchanges had been proportionate, and (2) the shareholder who received stock of lesser value than the property transferred made a gift or paid compensation or extinguished a debt to the shareholder who received the larger amount [Reg. Sec. 1.351-1(b)].

> **Example 4:** Alex and Ben organize a corporation with 1,000 shares of common stock. Alex transfers property worth $10,000 in exchange for 200 shares of stock while Ben transfers property worth $10,000 to the corporation in exchange for 800 shares of stock. No gain or loss is recognized. However, Alex is deemed to have transferred 300 shares (worth $6,000) to Ben. If Ben had worked for Alex, the disproportionate exchange would be taxed as compensation. If, say, Ben were Alex's son and the deemed transfer was gratuitous, it would be treated as a gift.

Corporation assumes shareholder's liability. The exchange is still tax-free even if the corporation assumes or acquires the property subject to a mortgage or assumes your liability. However, there are some exceptions. If the assumption has no real business purpose or the purpose is tax avoidance, the total liability is treated as a cash payment by the corporation. And if the total liabilities assumed plus amount of liability to which the property is subject exceeds your basis in the transferred property, the excess is treated as a gain from the sale of the property [IRC Sec. 357; Reg. Sec. 1.357-1, -2].

> **Example 5:** Baker transfers property with a $5,000 adjusted basis to his controlled corporation in exchange for stock worth $6,000. The corporation agrees to assume a $3,000 liability on the property and gives Baker $1,000 of cash. Thus, Baker received consideration worth $10,000. His realized gain is $4,000. But his recognized gain is $1,000 (cash received). If the exchange is tax-motivated, though, Baker's recognized gain is $4,000 (cash plus liability assumed).

Exchange with investment company. Gain or loss is recognized if you diversify your interests by transferring your property to an investment company. An investment company is a regulated investment company, a real estate investment trust or a corporation with substantial investment property [IRC Sec. 351(e); Reg. Sec. 1.351-1(c)(1)].

Basis determination. Your basis in the stock received is the same as the basis of the property exchanged, *increased* by any gain recognized on the transaction, and *decreased* by the fair market value of any other property or money you received in the exchange and any loss you recognized on the exchange [IRC Sec. 358(a); Reg. Sec. 1.358-1].

> **Example 6:** Trent transfers property to Sutton Corporation in exchange for its controlling stock worth $150,000. Trent's adjusted basis in the property was $100,000. His basis in the stock is $100,000.

> **Example 7:** Same facts as Example 6, except that Sutton gives Trent $5,000 in addition to the stock. Trent has a recognized gain of $5,000 (since the money is not covered by the nonrecognition provision). His basis in the stock is still $100,000 ($100,000 basis in stock less $5,000 cash received plus $5,000 recognized gain).

If the corporation receives property subject to a mortgage or assumes a liability, the person who transferred the property treats the liability as money. Thus, he subtracts it in figuring his basis [IRC Sec. 358(d)(1); Reg. Sec. 1.358-3]. Transfers of liabilities which would be deductible by the shareholder when paid (e.g., accounts payable) or of certain liquidating payments to a retiring partner [¶3429(b)] are not counted as liabilities [IRC Sec. 357(c)(3), 358(d)(2)].

> **Example 8:** Smith transferred property with an adjusted basis of $500,000 and subject to a mortgage of $100,000 to a controlled corporation in a nontaxable exchange. He received stock worth $550,000. His basis for the stock is $400,000 (the $500,000 adjusted basis of the property transferred less the $100,000 mortgage).

Corporation's basis. The corporation's basis in the property acquired from a controlling shareholder is the shareholder's basis in the property, increased by any gain recognized by the shareholder on the exchange [IRC Sec. 362].

Filing requirement. Both the shareholder and controlled corporation taking part in the exchange must file a statement describing the pertinent facts with their income tax returns for the year of the exchange [Reg. Sec. 1.351-3].

IDENTIFICATION OF BASIS

¶1622   **ALLOCATING BASIS**

Generally, when you purchase various kinds of property for a lump sum, your cost or other basis must be allocated among the assets in order to calculate depreciation deductions and gain or loss upon the disposition of each asset. The gain or loss on each part is the difference between the selling price and the basis allocated to that part [Reg. Sec. 1.61-6]. The allocation is usually made according to the relative value of each part in relation to the value of the whole.[1] If allocation is impractical, no gain or loss is realized until the cost of the entire property is recovered.[2]

(a) Corporate Securities Bought as a Unit. Suppose you purchase different classes of stock for a single lump-sum price. When practicable, the lump-sum is allocated in proportion to each security's respective value at the time of acquisition.[3] For a block of the same securities, the allocation is pro rata.[4]

If no reasonably accurate method of allocation exists, the purchased securities are treated as a unit for computing gain or loss. In particular, this would tend to occur with securities that are required to be resold as a unit.[5]

(b) Mixed-Use Property. When you put property to both personal and business/investment use, a basis allocation is required upon the disposition of the property. If you sell or trade in the property, the amount received for it is also allocated in the same manner. Thus, the disposition is treated as two separate transactions. As a result, you may have a gain on the depreciable business/investment portion with an adjusted basis, and a loss on the nondepreciable personal part of the property with a cost basis. This occurs most commonly when you use a car for both business and personal driving, use part of a home as a business office or own a multi-family home (part of which is used as a personal residence and the remainder as rental property).

> **NOTE:** In the case of a trade-in, a special rule applies in figuring the basis in the new car. You must recalculate your basis in the old car as if it had been used 100% for business—and depreciated accordingly. This increases the unrecognized gain on the trade-in and lowers the basis for your new car. The new car's basis is the purchase price less your unrecognized gain on the trade-in.

A gain you realize on the personal part is taxable, but a loss on that part is not deductible [IRC Sec. 165(c)].

> **Example 1:** Ms. Robinson purchased a car for $10,000. She used it 75% for business driving. Thus, her cost basis in the business portion of the car is $7,500, and her cost basis in the personal portion is $2,500. She has claimed $7,500 of depreciation deductions on account of business use. Therefore, her adjusted basis in the business portion is zero. Robinson sells the car for $2,000—$1,500 allocable to the business portion of the car and $500 to the personal portion. She has a $1,500 taxable gain on the disposition of the business part of the car and a $2,000 nondeductible loss ($2,500 basis less $500 sales proceeds) on the personal part.

> **Example 2:** Same facts as Example 1, except that Robinson trades in the car towards a new one selling for $12,000. She receives a $2,000 trade-in allowance and pays $10,000 in cash. New result: Assuming Robinson uses the new car at least 75% for business, the trade-in is a tax-free exchange of like-kind business property. Thus, she is not taxed on the gain. However, her basis in the new car is $10,000 ($12,000 less $2,000, since depreciation on the old car is computed as if it had a 100% business use). The $2,000 nondeductible loss has no effect on her basis in the new car.

> **Example 3:** Same facts as Example 2, except that Robinson uses the new car only 65% for business, instead of the 75% business use of the car she has traded in. Thus, 10% of the trade-in allowance is traceable to business property that is not being exchanged for like-kind property. Robinson is taxed on that portion of the gain—or $200. Her basis in the new car is $10,200 ($12,000 less $1,800 unrecognized gain).

(c) Bargain Sale to Charity. A basis allocation is required if you sell or exchange property to a qualified charitable organization for less than its fair market value. The allocation determines the amount of gain or loss on the transaction and the deductible charitable contribution [¶1917(d)].

(d) Stock Splits and Dividends. The additional shares of stock you receive on account of a stock split or dividend is not a taxable event. It generally does, though, require an allocation of your basis in the original shares among all the shares you come to own (¶1223) [IRC Sec. 307].

(e) Term Interests and Remainders. In general, when you sell a term interest (term of years, life interest or income interest in a trust) acquired by a gift or from a decedent, your basis for determining gain or loss is zero. Thus, the entire amount you realize from selling such an interest is a gain. However, the general rules for calculating basis apply to a term interest purchased for value or sold in the same transaction as the rest of the interests in the property (e.g., you inherit real estate and sell the right to use it for a term of years and the remainder interest to two separate individuals, but at the same time). In other words, both interests get a share of your basis [IRC Sec. 1001(e); Reg. Sec. 1.1001-1].

When a property's total basis is divided between term and remainder interests, the allocation is based on the relative values of each. IRS tables [Reg. Sec. 20.2031-7(f)] that take into account the length of the term (using life expectancies for life interests) or the passage of time until the remainder becomes a present interest are used. Purchased term interests undergo basis reductions on account of the passage of time. The cost basis is amortized over the length of the term [Reg. Sec. 1.1014-5]. The amortization deductions can offset taxable income from the property.

> **Example 4:** Patricia inherits a lifetime income interest. She sells it to Brian for $100,000. Patricia's gain is the full $100,000 since her basis had been zero. Brian's basis is $100,000. He recovers that basis through amortization deductions over Patricia's life expectancy. These amortization deductions offset income Brian receives from the property. The deductions also reduce his basis.

(f) Goodwill. A special rule applies when you buy a group of assets, constituting a business, and your basis in the assets is determined by reference to the purchase price. Your basis in the goodwill—and the amount the seller is deemed to receive for it—is the excess of the purchase price over the fair market value of all the assets other than goodwill [IRC Sec. 1060; Temp. Reg. Sec. 1.1060-1T].

(g) Easements. An easement is a limited right to use property (e.g., a right of way). The amount you receive for granting an easement reduces your basis in the property. If the amount you receive for the easement is more than your basis in the property, the gain is taxable.[6] If you lose all beneficial interest in the property, granting the easement is treated as a sale of the entire property.[7]

(h) Sports Franchises. The amount the buyer allocates to player contracts on a sale or exchange of a franchise cannot exceed what the seller allocates to the contracts. However, the tax law presumes that this is no more than 50%, unless a greater allocation is proven [IRC Sec. 1056].

¶1623   SHARES OF STOCK PURCHASED AT DIFFERENT PRICES

If you acquired shares of the same stock (including mutual funds) at different prices, and dispose of some of your holdings, you must identify which of the shares you have given up in order to determine your gain or loss. You can avoid the problem by keeping records that identify the stock sold.

If the stock is registered in your name, it can be identified by keeping a record of dates and prices by certificate numbers. If the stock certificate is in a broker's custody, or if you hold a single certificate representing stock from different lots, identification may be made by giving the broker instructions (confirmed by him or her in writing) as to which particular stock to sell [Reg. Sec. 1.1012-1(c)]. Stock identified in this manner is deemed to be stock sold, even though the broker delivers stock certificates from a different lot.[1] When the broker is authorized to sell without your prior approval, you may identify the particular shares sold before the settlement date (usually four business days after the trade date).[2] Special rules apply to identify Treasury bonds and notes[3] [Reg. Sec. 1.1012-1(c)(7)].

(a) First-In, First-Out Rule. When shares of stock are sold from lots bought at different dates or prices, and the identity of lots cannot be determined, the stock sold must be charged against the earliest purchase. The first-in, first-out rule also applies to bonds [Reg. Sec. 1.1012-1(c)].

> **Example 1:** Simms bought 100 shares of Phillips Co. stock on April 30, 1987, for $10 per share and another 100 shares of Phillips Co. stock on March 1, 1992, for $20 per share. On August 1, 1992, he sold 100 shares of the stock for $21 per share. It is assumed that the sale was from the earlier purchase. Thus, he recognizes a gain of $1,100 ($21 less $10, multiplied by 100 shares).

> **Example 2:** Same facts as Example 1, except that Simms identifies the stock he sells as the March 1, 1992, shares. He reduces his taxable gain to $100.

> ➤ **OBSERVATION** Identifying the shares at the time of disposition lets you do tax maneuvering. For example, you can defer tax on a big gain by selling the shares with a higher basis first. And you can reduce the tax on that gain by giving them to a relative in a low tax bracket (e.g., a child with college tuition bills) instead of selling the shares yourself and giving them the after-tax cash. The recipient of the gift takes over your basis in the shares [¶1610].

(b) Stock Received in Reorganization. The first-in, first-out rule does not apply to shares of stock received in a tax-free reorganization. Here the "average cost" rule is used.[4] The basis of each new share of stock you receive in exchange is determined by dividing your total cost of the old stock by the number of new shares received. However, if the new shares you receive in a reorganization can be traced to specific old shares, the "average cost" rule does not apply. So the cost of your new shares is the adjusted cost of your old shares with which they are identified.[5] If you receive new stock in a split-up, the first-in, first-out rule applies, unless you identify the new shares with purchases made before the split-up.[6] A split-up is defined in ¶3220.

¶1624   MUTUAL FUND SHARES

If you own shares in a mutual fund that were purchased at different prices, you may determine gain or loss on a sale by means of an average per share basis for all of your holdings in that fund [Reg. Sec. 1.1012-1(e)]. Alternatively, you may use the first-in, first-out method or identify the actual shares being sold[1] [¶1623(a)].

> **Example 1:** Mr. Barton owns 200 shares of Aggressive Investment Fund. He paid $10 per share for 100 of those shares and $16 for the other 100 shares. Barton's average basis per share is $13. If he sells 100 shares for $13 per share, Barton would have a $300 taxable gain using the first-in, first-out method. However, by opting for the average basis method, he would have no taxable gain.

(a) Dividend Reinvestment. Mutual funds commonly provide an automatic dividend reinvestment option for shareholders. If you elect this option, you do not receive cash dividends. Instead, the cash you normally would have received is used to purchase additional shares of the fund. The amount of cash that you could have received is includible in taxable income. And that same amount is your basis in the new shares.

> **Example 2:** Ms. Dalton owns 100 shares of Growth Fund. Her basis is $21 per share. Assume Growth Fund declares a dividend of $2 per share, and Dalton had chosen automatic dividend reinvestment. The fund purchases eight additional shares for Dalton. Her basis in the 100 original shares is still $21 per share. Her basis in the eight new shares is $200 ($2 dividend x 100 shares) or $25 per share.

(b) Undistributed Capital Gain. Your mutual fund can allocate its capital gain to you, but not actually pay it out as dividends. The mutual fund is taxed on that income. You also must include an allocable portion of the capital gain in your income. However, you can claim a credit for the tax paid by the fund. And your basis in the shares is increased by the difference between the undistributed gain and the amount of tax paid by the fund.[2]

SPECIAL RULES

[New tax legislation may affect this subject; see ¶1.]

¶1627   PROPERTY CONVERTED TO BUSINESS USE

You may deduct a loss on the disposition of personal-use property that has been converted to business or income-producing property. However, the property's basis for determining loss is the lesser of (1) your adjusted basis at the time of conversion or (2) the property's fair market value at the time of conversion. Appropriate adjustments are made in either case for the period after conversion to business or investment use [Reg. Sec. 1.165-9(b)]. The lower of fair market value or adjusted basis at the time of conversion is also the basis to be used for calculating depreciation deductions [Reg. Sec. 1.167(g)-1].

> **Example 1:** Robertson purchased a house in 1981 for $250,000. He used it as his residence through December 31, 1987. Starting in 1988, he turned the building into an office for his accounting practice. The house was worth $235,000 at that time. Since then, he has spent $30,000 on capital improvements and claimed depreciation deductions of $33,000. Robertson's basis for calculating loss on the sale of the house is $232,000 ($235,000 + $30,000 - $33,000).

Basis for gain. The basis for figuring gain on the sale of property converted from personal use is your adjusted basis at the time of conversion, adjusted from the date of conversion to the date of sale. If you have a gain when using the basis for loss and a loss when using the basis for gain, you realize neither gain nor loss.[1]

> **Example 2:** Same facts as Example 1. Robertson's basis for calculating gain is $247,000 ($250,000 + $30,000 - $33,000). If Robertson sells for between $232,000 and $247,000, he doesn't have a gain or a loss.

¶1628   INVENTORY

Manufacturers and large resellers must follow the so-called uniform capitalization rules to determine their basis in inventory. This means that the basis includes direct costs and many indirect costs of bringing the property to its sellable state (¶2714) [IRC Sec. 263A].

¶1629   ANNUITY CONTRACT

If an annuity contract is sold, the amounts recovered tax-free as a return of investment are subtracted from the cost basis of the annuity contract. However, the basis of the contract may not be reduced below zero (¶1522)[IRC Sec. 1021; Reg. Sec. 1.1021-1]. On the transfer of appreciated property for a private annuity, the investment in the contract is the transferor's basis in the property transferred; the gain (excess of the value of the annuity over the basis of the property transferred) is reported ratably over the annuitant's life expectancy.[1] For a secured private annuity, the Tax Court has held that the excess of the annuity's value, as determined under the actuarial tables, over the transferor's basis in the property exchanged is includible in income in the year of exchange.[2]

¶1630   PATENTS AND COPYRIGHTS

Your basis in a patent or copyright includes your purchase price (if purchased), governmental fees, cost of drawings, experimental models, attorney's fees and development or experimental expenses [Reg. Sec. 1.167(a)-6(a)]. If research and experimental expenditures have been deducted [¶2231], they are not included in your basis. The time you spent during the inventing process is not an element of cost.

¶1631   PARTNERSHIP INTEREST

In general, your basis in a partnership is the amount of money plus the adjusted basis of property you transferred to it. Adjustments are then made to take into account your share of partnership income, distributions, losses and certain expenditures (¶3419) [IRC Sec. 705].

Footnotes to Chapter 6

(For your added convenience, in brackets [] with the footnotes below, you will find citations to related paragraphs in the "RIA United States Tax Reporter"(USTR), "CCH Federal Tax Reporter" (CCH) and "RIA Federal Tax Coordinator 2d"(FTC) multi-volume services.)

FOOTNOTE ¶ 1600 [USTR ¶ 10,014 et seq.; CCH ¶ 29,625 et seq.; RIA ¶ P-1000, I-1950.]
(1) Treas. Dept. booklet "Your Federal Income Tax" (1991 Ed.), p. 88.
(2) Treas. Dept. booklet "Your Federal Income Tax" (1991 Ed.), pp. 89.
(3) Rev. Rul. 75-451, 1975-2 CB 330.
(4) Rev. Rul. 57-535, 1957-2 CB 513.
(5) Crane v. Comm., 331 U.S. 1, 67 SCt 1047, 35 AFTR 776.
(6) Treas. Dept. booklet "Tax Guide for Small Business" (1991 Ed.), p. 14.
FOOTNOTE ¶ 1601 [USTR ¶ 10,014.02; CCH ¶ 29,626; RIA ¶ P-1001].
FOOTNOTE ¶ 1604 [USTR ¶ 10,114; 10,124.03; CCH ¶ 29,685; RIA ¶ P-1100].
(1) McDonald, 28 BTA 64; Mountain Wholesale Co., 17 TC 870.
FOOTNOTE ¶ 1605 [USTR ¶ 10,314; CCH ¶ 29,626; RIA ¶ I-1000].

(1) Phila. Pk. Amusement Co. v. U.S., 126 F. Supp. 184, 46 AFTR 1293; Williams, 37 TC 1099; Rev. Rul. 57-535, 1957-2 CB 513; Rev. Rul. 55-27, 1955-1 CB 350.
(2) Countway v. Comm., 127 F2d 69, 29 AFTR 80; Myers, 1 TC 100.
(3) Williams Est. v. Comm., 1 AFTR 2d 834, 256 F2d 217.
(4) Alvary v. U.S., 9 AFTR 2d 1633, 302 F2d 790.
(5) Helvering v. Walbridge, 70 F2d 683, 13 AFTR 1062.
(6) Roe, ¶ 65,100 PH Memo TC.
(7) Acme Mills, Inc., 6 BTA 1065; Harris, 14 BTA 1259.
(8) General Securities Co., 38 BTA 330.
(9) Rev. Rul. 59-60, 1959-1, amplified by Rev. Rul. 83-120, 1983-2 CB 170.
(10) A & A Tool & Supply Co. v. Comm., 182 F2d 300, 39 AFTR 517.
(11) Rev. Rul. 67-107, 1967-1 CB 115.

FOOTNOTE ¶ 1606 [USTR ¶ 10,014; CCH ¶ 5507; 29,641; RIA ¶ I-1804].

FOOTNOTE ¶ 1607 [USTR ¶ 10,534; CCH ¶ 31,802; RIA ¶ P-1209].

FOOTNOTE ¶ 1610 [USTR ¶ 10,154; CCH ¶ 29,742; RIA ¶ P3100].

FOOTNOTE ¶ 1611 [USTR ¶ 10,414; CCH ¶ 31,702; RIA ¶ L-5101].

FOOTNOTE ¶ 1612 [USTR ¶ 10,144; CCH ¶ 29,730; RIA ¶ P-4000].

(1) Barkley Co. of Ariz., TC Memo 1988-324 Crane v. Comm., 35 AFTR 894; Comm. v. Tufts et al., 51 AFTR 2d 83-1132, aff'd 52 AFTR 2d 83-5759.

(2) McConnell, 29 BTA 710.

FOOTNOTE ¶ 1614 [USTR ¶ 10,314; CCH ¶ 31,508; RIA ¶ I-2720].

(1) Margolis, 337 F2d 1001, 14 AFTR 2d 5667.

(2) Rev. Rul. 74-7, 1974-1 CB 198.

(3) Rev. Rul. 82-166, 1982-2 CB 190.

(4) Rev. Rul. 90-34, 1990-1 CB 154.

FOOTNOTE ¶ 1615 [USTR ¶ 10,314; CCH ¶ 31,508; RIA ¶ I-2752].

FOOTNOTE ¶ 1616 [USTR ¶ 10,314.07; CCH ¶ 31,508; RIA ¶ I-1014].

FOOTNOTE ¶ 1617 [USTR ¶ 10,354; CCH ¶ 31,582; RIA ¶ I-1000].

(1) Rev. Rul. 73-124, 1973-1 CB 200.

FOOTNOTE ¶ 1618 [USTR ¶ 10,364; CCH ¶ 31,602; RIA ¶ P-5000].

(1) Clark v. Comm., 77 F2d 89, 15 AFTR 1343.

(2) Rev. Rul. 72-265, 1972-1 CB 222.

(3) Rev. Rul. 69-135, 1969-1 CB 198.

(4) Rev. Rul. 72-319, 1972-1 CB 224.

(5) Rev. Rul. 56-437, 1956-2 CB 507, Rev. Rul. 90-7, 1990-1CB 153.

(6) Rev. Rul. 69-20, 1969-1 CB 202.

FOOTNOTE ¶ 1619 [USTR ¶ 3514; CCH ¶ 16,405; RIA ¶ P-5016].

(1) Rev. Rul. 64-56, 1964-1 CB 133.

FOOTNOTE ¶ 1622 [USTR ¶ 10,124.55; CCH ¶ 5700; RIA ¶ P-5200].

(1) C.D. Johnson Lumber Corp., 12 TC 348.

(2) Atwell, 17 TC 1374.

(3) Hemphill, 25 BTA 1351.

(4) Bancitaly Corp., 34 BTA 494.

(5) Collin v. Comm., 32 F2d 753, 7 AFTR 8733.

(6) Rev. Rul. 70-510, 1970-2 CB 159.

(7) H.L. Scales, 10 BTA 1024; Rev. Rul. 70-510, 1970-2 CB 159.

FOOTNOTE ¶ 1623 [USTR ¶ 10,124.77; CCH ¶ 29,686; RIA ¶ P-5210].

(1) Rev. Rul. 61-97, 1961-1 CB 394.

(2) Rev. Rul. 67-436, 1967-2 CB 266.

(3) Rev. Rul. 71-21, 1971-1 CB 221; Rev. Rul. 73-37, 1973-1 CB 374.

(4) Rev. Rul. 55-355, 1955-1 CB 418.

(5) Letter Ruling, 9-1-55.

(6) Bloch v. Comm., 148 F2d 452, 33 AFTR 955.

FOOTNOTE ¶ 1624 [USTR ¶ 10,124 et seq.; CCH ¶ 29,686; RIA ¶ P-5213].

(1) Treas. Dept. booklet "Mutual Fund Distributions" (1991 Ed.), p. 5.

(2) Treas. Dept. booklet "Your Federal Income Tax" (1991 Ed.), p. 61.

FOOTNOTE ¶ 1627 [USTR ¶ 1674 et seq.; CCH ¶ 10,103; RIA ¶ P-1918].

(1) Treas. Dept. booklet "Your Federal Income Tax" (1991 Ed.), p. 90.

FOOTNOTE ¶ 1628 [USTR ¶ 263A4; CCH ¶ 13,807 et seq.; RIA ¶ I-4128].

FOOTNOTE ¶ 1629 [USTR ¶ 10,214; CCH ¶ 29,842; RIA ¶ P-1125].

(1) Rev. Rul. 69-74, 1969-1 CB 43.

(2) Estate of Bell, 60 TC 469.

FOOTNOTE ¶ 1630 [USTR ¶ 1624.025; CCH ¶ 11,016; RIA ¶ P-1176].

FOOTNOTE ¶ 1631 [USTR ¶ 7214; CCH ¶ 25,444; RIA ¶ B-1605].

GAIN OR LOSS—SALE OF RESIDENCE—CASUALTY—THEFT—CONDEMNATION

TABLE OF CONTENTS

SALE OF RESIDENCE

Generally, when you sell property for more than you originally paid for it, you must recognize gain on the difference and pay tax. You can, however, postpone part or all of the tax due on the sale of a principal residence if you buy a new residence within certain time limits. In addition, persons 55 or older get a once-in-a-lifetime break on the sale of their home. If you are at least 55 years old when you sell your principal residence, all or part of the gain (up to $125,000) can be tax-free even though you don't buy a replacement home.

¶1700   GENERAL RULE FOR SALE AND REPLACEMENT

-   Generally, you recognize gain on the sale or exchange of your residence if the amount you receive for the residence exceeds your adjusted basis [¶1702(d)].

But if you sell your principal residence and replace it within the statutory period—generally two years [¶1702(a)]—you recognize gain only to the extent that the "adjusted sales price" of the old residence exceeds the cost of the new residence [IRC Sec. 1034; Reg. Sec. 1.1034-1(a)]. In other words, you get a tax-free rollover of the gain as long as the cost of the new residence equals or exceeds the adjusted sales price of the old residence. The rollover treatment is mandatory; no election needs to be made to get it.

Example: Evan Kendrick sold his old residence for an adjusted sales price of $190,000 and realized a gain of $10,000 on the sale. Two months later in the year, he bought a new residence. The following table illustrates how the cost of the new residence affects the gain that will be recognized on the transaction.

Adjusted sales price	Realized gain	Cost of new residence	Recognized gain
$190,000	$10,000	$192,000	None
$190,000	$10,000	$188,000	$2,000
$190,000	$10,000	$190,000	None
$190,000	$10,000	$176,000	$10,000

➤ **OBSERVATION** You cannot deduct a *loss* on the sale of a residence [Reg. Sec. 1.165-1(e)]. However, if a former residence had been converted to income-producing property, the loss is deductible [¶2307].

¶1701   WHAT IS A PRINCIPAL RESIDENCE

For practical purposes, your principal residence is the place where you actually live. If you live in two residences, your principal residence is the one you live in most of the time. The residence need not be a conventional home to qualify you for this tax break. A condominium,[1] cooperative apartment, houseboat[2] or mobile home will also do [IRC Sec. 121(d)(3), 1034(f); Reg. Sec. 1.1034-1(c)(3)].

(a) More Than One Residence. If you have more than one residence, you may apply the special rule only to the sale of your principal residence. If you own a secondary residence and live in a rented residence, the special rule will not apply to the sale of the secondary residence. However, renting out your principal residence temporarily while attempting to sell it won't disqualify it as a principal residence.[3]

> **Example 1:** Perry Chasen owned two homes—one in New York and the other in Los Angeles. Since most of his work is in New York, he lives there ⅔ of the time and lives in the L.A. home for the other ⅓ of the year. If he sells the L.A. home at a gain, he will not be allowed to defer paying tax on the gain if he replaces it, since the L.A. home is not his principal residence.

> **Example 2:** Stan Shale, a trucker, spends most of the year in hotel rooms or in the cab of his truck. He lives in his home for only one month of the year. Since it is his principal residence, though, he will be allowed to defer the gain on the sale if he replaces it within the specified time limit, even though he lives in the house for only 1/12 of the year.

(b) Business or Investment Property. Property you use in a trade or business or hold for investment is not a residence. But property may still be considered a personal residence even if you temporarily rent it out.[4] Whether the property has lost its residential character as a result of the temporary rental depends on the facts and circumstances of each case—including your good faith regarding your intention to retain a particular residence as your principal residence [Reg. Sec. 1.1034-1(c)(3)].

> **Example 3:** Hubert buys a new residence before he sells his old one. He rents out the new residence for a few months while seeking a buyer for the old. The new property is still considered his new residence for this special rule.

> **Example 4:** Norman buys a new residence before he sells his old one. He moves into the new home and rents out the old residence while seeking a buyer for it. The old residence will qualify as his principal residence for this special rollover rule.

(c) Property Used Both for Residence and Business or Investment. You may use your property partly as a residence and partly for business or for the production of income. This frequently occurs when a storeowner or a professional providing services lives on the business premises—or maintains an office in his or her home. It may also occur when a person owns a multi-family dwelling, lives in one of the apartments and rents out the remaining apartments. In such cases, the special nonrecognition rule applies only to the part allocated to residential purposes (¶1702(j)) [Reg. Sec. 1.1034-1(c)(3)].

> **Example 5:** Ford owns a two-family house, which he purchased some years ago for $100,000. He lives in half of it and rents out the other half. Ford sold the house in 1991 for $250,000. One-half of the purchase and sales prices are allocable to Ford's principal residence. So Ford owes no tax on $75,000 of the gain ($125,000 selling price less $50,000 purchase price) if he purchases a new residence for at least $125,000.

> **NOTE:** No allocation is required if you no longer use the home for business in the year of sale.[5]

Example 6: In the past, Dr. Steele used two rooms of her home as an office where she saw and treated patients. She claimed depreciation and other business-type deductions for that office. However, she has since closed the office and converted the rooms back to personal use. Dr. Steele sold her home in 1992. Since none of the home was used for business in the year of the sale (1992), no allocation is necessary—despite the business use in previous years.

¶1702　　QUALIFYING FOR NONRECOGNITION

[New tax legislation may affect this subject; see ¶1.]

(a) Replacement Period. To qualify for nonrecognition of gain on the sale of a principal residence, you must buy or build another home and use it as your principal residence within two years before or after selling the old one. For a residence that is being constructed or improved, work may take place outside of this four-year period. However, only those costs attributable to the period qualify for the replacement break [IRC Sec. 1034(c)].

> ➤ **IMPORTANT** The tax-free rollover break can't be used more than once during a two-year period unless such multiple sales are job related [IRC Sec. 1034(d)]. If the sales are a result of commencing work at a new location *and* the requirements for the moving expense deduction are met [¶1935], you will be allowed a subsequent rollover.

Extension of replacement period for member of Armed Forces. The replacement period is suspended while you or your spouse is on extended duty (active duty for more than 90 days or indefinitely) with the U.S. Armed Forces. The suspension generally will not extend for more than four years from the date the old residence is sold. The suspension applies only when service begins before the end of the replacement period and only if the old and new residences are each used by you and your spouse as your principal residence [IRC Sec 1034(h); Reg. Sec. 1.1034-1(g)].

NOTE: The suspension period for members of the Armed Forces who are stationed outside the U.S. or who must live in remote government quarters can extend the replacement date to as long as eight years after the home sale [IRC Sec. 1034(h)(2)].

Persons living abroad. The period for replacing an old residence is suspended while your tax home is outside the United States or its possessions. The suspension only applies if your stay abroad began before the end of the replacement period. The replacement period, plus the suspension period, cannot extend for more than four years after the sale of your old residence [IRC Sec. 1034(k)].

(b) Amount Realized. The amount realized is generally the amount you receive in cash plus the fair market value of any property you receive. It also includes the amount of any mortgage or other debt to which the property remains subject, whether or not the buyer assumes such debt. If the consideration for the sale includes liabilities of the buyer to the seller (such as a personal note), the obligations are included at their face value.[1] However, to arrive at the amount realized, you subtract selling expenses from the amount received [Reg. Sec. 1.1034-1(b)(4)].

Selling expenses include real estate commissions, expenses of advertising the property for sale, preparing the deed, other legal services related to the sale, and "points" paid by the seller to obtain a mortgage for the buyer[2] [see also (e) below]. But when selling expenses are taken as a moving expense deduction, they cannot be used to reduce the sales price [IRC Sec. 217(e); Reg. Sec. 1.217-2(e)].

(c) Adjusted Sales Price. Your adjusted sales price is your amount realized [(b) above] reduced by your "fixing-up" expenses [IRC Sec. 1034(b)(1); Reg. Sec. 1.1034-1(b)(3)].

Fixing-up expenses are expenses for work performed on the old residence to make it saleable. Such work typically includes painting and papering. The expenses, however, must:

- be for work performed during the 90-day period ending on the date the sales contract is made,[3]
- be paid within 30 days after the sale date,
- be otherwise nondeductible in figuring taxable income,
- not be used in figuring the amount realized, and
- not be capital expenditures or improvements. [IRC Sec. 1034(b); Reg. Sec. 1.1034-1(b)].

Example 1: Mr. Bundy sold his old house for $100,000. He spent $8,000 in selling costs ($6,000 in commissions to his broker, $1,000 to his attorney, and $1,000 in "points" to help the seller finance the purchase of the property), and $2,000 in "fixing-up" expenses by painting the bedrooms and living room 60 days prior to the sale. Result: The adjusted sales price of the house is $90,000 ($100,000 sale price less both the $8,000 selling expenses and the $2,000 fixing-up expenses). Thus, he must spend at least $90,000 on another principal residence in order to avoid owing any current tax on the sale.

➤ **WATCH THIS** Fixing-up expenses are considered only in figuring the gain on which tax is postponed. They are not deductible in finding the actual profit on the sale of your old residence.

Example 2: If in Example 1 Bundy does not roll the proceeds over into another residence, he figures his taxable gain based on $92,000 ($100,000 less $8,000 in selling costs).

(d) Adjusted Basis of Old Residence. This is your old residence's original cost, including commissions and other expenses at the time of its purchase, *plus* the cost of subsequent improvements, *less* allowable depreciation, deductible casualty losses and gain on the sale of a previous residence on which tax was deferred [¶1702(g) below].

Example 3: Ms. Oswald purchased her first house in 1967 for $30,000. She sold it in 1977 for $50,000 and bought a new home for $60,000. Thus, her basis in the new home was $40,000 ($60,000 cost less $20,000 gain deferred from tax by rollover break). Oswald added a bedroom in 1982 and a sun deck in 1984 at costs of $10,000 and $3,000 respectively. While barbecuing on her deck in 1985, Oswald accidently started a fire that damaged the deck and house. Oswald deducted $4,000 on her 1985 tax return as a casualty loss. As a result, Oswald's adjusted basis is now $49,000 ($60,000 cost plus $10,000 bedroom, plus $3,000 sundeck, less $4,000 casualty loss and $20,000 gain deferred on previous home sale).

(e) Cost of New Residence. The cost of your new residence is more than the cash you pay and indebtedness you incur or assume as the purchase price. For example, the cost of your new residence includes closing costs and the cost of capital improvements you make on the new place within two years after the date of purchase [Reg. Sec. 1.1034-1(b),(c)(4)].[4] The cost of a tenant-stockholder's stock in a cooperative apartment house includes his share of the cooperative's mortgage.[5] The cost of a residence acquired by exchange is its fair market value at the time of the exchange [Reg. Sec. 1.1034-1(c)(4)].

If you acquire a new residence by gift or inheritance, the value of the new residence is not considered cost for determining your nonrecognized gain [IRC Sec. 1034(c)(2); Reg. Sec. 1.1034-1(b)(7),(c)(4)]. It is, of course, part of your basis for determining gain on subsequent transactions [¶1610; 1612]. However, amounts you spend on improving inherited or gift property may qualify as both: as cost for determining nonrecognition of gain [Reg. Sec. 1.1034-1(c)(4)] and basis for determining the gain on a later sale.[6]

(f) Basis of New Residence. The basis of your new residence is its purchase price, reduced by your nontaxable gain on the sale or exchange of your old residence. This reduction is made only after the old residence is sold [IRC Sec. 1034(e); Reg. Sec. 1.1034-1(e)].

(g) How to Figure Recognized Gain and Basis of New Home. This is illustrated below:

> **Example 4:** Trout sold the house he had used as his principal residence for ten years. Its adjusted basis was $167,000 and the selling price was $192,000. Selling expenses (broker's commissions) and fixing-up expenses were $5,000 each. Two months later, he bought a new residence for $175,000. Trout's recognized gain is $7,000, and his basis in the new home is $162,000 as follows:

Realized Gain

1. Selling price of old residence	$192,000
2. Less: Selling expenses	5,000
3. Amount realized on sale	$187,000
4. Less: Adjusted basis of old residence	167,000
5. Realized gain	$ 20,000

Adjusted Sales Price

6. Amount realized on sale (Line 3 above)	$187,000
7. Less: Fixing-up expenses	5,000
8. Adjusted sales price	$182,000

Recognized Gain

9. Adjusted sales price (Line 8 above)	$182,000
10. Less: Cost of new residence	175,000
11. Recognized gain	$ 7,000

Gain Not Recognized

12. Gain realized (Line 5 above)	$ 20,000
13. Gain recognized (Line 11 above)	7,000
14. Gain not recognized	$ 13,000

Basis of New Residence

15. Cost of new residence	$175,000
16. Less: Gain not recognized (Line 14 above)	13,000
17. Basis of new residence	$162,000

If you make capital improvements to the new residence within the replacement period, the amount expended will be added to the cost of purchasing your new residence, thereby reducing your taxable gain [IRC Sec. 1034(b)(7)].

> **Example 5:** Same facts as in Example 4, except that Trout adds on a $7,000 sun room a year after purchasing the new residence. As a result, Trout has no taxable gain. The adjusted sales price of the old house ($182,000) less the cost of the new residence ($175,000 purchase price and $7,000 addition) equals zero. Trout's basis in the new residence is $162,000 ($182,000 cost of new residence less $20,000 gain not recognized).

(h) Exchange. The sale-and-replacement break also applies if your old residence is *exchanged* for a new one within the allotted period [IRC Sec. 1034(c)(1); Reg. Sec. 1.1034-1(b)(8)].

(i) Installment Sale. The sale-and-replacement break applies even if you sell your residence on the installment plan [¶2903 et. seq.]. The recognized gain may be apportioned over the period of the installment transactions. The amount of recognized gain included in income is that portion of the installment payments received during the year which the total recognized gain bears to the total contract price.[7]

Example 6: Brady sold his principal residence for $200,000 and purchased a new home within two years for $180,000, thereby having to pay tax on a $20,000 gain. The deal was structured in a way that the $200,000 would be paid to him in equal installments over five years. As a result, he will have to include in income $\frac{1}{10}$ ($20,000 gain over $200,000 adjusted sales price) of each $40,000 annual payment, or $4,000, each year for the next five years.

(j) Part Residence, Part Business Use. If you use part of your residence for business or investment purposes (e.g., you maintain an office in your home), you will be treated as if you made two separate sales—a sale of your personal residence and a sale of your office. The sale profit from the office portion is not eligible for the rollover. As a result, any profit on the office portion will be taxable. Therefore, when you sell your home, you must make an allocation of basis and sales proceeds between the residence portion and the office portion.

Example 7: Dr. Casey purchased his old home in 1982 for $200,000, and sold it in 1992 for $300,000. He used $\frac{1}{4}$ of his home as an office where he treated patients. As a result, Dr. Casey must allocate the purchase and adjusted sales price of his old home to determine the amount of recognized gain on the office and residence portions. The results are as follows:

Dr. Casey will be treated as having paid $150,000 ($\frac{3}{4}$ of his $200,000 cost) for the residence portion, and $50,000 ($\frac{1}{4}$ of his $200,000 cost) for the office portion.

He will be treated as receiving $225,000 ($\frac{3}{4}$ of the $300,000 sales price) for the residence and $75,000 ($\frac{1}{4}$ of $300,000) for the office.

Dr. Casey's gain on the residence is $75,000 ($225,000 sales price less $150,000 cost). This gain is eligible for the sale-and-replacement break. He will owe no tax on it if he purchases a new residence for at least $225,000 within two years.

Casey's gain on the office is $25,000 ($75,000 sales price less $50,000 cost). This gain is not eligible for the rollover rules and is therefore taxable. (Any depreciation deductions taken in prior years reduce his cost basis in the office and thereby increase his gain on its sale.)

¶1703　HUSBAND AND WIFE SHARING IN NONRECOGNITION OF GAIN

[New tax legislation may affect this subject; see ¶1.]

Special rules apply if you and your spouse take title to your old and new residences in different forms (e.g., your spouse owns the old residence and you own the new one). If a you and your spouse both use the old and new residences as your principal residence, and if you elect, the sale-and-replacement rule for nonrecognition of gain on the sale or exchange of an old residence is applied to both as follows:

- Adjusted sales price of the old residence is the your or your and your spouse's adjusted sales price of the old residence.
- Cost of buying the new residence is the cost to you, or to your spouse, or to both of you, of buying the new residence, whether such new residence is held by you, your spouse, or both of you.
- The gain on the sale of the old residence that is not recognized, and the adjustment to the basis of the new residence, are allocated between you and your spouse [IRC Sec. 1034(g); Reg. Sec. 1.1034-1(f)].

➤ **OBSERVATION** This means you and your spouse acting singly or jointly benefit by the sale-and-replacement break, even if the one who sold the old residence is not the same as the one who bought the new residence, or the percentage interest of each of you in the new residence is not the same as it was in the old residence [Reg. Sec. 1.1034-1(f)(2)].

Example 1: Harvey individually owned a home which served as his and his wife's principal residence. It cost $50,000 (his adjusted basis). He sold it at an adjusted sales price of $100,000. Within a year after the sale, he and his wife contributed $50,000 each from their separate funds to buy their new principal residence, which they held as tenants in common. If they elect, the gain of $50,000 on the sale of the old residence will not be recognized to him, the adjusted basis of his interest in the new residence will be $25,000 and the adjusted basis of his wife's interest will also be $25,000.

Example 2: Norman and his wife, Bertha, own their principal residence as joint tenants. It has an adjusted basis of $20,000 to each of them ($40,000 together). They sold the house at an adjusted sales price of $80,000. Within a year after the sale, Bertha spent $80,000 of her own funds to buy a new principal residence for herself and Norman. She took title in her name only. If Norman and Bertha elect, the adjusted basis to Bertha of the new residence will be $40,000, and neither Norman's gain of $20,000 on the sale of the old residence nor Bertha's own gain is recognized.

Consent necessary. The allocation of nonrecognition and basis is available only if you and your spouse file your consent with the IRS. You make the election by attaching a statement to the Form 2119 filed in the year that the gain from the sale of the old residence is realized [IRC Sec. 1034(g); Reg. Sec. 1.1034-1(f)]. When one spouse dies after the sale of the old jointly-owned residence and before the purchase of the new residence, the surviving spouse's consent is sufficient to defer gain on the sale of the old residence [IRC Sec. 1034(g)(2)].

¶1704   CONDEMNATION OF A RESIDENCE

In the case of a seizure or condemnation of a residence, or if you transfer your residence as a result of its threat or imminence [¶1710(b)], you can elect to use the "sale-and-replacement" rules instead of the "condemnation" rules [¶1710 et seq.].

¶1705   WHEN NONRECOGNITION IS NOT AVAILABLE

Nonrecognition of gain on the sale of a residence may be denied in some instances.

(a) New Residence Sold Before Old. If you buy and sell another residence before you sell your old residence, the second residence is not treated as a new residence,. So the sale-and-replacement break does not apply to the appreciation of the second (or any subsequent) residence you purchase and sell within the two-year period [IRC Sec. 1034(c)(3); Reg. Sec. 1.1034-1(d)].

(b) More Than One New Residence. If you buy more than one residence within the time allowed, and you use it as your principal residence during the time for replacement after the old residence is sold, only the last residence so used is considered a new residence for rollover purposes [IRC Sec. 1034(c)(4)].[1] Furthermore, the sale-and-replacement break applies only to one sale or exchange within the replacement period preceding the last of the sales. However, nonrecognition applies to more than one sale within that period if the move was job-related, and the moving expenses could be deducted (¶1935 et. seq.) [IRC Sec. 1034(d)(2)].

Example 1: George Hand sold his old residence in January and bought a new residence a month later. During March, he sold the second residence and bought a third residence in April. Neither of these purchases were job-related. The gain on the sale of the old residence in January is not recognized, except to the extent that Hand's adjusted sales price of the old residence exceeds his cost of buying the third residence in April. Gain on the sale of the second residence in March is fully recognized. But since his basis in that residence is its full cost, Hand probably won't have any recognized gain on its sale in the following month.

Example 2: If in Example 1 Hand's moves were job-related, he could apply the nonrecognition rules to both the January and March sales.

(c) Title in New Residence Held by Another. The special sale-and-replacement break does not apply if the proceeds from the sale of your old residence are reinvested in a new residence to which another party, such as your child, holds title.[2]

¶1706   HOW TO REPORT THE SALE OF YOUR RESIDENCE

[New tax legislation may affect this subject; see ¶1.]

(a) Use of Basic Forms. You use Form 2119 to report *any gain* on the sale of a principal residence whether or not it was replaced with a new principal residence. Any taxable gain reported on Form 2119 must then be transferred to Schedule D of Form 1040. A loss is not deductible.

Let's say you sell or transfer your home as a result of seizure or condemnation (or threat thereof) and elect to use the "sale-and-replacement" rather than the "condemnation" rules [¶1704, 1710] for deferring gain. You must make the election by attaching a statement to your tax return showing the old residence's basis, adjusted sales price and the sale date. If you acquired a new residence before the election was made, the statement must show its price and occupancy and purchase dates [IRC Sec. 1034(i); Reg. Sec. 1.1034-1(h)(2)(iii)]. If no election is made, the general rules on involuntary conversions apply [¶1710 et seq.].

(b) Replacement Is Intended But Not Made by the Filing Date. If this happens and the replacement period has not expired, no gain is taxable in the year of sale. However, you must complete portions of Form 2119, which disclose the computation of gain on the old residence, and attach it to Form 1040 for the year of sale. You also indicate on Form 2119 that the replacement residence has not yet been bought.

When you purchase the new residence within the replacement period, you need to file again. If the new home costs at least as much as the old residence, file another Form 2119, giving the date you first lived in the new home and its cost. If the new residence costs less than the old residence, file Form 1040X for the year of sale along with Schedule D and a new Form 2119 showing the amount of gain that must be reported, plus interest on the additional tax.

(c) New Residence Not Bought or Built Within the Replacement Period. If you do not plan to replace your old home, you must complete Form 2119 and Schedule D and attach them to your tax return for the year of the sale. If you postponed gain on the sale of your old home and do not buy or build and live in a new home within the replacement period, you will have to file a second Form 2119 and an amended return (Form 1040X and Schedule D) for the year of the sale to report your gain.

(d) Unanticipated Replacement. If you already paid tax on the gain from the sale of your residence and later buy a new residence within the replacement period, you may file Form 1040X for the year of sale with Form 2119 to claim a refund.

(e) Home-Office Allocation. When calculating home office gain [¶1701(c)], use Form 4797 and attach it to Forms 1040 and 2119.

¶1707   SALES OF LOW-INCOME HOUSING PROJECTS

Under prior law, taxpayers who disposed of a qualified low-income housing project could take advantage of a sale-and-replacement break similar to the one available to homes. To qualify, however, the sale had to be to tenants of the project or to a condominium or cooperative association for their benefit. In addition, nonrecognition was available only if the property was replaced with similar low-income housing property within a year of the sale or any other period approved by the IRS. These rules applied only to housing projects constructed under FHA Sec. 221(d)(3) and Sec. 236 and certain state assisted programs. For depreciation recapture, see ¶1812 [IRC Sec. 1039; Reg. Sec. 1.1039-1].

> ► **TAX BREAK REPEALED** The nonrecognition break for low-income housing projects was repealed, generally as of November 5, 1990. However, since returns are open for three years, taxpayers should still be aware of the repeal. Important: The repeal does not apply to transactions or sales occurring before that date, even if they effect liability for periods ending after November 5, 1990.

¶1708   SPECIAL ONE-TIME EXCLUSION IF AGE 55 OR OVER

You may be able to elect to exclude the first $125,000 of gain on the sale of your principal residence ($62,500 if you are married and file a separate return). This exclusion is usually elected on a tax return for the year you would otherwise have recognized gain (either because you are not buying another residence or are buying a less expensive one). Certain age, ownership and occupancy requirements must be satisfied.

Example 1: Moe Fontana, age 60, sold his home for $245,000. His adjusted basis was $115,000. His selling expenses were $10,000. He elected the $125,000 exclusion. His amount realized is $235,000 (sales price less selling expenses). His realized gain is $120,000 [$235,000 (amount realized) less $115,000 (adjusted basis)]. Since the gain is less than $125,000, the entire gain is excludable.

NOTE: Gains on residences that are involuntarily converted (e.g, proceeds received on account of fire or condemnation) are eligible for the exclusion [IRC Sec. 121(d)(4)].

(a) Who Is Eligible. The first $125,000 of realized gain on the sale or exchange is not taxed if all the following requirements are met [IRC Sec. 121]:

- You were 55 or over before the date of the sale or exchange.
- You used the property as a principal residence for at least three years during the five-year period ending on the date of the sale.
- You or your spouse did not previously elect the exclusion. However, a taxpayer who sells a home and then marries later that same year can claim the exclusion on a joint return for the year, even if the spouse previously elected the exclusion.[1]

Three-year rule. You meet the three-year rule by using the residence for 36 full months or 1,095 days (3 × 365) during the five years prior to sale. Short temporary absences are counted as periods of use [Reg. Sec. 1.121-1(c)].

Periods during which an incapacitated homeowner lives in a nursing home or other qualified facility count as time lived in the residence being sold in meeting the three-year rule—provided he or she actually lived in the home for at least one year during the five-year period [IRC Sec. 121(d)(9)].

Once-in-a-lifetime. You can make the election to exclude the gain only once. Thus, if less than $125,000 of gain is excluded by one election, you cannot use the remainder by a subsequent election. However, you can revoke the election at any time as long as you can still file a refund claim for that year (generally, within three years). If you are married, the election or revocation must be made by both you and your spouse [IRC Sec. 121(c); Reg. Sec.1.121-4].

> **NOTE:** Before the $125,000 exclusion was enacted, there was an up-to-$35,000 exclusion that was tied to the sales price of the home. You can elect the present $125,000 exclusion even if you took the exclusion allowed under prior law [Reg. Sec. 1.121-2(c)].

(b) Allocation. Only the part of the property that is used as a principal residence qualifies. Gains from a rented unit or office would not qualify (¶1702(j)) [IRC Sec. 121(d)(5); Reg. Sec. 1.121-5(e)].

Unmarried persons 55 or over who sell their residence, which they hold as joint tenants or tenants in common, can get the exclusion in proportion to their undivided interest.[2]

(c) Surviving Spouse. Property qualifies for the exclusion even if disposed of by a surviving spouse as long as she or the deceased spouse met the ownership and use tests [IRC Sec. 121(d)(1), (2)]. The executor can make the election if the taxpayer died after signing the executory contract but before title to the property passed.[3]

(d) Sale of Residence by a Trust. A trust generally does not get the benefit of the $125,000 exclusion rule since it is not a person using property as a principal residence.[3] However, if the trust is a *grantor trust* [¶3523] (i.e., in other words, a trust where the grantor (creator) is considered to be the owner because he or she retains sufficient control over the trust or its assets), and the income is taxed to the grantor, the trust will be ignored and the grantor will be able to utilize the $125,000 home sale exclusion.[4] Since the sale profit is taxable to her, the exclusion is also available to her.

(e) Combining the Sale-and-Replacement Deferment Break With the $125,000 Exclusion. You can elect the deferment and exclusion breaks on the same sale if a replacement residence is bought or built within two years [Reg. Sec. 1.121-5(g)]. In figuring how much gain is deferred under the sale-and-replacement tax break, the excluded gain is treated like part of the cost of the new residence. Then the adjusted basis of the new residence is equal to the cost of the new residence less the gain not recognized due to electing the nonrecognition rules.

> **Example 2:** Mary Walker, age 59, sold her principal residence (which had an adjusted basis of $50,000) for $225,000. Selling expenses were $5,000. The fixing-up expenses were $4,000. She purchased a new residence for $75,000 and elected the $125,000 exclusion. Her recognized gain is $16,000, and her adjusted basis in the new residence is $46,000, computed as follows:

Realized Gain

1. Selling price	$225,000
2. Less: Selling expenses	5,000
3. Amount realized	220,000
4. Less: Adjusted basis of old residence	50,000
5. Realized gain	$170,000

Adjusted Sales Price

6. Amount realized	$220,000
7. Fixing-up expenses	4,000
8. Adjusted sales price	$216,000

Gain Not Excluded

9. Realized gain	$170,000
10. Less: The lesser of realized gain or $125,000	125,000
11. Gain not excluded	$ 45,000

Gain Recognized

12. Adjusted sales price		$216,000
13. Less: Line 10	$125,000	
Cost of new residence	75,000	200,000
14. Gain recognized		16,000

Gain Not Recognized or Excluded

15. Gain not excluded	$ 45,000
16. Less: Gain recognized	16,000
17. Gain not recognized or excluded	$ 29,000

Basis of New Residence

18. Cost of new residence	$ 75,000
19. Less: Gain not recognized or excluded	29,000
20. Basis of new residence	$ 46,000

CASUALTY—THEFT—CONDEMNATION

You may not have to pay tax when your property is destroyed, stolen, seized or condemned in whole or in part, and you are compensated by insurance or other reimbursement. You ordinarily must report the difference between the value of what you receive and your adjusted basis in the property lost as taxable gain. The gain may not be currently taxable if you reinvest the proceeds. Gains or losses from a casualty or theft are figured on Form 4684, while Form 4797 is used for condemnations.

¶1710　　　　　　　　　　GENERAL RULE

A so-called "involuntary conversion" occurs when your property is stolen, condemned or destroyed by casualty, and you receive an insurance payment or condemnation award of money or other property. You can avoid tax on the gain from an involuntary conversion if you reinvest the payment or award in "similar or related" property within a certain period of time—generally, two years before or after the date of the conversion [IRC Sec. 1033].

(a) Casualty and Theft. A casualty occurs when your property is destroyed by fire, storm, accident or some other sudden, unexpected or unusual event. The term "suddenness" has been defined quite liberally, and includes losses due to progressive deterioration. For example, the gain from having to cut and sell trees killed or infested by fungi or wood-destroying beetles may qualify as gain from involuntary conversion of property.[1]

Theft includes larceny, embezzlement and robbery (¶2304) [Reg. Sec. 1.165-8].

> **Example 1:** Brown's accountant, Smith, pledges Brown's common stock as collateral for Smith's personal loan without Brown's permission. This is theft under the involuntary conversion rules.

(b) Seizure and Condemnation. A seizure or condemnation occurs when a governmental body, in the exercise of its legal power, takes privately owned property for public use and pays a reasonable price for it. The taking of property for a limited time, however, is *not* an eligible conversion of property. Any compensation received is rent.[2]

Example 2: Gotham City, to install a new sewer system, digs up two acres of Mr. Wayne's land and replaces it one year later. This is not an involuntary conversion, and if Mr. Wayne received any money from the city, it would be taxable as rental income.

Sale or exchange due to a "threat or imminence" of condemnation.
There can also be an involuntary conversion when a sale or exchange takes place on account of a threat or imminence of condemnation. There is a threat or imminence of condemnation when you are informed by a public official who has the power to condemn the property, that a decision has been made to acquire the property, and you have reasonable grounds to believe that it will be condemned. A news media report that a condemnation is being *considered* is not a "threat or imminence." This occurs only when the condemning authority confirms that a decision has been made to condemn.[3]

Example 3: On Monday, Herman is informed by his neighbor that Herman's barn will soon be condemned. On Tuesday, Herman reads in the newspaper that the city is considering condemning his barn. On Thursday, Herman receives a visit from the mayor who tells Herman that his barn will be condemned to make way for a highway. Herman's barn was not under the "threat or imminence" of condemnation until he was informed by the mayor on Thursday.

(c) Livestock—Disease and Drought.
The destruction of livestock because of disease is treated as an involuntary conversion. Likewise, the sale or exchange of livestock on account of disease, in excess of what would ordinarily be sold or exchanged, is also an involuntary conversion [IRC Sec. 1033(d); Reg Sec. 1.1033(d)-1].

The sale or exchange of livestock (other than poultry) held for draft, breeding or dairy purposes, in excess of the number that would normally be sold, is treated as an involuntary conversion if sold or exchanged solely on account of drought [IRC Sec. 1033(e); Reg. Sec. 1.1033(e)-1].

(d) Property Used as Taxpayer's Principal Residence.
If your principal residence is seized, condemned, destroyed or sold under the threat or imminence of condemnation, you may elect to use either the involuntary conversion rules or the sale of residence rules (¶1700 et seq.) [IRC Sec. 1034(i); Reg. Sec. 1.1033(a)-3, 1.1034-1(h)]. You must use the involuntary conversion rules if your residence is destroyed (e.g., fire damage).

NOTE: The $125,000 exclusion (for those age 55 or over) can be used to shelter gain on an involuntary conversion [Reg. Sec. 1.121-5(g)].

(e) Use and Occupancy (Business Interruption) Insurance Proceeds.
If an insurance policy by its terms insures against loss of profits due to an involuntary conversion, the recovery is treated as income, equivalent to the earnings it replaced. If, however, the policy is of the valued type (i.e., it pays a fixed amount per week), the recovery under the policy is treated as proceeds of involuntary conversion.

(f) Sales Under Reclamation Laws.
The sale or exchange or other disposition of property in an irrigation project qualifies as an involuntary conversion [IRC Sec. 1033(c); Reg Sec. 1.1033(c)-1].

¶1711   GAIN OR LOSS ON INVOLUNTARY CONVERSION— GENERAL RULES

If property is converted *directly* into other similar or related property, no gain or loss is recognized [IRC Sec. 1033(a)(1)]. This may happen if a condemning governmental authority gives you property instead of a monetary award.

If you receive payment for property involuntarily converted and replace it with property that is similar or related in service or use, the following rules apply [IRC Sec. 1033(a)(2); Reg. Sec. 1.1033(a)-1(a)]:

1. If the amount realized *equals or is less than* the cost of the replacement property, no gain is recognized.

> **Example 1:** Mr. Drake receives $100,000 in insurance proceeds for property destroyed and buys similar replacement property for $200,000. No gain is recognized.

2. If the amount realized *exceeds* the cost of replacement, gain is recognized to the extent of the excess.

> **Example 2:** Mr. Drake receives $100,000 in insurance proceeds and spends only $20,000 on replacement property. Depending on Drake's basis in the old property, he may have to recognize up to $80,000 of the gain. (See ¶1714 for a detailed explanation of gain computations.)

3. A *loss* on an involuntary conversion is generally recognized (i.e., deductible) [¶1714(b)].

These rules for nonrecognition of gain do not apply unless (a) the replacement is made within a certain period of time (generally, two years) [¶1713], and (b) you elect to have the rules apply [IRC Sec. 1033 (a)(2); Reg. Sec. 1.1033(a)-2(c)].

> **NOTE:** Expenses you incur in connection with the conversion (e.g., legal, engineering and appraisal fees) reduce your amount realized and thereby reduce your involuntary conversion gain.[1]

¶1712   WHAT QUALIFIES AS REPLACEMENT PROPERTY

To avoid recognizing gain on an involuntary conversion, you must generally reinvest the proceeds in property that is similar or related in service or use to your old property [IRC Sec. 1033(a)(2)].

(a) "Similar or Related in Service or Use" Test. To qualify as "similar or related" property, the nature of the replacement property's service or use must be the same as that of the converted property.[1] The replacement property doesn't have to be identical to the converted property as long as it has the same general characteristics. That is, the replacement property must be functionally the same as the converted property. Thus a business vehicle must be replaced with another, and it must perform the same function.

> **Example 1:** Johnson's tractor is destroyed in a fire. If Johnson takes the insurance proceeds and purchases a pleasure boat, Johnson must recognize any gain from the proceeds. If Johnson uses the proceeds to purchase a thresher, the gain will not be recognized.

(b) If You Are an Owner-Lessor. In this situation, there must be similarity in the relationship to you of the services or uses of the original and replacement properties. Thus, new rental property can qualify to replace old, even though the tenant's functional uses differ.[2]

> **Example 2:** Adams leased part of his old building to lessees who used it as a movie theatre, and part to other lessees who sold groceries. If he leases the replacement building as a department store, it will qualify for the rollover. If he uses the new building as his personal residence, however, the replacement will not qualify.[3]

(c) Acquiring Control of a Corporation. Qualified replacement property can be bought, built, obtained directly or by acquiring control of a corporation owning similar property. Control of a corporation means you own at least 80% of the total combined voting power of all classes of stock and at least 80% of the total number of shares of all other classes of stock [IRC Sec. 1033(a)(2)(E)(i); Reg. Sec. 1.1033(a)-2(c)].

> **Example 3:** Glass owned a card shop that was destroyed by fire. Using the insurance proceeds, she acquired 80% of the stock of Ajax Company which owns a card shop similar to the one that burned down. Because she meets the "control" requirements, her gain from the proceeds will not be recognized.

(d) "Like-Kind" Test—Condemnation of Real Property. A special and more liberal rule applies to the replacement of real property that is held for investment or used in a trade or business. When such property is condemned (or is sold under its threat or imminence), gain is not recognized if you replace it with "like-kind" property [IRC Sec. 1033(g); Reg. Sec. 1.1033(g)-1].

For this purpose, "like-kind" has the same meaning as it has in the rule for nontaxable exchanges of property held for productive use or investment [¶1614(a)]. Thus improved and unimproved property would be of a "like-kind" in condemnation cases. This special rule does not apply to acquiring a controlling interest in a corporation, or to stock in trade or other property held primarily for sale. You can also elect to treat outdoor advertising displays as real property [IRC Sec. 1033(g)(3); Reg. Sec. 1.1033(g)-1(b)].

¶1713   TIME LIMIT ON REPLACEMENT

(a) Two Years. The period within which you must replace the converted property starts with the date of the disposition, or the date the threat or imminence of its condemnation began, whichever is earlier. The period ends two years after the conversion is realized [IRC Sec. 1033(a)(2)(B)(i)].

(b) Extension. The standard two-year time period may be extended upon request [Reg. Sec. 1.1033(a)-2(c)(3)].

(c) Prior Acquisition. If you make the replacement before the disposition of the converted property, the replacement property or stock must be held by you on the disposition.

(d) Three Years for Certain Real Property. For real property used in a trade or business, the time period for replacement is *three* years [IRC Sec. 1033(g)(4); Reg. Sec. 1.1033(g)-1(c)].

> ➤ **TAX-FREE CASH** Let's say you own an apartment house that burns down. There is no mortgage on the property. Your adjusted basis is $100,000, and the fair market value is $200,000. As a result of receiving $200,000 insurance proceeds, you have a $100,000 gain. You can avoid paying tax on that gain while retaining much of the cash proceeds by financing your purchase of the replacement property (i.e., taking out a mortgage for your purchase).

(e) Advance Payment to Contractor. A payment prior to construction of the replacement property is not timely unless the construction is completed before the end of the replacement period. The fact that a contract to construct replacement property is entered into does not fulfill the time requirements.[1]

¶1714 HOW TO FIGURE GAIN OR LOSS ON AN INVOLUNTARY CONVERSION

The following discussion shows how to apply the rules outlined in ¶1711 governing recognition of gain or loss on involuntary conversion [IRC Sec. 1033(a)(2)(A); Reg. Sec. 1.1033(a)-2(c)]:

(a) If There Is a Direct Conversion Into Other Property. In this situation, you do not recognize gain or loss.

(b) If the Basis of the Converted Asset Exceeds the Amount Realized. In this case, you recognize a loss if it's a (1) casualty or theft loss [¶2304; 2305] or (2) incurred in a trade, businesss or transaction entered into for profit [¶2302; 2303]. Thus, an involuntary conversion loss from a fire in a residence or business building is deductible. However, an involuntary loss from condemnation is deductible only for the business building; no loss is allowed for the residence [¶1700; 2304(b)].

(c) If There Is Gain on the Conversion and the Amount Realized Exceeds the Cost of Replacement. Here you must recognize gain to the extent of the excess. You may elect nonrecognition for the remainder of the gain [IRC Sec. 1033(a)(2)(A)].

(d) If the Cost of Replacement Exceeds the Amount Realized. If there is gain and the cost of the replacement exceeds the amount realized, you may elect nonrecognition of gain. You cannot take the excess of the cost of replacement over the amount received as a loss. It is treated as a capital expenditure [¶2203].

> **Example:** Akbar's manufacturing plant with an adjusted basis of $2,000,000 is destroyed by fire. The building is replaced at a cost of $2,250,000. The following table illustrates Akbar's choices under the rules in (b), (c) and (d) above, depending on the amount of insurance proceeds received and the cost of the replacement property. In all three cases, the amounts received include any liabilities assumed.[1]

	Adjusted basis	Amount received	Replacement cost	Recognized gain or loss
(b)	$2,000,000	$1,500,000	$2,250,000	($500,000)
(c)	$2,000,000	$2,500,000	$2,250,000	$250,000
(d)	$2,000,000	$2,150,000	$2,250,000	NONE

> **NOTE:** Under the second alternative (c), the realized gain is $500,000, but Akbar can elect to limit the taxable gain to $250,000 (the difference between the amount received and the replacement cost). Under the third alternative, gain is not taxed if Akbar so elects. However, if no replacement is made, the gain of $150,000 ($2,150,000 less $2,000,000) is taxable.

¶1715 BASIS OF REPLACEMENT PROPERTY ACQUIIRED IN INVOLUNTARY CONVERSION

Your basis in replacement property in an involuntary conversion depends on a number of factors, such as whether there is a direct conversion and whether or not a gain or loss is recognized [IRC Sec. 1033(b); Reg. Sec. 1.1033(b)-1].

(a) Direct Conversion. When you do not recognize gain because property is directly converted into other property similar or related in service or use, your basis in the new asset is the same as your adjusted basis in the old asset.

Example 1: Land owned by Betty, which had an adjusted basis of $50,000, was condemned by the county, and Betty received similar land from the county to replace her condemned land. The basis of the new land is $50,000.

(b) When Loss Is Recognized. In this situation, your basis in the new property is its replacement cost.

Example 2: Chester's factory with an adjusted basis of $1,000,000 was destroyed by fire. The insurance proceeds were $850,000. He bought a new plant for $1,200,000. A loss of $150,000 is recognized and the new factory's basis is $1,200,000.

(c) When No Gain Is Recognized Because Cost of Replacement Exceeds Amount Realized. Here, your basis in the replacement property is its cost *less* gain not recognized [¶1711; 1714(d)].

Example 3: Wilma's plant with a $1,100,000 adjusted basis was destroyed by fire. The insurance proceeds were $1,220,000. Wilma bought a new plant for $1,300,000. No gain is recognized. The basis of the new plant is $1,180,000, figured as follows:

Realized gain	$ 120,000
Recognized gain	0
Gain not recognized	$ 120,000
Cost of new plant	$1,300,000
Less: Gain not recognized	120,000
Basis of new plant	$1,180,000

(d) When Gain Is Recognized Because the Amount Realized Exceeds the Cost of Replacement. In this case, your basis in the replacement property is its cost *less* any gain not recognized [¶1711; 1714(c)].

Example 4: Goober owned a garage with an adjusted basis of $65,000 which the state condemned. He received a $75,000 award and bought a new garage for $70,000. His realized gain is $10,000 but only $5,000 of it is recognized (excess of condemnation proceeds over cost of new property). The new garage's basis is $65,000, figured as follows:

Realized gain	$10,000
Recognized gain	5,000
Gain not recognized	$ 5,000
Cost of new garage	$70,000
Less: Gain not recognized	5,000
Basis of new garage	$65,000

(e) If More Than One Property Is Bought. In this event, your basis is allocated to the properties in proportion to their respective costs.[1] Your basis in improved real property must be similarly allocated between the land and improvements, according to the value of each.[2]

Example 5: Wilbur owned a farm with an adjusted basis of $370,000 which the state condemned. He received a $420,000 award and bought two adjoining farms totaling about the same acreage as the condemned land. He paid $180,000 for farm 1 and $220,000 for farm 2. His realized gain is $50,000, but only $20,000 of it is recognized (excess of condemnation proceeds over new properties' total cost). The basis of each of the new properties is figured as follows:

Realized gain	$ 50,000
Recognized gain	20,000
Gain not recognized	$ 30,000
Cost of new property (both farms)	$400,000
Less: Gain not recognized	30,000
Basis of new property (both farms)	$370,000

Allocation:
  Basis of farm # 1: $180,000/400,000 × $370,000 = $166,500
  Basis of farm # 2: $220,000/400,000 × $370,000 = $203,500

(f) Basis in Partial Condemnation. If part of a property is condemned, your basis in the condemned part and your basis in the part retained must each be determined in order to figure your gain or loss from the condemnation. It is important to determine your basis in the retained part in case it is later sold or condemned. Allocating your basis presents a problem if the property is improved real estate that was purchased for a lump sum. In such a situation, the local tax authority's assessed valuation may be used to allocate basis.[3]

> **Example 6:** Land and building were bought for $60,000. Assessed valuations are: land—$18,000; building—$12,000. The land's basis is $36,000:
>
> $$\frac{\$18,000}{\$18,000 + \$12,000} \quad \times \quad \$60,000 \quad = \quad \$36,000$$
>
> The building's basis is $24,000 ($60,000 – $36,000). If one-third of the land was condemned, the basis of the condemned portion would be $12,000 ($36,000 ÷ 3).

¶1716   HOW TO MAKE THE REPLACEMENT AND ELECTION

You elect nonrecognition of gain treatment by reporting on your return only the portion of gain that is taxable after applying the involuntary conversion rules. If you don't replace the property within the time limit, or do so at a lower cost than anticipated, you must file an amended return recomputing the tax liability for the year of election.

(a) Who Must Make the Replacement. Generally, you or your agent must make the replacement. Tenants may replace leased property when they have to return it in the same condition as they receive it.[1] Replacement by your controlled corporation does not qualify.[2] Replacement of partnership property must be made by the partnership, not the individual partner.[3] A court has allowed a decedent's executor to make the replacement,[4] but the IRS disagrees.[5]

(b) Who Must Make the Election. Generally, the election is made by the taxpayer. The grantor of a reversionary trust must make the election if he is taxable on the income of the trust.[6] Partnerships must make the election, not the individual partners.[3]

(c) Information on the Return. When there is a gain on an involuntary conversion, you must report the details in a statement submitted with your return for the year the gain was realized. These details relate to the replacement of the converted property, the decision not to replace or the end of the replacement period. If you actually acquire replacement property in a later year, details of the replacement are reported on the return for that year [Reg. Sec. 1.1033(a)-2(c)(2)].

¶1717   SPECIAL BENEFIT ASSESSMENTS

These assessments may be levied against retained property when the property is benefited by the improvement for which the land was condemned. Such improvements often include the widening of streets or the installation of sewers. The assessments first reduce any severance damages. Any excess reduces the condemnation award.[1] Anything remaining is added to the property's basis. The reductions apply only if the assessment was actually withheld from the condemnation award.[1]

¶1718   SEVERANCE DAMAGES

Severance damages are compensation in addition to an award for the property condemned. They are paid to you where part of your property is condemned and the value of the property retained is decreased as a result of the condemnation.

Where it's not clearly shown that a condemnation award includes a specific amount for severance damages, it will be presumed that the proceeds were given in consideration of the property condemned only.[1]

There have been cases, however, where the Tax Court allowed allocations of condemnation awards to severance damages.[2]

Nonrecognition treatment of severance damages. Severance damages, if used to restore retained property (e.g., rebuilding of stone wall or fence) or purchase like property, can be accorded nonrecognition treatment [¶ 1710].[3]

Severance damages received must first be reduced by: (1) the expenses incurred in securing the severance damages and (2) the amount of any special assessment [¶1717] levied against the part of the property retained and withheld from the award by the condemning authority. Any balance of the proceeds you use to restore the retained property to its former use or to purchase similar use property is gain, eligible for nonrecognition treatment.

Any gain remaining after the application of Sec. 1033 is recognized to the extent it exceeds the basis of the retained property.[4]

> **Example:** Lori Smith receives a $10,000 condemnation award for part of her property taken by the state and uses the proceeds to purchase like property. She also receives $4,000 in severance damages for the decrease in value to the portion of the retained property. There is no special assessment, and Lori's basis in the retained property had been $1,000. She spends $1,500 to dig a new well on the retained property to replace the one on the condemned property, and incurs $1,000 in legal fees to obtain the severance damages. Result: Lori has $500 recognized gain ($4,000 severance damages less $1,000 legal fees incurred, less $1,500 cost of new well, less $1,000 basis in retained property) and a zero basis in the retained property.

Footnotes to Chapter 7

(For your added convenience, in brackets [] with the footnotes below, you will find citations to related paragraphs in the "RIA United States Tax Reporter"(USTR), "CCH Federal Tax Reporter" (CCH) and "RIA Federal Tax Coordinator 2d"(FTC) multivolume services.)

FOOTNOTE ¶ 1700 [USTR ¶ 10,344; CCH ¶4639.05; FTC ¶ I-3200].

FOOTNOTE ¶ 1701 [USTR ¶ 10,344; CCH ¶ 4639.067; FTC ¶ I-3207].

(1) Rev. Rul. 64-31, 1964-1 CB 300.

(2) Ltr. Rul. 8337050.

(3) Treas. Dept. booklet "Your Federal Income Tax" (1991 Ed.), p. 98.

(4) Andrews, ¶ 81,247 PH Memo TC; Bolaris v. Comm., 56 AFTR 2d 85-6472, 776 F.2d 1428, aff'g 81 TC 840.

(5) Rev. Rul. 82-26, 1982-1 CB 114.

FOOTNOTE ¶ 1702 [USTR ¶ 10,344; CCH ¶ 4639.051; FTC ¶ I-3219].

(1) Rev. Rul. 54-380, 1954-2 CB 155.

(2) Rev. Rul. 68-650, 1968-2 CB 78.

(3) Rev. Rul. 72-118, 1972-1 CB 227.

(4) Rev. Rul. 67-297, 1967-2 CB 87.

(5) Rev. Rul. 60-76, 1960-1 CB 296.

(6) Treas. Dept. booklet "Your Federal Income Tax" (1991 Ed.), p. 101.

(7) Rev. Rul. 75, 1953-1, CB 83.

FOOTNOTE ¶ 1703 [USTR ¶ 10,344; CCH ¶ 4639.08; FTC ¶ I-3225].

FOOTNOTE ¶ 1704 [USTR ¶ 10,344; CCH ¶ 4639; FTC ¶ P-1149, I-3007].

FOOTNOTE ¶ 1705 [USTR ¶ 10,344; CCH ¶ 4639.055; FTC ¶ I-3229].

(1) Rev. Rul. 77-371, 1977-2 CB 3808.

(2) Rev. Rul. 55-37, 1955-1 CB 347.

FOOTNOTE ¶ 1706 [USTR ¶ 10,344; CCH ¶ 4639.07; FTC ¶ I-3100].

FOOTNOTE ¶ 1707 [USTR ¶ 10,394; CCH ¶ 4645R.01; FTC ¶ I-3607].

FOOTNOTE ¶ 1708 [USTR ¶ 1214; CCH ¶ 1197; FTC ¶ I-3301].

(1) Rev. Rul. 87-104, 1987-2 CB 45.

(2) Rev. Rul. 67-234, 1967-2 CB 78; Rev. Rul. 67-235, 1967-2 CB 79.

(3) Rev. Rul. 82-1, 1982-1 CB.

(4) Rev. Rul. 85-45, 1985-1 CB 183.

FOOTNOTE ¶ 1710 [USTR ¶ 10,334; CCH ¶ 4625.01; FTC ¶ I-3000].

(1) Ltr. Rul. 8544001.

(2) Rev. Rul. 38, 1953-1 CB 16.

(3) Rev. Rul. 74-8, 1974-1 CB 200, modifying Rev. Rul. 63-221, 1963-2 CB 332.

FOOTNOTE ¶ 1711 [USTR ¶ 10,334; CCH ¶ 4625.0114; FTC ¶ I-3062].

(1) Treas. Dept. booklet "Sales and Other Dispositions of Assets " (1991 Ed.), p. 3.

FOOTNOTE ¶ 1712 [USTR ¶ 10,334; CCH ¶ 4625.0112; FTC ¶ I-3033, 3069].

(1) Rev. Rul. 64-237.

(2) Liant Records Inc. v. Comm., 9 AFTR 2d 1557, 303 F.2d 326.

(3) Rev. Rul. 70-466, 1970-2 CB 165; amplified by Rev. Rul. 76-84, 1976-1 CB 219.

FOOTNOTE ¶ 1713 [USTR ¶ 10,334; CCH ¶ 4625.0112; FTC ¶ I-3000].

(1) Rev. Rul. 56-300, 1956-1 CB 624.

FOOTNOTE ¶ 1714 [USTR ¶ 10,334; CCH ¶ 4625.0114; FTC ¶ I-3062].

(1) Comm. v. Fortee Properties, Inc., 211 F.2d 915, 45 AFTR 1347; but see Comm. v. Babcock, 2 AFTR 2d 5819, 259 F.2d 689.

FOOTNOTE ¶ 1715 [USTR ¶ 10,334; CCH ¶ 4625.011, 4627.01; FTC ¶ P-1149].

(1) Rev. Rul. 73-18, 1973-1 CB 368.

(2) Rev. Rul. 79-402, 1972-2 CB 297.

(3) Treas. Dept. booklet "Condemnations and Business Casualties and Thefts" (1989 Ed.), p. 3.

FOOTNOTE ¶ 1716 [USTR ¶ 10,334; CCH ¶ 4625.014; FTC ¶ I-3054].

(1) Adams, 16 BTA 497.

(2) Feinberg, 19 AFTR 2d 1366, 377 F.2d 21.

(3) Rev. Rul. 66-191, 1966-2 CB 300.

(4) Goodman v. Comm., 42 AFTR 877, 199 F.2d 895.

(5) Rev. Rul. 64-161, 1964-1 CB 298.

(6) Rev. Rul. 70-376, 1970-2 CB 164.

FOOTNOTE ¶ 1717 [USTR ¶ 10,334; CCH ¶ 4625.01; FTC ¶ I-3003].

(1) Treas. Dept. booklet "Sales and Other Dispositions of Assets" (1991 Ed.), p. 3.

FOOTNOTE ¶ 1718 [USTR ¶ 10,334; CCH ¶ 4625.01; FTC ¶ I-3068].

(1) Rev. Rul. 59-173, 1959-1 CB 201; Lapham v. U.S. 178 F.2d 994, 38 AFTR 1255; Allaben 35 BTA 327; Green v. U.S., 3 AFTR 2d 1461, 173 F.Supp. 868.

(2) L.A. Beeghly, 36 TC 154.

(3) Rev. Rul. 83-49, 1980-2 CB 191.

(4) Rev. Rul. 68-37, 1968-1 CB 359. Treas. Dept. booklet "Sales and Other Dispositions of Assets" (1991 Ed.), p. 3.

CHAPTER 8

CAPITAL GAINS AND LOSSES OF INDIVIDUALS

CAPITAL GAINS AND LOSSES

It is important for you to identify your capital gains and losses. To begin with, you net your capital gains and losses to figure taxable capital gain or deductible capital loss. And capital gain or loss is treated differently from ordinary gain or loss. There are special limits on the amount of deductible capital loss. And long-term capital gain gets tax-favored treatment not afforded other income.

¶1800   CAPITAL GAINS AND LOSSES IN GENERAL

Generally, a capital gain or loss results from disposing of a capital asset [¶1801] by a sale or exchange [¶1802]. When the property you sell or exchange is a capital asset, or treated like one, your next step is to figure how long you held it [¶1803-1806]. If you held the property for more than one year, a sale or exchange results in a long-term capital gain or loss. If you held the property for one year or less, its sale or exchange results in a short-term capital gain or loss.

Capital gains and losses can offset each other in full—regardless of whether they are short- or long-term. If you have a net capital loss for the year (capital loss exceeds capital gain), you can currently deduct only up to $3,000 of this loss against your other income (e.g., salary, interest, dividends). On the other hand, if your capital gains exceed your capital losses for the year, the tax treatment of your gain depends on whether the gain is long-term or short-term [¶1810].

Short-term gain is taxed at the same rates as other income. And that used to be the story for so-called "net capital gain"—the excess of net long-term capital gain over net short-term loss.

➤ **TAX RATE CAP** The maximum tax rate on net capital gain (net long-term gain over net short-term loss) is 28% [IRC Sec. 1(h)]. This rate cap, which benefits taxpayers in the regular 31% tax bracket (e.g., above $86,500 for joint filers), applies to "net capital gain" taxable after 1990—regardless of when the sale or exchange of the property took place. So the rate break applies to gain that's taxable after 1990 from installment sales made in 1990 or earlier years.

Here are the steps you follow in figuring your capital gains and losses:

1. Separate your capital gains and losses from your ordinary income and losses.

2. Segregate your long-term capital gains and losses from your short-term capital gains and losses.

3. Net your long-term capital gains and losses; likewise, net your short-term capital gains and losses.

4. Offset the net long-term figure against the net short-term figure to find the net gain or loss from the sale or exchange of capital assets.

5. Compute the tax on your net capital gain (the excess of net long-term gain over net short-term loss). This tax gets added to the tax on your other income.

6. Use the net loss as an offset against ordinary income—but the offset must be limited to only $3,000 in any one year [¶1810].

NOTE: Additional computations may be required if some business assets held for a required length of time are disposed of during the year [¶1811 et seq.].

¶1801   WHAT IS A CAPITAL ASSET

The principal capital assets are investment property (stocks and bonds held by an investor) and property held for personal use (jewelry, residence or automobile). Gain or loss from the sale or exchange of investment property is a capital gain or loss. Gain from a transaction involving property held for personal use is a capital gain, but losses are never deductible unless it is a casualty or theft loss [¶1813]. A capital asset is any property (whether or not connected with a trade or business), *except:*

*   Stock in trade or other inventory property.
*   Property held *primarily* for sale to customers in the ordinary course of the taxpayer's trade or business. "Primarily" means "of first importance" or "principally."[1]
*   Depreciable property used in a trade or business [but see ¶1811 et seq.].
*   Real property used in a trade or business [but see ¶1811; 1812(b)].
*   Copyrights; literary, musical or artistic compositions; a letter, memorandum or similar property held by (1) a taxpayer whose personal efforts created the property; or (2) a taxpayer for whom a letter, memorandum or similar property was prepared or produced; or (3) one receiving the property as a gift from the person who created it.
*   Accounts or notes receivable acquired in the ordinary course of trade or business (a) for services rendered, or (b) from the sale of stock in trade, inventory or property held for sale to customers.
*   Certain U.S. Government publications received free or at a reduced price [IRC Sec. 1221; Reg. Sec.1.1221-1].

(a) Stocks, Bonds, Notes, Debentures and Similar Securities. These items are capital assets, unless they fall under one of the above exceptions. Special rules apply to collapsible corporation stock [¶1820]. Small business stock and stock in a small business investment company are not considered capital assets if sold at a loss under certain conditions [¶1821]. Securities bought to get inventory or guarantee performance of a contract are not capital assets if the purpose for which they are acquired is accomplished and the securities are disposed of within a relatively short time after acquisition.[2] Gain on transfers of stock in controlled foreign corporations may be ordinary income [¶3828].

(b) Real Property. Real property not used in a trade or business is a capital asset—for example, your private residence. If property is used in a trade or business, it is not a capital asset. But homes purchased under a home-buying plan by a corporation to assist relocating employees in the sale of their personal residences are capital assets when later sold by the corporations. Thus, if there is a loss on the later sale, it is a capital ordinary loss.[3]

(c) Property Held for the Production of Income. If this property is not used in your trade or business, it is a "capital asset" [Reg. Sec. 1.1221-1(b)].

(d) Sales of Going Concerns. A sale of a going business for a lump sum is treated as a sale of each individual asset rather than of a single capital asset.[4] In order to figure the amount of gain or loss from each asset's transfer, the amount of goodwill that is being sold and the buyer's basis in the assets of the business, both the buyer and the seller must allocate the purchase price among the assets involved in the transaction. Except for the assets that are exchanged under the like-kind exchange rules [¶1614], the so-called residual method is used in making this allocation. Under the residual method, the purchase price is first reduced by the amount of cash, demand deposits and similar accounts transferred by the seller. Then the remaining amount is allocated in the following order: (1) to the marketable securities and similar items; (2) to all other tangible and intangible assets except going concern value and goodwill; and—whatever is left—(3) to goodwill and going concern value [Temp. Reg. Sec. 1.1060-1T].

> ▶ **INFORMATION REPORTING** For sales entered into after October 9, 1990, there is an infor-
> mation reporting requirement if a 10%-or-more business owner sells an interest in the business and
> the owner enters into an employment contract, covenant not to compete, royalty or lease agreement,
> or other agreement with the buyer. Both the seller (the 10% business owner) and the buyer are
> responsible to report to the IRS [IRC Sec. 1060(e)].

Both the buyer and seller involved in the sale of business assets must report the consideration's allocation among goodwill and the other business assets on Form 8594.

(e) Partnership Interest. The portion of an individual partner's partnership interest that is attributable to certain partnership noncapital assets (primarily accounts receivable and appreciated inventory) is an ordinary asset, while the remainder of his interest is a single capital asset.[5] Transfer of a partnership interest is discussed in ¶3426.

> **NOTE:** In some partnership distributions or transfers of interests, the allocation rules summarized in
> (d) above apply in valuing goodwill or going concern value [IRC Sec. 1060(d),(e)].

(f) Copyrights, Literary, Musical or Artistic Compositions, Letters or Memoranda and Similar Property. These items are not capital assets. "Similar property" includes a radio program created by a taxpayer's personal efforts, a theatrical production, a newspaper cartoon strip, or other property eligible for copyright protection. It does not include a patent, invention, or a design protected only under the patent law and not under the copyright law [Reg. Sec. 1.1221-1]. Letters and memoranda include manuscripts and any other writings or recordings of a business or personal nature. A letter or memorandum addressed to a person is considered as prepared or produced for him [Reg. Sec. 1.1221-1(c)(2)].

(g) Lease. Amounts received by a *tenant* for cancelling a lease are considered as received in exchange for the lease [IRC Sec. 1241; Reg. Sec. 1.1241-1]. This also applies to giving up a lease restriction.[6] The type of gain or loss depends on the lease's character. A nondepreciable leasehold is a capital asset. Part of a gain from the sale or exchange of the depreciable leasehold may be ordinary income to the extent the recapture rules apply [¶1812]. An amount received by the *landlord* for cancelling[7] or amending[8] a lease is ordinary income.

(h) Options. Gain or loss from the sale or exchange of an option to buy or sell property is treated the same as gain or loss from the sale or exchange of the property underlying the option. If the property that is the subject of the option is a capital asset, so is the option. If the loss results from failure to exercise the option, the option is considered to have been sold or exchanged on the day it expired [IRC Sec. 1234; Reg. Sec. 1.1234-1]. The rule does not apply to the following:

- An option that is part of your inventory or stock in trade.
- Gain from the sale of an option if income derived from the option would be treated as ordinary income without regard to the rule. For example, if gain on the sale of an employee stock option is in the nature of compensation, the gain is not treated

as a capital gain merely because the stock, if acquired, would be a capital asset in the employee's hands.

- Loss from failure to exercise a "put" bought on the same day as the stock used to fulfill the contract [¶1806].
- Gain resulting from the sale or exchange of an option acquired by you before March 1, 1954, if in your hands such option is a capital asset [Reg. Sec. 1.1234-1(e)].

A special rule applies to actively traded personal property acquired after June 23, 1981. This is property that would be a capital asset in the taxpayer's hands. Terminating rights or obligations in this property is treated as a sale or exchange [IRC Sec. 1234A]. Common examples of these transactions include cancelling forward contracts for currency or securities and regulated futures contracts (Sec. 1256 contracts).

NOTE: The capital gain or loss treatment from certain contract terminations does not apply to the retirement of any debt instrument whether or not through a trust or participation arrangement [IRC Sec. 1234A].

(i) Distributor's Agreement. Amounts received by a distributor of goods for cancelling a distributor's agreement (if the distributor has made a substantial capital investment) are considered received in exchange for the agreement. Such amounts usually receive capital gain treatment [IRC Sec. 1241; Reg. Sec. 1.1241-1].

(j) Patents. A patent you hold for investment is a capital asset. Long-term capital gain treatment may be granted to amateur or professional inventors or certain other holders who transfer *all substantial rights* in the patent regardless of the length of time the patent right was held. Payments may be spread over the duration of the transferred use of the patent or contingent on the patent's use [IRC Sec. 1235(a)]. IRS regulations say that all substantial rights are not being transferred when the patent is sold subject to restriction on its geographic use within the country [Reg. Sec. 1.1235-2(b)(1)], but the Tax Court disagrees.[9] Nor may there be limitations as to duration of use (shorter than the patent's remaining useful life) or fields of use. In addition, the transfer must not be made to certain related persons, including a trust in which the inventor is a grantor or beneficiary, certain partnerships, and a controlled corporation, but not including a brother or sister. An individual backer of an inventor who got his interest by investing money before the invention was completed also may be entitled to long-term capital gains. The IRS has ruled that patent transfers not qualifying for long-term capital gains treatment under Sec. 1235 may still qualify under other Code provisions.[10]

(k) Other Items. The following have been held to be capital assets: life estate;[11] bank account;[12] cotton acreage allotment.[13] The following have been held *not* to be capital assets: right to future dividend sold by stockholder;[14] employment contract sold by an employee;[15] trade acceptance received as incident to the sale of merchandise;[16] an exclusive or perpetual right to exploit and use one's name;[17] covenant not to compete;[18] a franchise, trademark or trade name, if the transferor retains any significant power, right or continuing interest [IRC Sec. 1253].

¶1802   NECESSITY FOR A SALE OR EXCHANGE

There is no capital gain or loss unless the asset disposed of was *sold or exchanged*. Some transactions that are not actually sales or exchanges are treated as such, since their effect is similar. These include:

- Involuntary conversion [¶1813].
- Cutting of timber [¶1814].
- Liquidating dividends [¶1229].
- Securities becoming worthless during the tax year [¶2308].
- Nonbusiness debts becoming worthless in the tax year [¶2357].
- Pension, profit-sharing and stock bonus distributions [¶1320].

HOLDING PERIOD

¶1803   FIGURING THE HOLDING PERIOD

Your records should show the exact date property was acquired and disposed of. In figuring the period held, exclude the date the property was acquired but include the day it was disposed of.[1] The reverse is true when figuring a prescribed period *before* a designated event (as in timber and coal transactions [¶1814; 1816]).[2] The holding period is figured by calendar months and fractions of months, not by days.[3] In other words, the day after the property was acquired is the start of the holding period and this same date in each succeeding calendar month is the start of a new month regardless of the number of days in the preceding month.[4]

> **Example 1:** Mr. Ames bought stock on June 26, 1992. He starts to count the holding period on June 27, 1992. Ames must sell the stock on or after June 27, 1993 to have held it more than one year.

Special Rules for Certain Property

Stock or securities. For securities traded on an established securities market, the holding period is measured by using the *trading date* as the date sold and not the settlement date. Gain or loss is also recognized on the trading date of the sale and not on the settlement date.[5]

For stock purchases in which the parties contracted for the sale, the date on which title is transferred, not the earlier contract date, governs.[6]

Real property. The holding period begins on the day after title passes or on the day after delivery of possession is made and the buyer assumes ownership privileges, whichever occurs first. A delivery of possession under a mere option agreement is without significance until a contract of sale takes place through exercise of the option.[7]

Newly erected building. Parts of a new building may be considered as having been completed before the entire building. Their holding period starts at their completion.[8]

Patents. The special rule under IRC Sec. 1235 [¶1801(j)] for long-term capital gain treatment on transfer of a patent applies regardless of the period held. If capital gain is sought under general capital gains rules, a patent's holding period runs from the earlier of either the date the invention is reduced to actual practice or the patent is issued.[9]

Community property. The holding period of a surviving spouse's share generally runs from the date the property was acquired by the deceased spouse.

Optioned property. The period during which you hold an option cannot be added to the period you own property acquired under the option.[10]

Commodity futures. A commodity future is a contract for the sale of some fixed amount of a commodity at a future date for a fixed price. If you accept delivery of a commodity in satisfaction of a commodity futures contract, the holding period of the commodity includes the period for which you held the futures contract if such commodity futures contract was a capital asset in your hands [IRC Sec. 1223(8); Reg. Sec. 1.1223-1(h)]. For short sale rules, see ¶1805(c).

The holding period of stock dividends and stock rights is given in ¶1223 and 1225; wash sales in ¶2321. For holding period of worthless securities, see ¶2308; 2362. See below for other special cases.

(a) Gifts. The holding period begins with the date the property was acquired by the donor. However, if the property had a value at the date of the gift lower than cost, and the sale results in a loss, the holding period begins on the date of the gift [IRC Sec. 1223(2); Reg. Sec. 1.1223-1(b)].

(b) Property Acquired by Bequest, Devise or Inheritance. Gains and losses from the sale or exchange of inherited property receive long-term treatment regardless of how long the property was held [IRC Sec. 1223(11)].

(c) Tax-Free Exchanges. The holding period you receive property in a nontaxable exchange includes the holding period of the property given in exchange, if the property exchanged was either a capital asset or depreciable property used in your trade or business and if the basis of the property you receive has the same basis, in whole or in part, as the property exchanged [IRC Sec. 1223(1); Reg. Sec. 1.1223-1(a)].

> **Example 2:** On December 13, 1992, Mr. Frank, a calendar year taxpayer, exchanged shares of Class A stock, bought July 12, 1992, for $1,200, for shares of Class B stock in a tax-free exchange. The holding period of the Class B shares began on July 13, 1992. He sells the Class B shares on August 3, 1993, for $1,000. Since his holding period of the Class B stock is more than one year, his $200 loss is a long-term loss.

(d) Partnership Interest. The holding period runs from the date the interest is acquired. A partner's death does not interrupt the holding period of the other partners' interest, as long as the business continues.[11]

(e) New Residence Replacing Old Residence. The holding period of a new residence that replaces one transferred without gain being recognized [¶1700; 1702] includes the old residence's holding period [IRC Sec. 1223(7); Reg. Sec. 1.1223-1(g)].

¶1804   FIRST-IN, FIRST-OUT RULE

In general, when shares of stock are sold from lots bought at different dates or prices and the identity of the lots cannot be determined, the stock sold is considered to have come from the earliest acquired lot [¶1623]. This is important in figuring the period held as well as fixing gain or loss.

¶1805   SHORT SALES

[New tax legislation may affect this subject; see ¶1.]

Selling short means selling property you do not own, borrowing property to cover the sale and repaying the lender (usually your broker) with substantially identical property, which you may have bought after the sale. Short sales involve two kinds of property: (1) stocks and securities, and (2) commodity futures. Gains or losses from short sales of property are considered gains or losses from sales or exchanges of capital assets to the extent that the property used to close the short sale (the property returned to the lender) is a capital asset in your hands [IRC Sec. 1233(a); Reg. Sec. 1.1233-1(a)]. For "put" and "call" options, see ¶1806.

The "wash sale" rule [¶2321], which disallows a loss deduction on the sale or disposition of certain stock or securities (including contracts or options to acquire or sell stock or securities), also applies to losses on a short sale if, within 30 days before or after the closing, the taxpayer sold or entered into another short sale of substantially identical securities [IRC Sec. 1091(e)]. Such short-sale losses are not deductible.

Background and purpose. Basically, short sales occur when speculators, believing that the price of certain stocks will fall, sell the stocks anticipating that they will be able to buy them back at a lower price than when they were sold. Short sellers must deliver the certificates to buyers like any other sellers. Since they may not have them, a broker borrows the stock for them and gives it to the buyer. Sellers close the short sale when they return the borrowed stock to the broker. If the stocks sold short decline in price, short sellers make a profit; if the price goes up, they have a loss. There are problems, however, in determining whether the gain or loss is short-term or long-term. If the date for measuring the holding period is simply the date the short sale is closed, a short sale might allow you to convert what is essentially a short-term holding period into a long-term holding period.

> **Example 1:** This example assumes Mr. Kraft owned no Yates stock and had no dealings in that stock except as stated.
> 2-4-92: Kraft buys 100 shares of Yates Co. stock for $1,000.
> 12-5-92: Kraft sells short 100 shares of Yates Co. stock for $1,400.
> 3-9-93: Kraft covers the short sale by delivering the stock bought on 2-4-92.
> When Kraft makes the short sale on December 5, 1992 for $1,400, he is assuring a $400 profit on stock that he has held less than the long-term period. Without the special rules explained in (a) below, Kraft would have converted what appeared to be a short-term capital gain into a long-term capital gain by holding the transaction open until March 9, 1993, when he covered the short sale (the holding period ran from February 4, 1992 to March 9, 1993—more than the minimum long-term period). However, under (a) below, the gain on the short sale is short-term because on the date of short sale (December 5, 1992), property substantially identical to that sold had not been held for more than one year.

(a) Special Rules for Short Sales. In general, the holding period on a short sale is figured by the length of time the seller holds the property that is eventually delivered to the lender to close the short sale. The following rules are aimed at closing what would otherwise be loophole situations:

1. If, on the date of the short sale, property substantially identical to that sold has been held for not more than one year or if such substantially identical property is acquired between the short sale and closing dates, any gain on the closing of a short sale is a short-term capital gain.

> **NOTE:** This rule applies regardless of when the property actually used to close the short sale was acquired, but it doesn't apply to that part of the property sold short that exceeds the substantially identical property.

> **Example 2:** On February 15, 1992, Mr. Latimer bought 100 shares of Jay stock for $1,000. On November 15, 1992, he sold short 100 shares of Jay stock for $1,500. On February 28, 1993, he closes the short sale by delivering the 100 shares of Jay stock bought on February 15, 1992. The gain of $500 ($1,500 less $1,000) is a short-term capital gain because on the date of the short sale (November 15, 1992) property substantially identical to that sold had not been held for more than a year.

2. If, as in Rule 1 above, on the date of the short sale, property substantially identical to the property sold short has been held for no more than one year or property substantially identical to the property sold short was acquired between the date of the short sale and the date the sale was closed, the holding period of such substantially identical property

begins on the earlier of (a) the date the short sale was closed or (b) the date the substantially identical property was either sold, gifted or otherwise disposed of.

> **NOTE:** This rule does not apply to that part of the substantially identical property that exceeds the amount sold short nor does it apply to short sales open no more than 20 days or to certain capital asset stock held by dealers.

> **Example 3:** On February 15, 1992, Mr. Latimer bought 100 shares of Jay stock for $1,000. On November 15, 1992, he sold short 100 shares of stock for $1,500. On February 20, 1993, he closes the short sale by delivering 100 shares of Jay stock that he had bought several days before for $1,500. On February 28, 1993, he sells the 100 shares he had bought on February 15, 1992 for $1,500. The $500 gain on the last sale ($1,500 less $1,000) is a short-term gain since the holding period of this substantially identical property, bought on February 15, 1992, didn't begin until the date of the short sale (November 15, 1992).

3. If substantially identical property has been held for more than one year as of the date of the short sale, any loss on the closing of the short sale is a long-term capital loss.

> **NOTE:** As in the case of Rule 1, this rule applies regardless of when the property actually used to close the short sale was acquired and doesn't apply to the part of the property sold short that exceeds the substantially identical property.

> **Example 4:** On February 15, 1992, Mr. Latimer bought 100 shares of Jay stock for $1,000. On February 28, 1993, he sells short 100 shares of Jay stock for $1,600. On March 16, 1993, he sells the 100 shares of Jay stock he had purchased on February 15, 1992 for $1,700. On the same day, he purchases 100 shares of Jay stock for $1,700 and uses this stock to cover the short sale. The gain of $700 on the sale of the stock originally purchased on February 15, 1992 ($1,700 less $1,000) is long-term gain because none of the above rules applied. The $100 loss on the closing of the short sale ($1,700 less $1,600) is a long-term loss because property substantially identical to the property sold short had been held for more than one year (February 15, 1992 to February 28, 1993), so Rule 3 applies.

What is substantially identical property depends on the circumstances of each case. Generally, preferred stocks or bonds are not identical to common stock of the same corporation. Securities of one corporation are not substantially identical to securities of another (except in special situations as, for example, securities of a corporation in reorganization).

When preferred stocks or bonds are convertible into common stock of the same corporation, the relative values and price changes may be so similar as to make them substantially identical to the common stock [Reg. Sec. 1.1233-1(d)].

Spouses included. The term "taxpayer" means the "taxpayer or his spouse." Consequently, if your spouse (not legally separated or divorced) holds stock substantially identical to that sold short by you, the three rules apply as if you owned the property [IRC Sec. 1233(e)(2)(C); Reg.Sec. 1.1233-1(d)(3)].

Short sale of small business investment company stock. If you are an investor in small business investment company stock, generally gains from the sale of such stock are capital gains but losses from such sale can be treated as ordinary losses. However, if you acquired the stock merely to close a short sale, you do not get ordinary loss treatment; it is a capital loss.[1]

(b) "When Issued" Transaction. Securities to be issued as a stock dividend, or in a reorganization or recapitalization, may be bought and sold on a "when issued" basis. A contract to sell stock or other securities on a "when issued" basis is a short sale, and the performance or assignment for value of the contract is a closing of the short sale [IRC Sec. 1233(e)(2)(A); Reg. Sec. 1.1233-1(c)(1)].

(c) Commodity Futures and Hedging Transactions. The short sale rules in (a) above apply to transactions in commodity futures that are capital assets [IRC Sec. 1233(b)]. A commodity future is a standard form contract to deliver a fixed quantity of a commodity (wheat, cotton, hides, etc.) in a future month for a fixed price. The purchase and sale of a commodity future results in capital gain or loss, unless the transaction is a hedge [IRC Sec. 1233(a), (g); Reg. Sec. 1.1233-1(b)]. A hedge generally is a form of price insurance to avoid the risk of change in the market price of commodities used in a business. The purchase and sale of futures acquired as hedges results in ordinary gain or loss.[2] However, the Revenue Service does not apply this to a short sale of currency to hedge against devaluation.[3]

In applying the short sale rules to capital transactions, futures that cover different commodities (corn and wheat), or that call for different delivery months (May wheat and July wheat) are not substantially identical. Futures obtained in different markets may be treated as substantially identical in particular cases. When a taxpayer engages in two futures transactions, one to deliver and the other to receive a substantially identical commodity in two different markets, only the excess quantity in either market is considered a short sale if both transactions are made the same day and closed the same day [IRC Sec. 1233(e); Reg. Sec. 1.1233-1(d)(2)].

(d) Commodity Tax Straddles. Straddles are offsetting positions as to personal property. The Code defines personal property as any personal property that is actively traded [IRC Sec. 1092(c)]. A position is an interest in personal property, including a futures contract, a forward contract, or an option. A simple commodity straddle would be constructed by you by taking equal long (buy) and short (sell) positions in a futures contract of a commodity with different delivery dates.

Generally, losses on straddle positions involving property not on the mark to market system (below) cannot be deducted in excess of the amount by which such losses exceed unrecognized gains on any offsetting straddle positions [IRC Sec. 1092].

Deferred losses carry over to the next year. They are subject to the application of the deferral rules in the later year. The losses on unidentified straddles are deferred until their offsetting positions are closed [IRC Sec. 1092; Temp. Reg. Sec. 1.1092(b)-1T(b)].

The loss deferral rules do not apply to losses on positions and straddles that you have clearly identified as straddles on your records on the day they were acquired. However, gain and loss on these identified positions must be netted. The positions must all have been acquired on the same day and either all closed on the same day or none closed by the end of the tax year.

Straddles composed entirely of futures contracts are not subject to the loss deferral rules, but they will be taxed under the mark-to-market system [IRC Sec. 1092]. For mixed straddles, however, where the position consists partly of Sec. 1256 contracts (below), a taxpayer may elect to exclude all of those positions from mark-to-market treatment. Once the exclusion is elected, the positions are eligible for the prescribed loss deferral, wash sale and short-term rules.

No deduction is allowed for interest and carrying charges allocable to property or positions belonging to straddle. They are treated as capital expenditures (¶2203) [IRC Sec. 263(g)].

The capitalization rule does not apply to any identified hedging transactions, any positions not part of a straddle, or qualified covered call options and optioned stock [IRC Sec. 1092(c)(4)(A)].

Mark to market (Sec. 1256 contracts). Gain or loss from "Sec. 1256 contracts" must be reported annually on a "mark to market" system. A Sec. 1256 contract is (1) any regulated futures contract; (2) any foreign currency contract; (3) any nonequity option and (4) any dealer equity option. Under the mark to market system, all of these contracts held at the end of the taxable year have to be treated as sold for fair market value on the last business day of that year.

Determining gain or loss. If a transaction is mark to market, 60% of the gain or loss that you would have had on a sale at that time is treated as a long-term capital gain or loss; the remaining 40% is treated as a short-term capital gain or loss. This is true regardless of the actual character and holding period of the property. When you later dispose of your Sec. 1256 property, you have to increase the gain or loss at that time by the gain or loss formerly recognized. The mark to market rules do not apply to hedging transactions unless the transactions were entered into by a syndicate.

You can elect to carry back commodity futures capital losses (called "net Sec. 1256 contract losses") for three years and apply them against net commodity futures capital gains (called "net Sec. 1256 contract gains") during that period. This carryback is available only after netting regulated futures contracts (and other positions subject to the mark to market rules) with capital gains and losses from other sources. The carryback is then available only if there is a net capital loss for the tax year, which, but for the election, would be a capital loss in the succeeding year [IRC Sec. 1212(c)].

¶1806   "PUT" AND "CALL" OPTIONS

Gain or loss from the sale of an option to buy or sell property is a capital gain or loss if the property optioned is a capital asset. Options are characterized as either "put" or "call" options. A "put" is an option that gives an investor (holder of the option) the right to sell stock to the maker of the option at a stated price within a limited time. A "call" is an option that gives the holder the right to buy stock from the maker of the option at a stated price within a limited time. The option's maker is paid a premium for his obligation to buy or sell the stock.

Background and purpose. Investors buy puts when they expect the value of the stock to fall. They then can sell the stock at the higher option price. If the market price goes up, they can sell the stock at the higher market price rather than exercise their option. Conversely, investors buy calls if they expect the value of the stock to rise. They can buy the stock at the lesser option price. If the market goes down, they can buy the stock at the market price rather than use the option. It is not unusual for one person to write or to acquire a "straddle" (i.e., offsetting put and call options on the same stock) at the same time.

(a) When Option Is Sold. Generally, capital gain or loss results from the sale or exchange of the option unless the taxpayer is a dealer (¶1801(h)) [Reg. Sec. 1.1234-1]. A dealer is one who trades in puts and calls written by others, but not someone who writes puts and calls for a premium.[1] The maker or writer of the put or call is not affected by the sale or exchange.

(b) When Option Is Exercised. The maker of a call option includes the premium received for the option with the option price to find the amount he realized on the exercise. The holder of the call adds the premium he paid to the property's cost in determining his basis for the stock.[1] When the holder sells a 30-day call option and reacquires it before the exercise period expires, the excess cost to reacquire over the option's selling price is added to the stock's basis.[2]

When a put option is exercised, the maker subtracts the premium he received for the option from the price paid for the stock to find his basis for the acquired stock.[1] The holder subtracts the premium he paid from the stock's price to determine the amount he realized on the sale.[3]

Gain or loss on the option's exercise is determined when the sale is closed. It is a capital gain or loss if the stock is a capital asset. The holding period runs from the time the option is exercised.

Short sales. Since a put is an option to sell, the holder generally is making a short sale when he acquires the put. The seller has a short-term capital gain when he exercises the option. The acquisition of a put is not a short sale if the holder owns substantially identical stock for more than one year before he buys the put. Accordingly, the holder can cover the put with this stock for a long-term capital gain or loss or cover it by other stock held less than a year for a short-term gain or loss. Also, the short sale rules do not apply when the put and the stock to be used to cover it are bought on the same day. A call is not "substantially identical" to the stock subject to the call [IRC Sec. 1233(c); Reg. Sec. 1.1233-1(c)].[4]

(c) When Option Lapses. For stock or commodity options granted after September 1, 1976, the option grantor realizes short-term capital gain or loss on a "closing transaction" or lapse of the option without exercise. A "closing transaction" means any end to the grantor's obligation other than by exercise or lapse of the option. This rule does not apply to dealers [IRC Sec. 1234(b)]. Prior to this rule, grantors of options realized ordinary income when they received a premium for the option. They would report as ordinary gain or loss the difference between the amount paid in the closing transaction and the premium received.

If the holder of a put or call lets his option expire without exercising it, he has a loss for the amount he paid for it. However, there is no loss if the put and the stock to cover it are bought at the same time. In that case, the amount paid for the put is added to the stock's cost [IRC Sec. 1233(c)]. A capital loss is a long-term loss if the put or call option was held more than one year; otherwise it's short-term.

FIGURING CAPITAL GAIN OR LOSS

¶1808   **HOW TO REPORT GAIN OR LOSS**

Capital gain or loss is reported on Schedule D of Form 1040. Take these steps to figure the capital gain or loss to be entered on Schedule D:

(a) Short-Term and Long-Term Transactions. Separate short-term capital asset transactions from long-term capital asset transactions.

(b) Find Net Short-Term Capital Gain or Loss. This is the difference between the gain and the loss on all short-term transactions [IRC Sec. 1222(1),(2),(5),(6); Reg. Sec. 1.1222-1].

Example 1: On May 4, 1993, Mr. Frank, a calendar year taxpayer, sells for $4,800 stock bought on October 28, 1992 for $3,600. The short-term capital gain is $1,200, since the shares had been held not more than one year. On August 6, 1993, Frank sold for $2,800 bonds bought November 29, 1992 for $3,000. The short-term capital loss was $200 since the bonds were held not over one year. His net short-term capital gain for 1993 was $1,000 ($1,200 less $200).

(c) Find Net Long-Term Capital Gain or Loss. This is the difference between the gain (in excess of any ordinary gain resulting from recapture) and the loss on all long-term transactions [IRC Sec. 1222(3), (4),(7),(8); Reg. Sec. 1.1222-1].

Example 2: On February 17, 1993, Mr. Frank in Example 1 sells for $15,700 stock bought on February 2, 1989 for $16,400. The loss is a long-term capital loss of $700, since the stock had been held for more than one year. On July 20, 1993, Frank sells for $10,000 stock bought on November 8, 1990 for $9,900. The gain is a long-term capital gain of $100, since the stock had been held for more than one year. His net long-term capital loss for 1993 is $600 ($700 less $100).

(d) Figuring Net Gain or Loss From Capital Asset Transactions. This is the total of the net figures arrived at in steps (b) and (c) above.

Example 3: In 1993, Mr. Frank had a net short-term capital gain of $1,000 and a net long-term capital loss of $600 (Examples 1 and 2 above). Frank's net short-term gain in that year from the sale or exchange of capital assets was $400 ($1,000 less $600).

(e) Net Gain or Loss on Return. Net gain from capital asset transactions is added to other income in figuring adjusted gross income. There may be special tax calculations for your post-1990 long-term capital gains. See ¶1809 below. If there's a net loss from capital asset transactions, the excess is deductible from ordinary income up to $3,000 [¶1810].

¶1809   INDIVIDUAL RATE ON CAPITAL GAIN

Short-term capital gain is taxed at the same rate as your other income. In 1990, long-term gain was also taxed at the same rate as other income. And for many taxpayers, that may still be true for long-term gains after 1990. But taxpayers whose marginal rate is 31% (top tax dollars taxed at 31%)—e.g., joint filers with taxable income over $86,500; singles over $51,900—can benefit from the tax law break.

➤ **CAPITAL GAIN RATE CAP** The maximum tax rate on an individual's "net capital gain" (excess of net long-term capital gain over net short-term capital loss) is 28% [IRC Sec. 1(h)]. Key point: This rate cap applies to all net capital gain that's taxable after 1990. So the rate cap applies to post-1990 installment payments received from a pre-1991 sale.

How the cap works: Generally speaking, taxpayers in the 31% bracket with net capital gain figure their tax by adding (1) a tax computed in the normal way on taxable income less net capital gain, plus (2) a tax of 28% on net capital gains. Here's a closer look at the special computation for the rate cap. Start the computation by checking to see if your taxable income (including your capital gain) exceeds:

- $51,900 if you are single.
- $86,500 if you are married filing jointly or a surviving spouse.
- $43,250 if married filing separately.
- $74,150 if a head of household.

If your taxable income, including capital gains, does exceed the threshold amount for your filing status, you figure your total tax liability as follows:

1. Enter your taxable income . . . . $ _____
2. Enter the capital gain included in taxable income . . . . $ _____
3. Subtract line 2 from line 1 . . . . $ _____
4. Enter your filing status threshold amount . . . . $ _____
5. Enter the larger of line 3 or line 4 . . . . $ _____
6. Subtract line 5 from line 1 . . . . $ _____
7. Figure tax on the amount on line 5 using the appropriate
       Tax Rate Schedules [¶1123] . . . . $ _____
8. Multiply the amount on line 6 by 28% (0.28) . . . . $ _____
9. Add lines 7 and 8. This is your total tax . . . . $ _____

> **Example:** In 1992, Mr. and Mrs. Byrne have a taxable income of $99,000, including a net capital
> gain of $20,000. Without the rate cap, their tax bill would be $23,441. But with the rate cap, their
> 1992 tax bill drops, determined as follows:

1. Taxable income $99,000
2. Less: Net capital gain 20,000
3. Balance $79,000
4. Threshold amount $86,500
5. Larger of line 3 or 4 . . . . $86,500
6. Line 1 less line 5 . . . . $12,500
7. Tax on amount on line 5 (Rate schedule—married filing jointly) $19,566
8. Plus: 28% of $12,500 3,500
9. Total of lines 7 and 8 . . . . $23,066

Tax savings: The Byrnes save $375 with the capital gain rate cap ($23,441 less $23,066).

High-income taxpayers: Despite the 28% rate cap, high-income taxpayers may still
have their long-term gains taxed at a rate higher than 28%. Reason: These taxpayers are
affected by the phaseout of their personal exemptions [¶1112] and the reduction of their
itemized deductions [¶1900]. Since these phaseouts are based on your adjusted gross
income, capital gains are included in determining if your income falls in the phaseout
ranges. In fact, it may be capital gain alone that pushes you into the phaseout ranges—
effectively raising the capital gains rate above 28%.

> **Example:** In 1992, Mr. Katz has salary income of $100,000 and a $50,000 capital gain. Katz's taxable
> income puts him in a 28% bracket for 1992. Since his total adjusted gross income is above the $105,250
> threshold for the itemized deduction phaseout, he will lose itemized deductions equal to $1,343 (3%
> of $44,750). The loss of those deductions means that Katz pays $376 of tax on his capital gains over
> and above the 28% tax of $14,000. Thus, the total tax on his long-term gains is $14,376, which is
> 28.75% of his $50,000 long-term gain.

There's a quick way to estimate the effect of the itemized deduction and personal
exemption phaseouts on a taxpayer's capital gains tax rate. Taxpayers in the 28% bracket
pay an additional 0.84% tax on every dollar of capital gain above the $105,250 itemized
deduction phaseout threshold. Taxpayers in the 31% bracket pay an extra 0.93% on those
dollars. Taxpayers who are also subject to the personal exemption phaseout feel an
additional 0.5% tax bite per personal exemption on each dollar of capital gains in that
phaseout range (which starts at $157,900 of AGI for joint filers).

¶1810   CAPITAL LOSS DEDUCTION

A net loss from capital asset transactions is partially or fully deductible from other income
in computing adjusted gross income [IRC Sec. 1211(b); Reg. Sec. 1.1211-1(b)]. Losses
from transactions of personal-use property are never deductible unless a casualty loss is
involved [¶1813].

(a) Amount of Loss Deductible. Capital losses fully offset capital gains. However, to the extent your capital losses exceed your capital gains, the net loss can only be deducted against $3,000 of ordinary income in any one year. (The limit is $1,500, instead, for marrieds filing separately.) Both long- and short-term capital losses offset ordinary income, dollar-for-dollar [IRC Sec. 1211(b)].

(b) Husband and Wife. A husband or wife filing separately is allowed to offset the excess of capital losses against only $1,500 of ordinary income. Neither spouse may use the other's loss in this case. On a joint return, they combine their capital gains and losses [Reg. Sec. 1.1211-1(b)(6)].

(c) Capital Loss Carryover. If your capital losses in the current year exceed the limits in (a) above, you may carry over the excess until completely exhausted. In finding the amount of the carryover, short-term losses are applied first even if incurred after a long-term loss. Then, if the capital loss limitation has not been reached, long-term losses are applied up to the limit. The character of the loss remains the same in the later years. Carried-over net short-term capital loss in excess of any net long-term capital gain is treated as a short-term loss in the later year; and net long-term capital loss in excess of any net short-term capital gain is treated as a long-term loss in the later year.

You carry over in full long-term capital losses. The capital loss carryovers are applied dollar for dollar against gains from the later years. Capital loss carryovers are calculated on Schedule D.

How to compute carryover. If your taxable income is sufficient to utilize the full $3,000/$1,500 loss deduction allowance in (a) above, your carryover is the excess of your capital loss over your capital gain for that year plus the allowance amount.

> **Example 1:** Sally Drake had $10,000 of capital loss in 1992 and $2,000 of capital gain. Thus her net capital loss was $8,000. She used $3,000 of it to shelter other income. Drake's carryover to 1993 is $5,000.

On the other hand, if your taxable income is a negative figure, your capital loss carryover is the amount of net capital loss in excess of the smaller of (1) the $3,000/$1,500 allowance or (2) taxable income increased by the $3,000/$1,500 allowance and the deduction for personal and dependency exemptions. In instances where deductions for the year exceed gross income, you can use negative taxable income to compute the amount in (2) [IRC Sec. 1212(b)(2)]. The purpose of this calculation is to prevent taxpayers with negative taxable incomes from losing some of the tax benefit of their capital loss.

> **Example 2:** Lou and Cecile Winston, a married couple without dependents, had $10,000 of long-term capital losses and $2,000 of short-term capital gains in 1992—or an $8,000 net capital loss. In 1992, they had $5,000 of deductions in excess of income. The Winstons' capital loss deduction for 1992 was limited to $5,000—$2,000 of gain plus the $3,000 applicable limit. However, their capital loss carryover to 1993 is $5,900. This is the excess of the $8,000 net capital loss over the sum of (a) the negative $5,000 taxable income plus (b) $3,000 loss allowance plus (c) $4,100 of exemptions.

Capital loss carryovers from separate returns must be combined if a joint return is filed for the current year. However, a capital loss carryover from any joint return can be deducted only on the separate return of the person who actually sustained the loss.[1]

DISPOSING OF BUSINESS PROPERTY

Certain assets qualify for an annual deduction related to their becoming worn out, exhausted or obsolete (depreciation). The idea is to spread their cost over the period of expected usefulness. These assets, called depreciable property, are specifically excluded from the capital asset category. Thus, their disposal would not normally result in capital gain or capital loss. However, under a special rule, a portion of the gain on the disposition of depreciable business property may be capital gain—while a loss on the same property would be an ordinary loss. Sales of business property are reported on Form 4797.

¶1811   **SALE OR EXCHANGE OF SEC. 1231 ASSETS**

It is the net result of all the sales or exchanges of Sec. 1231 assets that determines the tax treatment of each individual sale. If the net gains exceed the net losses, all the individual sale or exchange gains or losses are treated as long-term capital gains and losses. But if the net losses exceed the net gains, then the individual gains or losses are treated as ordinary gains or losses.

(a) What Property Is Involved. The special tax treatment applies to the following property known as "Sec. 1231 assets":

- Depreciable personal property used in a trade or business and held for more than one year.
- Real property used in a trade or business and held for more than one year.
- Property held for more than one year for the production of rents or royalties.
- Leaseholds used in a trade or business and held for more than one year [¶1801(g)].
- Timber under certain conditions [¶1814].
- Certain unharvested crops [¶1815(b)].
- Coal or domestic iron ore under certain conditions [¶1816].
- Cattle and horses acquired for draft, breeding, dairy or sporting purposes and held for 24 months or more [¶1815(a)].
- Livestock (except cattle, horses and poultry) acquired for draft, breeding, dairy or sporting purposes and held 12 months or more [¶1815(a)].
- Capital assets held for more than one year that have been involuntarily converted [¶1813].
- Business property held for more than one year that has been involuntarily converted [¶1813].

Inventory; property held for sale to customers; certain copyrights; artistic, musical, or literary compositions; letters or memoranda or similar property are not "Sec. 1231 assets." Also, certain U.S. Government publications received free or at a reduced price are not "Sec. 1231 assets" [IRC Sec. 1231(b)(1)].

(b) How to Figure the Computation. Since the net result of the sales or exchanges of "Sec. 1231 assets" determines the tax treatment of *each* individual sale, you must make a special computation. But before this can be completed, the following steps must be taken into account:

- First, you handle separately the portion of the gain that is "recaptured" as ordinary income. (Where depreciation was previously deducted as an offset to ordinary income, that much of the gain must be treated as ordinary income when the property is disposed of) [¶1812].

- You must net business casualty or theft gains and losses to find if they are to be included in the Sec. 1231 computation for further netting [¶1813].
- Sec. 1231 assets are segregated and netted:

1. If net gains exceed net losses, *all* the gains and losses are treated as long-term capital gains and losses.

2. If net losses exceed net gains, *all* the gains and losses are treated as ordinary.

Net Sec. 1231 gain is treated as ordinary income to the extent of the taxpayer's unrecaptured net Sec. 1231 losses for the five most recent prior years starting after 1981. Losses are recaptured in the chronological order they arose [IRC Sec. 1231(c)].

Personal casualty or theft gains or losses are not subject to Sec. 1231. Therefore, they are not netted with Sec. 1231 if personal casualty or theft gains exceed personal casualty or theft losses.

Example: Mr. West is a calendar-year accountant. In 1992, he received $20,000 in professional fees. On May 6, he had a $2,000 gain from the sale of stock held 14 months. On January 4, he sold a 15-month-old car used only in his practice for $2,700. The car had an adjusted basis of $2,200, and he had taken $400 depreciation on it. On July 2, he received royalties of $3,000 (in excess of his depletion basis) from coal lands he owned for six years. On August 13, he sold, at a gain of $1,000, a vacant lot held for four months as an investment. On September 17, he sold other depreciable investment property he owned for three years at a $500 loss. Sale of an office machine on October 8 (three months after purchase) resulted in a $200 loss.

	Gain	Loss	
Net professional fees			$20,000
Other business income (recapture of depreciation on car)			400
Less: Loss on office machine			(200)
Sec. 1231 transactions:			
Sale of car used in business	$ 100		
Coal royalties	3,000		
Sale of investment property	_____	$500	
Total gains	$3,100		
Total losses		$500	
Excess of gains over losses	$2,600		
Capital gain or loss:			
1. Net long-term capital gain ($2,600 + $2,000)			$4,600
2. Net short-term capital gain			1,000
3. Total			5,600
Adjusted gross income			$25,800

The net professional fees and $400 of the gain on the car sale are ordinary income. The gain on the stock sale is a long-term capital gain. The rest of the gain on the sale of the car, the coal royalties and the loss from the depreciable investment property are all Sec. 1231 gains and losses, resulting in a net Sec. 1231 gain of $2,600 (if the result were a net loss, the gains and losses would be ordinary gains and losses). The gain on the sale of the lot is a short-term capital gain. The loss on the office machine is an ordinary loss deductible in full from ordinary income. It is not a Sec. 1231 asset because it was held less than the holding period for long-term treatment [¶1803].

¶1812   RECAPTURE OF DEPRECIATION

Depreciation deductions for capital assets offset ordinary income. However, when you sell these assets, the recapture rules treat the part of gain attributable to recaptured depreciation as ordinary income rather than capital gain.

(a) Gain From Disposing of Certain Depreciable Property. If you dispose of depreciable personal or similar property ("Section 1245 property" below), any gain to the extent of depreciation taken after 1961 is treated as ordinary income. The rules for the treatment of gain on the sale or other disposition of Sec. 1245 property are the same for both ACRS and non-ACRS property [¶2112]. If a sale or exchange is not involved, gain is the excess of the property's fair market value over its adjusted basis at the time of disposition [IRC Sec. 1245(a); Reg. Sec. 1.1245-1]. If any part of the purchase price of property acquired after December 31, 1980 was deducted as an expense [¶2113] and not disallowed, that amount is treated as allowed for depreciation and therefore, recaptured as ordinary income [IRC Sec. 1245(a)(2)]. For installment sales, depreciation recapture income is fully recognized in the year of the sale, even if no principal payments are received in that year [IRC Sec. 453(i)].

"Section 1245 property" includes (1) personal property (both tangible and intangible); (2) other tangible property (except a building or its structural components) such as research, storage or structure facilities used as integral parts of specified business activities; (3) real property to the extent that its adjusted basis has been reduced by expenditures to remove architectural barriers to the handicapped and elderly, qualified tertiary injectant expenses and reforestation expenditures [¶2100]; (4) a single purpose agricultural or horticultural structure; (5) a storage facility used to distribute petroleum; and (6) railroad grading and tunnel bores [IRC Sec. 1245(a)(3); Reg. Sec. 1.1245-3].

Recomputed basis is the key factor. This is adjusted basis plus depreciation taken. The depreciation you add back must include any taken by another person if you have a carryover basis (such as gift property). Any gain up to the recomputed basis is Section 1245 ordinary income. Gain above recomputed basis is included in Sec. 1231 computations. Ordinary income is limited to actual gain on a sale or exchange for less than the full recomputed basis. If you can prove that the depreciation you took was lower than the maximum allowable, you can use the lower figure. But remember to keep permanent records to determine the recomputed basis [IRC Sec. 1245(a)(2); Reg. Sec. 1.1245-2].

> **Example 1:** Ramsey sold a business machine for $3,000 on February 4, 1992 that he bought on January 17, 1991. The machine had an adjusted basis of $2,380 and the depreciation deduction for 1990 was $420. Thus, the recomputed basis is $2,800. Ramsey's Sec. 1245 income is $420, figured as follows:
>
> | | |
> |---|---:|
> | Amount realized | $3,000 |
> | Adjusted basis | 2,380 |
> | Gain | $ 620 |
> | Recomputed basis ($2,380 + $420) | $2,800 |
> | Adjusted basis | $2,380 |
> | Section 1245 ordinary income | $ 420 |
> | Section 1231 capital gain | $ 200 |

Depreciation or amortization includes farmers' land clearing depreciation expenses [¶2101], certain costs of acquiring a leasehold and lessee's improvement costs [¶2101], the additional first-year depreciation, deductions taken under the Accelerated Cost Recovery System [¶2110; 2113], amortization of reforestation expenditures [¶2246] and expenditures to remove architectural barriers to the handicapped and elderly [¶2203].

(b) Gain From Disposing of Certain Depreciable Real Property. The treatment of gain from a sale or exchange of depreciable real property ("Section 1250 property") depends on how you've used the property, when you acquired it, whether you used an accelerated method of depreciation and whether the property is ACRS or non-ACRS [Ch. 11] property. Generally, you have ordinary income to the extent of a percentage of (1) gain or (2) excess depreciation (the amount that exceeds what would have been taken by straight line depreciation), whichever is less; any gain not recaptured as ordinary income gets Sec. 1231 treatment.

Recapture under ACRS. To recover the cost of Sec. 1250 depreciable property under ACRS, the following rules apply:

- If the property is nonresidential, any gain, up to the amount of deductions taken, is ordinary income; any excess is capital gain.
- If the property is residential, gain will be recaptured as ordinary income only to the extent that deductions under the accelerated method exceed those that would have been allowable if the straight line method of recovery had been used over the applicable recovery period.
- If the straight line method of recovery is used, any gain realized on the disposition of the property, whether residential or nonresidential, is capital gain.

➤ **OBSERVATION** You must use a straight line basis when you depreciate real estate placed in service after 1986. Therefore, when you dispose of this property, there is no recapture.

"Section 1250 property" is depreciable real property, which includes all real property that is subject to a depreciation allowance and is not depreciable personal property at any time [(a) above]. It also includes intangible real property such as a leasehold of land [IRC Sec. 1250(c)].

If Section 1250 property is acquired in certain tax-free transactions (other than like-kind exchanges or involuntary conversions), information, including depreciation deductions by prior owners, should be filed with the return for the year the property is acquired [Reg. Sec. 1.1250-2(f)].

Recapture involving non-ACRS property. The amount of the ordinary income is the applicable percentage of (1) the recognized gain, or (2) the excess depreciation, whichever is less [IRC Sec. 1250(a); Reg. Sec. 1.1250-1]. To determine what part of the gain is to be treated as ordinary income, the following steps must be taken:

➤ **IMPORTANT** The steps below apply to *property placed in service before 1981* (non-ACRS property). If property is placed in service *after 1980* (ACRS property), see "Recapture under ACRS" above.

Step 1.   Figure the amount of the gain.

NOTE: If the disposition is not a sale, exchange nor involuntary conversion, the gain is the fair market value less adjusted basis.

Step 2.   Find excess depreciation for periods after 1975.

Step 3.   Multiply the gain or excess depreciation, whichever is less, by the applicable percentage [see below].

Step 4.   Figure excess depreciation for periods after 1969 and before 1976.

Step 5.   Multiply the unabsorbed gain (amount remaining above the post-1975 depreciation) or excess depreciation for periods after 1969 and before 1976, whichever is less, by the applicable percentage [see below].

Commercial or industrial property. The applicable percentage on new or used property is 100%. This applies even though the property was acquired before 1970. There is no applicable percentage for used property acquired after 1969 since the depreciation deduction for this property must be computed under the straight line method [¶2103].

Residential rental property. The applicable percentage for this property (at least 80% of gross rents from dwelling units) is 100% until the property is held 100 full months; then it declines 1% for each full month of ownership.

Step 6.   Add Steps 3 and 5 to arrive at the gain to be treated as ordinary income.

Property sold with separate elements.   If real property disposed of has separate elements, the amount of ordinary gain is the total of the ordinary income figured for each element. A separate element can be: (1) a separate improvement; (2) units placed in service before the depreciable real property was completed; (3) depreciable real property plus improvements not considered as a separate improvement [IRC Sec. 1250(f); Reg. Sec. 1.1250-5].

A *separate improvement* is each improvement added to the property's capital account if the cost during a three-year period ending on the last day of any one tax year exceeds the greater of: (a) $5,000; (b) 25% of adjusted basis; or (c) 10% of unadjusted basis. The basis for (b) and (c) is figured as of the first day of the 36-month period, or the first day of the property's holding period, whichever is later. In applying the three-year period test, improvements in any of the three years are omitted entirely if for such year their total does not amount to the greater of: (a) $2,000, or (b) 1% of the property's unadjusted basis figured as of the start of the year or the property's holding period, whichever is later [IRC Sec. 1250(f)(4); Reg. Sec. 1.1250-5].

(c) Exceptions.   The recapture rule applies to most dispositions of depreciable personal or real property used in a trade or business, even if they would otherwise be without immediate tax consequences. Exceptions to this include [IRC Sec. 1245(b), 1250(d); Reg. Sec. 1.1245-4, 1.1245-6(b), 1.1250-1(a)(4), 1.1250-3]:

Gifts.   Gratuitous transfers of depreciable property do not give rise to depreciation recapture. However, the Sec. 1245 or 1250 potential is passed on to the person receiving the property. Thus, when the donee sells the property he or she must take into account the donor's depreciation deductions that are subject to the recapture rules.

Charitable contributions.   If depreciable business property is given to a charity, the donor realizes no income. However, the charitable contribution deduction is reduced by Sec. 1245 or 1250 income that would have resulted had the property been sold for its fair market value (¶1917) [IRC Sec. 170(e); Reg. Seg. 1.170A-4(b)(4)].

Transfers at death.   Both the decedent and his successor are completely free from the recapture rules once the property is transferred at death, except that the successor is subject to the rules for those amounts that would have been taxed to the decedent if he had remained alive and received them. Generally, this applies only to installment obligations [IRC Sec. 691, 1245(b)(2), 1250(d)(2); Reg. Sec. 1.1245-4(b), 1.1250-3(b)]. For basis of inherited property, see ¶1612.

Personal residence.   The depreciation recapture rules apply to gain on the part used in a trade or business, except to the extent a taxpayer can exclude the gain from income (¶1708) [IRC Sec. 1250(d)(7)(B); Reg. Sec. 1.1250-3(g)(1)(ii)].

Certain qualified low-income housing projects.   Special rules applied to ordinary income recaptured from the nonrecognition of gain when low-income housing was sold. These rules were repealed generally effective on November 5, 1990. However, transactions before that date can still be affected by the recapture rules.

Corporate or partnership contributions and distributions. Special rules apply to depreciation deductions taken before a new partner's admission to a partnership, partnership distributions [¶3420 et seq.], and to corporate distributions [¶3027].

(d) Nontaxable Exchanges. Generally, a like-kind exchange [¶1614] does not result in ordinary income when Sec. 1245 or 1250 property is disposed of unless "boot" is received. The *Sec. 1245 gain* is limited to the lesser of: (1) gain to the extent of depreciation taken since 1961, or (2) the gain recognized in a like kind exchange, plus the fair market value of the qualified property received that is not Sec. 1245 property. *Sec. 1250 gain* cannot exceed the greater of two limitations: (1) the total amount of the "boot," or (2) the amount of Sec. 1250 gain that would be recognized if the exchange was fully taxable, less the fair market value of the Sec. 1250 property received [IRC Sec. 1245(b)(4), 1250(d)(4); Reg. Sec. 1.1245-4(d), 1.1250-3(d)].

> **Example 2:** Old machine has an $8,000 adjusted basis and Sec. 1245 potential of $4,000. It's swapped for a new machine worth $10,000 and $1,000 cash. Although gain is $3,000, only $1,000 is recognized. It is all Sec. 1245 gain since it's less than the Sec. 1245 potential. If taxpayer sells the new machine for $10,000 before taking further depreciation deductions, he will then recognize an additional $2,000 of Sec. 1245 income.

The basis of property received in exchange. The rules are similar to those for involuntary conversions [(e) below].

Sale or exchange of Sec. 1250 property received in exchange. The unrecognized Sec. 1250 gain of property disposed of in a like kind exchange is carried over to the Sec. 1250 property received in the trade-in. This carryover is added to the "excess" depreciation taken after the exchange when the property is later disposed of. The holding period begins when the Sec. 1250 like kind property is acquired. To find the recognized gain on the resale, multiply the carryover gain and the "excess" depreciation by the applicable percentage [IRC Sec. 1250(d)(4)(E); Reg. Sec. 1.1250-3(d)].

(e) Involuntary Conversions. Gain that is generally not recognized in an involuntary conversion [¶1710] may be affected by the depreciation recapture rules when Sec. 1245 or 1250 property is disposed of. However, the amount taxed as ordinary income is limited to the unreinvested conversion proceeds [IRC Sec. 1245(b)(4), 1250(d)(4); Reg. Sec. 1.1245-4(d), 1.1250-3(d)].

Sec. 1245 gain cannot exceed the gain recognized in an involuntary conversion, plus the fair market value of qualified replacement property that is not Sec. 1245 property [IRC Sec. 1245(b)(4); Reg. Sec. 1.1245-4(d)]. Sec. 1250 gain cannot exceed the greater of two limitations: (1) the total amount of the unreinvested conversion proceeds increased by the value of controlling shares acquired in a corporation to get replacement property [¶1712]; or (2) the amount of Sec. 1250 gain that would be recognized if the proceeds were fully taxable less the cost of Sec. 1250 property acquired [IRC Sec. 1250(d)(4); Reg. Sec. 1.1250-3(d)].

The basis of replacement property acquired is cost reduced by the Sec. 1245 or 1250 gain not recognized on the conversion. If more than one piece of Sec. 1245 or 1250 replacement property is bought, the bases allocated to the properties are in proportion to their respective costs (see also ¶1715). If other replacement property also is bought, all the bases are combined to find the total cost of the replacement property. This amount is reduced by the gain not recognized under replacement rules [¶1714] and the Sec. 1245 or 1250 gain not taken into account. The total is then allotted in proportion to their respective costs [IRC Sec. 1245(b)(4), 1250(d)(4)(D); Reg. Sec. 1.1245-5(a), 1.1250-3(d)(2)].

> **Example 3**: Mr. Bailey's warehouse was condemned and he received an award of $90,000. He spent $10,500 to buy a storage shed and $31,500 for a garage. The land for the storage shed cost $12,000, and for the garage, $36,000. Assume that the unrecognized gain on the condemnation is $60,000 of which $10,000 is Sec. 1250 gain. The tentative total basis of the shed and the garage is therefore $32,000 ($42,000 property cost less $10,000 nonrecognized Sec. 1250 gain). The tentative basis of the shed is $8,000 ($32,000 × $10,500/$42,000), and the tentative garage basis is $24,000 ($32,000 × $31,500/$42,000). The basis of all the properties replaced is $30,000 figured as follows:

Cost (tentative basis) of shed		$ 8,000
Cost (tentative basis) of garage		24,000
Cost of land for shed		12,000
Cost of land for garage		36,000
Cost of properties bought		$80,000
Less: gain not recognized under replacement rules	$60,000	
Minus Sec. 1250 unrecognized gain	10,000	
		$50,000
Total basis of properties bought		$30,000

The total basis of $30,000 is allocated to each property:

Shed: $30,000 × ($8,000/$80,000)	$ 3,000
Garage: $30,000 × ($24,000/$80,000)	9,000
Land for shed: $30,000 × ($12,000/$80,000)	4,500
Land for garage: $30,000 × ($36,000/$80,000)	13,500
Total	$30,000

Sale or exchange of Sec. 1250 replacement property. These rules are similar to the sale or exchange of property received in a nontaxable exchange in (d) above.

¶1813   INVOLUNTARY CONVERSIONS

A recognized gain or deductible loss from the condemnation or involuntary conversion of property may be subject to Sec. 1231 [¶1811(b)]. Qualified property involves both business property and capital assets held over one year.

Special netting for business casualties or thefts. Recognized gains and deductible losses from fire, storm, shipwreck or other casualty or theft of the qualified business property are treated separately before the Sec. 1231 computation is made. A condemnation does not enter into the special netting of casualty or thefts. Unreinvested conversion proceeds for Sec. 1245 or 1250 property are ordinary income to the extent the recapture rules apply. These recapture rules apply to the assets before the separate netting of the casualty and theft gains and losses.

This special netting process involves property used in your trade or business or any long-term capital asset held in connection with a trade or business or a transaction entered into for profit. The separate "netting computation" applies whether or not the property is insured. It is made to find how all the business casualty or theft gains and losses will be treated on the return:

- Casualty or theft *gains* exceed casualty or theft losses: Make a further netting with Sec. 1231 gains or losses.
- Casualty or theft *losses* exceed casualty or theft gains: All the casualty or theft gains and losses are separately treated as ordinary income or deductible losses.

Netting of personal casualties or thefts. Personal casualty or theft gains and losses are not netted with Sec. 1231 gains and losses. Thus, Sec. 1231 is applied without regard to these gains or losses. See ¶2306 for separate netting of gains and losses from personal casualties or thefts.

The rules for personal casualties or thefts apply to capital assets held for personal purposes, such as a residence or automobile, but not a condemnation loss on a personal residence. Losses from condemnations of property held for personal use are not deductible.[1] A personal casualty or theft loss that exceeds 10% of adjusted gross income and the $100 floor [¶2304], and that is deductible as an ordinary loss, is an itemized deduction.

¶1814   TIMBER

The cutting of standing[1] timber, or disposal under certain contracts, if taxpayer retains an economic interest, may be treated as a sale of the timber. Gains or losses from these fictional sales come under Sec. 1231. Timber includes evergreen trees over six years old when cut down, and sold for ornamental purposes (for example, Christmas trees).

Cutting timber is treated as a sale if: (1) you owned the timber or the contract right to cut it on the first day of such year and for more than one year before the cutting; (2) it was cut for sale or for use in your trade or business; and (3) you so elect on your return [IRC Sec. 631].

In figuring gain or loss on this assumed sale, the basis is the adjusted basis for depletion. The fictional selling price is the fair market value of the timber as of the first day of the tax year. This market value also becomes the cost of the cut timber for future transactions.

(a) How to Elect. You make the election by reporting the gain or loss on the return and attaching a copy of the figures. It applies to all timber you own, or that you have a contract right to cut, and is binding for later years. It can be revoked with the IRS' permission on a showing of undue hardship. Any new election would then require IRS consent [IRC Sec. 631(a); Reg. Sec. 1.631-1].

> ➤ **OBSERVATION** Congressional action was originally designed to encourage investments in timber and to provide two instruments to enable the investor to get a favorable return: capital gain and depletion. Although tax-favored capital gains treatment has gone through a repeal in 1986 and a resurrection in 1990 [¶1800], the basic rules of depleting timber have remained the same.

(b) Disposal of Timber Under Contract. If you dispose of timber under a cutting contract, retaining an economic interest in the timber, the cutting can be considered a sale. You must have owned the timber for more than one year before disposal. The disposal date is the earlier of the cutting date, or when you are paid. Owner means any person who owns an interest in the timber, including a sublessor and a holder of a contract to cut timber. No election is needed. The difference between the amounts received for the timber in any tax year and the adjusted basis for depletion of the timber sold is considered gain or loss [IRC Sec. 631(b); Reg. Sec. 1.631-2].

¶1815   FARMERS' SEC. 1231 TRANSACTIONS

Gain or loss from the sale of livestock or unharvested crops may get Sec. 1231 treatment.

(a) Livestock. The provisions of Sec. 1231 apply to livestock held for draft, breeding, dairy, or sporting purposes; but the animals must be held for at least 12 months, except cattle and horses which must be held for 24 months or more. The holding period starts from the date of acquisition, not the date the animal was put to draft, breeding, dairy or sporting purposes. Livestock includes hogs, mules, donkeys, sheep, goats, fur-bearing animals, and other mammals, as well as cattle and horses. It does not include chickens, turkeys, pigeons, geese, other birds, fish, frogs, reptiles, etc. [IRC Sec. 1231(b)(3); Reg. Sec. 1.1231-2].

Held for Draft, Breeding, Dairy, or Sporting Purpose

An animal to be used for breeding is found to be sterile, and is sold "a reasonable time" afterwards.

A farmer retires from breeding or dairy business and sells his whole herd, including young animals never used for such purpose.

A farmer raises hogs for slaughter; customarily breeds sows once to get a litter which he raises for sale, and sells the brood sows after obtaining the litter. The sows are held for breeding purposes, even though intended for ultimate sale to customers in the ordinary course of the farmer's business.

A horse held for racing at a public track is used for sporting purposes.

Not Held for Draft, Breeding, Dairy, or Sporting Purpose

A person raises horses for sale to others, to be used by them for draft purposes. He uses the horses as draft animals on his own farm to train them. Since this use is incidental to his purpose of selling the horses, they are not held by him for draft purposes.

A taxpayer is in the business of raising registered cattle for sale to be used by the buyers for breeding. Business practice calls for such cattle to be bred before the sale to show their fitness for breeding. The test breeding does not, of itself, establish that the animal was held for breeding. (But any animal bred to add the calves to the taxpayer's herd would be held for breeding.)

The taxpayer's business is buying cattle and fattening them for slaughter. He buys cows with calf, and the calves are born while owned by him. These cows are not held for breeding.

(b) Unharvested Crops get Sec. 1231 treatment if (1) raised on land used in the trade or business and held for more than one year; (2) crop and land are sold (or exchanged or involuntarily converted) to the same person at the same time; and (3) no right or option is kept by the taxpayer, at the time of the sale, exchange, or conversion to acquire the land, directly or indirectly. (This does not bar rights under a mortgage or other security transaction.) The time the crop, as distinguished from the land, has been held does not matter [IRC Sec. 1231(b)(4); Reg. Sec. 1.1231-1(f)].

¶1816   COAL AND DOMESTIC IRON ORE

An owner (or sublessor) of a coal mine who disposes of coal (or lignite) under a royalty contract may get Sec. 1231 treatment for a gain or loss (except when recapture of exploration expenditures is involved [¶2242]). This can also apply to iron ore royalties. The coal or iron ore must be owned for more than one year before disposal (date of extraction). To figure the holding period, see ¶1803. In addition, an economic interest must be retained in the mineral. The difference between the amount realized and the adjusted depletion basis [¶2236] (plus certain disallowed deductions) is the gain or loss. The taxpayer is not entitled to percentage depletion, or Sec. 1231 treatment if involved in the mining operation [IRC Sec. 272, 631(c), 1231(b)(2); Reg. Sec. 1.272-1, 1.631-3].

For recapture of mine exploration expenses, see Chapter 12.

NOTE: In general, disposals of coal or domestic iron ore with a retained economic interest do not qualify for Sec. 1231 treatment. Royalties on such disposals, though, are eligible for percentage depletion.

¶1817   SALE OF DEPRECIABLE PROPERTY BETWEEN RELATED PARTIES

Sec. 1231 treatment does not apply to sales or exchanges of depreciable property between related parties. For this rule, related parties include: (a) you and all entities in which you own more than 50% either directly or indirectly, (b) entities more than 50% owned, directly or indirectly, by the same persons, (c) a trust and its beneficiary or the beneficiary's spouse, (d) a partner and the partnership in which the partner holds, directly or indirectly, over 50% of the capital or profits interest, and (e) an employer and an employer-controlled welfare benefits fund. The definition also covers other relationships that are covered under provisions disallowing losses on related party sales [IRC Sec. 1239].

SPECIAL RULES

¶1820   COLLAPSIBLE CORPORATIONS

A special rule prevents the use of a temporary (collapsible) corporation to convert what would be ordinary income to the corporation into capital gains for the stockholders. Gain from the sale of a collapsible corporation stock is generally ordinary income, rather than capital gain. Since capital gain is now taxed at a top rate of 28%, collapsible corporation tax treatment has, once again, become an important issue [IRC Sec. 341(a); Reg. Sec. 1.341-1].

A collapsible corporation is a corporation formed or used principally to [IRC Sec. 341(b); Reg. Sec. 1.341-2]:

- Manufacture, construct or produce property, or
- Buy "Sec. 341 assets," or
- Hold stock in such a corporation.

The corporation must have been formed to (1) allow the shareholders to realize gain through the sale or distribution of stock before the corporation realizes ⅔ of the taxable income from the property, and (2) allow the shareholders to realize gain from the property. Sec. 341 assets are property held for less than 3 years which is (a) stock in trade, (b) property held primarily for sale to customers, (c) unrealized receivables or fees, or (d) Sec. 1231 property [IRC Sec. 341(b); Reg. Sec. 1.341-2].

A corporation is presumed to be collapsible if the fair market value of its Sec. 341 assets is (1) 50% or more of the fair market value of its total assets (exclusive of cash, obligations that are capital assets, and stock in any other corporation) and (2) 120% or more of the adjusted basis of its Sec. 341 assets [IRC Sec. 341(c); Reg. Sec. 1.341-3].

¶1821   LOSS ON SMALL BUSINESS STOCK

A special rule allows ordinary loss treatment for the sale, exchange or worthlessness of certain small business stock (called "Section 1244 stock"). This applies even if the loss would be a capital loss under the general rules [IRC Sec. 1244]. Any amount not absorbed in the year sustained becomes part of the stockholder's net operating loss carryback and carryover [¶2342]. An ordinary loss is reported in Part II of Form 4797.

The rule applies to an individual, who must be the original buyer, either directly or through a partnership [IRC Sec. 1244(a); Reg. Sec. 1.1244(a)-1]. The maximum allowable as an ordinary loss in one tax year is $50,000. On a joint return, it is $100,000, whether the stock is owned by one or both spouses. Any excess loss is subject to capital-loss limitations [IRC Sec. 1244(b); Reg. Sec. 1.1244(b)-1].

(a) Qualification Requirements. For stock issued before July 19, 1984, only common stock can qualify as Sec. 1244 stock. Both common and preferred stock (voting or nonvoting) issued after July 18, 1984, can qualify as Sec. 1244 stock.

For stocks issued after November 6, 1978, (1) the corporation must be a "small business corporation" when the stock is issued, (2) the stock must be issued for money or property other than stock or securities and (3) over 50% of the corporation's gross receipts for the five most recent tax yers preceding the year of the loss must have come from sources other than royalties, rent, dividends, interests, annuities and sales or exchanges of stock or securities. [IRC Sec. 1244(c); Reg. Sec. 1.1244(c)-1].

For stocks issued before November 7, 1978, the requirements under (2) and (3) above apply except that the corporation need not be a small business when the plan is adopted—its status at the time of issue or of loss is immaterial—and the stock must be issued under a written plan to issue the stock within two years, and no other stock offering may be outstanding at the time of issue.

(b) What Is a Small Business Corporation. *For stocks issued after November 6, 1978,* a corporation will be treated as a small business corporation if the aggregate amount of money and other property received by the corporation for stock, as a contribution to capital, and as paid-in surplus, as of the time the stock is issued, does not exceed $1,000,000. The value of the "other property" is its adjusted basis to the corporation for figuring gain, reduced by any liability which the property is subject to, or was assumed by the corporation [IRC Sec. 1244(c); Reg. Sec. 1.1244(c)-2].

For stocks issued before November 7, 1978, a "small business corporation" is one which, when the plan is adopted, (a) has not more than $1,000,000 equity capital (assets, taken at basis for gain, less liabilities, except debt to stockholders); and (b) whose capital paid-in after June 30, 1958 does not exceed $500,000. In both cases, the amount of stock that can be offered under the plan is taken into account [IRC Sec. 1244(c)(2); Reg. Sec. 1.1244(c)-2].

The ordinary loss treatment of Sec. 1244 stock applies only if, for the five tax years ending before the loss, less than 50% of the corporation's gross receipts were from investment sources such as interest, dividends, rents, royalties, and stock or security gains. This limitation does not apply if deductions (excluding those for operating loss, partially tax-free interest, and dividends received) exceed gross income [IRC Sec. 1244(c)(1); Reg. Sec. 1.1244(c)-1]. However, the corporation must be largely an operating company [Reg. Sec. 1.1244(c)-1(g)(2)].

In general, stock received in a reorganization does not qualify. However, a stock dividend or stock received in a recapitalization or change of name, identity, etc., reorganization may qualify [IRC Sec. 1244(d)(2); Reg. Sec. 1.1244(d)-3].

If property with value less than basis is transferred tax-free to a corporation for Sec. 1244 stock, ordinary loss (but not total loss) is that value minus whatever is realized on disposition [IRC Sec. 1244(d)(1)(A); Reg. Sec. 1.1244(d)-1].

Example 1: Property valued at $1,000 and with a $3,000 basis is transferred tax-free to a small business corporation for all its stock. The stock becomes worthless. There is an ordinary loss to the extent of $1,000 and a capital loss of $2,000.

If, after acquiring Sec. 1244 stock, a stockholder's basis for his stock is increased (for example, by additional capital contribution), a loss on the stock is allocated [IRC Sec. 1244(d)(1)(B); Reg. Sec. 1.1244(d)-2].

Example 2: Mr. Smith paid $10,000 for shares of stock. Later on, she made a capital contribution of $2,000, thus increasing the basis to $12,000. She sold the stock for $9,000. Of the $3,000 loss, only $^{10}\!/_{12}$, or $2,500, is an ordinary loss.

Footnotes to Chapter 8

(For your added convenience, in brackets [] with the footnotes below, you will find citations to related paragraphs in the "RIA United States Tax Reporter"(USTR), "CCH Federal Tax Reporter" (CCH) and "RIA Federal Tax Coordinator 2d" (FTC) multi-volume services.)

FOOTNOTE ¶ 1800 [USTR ¶ 12,114; CCH ¶ 32,151 et seq.; FTC ¶ I-3900].

FOOTNOTE ¶ 1801 [USTR ¶ 12,214; CCH ¶ 32,222; FTC ¶ I-4000].

(1) Malat v. Riddell, 17 AFTR 2d 604, 383 US 569.

(2) Rev. Rul. 58-40, 1958-1 CB 275.

(3) Rev. Rul. 82-204, 1982-2 CB 192, Azar Nut Co. v. Comm., 94 TC 455.

(4) Williams v. McGowan, 152 F.2d 570, 34 AFTR 615.

(5) Comm. v. Shapiro, 125 F.2d 532, 28 AFTR 1079.

(6) Comm. v. Ray, 210 F.2d 390, 45 AFTR 334.

(7) Hort. v. Comm., 313 US 28, 25 AFTR 1207.

(8) Thorpe, 42 BTA 654.

(9) Rodgers, 51 TC 927.

(10) Rev. Rul. 69-482, 1969-2 CB 184.

(11) Bell's Estate v. Comm., 137 F.2d 454, 31 AFTR 411.

(12) Perkins, 41 BTA 1225.

(13) Rev. Rul. 66-58, 1966-1 CB 186.

(14) Rhodes' Est. v. Comm., 131 F.2d 50, 30 AFTR 220.

(15) Finch, ¶ 42,641 PH Memo TC.

(16) Hercules Motor Corp., 40 BTA 999.

(17) Rev. Rul. 65-261, 1965-2 CB 281.

(18) Beal Est. v. Comm., 82 F.2d 268, 17 AFTR 621.

FOOTNOTE ¶ 1802 [USTR ¶ 12,224.07; CCH ¶ 32,242.01; FTC ¶ I-3901].

FOOTNOTE ¶ 1803 [USTR ¶ 12,234.01; CCH ¶ 32,263; FTC ¶ I-5500].

(1) Rev. Rul. 66-5, 1966-1 CB 91; Rev. Rul. 70-598, 1970-2 CB 168.

(2) Rev. Rul. 66-6, 1966-1 CB 160.

(3) Rev. Rul. 66-5, 1966-1 CB 91.

(4) Rev. Rul. 66-7, 1966-1 CB 188; Caspe v. U.S., 694 F.2d 1116, 51 AFTR 2d 83-353.

(5) Treas. Dept. booklet "Your Federal Income Tax" (1991 Ed.), p. 96.

(6) Otto v. Comm., 101 F.2d 1017, 22 AFTR 620; Armstrong, 6 TC 1166.

(7) Rev. Rul. 54-607, 1954-2 CB 177.

(8) Paul v. Comm. 206 F..2d 763, 44 AFTR 319; Rev. Rul. 75-524, 1975-2 CB 342.

(9) Kronner v. U.S., 43 AFTR 574, 110 F.Supp. 730.

(10) Comm. v. San Joaquin Fruit and Investment Co., 297 US 496, 17 AFTR 470.

(11) Humphrey, 32 BTA 280; Lehman, 7 TC 1088, affd 165 F.2d 383, 36 AFTR 545.

FOOTNOTE ¶ 1804 [USTR ¶ 10,124.77; CCH ¶ 29,663.051; FTC ¶ P-5211].

FOOTNOTE ¶ 1805 [USTR ¶ 12,334; CCH ¶ 32,292; FTC ¶ I-4369].

(1) Rev. Rul 63-65, 1963-1 CB 142.

(2) Corn Products Refining Co. v. Comm., 350 US 46, 47 AFTR 1789.

(3) International Flavors & Fragrances, Inc., 62 TC 232; rev'd 36 AFTR 2d 75-6054.

FOOTNOTE ¶ 1806 [USTR ¶ 12,334.01; CCH ¶ 32,314; FTC ¶ I-4700].

(1) Rev. Rul. 58-234, 1958-1 CB 279.

(2) Rev. Rul. 78-182, 1978-1 CB 265.

(3) Rev. Rul. 71-521, 1971-2 CB 313.

(4) Rev. Rul. 58-384, 1958-2 CB 410.

FOOTNOTE ¶ 1808 [USTR ¶ 12,224; CCH ¶ 32,151 et seq.; FTC ¶ I-6000].

FOOTNOTE ¶ 1809 [USTR ¶ 12,009.01; CCH ¶ 32,151; FTC ¶ I-6010].

FOOTNOTE ¶ 1810 [USTR ¶ 12,114; CCH ¶ 32,190; FTC ¶ I-6013; I-6022].

(1) Treas. Dept. booklet "Your Federal Income Tax" (1991 Ed.), p. 104.

FOOTNOTE ¶ 1811 [USTR ¶ 12,344; CCH ¶ 32,275; FTC ¶ I-6008].

FOOTNOTE ¶ 1812 [USTR ¶ 12,454; CCH ¶ 32,509; 32,606; FTC ¶ I-6100].

FOOTNOTE ¶ 1813 [USTR ¶ 12,314.09; CCH ¶ 32,275; FTC ¶ I-6120].

(1) Treas. Dept. booklet "Nonbusiness Disasters, Casualties, and Thefts" (1991 Ed.), p. 1.

FOOTNOTE ¶ 1814 [USTR ¶ 6314.02; CCH ¶ 32,275.057; FTC ¶ I-6107; N-6200].

(1) Rev. Rul. 56-434, 1956-2 CB 334.

FOOTNOTE ¶ 1815 [USTR ¶ 12,314.11; CCH ¶ 32,275; FTC ¶ I-6107].

FOOTNOTE ¶ 1816 [USTR ¶ 2724; CCH ¶ 24,706; 32,222.352; FTC ¶ N-7000].

FOOTNOTE ¶ 1817 [USTR ¶ 12,394; CCH ¶ 32,433; FTC ¶ I-6150].

FOOTNOTE ¶ 1820 [USTR ¶ 3484.21; CCH ¶ 16,315; CCH ¶ 2486; FTC ¶ I-6200].

FOOTNOTE ¶ 1821 [USTR ¶ 12,444.01; CCH ¶ 32,500; FTC ¶ I-6200].

MAXIMIZING DEDUCTIONS AND CREDITS

CHAPTER
9

PERSONAL DEDUCTIONS

TABLE OF CONTENTS

¶1900   ITEMIZED DEDUCTIONS IN GENERAL

[New tax legislation may affect this subject; see ¶1.]

Deductions play a critical part in slashing your tax bill since they reduce the amount of income subject to tax. The expenses you subtract from your adjusted gross income are called itemized deductions. They are claimed in lieu of the standard deduction. The most common itemized deductions are qualified residence interest, state and local taxes, unreimbursed medical expenses and miscellaneous expenses.

Certain itemized deductions are allowed only to the extent that the expense amount you incurred during the tax year exceeds a specified percentage of your adjusted gross income. For example, medical expenses are deductible only to the extent that they exceed 7.5% of your adjusted gross income [¶1931].

> **DEDUCTION LIMITS** You may lose part of the tax benefit from your itemized deductions. Reason: Your itemized deductions can be reduced once your adjusted gross income exceeds certain amounts. In 1992, the amounts are $105,250 ($52,625 for married persons filing separately).

NOTE: These income levels are adjusted for inflation. And unless Congress takes action, the deduction cutback disappears after 1995.

How the cutback works: The general rule is that your total 1992 itemized deductions are reduced by 3% of the amount of your adjusted gross income above $105,250 ($52,625 if married filing separately). But you may not actually lose that much—and for two reasons: (1) The cutback does not apply to the deductions for medical expenses, gambling, theft and casualty losses, and investment interest. (2) Of the remaining itemized deductions—the ones affected by the cutback—you never lose more than 80% of your deductions [IRC Sec. 68].

➤ **BOTTOM LINE** No matter how high your income is, you can always deduct your medical expenses, gambling losses, casualties, thefts and investment interest, plus 20% of all other itemized expenses.

Key point: This itemized deduction reduction is figured only after applying any regular limitations on itemized deductions. For example, the 2%-of-AGI floor is applied to your miscellaneous expenses [¶1942] before they are subject to the the cutback calculation.

A simple way to figure your 1992 itemized deduction reduction would be to use the following worksheet:

Itemized Deduction Reduction Worksheet

1. Enter your total itemized deductions .... _____
2. Enter the amount included in line 1 for medical and dental expenses, investment
   interest, casualty or theft losses, and gambling losses .... _____
3. Subtract line 2 from line 1 .... _____
4. Multiply the amount on line 3 by .80 .... _____
5. Enter your adjusted gross income .... _____
6. Enter $105,250 ($52,625 if married filing separately) .... _____
7. Subtract line 6 from line 5 .... _____
8. Multiply the amount on line 7 by .03 .... _____
9. Enter the smaller of line 4 or line 8. This is your itemized deduction reduction for
   the year .... _____
10. Subtract line 9 from line 1 to get your 1992 itemized deduction .... _____

Example 1: Ms. West has 1992 adjusted gross income of $117,000. She has $22,000 of total itemized deductions in 1992 (consisting only of mortgage interest, taxes and charitable contributions). *Result:* The new rules cost Ms. West $352.50 of her itemized deductions—she can deduct only $21,647.50 of her allowable itemized expenses on her 1992 return.

1. Total itemized deductions $22,000.00
2. Amount included in line 1 for medical and dental expenses, investment
   interest, casualty or theft losses, and gambling losses $0
3. Subtract line 2 from line 1 .... $22,000.00
4. Multiply the amount on line 3 by .80 .... $17,600.00
5. AGI $117,000.00
6. $105,250 threshold $105,250.00
7. Subtract line 6 from line 5 .... $ 11,750.00
8. Multiply the amount on line 7 by .03 .... $ 352.50
9. Itemized deduction reduction (the smaller of line 4 or line 8) .... $ 352.50
10. Remaining itemized deduction (subtract line 9 from line 1) .... $ 21,647.50

Example 2: In 1992, Mr. and Mrs. White have an adjusted gross income of $950,000. They have total itemized deductions of $24,000 (state income taxes, $15,000; charitable contributions, $3,000; investment interest, $6,000). *Result:* The Whites's allowable itemized deductions are $9,600 ($24,000 less $14,400).

1. Total itemized deductions .... $ 24,000.00
2. Amount included in line 1 for medical and dental expenses, investment interest, casualty or theft losses, and gambling losses 6,000.00
3. Subtract line 2 from line 1 .... $ 18,000.00
4. Multiply the amount on line 3 by .80 .... $ 14,400.00
5. AGI $950,000.00
6. $105,250 threshold $105,250.00
7. Subtract line 6 from line 5 .... $844,750.00
8. Multiply the amount on line 7 by .03 .... $ 25,342.50
9. Itemized deduction reduction (the smaller of line 4 or line 8) .... $ 14,400.00
10. Remaining itemized deduction (subtract line 9 from line 1) .... $ 9,600.00

For purposes of the alternative minimum tax, the cutback on itemized deductions is disregarded. See ¶2600 et seq.

For purposes of determining the tax treatment of state income tax refunds and other similar payments, the usual tax benefit rules apply. See ¶1244.

Tax return tip. Your itemized deductions are entered on Schedule A of Form 1040.

INTEREST

¶1901   INTEREST EXPENSE DEDUCTION IN GENERAL

Interest is the amount you must pay for the use of money you borrow.[1] You may deduct the interest you pay, subject to special limitations, as explained in the following paragraphs.

To be a deductible interest expense, a true debtor-creditor relationship must exist between you and the lender.[2] Both of you must intend that the loan be repaid. In addition, no deduction is permitted unless you are legally responsible for the debt [IRC Sec. 163(a); Reg. Sec. 1.163-1].

Exceptions: You can deduct mortgage interest attributable to real estate if you are the legal or equitable owner, even if you are not directly liable on the note [Reg. Sec. 1.163-1(b)]. Tenant-shareholders of a cooperative housing corporation can deduct amounts paid to the corporation that represent interest on the corporation's mortgage [IRC Sec. 216; Reg. Sec. 1.216-1(d)].

(a) Interest and Dividends Distinguished. Payments by a corporation on its stock are nondeductible dividends. Payments made on its debt (e.g., bonds or promissory notes) are deductible interest. In some situations, it is difficult to classify the nature of the instrument on which the payments are made. Several factors must be weighed on a case-by-case basis.

Factors distinguishing stock and debt include: (1) name; (2) intent; (3) maturity date; (4) certainty of payment; (5) rate of payment; (6) right to share in profits; (7) voting rights; (8) remedy on default; and (9) business purpose other than tax avoidance. The characteristic features of stock are the rights to participate in net profits beyond a fixed rate, to participate in management through voting power, and to share in the distribution of net assets on liquidation. Debt generally represents a definite promisor's unconditional promise to pay, to a definite promisee, a definite ascertainable amount, at a fixed or definite maturity date. Of course, both stock and debt may, and usually do, have other features. The weight to be given to any one feature depends on its relative importance to all the other factors in proof. A feature may be significant in one case and not in another.[3]

(b) Interest Expense Classifications. There are five categories of interest for tax purposes. Your deduction for interest you pay depends on how the interest is categorized.

You must trace the loan proceeds to specific expenditures in order to categorize the interest. Exception: For qualified residence interest, the loan collateral determines the tax treatment. The categories of interest are: Personal interest [¶1902]; qualified residence interest [¶1903]; investment interest [¶1904]; trade or business interest [¶2224]; and passive activity interest [¶2326].

Allocation of interest expense. For a debt (other than qualified residence loans) that has been applied to mixed uses, an allocation must be made to determine the amount of interest falling into each category. The allocation is made by tracing the loan to the specific expenses [See ¶2845(d)].

> **Example:** In 1993, Mr. Parker borrows $40,000 at a 10% interest rate. Half of the loan is for buying a new office computer system for his business. He uses $15,000 to purchase his dream car. The remaining $5,000 is invested in a hot, new stock. Because the loan was put to mixed uses, Parker must trace the loan proceeds to the specific expense to determine his interest expense deduction. Parker's yearly interest is $4,000 ($40,000 × 10%). His interest allocation is as follows: business interest $2,000 ($20,000/$40,000 × $4,000); personal interest $1,500 ($15,000/$40,000 × $4,000); investment interest $500 ($5,000/$40,000 × $4,000). The amount of his deduction is determined by the interest rules for each of the respective categories.

> ➤ **OBSERVATION** To facilitate allocating interest among the various categories, you can (1) maintain separate loans or loan accounts for separate expenditures, (2) avoid commingling borrowed funds with unborrowed funds (e.g., savings) and (3) try not to finance several expenditures with one loan.

Where to deduct. You report investment interest expenses and qualified residence interest on Schedule A, Form 1040 [¶1900]. Personal interest is no longer deductible (see below).

¶1902   PERSONAL INTEREST

Until 1991, you were entitled to deduct a portion of your personal interest expense. The deduction was phased out gradually over five years, starting in 1987. As late as 1990, you could still deduct 10% of your personal interest. Since 1991, however, you can no longer deduct personal interest [IRC Sec. 163(h)(5)].

What is personal interest? This is a catchall category for interest that does not fit into another category. Below is a list of the most common sources of personal interest:

- Credit card finance charges
- Automobile loans
- Installment plan interest
- Finance charges
- Mortgage on a third home
- College loans
- Deferred payment transactions

> ➤ **TAX STRATEGY** Within generous limits, you can deduct interest on loans secured by your primary residence plus one other home [¶1903]. Therefore, take out a home equity loan to pay for that new car, boat, vacation or college education. Provided you are within the qualified residence limitations, you end up with a full deduction and you will probably pay interest at a lower rate.

Special rule for long-term payments. Sellers can mask interest charges as part of the sales price in deferred payment transactions. When payment is due long after the purchased goods or services are delivered, interest may be imputed unless the contract calls for adequate interest to be paid currently (see ¶1217) [IRC Sec. 483; Reg. Sec. 1.483-1].

¶1903   QUALIFIED RESIDENCE INTEREST

Qualified residence interest is interest you pay during the year on debt that is secured by your primary and one other residence [IRC Sec. 163(h)(3)]. Qualified residence interest is also called home mortgage interest.

(a) What Is a Qualified Residence? Qualified residences include your main home and your second home (e.g., vacation home) [IRC Sec. 163(h)(4)(A)]. The home may be a house, cooperative apartment, condominium or a house trailer. A boat will qualify as a second home provided it has sleeping space, toilet, cooking facilities and basic living accommodations. A second home may be one that is not occupied, a home occupied part of the year or a home that is rented out.

> **NOTE:** To be a qualified residence, a home that is rented out must be used as a personal residence for at least the greater of 14 days or 10% of the days it is rented out. Otherwise, it is deemed to be rental property, subject to the passive loss rules (¶2328) [IRC Sec. 163(h)(4)(A)].

Deduction available for only two homes. If you own more than two homes, you may choose the property that you want to consider as your second home, and take an interest deduction on that property. (Your main home is generally the one where you spend the most time.) In addition, once a year you may change the property that you wish to consider as your second qualified home [Temp. Reg. Sec. 1.163-10T(p)(3)(iv)].

> **Example 1:** Mr. Smith owns three homes—Whiteacre, Blackacre, and Greyacre, with outstanding mortgages on all of these properties. Smith lives in Whiteacre, his main home. Smith chooses to designate Greyacre as his qualified second home in 1992. Provided the rules on deductible home mortgage interest are met, Smith may deduct all of the mortgage interest he pays on Whiteacre and Greyacre. The interest paid on Blackacre is not deductible personal interest [¶1902]. In 1993, Smith designates Blackacre as his second home. As a result, he may deduct mortgage interest on Blackacre that year. The interest paid on Greyacre in 1993 does not come under the qualified residence interest rules.

(b) Home Mortgage Interest Deduction Limitations. Home mortgage debt falls into one of two categories: acquisition indebtedness or home equity indebtedness. Your mortgage interest deduction limitation depends on how the loan is categorized [IRC Sec. 163(h)(3)(A)].

Acquisition indebtedness. You are entitled to deduct interest on up to $1,000,000 of "acquisition indebtedness." To be classified as acquisition indebtedness, the loan must be used to purchase, construct, or substantially improve a qualified residence. In addition, the debt must be secured by the acquired qualified residence [IRC Sec. 163(h)(3)(B)]. Refinanced mortgages are also covered by the rules of acquisition indebtedness. To be deductible, the refinanced amount cannot exceed the existing outstanding debt immediately prior to the refinancing [IRC Sec. 163(h)(3)(B)(i)]. However, the excess debt may be eligible for deduction under another interest expense category.

> **Example 2:** Mr. Roberts purchased his home in December 1989 for $150,000. In 1993, when the mortgage was $80,000, Robert refinanced the mortgage. The new mortgage is $95,000. The excess ($15,000) is not eligible to be deducted as acquisition indebtedness. The additional $15,000 of debt may be deductible as home equity indebtedness (see below) or treated as personal, business or investment interest, depending on Roberts' use of the funds.

Home equity indebtedness. You are entitled to deduct up to $100,000 of other indebtedness that is secured by a qualified residence. However, the amount of the home equity loan cannot cause the total indebtedness on the home to be greater than its fair market value [IRC Sec. 163(h)(3)(C)].

> **Example 3:** Ms. Johnson purchased a home in 1990 for $300,000 with a mortgage of $150,000. In 1992, Johnson secured a home equity loan for $80,000. Johnson is entitled to deduct the interest on the home equity loan (as well as the interest on the original $150,000 mortgage).

> **NOTE:** Part of a debt may qualify as acquisition indebtedness and part of the same debt may be home equity indebtedness.[1]

Transitional rules for pre-October 13, 1987 mortgages.
You can fully deduct the interest on all qualified residence mortgages obtained prior to October 13, 1987. These loans are considered to be debts to purchase homes (i.e., acquisition indebtedness)—even if the loans were taken out long after the home was purchased. What's more, these pre-October 13, 1987 debts are not subject to the $1,000,000 interest limitation. However, if you acquire a new debt, you total all your home debts to see if you exceed the 1,000,000 debt limit [IRC Sec. 163(h)(3)(D)].

> **Example 4:** Ms. Caroll purchased her home in 1986 with a mortgage of $1,500,000 on the residence. In September 1987, she took out a $200,000 home equity loan. Both loans are now classified as acquisition indebtedness. And her 1992 interest payments on both the mortgages are fully deductible. Caroll sells her home in 1993 and purchases another residence with a $2,500,000 mortgage. Only interest on $1,000,000 of indebtedness is deductible as acquisition interest.

> **Example 5:** Mr. James has $800,000 of indebtedness remaining on his home from a 1986 mortgage. In 1992 he takes out a $300,000 second mortgage. He can deduct interest on only $900,000 of the $1,100,000 loans in 1992. That's the $800,000 pre-October 13, 1987 loan and $100,000 of the home equity loan.

> **NOTE:** Your refinancing of a pre-October 14, 1987 mortgage is considered acquisition debt. Key limits: The refinancing can't exceed the outstanding balance as of the refinance date, and it can't extend beyond the term remaining on your original loan (unless the old loan called for a balloon payment). Interest you pay on a refinancing in excess of those two limits is considered home equity debt [IRC Sec. 163(h)(3)(D)(iv)].

(c) Types of Qualified Residence Interest. The following types of payments can qualify as interest on your residence: mortgage interest (including second mortgages), "points" (see below), mortgage prepayment penalties, home equity line of credit interest, home equity loan interest, and charges on late mortgage payments (unless for a specific service).

> ➤ **RAW LAND** In some cases, the interest you pay on debt to purchase raw land can qualify for the residence interest deduction. In a ruling, the IRS allowed homeowners to treat a loan to purchase five acres of land adjacent to the home site as residential acquisition indebtedness—and the interest payments were fully deductible. Reason: The homeowners intended to clear the acreage and landscape it as part of their residence.[2]

The term "points" is sometimes used to describe certain charges you pay as a borrower. They are also called loan origination fees, maximum loan charges, or premium charges. If the payment of any of these charges is only for the use of money, it is interest. A loan processing fee you pay as a bonus or premium to get a conventional mortgage loan is deductible as interest.[3] However, a loan origination fee you pay instead of specified service charges in connection with a loan (such as a VA loan) is a charge for service rendered and is not deductible as interest. And a loan placement fee paid by a seller to get a loan for the buyer (such as an FHA loan) is also not deductible. However, the placement fee will reduce the amount realized on the sale of the residence.[4]

> ➤ **WHEN TO DEDUCT** You can deduct in full "points" you pay in connection with buying or improving your principal residence in the year of payment [IRC Sec. 461(g)(2)]. If you pay points to refinance an existing home mortgage, the IRS says these points must be deducted over the loan period. However, the Eighth Circuit Court of Appeals has allowed a current deduction for points paid

to refinance a short-term balloon that has been taken out to purchase a principal residence.[5] Under the IRS position, each year, you can either (1) deduct the portion of the points allocable to the use of the mortgage balance for that year, or (2) write off a ratable portion of the points.[6]

Important: The IRS has announced that any cash paid in connection with the purchase of a principal residence can help the buyer get a current deduction for points.[7] In other words, you don't have to write out separate checks to pay points. The IRS has also provided guidance on how to nail down full current deductions for mortgage points. The following requirements must be met: (1) The bank charges points; (2) The points must be clearly shown on the title statement; (3) The points must be shown not only as a dollar amount but also as a percentage of the total amount borrowed; and (4) You must pay at least that many dollars as a downpayment or other home purchase cost.[8]

Further IRS guidance in this area discusses the following two items: (1) To be currently deductible, the points must be paid directly by the buyer, using his or her own money. So points paid by a seller on behalf of the buyer are not currently deductible. (But the IRS says it will try to allocate amounts paid by the seller to other expenses before treating them as a payment to cover the buyer's points, as long as the buyer and seller have not expressly allocated the payment to points.) (2) Amounts designated on the title statement as "loan origination fees" on Veterans Affairs (VA) and Federal Housing Administration (FHA) loans can qualify as currently deductible points.[9]

NOTE: High-income taxpayers can lose up to 80% of their deduction for mortgage interest. See ¶1900.

¶1904   INVESTMENT INTEREST

Investment interest is interest on loans you use to purchase or carry property held for investment purposes (e.g., interest on margin accounts) [IRC Sec. 163(d)(3)(A)]. Investment interest does not include qualified residence interest or interest from a passive activity [IRC Sec. 163(d)(3)(B)].

(a) Deductible Investment Interest Expense. You can fully deduct investment interest to the extent of your "net investment income" [IRC Sec. 163(d)(1)]. But since 1991, there is no deduction for any investment interest in excess of investment income.

Your net investment income is equal to your investment income less deductible investment expenses. (To be deductible, investment expenses must exceed 2% of your adjusted gross income [¶1942]. Sources of investment income include: income from interest, dividends, rents, and royalties; and gain from the sale of investment property. Investment expenses are costs directly related to the production of investment income. Investment expenses include depreciation, depletion, attorney fees and accounting fees [IRC Sec. 163(d)(4)(C)].

NOTE: The reduction in itemized deductions for high-income taxpayers does not apply to investment interest. See ¶1900.

➤ **CARRYFORWARD ALLOWED** You may carry forward investment interest that is not currently deductible. The carried-over excess can be deducted only if sufficient investment income exists in a subsequent year [IRC Sec. 163(d)(2),(6)].

Tax return tip. Investment interest is deducted on Form 4952.

¶1905   NONDEDUCTIBLE INTEREST

There are special provisions that disallow or limit your allowable interest deduction. These disallowances serve to eliminate unintended double tax benefits and to prevent abuses.

> ➤ **OBSERVATION** As noted earlier, personal interest is no longer deductible.

(a) Interest Relating to Tax-Exempt Income. You cannot deduct interest charges on indebtedness to purchase or carry tax-exempt obligations [IRC Sec. 265(2)(a); Reg. Sec. 1.265-2(a)]. These include zero-coupon bonds, municipal bonds and tax-free United States obligations. The IRS has broadly interpreted the meaning of "carrying" tax-exempt obligations. In their view, loans can be treated as "carrying" tax exempts even where there is no direct link between the loan and the obligation.[1]

> **Example 1:** Mr. Jones held taxable and tax-free securities in separate brokerage accounts. He financed some of the taxable securities with a margin account. Jones loses his deduction even though the loan proceeds went directly to purchase taxable securities. Reason: Jones chose to incur debt instead of liquidating his investment in the tax-free obligations. As a result, the loan helped Jones carry tax-exempt investments.

> **Example 2:** Ms. Hall owns municipal bonds. She borrows money for her business expansion. Hall's interest is deductible if she can demonstrate that business reasons, unrelated to owning tax-exempt bonds, dominated the transaction.

The IRS has said that you cannot deduct interest if you could have foreseen, at the time you purchased the tax-exempts, that a business loan would be needed in the future to meet business demands.[2] On the other hand, it allowed the deduction where money that was borrowed for working capital needs was temporarily invested in tax-exempt securities.[3]

> **Example 3:** ABC Corp. issues long-term bonds to finance new plant construction. The construction will take two years. The proceeds from the bond sale, in excess of immediate cash needs, are invested in short-term tax-exempt securities. ABC Corp. is entitled to an interest expense deduction.

You can also take a deduction for interest if you borrowed the money to buy a personal residence.[4]

Suppose only a portion of the loan proceeds is attributable to uses for which the interest deduction is disallowed. In that case, the interest is allocated on a proportionate basis— and the interest deduction is disallowed accordingly.

Housing allowance. Members of the clergy or Armed Forces who receive tax-free housing allowances are still entitled to deduct mortgage interest and property taxes on the property [IRC Sec. 265(a)(6)].

(b) Loan to Buy or Carry Single Premium Insurance Contract. You cannot deduct interest on a debt to finance a single premium life insurance or endowment contract, or a single premium annuity contract. This includes a contract on which (1) you pay substantially all the premiums within four years from the purchase date or (2) you deposit an amount with the insurer for paying a substantial number of future premiums [IRC Sec. 264; Reg. Sec. 1.264-2].

(c) Loan to Buy or Carry Insurance. You also cannot claim interest deductions as to insurance contracts you purchase under a plan involving systematic borrowing of the policy's cash value. This applies to life insurance, endowment and annuity contracts bought after August 6, 1963. Exceptions: The deduction is not disallowed if (1) the annual interest is $100 or less, (2) you incur the loan due to unforeseen financial difficulties, (3) the loan is for business purposes, or (4) you pay no part of four of the first seven annual premiums with funds borrowed under the plan [IRC Sec. 264]. You can take interest deductions until four of the first seven premiums are paid by debt. The deductions will then be disallowed for the earlier years, if open [Reg. Sec. 1.264-4(b)].

Applying loan proceeds. You first apply borrowed funds used to pay more than one annual premium payment to the premium for the current policy year. You then apply the remaining loan amount to premiums for previous policy years (beginning with the most recent year). However, the loan is not applied to any previous year when you already have borrowed for the premium payment. When the borrowed amounts exceed the premiums for the current and prior years and you have already paid your current premium (i.e., in advance of the due date), the borrowing is debt used to carry the contract. The excess loan amount is applied to succeeding premium years (beginning with the next year). This rule does not apply to single premium contracts since they are paid for up-front [Reg. Sec. 1.264-4(d)(1)(ii)].

(d) Loans to Key Employees. Company owners and certain other employees cannot deduct interest paid on loans borrowed from company retirement plans [¶1325].

(e) Miscellaneous Disallowances. Special rules deny or limit an interest deduction for certain: (1) carrying charges chargeable to a capital account; (2) corporate acquisition indebtedness [IRC Sec. 279]; (3) related party transactions (deduction postponed) [¶2860]; (4) debt incurred to carry market discount bonds (deduction limited) [¶1217(d)]; and (5) interest attributable to deferred payment agreements [¶1217(f)].

(f) Other Nondeductible Interest Expenses. The following items are not deductible as interest: "points" paid by the seller; nonredeemable ground rents; service charges; loan fees; credit investigation fees; penalties; and premiums on convertible bonds.[5]

TAXES

¶1906　　　　　　　　　**DEDUCTIBLE TAXES IN GENERAL**

[New tax legislation may affect this subject; see ¶1.]
A tax is imposed by an authorized government body to raise revenue. Certain state, local and foreign taxes are deductible if you itemize your deductions. To be deductible, the tax must be specifically named as such in the tax law, imposed on you and paid during the tax year. The deductible taxes are:

- State, local and foreign real property taxes [(d) below];
- State, local and foreign income, war profits and excess profits taxes [(b) below; ¶1907];
- State and local personal property taxes [(c) below];
- Environmental taxes; and
- Generation skipping transfer taxes.

Where to deduct. You report most tax payments on Schedule A, Form 1040 [¶1900]. Taxes attributable to property producing rent or royalty, though, are deducted on Schedule E.

> **NOTE:** High-income taxpayers may lose part of their itemized deductions, including taxes. See ¶ 1900.

(a) State and Local Taxes are imposed by one of the 50 states, the District of Columbia, a U.S. possession, or any of their political subdivisions (e.g., a school district or city) [IRC Sec. 164(b)(2); Reg. Sec. 1.164-3(a)].

(b) Foreign Taxes are imposed by a foreign country or any of its political subdivisions [IRC Sec. 164(b)(3); Reg. Sec. 1.164-3(d)].

(c) Personal Property Taxes are deductible as long as the tax is based on the value of the personal property. You cannot deduct a tax that is based on criteria other than value (for example, the weight of a car). If a tax is based on both value and another measure, you can deduct the portion of the tax calculated as to value; you cannot deduct the remainder. In addition, the tax must be assessed on a yearly basis. However, it may be collected more or less often [IRC Sec. 164(b)(1); Reg. Sec. 1.164-3(c)].

> **Example 1:** A state charges a yearly motor vehicle registration tax of 1% of value of the car plus 50 cents per hundred weight. Mr. Taylor, a resident of State XYZ, paid $300 personal property tax based on the value of his car ($30,000), and $10 based on the 2,000 pound weight of the car. Mr. Taylor may deduct the $300 as personal property tax, since it is based on value. However, he may not deduct the $10 paid on the weight of the vehicle.

(d) Real Property Taxes are levied for the general public welfare. Assessments for sidewalks and other improvements directly traceable to the particular parcel of realty do not qualify as deductible real property taxes. However, levies for the maintenance of such local benefits and interest charges for them are deductible [Reg. Sec. 1.164-3(b), 1.164-4(a)].

Tenant-shareholders in a cooperative housing corporation. As a tenant-shareholder, you can deduct your portion of the real estate taxes the corporation paid or incurred on the property. However, if the corporation leases the land and building and pays the real estate taxes under the terms of a lease agreement, you are not entitled to a real estate tax deduction.[1]

> **Example 2:** Mr. Michaels is a 2% tenant-shareholder in a cooperative housing corporation. The cooperative pays $100,000 of real estate taxes. Michaels can deduct his $2,000 share of the corporation's real estate taxes on his tax return.

¶1907   INCOME TAXES

State and local income taxes you pay during the tax year are deductible. These include amounts withheld from paychecks, estimated taxes and any funds you paid when you filed your 1991 tax return in 1992 [IRC Sec. 164(a)(3); Reg. Sec. 1.164-1].[1]

Employee contributions to state disability and unemployment funds. Mandatory contributions to state disability benefit funds that provide against loss of wages are deductible. Currently California, New Jersey, New York and Rhode Island have such funds.[2] Employee contributions to the West Virginia Unemployment Trust Fund are also deductible.[3]

NOTE: Employee contributions to private or voluntary disability plans are not deductible.

¶1908   TAXES DEDUCTIBLE AS EXPENSES OF PRODUCING INCOME

You may still be able to deduct certain state and local taxes not included in those listed in ¶1906. You can deduct taxes if they are trade or business expenses or expenses for the production of income. However, you must capitalize state and local taxes usually deductible as an expense of business or producing income if you incur them in the acquisition or disposition of property. These taxes are treated as part of the property's cost on acquisition or as a reduction in the amount realized on disposition [IRC Sec. 164(a)].

¶1909   WHO MAY TAKE THE DEDUCTION

Generally, you may deduct only taxes that are imposed on you [Reg. Sec. 1.164-1(a)]. In some situations, an allocation must be made to determine upon whom the tax has been imposed.

Apportionment of taxes when real estate is sold. When there is a change in the ownership of real estate, the deduction for taxes is divided between the buyer and seller according to the number of days each owned the property during the real property tax year. As a general rule, the seller pays the taxes up to the day before the date of sale, and the buyer pays the taxes beginning with the date of the sale [IRC Sec. 164(d)(1); Reg. Sec. 1.164-6(a),(b)].

NOTE: Cash-basis taxpayers are deemed to pay their share of taxes when they sell the property, provided the buyers are liable for the tax. Thus, sellers can deduct taxes they do not actually pay [IRC Sec. 164(d)(2); Reg. Sec. 1.164-6(b)].[1]

Example 1: Mr. and Mrs. Thurston's real property tax year is the calendar year, with payment due August 1, 1992. The tax on their old home, sold May 6, 1992 was $2,000 and the tax on their new home, bought May 4, 1992 was $2,500. They are entitled to the following real estate tax deductions in 1992: Old property: Property was held for 126 days (January 1 to May 5—the day before the sale). Deduction = $689 (126/366 × $2,000). New property: Property was held for 242 days (May 4 to December 31—including the date of purchase). Deduction = $1,658 (242/365 × $2,500). Total real estate tax deduction: $689 + $1,658 = $2,347.

Adjustment of amount realized by seller and basis to buyer. When the tax deduction is divided between buyer and seller, regardless of who pays the tax, adjustments may have to be made to the amount realized by the seller and the cost basis to the buyer.

If buyer pays the tax. The tax treated as imposed on the buyer is not considered part of cost [IRC Sec. 1012; Reg. Sec. 1.1012-1(b)]. But the part of the tax paid by the buyer and treated as imposed on the seller is considered part of the amount realized by the seller and is an additional cost of the property to the buyer [IRC Sec. 1001(b)(2); Reg. Sec. 1.1001-1(b)].

Example 2: On April 4, 1993, Mr. Sellers sells Mr. Beyers real property. The price is $100,000. On January 1, 1993, annual state property taxes of $3,650 became a lien on the property for the calendar year 1993. The tax, however, is not due until December 31, 1993. Beyers pays the entire tax when it is due. Sellers can deduct $900 (90/365 × $3,650) and Beyers, $2,750 (275/365 × $3,650) for taxes. The amount realized by Sellers and the purchase price of Beyers is $100,900 ($100,000 + $900).

If seller pays the tax. The tax treated as imposed on the seller is not considered part of the amount realized. However, the part of the tax paid by the seller and treated as imposed on the buyer reduces both the amount realized by the seller and the basis of the property to the buyer.

> **Example 3:** Assume the same facts as in Example 2 except that the tax is due on January 15, 1993 and that Sellers pays the tax when it is due. The tax deduction for Sellers is $900, and the amount realized by Sellers (and the cost to Beyers) is $97,250 ($100,000 less $2,750).

However, if the buyer reimburses the seller for the taxes paid by the seller but deductible by the buyer, the amount realized by the seller and the cost to the buyer is the unadjusted sale price [IRC Sec. 1001(b)(1); Reg. Sec. 1.1001-1(b)].

> **Example 4:** Assume in Example 3 Beyers reimburses Sellers for $2,750, representing the portion of the tax paid by Sellers and deductible by Beyers. Sellers still deducts $900 and Beyers, $2,750 for taxes. However, the amount realized by Sellers and the cost to Beyers is $100,000.

There is one exception to this rule. If the seller paid the tax before the year of the sale and elected to capitalize it, then he must increase the amount realized by the reimbursement [Reg. Sec. 1.1001-1(b)].

> **NOTE:** High-income taxpayers can lose up to 80% of their itemized deductions, including their deduction for taxes. See ¶1900.

¶1910   NONDEDUCTIBLE TAXES

The following taxes are not deductible as itemized deductions:[1]

General sales taxes

Federal income taxes

Social Security taxes

Federal excise taxes or customs duties

Fines

Federal estate and gift taxes (except if allocable to the taxable income in respect of a decedent)

Motor vehicle taxes

State inheritance or gift taxes

CHARITABLE CONTRIBUTIONS

¶1914   CHARITABLE CONTRIBUTIONS IN GENERAL

A charitable contribution is a gift, of cash or property, to or for the use of a qualified organization. Subject to certain limitations, you can deduct charitable contributions if you itemize your deductions [IRC Sec. 170(a)(1),(c)].

> **NOTE:** The value of the time or services that you contribute to a qualified organization is not deductible [Reg. Sec. 1.170A-1(g)].

Qualified organizations. You may deduct a contribution to an organization only if the organization meets the following qualifications and, in some cases, if the gift is used for a stated purpose [IRC Sec. 170(c)]:

- *Community chest, corporation, trust, fund or foundation.* These organizations must be created under federal or state laws or laws of U.S. possessions and operated exclusively for religious, charitable, scientific, literary or educational purposes, or to prevent cruelty to children or animals.
- *Veterans' organizations.* A post, group, or a trust or foundation for war or "non-war" veterans' organizations must be organized in the U.S. or its possessions [IRC Sec. 501(c)(19)].
- *Fraternal organizations.* Only contributions used for the same religious, charitable, etc., purposes as community chests or funds (above) qualify as deductible contributions. The society, order or association must be a domestic organization operating under the lodge system.
- *Cemetery organizations.* This must be company owned and operated solely for the benefit of its members or a nonprofit corporation chartered solely for burial purposes and no other business.
- *Governmental units.* Only contributions made exclusively for a public purpose (i.e., not to influence legislation and not campaign contributions) may be deducted. They may be made to a state, U.S. possession, or any political subdivision, or the U.S. or District of Columbia.

NOTE: You can deduct donations you make to foster national or international amateur sport competition, whether or not the organization furnished athletic facilities or equipment. An organization would generally lose its exemption for trying to influence legislation or by taking part in getting involved in a political campaign for any candidate [IRC Sec. 170(a),(c), 501(h),(j); Reg. Sec. 1.170A-1(h)]. But special elective rules permit a limited amount of lobbying activities [¶3336(d)].

Qualified organizations include: Churches and synagogues, Salvation Army, Red Cross, CARE, Goodwill Industries, United Way, Girl Scouts and Boy Scouts, Boys Club of America,[1] American Heart Association, Juvenile Diabetes Association, Cancer associations, veterans' organizations, public parks.

NOTE: To be certain of the deductibility of a contribution, contact the organization directly to determine if it is qualified.

Nondeductible contributions. You cannot deduct contributions to Communist organizations, foreign organizations, social clubs, civic leagues and political parties or candidates. Funds paid directly to your children to support their work as unpaid, full-time missionaries for a qualified church are nondeductible.[2] Also, donations of time, personal services and blood, as well as gifts given directly to needy individuals, do not qualify as deductible charitable contributions.[3]

Where to deduct. You report charitable contributions on Schedule A, Form 1040 [¶1900].

NOTE: High-income taxpayers may lose part of their itemized deductions, including their deduction for charitable contributions. See ¶1900.

¶1915   BENEFITS RECEIVED FOR CONTRIBUTIONS

You cannot deduct, or may only partially deduct, payments to qualified organizations, if you receive a future benefit. No deduction is permitted if your expected benefit's value equals or exceeds the payment. If the value of your payment exceeds your benefit, the excess is deductible.

Example 1: Mr. Gillian paid $20 for a picnic box lunch at a Juvenile Diabetes Association picnic. The Association gives Gillian a receipt indicating that the lunch plus the entertainment has a fair market value of $6. The excess paid ($14) is a deductible contribution to the charity provided all the proceeds of the picnic go to the organization.

If you contribute to your alma mater's athletic programs, you may receive, in exchange, the right to purchase season tickets, or purchase advance tickets to athletic events. While the price of the ticket is not deductible, 80% of the contribution is [IRC Sec. 170(l)].

Example 2: Mr. Jobe contributes $300 to his alma mater's athletic scholarship program. In exchange, he becomes a "member" of the program. The membership fee is paid annually. Jobe is entitled to purchase a season ticket to the university's home football games in a desirable area of the stadium (i.e., excellent seats) for $120. Only 80% of the $300 is eligible for deduction as a charitable contribution.

Example 3: Assume same facts as above, except the $300 contribution includes the price of the ticket. Jobe is allowed a deduction of $144 [($300 less $120) × 80%].

¶1916   OUT-OF-POCKET EXPENSES

Although you cannot deduct the value of your donated service to a qualified organization, you can take a deduction for some amounts paid in providing those services. These include such items as the cost and upkeep of uniforms, out-of-pocket expenses (not depreciation) and travel costs. For the incidental expenditures to be deductible, however, they must be made in connection with your own performance of services.[1]

NOTE: You may use a standard rate of 12 cents per mile to determine your deduction for the expense of using your car for charitable purposes [IRC Sec. 170(i); Reg. Sec. 1.170A-1(g)].

➤ **TRAVEL EXPENSE RESTRICTIONS** You cannot claim the cost of transportation, meals, and lodging expenses as deductible charitable donations if there is a significant element of personal pleasure, recreation, or vacation in the travel. Furthermore, you can deduct only 80% of the cost of most meals that are otherwise allowable as a charitable travel expense deduction (¶2001) [IRC Sec. 170(j), 274(n)].

Example 1: Ms. Baker works on an archeological excavation sponsored by a qualified charitable organization. She works several hours each morning. The rest of the day is free for recreation and sightseeing. No charitable deduction is allowed, even if she worked hard all morning.

Example 2: Mr. Taylor spends the entire day attending a qualified charitable organization's regional meeting. In the evening, he attends the theater. He may claim his travel expenses—but not the theater ticket, of course—as charitable contributions. Taylor's deduction for meals is limited to 80% of his cost.

➤ **FAMILY VACATION** Provided there is no "significant element" of vacation for you, you can get the same deductions for your travel costs even if your spouse accompanies you. No allocation of travel and lodging costs between family members is necessary if the expenses would be the same whether your family comes along or not.

Example 3: Same facts as in Example 2 except that Mr. Taylor drives to the city where the meeting is held and brings along his wife and child. Result: Taylor deducts the full amount of travel expenses (since it would cost the same to drive alone), the cost of the hotel room based on a single person occupancy rate and 80% of his meals.

Unrelated student living in taxpayer's home. You are permitted to take a deduction if you pay the expenses of a student who lives in your home. The person must be a full-time student in the 12th or lower grade of a school located in the U.S. The deduction is limited to a maximum of $50 for each calendar month the student is attending school for 15 or more days. The student may be foreign or American, but may not be your dependent or relative. The student must be a member of your household, under a written agreement between you and a qualified organization. The purpose of the agreement must be to provide educational opportunities for the student. Expenses that qualify for the deduction include books, food, clothing, entertainment and medical or dental care.[2]

No deduction is permitted if you are compensated or reimbursed for any portion of the costs of having a student live with you [IRC Sec. 170(g); Reg. Sec. 1.170A-2]. For example, if you receive $30 a month for student costs, any additional costs incurred by you on account of the student are not deductible.

¶1917   CONTRIBUTIONS OTHER THAN MONEY

[New tax legislation may affect this subject; see ¶1.]

If you donate property other than money (e.g., stocks, bonds, paintings, furniture, etc.), you deduct the property's fair market value at the time of the contribution [Reg. Sec. 1.170A-1(c)(1)]. However, if the property has increased in value, certain adjustments are made to determine the allowable amount of the contribution deduction [IRC Sec. 170(e); Reg. Sec. 1.170A-4]. In certain cases, an independent appraisal is necessary to establish the fair market value of the contributed property [Reg. Sec. 1.170A-1(c)].

Tax return tip: If you claim a charitable deduction for noncash gifts totalling more than $500, you must file Form 8283.

(a) Used Clothing and Household Goods. Generally, the fair market value of used clothing and household goods (e.g., furniture) is the price that buyers of used items actually pay in used clothing stores.[1]

(b) Cars, Boats, and Aircraft. Assuming you are not a dealer of such property, its fair market value is determined by outside sources.

> **NOTE:** A qualified appraisal is required to deduct a charitable contribution of property worth more than $5,000 [¶1922(b)].

(c) Gifts of Appreciated Property. If you donate appreciated property (i.e., its fair market value is more than your basis in the property), you generally get a deduction for the property's full fair market value. However, in some instances, your deduction is reduced. Also, a special percentage-of-adjusted-gross-income limitation puts a cap on the amount you may deduct in the year the contribution is made [IRC Sec. 170(e)(1); Reg. Sec. 1.170A-4(a)].

Ordinary income property. The first limitation applies if you contributed appreciated property that would produce something other than long-term capital gain if you had sold it. Your deduction is limited to the fair market value of the property less the amount of profit that would *not* be long-term capital gain [Reg. Sec. 1.170A-4(a)(1)]. The following types of property fall into this category: inventory, depreciated property, a work of art created by the donor and capital assets held for no longer than one year.

Example 1: Mr. Meyer donates, to a qualified charity, shares of stock that he purchased five months ago for $1,000. The stock is worth $1,200 at the time the contribution is made. Meyer's deduction is limited to $1,000. That's the $1,200 fair market value less the $200 that would be short-term capital gain had he sold the shares.

Long-term capital gain property. In general, you can deduct the fair market value of donations of property that would produce long-term capital gain if you had sold the item instead of donating it. However, an exception applies to donations (1) of tangible personal property that are put to use unrelated to the purpose or function of the charitable organization or (2) donations to or for the use of a private foundation. Your charitable deduction, in these cases, is limited to your basis in the property.

Example 2: Mr. Nelson donated to his college a painting worth $22,000 that he bought years ago for $2,000. The college immediately sold the painting at an auction for $22,000. Since the use was unrelated to education, Nelson's deduction is limited to $2,000, his basis.

Example 3: Suppose in Example 2 Nelson required the college to use the painting in art classes where students could study it. His charitable deduction is $22,000 (assuming it's within the percentage limitation explained at ¶1919).

Example 4: Suppose in Example 2 Nelson gave the painting to a private foundation. His deduction is limited to $2,000, regardless of how the foundation uses it.

➤ **OBSERVATION** The deduction allowed may be further limited by the percentage of adjusted gross income caps on charitable deductions [¶1919].

Deduction for Appreciated Property Contributions

Type of property contributed	Donee	Deduction
1. Property, if sold, would result in ordinary income only (e.g., inventory and short-term capital assets).	Any qualified organization	Basis
2. Property, if sold, would result in portion of ordinary income (e.g., Sec. 1245 assets).	Any qualified organization	Fair market value less amount recaptured if sold
3. Certain appreciated stock, if held over one year.	Qualified organizations, including private nonoperating foundations	Fair market value
4. Tangible personal property put to unrelated use by donee and, if sold, would result in long-term capital gain (e.g., work of art contributed by donor not creator).	Any qualified organization	Basis
5. Property, if sold, would result in long-term capital gain (other than 3. and 4.) if 50% limit elected [¶1919(b)].	Any qualified organization	Basis
6. Other property, if sold, would result in long-term capital gain and not described in 3., 4. or 5.	Any qualified organization	Fair market value

Alternative minimum tax. The alternative minimum tax is figured on the benefits received in the form of deductions, lower tax rates and exclusions from tax. These benefits are called "tax preferences" since they result from the preferential treatment given in the tax law. Donating appreciated capital gain property can result in a tax preference for the alternative minimum tax. If you donate long-term capital gain property, such as stocks, real estate or tangible personal property that is used in a manner related to the charity's tax-exempt function, the property's appreciation is a tax preference (¶ 2603(a)) [IRC Sec. 57(a)(6)(A)].

> **SPECIAL BREAK** The appreciation of donated long-term tangible personal property that meets the related-use test is not a tax preference for donations made by June 30, 1992 [IRC Sec. 57(a)(6)(B)]. *Note:* The appreciation in value on other kinds of charitable gifts—for example, donated stock—continues to be a tax preference.

If you make a special election to reduce the amount of the deduction for donating capital gain property [¶1919(b)], there is no tax preference [IRC Sec. 57(a)(6)(B)].

(d) Bargain Sales to Charity. A bargain sale is a sale or exchange of property to a qualified charitable organization for less than its fair market value. The transaction is treated as partly a sale or exchange and partly a charitable contribution. If the transaction qualifies for a charitable contribution deduction, you must allocate the property's basis between the part of the property that was sold and the part contributed. This is necessary to calculate the gain from the sale and the deductible donation [IRC Secs. 170(e)(2), 1011(b)].

To determine if a deductible contribution has been made, you reduce the property's fair market value by (1) the sales proceeds and (2) the appreciation that would be subtracted out in determining the deduction under (c), above, had the transaction been a straight donation.

Once it is determined that the bargain sale is eligible for a charitable contribution deduction, you calculate your basis and appreciation allocable to the sold and contributed portions of the property as follows:

Allocation to the part of the property sold. Multiply the item involved (adjusted basis, ordinary gain or long-term capital gain) by this fraction: proceeds from sale divided by the fair market value of the entire property at the time of sale.

Allocation to the part of the property contributed. Multiply the basis or gain by the following fraction: fair market value of the entire property at the time of the sale less the proceeds from the bargain sale, divided by the fair market value [Reg. Sec. 1.170A-4(c)].

> **OBSERVATION** Your deduction may be further limited by the percentage-of-adjusted-gross-income caps on charitable deductions [¶1919].

Example 5: Mr. Dobbs bought stock two years ago for $4,000. He sold it to the United Way in 1992 for $4,000. The stock was worth $10,000 at the time of the bargain sale.

Result: Dobbs' deductible contribution is $6,000 ($10,000 FMV less $4,000 sales price). So 60% of the stock's FMV is allocated to the donation and 40% is allocated to the sale. Dobbs' taxable profit on the sale portion is $2,400—$4,000 sales price less $1,600 basis allocable to the sale ($4,000 total basis × 40% allocation to the sale).

(e) Reduction for Certain Interests. A special rule prevents a double deduction—interest expense and charitable donation—if you donate property on which there is an outstanding loan. You must reduce the amount of your charitable deduction by the amount of interest payments attributable to the post-contribution period. In addition, if the property is a bond or other debt instrument, the value is further reduced by any interest paid that is attributable to the pre-contribution period [IRC Sec. 170(f)(5); Reg. Sec. 1.170A-3].

¶1918 CONTRIBUTIONS OF PARTIAL INTERESTS

With certain major exceptions, you may not deduct donations of less than your entire interest in property (e.g., an income or remainder interest). You can claim a deduction for a contribution of a partial interest in property only if the interest is your entire interest in the property or the donation is in trust and meets the requirements specified below [IRC Sec. 170(a)(3),(f)(3); Reg. Sec. 1.170A-5(a)(1),(7)]. However, in no case can you deduct gifts of future interests in tangible personal property as long as you or someone related to you [¶2323] has any interest in, or right to actual possession or enjoyment of the property; the deduction may be taken when these rights or interests terminate [IRC Sec. 170(a)(3); Reg. Sec. 1.170A-5(a)(1)].

> **Example 1:** Mr. Hill gives securities to Murray Hill for life, with the remainder interest to Allen Hill. Allen makes a charitable contribution of his remainder interest to a qualified organization. Allen gets a deduction for the present value of his remainder interest in the securities. Reason: Allen has donated the entire interest he has in the property.

> **NOTE:** A deduction is permitted even though the charity's right to receive the property in the future may be defeated by the performance of some act or the happening of an event. However, on the date of the gift, it must appear that the possibility of such an event or act is so remote as to be negligible [Reg. Sec. 1.170A-7(a)(3)].

> **Example 2:** Mrs. Robin, a naturalist, transfers four acres of land to Guernsey City for as long as the land is used by the city for a public park. If on the date of the gift, the city does plan to use the the land for a park, and if the possibility that the city will not use it for that purpose is remote, Robin will be allowed the charitable deduction.

When contributions of partial interests are deductible: You can deduct a contribution of less than your entire interest on the property if it takes any of the following forms: (1) a contribution of a remainder interest in a personal residence or farm, (2) a contribution of an undivided portion of your entire interest in property (e.g., giving a museum the right to take possession of paintings for a portion of each year[1]) or (3) a qualified conservation contribution [IRC Sec. 170(f)(3)(B),(h); Reg. Sec. 1.170A-7(b)].

> **Example 3:** Ms. Jones contributed an undivided one-half interest in 100 acres of land to her church. The church and Jones are to share the economic benefits of the property as tenants in common. Jones is allowed a deduction for the value of the property at the time of contribution.

(a) Transfers for Conservation Purposes. You can deduct certain partial real property interests contributed to a qualified organization exclusively for conservation purposes (i.e., keeping real estate of ecological or historical value in its present form). These interests include: (1) your entire interest other than subsurface mineral interests, (2) a remainder interest and (3) certain permanent restrictions on the use of real property such as easements or restrictive covenants [IRC Sec. 170(f)(3)(B), (h)].

> **NOTE:** You can deduct contributions of qualified conservation property even though surface mining is not precluded. However, two conditions must be met: (1) the surface estate and mineral interest in the property must have been separated at all times after June 12, 1976 and (2) the probability of surface mining on the property must be remote [IRC Sec. 170(h)(5)(B)].

> **Example 4:** Mr. Baker owns a residence in an area that has historic significance. He formally commits himself to keep his home as it is by giving a local agency a "scenic easement" in his property. This gives the agency the perpetual power to restrict any alteration or remodeling of the property. Even though Baker had intended to preserve the home, he is entitled to a charitable deduction for the decrease in value of the property after the easement is given.[2]

(b) Transfer in Trust of Income Interest. You can deduct the present value of an income interest you donate to a charity. With this arrangement, you put assets in a trust that makes distributions to a charity for a term of years or an individual's lifetime. After that, you get the property back. The charity must receive either a guaranteed annuity interest (the right to a specified sum payable at least annually) or a unitrust interest (payment, at least annually, of a specified percentage of the fair market value of the trust assets, determined annually) [Reg. Sec. 1.170A-6(c)]. The amount of your deduction is determined by a table issued and revised monthly by the IRS [Reg. Sec. 25.2512-5(f)].

Example 5: Mr. Green has been contributing $5,000 to his favorite charity each year. Instead of making these annual gifts, suppose he contributes funds to a trust that produce $5,000 of income each year. The trust is designated to pay the $5,000 to the charity annually for ten years. After that, the assets revert to Green. Result: Green gets an upfront deduction equal to the present value of the ten $5,000 payments to the charity [Reg. Sec. 25.2512-5(f), Table B].

(c) Transfer in Trust of Remainder Interest. The holder of a remainder interest does not get possession of the property until another interest terminates. You cannot claim an income tax deduction for the transfer in trust of a charitable remainder unless the trust is an annuity trust, a unitrust or a pooled income fund [IRC Sec. 170(f)(2)(A); Reg. Sec. 1.170A-6(b)].

With an annuity trust, the charity gets what is left after a specified amount is paid at least annually to someone for life or a term of years. The amount paid to the noncharitable organization must be at least 5% of the value of the property put in trust, measured at the time it is put in the trust [IRC Sec. 664(d)(1)].

When a charitable remainder unitrust is used, the amount paid out at least annually is a fixed percentage (at least 5%) of the value of the trust assets, valued annually. Thus, the payout varies with the investment experience of the unitrust. As with the annuity trust, the charity gets what is left after these payments have been made for a term of years or the other party's life [IRC Sec. 664(d)(2)].

With a pooled income fund, you transfer assets to a trust and retain an income interest for life. The trust can accept assets only under an arrangement whereby they go to a charity upon the termination of the income interest [IRC Sec. 642(c)(5)].

(d) Right to Use Property. You cannot deduct a contribution of the right to use property for a period of time (unless the contribution is made through a transfer in trust) [IRC Sec. 170(f)(3)(A); Reg. Sec. 1.170A-7(a)(1)].

¶1919 LIMITATIONS ON CHARITABLE CONTRIBUTIONS

Your charitable contributions deduction may be limited by three ceilings: 20%, 30% or 50% of your adjusted gross income. The particular ceiling depends on the type of property donated and the type of organization receiving the donation. Amounts in excess of the 20%, 30% or 50% ceilings may be carried forward for five years [IRC Sec. 170(b); Reg. Sec. 1.170A-8].

NOTE: If all your qualified charitable contributions for the year do not add up to more than 20% of your adjusted gross income, you are not affected by these limits. Thus, you need not do the calculations in ¶1920; your contributions are fully deductible.

NOTE: High-income taxpayers may lose part of their itermized deductions, including their deductions for charitable contributions. See ¶1900.

(a) 50% Limit. Your annual deduction for contributions to certain charities is limited to 50% of your adjusted gross income. The following charities qualify as "50 percent charities" [IRC Sec. 170(b)(1); Reg. Sec. 1.170-8(b)]:

- A church, or a convention or association of churches.
- An educational organization that maintains a regular faculty and curriculum, and has a regularly enrolled student body.
- An organization providing medical or hospital care.

- A medical research organization directly engaged in the continuous active conduct of medical research in conjunction with a hospital, if certain conditions are met.
- A governmental unit.
- A state university fund.
- A corporation, trust, fund, community chest or foundation that gets a substantial part of its support, directly or indirectly, from a governmental unit or from the general public.
- Certain private foundations, including: (1) private operating foundations [IRC Sec. 4942(j); Reg. Sec. 53.4942(b)-l]; (2) private nonoperating foundations that distribute contributions within 2-1/2 months after the year of receipt, provided the distribution is treated as a distribution of corpus [Reg. Sec. 1.170A-9(g)]; and (3) a pooled income fund [IRC Sec. 170(b)(1)(E)].
- Exempt charitable organizations that normally receive more than ⅓ their support from the general public and ⅓ or less from gross investment income. Other charitable organizations set up for and controlled by "⅓ charitable organizations" are also allowed the 50% limitation [IRC Sec. 509(a)(2),(3); Reg. Sec. 1.509(c)-2].
- Certain community trusts if they meet the tests specified in the regulations [Reg. Sec. 1.170A-9(e)(10)].

Example 1: Mr. Sifis, a retired physician, donates $60,000 to the kidney research center in the hospital where he used to practice. His adjusted gross income for this year is $100,000. His current charitable deduction is limited to $50,000 ($100,000 × 50%). The $10,000 ($60,000 – $50,000) Sifis cannot deduct this year may be carried over to future years [¶1920].

On a joint return, the percentage limits apply to the total adjusted gross income of you and your spouse [Reg. Sec.1.170-2(a), 1.170A-8(a)].

(b) 30% Limit. The 30% limit applies in either of two situations:

1. Contributions to 30% charities. All qualified charities other than 50% charities are 30% charities [IRC Sec. 170(b)(1)(B)]. Examples of 30% charities include veterans' organizations, fraternal societies and private nonoperating foundations. Your current deduction for contributions to 30% charities (other than contributions of long-term capital gain property) is limited to 30% of your adjusted gross income.

Example 2: Same facts as Example 1, except Sifis gives the $60,000 to a local veteran's organization. Now his current charitable deduction is limited to $30,000 ($100,000 × 30%). The $30,000 Sifis cannot deduct currently may be carried over to future years [¶1920].

2. Contributions of appreciated property. Your current deduction for contributions of appreciated long-term capital gain property to 50% charities is limited to 30% of your adjusted gross income. However, the 30% ceiling will not apply if your deduction is limited to your basis in the property (¶1917) [IRC Sec. 170(b)(1)(C)].

Example 3: Same facts as Example 1, except Sifis gives his alma mater a painting worth $60,000 to display in its art museum. Sifis bought the painting 15 years ago, and his basis in it is $40,000. Since the college uses the painting for a purpose related to its tax-exempt function, the full fair market value is deductible. However, the deduction is subject to the 30% ceiling. In this case, Sifis can currently deduct $30,000 ($100,000 × 30%). He can carry over the remaining $30,000 and deduct it next year, subject to the 30% ceiling.

Example 4: Same as Example 3, except Sifis gives the college the painting to sell in order to raise money for a scholarship fund. Only Sifis' basis in the painting is deductible, but the more generous 50% ceiling applies. In this case, Sifis can currently deduct $40,000 (his basis in the painting) because the 50% ceiling ($50,000) was not reached.

Special election to take 50% limit. Even if your deduction for long-term capital gain property donated to a 50% charity is not automatically limited to your basis in the property [¶1917] you may still be able to use the 50% ceiling instead of the 30% ceiling. How to do it: You elect to use your basis rather than the property's fair market value as the amount of your contributions of appreciated long-term capital gain property for the year [IRC Sec. 170(b)(1)(C)(iii)].

> **Example 5:** Same as Example 3, except Sifis elects to have his donations valued at his basis. Now, Sifis can deduct his basis in the donated property ($40,000) currently since the 50% ceiling ($50,000) was not reached. Of course, he does not get any carryover deduction next year.

You make the election by filing a statement with your tax return for the year of the election [Reg. Sec. 1.170A-8(d)(2)].

(c) 20% Limit. Your current deduction for contributions of long-term capital gain property to 30% charities is limited to 20% of your adjusted gross income. There is no election out of the 20% ceiling corresponding to the election out of the 30% ceiling. Still, the value of your contributions that exceeds the 20% ceiling may be carried over to future years (¶1920) [IRC Sec. 170(b)(1)(D)].

¶1920   CALCULATING THE CHARITABLE DEDUCTION

The way you figure your charitable deduction for the year depends on the kind of property you donated, the kind of charity to whom you made your donations and, if you have excess contributions from the prior five years, the kind of contributions to which they relate.

(a) Current Contributions. Your maximum charitable deduction is limited to 50% of your adjusted gross income [IRC Sec. 170(b)(1)(A); 170(b)(1)(B)(ii)]. If the value of all your contributions does not exceed this limit, and you have not exceeded the 50%, 30% or 20% limits on specific types of contributions [¶1919], you may deduct the full value of all your contributions. If your contributions exceed any of these limits, however, you deduct your contributions—up to 50% of your adjusted gross income—in the following order:[1]

     1. Contributions qualifying for the 50% limit.

     2. Contributions (other than long-term capital gain property) qualifying for the 30% limit to the extent of the lesser of:

- 30% of adjusted gross income or
- 50% of adjusted gross income minus contributions to 50% limit organizations (including contributions of long-term capital gain property donated to 50% charities).

     3. Contributions of long-term capital gain property donated to 50% charities (up to 30% of adjusted gross income).

     4. Contributions qualifying for the 20% limit to the extent of the lesser of:

- 20% of adjusted gross income or
- 30% of adjusted gross income minus contributions of long-term capital gain property to which the 30% limit applies.

Example 1: Mr. Smith's adjusted gross income is $50,000 for 1992. During the year, he gave his church $2,000 cash and land with a fair market value of $30,000. He purchased the land in 1988 and its basis is $22,000. He held the land for investment purposes. The deduction for the gift of land does not have to be reduced by the appreciation in value. He also gives $5,000 cash to a private foundation to which the 30% limit applies.

The $2,000 cash donated to the church is considered first and is fully deductible. Smith's contribution to the private foundation is considered next. However, because his contributions to 50% limit organizations ($2,000 + $30,000) are more than $25,000 (50% of $50,000), his contribution to the private foundation is not deductible. It may be carried over to later years. The deduction for the gift of land is limited to $15,000 (30% × $50,000). The unused part ($15,000) may be carried over. Therefore, in 1992, Smith's deduction is $17,000 ($2,000 + $15,000).

(b) Carryover Amounts. You can carry over for up to five years the amount you could not deduct currently because of the percentage of adjusted gross income deduction limits.

50% property. You may treat the amount of your carryover contributions that exceeded the 50% limit in a prior year as contributed this year to the extent your actual contributions for this year are less than 50% of your adjusted gross income [IRC Sec. 170(d)(1)(A); Reg. Sec. 1.170A-10(b)(2)].

Example 2: Mr. Jones has an adjusted gross income of $40,000 in 1991 and $60,000 in 1992. In 1991, Jones gave $24,000 in cash to the American Society for the Prevention of Cruelty to Animals (a 50% charity). In 1992, he gave the ASPCA $28,000. Jones can claim a $20,000 ($40,000 × 50%) charitable deduction in 1991. The remaining $4,000 he can carry over for the next five years. In 1992, Jones can claim a deduction of $30,000 ($60,000 × 50%). The deduction includes his $28,000 contribution for 1992 and $2,000 ($30,000 less $28,000) of his excess from 1991. He can carry over the remaining $2,000 ($4,000 less $2,000) for the next four years.

Other property. If the maximum deduction has not been reached after considering excess contributions of property to which the 50% limit applies, you may consider excess contributions of other property donated in the five preceding years. For example, excess contributions of long-term capital gain property to 50% charities that exceeded the 30% limit in the year they were donated may be treated as contributed in 1992, up to the extent that your 1992 contributions of such property are less than 30% of your adjusted gross income for 1992 and to the extent that the total deduction does not exceed the maximum allowable deduction (i.e., 50% of your adjusted gross income) [Reg. Sec. 1.170A-10(c)(2)].

Your excess contributions are also carried over and deducted subject to analogous rules [IRC Sec. 170(b)(1)(C)(ii), 170(b)(1)(D)(ii)].

Change to joint returns in carryover years. If you have a contribution carryover and change to a joint return (or a spouse changes from a joint to a separate return) in a later year, you must specially compute the carryover deduction. An unused carryover of a deceased spouse can be applied only on a return (separate or joint) of the year the spouse dies [Reg. Sec. 1.170A-10(d)(4)]. After that, the carryover is lost.

(c) Special Election Property. Suppose you elect to reduce your deductions for all of your contributions of capital gain property in a tax year and apply the 50% instead of the 30% limitation [¶1919(b)]. Then you must continue to apply the 50% limit to any excess in carryover years. If you carry over contributions of long-term capital gain property from a year the election was not in effect to a year the election is in effect, you must use the property's basis as the value of the contribution and recalculate your carryover using the higher 50% limit [IRC Sec. 170(b)(1)(C)(iii); Reg. Sec. 1.170A-8(d)(2)(B)].[2]

Example 3: In 1991, your adjusted gross income was $50,000 and you contributed capital gain property valued at $30,000 to a 50% limit organization and did not choose to use the 50% limit. Your basis in the property was $20,000. Your deduction was limited to $15,000 and $15,000 was carried over. In 1992, your adjusted gross income is $80,000 and you contribute capital gain property valued at $25,000 to a 50% limit organization. Your basis in the property is $20,000 and you choose to use the 50% limit. You must refigure your carryover as if you *not* had taken the appreciation into account in 1991 as well as in 1992. Because your deduction in 1991 would have been $20,000 instead of the $15,000 you actually deducted, your refigured carryover is $5,000 ($20,000 less $15,000). Your total deduction in 1992 is $25,000 (your $20,000 current contribution plus your $5,000 carryover). If you do not itemize deductions in any of the carryover years, you must reduce the carryover by the amount that would have been deductible had you itemized your deductions.[3]

Example 4: You have a contribution carryover of $500 from 1991 to 1992. In 1992, your adjusted gross income is $10,000, your deductible contributions are $300, and you do not itemize deductions. If you had itemized your deductions, the total of your contributions paid during 1992 plus the carryover from 1991 would have fallen below 50% of your adjusted gross income and would have been deductible. Therefore, you must consider that your carryover is used up in 1992.

(d) Net Operating Loss Carryover. Once you make an excess contribution, a net operating loss carryback [¶2341] from later years does not change the contribution carryover amount; but a net operating loss carryover to the contribution year reduces the contribution carryover to the extent it increases the net operating loss carryover to later years [Reg. Sec. 1.170-2(g), 1.170A-10(d)(2),(3)].

¶1921   WHEN TO CLAIM A DEDUCTION

You can deduct contributions only in the year you actually pay for them. In general, this applies whether you use a cash or accrual method of accounting. However, an accrual corporation may claim a deduction even if payment is made as late as 15 days after the close of the year, provided the board of directors had authorized the contribution before the end of the year [IRC Sec. 170(a)(2)].

NOTE: You are deemed to have made payment on the date a check is mailed if it clears the bank in due course.

Example: On December 31, 1992, Mr. Smith mails a check for $100 to the American Heart Association, a qualified organization. The check is received on January 3, 1993 and clears Smith's bank soon afterwards. Smith can deduct the contribution on his 1992 tax return.

NOTE: You are deemed to have paid qualified contributions in trust when you transfer the assets to the irrevocable trust.

¶1922   RECORDKEEPING AND REPORTING REQUIREMENTS
[New tax legislation may affect this subject; see ¶1.]

You must keep records to substantiate the amount of all your cash or noncash charitable contributions [Reg. Sec. 1.170A-13(a)].[1]

(a) Cash Contributions. You can substantiate a charitable contribution of money by a cancelled check, or a receipt or letter from the organization showing the organization's name, and the contribution's date and amount.

> ▶ **OBSERVATION** Organizations to which you have contributed a total of $3,000 or more in cash must be reported separately on Schedule A of Form 1040. Otherwise, you must lump together cash contributions, with the total reported on Schedule A [¶1900].

(b) Noncash Contributions. For each noncash contribution, you must keep a receipt from the charitable organization showing: (1) the organization's name, (2) the contribution's date and location, and (3) a reasonably detailed description of the donated property [Reg. Sec. 1.170A-13(b)(1)].

A letter (or other written communication) from the charitable organization acknowledging receipt of the contribution, containing the above information, is considered adequate documentation [Reg. Sec. 1.170A-13(b)(1)].

In addition, you must keep written records of:[1]

- The property's fair market value and how it was figured. If you used an appraisal, keep a signed copy.
- The property's cost or other basis. If you must reduce the fair market value of the property by the amount of appreciation [¶1917(c)], keep a record of the amount of the reduction and how you figured it. If you make the special election to use the 50% limit rather than the 30% limit [¶1919(b)], also keep a record of the years you made the election, your current contributions of such property and the excess amount you carried over to deduct in the current year.
- The amount you claim as your deduction. Special rules apply for donations of partial interests.
- Any conditions attached to your donation.
- The fair market value of the underlying property before and after the giving, if you make a qualified conservation contribution [¶1918(a)].

Deductions over $500. If your deduction for noncash charitable contributions exceeds $500, you must also keep records of:[2]

1. How you acquired the property (e.g., by purchase, gift, bequest, inheritance or exchange).

2. The approximate date you got the property or, if it was made by or for you, the approximate date the property was substantially completed.

3. The cost or other basis, and any adjustments to the basis, of property held less than 12 months and, if you have the information, the cost or other basis of property held 12 months or more. This requirement, however, does not apply to publicly traded securities.

If you claim a charitable deduction of over $500 (but not over $5,000), you must complete Section A of Form 8283.[2]

Deductions over $5,000. If you claim a charitable deduction of more than $5,000, you must complete Section B of Form 8283. If your deduction for noncash charitable contributions is over $5,000, you are also required to keep a written appraisal of the donated property from a qualified appraiser.[2] When you file your tax return to claim the deduction, you have to attach an appraisal summary [Reg. Sec. 1.170A-13(c)(2)(B)].

A qualified appraisal contains the following [Reg. Sec. 1.170A-13(c)(3)(ii)]:

1. A detailed description of the property;

2. A description of the physical condition of tangible property;

3. The method of valuation used to determine the property's fair market value (e.g., income approach; market data approach; replacement-cost-less-depreciation approach);

4. The specific basis for the valuation (e.g., comparable sales);

5. The date on which the property was appraised and contributed;

6. The terms of any agreement regarding the property's use or disposition by the donee;

7. The appraiser's name, address, identifying number and qualifications;

8. A statement that the appraisal was prepared for tax purposes;

9. The appraiser's signature.

NOTE: If you don't use a qualified appraiser to value the donated property, you won't get the charitable contribution as to that property.

Generally, qualified appraisers are those who hold themselves out to the public as appraisers or perform appraisals on a regular basis [Reg. Sec. 1.170A-13(c)(5)].

(c) Sale of Donated Property. If the charity sells, within two years after receiving it, property for which an appraisal is required, the charity must file an information return on the sale with the IRS and furnish a copy to you [IRC Sec. 6050L].

MEDICAL EXPENSES

¶1931　　　　　　MEDICAL EXPENSE DEDUCTION IN GENERAL

You may claim unreimbursed medical expenses as itemized deductions if you paid them during the tax year. The medical care must be for you, your spouse, or one of your dependents. It does not matter when the injury occurred, so long as you actually pay the medical expenses during the tax year [IRC Sec. 213(a); Reg. Sec. 1.213-1(a)].

➤ **DEDUCTION FLOOR** You can deduct unreimbursed medical expenses only to the extent that they exceed 7.5% of your adjusted gross income [IRC Sec. 213(a)]. The reduction in allowable itemized deductions for high-income taxpayers does not apply to medical expenses. See ¶1900.

Example 1: Mr. Frank has an adjusted gross income of $60,000 for 1992. He spent $5,200 on medical care during the year. He received $400 from his insurance company on account of some of those costs. Thus, Frank has $4,800 of unreimbursed medical expenses. And he gets a medical deduction of $300 [$4,800 less $4,500 (which is 7.5% of $60,000)].

NOTE: If you file a joint tax return, the 7.5% floor is applied to the combined incomes of both you and your spouse. Therefore, if you or your spouse have high medical bills this year, you may come out ahead by filing separately rather than jointly.

Example 2: Mr. Cooper has an adjusted gross income (AGI) of $115,000, and Mrs. Cooper has an AGI of $35,000, for a combined total of $150,000 in 1992. Mrs. Cooper has $10,000 of unreimbursed medical bills resulting from back surgery. If the Coopers file a joint return, Mrs. Cooper's medical expenses will be deductible only to the extent they exceed $11,250 (7.5% of $150,000 combined AGI). Based on these facts, the Coopers will get no deduction for the $10,000 of medical expenses. By filing separate returns, Mrs. Cooper can deduct $7,375 of her medical expenses. That's because the 7.5% floor on her separate AGI of $35,000 is only $2,625. And $10,000 − $2,625 = $7,375.

¶1932　　　　　　WHAT ARE DEDUCTIBLE MEDICAL EXPENSES

[New tax legislation may affect this subject; see ¶1.]

These amounts include more than just doctor bills. Medical expenses include a wide variety of costs associated with diagnosising, curing, mitigating, treating, or preventing disease. The medical expense deduction is also available for the cost of related transportation and health insurance [IRC Sec. 213(d)].

(a) Fees for Services. In determining if fees paid for health-related services are deductible, you must look to the nature of the service provided. The deductibility of these expenses is not based on the experience, qualifications, or the title of the person performing those services.[1] The following is a sampling of what are—and are not—deductible fees and services:

Deductible Fees for Services

Fees for doctors, dentists and other services. These include fees of surgeons, eye doctors, authorized Christian Science practitioners, chiropodists, chiropractors, osteopaths, qualified psychologists;[2] practical or registered nurses (including cost of nurses' board and social security taxes[3] where paid by taxpayer); cost of clerk in family business to let wife perform nursing services;[4] fees for healing services, laboratory, x-ray, fees to health institutes if prescribed by physician as necessary to health;[5] membership fees in association furnishing medical services, hospitalization and clinical care; part of lump-sum tuition or retirement hotel (or home) fees allocated to medical care if breakdown is provided or is readily obtainable;[6] a portion of housekeeper's salary where duties include medical care;[7] obstetrical expenses; therapy treatment; cost of operation, including legal abortion or vasectomy;[8] legal fees paid in guardianship proceeding to commit an incompetent;[9] cost of acupuncture.[10]

Hospitalization and institutional costs. These include hospital fees; cost of renting and equipping an apartment in lieu of hospitalization;[4] cost of special schools or institutions for mentally or physically handicapped (including board, lodging and ordinary education incidental to special services) if medical resources of institution are primary reasons for being there[11] [Reg. Sec. 1.213-1(e)]; and also the cost of keeping a mentally retarded patient in a specially selected home to aid in his adjustment to community life after institutional care.[12] The Tax Court has held that tuition for special training may be deductible, although not the cost of board and lodging.[13]

Not Deductible

Cost of illegal operation; cost of personal analysis required by students in psychoanalytic training schools;[14] fees for practical nurses hired to care for motherless but healthy child[15] (but see below); cost of dancing lessons even though recommended by doctors;[16] funeral and burial expenses;[17] and expenses for ear piercing or tattoos.[18]

Child care expenses as medical expense. If an expense (such as a nurse's fee) qualifies both as a credit-eligible child care expense [¶2401] and as a medical expense, you cannot claim both tax benefits for the same dollars spent. In other words: (1) you cannot also treat that part allowed as a child care expense as a medical expense; and (2) the amount you treat as a medical expense for determining the medical expense deduction cannot also be allowed as a child care expense [IRC Sec. 213(e)].

Cosmetic surgery. For years, the cost of cosmetic surgery was deductible, even though the surgery was purely for non-medical reasons—such as a rhinoplasty or face lift done just to improve appearance.[19] However, since 1991, the cost of cosmetic surgery is no longer a deductible medical expense. Exceptions: The cost is deductible if the surgery or procedure corrects a (1) deformity related to a congenital abnormality, (2) a personal injury from an accident or trauma, or (3) a disfiguring disease. For this purpose, cosmetic surgery is any procedure to improve the patient's appearance without promoting the proper function of the body or prevent or treat illness or disease [IRC Sec. 213(d)(9)].

If the cosmetic surgery expenses are not deductible, then the premiums for insurance coverage for such expenses are also not deductible medical expenses. And any reimbursement from a health plan for nondeductible cosmetic surgery is taxable income.

(b) Cost of Medicines or Drugs. Amounts you pay for prescription medicines or drugs (including insulin) are deductible as a medical expense [IRC Sec. 213(b); Reg. Sec. 1.213-1(e)(2)]. The cost of special foods and beverages prescribed by doctors for medicinal purposes in addition to the normal diet is also counted as a medicine and drug expense.[5]

(c) Transportation Expenses. You can deduct the cost of getting to and from a deductible medical treatment as well. This includes payments for:

- Bus, taxi, plane fare, or ambulance service;
- Out-of-pocket expenses of driving (e.g., gas, oil, parking fees, tolls);

NOTE: You cannot, however, take a deduction for depreciation, insurance, general repair, and maintenance expenses. Instead of deducting the actual amount of out-of-pocket expenses, you can claim a deduction based on simply the number of medically-connected miles you drive. The deduction is computed at a rate of 9 cents per mile (plus tolls and parking fees). If you use this flat rate, you need not keep records of your expenses.

- Transportation expenses of a parent accompanying a child who is traveling to receive medical care, if the parent's presence is necessary.[17]

▶ **TRAVEL TO VACATION RESORT** If you travel to a more healthful climate on a doctor's advice to alleviate a specific chronic ailment, you can deduct the transportation expenses incurred. In addition, you can deduct the transportation expense for your spouse, if the spouse's presence is necessary. However, there is no deduction for lodging expenses or the cost of meals [Reg. Sec. 1.213-1(e)(1)(iv)].

(d) Lodging Away From Home. You can deduct lodging expenses you incur while away from home receiving care. The medical care must be provided by a physician in a licensed hospital or equivalent medical care facility. The lodging cannot be lavish or extravagant, and there must be no significant element of personal pleasure, recreation or vacation in the travel away from home.

▶ **DOLLAR CAP** The medical care lodging expense deduction is limited to $50 per person per night [IRC Sec. 213(d)(2)].

(e) Capital Expenses. Generally, you can write off capital expenses only through depreciation deductions—which are spread out over a number of years. However, a favorable exception—permitting a full current writeoff—applies to capital expenses incurred primarily for medical care. Examples of these deductible capital expenses include the cost of eyeglasses, a seeing eye dog, artificial teeth and limbs, a wheelchair and crutches [Reg. Sec. 1.213-1(e)(1)(iii)].

Home improvements. A capital expenditure for the permanent improvement of property may qualify as a medical expense if the particular expense is directly related to medical care. In general, your deduction is limited to the improvement's cost less the property's increase in value on account of it (if any).

The cost of operating and maintaining the capital asset will also qualify for the deduction if the capital expense qualifies as a medical expense. The *entire* amount of the operation and maintenance is deductible even if none or only part of the capital asset's original cost qualifies for the deduction.

Example: In 1992, Mr. Jones installed an elevator in his home because his wife, who has a heart condition, had difficulty climbing the stairs of their home. The cost of installing the elevator was $3,500. That year, maintenance and operation cost (electricity and maintenance checkup) was $150. The increase in the value of their residence was determined to be $2,500. The difference of $1,000, which is the amount in excess of the value enhancement, is deductible as a medical expense—as well as the entire amount of the operation and maintenance ($150).

➤ **SPECIAL BREAK** You can fully deduct some improvements regardless of the effect their installation has on the underlying property's market value. In other words, they are treated as adding no value to the home.[20]

Fully deductible improvements: Constructing entrance or exit ramps to home; widening doorways at entrances or exits to the home; widening or otherwise modifying halls and interior doorways; installing railings, support bars or other modifications to bathrooms; lowering of or making other modifications to kitchen cabinets and equipment; altering the location of or otherwise modifying electrical outlets and fixtures; installing porch lifts and other forms of lifts (this does not include elevators since they may increase the value of your home); modifying fire alarms, smoke detectors and other warning systems; modifying stairs; adding handrails and grab bars, whether or not in bathrooms; modifying hardware on doors; modifying areas in front of entrance and exit doorways.

(f) Medical Care Insurance. You can deduct as a medical expense, the cost of insurance that provides reimbursement for medical care and prescription drugs [IRC Sec. 213(d); Reg. Sec. 1.213-1(e)(4)].

➤ **WATCH OUT** If a policy covers both medical care and something else (e.g., accidental loss of life), you cannot deduct any part of the premium unless the policy specifies the amount attributable for medical coverage. No deduction is allowed if the charge for medical insurance is unreasonably large in relation to the total charges under the contract [IRC Sec. 213(d)(6); Reg. Sec. 1.213-l(e)(4)]. And since 1991, amounts paid for insurance coverage for unnecessary cosmetic surgery are not deductible [IRC Sec. 213(d)(9)].

Self-employed taxpayers and 2% S corporation shareholders. If you are self-employed or a 2% S corporation shareholder, you are eligible to deduct from your gross income up to 25% of the cost of medical insurance premiums paid for yourself and your family [IRC Sec. 162(l)]. Since this writeoff is not an itemized medical expense deduction, the 7.5% of adjusted gross income floor does not apply. You may include the balance of the premiums with other medical expenses subject to the 7.5% limitation. Your deduction is limited to 75% of your earned income for the year. No deduction is permitted if you or your spouse can participate in another health plan.

This deduction had been scheduled to expire on December 31, 1991. But the 25% deduction for medical insurance premiums has been extended—it applies to premiums paid and insurance coverage provided by June 30, 1992 [IRC Sec. 162(l)(6)].

Premium prepayments. If you are below age 65, you may deduct certain medical premium prepayments. The insurance must cover you, your spouse or your dependents and must take effect after you reach age 65. To be eligible for this deduction, the premiums must be payable on a level basis for a period of at least the lesser of 10 years or until you attain age 65. However, in no case may the period be less than 5 years [IRC Sec. 213(d)(7)].

NOTE: You cannot deduct the hospital insurance portion of the FICA tax paid on your earned income. However, the voluntary Medicare Part B monthly premiums paid by those receiving Medicare health benefits are deductible.

Supplemental earned income credit for health insurance premiums. Any expenses eligible for the medical deduction are reduced dollar-for-dollar by the amount of supplemental earned income credit claimed by you (¶2402(c)) [IRC Sec. 213(f)].

(g) Special Aids and Supplies. You can include facilities and supplies purchased to alleviate a physical defect or provide relief for an ailment with other medical expenses.

Deductible Expenses

These include artificial limbs and teeth; braces and crutches; dental supplies (but not toothpaste or toothbrushes[21]), eyeglasses (or contact lenses), including examination fees; hearing aids;[17] oxygen and oxygen equipment;[5] iron lung and operating expenses[5]; special mattress and plywood boards for arthritic condition,[5] air conditioning units (less resale or salvage value) and operating expenses, if primarily for illness and they do not become a permanent part of dwelling;[5] cost of "seeing eye" dog and its maintenance;[17] wheel chair [Reg. Sec. 1.213-1(e)] or "autoette" and its costs to operate and maintain[22] if used primarily to alleviate sickness or disability and not merely as transportation to work;[23] cost of special equipment for physically handicapped to enter and operate automobile;[24] excess cost of auto specially designed to accommodate wheelchair passengers;[25] special aids (special typewriter, tape recorder, etc.) to assist in educating child becoming progressively blind[26]; clarinet and lessons recommended by orthodontist to help correct teeth[27]; fees for notetaker for deaf child at college;[13] cost and repair of special equipment for deaf person to communicate effectively over a regular telephone.[28]

Not Deductible

Personal expenses. Maternity clothing, diaper service, and similar personal expenses. Generally wigs, unless ordered by doctor as essential to health.[29]

¶1933   ELIGIBLE RECIPIENT OF DEDUCTIBLE MEDICAL CARE

You may deduct those medical expenses you incur for yourself, your spouse or your dependents. The status of an individual as a "spouse" or a "dependent" may be met either at the time the services were rendered or when you pay the expenses [IRC Sec. 213(a); Reg. Sec. 1.213-1(e)(3)].

➤ **LEGALLY SEPARATED** No deduction is permitted for medical expenses paid by you for medical care your spouse received after you were legally separated under a decree of separate maintenance [Reg. Sec. 1.213-1(e)(3)].

Example 1: Barry and Nancy Hall were married on January 1, 1992. Barry may deduct payments he made in 1992 for medical treatment Nancy received in 1991. On November 30, 1993, Barry and Nancy were legally separated. Barry may deduct the medical bills he pays for Nancy in December only if they are attributable to care she received before December.

Who is a dependent? Your "dependent" for medical expense deduction purposes is an individual who satisfies the support, relationship, and citizenship or residency dependency tests (see ¶1115 et seq.) [IRC Sec. 152]. The income limitation test need not be met.

Example 2: Mr. Block provides more than half of his parents' support—including the payment of their medical bills. However, he cannot claim them as dependents on his tax return because their income exceeds the exemption amount. Nonetheless, he may claim the medical expenses he pays for them.

Divorced parents with a child. Medical expenses of a child paid by a divorced or legally separated parent are deductible by that parent, whether or not he or she is entitled to the dependency exemption [IRC Sec. 213(d)(5)].

¶1934   EFFECT OF REIMBURSEMENT

When calculating the medical expense deduction, expenses are reduced by reimbursements received during the year. Thus, there is no deduction if reimbursements exceed expenses. Generally, though, this excess is not included in your gross income [IRC Sec. 213(a)].

> **TAXABLE EXCEPTION** If medical insurance premiums are paid in part by your employer, you must include in gross income the pro rata share of the excess reimbursement [¶1516].

NOTE: Reimbursements for unnecessary cosmetic surgery under an employer-provided health plan (including a flexible spending arrangement) are taxable income.

Reimbursement in a later year. If you receive insurance reimbursements in a year after a medical expense deduction was taken (e.g., deduction taken in 1992; reimbursement received in 1993), you must include all or part of the reimbursement in gross income (e.g., in 1993) [Reg. Sec. 1.213-1(g)]. The amount taxable is the lesser of the reimbursement or the deduction allowed [¶1244(c)].

MOVING EXPENSES

¶1935   MOVING EXPENSE DEDUCTION IN GENERAL

[New tax legislation may affect this subject; see ¶1.]

When you move your residence as a result of starting work at a new location, you may be able to deduct certain moving expenses. The work may be a new job or the result of a job transfer. In general, you must incur the expenses within one year of beginning that work. The deduction is available to both employees and self-employeds [IRC Sec. 217(a); Reg. Sec. 1.217-2(a)(3)]. Self-employed individuals are treated as having obtained employment when they make substantial arrangements to commence work in the new location (e.g., lease or purchase workspace and equipment, make arrangements to purchase inventory and make arrangements to contact customers) [Reg. Sec. 1.217-2(f)(2)].

NOTE: High-income taxpayers may lose part of their deduction for itemized expenses, including moving expenses. See ¶1900.

To qualify for the deduction, you must pass distance and time tests [¶1936; 1937], and the expense must fall into one of the following categories:

- Moving household goods and personal effects from old to new residence.[1]

NOTE: If you travel by a car to your new home or use the car for transporting household goods or for househunting, you may deduct your actual expenses or nine cents a mile.[2] Depreciation on the car cannot be deducted.[3]

- Traveling (including lodging and 80% of meal costs) to your new residence.
- Traveling (including lodging and 80% of meal costs) after obtaining employment, to and from your old residence to the general area of your new job to search for a residence.
- Lodging in temporary quarters and 80% of meal costs in the new job site's general area for up to 30 days (90 days for a foreign move) while waiting to move into your new residence after obtaining employment.
- Certain expenses of selling your old residence and buying your new one, as well as the expenses of settling your old lease and acquiring your new one [(b) below].

NOTE: Except for travel expenses after obtaining employment and temporary living expenses, you can deduct moving costs even if you move before making your new work arrangements [Reg. Sec. 1.217-2(a)(3)].

The moving expenses of a member of your household can also be deducted if that person resided with you before and after the move. However, your spouse is the only member of your household eligible for the sale, purchase and lease expense deduction. In addition, none of the moving expenses of a tenant in your residence, or an individual such as a servant, governess, chauffeur, nurse, valet, or personal attendant are deductible [IRC Sec. 217(b); Reg. Sec. 1.217-2(b)(10)].

Reimbursements. If you are reimbursed for moving expenses by your employer (or if your employer pays the moving bills directly to the moving company), you must include the reimbursement in gross income [IRC Sec. 82]. The moving expense deduction acts as an offset against this income.

A retroactive law change applies to reimbursed move-connected meal expenses. Under prior law, the 80% limit on the meal expense deduction did not affect you if you were reimbursed for your moving costs by your employer. The 80% limit applied to your employer's deduction, not yours. Now the roles are reversed—you, and not your employer, are subject to the 80% limit. This change applies retroactively, back to 1987 [IRC Sec. 274(n)(2)(E)].

When to claim the deduction. You may claim the moving expense deduction either (1) on your original tax return for the year you incurred the expenses, or (2) on an amended return for that year, filed when the time test is actually satisfied. Thus, suppose you start work too late in the year to have worked 39 weeks by the tax return filing deadline, but you expect to meet the time test later on. You may claim the moving expense deduction right away. Recapture rules apply if you later stop working in the locale and fail to meet the time test. You take into income the amount previously deducted in the year you fail the test [IRC Sec. 217(d)(2), (3); Reg. Sec. 1.217-2(d)(2), (3)].

Where to deduct. You report moving expenses on Form 3903. You then enter the total deduction on Schedule A of Form 1040.

(a) Dollar Limits on Indirect Moving Expenses. Your direct moving expenses are fully deductible. However, your aggregate deduction for each job move for the indirect expenses of househunting trips, temporary quarters and acquiring, leasing or disposing of a residence is limited to $3,000 ($6,000 for a foreign move). Furthermore, your deduction for househunting trips and temporary quarters cannot exceed $1,500 [IRC Sec. 217(b)(3); Reg. Sec. 1.217-2(h)].

You cannot take any deduction for other indirect expenses, such as the expenses of refitting rugs and draperies [Reg. Sec. 1.217-2(b)(3)]. You may deduct any combination of deductible indirect expenses within the dollar limits. Note that you may use those costs of acquiring and disposing of residences not treated as moving expenses to offset the amount realized from a sale or increase the basis of a purchased residence [(b) below; ¶1700].

Married couples. The dollar limits are halved if you and your spouse file separately. The limits remain at the $1,500-$3,000 level when you and your spouse file jointly and both start work in the same general location [IRC Sec. 217(b)(3)(B)]. However, the dollar limits are not split for separate filers if: (1) only one spouse makes the job change; or (2) both spouses make job changes—but you live apart and work at sites at least 35 miles apart. Also, if you and your spouse meet the conditions of (2) above and file a joint return, you get the benefit of a $3,000-$6,000 limitation.

(b) Deductible Sale, Purchase and Lease Expenses. Deductible sale-related expenses are those that would be offset against the amount realized on the sale of your residence [¶1700]. These include the real estate agent's commission, escrow fees, expenses of advertising the property for sale, the cost of preparing the deed and other legal expenses related to the sale, "points" paid to obtain an FHA mortgage for the buyer, and state transfer taxes paid or incurred in the sale or exchange. You cannot deduct the expense of fixing up your home or any loss sustained on the sale. Deductible purchase-related expenses include the cost of a loan and those expenses that would be added to the basis of your new residence, such as legal fees, title costs and appraisal fees. You may also treat as deductible moving expenses the expenses of settling a lease and acquiring a new one. However, you cannot deduct payments or prepayments of rent on a lease for the new residence [IRC Sec. 217(b)(2); Reg. Sec. 1.217-2(b)(7)].

> **NOTE:** To prevent a double benefit, you cannot use selling expenses taken as a moving expense deduction to reduce the amount realized on the sale of your old residence.Nor can you add deducted purchase expenses to the cost basis of your new residence [IRC Sec. 217(e); Reg. Sec. 1.217-2(e)].

¶1936   THE DISTANCE TEST

Taxpayers are divided into two groups for satisfying the minimum distance requirement: (1) those changing job locations and (2) those beginning work for the first time or returning to full-time employment (e.g., college graduate or mother returning to work).

*   If you are changing job locations, a move will satisfy the minimum distance requirement if the distance between your former residence and the new principal job location is at least 35 miles more than the distance between the former residence and former job location [IRC Sec. 217(c)(1)(A); Reg. Sec. 1.217-2(c)(2)(i)].
*   If you are entering the workplace for the first time or reentering the job market after a period of absence, the distance requirement is satisfied if the distance between your former residence and the new principal place of work is at least 35 miles [IRC Sec. 217(c)(1)(B); Reg. Sec. 1.217-2(c)(2)(ii)].

> **NOTE:** The distance between two points is the shortest of the more commonly traveled routes between the two points, regardless of the route selected by you [IRC Sec. 217(c); Reg. Sec. 1.217-2(c)(2)(iii)].

> **Example:** Ms. Taylor moved to a new home after receiving a job transfer by her employer. Taylor's old job was three miles from her former home. Her new job is 40 miles from the former home. Because her new job is 37 miles farther from her former home than the distance from her former home to her old job, she satisfies the 35 mile distance requirement. Assuming the other criteria are established, she is entitled to a moving expense deduction for the expenses incurred.

> **NOTE:** There is no requirement that your old and new homes be at least 35 miles apart.

> ➤ **EXCEPTION FOR ARMED FORCES PERSONNEL**   Armed forces personnel who must move because of a permanent change of station are not required to satisfy the distance test [IRC Sec. 217(g)].

Principal place of work.   Your principal place of work is the place where you spend most of your time—at the plant, office, shop, store or other property. Your principal place of work can also be where your business activities are centered (a home base) if there is no one place where you spend a substantial portion of your working time (e.g., a railroad terminal for a train conductor) [Reg. Sec. 1.217-2(c)(3)(i)].

> ➤ **DOUBLE DEDUCTION DENIED**   You cannot take a moving and business expense deduction for the same expense. A deduction is permitted under only one category [Reg. Sec. 1.217-2(c)(3)(iii)].

¶1937   THE TIME TEST

You must work in the new locale for a specific length of time to qualify for the moving expense deduction. Different time requirements apply to employees and self-employeds.

Time test for employees. To be eligible for a deduction, employees must work full-time for at least 39-weeks during the first year after arriving in the area of the new job [IRC Sec. 217(c)(2)(A); Reg. Sec. 1.217-2(c)(4)(a)]. The time is measured from the arrival date in the new job's general location.

> ➤ **EMPLOYMENT CHANGE PERMITTED** You do not have to remain in the employ of the same employer for the 39-week period. To be eligible for the moving expense deduction, you only must be employed in the same general location of the new job [Reg. Sec. 1.217-2(c)(4)(iii)]

Time test for the self-employed. A self-employed taxpayer must work full time for at least 39 weeks during the first year and for a total of at least 78 weeks during the first two years after arriving in the area of the new workplace [IRC Sec. 217(c)(2)].

> **NOTE:** If you are both an employee and self-employed, your principal activity will determine if the 39- or 78-week test is applicable [Reg. Sec. 1.217-2(c)(4)(a)].

Seasonal employees. If your work is seasonal, you are considered to be working full-time during the off season, if the employment contract covers an off-season period of less than six months [Reg. Sec. 1.217-2(c)(4)(b)(iv)].

> **Example 1:** A school teacher on a 12-month contract, who teaches full-time for more than six months, is considered a full-time employee for 12 months.

> **Example 2:** A self-employed motel owner in a resort area that closes down for five months of the year is deemed to work all year even though the motel is closed during the off-season.

> ➤ **JOINT FILERS** Either you or your spouse may satisfy the minimum period of employment, if you file a joint tax return. Let's say you are an employee and your spouse is self-employed. You must satisfy the time test applicable to your employee status, or your spouse must satisfy the test applicable to her own situation [Reg. Sec. 1.217(c)(4)(b)(v)].

> **Example 3:** Mr. Albert is an electrician residing in New York City. He moves himself, his family, and his household goods and personal effects, at his own expense, to Denver. He commences work with ABC Aircraft Inc. After working 30 weeks, Albert leaves the job. He moves to and commences work in Los Angeles. Employment lasts for more than 39 weeks. No moving expense deduction is permitted for expenses incurred from New York City to Denver because Albert was not employed in the general location of ABC Aircraft in Denver for at least 39 weeks. A moving expense deduction is permitted (if all other conditions are met) for the expenses incurred in relocating from Denver to California.

> **Example 4:** Same facts as Example 3. Assume Albert and his wife, Mary, file a joint tax return. Mary began working in Denver at the same time as Mr. Albert. Mary continued working in Denver for 10 weeks after he left for California. The moving expenses incurred in the move from New York City to Denver are deductible (assuming all criteria are met) because Mary has satisfied the 39 week requirement in Denver. If they filed separate tax returns, only Mary would be entitled to the moving expense deduction based on the New York to Denver move.

Exceptions to the time test requirement. The time test requirement is waived if the taxpayer dies, becomes disabled or is involuntarily separated from service, other than for willful misconduct [IRC Sec. 217(d)(1)(B)].

Retirees. If you retire from a workplace outside of the United States and had maintained a foreign residence as well, you may treat the cost of moving to the United States in connection with retirement as job-related moving expenses. No post-move time test applies. Similarly, a spouse or dependent of a decedent who had worked outside of the United States may deduct the cost of moving to the United States within six months after the decedent's death [IRC Sec. 217(i)].

Military personnel. Members of the United States armed forces are not required to meet the 39-week time test if a subsequent move is on account of a military order or permanent change of station [IRC Sec. 217(g)].

DEDUCTION FOR MISCELLANEOUS EXPENSES

¶1942   MISCELLANEOUS ITEMIZED DEDUCTIONS IN GENERAL

[New tax legislation may affect this subject; see ¶1.]
You can claim expenses that are reported as miscellaneous deductions on Schedule A, Form 1040 [¶1900] only if you itemize your deductions. You can deduct most of these expenses only to the extent that they exceed 2% of your adjusted gross income [IRC Sec. 67].[1]

➤ **HOW TO FIGURE THE DEDUCTION** Your deduction is equal to the total of all allowable miscellaneous expenses reduced by 2% of your adjusted gross income. Generally, you apply the 2% limit after any other deduction limitation (for example, the 80% limit on meals and entertainment [¶2008]) is figured. However, high-income taxpayers may lose part of their itemized deductions, including miscellaneous expenses (in excess of 2% floor). See ¶1900.

For passthrough entities (i.e., partnerships, S corporations and grantor trusts), the 2% floor is applied at the investor level. Thus, as an investor, you are deemed to have incurred an allocable share of these types of expenses—which are subject to your 2%-of-adjusted-gross-income floor [Temp. Reg. Sec. 1.67-2T].

Miscellaneous Expenses Subject to the 2% Deduction Limit

Tax preparation fees [¶1943(c)].

Dues to unions or professional societies.

Safe deposit box rental.

Employment-related education [¶2228].

Certain appraisal fees.

Certain legal fees (e.g., those incurred in connection with employment or to recover unpaid alimony).

Clerical help and office rent in caring for investments, including the cost of a computer.

Custodial fees in connection with property held for producing income.

Expenses incurred for management of undeveloped land and other property held for appreciation.

Fees to collect interest and dividends.

Hobby expenses, but generally not more than hobby income. Note that the hobby income limitation is applied before the 2% rule [¶2325].

Investment counsel and seminar fees.

Liquidated damages paid to former employer for breach of employment contract.

Looking for a new job (including fees paid to employment agencies and resume printing and mailing costs).

Employee's malpractice insurance premiums.

Medical examinations required by employer.

Occupational taxes.

Part of home used regularly and exclusively in work [¶2227].

Research expenses of a college professor.

Small tools and supplies used in the taxpayer's work.

Subscriptions to professional journals and trade magazines related to work.

Tax professionals' fees to prepare IRS ruling requests.[2]

Travel and entertainment expenses directly related to or associated with an employee's job [Ch. 10].

Travel expenses in connection with the management of investments.

Union dues and expenses.

User fee to request IRS rulings.[2]

Work clothes and uniforms.

➤ **OBSERVATION** If you or your spouse have a lot of miscellaneous expenses subject to the 2% floor, you may be better off filing separately rather than jointly this year. That way the 2% floor is applied separately to each spouse's adjusted gross income (AGI).

Miscellaneous Expenses Not Subject to the 2% Limit

Amortizable bond premiums on bonds bought before October 23, 1986 [¶1948].

Certain annuity payments.

Gambling losses to the extent of gambling winnings [¶2324].

Jury duty pay surrendered to employer [¶2226].

Unrecovered investment in pension.

Impairment-related work expenses of a handicapped individual.

Federal estate tax on income in respect of a decedent.[1]

Nondeductible Expenses

Adoption expenses for children with special needs.

Burial or funeral expenses.

Campaign expenses.

Commuting expenses (but see ¶2000 for taxpayers who have two jobs).

Fees and licenses, such as car licenses (but see ¶1906 for fees that are personal property taxes), marriage licenses and dog tags.

Fines and licenses, such as parking tickets.

Home repairs, insurance and rent (but see ¶2227 for home offices).

Life insurance.

Losses from the sale of a residence or personal car.

Lunches and meals while working late.

Personal legal expenses

Personal, living or family expenses.

Political contributions.

Self-improvement expenses.

¶1943   COMMON TYPES OF MISCELLANEOUS EXPENSES

What are probably the most common types of deductible miscellaneous expenses fall into three groups: Employee business expenses, investment expenses and expenses of determining tax liability.

(a) Employee Business Expenses. Employee business expenses are generally miscellaneous expenses that are subject to the 2% of adjusted gross income floor. However, special rules apply when you are reimbursed by your employer for these costs. The tax treatment of your reimbursed employee business expenses depends on how your employer treated the reimbursement and if you adequately accounted to your employer (i.e., submitted records substantiating expenses) under a so-called "accountable plan."

Accountable plans. An accountable plan [¶2003(a)] is any expense arrangement that satisfies three requirements: (1) Payments cover only job-related expenses you could have otherwise deducted, (2) you must substantiate to the company the expense's date, time, place, amount and business purpose, and (3) you must return any amount not substantiated within a reasonable time period.

➤ **TIME-SAVING EXCEPTION** If you use one of the so-called "automatic" allowances, you meet the substantiation requirement as long as the allowance is within IRS-approved limits. These allowances include a mileage allowance (28 cents or less in 1992) for employees who use their cars for business travel [¶2007(d)] and a per diem allowance for meals and/or lodging for employees traveling away from home on business [¶2003(c)]. If you meet the accountable plan requirements, and the reimbursement is not included on Form W-2, you need not report the expenses and reimbursement on your tax return—unless you want to deduct your employee business expenses in excess of the reimbursement.

Otherwise, you report the expenses and reimbursements on Form 2106 [¶2002]. You transfer any expenses in excess of reimbursements to Schedule A of Form 1040 [¶1900]. You subtract reimbursements that were not included on Form W-2 from the expenses on Form 2106. You can deduct expenses up to the amount of reimbursements that were included on Form W-2 as an adjustment to your gross income (they offset the additional reimbursement income). You may claim unreimbursed expenses as a miscellaneous itemized deduction, subject to the 2% of adjusted gross income floor.

> **NOTE:** The rules for deducting business travel and entertainment expenses are discussed in Chapter 10. Other business expenses are covered in Chapter 12.

(b) Investment Expenses. The miscellaneous itemized deduction category includes expenses you incur to produce, or collect income, and to manage or maintain property held for the production of income. The income must be taxable (e.g., expenses associated with investments in tax-exempt municipal bonds are not deductible) [IRC Sec. 212; Reg. Sec. 1.212-1(a),(d)].

> **NOTE:** You report expenses incurred in the rental of property or in the production of royalty income (including depreciation, repairs, taxes and interest) on Schedule E, Form 1040. These expenses are deductions *for* adjusted gross income.

(c) Expenses of Determining Tax Liability. You can claim the cost of determining the amount of tax due, seeking a refund or contesting an assessment as a miscellaneous itemized deduction. The taxing authority may be federal, state, or municipal.

> ➤ **NEW TAX BREAK** The IRS has ruled that the cost of tax return preparation and tax litigation connected with a sole proprietorship or rental income can be written off as a deduction to arrive at adjusted gross income. In other words, these expenses are not considered miscellaneous itemized expenses. So the deduction for these expenses is not subject to the 2%-of-AGI floor.[1]

SPECIAL SITUATIONS

¶1946   ALIMONY

You can deduct alimony you paid during the tax year as an adjustment to gross income (See ¶1235 for details on alimony) [IRC Sec. 62(a)(10), 215(a)].

¶1947   PENALTY FOR PREMATURE WITHDRAWAL FROM BANK CERTIFICATE OF DEPOSIT

Banks generally impose a penalty if you withdraw funds from a certificate of deposit or other time savings account before the maturity date. You deduct this penalty, or forfeiture of interest, as an adjustment to gross income [IRC Sec. 62(a)(9)]. Thus, you can claim it regardless of whether or not you itemize your deductions.

¶1948   BOND PREMIUMS

When your purchase price (or other basis for purposes of determining loss on sale or exchange) for a bond is more than the bond's face value, the difference between the purchase price and the face value is called the bond premium [IRC Sec. 171(b)(1)]. The bond premium represents the amount of interest you receive from the bond that is really a return of your investment (rather than taxable income). Thus, receipt of the bond premium reduces your basis in the bond and, if you include interest from the bond in income, you may write off the amount of the bond premium.

Normally, you treat bond premiums as received in the year the bond matures. However, certain bond premiums may be "amortized," that is, treated as an offset against the interest received each year over the life of the bond. The amount of the bond premium allocated to each year is called the amortizable bond premium [IRC Sec. 171(b)(2)].

(a) Taxable Bonds. You are allowed to write off an amount representing your amortizable bond premium for each year you receive interest from a taxable bond [IRC Sec. 171(a)(1)]. Because the amortizable bond premium is a return of your investment, you must also reduce your basis in the bond by the amount you deduct [IRC Sec. 1016(a)(5)]. How you handle the deduction and basis reduction depends on the year you acquired the bond.

Bonds acquired after 1987 are handled in one of two ways:

1. You may elect to amortize the bond premium by offsetting your interest income from the bond with a proportional deduction (reducing your basis by the amount of the deduction) in each year you hold the bond [IRC Sec. 171(c)(1), (e)].

If an election is made for any particular bond issue, it applies to all bonds owned at the date of election and all bonds later acquired. The election must be made by claiming the offset on your return. It is binding for all future years, unless it is revoked on application to the IRS [IRC Sec. 171(c)(2)]. Elections made in a refund claim after the return is filed are not recognized.[1]

2. You can forgo your opportunity to elect amortization [Reg. Sec. 1.171(a)(2)]. You will be allowed a deductible loss for the amount of the bond premium in the year you redeem or dispose of the bond, pursuant to the regular rules for capital losses [Ch. 8].

Bonds acquired after October 22, 1986 but before 1988. In addition to the two options explained above, you may elect to amortize the bond premium and deduct the allowable amount as an interest expense (¶1901) [IRC Sec. 171(e)]. Thus, you get no tax benefit unless you itemize your deductions. Furthermore, your write off would be subject to the limits on investment interest deductions [¶1904]. If you elect to use this method, your basis must be reduced by the amount of the deduction, even if you decide not to itemize your deductions [Reg. Sec. 1.171-1(b)(5)].

Bonds acquired before October 23, 1986. You may elect to amortize the bond premium as a miscellaneous deduction not subject to the 2%-of-adjusted-gross-income limit [¶1942]. This type of deduction is not subject to the investment interest deduction limit. However, you do reduce your basis by the amount of the deduction. Alternatively, you may forgo the opportunity to amortize and have the bond premium treated as a capital loss.

(b) Tax-Exempt Bonds. Tax-exempt bonds must be amortized. Because the interest is tax exempt, you may not write off the amount of the amortizable bond premium. Still, you must reduce your basis in the bond by the amount of the premium you would have otherwise deducted [IRC Sec. 171(a)(2), 1016(a)(5); Reg. Sec. 1.171-1(b), 1.1016-5(b)].

(c) Figuring the Amortizable Bond Premium. You have a choice of methods for calculating your amortizable bond premium for the year.

Under the general rule, you use your yield to maturity with semiannual compounding. The amortizable premium is the difference between the interest actually paid on the bond and the earnings based on the yield to maturity [IRC Sec. 171(b)].

Example 1: Ms. Burger buys a $10,000 bond that pays 11% interest—or $550 every six months—for $12,000. Thus, she paid a $2,000 premium. Since Burger will receive only $10,000 when the bond matures, her yield to maturity is less than 11%—the exact yield depends on the remaining term of the bond. Assume the actual yield comes to 8% compounded semiannually. For the first six months, an 8% yield on the $12,000 basis is $480. The $70 difference between this and the $550 interest payment she receives is the amortizable bond premium.

For the next six months, her basis is $11,930. An 8% annual yield on that for six months is $477. Thus, Burger's amortizable bond premium and basis reduction for this period is $73 ($550 – $477).

Alternatively, you can use a straight-line type of amortization method. You divide the number of months you owned the bond during the year by the number of months from your acquisition date until the maturity date. Then you multiply the result by the premium you had as of the acquisition date. Fractional parts of a month are disregarded, unless they are more than half a month. In that case, they are treated as full months [Reg. Sec. 1.171-2(d)(f)].

Example 2: Mr. Crown buys a $10,000 bond on March 20, 1992 for $11,000. The bond will mature on July 31, 2000. Thus, the bond has 100 months until maturity (not counting the fractional month of March 1992). Crown's amortizable bond premium for 1992 is $90 (9 months in 1992 ÷ 100 months × $1,000). If Crown holds the bond throughout 1993, his amortizable bond premium for that year is $120 (12 ÷ 100 × $1,000).

(d) Special Situations. The following situations utilize special rules:

Callable bonds. The premium on taxable bonds is amortized to either the maturity date or an earlier call date, whichever results in a smaller deduction [IRC Sec. 171(b)(1)]. If a bond is called before a premium is fully amortized, you can deduct the portion not yet amortized in the year of the call [IRC Sec. 171(b)(2)].

Convertible bonds. Convertible bonds may be amortized if the bondholder has the right to decide whether or not to convert the bond on a specified date. However, the extra amount paid for the conversion privilege cannot be amortized. The amount of the premium that represents the conversion feature may be found by getting the yield on similar bonds without conversion features selling on the open market, and adjusting the price of the convertible bond to this yield. This adjustment may be made by using standard bond tables [Reg. Sec. 1.171-2(c)].

Capitalized expenses. You generally may amortize capitalized expenses (such as buying commissions) as part of the bond premium, unless the premium is made up entirely of capitalized expenses. In that case, you may choose to amortize your capitalized expenses, but you are not required to do so [Reg. Sec. 1.171-2(d)].

Footnotes to Chapter 9

(For your added convenience, in brackets [] with the footnotes below, you will find citations to related paragraphs in the "RIA United States Tax Reporter"(USTR), "CCH Federal Tax Reporter" (CCH) and "RIA Federal Tax Coordinator 2d"(FTC) multi-volume services.)

FOOTNOTE ¶ 1900 [USTR ¶ 684; 684.01; 684.02; CCH ¶ 6081; FTC ¶ A-2704].

FOOTNOTE ¶ 1901 [USTR ¶ 1634; CCH ¶ 9104; FTC ¶ K-5000].

(1) Old Colony R.R. Co. v. Comm., 284 US 552, 52 SCt. 211, 10 AFTR 786; Deputy v. DuPont, 308 US 488, 60 SCT 363, 23 AFTR 808.

(2) Knetsch v. U.S., 6 AFTR 2d 5851, 364 US 361.

(3) Bettendorf, 3 BTA 378.

FOOTNOTE ¶ 1902 [USTR ¶ 1634; CCH ¶ 9400A; FTC ¶ K-5160; 5162].

FOOTNOTE ¶ 1903 [USTR ¶ 1634; CCH ¶ 9402; FTC ¶ K-5377 et seq.].

(1) IR-88-99, 6-17-88.

(2) Ltr. Rul. 8940061.

(3) Rev. Rul. 69-188, 1969-1 CB 54, amplified by Rev. Rul. 69-582, 1969-2 CB 29.

(4) Rev. Rul. 67-297, 1967-2 CB 87; Rev. Rul. 68-650, 1968-2 CB 78; Rev. Rul 69-188, 1969-1 CB 54, amplified by Rev. Rul. 69-582, 1969-2 CB 29.

(5) Rev. Proc. 87-15, 1987-1 CB 624; Huntsman, USCA 8, No. 89-1672.

(6) Rev. Rul. 87-22, 1987-1 CB 146.

(7) Notice 90-70, 1990-2 CB 351.

(8) Rev. Proc. 92-12, IRB 1992-3.

(9) Rev. Proc. 92-12A.

FOOTNOTE ¶ 1904 [USTR ¶ 1634; CCH ¶ 9403; FTC ¶ K-5310 et seq.].

FOOTNOTE ¶ 1905 [USTR ¶ 2654; 2644; CCH ¶ 14,054; FTC ¶ K-5235; 5368].

(1) Ltr. Rul. 8624017.

(2) Ltr. Rul. 8624017.

(3) Ltr. Rul. 8632037.

(4) Rev. Proc. 72-18, 1972 CB 704.

(5) Treas. Dept. booklet "Your Federal Income Tax" (1991 Ed.), p. 134.

FOOTNOTE ¶ 1906 [USTR ¶ 1644; CCH ¶ 9502; FTC ¶ K-4000 et seq.].

(1) Treas. Dept. booklet "Your Federal Income Tax" (1991 Ed.), p. 128.

FOOTNOTE ¶ 1907 [USTR ¶ 1644; CCH ¶ 9502; FTC ¶ K-4400].

(1) Treas. Dept. booklet "Your Federal Income Tax" (1991 Ed.), p. 128.

(2) Treas. Dept. booklet "Your Federal Income Tax" (1991 Ed.), p. 128.

(3) Rev. Rul. 89-16, 1989-2 CB 208.

FOOTNOTE ¶ 1908 [USTR ¶ 1644; CCH ¶ 9502; FTC ¶ K-4502].

FOOTNOTE ¶ 1909 [USTR ¶ 1664; CCH ¶ 9502; FTC ¶ K-4100].

(1) Treas. Dept. booklet "Your Federal Income Tax" (1991 Ed.), pp. 128.

FOOTNOTE ¶ 1910 [USTR ¶ 1644; CCH ¶ 9502; FTC ¶ K-4000].

(1) Treas. Dept. booklet "Your Federal Income Tax" (1991 Ed.), p. 129, 130.

FOOTNOTE ¶ 1914 [USTR ¶ 1704; CCH ¶ 11,690; FTC ¶ K-3000].

(1) Treas. Dept. booklet "Your Federal Income Tax" (1991 Ed.), p. 135.

(2) Davis v. U.S., 65 AFTR 2d 90.

(3) Treas. Dept. booklet "Your Federal Income Tax" (1991 Ed.), p. 137.

FOOTNOTE ¶ 1915 [USTR ¶ 1704; CCH ¶ 11,690; FTC ¶ K-3205].

FOOTNOTE ¶ 1916 [USTR ¶ 1704; CCH ¶ 11,690; FTC ¶ K-3003].

(1) Davis v. U.S., 65 AFTR 2d 90.

(2) Treas. Dept. booklet "Charitable Contributions" (1991 Ed.), p. 2.

FOOTNOTE ¶ 1917 [USTR ¶ 1704; CCH ¶ 11,690; FTC ¶ K-3311].

(1) Treas. Dept. booklet "Your Federal Income Tax" (1991 Ed.), p. 138.

FOOTNOTE ¶ 1918 [USTR ¶ 1704; CCH ¶ 11,690; 11698; FTC ¶ K-3361 et seq.].

(1) Winokur, 90 TC 733.

(2) Ltr. Rul. 8032013.

FOOTNOTE ¶ 1919 [USTR ¶ 1704; CCH ¶ 11,690; FTC ¶ K-3200 et seq.].

FOOTNOTE ¶ 1920 [USTR ¶ 1704; CCH ¶ 11,690; FTC ¶ K-3644 et seq.].

(1) Treas. Dept. booklet "Charitable Contributions" (1991 Ed.), p. 5.

(2) Treas. Dept. booklet "Charitable Contributions" (1991 Ed.), p. 6.

FOOTNOTE ¶ 1921 [USTR ¶ 1704; CCH ¶ 11,690; FTC ¶ K-3002 et seq.].

FOOTNOTE ¶ 1922 [USTR ¶ 1704; CCH ¶ 11,699; FTC ¶ K-3800 et seq.].

(1) Treas. Dept. booklet "Your Federal Income Tax" (1991 Ed.), p. 138, 139.

(2) Treas. Dept. booklet "Charitable Contributions" (1991 Ed.), p. 5.

FOOTNOTE ¶ 1931 [USTR ¶ 2134; CCH ¶ 12,543; FTC ¶ K-2300 et seq.].

FOOTNOTE ¶ 1932 [USTR ¶ 2134; CCH ¶ 12,543; FTC ¶ K-2102 et seq.].

(1) Dodge Est., ¶61,346 PH Memo TC.

(2) Rev. Rul. 143, 1953-2 CB 129.

(3) Rev. Rul. 57-489, 1957-2 CB 207.

(4) Ungar, ¶63,159 PH Memo TC.

(5) Rev. Rul. 55-261, 1955-1 CB 307.

(6) Rev. Rul. 54-457, 1954-2 CB 100; Rev. Rul. 67-185, 1967-1 CB 70.

(7) Hentz, ¶53,110 PH Memo TC.

(8) Rev. Rul. 73-201, 1973-1 CB 140.

(9) Rev. Rul. 71-281, 1971-2 CB 165.

(10) Rev. Rul. 72-593, 1972-2 CB 180.

(11) Rev. Rul. 58-280, 1958-1 CB 157.

(12) Rev. Rul. 69-499, 1969-2 CB 39.

(13) Baer, ¶67,034 PH Memo TC.

(14) Rev. Rul. 56-263, 1956-1 CB 135.

(15) Wendell, 12 TC 161.

(16) Thoene, 33 TC 62.

(17) Treas. Dept. booklet "Your Federal Income Tax" (1991 Ed.), p. 124.

(18) Rev. Rul. 82-111, 1982-1 CB 48.

(19) Rev. Rul. 76-332, 1976-2 CB 81.

(20) Conference Report 99-841, p. 21, 99th Cong. 2nd Sess.

(21) Rev. Rul. 66-216, 1966-2 CB 100.

(22) Rev. Rul. 67-76, 1967-1 CB 70.

(23) Rev. Rul. 58-8, 1958-1 CB 154.

(24) Rev. Rul. 66-80, 1966-1 CB 57.

(25) Rev. Rul. 70-606, 1970-2 CB 66.

(26) Rev. Rul. 58-223, 1958-1 CB 156.

(27) Rev. Rul. 62-210, 1962-2 CB 89.

(28) Rev. Rul. 71-48, 1971-1 CB 99.

(29) Rev. Rul. 62-189, 1962-2 CB 88.

FOOTNOTE ¶ 1933 [USTR ¶ 2134; CCH ¶ 12,543; FTC ¶ K-2300 et seq.].

FOOTNOTE ¶ 1934 [USTR ¶ 2134; CCH ¶ 12,543; FTC ¶ K-3600 et seq.].

FOOTNOTE ¶ 1935 [USTR ¶ 2174; CCH ¶ 12,623; FTC ¶ L-3600 et seq.].

(1) Rev. Rul. 70-625, 1970-2 CB 67.

(2) Rev. Proc. 85-49, 1985-2 CB 716 modifying Rev. Proc. 84-72, 1984-2 CB 735, Rev. Proc. 83-74, 1983-2 CB 593 and Rev. Proc. 82-61, 1982-2 CB 849.

(3) Rev. Rul. 70-656, 1970-2 CB 67.

FOOTNOTE ¶ 1936 [USTR ¶ 2174; CCH ¶ 12,623; FTC ¶ L-3616].

FOOTNOTE ¶ 1937 [USTR ¶ 2174; CCH ¶ 12,623; FTC ¶ L-3602].

FOOTNOTE ¶ 1942 [USTR ¶ 674; CCH ¶ 6064; FTC ¶ A-2700 et seq.].

(1) Treas. Dept. booklet "Your Federal Income Tax" (1991 Ed.), p. 171.

(2) Rev. Rul. 89-68, 1989-1 CB 82.

FOOTNOTE ¶ 1943 [USTR ¶ 2124; CCH ¶ 6005; 12,523; FTC ¶ A-2709].

(1) Rev. Rul. 92-29, IRB 1992-16.

FOOTNOTE ¶ 1946 [USTR ¶ 2154; CCH ¶ 12,573; FTC ¶ K-6036 et seq.].

FOOTNOTE ¶ 1947 [USTR ¶ 624; CCH ¶ 6005; FTC ¶ A-2618].

FOOTNOTE ¶ 1948 [USTR ¶ 1714; CCH ¶ 11,855; FTC ¶ D-2817].

(1) Barnhill, 241 F.2d 496, 50 AFTR 1675.

TRAVEL AND ENTERTAINMENT DEDUCTIONS

TABLE OF CONTENTS

TRANSPORTATION AND TRAVEL EXPENSES

¶2000   TRAVEL AND TRANSPORTATION EXPENSES

You can deduct transportation costs if they are ordinary and necessary expenses incurred in connection with your trade or business or for the production of income. Travel expenses are also deductible if they satisfy an additional requirement: You incur them while you are "away from home" [IRC Sec. 162(a)(2)].

Transportation expenses are the direct cost of going from one place to another (e.g., cab fares, car expenses). Travel expenses include transportation costs and living expenses you incur when you are away from home. Travel expenses cover:

- Air, rail and bus fares;
- The cost of operating and maintaining a car or an airplane;
- Taxi fares or other transportation costs between an airport or station and a hotel, between business meetings, and from a business meeting to a hotel or restaurant;
- Meals at restaurants;
- Hotel charges or other lodging costs;
- Cleaning and laundry services;
- Telephone and telegraph expenses;
- Public stenographers' fees; and
- Tips incidental to any of the above expenses.

The deduction for transportation and travel expenses is available to corporations, partnerships, sole proprietors and to employees who incur these expenses in connection with their employment. For example, if an employer reimburses an employee for expenses incurred while away from home on business, the employer can deduct the reimbursement as a travel expense. And the reimbursement is tax free to the employee so long as a proper record of the expenses is submitted to the employer [¶2003].

(a) Away From Home. Generally, you can deduct the cost of meals, lodging and other travel expenses when you are away from your tax home on business overnight or for a period long enough to require sleep or rest. If you do not satisfy the sleep-or-rest requirement, you do not get a travel deduction.[1] On the other hand, you can deduct business transportation expenses whether or not you are away from home.

> **Example 1:** Mr. Baker lives and works in Los Angeles. He flies to San Francisco on business and returns the same day. Results: (1) He can deduct the cost of his airfare as a transportation expense. (2) He cannot deduct the cost of his meals in San Francisco because this is a travel expense, and Baker was not away from home overnight. However, if Baker stays in San Francisco overnight and returns the next day, his hotel and meal expenses in San Francisco are deductible.

Your tax home is the location of your business or employment, regardless of where you live.[2] The entire city or general area in which the business or employment is located is your tax home.

> **Example 2:** Ms. Lawrence's residence is in Boston. But she works in New York where she stays in a hotel and eats her meals in a local restaurant. She returns to Boston every weekend to be with her family. She cannot deduct any of her expenses of traveling to and from New York and while in New York because it is her tax home. Additionally, she cannot deduct the cost of traveling to and from Boston because these trips are not for a business reason.

Two places of business. If you have two or more regular work locations, your main place of work is considered your tax home. In determining which location is the main place of work, you have to take into account such factors as the total time spent at each location, the degree of business activity there and the amount of income derived there.[3] You can deduct the cost of business travel from your primary work location to a secondary location, even if your family residence is in the area of the secondary location. You can also deduct a portion of your family living expenses to the extent they are attributable to your presence while conducting business at the secondary location.[4]

> **Example 3:** Mr. Mason works three weeks a month in Detroit and one week in Chicago. Mason's family lives in Chicago. Mason can deduct his travel expenses to and from Chicago because he is away from home (Detroit) on business. And, for the same reason, he can also deduct an allocable portion of his family's meal and lodging expenses while in Chicago. He cannot, however, deduct his living expenses in Detroit; that is his tax home.

No regular place of work. It is possible that you have no regular place of work (e.g., an outside salesperson). In that case, your principal residence is treated as your tax home if all of the following tests are met:

- You do some work in the area of the principal residence and stay at the residence while working in the area;
- You have duplicate living expenses when away from the residence on business; and
- You have not abandoned the residence (e.g., your family lives there).[5]

If you satisfy only one of the three tests, you have no real tax home. Your tax home is wherever you happen to be at the time, and no deductions for travel expenses are allowed. If you meet two of the three tests, then your principal residence may be considered your tax home, depending on the circumstances.

Temporary v. permanent place of work. Once your tax home has been established, you can deduct travel expenses away from the tax home to a temporary work location. However, your employment at the new work location must be of a definite, limited duration. If the employment is of an indefinite duration, the new work location becomes your new tax home and you cannot deduct travel expenses (but you may be entitled to a moving expense deduction [¶1935 et seq.]).

In determining whether a new work assignment is temporary, the Revenue Service uses three general rules:[6]

1. Assignments of less than one year are usually considered temporary.

2. Assignments of one to two years are presumed to be a permanent change of tax homes. But that presumption can be overcome if you can show that (a) the assignment was realistically expected to last for less than two years (after which you would return to the claimed tax home) and (b) the claimed tax home is your regular place of abode in a real sense (e.g., you maintain a residence there and vote there).

3. If an assignment is expected to last two years or more (or in fact, lasts that long), then it is not considered temporary under any circumstances.

If you interrupt a temporary assignment to make a personal trip home, you cannot deduct expenses incurred during your personal stay at home. That is because you are no longer away from home during that period. However, you can deduct travel expenses en route to and from your home. But the deduction cannot exceed what it would have cost you to remain at your temporary assignment location.[7]

Example 4: Ms. Parker is away from home for two weeks on business. On Friday of the first week, she travels back home to be with her family. On Sunday she returns to her temporary assignment location. Her airfare to and from home is $280. If Parker had stayed at her temporary assignment location for the weekend, her meal and lodging costs would have been $250. Result: Parker can deduct $250 of her airfare.

(b) Mixing Business and Personal Travel. If you travel to a destination for both business and personal reasons, you can deduct travel expenses to and from the destination only if the primary purpose of your trip is business [Reg. Sec. 1.162-2(b)(1)]. However, even when the trip is not primarily business-connected, you can still deduct business expenses at the destination.

Whether a trip is primarily related to business depends on the facts and circumstances of each situation. The amount of time you spend on business activities compared with the time you spend on personal activities is an important determining factor [Reg. Sec. 1.162-2(b)(2)].

Example 5: Mr. Brown travels from New York to Florida for a two-week vacation. On two days, he interrupts his vacation to meet with customers of his company. Result: Brown cannot deduct his travel expenses between New York and Florida because the trip is primarily personal. However, he can deduct expenses allocable to the two-day business portion of the trip.

Example 6: Ms. Smith has to go from her home in Chicago to Los Angeles on business for her company. She spends one week in Los Angeles meeting with her company's customers. She then decides to stay on another three days to go sightseeing. Result: Smith's trip is primarily for business. So she can deduct 100% of her expenses en route to and from Los Angeles and her expenses during the one-week business portion of her stay. What she spends during the other three days is personal and nondeductible.

Bonus deduction for weekend days. A special tax rule says that weekends count as business days for purposes of claiming a travel deduction. Result: If your business trip flanks a weekend, you can claim a travel deduction for the cost of your hotel room, meals and other living expenses during the weekend. You get the deduction even if you spend the weekend sightseeing, visiting friends or pursuing other leisure activities. However, your out-of-pocket cost for leisure activities is not deductible.

Similarly, you can get a deduction break when you conclude your business discussions on Friday, but you stay over an extra day to take advantage of low weekend airfares. You can claim a travel deduction for your hotel room, meals and other living expenses for that extra day, provided your extra expenses are at least offset by your savings on the airfare.

The cost of traveling to a convention or other meeting may constitute an ordinary and necessary business expense. You are entitled to a deduction if there is a sufficient relationship between your business and the convention so that your attendance benefits your business [Reg. Sec. 1.162-2(d)].

When your spouse accompanies you on a business trip, your spouse's expenses are usually considered personal and nondeductible. However, a deduction for a spouse's expenses is allowed if his or her presence on the trip serves a bona fide business purpose [Reg. Sec. 1.162-2(c)]. For example, deductions have been allowed when an employee's spouse was required to attend trade association meetings to help establish personal contacts and the spouse's activities were devoted solely to the association meetings.[8]

➤ **OBSERVATION** Even where your spouse's attendance does not serve a bona fide business purpose, you can still deduct the entire cost of traveling as if you were alone. In other words, you are not necessarily limited to a deduction of 50% of the travel expenses of you and your spouse.

Example 7: Mr. Nolan drives from Denver to San Francisco solely for business reasons. Mrs. Nolan goes with him. Result: Nolan can deduct all of the auto expenses of the trip because the expenses would have been the same whether Mrs. Nolan accompanied him or not. And if the hotel rooms in San Francisco are $125 a day for singles, and $150 for doubles, Nolan can deduct $125.[9]

(c) Commuting. The cost of transportation between your family residence and place of business or employment generally is not deductible [Reg. Sec. 1.162-2(e)]. Since the cost stems from your personal choice to maintain your residence distant from work, it is not considered a business expense.[10]

➤ **TAX-SAVING EXCEPTION** Any time you go from your home to a temporary workplace or from a temporary workplace to your home, your transportation expenses are deductible.[11]

The key here is "temporary." As long as your destination is not a place to which you routinely go (e.g., daily trips to deposit funds at your bank or to pursue a long-term course of study at college), you get a deduction.

Example 8: In the morning, Ms. Wilson drives from her home to a client's office. She stops by her own office during lunch, returns to the client's office in the afternoon and then heads home. The client's office qualifies as a temporary workplace, so 100% of Wilson's driving for the day is deductible.

The temporary workplace exception can apply to more situations than a client's office. For example, a restaurant where you discuss business over dinner can constitute a temporary work location. Assuming you discuss business at the restaurant, all the miles between the restaurant and your home become deductible.

The cost of transportation between two or more permanent work locations is deductible as well. However, the trips directly between your residence and the first permanent location and between the last permanent location and your residence are considered nondeductible commuting.[12]

Example 9: Mr. Hargrove is an executive with XYZ, Inc. In the evenings, he also teaches business courses at a local college. He cannot deduct the trips between his home and XYZ's office and the trips between the college and his home. Since Hargrove is employed by the college on a regular basis, he cannot take advantage of the temporary workplace exception. But he can deduct the trips between XYZ's office and the college.

Where you maintain a secondary office in your home, deductions have usually been denied for trips between the home office and your principal office. That's because you would have made these trips anyway and cannot convert commuting trips into business trips simply by locating another office in the home.[13] However, deductions have been allowed where your principal office is in your home and you make trips to secondary work locations.[14]

(d) Education-Related Travel. You can deduct the cost of education that maintains or improves skills needed in your business or employment or that is required to retain your current job or pay rate (¶2228) [Reg. Sec. 1.162-5(a)]. If you travel away from home overnight to obtain education that is deductible, then your travel expenses (including meals and lodging) are also deductible [Reg. Sec. 1.162-5(e)]. However, travel itself is not deductible as a form of education [IRC Sec. 274(m)(2)].

Example 10: Ms. Graham is a Spanish teacher who takes a sabbatical leave to travel to Spain to improve her understanding of the language and culture. Graham's travel costs are not deductible.

Example 11: Mr. Blaine is a history teacher. He goes to Paris to do research on an article he is writing on French history for a periodical. Assuming his nontravel research expenses are deductible, his travel expenses are deductible too.

(e) Investment-Related Travel. You can deduct ordinary and necessary expenses related to the production of income or for the management and conservation of property held for the production of income [IRC Sec. 212]. Deductible "nonbusiness" expenses include travel and transportation expenses you incur in looking after your investments. However, you cannot deduct the cost of attending a convention or seminar relating to investments, financial planning or other activities related to the production of income [IRC Sec. 274(h)(7)]. Additionally, you cannot claim a deduction for travel expenses you incur for investigating new investments.[15]

Deductions allowed. Aircraft rental incurred by a taxpayer to attend board and shareholder meetings of corporation in which he was a major stockholder;[16] travel expenses incurred by a taxpayer in going from St. Louis to Charlotte twice a year to maintain three unimproved lots owned by taxpayer;[17] trips by a taxpayer to manage rental property located 30 miles from the taxpayer's home.[18]

Deductions disallowed. A taxpayer's travel expenses incurred for inspecting rental property when the main purpose of trip was to visit relatives;[19] trips to plants of corporations in which a taxpayer held stock when the costs involved did not bear a reasonable relationship to investments;[20] transportation costs incurred to attend stockholder meetings when a taxpayer is attending to get useful information for future investments.[21]

> ➤ **OBSERVATION** There is often a fine line between nondeductible investment travel and deductible business travel. For example, a taxpayer who owned 21 rental apartments went to Palm Springs to investigate the purchase of additional real estate. The taxpayer was allowed to deduct the trip to Palm Springs because he was in the business of owning rental real estate.[22]

¶2001   SPECIAL RESTRICTION ON TRAVEL DEDUCTIONS

Even when your travel away from home is an ordinary and necessary business expense, no deduction or only a partial deduction may be allowed. The tax law imposes limits on deductions for certain kinds of travel expenses [IRC Sec. 274].

(a) Meals. You generally may deduct only 80% of the cost of meals while away from home on business [IRC Sec. 274(n)(1)]. Taxes and tips related to the meals are also subject to the 80% limit, but transportation to and from the meal location is not.[1]

> **Example 1:** Mr. Green is away from home on business. One evening he goes out to dinner. His expenses: $6 for the taxi to and from the restaurant, $20 for the meal, $1 sales tax, and $4 for tips. Result: Green can deduct $26—his $6 taxi ride plus 80% of his other $25 of expenses.

If you incur charges for goods and services while traveling and part of the charges are attributable to meals, you must make a reasonable allocation between the meal and nonmeal portion. For example, if the room rate at a hotel includes one or more meals, then you must segregate the meal costs from the lodging costs. The lodging costs are fully deductible, but only 80% of the meal costs are deductible.

If you are reimbursed for the cost of business meals by your employer, only the company is subject to the 20% disallowance; its deduction is limited to 80% of the reimbursement [IRC Sec. 274(n)(2)(A)]. The reimbursement is tax-free to you, provided recordkeeping requirements are met [¶2003]. If the reimbursement is in the form of a per diem allowance (covering meals and lodging), your employer is required to separate out the meal portion on a "reasonable basis" to compute the 20% disallowance.

> ➤ **SAFE HARBOR** The IRS has authorized a mechanical way for your employer to separate out the meal portion of a per diem travel allowance: (1) It can allocate 40% of the allowance to meals if the allowance is less than the per diem travel rate paid to federal employees for that locality [¶2003(c)]. (2) It can allocate an amount equal to the federal meals and incidental expense rate to meals if the allowance equals or exceeds the per diem travel rate paid to federal employees.[2]

> ➤ **OBSERVATION** If an employer intends to pay a travel allowance at a rate less than or equal to the federal lodging rate, the employer should pay an allowance for lodging only. Additionally, if a travel allowance is higher than the federal lodging rate but less than the combined lodging and meals rate, the employer may want to pay two allowances: a lodging allowance at the maximum federal lodging rate and a separate meals allowance to cover the additional cost of eating away from home. That way, the employer reduces the impact of the 80% deduction limit for meals.

NOTE: The 20% disallowance also applies when you are reimbursed by a third party who is not your employer (e.g., a business colleague). The party who reimburses you is subject to the disallowance [IRC Sec. 274(e)(3)].

(b) Foreign Business Travel. When you travel outside the United States for both business and personal reasons, you may not be able to deduct full travel costs to and from the foreign destination, even though the trip is primarily business related [IRC Sec. 274(c)(1)]. (If the trip is primarily personal, no deduction is allowed for travel costs en route to and from the destination, under the same rule that applies to domestic travel.)

Except as provided below, when you travel to a foreign destination primarily for business and you engage in both personal and business activities, you must allocate your travel expenses to and from the destination between the days spent on personal activities and the days spent on business activities. You can deduct only the portion attributable to business days. For this purpose, the actual days spent traveling to and from the foreign destination are considered business days [Reg. Sec. 1.274-4(2)(i)].

Example 2: Ms. Claiborne travels from New York to London by plane. She spends the next five days on business matters and then spends the following three days sightseeing. On the tenth day, she returns to New York. Her round-trip airfare is $1,000. Result: Seventy percent of Claiborne's travel expense is allocable to business (seven days out of ten). So Claiborne can deduct $700 of her airfare.

> ➤ **OBSERVATION** Suppose Claiborne is an employee and her employer reimburses her $1,000 for the airfare. Then the employer may deduct the entire $1,000. And assuming the reimbursement is provided under an accountable plan [¶2003], the employer need only report $300 as income on Claiborne's W-2 form.

If your principal activity during working hours is business-related, then the day is considered a business day [Reg. Sec. 1.274-4(d)(2)(iii)]. Weekends and holidays are considered business days if they fall between regular business days. However, if you have completed your business activities and remain at the foreign location for personal reasons, weekends and holidays are treated as personal days [Reg. Sec. 1.274-4(d)(2)(v)].

"Foreign" travel includes any travel outside of the 50 states and the District of Columbia (for example, a business trip to Puerto Rico or Canada would be considered foreign travel) [Reg. Sec. 1.274-4(a)]. However, if one leg of the trip involves travel between two points in the U.S., that portion of the travel expenses does not have to be allocated between business and personal days [Reg. Sec. 1.274-4(e)].

Example 3: Mr. Robinson travels by plane from Chicago to Puerto Rico on business. If the plane flies nonstop, the entire airfare is considered a foreign travel expense. But if the plane makes a stop in Miami, only the cost of the Miami-Puerto Rico leg is considered a foreign travel expense.

If the nonbusiness activity on your foreign trip takes place at or beyond your business destination, the travel expenses subject to allocation are the round-trip expenses to your business destination. If the nonbusiness activity takes place en route to or from your business destination, then the expenses subject to allocation are only the round-trip expenses to your nonbusiness destination [Reg. Sec. 1.274-4(f)].

Example 4: Ms. Carson travels from New York to Rome on business. She spends two weeks in Rome and then takes a one-week vacation before returning to New York. If she spends the vacation week in Greece, she must allocate the round-trip cost from New York to Rome (two-thirds business, one-third personal). The trip from Rome to Greece is entirely personal and nondeductible. However, if she spends the vacation week in Paris, the allocation applies to a round-trip fare from New York to Paris. The added cost of going to Rome is a fully deductible business expense.

Exceptions. Not all foreign business trips are subject to the allocation rule. You do not have to allocate your travel expenses to and from a foreign destination if:

- You are not traveling outside the United States for more than one week [IRC Sec. 274(c)(2)(A); Reg. Sec. 1.274-4(c)]. For this purpose, one week means seven consecutive days. The day in which the trip outside the U.S. begins does not count, but the day you return to the U.S. does count. For example, if you leave the U.S. on Wednesday morning and return in the evening of the following Wednesday, you are considered to have been outside the U.S. for seven days, and no allocation is necessary.
- Your nonbusiness activities outside of the U.S. constitute less than 25% of the total travel time [IRC Sec. 274 (c)(2)(B); Reg. Sec. 1.274-4(d)]. This determination is made in the same way you allocate travel expenses when an allocation is required (i.e., business days versus nonbusiness days).

Example 5: Mr. Gregory flies from Los Angeles to Mexico City on Wednesday. On Thursday and Friday, he has business meetings. He spends the weekend on nonbusiness activities and on Monday and Tuesday, he has more business meetings. On Wednesday and Thursday, he again has nonbusiness activities and flies back to Los Angeles on Friday. Result: No allocation is required. Of his ten travel days, eight are considered business days (four days of business meetings, two days of the intervening weekend and two days en route). So less than 25% of his total travel time is spent on nonbusiness activities.

- You do not have substantial control over arranging the trip [Reg. Sec. 1.274-4(f)(5)(i)]. For this purpose, you are not treated as having substantial control over the arrangements simply because you have control over the timing of the trip. If you travel as an employee under a reimbursement or expense account arrangement with your employer, you are considered not to have substantial control unless you (1) are a managing executive who can authorize the trip without effective veto procedures or (2) have a more-than-10% ownership interest in the employer.
- You did not have a vacation as a major consideration in making the trip [Reg. Sec. 1.274-4(f)(5)(ii)]. This is determined on the basis of the facts and circumstances of your individual situation. For example, suppose you have no intention of doing any vacationing when you make your foreign travel plans. But your business at the foreign destination is unexpectedly cut short for some reason. So you stay on for a few extra days of sightseeing. The Revenue Service may determine that your vacation was not a major consideration in making the trip.

(c) Foreign Conventions. You cannot claim any deduction for the expenses of attending a convention, seminar or similar meeting held outside the "North American area" unless (1) the meeting is directly related to the active conduct of your trade or business and (2) it is as reasonable to hold the meeting outside of the North American area as it is to hold it within the North American area [IRC Sec. 274(h)(1)].

In determining the reasonableness of holding the meeting outside North America, the following factors are taken into account: (1) the purpose of the meeting and the activities taking place at the meeting; (2) the purposes and activities of the sponsoring organization or groups; (3) the residences of the organization's active members and the places at which their other meetings have been or will be held; and (4) other relevant factors.

The North American area includes the U.S., its possessions (Puerto Rico, Guam, the U.S. Virgin Islands), Trust Territory of the Pacific Islands, Canada and Mexico [IRC Sec. 274(h)(3)(A)]. It also includes the Marshall Islands and the Federated States of Micronesia, Jamaica and any other noncommunist Caribbean Basin country (or Bermuda) that has an agreement with the U.S. to exchange tax information and that doesn't discriminate against U.S. conventions [IRC Sec. 274(h)(6)].

If your employer reimburses you for foreign convention expenses, the employer's deduction for the reimbursement will not be subject to the disallowance rule if it's reported on your Form W-2 as income [IRC Sec. 274(h)(4)(B)]. However, your offsetting deduction to the taxable income will be treated as a miscellaneous itemized expense. And your miscellaneous expenses are deductible only to the extent they total more than 2% of your adjusted gross income.

(d) Conventions on Cruise Ships. Generally, you cannot claim a deduction for expenses you incur in connection with a business convention, seminar or similar meeting held on a cruise ship. However, you can claim a deduction for up to $2,000 of cruise expenses per year if (1) the ship is a U.S. flagship, and (2) all ports of call are located in the U.S. or its possessions [IRC Sec. 274(h)(2)].

(e) Luxury Water Transportation. There is a limit on the amount of expenses you can deduct when using an ocean liner, cruise ship or other "luxury water transportation" to reach a business destination. Your deduction for each day on the boat cannot exceed twice the highest per diem amount paid by the U.S. government to employees traveling in the U.S. [IRC Sec. 274(m)(1)(A)]. You are not subject to this limit if you attend a convention, seminar or other business meeting while on a cruise ship (see (d) above for special limits). Also, if you are reimbursed by your employer or client, you are not subject to the per diem limit. But the employer or client's deduction for the reimbursement is limited to twice the U.S. government per diem rate [IRC Sec. 274(m)(1)(B)].

(f) Investment Seminars. You cannot deduct the cost of attending conventions, seminars or similar meetings in connection with investments [IRC Sec. 274(h)(7)]. This disallowance covers transportation costs, registration fees and meals and lodging expenses.

¶2002   SUBSTANTIATION AND REPORTING OF TRAVEL EXPENSES

There are special substantiation requirements if you deduct expenses for travel away from home [IRC Sec. 274(d)]. However, your expenses for local transportation are not subject to the special substantiation requirements, unless your auto is used.

(a) What Has to Be Proved. In general, you must substantiate the following elements of each expense:

*   **Amount.** You must show the amount of each separate travel expense. At your option, you can aggregate the total daily amount of certain expenses like meals and taxi fares if the expenses are repetitious or concurrent. You can also aggregate tips with the underlying expenses [Temp. Reg. Sec. 1.274-5T(b)(2)(i), (b)(3)(i), (c)(6)(i)].
*   **Time and place.** You must show the date of departure and return for each trip, the number of days away from home and the travel destination [Temp. Reg. Sec. 1.274-5T(b)(3)(ii)].
*   **Business purpose.** You must show the business reason for the travel away from home.

(b) How the Elements Are Proved. You must substantiate each element of an expense either by adequate records or by sufficient evidence corroborating your own statement. However, written evidence has more value as proof than oral evidence. In addition, the value of written evidence is greater the closer in time the writing is to the time you incur the expense [Temp. Reg. Sec. 1.274-5T(c)(1)].

Adequate records. To meet the "adequate records" requirement, you must maintain (1) an account book, diary, log, statement of expense, trip sheets or similar records and (2) documentary evidence that, in combination, proves each required element [Temp. Reg. Sec. 1.274-5T(c)(2)]. You must make the record in the account book, diary, etc. at or near the time you incur the expense so that you have present knowledge of each of the required elements [Temp. Reg. Sec. 1.274-5T(c)(2)(ii)].

You must have documentary evidence (e.g., receipts or paid bills) for (1) any lodging expense and (2) any other travel expense of $25 or more. However, no documentary evidence is required for transportation charges away from home if it is not readily available. Documentary evidence may, by itself, be sufficient to prove the required elements. For example, a hotel receipt is sufficient to substantiate travel expenses if it contains the name, date, location and separate amounts for charges such as lodging, meals and telephone [Temp. Reg. Sec. 1.274-5T(c)(2)(ii)].

In unforeseen instances, such as the loss or destruction of records due to a fire, you can substantiate expenses by reasonable reconstruction of the records [Temp. Reg. Sec. 1.274-5T(c)(5)].

(c) Standard Meal Expense Deduction. You can deduct a flat dollar amount for meals and incidental expenses you incur while traveling away from home overnight on business. You do not have to record the amount of your actual expenses or keep any receipts. You only have to prove the time, place and business purpose of the travel. The standard meal deduction is $34 per day for meals in designated high-cost cities and $26 for the rest of the country.[1]

> **NOTE:** There is no standard deduction for lodging or combined meals and lodging expenses as there is with travel allowances [¶2003(c)].

(d) How to Report Travel Expenses on the Return. Business travel and transportation expenses incurred by self-employed individuals are deductions for adjusted gross income and are reported on Schedule C of Form 1040 [¶2226]. Travel and transportation expenses incurred by employees are miscellaneous itemized deductions [¶1943(a)] deductible from adjusted gross income on Form 2106 and Schedule A of Form 1040.

You generally can deduct travel expenses you incur in connection with investments as a miscellaneous itemized expense. However, travel expenses related to rental or royalty property are deductions for adjusted gross income [¶1102(b)(5)].

¶2003   TRAVEL ALLOWANCES AND REIMBURSEMENTS

If, as an employee, you receive a travel allowance or reimbursement under an "accountable plan," you need not report your employer's payment as income on your tax return or claim an offsetting deduction for the business travel expenses. In short, an allowance paid under an accountable plan is income and payroll tax-free to you [IRC Sec. 62(a)(2)(A), (c); Reg. Sec. 1.62-2].

In contrast, a travel allowance provided under something other than an "accountable plan" is considered taxable wages. Your employer must withhold on the payments and report them as income on your Form W-2. You treat the payments as income on your tax return and claim an offsetting deduction for the actual travel expenses [Reg. Sec. 1.62-2(c)(5)].

> ➤ **OBSERVATION** Your expenses under a nonaccountable plan must be treated as a miscellaneous itemized deduction. You can deduct miscellaneous expenses only to the extent their total for the year exceeds 2% of your adjusted gross income [¶1942 et seq.]. Net result: If your miscellaneous expenses don't reach the 2% mark, you end up with no deduction to offset the taxable allowance. What's more, your deduction can be further reduced if your 1992 adjusted gross income exceeds $105,250 ($52,625 for married filing separately). See ¶1900.

(a) Accountable Plan Requirements. A travel allowance is provided under an accountable plan if it satisfies four key requirements: (1) business connection; (2) substantiation; (3) return of unspent amounts; and (4) timeliness.

Business connection. The allowance must be limited to job-related expenses that you could claim as an employee deduction if you paid for them out of your own pocket. An advance payment qualifies only if it is for business expenses that you are reasonably expected to incur. For example, a "travel" advance to an employee who never travels is subject to withholding when it is paid, even though the employee later returns the entire amount [Reg. Sec. 1.62-2(d)].

Suppose a single plan covers deductible business expenses as well as other bona fide expenses related to your employer's business that are not deductible. Then, the advance is considered to be paid under two separate plans: one that satisfies the business connection requirement and is tax-free and one that does not and is taxable [Reg. Sec. 1.62-2(d)(2)].

> **Example 1:** Ms. Lane is an employee of Acme, Inc. She frequently travels out of town on company business. Sometimes, she stays away overnight. At other times, Lane returns home on the same day. Acme provides her with an advance for all her anticipated meal and lodging expenses, even though Lane could not deduct the day trip travel expenses if she had paid them out of her own pocket.

Result: The portion of each advance that covers overnight meals and lodging expenses (the "business" portion) is tax-free. However, the portion covering the day trips ("personal" portion) is taxable.

> ➤ **OBSERVATION** Even the personal portion of a reimbursement or advance must be paid for expenses that are, in some way, business related. An employer payment that covers strictly personal expenses could render the whole plan nonaccountable. What's more, a payment can be provided only for expenses your employer reasonably expects you and other employees to incur. Suppose your

employer provides travel advances to a group of employees, and even a few of the group's members are not likely to travel on business. Then the entire plan fails the business connection requirement [Reg. Sec. 1.62-2(j)].

Substantiation. Your employer must require you to turn over the same detailed expense records that would be required if you had to substantiate deductions on your own return (¶2002(b)) [Reg. Sec. 1.62-2(e)]. However, your employer does not have to require you and other employees to substantiate miscellaneous expenses, provided the payments covering miscellaneous expenses are separated from payments made under your employer's accountable plan. In this case, the payment covering the miscellaneous expenses is treated as paid under a nonaccountable plan, but the payments covering substantiated expenses are tax-free.

➤ **EXCEPTION** If you use one of the so-called "automatic" allowances, you do not have to substantiate amounts. The allowances automatically are tax-free to the extent they are within IRS-approved limits. The allowances include a mileage allowance for employees who use their cars for business travel [¶2007(d)] and a per diem allowance for meals and/or lodging for employees traveling away from home on business ((c) below).

Return of unspent amounts. Your employer must require you and other employees to return any advance payments over your substantiated amounts. If you must return excess amounts, but do not, the arrangement is still an accountable plan to the extent of the substantiated amount. Only the excess amount is taxable [Reg. Sec. 1.62-2(f)].

➤ **EXCEPTION** Your allowance may often be based on the number of days away from home or miles driven. In this situation, your employer can let you keep any amount that exceeds your actual expenses as long as you actually travel the number of days or drive the number of miles that the allowance specifies.

Example 2: Mr. Mason drives his luxury car about 3,000 business miles per month. His company pays him 50 cents for each of those miles (his approximate cost of driving the car). This gives Mason a total monthly advance of $1,500. The IRS-approved mileage allowance is 28 cents per mile in 1992 [¶2004(b)]. So Mason can get a tax-free car allowance of $840 per month. What's more, he does not have to return the remaining $660 since his company pays him in the form of a mileage allowance (although he is taxed on it). Suppose, however, Mason drives only 2,000 business miles in one month. Here, he must return $500 of his monthly advance. That is the amount paid to him for business miles not actually driven.

Timeliness. You must substantiate your expenses and return unsubstantiated amounts within a reasonable period of time after you incur the expenses. What constitutes a "reasonable" period of time depends on the individual facts and circumstances of each situation [Reg. Sec. 1.62-2(g)]. For example, if you were on a month-long assignment out of town, you can have more time to substantiate expenses than if you were on an overnight trip.

The IRS does provide two escape hatches. Under the first, you automatically meet the timeliness requirement if you: (1) get an advance payment no more than 30 days before you incur the expenses; (2) substantiate the expenses to your employer no more than 60 days after you incur the expenses; and (3) return the unsubstantiated amount no more than 120 days after you incur the expenses. The second safe harbor requires your employer to provide statements (at least once a quarter) to you and other employees that detail the advances that have not yet been substantiated. You have up to 120 days following the receipt of the statement to either substantiate expenses or return the unsubstantiated amount.

A sample employee travel expense voucher appears on page 2015. You can use your own records and receipts to fill out the voucher and submit it to your employer at the end of each trip. By requiring employees to use this type of arrangement, your employer can make sure its travel allowances and reimbursements satisfy the tough accountable plan requirements.

(b) Actual Expenses Exceed Allowance. If you receive an allowance or reimbursement that does not fully compensate you for your actual expenses, you may claim a deduction on your tax return. To get the deduction, however, you must (1) report any allowance you receive as income and (2) deduct all your actual expenses. You cannot simply claim a deduction for the excess amount that is not covered by the allowance.

> **Example 3:** Ms. Eller is a salesperson with an adjusted gross income of $80,000 per year. She drives 30,000 business miles during the year and receives 7½ cents from her employer for each business mile she drives. Her total mileage allowance comes to $2,250. Eller keeps a record of all her auto expenses and calculates that her actual expenses (including depreciation) run about 30 cents per mile or $9,000.
>
> *Result:* Ms. Eller has a choice. She can ride along with the tax-free allowance and report nothing on her tax return. Or she can report the $2,250 allowance as income and claim the $9,000 of actual expenses as a miscellaneous itemized deduction. As such, the actual expenses are deductible to the extent her total miscellaneous deductions exceed $1,600 (2% of her adjusted gross income).
>
> **NOTE:** If Eller wants to deduct her actual auto expenses, she must report any other allowance she receives (e.g., meals and lodging, entertainment, etc.) and deduct her actual expenses for these as well.

(c) Per Diem Travel Allowances. Employers can provide tax-free per diem travel allowances for meals and lodging, just lodging or just meals. These allowances can be based on what the federal government pays its own employees, or they can be based on "high-low" rates.[1]

Meals and lodging allowance. A per diem allowance for meals, lodging and other incidental expenses is 100% tax-free to you to the extent it does not exceed the rate the federal government provides its own employees when they are on travel status. However, there are many different federal rates, depending on where you travel. For example, the 1992 per diem rates range from $67 in low-cost places like Anniston, Alabama, to $174 in high-cost places like New York City. All in all, there are separate rates for nearly 500 cities.[1]

> ▶ **HIGH-LOW ALTERNATIVE METHOD** For 1992, employers can reimburse employees at a per diem rate of up to $147 for meals and lodging expenses incurred in any travel destination designated as a "high-cost" locality. The rate for travel anywhere else in the continental United States is $93 per day. The cities listed below qualify for the high $147 per diem. Note: The $147 per diem rate also applies to the county in which the cities below are located (for starred cities, the rate also applies to certain surrounding counties).
>
> | | |
> |---|---|
> | Aspen, Colorado | Martha's Vineyard/Nantucket, |
> | Atlantic City, New Jersey | Massachusetts |
> | Bala-Cynwyd, Pennsylvania | Newark, New Jersey * |
> | Boston, Massachusetts | Newport, Rhode Island |
> | Chicago, Illinois * | New York, New York * |
> | Columbia, Maryland | Ocean City, Maryland |
> | Death Valley, California | Philadelphia, Pennsylvania |
> | Hilton Head, South Carolina | San Francisco, California |
> | Keystone/Silverthorne, Colorado | Vail, Colorado |
> | Key West, Florida | Washington, D.C. * |
> | Los Angeles, California * | White Plains, New York |

Note: The IRS has considerably shortened the list of cities that qualify as high-cost travel destinations as of March 1, 1992. The following cities are no longer on the list: San Diego and Santa Barbara, California; Atlanta, Georgia; Annapolis, Maryland; Andover, Lowell, Quincy and Plymouth, Massachusetts; Detroit, Michigan; and Princeton and Trenton, New Jersey.

Lodging-only rate. Your employer can provide an allowance for lodging only. The allowance is tax-free to you to the extent it does not exceed the federal travel rate for the locality less the meal and incidental expense rate for that locality.

There is also a high-low option for lodging per diems: $113 a day for travel to any "high-cost" locality (see above list) and $67 for anyplace else in the continental United States.[1]

Meals-only rate. Similarly, your employer can provide a tax-free allowance for meals only that is tied to what federal employees receive. The allowance is $34 for meals in certain designated cities in the United States and $26 for the rest of the country (see the above list).

Instead of using the federal rates for meals-only, your employer can opt to use high-low rates. Your employer can provide a tax-free allowance of $34 per day for meals eaten in any "high-cost" locality. The meals-only rate is $26 for anywhere else in the United States.

Your employer can use the federal per diem rates for some employees and the high-low rates for others. But the same employee cannot be reimbursed for some travel cities by one method and some cities by the other method. Your employer can, however, reimburse the same employee at the high-low rate for travel in the continental U.S. and at the federal rate for foreign travel.

> ➤ **IMPORTANT** You cannot use the automatic travel allowances if you own more than a 10% interest in your company. In that situation, you must substantiate your actual expenses under the accountable plan rules or the allowances are fully taxable.[1]

(d) Employer-Designed Travel Allowances. Your employer may use travel allowances that are tailored to its individual travel circumstances. The allowances can be based on a flat rate or on a stated schedule set by the employer. For example, your employer could provide a cents-per-mile meal allowance for employees who spend most of their travel time on the road.

The rate or schedule must be "reasonably calculated" not to exceed your actual expenses. It must also be "consistently applied" and "in accordance with reasonable business practice."[1]

(e) Excess Per Diem Allowances. If you receive a per diem allowance in excess of an IRS-approved rate, you pay tax only on the excess. If you receive a total per diem amount before the trip and it exceeds the approved rate, your employer does not have to require you to return the excess. The plan is still treated as accountable as long as you are required to return any portion allocable to days not actually traveled [Reg. Sec. 1.62-2].

> **Example 4:** Ms. Hill is a manager for the L&M Co. She goes to New York City on business. She receives a $560 advance for her meals, based on a meal per diem of $40 per day for an expected 14-day stay. The federal per diem meal rate for New York is $34. Hill stays in New York City for only 12 days. L&M must require Hill to return $80 ($40 × 2), the amount of the allowance attributable to the two days she was not traveling. L&M does not have to require her to return the $72 [($40 less $34) × 12] excess for the 12 days she was actually in New York. However, Hill must pay income and payroll taxes on the $72 excess amount. What's more, if Hill does not return the $80 for the two extra days, that is also taxable to her.

> ➤ **TAX-SAVING IDEA** If your employer pays a per diem allowance in excess of the approved rates, it can permit you to substantiate your actual expenses. That way, if the substantiated expenses exceed the approved rate, only the allowance in excess of your actual expenses is taxable to you.

> **Example 5:** Same facts as Example 4, except Hill's actual meal expenses in New York City ran to $540. If she substantiates this amount to L&M, then only $20 (the $560 allowance less $540 expenses) is taxable, not $72.

Travel Expense Voucher

Name _____

Department _____

For Period Beginning _____   Ending _____

Date								Total
Destination From								
To								
Purpose of Business Trip:								

Transportation

Car Travel	Mileage							
	Rate X Miles							
	Car Rental							
	Parking							
	Tolls							
Air Fare								
Rail Fare								
Carfare & Bus								
Limousine/Taxi								
Tips								

Hotel

Room Charge								
Hotel Tips								

Meals (inc. Tips)

Personal Meals	Breakfast							
	Lunch							
	Dinner							
Business Meals (explain on reverse)	Breakfast							
	Lunch							
	Dinner							

Misc.

Postage								
Telephone/Telegrams								
Laundry								
Other, Attach Statement								
Total								

	Less Amount Advanced
	Balance Due

I certify these travel expenses were incurred by me in the transaction of authorized company business

Signature _____

DEDUCTIONS FOR BUSINESS CARS

¶2004   AUTO EXPENSES IN GENERAL

You can deduct your automobile expenses to the extent the auto is used for ordinary and necessary business purposes. The deduction is available to self-employeds, employees who use their cars in their jobs and employers who provide their employees with cars.

If you use your car solely for business purposes, you can write off 100% of your automobile expenses. If you are like most taxpayers, however, you put some business miles and some personal miles on the car. In this situation, you can deduct only the portion of your auto expenses allocable to the business use. When you use a car solely for personal transportation, no business deduction generally is allowed.

> **NOTE:** Even when you do not drive any business miles in your car, you can still claim itemized deductions for any personal property taxes you pay on the auto [¶1906]. In addition, you may be able to write off car expenses connected with medical treatment [¶1932] or charitable work [¶1916].

Deductible car expenses generally are computed in one of two ways: You can deduct (1) the actual costs for operating and maintaining a business car or (2) the standard mileage rate.

(a) Actual Expenses. Expenses that can be deducted for the business use of a car include the costs of gas, oil, tires, repairs, insurance, depreciation [¶2005], interest to buy the car, property taxes, licenses, garage rent, parking fees and tolls.[1] If you lease a business car, your lease payments can be deducted to the extent allocable to business use.[2]

> ➤ **IMPORTANT** (1) If you use a car in your job as an employee, interest you pay on a car loan is not considered deductible business interest. Instead, it is treated as nondeductible personal interest [IRC Sec. 163(h)(2)]. (2) Sales taxes you pay on the purchase of a business car must be capitalized and recovered through depreciation [IRC Sec. 164(a)].

When you use a car for both business and personal reasons, the car's expenses must generally be allocated on the basis of mileage [Temp. Reg. Sec. 1.280F-6T(3)]. Your deductible portion of the expenses is determined by dividing your business mileage for the year by your total mileage. However, you must allocate parking fees and tolls on a per trip basis.

> **Example 1:** Mr. Hardy drives 10,000 miles on business-connected trips during the year and 5,000 miles on personal trips. He incurs $800 in parking and toll expenses on his business trips and $200 on his personal trips. His other car expenses come to $6,000. Result: Hardy can deduct $800 for the business parking and tolls plus two-thirds (10,000 ÷ 15,000) of his other expenses. Total deduction: $4,800.

For purposes of making the allocation between your business and personal mileage, you use the same rules that apply to the deductibility of transportation costs in general [¶2000]. For example, if you drive from home to work, that is not considered business mileage. But driving between two work locations or between home and a temporary workplace is considered business related.

Employer-provided cars. If your employer provides you with a car, your employer ordinarily can deduct the entire cost of the car, including an allowance for depreciation. Even if you use the car for both business and personal driving, your use is considered entirely business connected, insofar as your employer's deductions are concerned.

Your employer's cost attributable to your business use is deductible as a business expense. And your employer's cost attributable to your personal use can be written off as compensation, as long as your employer reports the value of the personal use as income to you [¶1400].

Employee-owned cars. As an employee, you can write off your business auto expenses as a miscellaneous itemized deduction. That means you can deduct the expenses to the extent your total miscellaneous expenses exceed 2% of your adjusted gross income.

> **Example 2:** Ms. Steed is an employee of Texxon Corporation who earns $100,000 per year. She drives 15,000 business miles per year, and her business auto expenses (including depreciation) come to about $3,000. Steed has no other miscellaneous expenses eligible for a deduction. Result: Steed can deduct only $1,000 of her business auto expenses. The first $2,000 of the expenses are counted in meeting the deduction threshold.

> **NOTE:** If you are self-employed, you are not subject to the 2% floor and can deduct 100% of your business auto expenses.

Investment use of auto. You can deduct auto expenses you incur while managing and maintaining property held for the production of income [IRC Sec. 212].

> **Example 3:** Mr. Hackett drives 12,000 business miles during the year. He drives an additional 3,000 miles to oversee the upkeep and management of an apartment building he owns. He also drives 5,000 personal miles. Hackett's car expenses for the year total $10,000. Result: Hackett can deduct $6,000 as a business auto expense (12,000 business miles ÷ 20,000 total miles × $10,000). Additionally, he can deduct $1,500 as an investment expense (3,000 investment miles ÷ 20,000 total miles × $10,000).

(b) Standard Mileage Rate. In lieu of deducting actual expenses, you may deduct an IRS-approved amount based on the number of miles you drive. For expenses incurred in 1992, you may deduct 28 cents for each business mile you drive.[3] For example, if you drive 50,000 business miles during the year, you can deduct $14,000.

> ➤ **OBSERVATION** With the actual expense method, you will be hard pressed to get a $14,000 deduction no matter how many business miles you drive. Reason: The 28 cents figure includes an amount for depreciation—which keeps adding up as you drive more miles. On the other hand, the depreciation writeoffs under the actual expense method are subject to strict dollar caps—the deduction is the same whether you drive 5,000 or 50,000 miles (assuming your percentage of business use is the same).

The standard mileage rate contains a depreciation element that must be taken into account when determining your taxable profit or loss when the car is eventually sold [¶1600]. For example, depreciation was allowed at a rate of 11½ cents per business mile in 1992. So you must reduce your adjusted basis in the car by 11½ cents for each business mile you drove that year.

> ➤ **OBSERVATION** The standard mileage rate applies to more than your business driving. You also can use the standard mileage rate to deduct miles you drive for deductible investment, charitable, medical or moving activities. For 1992, you can deduct 28 cents for each investment mile, 12 cents for each charitable mile and 9 cents for each medical or moving mile.

Eligibility. To use the standard mileage rate, you must: (1) own the car; (2) not use the car for hire (e.g., as a taxi); and (3) not operate two or more cars simultaneously in the same business.[4]

If you want to use the standard mileage rate, you must elect it in the first year you use the car for business. If you use the actual expense method in the first year, you must continue using it for all future years for the car.

If you switch from the standard mileage rate to the actual expense method, you cannot compute your depreciation deductions under the Modified Accelerated Cost Recovery

System (MACRS) [¶2005]. Instead, you must estimate the car's remaining useful life and claim straight line depreciation over that period.

> ➤ **OBSERVATION** The useful life of your car may be shorter than the five-year depreciation period allowed under MACRS. So, in some cases, it may be beneficial for you to elect the standard mileage rate for the first year and then switch to the actual expense method in subsequent years. You could write off the car's cost over a shorter period of time.

¶2005   DEPRECIATION DEDUCTIONS FOR CARS

Cars placed in service after 1986 are depreciated using the Modified Accelerated Cost Recovery System (MACRS) [¶2110].

(a) General Rules. Under MACRS, you can write off the adjusted basis (generally cost less prior depreciation deductions) of your car by claiming annual depreciation deductions. The amount of your annual deduction is based on three factors: (1) the applicable recovery period (i.e., the number of years required to fully depreciate the car); (2) the applicable depreciation method (i.e., accelerated or straight line); and (3) the applicable convention (i.e., when you are deemed to place the car in service) [IRC Sec. 168(a)].

- **Recovery period.** Under MACRS, you generally write off cars over a five-year cost recovery period [IRC Sec. 168(e)(3)(B)]. However, the five-year period is not based on tax years. Instead, it straddles six tax years.
- **Depreciation method.** The usual way you write off your car's cost is to claim accelerated depreciation using the 200% declining balance method and switching to the straight line method when that yields a bigger deduction [IRC Sec. 168(b)(1)]. Under the 200% declining balance method, your annual depreciation deduction is 40% of the car's adjusted basis (200% divided by five years).

In the fifth year of the recovery period, straight line depreciation will yield a larger deduction than the 200% declining balance method. So you should switch over to straight line at this point. To calculate your depreciation deduction under the straight line method, you multiply your applicable depreciation percentage by the car's adjusted basis. The applicable depreciation percentage is: 1 ÷ (remaining years in the recovery period + 0.5).

> **NOTE:** You can elect to use straight line depreciation during the entire recovery period. Of course, this will produce smaller writeoffs than the declining balance method in early years and larger writeoffs later on [IRC Sec. 168(b)(5)].

- **Applicable convention.** You generally use the half-year convention to determine when you are deemed to place the car in service. Under this convention, a car put in service at any time during the year is treated as being placed in service at the midpoint of the year. So your depreciation deduction for the first year is one-half of what would be allowed for a full year [IRC Sec. 168(d)(1), (4)].

> ➤ **OBSERVATION** The half-year convention means you normally write off the car over six tax years: a half year of depreciation in the year you start using it, a full year of depreciation in each of years two through five, and a half year of depreciation in the sixth year (after which the car is fully depreciated).

Depreciation tables. In most situations, you can determine your depreciation deduction without going through the arithmetic calculations described above. An IRS table expresses the annual writeoffs as a percentage of the car's basis. You can write off 20% of your car's original basis in the first year you place it in service, 32% of the car's original basis in the second year, 19.2% in the third year, 11.52% each in the fourth and fifth years and 5.76% in the sixth year. If you elect to use straight line depreciation for the entire recovery period, you generally can write off 10% of the original basis in the first year, 20% each in years two through five and 10% in the sixth year.

> **Example 1:** Mr. Nolan sells his old car and buys a new one for $13,000 that he uses exclusively for business. His basis in the car is $13,000, and his first-year depreciation deduction is 20% of that basis, or $2,600, whether he puts the car in service on January 1 or December 31. His second-year depreciation deduction is 32% of his original basis, or $4,160.

If your car is used for both business and personal travel, your depreciation deduction is figured only on the portion of your adjusted basis allocable to your business travel. But in computing subsequent deductions, you must reduce your adjusted basis by what you could have deducted had the car been used 100% for business [IRC Sec. 280F(d)(2)].

> **Example 2:** Same facts as before, except that Nolan's business mileage each year is 60% of his total mileage. Result: His first-year depreciation deduction is 60% of $2,600, or $1,560. However, his adjusted basis in the car is reduced by the full $2,600.

If you make a capital improvement to your car, the improvement is depreciated separately from the car. But you must use the same recovery period, depreciation method and convention as you would if the car itself had been placed in service at that time.[1] So you generally use a five-year recovery period for the improvement, regardless of what kind it is.

(b) Special Depreciation Rules. There are a number of exceptions to the general depreciation rules that can affect the amount of your automobile writeoffs.

Mid-quarter convention. The most important exception comes into play when you place more than 40% of your business property (excluding real estate) in service during the last quarter of the tax year [IRC Sec. 168(d)(3)]. Under this rule, you must use a mid-quarter convention to calculate your depreciation writeoffs instead of the usual half-year convention. This rule prevents you from placing the bulk of your business property in service at the end of the year and then claiming a half-year of depreciation.

With the mid-quarter convention, a car placed in service during any quarter of the year is treated as if it was placed in service at the midpoint of that quarter [IRC Sec. 168(d)(4)(C)]. Instead of getting a half-year of depreciation, you get 10½ months' worth if you place the car in service in the first quarter, 7½ months if you place the car in service in the second quarter, 4½ months if you place the car in service in the third quarter and only 1½ months if you place the car in service in the last quarter. For a complete discussion of the mid-quarter convention, see ¶2112(g).

> **Example 3:** Ms. Kirk buys a business car for $11,000 in October. She uses the car exclusively for business and buys no other business property during the year. Result: Kirk must use the mid-quarter convention to compute her automobile depreciation deduction. Since she placed the car in service during the fourth quarter of the year, her 1992 depreciation percentage is 5% [40% full year's depreciation × (1.5 ÷ 12 months)]. So she can claim a depreciation deduction of $550 (5% of her $11,000 cost).
>
> ➤ **OBSERVATION** October 1 is a key date for calendar-year business car buyers. If you buy before October 1, you can get a much larger first-year depreciation deduction than if you buy on or after October 1. For example, if Kirk had put her new car in service in September instead of October, her 1992 deduction would have been $2,200.

Calculating the adjusted basis. Your depreciation deduction each year is a percentage of your adjusted basis in the car. Under the usual rule, your adjusted basis in the year you buy the car is its cost (plus tax and registration). For depreciation purposes, your adjusted basis in subsequent years is your original cost less the depreciation you could have claimed in prior years had you used the car 100% for business [IRC Sec. 280F(d)(2)].

In some situations, however, you must modify the original cost figure to determine your adjusted basis. If you trade in your existing car, your adjusted basis in the old car is carried over to your new car. So if you have a loss on the trade-in, this loss is added on to your basis in the new car and can increase the size of your depreciation deductions. You have a loss if your adjusted basis in the old car exceeds the amount the dealer credits you for it. Similarly, you have a profit if the amount the dealer credits you exceeds your adjusted basis. A profit reduces your basis in the new car and can decrease your depreciation deductions.

Example 4: Mr. Johnson bought a car in 1990 for $10,000 that he uses exclusively for business. In 1990 and 1991, the claimed depreciation deductions that totaled $5,200. So his adjusted basis in the car is $4,800 ($10,000 cost less $5,200 accumulated depreciation). In 1992, Johnson decides to trade in his existing car for a new $11,000 car. However, the dealer gives him an allotment of only $3,000 for his old car—$1,800 less than his adjusted basis. Result: Johnson has an $1,800 tax loss on his old car. This loss is added to the $11,000 cost of his new car, which gives him a basis in the new car of $12,800. In 1992, Johnson can claim a depreciation deduction of $2,560 (20% of $12,800).

Using the family car on business. If you start using a personal car for business driving, you can claim a depreciation deduction for that car. However, your adjusted basis for the deduction is the lesser of (1) the adjusted basis on the date of conversion or (2) the fair market value on the date of conversion [Reg. Sec. 1.167(g)(1)].

Example 5: Ms. Smith gets a new job that requires her to use her personal car for business driving. Smith bought the car several years ago for $15,000 and until now, she only used it for personal driving. The car is now worth about $5,000. Result: Smith can claim a depreciation deduction for the car in 1992, but her deduction is computed on the car's current $5,000 value.

(c) Dollar Caps on Depreciation. There are special limits on the amount of depreciation that may be claimed in any one year for a luxury car [IRC Sec. 280F(a)]. If you purchased a car that cost more than $13,700 in 1992 ($13,400 in 1991, $13,100 in 1989 or 1990, $12,800 in 1987 or 1988), these limits effectively reduce the depreciation you would otherwise be allowed to claim during the normal five-year recovery period.[2] And for cars of any price, the limits also restrict the amount you can claim as an expensing deduction [IRC Sec. 179].

If you placed a car in service during 1992, your depreciation deduction cannot exceed $2,760 for 1992, $4,400 for 1993, $2,650 for 1994 and $1,575 for each additional year.

If you placed a car in service during 1991, your depreciation deduction cannot exceed $2,660 for 1991, $4,300 for 1992, $2,550 for 1993 and $1,575 for each additional year.

If you placed a car in service during 1989 or 1990, your depreciation deduction cannot exceed $2,660 during the first year of the recovery period, $4,200 during the second year of the recovery period, $2,550 during the third year and $1,475 for each additional year.

If you placed a car in service during 1987 or 1988, your depreciation deduction cannot exceed $2,560 during the first year of the recovery period, $4,100 during the second year, $2,450 during the third year and $1,475 for each additional year [IRC Sec. 280F(a)(2)].

NOTE: The dollar limits are increased periodically for inflation [IRC Sec. 280F(d)(7)].

Example 6: Mr. Bartlett buys a new car in 1992 for $15,000. He puts 10,000 miles on the car during the year, all of which are business-connected. Here is how Bartlett figures his depreciation deduction for 1992:

Step 1: Bartlett multiplies his original basis ($15,000) by 20%. That comes to $3,000.

Step 2: Since $3,000 exceeds the $2,760 dollar limit for the first recovery year, Bartlett's depreciation deduction is limited to $2,760.

Example 7: Same facts as Example 6 except that Bartlett drives only 6,000 business miles and 4,000 personal miles. Now Bartlett has an additional step: His depreciation deduction is 60% of the $2,760 dollar cap, or $1,656.

NOTE: In computing his adjusted basis for the following year, Bartlett does not reduce his basis by the $3,000 deduction for 100% business use. Even if there had been a 100% business use, the dollar limits would have allowed him to deduct only $2,760. So his adjusted basis for 1992 is $15,000 less $2,760—or $12,240 [Temp. Reg. Sec. 1.280F-4T(a)(2)].

➤ **OBSERVATION** The dollar limits are computed separately for each car you use in business. So if you are a two-car family, you may be better off dividing your business mileage between the two cars instead of using one exclusively for business. For example, if you drive 15,000 business miles on one car and 10,000 personal miles on the other, your maximum first-year deduction is $2,760. But if you split your business and personal mileage evenly between the cars, you can deduct $1,656 for each car (15,000 business miles ÷ 25,000 total miles × $2,760 × 2 cars). That yields a combined deduction of $3,312.

Unrecovered basis. Depreciation disallowed during the normal five-year recovery period because of the dollar limits can be deducted after the recovery period. Starting in the year after the close of the recovery period, you may deduct your "unrecovered basis," subject to the $1,575 annual dollar limit [IRC Sec. 280F(a)(2)(B)]. The unrecovered basis is your adjusted basis at the close of the recovery period [IRC Sec. 280F(d)(9)]. You can deduct the unrecovered basis in the years following the recovery period only to the extent that a depreciation deduction would have been allowed in these years (e.g., your depreciation deduction is cut back by your personal use of the car) [Temp. Reg. Sec. 1.280F-2T(c)(3)].

Example 8: Mr. Mason purchases a $30,000 car in 1992. During the normal recovery period (1992-1997), 80% of Mason's mileage each year is business related. Under the dollar limits, Mason is entitled to claim a total of $11,628 of depreciation during the normal recovery period. Had he used the car exclusively for business, his deductions would have amounted to $14,535. So his unrecovered basis is $15,465 ($30,000 less $14,535). That is the amount he can write off after the end of the recovery period in 1997. If he uses the car 80% for business in 1998, he can deduct $1,260 (80% of $1,575) of his unrecovered basis in that year.

➤ **OBSERVATION** When Mason sells the car, he can write off his unrecovered basis in the business portion of the car to the extent it exceeds the sales price attributable to that part. On the other hand, if Mason trades in the car, he gets no current writeoff; instead, his unrecovered basis is taken into account in calculating his basis in the new car [¶1622(b)].

(d) Expensing Deduction. In lieu of depreciation, you may elect to "expense" (i.e., currently deduct) up to $10,000 of the cost of depreciable personal property in the year it is placed in service in your business [IRC Sec. 179]. The remaining cost can then be depreciated under the normal depreciation rules.

Expensing is available on business cars (but it is not available to the extent you use the car for investment purposes). However, an expensing deduction is treated as depreciation for purposes of the dollar limits on depreciation deductions [IRC Sec. 280F(d)(1)]. So your expensing deduction cannot exceed the appropriate depreciation limit for the first year the car is placed in service. And, after you apply the dollar limit, you must reduce your expensing deduction by the amount allocable to personal use.

Example 9: Mr. Winslow purchases a new car for $12,000 in September 1992. His business mileage for the year is 60% of his total mileage. If he does not expense, his regular depreciation deduction for 1992 is $1,440 ($12,000 × 20% depreciation percentage × 60% business use percentage). If he elects expensing, he can deduct $1,656 (60% of $2,760).

➤ **CAUTION** If you elect expensing, do not use the IRS' optional depreciation table. Under the table, you deduct 20% of your unadjusted cost in the first year and the remaining 80% over the rest of the recovery period. If you expense the first year instead of claiming depreciation, the table will permit you to deduct only 80% of your unadjusted basis less expensing over the recovery period. Bottom line: You will end up with an unrecovered cost at the end of the recovery period, even when your car is not subject to the depreciation caps.

(e) Mixed Use. If your "qualified business use" of a car does not exceed 50% of the total use, there are special restrictions: (1) You must use straight line depreciation and (2) you cannot claim an expensing deduction [IRC Sec. 280F(b)(2), (d)(1)].

Qualified business use is any use of the car in your trade or business. It does not include investment use[3] [Temp. Reg. Sec. 1.280F-6T(d)(2)(i)].

> **Example 10:** Ms. Barker, an employee of XYZ, Inc. buys a new car for $12,000 in August 1992. During the rest of the year, she drives 4,000 miles for business reasons, 2,000 miles for investment reasons and 4,000 miles for personal reasons. Result: Since Barker's qualified business use did not exceed 50% of her total use, she must use straight line depreciation. The car's adjusted basis allocable to her combined business/investment use is $7,200. So in 1992, she can write off $720 ($7,200 × 10%).

Employer-provided cars. Qualified business use generally includes all use by employees of employer-owned cars. Your use of your employer's car for personal trips is treated as qualified business use for purposes of computing your employer's depreciation, as long as the value of the personal use is reported on your Form W-2 [Temp. Reg. Sec. 1.280F-6T(d)(2)(ii)(3)].

Exception. If you own a 5% or greater interest in your employer, your personal use is not considered qualified business use, even though your employer treats your personal use as taxable compensation [Temp. Reg. Sec. 1.280F-6T(d)(2)(ii)(2)].

> **Example 11:** Same facts as in Example 10, except that XYZ owns the car that Barker is using and she is a 5% shareholder of XYZ. Result: XYZ's adjusted basis for computing depreciation includes both the portion allocable to business use and the portion allocable to nonbusiness use. So its depreciable basis is $12,000. However, only 40% of Barker's use is connected with her job at XYZ; the other 60% is personal use excluded for purposes of the 50% test. So XYZ must use straight line depreciation to write off the $12,000 adjusted basis.

> ➤ **OBSERVATION** Getting over the 50% business use mark is important, particularly in the year you place the car in service. The first-year deduction under straight line depreciation is only half of what you would get under MACRS. So, at year end, if you find out you are a few miles short of 50%, it may be worth-while to accelerate a business trip you had been planning.

Recapture. If your business use exceeds 50% in the year the car is placed in service, but falls to 50% or less in a subsequent recovery year, a special recapture rule applies. In the subsequent year, you must include in income the difference between (1) the expensing and depreciation deductions you claimed in prior years and (2) the depreciation deductions that you could have claimed had you used straight line depreciation.

> **Example 12:** Mr. Latimer purchased a $12,000 car in June 1991. He used the car 75% for business in 1991 and claimed a depreciation deduction of $1,800 ($12,000 × 20% × 75%). In 1992, his business use drops to 40% and he is subject to the recapture rule. If Latimer had used straight line depreciation in 1991, his deduction would have been $900 ($12,000 × 10% × 75%). So he has to include $900 ($1,800 less $900) in income in 1992.

(f) Employee Use. As an employee, your own use of your car is not considered depreciable business use unless the use is for the convenience of your employer and required as a condition of employment [IRC Sec. 280F(d)(3)]. That means your use of the car must be required in order for you to perform the duties of your employment properly. The presence or absence of your employer's statement requiring the use of the car is not decisive [Temp. Reg. Sec. 1.280F-6T(a)(2)(ii)].

¶2006　　　LEASED CARS

The dollar limits for depreciation on expensive cars have their equivalent for leased cars [IRC Sec. 280F(c)]. There is no limit on your deduction for your lease payments. However, if you lease a car for more than 30 days in 1992 and the fair market value at the start of the lease exceeds $13,700 (lower amount for earlier years), you must report an "inclusion amount" in your gross income each year of the lease. This has the effect of offsetting your lease payment deduction and limiting the net tax benefit you get from the deduction.

The IRS periodically releases Lease Tables that specify the inclusion amounts for leased automobiles. The Lease Tables for cars leased since 1987 are reproduced on the following pages.

You use a four-step process to figure your inclusion amount for any given tax year:

Step 1: Find the fair market value of your leased car on the first day of the lease in the first column. Make sure you are using the correct table. Table I is for lease terms beginning in 1992. Table II is for lease terms beginning in 1991. Table III is for lease terms beginning in 1989-1990. Table IV is for lease terms beginning in 1987-1988.

Step 2: Then go to the right to the appropriate column for the tax year of the lease. For example, if the lease started in 1991, you would use Table II and the column labeled "2nd" to find your inclusion amount for 1992. If you are computing your inclusion amount for the last tax year of the lease, use the column for the preceding year. For example, if your lease runs from 1991 to 1993, you would use the "2nd" column for both your 1992 and 1993 inclusion amounts.

Step 3: Prorate the inclusion amount listed in the table by the number of days of the lease term included in the tax year. For example, if you lease a car in 1992 for 180 days, the inclusion amount would only be 49.2% (180/366) of the amount found in the "1st" column.

Step 4: If you do not use the leased car exclusively for business and investment purposes, multiply the result in Step 3 by the percentage of business and investment use.

> **Example:** Ms. Franklin leases a car on August 1, 1992. The car has a fair market value of $29,500 at the start of the lease, and the lease runs for two years. Her business mileage each year is 60% of her total mileage. For a $29,500 car first leased in 1992, the Lease Table inclusion amount is $133. So Franklin includes $33 in her income for 1992 ($133 × 153/366 × 60%). For 1993, her inclusion amount is $175 ($291 × 365/365 × 60%). In 1994, her inclusion amount is $101 ($291 × 212/365 × 60%). Note: Since 1994 is the last year of the lease, Franklin uses 2nd year column to determine the inclusion amount for that year.

¶2007　　REPORTING AND SUBSTANTIATION OF AUTO EXPENSES

No deduction is allowed for a business car unless you meet special substantiation requirements [Temp. Reg. Sec. 1.274-5T].

(a) What Must Be Proved. If you are deducting your actual auto expenses, you must be able to prove:

- The amount of each expense;
- The mileage for each business or investment use of the car, plus the total mileage for the car during the year;

- The date each business/investment use occurred or expense was incurred;
- The business/investment purpose of each use or expense [Temp. Reg. Sec. 1.274-5T(b)(6)].

If you use the standard mileage rate, you do not have to prove your expenses. But you do have to prove the date and purpose of your driving, as well as the amount of your mileage.

(b) How to Prove It. You must generally substantiate each car expense or use of the car by adequate records or by sufficient evidence corroborating your own statement [Temp. Reg. Sec. 1.274-5T(c)(1)]. You are not required to keep a contemporaneous log of each use or expense. But a record made at or near the time of the use or expense has a much higher value as proof than one made weeks or months later.

Table I: Dollar Amounts For Automobiles With A Lease
Term Beginning In Calendar Year 1992

Fair Market Value of Automobile		Year of Lease*				
Over	Not Over	1st	2nd	3rd	4th	5th and Later
$13,700	$14,000	0	2	2	2	4
14,000	14,300	3	7	10	13	15
14,300	14,600	5	13	18	23	26
14,600	14,900	8	18	27	32	38
14,900	15,200	11	23	35	43	49
15,200	15,500	13	29	44	52	61
15,500	15,800	16	35	51	62	72
15,800	16,100	18	40	60	72	84
16,100	16,400	21	46	68	82	95
16,400	16,700	23	52	76	92	106
16,700	17,000	26	57	84	102	118
17,000	17,500	29	65	95	115	133
17,500	18,000	33	74	109	132	152
18,000	18,500	38	83	123	148	171
18,500	19,000	42	92	137	164	190
19,000	19,500	46	102	150	181	209
19,500	20,000	50	111	164	198	228
20,000	20,500	55	120	178	214	247
20,500	21,000	59	129	192	230	267
21,000	21,500	63	139	205	247	285
21,500	22,000	67	148	219	263	305
22,000	23,000	74	162	239	288	333
23,000	24,000	82	180	268	321	371
24,000	25,000	90	199	295	354	409
25,000	26,000	99	217	323	387	447
26,000	27,000	107	236	350	420	485
27,000	28,000	116	254	378	453	523
28,000	29,000	124	273	405	486	561
29,000	30,000	133	291	433	518	600
30,000	31,000	141	310	460	552	637
31,000	32,000	150	328	488	584	676
32,000	33,000	158	347	515	618	713
33,000	34,000	167	365	543	650	752
34,000	35,000	175	384	570	684	789
35,000	36,000	184	402	598	716	828
36,000	37,000	192	421	625	750	865
37,000	38,000	200	440	652	783	904
38,000	39,000	209	458	680	816	942
39,000	40,000	217	477	707	849	980
40,000	41,000	226	495	735	882	1,018
41,000	42,000	234	514	762	915	1,056
42,000	43,000	243	532	790	948	1,094
43,000	44,000	251	551	817	981	1,132

Fair Market Value of Automobile		Year of Lease*				
		1st	2nd	3rd	4th	5th and Later
Over	Not Over					
44,000	45,000	260	569	845	1,013	1,171
45,000	46,000	268	588	872	1,047	1,208
46,000	47,000	277	606	900	1,079	1,247
47,000	48,000	285	625	927	1,113	1,284
48,000	49,000	293	644	955	1,145	1,323
49,000	50,000	302	662	982	1,179	1,360
50,000	51,000	310	681	1,010	1,211	1,399
51,000	52,000	319	699	1,037	1,245	1,436
52,000	53,000	327	718	1,065	1,277	1,475
53,000	54,000	336	736	1,092	1,311	1,513
54,000	55,000	344	755	1,120	1,343	1,551
55,000	56,000	353	773	1,147	1,377	1,589
56,000	57,000	361	792	1,175	1,409	1,627
57,000	58,000	370	810	1,202	1,442	1,666
58,000	59,000	378	829	1,230	1,475	1,703
59,000	60,000	386	848	1,257	1,508	1,741
60,000	62,000	399	875	1,299	1,557	1,799
62,000	64,000	416	912	1,354	1,623	1,875
64,000	66,000	433	949	1,409	1,689	1,951
66,000	68,000	450	987	1,463	1,755	2,027
68,000	70,000	467	1,024	1,518	1,821	2,103
70,000	72,000	484	1,061	1,573	1,887	2,179
72,000	74,000	501	1,098	1,628	1,953	2,255
74,000	76,000	518	1,135	1,683	2,019	2,331
76,000	78,000	535	1,172	1,738	2,085	2,407
78,000	80,000	551	1,209	1,794	2,150	2,484
80,000	85,000	581	1,274	1,889	2,267	2,617
85,000	90,000	623	1,367	2,027	2,431	2,807
90,000	95,000	666	1,459	2,165	2,595	2,998
95,000	100,000	708	1,552	2,302	2,761	3,188
100,000	110,000	771	1,691	2,508	3,008	3,474
110,000	120,000	856	1,876	2,783	3,338	3,854
120,000	130,000	940	2,062	3,058	3,668	4,234
130,000	140,000	1,025	2,247	3,333	3,997	4,616
140,000	150,000	1,110	2,432	3,608	4,327	4,996
150,000	160,000	1,194	2,618	3,883	4,656	5,377
160,000	170,000	1,279	2,803	4,158	4,986	5,758
170,000	180,000	1,363	2,988	4,434	5,316	6,138
180,000	190,000	1,448	3,174	4,708	5,645	6,519
190,000	200,000	1,532	3,359	4,983	5,976	6,899
200,000	210,000	1,617	3,544	5,258	6,305	7,280
210,000	220,000	1,702	3,729	5,533	6,635	7,661
220,000	230,000	1,786	3,915	5,808	6,965	8,041
230,000	240,000	1,871	4,100	6,083	7,294	8,422
240,000	250,000	1,955	4,286	6,358	7,624	8,802

* For the last tax year of the lease, use the dollar amount for the preceding year.

Table II: Dollar Amounts For Automobiles With A Lease Term Beginning In Calendar Year 1991

Fair Market Value of Automobile		Year of Lease*				
		1st	2nd	3rd	4th	5th and Later
Over	Not Over					
$13,400	$13,700	2	4	6	6	6
13,700	14,000	5	10	16	18	18
14,000	14,300	8	17	25	29	32
14,300	14,600	11	23	35	41	45

Fair Market Value of Automobile		Year of Lease*				
Over	Not Over	1st	2nd	3rd	4th	5th and Later
14,600	14,900	14	30	44	52	58
14,900	15,200	17	36	54	64	71
15,200	15,500	20	43	63	75	85
15,500	15,800	23	49	73	87	98
15,800	16,100	26	55	83	98	112
16,100	16,400	29	62	92	110	124
16,400	16,700	32	68	102	121	138
16,700	17,000	35	75	111	133	151
17,000	17,500	39	83	125	147	169
17,500	18,000	44	94	140	167	191
18,000	18,500	49	105	156	186	213
18,500	19,000	54	116	172	205	235
19,000	19,500	59	126	189	224	257
19,500	20,000	63	138	204	243	279
20,000	20,500	68	148	220	263	301
20,500	21,000	73	159	236	282	323
21,000	21,500	78	170	252	301	345
21,500	22,000	83	180	269	319	368
22,000	23,000	90	197	292	348	401
23,000	24,000	100	218	324	387	445
24,000	25,000	110	240	356	425	489
25,000	26,000	120	261	388	463	534
26,000	27,000	130	283	419	502	578
27,000	28,000	140	304	452	540	622
28,000	29,000	149	326	484	578	666
29,000	30,000	159	347	516	617	710
30,000	31,000	169	369	547	655	755
31,000	32,000	179	390	580	693	799
32,000	33,000	189	412	611	732	843
33,000	34,000	199	433	644	769	888
34,000	35,000	208	455	676	808	931
35,000	36,000	218	477	707	846	976
36,000	37,000	228	498	739	885	1,020
37,000	38,000	238	519	772	923	1,064
38,000	39,000	248	541	803	961	1,109
39,000	40,000	258	562	835	1,000	1,153
40,000	41,000	267	584	867	1,038	1,197
41,000	42,000	277	606	899	1,076	1,241
42,000	43,000	287	627	931	1,115	1,285
43,000	44,000	297	649	962	1,153	1,330
44,000	45,000	307	670	995	1,191	1,374
45,000	46,000	317	692	1,026	1,230	1,418
46,000	47,000	326	714	1,058	1,268	1,462
47,000	48,000	336	735	1,091	1,306	1,506
48,000	49,000	346	756	1,123	1,344	1,551
49,000	50,000	356	778	1,154	1,383	1,595
50,000	51,000	366	799	1,187	1,421	1,639
51,000	52,000	376	821	1,218	1,459	1,684
52,000	53,000	385	843	1,250	1,498	1,727
53,000	54,000	395	864	1,282	1,536	1,772
54,000	55,000	405	886	1,314	1,574	1,816
55,000	56,000	415	907	1,346	1,613	1,860
56,000	57,000	425	929	1,378	1,650	1,905
57,000	58,000	435	950	1,410	1,689	1,949
58,000	59,000	444	972	1,442	1,727	1,993
59,000	60,000	454	993	1,474	1,766	2,037
60,000	62,000	469	1,026	1,521	1,824	2,103
62,000	64,000	489	1,068	1,586	1,900	2,192
64,000	66,000	508	1,112	1,649	1,977	2,280
66,000	68,000	528	1,155	1,713	2,053	2,369
68,000	70,000	548	1,198	1,777	2,130	2,457
70,000	72,000	567	1,241	1,841	2,206	2,546
72,000	74,000	587	1,284	1,905	2,283	2,634
74,000	76,000	607	1,327	1,969	2,359	2,723

Fair Market Value of Automobile		Year of Lease*				
		1st	2nd	3rd	4th	5th and Later
Over	Not Over					
76,000	78,000	626	1,370	2,033	2,436	2,811
78,000	80,000	646	1,413	2,097	2,512	2,900
80,000	85,000	680	1,489	2,208	2,647	3,054
85,000	90,000	730	1,596	2,368	2,838	3,276
90,000	95,000	779	1,704	2,528	3,029	3,497
95,000	100,000	828	1,812	2,687	3,221	3,718
100,000	110,000	902	1,973	2,927	3,508	4,049
110,000	120,000	1,000	2,188	3,247	3,891	4,492
120,000	130,000	1,098	2,404	3,566	4,274	4,934
130,000	140,000	1,197	2,619	3,885	4,658	5,375
140,000	150,000	1,295	2,834	4,205	5,041	5,817
150,000	160,000	1,393	3,050	4,524	5,424	6,259
160,000	170,000	1,492	3,265	4,844	5,806	6,702
170,000	180,000	1,590	3,480	5,164	6,189	7,144
180,000	190,000	1,688	3,696	5,483	6,572	7,586
190,000	200,000	1,787	3,911	5,802	6,955	8,029
200,000	210,000	1,885	4,126	6,122	7,338	8,471
210,000	220,000	1,983	4,342	6,441	7,721	8,913
220,000	230,000	2,081	4,557	6,761	8,104	9,355
230,000	240,000	2,180	4,772	7,080	8,487	9,798
240,000	250,000	2,278	4,988	7,399	8,870	10,240

* For the last tax year of the lease, use the dollar amount for the preceding year.

Table III: Dollar Amounts For Automobiles With A Lease Term Beginning In Calendar Year 1989 or 1990

Fair Market Value of Automobile		Year of Lease*				
		1st	2nd	3rd	4th	5th and Later
Over	Not Over					
$12,800	$13,100	0	0	0	1	2
13,100	13,400	0	2	3	5	9
13,400	13,700	3	11	15	21	26
13,700	14,000	8	19	29	37	45
14,000	14,300	12	29	42	53	64
14,300	14,600	16	38	55	70	83
14,600	14,900	20	47	69	86	101
14,900	15,200	24	56	83	102	120
15,200	15,500	28	65	97	118	139
15,500	15,800	33	74	110	134	158
15,800	16,100	37	83	123	151	176
16,100	16,400	41	93	136	167	195
16,400	16,700	45	102	150	183	213
16,700	17,000	49	111	164	199	232
17,000	17,500	55	123	182	220	258
17,500	18,000	62	138	204	248	289
18,000	18,500	69	153	227	275	319
18,500	19,000	76	168	250	301	351
19,000	19,500	83	184	271	329	382
19,500	20,000	90	199	294	356	413
20,000	20,500	97	214	317	382	445
20,500	21,000	104	229	339	410	476
21,000	21,500	111	244	362	437	507
21,500	22,000	117	260	384	464	538
22,000	23,000	128	282	419	504	585
23,000	24,000	142	313	463	558	647
24,000	25,000	156	343	508	613	709

Fair Market Value of Automobile		Year of Lease*				
		1st	2nd	3rd	4th	5th and Later
Over	Not Over					
25,000	26,000	170	373	554	666	772
26,000	27,000	183	404	599	720	834
27,000	28,000	197	435	643	774	897
28,000	29,000	211	465	688	829	958
29,000	30,000	225	495	734	882	1,021
30,000	31,000	239	526	778	936	1,084
31,000	32,000	253	556	824	990	1,146
32,000	33,000	267	586	869	1,044	1,209
33,000	34,000	281	617	913	1,099	1,270
34,000	35,000	295	647	959	1,152	1,333
35,000	36,000	309	677	1,004	1,206	1,396
36,000	37,000	322	708	1,049	1,260	1,458
37,000	38,000	336	738	1,094	1,315	1,520
38,000	39,000	350	769	1,139	1,368	1,583
39,000	40,000	364	799	1,184	1,423	1,664
40,000	41,000	378	829	1,230	1,476	1,707
41,000	42,000	392	860	1,274	1,530	1,770
42,000	43,000	406	890	1,319	1,585	1,832
43,000	44,000	420	920	1,365	1,638	1,894
44,000	45,000	434	952	1,409	1,693	1,956
45,000	46,000	448	981	1,454	1,747	2,019
46,000	47,000	461	1,012	1,499	1,801	2,081
47,000	48,000	475	1,042	1,545	1,854	2,144
48,000	49,000	489	1,073	1,589	1,909	2,205
49,000	50,000	503	1,103	1,634	1,963	2,268
50,000	51,000	517	1,133	1,680	2,016	2,331
51,000	52,000	531	1,164	1,724	2,071	2,393
52,000	53,000	545	1,194	1,770	2,124	2,455
53,000	54,000	559	1,224	1,815	2,179	2,517
54,000	55,000	573	1,255	1,859	2,233	2,580
55,000	56,000	587	1,285	1,905	2,286	2,643
56,000	57,000	600	1,316	1,950	2,340	2,705
57,000	58,000	614	1,346	1,995	2,395	2,767
58,000	59,000	628	1,376	2,041	2,448	2,829
59,000	60,000	642	1,407	2,085	2,502	2,892
60,000	62,000	663	1,452	2,153	2,584	2,985
62,000	64,000	691	1,513	2,243	2,691	3,110
64,000	66,000	719	1,574	2,332	2,800	3,325
66,000	68,000	746	1,635	2,424	2,907	3,360
68,000	70,000	774	1,695	2,514	3,015	3,484
70,000	72,000	802	1,756	2,603	3,124	3,609
72,000	74,000	830	1,817	2,693	3,232	3,733
74,000	76,000	858	1,877	2,784	3,340	3,858
76,000	78,000	885	1,939	2,873	3,448	3,983
78,000	80,000	913	1,999	2,964	3,556	4,107
80,000	85,000	962	2,106	3,121	3,745	4,325
85,000	90,000	1,031	2,258	3,346	4,015	4,638
90,000	95,000	1,101	2,409	3,572	4,285	4,949
95,000	100,000	1,170	2,562	3,796	4,556	5,261
100,000	110,000	1,275	2,789	4,135	4,960	5,729
110,000	120,000	1,414	3,093	4,585	5,501	6,352
120,000	130,000	1,553	3,397	5,036	6,040	6,976
130,000	140,000	1,692	3,701	5,486	6,580	7,600
140,000	150,000	1,831	4,004	5,937	7,121	8,223
150,000	160,000	1,970	4,308	6,388	7,660	8,847
160,000	170,000	2,109	4,612	6,838	8,201	9,469

Fair Market Value of Automobile		Year of Lease*				
		1st	2nd	3rd	4th	5th and Later
Over	Not Over					
170,000	180,000	2,248	4,916	7,288	8,741	10,093
180,000	190,000	2,387	5,220	7,739	9,281	10,716
190,000	200,000	2,526	5,524	8,189	9,821	11,340
200,000	210,000	2,665	5,828	8,639	10,362	11,963
210,000	220,000	2,804	6,131	9,091	10,901	12,587
220,000	230,000	2,943	6,435	9,541	11,442	13,210
230,000	240,000	3,082	6,739	9,992	11,981	13,834
240,000	250,000	3,221	7,043	10,442	12,522	14,457

*For the last tax year of the lease, use the dollar amount for the preceding year.

Table IV: Dollar Amounts For Automobiles With A Lease Term Beginning In Calendar Year 1987 or 1988

Fair Market Value of Automobile		Year of Lease*				
		1st	2nd	3rd	4th	5th and Later
Over	Not Over					
$12,800	$13,100	2	5	7	8	9
13,100	13,400	6	14	20	24	28
13,400	13,700	10	23	34	41	47
13,700	14,000	15	32	47	57	65
14,000	14,300	19	41	61	73	84
14,300	14,600	23	50	74	89	103
14,600	14,900	27	59	88	105	122
14,900	15,200	31	68	101	122	140
15,200	15,500	35	77	115	138	159
15,500	15,800	40	87	128	154	178
15,800	16,100	44	96	142	170	196
16,100	16,400	48	105	155	186	215
16,400	16,700	52	114	169	203	234
16,700	17,000	56	123	182	219	253
17,000	17,500	62	135	200	240	277
17,500	18,000	69	150	223	267	309
18,000	18,500	76	166	246	294	340
18,500	19,000	83	181	268	321	371
19,000	19,500	90	196	291	348	402
19,500	20,000	97	211	313	375	433
20,000	20,500	104	226	336	402	465
20,500	21,000	111	242	358	429	496
21,000	21,500	117	257	381	456	527
21,500	22,000	124	272	403	483	558
22,000	23,000	135	295	437	524	605
23,000	24,000	149	325	482	578	667
24,000	25,000	163	356	527	632	729
25,000	26,000	177	386	572	686	792
26,000	27,000	190	416	617	740	854
27,000	28,000	204	447	662	794	917
28,000	29,000	218	477	707	848	979
29,000	30,000	232	507	752	902	1,041
30,000	31,000	246	538	797	956	1,104
31,000	32,000	260	568	842	1,010	1,166
32,000	33,000	274	599	887	1,064	1,228
33,000	34,000	288	629	933	1,118	1,291
34,000	35,000	302	659	978	1,172	1,353
35,000	36,000	316	690	1,023	1,226	1,415
36,000	37,000	329	720	1,068	1,280	1,478
37,000	38,000	343	751	1,113	1,334	1,540
38,000	39,000	357	781	1,158	1,388	1,602
39,000	40,000	371	811	1,203	1,442	1,665

| 40,000 | 41,000 | 385 | 842 | 1,248 | 1,496 | 1,727 |

Fair Market Value of Automobile		Year of Lease*				
		1st	2nd	3rd	4th	5th and Later
Over	Not Over					
41,000	42,000	399	872	1,293	1,550	1,789
42,000	43,000	413	902	1,338	1,604	1,852
43,000	44,000	427	933	1,383	1,658	1,914
44,000	45,000	441	963	1,428	1,712	1,976
45,000	46,000	455	994	1,473	1,766	2,039
46,000	47,000	468	1,024	1,518	1,820	2,101
47,000	48,000	482	1,054	1,563	1,874	2,164
48,000	49,000	496	1,085	1,608	1,928	2,226
49,000	50,000	510	1,115	1,653	1,982	2,288
50,000	51,000	524	1,146	1,698	2,036	2,351
51,000	52,000	538	1,176	1,743	2,090	2,413
52,000	53,000	552	1,206	1,788	2,144	2,475
53,000	54,000	566	1,237	1,834	2,198	2,538
54,000	55,000	580	1,267	1,879	2,252	2,600
55,000	56,000	594	1,297	1,924	2,306	2,662
56,000	57,000	607	1,328	1,969	2,360	2,725
57,000	58,000	621	1,358	2,014	2,414	2,787
58,000	59,000	635	1,389	2,059	2,468	2,849
59,000	60,000	649	1,419	2,104	2,522	2,912

* For the last tax year of the lease, use the dollar amount for the preceding year.

You can aggregate separate uses of a car if part of an overall, uninterrupted business use. For example, if you make a sales trip out of town to see customers, a single record of the miles travelled is sufficient [Temp. Reg. Sec. 1.274-5T(c)(6)(C)]. Likewise, you can aggregate expenses such as gasoline and repairs. You have to keep a record of the amount and date of each expense, but you do not have to record the business purpose. Instead, you can simply prorate the expenses based on business mileage [¶2004].

Here is a sample of a page from a diary of auto use that you might keep:

List all auto expenses:

DATE	DESCRIPTION	AMOUNT
11/18	gasoline	26 50
	tolls	7 50
11/18	parking	24 00
11/20	oil change, filter	20 00
11/21	gas	19 25
11/22	gas	10 00
	tolls	5 60
	parking BALT.	15 00
Total parking & tolls		52 10
Total other expenses		75 75

List all business trips:

DATE	TRIP BETWEEN—	BUSINESS PURPOSE	MILES
11/18	Phila. & NYC & back	conference with client XYZ Inc.	180
11/19	office & ad agency & back	review ad campaign	16
11/20	office & factory & back	check product packaging	66
11/22	Phila. & Baltimore & back	company's annual marketing conference	192
		TOTAL	454

Sampling. You can maintain an adequate record of your business/investment use for only part of the year if you can show that that part is representative of the year as a whole [Temp. Reg. Sec. 1.274-5T(c)(3)(ii)].

Example: Ms. Bowen runs a business out of her home. She uses the automobile for trips around town to visit customers and suppliers. She maintains adequate records for the first three months of 1992 that indicate 75% of the use of the car was in her business. Her business records (e.g., invoices, billings, etc.) show that the level of her business activity was fairly uniform throughout 1992. So she will be considered to have adequate records to support a 75% business use rate for the entire year.

(c) Employer-Provided Cars. Your employer should require you and other employees who drive company-owned cars to submit a record of your automobile use. The record should satisfy the accountable plan rules [¶2003]. Specifically, each employee's record must state the date, business purpose and mileage of each trip, and it must be submitted to the employer in a timely manner.

In lieu of receiving a detailed record from you, your employer can accept a statement summarizing your use. But, in this case, you are required to retain adequate records supporting the statement [Temp. Reg. Sec. 1.274-5T(e)(2)].

If the accountable plan requirements are satisfied, your employer generally can write off 100% of its automobile expenses, and you are not taxed on your business use of the automobile. Only the value of your personal use, if any, is taxed to you as compensation.

If the accountable plan rules are not satisfied, your employer must report 100% of the car use as taxable compensation on your Form W-2. You can claim an offsetting deduction for the business use, but only to the extent the auto deduction, when combined with your other employee business expenses and miscellaneous deductions, exceeds 2% of your adjusted gross income [¶1942].

NOTE: In the past, your employer could treat 100% of your car use as taxable compensation, and your offsetting deduction would not be subject to the 2%-of-adjusted-gross-income floor. Since 1990, however, the 2% floor does apply to your deduction.

Cars not used for personal travel. An employer does not have to meet the substantiation requirements for cars that are not used for personal driving [Temp. Reg. Sec. 1.274-6T(a)(2)]. The following conditions have to be met:

* The employer must have a policy statement in writing that specifically prohibits employees from using the car for personal driving (other than incidental personal use, such as stops for lunch);
* The employer reasonably believes that its written policy statement is being honored by employees;
* The cars are kept on the employees' premises when not in use; and
* No employee using a vehicle lives on the employer's business premises.

Cars not used for personal travel other than commuting. An employer is exempt from the substantiation requirements for cars used only for business and commuting purposes if the following conditions are met:

* For bona fide noncompensatory reasons, the employer requires an employee to commute to and from work in the car;
* The employer has a written policy statement prohibiting personal use other than commuting, and the employer reasonably believes that this policy is being carried out;
* The employer reports the value of the commute in the employee's wage statement;
* The employee is not an officer or director of the employer or does not own a 1%-or-more interest in the employer [Temp. Reg. Sec. 1.274-6T(a)(3)].

(d) Automobile Allowances and Reimbursements. You may receive an automobile allowance or reimbursement under an accountable plan [¶2003]. If so, you need not report the employer payment as income on your tax return or claim a deduction for your offsetting expenses [Reg. Sec. 1.62-2].

If, however, your expenses exceed the reimbursement and you have an adequate record of your expenses, you can report the reimbursement as income and deduct the excess auto expenses. The expenses are combined with your other employee business expenses and miscellaneous deductions, and the total is deductible to the extent it exceeds 2% of your adjusted gross income [¶1942].

Mileage allowance. You do not have to substantiate your actual automobile expenses to your employer to the extent you receive a mileage allowance of 28 cents or less in 1992 (this figure is adjusted periodically by the IRS). You can get by with a record of the date, business purpose and mileage of each trip. The IRS has said that an employer can use the automatic mileage allowance to figure the tax-free portion of a reimbursement—even if the employer uses another method (e.g., fixed costs of maintaining a car) to calculate the reimbursement itself.[1]

> ➤ **CAUTION** If you receive an allowance or reimbursement below the 28-cents-a-mile rate, you may report the reimbursement on your return and deduct your actual expenses or 28 cents per mile. However, your automobile deduction is grouped with your other employee business expenses and miscellaneous deductions, and the total is deductible only to the extent it exceeds 2% of your adjusted gross income.

FAVR allowance. You may be able to receive a fixed and variable rate (FAVR) allowance. Like the mileage allowance, you do not keep track of your actual expenses; you can get by with a minimum record of the date, business purpose and mileage of each trip. Unlike the mileage allowance, however, you are not limited to 28 cents per mile or any other set figure.[2]

A FAVR allowance is made up of two parts: (1) a periodic flat payment covering fixed costs for depreciation, insurance, registration, and license fees and (2) a periodic variable payment covering operating costs for gas, oil, tires, and routine maintenance and repairs.

There are restrictions on who can receive a FAVR allowance. Officers and directors cannot receive it, nor can employees who own at least 1% of the employer. Additionally, no one can get the allowance unless (1) at least 15 employees are covered by the FAVR at all times and (2) at least 50% or more of the employees covered by the FAVR are non-management.

> ➤ **IMPORTANT** FAVR allowances are too complicated for most employers to set up and administer by themselves; they will need outside help—which can be costly.

(e) Reporting Car Expenses on Your Tax Return. You deduct car expenses in the same manner as other transportation expenses [¶2002].

BUSINESS ENTERTAINMENT DEDUCTIONS

¶2008   ENTERTAINMENT DEDUCTIONS IN GENERAL

You can deduct 80% of the expenses you incur for entertaining if the expenses (1) are ordinary and necessary business [IRC Sec. 162] and (2) meet special tax law requirements (¶2009) [IRC Sec. 274].

(a) What Is Entertainment? It's more than amusement or recreation. It includes entertaining at night clubs, cocktail lounges, theaters, country and athletic clubs, sporting events, and hunting and fishing trips. Entertainment also covers personal living expenses, such as providing a hotel room or car for a customer [Reg. Sec. 1.274-2(b)(1)]. However, in general, no deduction is allowed for the cost of providing meals to someone else unless you (or your employee) are present [IRC Sec. 274(k)(1)].

Your trade or business is taken into account when determining if an activity is entertainment. For example, going to a theater is not entertainment to a theater critic. And if a dress designer puts on a fashion show to introduce a new line, it would not be treated as entertaining customers.

(b) Ordinary and Necessary. You cannot deduct an entertainment expense unless it's incurred with an intent to obtain a specific business benefit, is customary in your trade or business and isn't lavish or extravagant. For example, if you are a self-employed professional who depends on referrals from other professionals, the cost of entertaining them is usually considered an ordinary and necessary expense. The same applies to your employer's reimbursements to you for the cost of entertaining customers. However, no deduction is generally allowed for entertainment designed to expand your circle of acquaintances in the hope that some extra business might result.

Entertaining employees through picnics, holiday parties and the like is usually considered an ordinary and necessary expense because the employer benefits through improved employee morale. But including a few employees in a large social gathering does not convert personal expenses into business expenses.

Entertainment expenses of employees. If you, as an employee, claim deductions for unreimbursed business entertainment, you must do more than show that the expenses are ordinary and necessary business expenses. You must show the expenses are ordinary and necessary in your business as an employee. You must be expected to incur these expenses as part of your duty or position. Or your income must be dependent on the entertainment. For example, if a salesperson on commission entertains a customer of the company, that would generally be considered an ordinary and necessary expense. But if the personnel director of the same company entertains the customer, it probably is not treated as an ordinary and necessary expense.

The fact that your employer does not reimburse you may indicate that it is not an ordinary and necessary expense. On the other hand, if you can be reimbursed for entertainment expenses, but choose not to be, the expenses are considered nondeductible personal expenses.

Personal expenses. As a general rule, when you incur ordinary personal living expenses in your business, you can only deduct the portion in excess of what you would normally pay. For example, according to the rule, if your lunch expenses usually run around $10, but your meal costs $25 when you entertain a customer, only $15 would be an ordinary and necessary business expense. But the IRS says this rule will not be enforced except in abusive situations.[1] So the full cost of your meal, as well as your customer's, is treated as an ordinary and necessary expense.

Personal guests. When you entertain both business guests and nonbusiness guests, you must allocate your expenses between the business portion and the personal portion. For example, if you entertain three customers and three social acquaintances at a restaurant, only 4/7 of the restaurant tab is considered an ordinary and necessary expense: the portion allocable to your meal and the meals of your three customers.

When your spouse and a customer or client's spouse attend the entertainment activity, their expenses are considered ordinary and necessary if you have a clear business purpose for the entertainment.

> **Example 1:** Mr. Soden, a good customer of XYZ Company, is in town for business discussions. Mrs. Soden is with him. Mr. Brown, an employee of XYZ, invites Soden to dinner at a restaurant. Because it would be impractical for Soden to dine without his wife, Mrs. Soden also comes to the restaurant. And because Mrs. Soden is there, Brown asks his wife to come too. XYZ picks up the tab. Result: XYZ's entire cost is considered an ordinary and necessary expense.

(c) 80% Deduction Limit. You can deduct only 80% of the cost of an otherwise allowable entertainment expense [IRC Sec. 274(n)(1)]. This limit applies not only to the actual cost of your entertainment activity, but to taxes, tips and other related charges (e.g., nightclub cover charges, parking fee at the entertainment site, etc.). However, it does not include transportation to and from the location of the entertainment; that cost is fully deductible.

> **Example 2:** Mr. Burke pays a $10 cab fare to meet a client for dinner. The dinner bill comes to $80, plus $5 tax and a $15 tip. Result: Assuming the expenses qualify as deductible, Burke can write off $90 (80% of the total restaurant charges, plus the $10 cab ride).

If your employer reimburses you for entertainment expenses, only your employer is subject to the 80% deduction limit [IRC Sec. 274(e)(3)].

For example, if Burke (Example 2) is reimbursed in full by his employer, the employer can only deduct $90 of the reimbursement. And Burke excludes 100% of the reimbursement from his taxable income as long as the reimbursement is provided under an accountable plan [¶2003]. If you are not fully reimbursed for entertainment expenses, the 80% deduction limit applies at your employer's level to the extent of any reimbursement. But the 80% deduction limit applies at your level to determine how much of the excess entertainment expenses you can write off. Your deduction is then subject to the 2%-of-adjusted-gross-income deduction floor [¶1942].

Exceptions. Certain types of expenses are not subject to the 80% limit and are deductible in full [IRC Sec. 274(n)(2)]. These include:

- Amounts treated as compensation. If your employer reports an entertainment reimbursement as compensation on your W-2, the reimbursement is fully deductible by your employer. You then take the reimbursement into income, and your deduction for the entertainment expense is subject to the 80% limit and the 2%-of-adjusted-gross-income deduction floor.
- De minimis fringe benefits. These are items that are provided by your employer and excluded from your income (e.g., subsidized company cafeteria, holiday gifts of turkeys, etc.) [IRC Sec. 132].
- Employer-provided recreation. This covers holiday parties, summer picnics and similar recreational and social activities for you and other employees.
- Items made available to the public as samples or promotional materials.
- Entertainment sold to customers. If you charge a customer the full fair market value for an entertainment-type activity, your expenses are fully deductible. For example, a nightclub can write off 100% of the cost of its floorshow.
- Sporting activities. The cost of business entertainment at a sporting event is not subject to the 80% limit; it's fully deductible if: (1) the event's primary purpose is to benefit a charity; (2) the entire net proceeds go to the charity; and (3) the event uses volunteers to perform substantially all of the work needed for the event. Golf

tournaments for charity are a prime example of this kind of business entertainment activity.

Tickets. If you buy tickets to an entertainment event (e.g., Broadway show, baseball game), your deduction cannot exceed 80% of the face value of the ticket [IRC Sec. 274(l)(1)]. No deduction is allowed for the premium paid a "scalper," nor is any deduction permitted for the fee paid a ticket agency.

Skybox rentals. A special limit applies to deductions for using skyboxes or other private luxury boxes for business entertainment. If you rent the box for more than one event, your deduction cannot exceed 80% of the face value of the same number of nonluxury box seats [IRC Sec. 274(1)(2)].

¶2009   SPECIAL ENTERTAINMENT DEDUCTION RULES

[New tax legislation may affect this subject; see ¶1.]

In addition to being ordinary and necessary, you can deduct an entertainment expense only if it's directly related to or associated with the active conduct of your trade or business [IRC Sec. 274(a)].

(a) Entertainment Directly Related to Business. Entertainment is generally directly related to your business if, during the entertainment period, you hold active discussions or negotiations with an eye on a specific business benefit. To qualify an expense as directly related to business, you must meet three basic conditions [Reg. Sec. 1.274-2(c)(3)]:

1. There is more than a general expectation of deriving income or other business benefit from providing the entertainment. For example, a discussion at dinner about the general state of the economy is not considered directly related to business. However, you are not required to show that new income or a specific benefit actually resulted from each and every expense. If the business discussion is fruitless, a deduction is still allowed.

2. You actively engaged in a discussion, negotiations or a transaction during the entertainment. However, expenses may still be deductible if you expected to talk business, but no business was actually discussed for reasons beyond your control.

3. The principal character of the combined entertainment/business activity was the active conduct of your business. This doesn't mean, for example, that you and a customer have to talk business all the way through lunch. But an incidental business discussion isn't sufficient.

An expense automatically qualifies as directly related to business if it occurs in a clear business setting and is designed to further your business [Reg. Sec. 1.274-2(c)(4)]. A clear business setting is one in which the recipient of the entertainment could reasonably conclude that you have no motive for providing the entertainment other than business. For example, if a company operates a hospitality room at a convention to display its products, that would be considered a clear business setting.

Entertainment is presumed to fail the "directly related" test if you hold it under circumstances where there is little or no possibility that business can be discussed [Reg. Sec. 1.274-2(c)(7)]. The Revenue Service says these circumstances include hunting and fishing trips and outings on yachts and other pleasure boats.[1] However, in some cases, taxpayers have been allowed deductions for these types of expenses.[2]

(b) Entertainment Associated With Business. Entertainment is associated with your business if (1) there is a clear business purpose to the expenditure, such as soliciting business or improving an existing business relationship and (2) it directly precedes or follows a substantial and bona fide business discussion [Reg. Sec. 1.274-2(d)(1)].

Whether or not a discussion is substantial or bona fide depends on the facts and circumstances of each situation. Generally, you must show that you are engaged in a business discussion, conference meeting or negotiation that had a business or income-producing goal. The meeting does not have to last any specific length of time, and it does not have to last longer the entertainment that precedes or follows it. But you must show that the principal character of the combined business/entertainment activity is business [Reg. Sec. 1.274-2(d)(3)(i)(a)].

> **Example 1:** Dr. Gilbert, a family practitioner, refers patients to Dr. Moss, a surgeon. One morning, Gilbert and Moss discuss patients' cases. Then Moss takes Gilbert out to lunch at a restaurant. After that they go for a round of golf, and Moss pays the greens fees. Result: The meal and golfing are generally considered associated with the active conduct of Moss's practice.

A professional conference or convention qualifies as a substantial business discussion, assuming you can deduct the cost of attending the conference or convention [Reg. Sec. 1.274-2(d)(3)(i)(b)]. For example, if you entertain a customer following a convention session, you can deduct 80% of your cost, even though it's strictly for goodwill and no business is discussed.

Generally speaking, a business discussion directly precedes or follows an entertainment activity if both occur on the same date. If they occur on different days, the entertaining may be considered associated with business if the facts and circumstances warrant it [Reg. Sec. 1.274-2(d)(3)(ii)].

> **Example 2:** Mr. Morton, a customer of XYZ, and Mrs. Morton fly in from out of town. Mr. Pickford, a sales executive with XYZ, has the Mortons over to his home for dinner. Afterwards, they go to the theater. The following day Morton and Pickford spend several hours at XYZ's office negotiating a sales contract. Result: The cost of the dinner and theater tickets is considered associated with Pickford's business.

(c) Entertainment Facilities. In general, you cannot deduct expenses with respect to a facility used for entertainment [IRC Sec. 274(a)]. An entertainment facility includes yachts, hunting lodges, fishing camps, swimming pools, automobiles and other items of personal or real property owned, rented or used in connection with business entertainment [Reg. Sec. 1.274-2(e)(2)]. Disallowed deductions include those for depreciation, rents, repair expenses, utility charges, and a loss on the sale of the facility [Reg. Sec. 1.274-2(e)(3)(i)].

The disallowance rule does not apply to the expenses that could be deducted even if the facility was not used for business entertainment [Reg. Sec. 1.274-2(e)(3)(iii)(c)]. So property taxes, mortgage interest and casualty losses on an entertainment facility may be deductible. And you can also deduct expenses attributable to the business use of a facility for other than entertainment [Reg. Sec. 1.274-2(e)(3)(iii)(b)]. For example, if you let a customer use your business car for entertainment purposes, you can still claim deductions for other nonentertainment business use of the car. In addition, you can write off out-of-pocket entertainment expenses at a facility, as long as they are otherwise deductible [Reg. Sec. 1.274-2(e)(3)(iii)(a)]. For example, if you take a client fishing on your boat following a business discussion, you can deduct 80% of what you spend for gas, bait and so forth.

(d) Entertaining at Clubs. You can deduct 80% of your out-of-pocket cost of entertaining a customer or client at your country, social or athletic club, provided the entertainment activity is directly related to or associated with your business. For example, after a morning business meeting, you treat a client to lunch and golf at your club. Result: You can deduct 80% of what you spend on meals and drinks in the club dining room as well as 80% of the greens fees and golf cart rental.

What's more, if you use the club *primarily* for business, you can also deduct the portion of club dues allocable to directly related entertainment at the club [IRC Sec. 274(a)(2)]. Your club use is primarily for business if more than 50% of the total days you and your family use the club are so-called business days. A day of use is a business day if the primary use of the club that day is considered ordinary and necessary to your business. In other words, even though the out-of-pocket cost for an entertainment activity may not be deductible (because the cost is not directly related or associated with business), the activity can still qualify as a business use of the club. A day is automatically a business day, even though there is personal or family use, if you have a substantial and bona fide business discussion at the club [Reg. Sec. 1.274-2(e)(4)(iii)(b)].

Example 3: Mr. Wilson and his family use his club 60 days during the year for personal reasons. On another 40 days, Wilson uses the club for "directly related" or "associated with" entertaining (i.e., he has business discussions at the club or entertains customers before or after substantial business discussions). On another 25 days, Wilson uses the club for strictly goodwill entertaining—no business is discussed before, after or during the entertainment. Result: Wilson uses his club primarily for business. More than 50% of his total use (65 days out of 125 days) is considered an ordinary and necessary business use.

➤ **OBSERVATION** A few extra business meals or rounds of golf with a customer at your club can make a big difference. If you find yourself falling short of the 50% business use mark at year end, schedule some business meals with your good customers or clients. Remember, you don't have to talk business for it to count as a business day, and it may be enough to get you over the 50% mark.

Directly related use. Once you have established that a social, athletic or country club is used primarily for business, your dues are deductible to the extent the club use is directly related to business ((a) above) [Reg. Sec. 1.274-2(a)(2)(ii)(b)].

Example 4: Mr. Wallace and his family use the club for a total of 100 days during the year. On 25 days, Wallace uses it for entertainment directly related to his law practice. On another 35 days, he entertains for goodwill purposes. On the remaining 40 days, the club is used by his family. Wallace's annual club dues are $3,000. Result: One-quarter of Wallace's club use is directly related to his business. So he can deduct 80% of one-quarter of his dues, or $600.

➤ **IMPORTANT** While a quiet business meal in the club dining room is not deductible, it can help you nail down a club dues deduction by pushing you over the 50% mark.[1]

(e) Exceptions. You can forget about the complicated restrictions for some business entertainment expenses [IRC Sec. 274(e); Reg. Sec. 1.274-2]. They can be deducted, whether or not they are directly related or associated with business. These are:

1. Food and beverages furnished to employees on the employer's premises. This includes executive dining rooms and company cafeterias, and applies even though business guests may occasionally be served.

2. Amounts treated as compensation. The cost of the entertainment activity or facility must be deducted as compensation on the employer's original tax return, and the value must be included in the employee's wages for withholding and reporting purposes. In other words, you cannot go back and change an entertainment expense to compensation on an amended return.

3. Reimbursed expenses. The purpose here is to apply the disallowance rule to either the employee incurring the expense or the employer on whose behalf the expense is incurred—but not both. If the amount received is treated as a reimbursement and the

employee substantiates the expenses under an accountable plan [¶2003], the employer is subject to the disallowance rules (i.e., the employee may offset the expense against the reimbursement); if a payment to the employee is treated as compensation, the employee suffers the loss of deductions (i.e., the compensation is deductible by the employer, but the employee cannot claim a deduction to offset the taxable compensation).

4. Recreational activities or facilities primarily for the benefit of employees. This exception does not apply to expenditures made mainly for the benefit of officers, other highly compensated employees, shareholders or business owners.

> ➤ **IMPORTANT** Once it is established that a facility is used primarily (more than 50%) for the benefit of employees, then all of the use of the facility is exempt from the disallowance rules (including the 80% deduction limit). So if you also entertain customers at the facility, you can write off all the expenses attributable to that use as well.[3]

5. Shareholder or employee business meetings. Here the primary purpose of the meeting must be to transact business.

6. Expenses of attending business meetings or conventions of tax-exempt organizations. This includes business organizations and chambers of commerce.

7. Items made available to the general public. This covers the distribution of samples to the public and maintenance of recreational facilities for public use.

8. Entertainment sold to customers in bona fide transactions.

9. Entertainment provided as compensation or a prize to someone who is not an employee.

¶2010   BUSINESS GIFTS

Gifts to customers, clients, or even the general public may be both a deductible goodwill expense for the donor and excludable from the recipient's income as a tax-free gift. In such a case, your deduction for business gifts you make cannot exceed $25 per recipient per year [IRC Sec. 274(b)(1)]. But you can deduct any amount up to $25 in full; there is no 20% disallowance as there is with entertainment.

Example: XYZ, Inc. sends out hams at Christmas to its customers. The cost of each ham is $40. XYZ can deduct $25. If the hams cost $20, XYZ could deduct the $20 in full.

For purposes of the deduction limit, a business gift does not include:

* Amounts other than gifts that are excludable from income (e.g., scholarships);
* An item having a cost of $4 or less on which your name or company name is clearly and permanently imprinted, and which is one of a number of identical items you distribute generally; or
* A sign, display rack or other promotional material to be used on the business premises of the recipient [Reg. Sec. 1.274-3(b)].

In figuring the amount subject to the $25 limit, you do not have to include incidental costs, such as engraving, packaging or mailing [Reg. Sec. 1.274-3(c)]. A gift to the spouse of a customer or client is considered an indirect gift to the customer or client (unless you have independent business dealings with the spouse). So if you give the spouse a $25 gift, you cannot deduct any additional gifts to the customer for the year [Reg. Sec. 1.274-3(d)(i)]. By the same token, you and your spouse are treated as one taxpayer for purposes of the deduction limit. If you and your spouse each give a $25 gift to a customer or client, your total deduction is limited to $25 [IRC Sec. 274(b)(2)].

A gift of tickets to an event is considered entertainment if you accompany the recipient. However, if you don't attend, you may treat the tickets as either entertainment or a gift [Reg. Sec. 1.274(b)(1)(iii)(b)(2)].

> ➤ **OBSERVATION** If the event does not qualify as associated with or directly related entertainment [¶2009], you obviously want to treat the tickets as gifts; otherwise you get no deduction. On the other hand, if the event does qualify as directly related or associated with entertainment, you should elect to treat the tickets as entertainment if they cost more than $31.25. Above the $31.25 level, your 80% deduction as entertainment exceeds the $25 limit on gifts.

¶2011   REPORTING AND SUBSTANTIATION

If you are self-employed and incur deductible entertainment expenses, you claim the expenses as deductions for adjusted gross income [¶1102]. If you are an employee and receive an entertainment allowance or reimbursement, you do not have to pay tax on your employer's payment if it is made under an accountable plan [¶2003]. However, your unreimbursed or unsubstantiated entertainment expenses (or expenses in excess of reimbursements) are miscellaneous itemized deductions, subject to the 2%-of-adjusted-gross-income floor [¶1942].

(a) Substantiation. To claim a deduction for an entertainment expense that is directly related to business, you must be able to prove:

1. The amount of each expense for entertainment;
2. The date of the entertainment;
3. The name, address or location of the site of the entertainment (including a designation of the type of entertainment if not readily apparent from the name of the place);
4. The business reason for the entertainment or the nature of the business benefit to be derived and the nature of any business discussion or activity; and
5. The name, title or other designation of the person being entertained, sufficient to establish his or her business relationship to you [Temp. Reg. Sec. 1.274-5(b)(3)].

For entertainment deducted as an expense associated with your business (i.e., a substantial business discussion precedes or follows it), you must prove all of the items above; plus—

1. The date and duration of the business discussion;
2. The place of the business discussion;
3. The nature of the discussion; and
4. The identification of the participants in the discussion [Temp. Reg. Sec. 1.274-5T(b)(4)].

The items that must be proved in the case of deductions for business gifts are

1. The cost of the gift;
2. The date of the gift;
3. A description of the gift;
4. The business reason for the gift or the business benefit expected to be derived; and
5. The name, title or other designation of the recipient sufficient to establish your business relationship with the recipient [Temp. Reg. Sec. 1.274-5T(b)(5)].

You must substantiate the items above by adequate written records or by sufficient evidence corroborating your own statement [Temp. Reg. Sec. 1.275-5T(c)(1)]. "Adequate records" include an account book, diary, log or similar record, prepared at or near the time each expense is incurred, that is sufficient to establish each required item of proof [Temp. Reg. Sec. 1.274-5T(c)(2)]. A sample diary page of entertainment expenses appears below.

DATE	MEALS AND ENTERTAINMENT	PLACE	AMOUNT	BUSINESS PURPOSE/RELATIONSHIP
TOTAL				

In addition to the adequate—records requirement, you must keep receipts or other documentary evidence for entertainment expenses in excess of $25 [Temp. Reg. Sec. 1.274-5T(c)(iii)].

(b) Allowances and Reimbursements. If you are an employee who receives an entertainment allowance or reimbursement, you must keep records that satisfy (a) above, plus you must be required to submit a record of your expenses to your employer under an accountable plan [¶2003]. This is the only way for you to avoid the 2%-of-adjusted-gross-income deduction floor [¶1942 et seq.].

Footnotes to Chapter 10

(For your added convenience, in brackets [] with the footnotes below, you will find citations to related paragraphs in the "RIA United States Tax Reporter"(USTR), "CCH Federal Tax Reporter"(CCH) and "RIA Federal Tax Coordinator 2d" (FTC) multi-volume services.)

FOOTNOTE ¶ 2000 [USTR ¶ 1624; CCH ¶ 8500; 8520; FTC ¶ L-1600; L-1700].

(1) U.S. v. Correll [1967], 389 U.S. 299, 20 AFTR 2d 5845; Rev. Rul. 75-170, 1975-1 CB 60.

(2) Rev. Rul. 71-247, 1971-1 CB 54; Newman, ¶ 89,672 PH Memo TC.

(3) Treas. Dept. booklet "Travel, Entertainment and Gift Expenses" [1991 Ed.], p. 2.

(4) Edward Andrews, 931 F.2nd 132 [1st Cir.].

(5) Rev. Rul. 73-529, 1973-2 CB 37.

(6) Rev. Rul. 83-82, 1983-2 CB 45.

(7) Rev. Rul. 54-497, 1954-2 CB 75.

(8) Bank of Stockton, ¶ 77,024 PH Memo TC.

(9) Treas. Dept. booklet "Travel, Entertainment and Gift Expenses" [1991 Ed.], p. 3.

(10) Comm. v. Flowers, 326 U.S. 465, 34 AFTR 301.

(11) Rev. Rul. 90-23, 1990-1 CB 28.

(12) Chandler et al. v. Comm., 48 AFTR 273.

(13) Leroy Bloomberg, ¶ 79,050 PH Memo TC.

(14) Mark McKinsey, ¶ 84,514 PH Memo TC.

(15) Treas. Dept. booklet "Your Federal Income Tax" [1991 Ed.], p. 155.

(16) Weinstein v. U.S., 25 AFTR 2d 70-474.

(17) Duane Stranahan, ¶ 82,151 PH Memo TC.

(18) Otho Harris, ¶ 78,332 PH Memo TC.

(19) Louis H. Mayer, ¶ 51,175 PH Memo TC.

(20) Lloyd I. Holmes, ¶ 83,442 PH Memo TC.

(21) William R. Kinney, 66 TC 122.

(22) Treas. Dept. booklet "Travel, Entertainment and Gift Expenses" [1991 Ed.], p. 6.

FOOTNOTE ¶ 2001 [USTR ¶ 2744; CCH ¶ 14,417; FTC ¶ L-2101].

(1) Treas. Dept. booklet "Travel, Entertainment and Gift Expenses" [1991 Ed.], p. 9.

(2) Rev. Proc. 90-15, 1990-1 CB 476.

FOOTNOTE ¶ 2002 [USTR ¶ 2744; CCH ¶ 14,417.122; FTC ¶ L-4600].

(1) Treas. Dept. booklet "Travel, Entertainment and Gift Expenses" [1991 Ed.], p. 4.

FOOTNOTE ¶ 2003 [USTR ¶ 624; CCH ¶ 8500 et seq.; FTC ¶ L-4700].

(1) Rev. Proc. 92-17, 1992-8 IRB 16, modifying and amplifying Rev. Proc. 90-60, 1990-2 CB 651.

FOOTNOTE ¶ 2004 [USTR ¶ 1624; CCH ¶ 8540; FTC ¶ L-1900].

(1) Treas. Dept. booklet "Business Use of a Car" [1991 Ed.], p. 2.

(2) Treas. Dept. booklet "Business Use of a Car" [1991 Ed.], p. 8.

(3) Rev. Proc. 90-59, 1990-2 CB 644, as amplified and modified by Rev. Proc. 91-67, IRB 1991-52.

(4) Treas. Dept. booklet "Business Use of a Car" [1991 Ed.], p. 3.

FOOTNOTE ¶ 2005 [USTR ¶ 1684; CCH ¶ 8540.02; FTC ¶ L-1902; L-8004].

(1) Rev. Proc. 87-57, 1987-2 CB 687.

(2) Rev. Proc. 92-43, 1992-23 IRB 23, as modifying and amplifying Rev. Proc. 91-30, 1991-1 CB 563.

(3) Treas. Dept. booklet "Business Use of a Car" [1991 Ed.], p. 7.

FOOTNOTE ¶ 2006 [USTR ¶ 280F4; CCH ¶ 8540 et seq.; FTC ¶ L-8040].

FOOTNOTE ¶ 2007 [USTR ¶ 2744; CCH ¶ 8540 et seq.; FTC ¶ L-4644].

(1) Ltr. Rul. 9117052.

(2) Rev. Proc. 91-67, IRB 1991-52, modifying and superseding Rev. Proc. 90-59, 1990-2 CB 644.

FOOTNOTE ¶ 2008 [USTR ¶ 1624; 2744; CCH ¶ 14,417 et seq.; FTC ¶ L-2100].

(1) Rev. Rul. 63-144, 1963-2 CB 129.

FOOTNOTE ¶ 2009 [USTR ¶ 2744; CCH ¶ 14,417 et seq.; FTC ¶ L-2149].

(1) Treas. Dept. booklet "Travel, Entertainment and Gift Expenses" [1991 Ed.], p. 8.

(2) Detko, ¶ 87,099 PH Memo TC.

(3) Ltr. Rul. 8321003.

FOOTNOTE ¶ 2010 [USTR ¶ 2744; CCH ¶ 14,417.09; FTC ¶ L-2300].

FOOTNOTE ¶ 2011 [USTR ¶ 2744; CCH ¶ 14,417.09; FTC ¶ L-4644].

CHAPTER 11

DEPRECIATION

DEPRECIATION IN GENERAL

A deduction for depreciation may be claimed each year for property with a limited useful life that's used in a trade or business or held for the production of income. This deduction allows taxpayers to recover their costs for the property over a period of years.

¶2100   GENERAL RULES

When figuring your tax bill, you can subtract from your income the costs you incurred to produce that income. Among these deductible costs are the expenses of income-producing assets.

You cannot, however, deduct the entire cost of such as assets all at once. Rather, you are permitted to deduct a portion of the asset's cost over a period of time--in the form of an annual allowance for depreciation [IRC Sec, 167, 168]. This deduction reflects the fact that an income-producing asset does not last forever, but eventually wears out or ceases to be useful to you.

Your annual depreciation deduction is generally a fraction or percentage of your depreciable basis, computed according to the method of depreciation used. Your depreciation deductions are computed under one of three different methods or systems: (1) the Modified Accelerated Cost Recovery System, (2) the Accelerated Cost Recovery System or (3) the useful-life (or facts-and-circumstances) system. Which system controls depreciation on a particular property depends on when you originally placed the property in service. In other words, once you place the property in service, you continue to figure your depreciation under the system in effect at that time.

Depreciation for most property placed in service after 1980 is governed by a strict statutory scheme, controlling the rate and period over which you can depreciate specific property. You compute your depreciation for property placed in service after 1986 under the Modified Accelerated Cost Recovery System (MACRS) [¶2110]. For property placed in service after 1980 and before 1987, you determine your depreciation under the Accelerated Cost Recovery System (ACRS) [2120]. The depreciation deduction allowed under MACRS and ACRS is also known as a cost recovery deduction.

The depreciation system for property placed in service before 1981 is less specific than MACRS or ACRS. It permits you a reasonable allowance for depreciation based on the particular facts and circumstances [¶2121]. You also use this system to figure depreciation on certain property you placed in service after 1980 that is ineligible for MACRS or ACRS.

¶2101   WHAT PROPERTY CAN BE DEPRECIATED

[New tax legislation may affect this subject; see ¶1.]

In general, you can claim depreciation for all property with a limited useful life of more than one year that you use in your trade or business (which includes most so-called Section 1231 assets; see ¶1811) or property held for the production of income (which falls into the category of capital assets). (You can usually currently deduct the entire cost of business property with a useful life of one year or less; see ¶2203.) Common examples of depreciable property include business machinery, office furniture, autos used in business and commercial buildings. Note: The IRS has said that when recyclable materials (which aren't depreciable) represent more than 50% of the cost of property, they must be accounted for separately. The remaining cost of the property can be depreciated.[1]

You can depreciate property available for use in your business, even though it's not actually used in the business [¶2104]. By the same token, you may be able to claim depreciation for property you hold for the production of income, although income is never produced. For example, you can depreciate a residence advertised and maintained for rental use, despite the fact that it is not rented.[2]

(a) Land. You cannot depreciate land, regardless of how it is used [IRC Sec. 167(a)(2)]. So, for example, the cost of enclosing and filling in part of a lake to create additional land for industrial facilities is considered a land acquisition cost and is not depreciable.[3]

You can, however, depreciate improvements to land. Here are some examples of depreciable improvements:

* Excavation, grading and removal costs directly associated with construction of buildings and paved roadways;[4]
* Tunnels between buildings;[5]
* Sidewalks, gutters and drains added to a mill;[6]
* Construction costs of earthen dam;[7]
* Irrigation system for citrus grove.[8]

(b) Inventories and Other Property Held for Sale. You cannot claim a depreciation deduction for property you hold for sale. You must account for decreases in the value of inventory items through inventory valuation [¶ 2710].

(c) Intangibles. Depreciation of intangible assets is commonly referred to as amortization. You may claim an amortization deduction for intangibles with limited useful lives that can be estimated with reasonable accuracy [Reg. Sec. 1.167(a)(3)]. For example, patents and copyrights are amortizable.

You cannot claim a deduction for customer goodwill you purchase from the seller of a business. That's because the goodwill has an indefinite duration. But you can amortize a payment made to a seller for a covenant not to compete.

> **NOTE:** The IRS issued an Industry Specialization Program position paper saying that intangible assets that represent "customer structures" are inseparable from any goodwill of an acquired business. In other words, if the acquired business has any goodwill, customer lists or accounts automatically become part of that nondeductible goodwill. However, the Eleventh Circuit Court of Appeals has contradicted the IRS position. Based on this case, a company that buys another business may be in a position to write off assets that are closely associated with goodwill.[9]

> ► **OBSERVATION** If you are buying a business and the seller is giving a covenant not to compete, you should be sure that (1) a separate valuation is put on the covenant and (2) the covenant is limited to a definite period of time. If these requirements are met, you can write off a portion of the covenant price annually over the fixed period.

(d) Home Office. Generally speaking, you cannot claim depreciation for any portion of a residence used for business purposes unless the portion is (1) used regularly and exclusively as (2) the principal place of your business or a place for meeting with customers, clients or patients [¶2227].

¶2102   WHO CAN DEDUCT DEPRECIATION

Taxpayers (e.g., individuals, corporations, trusts and estates) are entitled to depreciation if they will suffer the economic loss when the property depreciates in value. Ordinarily, owners meet this requirement and their deduction will not be challenged. However, bare legal title does not, by itself, guarantee the deduction. For example, a mortgagee who holds title merely for security cannot claim depreciation.

Purchased property. If you are buying depreciable property but do not yet have title, you can claim depreciation if you have assumed the benefits and burdens of ownership. Whether that assumption has occurred depends on various factors, such as: (1) how you and the seller treat the transaction; (2) whether you have acquired any equity in the property; (3) the extent of your control over the property; (4) whether you bear the risk of damage to the property; (5) whether you will receive any benefit from the operation or disposition of the property.[1]

Leased property. You cannot take depreciation on property you are leasing. However, you can depreciate improvements to the property. For example, if you construct a building on land you lease, you may claim depreciation on the building.

Life estates and remainders. You may have the right to use depreciable property during your lifetime (i.e., life estate). After you die, the property goes outright to someone else. This is known as the remainder interest.

As the holder of the life estate, you can depreciate the property as if you were the absolute owner. After your death, the holder of the remainder interest can write off any unrecovered amount [IRC Sec. 167(h)].

If you buy a life estate in nondepreciable property (e.g., land), you can amortize your cost over your remaining life expectancy. However, no amortization deduction is allowed for life estates acquired after July 27, 1989, if the remainder interest is held by a member of your family or any other related taxpayer [IRC Sec. 167(r)]. In addition, you cannot claim a deduction if you acquire a life estate by gift or inheritance [IRC Sec. 273].

¶2103   HOW MUCH CAN BE DEPRECIATED

Your annual depreciation deduction is a fraction or percentage of your "depreciable basis." Your depreciable basis, in turn, depends on which depreciation system you are using. For example, under MACRS [¶2110], your depreciable basis is generally the same as your basis for figuring gain or loss on a sale [¶1600], unadjusted for prior depreciation.

(a) Conversion of Personal Property to Business Property. A special rule applies when you convert property from personal-use property to business-use property. Your basis for figuring depreciation is the lower of (1) the property's fair market value at the time of conversion or (2) its adjusted basis [¶1600(b)] when converted [Reg. Sec. 1.167(g)-1; Prop. Reg. Sec. 1.168-2(j)(6)(ii)].

> **Example 1:** In 1992, Mr. Brown purchases a personal residence for $100,000. In 1993, he vacates the residence and rents it out. At that time, the house is worth $110,000. Result: Since Brown's adjusted basis at the time of conversion is lower than the fair market value, his basis for depreciation is $100,000.

> **Example 2:** Same facts as before, except the value of the home has declined to $90,000 in 1993. Result: Brown's basis for depreciation is $90,000.

(b) Allocation of Basis. If you purchase both depreciable and nondepreciable property for a lump sum, you must allocate your basis (cost) between the two to figure your depreciation. The depreciable part must bear the same ratio to the lump sum that the fair market value of the depreciable property bears to the entire property [Reg. Sec. 1.167(a)(5)].

> **Example 3:** Ms. Johnson purchases a small apartment house. The fair market value of the building is $200,000 and the land is worth $50,000. But Johnson is able to purchase the property for only $225,000. Result: Since 20% of the total fair market value of the property is allocable to the land, Johnson must allocate 20% of her cost—$45,000—to the land. So her basis for figuring depreciation on the building is $180,000 ($225,000 less $45,000).

> ➤ **WHAT TO DO**   Get an expert appraisal of the separate properties when you buy. Then spell out in the sales contract exactly how much of the purchase price is allocable to the depreciable property and how much to the nondepreciable.

You must make a similar allocation when you use property for both business and personal purposes. For example, when you use an auto for both personal and business travel during the year, you compute depreciation on the basis of mileage, i.e., what portion of total annual mileage is business-connected [¶2003]. When you use a house both as a personal residence and business office, your allocation is based on the number of rooms or floor space [¶2227].

(c) Self-Constructed Property. If you are building depreciable property for use in your business, your basis for the property is the cost of construction, including depreciation on the equipment used to build it. To the extent the depreciation on that equipment is allocable to the construction of the new property, you cannot deduct it currently. Instead, it must be added to the basis of the new property and depreciated along with it.[1]

¶2104   WHEN CAN YOU DEPRECIATE

Depreciation begins when an asset is "placed in service" [Reg. Sec. 1.167(a)-10(b)]. Property is considered to be placed in service in the year it is ready and available to perform the function it was designed to do. (Special "conventions" usually apply in determining at what point during the year the property is placed in service; see ¶2112(b),(g).)

> **Example 1:** XYZ, Inc. begins construction of a manufacturing building in November 1991. The building is completed in August 1992. Equipment used in the production line process is installed during September and October 1992. It is tested in November 1992. Equipment used in the finishing line process is installed in December and January 1993. All of the equipment is tested during February 1993. Production actually begins in April 1993. Result: The building is considered placed in service in August 1992, when it becomes available for the installation of equipment. So XYZ can claim a depreciation deduction for the building in 1992. None of the equipment, however, is considered placed in service until 1993. That's when the equipment first became available to produce an acceptable product.[1]

> **Example 2:** In October 1992, Mr. Crane installs new equipment in four retail stores he owns. Two of the stores are being remodeled, but remain open during the remodeling. The other stores are newly constructed and do not open for business until early 1993. Result: Crane can deduct depreciation in 1992 on the equipment installed in the remodeled stores. That's because the equipment became available for use immediately upon installation. But no depreciation can be claimed on the equipment put in the new stores until 1993. Until the stores open for business, the equipment cannot be used.[2]

When depreciation ends depends on which depreciation system you use, the type of property, the depreciation method, etc. (see below). But in no case can you claim a deduction after the property has been retired from service or has been fully depreciated.

Once you write off your cost for the property, depreciation ceases—even though the property may still be in use [Reg. Sec. 1.167(a)-1(a), 1.167(a)-10(b)].

> ▶ **OBSERVATION** You should always be sure that the correct deduction is claimed in the proper year. Once property is placed in service, you cannot accumulate depreciation and then deduct the accumulated amount in later years. Your basis in the property will be reduced each year by your allowable depreciation, even though you never actually deduct it [Reg. Sec. 1.167(a)-10(a)].

¶2105   TAX RETURNS AND RECORDKEEPING

If you report depreciation and amortization deductions, you must figure your deductions on Form 4562. (Exception: An employee claiming depreciation on a car used in his job computes depreciation on Form 2106.) You then enter the total on the appropriate expense line of the return. Individuals and fiduciaries claiming depreciation on rental property enter their Form 4562 amount on Schedule E of Form 1040. Self-employed business and professional people and fiduciaries claiming depreciation on business property report their Form 4562 amount on Schedule C of Form 1040. Unreimbursed employees claim depreciation as a miscellaneous itemized expense on Schedule A of Form 1040.

Your records should be complete and detailed enough to support and permit verification of the depreciation deductions you claim. Your regular accounting books need not reflect the same depreciation as your depreciation for tax purposes—as long as permanent auxiliary records are maintained to reconcile the differences.[1]

MODIFIED ACCELERATED COST RECOVERY SYSTEM

¶2110   MACRS IN GENERAL

The Modified Accelerated Cost Recovery System basically applies to property placed in service after 1986 [IRC Sec. 168]. With limited exceptions, the use of MACRS is mandatory. Eligible property generally must be written off in accordance with the following rules:

- *Applicable recovery period*: Depreciable assets are divided into several classes, based on how long it takes to write off an asset. For example, the "applicable recovery period" for automobiles is five years.
- *Applicable convention*: Under depreciation conventions, all property you place in service during a period is treated as placed in service at a specified point in the period. And depreciation is allowed only from that point on. MACRS real estate, for example, uses the mid-month convention. For purposes of figuring your deduction, real estate you place in service any time during a month is depreciable starting at the middle of the month. Thus, the owner of a factory building actually placed in service on November 1 is entitled to a depreciation deduction for only 1½ months on a calendar-year return.
- *Applicable depreciation method:* This is the rate at which a property is depreciated. If more than half of the cost is written off during the first half of the recovery period,

the depreciation is said to be "accelerated." MACRS generally provides for accelerated methods of depreciation.

¶2111   WHAT PROPERTY IS ELIGIBLE

MACRS applies to most tangible depreciable property, new and used, personal and real property, placed in service after 1986. (Taxpayers were given the option of electing MACRS for property placed in service on or after July 1, 1986 and before 1987.)

MACRS does not apply to an automobile if you use the standard mileage rate to compute your deductions for business-connected transportation [¶2004(b)], intangibles [¶2101(c)], and films and video tapes.

(a) Antichurning Provisions. There are special rules designed to prevent you from "churning" property you placed in service before 1987—engaging in transactions that would place the property in service after 1986 simply to make it eligible for MACRS [IRC Sec. 168(f)(5)]. MACRS does not apply to equipment and other personal property if it (1) was owned or used at any time during 1986, (2) the property is acquired from a person who owned it at any time during 1986 and (3) as part of the transaction, the user of the property did not change, or the taxpayer leased the property to a person who owned or used the property during 1986. You are not subject to the antichurning rules if they would give you a bigger deduction than you would get under MACRS [IRC Sec. 168(f)(5)(B)]. There are no MACRS antichurning rules for real estate.

(b) Tax-Free Transactions. The antichurning rules do not fully apply to all transactions. If the transferor put the property into service before 1987, you are not eligible to use MACRS on the property to the extent of the transferor's undepreciated basis. However, to the extent your basis exceeds the transferor's basis, you are eligible for MACRS.

Transactions subject to the antichurning rule are the type where no gain or loss is recognized because of a special Internal Revenue Code provision. They include: (1) transfers to controlled corporations [¶1619], (2) liquidations of subsidiary corporations [¶3235], (3) contributions to partnership by partners [¶3418], and (4) distributions by partnerships to partners [¶3420]. Note: Tax-free exchanges of like-kind property [¶1614] are not included in this list. If you acquire property after 1986 in a like-kind exchange, you must use MACRS, even though the transferor put the property into service before 1987.

(c) Depreciation Not Based on Years. MACRS does not apply to any property that (1) you can properly depreciate under a method not expressed in terms of years and (2) you elect to exclude it from MACRS [IRC Sec. 168(f)(1)]. You must make this election for the year the property is placed in service [Temp. Reg. Sec. 5h.5(a)].

Unit-of-production method. Under the unit-of-production method, your depreciation deduction is based on the estimated number of units that depreciable property will produce before it wears out [Reg. Sec. 1.167(b)-0(b)].

> **Example 1:** A machine costs $10,000. You estimate that the machine will produce 20,000 units before it is no longer useful. If it produces 2,500 units during 1992, your depreciation deduction is $1,250 ($10,000 × 2,500/20,000).

The unit-of-production method is especially suitable for figuring depreciation of equipment used in mining, oil wells and timber working.

Operating-day method. The operating-day method allows you to figure depreciation based on the number of days of life the equipment is expected to have.

> **Example 2:** You buy a machine for $15,000. The life of the machine is estimated to be 1,000 days. If you use it on 200 days during 1992, your deduction is $3,000 ($15,000 × 200/1,000).

This method may be used on rotary drilling equipment and other machinery where the major depreciation factor is the wear and tear from use.[1]

Income forecast method. You can write off the cost of leased TV films and similar property under the income forecast method of depreciation. Your deduction for any given year is computed by dividing the income produced by the property during the year by the total estimated income it will produce. This fraction is then multiplied by the cost of the property.

> **Example 3:** The cost of a TV film is $100,000 and the total estimated income to be derived from it is $150,000. Income from the film is $120,000 in 1992 and $30,000 in 1993. Your depreciation deduction is $80,000 in 1992 ($100,000 × $120,000/$150,000) and $20,000 in 1993 ($100,000 × $30,000/$150,0000.

(d) Public Utility Property. MACRS is not available to public utility property unless the benefits of MACRS are "normalized" in setting rates charged customers [IRC Sec. 168(f)(2)]. This means that the tax savings from MACRS' accelerated depreciation cannot flow to customers. Instead, they must be put in a reserve account. The reserve account is drawn upon when MACRS produces smaller deductions than a slower depreciation method. If the tax savings are not normalized, then a public utility must use the same depreciation method used in its regulated books of account.

¶2112   MACRS AND PERSONAL PROPERTY

The applicable recovery period for equipment, machinery and other personal property ranges from 3 years to 20 years, depending on the type of property [IRC Sec. 168 (b)(1)]. The applicable depreciation convention is the half-year (or midyear) convention ((b) below) [IRC Sec. 168(d)(1),(4)(A)]. The applicable depreciation method is a combination of the declining balance method and the straight line method [IRC Sec. 168(b)(1), (2)]. You have a choice of computing your allowable depreciation deduction yourself or using optional tables issued by the IRS [(e) below].

(a) Recovery Period. How quickly you can write off property depends on what the MACRS recovery period is for the property. MACRS contains six different recovery periods for personal property: 3, 5, 7, 10, 15 and 20 years. Which recovery period applies to a particular item depends on what its class life was under the Asset Depreciation Range (ADR) system.

The ADR system was an optional depreciation system used before 1981. Under ADR, the Revenue Service separated tangible property into classes and gave a range of allowable useful lives for each class.[1]

For example, with ADR, equipment used in the manufacture of glass produces could be depreciated in as little as 11 years or as long as 17 years, with 14 years being the midpoint.

MACRS generally keys its recovery periods into the midpoint class lives under ADR.

3-year property. Property falls into this category if it has an ADR midpoint life of 4 years or less. Under ADR, property with a midpoint life of 4 years or less includes: special handling devices for the manufacture of food and beverages, special tools and devices for the manufacture of rubber products, special tools for making finished plastic, fabricated metal products or motor vehicles.

While cars had a midpoint ADR life of 3 years and light trucks had one of 4 years, both are expressly excluded from MACRS' 3-year property category. Cars and light trucks are treated as 5- year property under MACRS. But racehorses more than 2 years old when placed in service and any other horses more than 12 years old when placed in service are considered 3-year property.

5-year property. This class consists of property with an ADR midpoint of more than 4 years and less than 10 years. This includes assets such as computers, typewriters, copiers, duplicating equipment, heavy purpose trucks, trailers, cargo containers and trailer-mounted containers. The category also contains cars, light-duty trucks, computer-based telephone office switching equipment, semiconductor manufacturing equipment and equipment used with research and experimentation.

7-year property. This class includes any property with a midpoint of 10 years or more and less than 16 years, including office furniture, fixtures, railroad track and single-purpose agricultural structures. Any property not assigned an ADR life is also contained here.

10-year property. This category covers property with an ADR midpoint of 16 years or more and less than 20 years. For example, this class includes barges and similar water transportation vessels, petroleum refining equipment and property used in manufacturing tobacco and certain food products.

15-year property. This class consists of property with an ADR midpoint of 20 years or more and less than 25 years. This covers sewage treatment plants, telephone distribution plants and comparable equipment used by nontelephone companies for voice and data communications.

20-year property. This covers municipal sewers and other property with an ADR midpoint of 25 years or more.

The Revenue Service generally has the power to change the ADR life—and thus possibly the MACRS recovery period—of any property [IRC Sec. 168(i)(1)]. Likewise, it can assign an ADR life to property that currently does not have one.

(b) Half-Year Convention. MACRS uses the half-year convention for personal property [IRC Sec. 168(d)(1)]. This treats all property placed in service or disposed of during a year as placed in service or disposed of at the year's midpoint. This means that you can claim a half-year's worth of depreciation in the first year you place property in service, regardless of when during the year you actually placed the property in service. Likewise if you dispose of property before the end of the recovery period, you can claim a half-year of depreciation for the disposition year.

One practical effect of the half-year convention is that you must wait until the year after the end of the recovery period to fully depreciate the property. The half year of depreciation not allowed in the first year is tacked on after the end of the recovery period.

For example, suppose you place an item of three-year property into service on April 1, 1992. You can claim only a half-year of depreciation in 1992 (even though the property is used for three-fourths of the year). In 1993 and 1994 you can claim a full year of depreciation. The remaining half year is written off in 1995—the fourth year you have claimed depreciation.

If you have a short tax year, the depreciation allowed under the half-year convention is correspondingly reduced. For example, if your tax year is only four months long, any personal property placed in service during the year would be allowed two months of depreciation.[2]

(c) Depreciation Method. MACRS property is initially depreciated under the declining balance method. For all but 15-year and 20-year property, the 200% declining balance method is used; for 15-year and 20-year property, the 150% declining balance method is used.

These methods have the effect of allowing you to recover the bulk of your cost in the first half of the recovery period. However, if you continue to use the declining balance methods over the entire recovery period, you would still have unrecovered basis at the end of the period. So, under MACRS, you switch to the straight line depreciation method at the point where it produces a larger deduction than the declining balance method.

Straight line method. Under straight line depreciation, you deduct an equal amount in each of the remaining years of the recovery period. But your *rate* of depreciation changes each year. Your rate is one divided by the number of years left in the recovery period. For example, if you have four years left, your depreciation deduction is one-fourth of your adjusted basis for the current year, one-third of your adjusted basis for the following year and so on.

Declining balance method. With the declining balance, your rate stays the same each year, but the amount of your deduction changes. Your rate is (1) one divided by the number of years in the recovery period, multiplied by (2) either 200% or 150%, depending on which declining balance method is allowed. For example if you have a five-year asset, your depreciation rate is 40%—one-fifth multiplied by 200%. This same rate is applied each year to your adjusted basis for that year.

Special elections. You can choose less accelerated methods of depreciation if you wish. You may elect to use either (1) straight line depreciation over the regular MACRS recovery periods or (2) 150% declining balance switching to straight line over the recovery periods provided in the Alternative Depreciation System [(f) below]. An election is made separately for each recovery class and covers all property in the class you put in service during the year. You must make the election by the tax return due date (including extensions) for the years.

(d) How to Figure Your MACRS Deduction. Assuming you are not electing one of the slower methods of depreciation, here is how you figure your MACRS deduction on personal property:

- Determine your declining balance rate (one divided by your recovery period);
- Multiply the basic rate by the percentage allowed for the class of property being depreciated (either 200% or 150%);
- Multiply the property's adjusted basis by the result above;

- Apply the half-year convention to figure the first year's depreciation;
- In the second year, adjust the basis for the depreciation taken for the first year;
- Multiply the adjusted basis by the same rate used in the first year;
- Continue the process until your deduction for a year figured under the declining balance method falls to that allowed under the straight line method;
- At that point switch to the straight line method until the end of the recovery period;
- In the year following the end of the recovery period, deduct your remaining adjusted basis (i.e., a half year of depreciation).

Example 1: Mr. Nolan buys office furniture (7-year property) on August 11, 1992 for $10,000. Here is how Nolan computes his depreciation deductions:

1. Nolan divides 1 by 7 to get his basic declining balance rate of 14.29%.
2. He doubles this rate to get his 200% declining balance rate of 28.58%.
3. He then multiplies his $10,000 adjusted basis by 28.58% to get $2,858, the amount of a full year's depreciation.
4. Since the half-year convention applies for 1992, the year the furniture is placed in service, his deduction for 1992 is half of $2,858—or $1,429.
5. In 1993, his depreciation deduction is $2,450—his $8,571 adjusted basis ($10,000 less $1,429) multiplied by 28.58%.
6. For 1994, his deduction is $1,749 ($6,121 adjusted basis × 28.58%).
7. For 1995, his deduction is $1,250 ($4,373 adjusted basis × 28.58%).
8. For 1996, his deduction is $892 ($3,122 adjusted basis × 28.58%.)
9. For 1997, his deduction under the 200% declining balance method would be $637 ($2,230 adjusted basis × 28.58%). Under the straight line method, his rate would be 40% (1 divided by 2.5 remaining years of depreciation) and his deduction would be $892 ($2,230 × 40%). So Nolan switches to the straight line method and deducts $892.
10. For 1998, his straight line rate is 66.66% (1 divided by 1.5 years) and he deducts $892 (66.66% × $1,338).
11. For 1999, he deducts his remaining adjusted basis—$446—to recover the total $10,000 cost of the furniture.

(e) Optional MACRS Table. Instead of figuring your MACRS deduction as described above, you have the option of using a table issued by the Revenue Service.[3]

The table gives you the percentage depreciation rate to be used each year for each class of property and reflects half-year convention and the switch from the declining balance method to the straight line method. The rate is to be applied to the property's basis unadjusted for prior depreciation. However, you reduce the basis by any expensing deduction [¶2113] you claim for the property.

You can use the table for some items of personal property and not others, even within the same class. But once you begin using the table for an item, you must continue to use the table for the entire recovery period. However, if there is a reduction in an item's basis because of a casualty, you can no longer use the table. Beginning with the year of the casualty adjustment, you must figure your deduction the long way.

The optional table is reproduced on the next page.

If the Recovery Year is:	3-year	5-year	and the Recovery Period is: 7-year	10-year	15-year	20-year
			the Depreciation Rate is:			
1	33.33	20.00	14.29	10.00	5.00	3.750
2	44.45	32.00	24.49	18.00	9.50	7.219
3	14.81	19.20	17.49	14.40	8.55	6.677
4	7.41	11.52	12.49	11.52	7.70	6.177
5		11.52	8.93	9.22	6.93	5.713
6		5.76	8.92	7.37	6.23	5.285
7			8.93	6.55	5.90	4.888
8			4.46	6.55	5.90	4.522
9				6.56	5.91	4.462
10				6.55	5.90	4.461
11				3.28	5.91	4.462
12					5.90	4.461
13					5.91	4.462
14					5.90	4.461
15					5.91	4.462
16					2.95	4.461
17						4.462
18						4.461
19						4.462
20						4.461
21						2.231

(f) Alternate Method. You may elect an Alternative Depreciation System (ADS) for most property [IRC Sec. 168(g)(7)]. ADS is a less accelerated depreciation system than regular MACRS, and might be elected, for example, by a new company that wants to conserve depreciation deductions for future use—when its income is more highly taxed. Under ADS, you use straight line depreciation and, in many cases, longer recovery periods than the standard MACRS periods. The regular depreciation conventions apply—either half-year or midquarter [(b), (g) below] for the year the property is placed in service and disposed of. The recovery periods for ADS are:

- 5 years for cars, light trucks, qualified technological equipment and semiconductor manufacturing equipment,
- 9.5 years for computer-based telephone central-office switching equipment,
- 10 years for railroad track,
- 12 years for personal property with no class life,
- 15 years for single-purpose agricultural and horticultural structures,
- 24 years for municipal waster water treatment plants and telephone distribution plants and other equipment used for 2-way exchange of voice and data communications,
- 50 years for municipal sewers, and
- For all other property, the midpoint of its class life [(a) above].

You make a separate ADS election for each class of recovery property. And you can make an ADS election for a particular class one year and not the next. But once an election is made it is irrevocable.[4]

ADS required. In some situations, the use of ADS is mandatory, not elective. You must use ADS for (1) certain "listed" property [(h) below], (2) tangible property used predominantly outside of the U.S., (3) property leased, used, or financed by a tax-exempt organization, and (4) property imported from a foreign country that maintains discriminatory trade practices [IRC Sec. 168(g)(1)]. You also use ADS for computing earnings and profits in determining how much of a corporate distribution is a taxable dividend [¶ 1218 (a)].

(g) Special Mid-Quarter Convention. If a large portion of the depreciable personal property you place in service during a year is placed in service in the last calendar quarter, you may not be permitted to use the half-year convention. You must use a "mid-quarter" convention if the combined bases of property placed in service during the last three months of the tax year exceed 40% of the combined bases of personal property put in service during the entire year [IRC Sec. 168(d)(3)].

> **IRS REGULATIONS** The IRS has issued proposed regulations that explain the rules for applying the 40% mid-quarter convention test. Property that you do not depreciate under MACRS (for example, certain public utility property, films and video tapes, and sound recordings) should not be counted when applying the 40% test. On the other hand, you should take into account "listed property" (for example, cars, entertainment property, computers and cellular phones) [Prop. Reg. Sec.1.168(d)-1]. Note: The regs also say that you reduce the basis of property placed in service during the year by any expensing deduction claimed for the property. The proposed regulations apply to property placed in service in tax years ending after January 30, 1991.

Under the mid-quarter convention, all property you place in service or sell or otherwise dispose of during any quarter of a tax year is treated as placed in service or disposed of at the quarter's midpoint. This has the effect of increasing your depreciation deduction for property placed in service in the first two quarters of the year and decreasing your deduction for property placed in service in the last quarter. Instead of deducting 50% of a full year's depreciation for all property placed in service during the year, the mid-quarter convention gives you an 87.5% deduction for property placed in service in the first quarter, 62.5% deduction for second quarter property, 37.5% for third quarter property and 12.5% for fourth quarter property.

Whether the mid-quarter convention benefits you or hurts you depends on how much property you place in service in each quarter.

Example 2: Alpha Corp., a calendar-year taxpayer, placed two items of property into service during 1992—both five-year properties. The first item cost $40,000 and was placed in service in February. The other item cost $30,000 and was placed in service in December. Result: Since more than 40% of total bases of property put in service in 1992 was put in service during the fourth quarter ($30,000 of $70,000 total), Alpha must use the mid-quarter convention. For the $40,000 item, a full year's depreciation would be $16,000 (40% rate for five-year property × $40,000), assuming Alpha doesn't use ADS. So Alpha can deduct $14,000 (87.5% of $16,000). For the $30,000 item, the full year deduction would be $12,000, so Alpha can deduct $1,500 (12.5% of $12,000). Total 1992 depreciation deduction: $15,500. By comparison, with the half-year convention, Alpha's total deduction would be only $14,000.

Example 3: Beta Corp., also a calendar year taxpayer, makes the same purchases as Alpha Corp., except that it puts the $40,000 item in service in July. Result: Beta also is subject to the mid-quarter convention. But it only gets a 1992 deduction of $6,000 for the $40,000 item (37.5% of $16,000). So its total 1992 depreciation for the two items is $7,500—$8,000 less than Alpha's and $6,500 less than with the half-year convention.

> **OBSERVATION** Timing your equipment and machinery purchases is crucial if you are dealing with the mid-quarter convention. For example, if Beta had simply waited until January 1993 to place the $30,000 item into service, it would not have been subject to the mid-quarter convention and its 1992 depreciation would have been $500 higher. Or if it had accelerated the purchase—putting the $30,000 item into service before the fourth quarter—its deduction would have been $6,500 higher.

Tax-free transfers. A special rule applies if you place property in service and later in the same year you transfer the property to a related party in a tax-free transfer [¶2111(b)]. For purposes of determining whether your transferee meets the 40% threshold, the date of the transfer between you two is the date the transferee is deemed to place the property into service. However, if the transferee is subject to the mid-quarter convention, the allowable depreciation is governed by the date the property was originally placed in service by you.[5]

Example 4: The sole owner of a calendar-year corporation puts property into service on February 1 and then transfers it to the corporation on November 1. For purposes of determining whether or not the corporation is subject to the mid-quarter convention, the property is considered placed in service on November 1. But if the corporation must use the mid-quarter convention, allowable depreciation is computed from the midpoint of the first quarter.

Optional tables. The Revenue Service has issued four tables that may be used to compute depreciation for property subject to the mid-quarter convention.[6] The tables, one for each quarter during the year property is placed in service, are reproduced starting below.

(h) Listed Property. A special depreciation rule applies to "listed" property. Listed property includes cars and other property used for transportation, computers, cellular phones placed in service after 1989, and any other property generally used for entertainment, recreation and amusement (e.g., phonographs, video recording equipment, etc.). Under the special rule, listed property is not eligible for either regular MACRS depreciation or the expensing deduction [¶2113] unless you use it more than 50% of the time in qualified business use (see below) [IRC Sec. 280F]. If the business use is 50% or less, you must depreciate the property on a straight-line basis under ADS [(f) above]. Automobiles (but not other listed property) are also subject to special dollar limits on depreciation [¶2005(c)].

If the Recovery Year is:	Property Placed in Service in the 1st Quarter and the Recovery Period is:					
	3-year	*5-year*	*7-year*	*10-year*	*15-year*	*20-year*
	the Depreciation Rate is:					
1	58.33	35.00	25.00	17.50	8.75	6.563
2	27.78	26.00	21.43	16.50	9.13	7.000
3	12.35	15.60	15.31	13.20	8.21	6.482
4	1.54	11.01	10.93	10.56	7.39	5.996
5		11.01	8.75	8.45	6.65	5.546
6		1.38	8.74	6.76	5.99	5.130
7			8.75	6.55	5.90	4.746
8			1.09	6.55	5.91	4.459
9				6.56	5.90	4.459
10				6.55	5.91	4.459
11				0.82	5.90	4.459
12					5.91	4.460
13					5.90	4.459
14					5.91	4.460
15					5.90	4.459
16					0.74	4.460
17						4.459
18						4.460
19						4.459
20						4.460
21						0.557

Property Placed in Service in the 2nd Quarter
and the Recovery Period is:

If the Recovery Year is:	3-year	5-year	7-year	10-year	15-year	20-year
			the Depreciation Rate is:			
1	41.67	25.00	17.85	12.50	6.25	4.688
2	38.89	30.00	23.47	17.50	9.38	7.148
3	14.14	18.00	16.76	14.00	8.44	6.612
4	5.30	11.37	11.97	11.20	7.59	6.116
5		11.37	8.87	8.96	6.83	5.658
6		4.26	8.87	7.17	6.15	5.233
7			8.87	6.55	5.91	4.841
8			3.33	6.55	5.90	4.478
9				6.56	5.91	4.463
10				6.55	5.90	4.463
11				2.46	5.91	4.463
12					5.90	4.463
13					5.91	4.463
14					5.90	4.463
15					5.91	4.462
16					2.21	4.463
17						4.462
18						4.463
19						4.462
20						4.463
21						1.673

Property Placed in Service in the 3rd Quarter
and the Recovery Period is:

If the Recovery Year is:	3-year	5-year	7-year	10-year	15-year	20-year
			the Depreciation Rate is:			
1	25.00	15.00	10.71	7.50	3.75	2.813
2	50.00	34.00	25.51	18.50	9.63	7.289
3	15.57	20.40	18.22	14.80	8.66	6.742
4	8.33	12.24	13.02	11.84	7.80	6.237
5		11.30	9.30	9.47	7.02	5.769
6		7.06	8.85	7.58	6.31	5.336
7			8.86	6.55	5.90	4.936
8			5.53	6.55	5.90	4.566
9				6.56	5.91	4.460
10				6.55	5.90	4.460
11				4.10	5.91	4.460
12					5.90	4.460
13					5.91	4.461
14					5.90	4.460
15					5.91	4.461
16					3.69	4.460
17						4.461
18						4.460
19						4.461
20						4.460
21						2.788

If the Recovery Year is:	3-year	5-year	Property Placed in Service in the 4th Quarter and the Recovery Period is: 7-year	10-year	15-year	20-year
			the Depreciation Rate is:			
1	8.33	5.00	3.57	2.50	1.25	0.938
2	61.11	38.00	27.55	19.50	9.88	7.430
3	20.37	22.80	19.68	15.60	8.89	6.872
4	10.19	13.68	14.06	12.48	8.00	6.357
5		10.94	10.04	9.98	7.20	5.880
6		9.58	8.73	7.99	6.48	5.439
7			8.73	6.55	5.90	5.031
8			7.64	6.55	5.90	4.654
9				6.56	5.90	4.458
10				6.55	5.91	4.458
11				5.74	5.90	4.458
12					5.91	4.458
13					5.90	4.458
14					5.91	4.458
15					5.90	4.458
16					5.17	4.458
17						4.458
18						4.459
19						4.458
20						4.459
21						3.901

For purposes of the 50% test, qualified business use is any use of the property in a trade or business, *except*:

- The leasing of the property to someone who has a 5% or more ownership in the business;
- The use of the property as compensation for services unless the amount of the compensation is reported on the appropriate information return (and, where required, income tax is withheld on the compensation);
- The use of the property as compensation to someone who has a 5% or more ownership interest in the business—even when the compensation is properly reported on an information return; and
- The use of property for investment purposes.

Example 5: Mr. Johnson is a 50% owner of XYZ, Inc. XYZ provides Johnson with a home computer. Johnson uses the computer 45% of the time in XYZ's business, 30% of the time for personal investing, and 25% for entertainment purposes. As required, XYZ reports the value of Johnson's 55% nonbusiness use on his Form W-2 and withholds income tax on it. Result: Only 45% of the computer's use is considered a qualified business use. So XYZ must use straight-line depreciation under ADS to compute its deductions.

Employee-owned listed property. If you own listed property for use in your employer's business, you may claim depreciation on the property only if your use is (1) for the convenience of your employer and (2) required as a condition of employment [IRC Sec. 280F(d)(3)]. Your use of the property is regarded as for your employer's convenience only if your use is for a substantial business reason of your employer. Your use is considered a condition of employment only if it is required for you to properly perform your duties.

Example 6: Mr. Nelson is an inspector for a construction company with many construction sites in the local area. Nelson is required to travel to the various construction sites on a regular basis. The company does not furnish Nelson an automobile and does not explicitly require him to use one. However, the company reimburses him for his expenses in traveling to the various sites. Result: Nelson's use of the car is for the convenience of his employer and is required as a condition of his employment. So he may claim depreciation on the car to the extent of the business use.

Example 7: Ms. Bronson is a sales manager for a manufacturing company. She frequently takes work home at night. She buys a home computer to help her track sales, do departmental budgets, write reports and so forth. Result: Bronson does not meet the convenience-of-employer or the condition-of-employment requirements. So she may not claim depreciation on her computer.

➤ **OBSERVATION** The Revenue Service has ruled that no depreciation is allowed for a computer unless there is a clear showing that the employee cannot properly perform the duties of employment without it.[7] However, the Tax Court has taken a more liberal position. The Court allowed a couple without access to a computer at work to write off their home computer because it "substantially aided" them in the performance of their job.[8]

Recapture. If you meet the 50% requirement in the first year of use and fail to meet it in a subsequent year, you must begin using ADS in that subsequent year. In addition, you must include in income in that year, your "excess depreciation" claim in the prior year(s). Excess depreciation is (1) the amount of depreciation (including any expensing deduction) [¶2113] you actually claimed during the prior year(s), less (2) the amount of depreciation that you would have been allowed using straight line depreciation under ADS.

Example 8: Ms. Lester, a sole proprietor, bought a $10,000 computer in September 1991. (Computers have a five-year recovery period under both regular MACRS and ADS.) During the year, she used it 60% of the time for business purposes and 40% for personal purposes. Using regular MACRS, she claimed a depreciation deduction of $1,200 ($6,000 × 40% rate for 5-year property × ½). With ADS, her straight line deduction would have been $600 ($6,000 × 20% × ½). If Lester's business use falls to 50% or less in 1992, she must include $600 ($1,200 less $600) in income.

(i) Dispositions. A disposition is the permanent withdrawal of property from use in your trade or business. A disposition may be made by sale, exchange, retirement, abandonment or destruction.

If you dispose of property before you have fully recovered your cost, you are entitled to a depreciation deduction in the year of disposition. Your deduction is determined as if you disposed of the property in the middle of the year or the middle of the quarter, depending on the convention that was used when the property was originally placed in service.

Example 9: Mr. Foley placed a business car in service on December 1, 1990. It was the only item of business property placed in service in 1990. Therefore, Foley was required to use the mid-quarter convention to compute his 1990 depreciation deduction on the car. Foley disposes of the car on July 10, 1992 and acquires a new one. Result: Under the mid-quarter convention, Foley is considered to have disposed of his old car at the midpoint of the third quarter. So he is entitled to a 1992 depreciation deduction equal to 62.5% of a full year's deduction. And, assuming the half-year convention applies to the new car, he also gets 50% of a full year's deduction on the new car.

If you transfer property to a related party in a tax-free transfer [¶2111(b)], the normal rule for dispositions does not apply. Instead, you compute your depreciation deduction as if you retained the property for the entire year. Then the full year's deduction is allocated between you and your related-party transferee, according to which portion of the year each of you held the property.[8]

(j) Mass Asset Accounts. You may elect to treat all property of one MACRS class placed in service during a year as a single asset [IRC Sec. 168(i)(4)]. You claim one deduction for the mass asset account, computed on the combined adjusted bases of the individual properties. If you dispose of an item from the mass account, any proceeds you receive are fully taxable. The adjusted basis of the asset you disposed of remains in the account and continues to be depreciated after you dispose of it.

¶2113　　　　　　　　　　**EXPENSING DEDUCTION**

[New tax legislation may affect this subject; see ¶1.]

Instead of depreciating tangible personal property under MACRS, you may elect to treat all or part of the cost of the property as a currently deductible expense [IRC Sec. 179].

Your expensing deduction (also known as a Sec. 179 deduction) cannot exceed the lesser of $10,000 or your taxable income for the year. The $10,000 maximum can be allocated among more than one asset in whichever way you choose. If only one asset is placed in service during the year and its cost is less than the maximum, the deduction is limited to that cost. Expensing deductions that are disallowed because of the taxable income limit are carried over to succeeding tax years. You use carryover deductions on a first-in-first-out basis—that is, carryovers from earlier years are used first [Prop. Reg. Sec. 1.179-3]..

If your combined cost of items placed in service during the year exceeds $10,000, you can write off each item's non- expensed cost through MACRS. The amount you expense of each item must be subtracted from the item's basis. This reduced basis is the amount you use to compute your MACRS deduction. Therefore electing the expense deduction reduces your MACRS deduction.

Example 1: In 1992, Mr. O'Connor purchases a forklift for $40,000 and welding equipment for $1,200 for use in his construction business. He elects to expense the entire $1,200 cost of the welding equipment and $8,800 of the cost of the forklift. Since the welding equipment is completely expensed, there is no MACRS deduction for it. O'Connor can claim an MACRS deduction for the forklift. But his adjusted basis for computing his deduction is $31,200 ($40,000 less $8,800).

➤ **OBSERVATION** Under proposed IRS regulations, the expensing deduction can be a way to avoid the effect of the mid-quarter convention [¶2112(g)]. Reason: Property expensed is not included in determining whether the mid-quarter convention applies.

Example 2: XYZ, Inc., a calendar-year taxpayer, puts two items of personal property into service in 1992, each costing $10,000. One is put into service in February 1992 and the other in November 1992. If XYZ expenses the February item, it will get a $10,000 expensing deduction, but it's depreciation deduction is subject to the mid-quarter rules and its deduction for the November item will be only 12.5% of a full year's deduction (one-half of a quarter). On the other hand, if it expenses the November item, it will get a $10,000 deduction and the mid-quarter rules don't apply. So it gets a half-year's depreciation on the February item.

Limitations. Several restrictions are imposed on the use of the expensing deduction:

1. If the combined cost of personal property you place in service during the year exceeds $200,000, then the $10,000 maximum is reduced dollar-for-dollar by the excess over $200,000. So your expensing deduction is completely phased out if you place in service more than $210,000 of personal property during the year.

2. Married couples (whether filing jointly or separately) are subject to the same $10,000/$200,000 limitations as single taxpayers. The same is true for a group of controlled corporations. In partnerships and S corporations, the limitations apply both to the partnership or corporation and to the individual partners and shareholders. You cannot carry over to future years any unused expense deductions due to the dollar limit on property.[1]

NOTE: To ease recordkeeping and reporting burdens, the cost of property placed in service by an S corporation or partnership is not attributed to the shareholders or partners. Thus, once the S corporation or partnership has applied the $200,000 limit, its costs for Sec. 179 property won't be counted again at the shareholder or partner level [Prop. Reg. Sec. 1.179-2(b)(3),(4)].

3. If you acquire property in a nontaxable like-kind exchange, the adjusted basis of the old asset is excluded in computing your expense deduction for the new asset.

4. You can expense property only if you use it in an active trade or business. The expensing deduction is not available for investment property you hold for the production of income.

5. Your expensing deduction cannot exceed the taxable income you derive from any trade or business during the year.

> **NOTE:** If you are an employee, you are considered to be engaged in the active conduct of the trade or business of your employment. So wages or other compensation you receive as an employee count as your business income [Prop. Reg. Sec. 1.179-2(c)(5)(iv)].

6. You cannot expense property that you acquire by gift or from a decedent or a "related" party (e.g., your parents or children or a corporation in which you own more than 50% of the stock).

7. You cannot expense "listed" property [¶2112(h)] if you do not use the item predominantly (i.e., more than 50%) for business purposes.

Recapture. If you dispose of expensed property before the end of the MACRS recovery period for the property, you must recapture the tax benefit you received from the expensing deduction. You must include in income the difference between (1) the expensing deduction (and depreciation deductions, if any) you have claimed before the year of disposition and (2) the deductions you would have been allowed under regular MACRS without expensing. Recapture also applies where there is no disposition, but your business use of the property falls below 50% of your total use. For example, if you expense an item and later convert it to personal use, you would be subject to recapture. (Note: There are different recapture rules for listed property [¶2112(h)].)

Election. Your election to expense property must specify the assets it applies to and the portion of the cost of each item to be currently deducted. You must make the election by the due date (including extensions) of the return for the tax year in which you placed the property in service. Once you make the election, you may not revoke it without IRS consent.

¶2114   MACRS AND REAL ESTATE

[New tax legislation may affect this subject; see ¶1.]

Real estate is divided into two classes for figuring MACRS depreciation: residential rental real estate and nonresidential real estate [IRC Sec. 168(b), (c)]. A building is considered residential rental property only if 80% or more of the gross rents come from dwelling units. A dwelling unit is a house or apartment used to provide living accommodations. It does not include a unit of a hotel, motel or any other establishment where more than half of the units are used on a transient basis.

If you own a building and use one of the units as a personal residence, you include that unit's rental value in determining if the 80% test is met.

> **Example 1:** Ms. McDonald owns a six-unit building, five residential apartments and one professional office. She lives in one unit and rents out the other four apartments and the office. Gross annual rent from the office: $15,000. Gross rent from each apartment: $12,000. Result: Assuming the rental value of McDonald's apartment is also $12,000, her building is considered a residential rental property—even though less than 80% of her actual rents come from the apartments. When you figure in the rental value of her apartment, exactly 80% ($60,000/$75,000) comes from residential rents.

(a) How to Figure Your Depreciation Deduction. For real estate subject to MACRS, the recovery period for residential rental property is 27.5 years; for nonresidential property, it's 31.5 years [IRC Sec. 168(c)]. There is no accelerated depreciation for MACRS real estate. You must use straight line depreciation [IRC Sec. 168(b)(3)].

> ➤ **OBSERVATION** Anything with an ADR class life [¶2112(a)] of less than 27.5 years is *not* considered real estate. Since land improvements—for example, parking lots, sidewalks, roads, and fences—have a 20-year ADR life,[1] you can depreciate them more rapidly than real estate. They qualify as 15-year property and you can write them off using the 150% declining balance method of depreciation.

The applicable depreciation convention for real estate is the mid-month convention. (Unlike personal property, there is no special rule for substantial fourth-quarter purchases of real estate.) Any real property, residential or nonresidential, you place in service during a year is depreciable from the midpoint of the month it is placed in service. (The mid-month convention also applies in the year of disposition.) So, unlike personal property with its half-year convention, the size of your first-year deduction depends on when you place the property in service.

Example 2: Mr. Green buys an office building for $240,000, $40,000 of which is allocable to the land. He places the building in service on October 8, 1992. His depreciation deduction for a full year would be $200,000 divided by the 31.5 year recovery period, or $6,350. Since he is considered to have placed the building in service in mid-October, he is entitled to 2½ months of depreciation for 1992. So his deduction is $1,323 (5/24 × $6,350).

Example 3: Same facts as before, except that Green puts the property into service on April 10, 1992. Now he is entitled to 8½ months of depreciation in 1992. So his deduction is $4,498 (17/24 × $6,350).

Since the mid-month convention applies, you do not have to make any adjustment in your real estate depreciation for short tax years.

(b) Optional Tables. Instead of computing depreciation as described in (a), you may use optional tables issued by the IRS.[2]

There are separate tables for residential rental and nonresidential properties. Each table lists the percentage depreciation to be applied to the unadjusted basis of a property in each taxable year and varies according to which month the property was first placed in service. The tables are on the next page.

Residential Rental Property

And the Month in the First Recovery Year the Property is Placed in Service is:

If the Recovery Year is:	1	2	3	4	5	6	7	8	9	10	11	12
						the Depreciation Rate is:						
1	3.485	3.182	2.879	2.576	2.273	1.970	1.667	1.364	1.061	0.758	0.455	0.152
2	3.636	3.636	3.636	3.636	3.636	3.636	3.636	3.636	3.636	3.636	3.636	3.636
3	3.636	3.636	3.636	3.636	3.636	3.636	3.636	3.636	3.636	3.636	3.636	3.636
4	3.636	3.636	3.636	3.636	3.636	3.636	3.636	3.636	3.636	3.636	3.636	3.636
5	3.636	3.636	3.636	3.636	3.636	3.636	3.636	3.636	3.636	3.636	3.636	3.636
6	3.636	3.636	3.636	3.636	3.636	3.636	3.636	3.636	3.636	3.636	3.636	3.636
7	3.636	3.636	3.636	3.636	3.636	3.636	3.636	3.636	3.636	3.636	3.636	3.636
8	3.636	3.636	3.636	3.636	3.636	3.636	3.636	3.636	3.636	3.636	3.636	3.636
9	3.636	3.636	3.636	3.636	3.636	3.636	3.636	3.636	3.636	3.636	3.636	3.636
10	3.637	3.637	3.637	3.637	3.637	3.637	3.636	3.636	3.636	3.636	3.636	3.636
11	3.636	3.636	3.636	3.636	3.636	3.636	3.637	3.637	3.637	3.637	3.637	3.637
12	3.637	3.637	3.637	3.637	3.637	3.637	3.636	3.636	3.636	3.636	3.636	3.636
13	3.636	3.636	3.636	3.636	3.636	3.636	3.637	3.637	3.637	3.637	3.637	3.637
14	3.637	3.637	3.637	3.637	3.637	3.637	3.636	3.636	3.636	3.636	3.636	3.636
15	3.636	3.636	3.636	3.636	3.636	3.636	3.637	3.637	3.637	3.637	3.637	3.637
16	3.637	3.637	3.637	3.637	3.637	3.637	3.636	3.636	3.636	3.636	3.636	3.636
17	3.636	3.636	3.636	3.636	3.636	3.636	3.637	3.637	3.637	3.637	3.637	3.637
18	3.637	3.637	3.637	3.637	3.637	3.637	3.636	3.636	3.636	3.636	3.636	3.636
19	3.636	3.636	3.636	3.636	3.636	3.636	3.637	3.637	3.637	3.637	3.637	3.637
20	3.637	3.637	3.637	3.637	3.637	3.637	3.636	3.636	3.636	3.636	3.636	3.636
21	3.636	3.636	3.636	3.636	3.636	3.636	3.637	3.637	3.637	3.637	3.637	3.637
22	3.637	3.637	3.637	3.637	3.637	3.637	3.636	3.636	3.636	3.636	3.636	3.636
23	3.636	3.636	3.636	3.636	3.636	3.636	3.637	3.637	3.637	3.637	3.637	3.637
24	3.637	3.637	3.637	3.637	3.637	3.637	3.636	3.636	3.636	3.636	3.636	3.636
25	3.636	3.636	3.636	3.636	3.636	3.636	3.637	3.637	3.637	3.637	3.637	3.637
26	3.637	3.637	3.637	3.637	3.637	3.637	3.636	3.636	3.636	3.636	3.636	3.636
27	3.636	3.636	3.636	3.636	3.636	3.636	3.637	3.637	3.637	3.637	3.637	3.637
28	1.970	2.273	2.576	2.879	3.182	3.485	3.636	3.636	3.636	3.636	3.636	3.636
29	0.000	0.000	0.000	0.000	0.000	0.000	0.152	0.455	0.758	1.061	1.364	1.667

Nonresidential Real Property

And the Month in the First Recovery Year the Property is Placed in Service is:

If the Recovery Year is:	1	2	3	4	5	6	7	8	9	10	11	12
						the Depreciation Rate is:						
1	3.042	2.778	2.513	2.249	1.984	1.720	1.455	1.190	0.926	0.661	0.397	0.132
2	3.175	3.175	3.175	3.175	3.175	3.175	3.175	3.175	3.175	3.175	3.175	3.175
3	3.175	3.175	3.175	3.175	3.175	3.175	3.175	3.175	3.175	3.175	3.175	3.175
4	3.175	3.175	3.175	3.175	3.175	3.175	3.175	3.175	3.175	3.175	3.175	3.175
5	3.175	3.175	3.175	3.175	3.175	3.175	3.175	3.175	3.175	3.175	3.175	3.175
6	3.175	3.175	3.175	3.175	3.175	3.175	3.175	3.175	3.175	3.175	3.175	3.175
7	3.175	3.175	3.175	3.175	3.175	3.175	3.175	3.175	3.175	3.175	3.175	3.175
8	3.175	3.174	3.175	3.174	3.175	3.174	3.175	3.175	3.175	3.175	3.175	3.175
9	3.174	3.175	3.174	3.175	3.174	3.175	3.174	3.175	3.174	3.175	3.174	3.175
10	3.175	3.174	3.175	3.174	3.175	3.174	3.175	3.174	3.175	3.174	3.175	3.174
11	3.174	3.175	3.174	3.175	3.174	3.175	3.174	3.175	3.174	3.175	3.174	3.175
12	3.175	3.174	3.175	3.174	3.175	3.174	3.175	3.174	3.175	3.174	3.175	3.174
13	3.174	3.175	3.174	3.175	3.174	3.175	3.174	3.175	3.174	3.175	3.174	3.175
14	3.175	3.174	3.175	3.174	3.175	3.174	3.175	3.174	3.175	3.174	3.175	3.174
15	3.174	3.175	3.174	3.175	3.174	3.175	3.174	3.175	3.174	3.175	3.174	3.175
16	3.175	3.174	3.175	3.174	3.175	3.174	3.175	3.174	3.175	3.174	3.175	3.174
17	3.174	3.175	3.174	3.175	3.174	3.175	3.174	3.175	3.174	3.175	3.174	3.175
18	3.175	3.174	3.175	3.174	3.175	3.174	3.175	3.174	3.175	3.174	3.175	3.174
19	3.174	3.175	3.174	3.175	3.174	3.175	3.174	3.175	3.174	3.175	3.174	3.175
20	3.175	3.174	3.175	3.174	3.175	3.174	3.175	3.174	3.175	3.174	3.175	3.174
21	3.174	3.175	3.174	3.175	3.174	3.175	3.174	3.175	3.174	3.175	3.174	3.175
22	3.175	3.174	3.175	3.174	3.175	3.174	3.175	3.174	3.175	3.174	3.175	3.174
23	3.174	3.175	3.174	3.175	3.174	3.175	3.174	3.175	3.174	3.175	3.174	3.175
24	3.175	3.174	3.175	3.174	3.175	3.174	3.175	3.174	3.175	3.174	3.175	3.174
25	3.174	3.175	3.174	3.175	3.174	3.175	3.174	3.175	3.174	3.175	3.174	3.175
26	3.175	3.174	3.175	3.174	3.175	3.174	3.175	3.174	3.175	3.174	3.175	3.174
27	3.174	3.175	3.174	3.175	3.174	3.175	3.174	3.175	3.174	3.175	3.174	3.175
28	3.175	3.174	3.175	3.174	3.175	3.174	3.175	3.174	3.175	3.174	3.175	3.174
29	3.174	3.175	3.174	3.175	3.174	3.175	3.174	3.175	3.174	3.175	3.174	3.175
30	3.175	3.174	3.175	3.174	3.175	3.174	3.175	3.174	3.175	3.174	3.175	3.174
31	3.174	3.175	3.174	3.175	3.174	3.175	3.174	3.175	3.174	3.175	3.174	3.175
32	1.720	1.984	2.249	2.513	2.778	3.042	3.175	3.174	3.175	3.174	3.175	3.174
33	0.000	0.000	0.000	0.000	0.000	0.000	0.132	0.397	0.661	0.926	1.190	1.455

(c) Alternative Depreciation System. In lieu of regular MACRS depreciation, you may elect to use the Alternative Depreciation System (ADS) to depreciate real estate. You can make this election on a property-by-property basis. For example, if you put two apartment buildings into service in one year, you can use regular MACRS on one and elect ADS on the other. You must make the election to use ADS in the year you place the property in service. Once you make the election, it is irrevocable.

Under ADS, you write off the cost of your property using the straight line method, the mid-month convention and a 40-year recovery period. The same recovery period is used for both residential and nonresidential properties.

(d) Additions or Improvements. You treat an addition or improvement to a building as a separate property under MACRS. You do not simply add it to the depreciable basis of the building. Instead, you must depreciate the addition or improvement separately, using straight line depreciation, the mid-month convention and appropriate recovery period (e.g. 27.5 years for an improvement to a residential rental property). Depreciation begins on the later of (1) the date on which you place the addition or improvement in service or (2) the date on which you place the building in service [IRC Sec. 168(j)(6)].

If you are leasing property and make an improvement to it, you must use the normal MACRS recovery period for the improvement—regardless of the length of the lease. For example, if you lease land for 20 years, and erect a nonresidential building on it, you must use a 31.5-year recovery period to figure your depreciation deductions.

OTHER DEPRECIATION SYSTEMS

¶2120　　　　　　ACCELERATED COST RECOVERY SYSTEM

The Accelerated Cost Recovery System (ACRS) applies to depreciable property placed in service after 1980 and before 1987. ACRS has been replaced by MACRS [¶2110], but it continues to govern current deductions for property you originally placed in service in those years.

In many ways, ACRS is similar to MACRS. They both allow accelerated depreciation of property over a fixed period specified by law. But in several key respects, ACRS differs from MACRS:

- ACRS has no 7-or 20-year property classes.

Cars and trucks are in the 3-year class rather than the 5-year class.

The recovery period for real estate is much shorter under ACRS than MACRS.

Instead of MACRS-prescribed depreciation methods (with depreciation tables optional), ACRS mandates the use of tables.

ACRS does not permit a depreciation deduction in the year personal property is disposed of.

- ACRS has no special depreciation rule that applies when a large amount of property is placed in service in the last quarter of the year.

(a) Recovery Period for Personal Property. The cost of equipment, machinery and other personal property you placed in service under ACRS is generally written off over 3, 5, 10 or 15-year periods. The precise period depends on what ACRS class your property falls in [IRC Sec. 168(c); note that all ACRS references to the Internal Revenue Code are to the Code as it existed prior to the Tax Reform Act of 1986].

3-year property includes cars, light-duty trucks, property used in research and experimentation, and all other property with an ADR midpoint life [¶2112(a)] of four years or less.

5-year property covers all depreciable personal property not included in any other class, such as most kinds of production machinery, office furniture and equipment and heavy-duty trucks.

10-year property includes railroad tank cars, mobile and prefab homes, certain coal burning equipment, public utility property with an ADR midpoint life of 18½ to 25 years and real estate with an ADR midpoint life of 12.5 years of less (e.g. theme park structures).

15-year property covers public utility property with an ADR midpoint life of more than 25 years.

(b) Depreciation Methods for Personal Property. You find your ACRS deduction for each year of the recovery period by multiplying the unadjusted basis of the property (less any expensing deduction claimed) by a percentage prescribed by law. The applicable percentage depends on the property's class and the number of years since you placed the property in service [IRC Sec. 168(b)(1)]. The prescribed percentages are reproduced on the next page.

The applicable percentage for the class of property is:

If the recovery year is:	3-year	5-year	10-year	15-year public utility
1	25	15	8	5
2	38	22	14	10
3	37	21	12	9
4		21	10	8
5		21	10	7
6			10	7
7			9	6
8			9	6
9			9	6
10			9	6
11				6
12				6
13				6
14				6
15				6

Example 1: In November 1986, Mr. Baker bought a mobile home for $47,000 that he rented out. The mobile home is 10-year property under ACRS. Since 1992 is the seventh depreciation year for the item, Mr. Baker can claim a 1992 depreciation deduction of $4,230 for the mobile home (9% of $47,000).

NOTE: The depreciation percentages for each year are based on a 150% declining balance method of depreciation in the early years of the recovery period and a switch to straight line in the later years [¶2112(c)]. They are figured under a half-year depreciation convention for the year the property was placed in service [¶2112(b)]. So, as with MACRS, your first-year deduction under ACRS was the same no matter when property is placed in service during a year.

If you dispose of ACRS property before the end of its last depreciation year, you cannot claim a deduction for the year of disposition [IRC Sec. 168(d)(2)].

Alternate depreciation method. ACRS provides a straight line depreciation method [¶2112(c)] in lieu of the specified depreciation percentages. ACRS also allows alternate recovery periods [IRC Sec. 168(b)(3)] as follows:

Type of Property	*Recovery Periods Available*
3-year property	3, 5 or 12 years
5-year property	5, 12 or 25 years
10-year property	10, 25 or 35 years
15-year public utility property	15, 35 or 45 years

The straight-line method and alternate recovery periods had to be elected in the year you originally placed the property into service (i.e., before 1987). If you elected the alternate method, you use the half-year convention in both the year the property was placed in service and in the year following the end of the recovery period. Like regular ACRS, no deduction is allowed in the year you dispose of the property. And you cannot revoke your election without IRS consent.

Example 2:

(c) ACRS and Real Estate. You generally depreciate all real estate, both residential and nonresidential, in the same way under ACRS (unlike MACRS where residential and nonresidential properties have different recovery periods). Like ACRS personal property, you find your percentage depreciation rate for each year from a table prescribed by law [IRC Sec. 168(b)(2)]. The percentages are based on a 175% declining balance method switching to straight line [¶2112(c)]. However, because of statutory changes made in the recovery period and depreciation convention during the years ACRS was in effect, there are four different tables. The one you use depends on when your property was placed in service:

- For real estate placed in service after 1980 and before March 16, 1984, the table percentages are based on a 15-year recovery period. And any property placed in service during a year is depreciated from the first day of the month you place it into service.
- For real estate placed in service after March 15, 1984 and before June 23, 1984, the recovery period is 18 years. But property continues to be depreciable from the first day of the month it is placed in service.
- For real estate placed in service after June 22, 1984 and before May 9, 1985, the recovery period is 18 years, but a mid-month convention applies. Property placed in service during any month is depreciable from the midpoint of that month.
- For real estate placed in service after May 8, 1985 and before 1987, the recovery period is 19 years with a mid- month depreciation convention.

The ACRS real estate tables are reproduced below.

Table I   15-year Real Property (other than low-income housing)

Year	Month Placed in Service											
	1	2	3	4	5	6	7	8	9	10	11	12
1st	12%	11%	10%	9%	8%	7%	6%	5%	4%	3%	2%	1%
2nd	10%	10%	11%	11%	11%	11%	11%	11%	11%	11%	11%	12%
3rd	9%	9%	9%	9%	10%	10%	10%	10%	10%	10%	10%	10%
4th	8%	8%	8%	8%	8%	8%	9%	9%	9%	9%	9%	9%
5th	7%	7%	7%	7%	7%	7%	8%	8%	8%	8%	8%	8%
6th	6%	6%	6%	6%	7%	7%	7%	7%	7%	7%	7%	7%
7th	6%	6%	6%	6%	6%	6%	6%	6%	6%	6%	6%	6%
8th	6%	6%	6%	6%	6%	6%	5%	6%	6%	6%	6%	6%
9th	6%	6%	6%	5%	5%	6%	5%	5%	5%	6%	6%	6%
10th	5%	6%	5%	6%	5%	5%	5%	5%	5%	5%	6%	5%
11th	5%	5%	5%	5%	5%	5%	5%	5%	5%	5%	5%	5%
12th	5%	5%	5%	5%	5%	5%	5%	5%	5%	5%	5%	5%
13th	5%	5%	5%	5%	5%	5%	5%	5%	5%	5%	5%	5%
14th	5%	5%	5%	5%	5%	5%	5%	5%	5%	5%	5%	5%
15th	5%	5%	5%	5%	5%	5%	5%	5%	5%	5%	5%	5%
16th	—	—	1%	1%	2%	2%	3%	3%	4%	4%	4%	5%

Table II

18-year Real Property
(placed in service after March 15, 1984 and before June 23, 1984)

Year	Month Placed in Service										
	1	2	3	4	5	6	7	8	9	10-11	12
1st	10%	9%	8%	7%	6%	6%	5%	4%	3%	2%	1%
2nd	9%	9%	9%	9%	9%	9%	9%	9%	9%	10%	10%
3rd	8%	8%	8%	8%	8%	8%	8%	8%	9%	9%	9%
4th	7%	7%	7%	7%	7%	7%	8%	8%	8%	8%	8%
5th	6%	7%	7%	7%	7%	7%	7%	7%	7%	7%	7%
6th	6%	6%	6%	6%	6%	6%	6%	6%	6%	6%	6%
7th	5%	5%	5%	5%	6%	6%	6%	6%	6%	6%	6%
8-12th	5%	5%	5%	5%	5%	5%	5%	5%	5%	5%	5%
13th	4%	4%	4%	5%	5%	4%	4%	5%	4%	5%	5%
14-18th	4%	4%	4%	4%	4%	4%	4%	4%	4%	4%	4%
19th	—	—	1%	1%	1%	2%	2%	2%	3%	3%	4%

Table III

18-year Real Property
(placed in service after June 22, 1984 and before May 9, 1985)

Year	Month Placed in Service											
	1	2	3	4	5	6	7	8	9	10	11	12
1st	9%	9%	8%	7%	6%	5%	4%	4%	3%	2%	1%	0.4%
2nd	9%	9%	9%	9%	9%	9%	9%	9%	9%	10%	10%	10%
3rd	8%	8%	8%	8%	8%	8%	8%	8%	9%	9%	9%	9%
4th	7%	7%	7%	7%	7%	8%	8%	8%	8%	8%	8%	8%
5th	7%	7%	7%	7%	7%	7%	7%	7%	7%	7%	7%	7%
6th	6%	6%	6%	6%	6%	6%	6%	6%	6%	6%	6%	6%
7th	5%	5%	5%	5%	6%	6%	6%	6%	6%	6%	6%	6%
8-12th	5%	5%	5%	5%	5%	5%	5%	5%	5%	5%	5%	5%
13th	4%	4%	4%	5%	4%	4%	5%	4%	4%	4%	5%	5%
14-17th	4%	4%	4%	4%	4%	4%	4%	4%	4%	4%	4%	4%
18th	4%	3%	4%	4%	4%	4%	4%	4%	4%	4%	4%	4%
19th	—	1%	1%	1%	2%	2%	2%	3%	3%	3%	3%	3.6%

Table IV

19-year Real Property

Year	Month Placed in Service											
	1	2	3	4	5	6	7	8	9	10	11	12
1st	8.8	8.1	7.3	6.5	5.8	5.0	4.2	3.5	2.7	1.9	1.1	0.4
2nd	8.4	8.5	8.5	8.6	8.7	8.8	8.8	8.9	9.0	9.0	9.1	9.2
3rd	7.6	7.7	7.7	7.8	7.9	7.9	8.0	8.1	8.1	8.2	8.3	8.3
4th	6.9	7.0	7.0	7.1	7.1	7.2	7.3	7.3	7.4	7.4	7.5	7.6
5th	6.3	6.3	6.4	6.4	6.5	6.5	6.6	6.6	6.7	6.8	6.8	6.9
6th	5.7	5.7	5.8	5.9	5.9	5.9	6.0	6.0	6.1	6.1	6.2	6.2
7th	5.2	5.2	5.3	5.3	5.3	5.4	5.4	5.5	5.5	5.6	5.6	5.6
8th	4.7	4.7	4.8	4.8	4.8	4.9	4.9	5.0	5.0	5.1	5.1	5.1
9th	4.2	4.3	4.3	4.4	4.4	4.5	4.5	4.5	4.5	4.6	4.6	4.7
10-19th	4.2	4.2	4.2	4.2	4.2	4.2	4.2	4.2	4.2	4.2	4.2	4.2
20th	0.2	0.5	0.9	1.2	1.6	1.9	2.3	2.6	3.0	3.3	3.7	4.0

You can claim a depreciation deduction in the year you dispose of the real estate. But you must apportion the deduction to reflect the months the property is actually in service during the disposition year [Prop. Reg. Sec. 1.168-2(g)(3)(iv)(B)].

Example 3: XYZ, Inc. put an office building into service in December 1986. The building cost $400,000, $100,000 of which was allocable to the nondepreciable land. XYZ sold the building on July 10, 1992. Under ACRS, the building is 19-year property. The depreciation percentage for the seventh year of property placed in service in December is 5.6%. So if XYZ had kept the property for all of 1992, its deduction would be $16,800. But, since it sold the property in July, it is entitled to only 6½ months of depreciation. So its deduction is $9,100 (6.5/12 × $16,800).

Alternate depreciation method. Straight line depreciation could have been elected for ACRS real estate in the year a property was placed in service. For 15-year property, ACRS allows alternate recovery periods of either 15, 35 or 45 years. For 18-year property, the recovery periods are 18, 35 or 45 years. And for 19-year real estate, the periods are 19, 35 or 45 years.

Improvements to ACRS real estate. If you make an improvement or addition to property being depreciated under ACRS, you cannot write off the improvement or addition under ACRS. As long as the improvement or addition was placed in service after 1986, you must depreciate it using a longer recovery period and the straight line method under MACRS [¶2114].[1]

Example 4: Mr. Varner put a two-family rental house into service in 1981. He has been depreciating it as 15-year ACRS real estate. In April, 1991, he put a new roof on the house. The roof must be depreciated as residential MACRS real estate. That means he must use straight line depreciation and a 27½ year recovery period.

¶2121 USEFUL LIFE DEPRECIATION SYSTEM

You write off depreciable personal and real property placed in service before 1981 under the useful life (or facts and circumstances) system. You generally recover the cost of the property over the estimated useful life of the property, using a reasonable depreciation method [Reg. Sec. 1.167(a)-1]. However, for property placed in service after 1970, you were allowed to elect the Asset Depreciation Range (¶2112(a)) [Reg. Sec. 1.167(a)-11(a)] [¶2112(a)].

(a) Useful Life. The useful life of a property is an estimate of how long you can expect to use it in your trade or business. It is not how long the property will last, but how long it will continue to be useful to you, taking into account the frequency of use, your repair policy, and the conditions in the area surrounding the property.

Suppose you placed property into service before 1981 and the facts on which you based your estimated useful life have now changed significantly. You may revise your estimate if (1) there is a clear and convincing basis for your change and (2) the change in the estimate is significant [Reg. Sec. 1.167(a)-1(b)].

(b) Depreciation Methods. Straight line and declining balance methods of depreciation [¶2112(c)] are permitted under the useful life system. However, you may use 200% declining balance only for property that was new when you placed it in service and had a useful life of more than three years or more. And used depreciable real property is generally limited to 125% declining balance (for residential rental property) or straight line (for other real estate).

If you want to change the depreciation method you have been using, you generally must file Form 3115 with the Revenue Service. You must file the form in the first 180 days of the tax year the change is to take effect.

➤ **OBSERVATION** If you have been depreciating property under the declining balance method, you may now want to switch to the straight line method. The declining balance method will leave you with a portion of your cost unrecovered at the end of the property's useful life; the straight line method won't. Note: You can make a switch from the declining balance method to the straight line method without filing Form 3115.

(c) Salvage Value. The salvage value is the second hand value of property at the expected time of disposition. The total amount that can be written off under the useful life system is ordinarily the adjusted basis of the property less the property's salvage value. Once determined, salvage value doesn't change due to price fluctuations. However, it may be changed if you revise a property's useful life [¶2121(a)]. You may ignore salvage value to the extent of 10% of the cost of the property. (Note: Salvage value is ignored completely under ACRS and MACRS.)

Footnotes to Chapter 11

(For your added convenience, in brackets [] with the footnotes below, you will find citations to related paragraphs in the "RIA United States Tax Reporter"(USTR), "CCH Federal Tax Reporter"(CCH) and "RIA Federal Tax Coordinator 2d"(FTC) multivolume services.)

FOOTNOTE ¶ 2100 [USTR ¶ 1674; CCH ¶ 11,001; FTC ¶ L-7500 et seq., 9507].

FOOTNOTE ¶ 2101 [USTR ¶ 1674.006; CCH ¶ 11,007; FTC ¶ L-7751, 7772].

(1) Rev. Rul. 90-65, 1990-2 CB 41.

(2) Robinson, 2 TC 305; Ltr. Rul. 8030017.

(3) Rev. Rul. 77-270, 1977-2 CB 79.

(4) Rev. Rul. 65-265, 1965-2 CB 52.

(5) Edwards, 23 AFTR 730.

(6) Clinton Cotton Mills, Inc., 16 AFTR 380.

(7) Fancher, 10 AFTR 2d 5925.

(8) Rev. Rul. 80-25, 1980-1 CB 65; Rev. Rul. 83-128, 1983-2 CB 57.

(9) Citizens & Southern Corp., 900 F.2d 266 (11th Cir.).

FOOTNOTE ¶ 2102 [USTR ¶ 1674.002; CCH ¶ 11.004.10; FTC ¶ L-7650 et seq.].

(1) Houchins, 79 TC 570.

FOOTNOTE ¶ 2103 [USTR ¶ 1674.037; CCH ¶ 11,001; FTC ¶ L-7851 et seq.].

(1) Idaho Power Co., 34 AFTR 2d 74-5244.

FOOTNOTE ¶ 2104 [USTR ¶ 1674.085; CCH ¶ 11,025; FTC ¶ L-7550 et seq.].

(1) Rev. Rul. 76-238, 1976-1 CB 55.

(2) Piggly Wiggly Southern, Inc., 59 AFTR 2d 87-304, 803 F.2d 1572 (USCA 11), aff'g. 84 TC 739.

FOOTNOTE ¶ 2105 [USTR¶ 1674.058; CCH ¶ 11,001 et seq.; FTC ¶ L-9816, 9817].

(1) Rev. Rul. 59-389, 1959-2 CB 89.

FOOTNOTE ¶ 2110 [USTR ¶ 1684; CCH ¶ 11,256; FTC ¶ L-9500 et seq.].

FOOTNOTE ¶ 2111 [USTR ¶ 1684; CCH ¶ 11,258; FTC ¶ L-7830,7848].

(1) Rev. Rul. 56-652, 1956-2 CB 125.

FOOTNOTE ¶ 2112 [USTR ¶ 1684.01; CCH ¶ 11,258; FTC ¶ L-7851, 7871].

(1) Rev. Proc. 83-85, 1983-1 CB 745.

(2) Rev. Proc. 89-15, 1989-1 CB 816.

(3) Rev. Proc. 87-57, 1987-2 CB 687; Treas. Dept. booklet "Depreciation" (1991 Ed.), p. 24.

(4) Rev. Proc. 87-57, 1987-2 CB 687; Treas. Dept. booklet "Depreciation" (1991 Ed.), p. 68.

(5) Ltr. Rul. 8948015.

(6) Treas. Dept. booklet "Depreciation" (1991 Ed.), p. 25.

(7) Rev. Rul. 86-129, 1986-2 CB 48; Ltr. Rul. 8725067.

(8) Ltr. Rul. 8948015.

FOOTNOTE ¶ 2113 [USTR¶ 1794; CCH ¶ 12,126; FTC ¶ L-7961 et seq.].

(1) Treas. Dept. booklet "Depreciation" (1991 Ed.), p. 5.

FOOTNOTE ¶ 2114 [USTR ¶ 1684.02; CCH ¶ 11,258; FTC ¶ L-7851, 7901, 7902].

(1) Rev. Proc. 87-56, 1987-2 CB 674.

(2) Rev. Proc. 87-57, 1987-2 CB 687; Treas. Dept. booklet "Depreciation" (1991 Ed.), p. 27.

FOOTNOTE ¶ 2120 [USTR ¶ 1688.400; CCH ¶ 11,258; FTC ¶ L-7851, 7902].

(1) Treas. Dept. booklet "Depreciation" (1991 Ed.), p. 8.

FOOTNOTE ¶ 2121 [USTR ¶ 1674.040; CCH ¶ 11,029; FTC ¶ L-7501 et seq.].

CHAPTER 12

BUSINESS DEDUCTIONS

BUSINESS EXPENSES IN GENERAL

A broad variety of costs qualify as deductible business expenses. Some of these are discussed in other chapters: For example, retirement plan contributions are covered in Chapter 3, travel and entertainment in Chapter 10 and depreciation in Chapter 11. This chapter brings together a diverse group of deductible expenses incurred in business by companies, self-employeds and employees alike. The writeoffs range from compensation, insurance, home offices and education to depletion and farming expenses.

¶2201   WHAT IS A DEDUCTIBLE EXPENSE

An expense, to be deductible, must be: (1) ordinary and necessary; (2) paid or incurred during the tax year; and (3) related to carrying on a trade or business [IRC Sec. 162; Reg. Sec. 1.162-1].

(a) Ordinary and Necessary. An *ordinary* expense is one that is commonly incurred in your trade or business. It may vary, depending on the time, place and circumstances under which it is incurred.[1] A *necessary* expense need not be "essential." It may be necessary if it is "appropriate and helpful" to your business or occupation.[2]

Among items included as business expenses are: management expenses; commissions; labor; supplies; incidental repairs; operating expenses of automobiles used in the trade or business; traveling expenses while away from home in the pursuit of a trade or business; advertising and other selling expenses; insurance premiums against fire, storm, theft, accident, or other similar losses as to a business; and rental for using business property [Reg. Sec. 1.162-1(a)].

(b) How Treated on Return. Business expenses are generally deductions for adjusted gross income [IRC Sec. 62(a)(1)]. If you are the sole owner of an unincorporated business, you must report business income and expenses on Schedule C (Form 1040). Partnerships are required to file Form 1065 and a Schedule K listing the total of the partners' share of income, deductions, credits, etc. Each partner's distributive share of specially allocated items is shown on the appropriate line of his or her Schedule K-1.

A corporation's business expenses are deductions from gross income. Corporations file either Form 1120 or short Form 1120-A, and S corporations file Form 1120-S. For employee business expenses, see ¶2226.

¶2202 EXPENSES INCURRED IN TRADE, BUSINESS OR PROFESSION

Expenses paid or incurred by a self-employed individual in a trade, business or profession are deductions for adjusted gross income [IRC Sec. 62(a)(1); Reg. Sec. 1.62-1]. They are not limited to actual out-of-pocket "expenses," but may also include losses, bad debts, depreciation, etc. To be deductible as ordinary and necessary expenses of a trade, business or profession, the expenses must be:

- *Directly* connected with your trade, business or profession [IRC Sec. 162(a); Reg. Sec. 1.162-1]; and
- *Reasonable* in amount.[1]

State income taxes on gross income from a trade or business are deductible in computing adjusted gross income. Those taxes on *net income* from business , however, are *not* deductible in computing adjusted gross income.[2] Both the Tax Court and IRS hold that state income taxes are business expenses for the net operating loss deduction.[3]

¶2203   TAX TREATMENT OF CAPITAL EXPENDITURES

A capital expenditure is an outlay to acquire property or make a permanent improvement that extends beyond the tax year. Such an expenditure, generally, is not fully deductible in the year incurred [IRC Sec. 263(a); Reg. Sec. 1.263(a)-1]. Instead, the cost is written off through a series of depreciation or amortization deductions over a number of years. Some examples of capital expenditures are: (1) commissions paid in buying securities; (2) the cost of defending or perfecting title to property; (3) amounts expended for an architect's services; (4) the cost of good will as to acquiring the assets of a going concern [Reg. Sec. 1.263(a)(2)]; and (5) certain stock redemption payments [IRC Sec. 162(k)]. Depreciation and amortization expenses are reported on Form 4562 [¶2105].

Commissions paid in selling securities are generally offset against the sales price. However, a dealer in securities may treat these commissions as ordinary and necessary business expenses [Reg. Sec. 1.263(a)-2].

Deductible as Expenses

Expenses of installing accounting and cost system;[1] moving machinery;[2] cost of automobile worn out and junked by company in 6 months.[3]

Special Rules

Costs of investigating a new business are capital expenditures generally recoverable only on sale or final disposition of the business. If the taxpayer actually enters into a project for profit and the project is later abandoned, the expenses are deductible as a loss in the year of abandonment.[4]

Payments to eliminate competition. If the restraint is for a definite term, the cost may be written off over that time period. However, if the restriction is permanent or indefinite, no deduction is allowed. If an agreement not to compete is part of indivisible contract for sale of all assets of a business, no deduction is allowed.[5]

Dissolution and liquidation expenses of a corporation are deductible as ordinary and necessary business expenses in the year dissolution occurs.[6]

Expenses for handicapped. Costs up to $15,000 to make any facility or vehicle used in a trade or business more accessible to the handicapped or elderly are currently deductible [IRC Sec. 190]. See also ¶ 2411 for availability of tax credit .

Payments to cancel supply contract. The payment to terminate a long-term supply contract is a currently deductible business expense if it eliminates future expenses. The payment must be capitalized if it is linked to future income.[7]

Trademark expense. You must generally capitalize trademark and trade name expenditures. You can recover these expenditures when you dispose of the asset.

A business expense deduction can be taken for amounts paid or incurred on selling or transferring a franchise, trademark or trade name that is contingent on its productivity, use or disposition. However, if you retain any significant power, right or continuing interest in the property, the writeoff may have to be spread out over a number of years [IRC Sec. 1253; Prop. Reg. Sec. 1.1253-1(c)(1)].

Business start-up expenses. No deduction is allowed for start-up expenses. However, you can elect to amortize business start-up expenses over a period of not less than 60 months [IRC Sec. 195]. Start-up expenses include: (1) those that you have in connection with setting up an active trade or business, or for investigating the possibility of creating or acquiring an active trade or business: (2) amounts incurred in any activity engaged in for profit in anticipation of the activity becoming an active business, which are not currently deductible as interest [IRC Sec. 163(a)], taxes [IRC Sec. 164] or research and experimental expenses [IRC Sec. 174]; (3) pre-opening costs which, if paid or incurred in the operation of an existing business, would be allowable as a deduction for the year paid or incurred; and (4) expenses for the production of income incurred before business activities start. If the trade or business is disposed of before the end of the amortization period, any unamortized start-up expenses may be deducted as losses [IRC Sec. 195(b)(2)].

The IRS has adopted a three-prong test for determining when a company starts doing business. A company first functions as a "going concern" when it (1) acquires the assets it needs to conduct business; (2) the assets are put to productive use; and (3) the business is producing income.[8]

¶2204   EXPENSES FOR TAX-EXEMPT INCOME

Business expenses allocable to tax-exempt income are not deductible [IRC Sec. 265(a)(1)]. In addition, no deduction is allowed for interest on a loan to buy or carry tax-exempt securities [¶1905].

Example: Lee paid a $4,000 service fee to manage investments that produced $16,000 of income—$2,000 of which was tax-exempt interest. One-eighth of the fee ($2,000/$16,000 x $4,000) or $500 is disallowed.[1]

An unrecognized involuntary conversion gain [¶1711] is not tax-exempt income for this purpose.[2] Likewise, tax-free parsonage or off-base military housing allowances do not cause the disallowance of deductions for home mortgage interest and property taxes.

¶2205   EXPENSES FOR DONATED INVENTORY

In general, you deduct your cost or other basis of inventory donated to charity. However, there are special rules that provide corporations (other than S corporations) with a bigger deduction for donations of inventory used for the care of the ill, needy or infants. The deduction is the corporation's basis plus one-half the appreciation—but the deduction cannot exceed twice the basis (¶2701; 2720(c)) [IRC Sec. 170(e)(3)].

¶2206   EXPENSES FOR POLITICAL PURPOSE

Generally no business deduction is allowed for direct or indirect payments for political purposes. Indirect contributions include: (1) admission to a dinner or program where the proceeds of the affair would benefit a political party or candidate; (2) admission to an inaugural ball, parade, concert, or similar event that is identified with a candidate or party; and (3) advertising in a publication (including a convention program) where the proceeds benefit a party or candidate [IRC Sec. 276].

¶2207   ILLEGAL BUSINESS OR PAYMENT

Operating expenses of an illegal or questionable business are deductible.[1] But expenses of an inherently illegal nature, such as bribery and protection payments, are not deductible[2] [IRC Sec. 162(c), (f), (g); Reg. Sec. 1.162-18, 1.162-21]. No deductions or credits are allowed for amounts paid for illegal trafficking in drugs listed in the Controlled Dangerous Substances Act or the law of the state where the activity is conducted [IRC Sec. 280E]. However, the general disallowance of deductions doesn't affect the deduction from gross receipts for cost of goods sold. A deduction for payments to foreign government employees is disallowed only if it violates the Foreign Corrupt Practices Act [IRC Sec. 162(c)(1)]. Formerly, the deduction would be disallowed if it would be illegal under any U.S. law. The 6th Circuit has allowed a deduction for legal kickback payments that meet the "ordinary and necessary" business expense test.[3]

COMPENSATION FOR SERVICES

¶2210   DEDUCTION FOR COMPENSATION

You may deduct what you pay for personal services actually rendered for you in connection with your trade, business or profession provided the payment is reasonable (¶2211)[IRC Sec. 162(a); Reg. Sec. 1.162-7]. Wages paid *solely* for services that are personal to the employer (for example, to domestics) are not deductible [IRC Sec. 262; Reg. Sec. 1.262-1]. For when you can claim the deduction, see ¶2840.

Child employed by parent. Wages (except the cost of meals and lodging) you pay to your minor child for services actually rendered as a bona fide employee in your business are deductible even if the child uses the wages for part of his or her own support.[1]

> ▶ **INCOME-SHIFTING OPPORTUNITY** Unlike unearned income (e.g., interest and dividends), wages received by your under-age-14 child are taxed in the child's own tax bracket—not at your higher tax rate [¶ 1240]. This is true even if you are the employer. This, in effect, provides an opportunity to shift business profits into your child's low tax bracket.

¶2211 REASONABLENESS OF COMPENSATION

The question of reasonableness of compensation generally arises only if there is some relationship between the parties in addition to that of employer and employee; for example, if the employee is also a stockholder of a corporate employer or if he is the proprietor's child or parent.

There is no precise rule to determine the exact amount of compensation that is considered reasonable. It is an amount that would ordinarily be paid for like services by like enterprises under like circumstances [Reg. Sec. 1.162-7(b)(3)]. The facts in each case control. For example, a company is justified in paying more to an owner-employee who is instrumental in boosting company profits.[1]

Factors of reasonableness are the character and amount of responsibility, difficulty of the work itself, time required, working conditions, future prospects, general cost of living in the locality, individual ability, technical training, profitability to the employer of the services rendered and the number of available persons capable of performing the duties of the position.

> ➤ **OBSERVATION** The IRS may examine a situation in which an officer-stockholder with a controlling interest in a corporation gets a large payment of compensation, especially if the corporation has a history of paying small dividends.

¶2212 PAYMENT FOR SERVICES

In addition to being reasonable, the compensation, to be deductible, must be paid purely for services. If the purported compensation is actually a payment for the transfer of property by the employee, then it is a nondeductible capital expenditure. A payment may be a dividend if it is excessive and bears a close relationship to the employee's stockholdings [Reg. Sec. 1.162-7, 1.162-8].

¶2213 COMMISSIONS

Amounts paid for services are deductible, the same as ordinary salaries [Reg. Sec. 1.162-1].

(a) Advances to Salespersons. These amounts, originally intended as loans, but later considered paid by the employer, are compensation to the salespersons and deductible by the employer in the year charged off.[1]

(b) Buying and Selling Commissions. Commissions paid in buying and selling property, such as securities and real estate, are generally not deductible by the investor, trader or dealer. These are either added to the property's cost or offset the selling price, and thereby determine the gain or loss on the property's later sale.[2] However, a dealer may deduct commissions as an expense [Reg. Sec. 1.263(a)-2]. Selling commissions deducted for estate tax purposes can *not* be offset against the selling price [IRC Sec. 642(g)]. Commissions paid for buying or selling a residence can be deducted if they qualify as moving expenses of an employee or self-employed person [¶1935 et seq.].

¶2214   BONUSES AND OTHER ADDITIONAL COMPENSATION

Compensation paid to employees in addition to their regular salary or wage, is deductible by the employer only if the total compensation package is reasonable. Any excess (unreasonable) amount is not deductible [Reg. Sec. 1.162-9]. For fringe benefits, see Chapter 4.

(a) Wages During Military Reserve Leaves. Amounts paid by employers to employees while they are on leave to attend National Guard or Army and Navy Reserve training are additional compensation and are deductible.[1]

(b) Employee Benefits. Amounts paid for dismissal wages, unemployment benefits and guaranteed annual wages are deductible.

Payments to an employee because of injuries (even if paid in a lump sum) are deductible to the extent not compensated for by insurance or otherwise [Reg. Sec. 1.162-10].

Amounts paid under sickness, accident, hospitalization (including reimbursement of Medicare premiums to active or retired employees and contributions to welfare fund for these premiums[2]), recreational, welfare or similar benefit plans are also deductible. If, however, these amounts may be used to provide benefits under a deferred compensation pension, or profit-sharing plan, they are deductible under the rules covering such plans [Reg. Sec. 1.162-10].

Contributions to retirement plans may be deductible. The tax rules are covered in Chapter 3.

(c) Employer's Deduction for Restricted Property. An employer who gives restricted property as compensation to his employee may claim a deduction equal to the amount included in the employee's gross income. The deduction is allowed in the employer's accounting period including the close of the tax year in which the employee treats the restricted property as income (¶1208(a))][IRC Sec. 83(h); Reg. Sec. 1.83-6].

¶2215   COMPENSATION FOR SERVICES PERFORMED IN PRIOR YEARS

Reasonable payments for services performed in prior years are deductible.[1] However, payment must be authorized in the year that the deduction is claimed.[2]

¶2216   FEES TO ATTORNEYS, ACCOUNTANTS AND OTHER PROFESSIONALS

Fees you pay to attorneys and other professionals are deductible if incurred [IRC Sec. 212(3); Reg. Sec. 1.162-1, 1.212-1]:
- In a transaction directly connected with, or closely resulting from, your trade, business or profession, or
- In producing or collecting income, or managing, conserving or maintaining property held for the production of income, or
- In the determining, collecting or refunding of any tax.

Deductible fees include reasonable administration expenses of an estate or trust as well as fees you pay for legal advice as to investments, loans to protect stockholdings and advice on the rearrangement of an estate.[1]

The Supreme Court has held that legal fees paid in defending a criminal action are deductible if they are an ordinary and necessary business expense, even if the defense is unsuccessful.[2] A disallowance of the deduction must be supported by some governmental statement of a national or state public policy considered to be frustrated.

Deductible

Fees for defense of malpractice suit, disbarment proceedings, mail fraud proceedings,[3] suit against a director of a corporation,[4] expense of defending against a court martial;[5] attorney's fees in connection with additional income tax on taxpayer's (or transferor's) business,[6] or in suit to recover income tax deficiencies assessed on property held for production of income,[7] or in will contest resulting in increase of taxpayer's share of trust income;[8] legal and accounting fees in contesting income tax deficiency and fraud penalties and effecting compromise settlement;[9] tax or investment counseling fees paid by a corporation for the benefit of its executives;[10] legal fees in suit for negligent destruction of rental property.[11]

Nondeductible

Fees in suing for slander[12], or libel[13] (unless livelihood threatened);[14] fees to recover nontaxable damages for personal injuries suffered on business trip;[15] defense of contested election by public officer;[16] defense of title to property;[17] legal advice as to selection of securities for gift; preparation of a will; obtaining or defending a suit for divorce or separate maintenance,[18] even if expenses are to conserve income-producing property;[19] (but fees are deductible if incurred for the production or collection of alimony or separate maintenance payments that are includible in gross income [Reg. Sec. 1.262-1]); defense of assault or bribery charges (neither business connected).[20]

Capital expenditures. Occasionally, an attorney's fee may be a capital expenditure. Examples: Fees paid to secure a long-term lease of real estate;[21] fees for reducing an assessment for a local benefit;[22] and fees for tax advice on changing corporate capital structure (merger, stock split and proposed redemption).[23]

Cost of corporate takeover attempt: The IRS has said that takeover costs incurred during a hostile takeover for advisors (attorneys, accountants, etc.) are currently deductible by a target company if the costs do not create a long-term benefit.[24] However, takeover costs paid to the acquiring company (greenmail, cost of repurchasing stock, etc.) are always treated as capital costs and must be written off over a period of years. And the U.S. Supreme Court has said that financial and legal expenses a company incurred to facilitate its own takeover are capital expenses.[25]

¶2217   GOLDEN PARACHUTE PAYMENTS

"Parachute payments" are usually additional compensation given to key executives by a corporation that is the target of a takeover attempt. Effective for agreements entered into after June 14, 1984, there is generally no deduction allowed for payments in money or property in excess of the "base amount" under a "golden parachute" agreement [IRC Sec. 280G; Prop. Reg. Sec. 1.280G-1]. There is a 20% nondeductible excise tax on the excess amount, as well as social security tax [IRC Sec. 4999].

A golden parachute agreement is an agreement: (1) That calls for payments or property transfers contingent on a change in the corporate ownership or control or a significant portion of its assets; (2) under which payments are to be made to a "disqualified individual," i.e., officer, shareholder, highly compensated employee, independent contractor, or personal service corporation performing services for the corporation; (3) if the aggregate present value of the payments equals or exceeds three times the "base amount" (below); (4) if at least some part of the payments isn't reasonable compensation for services actually rendered.

NOTE: For purposes of the "disqualified individual" rules: (1) A company cannot have more than 50 employees (or, if less, the greater of three employees or 10% of the corporation's employees) who are "officers." (2) A "shareholder" is an owner holding at least $1 million in company stock or 1% of all the outstanding stock. (3) A "highly compensated individual" is a member of the highest paid 1% of employees of the corporation (or top-paid 250 employees, if less); the annual compensation, though, must be at least $75,000 [Prop. Reg. Sec. 1.280G-1] .

"Base amount" is the disqualified individual's average annualized compensation from the corporation during the five-year period preceding the change in ownership or control.

Example: Howard Kohl was a director of Corp. A which was taken over by Corp. Z. Under an agreement, Corp. A paid Howard $500,000 on the date of the takeover. Howard's base amount was $120,000. The $500,000 payment to Howard was an excess parachute payment because it exceeded $360,000 (3 x $120,000 base amount). The excess payment not deductible by Corp. A is $380,000 ($500,000 less $120,000). Also, Howard must pay the excise tax of $76,000 (20% x $380,000).

➤ **OBSERVATION** Excluded from the term "parachute payments" are payments to (or for the benefit of) a disqualified individual relating to (1) a small business corporation, or (2) a corporation whose stock was not readily tradeable on an established securities market, provided that shareholder approval was obtained for the payment. For the tradeable stock test, the term "stock" does not include any stock that is nonvoting, nonconvertible, limited and preferred as to dividends and loss redemption and liquidation rights limited to its issue price provided the parachute payments do not affect the shareholder's redemption rights [IRC Sec. 280G(b)(4), (5); Prop. Reg. Sec. 1.280G-1].

REPAIRS, RENT, ADVERTISING, INSURANCE

¶2220   **REPAIRS**

The cost of repairs to property used in a trade, business or profession and of repairs to property held for the production of income is deductible as an ordinary and necessary expense [IRC Sec. 162(a); Reg. Sec. 1.162-4; 1.212-1]. The cost of repairs to your residence is not deductible. If the property is held by you as rental property, the cost of repairs is deductible even though it was formerly your residence [Reg. Sec. 1.212-1(h)]. This rule applies even though the property is not actually rented, if it has been abandoned as a residence and is listed for rent or sale, or for sale only.

(a) Distinction Between Capital Expenditures and Repairs. For business property and property held for production of income, the question is whether the expenditure is an expense (deductible in the year paid or incurred) or a capital expenditure (recoverable usually through annual depreciation deductions spread over a period of time; see Chapter 11) [IRC Sec. 162(a); Reg. Sec. 1.162-4]. The distinction between improvements (capital expenditures) and repairs (expenses) is not always clear. But here is a useful general guide: "A repair is an expenditure for the purpose of keeping the property in an ordinarily efficient operating condition. It does not add to the value of property, nor does it appreciably prolong its life. It merely keeps the property in an operating condition over its probable useful life for the uses for which it was acquired. Expenditures for repair purposes are distinguishable from those for replacements, alterations, improvements or additions that prolong the life of the property, increase its value, or make it adaptable to a different use. The one is a deductible maintenance charge, while the others are additions to capital investment that should not be applied against current earnings."[1]

Examples relating to business property. The cost of a new roof is a capital expenditure, but the cost of repairing the roof is an expense;[2] the cost of a new concrete floor and a new foundation for machinery is a capital expenditure;[3] however, the cost of a concrete lining added to a basement floor and walls is an expense.[4]

(b) Simultaneous Repairs and Improvements. Repairs and improvements are often made at the same time. If the repair items are merely part of the general plan of improvements, cases hold that the *entire* amount spent for both repairs and improvements must be treated as a capital expenditure.[5] Even if the repairs and improvements are not part of a general plan of improvement, the repairs are not a deductible expense unless they are segregated from the nondeductible improvements.[6] When the exact cost of repairs is not shown, some deduction may be allowed depending on the evidence submitted.[7]

¶2221   RENT

Tenants can deduct rent for property they use to the extent it is used in their trade, business or profession [IRC Sec. 162(a)(3), 212]. Payments for leasing machinery and equipment can also be deducted.

(a) Advance Rental. Payments are generally not deductible when paid. Only the portion allocable to the particular tax year is deductible.[1] The Tax Court has not been following the "one-year rule" (adopted by the 9th Circuit), which allows a present deduction for rent paid on a lease that extends no more than 12 months beyond the close of the tax year.[2] Some jurisdictions have applied a 3-prong test for allowing a current deduction for advance rental payments:[3] (1) actual payment of the item; (2) a substantial business reason for making the payment; and (3) the item's prepayment cannot cause a material distortion in the taxpayer's taxable income.

> **Example:** Ed Dolan paid $25,000 rent in 1992 for use of a store under a lease covering the years 1992-1996 inclusive. $25,000 is not deductible in full in 1992, but $5,000 is deductible in each of the five years.

(b) Lease Cancellation Payments. Amounts paid by a landlord for cancelling a lease are capital expenditures.[4] If the sum is paid by the tenant for cancelling his lease, the total cost of cancelling the lease and any unamortized improvements to the leasehold are deductible in the year of cancellation.[5]

(c) Payments Under Lease. Payments for using machinery and equipment under lease agreements are deductible as rent if there is compelling evidence of a true rental and not a sale. Otherwise, the payments (except for interest and other charges) are part of the purchase price and are not deductible (but you are allowed depreciation on the property).

Lease agreement treated as purchase or sale. To determine if your payments are rent, you must first establish that your agreement is a lease rather than a conditional sales contract. If you acquire title to or equity in the property, the agreement should be treated as a conditional sales contract. Any one or more of the following conditions indicate that the so-called lease is really a purchase or sale:

- Portions of periodic payments apply specifically to an equity to be acquired by the lessee.
- Lessee will acquire title on payment of a stated amount of "rent" that must be paid in any event.
- Total amount that the lessee must pay for a relatively short period of use is very large compared with the amount needed to get transfer of title.
- Periodic payments materially exceed current fair rental value.
- Property may be bought under an option at a price that is (a) nominal in relation to value of property at time option may be exercised, or (b) relatively small compared with total required payments.
- Part of the "rent" is specifically designated interest, or is easily recognizable as the equivalent of interest.
- Total rental payments plus option price approximate price at which property could have been bought plus interest and carrying charges.

Transfer of title not essential. The fact that the agreement does not provide for the transfer of title or specifically precludes transfer of title does not prevent the contract from being a sale of an equitable interest in the property. Thus, the agreement is a sale if (1) total rents over a relatively short period approximate the price at which the property could have been bought plus interest and carrying charges, and (2) the lessee may continue to use the property over its entire useful life for relatively nominal or token payments, even if there is no provision for the passage of title.[6]

¶2222　　　　　　　　ADVERTISING EXPENSES

Advertising expenditures (except indirect political contributions [¶2206]) are deductible as business expenses, if they are ordinary and necessary and bear a reasonable relation to the business activities of the taxpayer. The cost of goodwill advertising that keeps the advertiser's name before the public is deductible. But the cost of advertising intended to promote or defeat legislation is not deductible. Advertising that encourages charitable contributions or the buying of U.S. savings bonds qualifies as a deductible expense [Reg. Sec. 1.162-20].

Deductible

Expenses of car dealer for sponsoring sports car racing;[1] of slaughterhouse for sponsoring race car displaying company name;[2] of auto agency outfitting and supporting local youth baseball team;[3] of professional sports club for financing construction of local hall of fame;[4] of slot machine leasing company for furnishing pencils, balloons, calendars, etc. to clubs and lodges that leased machines from company.[5]

Nondeductible

Expenses of lock and safe business for maintaining parade horses that did not link company name with show entries;[6] of tax expert for maintaining yacht which flew pennant bearing numerals "1040";[7] of realtor for maintaining moorish "castle" as residence;[8] of restaurant intending to promote or defeat legislation, political parties or candidates.[9]

¶2223   INSURANCE PREMIUMS

[New tax legislation may affect this subject; see ¶1.]
The following rules prevail:

(a) Life Insurance Premiums are nondeductible if paid by the person insured [IRC Sec. 262; Reg. Sec. 1.262-1]. Such premiums are personal rather than business or "nonbusiness" expenses. For example, premiums you pay on an ordinary life policy you take out on your life (with your wife or other dependents as beneficiaries) are not deductible.

Premiums you pay on the life of an officer, employee, or other person financially interested in your business are not deductible, when you are directly or indirectly a beneficiary under the policy [IRC Sec. 264(a)(1); Reg. Sec. 1.264-1]. Thus, premiums paid by an employer on the life of any employee are not deductible while the employer is a beneficiary, even if only to the extent of the cash surrender value.[1]

However, premiums you pay on the life of an officer or employee *are* deductible if you are neither directly nor indirectly a beneficiary *and* the premium is an ordinary and necessary business expense.[2]

> **Example:** The Blaine Corp. insured the life of John Watson, its treasurer, for $50,000. The premiums were $2,000 a year. Watson, who earns $25,000 annually, named his wife as beneficiary. The $2,000 is considered additional compensation. If the total compensation ($25,000 plus $2,000 insurance premium) is reasonable in amount, it is deductible in full.

Group insurance premiums. Premiums paid by an employer on group-permanent and group-term life insurance are deductible[2] [¶1407]. For taxability to the employee, see ¶1207(a).

Loan insurance. If you insure your own life to get a loan for business purposes (policy in favor of lender), you may not deduct the premiums. The proceeds would be used to liquidate the debt, so you are indirectly a beneficiary.[3]

Certain partnership insurance. A partner cannot deduct premiums on insurance on his own life, irrevocably naming his co-partners as sole beneficiaries to induce them to stay in the business. (In accomplishing his purpose, jeopardy to a taxpayer's interest in the partnership is removed and his interest in the business is favorably affected.[4]) [Reg. Sec. 1.264-1(b)].

Split-dollar life insurance plan. An employer cannot deduct its share of premiums paid on the life of an employee under a so-called split-dollar plan[5] [¶1207(a)].

(b) Premiums on Insurance Other Than Life—Fire, Burglary, etc. Premiums on fire,[6] burglary, storm, theft and accident insurance covering property used in a trade, business or profession, or in connection with the production of income or the management, conservation or maintenance of property held for the production of income, are deductible [IRC Sec. 162(a), 212; Reg. Sec. 1.162-1, 1.212-1]. The Tax Court has held that premiums paid after a business use ends and the property is offered for sale must be capitalized.[7] Insurance on property used for personal purposes, for example, fire insurance on your home, is a nondeductible personal expense [IRC Sec. 262; Reg. Sec. 1.262-1]. Premiums paid to insure against your sudden dismissal from employment for reasons other than your own actions or disability are deductible.[8]

Employers' liability, etc. Premiums on other insurance such as public liability, worker's compensation, credit, fidelity, indemnity bonds, use and occupancy, and the like, are deductible, if incurred in (1) carrying on a trade, business or profession, (2) the production or collection of income, or (3) the management, conservation or maintenance of property held for the production of income. Some premiums may have to be capitalized [¶2203].

Premiums on overhead insurance that reimburses the taxpayer for business overhead expenses incurred during prolonged periods of disability are deductible, if the policy expressly states that it is overhead insurance.[9]

Health, accident and disability. If an employer buys group hospitalization and surgical insurance for employees and their families, the premiums paid are deductible as ordinary and necessary business expenses. The purchase must be in consideration of services rendered.[10]

Employers cannot deduct contributions to any group health plan unless all of the employer's group health plans provide continuation coverage to employees and their beneficiaries.

> **OBSERVATION** An employer's highly compensated employees cannot exclude from their gross income contributions made by the employer to a group health plan unless all of the employer's group health plans provide continuation coverage.

To meet the continuation coverage requirement, a plan must provide employees and their qualified beneficiaries the choice of continuing to be covered by the employer's group health plan if they experience a qualifying event. A qualifying event is a covered employee's death, termination, divorce, and eligibility to receive Medicare benefits. A qualifying event can also involve the end of coverage eligibility for a dependent child under the plan guidelines or a bankruptcy proceeding involving the employer [IRC Sec. 4980B(f)].

If any of the qualifying events occur, the plan must provide an election period of at least 60 days to covered employees, their spouses, and their dependent children during which they may choose to continue coverage under the plan [IRC Sec. 4980B(f)(5)].

If an employer's group health plan fails to make continuation coverage available to qualified beneficiaries, the employer will be subject to an excise tax. In general, the tax is $100 per day during the noncompliance period for each failure. For certain combined groups of beneficiaries, $200 per day is the maximum tax that can be imposed [IRC Sec. 4980B].

NOTE: Any governmental or church plan is excluded from the tax. What's more, the tax doesn't apply to a group health plan that fails to meet the continuing coverage requirements, if the qualifying event occurred in a calendar year right after a calendar year during which the employer usually had fewer than 20 employees on a typical business day [IRC Sec. 401(d), (e), 4980B(d)].

Health insurance payments of self-employeds and certain S-corporation shareholders. S-corporation shareholders who own more than 2% of the stock or voting power and self-employeds can take a business expense deduction for 25% of the amount paid for medical insurance covering themselves, their spouses and dependents [IRC Sec. 162(l)]. This is a deduction for adjusted gross income—rather than an itemized medical expense deduction. The remaining 75% of medical insurance payments can, however, be deducted as part of their medical expenses on Schedule A, Form 1040. The deduction cannot exceed net earnings from the business. And the 25% deduction is not available if you are eligible to participate in a health insurance plan maintained by an employer from any other job you hold or in a plan maintained by your spouse's employer. This deduction is not considered a medical expense [¶1931 et seq.]. The amount deductible under this rule is not taken into account in figuring if the threshold for the itemized medical expense deduction is met.

> **TAX BREAK EXTENDED** This deduction, which was set to expire as of December 31, 1991, has been extended by the Tax Extension Act of 1991. You can claim the 25% deduction for premiums paid and insurance coverage provided before July 1, 1992.

¶2224   INTEREST EXPENSES

Business-connected interest charges are generally deductible in full [IRC Sec. 163(a)].

Insurance policy loans. A special restriction applies to loans on policies insuring the life of an officer, employee or owner of the business. If the aggregate of loans on policies, purchased after June 20, 1986, insuring such an individual exceeds $50,000, the company's interest deduction is limited to interest allocable to the first $50,000 of indebtedness [IRC Sec. 264(a)(4)].

Amortization of realty construction period interest. Interest paid or incurred after 1986 and during the production period of certain types of property must be capitalized [IRC Sec. 263A]. Property subject to the interest capitalization rule includes property produced by the taxpayer for use in its trade or business, or in an activity for profit; but only if it: (1) is real property, (2) is personal property with an estimated production period exceeding two years (one year if the property's cost exceeds $1 million), or (3) has a class life for depreciation purposes of 20 years or more. For real property, the production period begins when physical activity is first performed on the property. This includes the grading or clearing of land and the excavation of foundations or utility lines. For all other property, the production period starts when 5% of the total estimated production costs are incurred, and ends when the property is ready to be placed in service or held for sale.[1]

MISCELLANEOUS TRADE OR BUSINESS EXPENSES

¶2225   EXPENSES OF SELF-EMPLOYEDS

Certain types of business expenses are generally associated with self-employed business and professional people. They are claimed on Schedule C of Form 1040. The IRS has said that so-called "statutory employees"—a hybrid group of workers that includes outside salespeople, truck drivers, insurance salespeople, etc.—are not employees for income tax purposes. They are treated as self-employeds and deduct their business expenses on Schedule C.[1]

Membership dues in technical or professional societies, chambers of commerce, unions etc., may be deducted.

Magazines and books. The cost of magazines and newspapers is usually a personal expense. Physicians and dentists can deduct the cost of magazines and newspapers kept in their waiting rooms. The cost of technical magazines, newspapers and looseleaf services is deductible. The cost of technical books is not immediately deductible in full, but the professional person may deduct a proportionate amount for each year's depreciation of technical books.

Fees for right to practice. The following items are *not* deductible: bar examination fees and other expenses incurred in securing admission to the bar; similar fees and expenses incurred by physicians, dentists, accountants and others for securing the right to practice their professions [Reg. Sec. 1.212-1(f)]; fees paid to hospital to practice as staff member (capital expenditure).[2]

¶2226   EXPENSES INCURRED IN TRADE OR BUSINESS BY EMPLOYEE

In general, employees can deduct the same types of expenses as self-employeds. Employee business expenses are claimed on Form 2106. Any expense incurred by an employee is not deductible unless it is required by the employment agreement,[1] or is incident to performing his or her duties.[2] For example, as noted earlier, an employee can take a home-office deduction only if the office's exclusive use is for the employer's convenience [IRC Sec. 280A(c); Prop. Reg. Sec. 1.280A-2(b)].

Deductible

Employment agency fees and other expenses in seeking employment in the same trade or business even if employment is not secured, but not if employment is sought in new trade or business.[3]	**Cost of medical examination** required as condition of employment.[4]
	Cost of meals eaten by state troopers, while on duty, at a public restaurant adjacent to the highway they were patrolling.[5]

Reimbursed expenses. The fact that employees have been reimbursed for certain expenses does not, of itself, convert an item to deductible status. The expense must be justified by the Code. For example, a reimbursement could be a disguised form of compensation.

How treated on return. Generally, reimbursements or other expense allowances made under an "accountable plan"—where the employee substantiates the expenses and must return excess allowances to the employer—need not be reported an the employee's tax return. And the employee does not have to claim an offsetting deduction for his or her expenses [¶2003]. However, reimbursements or allowances not from an accountable plan must be reported on the employee's return. The employee can then deduct his or her business expenses—but only as a miscellaneous itemized deduction. And miscellaneous expenses are deductible only to the extent their total exceeds 2% of the employee's adjusted gross income [¶1942 et seq.]. Net result: If the employee's miscellaneous expenses don't reach the 2% mark, he or she has no deduction to offset the taxable reimbursement.

Reimbursement must be claimed. Employees get no deduction for amounts for which their employer would have reimbursed them had they made a claim.[6]

Reporting requirements. The employee's method of reporting business expenses on the return depends on whether or not an accounting is made to the employer. Form 2106 is used to report an employee's business deductions on the return. No accounting, reporting or recordkeeping is required for incidental expenses [Reg. Sec. 1.162-17, 1.274-5].

Per diem arrangements. An employer can provide its employees with per diem travel allowances for away-from-home travel at a fixed per diem rate [¶2002]. If the allowance does not exceed the government-approved maximum, the expenses are considered accounted for provided the employee is required to (1) keep a record of time, place, and his expenses' business purpose, and (2) give the same information to the employer. The employee does not have to keep track of actual expenses for travel, lodging or meals.

If an employee receives a per diem allowance in excess of the approved rate, only the excess is taxable. In other words, the expenses are deemed to be substantiated to the extent of the maximum rate. If an employee receives a total per diem amount before the trip and it exceeds the approved rate, the employer does not have to require the employee to return the excess. The plan is still treated as accountable as long as the employee is required to return any portion allocable to days not actually traveled.

Example 1: The Orwell Welding Company provides its manager David Dean with a per diem travel allowance of $120 per day for five days. Assume the applicable government-approved maximum rate is $100 per day. As long as Dean meets the above per diem requirements, only the excess ($20 per day) will be taxable to him as compensation and thus subject to payroll and income taxes.

Example 2: Dean is given a per diem allowance equal to the government rate: $100 per day. His away-from-home meetings were productive and he wraps up his business in only four days (though provided with a five-day allowance). As long as Orwell Welding Co. required him to return the amount attributable to the day he was not traveling, only that amount (if not returned) will be taxable to him as compensation.

Employee expense arrangements, for tax purposes, are divided into two categories: "accountable plans" and "nonaccountable plans." An allowance paid under an accountable plan is generally tax-free to the employee. It is not subject to payroll taxes, nor is it reported on the employee's tax return. The employee only reports the employer payment as income if expenses exceed the allowance and the employee wants to deduct the difference. In contrast, payments under a nonaccountable plan are considered taxable wages. The employer must withhold on the payments and report them on the employee's Form W-2 [¶2004].[7]

Any expenses incurred by the employee in excess of amounts reimbursed are deductible by the employee, but only to the extent that, when combined with other miscellaneous expenses, they exceed 2% of the taxpayer's adjusted gross income.

Proving expenses. Employees who receive payments under an accountable plan ordinarily will not be called on to prove their expenses unless [Reg. Sec. 1.162-17(d)(1), 1.274-5]:

- They claim a deduction for an excess of expenses over reimbursements; or
- They are related to the employer [¶2323]; or
- It is determined that the employer's accounting procedures for reporting and substantiating employees' expenses were not adequate.

What is "adequate accounting?" To "adequately account" to an employer, the employee must submit a record describing the business nature and the amount of each expense. For travel, entertainment and gift costs, the employee must substantiate the amount, date, place (or description of the item, for gifts) business purpose and business relationship of the expenditure that has been recorded at or near the time of the expenditure. There must also be supporting documentary evidence. Only this kind of proof will qualify as "adequate accounting," except when records were destroyed or if it is impossible to get the evidence (¶2003) [Reg. Sec. 1.162-17(b)(4); 1.274-5].

Jury duty pay. Suppose employees serving on a jury must give their employer all or part of their jury duty pay in return for receiving their regular pay during the jury service period. Then, the jury duty pay turned over to the employer is a deduction for adjusted gross income [IRC Sec. 62(a)(13)].

¶2227   BUSINESS USE OF HOME

[New tax legislation may affect this subject. See ¶1.]

You can take a deduction for the expenses related to the business use of your home if a specific part of the home is set aside and used exclusively on a regular basis as: (a) the principal place of *any* business; or (b) a place used to meet with patients, clients or customers; or (c) a separate structure used in a trade or business and not attached to your dwelling. Added requirement: If you are an employee, your business use must be for your employer's convenience and not merely appropriate or helpful [IRC Sec. 280A].

On the return: Self-employed taxpayers who file Schedule C (Form 1040) must figure the business use of their home on Form 8829.

> ▶ **OBSERVATION** You can deduct office-at-home expenses incurred in maintaining the principal office for *any* business [IRC Sec. 280A(c)(1)]. In addition, the Tax Court has ruled that "exclusive use" does not mean the home-office must be in a separate room. The home-office qualifies as long as the office is a specific portion of a room used exclusively and on a regular basis for business.[1]

Example 1: Peggy is a high school teacher. She also engages in a retail sales business. Peggy uses a part of her home as the principal place of business for her retail business. She can deduct expenses for business use of her home. This is so, even though as a teacher, her principal place of business is the school.

NOTE: Both the Tax Court and the Fourth Circuit Court of Appeals have applied a more liberal test when granting home-office deductions. These courts have said that you merely have to establish that (1) the home office was essential to your business, (2) you spent a substantial amount of time in the office, and (3) there was no other location available to perform the office functions of your business.[2]

To figure the percentage of the home used for business, compare the square feet of space used for business to the total square feet in your home. Or, if the rooms in the home are about the same size, the percentage may be determined by comparing the number of rooms used for business to the total number of rooms in the home. The business part of the expenses is figured by applying the percentage to the total of each expense.[3]

If you carry on a business from your residence, you can take deductions for space in your home that is used regularly for storing inventory. In this case, your home must be the sole fixed location for the business [Prop. Reg. Sec. 1.280A-2(e)].[4]

The deduction limitation for the home's business use is based on the gross income from the business use. Your business deductions for the business use of your home are taken in the following order [Prop. Reg. Sec. 1.280A-2(i)(5)]:

1. Business percentage of the expenses that would otherwise be allowable as deductions, without regard to the business use (mortgage interest, real estate taxes, and deductible casualty losses);

2. Direct expenses for your business in your home, that are not allocable to the use of the unit itself (for example, expenses for supplies and compensation); and

3. Other business expenses for the business use of your home that are allocable to the use of the unit itself (like maintenance, utilities, insurance and depreciation). Deductions that adjust the home's basis are taken last.

> ▶ **OBSERVATION** Deductions for the business use of your home will not create a business loss or increase a net loss from your business.

Tough rule if two business locations involved: If you do business in two locations—at a regular business office and at a home office—you may not be able to deduct any of your home office expenses, even though you have substantial income from that office. It's due to the special calculations required on Form 8829. Your deduction limitation is figured using only the part of your business income attributable to the home office. Yet you must still subtract out 100% of your business expenses (other than those for the home office).

Example: Dr. Johnson took in $200,000 of gross receipts for the year. Johnson worked in his home office two days a week. For the other three days, he worked in an office in a professional building. His general business expenses came to $80,000. He also had $5,000 of home office expenses.

Since Johnson worked in his home office 40% of the time, $80,000 of his gross income is attributable to the use of his home office. But this amount is reduced to $0 by his $80,000 of general business expenses. So Johnson cannot write off his $5,000 of home office expenses, even though he really has $115,000 of net business income.

> ▶ **TAX-SAVING MOVE** You can get around the tough deduction limit by treating the in-home activities as a separate business from the outside activities. This requires keeping separate records and filing separate Schedule Cs.

A carryforward is allowed for any deduction that is disallowed by the gross income limit. Deductions carried over continue to be allowable only up to the income from the business from which the expenses arose, whether or not the dwelling unit is used as a residence during the tax year [IRC Sec. 280A(c)(5)].

Example 2: Baker operates a retail sales business from his home. His use meets the requirements for deducting expenses for the home's business use. His use is 20% of the home for business. In 1992, his gross income, expenses for the business, and computing the expenses for the business use of the home are as follows:

Gross income from business use of home	$12,000
Total expenses:	
1. Business percentage (20%) of mortgage interest and real estate taxes	$2,000
2. Expenses for business in home not allocable to the home itself (cost of goods sold, telephone, supplies, labor, etc.)	9,000
3. Other expenses attributable to home's business use:	
a) Maintenance, insurance, utilities (20%)	800
b) Depreciation (20%)	1,600
Gross income limitation:	
Total of (1) and (2) (allowable in full)	11,000
Limit on further deductions	$ 1,000
Subtract expenses in (3)(a)	$ 800
Limit on further deductions	$ 200
Depreciation ((3)(b))	$ 1,600
Depreciation allowable	$ 200
Carryover expenses in 1992 (subject to income limit in 1993)	$ 1,400

NOTES: Tenants who meet the office-at-home rules can deduct an allocable portion of their rent payments (instead of depreciation, taxes and the like). Employees cannot claim landlord-type deductions (e.g., depreciation) on account of renting a home-office to their employer [IRC Sec. 280A(c)(6)].

Day care services. A home-office deduction is allowed for licensed day-care services (for children, the elderly or those incapable of caring for themselves) regularly provided in the home for compensation. The portion of the home used for day care need not be used exclusively for business purposes. When home-office deductions are claimed for day care provided in portions of the home that are also put to nonbusiness use, two allocations are necessary. However, the Revenue Service has said that you are not required to keep detailed records of the number of hours a given room is used for day care. A room that is available for day care use throughout the business day and is regularly used as part of the day care routine can be treated as used for day care during all business operation hours. The deduction is figured as follows [IRC Sec. 280A(c)(4)]: [5]

1. Multiply the annual home expenses (mortgage interest, taxes, utilities, etc.) by a fraction–the square footage of the home available for day care divided by the home's total square footage.

2. Next, multiply the amount in (1) above by a second fraction–the total hours during the year the day care business is operated (including preparation and cleanup time) divided by the total number of hours in the year (8,760).

Example 3: Joan Brown, a licensed day care provider, uses her home 250 days a year for day care. She spends 11 hours daily on this plus another hour each day for preparation and cleanup [3,000 hours (12 hours x 250 days per year)]. The Browns' home has a total of 1,600 square feet with personal living area totaling 400 square feet. The Browns' total annual home expenses come to $10,000 for 1992. Joan Brown figures her deduction for day services as follows:

1. $10,000 home expenses x 1,200/1,600 = $7,500

2. $7,500 x 3,000 hours/8,760 hours = $2,568.49

NOTE: Form 8829 has special lines for day care providers to calculate the area of the home that is used for day care, as well as the percentage of hours devoted to day care. If, in Example 3 above, Joan Brown's day care business was in operation for only part of the year, the 8,760 hour figure would have to be adjusted to take into account only the total number of hours in that part of the year.

¶2228   EDUCATION EXPENSES

You can deduct education expenses as ordinary and necessary business expenses if the education either:

- *Maintains or improves* skills required in your job; or
- *Meets new requirements* of your employer or the law, to *keep* your job or rate of pay [Reg. Sec. 1.162-5(a)].

However, even if any of the above requirements are met, expenses are not deductible if the education either:

- *Meets minimum educational requirements* for your present job; or
- *Qualifies you for a new trade or business* [Reg. Sec. 1.162-5(b)].

Example 1: Steele, who is an attorney licensed to practice in Ohio, takes a review course to prepare for the Kentucky bar exam. This expenditure is not deductible. Passing the bar is the minimum educational requirement for the practice of law in each individual state.

Maintaining or improving skills. Deductible educational costs to maintain or improve skills include those refresher courses or courses dealing with current developments as well as academic and vocational courses [Reg. Sec. 1.162-5(c)].

Example 2: Attorney Steele has a general practice. He enrolls in a program to get a graduate law degree in federal income taxation. The expense is deductible. The education sharpens Steele's skills in his current profession.

Requirements of employer. If, after meeting the minimum educational requirements for the job, you must obtain additional education to keep your present job status or pay rate, those expenses are deductible. Education that also allows advancement in the employer-firm will not necessarily be disallowed under the "requirements of employer" criterion. The deduction is allowed if education resulting in advancement is required for you to be kept as an employee at your present level [Reg. Sec. 1.162-5(c)]. Important: The fact that you hold a job is not absolute proof that you have met the minimum requirements of that trade or business. The cost of subsequent education may still be nondeductible even though it is required by your employer.

Example 3: Allison Parke, who has completed two years of a normal three-year law school course leading to a law degree, is hired by a law firm to do legal research and perform other functions on a full-time basis. As a condition to continued employment, Ms. Parke is required to obtain the degree and pass the state bar exam. Parke completes her law school education by attending night school and she takes a bar review course in order to prepare for the state bar exam. The law courses and bar review course constitute education required to meet the minimum educational requirements for qualification in Parke's trade or business and thus, the expenditures for such courses are not deductible [Reg. Sec. 1.162-5(b)(2)].

The following chart provides a bird's-eye view of whether your education expenses are deductible:

(a) What Expenses Are Deductible. Deductible education expenses include amounts spent for tuition, books, supplies, typing, lab fees, and similar items as well as certain travel and transportation costs.[1]

Travel and transportation expenses. The school where you take job-related classes is considered to be a work location and thus subject to the general work-related travel rules [¶2000]. And that means you can deduct the costs of the one-way trips from work to class. Whether you can deduct the costs incurred to travel between your home and class, however, depends on whether the school is a "temporary work location."[1]

For travel within your city or locality, the school is considered "temporary" if you attend the classes on a short-term basis (generally a matter of days or weeks). So any course of study that lasts beyond one semester is probably "regular" (as opposed to temporary) and therefore nondeductible.

For travel outside your city or locality, the school is considered temporary (and thus deductible) if the education lasts less than one year.[2]

➤ **OBSERVATION** If your main office is in your home, the expenses incurred between your home office and school are considered to be expenses incurred to go between two work locations. Therefore, they are deductible.

The cost of travel for personal reasons is not deductible [Reg. Sec. 1.162-5(d)].

No deduction is allowed for travel expenses by teachers and others when their travel is a form of education [IRC Sec. 274(m)(2)]. But deductions for travel that is necessary to engage in activities that give rise to deductible education continue to be deductible.

(b) Teachers. The education expenses of teachers are often deductible. The minimum educational requirements for a position in an educational institution is the minimum level of education (in college hours or degree) normally required when persons are first employed. If there is no minimum level, a teacher is considered to meet the minimum educational requirements (as to the deductibility of expenses) when he or she becomes a faculty member. All teaching and related duties are considered to be the same general type of work. Thus, education expenses incurred by a classroom teacher for a change from elementary to secondary school, or from one subject to another or from teacher to principal would be deductible. Expenses incurred to qualify for a permanent certificate to teach in another state would also be deductible[2] [Reg. Sec. 1.162-5(b), (2), (3)]. A teacher has been allowed an education expense deduction for full-time graduate study, even though not actively employed at the time.[3] The IRS limits this to a suspension of a year or less to qualify for the deduction.[4]

Example 4: Joe Frank, who holds a bachelor's degree, is employed by UPI University as an instructor in economics. He enrolls in graduate courses as a candidate for a graduate degree. Joe may become a permanent faculty member only if he obtains a graduate degree. He may continue as an instructor only so long as he shows satisfactory progress toward obtaining his degree. The costs of the graduate courses are not deductible, since they constitute education required to meet the minimum educational requirements for qualification in Joe's trade or business.

(c) Education Expenses Paid by Employer. If your employer pays the tuition and expenses for courses you take that are not required for the job or that are not job-related, these payments must be treated as taxable income by you. Your employer takes the corresponding deduction. If you pay the expenses and are reimbursed by your employer, the reimbursement is likewise taxable if the educational expenses are not job-related. Your employer takes the corresponding deduction [¶2226].

Note: Employer reimbursements for non-job-related courses under an educational assistance plan may be tax-free [¶1414].

¶2229   UNIFORMS AND EQUIPMENT

You can deduct the cost of equipment that is especially required by your business or profession. The cost of work clothes and uniforms is deductible only if they are not suitable for everyday use and required as a condition of employment. For example, uniforms worn by nurses and police officers, as well as safety shoes and hard hats can qualify for the deduction. Clothes with the company logo have also qualified for the deduction.[1] Generally, armed forces uniforms may not be deducted by those on active duty. However, reserve personnel on inactive duty can deduct the excess of these costs over a uniform gratuity received for uniforms required for training and drills.[2]

SPECIAL PROBLEMS

¶2230   LEASEHOLDS

If you must pay a specified sum to acquire a lease for business reasons, you can deduct a proportionate part of that sum each year of the lease [Reg. Sec. 1.162-11]. Lease-acquisition costs may be amortized over the lease term [IRC Sec. 178; Reg. Sec. 1.178-1, 1.178-3]. However, any lease renewals (including renewal options and any other period for which you reasonably expect the lease to be renewed) must be included in figuring the amortization period, but only if less than 75% of the lease-acquisition cost is for the lease's remaining term (excluding any renewal period remaining on the lease acquisition date).

¶2231   RESEARCH AND EXPERIMENTAL EXPENDITURES

[New tax legislation may affect this subject; see ¶1.]

Research and experimental expenditures of an existing [1] trade or business may be deducted in the year paid or incurred, or over a period of 60 months or more. A new venture is allowed a deduction for the costs of a new product even though the product is not finished or marketable the year the expenses are incurred.[2] It is not necessary that the expenses be related to the current product lines or manufacturing processes of the trade or business; they may be for new products or processes.[3] This rule applies whether the research and experiments were made by the taxpayer, or by another for him (such as an institute or foundation). If neither method is used, the expenditures must be capitalized [IRC Sec. 174; Reg. Sec. 1.174-1, 1.174-2].

> **NOTE:** Certain 1992 research expenses qualify for a tax credit—a dollar-for-dollar reduction in tax. The credit is equal to 20% of the increase in current research expenses over the average in the three four preceding years [¶2409].

> ➤ **CREDIT EXTENDED** The research credit, which had been scheduled to expire on December 31, 1991, was extended. The credit is available for expenses paid or incurred through June 30, 1992.

(a) Deductible in Year Paid or Incurred. If this method is elected, the expenses are not chargeable to capital account. However, they may be deducted currently regardless of how they are recorded on the books.[4]

Election of method. This method can be adopted without IRS consent if the deduction is claimed on the return in the first tax year the expenditures are paid or incurred.

Consent is required for adoption at any other time. The request should be in writing and addressed to the Commissioner, Att: T: R, Washington, D.C. It must be filed by the end of the first tax year for which the request is made [Reg. Sec. 1.174-3(b)(2)]. Once adopted, this method applies to *all* research and experimental expenditures regularly incurred, starting with the election year [Reg. Sec. 1.174-3(a), (b)(2)]. The method must be followed unless the Commissioner consents to a change for all or a part of the expenditures [IRC Sec. 174(a); Reg. 1.174-3(a)]. You may request authorization to capitalize research and experimental expenditures for a special project [Reg. Sec. 1.174-3(a)].

Change of method. You must file the application for change by the end of the first tax year to which the change applies. You must attach a copy of the letter of permission to the return for the first tax year to which the change applies [Reg. Sec. 1.174-3(b)(3)].

(b) Deferred Expenses. If you defer your research and experimental expenditures and charge them to capital account, you must deduct them ratably over a period of 60 months or more. You start with the month you first benefit from the expenditures. If there are two or more projects, different periods may be selected for each. If, however, the property resulting from such expenditures has a determinable useful life, such capitalized expenditures are recoverable by way of depreciation or depletion. Also, if the expenditures which you elected to defer result in the development of depreciable property, the unrecovered costs from the time the asset first becomes depreciable must be recovered by way of depreciation. Rapid writeoffs, to the extent they exceed the amount allowable had the research and experimental expenditures been capitalized and deducted ratably over 10 years, are considered adjustments for determining the alternative minimum tax (¶2601) [IRC Sec. 56(b)(2), 174(e)(1)].

Election of method. You must make the election no later than the time for filing the return for the tax year (including extensions) the expenditures are paid or incurred. You make the election by a signed statement attached to the return [Reg. Sec. 1.174-4(b)(1)]. The election cannot be made simply by claiming the deduction on the return.[5] The election does not apply to an expenditure paid or incurred before the year of election [IRC Sec. 174(b); Reg. Sec. 1.174-4].

Change of method. Once adopted, this method must be followed unless IRS consents to a change. You must file the application by the end of the first tax year for which the change applies. You must attach a copy of the permission to the return for the first tax year to which the change applies [Reg. Sec. 1.174-4(b)(2)].

(c) Exceptions. Generally, the option to defer the expenses or deduct them in the year paid or incurred does not apply to: (1) expenditures for land or depreciable or depletable property, even if it is to be used in research or experimentation (but depreciation and depletion on such property are considered research and experimental expenditures); or (2) exploration expenditures incurred for minerals, oil or gas [IRC Sec. 174(c)(d); Reg. Sec. 1.174-2(b), (c)]. However, research and experimental expenditures, themselves, are deductible in the year paid or incurred even if they result (as a product of the research and experimentation) in depreciable property to be used in your trade or business. If the expenditures are for the construction or manufacture of depreciable property by another, they are deductible only if incurred at your order or risk.

(d) Adjustment of Basis. Expenses deferred (under (b) above) are included in figuring the adjusted basis of the property for which they are paid or incurred. The adjusted basis, however, must be reduced by the deferred expenses allowed as deductions to the extent there is a tax benefit (but not less than the amount allowable for the tax year and prior years) [IRC Sec. 1016(a)(1), (14); Reg. Sec. 1.1016-5(j)].

DEPLETION DEDUCTION

¶2233   WHAT IS DEPLETION

Minerals, oil and gas, other natural deposits (including soil in place[1]), and timber are known as wasting assets. The gradual reduction of the original amount by removal for use is known as "depletion." The theory is that the annual deduction for depletion and depreciation, in the aggregate, will return the cost or other basis of the "property" (see definition, below) plus later allowable capital additions [Reg. Sec. 1.611-1, 1.611-5].

"Property" means each separate interest you own in each mineral deposit in each separate tract or parcel of land. It includes working or operating interests, royalties, overriding royalties, production payments and net profits interests. Contiguous areas acquired at the same time from the same owner constitute a single separate tract or parcel of land. Areas included in separate conveyances or grants from separate owners are separate tracts or parcels, even if the areas are contiguous [IRC Sec. 614(a); Reg. Sec. 1.614-1].

¶2234   WHO IS ENTITLED TO THE DEDUCTION FOR DEPLETION

(a) **Owner of an Economic Interest.** To qualify for depletion deductions, you must own an "economic interest" in the property. This means you have an interest in the mineral deposit or timber and must look solely to income from production for a return of your capital [Reg. Sec. 1.611-1(b)(1)].

The Supreme Court has ruled that contract coal miners have no economic interest in the coal they mine.[1]

> **Example 1:** An adjacent upland owner who provides the only available drilling site for oil from submerged coastal lands is entitled to depletion on the share of net profits received from the producer for use of the lands.[2]

> **Example 2:** A processor under contracts with oil producers to extract casinghead gasoline from natural gas they deliver to it is not entitled to depletion, since it has no capital investment in the mineral deposit being depleted.[3]

For an individual taxpayer, the deduction is subtracted from gross income to arrive at adjusted gross income.

(b) **Lessor and Lessee.** No specific rule can be laid down for making the apportionment, and each case must be decided on its own merits.

If the value of any leased mineral or timber property must be ascertained to figure the basis for depletion, the value of the interests of the lessor and lessee may be found separately. If they are figured as of the same date, they may not exceed the value of the property as a whole on that date [Reg. Sec. 1.611-1(c)].

Minimum royalties. If lessees agree that they will pay a minimum royalty to be applied against the price or royalty per unit, lessors take depletion even if the minerals covered by that royalty are not extracted. The depletion is computed as if the minerals had been removed. No further deduction is allowed, of course, when actual removal takes place [Reg. Sec. 1.612-3(b)(1)]. If all the minerals are not extracted, and the lease is ended, lessors must adjust their capital account by restoring the depletion deductions taken in prior years for the minerals paid for in advance, *but not extracted.* The same amount must be reported as income [Reg. Sec. 1.612-3(b)(2)].[4]

Overriding royalties. Lessees who transfer their interest in the property, but retain their royalty interests, share an equitable portion of the depletion allowance with the lessor. It is immaterial whether the transfer is by assignment or by a sublease, since an economic interest in the property has been retained.[5]

Delay rentals. Amounts paid for the privilege of deferring development are ordinary income to the lessor and not subject to depletion [Reg. Sec. 1.612-3(c)(1)].

Shut-in royalties are treated the same as delay rentals.[6]

(c) Life Tenant and Remainderman. The life tenant gets depletion until his death. Then the remainderman gets it [Reg. Sec. 1.611-1(c)(3)].

(d) Sale of Entire Economic Interest. If you lease or transfer property subject to depletion, but retain an economic interest in that property, you are entitled to the deduction.

If you sell the property or your entire economic interest (for example, an interest in an oil and gas lease, or a mineral deposit), no subsequent depletion deduction is allowed.

(e) Mineral Production Payments. A production payment is a right to a share of the production from a mineral property (or a sum of money in place of the production) when that production occurs.

1. *Carved-out payments* are created when owners of mineral property sell—or carve out—a portion of their future production. They are treated as mortgage loans rather than economic interests in the mineral property [IRC Sec. 636(a); Reg. Sec. 1.636-1(a), 1.636-3]. Income will be taxable to the property owner, subject to depletion, as income is derived from the property.

2. *Retained payments* are created when owners of a mineral interest sell the working interest, but retain production payments for themselves. Retained payments are treated as purchase-money mortgage loans rather than economic interests in the mineral property [IRC Sec. 636(b); Reg. Sec. 1.636-1(c)]. The production payment is part of the sales proceeds entering into the seller's gain or loss. The income from the property used to satisfy the payment is taxable to the buyer and is subject to depletion; he can deduct operating costs.

3. *Payments retained by lessors* on leases of mineral interests are treated by the lessee as a bonus payable by him in installments; the lessee capitalizes the payments and recovers them through depletion. The lessor treats the production payments as depletable income [IRC Sec. 636(c); Reg. Sec. 1.636-2(b)].

¶2235   FIGURING THE DEPLETION DEDUCTION

There are two methods for calculating depletion—cost depletion and percentage depletion. Under the cost depletion method, each year's deduction is a portion of your depletable basis in the property. With percentage depletion, deductions are a specified percentage of your income from the property [IRC Sec. 613(b); Reg. Sec. 1.613-2]. Consequently, your cumulative percentage depletion deductions may exceed your purchase price for the property.

Tax return entry. Depletion is generally claimed on Schedule E of Form 1040. However, depletion on an operating oil and gas interest is claimed on Schedule C.

¶2236   COST DEPLETION

This method, also known as valuation depletion, applies to all types of property subject to depletion. Under it, the basis is the same as that for figuring gain on the sale of the property, and may be more or less than cost. The basis is divided by the estimated number of units (tons of ore, barrels of oil, thousands of cubic feet of natural gas, feet of timber) in the ground to arrive at the depletion unit. The deduction for a tax year is the depletion unit multiplied by the number of units sold within the year.

(a) How to Figure Cost Depletion. The basis for depletion under the cost method is the adjusted basis for determining gain on a sale [IRC Sec. 612; Reg. Sec. 1.612-1]. If you can use percentage depletion, you should still figure out what your deduction would be under the cost depletion method. That way, if the cost depletion deduction turns out to be larger, you can claim it.

Depletion under the cost method is figured as follows [Reg. Sec. 1.611-2]:

(Adjusted basis/total remaining mineral units) × number of units sold.

> ➤ **OBSERVATION** It is the number of units sold (not the number produced) that determines the allowance.

Example 1: On January 1, the Russell Co. owned property subject to depletion, with a basis in its hands of $1,000,000. The recoverable reserves (the total remaining mineral units) were estimated at 100,000 units. The unit cost was $10, and if 5,000 units were sold during the year, the depletion deduction would be $50,000 (assuming no capital additions).

Important exceptions to the cost method are considered in ¶2237; 2238; 2240.

(b) Determining Adjusted Basis. In general, the property's adjusted basis, for cost depletion purposes, is figured by following the same rules as apply when determining gain from the sale of the property (see ¶ 1600) [IRC Sec. 612]. The exceptions to this rule are explained below.

(c) Charges to Capital Account. In figuring the adjusted basis, certain additions must be made to capital account. In the case of mines and oil and gas properties, capital expenditures allocable to the mine or well itself are recoverable through depletion; capital expenditures allocable to plant or equipment are recoverable through depreciation.

Capital additions to mines. Expenditures for plant and equipment (except maintenance and repairs) are ordinarily recoverable through depreciation. But in certain cases, expenditures for equipment necessary to maintain normal output are chargeable to expense (deductible) [Reg. Sec. 1.612-2]. For operating oil and gas properties, depreciation is allowed on machinery, tools, pipes, and similar items, and also on installation costs if they are not deducted as intangible drilling expenses [Reg. Sec. 1.611-5(b)(4)].

Intangible drilling costs. An operator can either charge intangible drilling and development costs to capital, recovering them through depletion or depreciation (depending on the nature of the expenditure), or deduct the costs as expenses. A binding election must be made on the return for the first tax year the costs are sustained. If the costs are not deducted on this return, you are considered to have elected to capitalize them [IRC Sec. 263(c); Reg. Sec. 1.612-4]. There are exceptions to the general rule denying current deductions for capital expenditures. Examples are intangible drilling and development costs for oil and gas wells, and geothermal wells, and the like [IRC Sec. 263(c)]. Cash basis taxpayers can only deduct their intangible drilling and development costs in the year in which the payment is required under a drilling contract, not in a prior year.[1]

If the operator has elected to capitalize intangible drilling and development costs, an additional option is available. This option permits deduction as an ordinary loss of the intangible drilling and development costs incurred in drilling a nonproductive well [Reg. Sec. 1.612-4(b)].

Intangible drilling and development costs of oil and gas wells must be capitalized and amortized ratably over 60 months for computing a corporation's earnings and profits starting with the month production begins [IRC Sec. 312(n)(2)].

A portion of intangible drilling costs may be a tax preference item for the alternative minimum tax. Specifically, the amount of excess intangible drilling costs is a tax preference item to the extent it exceeds 65% of your net income from oil, gas or geothermal properties (¶2603) [IRC Sec. 57(a)(2)]. Net oil and gas income is found without deducting excess intangible drilling costs. Excess intangible drilling costs are the amount of the regular deduction over the amount that would have been allowable if the costs had been amortized over 120 months on a straight line basis or through cost depletion. You can avoid the tax preference treatment by capitalizing the intangible drilling costs and amortizing them over 10 years (a 5-year writeoff option also exists for costs not attributable to a limited partnership interest) [IRC Sec. 59(e)].

Example 2: Mr. Able has $1,000 of net oil income (disregarding excess intangible drilling costs) and $800 of excess intangible drilling costs. He must treat $150 as a tax preference item [$800 excess intangible drilling costs less $650 (65% of $1,000 net oil income)].

Intangible drilling and development costs include the cost to operators of any drilling or development work (excluding amounts payable only out of production or the gross proceeds of production, and amounts properly allocable to cost of depreciable property) done for them by contractors under any form of contract, including turnkey contracts [Reg. Sec. 1.612-4(a)].

Intangible drilling costs incurred in drilling a well in consideration of an assignment of an interest in a lease are capital expenditures, and may not be deducted as business expenses.[2] However, intangible drilling and development expenses incurred in acquiring an *operating or working interest* may be treated as deductible expenses [Reg. Sec. 1.612-4(a)].

The deductions for depletion which reduced the adjusted basis of the property are recaptured if the property is disposed of. The amounts previously deducted are treated as ordinary income to the extent they exceed the amounts that would have been deducted had the costs been capitalized. The recapture rules are similar to those involving Sec. 1245 property (¶1812) [IRC Sec. 1254].

Special energy deduction. For tax years starting after 1990, taxpayers (other than integrated oil companies) can take a special energy deduction for computing their

2227 Chapter 12—Business Deductions ¶2237

alternative minimum tax. This deduction is calculated by determining the taxpayer's oil and gas related tax preference items, including the intangible drilling cost preference. See ¶ 2604. An integrated oil company is one that does not qualify as a small producer or royalty owner (¶ 2237(a))[IRC Sec. 56(h)].

This special tax break given to oil and gas investors is designed to offset a portion of oil and gas tax preferences (percentage depletion and intangible drilling costs) in computing the AMT.

Reduction of benefits. Every corporation that is an integrated oil company [see ¶ 2237(a)] must reduce its deduction for intangible drilling costs to 70% of what it could otherwise deduct. The remaining 30% must be deducted ratably over a 60-month period starting with the month the costs are paid or incurred [IRC Sec. 291(b)].

(d) Incorrect Estimate of Remaining Units. If it is discovered that the remaining units have been incorrectly estimated, the annual depletion allowance for the tax year and later years will be based on the revised estimate [IRC Sec. 611(a); Reg. Sec. 1.611-2(c)].

Example 3: The United Coal Co. bought mineral property on January 1, 1991 for $3,000,000 when the recoverable reserves (remaining units) were estimated at 300,000 units. United did not use percentage depletion. 40,000 units were extracted during the year but only 25,000 were sold. The depletion deduction is $250,000 (($3,000,000/300,000) × 25,000).

Example 4: In Example 3, suppose on January 1, 1992 it is discovered that the property actually contains 500,000 units. Assuming that no capital additions are to be made, the adjusted basis would be $2,750,000 ($3,000,000 – $250,000 depletion taken in 1991), and if 30,000 units were sold during 1992 the depletion deduction would be $165,000 (($2,750,000/500,000) × 30,000). Note that the revision in the remaining units does not affect the basis for depletion. It would have been $2,750,000 (assuming no capital additions), if the revised estimate of the remaining units had not been made.

¶2237 PERCENTAGE DEPLETION

Your percentage depletion allowance is a specified percentage of the "gross income from the property" subject to the limitation that it generally may not exceed 50% (100% for oil and gas properties) of the "taxable income from the property" (figured without depletion allowance). But see (a) below [IRC Sec. 613(a); Reg. Sec. 1.613-1]. The percentage method applies to geothermal wells and deposits, oil and gas wells, coal mines, metal mines, and certain other deposits, but not to timber. For those properties to which the percentage method applies, the deduction should be figured under both the cost method and the percentage method, and the larger deduction taken [IRC Sec. 612(a); Reg. Sec. 1.613-1]. Also, the basis of the property must be reduced by the larger allowance [Reg. Sec. 1.1016-3(b)].

▶ **BIGGER DEPLETION ALLOWANCE** The 50%-of-taxable income limitation has been raised to 100% for oil and gas properties, for tax years starting after 1990. The 100% net income limitation applies to all oil and gas properties with respect to which percentage depletion is allowed.

Example 1: Acme Drilling Co. is a small independent producer. During 1992, the company generated $300,000 of gross income from crude oil produced from its Field X. Its operating costs for the year, before depletion, totaled $250,000. Acme can claim a percentage depletion of $45,000 (15% of $300,000)(assuming other limitations did not apply). *Note:* Under prior law, Acme would have been limited to depletion of $25,000 (50% of $50,000 net income).

Example 2: Assume the same facts as in Example 1, except that Acme also owns Field Y from which it has $100,000 of gross income and pre-depletion net income of $10,000. Acme's percentage depletion allowance for its Field Y income is limited to $10,000.

Alternative minimum tax. The depletion deduction can result in an additional tax called alternative minimum tax. This tax is figured on benefits received (like the depletion deduction), lower tax rates and tax exclusions. Since some income and deductions receive special tax treatment, they are considered tax preferences. These tax preferences are used to figure the alternative minimum tax. The excess of the depletion deduction over the property's adjusted basis is a tax preference item (¶2603) [IRC Sec. 57(a)(1)].

(a) Oil, Gas and Geothermal Wells. Percentage depletion is permitted only for (1) certain domestic gas wells and (2) small independent producers and royalty owners. In general, the percentage depletion rate for oil and gas is 15% of the gross income from the property.

Domestic gas production. Geothermal wells, which consist of natural heat stored in rocks or aqueous liquid or vapor, are eligible for percentage depletion on wells commenced after September 30, 1978. The depletion allowance is 15%. The well must be located in the U.S. or its possessions [IRC Sec. 613(e)].

Grandfather rule. Producers of gas sold under a "fixed contract" regarding any geothermal deposit in the U.S. or its possessions that is determined to be a gas well, can take a depletion allowance equal to 22% of the gross income from the property's domestic production. A *"fixed contract"* is a contract in effect on February 1, 1975 (and at all times thereafter before such sale), under which the price cannot be adjusted to reflect any increase in seller's tax resulting from the repeal of percentage depletion [IRC Sec. 613A(b)].

Small producers and royalty owners. The test to qualify for percentage depletion is based on "average daily production" for the tax year from domestic oil and gas wells. This is the result of dividing aggregate production by the number of days in the tax year. The amount of your average daily production to which depletion applies is the amount of average daily production that doesn't exceed 1,000 barrels or 6 million cubic feet of natural gas. For production that includes both oil and gas, the exemption is allocated between the two [IRC Sec. 613A(c)].

The small producer's exemption is not available to any producer who owns or controls a retail outlet for the sale of oil or gas or petroleum products; who engages (directly or through a related person) in refining oil if, on any one day during the tax year, the refinery exceeds 50,000 barrels; or for any proven oil or gas property transferred after 1974 except transfers by reason of death and certain other transfers. A "retailer" is a taxpayer with gross receipts of over $5 million for the tax year from the sale of these products. Also, a change of a trust's beneficiaries is not considered a "transfer" if it occurs only for death, birth or adoption of any beneficiary if the transferee was a beneficiary under the trust before any of those events. Special basis rules apply to the partnership depletion allowance (¶3427(c)) [IRC Sec. 613A(c)].

NOTE: The restriction on claiming percentage depletion on transferred proven property was repealed for transfers occurring after October 11, 1990.

The tax year's percentage depletion deduction for small producers and royalty owners is subject to two limitations. It may not exceed 100% of the taxable income from the property (see above), figured without the depletion allowance [IRC Sec. 613(a)]. Nor may it exceed 65% of your taxable income from all sources (computed without regard to percentage depletion under the small producer's exemption, capital loss or net operating loss carrybacks and trust distributions to a beneficiary other than certain family members). A disallowed deduction may be carried over [IRC Sec. 613A(d)].

➤ **HIGHER DEPLETION RATE** The 15% rate increases for marginally producing oil and gas wells for tax years starting after 1990. The increase is 1% for each whole dollar that the average domestic wellhead price of crude oil sinks below $20 per barrel (subject to a maximum 25% depletion rate). Marginal production is production from stripper wells and from property that produces substantially all heavy oil [IRC Sec. 613A(c)(6)].

NOTE: For tax years starting after 1990, taxpayers (other than integrated oil companies) can take a special energy deduction for computing their AMT. This deduction is calculated by determining your oil and gas related tax preference items, including the marginal production depletion preference. See ¶ 2604. An integrated oil company is one that does not qualify as a small producer or royalty owner [IRC Sec. 56(h)].

Gross income from the property generally is the amount for which you sell the oil or gas in the immediate vicinity of the well. If the oil or gas is processed or transported or both, gross income is figured using the average market or field price before processing or transportation [Reg. Sec. 1.613-3(a)].

In figuring gross income for percentage depletion, a lessee must exclude from actual gross income the amount of rents and royalties paid to the lessor [IRC Sec. 613(a); Reg. Sec. 1.613-2(c)(5)]. If royalties in the form of bonus payments have been paid in any year, lessees must exclude from gross income the part of the payments that are allocable to the products sold during the tax year.[1] Percentage depletion is not allowed for lease bonuses or advance royalties for oil, gas or geothermal properties—regardless of the actual production of the property [IRC Sec. 613(e)(4), 613A(d)(5)].

Taxable income from the property is "gross income from the property," less the allowable deductions directly related to the mineral property on which depletion is claimed. Deductions not directly related to the property are fairly allocated [Reg. Sec. 1.613-5]. The charitable contribution deduction is not subtracted.[2] This applies to qualifying gas well production.

(b) Other Depletable Mineral Interests. The percentage of gross income depletion for mines, wells and other natural deposits ranges from 22% (e.g., sulfur and uranium) to 5% (e.g., gravel, peat[3] and clay) depending on whether the location is within or outside the U.S. [IRC Sec. 613(b); Reg. Sec. 1.613-2].

An amount equal to any rents and royalties paid or incurred for the property must be excluded in determining gross income [IRC Sec. 613(a); Reg. Sec. 1.613-2(c)(5)].

Gross income from property in connection with percentage depletion for mines means gross income *from mining*. Mining includes more than merely the extraction of ores or minerals from the ground. Mining also includes (1) the treatment processes considered as mining to the extent they are applied by the mine owner or operator to the mineral or the ore, and (2) the transportation of ores or minerals from the point of extraction to the plants or mills where the ordinary treatment processes are applied, but not in excess of 50 miles (unless the Revenue Service rules otherwise) [IRC Sec. 613(c); Reg. Sec. 1.613-4(h)]. Any process that is not necessary to bring the minerals to shipping form is not part of the treatment process.[4] The Supreme Court holds that a lessee of mining property must deduct ad valorem and royalty taxes it paid before figuring gross income from property for percentage depletion purposes.[5]

NOTE: Percentage depletion is to be based on the constructive income from the raw product if marketable in that form (whether or not marketable at a profit), and not on the value of the finished product.[6]

The percentage depletion on oil shale is figured on its value after the extraction and retorting of the shale oil, but before hydrogenating and refining [IRC Sec. 613(c)].

Cash or trade discounts actually allowed by a taxpayer must be subtracted from the sales price in determining "gross income from the property" [Reg. Sec. 1.613-4(e)].

> **NOTE:** The "extraction of ores or minerals from the ground" includes the extraction by *mine owners or operators* of ores or minerals from the waste or residue of their prior mining such as a tailing dump, or a culm bank. This does not apply to a buyer of the waste or residue or a buyer of the rights to extract ores or minerals from the waste or residue [IRC Sec. 613(c); Reg. Sec. 1.613-4(i)].

The depletion deduction may be figured (without regard to any election) either on the percentage basis, or on the general rule basis, whichever gives the greater deduction [IRC Sec. 613(a); Reg. Sec. 1.613-1].

Business interruption insurance. Proceeds from a policy insuring against loss of mining profits are not taken into account in figuring percentage depletion, since they are not considered gross income from mining.[7]

Taxable income from the property generally has the same meaning as in (a), above. However, the deduction for mining expenses is reduced by gain on sale of depreciable property [¶1812] that is taxed as ordinary income, and which is allocable to the property. Records must be kept in determining the gain on the property [IRC Sec. 613(a); Reg. Sec. 1.613-5(b)(5)].

Reduction of benefits. The amount allowable as a deduction for coal and iron ore percentage depletion by corporations is reduced by 20% of the amount of the excess of the deduction over the property's adjusted basis [IRC Sec. 291].

(c) Percentage Depletion Allowed Though No Cost Basis. It is possible and not unusual for a taxpayer to recover tax-free, through percentage depletion, an amount greater than the property's cost. It follows that you may recover a larger amount tax-free through depletion than you could through a sale or other disposition of the property. These inequalities are ignored. The law allows the deduction although the cost has been recovered.[8] However, any depletion above the cost basis is a tax preference item subject to the alternative minimum tax [¶2603].

¶2238   TREATMENT OF BONUSES AND ROYALTIES

If a lessor receives a bonus in addition to royalties, a cost depletion deduction for the bonus is figured as follows [Reg. Sec. 1.612-3(a)]:

$$\text{Basis for depletion} \times \frac{\text{Bonus}}{\text{Bonus} + \text{Expected Royalties}} = \text{Depletion deduction}$$

The depletion allowance figured above is deducted from the lessor's basis for depletion; the remainder of the basis is recoverable through depletion deductions as the royalties are received later.

> **Example:** Assume that the lessor's basis for depletion is $2,000,000, that he receives a bonus of $1,000,000 and that he is to receive a royalty of one-fourth of the minerals produced by the lessee, it being estimated that the royalty payments will amount to $3,000,000. The depletion deduction on account of the receipt of the bonus would be $500,000, figured as follows:
>
> $2,000,000 x $1,000,000 / ($1,000,000 + $3,000,000) = $500,000

SPECIAL DEPLETION PROBLEMS

¶2240   **DEPLETION OF TIMBER**

This depletion is based on the adjusted basis for figuring gain on a sale. It does not include any part of the land's cost. Depletion occurs when the timber is cut and is figured by the cost method only. The deduction each year is the number of timber units cut multiplied by the depletion unit. The unit is figured as follows [IRC Sec. 611; Reg. Sec. 1.611-3(b)(2)]:

$$\frac{C + P + A}{U + (\text{or}-) \ YX + (\text{or}-)} = \text{depletion unit}$$

   C equals the capital sum remaining at the beginning of the year.
   P equals the cost of any purchases during the year.
   A equals capital additions during the year other than purchases.
   U equals total units of timber at the beginning of the year.
   X equals the units to be added or deducted in order to adjust the total remaining units (U) to conform to the actual quantity of units remaining.
   Y equals the units added through purchase or deducted on account of sale en bloc.
   The loss to be deducted for forest fire is found the same way. If timber contains turpentine, that portion of the total cost or other basis reasonably allocable to turpentine may be amortized or recovered through depletion deductions on any reasonable basis over the period of actual turpentining.

> **NOTE:** A map and statement (Form T) giving the data required by the regulations must be attached to the return if depletion of timber is claimed [Reg. Sec. 1.611-3(h)].

¶2241   **BOOKS OF ACCOUNT**

Separate accounts should be kept in which there should be recorded the basis of the property, any allowable capital additions, and all other adjustments. The annual depletion deduction should be credited to the mineral property accounts or to the depletion reserve accounts [Reg. Sec. 1.611-2(b)]. It is not necessary to adopt any particular method of bookkeeping, but records must be accurate.

As to timber, there are special requirements for the books of account [Reg. Sec. 1.611-3(c)], and, as a general rule, separate accounts must be kept for each "block" of timber [Reg. Sec. 1.611-3(d)].

MINING EXPENSES

¶2242   **MINE EXPLORATION EXPENDITURES**

Exploration expenditures are those expenses incurred in ascertaining the existence, extent, quality or quantity of a new mineral deposit. You may elect to deduct domestic exploration expenditures incurred in hard mineral operations [IRC Sec. 617; Reg. Sec. 1.617-1]. Expenses to *discover* oil and gas deposits, called geological and geophysical expenses, must be capitalized.

Expenditures for capital equipment or improvements used in exploration are not exploration expenditures if the cost is recoverable through depreciation. However, the depreciation is an exploration expenditure [Reg. Sec. 1.617-1(b)(2)].

You may elect an unlimited deduction of exploration expenditures paid during the tax year as to any *domestic* mineral deposit (other than oil and gas) subject to the depletion allowance [Reg. Sec. 1.617-1(a), 1.617-2(b)(1)]. If this election is made, the capitalized exploration costs must therefore be deductible only on abandoning the exploration project or the property.

Mining exploration costs are an adjustment in figuring the alternative minimum tax (¶2601) [IRC Sec. 56(a)(2)]. The costs that are deducted for regular tax purposes must be recovered through 10-year straight line amortization for the alternative minimum tax.

Example: Blake incurred a one-time mining exploration expense of $1,000. He gets a deduction for that amount on his return. For alternative minimum tax purposes, he must spread $1,000 over a 10-year period starting with the year the expenditure was incurred.

Recapture. Once the property reaches the development stage, all previously deducted exploration expenditures must be recaptured. You have two choices about the recapture: (1) You can elect, as to all mines reaching the production stage during the tax year (on which deductions have been allowed) to include in gross income an amount equal to the adjusted exploration expenditures. Or, (2) If you do not so elect, you cannot take otherwise deductible depletion allowances until the sum of the allowances not taken equals the adjusted exploration expenditures. Adjusted exploration expenditures are those which produced a tax benefit. Therefore, depletion allowances not taken reduce total adjusted exploration expenditures. You must make this election annually [IRC Sec. 617(b); Reg. Sec. 1.617-3].

Recapture also applies to sales and assignments, causing ordinary gain to the extent of the deducted exploration expenditures. Transferees in tax-free exchanges will eventually have to recapture the deductions [Reg. Sec. 1.617-4]. Partnerships are subject to special rules [IRC Sec. 617(g)].

The above rules do not apply to expenditures: (1) to acquire or improve depreciable property (although depreciation on such property qualifies as an expenditure); (2) that are deductible without regard to these provisions; (3) that are part of the acquisition cost [IRC Sec. 616, 617; Reg. Sec. 1.616-1(b)].

Adjusted basis of mine or deposit is not reduced by depletion disallowed when the unlimited exploration expenditure is elected [IRC Sec. 617(e)].

Reduction of benefits. For corporations, 30% of domestic mining exploration costs must be amortized ratably over a 60-month period. The remaining 70%, together with similar costs of noncorporate taxpayers, is eligible for expensing [IRC Sec. 291(b)].

How treated on return. An individual's deductible exploration expense is a deduction for adjusted gross income.

¶2243   MINING DEVELOPMENT EXPENDITURES

Expenses for the development of a mine or natural deposit (other than an oil or gas well) that contains commercially marketable quantities of the ore or mineral, are deductible as follows:

1. The expenses can be deducted in the year paid or incurred [IRC Sec. 616(a); Reg. Sec. 1.616-1]; *or*

2. You may elect to deduct the expenses proportionately as the ore or mineral benefited by them is sold (deferred expense). While the mine or deposit is in the development stage, this election is limited to the development expenses in excess of the net receipts from production within the tax year. (Expenditures not in excess of such receipts are deductible in full.) This election is not binding on future years. It may be made on the return or by a statement filed with the timely filed return (including extensions) for the tax year to which the election applies [IRC Sec. 616(b); Reg. Sec. 1.616-2].

3. The expenses can be amortized over 10 years [IRC Sec. 59(e)(4)].

Example 1: Mine A was in the development stage throughout the year 1992. If the development expenses incurred during the year are $5,000, the whole amount is either deductible in 1992, or, at your election, deferred to be deducted ratably as the ore or mineral is sold.

Example 2: Mine C was in the development stage from January to August 1992. From August to December 1992, it was in the productive stage. Development expenses from January to August amounted to $5,000 and from August to December, $1,000. If the net receipts from the sale of minerals produced in 1992 is $3,000, you have an option to—
  (1) deduct $6,000 in 1992, or
  (2) deduct $3,000 in 1992 and defer $3,000 to be deducted ratably as the ore or mineral is sold.
(The $3,000 to be deducted in 1992 represents your $5,000 preproduction development expenses not in excess of the $3,000 net receipts. The $3,000 to be deferred represents the $1,000 development expenses incurred in the productive stage plus the $2,000 which is the excess of your $5,000 of preproduction development expenses over the $3,000 of net receipts.)

The above rules do not apply to expenditures: (1) to acquire or improve depreciable property (although depreciation on such property qualifies as an expenditure); (2) that are deductible without regard to these provisions; (3) that are part of the acquisition cost [IRC Sec. 616, 617; Reg. Sec. 1.616-1(b)].

Mining development costs are an adjustment in figuring the alternative minimum tax (2603) [IRC Sec. 56(a)(2)]. The costs that are deducted for regular tax purposes must be recovered through 10-year straight line amortization for the alternative minimum tax.

Reduction of benefits. For corporations, 30% of domestic mining exploration costs must be amortized ratably over a 60-month period. The remaining 70%, together with similar costs of noncorporate taxpayers, is eligible for expensing [IRC Sec. 291(b)].

Adjusted basis of mine or deposit. Deferred development expenses are included in figuring the adjusted basis when the mine or deposit is sold. The adjusted basis is reduced by the deferred deductions to the extent they reduced tax liability (but not less than the amount *allowable*). These expenses are not factors in figuring the adjusted basis for depletion purposes [IRC Sec. 616(c), 617(i); Reg. Sec. 1.1016-5(f)].

FARMERS' EXPENSES

¶2244 EXPENSES OF FARMERS

The expenses of preparing, developing and operating your farm are either ordinary and necessary current business expenses or capital expenditures. Your income and expenses are reported on Schedule F of Form 1040, 1041, or 1065. (A sample Schedule F can be found on pages 2230 and 2231.) Special rules limit the deductions available to farm syndicates. See (d) below. Losses of farmers are discussed in ¶2311.

(a) Business Expenses. During the productive period of the farm, the ordinary and necessary current expenses of farming are deductible [Reg. Sec. 1.162-12].

Examples of Deductible Expenses[1]

Rations bought and furnished to sharecroppers

Feed purchased (grain, hay, silage, mill feeds, concentrates and other roughages, and cost of grinding, mixing, and processing feed) [but see (d) below]

Machine hire (payments for use of threshing, combining, silo filling, baling, ginning, and other machines)

Seeds and plants bought (but see (d) below)

Supplies purchased (spray material, poisons, disinfectants, cans, barrels, baskets, egg cases, bags, etc.)

Repairs and maintenance of farm machines and equipment

Breeding fees

Fertilizers and lime (cost of commercial fertilizers, lime and manure purchased during the year, the benefit of which is of short duration) [see also election]

Veterinary and medicine for livestock

Storage and warehousing expense

Insurance on farm property, except farmer's dwelling (buildings, improvements, equipment, crops and livestock)

Water rent (farm share of expense)

Blacksmith and harness repair

Examples of Nondeductible Expenses[1]

Value of products raised by farmer and used for board of hired help

Expense of raising products consumed by farmer and his family

Cost of producing or acquiring donated products[2] [see ¶2205]

Value of labor of farmer, his wife, or minor children (but reasonable wages paid to child for service on farm are deductible)

Cotton acreage allotments[3]

Expenses of planting and developing citrus groves (see below)

During the development of the farm, you may elect to capitalize ordinary and necessary expenses incidental to current operation instead of deducting them [Reg. Sec. 1.162-12].

Citrus and almond grove expenses. In general, the costs of planting, cultivating, maintaining and developing citrus and almond groves must be capitalized if they have a preproduction period of more than two years. However, an election can be made to deduct all these preproductive costs [IRC Sec. 263A(d)]. The election does not apply under certain circumstances. For example, it does not apply to the cost of planting, cultivating, maintaining, or developing any citrus or almond grove incurred before the end of the fourth tax year after the trees were planted. The costs of replanting a grove lost by disease, freeze or other casualty generally are deducted currently [IRC Sec. 263A(d)(2)].

Election to deduct fertilizer and lime expenditures. You may elect to treat as a deductible expense expenditures for fertilizer, lime, ground limestone, marl, or other materials used to enrich, neutralize, or condition his farmland, or for the application of these materials. You make the election by taking the deduction on a timely filed return for the year. It may not be revoked without consent of the Revenue Service [IRC Sec. 180; Reg. Sec. 1.180-1, 1.180-2].

(b) Capital Expenditures. Expenditures during the preparatory period, when the property is made ready for development, are not deductible as business expenses. They are capital expenditures[1] (¶2101; 2203) [Reg. Sec. 1.162-12], except for fertilizer and lime expenditures (above) the farmer elects to deduct.

The cost of farm machinery, equipment, and buildings (other than dwellings) whether incurred in the preparatory period or another period, is not deductible as an expense, but is a capital expenditure, and deduction is allowed for depreciation. Likewise, amounts spent to buy work, breeding or dairy animals are regarded as investments of capital, and depreciation is allowed, unless the animals are included in inventory [Reg. Sec. 1.162-12].

(c) Farming for Pleasure. If you operate a farm for recreation or pleasure and not on a commercial basis, and farm expenses exceed farm receipts, you need not include in income the receipts from the sale of farm products. The expenses will be treated as personal expenses, that is, not deductible [Reg. Sec. 1.162-12(b)]. Farm expenses in excess of receipts are deductible only if the farming is engaged in for profit [¶2325].

(d) Farming Syndicates. Farm syndicates can only deduct during the tax year feed, seed, seed fertilizer and other similar farm supplies when actually used or consumed. The cost of poultry (including egg-laying hens and baby chicks) must be capitalized and deducted ratably over the lesser of 12 months or their useful life in the trade or business. The cost of poultry purchased for sale must be deducted in the year the poultry is sold or otherwise disposed of [IRC Sec. 464(b)].

What are farming syndicates. A farm syndicate is a partnership or any other enterprise (other than C corporations [¶3100]) that engages in farming and has registered securities for sale with a federal or state agency. It also includes a partnership or any other enterprise (other than a C corporation) that allocates more than 35% of its losses to a limited entrepreneur (someone who does not actively participate in the enterprise's management) or limited partner. However, an individual can avoid being treated as a limited partner or entrepreneur by actively participating in the management for at least 5 years or by living on the farm [IRC Sec. 464(c)].

Cash basis taxpayers who are in the trade or business of farming are also limited in deducting prepaid amounts for feed, fertilizer, and other similar farm supplies. The limitation applies to the extent that prepaid expenses exceed more than 50% of the person's farming expenses paid during the tax year (other than prepaid farm supplies). These may be deducted only in the tax year when actually used or consumed. An exception is provided for those "qualified farm-related taxpayers" who satisfy the 50% test on an aggregated basis for the past three years or whose failure to satisfy the 50% test is due to a change in business operations directly attributable to extraordinary circumstances. "Farm related taxpayers" include: (1) any person whose principal residence is on the farm; (2) any person with a principal occupation of farming; or (3) any family member of the above [IRC Sec. 464(f)].

¶2245   SOIL AND WATER CONSERVATION EXPENDITURES

You can deduct in the tax year paid or incurred expenses for soil and water conservation and the prevention of erosion of land used in farming [IRC Sec. 175; Reg. Sec. 1.175-1]. The deduction cannot be more than 25% of your gross income from farming during the tax year (see (a) below). The expenditure must be made to further the business of farming and, if not deducted, must be capitalized [Reg. Sec. 1.175-1, 1.175-2]. Examples of deductible expenditures include the treatment and moving of earth. However, you may not deduct expenditures to buy, construct, install or improve depreciable structures or facilities.

The deduction applies to land used by you or your tenants for the production of crops, fruits or other agricultural products or for the sustenance of livestock [IRC Sec. 175(c)(2)]. It does not apply when you rent farm land at a fixed rental (unless you materially help manage or operate the farm), engage in forestry or timber growing, or run a farm as a hobby [Reg. Sec. 1.175-3]. If the expenditures are made for newly acquired farm land, the deduction applies if the land is put to the same type of farming use as that immediately preceding its acquisition. However, if land will be put to a different use (i.e., pasture or timber land cultivated for crops) the expenditures are preparatory expenses and must be capitalized [Reg. Sec. 1.175-4].

> **NOTE:** Expenditures that can be deducted currently are limited to amounts incurred that are consistent with a conservation plan approved by the Department of Agriculture's Soil Conservation Service. [IRC Sec. 175(c)(3)].

Deductible

Expenditures for treating and moving earth (including—but not limited to—leveling, conditioning, grading, terracing, contour furrowing, and restoring soil fertility); eradication of brush; planting of windbreaks; construction, control and protection of diversion channels, drainage ditches, irrigation ditches, earthen dams, watercourses, outlets and ponds[IRC Sec. 175(c)(1), Reg. Sec. 1.175-2].

Not Deductible

Expenditures to buy, construct, install, or improve depreciable structures, appliances, or facilities, or any amount deductible under other provisions. Expenditures for depreciable property include cost of materials, supplies, wages, fuel, hauling and dirt moving for structures such as tanks, reservoirs, pipes, conduits, canals, dams, wells or pumps made of masonry concrete, tile, metal or wood [IRC Sec. 175(c); Reg. Sec. 1.175-2]. For deductibility of assessments for depreciable property, see (c) below.

(a) Limitation. 1. The amount deductible for the tax year cannot exceed 25% of gross income from farming during the tax year. "Gross income from farming" means gross income from *all* of your farms. It does not, however, include gains from sale of assets such as farm machinery or gains from the disposition of land [Reg. Sec. 1.175-5].

2. Expenditures over the amount allowable for any tax year can be carried over to the following tax year, and considered the first expenditure in that year. However, the total deduction for each succeeding year (carryover plus actual expenditures made during the tax year) is still limited to 25% of gross income from farming during the tax year.

> **Example 1:** Mr. McDonald had $12,000 gross income from farming in 1992. His soil and water conservation expenditures were $3,500. McDonald can deduct $3,000 (.25 x $12,000) for 1992. The balance, $500, can be carried over to 1993 and considered the first such expenditure in that year.

> **Example 2:** Assume McDonald had $10,000 gross income from farming in 1993, and that his soil and water conservation expenditures were $2,100. He can deduct $2,500 for 1992, and his carryover to 1993 would be $100, figured as shown below:

Carryover from 1992	$ 500
Expenditures in 1993	2,100
Total	$2,600
Deduction (limited to .25 x $10,000)	2,500
Carryover to 1993	$ 100

Amounts deducted either in the year paid or incurred or a carryover year are considered in figuring a net operating loss (¶2341 et seq.) [Reg. Sec. 1.175-5(a)(3)].

(b) Election to Expense or Capitalize. The method (deduction or capitalization) can be adopted without consent for the first tax year the expenditures are paid or incurred. For adoption at any other time, IRS consent is required. Once adopted, the method applies to all soil and water conservation expenditures for the tax year and later tax years, and must be followed consistently, unless the IRS consents to a change. However, you may request authorization to capitalize (or, if the election to deduct is not made, to deduct) soil and water conservation expenditures for a special project or a single farm.

The request for adoption (or a change) must be filed not later than the time required for filing the return [IRC Sec. 175(d); Reg. Sec. 1.175-6].

> ➤ **OBSERVATION** You should distinguish between (1) soil and water conservation *expenditures* and (2) expenses for *maintenance and repair* of structures built for soil and water conservation purposes or to prevent erosion. Expenses for maintenance and repair are deductible when paid or incurred without limit. They cannot be carried over and deducted in a succeeding year.[1]

(c) Assessments. Amounts paid to a soil or water conservation or drainage district are deductible to the extent they are (1) not otherwise allowable as a deduction and (2) they defray expenses by such a district, which, if made by you, would be deductible as soil or water conservation expenditures [IRC Sec. 175(c); Reg. Sec. 1.175-2(c)]. Also, a limited deduction is allowed for assessments levied by a district to acquire depreciable property used in the district's conservation or drainage activities. The deduction for any one member of a district is limited to 10% of the depreciable cost of the property to the district (any balance is capitalized as land cost). Payment in any year is deductible currently only to the extent of 10% of a member's assessment for equipment cost to the district; the balance is spread over nine succeeding years if it exceeds 10% of the assessment plus $500 [IRC Sec. 175(c),(f)]. If members sell their land before they have taken the full allowable deduction, the unwritten amounts enter into their gain or loss. If they die, the amount not written off is deductible on their last returns but subject to the 25% limit in (a) above [IRC Sec. 175(f); Reg. Sec. 1.175-5].

¶2246   AMORTIZATION OF REFORESTATION EXPENDITURES

You can elect to amortize certain capital costs involved in the seeding or planting of land held for timber production. The election covers a maximum of $10,000 of qualified expenditures incurred during the year. These costs are amortized over a period of 84 months (7 years). Qualified expenditures are those incurred in connection with planting or seeding, including the cost of (1) site preparation, (2) seeds or seedlings, and (3) labor and tools [IRC Sec. 194] . Amounts deducted as amortization are subject to recapture under Sec. 1245 if the property is sold prematurely [¶1812] .

Footnotes to Chapter 12

(For your added convenience, in brackets [] with the footnotes below, you will find citations to related paragraphs in the "RIA United States Tax Reporter"(USTR), "CCH Federal Tax Reporter"(CCH) and "RIA Federal Tax Coordinator 2d"(FTC) multi-volume services.)

FOOTNOTE ¶ 2201 [USTR ¶ 1624; CCH ¶ 8470; FTC ¶ L-1100].

(1) Welch v. Helvering, 290 US 111, 54 SCt. 8, 12 AFTR 348, Dunn & McCarthy, Inc. v. Comm.,
139 F.2d 242, 31 AFTR 1043; Cf. Kentucky Util. Co. v. Glenn, 21 AFTR 2d 1263, 394 F.2d 631.

(2) Comm. v. Heininger, 320 US 467, 64 SCt. 249, 31 AFTR 783.

FOOTNOTE ¶ 2202 [USTR ¶ 1624; CCH ¶ 8470; FTC ¶ L-1000].

(1) Comm. v. Lincoln Elec. Co., 176 F.2d 815, 38 AFTR 411.

(2) Rev. Rul. 70-40, 1970-1 CB 50.

(3) Rev. Rul. 70-40, 1970-1 CB 50, Reise, 9 AFTR 2d 887, 299 F.2d 380, acq. 1969-2 CB XXV.

FOOTNOTE ¶ 2203 [USTR ¶ 1634; CCH ¶ 13,709; FTC ¶ L-5600].

(1) Schlosser Bros., 2 BTA 137.

(2) MacAdam & Foster, Inc., 8 BTA 542.

(3) Harbeson Lumber Co., 24 BTA 542.

(4) Rev. Rul. 57-418, 1957-2 CB 143; Rev. Rul. 77-254, 1977-2 CB 63; Finch v. U.S. (DC Minn. 6-30-66), 18 AFTR 2d 5259.

(5) Babbitt, 32 BTA 693; The Toledo Blade Co., 11 TC 1079.

(6) Idaho Power Co. v. Comm., 34 AFTR 2d 74-5244, 94 SCt. 2757.

(7) Ltr. Rul. 9123004.

(8) Ltr. Rul. 9047032.

FOOTNOTE ¶ 2204 [USTR ¶ 2654; CCH ¶ 14,054; FTC ¶ K-9000].

(1) Herbst, ¶ 43,309 PH Memo TC.

(2) Cotton States Fertilizer Co., 28 TC 1169

FOOTNOTE ¶ 2205 [USTR ¶ 1704; CCH ¶ 11,690.03; FTC ¶ K-3481 et seq.].

FOOTNOTE ¶ 2206 [USTR ¶ 2764; CCH ¶ 2296B; FTC ¶ L-2400].

FOOTNOTE ¶ 2207 [USTR ¶ 1624; CCH ¶ 8904; FTC ¶ L-2207].

(1) Comm. v. Sullivan, 1 AFTR 2d 1158, 356 US 27, 78 SCt. 512.

(2) Comeaux, G.A., 10 TC 201; Excelsior Baking Co. v. U.S., 82 F. Supp. 423, 37 AFTR 1066.

(3) Raymond Bertolini Trucking Co. v. Comm., 54 AFTR 2d 84-5413.

FOOTNOTE ¶ 2210 [USTR ¶ 1624; CCH ¶ 8586; FTC ¶ H-2600].

(1) Rev. Rul. 72-23, 1972-1 CB 43; Rev. Rul. 73-393, 1973-2 CB 33.

FOOTNOTE ¶ 2211 [USTR ¶ 1624; CCH ¶ 8587; FTC ¶ H-2700 et seq.].

(1) Hendricks Furniture, Inc., TC Memo 1988-133.

FOOTNOTE ¶ 2212 [USTR ¶ 1624; CCH ¶ 8586; FTC ¶ H-1500 et seq.].

FOOTNOTE ¶ 2213 [USTR ¶ 1624; CCH ¶ 8686; 13,709; FTC ¶ H-3020 et seq.].

(1) Rev. Rul. 69-465, 1969-2 CB 27.

(2) Treas. Dept. booklet "Basis of Assets" (1991 Ed.), p. 1.

FOOTNOTE ¶ 2214 [USTR ¶ 1624; CCH ¶ 8592; 8702; FTC ¶ H-2603].

(1) Treas. Dept. Press Release, 6-2-47.

(2) Rev. Rul. 67-315, 1967-2 CB 85.

FOOTNOTE ¶ 2215 [¶ 1624; CCH ¶ 8585; FTC ¶ H-3015].

(1) Lucas v. Ox Fibre Brush Co., 281 US 115, 50 SCt. 273, 8 AFTR 10901; Associated Theatres Corp., 14 TC 313.

(2) Reub Isaacs & Co., Inc., 1 BTA 45.

FOOTNOTE ¶ 2216 [USTR ¶ 2124; CCH ¶ 8584; FTC ¶ L-4100 et seq.].

(1) Bagley, 8 TC 130.

(2) Comm. v. Tellier, 17 AFTR 2d 633, 86 SCt. 118, 383 U.S. 687.

(3) Comm. v. Heininger, 320 US 467, 64 SCt. 249, 31 AFTR 783. See ¶ 1808.

(4) Hurt, 30 BTA 653; Hochschild, 161 F.2d 817, 36 AFTR 1373.

(5) Howard v. Comm., 202 F.2d 28, 43 AFTR 249.

(6) O'Neal, 18 BTA 1036; Kelley, 38 BTA 1292.

(7) Commack, 5 TC 467.

(8) Tyler, 6 TC 135.

(9) Greene Motor Co., 5 TC 314.

(10) Rev. Rul. 73-13, 1973-1 CB 42.

(11) U.S. v. Pate, 254 F.2d 480, 1 AFTR 2d 1530.

(12) Lloyd, 22 BTA 674, aff'd 55 F.2d 842, 10 AFTR 1195.

(13) Kleinschmidt, 12 TC 921.

(14) Draper, 26 TC 201.

(15) Murphy, 48 TC 569.

(16) Rev. Rul. 1, 1953-1 CB 36. ·

(17) Bowers v. Lumpkin, 140 F.2d 927, 32 AFTR 201; Coughlin, 3 TC 420.

(18) Robins, 8 BTA 523.

(19) Gilmore, 372 US 39, 11 AFTR 2d 758; Patrick, 372 US 53, 11 AFTR 2d 764.

(20) Nadiak v. Comm., 17 AFTR 2d 396, 356 F.2d 911; Margoles, ¶ 68,058 PH Memo TC.

(21) Davidson, 27 BTA 158.

(22) Rev. Rul. 70-62, 1970-1 CB 30.

(23) Rev. Rul. 67-125, 1967-1 CB 31.

(24) Ltr. Rul. 9144042.

(25) National Starch, US S.Ct., No. 92-1849 (2/27/92).

FOOTNOTE ¶ 2217 [USTR ¶ 28064; CCH ¶ 15,152; FTC ¶ H-2732 et seq.].

FOOTNOTE ¶ 2220 [USTR ¶ 1624; CCH ¶ 8580; FTC ¶ L-6100 et seq.].

(1) Illinois Merchants Trust Co., Ex., 4 BTA 103, 106.

(2) Munroe Land Company, ¶ 66,002 PH Memo TC.

(3) Parkersburg Iron & Steel Co. v. Burnet, 48 F.2d 163, 9 AFTR 1078.

(4) Midland Empire Packing Co., 14 TC 635.

(5) Cowell, 18 BTA 997; University Nat'l Bk., 21 BTA 71.

(6) Modesto Lumber Co., 5 BTA 598.

(7) Markovits, ¶ 52,245 PH Memo TC.

FOOTNOTE ¶ 2221 [USTR ¶ 1624; CCH ¶ 8704; FTC ¶ L-6600 et seq.].

(1) Baton Coal Co., 19 BTA 169, aff'd 51 F.2d 469, 10 AFTR 270.

(2) Zaninovich v. Comm., 45 AFTR 2d 80-1442, 616 F.2d 429.

(3) Grynberg, 83 TC 255.

(4) Miller, 10 BTA 383.

(5) Cassatt v. Comm., 137 F.2d 745, 31 AFTR 576.

(6) Rev. Rul. 55-540, 1955-2 CB 39.

FOOTNOTE ¶ 2222 [USTR¶ 1624; CCH ¶ 8801; FTC ¶ L-2200 et seq.].

(1) The Lang Chevrolet Co., ¶ 67,212 PH Memo TC.

(2) Duane O. Hestness, ¶83,727 PH Memo TC, aff'd by unpublished order (7 Cir.; 4-11-85), cert. den. 10-15-85.

(3) Julia Dahl, 24 BTA 1167.

(4) Rev. Rul. 66-277, 1966-2 CB 42.

(5) Ohio Novelty Co., ¶ 47,293 PH Memo TC.

(6) Lucien W. Rolland, 7 AFTR 462, 285 F.2d 760.

(7) Robert Lee Henry, 36 TC 879.

(8) Daniel B. Kenerly, ¶ 84,117 PH Memo TC.

(9) Pickwick v. U.S., 16 AFTR 2d 5277.

FOOTNOTE ¶ 2223 [USTR¶ 2624; CCH ¶ 13,603; 14,004; FTC ¶ H-2915].

(1) Rev. Rul. 66-203, 1966-2 CB 104.

(2) Treas. Dept. booklet "Tax Guide for Small Business" (1991 Ed.), p. 60.

(3) Rev. Rul. 68-5, 1968-1 CB 99.

(4) Rev. Rul. 73, 1953-1 CB 63.

(5) Treas. Dept. booklet "Tax Guide for Small Business" (1991 Ed.), p. 61.

(6) Bell, 13 TC 344.

(7) Lenington, ¶ 66,264, PH Memo TC.

(8) Ltr. Rul. 8321074.

(9) Rev. Rul. 55-264, 1955-1 CB 11.

(10) Treas. Dept. booklet "Business Expenses" (1991 Ed.), p. 25.

FOOTNOTE ¶ 2224 [USTR ¶ 1634; CCH ¶ 9104; 14,102.015; FTC ¶ K-5000 et seq.].

(1) Treas. Dept. booklet "Business Expenses" (1991 Ed.), p. 29, 30.

FOOTNOTE ¶ 2225 [USTR¶ 1624; CCH ¶ 8474 et seq.; FTC ¶ L-4100 et seq.].

(1) Rev. Rul. 90-93, 1990-2 CB 33.

(2) Heigerick, 45 TC 475.

FOOTNOTE ¶ 2226 [USTR¶ 280A4; CCH ¶ 8474 et seq.; FTC ¶ L-3900 et seq.].

(1) Magill, 4 BTA 272.

(2) Tyler, 13 TC 186.

(3) Cremona, 58 TC 219; Rev. Rul. 75-120, 1975-1 CB 55; Rev. Rul. 77-16, 1977-1 CB 37.

(4) Rev. Rul. 58-382, 1958-2 CB 59.

(5) Pillsbury v. U.S., 841 F.2d 809, 61 AFTR 2d 769.

(6) Podems, 24 TC 21; Kennelly, 56 TC 936, aff'd 29 AFTR 2d 72-855.

(7) Treas. Dept. booklet "Your Federal Income Tax" (1991 Ed.), p. 161.

FOOTNOTE ¶ 2227 [USTR ¶ 280A4; CCH ¶ 14,854; FTC ¶ L-1300 et seq.].

(1) Weightman, ¶ 81,301 PH Memo TC.

(2) Soliman v. Comm., 94 TC 20, aff'd 67 AFTR2d 91-1112.

(3) Treas. Dept. booklet "Your Federal Income Tax" (1991 Ed.), p. 172.

(4) Garvey, ¶ 82,176 PH Memo TC.

(5) Rev. Rul. 92-3, IRB 1992-3.

FOOTNOTE ¶ 2228 [USTR ¶ 1624; CCH ¶ 8582; FTC ¶ L-3700 et seq.].

(1) Treas. Dept. booklet "Your Federal Income Tax" (1991 Ed.), p. 170; McCulloch, ¶ 88,084 PH Memo TC; Johnson, ¶ 88,177 PH Memo TC.

(2) Comm. v. Stidger, 19 AFTR 2d 959, 386, US 287, 87 SCt. 1065.

(3) Rev. Rul. 55-572, 1955-2 CB 45.

(4) Rev. Rul. 55-109, 1955-1 CB 261.

FOOTNOTE ¶ 2229 [USTR ¶ 1624.067, 1625.077; CCH ¶ 8474.2646; FTC ¶ A-2400].

(1) Williams, TC Memo 1991-317.

(2) Treas. Dept. booklet "Your Federal Income Tax" (1990 Ed.), p. 173.

FOOTNOTE ¶ 2230 [USTR ¶ 1624; CCH ¶ 8704; 12,105; FTC ¶ D-7151].

FOOTNOTE ¶ 2231 [USTR¶ 1744; CCH ¶ 12,047; FTC ¶ L-3117].

(1) Koons, 35 TC 1092; Mayrath v. Comm., 17 AFTR 2d 375, 357 F.2d 209.

(2) Snow v. Comm., 33 AFTR 2d 74-1251, 416 US 500.

(3) Rev. Rul. 71-162, 1971-1 CB 97.

(4) Rev. Rul. 58-78, 1958-1 CB 148.

(5) Rev. Rul. 76-324, 1976-2 CB 77.

FOOTNOTE ¶ 2233 [USTR ¶ 6114; CCH ¶ 24,501 et seq.; FTC ¶ N-2002].

(1) Rev. Rul. 78, 1953-1 CB 18.

FOOTNOTE ¶ 2234 [USTR ¶ 6114.001; CCH ¶ 24,524; FTC ¶ H-3110 et seq.].

(1) Paragon Jewel Coal Co., Inc., v. Comm., 380 US 624, 15 AFTR 2d 812.

(2) Comm. v. Southwest Exploration Co., 350 US 308, 48 AFTR 683.

(3) Helvering v. Bankline Oil Co., 303 US 362, 20 AFTR 782.

(4) Douglas v. Comm., 322 US 275, 32 AFTR 358.

(5) Palmer v. Bender, 287 US 551, 11 AFTR 1106.

(6) Johnson v. Phinney, 7 AFTR 2d 860, 287 F.2d 544.

FOOTNOTE ¶ 2235 [USTR ¶ 6114; CCH ¶ 24,501 et seq.; FTC ¶ N-2930].

FOOTNOTE ¶ 2236 [USTR ¶ 6114; CCH ¶ 24,524; FTC ¶ N-2202].

(1) Hardesty v. Comm., 127 F.2d 843, 29 AFTR 420; Comm. v. Rowan Drilling Co., 130 F.2d 62, 29

AFTR 1050; Hunt v. Comm., 135 F.2d 697, 31 AFTR 49.

(2) Rev. Rul. 71-579, 1971-2 CB 225.

FOOTNOTE ¶ 2237 [USTR ¶ 6124; CCH ¶ 24,563; FTC ¶ N-2002].

(1) Canadian River Gas Co. v. Higgins, 151 F.2d 954, 34 AFTR 411.

(2) Rev. Rul. 60-74, 1960-1 CB 253.

(3) Rev. Rul. 57-336, 1957-2 CB 325.

(4) Rev. Rul. 62-5, 1962-1 CB 88; Rev. Rul. 64-49, 1964-1 CB 218.

(5) U.S. Steel Corp. v. U.S., 19 AFTR 2d 1493, 270 F.Supp. 253, aff'd 28 AFTR 2d 71-5053, 445 F.2d 520.

(6) U.S. v. Cannelton Sewer Pipe Co., 364 US 76, 5 AFTR 2d 1773, 80 SCt. 1581.

(7) Guthrie v. U.S., 12 AFTR 2d 5666, 323 F.2d 142.

(8) Comm. v. Elliott Petroleum Corp., 82 F.2d 193, 17 AFTR 595; Louisiana Iron & Supply Co., Inc., 44 BTA 1244.

FOOTNOTE ¶ 2238 [USTR ¶ 6114; CCH ¶ 24,538; FTC ¶ N-2207; 2208].

FOOTNOTE ¶ 2240 [USTR ¶ 6112.03; CCH ¶ 24,529; FTC ¶ N-6100 et seq.].

(1) Income Tax Information Release No. 1, 12/28/49.

FOOTNOTE ¶ 2241 [USTR ¶ 6114; CCH ¶ 24,530; FTC ¶ N-3203].

FOOTNOTE ¶ 2242 [USTR ¶ 6174; CCH ¶ 24,665; FTC ¶ N-3301].

FOOTNOTE ¶ 2243 [USTR ¶ 6114; CCH ¶ 24,644; FTC ¶ N-3300].

FOOTNOTE ¶ 2244 [USTR ¶ 1624; CCH ¶ 8796; FTC ¶ N-1300 et seq.].

(1) Treas. Dept. booklet "Farmers' Tax Guide" (1991 Ed.), p. 16.

(2) Rev. Rul. 55-531, 1955-2 CB 520.

(3) Rev. Rul. 66-58, 1966-1 CB 186.

FOOTNOTE ¶ 2245 [USTR ¶ 1734; CCH ¶ 12,068; FTC ¶ N-1450 et seq.].

(1) Treas. Dept. booklet "Farmers' Tax Guide" (1991 Ed.), p. 23.

FOOTNOTE ¶ 2246 [USTR ¶ 1944; CCH ¶ 12,335; FTC ¶ N-6211 et seq.].

CHAPTER 13

LOSSES AND BAD DEBTS

TABLE OF CONTENTS

LOSSES IN GENERAL

You can deduct losses and bad debts in appropriate circumstances. The specific deduction rules depend on such factors as whether the loss or bad debt arose in connection with your business investments or is personal. The rules are explained in this chapter. Capital losses of individuals are discussed in Chapter 8; for corporate capital losses, see ¶3020.

¶2300   DEDUCTIBLE LOSSES

In one sense, you suffer a loss each time your wealth decreases in value. But you get no writeoff unless certain requirements are met. For example, if stock you own is worth less than you paid for it, you generally get no deduction until you sell the shares.

For individuals, only the following losses are eligible for a deduction [IRC Sec. 165(c); Reg. Sec. 1.165-1(e)]:

- Losses incurred in a trade or business.
- Losses incurred in a transaction entered into for profit.
- Losses from fires, storms, shipwreck, other casualty or theft, whether or not connected with a trade or business or incurred in a transaction entered into for profit.

Example 1: Mr. Edwin is a self-employed real estate agent. During the year, he sold his auto at a loss and bought a new one. To the extent Edwin's auto is used for business, he is entitled to deduct the loss. But to the extent Edwin uses the auto for personal travel, he gets no deduction.

A corporation is not subject to these limitations, so all its losses generally are deductible. Consequently, a corporate taxpayer does not need a business or profit connection to write off a loss. In fact, a corporation may be able to deduct a loss when it disposes of nonbusiness property used by stockholders for personal purposes.

Of course, the corporate deduction can be limited by other tax rules, such as the prohibition for writeoffs on entertainment facilities [¶2009(c)].

A related deduction is allowed for bad debts. If someone owes you money and does not pay, you may be entitled to a deduction [IRC Sec. 166; Reg. Sec. 1.166-1].

> **Example 2:** Mr. Edwin, a real estate agent, lends $5,000 to a client for the purpose of using the proceeds as the downpayment on a house Edwin wants to sell. When the debt comes due several years later, the client has no property and is unable to pay. Edwin can deduct $5,000 as a business bad debt in the year the debt is due.

> **NOTE:** It is possible for a deduction to be allowed under the loss rules as well as the bad debt rules. In this situation, you must treat the deduction as a bad debt and not as a loss.[1]

You can deduct voluntary as well as involuntary losses. For example, losses from the voluntary sale of business property are deductible. Also, you can deduct an involuntary loss, such as from theft or a casualty.

To be deductible, your losses must be due to closed and completed transactions, fixed by identifiable events. Your losses must be real losses that are actually sustained during the tax year for which claimed [Reg. Sec. 1.165-1(b)].

Special rules apply to certain losses, such as loss on the sale of income-producing property that was formerly used as a residence, loss from worthless stock, loss from voluntary removal of buildings, loss due to obsolescence of nondepreciable property and losses of farmers [¶2307-2311].

Some losses are specifically disallowed, such as loss on "wash sales," loss on sales to certain related taxpayers, losses from passive activities, gambling losses in excess of winnings, losses from the rental of a vacation home that is also used as a personal residence and hobby losses [¶2321 et seq.].

You may be able to offset business, casualty and theft losses of the current year against income from past and future years. This is the "net operating loss" deduction [¶2341 et seq.].

You can generally deduct losses from passive activities (i.e., activities you do not materially participate in) and vacation home rentals only to the extent of your passive income. But can carry over losses that are disallowed in the year incurred and deduct them against passive and vacation home income in future years. Additionally, you can deduct these losses against your salary, interest, dividend and other income once you dispose of the passive activity.

¶2301   AMOUNT DEDUCTIBLE

In general, the amount of your loss deduction is figured the same way as a loss on a sale [IRC Sec. 165(b)]. It is the difference between your amount realized and your adjusted basis of the property [¶1600]. In any event, the amount of your loss cannot be more than your adjusted basis of the property [Reg. Sec. 1.165-1(c)]. Insurance, salvage value and other recoveries reduce your deductible loss [IRC Sec. 165(a); Reg. Sec. 1.165-1(c)].

Example: Ms. Juliet owns a ski shop. She purchased 10 pairs of skis at a total cost to her of $2,000. She hoped to sell the skis for $4,000, but market conditions forced her to sell them at a bargain price of only $1,000. Her amount realized (selling price) is $1,000, while her adjusted basis (what she paid) is $2,000. Her deductible loss is the difference between the two, or $1,000.

NOTE: You do not necessarily have a deductible loss when you sell property for less than you intended or for less than its market value. To have a loss, you must sell·for less than your basis.

There are special rules that apply to personal casualty and theft losses and losses of business property by casualty and theft [¶2306].

LOSSES IN BUSINESS OR PROFIT TRANSACTIONS

¶2302　　LOSS INCURRED IN TRADE OR BUSINESS

A trade or business is a regular occupation or calling you carry on for a living or for profit. The loss does not have to be incurred in your principal trade or business if you are engaged in several occupations. An isolated activity or transaction generally is not a trade or business.

Example 1: Mr. Smith bought a new refrigerator for his home and sold it at a loss after deciding it was not big enough for his needs. He is not entitled to a deduction. Mr. Jones is a butcher who bought a refrigerator for his store and sold it at a loss because it did not fit his requirements. He has a deductible loss.

You cannot claim a loss deduction on the sale of your business or investment property (e.g., a business car) to the extent your property is used for personal reasons [¶2307]. And you cannot deduct a loss on the sale of an entertainment facility, even if you used it exclusively for business entertainment purposes [¶2009(c)].

(a) Anticipated Profits or Wages. You cannot take a deduction for loss of anticipated profits or wages. Of course, the lost profits or wages are not taxed to you in the first place.

Example 2: As a result of personal injuries, Ms. Green lost anticipated income from writing. Green cannot take a deduction for expected income not yet earned.[1]

(b) Legal Damages. You can deduct damages you pay under a judgment to settle a suit or claim arising out of trade or business, or transaction entered into for profit. However, you cannot deduct damages for personal losses.

Payment by a corporate president and director to settle suit for mismanagement is deductible.[2] Payments to a bank as restitution for nephew's embezzlement are nondeductible gifts.[3] Damages paid for the fraudulent claim of fire loss are not deductible when it frustrates public policy.[4]

➤ **OBSERVATION** Business expense deductions are not disallowed for being in violation of public policy, unless the type of expense is specifically disallowed by a provision of the tax law (e.g., bribing government officials) [IRC Sec. 162(c), (f), (g)]. On the other hand, loss deductions can be denied on the ground of frustrating public policy.[5]

(c) Repayment of Embezzled Funds. An embezzler who includes embezzled income on his or her tax return is entitled to a deduction for reimbursing the victims in the year in which restitution is made. But the amount of the deduction cannot exceed the amount embezzled. The deduction is not based on the value of any assets which the embezzler may have purchased with the embezzled funds.[6] Payments to a bank as restitution for a relative's embezzlement, though, are nondeductible gifts.[7]

(d) How Treated on Return. You deduct your losses from your trade or business from gross income to arrive at your adjusted gross income. This type of deduction (called deductions *for* adjusted gross income) should be distinguished from your *personal* casualty losses, which you claim as itemized deductions [¶1102(d)]. You report a sale, exchange or involuntary conversion of property used in your trade or business on Form 4797. However, you report involuntary conversions of property due to casualty or theft on Form 4684.

¶2303   TRANSACTION ENTERED INTO FOR PROFIT

You can deduct a loss incurred in any transaction entered into for profit, even though not connected with your trade or business [IRC Sec. 165(c)(2); Reg. Sec. 1.165-1(e)]. Profit is used in its ordinary and usual sense. It has been defined as the gain on invested capital or the receipt of money in excess of the amount spent. It must be of a tangible or pecuniary nature and capable of measurement.

> **Example 1:** You cannot deduct a payment you make on a promise to a relative to repay him for any loss sustained on securities he bought. This is not a transaction entered into for profit. However, the loss on sale of a residence you converted to rental use is a transaction entered into for profit and is deductible.[1] Penalties for a premature withdrawal of funds from a time savings account, including amounts that exceed interest accrued or already paid on the account, are allowable loss deductions.[2] [¶1947].

(a) Sale of Gift and Inherited Property. A sale of property you acquired by gift or inheritance may be a transaction for profit that gives rise to a deductible loss. It depends on how you use the property. Ordinary investment property is treated as held for profit unless your conduct shows contrary intent.

> **Example 2:** The loss was allowed where a taxpayer inherited a private residence and planned to rent or sell it from time of acquisition. A joint owner was also allowed to deduct the loss on the sale of personal residence when there was an intention to sell it after it was inherited from the co-owner.[3] A loss on the sale of an inherited necklace was deductible when the taxpayer had no intention of using the necklace, but always intended to dispose of it at the best possible price. A loss deduction was allowed on the sale of an inherited yacht never used for personal purposes, when there was no intent to use it for such purposes.

(b) Sale of Stock. Under ordinary conditions, the purchase of stock shows an intention to receive profits, and a loss on its sale is allowed. But the loss may not be deductible if you have a nonprofit motive when the stock is acquired.[4]

> **Example 3:** Loss on sale of stock in country club is not deductible when you buy the stock to become a member. Nor can you deduct the loss on the sale of stock you knew to be worthless when you bought it [¶2308].

(c) How Treated on Return. Deductible losses in any transaction entered into for profit, even though not for your trade or business, are deductions *for* adjusted gross income if (1) you held the property for the production of rents or royalties, or (2) the loss is from the sale or exchange of capital assets (deduction is subject to capital loss limitation), or (3) the loss is due to securities becoming worthless (subject to capital loss limitation). You report a loss on the sale or exchange of property held for the production of rents or royalties on Form 4797 [¶1811]. You report a loss on the sale or exchange of capital assets and a loss on securities that become worthless on Schedule D of Form 1040.

CASUALTY AND THEFT LOSSES

¶2304   CASUALTY LOSSES

[New tax legislation may affect this subject; see ¶1.]

You can deduct losses from fire, storm, shipwreck or other casualty, even though not incurred in your trade or business or in a transaction entered into for profit [IRC Sec. 165(c)(3); Reg. Sec. 1.165-7]. A "casualty" is an event due to some sudden, unexpected or unusual cause. Generally, this means an accident or some sudden invasion by a hostile agency. It need not be due to natural causes. The progressive deterioration of your property through a steadily operating cause is not a casualty; nor is it a casualty when you lose an article through your own negligence or carelessness. A casualty loss may arise from the demolition or evacuation of your home in a disaster area [¶2309].

(a) Deduction Limited to Property Losses. Your deduction is limited to *property* losses, and the loss must be of your own property.

> **Example 1:** Damages paid by Mr. Brown for injuries to Ms. White's property are not deductible by Brown unless the damages arose out of Brown's business.

The Revenue Service and most courts have determined that a loss is allowed only for the actual physical damage resulting from the casualty.[1]

> **Example 2:** Mr. Smith's cottage on the shore escaped damage when a hurricane demolished neighboring cottages. But the value was reduced because the area might suffer again from hurricanes. No loss is allowed for the reduction in value.

However, one court has allowed a deduction for loss in value of property resulting from a casualty even though there was no physical damage to the property.[2]

> **Example 3:** Ms. Muller's home built on a bluff was partially isolated when the bluff suddenly slid and the home's value declined because of poor access to it. The loss in value was allowed even though the home itself was not physically damaged.

The expenses of taking care of personal injuries and the cost of temporary lights, fuels, moving, or rental of temporary quarters are not a part of the casualty loss deduction. But the cost of cleaning up can be [(c) below].

(b) Deductible Whether Business or Personal. You can deduct casualty losses from business, personal or investment property are deductible. However, the type of property determines the amount of your deduction [(c) and (d) below] [IRC Sec. 165(c); Reg. Sec. 1.165-7].

> ➤ **OBSERVATION** You can deduct a loss from the destruction of your personal-use property only if the loss is from a casualty. However, you can deduct a loss from the destruction of business or investment property, even though it fails to qualify as a casualty [¶2302; 2303]. For example, a condemnation loss of business or investment property is deductible; a condemnation loss of personal-use property, such as a residence, is not.

Deductible

Automobile damages to your pleasure car caused by faulty driving (but not your wilful act or wilful negligence); damages to your auto from faulty driving by operator of another auto [Reg. Sec. 1.165-7(a)(3)].

Drought damages if unusual in area (not from normal dry spell); foundation of residence weakened by subsoil shrinkage due to unusually severe drought.[3]

Sonic boom damage caused by airplane breaking the sound barrier.[4]

Vandalism damage.[5]

Damage to exterior house paint from sudden and severe smog containing high chemical fume concentration.[6]

Attorney's fees and court costs paid from award in suit to recover casualty losses, if court finds a deductible casualty.[7]

Losses from deposits or accounts in certain insolvent financial institutions [IRC Sec. 165(l)].

Not Deductible

Damages paid to another to cover personal injury by your car (unless used for business purposes).[8] **Moth damage** to fur coat.[9]

Loss of livestock from disease (does not meet the suddenness test).[10]

Tree and shrub damage on residential property caused by disease or insects (but damage by freeze and mass attack by southern pine beetles is deductible).[11]

Loss of purse, package or other article left on a bus or train; loss of valuable ring that slipped from finger.

Termite damage (unless it meets suddenness test).[12]

Loss on sale of residence due to condemnation of property as part of a site for flood prevention construction.[13]

(c) Amount Deductible as Personal Casualty Loss. The amount of your personal casualty loss deduction is the lesser of: (1) *the sustained loss*—that is, the property's value just before the casualty less its value immediately afterward—or (2) *the adjusted basis of the property* for figuring loss on a sale [IRC Sec. 165(h); Reg. Sec. 1.165-7(b)]. This amount eligible for a deduction is reduced by:

- Insurance;
- Amounts received from an employer or disaster relief agencies to restore the property;
- Other compensation for lost property;
- $100.
- After these reductions are made for each casualty, the remaining loss amounts are added up for the year. You can write off this aggregate figure to the extent it exceeds 10% of your adjusted gross income.

Example 4: Mr. Green has an adjusted gross income of $80,000. A fire in his home results in a $48,000 loss. Green recovers $40,000 in full settlement from his insurance company. The $8,000 net loss must be reduced by the $100 limitation. The $7,900 balance is not deductible since it does not exceed 10% of Green's adjusted gross income ($8,000). But suppose Green also has another uninsured loss of $1,200. After the $100 reduction, his total casualties for the year ($7,900 plus $1,100) will exceed 10% of his adjusted gross income ($8,000). So he can deduct $1,000 resulting from the second loss.

Example 5: Ms. Johnson's personal summer residence was wrecked by a hurricane. The home, bought for $40,000, was worth $80,000 just before the storm, but only $10,000 afterward. It was not insured against loss by hurricane. Her adjusted gross income for the year was $100,000.

1. Value before casualty $80,000
2. Value after casualty 10,000
3. Difference $70,000
4. The property's cost (adjusted basis) $40,000
5. Lesser of (3) or (4) $40,000
6. Casualty loss $40,000
7. Less $100 reduction 100
8. Total $39,900
9. Less $10,000 (10% of AGI) 10,000
10. Deductible loss $29,900

Example 6: Mr. Smith owned residential property that cost $100,000 and had a value before the casualty of $180,000. Earlier this year, it was completely destroyed. Smith received a $70,000 insurance payment. Smith's adjusted gross income for the year is $200,000.

1. Value before casualty $180,000
2. Value after casualty 0
3. Difference $180,000

4. The property's cost (adjusted basis) $100,000
5. Lesser of (3) or (4) $100,000
6. Less: Insurance recovery . . . . $ 70,000
7. Casualty loss . . . . $ 30,000
8. Less $100 reduction   100
9. Total . . . . $ 29,900
10. Less $20,000 (10% of AGI)   20,000
11. Deductible loss . . . . $ 9,900

For losses sustained on your personal-use property, you can claim a deduction only to the extent your damages are not covered by insurance and only if you file a timely insurance claim. In other words, you cannot deduct a loss covered by insurance if you choose not to make a claim.

➤ **OBSERVATION** The above limitation does not apply to a casualty loss of business or investment property. In some instances, you can come out ahead by forgoing an insurance claim—if your premium payments will increase—and taking the tax deduction in its place [IRC Sec. 165(h)(4)(E)].

Your deductible loss is not reduced by food, medical supplies and other forms of subsistence received that are not replacements of lost property. Nor is your loss reduced by unrestricted cash gifts.

If the insurance proceeds you receive exceed your loss and you replace the property, you have taxable income only to the extent that your amount realized exceeds your replacement cost.

If you sustain more than one loss from a single event, only one $100 reduction is made. If you and your spouse file jointly, you are treated as one taxpayer. Separate losses sustained by the same act, therefore, bring only one reduction [Reg. Sec. 1.165-7(b)(4)].

Exclusion of insurance proceeds. You may receive insurance proceeds for expenses incurred while your principal residence is not useable because of fire, storm or other casualty. To the extent the insurance compensates you for extraordinary living expenses, the proceeds are income tax-free. Your extraordinary expenses are defined as the actual expenses you incur to live away from your residence less the normal expenses you would incur had you been able to stay there.

Insurance proceeds you receive when a government authority forces you to evacuate your residence because of a fire, storm or other casualty are also tax-free. However, you do owe tax on payments you get for the loss of rental income or damage to the property. The tax-free break also does not apply to the extent your residence is used for business purposes [IRC Sec. 123; Reg. Sec. 1.123-1].

How to prove loss in value. You should use competent appraisals to prove the difference between the value of the property immediately before and immediately after the casualty. The reasonable cost of repairs necessary to restore your damaged property to its condition immediately before the casualty may be acceptable evidence of the loss of value. However, your loss is measured by the difference in value, not your repair bill. Repairs must be limited to damage sustained [Reg. Sec. 1.165-7(a)(2)].

A loss involving both realty and improvements (buildings, ornamental trees and shrubbery) is treated as a single loss that is measured by the actual decrease in the entire property's value [Reg. Sec. 1.165-7(b)]. And the cost of clearing property of debris is part of the loss deduction. However, when more than one item of *personal* property is involved, the decrease in fair market value or adjusted basis is figured separately for each item and then combined to find the deduction.

Sentimental values are not considered in determining loss on the destruction, damage or theft of family portraits, heirlooms or keepsakes.

(d) Figuring Business Casualty Loss. The amount of your business casualty loss depends on whether the property is *completely* destroyed or only *partially* destroyed. If the property is entirely destroyed, your loss is your adjusted basis for determining loss on a sale [Ch. 6] less any insurance, salvage value or other recovery [IRC Sec. 165(b); Reg. Sec. 1.165-7(b)(1)].

> **Example 7**: Mr. Flynn's insured shop was demolished by hurricane. Flynn originally purchased the shop for $100,000 but had taken $15,000 worth of depreciation writeoffs. Thus his adjusted basis was $85,000. Flynn received $80,000 from his insurance company. Thus his deduction is $15,000 ($85,000 - $80,000), the difference between the adjusted basis and the insurance recovery.

If only part of the property is destroyed, your loss is measured by the decrease in the property's fair market value, up to your adjusted basis in the property. You can generally use the cost of reasonable repairs to determine how much the property has declined in value [Reg. Sec. 1.165-7(a)(2)(ii)].

Allocation of loss. You must figure the loss for each part of the business property destroyed separately. For example, you must compute separately damage to a building and damage to the surrounding shrubbery [Reg. Sec. 1.165-7(b)(2)(i)].

(e) When to Deduct a Casualty Loss. The time to deduct a casualty loss is the tax year in which you *actually sustain* the loss.

If you do not collect insurance or other reimbursement in the loss year, but there is a reasonable prospect of recovery by insurance or reimbursement, the loss is not sustained until it can be determined with reasonable certainty whether the reimbursement will be received. If a portion of the loss is not covered by insurance or reimbursement, the loss on that portion is sustained in the year the casualty occurs.

> **Example 8**: Ms. Smith's business property with a $10,000 basis, insured for $8,000, is destroyed in 1992. Smith expects the $8,000 insurance claim to be paid in full in 1993. She has a $2,000 loss in 1992. If she recovers only $7,500 in 1993 with no chance of getting the full $8,000, she has a $500 loss in 1993.

If you deduct a loss in one year and are compensated for it in a subsequent year, you do not recompute your tax for the earlier year. Instead, the amount you receive for the loss is taxed to you as income in the year you receive it, but only to the extent your taxable income was actually reduced by a deduction in the earlier year [Reg. Sec. 1.165-1(d)(2)].

> **Example 9**: In 1992, Mr. Parker has an adjusted gross income (AGI) of $60,000 and suffers a $10,000 personal casualty loss. The insurance company refuses to pay his claim, so Parker is entitled to a deduction. After subtracting $100 and 10% of Parker's AGI (the limitations for personal losses), only $3,900 is actually deductible. The insurance company finally does investigate Parker's claim in 1993 and pays him the full $10,000. Result: Since Parker only gets a loss deduction of $3,900 in 1992, he treats only $3,900 of the proceeds as income in 1993.

Special rule for some disaster losses. You can elect to deduct losses from some disasters on your return for the tax year immediately preceding the tax year in which the disaster occurred. This applies only to losses occurring in a location the President declares a disaster area entitled to federal assistance. The loss is measured as of the date of the disaster. Otherwise, you deduct the loss in the year sustained [IRC Sec. 165(i); Reg. Sec. 1.165-11].

(f) Carrybacks and Carryovers. When your deductible casualty losses exceed your income for the tax year, the excess is considered a net operating loss. As such, you may carry back the loss to offset income of prior years and carry over the loss to offset income of future years under the net operating loss provisions [IRC Sec. 172(d)(4)(C)]. All casualty losses qualify even though the property involved is personal, and you are not in business [Reg. Sec. 1.172-3(a)(3)(iii)]. See ¶2341 et seq.

¶2305 THEFT

Losses from theft or embezzlement are deductible if proven [IRC Sec. 165; Reg. Sec. 1.165-8]. The cost of recovering stolen property is deductible as a theft loss.

(a) Amount Deductible. Theft losses are generally treated as casualty losses for tax purposes. For personal property, each theft loss is deductible only to the extent it exceeds $100. And, no deduction is allowed if total casualty losses (including thefts) for the year are 10% or less of adjusted gross income [IRC Sec. 165(h)]. In applying the casualty loss rules to thefts, your fair market value of the property immediately after a theft is considered to be zero [Reg. Sec. 1.165-8(c)]. Your loss must be reduced by (1) amounts you receive from an insurance company, or the value of your claim against the company; and (2) surety or fidelity bond proceeds, or amount of claim against the bonding company. You cannot take a theft deduction for unreported income that has been embezzled from you. You may deduct, as a theft loss, amounts loaned to a corporation as a result of the corporation's fraudulent financial reports before it became bankrupt.

If your property is protected by insurance, you cannot deduct a personal theft loss unless you file a timely claim.

(b) When to Deduct Theft Loss. You can generally deduct casualty losses in the year sustained. However, for embezzlements and other thefts, you may not find out about the loss until it's too late to amend a return for the year the loss was sustained. So that the deduction is not lost, a special rule applies: Theft losses are considered "sustained" and deductible in the year discovered [Reg. Sec. 1.165-8(a)(2)].[1]

¶2306 SPECIAL TAX RETURN RULES FOR CASUALTIES AND THEFTS

Generally, the way you report casualties (including thefts) depends on whether you have a net gain or loss from casualties and whether you held the property for personal purposes or for business or investment purposes.

You may have a gain from a casualty when an insurance recovery or other reimbursement exceeds your loss.

(a) Personal Casualty and Theft Losses. If you had only one loss, and no gains, during the year and the loss was on a single item, you can report the loss on Schedule A, Form 1040. If there was more than one casualty or theft, or if more than one item was involved, you use Form 4684, Casualties and Thefts, to figure the loss. The final amount gets transferred to Schedule A.

Allocation of loss. You must allocate losses on property used for *both* business and pleasure before deducting them. Your business losses are wholly deductible for adjusted gross income, but your personal losses are deductible only above $100 per loss and 10% of adjusted gross income on all of your combined casualty and theft losses for the year.

> **Example 1:** Ms. Syms had an adjusted gross income of $50,000. Her car, which she used 75% of the time for business and 25% for pleasure, was totally destroyed in an accident on June 5, 1992. After receiving an insurance settlement, Syms still had a remaining theft loss of $1,200. Syms can deduct $900 on her return. There is a $900 business casualty loss (75% × $1,200), but no personal casualty loss, because the loss didn't exceed the threshold limit ($100 and 10% of adjusted gross income).

(b) Gains and Losses From Casualties or Thefts. When you have both gains and losses from casualties or thefts, a special computation is made on Form 4684, Casualties and Thefts.

Special netting of personal casualty and theft gains and losses. You must net gains and losses from personal casualties or thefts. If your recognized gains exceed your recognized losses from these transactions, then you treat all of these gains and losses as capital gains and losses. In this case, your losses will not be subject to the 10% of adjusted gross income floor. However, you must apply the $100 floor before the netting computation is made. If your recognized losses exceed recognized gains, your losses are fully deductible to the extent of your gains. Losses in excess of gains are subject to the 10% of adjusted gross income floor [IRC Sec. 165(h)(2); 1231(a)].

> **Example 2:** In 1992, Mr. Smith has an adjusted gross income of $100,000 (exclusive of any personal casualty losses). During the year, Smith had a $50,000 gain from an insurance recovery for the destruction by fire of his personal residence. He also had a $40,000 casualty loss after applying the $100 floor. Smith treats all his casualties as capital gains and losses. He can disregard the 10% adjusted gross income rule.
>
> **Example 3:** Assume the same facts as in Example 2 except that Smith's casualty losses for the year are $70,100 (not $40,000). The first $50,000 of losses will be allowed as a deduction in full against Smith's gain. Of the remaining $20,000 (after subtracting the $100 floor), $10,000 is deductible—$20,000 less the 10%-of-AGI floor.

IRC Sec. 1231 property and separate netting of gains and losses. You do not net casualty gains and losses on property used in business with personal casualties. Instead, you net business casualties with gains or losses from "IRC Sec. 1231 property" (i.e., property used in your trade or business, or held for the production of rents or royalties and held for more than one year). If your gain on the casualty is subject to depreciation recapture, you do not include the recaptured gain in the netting computation. You then net the gains not subject to recapture and the losses separately from *other* gains and losses from IRC Sec. 1231 assets. If the result is a net gain, you net the gain again with the gains and losses from other IRC Sec. 1231 assets. If this also results in a net gain, you treat the casualty gains and losses as capital gains and losses (except to the extent the recapture rules apply); if it results in a net loss, you treat the casualty gains and losses as ordinary gains and losses [¶1813].

If the result of the separate netting of the business casualty gains and losses is a net loss, you keep the casualty or theft gains and losses separate from any gains and losses from other IRC Sec. 1231 assets. You treat the losses as fully deductible ordinary losses, and the gains as ordinary gains.

SPECIAL RULES

¶2307   PROPERTY CONVERTED TO BUSINESS USE

Generally, you cannot deduct a loss on the sale of property used for personal purposes.

When you convert personal-use property to business or income-producing property, you can deduct any loss on a sale. Your basis for loss when you sell the property is the lesser of the fair market value or your adjusted basis in the property on the conversion date [¶1627].

¶2308   WORTHLESS STOCK

If you own worthless stock, you are entitled to a deduction in the year the stock becomes worthless [Reg. Sec. 1.165-5]. Your basis for figuring the deduction is the same as for a loss on a sale. You cannot claim a deduction until the stock is completely worthless [Reg. Sec. 1.165-4, 1.165-5(f)]. If you owe money on the purchase price, you cannot take a deduction until the money owed is paid. You may may establish the loss by a *bona fide* sale before the stock becomes entirely worthless. You can also deduct losses on worthless bonds. See ¶2362.

Loss as capital loss. Generally, loss on worthless stock is a capital loss on the last day of the tax year it becomes worthless [IRC Sec. 165(g); Reg. Sec. 1.165-5(c)].

Stock of corporate subsidiary. Worthless stock is not a capital loss for a domestic corporation that sustains the loss on stock of an affiliated corporation (as specially defined) [IRC Sec. 165(g)(3); Reg. Sec. 1.165-5(d)]. As a result, the loss can be deducted to offset the tax on ordinary income.

Bank stock owned by another bank. If a bank owns directly at least 80% of each class of stock of another bank, loss sustained on the stock of the other bank is not a capital loss [IRC Sec. 582(b); Reg. Sec. 1.582-1].

Small business stock. Loss on small business stock or small business investment company stock is not a capital loss [¶1821]. This does not apply to the loss on the closing of a short sale of small business investment company stock.

¶2309   DEMOLITION OF BUILDINGS

Generally, you must add losses incurred in connection with the demolition of buildings to your basis in the land upon which the demolished building was located [IRC Sec. 280B]. This means you get no deduction until you dispose of the land.

Demolition of home in a disaster area. You can take a casualty loss deduction when you are forced to abandon or demolish your residence due to a disaster if (1) the residence is located in a federally declared disaster area, (2) demolition or evacuation is ordered by the state or local government within 120 days of the federal determination and (3) the residence has been rendered unsafe because of the disaster [IRC Sec. 165(k)].

¶2310   ABANDONMENT LOSSES

You can deduct a loss arising from the *sudden* end of usefulness of nondepreciable business or investment property if the abandonment is permanent. If it is not permanent, you may still take a deduction for obsolescence. Losses from sales or exchanges, or from casualties, are not included. The deduction is not allowed for stock in trade or property held in inventory. You take the deduction in the year the loss is actually sustained. This is not necessarily the tax year when the act of abandonment or the loss of title to the property occurs [Reg. Sec. 1.165-2].

Example: Amounts spent in drilling test holes to find water for a business are capital expenditures. However, if sufficient water is not found and the project is abandoned, the entire cost is deductible as a loss.[1]

A loss deduction is available for goodwill allocable to the abandoned part of a business.[2]

¶2311   LOSSES OF FARMERS

Generally, you can deduct losses incurred in the operation of a farm as a business enterprise [Reg. Sec. 1.165-6].

(a) Deterioration of Crops in Storage. You cannot claim a deduction for deterioration or shrinkage in weight or decrease in value of farm products held for favorable markets. However, the shrinkage can be reflected in inventory for farmers who use an inventory method of accounting [Reg. Sec. 1.165-6(b)].

(b) Destruction of Prospective Crops. You cannot deduct a loss due to destruction by frost, storm, flood or fire. This is a loss of anticipated profits [Reg. Sec. 1.165-6(c)]. See ¶2302(a).

(c) Destruction of Livestock. If you raise and sell livestock, you cannot deduct a loss for the value of animals that were raised on the farm and die, except as loss reflected in inventory. This again is simply a loss of anticipated profits. A loss not reflected in inventory that results from the death of any *purchased* livestock may be deducted like any other business casualty loss if it is not compensated for by insurance or otherwise. This applies when death is the result of disease, exposure, injury or an order of state or federal authorities. Your deductible amount is your actual purchase price less any depreciation allowable. The cost of any feed, pasture or care that has been deducted as an expense of operating cannot be included as part of the cost of the stock to determine the loss [Reg. Sec. 1.165-6(d)].

> **NOTE:** If a state or the federal government pays for livestock killed or other property destroyed for which a loss was claimed in a prior year, you must include the amount received as income in the year the payment is made.

(d) Loss Reflected in Inventory. If your gross income is determined by the use of inventories, you cannot take a deduction separately for livestock or products lost during the year, whether bought for resale or produced on the farm. These losses will be reflected in your inventory by reducing the livestock or products on hand at the close of the year. This reduces your gross income from your business by the amount of the loss [Reg. Sec. 1.165-6(f)(2)].

(e) Operating a Farm and Another Business. If you own and operate a farm and also have another trade, business or calling, you can deduct farm operation losses from gross income you receive from other sources only if (1) you engaged in the farming for profit [¶2325] and (2) only to the extent allowed by the passive loss rules if you do not materially participate in the farming activity [¶2326].

(f) How Treated on Return. You take farm operating losses as deductions *for* adjusted gross income if you operate the farm as a business or you hold the property for the production of rents or royalties. If you operate the farm yourself, report an operating loss on Schedule F of Form 1040. (See sample Form F at ¶2244.) If you rent farm land out for a flat fee, report any loss from the rental activity on Schedule E of Form 1040. If your rental income is based on farm production or crop shares, report any rental activity loss on both Schedule E and Form 4835.

¶2312   LOSS DISTINGUISHED FROM CAPITAL EXPENDITURE

Some items that seem like losses are really nondeductible contributions of capital.

(a) Contributions to Corporation or Partnership. As a stockholder, you get no loss deduction for voluntary capital contributions to a corporation. These are treated as capital expenditures that increase the stock's basis. But you have a loss if you are forced to make advances to the corporation from which you can expect no return.[1] Advances by partners to partnerships are generally treated the same as advances by stockholders to corporations [¶3006].

(b) Surrender of Stock to Corporation. You can make a capital contribution by surrendering part of your stock to a corporation. Generally, the cost of the surrendered stock increases the retained stock's basis, so you get no "loss" deduction.

DISALLOWED LOSSES

¶2321   WASH SALES

A wash sale occurs when you buy substantially identical stock or securities within 30 days before or after the sale of such securities. You cannot currently deduct losses on wash sales. Instead, you add the disallowed loss to your basis in the newly acquired securities, which increases your loss or reduces your gain when you eventually sell them [IRC Sec. 1091; Reg. Sec. 1.1091-1, 1.1091-2]. Thus, while you cannot prematurely claim losses, you can receive an investment return that is partially or wholly tax-free. Options to purchase or sell securities are securities in their own right and are subject to the wash sale rules.

Example 1:

Item	Date of Purchase	Cost	Date of Sale	Selling Price	Indicated Loss
(A) 100 shares of X stock	1-5-87	$10,000	2-9-92	$8,500	$1,500
(B) 100 shares of X stock	2-2-92	$ 9,000			

The indicated loss of $1,500 on the sale of the 100 shares in lot A is disallowed because within 30 days before the sale, identical stock (lot B) was bought. The basis of stock in lot B becomes $10,500 ($9,000 + $1,500). The result would be the same if identical securities were bought within 30 days after the sale.

Your loss on the sale of securities will also be disallowed if your spouse, your controlled company or another related taxpayer buys replacement securities within the prohibited time period.

The wash sales provisions do not apply to sales of stock or securities that result in a profit. Nor do they apply to commodity futures contracts since these are not considered stock or securities. Shares acquired within the 61-day period need not be in the same quantity as the shares sold for the wash sale provisions to apply. But you can deduct a loss to the extent the number of shares sold exceed the number purchased.

Short sales. Rules similar to the general wash sale rules apply to losses realized on the closing of a short sale of stock or securities if you either sell or sell short substantially identical stock or securities. The 30-day period is measured from the date of the closing [IRC Sec. 1091(e)].

(a) The Holding Period for securities bought in connection with a wash sale includes the period for which you held the original securities [IRC Sec. 1223(4); Reg. Sec. 1.1223-1].

Example 2:

	Item	Date of Purchase	Cost	Date of Sale	Selling Price	Indicated Loss
(C)	100 shares of X stock	3-2-92	$5,000	8-31-92	$4,500	$500
(D)	100 shares of X stock	9-14-92	$4,600	5-1-93	$4,200	$400

The indicated loss of $500 on the sale of 100 shares in lot C is disallowed because within 30 days after the sale, identical stock or securities (lot D) were bought. The basis of the securities in lot D becomes $5,100 ($4,600 plus $500). The recognized loss on the sale of lot D is $900 ($5,100 less $4,200). The period held is counted as follows: From 3-2-92 to 8-31-92 and 9-14-92 to 5-1-93. Thus, the securities in lot D were held more than one year, and the loss is treated as long-term capital loss. Note: The original securities (lot C) were not held from 9-1-92 to 9-14-92, so that period cannot be included in the holding period.

(b) Substantially Identical Stock or Securities. The wash sales provisions apply only when you purchase securities that are substantially identical to those sold. The securities must be the same in all important particulars. Any significant difference in the securities purchased and those sold, such as bonds with different interest rates or stock in different corporations, renders the wash sale rules inapplicable.

(c) Dealers. The wash sale rules do not apply if you are a dealer in stock or securities and the loss is sustained in a transaction made in the ordinary course of your business [IRC Sec. 1091(a)].

¶2322   SHAM SALES

While you can sell property for the sole purpose of writing off a loss, you get a deduction only if the sale is bona fide. A sham transaction made only for the record will not do. For example, if there is a repurchase agreement, the sale is termed a sham and your loss deduction disallowed. The IRS considers the following circumstances in determining whether there is a repurchase agreement: (a) the relationship, business association or friendship between you and purchaser; or (b) actual repurchase of the property.[1] What's more, a loss on a real sale to a related taxpayer may be disallowed [¶2323].

¶2323   SALES TO RELATED TAXPAYERS

No loss deduction is allowed when you sell property to certain related taxpayers. If the related taxpayer later sells the property, his gain is reduced by the amount of your disallowed loss. The following rules apply to losses from sales or exchanges of property other than those resulting from distributions in corporate liquidations [IRC Sec. 267].

(a) Family Losses. No deduction is allowed for a sale or exchange made, directly or indirectly, between:

- Husband and wife;
- Brothers and/or sisters (whole or half blood);
- Ancestors and lineal descendants [IRC Sec. 267(b), (c); Reg. Sec. 1.267(b)-1].

The loss is disallowed even if the sale is made indirectly. The sale of stock on a stock exchange by one family member followed the same day by the purchase of the same number of shares of the same stock at similar prices by another family member is considered an indirect sale between members of the family.

A forced sale is treated the same as a voluntary sale. For example, a loss sustained by a mortgagor on foreclosure sale to a family member as mortgagee is not deductible.

The no-deduction rule does not apply to any transfer incident to a divorce [IRC Sec. 267(g)].

(b) Sales Between Corporation and Shareholders. No deduction is allowed if a sale is made, directly or indirectly, between you and your corporation if you own more than 50% in value of the outstanding stock, directly or indirectly [IRC Sec. 267(b)(2); Reg. Sec. 1.267(c)-1].

(c) Sales Between Taxpayer and Exempt Organization. No deduction is allowed if you sell property to a tax-exempt organization controlled by you or your family [IRC Sec. 267(b)(9); Reg. Sec. 1.267(b)-1].

(d) Constructive Ownership of Stock. In applying the above rules, you are considered to own not only the stock registered in your name, but stock you constructively own under rules explained below [IRC Sec. 267(c); Reg. Sec. 1.267(c)-1].

1. Stock ownership rule. Stock owned, directly or indirectly, by or for a corporation, partnership, estate or trust, is considered as being owned proportionately by or for its shareholders, partners, or beneficiaries.

> **Example 1:** Mr. Albert owns 60% of Corp. P's stock, and Corp. P owns all the stock of Corp. Q. Albert is the constructive owner of 60% of Corp. Q's stock. Since Albert owns more than 50% in value of the stock of Corp. Q, a loss on the sale of property to the corporation would be disallowed. Furthermore, a loss on property sold by the corporation to Albert would also be disallowed.

> **Example 2:** Mr. Crowley and Mr. Dillon are members of the C&D Partnership that owns 4,000 of the 5,000 shares of Corp. U. Crowley's proportionate interest in the partnership is 60%. In addition, Crowley personally owns 500 shares of stock of Corp. U. Dillon, a 40% partner, does not personally own any shares of Corp. U. Crowley is the constructive owner of 2,400 shares of U stock (60% of 4,000) and the actual owner of 500 shares. Since Crowley is the owner of more than 50% in value of the outstanding stock of Corp. U, a loss would be disallowed on any sale of property between the partnership and Crowley.

2. Partnership rule. If you actually or constructively own stock of a corporation, you are considered as owning the stock owned, directly or indirectly, by or for your partner.

> **Example 3:** Same facts as in Example 2. Under rule (1) above, Mr. Dillon is treated as the owner of 40% of the shares owned by C&D Partnership—or 1,600 shares. And since he is the constructive owner of these shares, he is also treated as owning the 2,900 shares actually and constructively owned by Crowley. Since this makes Dillon a more-than-50% owner of U, any loss on a sale of property between Dillon and U is not deductible.

3. Family rule. You are considered as owning the stock owned, directly or indirectly, by or for your family (spouse; brothers and sisters, whether by the whole or half blood; ancestors and lineal descendants).

> **Example 4:** Mr. Easton owns 30%, his wife 10%, and his wife's brother (Easton's brother-in-law) 20% of the stock of corporation V. Easton is the constructive owner of 10% of V stock and the actual owner of 30% (40% in all). Since Easton is the owner of less than 50% in value of the outstanding stock of corporation V, a loss would be allowed on a sale of property between them.
>
> Mrs. Easton is the constructive owner of 50% of V stock (the 30% owned by Mr. Easton plus the 20% owned by her brother) and the actual owner of 10% (60% in all). Since Mrs. Easton is the owner of more than 50% in value of the outstanding stock of corporation V, a loss would be disallowed on a sale of property between them.

(e) Recognized Gain on Resale. If your loss on a sale to a related taxpayer is disallowed and the related taxpayer later sells the property at a gain, a special rule limits the income tax consequences. The related taxpayers pays tax on the gain from the sale of the property only to the extent that it exceeds your disallowed loss [IRC Sec. 267(d); Reg. Sec. 1.267(d)-1].

> **Example 5:** Mr. Clark bought stock for $7,500 and sold the stock to his wife, Martha, for $5,000. The $2,500 loss is disallowed. Martha sells the stock for $8,000. Her recognized gain is $500 figured as follows:

Martha's selling price	$8,000
Her basis	5,000
Gain	$3,000
Disallowed loss	2,500
Excess of gain over disallowed loss (gain taxed)	$ 500

There is a similar result when losses are disallowed under the wash sales provisions [¶2321].

Divisible property. Suppose you sell property at a loss to a related taxpayer and the relative later sells a part. A proportionate part of your disallowed loss is allocated to the partial sale and reduces the relative's taxable gain.

> **Example 6:** Mrs. Harry sold class A stock which had cost her $1,100 and common stock which had cost her $2,000 to her spouse for a lump sum of $1,500. The loss of $1,600 ($3,100 less $1,500) was disallowed. When the spouse bought the stocks, the value of class A stock was $900 and the value of the common stock was $600. The spouse later sold the class A stock for $2,500. His gain is $1,400, determined as follows:

Selling price by spouse of class A stock		$2,500
Less: Basis allocated to class A stock ($900/$1,500 x $1,500)		900
Gain		$1,600
Less: Disallowed loss sustained by Harry on class A stock sale:		
Basis of class A stock to Harry	$1,100	
Amount realized by Harry on class A stock		
($900/$1,500 x $1,500)	900	
Disallowed loss to Harry on class A stock sale		200
Taxable gain on sale of class A stock by spouse		$1,400

Exchange or gift of property by buyer. Suppose your relative exchanges the property for other property in a *nontaxable* exchange, and then sells the other property. The gain on the sale of the other property is reduced by your disallowed loss, just as though the property sold were the original property bought from you. But only the person who bought the original property gets the benefit of the rule. Thus, if your relative gives the property to another person, the other person would have to pay the full tax if he sold the property at a gain.

¶2324   GAMBLING LOSSES

You can deduct losses from wagering transactions only to the extent of your gambling winnings [IRC Sec. 165(d); Reg. Sec. 1.165-10].

> **Example:** Mr. Carson, whose gambling transactions result in losses of $500 and winnings of $400, must report the $400 winnings to obtain a deduction for $400 of the loss. The $100 excess is not deductible. If the winnings are $500 and the losses $400, the $100 excess of winnings over losses is taxable.

How treated on return. If gambling is your trade or business, you get a loss deduction for adjusted gross income up to the amount of gambling winnings. If it is not your trade or business, you can deduct the losses, up to the amount of your gains, as a miscellaneous itemized deduction on Schedule A of Form 1040.

> **NOTE:** Certain miscellaneous deductions can be written off only to the extent they, when added together, exceed 2% of your adjusted gross income [¶1942]. However, this limitation does not apply to your gambling losses [IRC Sec. 67].

¶2325   HOBBY LOSSES AND EXPENSES

If you are engage in an activity not carried on for profit (e.g., stamp collecting), you get no deduction for that activity except for (1) deductions that you could claim whether or not the activity was carried on for profit (for example, mortgage interest, state and local property taxes); and (2) deductions that you could claim if the activity was carried on for profit (for example, maintenance and depreciation), but only to the extent your gross income from the activity for the tax year exceeds your allowable deductions in (1) [IRC Sec. 183; Reg. Sec. 1.183-1(b)(1)]. You claim your hobby expenses as a miscellaneous itemized deduction, subject to the 2%-of-adjusted-gross-income floor. However, hobby expenses that are attributable to rental or royalty income (e.g., renting out your yacht) generally are deductible up to the amount of your hobby income—these expenses are not subject to the 2% floor [IRC Sec. 62, 67; Reg. Sec. 1.62-1T, 1.67-1T].

Note: The hobby loss rules also apply to an S corporation [Ch. 21] engaged in activity not carried on for profit.

An activity is presumed to be "engaged in for profit" if it produces a profit in any three or more tax years out of five consecutive years ending with the current year [IRC Sec. 183(d); Reg. Sec. 1.183-1(a)]. For the breeding, training, showing or racing of horses, there must be a profit in two out of seven consecutive years [Reg. Sec. 1.183-1(c)(1)]. You can elect to suspend the presumption until five (or seven) tax years from the time the activity is started. Generally, this election is made by filing Form 5213 with the Revenue Service no later than three years after the return due date for the year the activity is started [IRC Sec. 183(e); Temp. Reg. Sec. 12.9]. By making the election, you automatically extend the statute of limitations for a deficiency during any year in the suspension period to at least two years after the return's due date for the last year in the five (or seven) year period. For this purpose, the due date does not include extensions of time to file [IRC Sec. 183(e)(4)].

¶2326   PASSIVE LOSSES

[New tax legislation may affect this subject; see ¶1.]

There are special rules governing loss deductions from "passive" activities. These rules are designed primarily to prevent you from using losses from a tax shelter to offset income from other sources. Under the passive loss provisions [IRC Sec. 469; Reg. Sec. 1.469-1T], you can generally deduct a loss from a passive activity only to the extent of income from other passive activities. The loss cannot be deducted against "active" income (e.g., your salary or self-employment earnings) or "portfolio" income (e.g., your dividends or interest).

Passive activities include any trade or business in which you do not materially participate and any rental activity whether or not you materially participate [IRC Sec. 469(c); Reg. Sec. 1.469-1T(e)]. But a working interest in an oil or gas property is not a passive activity, even if you do not materially participate [IRC Sec. 469(c)(3); Reg. Sec. 1.469-1T(e)(4)].

How the passive loss rule works. Your taxable income from profitable passive activities is netted against your losses from other passive activities. If the losses exceed the income, you cannot currently deduct the net overall loss. Instead, you carry the loss forward (but not backward) and use it to offset your net passive income in future years. Additionally, you can generally deduct in full suspended passive losses when you sell or otherwise dispose of the activity. If your income from profitable passive activities exceeds your losses, your net income is taxed like other income (and can be offset by losses from nonpassive activities).

Taxpayers affected. The passive loss rules apply to individuals, estates, trusts and personal service corporations. They also apply in a limited fashion to other closely held corporations. A closely held corporation cannot deduct passive losses against portfolio income. But it *can* deduct passive losses as an offset to its active business income [IRC Sec. 469(a)(2), (e)(2); Reg. Sec. 1.469-1T(g)(5)].

The passive loss rules generally apply to tax years beginning after 1986. However, there was a five-year phase-in for interests in passive activities held on October 22, 1986. But since 1991, the passive loss rules apply all interests, regardless of when they were acquired.

Passive activity. To determine if your participation in an activity is sufficient to avoid the passive loss rules, you must first determine how many activities you are involved in. How you go about making this determination depends on when your tax year ends.

Tax years ending on or before May 10, 1992: You apply certain intricate and mechanical tests for defining your activities. Generally, all your operations at a single location are one activity regardless of the similarity or diversity of the operations. On the other hand, a rental operation is generally treated as a separate passive activity even if conducted at the same location as a nonrental operation. However, you must treat the rental and nonrental operations as a single activity if either operation generates more than 80% of the income from that location [Temp. Reg. Sec. 1.469-4T].

Tax years ending after May 10, 1992: The IRS has proposed rules on defining an activity that contains no mechanical rules, no detailed examples and no numerical tests. Instead, the new rules distill the entire inquiry into two general rules, five special limitations and a new break [Prop. Reg. Sec. 1.469-4].

- Under the proposed regulation, one or more trade or business or rental activities can be grouped together or treated as separate activities if: (1) Each resulting activity constitutes an "appropriate economic unit" for measuring gain or loss; and (2) your grouping is justified by all the relevant facts and circumstances. You may use any reasonable method of applying the facts and circumstances in grouping activities. The following factors will be given the greatest weight in deciding whether a grouping of activities is an appropriate economic unit: similarities and differences in types of business; the extent of common control; the extent of common ownership; geographical location; and interdependencies between the activities (e.g., whether the activities purchase and sell goods among themselves, involve related products or services, have the same customers, have the same employees, or keep one set of books).
- The proposed regulation contains five special limitations on activity groupings: (1) A rental activity cannot be grouped with a trade or business activity unless one of those activities is "insubstantial" in relation to the other. (2) An activity involving the rental of real property and an activity involving the rental of personal property (other than personal property provided in connection with the real property) cannot be treated as a single activity. (3) Activities held as a limited partner or limited entrepreneur generally cannot be grouped with other activities. (4) Once you have grouped particular activities, those activities may not be regrouped in later tax years unless there has been a material change in facts and circumstances. (5) The IRS has the final call. It may regroup your activities if your grouping does not reflect appropriate economic units and one of the primary purposes is to circumvent the passive loss rules.
- New break: Under the proposed regulation, if you dispose of a substantial part of an activity, you may treat that part as a separate activity for the tax year, thus triggering suspended losses from that part.

▶ **TAX CHOICE FOR '92** You may continue to apply the old temporary regulations for a 1992 tax year that includes May 10, 1992.

Material participation. You are considered a material participant in a trade or business (and your losses are not passive) if you meet any of the following tests [Reg. Sec. 1.469-5T(a)]:

- You participate in an activity for more than 500 hours during the year.
- Your participation for the year constitutes substantially all of the participation by anyone in the activity for the year.
- Your participation was more than 100 hours and was not less than the participation of any other person.
- You participated in the activity for more than 500 hours per year for any five of the ten preceding years.
- Your aggregate participation in two or more activities exceeds 500 hours and your participation in each individual activity exceeds 100 hours, but is less than 500 hours.
- You participated in a personal service activity for more than 500 hours per year in any three preceding tax years (whether or not consecutive).
- You materially participate based on all the facts and circumstances. For this purpose, your participation in the management of an activity isn't taken into

account if there's a paid manager or if your management services are exceeded by another individual.

As a general rule, a limited partner cannot be treated as materially participating in a partnership activity. But this rule doesn't apply if the limited partner participates for more than 500 hours during the year or materially participates under the five-out-of-ten-year test or the three-year personal service test.

Significant participation. A special rule applies to activities in which you "significantly participate." You are considered to significantly participate if your time devoted to the activity exceeds 100 hours but doesn't reach the level of material participation.

Under the special rule, you first combine your income from profitable significant-participation activities with your losses from other significant-participation activities. If your losses exceed the income, then your net loss from significant-participation activities is included with other passive losses (and is used to offset passive income). However, if your income exceeds your losses, then your net income from significant-participation activities is not treated as passive income. Instead, the net income is considered active income and cannot be offset by any other passive losses [Reg. Sec. 1.469-2T(f)(2)].

With a significant-participation activity, you are in a no-win situation. If the activity generates a profit, the tax law classifies it as active income that can't be sheltered by your other passive losses. But if the activity operates in the red, you have a passive loss that can't offset your other active (e.g., salary) income.

> **IDEA IN ACTION** If the activity generates a profit, try to cut back your involvement so that you don't reach the 100-hour mark. That way, your income will be passive, and you can use it to soak up your passive losses, such as from rental real estate.

Rental activity. In a passive rental activity, you derive income by leasing tangible property to others. As a general rule, your income or loss from a rental activity is considered passive whether or not you materially participate. However, there are exceptions [Reg. Sec. 1.469-1T(e)(3)]. For tax purposes, you are not engaged in a rental activity if:

- The average period for which each customer uses the property is seven days or less, which excludes short-term rentals of cars, video cassettes, tuxedos, hotel rooms, etc., from the passive activity rules.
- The average use for each customer exceeds seven days but is less than 30 days, and significant personal services are provided. This excludes hotels.
- Extraordinary personal services are provided by or on your behalf to make the property available to customers. The customers' use of the property must be incidental to the services provided. This exception applies even if the average period of use is more than 30 days. This rule excludes hospitals and nursing homes.
- The rentals are incidental to certain nonrental activities. This exception applies if the rental income is insubstantial; the rented property is lodging provided for your employees and for your convenience; or the property is held for sale in the ordinary course of business and is sold during the year.
- You customarily make the property available to various customers on a nonexclusive basis during defined business hours. As a result, golf courses generally would be excluded.

- The property is used in a nonrental activity of a partnership, S corporation or joint venture in which you own an interest.

➤ **SPECIAL BREAK** You may use up to $25,000 of losses from passive real estate rental activities to offset nonpassive income if (1) you "actively participate" in the rental activity and (2) your income doesn't exceed certain limits [IRC Sec. 469(i)].

The active participation standard for rental real estate is more liberal than the material participation standard. All that's required is that you participate in a bona fide sense. For example, making management decisions, such as approving tenants, lease terms and repairs is sufficient even if an agent handles the day-to-day affairs of the rental activity. However, you cannot be an active participant if you are a limited partner or hold less than a 10% interest in the rental activity.[1]

The special $25,000 allowance is available in full if your adjusted gross income (AGI) does not exceed $100,000. The allowance is reduced by one dollar for each two dollars that your AGI exceeds the $100,000 mark. So, for example, if your AGI is $125,000, up to $12,500 of your active participation passive losses can be deducted against your salary, interest and dividend income. And if your AGI equals or exceeds $150,000, there is no special allowance at all.

NOTE: The $25,000 allowance is available in an equivalent form for the rehabilitation and low-income housing credits. The AGI restriction on getting the credits is more liberal. The rehabilitation credit phases out at AGI in the $200,000 to $250,000 range [¶2406; 2407]. And in the case of the low-income housing credit, there is no AGI cap for property placed in service after 1989. (There was a $250,000 AGI cap for property placed in service prior to 1990.) [IRC Sec. 469(i)(3)(C)].

¶2327   AT RISK RULES

Like the passive loss rules [¶2326], the "at risk" rules are designed to limit tax shelter losses. Under these rules, your loss deductions cannot exceed the amount you have "at risk" in each activity at the end of the tax year. Any loss disallowed because it exceeds your amount at risk may be deducted in the succeeding tax years, subject to the at risk limits in each of those years [IRC Sec. 465]. The amount of loss deductible in a particular year reduces your risk investment (but not below zero) for that activity for subsequent tax years. Thus, if a loss exceeds your risk amount, it will not be allowed in the next year unless your risk amount is increased.

Amount considered at risk. You are at risk for an investment to the extent of money or your adjusted basis in other property you contribute to the activity. In addition, you are at risk for loans on which you are personally liable or for which property has been pledged (other than property used in the activity). You are not at risk for amounts protected against loss by insurance, nonrecourse financing (i.e., no personal liability), guarantees, stop loss agreements or similar arrangements [IRC Sec. 465(b)]. However, there is an exception for real estate: Real estate bought with nonrecourse debt is exempt from the at risk rules if the financing comes from a bank, the government or is insured by the government.

Interplay with passive loss rules. The at risk rules are applied before the passive loss rules. This means your maximum possible deduction is the amount you have at risk in the investment, regardless of how much passive income you have from other activities.

On the other hand, your at risk amounts are reduced by losses allowed by the at risk rules, even though they are not deductible under the passive loss rules.

Example: This year Mr.Berry invests $5,000 in a limited partnership. The partnership borrows $45,000 and invests the $50,000 total in a farming operation. Due to the high degree of leverage, the partnership generates $7,500 worth of tax losses for Berry. Since Berry has only $5,000 at risk in the investment, his loss deduction cannot exceed that amount. Berry's deduction is further reduced by the passive loss rules. If he has only $500 of passive income, he can deduct only $500 of the loss.

Recapture. Losses you previously deducted must be recaptured when your at risk amounts fall below zero. This can happen if you receive a distribution, your nonrecourse debt increases or you receive a loan guarantee. When your loss is recaptured, you have taxable income to the extent your at risk basis is reduced below zero [IRC Sec. 465(e)].

Example: Ms. Smythe invests $50,000 in a business venture subject to the at risk rules. Smythe is not personally liable for any of the debts of the business, so her at risk amount is her original investment of $50,000. Over the course of several years, she deducts losses of $25,000. Smythe subsequently borrows $35,000 in nonrecourse debt from the local bank. The debt is secured by business property. Smythe must recapture $10,000 of the loss deductions, since her at risk amount ($50,000 less $25,000 less $35,000) is reduced below zero.

Important limitation: The amount you recapture in any year is limited to the excess of losses you previously claimed over amounts you previously recaptured. This means Smythe would not have to recapture more than $15,000 in future years unless she takes additional loss deductions.

Finally, you may deduct recaptured income in a subsequent year to the extent your at risk amount increases above zero. So, for example, if Smythe were to make an additional contribution to the business of $10,000 or more, she would be allowed to deduct the recaptured $10,000.

¶2328   LOSSES FROM VACATION HOME RENTALS

[New tax legislation may affect this subject; see ¶1.]

If you rent out your vacation home or other dwelling unit, any losses you incur on the rental activity may not be currently deductible. A special provision disallows losses attributable to rental-type expenses (e.g., depreciation and maintenance) if a vacation home is also used as your residence during the year. Deductible expenses unrelated to the rental (e.g., property taxes, mortgage interest) are not affected by this provision. So you can deduct them in full against your other income [IRC Sec. 280A(b)].

For purposes of this disallowance rule, you are considered to have used the vacation home as a residence if you used the property during the year for personal purposes for the greater of (1) 14 days or (2) 10% of the days the property is rented out [IRC Sec. 280A(d)(1)]. If your personal use falls below these levels, then any loss is fully deductible (subject to the passive loss rules [¶2326] and the hobby loss rules [¶2325]).

➤ **OBSERVATION** If you reach the 10%/14-day limits, the mortgage interest and property taxes attributable to your personal use of one vacation home are fully deductible. Your expenses and depreciation attributable to rental use are deductible up to the amount of your rental income (after subtracting out mortgage interest and property taxes attributable to the rental) [IRC Sec. 280A(c)(5)]. What's more, your writeoffs are not subject to the passive loss rules [IRC Sec. 469(j)(10)]. If your personal use falls below the 10%/14-day level, then the mortgage interest is subject to the deduction restriction for passive losses. So, in some cases, you may be better off if your vacation home is treated as a residence for tax purposes.

Special rule. If your vacation home is rented for fewer than 15 days during the year, then the rental is ignored for tax purposes. In other words, your rental income is tax-free and your rental expenses are not deductible [IRC Sec. 280A(g)].

Personal use. In computing personal use of a vacation home, you must count one personal day for every day or part of a day that the home is used by you or your family members for personal purposes. Any day spent doing repair or maintenance work isn't counted as a personal day, but any day that the home is rented for less than a fair market rental is counted as a personal day.

A special rule applies where you rent your principal residence (or hold for rental) at a fair market rental for a consecutive period of 12 months or more. Your use of the property as your principal residence for a part of any tax year during which the rental period extends is not treated as personal use. The rental period may be less than 12 months if the property is sold or exchanged at the end of the period [IRC Sec. 280A(d)(4)]. This rule is helpful if you move to a new residence before selling your old one. You can get full tax savings from renting out the old home while seeking a buyer—even though you lived in the home for more than 14 days during the year.

Computing rental expense deductions. When you use your home and also rent it out, you figure your deductions by first allocating expenses between the days the home is rented and the days the home is used for personal purposes [IRC Sec. 280A(e)]. Three allocations must be made on this basis—one for operating expenses, one for depreciation and one for interest, taxes and other expenses. Then deductions allocable to the rental period are taken in the following order [Prop. Reg. Sec. 1.280A-3(d)(3)]:

1. Interest, taxes, etc., allocable to the rental period.

2. Operating expenses (maintenance, repairs, utilities) are only deductible to the extent the rental income from the home exceeds the deductions in (1).

3. Depreciation is deductible only to the extent the rental income exceeds the deductions in (1) and (2).

You claim the interest, taxes and other expenses detailed above, to the extent deductible, on Schedule E, Form 1040. You deduct interest and taxes attributable to your personal use period on Schedule A. Operating expenses and depreciation attributable to the personal use period are, of course, not deductible.

Example: Mr. and Mrs. Smith own a second home that they rented out during the year for 100 days and occupied themselves for 25 days. During the year, they spent $5,200 for interest and taxes, $4,000 maintaining the property, and they have $2,000 in depreciation. Their gross rental income is $6,300. Under the allocation formula, 80% of their expenses are attributable to the rental period (100 days out of 125 days)—$4,160 of the interest and taxes, $3,200 of the maintenance and $1,600 of the depreciation. The Smiths can deduct the $4,160 interest and taxes in full. They can deduct $2,140 of their maintenance expenses ($6,300 less $4,160). The remaining maintenance expenses, as well as the depreciation, are not deductible. The Smiths can also deduct the $1,040 of interest and taxes allocable to the personal use period.

▶ **OBSERVATION** The result in the example is based on the IRS position for allocating interest and taxes on a rental vacation home. The Tax Court and the Ninth and Tenth Circuit Courts have adopted a different position.[1] These courts maintain that the proper allocation of interest and taxes to the rental period should be: the number of rental days to the number of days in the whole year. Under this approach, you could be entitled to deduct more of your operating expenses and depreciation.

For example, with this more liberal rule, the Smiths in the above example would allocate only $1,425 of their interest and taxes to the rental of the second home. That would allow them to deduct $4,000 of their maintenance expenses and $875 of depreciation. Result: An extra $2,735 of deductions.

NET OPERATING LOSS DEDUCTION

¶2341   SPECIAL TREATMENT OF NET OPERATING LOSS (NOL)

If the operations of a business are in the red for a year, the tax law offers some relief. When there is a so-called net operating loss (NOL), you can use the losses of a bad year to offset the profits of a good year [IRC Sec. 172; Reg. Sec. 1.172-1—1.172.8].

Thus, you may use a NOL to cut your taxable income in other years. Here's how: You can carry it back and deduct it from income earned in earlier years, and you can carry it forward and deduct it from income in later years. If you carry back a NOL, you must refigure your tax for the carryback year. Then, if it turns out that you owe less tax for that year, you can get a refund. Note: You may disregard the carryback period and simply carry the NOL forward—if that's to your tax advantage.

There are special rules that restrict your deductible operating loss. Thus, in computing the NOL and the carrybacks and carryovers, you may have to adjust (modify) deductions and income for the years involved.

> **NOTE:** The loss must be from the operation of your trade, business or profession, or from casualty or theft. A loss due to confiscation of a business by a foreign government can also qualify for the net operating loss.[1]

(a) Years to Which NOL May Be Carried. You can use the net operating loss to offset profits in the three years before the loss. If any of the loss remains after this carryback, you can use it to offset profits in the 15 years following the year the loss was sustained [IRC Sec. 172(b)(1); Reg. Sec. 1.172-4]. The loss must first be carried to the earliest year and then to the next earliest year, and so on.

Election to forgo carryback. You can elect not to carry back the NOL. Instead, you may use it only in the 15-year carryover period. To make this choice, you must attach a statement to your tax return for the NOL year showing that you elect to forgo the carryback [IRC Sec. 172(b)(3)]. The election must be made by the due date of the return (including extensions). Once you make the election for any NOL year, you cannot change it. Thus, the carryover for a 1992 NOL election would be to 1993-2007 only.

(b) Who Is Entitled to NOL Relief. All taxpayers are entitled to the net operating loss deduction. It can be taken even if you are not in business during the carryback or carryover year [IRC Sec. 172; Reg. Sec. 1.172-1]. Although corporations are also allowed to write off NOLs, a special tax rule has been designed to prevent profitable corporations from acquiring unprofitable corporations merely to take advantage of their loss writeoffs [¶3031 et seq.].

Special rules apply to partnerships [¶3407], estates and trusts [¶3515], corporations [¶3031 et seq.], real estate investment trusts [¶3329] and so-called "S" corporations [¶3110].

¶2342   DETERMINING NET OPERATING LOSS

A net operating loss is computed the same way as taxable income. Deductions are made from gross income and if the deductions are more than gross income, you have a net operating loss.

However, special rules limit what you can deduct in computing a net operating loss. In general, the rules do not allow you to deduct net capital losses or nonbusiness losses in computing the net operating loss.[1]

(a) Business and Nonbusiness. It is necessary first to separate business from nonbusiness items of income and expense.

Business income is income from your trade or business. Salary or wages you earn as an employee are also considered business income. Also, gain from the sale or exchange of depreciable property or real estate you use in your business is included in business income.

Business deductions are deductions from your trade or business. Personal casualty and theft losses are also business deductions. So are moving expenses and employee business expenses such as travel, transportation, union dues and work clothes required for work. Individual stockholder losses from S corporations are also business deductions.[1]

Nonbusiness income is income that is not from your trade or business. Examples are dividends, annuities, income from an endowment, interest on investments and income from S corporations.

Nonbusiness deductions are those not from your trade or business, or are not related to employment. These include medical expenses, alimony, charitable contributions and contributions to a personal retirement plan. If you do not itemize deductions, nonbusiness deductions include the standard deduction.

(b) Adjustments in Figuring NOL. If your deductions exceed your income so that your tax return shows a loss for the year, certain adjustments have to be made in the loss figure shown on the return. The resulting amount is your net operating loss.

The following items reduce the amount of your loss [IRC Sec. 172(d); Reg. Sec. 1.172-3]:

- Net operating loss from any other year.
- Deduction for personal exemptions.
- Nonbusiness capital losses are deductible only up to nonbusiness capital gains. Any excess cannot be deducted.
- Nonbusiness deductions may be subtracted only from nonbusiness income, including any nonbusiness capital gains that remain after deducting nonbusiness capital losses. Any excess of nonbusiness deductions over nonbusiness income cannot be deducted.
- Business capital losses may be deducted only up to the total business capital gains plus any nonbusiness capital gains that remain after deducting nonbusiness capital losses and other nonbusiness deductions. A net capital loss cannot be deducted.
- Contributions for a self-employed person to a self-employment retirement plan [¶1350].

Example: The following illustrates how net operating loss is computed. Mr. Miller owns a small store and he has the following 1992 income and deductions:

Income:	
Salary earned as part-time salesman	$26,225
Interest on savings	425
Net long-term capital gain on sale of real estate in business	2,050
Total income	$28,700
Deductions:	
Net loss from small business (sales of $67,000 minus expenses of $97,000)	$30,000
Net short-term capital loss on sale of stock	900
Net loss from rental property	50
Personal exemption	2,300
Small business investment company stock loss	300
Loss on small business stock	620
Total deductions	$34,170

Miller's deductions exceed his income by $5,470 ($34,170 -- $28,700). However, to compute Miller's net operating loss, certain of his deductions must be modified. He cannot deduct the following:

Nonbusiness net short-term capital loss	$ 900
Personal exemption	2,300
Total adjustments to net loss	$3,200

When these items are eliminated, total deductions are $30,970 ($34,170--$3,200). Total deductions then exceed income by $2,270 ($30,970--$28,700). This is Miller's NOL.

(c) Capital Loss Carryover. Because of the distinction between business and non-business capital gains and losses, you must find how much of any capital loss carryover is a business capital loss and how much is a nonbusiness capital loss [Reg. Sec. 1.172-3(b)].

¶2343 CARRYOVER OF UNUSED PORTION OF NET OPERATING LOSS

Your net operating loss (as adjusted above) is used first to reduce your income of the third preceding year. If any loss remains, it is carried to the second preceding year, then to the first preceding year, and then it is carried forward to future years, as described in ¶2341(a). However, you must make adjustments to the taxable income for each year to which the loss is applied [IRC Sec. 172(b)(2); Reg. Sec. 1.172-4(b)].

Important: You can elect to waive the three-year carryback and have your NOL apply against only future operating income [IRC Sec. 172(b)(3)]. If you make this election, it must apply for both regular tax and alternative minimum tax purposes.[1]

(a) Determining the Carryover. After determining the year to which you will initially carry your net operating loss, you need to calculate how much of it you can carry back or forward to that year.

If your net operating loss is *less than* the taxable income of the first year to which it is carried, you simply subtract the loss from the taxable income in that year.

Example 1: Mike Miller suffers a $12,000 net operating loss (as adjusted) in 1993 that he carries back to 1990. When he filed his return for that year, his taxable income was $30,000. Mike offsets the $30,000 of income by the full $12,000 loss, so his taxable income now drops to $18,000. Mike files an amended return and claims a refund for 1990.

If your net operating loss is *more than* your taxable income of the first year to which it is carried, you must adjust that year's taxable income to see how much of the loss will be used up then and how much will be carried over to the following year [IRC Sec. 1.172-5]. These are the key adjustments you must make:

- Capital losses are only deductible to the extent of your capital gains. A net capital loss is not allowed.
- Deduct any prior net operating loss carrybacks or carryovers. The earliest losses are deducted first.
- Recompute your deductions that are dependent on your adjusted gross or taxable income. This applies, for example, to medical expenses (deductible only to the extent they exceed $7\frac{1}{2}\%$ of your adjusted gross income) and to charitable contributions (generally deductible to the extent they don't exceed 50% of your adjusted gross income). Special rule: For charitable contributions only, you must add back any carrybacks or carryovers deducted in the previous step.
- You cannot claim personal or dependency deductions.

Example 2: Mr. Smith suffers a $30,000 net operating loss (as adjusted) in 1993 that he carries back to 1990. His 1990 tax return, as a single taxpayer with no dependents, looked like this:

Salary	$30,000
Taxable interest and dividends	5,000
Total	$35,000
Less: Net capital loss	(1,000)
Adjusted gross income (AGI)	$34,000
Less: Itemized deductions:	
$20,000 charitable gift—deduction limited to 50% of AGI	17,000
$3,000 medical expenses—only amount above $7\frac{1}{2}\%$ of AGI deductible	450
Taxes, mortgage interest, etc.	3,450
Personal exemption	2,050
Taxable income	$11,050

Because the $30,000 operating loss carried back to 1990 exceeds the taxable income for that year, it is necessary to adjust Smith's 1990 taxable income as follows:

Salary	$30,000
Taxable interest and dividends	5,000
Net capital loss not allowed	0
Modified adjusted gross income	$35,000
Less: Itemized deductions:	
Recomputed charitable gift	17,500
Recomputed medical expenses	375
Taxes, mortgage interest, etc.	3,500
Personal exemption not allowed	0
Modified taxable income	$13,625

The adjustments give Smith a higher 1990 taxable income. His 1993 operating loss offsets 100% of this income, so Smith is entitled to a refund of any tax paid for that year. The remaining $16,375 of the 1993 loss is carried forward to be used against 1991 and later years' income as needed. Note: If Smith's 1991 taxable income is insufficient to absorb 100% of the remaining loss, it will be necessary to adjust that year's income in the same manner as for 1990.

(b) Refund Claim. If you carry a NOL back to a prior year, you can get a tax refund for that year by filing an amended return on Form 1040X with the appropriate supporting evidence [¶3736; 3740]. Your refund can be speeded up, however, by filing Form 1045, Application for Tentative Carryback Adjustment. For special refund period, see ¶3738.

(c) How Treated on Return. You enter a prior year's NOL carried forward to the current year on Form 1040 as a minus figure on the line showing "other income." Whether you carry the NOL back or forward, you must attach a statement to your tax return in the year the loss is incurred. Your statement should include how much was deducted and how you figured the NOL. If more than one NOL is deducted in the same year, your statement must cover each of them.

¶2344   CARRYOVERS OR CARRYBACKS FROM MORE THAN ONE YEAR

Since a net operating loss generally can be carried back three years and then forward 15 years, your net operating loss deduction for a particular year may involve carryovers or carrybacks from more than one year. When this happens, your carryovers and carrybacks are added together, with the older ones being used up first [IRC Sec. 172(a); Reg. Sec. 1.172-1(a)].

BAD DEBT DEDUCTION IN GENERAL

¶2351   THE DEDUCTION FOR BAD DEBTS

This deduction comes into play when you loan money to others or have included in gross income debts due from others for property sold or services rendered. You can deduct the loss resulting from the worthlessness or uncollectibility of these debts, provided the debts had a value when acquired or created.[1] If a worthless debt arises from unpaid wages, salaries, rents, fees or commissions, etc., you cannot deduct the loss unless the unpaid amount has been included in your income [IRC Sec. 166; Reg. Sec. 1.166-1].

When and how deductible. You deduct bad debts in the year they become worthless. Your corporation generally may claim the full amount of the loss as an ordinary deduction, but a special rule applies for worthless bonds [¶2362]. You also may claim the full amount of the loss as an ordinary deduction, if the debt is business connected. Special rules apply to nonbusiness bad debts [¶2357].

You may claim a deduction for a partially worthless business bad debt. Your corporation may also claim a deduction for a partially worthless debt, whether connected to its business or not.

A corporate bond that becomes worthless is not considered a bad debt. But a deduction may still be claimed as a capital loss [¶2362].

¶2352   EXISTENCE OF DEBT

In order for a bad debt to be deductible, there must be a valid, real debt. There must also be a debtor-creditor relationship. This exists when one person, by contract or law, is obliged to pay another an amount of money, certain or uncertain, either currently or at some future date. There is no debt, however, if the obligation to repay is subject to a contingency and that contingency has not occurred.

Banks, but not other taxpayers, can deduct a worthless debt owed by a political party. The debt must be created under the bank's usual commercial practice [IRC Sec. 271; Reg. Sec. 1.271-1]. For example, a debt motivated only by a bank officer's political interest would not qualify.

¶2353   AMOUNT DEDUCTIBLE

The amount deductible is your adjusted basis in the debt for determining loss from a sale or exchange [IRC Sec. 166(b); Reg. Sec. 1.166-1(d)]. This may or may not be the same as the face amount of the debt. See ¶1600 et seq. No deduction is allowed when your basis cannot be proven.[1]

> **Example:** Ames buys a $1,000 note for $700. His basis in the note is $700, and that is the amount deductible if the debt becomes worthless.

WHAT BAD DEBTS ARE DEDUCTIBLE

¶2355   BUSINESS BAD DEBTS

A bad debt you hold is considered a business bad debt only if it was created or acquired in the course of your trade or business or the debt became worthless in the course of your trade or business [Reg. Sec. 1.166-5(b)(2)]. Your motivation for making the debt must be primary and dominant to your trade or business; significant motivation is not sufficient.[1] A business bad debt is a deduction *for* adjusted gross income [Reg. Sec. 1.166-1].

You can deduct business bad debts in full to the extent they become partially or completely worthless. Whether a debt is worthless depends on the facts and circumstances of each situation, including the value of any collateral and the financial condition of the debtor [Reg. Sec. 1.166-2(a)].

Factors Indicating Debt Worthless

Bankruptcy generally indicates that at least part of an unsecured and unpreferred debt is worthless [Reg. Sec. 1.166-2(c)]. The deduction is limited to the difference between the claim and the amount received on distribution of the bankrupt's assets [Reg. Sec. 1.166-1(d)(2)].

Statute of limitations having run on the debt is strong, but not conclusive, evidence of worthlessness.[2]

Other factors. The availability or value of collateral, debtor's disappearance, insolvency, ill health, receivership, debtor with-out assets or out of business, foreign expropriation [IRC Sec. 1351(b)].

Factors Indicating Debt Not Worthless

No serious effort to collect, but legal action against debtor is not necessary if it would be futile; debtor still in business or earning substantial income.[3]

¶2356   PARTIALLY WORTHLESS BUSINESS DEBTS

A debt need not be completely worthless before you claim a deduction. If a business debt is partially worthless, you can deduct the part you charge off on your books for the year [IRC Sec. 166(a)(2); Reg. Sec. 1.166-3(a)]. However, partial deductions are allowed for specific debts only. For example, you cannot deduct a percentage of the total of certain accounts.

Charge-off not mandatory. The charge-off does not have to be made in the tax year the debt became partially worthless [Reg. Sec. 1.166-3]. For instance, if a debt became partially worthless in 1991, you can make the charge-off in 1992, and take a deduction on your 1992 return.

Failure to claim partial worthlessness as a deduction in one year does not preclude you from taking a deduction for partial worthlessness of a greater amount—or for total worthlessness—in a later year.[1] But no deduction is allowed after the year the debt becomes totally worthless.

➤ **OBSERVATION** Partial charge-offs allow you to take the deduction in the year it will do the most good.

Example: The Expo Corporation manufactures computer terminals and sells them to 18 regional distributors across the country. In 1992, one of Expo's distributors purchased $50,000 worth of terminals on account but failed to pay any money when due. The distributor promises to pay $20,000 toward the debt in 1993. Expo has record profits in 1992 that it wants to shelter from tax. The company decides to charge off $30,000 worth of the delinquent sale proceeds on its 1992 tax return since it will probably never receive them.

Collateral need not be liquidated. Generally, the collateral securing a debt need not be liquidated to establish the worthless part of the debt.

¶2357   NONBUSINESS BAD DEBTS

These are debts that are not related to your trade or business when they are created, acquired or become worthless. So, even if a debt arose in your trade or business, it is a nonbusiness debt in the hands of a donee, executor or transferee who was not in your trade or business when the debt arose. No deduction is allowed for a *partially worthless* nonbusiness bad debt [IRC Sec. 166(d); Reg. Sec. 1.166-5].

NOTE: Debts owed to corporations are business debts by definition.

Example 1: During 1992, Mr. Lane, a sole proprietor, made the following loans:

To	Amount	Type	Unrecoverable
Sister	$2,000	Nonbusiness	$1,000
Mother	$1,000	Nonbusiness	$1,000
Customer 1	$3,000	Business	$1,000
Customer 2	$5,000	Business	$2,000

Mr. Lane can deduct $4,000 for bad debts in 1992: $1,000 that his mother owes him, $1,000 of the $3,000 that Customer 1 owes him and $2,000 of the $5,000 that Customer 2 owes him. Mr. Lane gets no deduction for the $1,000 that his sister owes him because partially worthless nonbusiness bad debts are not deductible.

(a) Loans by Officers or Employees. Uncollectible loans made by corporate officers or employees are generally nonbusiness bad debts. The business of the corporation is not the business of its employees or officers. However, a loan may be a business debt if it was required as a condition of your employment, not just to protect your investment in the company. In one case, the Tax Court allowed a corporate president to take a business bad debt deduction for a loss on a business-related guarantee of the corporation debt. The court said his primary motivation was to protect his job.[1]

(b) Loans by a Stockholder. Stockholders who lend money to their corporations are not in business when their only return is that of an investor. This applies even if the return on a loan to the corporation is substantially due to their services. Any loss is a nonbusiness bad debt. Similarly, loans by a stockholder-employee do not receive business bad debt treatment unless the dominant motivation for making the loan was business oriented. A sole shareholder's worthless loan to a client of his corporation may be deducted as a business bad debt if the primary motivation for loaning the money was to maintain a high income level as a corporate employee.[2]

(c) Nonbusiness Bad Debt as Short-Term Capital Loss. You treat a nonbusiness bad debt as a short-term capital loss in the year of worthlessness. (Since debts owed to corporations are always business debts, this restriction does not apply to them.)

> **Example 2:** Ms. Zale had a nonbusiness bad debt of $3,200 owed to her which became worthless in 1992. The debt of $3,200 is considered a short-term capital loss. If Zale had no other capital gains and losses in 1992, the debt is deductible only to the extent of $3,000, and the balance ($200) is carried over to 1993.

¶2358   ADVANCES TO RELATIVES

First, you must establish whether the advance to a relative is actually a gift or a loan. There is no bad debt deduction for gifts, since no debtor-creditor relationship exists. Even if the advance is a loan, it may be a nonbusiness debt. It depends on whether the debt was created in your trade or business, or the loss from the worthless debt is related to your trade or business.

¶2359   ADVANCES TO CORPORATIONS BY STOCKHOLDERS

These advances may be loans or capital contributions (additional investment). If the advance is in fact a loan, it is subject to the rules governing bad debts.

¶2360   DEPOSITS IN CLOSED BANKS

You can claim a bad debt deduction for funds deposited in a bank or other financial institution that becomes insolvent. Your deduction is reduced to the extent you are compensated by deposit insurance. Your deposit is simply treated as a loan to the bank.

However, deposits not made in the course of your business are subject to the usual rule for nonbusiness bad debts and are treated as short-term capital losses [IRC Sec. 166(d)(1); Reg. Sec. 1.166-5]. Your total net capital losses (for the current year and any carryovers) can offset up to $3,000 of your salary, dividends and other income for the year.

Election to treat as a deductible loss. You may elect to deduct a deposit the bank will not repay as an ordinary loss [IRC Sec. 165(l)]. A special rule allows you to get a full deduction up to a maximum amount of $20,000 per year ($10,000 for married taxpayers filing separately).

However, you may not make this election if any part of the deposit is insured under federal law. Additionally, you must reduce the $20,000 ceiling by the amount of insurance proceeds you reasonably expect to receive under state law.

You may also elect to treat your deposit as a casualty loss. As with other nonbusiness casualty losses, your deposit must first be reduced by $100, and the remainder is only deductible to the extent your total casualty losses for the year exceed 10% of your adjusted gross income.

> **NOTE:** If you own 1% or more of the financial institution or are an officer, you cannot elect to treat your deposit as an ordinary loss or a casualty loss. You also cannot make an election if you are related to an owner or officer.

¶2361   DEDUCTING BAD DEBTS

Under the current rules, you must deduct bad debts by using the specific charge-off method, which means you write them off on a debt-by-debt basis. Before 1987, you could write off bad debts by using the reserve method of accounting, which allowed you to set up an expected reserve to cover anticipated bad debts and deduct each year how much you added to the reserve to bring it up to the necessary level.

¶2362   WORTHLESS BONDS

The bad debt rules do not apply to bonds issued by corporations or governments [IRC Sec. 165(g)]. This is true whether the holder of the bond is a corporate or noncorporate taxpayer. However, as with any worthless security, you may be entitled to a capital loss deduction.

Exception. Worthless securities held by a bank or trust company are treated as bad debts [IRC Sec. 582]. And there is a conclusive presumption of complete or partial worthlessness when a bank or trust company must charge off a debt in whole or in part in obedience to specific orders of the banking authorities.

SPECIAL PROBLEMS

¶2365   BAD DEBT AND LOSS DISTINGUISHED

The difference between a bad debt and loss may be important for two reasons: (1) you cannot take a deduction for property that declines in value (e.g., stock certificates) without a sale or exchange, but you may be able to deduct partially worthless business bad debts; and (2) ordinarily, the statute of limitations for you to file a refund claim for a loss deduction is three years after you filed the return. The statute of limitations is seven years for a bad debt.

(a) Voluntary Cancellation or Forgiveness of a debt does not give rise to a deductible *loss*. However, you may be able to take a bad debt deduction if the debt is actually worthless. That deduction may be allowed because the debt is worthless, not because it is forgiven. For example, you can deduct the difference between a note's face value and the amount received in compromise *if* your debtor has no assets out of which the entire amount can be collected by suit. In some cases, even though the debt was *not* worthless when you forgave it, you can take a loss deduction when there is some payment in exchange for the forgiveness.

Deductible as a Loss

Consideration. The debt cancellation is a loss when made in exchange for a security interest (or lien) for other debts previously unsecured.[1]

Compromised accounts. A loss resulting from a dispute over the correctness of book charges and credits in connection with business transactions is deductible in the year in which settled by compromise or otherwise.[2]

Composition agreement. Loss under composition agreement is deductible in the year the agreement was made.[3]

Not Deductible

Capital transaction. If a shareholder gratuitously forgives a debt owed to him by the corporation, the transaction amounts to a contribution to the capital of the corporation [Reg. Sec. 1.61-12]. No loss deduction is allowed.

(b) Endorsers and Guarantors. If you incur a loss from a loan guaranty, you receive the same treatment as if you had made the loan directly. Thus, you can generally deduct the loss generally in full if the guaranty is connected with the your trade or business. If you entered into a guaranty for profit, the loss is a short-term capital loss. If you operate on the cash basis of accounting, you get no bad debt deduction until you pay the note.

> **Example 1:** Francis endorses John's note. John defaults and Francis has to pay. Ordinarily, John owes Francis the amount paid. If this debt is worthless, Francis may take a deduction.

The deduction may be disallowed if the endorser cannot prove he intended to collect the debt.

> **Example 2:** Father endorsed his son's note, without investigating the son's financial prospects. Father made no effort to collect from the son when he had to pay the son's debt. The bad debt deduction is denied on the ground that the transaction was in effect a gift to the son.

¶2366   RECOVERY OF BAD DEBTS

In the year you recover part or all of a bad debt previously deducted, you must include the recovery in your income to the extent that it reduced your tax in an earlier year. A recovery is a return of an amount you deducted or took a credit for in an earlier year. Generally, you must include part or all of the recovered amounts in income in the year you receive the recovery.

> **Example:** In 1991, Mr. Stone's tax return showed a short-term capital loss deduction of $300 when his debtor failed to pay a $300 debt. In 1992, the debtor paid Stone the $300. Stone includes the $300 in gross income for 1992. He does not make the adjustment by filing an amended return for 1991.

Tax benefit rule. This rule comes into play if you deducted a bad debt from your gross income and later collect all or part of the debt. Your recovery is included in your income only to the extent that the deduction reduced your tax (by any amount) in an earlier year. The recovery amount is excludable from income if the deduction reduced your *taxable income* but did not reduce your *tax liability* [¶1244].

¶2367   LOSS ON SALE OF PLEDGED PROPERTY OTHER THAN ON PURCHASE MONEY MORTGAGE

If a mortgagor makes a voluntary conveyance of property to the mortgagee, the property's fair market value is considered as payment of the unpaid balance of the obligation. If the fair market value of the property is less than the amount owed, the difference, if uncollectible, is a bad debt deductible by the mortgagee. If there is a foreclosure and someone other than the mortgagee bids on the property for less than the obligation, the mortgagee has a bad debt deduction for the difference between the obligation and the amount received. If the mortgagee bids on the property, the deduction is the difference between the obligation and the bid price [Reg. Sec. 1.166-6]. For repossessions of installment sale property, see Chapter 19.

Footnotes to Chapter 13

(For your added convenience, in brackets [] with the footnotes below, you will find citations to related paragraphs in the "RIA United States Tax Reporter"(USTR), "CCH Federal Tax Reporter" (CCH)" and "RIA Federal Tax Coordinator 2d" (FTC) multi-volume services.)

FOOTNOTE ¶ 2300 [USTR ¶ 1654; CCH ¶ 9804 et seq.; FTC ¶ M-1001].

(1) Rev. Rul 69-458, 1969-2 CB 33.

FOOTNOTE ¶ 2301 [USTR ¶ 1645.092; CCH ¶9806; FTC ¶ M-1001].

FOOTNOTE ¶ 2302 [USTR ¶ 1654.061; CCH ¶ 9808; FTC ¶ M-1501].

(1) Greenway, ¶ 80,097 PH Memo TC.

(2) The Great Island Holding Corp., 5 TC 150.

(3) Dickey, 14BTA 1295, aff. 56 F.2d 917, 10 AFTR 1449.

(4) O'Brien, 12 AFTR 2d 5411, 321 F.2d 227, aff'g 36 TC 957 on other grounds.

(5) Rev. Rul. 82-74, 1982-1 CB 110; Rev. Rul. 77-126, 1977-1 CB 47.

(6) Greenman v. U.S., 65 AFTR 2d 90-923.

(7) Lingham, ¶ 77,152 PH Memo TC.

FOOTNOTE ¶ 2303 [¶1654.062; CCH ¶ 9900; FTC ¶ M-1502].

(1) Heiner v. Tindle, 276 US 582, 6 AFTR 7366.

(2) Rev. Rul. 82-27, 1982-1 CB 32.

(3) Miller, ¶ 67,044 PH Memo TC.

(4) Weir, 109 F.2d 996, 24 AFTR 453; Albechten, ¶ 71,229 PH Memo TC; Dresser, 55 F.2d 499, 10 AFTR 1096.

FOOTNOTE ¶ 2304 [USTR ¶ 1654.300; CCH ¶ 10,005; FTC ¶ M-1700 et seq.].

(1) Treas. Dept. booklet "Nonbusiness Disasters, Casualties and Thefts" (1991 Ed.), p. 2; West 2 AFTR 2d 6003, 259 F.2d 704; Peterson, 30 TC 660; Rev. Rul. 70-16, 1970-1 CB 441.

(2) Stowers v. U.S., 3 AFTR 2d 505, 169 F. Supp. 246.

(3) Rev. Rul. 54-85, 1954-1 CB 58.

(4) Rev. Rul. 60-329, 1960-2 CB 67.

(5) Davis, 34 TC 586.

(6) Rev. Rul. 71-560, 1971-2 CB 126.

(7) Hayutin, ¶ 72,127 PH Memo TC.

(8) Anderson v. Comm., 81 F.2d 457.17 AFTR 369.

(9) Rev. Rul. 55-327, 1955-1 CB 25.

(10) Rev. Rul. 61-216, 1961-2 CB 134.

(11) Lloyd v. U.S., (DC, Wash.; 8-22-61) 8 AFTR 2d 5586; Nelson, ¶ 68,035 PH Memo TC.

(12) Rev. Rul. 63-232, 1963-2 CB 97.

(13) Rev. Rul. 70-16, 1970-1 CB 36.

FOOTNOTE ¶ 2305 [USTR ¶ 1654.350; CCH ¶ 10,101; FTC ¶ M-2100 et seq.].

(1) Allison v. U.S., 344 US 167, 73 SCt. 191, 42 AFTR 660; Gwinn Bros. & Co., 7 TC 320.

FOOTNOTE ¶ 2306 [USTR ¶ 1654.304; CCH ¶ 9804; FTC ¶ M-1800].

FOOTNOTE ¶ 2307 [USTR ¶ 1654.420; CCH ¶ 10,105; FTC ¶ M-1501].

FOOTNOTE ¶ 2308 [USTR ¶ 1654.200; CCH ¶ 9802 et seq.; FTC ¶ M-3400 et seq.].

FOOTNOTE ¶ 2309 [USTR ¶ 1654.180, .302; CCH ¶ 9904 et seq.; FTC ¶ M-2200].

FOOTNOTE ¶ 2310 [USTR ¶ 1654.092, .150; CCH ¶ 9901 et seq.; FTC ¶ M-2300].

(1) Rev. Rul. 61-206, 1961-2 CB 57.

(2) Strauss v. U.S., 8 AFTR 2d 5952, 199 F.2d 845.

FOOTNOTE ¶ 2311 [USTR ¶ 1654.250; CCH ¶ 8706; FTC ¶ I-1207; 1314].

FOOTNOTE ¶ 2312 [¶ 1654.021, .050; CCH ¶ 13,705 et seq.; FTC ¶ M-1008; 1009].

(1) Kohler, 37 BTA 1019.

FOOTNOTE ¶ 2321 [USTR ¶ 10,914; CCH ¶ 32,083; RIA ¶ I-2701].

FOOTNOTE ¶ 2322 [USTR ¶ 1654.410; CCH ¶ 9900.738; FTC ¶ M-1017].

(1) Shoenberg v. Comm., 77 F.2d 446, 16 AFTR 95.

FOOTNOTE ¶ 2323 [USTR ¶ 1654.410; CCH ¶ 2150.45; 14,150; FTC ¶ M-1017].

FOOTNOTE ¶ 2324 [USTR ¶ 1654.500; CCH ¶ 10,105; FTC ¶ M-6000 et seq.].

FOOTNOTE ¶ 2325 [USTR ¶ 1834.01; CCH ¶ 12,177; FTC ¶ M-1515].

FOOTNOTE ¶ 2326 [USTR ¶ 4694; CCH ¶ 21,966; FTC ¶ M-5400].

(1) Conf. Rept. No. 99-841 (P.L. 99-54).

FOOTNOTE ¶ 2327 [USTR ¶ 4654; CCH ¶ 21,893; FTC ¶ M-5502].

FOOTNOTE ¶ 2328 [USTR ¶ 280A4; CCH ¶ 14,854; FTC ¶ M-5833, 5843].

(1) Bolton, 51 AFTR 2d 83-305, 694 F.2d 556, aff'g 77 TC 104; McKinney, 53 AFTR 2d 83-6281, 732 F.2d 414.

FOOTNOTE ¶ 2341 [USTR ¶ 1724; CCH ¶ 12,014; FTC ¶ M-4400].

(1) Alvary v. U.S., 9 AFTR 2d 1633, 302 F.2d 790.

FOOTNOTE ¶ 2342 [USTR ¶ 1724; CCH ¶ 12,014; FTC ¶ M-4402].

(1) Treas. Dept. booklet "Tax Guide for Small Business" (1991 Ed.), p. 68.

FOOTNOTE ¶ 2343 [USTR ¶ 1724; CCH ¶ 12,014; FTC ¶ M-4300].

(1) Plumb, 97 TC No.44.

FOOTNOTE ¶ 2344 [USTR ¶ 1724; CCH ¶ 1921; FTC ¶ M-4301].

FOOTNOTE ¶ 2351 [USTR ¶ 1664; CCH ¶ 10,550 et seq.; FTC ¶ M-2400].

(1) Eckert v. Burnet, 283 US 140, 51 SCt. 373, 9 AFTR 1413.

FOOTNOTE ¶ 2352 [USTR ¶ 1664; CCH ¶ 10,550 et seq.; FTC ¶ M-2401].

FOOTNOTE ¶ 2353 [USTR ¶ 1664; CCH ¶ 10,550 et seq.; FTC ¶ M-2410].

(1) Skinner v. Eaton, 34 F.2d 576, 7 AFTR 9394, affd 44 F.2d 1020, 9 AFTR 491.

FOOTNOTE ¶ 2355 [USTR ¶ 1664; CCH ¶ 10,501; FTC ¶ M-2600].

(1) U.S. v. Generes, 405 U.S. 93, 29 AFTR 2d 72-609.

(2) Nichols, 17 BTA 580.

(3) American Trust Co. v. Comm., 31 F.2d 47, 7 AFTR 8537.

FOOTNOTE ¶ 2356 [USTR ¶ 1664; CCH ¶ 10,501; FTC ¶ M-2706-2708].

(1) Moock Electric Supply Co., 41 BTA 1209.

FOOTNOTE ¶ 2357 [USTR ¶ 1664; CCH ¶ 10,600; FTC¶ M-2601].

(1) Rosati, ¶ 70,343 PH Memo TC.

(2) Bowers v. Comm., 50 AFTR 2d 82-5014; Litwin, 67 AFTR2d 91-1098.

FOOTNOTE ¶ 2358 [USTR ¶ 1664; CCH ¶ 10,550.6569 et seq.; FTC ¶ M-2501].

FOOTNOTE ¶ 2359 [USTR ¶ 1664; CCH ¶ 10,550.73; FTC ¶ M-2403].

FOOTNOTE ¶ 2360 [USTR ¶ 1664; CCH ¶ 10,550.065; FTC ¶ M-2500].

FOOTNOTE ¶ 2361 [USTR ¶ 1664; CCH ¶ 10,571; FTC ¶ M-3017].

FOOTNOTE ¶ 2362 [USTR ¶ 1664; CCH ¶ 10,001; FTC ¶ M-3300].

FOOTNOTE ¶ 2365 [USTR ¶ 1664; CCH ¶ 10,501; FTC ¶ M-3200].

(1) First National Bank of Durant, Okla., 6 BTA 545.

(2) Kansas City Pump Co., 6 BTA 938.

(3) Pacific Novelty Co., 5 BTA 1017.

FOOTNOTE ¶ 2366 [USTR ¶ 1664; CCH ¶ 10,501 et seq.; FTC ¶ M-5600].

FOOTNOTE ¶ 2367 [USTR ¶ 1664; CCH ¶ 10,650; FTC ¶ M-3800].

CHAPTER 14

TAX CREDITS—ESTIMATED TAX FOR INDIVIDUALS

PERSONAL TAX CREDITS

[New tax legislation may affect this subject; see ¶1.]

¶2401   EXPENSES OF CHILD CARE AND CARE OF DISABLED DEPENDENT OR SPOUSE

If you pay someone to care for your dependent child, your disabled spouse or other disabled dependent, you may be able to get a tax credit of up to 30% of your expenses. To qualify, you must pay these expenses so you can work or look for work. If you file Form 1040A, you claim the credit by completing a schedule right on that form; you must complete Form 2441 if you file Form 1040.

(a) Who May Take the Credit. You can take the credit if you maintain a household (pay more than 50% of the expenses) for any of the following individuals: a person under the age of 13 for whom you can claim a dependency exemption; a dependent of yours (regardless of age) who is incapable of self-care; and a spouse who is incapable of self-care [IRC Sec. 21(b)(1),(e)(1)].

If you are claiming the part of the earned income credit that is an extra credit for a young child [¶ 2402], then you cannot claim the child care credit for that child. However, you can claim the child care credit if you have eligible child care expenses for another qualifying child.

(b) What Expenses Qualify. You must incur the expenses to enable you to be gainfully employed. Your work can be for others or in your own business. It can be either full time or part time. Work also includes actively looking for work. However, if you do not find a job and have no earned income for the year, you cannot take the credit.

Expenses for services outside your home qualify for the credit if you incur them for the care of a dependent under age 13. If you have a child who turns 13 in mid-year, you can still claim a credit for expenses in that year, but only for those expenses you incur prior to the child's thirteenth birthday. However, the expense of sending a child to overnight camp does not qualify for the credit.

You can also claim a credit for expenses for the out-of-home care of an individual, other than a child, if (1) the individual spends at least 8 hours a day in your household and (2) the care is provided in a qualified dependent care center [IRC Sec. 21(b)(2)].

The social security and federal unemployment tax you pay on household and dependent care wages are considered to be part of the total amount paid for household and dependent care.[1]

(c) Amount of Credit. You may be able to take a credit of up to 30% of the work-related expenses you pay during the tax year. However, these work-related expenses are limited to $2,400 for one qualifying person or $4,800 for two or more qualifying persons [IRC Sec. 21(c)]. The 30% credit applies to taxpayers whose adjusted gross income is $10,000 or less. The 30% is reduced by 1% for each $2,000 of adjusted gross income above $10,000. The following table shows the maximum credits:

Adjusted Gross Income	Applicable Percentage	Credit Limitation One Person	Two or More Persons
> 0 to $10,000	30%	$720	$1,440
$10,001 to 12,000	29	696	1,392
12,001 to 14,000	28	672	1,344
14,001 to 16,000	27	648	1,296
16,001 to 18,000	26	624	1,248
18,001 to 20,000	25	600	1,200
20,001 to 22,000	24	576	1,152
22,001 to 24,000	23	552	1,104
24,001 to 26,000	22	528	1,056
26,001 to 28,000	21	504	1,008
28,001 and above	20	480	960

The amount of your work-related expenses during the tax year may not exceed your earned income for the year. If you are married, the expenses may not exceed the lower-paid spouse's earnings for the year.

If one spouse is a full time student or is incapable of self-care and so has no earned income, he or she is treated as having earnings of $200 a month if there is one dependent or $400 a month for two or more dependents [IRC Sec. 21(d)(2)].

There is an overall limit on the child care credit and the credit for the elderly and permanently disabled [¶2403]. These combined credits are allowed to the extent they do not exceed your tax liability.

Example: Ms. Smith, a single parent, maintains a home for herself and her two pre-school children for whom she claims dependency exemptions. Her earned income (adjusted gross income) for the year is $25,000. During the year, she paid work-related expenses of $3,000 for a housekeeper to care for her two children at home and $2,200 for child care at a nursery school. Smith can take a child care credit of $1,056, figured as follows:

In-home child care	$3,000
Nursery school costs	2,200
Total work-related expenses	$5,200
Maximum allowable expenses for two qualifying persons	$4,800
Amount of credit (22% of $4,800)	$1,056

(d) Payments to Relatives. The credit is available for child care payments you make to a relative, provided you are not eligible to claim a dependency exemption for the relative. If the relative is your child, the child must be at least 19 [IRC Sec. 21(e)(6); Reg. Sec. 1.44A-4 (a)(1)].

(e) Information Requirement. To claim the credit, you must report on your tax return the name, address and taxpayer identification number (social security number for individuals; employer identification number for organizations) of the dependent care provider. To get this information, have the provider fill out Form W-10. If you are unable to furnish this information, you may still claim the credit if you can show to the IRS that you made a genuine effort to provide the information (for example, you retained a copy of the baby sitter's social security card on recently printed letterhead) [IRC Sec. 21(e)(9)].

(f) Special Rules. Married couples are allowed the credit only if they file a joint return. However, married taxpayers living apart are not considered married for this rule, if the absent spouse was not a member of the household during the last six months of the tax year. So the spouse incurring the child care expenses can claim the credit even though a joint return is not filed, as long as he or she furnishes more than 50% of the cost of maintaining a household that was the principal place of abode of a qualifying individual for over one-half of the tax year [IRC Sec. 21(e)]. For a child of divorced parents, the custodial parent can claim the credit even if that parent agrees to let the noncustodial parent claim the child's dependency exemption.

You can exclude amounts paid or incurred by your employer for furnishing dependent care assistance to you under a written dependent care assistance program. Any expenses covered by your employer plan (¶1415) [IRC Sec. 129] reduce the dollar cap on expenses eligible for the credit ((c) above) [IRC Sec. 21(c)].

> **Example:** In 1992, the Robinsons incur $7,000 of baby sitting expenses for their only child, $2,000 of which is reimbursed under a qualified employer-provided plan. As a result, only $400 of expenses ($2,400 less $2,000) is now eligible for the credit.

> ➤ **TAX TIP** If your employer has a plan that lets you put pre-tax dollars in a child care reimbursement account, you need to choose between participating in that plan and claiming the credit. The employer's plan has this edge: (1) The plan dollar limits are higher (up to $5,000, even if you have one child); and (2) the employer's plan exclusion gives a tax benefit at your highest tax rate (28% or 31%), while the child care credit for you will probably be limited to 20% (if your adjusted gross income exceeds $28,000).

¶2402   EARNED INCOME CREDIT

[New tax legislation may affect this subject; see ¶1.]

The earned income tax credit (EITC) is intended to give tax relief to low-income working parents. There are actually three parts to the earned income credit: (1) the basic credit; (2) the supplemental young child credit; and (3) the credit for health insurance premium expenses [IRC Sec. 32].

To be eligible for the earned income credit, you must have a "qualifying child." A qualifying child is someone who satisfies all of the following tests [IRC Sec. 32(c)(3)]:

- **Relationship test:** The child must be the your son, stepson, daughter, stepdaughter, or one of their descendants, or a foster or adopted child.
- **Residency test:** The child must have the same principal place of abode as you for more than half the tax year (the entire year for foster children).

> ➤ **OBSERVATION** The residency test uses rules similar to those that apply to head of household status [¶ 1106]. Thus, for example, certain temporary absences due to education or illness are disregarded in determining if you satisfy the principal-place-of-abode test.

- **Age test:** This test is satisfied if the child (1) has not reached age 19 at the end of the tax year; or (2) is a full-time student who has not reached age 24 by year's end; or (3) is permanently and totally disabled.

> ➤ **OBSERVATION** A child is a full-time student if he or she meets the rules that apply to the dependency exemption [¶ 1116 (c)].

> ➤ **TAX SAVING POINT** Unlike most tax credits, the earned income credit is refundable. Thus, if the credit exceeds your tax liability, you will get the difference as a refund. And if you are eligible for the credit you should file a return to obtain payment, even if your income is low enough that filing is not required.

Taxpayer identification number. You must supply a taxpayer ID number for each qualifying child who has reached age one as of the end of the tax year [IRC Sec. 32(c)(3)(D)].

(a) What Earned Income Qualifies. Earned income includes wages, salaries, tips and other employee compensation. Compensation includes items which can be excluded from gross income, such as meals and lodging furnished for the employer's convenience [¶1410]. Earned income also includes any net earnings from self-employment. Pension and annuity payments cannot be included [IRC Sec. 32(c)(2)].

(b) Computing the Credit. You can compute your earned income credit by using the Revenue Service tables for each of three types of credits. No arithmetical computation is required. You use Schedule EIC (Forms 1040 or 1040A) to claim the credits.

Basic earned income credit. This part of the earned income credit is based on how many qualifying children live with you. For 1992, the maximum basic credit is $1,324 for one qualifying child and $1,384 for two or more qualifying children. The credit begins to phase out once your adjusted gross income (or earned income, if greater) exceeds $11,840. This phaseout is complete at the $22,370 income threshold. These amounts are indexed for inflation.

If you and someone else both take care of a qualifying child, then only the one with the higher adjusted gross income may be eligible to claim the credit for that child. If you are the eligible party but you cannot claim the credit (say, because your earned income is too high), then no one can claim the credit for the child.

Example 1: Bob Cole and his son lived with Bob's mother. Bob, age 25, had a part-time job with earnings and adjusted gross income from the job of $3,000. Bob's mother worked and had $11,000 of earned income and AGI. Bob and his mother both qualify for the earned income credit. However, only one is eligible to take the credit—Bob's mother who has the higher AGI for the year.

Example 2: Assume the same facts as in Example 1, except that the mother has an AGI of $50,000. Again, only the mother is entitled to the credit. But she cannot claim the credit since her AGI exceeds the phaseout amount (see below). Result: No credit can be claimed for the child.

NOTE: This rule does not apply if the other person is your spouse and you file a joint return.

Supplemental young child credit. If you have a qualifying child who has not reached his or her first birthday by the end of the calendar year, you can elect to claim a supplemental earned income credit. For 1992, the maximum amount of this part of the earned income credit is $376. This credit phases out at income levels above $22,370.

Example 3: Dina had a baby born on June 26, 1992. She files a joint return with her husband Don. Dina and Don have no other children. Based on their income level, they are entitled to a basic credit of $1,324. In addition, they can choose to take the supplemental credit of $376 for the birth this year of their child.

➤ **TAX TIP** If you claim the supplemental young child credit, you are not eligible to take the child care credit for the same child. So if you qualify for both the child care (or the exclusion of employer-provided dependent care benefits) [¶1415; 2401] and the supplemental young child credit, you should compare the amounts computed for each credit.

Additional credit for health insurance premium expenses. You can claim a credit for health insurance premiums that include coverage for one or more qualifying children. In 1992, the maximum credit is $451. However, the credit cannot be more than what you actually paid during the year for premiums [IRC Sec. 32(b)(2)].

This credit is completely phased out at 1992 income levels above $22,370.

Only those expenses relating to premium costs qualify for the credit. What you pay for co-payments, deductibles or other out-of-pocket medical expenses do not qualify. Amounts paid to an employer-sponsored health plan on a pre-tax basis (that is, through a cafeteria plan) do not qualify for this credit [IRC Sec. 32(b)(2)].

➤ **OBSERVATION** You must subtract the amount of this credit from your medical expenses eligible for the medical expense deduction [IRC Sec. 213(f)].

Example 4: In 1992, Mr. Ames pays a $3,000 premium for health insurance coverage for himself and his family, including his qualifying child. Ames is entitled to a $200 health insurance credit. Assuming Ames has no other medical expenses for the year, Ames' deduction for medical expense purposes is $2,800 ($3,000 less $200 EIC).

Suppose you are self-employed and are eligible to take a deduction for up to 25% of the amount paid for health insurance [¶ 1932(f)]. Then you must subtract from this deduction the amount of any health insurance credit that you may claim [IRC Sec. 162(l)(3)(B)].

(c) Advance Payments. You may be able to get advance payments of the earned income credit from your employer. You must submit a certificate (Form W-5) to your employer stating that you believe that you are eligible for the credit (¶ 2514) [IRC Sec. 32(g), 3507, 6012, 6051; Reg. Sec. 31.3507-1, 2]. Important: The credit amount that you can receive on an advance basis is limited to the basic credit that you could receive if you had only one qualifying child.

¶2403   CREDIT FOR THE ELDERLY AND PERMANENTLY DISABLED

You can qualify for this special credit if you're a U.S. citizen or resident and you are: (1) Age 65 or older by the end of the tax year or (2) under age 65 at the tax year's end and you (a) are retired on permanent and total disability, (b) did not reach mandatory retirement age before the current year and (c) received taxable disability benefits in the current year [IRC Sec. 22(b)].

The credit is equal 15% of your eligible income. The maximum credit for a married couple where both are over age 65 is $1,125 [IRC Sec. 22(a)].

(a) Figuring the Credit. To figure the credit, you must first determine your base amount. Then you subtract from your base amount: (1) any nontaxable social security or other nontaxable pension and disability benefits and (2) part of your adjusted gross income, depending on the level of your income.

Base amounts: The following base amounts apply:

If your filing status is:	*Your base amount is:*
1. Single, a head of household, or a surviving spouse, and	
• 65 or older	$5,000
• under 65 and retired on permanent and total disability	5,000
2. Married filing jointly and	
• both you and your spouse are 65 or older	7,500
• both you and your spouse are under 65 and one of you retired on permanent and total disability	5,000
• both you and your spouse are under 65 and both of you retired on permanent and total disability	7,500
• one of you is 65 or older, and the other is under 65 and retired on permanent and total disability	7,500
• one of you is 65 or older, and the other is under 65 and *not* retired on permanent and total disability	5,000
3. Married filing separately and did not live with your spouse at any time during the year and	

- 65 or older $3,750
- under 65 and retired on permanent and total disability 3,750

The base amount for taxpayers under 65 is limited to the amount received as disability income. On joint returns, if one spouse is over 65, but both are qualified individuals, the initial amount is increased to a maximum of $5,000 plus the amount received as disability income by the younger spouse.

Base amount reductions: Your credit base must be reduced by nontaxable social security, railroad retirement benefits or other exempt pension benefits you receive. The base amount is also reduced by one-half of the amount of your adjusted gross income above the following income levels: $7,500 for single persons; $10,000 for married persons filing jointly; or $5,000 for married persons filing separately [IRC Sec. 22(c),(d)].

NOTE: "Nontaxable social security" includes disability benefits, any amounts that are withheld to pay premiums on supplementary Medicare insurance, and any reduction because of receiving a benefit under workers' compensation.

Example: Ezra Peters, age 65 and single, received the following amounts during 1992: social security payments $1,400, taxable pension benefits $3,000, nontaxable pension benefits $750, and wages from a part-time job $5,400. His adjusted gross income is $8,400. Since he does not itemize, he takes the following deductions: one personal exemption of $2,300, the regular standard deduction of $3,600, and the additional standard deduction for the elderly of $900. Ezra's taxable income is $1,600, and his 1992 tax is $240—the same as his credit for the elderly, computed as follows:

Maximum credit base		$5,000
Deduct: Social security payments	$1,400	
Nontaxable pension benefits	750	
One-half of adj. gross income over		
$7,500 [½ × ($8,400 – $7,500)]	450	$2,600
Balance		$2,400
Tentative credit (15% of $2,400)		360
Tax		240
Credit		$ 240

Your credit may be limited by the alternative minimum tax [¶ 2607]. The limit could apply if you filed certain schedules (Schedules C, D, E, or F (Form 1040)) and your total income exceeds $30,000 if you're single or a head of household, $40,000 if you are married filing joint or a surviving spouse, or $20,000 if you're married filing separately. The limit on your credit is the smaller of: (1) your credit as computed, or (2) your regular credit minus: (a) any child care credit, and (b) AMT exemption phaseout amount [¶2605].

(b) Husband and Wife. Generally, the credit is available to married couples only if you file a joint return. The credit is figured on your combined income, and the credit base is reduced by the total exempt pension income above the permitted level. Certain married taxpayers living apart can qualify for the credit [IRC Sec. 22(e)].

GENERAL BUSINESS CREDIT

All related business credits are combined into a single general business credit. This means that the research credit, targeted jobs credit, alcohol fuels credit, the low-income housing credit, the enhanced oil recovery credit and the disabled access credit are grouped together with the same tax liability limitations and carryover rules (see below).

¶2405   FIGURING THE GENERAL BUSINESS CREDIT

You compute the general business credit using these 3 steps: (1) You figure each of the business credits (investment credit, targeted jobs credit, alcohol fuels credit, low-income housing credit, the research credit, enhanced oil recovery credit, and the disabled access credit) separately and then combine them into a single, general business credit (including any carrybacks and carryovers); (2) You apply the combined credit dollar-for-dollar against the first $25,000 of net tax liability ($12,500 for a married person filing separately, unless your spouse is not entitled to any business credit) and 75% of any excess; (3) You carry any unused combined credit back 3 years and forward 15 years, applying it on a first-in, first-out (FIFO) basis [IRC Sec. 38, 39].

> NOTE: When any of the general business credit is carried to other years, the particular types of credits being used or carried are determined by means of the following ordering: (1) the investment credit, (2) the targeted jobs credit, (3) the alcohol fuels credit, (4) the research credit, (5) the low-income housing credit, (6) the enhanced oil recovery credit and (7) the disabled access credit [IRC Sec. 38(d)].

Net tax liability. This generally means the tax liability imposed for the year reduced by the foreign tax credit and other nonrefundable credits. Tax liability does not include the alternative minimum tax imposed on corporations, the additional tax on certain distributions, an additional tax on income from certain retirement accounts, personal holding company tax, the tax on recoveries of foreign expropriation losses, accumulated earnings tax, tax on S corporations' capital gains and tax on S corporations for certain passive income [IRC Sec. 26(b)].

> NOTE: A deduction is allowed for the unused portion of the business credits. The deduction equals the amount of the credit that has not been used to reduce tax liability by the earlier of (1) the end of the 15-year carryover period or (2) date the taxpayer dies or ceases to exist [IRC Sec. 196].

Tax return tip. If you have two or more of the general business credits or a carryover from an earlier year of any of the credits, file Form 3800 with your return.

¶2406   INVESTMENT CREDIT

The investment credit consists of the regular credit, the rehabilitation credit and the energy credit. The regular investment credit was repealed for property placed in service after 1985, but it may possibly still be available for transition property, certain qualified progress expenditures for periods before 1986 and certain timber property [IRC Sec. 46].

The depreciable basis of transition property placed in service after 1985 and eligible for the credit under transition rules must be reduced by the full amount of the investment credit.

Transition property.   Transition property is any property placed in service after 1985 if by December 31, 1985, you already had a binding contract to acquire, construct or reconstruct the property.

(a) Credit Recapture. Despite the repeal of the regular investment credit, the recapture rules can still affect the open years for some taxpayers. If qualified property on which you took an investment credit was disposed of prematurely, part or all of this credit may be recaptured. Recapture can also apply if the property ceased to be qualified. Recapture means that you must add back to the tax due in the year of disposition a certain amount of the credit previously claimed. The recaptured amount is the difference between the credit taken (including carrybacks and carryforwards) and the credit allowed for actual use [IRC Sec. 50(a)].

In general, the recaptured amount decreases ratably over time. If the property was disposed of within one year after being placed in service, all of the credit is recaptured. If the property was disposed of in later years, the amount of the credit recaptured is as shown below [IRC Sec. 50(a)(1)(B)]:

If disposed of:	*The recapture percentage is:*
Within one year	100%
After one year	80%
After 2 years	60%
After 3 years	40%
After 4 years	20%
After 5 years	none

Tax return tip. Investment credit recapture is computed on Form 4255.

(b) Energy Property. You can take a 10% business energy investment credit for solar and geothermal equipment. To qualify as energy property, the property must be new [IRC Sec. 48].

> ➤ **CREDITS EXTENDED** The business energy credits for solar and geothermal energy property had been scheduled to end for property placed in service after December 31, 1991. But these business energy credits were extended, and are available for qualifying property placed in service by June 30, 1992.

(c) Rehabilitation Expenditures. The credit for rehabilitation expenditures is provided to encourage businesses to remain in the "center cities" instead of relocating into newer buildings. You can take a separate percentage of the investment credit for the cost of rehabilitating qualified existing buildings. Generally, for qualified property placed in service after 1986, a two-tier rehabilitation credit applies for qualified rehabilitation expenditures: (1) 20% for rehabilitation of certified historic structures and (2) 10% for rehabilitation of buildings (other than certified historic structures) originally placed in service before 1936. The 20% credit is available for both residential and nonresidential buildings. However, the 10% credit is limited to nonresidential property [IRC Sec. 47(a)]. No expenditure is eligible unless you elect to recover rehabilitation costs under the straight-line method. The credits require a full basis adjustment for both the 10% and 20% credits. Transitional rules are available generally for property you placed in service after 1986, but before 1994, if the property is acquired and undergoing rehabilitation under a pre-March 2, 1986 contract. Property qualifying under a transitional rule and placed in service after 1986 is eligible for reduced credits (25% to 20%; 20% to 13%; and 15% to 10%) and a full basis adjustment is required.

> **Example:** Ames spent $15,000 rehabilitating a 60-year old building in 1992. The credit allowed is $1,500 (10% of $15,000). Depreciation deductions are allowed for only $13,500 of his expenses.

A rehabilitation is substantial if expenditures during the 24-month period selected by you and ending with or within the tax year exceed the greater of (1) $5,000, or (2) the adjusted basis of the building as of the first day of the 24-month period. However, a 60-month period may be used if the rehabilitation is reasonably expected to be carried out in phases which are set out in architectural plans and specifications completed before the rehabilitation began [IRC Sec. 47(c)].

A certified historic structure is any building which is listed in the National Register, or is located in a registered historic district, and is certified by the Secretary of the Interior to the Secretary of the Treasury as being of historic significance to the district.

Qualified rehabilitation expenditures do not include the costs of acquiring the property or enlarging a building. No expenditures are covered unless at least 75% of the external walls are retained, including at least 50% as external walls, as well as at least 75% of the building's internal structural framework [IRC Sec. 47(c)]. Completely gutted buildings cannot qualify.

> **NOTE:** The Tax Court has taken the position that if you rehab an historic structure and then donate a scenic easement to charity, you cannot claim the credit for rehabilitating the portion of the building given away. Your rehab expenses must be reduced by the charitable donation.[1]

¶2407   LOW-INCOME HOUSING CREDIT

[New tax legislation may affect this subject; see ¶1.]

If you build or rehabilitate housing for low-income tenants, you are entitled to a tax credit each year over a ten-year period [IRC Sec. 42]. You may also claim the credit on eligible property placed in service as much as two years after the allocation is made. However, you must incur at least 10% of the project's costs in the allocation year. You calculate the credit by multiplying the qualified basis of the low-income property by a given percentage.

> ➤ **CREDIT EXTENDED** The low-income housing credit had been scheduled to expire for buildings placed in service after December 31, 1991. But the credit was extended, and is available for buildings placed in service through June 30, 1992.

Election to accelerate credit. Taxpayers who held an interest in a low-income housing property before October 26, 1990, could elect to claim a credit that's 150% of the regular low-income housing credit for the first tax year ending after October 24, 1990. If you made that election, your credit for subsequent years must be reduced on a pro rata basis by the amount of the increased credit.

Definitions. A qualified low-income housing project is one that meets minimum set-aside requirements. This means that (1) 20% or more of the combined residential rental units in the project are occupied by those with incomes of 50% or less of area median income (as adjusted for family size); or (2) 40% or more of the combined residential rental units are occupied by those with incomes of 60% or less of area median income (as adjusted for family size). [IRC Sec. 42(g)].

Eligible residential units must be used by the general public, and all of the units in a project must be used on a nontransient basis. Generally, a unit is nontransient if the initial lease term is six months or greater. Additionally, no hospital, nursing home, sanitarium, lifecare facility, retirement home, or trailer park can be a qualified low-income project. However, the portion of the building used to provide supportive services for the homeless does qualify.

The *qualified basis* of a low-income housing building is the lesser of (1) or (2) [IRC Sec. 42(c)(1)]:

(1) Eligible basis   × $\dfrac{\text{Low-income housing units in bldg.}}{\text{All units in bldg.}}$

(2) Eligible basis   × $\dfrac{\text{Total floor space in low-income housing units}}{\text{Total floor space of all units}}$

Eligible basis is the new building's adjusted basis but not the land's cost. Eligible basis for an existing building is your acquisition cost plus any capital improvements you made by the end of the first tax year of the credit period [IRC Sec. 42(d)].

A resident manager's unit is included in figuring the building's eligible basis under IRC Sec. 42(d), but excluded from the fraction under IRC Sec. 42(c).[1]

Your depreciable basis for the project is not reduced by the low-income housing credit.

To encourage the construction of low-income housing in certain high-cost areas, the eligible basis of a new building or the eligible basis of an existing building undergoing substantial rehabilitation can be 130% of the basis claimed for depreciation. This exception, however, does not apply to federally subsidized buildings other than HUD Community Development Block Grants.

Credit percentage. The annual credit percentage is set to yield a present value, over a ten-year period, of 70% of new buildings and substantial rehabilitations that are not federally subsidized and a present value of 30% of existing buildings and federally subsidized buildings. As for existing buildings, after 1989, they can qualify for the credit only if they undergo substantial rehabilitations [IRC Sec. 42(b)(2)].

For buildings placed in service after 1987, the low-income credit depends upon the applicable rate (tax credit percentage adjusted each month by the IRS) for the earlier of (1) the month in which the building is placed in service, or (2) at your election, the month in which a binding agreement between you and the state housing credit agency is reached [IRC Sec. 42(b)(2)].

The applicable monthly rate is determined using a complex set of rules but approximates: (1) 9% for new construction and rehabilitation costs that are not federally subsidized and (2) 4% for new construction and rehabilitation costs that are federally subsidized, and acquisition costs for existing buildings.

For buildings that are 70% or more financed by tax-exempt bonds, you may elect to use the month in which the bonds are issued. You must file this irrevocable election, as well as the election concerning the applicable rate, with the IRS by the fifth day of the month following the date the binding agreement is made or the taxable bonds are issued [IRC Sec. 42(b)(2)].

For buildings placed in service during 1987, the following low-income credits apply:

- Qualified new construction and rehabilitation costs that are not federally subsidized (9%),
- Qualified new construction and rehabilitation costs that are federally subsidized (4%) and
- Acquisition costs for existing buildings (4%) [IRC Sec. 42(b)(1)].

To qualify, there must be a period of at least ten years between the acquisition date and the date the property was placed in service or substantially rehabilitated by the previous owner. This ten-year requirement is ignored if the current owner acquired the property: (1) in a transaction involving a carryover basis; (2) from a decedent; (3) from a governmental unit or nonprofit organization; (4) through a foreclosure, under certain circumstances; (5) for use as a principal residence [IRC Sec. 42(d)(2)(D)(ii)]. The credit allowed for *each* tax year in the "credit period" is computed as follows [IRC Sec. 42(a)]:

Qualified basis for each   ×   Applicable credit percentage
qualified low-income bldg.

The *credit period* is ten tax years, starting with the year the building is placed in service or, if you choose, the following year [IRC Sec. 42(f)(1)].

Substantial rehabilitation. As already pointed out, there is a substantial rehabilitation requirement for existing buildings. To meet this requirement, the rehabilitation expenditure must be made for the benefit of the low-income tenants or to common areas which benefit low-income tenants. During any 24-month period, the expenditures must equal the greater of $3,000 per low-income unit or 10% of the unadjusted basis of the building. If these tests are met and there is no federal subsidy for the substantial rehabilitation expenditures, the rehabilitation expenditures become eligible for the 70% present value credit limitation; the rest of the existing building, however, remains subject to the 30% limitation.

A 30% present value credit may be claimed on a building you acquire from a governmental agency if the expenditures are at least $3,000—even if that is less than 10% of the unadjusted basis.

Shared low-income-housing credits. If you dispose of the building during the tax year, the credit has to be shared between you and the new owner on the basis of the number of days you each held the building. Likewise, for estates and trusts, the low-income housing credit has to be allocated between the trust, the estate and the beneficiaries, on the basis of the interest held by each.

Credit recapture. Even though the low-income credit is spread over a ten-year period, the compliance period for qualifying as low-income housing is generally 15 years. If a building fails to qualify as low-income housing during the entire 15-year period, there's a discrepancy between the credit claimed and the credit to which you are entitled. The difference between the credit actually claimed and the amount that would have been claimed had the credit been spread over a 15-year period, plus interest, is subject to recapture. The disposition of property can also trigger the recapture requirement.

Passive loss restriction eased. In general, losses from rental and other so-called passive activities cannot be used to offset income from non-passive activities from tax [IRC Sec. 469]. However, if you participate in rental real estate activity, you can deduct up to $25,000 of passive activity losses and the deduction equivalent amount of credits attributable to rental real estate. For property placed in service prior to 1990, the $25,000 allowance was reduced by one-half of your adjusted gross income in excess of $200,000. This meant that the allowance would be phased out completely once your adjusted gross income was greater than $250,000. The phase-out no longer applies to the low-income housing credit [IRC Sec. 469 (i)(3)].

No hobby loss problems: The IRS has released proposed regulations that exempt the low-income housing credit from the hobby loss rules (which state that writeoffs from a hobby cannot exceed income from the activity) [Prop. Reg. 1.42-4(a)]. So taxpayers who invest in low-income housing can now claim the credit even if they don't expect to make a profit from the investment.

Tax return tip. You use Form 8586 to claim the low-income housing credit. You must also attach Form 8609 concerning credit allocation certification along with Schedule A (Form 8506). You (the building owner) must complete this schedule each year of the 15-year compliance period, regardless of whether you claimed a credit for the tax year. You use Form 8611 to calculate the recapture portion of a low-income housing credit taken in a previous year and later disallowed.

NOTE: Suppose you are a recipient of a credit from a flow-through entity (partnership, S corporation, estate or trust). Then Form 8586 is the only form necessary to claim the credit. The flow-through entity completes an additional Form 8586 and attaches that form and Form 8609 to its return.

¶2408   TARGETED JOBS CREDIT

[New tax legislation may affect this subject; see ¶1.]

The targeted jobs credit provides an incentive for employers to hire persons from certain targeted groups that have a high unemployment rate or other special employment needs. The employer's deduction for wages is reduced by the amount of the credit [IRC Sec. 51].

▶ **CREDIT EXTENDED** The targeted jobs credit had been scheduled to expire on December 31, 1991. But the credit was extended, and covers wages paid to employees hired through June 30, 1992.

(a) Amount of Credit. The credit is equal to 40% of the first $6,000 ($3,000 for summer youth employees) of first-year qualified wages, for each eligible employee [IRC Sec. 51(a),(b)].

Your deduction for an employee's wages is reduced by the dollar amount of the jobs credit. You may elect not to have the credit apply for any tax year. If you do not choose to take advantage of the credit, you are not required to reduce your deduction for wages paid [IRC Sec. 51 (j), 280C].

(b) Limitations. For wages to be qualified, at least half must be paid for services in your trade or business Thus, wages paid to household employees aren't eligible for the credit [IRC Sec. 51(f)]. The targeted jobs credit is combined with other business-related credits for the tax liability limitations and the carryover rules [¶2405].

The credit is not available for wages paid to employees who perform the same or substantially similar services as those affected by a strike or lockout at the employer's facility [IRC Sec. 51(C)(3)].

(c) Targeted Groups. An eligible employee must be a member of one of the following groups [IRC Sec. 51(d)]: (1) vocational rehabilitation referrals; (2) economically disadvantaged youths (ages 18 to 22); (3) Vietnam veterans from economically disadvantaged families; (4) SSI recipients; (5) general assistance recipients; (6) economically disadvantaged ex-convicts; (7) cooperative education students from economically disadvantaged families; (8) eligible work incentive employees; and (9) 16- and 17-year-old economically disadvantaged summer workers.

Eligible employees. Your close relatives or dependents [¶1117] (or those of your company's major stockholder [¶2323]) are not eligible employees. In addition, someone, once employed while not a member of a qualified group, cannot be rehired by you and have the wages qualify for the credit [IRC Sec. 51(i)].

An individual is not considered an eligible employee unless, on or before his first day at work, you have received or requested in writing a certification from the designated local agency indicating that the individual is a member of the targeted group. When requesting certification, you must specify the targeted group or groups (not more than two) in which the employee belongs. Also, you must provide a statement showing that a good-faith effort had been made to determine eligibility [IRC Sec. 51(d)(16)].

No wages paid to a targeted group member will be taken into account if the individual (1) is employed by you less than 90 days (14 days for economically disadvantaged summer youth employees) or (2) has completed less than 120 hours of work (20 hours for summer employees) [IRC Sec. 51(d)].

Tax return tip. You claim the targeted jobs credit on Form 5884.

¶2409   CREDIT FOR RESEARCH EXPENSES

[New tax legislation may affect this subject; see ¶1.]

The research credit is designed to encourage businesses to increase the amounts they spend on research and experimental activities. The credit consists of two parts: (1) the regular or incremental credit and (2) the basic research credit. The regular or incremental credit is based on research expenses incurred by you as part of your trade or business; the basic research credit is based on basic research done for you by a university or tax-exempt research organization [IRC Sec. 41].

➤ **CREDITS EXTENDED** Both credits had been scheduled to expire on December 31, 1991. But they have were extended and cover expenses paid or incurred through June 30, 1992.

(a) Regular Credit. A 20% tax credit is allowed to the extent that your qualified research expenditures for the current year exceed your base amount for that year. The base amount for the current year is computed by multiplying your "fixed base percentage" by the average amount of your gross receipts for the four preceding years.

NOTE: The base amount cannot be less than 50% of the current year's qualified research expenditures. Thus, the credit cannot apply to more than half of the year's research cost.

Fixed base percentage. This is the ratio of (1) your total qualified research expenses for taxable years beginning after 1983 and before 1989 to (2) your total gross business receipts for that period. This ratio cannot be more than 16%. If you do not have qualified research expenses and gross receipts in at least three years during that time period, you are assigned a fixed base percentage of 3%.

Eligible expenses. To be eligible for the regular credit, research expenses must qualify for expensing or amortization under IRC Sec. 174 [¶2231], be conducted in the U.S. and be paid by you (e.g., not funded by government grant). In addition, the expenses must be for research and development in the experimental or laboratory sense and must pass a three-part test:

1. Research must be undertaken to discover information that is technological in nature. It must fundamentally rely on the principles of the physical, biological, engineering, or computer sciences.

2. Substantially all of the research activities must involve elements of a process of experimentation relating to a new or improved function, performance, or reliability or quality. Research involves a process of experimentation only if the design of the item as a whole is uncertain at the outset. Examples: Developing and testing a new drug or designing a new computer system.

3. The application of the research is intended to be useful in the development of a new or improved business component. This includes a product, process, software, technique, formula or invention to be sold, leased or licensed or used by you in a trade or business. Research is conducted for a qualified purpose if it relates to (1) a new or improved function; (2) performance; (3) reliability or quality or (4) reduced cost.

The three requirements are applied first at the product level. If the product as a whole does not qualify for the credit, then subsets of the product are examined to see whether a portion of the total cost qualifies. For example, even if research on a new computer system as a whole does not satisfy all the tests, the development of a specific component (e.g., a new integrated chip or circuit) may qualify.

Stock options are eligible for the credit: The Tax Court has allowed a company to claim the credit for stock options that had been issued to research employees in the company's early years.[1]

Special rules for internal use computer software. Software developed primarily for your internal use qualifies for the credit only if it is used in qualified research (other than the development of the software itself) or in a production process that involves a credit-eligible component. The development of internal use software for general or administrative functions (such as payroll or accounting) is ineligible for the credit.

Ineligible expenses. Research expenses related to the following items do not qualify for the credit:

- Style, taste, cosmetic or seasonal design factors.
- The social sciences, arts, or humanities.
- Efficiency surveys, management studies, market research (including advertising and promotion), routine data collection and routine quality-control testing or inspection.
- Expenses incurred after commercial production has begun.
- The costs of ascertaining the existence, location, extent, or quality of any ore or mineral deposit (including oil and gas). *Note:* Expenses of developing new or innovative methods of extracting minerals qualify.
- Development of any plant process, machinery, or technique for the commercial production of a business component, unless the process is technologically new or improved.
- Adaptation of a business component to suit a particular customer's needs.
- Partial or complete reproduction of an existing business component from plans, specifications, a physical examination, or publicly available information.
- The costs of developing and play-testing games.[2]

➤ **OBSERVATION** Although an expense is not eligible for the credit, it may qualify for expensing [¶2113] or 60-month amortization (¶2231) [IRC Sec. 174].

(b) Basic Research Credit. This is equal to 20% of all payments you make to qualified organizations for basic research expenses in excess of a special base amount. The credit is available to any corporation other than a service corporation [IRC Sec. 414(m)(3)], an S corporation, or a personal holding company. Basic research consists of any original investigation for the advancement of scientific knowledge not having a specific commercial objective. The research does not have to be conducted in the same field as your trade or business. The expenses are not deductible until you actually pay them in cash under a written agreement between you and the qualifying organization. The term qualified organizations includes most colleges, universities, tax-exempt scientific research organizations, and certain tax-exempt conduit or grant organizations (other than private foundations) [IRC Sec. 41(e)].

How to figure the 20% tax credit for basic research expenses. The credit is equal to 20% of the excess of qualifying basic research expenses over a special floor that consists of the minimum basic research amount, plus the maintenance-of-effort amount.

The minimum basic research amount is the greater of: (a) the average of contract research expenses during the base period (contract research expenses were the old-law equivalent of basic research expenses), or (b) 1% of the average of in-house research expenses, contract research expenses, and credit-eligible basic research expenses during the base period.

In general, the base period is the three-tax-year period ending with the tax year immediately preceding your first tax year beginning in 1984.

The maintenance-of-effort amount is the average of all nondesignated university contributions made during the base period, adjusted by a cost-of-living factor, less university contributions.

(c) Interplay of Regular and Basic-Research Credits. Basic-research expenses eligible for the 20% credit are not eligible for and do not figure into the computation of regular 20% credit (i.e., they are not included in base-period research expenses). However, basic-research expenses that are ineligible for the 20% credit because of the special floor do count as expenses eligible for the regular 20% credit.

> **Example 1**: ABC Corp.'s qualified research expenses exceed base-period research expenses by $80,000. It has a total of $60,000 in basic research expenses. Assume the basic research floor amount is $20,000. Result: ABC may claim an $8,000 credit for basic research ($60,000 less $20,000 times 20%). It may also claim a $20,000 credit for qualified research expenses ($80,000 of qualified research expenses, plus $20,000 of basic research expenses for which the new credit was not claimed, times 20%). Total research credit: $28,000.

Coordination of research credit with research deductions. Aside from the credit, you may write off research expenditures through deductions permitted by various provisions in the tax code.

Election to take a reduced credit. The amount of research expenses that you may deduct is reduced by the amount of the credit. Prior to 1990, if you found it more profitable to take the deduction rather than the credit, you could elect out of using the research credit. This option is no longer available. However, an election to take a reduced credit is available. Under the election, the credit is reduced by the highest corporate tax rate (34% in 1992) [IRC Sec. 280C(c)].

> **Example 2**: XYZ, Inc. incurs $10,000 of expenses eligible for the 20% research credit. It may either (1) take a $2,000 credit and $8,000 of deductions or (2) make an election to claim a reduced credit of $1,320 ($2,000 less 34% of $2,000) and $8,680 of deductions.

Other limitations. The research credit is subject to the overall limitation that applies to general business tax credits (credits can offset only 75% of tax liability over $25,000) [¶2405].

Tax return tip. You claim the credit for research activities on Form 6765.

¶2410   ENHANCED OIL RECOVERY CREDIT

A credit is available for costs related to enhanced oil recovery (EOR) projects, also called tertiary recovery projects [IRC Sec. 43]. The credit is 15% of qualified enhanced oil recovery costs. If you claim the credit, you must reduce the amount otherwise deductible or recoverable through depreciation, depletion or amortization as to these costs [IRC Sec. 43(d)(1)]. In other words, there is no double benefit for the same item. You can't claim both a credit and a deduction for the same costs.

The enhanced oil recovery credit is part of the general business credit [¶ 2405]. Thus, the same limitations and carryover rules of that credit apply to the enhanced oil recovery credit. However, any unused portion of your general business credit due to the enhanced oil recovery credit cannot be carried back to a tax year that started before January 1, 1991.

Tax return tip. You claim the enhanced oil recovery credit on Part I of Form 8830, Enhanced Oil Recovery Credit. You use Part II of this Form to apply the limit on general business credits.

You can elect not to claim this credit for any tax year. The election can be made (or revoked) at any time within three years of the tax return due date for the year (not including extensions) [IRC Sec. 43(e)].

Suppose property qualifies as an integral part of more than one qualified enhanced oil recovery project. Then you can include that project's cost in the credit base only once.

> **Example:** The price of domestic crude oil in the prior calendar year is $29. Then the credit for the current year's qualified costs is 12.5% [($34 less $29)/($34 less $28) x 15%].

(a) Enhanced oil recovery costs. These include costs paid or incurred on a qualified enhanced oil recovery project located in the U.S. and involving one or more tertiary recovery methods. The credit can be as much as 15% of the following types of costs [IRC Sec. 43(c)]:

- Depreciable or amortizable tangible property that is an integral part to the project;
- Intangible drilling and development costs [¶ 2236(c)];

> **NOTE:** For an integrated oil company, the credit base includes the intangible drilling costs that taxpayers must capitalize under IRC Sec. 291(b)(1).

- Costs of tertiary injectants for which an amortization deduction can be claimed.

(b) At-risk limit. Enhanced oil recovery project costs eligible for the credit are limited to the amount for which you are at-risk in the project [IRC Sec. 43(c)(3)]. This means that any item's credit base will be reduced to the extent it was financed with nonqualified nonrecourse financing.

(c) Phase-out of credit The credit is reduced in a tax year following a calendar year where the average domestic crude oil price exceeds $28 (adjusted for inflation) per barrel. The credit will be reduced ratably over a $6 phase-out range. So there is no credit once the price exceeds $34.

¶2411   DISABLED ACCESS CREDIT

Costs you incur to make your business premises accessible to the handicapped can result in tax benefits. Your business can elect to take a deduction of up to $15,000 each year for certain improvements [¶ 2203]. In place of this deduction, your business can choose to take a disabled access credit.

A credit is available to certain small businesses for similar expenses. The credit is designed to reduce the cost of complying with the Americans With Disabilities Act of 1990. This law requires that your business make accommodations for your disabled workers and customers [IRC Sec. 44(b)]. The credit applies to expenditures you pay or incur after November 5, 1990.

The nonrefundable credit is equal to 50% of the amount of the eligible expenses that exceed $250, but not more than $10,250. Thus, the maximum credit allowable is $5,000 [50% of $10,000 ($10,250 less $250)]. You claim the credit on Form 8826 and attach it to your tax return.

(a) Eligible Small Business. An eligible small business is any person engaged in the trade or business of operating a public accommodation. It must be a business that is required by federal law to make its accommodations accessible to, or usable by those with disabilities.

An eligible small business is one that has either (1) gross receipts for the prior tax year of not more than $1 million or (2) no more than 30 full-time employees during the tax year. (Full-time employees work at least 30 hours a week for at least 20 weeks during the year.) [IRC Sec. 44(b)].

(b) Eligible Public Accommodations Access Expenses. Qualified expenses include amounts you pay or incur:

- To remove architectural, communication, physical or transportation barriers that keep the handicapped from gaining access to the premises.
- To provide qualified interpreters or other effective methods of making aurally delivered materials available to the hearing-impaired.
- To provide qualified readers, taped texts and other effective methods of making visually delivered materials available to the visually impaired.
- To acquire or modify equipment or devices for the disabled.
- To provide other similar services, modifications, materials or equipment [IRC Sec. 44(c)(2)].

These costs must meet certain standards set by the IRS in regulations to be issued [IRC Sec. 44(c)].

(c) Special Rules. In determining the credit and if the limitations are met, all members of a corporation's controlled group are treated as one person. For a partnership, the $10,250 annual limit applies at both the partnership and partner levels. A similar rule applies for an S corporation [IRC Sec. 44(d)].

You cannot get a double benefit for expenses you incur to remove barriers to the handicapped. So expenses you claim for the credit cannot also be claimed for the up-to-$15,000 deduction.

▶ **OBSERVATION** The deduction is available to all businesses—not just small businesses as with the credit. You should figure the credit before taking the deduction. *Reason:* The credit reduces your tax liability dollar-for-dollar, while the deduction only reduces your income subject to tax. But expenditures in excess of the credit qualify for the deduction.

The amount of the credit is not included in the adjusted basis of any property with respect to which a credit is determined [IRC Sec. 44(d)(7)].

The disabled access credit is part of the general business credit [¶ 2405]. Thus, the same limitations and carryover rules apply. The portion of the unused business credit for any tax year that is due to the disabled access credit cannot be carried back to any tax year ending before November 5, 1990.

OTHER TAX CREDITS

¶2412　　　CREDITS FOR CERTAIN USES OF GASOLINE AND SPECIAL FUELS

Generally, you can claim a credit for the federal excise taxes on the non-highway use of gasoline and special fuels. These include gasoline or special fuels used in farming and special fuels used in local transit systems and for aviation or commercial fishing purposes. Quarterly refund payments are allowed for claims of at least $1,000 [IRC Sec. 34, 6420, 6421, 6424, 6427]. Examples of non-highway use include operating a power lawn mower, stationary engines or engines for use in construction, mining or timbering projects.

Any individual, estate, trust or corporation claiming the credit must file and attach Form 4136 to their income tax return.

¶2413　　　FUEL PRODUCTION CREDITS

There are two tax credits for the production of certain types of fuel.

(a) Fuel From Nonconventional Sources. An income tax credit is available for the production of fuel from nonconventional sources, such as oil shale [IRC Sec. 29]. Subject to a phaseout based on oil prices, the amount of credit is $3 for each quantity of fuel that would yield energy equal to that of a barrel of oil. Additionally, the credit is adjusted upward for inflation under a formula keyed to the Commerce Department's GNP deflator. The credit is effective for sales to an unrelated party in tax years before 2003.

> **NOTE:** You must reduce this credit by any excess of the enhanced oil recovery credit for the tax year and any prior tax year over the aggregate recaptured amount of the enhanced oil recovery credit [IRC Sec. 29(b)(5)]. You can avoid this offset by electing not to claim the enhanced oil recovery credit.

(b) Alcohol Fuels Credit. Producers, sellers and users of alcohol fuels suitable for use in an internal combustion engine can get an income tax credit for alcohol sold or used before 2001 [IRC Sec. 40]. To qualify, the fuel must contain alcohol that is at least 150 proof and not made from petroleum, natural gas or coal. The amount of the credit is 54 cents (60 cents for tax years starting before 1991) for each gallon of alcohol sold or used as a fuel, or blended into a fuel mixture. The credit is reduced to 40 cents (45 cents for tax years starting before 1991) for alcohol between 150 and 190 proof [IRC Sec. 40(b), (d)]. The amount of credit must be included in gross income in the year it is allowed [IRC Sec. 87].

Small ethanol producers can take a credit of 10 cents per gallon for each gallon of qualified ethanol fuel production—up to a maximum of 15 million gallons. A small producer is any fuel ethanol producer with productive capacity to produce less than 30 million gallons of alcohol per year [IRC Sec. 40(b)(4), (g)].

The alcohol fuels credit is combined with other business-related credits for the tax liability limitations and the carryover rules [¶2405].

¶2414　　　　　MORTGAGE CREDIT CERTIFICATES

[New tax legislation may affect this subject; see ¶1.]

States and localities can issue so-called mortgage credit certificates to qualified first-time homebuyers. These are certificates issued under a qualified mortgage certificate program by the state or political subdivision with authority to issue qualified mortgage bonds to provide financing on a taxpayer's residence. Qualified homebuyers will receive a mortgage credit certificate indicating the portion of the principal debt that qualifies for the credit and the credit percentage rate. It allows you a credit against your federal income tax for a portion of the mortgage interest you paid during the year in which the qualified residence is used as your principal residence [IRC Sec. 25].

> ➤ **CREDIT EXTENDED** The mortgage credit certificate and qualified mortgage bond programs had been scheduled to expire on December 31, 1991. However, they were extended through June 30, 1992.

The percentage of mortgage interest eligible for this credit must be at least 10%, but not more than 50% (25% for assumptions). If the credit rate in the mortgage credit certificate exceeds 20%, the maximum credit is $2,000 per year. Your deduction for interest on the qualifying mortgage is reduced by the amount of the credit [¶1902]. The credits allowed are nonrefundable. However, you may carry over excess credits to the next three years [IRC Sec. 25(a), (d), (e)]. You figure the credit on Form 8396.

> **Example:** Mr. Smith received a mortgage credit certificate specifying a 50% credit rate. For the tax year, he pays mortgage interest of $5,000. Of this amount, he is entitled to the maximum mortgage credit of $2,000 plus an interest deduction for the remaining $3,000.

Mortgage credit certificates may be used only in connection with buying single family residences that are expected to become the borrowers' principal residences within a reasonable time. The cost of the residence cannot exceed 90% (110% in targeted areas) of the average area purchase price for a single family residence. At least 20% of the mortgage credit certificates issued must finance purchases in targeted areas for at least one year [IRC Sec. 25(c)(2); 143(e)].

Generally, only new mortgages are eligible for mortgage credit certificates. However, certain loans for qualified rehabilitations, improvements and assumptions may also be eligible [IRC Sec. 25(b)(2)].

PAYMENT OF ESTIMATED TAX BY INDIVIDUALS

¶2416　　　　　WHAT IS ESTIMATED TAX

Estimated tax is the method you use to prepay tax on income not subject to withholding. Such income includes earnings from self-employment, interest, dividends, alimony, rent and gains from the sale of assets. You may also pay estimated tax if the amount of withholding from your salary, pension or other income is insufficient to satisfy your current tax liability. In broad terms, estimated tax is the amount of income tax (including the alternative minimum tax [¶ 2600]) that you anticipate owing, plus any self-employment tax, less any credits [IRC Sec. 6654(g)]. Estimated tax must be paid by those with an estimated tax liability of $500 or more.

Payment procedures. If you must make estimated tax payments, use Form 1040-ES payment vouchers. Each payment voucher has a date when the voucher is due for the calendar year. Except for the first-time filers, each voucher is preprinted by the IRS with your name, address and social security number. When payment is due, you send the appropriate voucher and payment to the IRS Center listed in the instructions to the form.

¶2417   WHO MUST MAKE ESTIMATED TAX PAYMENTS

[New tax legislation may affect this subject; see ¶1.]

You must pay estimated tax if you expect to owe, after withholding and credits, at least $500 for a tax year; *and* expect that your annual withholding payment will be below the lesser of: (1) 90% of the tax shown for a current tax year, or (2) 100% of the tax shown for the preceding tax year (but only if the return covered 12 full months). If this test is met, the required installment or estimated tax payment for each of the four payment periods [¶2418] should be 25% (¼) of the required annual payment. An underpayment penalty can be imposed for failing to pay the required installment[1] (¶2420) [IRC Sec. 6654(d)].

> ➤ **NEW FOR 1992** Many taxpayers keep their estimated tax payments to a minimum by taking advantage of the 100%-of-last-year's-tax escape hatch. They comply with the estimated tax requirements simply by paying an amount equal to their prior year's tax. But there is a new change here: Starting in 1992, higher income taxpayers whose incomes take a substantial jump from the previous year cannot take advantage of this escape hatch. See ¶ 2420.

You do not have to pay estimated tax if your current tax year income tax return will show (1) a refund, (2) an estimated tax liability of less than $500, or (3) you are a U.S. citizen or resident and had no liability for the full 12-month preceding tax year.[2]

> **Example 1:** In April 1993, Ms. Richards completes her income tax return for tax year 1992. She properly computes her tax liability to be $12,000. Since her 1992 withholding was $9,000, Richards still owes $3,000. Her 1991 tax liability was only $8,000, so Richards pays no penalty for 1992. Reason: Her 1992 withholding was more than 100% of her 1991 tax. The $9,000 withholding amount is treated as estimated tax payments made in four equal installments on the due date for each quarterly payment.

> **Example 2:** In 1993, Richards expects to owe taxes of $15,000. Halfway through 1993, only $5,000 had been withheld from her pay, and she has made no estimated tax payments. At this rate, she will have to pay an underpayment penalty. Suppose, however, Richards increases her wage withholding so that by the end of the year, $12,000 has been withheld from her pay. Her withholding for the year equals 100% of her 1992 tax liability. Withholding is treated as having been made in equal installments throughout the year. Thus, there is no penalty.

> ➤ **TAX SUGGESTION** If, toward the end of the year, you have underpaid estimated tax, you can increase the amount of wage withholding by claiming fewer allowances. If you already claim no allowances, you can request your employer to withhold an additional amount. The result: You can avoid the penalty for an underpayment that occurred earlier in the year.

Estates and trusts. A fiduciary of an estate or trust must make estimated income tax payments on Form 1041-ES in the same manner as individuals. A new estate, however, need not pay estimated tax in its first two years [IRC Sec. 6654]. Fiduciaries are allowed to assign any amounts of a trust's quarterly payments to the beneficiaries. The election is made on the tax return of the trust. Since the return (Form 1041-W) must be filed within 65 days after the end of the trust's tax year, the amount of the credits assigned to the beneficiaries is considered a distribution under the 65-day rule [¶3506]. Thus, the beneficiaries are considered to have received the distribution on the first day of the trust's year. The amount considered distributed won't be treated as a payment of the trust's estimated tax, but are treated as a payment of the beneficiary's estimated tax on the January 15 following the tax year. This election is available only to the extent the trust's total estimated tax payments for the year exceeds its own tax liability. The beneficiaries, on the other hand, treat the credit as received at the time the election is made for their estimated taxes. [IRC Sec. 643(g)].

¶2418   WHEN TO PAY ESTIMATED TAX

Your first estimated tax payment (either in full or in an installment) is due for a current tax year when you (as a calendar-year taxpayer) file your income tax return for the prior year. Payment is sent with a payment-voucher included in the Form ES. Payment due dates that apply for you and other calendar-year taxpayers are detailed in (a) below. However, special payment due dates apply for farmers and fishermen and for fiscal year taxpayers (b) and (c) below.

(a) Payment for 1993. You pay estimated tax in quarterly installments by filing the appropriate Form 1040-ES payment voucher with the IRS Service Center listed in the instructions to the form. The payments dates are as follows [IRC Sec. 6654(c)]:

Required installments for 1993 calendar year	Required payment due dates for 1993 calendar year
1st	April 15, 1993
2nd	June 15, 1993
3rd	Sept. 15, 1993
4th	Jan. 17, 1994

If you must pay by April 15, you may pay the entire year's estimated tax then or pay 25% on each of these dates: April 15, June 15, Sept. 15 or the following Jan. 17. Your installment payments may be lowered if income is annualized, or if you base installment payments on the amount of your last year's tax [IRC Sec. 6654(d)].

If the payment due date falls on Saturday, Sunday or legal holiday, the next business day is the due date.

You may apply a credit for overpayment of your previous year's income tax against your current year's first installment or equally divide the credit among all the installments.[1] You must elect to apply the overpayment against a later installment. You make the election by attaching a statement to the return showing the overpayment and indicating which installment it should be applied against. Also, you may elect to credit the overpayment to an estimated tax payment arising after the overpayment arose but before the election is made.[2]

Example 1: Mr. Roberts makes an estimated tax payment of $10,000 for 1992, and receives an extension to file his 1992 return until August 16, 1993. When the return is filed on August 16, 1993, it shows a tax liability of only $8,000. Al may elect to credit the $2,000 overpayment to the April 15, 1993 estimated tax payment.

Return as last installment. If you (and other calendar-year taxpayers) first come within the estimated tax requirements after September 1, 1993, you may file the annual income tax return by January 31, 1994, and pay the balance of tax due.

How to amend. You may use the *Amended Estimated Tax Schedule* on page 2 of Form 1040-ES instructions to figure if your estimated tax needs to be increased or decreased. You may pay the estimated tax, or the rest of the tax in equal installments on the remaining payment dates. If you make the amendment after September 15 of the tax year, your payment must be made by January 15 of the next year.

> **Example 2:** Mr. Jones figured a 1993 estimated tax of $800 when he filed his 1992 income tax return on April 15, 1993. Later, on September 15, 1993, he discovered that his estimated tax should be reduced by $150. The amount payable on January 17, 1994, will be $50 computed as follows:
>
> 1. Amended estimated tax $650
> 2. Less estimated tax payments:
>   April 15, June 15, and September 15, at $200 each 600
> 3. Unpaid balance . . . . $ 50
> 4. Amount to be paid on January 17, 1994 . . . . $ 50

(b) Farmers and Fishermen are allowed to pay their estimated tax (for a calendar year) by January 15 of the next year when at least two-thirds of their estimated gross income comes from farming or fishing for the preceding or current tax year. They can also file an income tax return and pay the tax by March 1 of the next year instead of making estimated tax payments.[3]

(c) Fiscal-Year Taxpayers substitute corresponding months in their fiscal year instead of those indicated for paying the installments by calendar year taxpayers.[2] Thus, for a fiscal year starting July 1, the month corresponding to April would be October (fourth month of fiscal year).

> **Example 3:** Ms. Holt's fiscal year begins October 1, 1993. Her quarterly installment payment of estimated tax is due January 17, 1994. The other three installments are due March 15, June 15 and October 17, 1994.

(d) Extension of Time. The District Director may extend the due date for filing and payment. It is limited to six months, except when you are abroad [IRC Sec. 6081(a); Reg. Sec. 1.6081-(a)]. No interest is charged [IRC Sec. 6601(f); Reg. Sec. 301.6601-1(f)(5)].

(e) Nonresident Aliens who must pay estimated tax use Form 1040-ES (NR) and file it with the IRS Center, Philadelphia, Pa. 19162-0825.

(f) Social Security Benefits. Part of these benefits may be taxable income. To that extent, they must be included in the estimated tax base as taxable income. To figure the taxable part, see ¶1526.

¶2419   HOW TO FIGURE ESTIMATED TAX

[New tax legislation may affect this subject; see ¶1.]

In figuring your estimated tax payments, you must estimate your tax for the year and reduce it by estimated withholding and other credits against your tax. You should consider all available facts that will affect your income, deductions, and credits during the year.[1] In estimating your tax before reducing it for estimated withholding and other credits, you may be able to use last year's tax (including self-employment and alternative minimum taxes), or annualize income. For the lowest amount of estimated taxes that must be paid to avoid penalties, see ¶2420.

> ➤ **OBSERVATION** You must be careful to make adjustments both for changes in your own situation and recent changes in the tax law. For example, employers were required as of March 1, 1992, to use withholding tables that reduced the amount withheld for all single employees earning up to $53,200 and for all married employees earning up to $90,200. As a result, some of these employees may have fallen below the estimated tax requirements unless they increased their payments.

A worksheet is provided on Form 1040-ES for you to compute your estimated tax liability. Although you do not file the worksheet with the payment voucher, it is almost a necessity to figure your estimated taxes.[1]

(a) Figuring Your Adjusted Gross Income. Your expected AGI for the year is your expected total income less your expected adjustments to income.

You include in your total income everything you expect to receive during the year, even if it is subject to withholding. However, you can exclude income that is tax-exempt, like interest from municipals.

You reduce your total income by adjustments you expect to take on your income tax return. These may include deductions for IRA or Keogh contributions. If you expect to have self-employment income, figure your self-employment tax first and then subtract half of it as an adjustment [¶ 2539].

(b) Figuring Your Expected Taxable Income. Your expected AGI is reduced by either your expected itemized deductions [¶ 1900] or the standard deduction [¶ 1107] and by your personal exemptions [¶ 1111; 1115].

> ➤ **OBSERVATION** Your expected itemized deductions include all those deductions claimed on your Form 1040 Schedule A.

Limit on itemized deductions. High-income taxpayers will find that their total itemized deductions may be limited [¶ 1900]. For 1992, if your adjusted gross income exceeds $105,250 ($52,625 if you are married filing separately), you are subject to a limit on yourr itemized deductions. (These thresholds are adjusted each year for inflation.).

Suppose your expected adjusted gross income exceeds the threshold amount. Then you follow these steps: (1) Reduce that AGI by the applicable threshold; (2) Figure your anticipated itemized deductions, excluding medical expenses, investment interest, casualty, theft or gambling losses; (3) Apply 80% to the itemized deductions determined in (2); (4) Multiply the amount determined in (1) by 3% (.03); (5) Subtract the smaller of (3) or (4) from your expected itemized deductions. The result is the amount of itemized deductions you can use to reduce your anticipated AGI.

Phase out of personal and dependency exemptions. After you reduce your AGI by anticipated itemized deductions or the standard deduction, you subtract the total amount for each exemption to which you are entitled [¶ 1111; 1115]. For 1992, each exemption is worth $2,300 (adjusted each year for inflation). However, a phase-out applies to high income taxpayers. See ¶ 1112. In general, the phase-out for high-income taxpayers reduces 2% of each exemption for each $2,500 (or any fraction of that amount) that their AGI exceeds a threshold amount (also adjusted each year for inflation).

(c) Figuring Your Expected Taxes and Credits. You use the tax rates that apply to 1993 to compute your tax liability for 1993 estimated tax purposes.

➤ **OBSERVATION** You may not owe any estimated tax penalty if the total of your withholding and estimated tax payments for each estimated tax payment period is at least one-fourth of the total tax shown on your prior year's return. However, starting in 1992, this escape hatch is not available to higher-income taxpayers whose income jumped substantially from the prior year. See ¶ 2420.

Tax on net capital gain. Suppose your adjusted gross income includes a net long-term capital gain. Then, in determining your tax liability, you will have to consider the special computation for figuring the tax on the net capital gain. Reason: A 28% maximum rate applies to the taxpayer's net long-term capital gain. See ¶1809.

Self-employment and other taxes. In determining your estimated tax, you must take into account expected additional taxes, such as the tax on lump-sum distributions [¶ 1320]. Also, you must add in any expected self-employment tax [¶ 2539].

➤ **IMPORTANT** The social security wage base is split into two parts. For 1992, the OASDI portion has a $55,500 maximum and the Medicare portion has a $130,200 maximum (these amounts are indexed for inflation).

Expected credits. The computation of your estimated taxes must consider your anticipated credits, such as the child care credit.

Example 1: In 1993, Mr. and Mrs. Brock expect to have an adjusted gross income of $320,000 (wages, $230,000; self-employment income, $75,000; net capital gains, $15,000). They expect to have total itemized deductions before any reduction of $58,000 (taxes and mortgage interest, $50,000; investment interest, $8,000). Their personal and dependency exemptions should total $9,200. Bob estimates that $50,000 will be withheld from his wages. The Brocks' 1992 tax liability was $78,250. Their estimated tax payable for 1993 is computed as follows (assume that 1992 rates, thresholds and exemptions apply):

Estimated Tax Worksheet

1. Estimated adjusted gross income $320,000
2. Less: Itemized deductions (see below)   51,557
3. Balance $268,443
4. Less: Exemptions (see below) . . . . $ 0
5. Balance $268,443
6. Tax liability (see below) . . . . $ 75,518
7. Plus: Additional taxes . . . . $ 0
8. Total . . . . $ 75,518
9. Less: Credits . . . . $ 0
10. Balance . . . . $ 75,518
11. Plus: Self-employment tax (see below) . . . . $ 8,891
12. Other taxes . . . . $ 0
13. Total (Lines 10-12) . . . . $ 84,409

Required annual payment: Lesser of $75,968 (90% of $84,409) or $78,250 (100% of 1991 tax) . . . . $ 75,968

Less: Estimated withholding on wages . . . . $ 50,000

Estimated tax payable . . . . $ 25,968

Since the balance owed is more than $500, the $25,968 is payable in four equal installments of $6,492 each on April 15, June 15, September 15, 1993 and January 17, 1994. Note: The Brocks may not be able to consider their prior year's tax when figuring their required estimated tax payments. See ¶ 2420.

The following worksheets show how the Brocks computed their allowable itemized deductions (Line 2); personal exemptions (Line 4); tax liability (Line 6); and self-employment taxes (Line 11):

Limit on Itemized Deductions
(Line 2)

1. Enter the amount from line 1 of the Estimated Tax Worksheet $320,000
2. Enter $105,250 ($52,625 if married filing separately   105,250

3. Subtract line 2 from line 1 . . . . . . $214,7500
4. Enter the estimated total of your itemized deductions . . . . $ 58,000
5. Enter the amount included in line 4 for medical and dental expenses, investment interest, casualty or theft losses, and

	gambling losses	8,000
6.	Subtract line 5 from line 4	$ 50,000

Note: If the amount on line 6 is zero, stop here and enter the amount from line 4 on line 2 of the Estimated Tax Worksheet.

7.	Multiply the amount on line 6 by .80	$ 40,000
8.	Multiply the amount on line 3 by .03	$ 6,443
9.	Enter the smaller of line 7 or line 8	$ 6,443
10.	Subtract line 9 from line 4. Enter the result here and on line 2 of the Estimated Tax Worksheet	$ 51,557

Tax Liability
(Line 6)

1.	Enter the amount from line 5 of your Estimated Tax Worksheet	$268,443
2.	Enter net capital gain included in line 1 of your Estimated Tax Worksheet . .	15,000
3.	Subtract line 2 from line 1	$253,443
4.	Enter: $51,900 if single $86,500 if married filing jointly or qualifying widow(er) $43,250 is married filing separately $74,150 if head of household	$ 86,500
5.	Enter the larger of line 3 or line 4 . .	$253,443
6.	Subtract line 5 from line 1	$ 15,000
7.	Figure the tax on the amount on line 5 using the 1992 Tax Rate Schedules, and enter the result	$ 71,318
8.	Multiply the amount on line 6 by .28	$ 4,200
9.	Add line 7 and line 8. Enter the result here and on line 6 of your Estimated Tax Worksheet	$ 75,518

Exemption Phaseout
(Line 4)

1.	Enter the amount from line 1 of your Estimated Tax Worksheet	$320,000
2.	Enter: $105,250 is single $157,900 if married filing jointly or qualifying widow(er)	

	$78,950 if married filing separately $131,550 if head of household . . .	157,900
3.	Subtract line 2 from line 1	$162,100
4.	Divide the amount on line 3 by $2,500 ($1,250 if married filing separately). If the result is not a whole number, increase to next whole number	$ 65
5.	Multiply the number on line 4 by .02. Enter the result as a decimal, but not more than 1	1.00
6.	Multiply $2,300 by the number of exemptions you plan to claim	$ 9,200
7.	Multiply the amount on line 6 by the decimal on line 5	$ 9,200
8.	Subtract line 7 from line 6. Enter the result here and on line 4 of your Estimate Tax Worksheet	$ –0–

Self-Employment Tax
(Line 11)

1.	Enter your expected income and profits subject to self-employment tax . . .	$ 75,000
2.	Multiply the amount on line 1 by .9235	69,263
3.	Medicare tax maximum income . . .	$130,200
4.	Enter your expected wages (if subject to Medicare tax)	$ –0–
5.	Subtract line 4 from line 3	$130,200

Note: If line 5 is zero or less, enter –0– on line 7 and skip to line 9.

6.	Enter the smaller of line 2 or line 5	$ 69,263
7.	Multiply the amount on line 6 by .029	2,009
8.	Social Security tax maximum income	$ 55,500
9.	Enter your expected wages (if subject to Social Security tax)	$ –0–
10.	Subtract line 9 from line 8	$ 55,500

Note: If line 10 is zero or less, enter –0– on line 12 and skip to line 13.

11.	Enter the smaller of line 2 or line 10	$ 55,500
12.	Multiply the amount on line 11 by .124	$ 6,882
13.	Add line 7 and line 12. Enter the amount here and on line 11 of your Estimated Tax Worksheet	$ 8,891

¶2420   PENALTY FOR UNDERPAYING ESTIMATED TAXES

[New tax legislation may affect this subject; see ¶1.]

The penalty for not paying enough estimated tax is interest charged at the current underpayment rate.[1] The penalty is based on the federal short-term interest rate plus three percentage points [IRC Sec. 6621]. Since this rate is adjusted every calendar quarter, you calculate the penalty separately for each estimated tax installment. Normally, you would have to compound interest daily, but this would render the calculations extremely complex. A special exception allows you to ignore the compound interest requirement for the estimated tax penalty [IRC Sec. 6622].

The penalty, which is not deductible interest, can be avoided if the amount of each *required installment* is 25% of the *required annual payment.* For many or most individuals, the required annual payment is the lesser of (1) 90% of the tax shown on the current year's return (or if no return was filed, 90% of the tax for the year) or (2) 100% of the tax shown on the preceding tax year's return (if the tax year consisted of 12 months and a return was filed for that year) [IRC Sec. 6654(d)].

If your tax liability less withholding is under $500, the penalty does not apply. Also you don't have a penalty for a current year's underpayment if you had no tax liability in the prior year and you were a U.S. citizen or resident for the entire year. The prior tax year must have been a 12-month period [IRC Sec. 6654(e)].

The year's withholdings are equally divided among the installment periods, unless you prove a different allocation, or unless more than one tax year begins in a calendar year [IRC Sec. 6654(g)]. This allows you to adjust your withholding to avoid a penalty.

Example 1: For 1992, Smith paid income tax of $3,000. In 1993, his tax liability is $6,000. He pays no estimated tax for 1993 but plans to pay the 1993 tax when he files the return on April 15 of 1994. Smith's underpayment penalty is computed on 25% of the lesser of 90% of the tax shown on the 1993 return (90% × $6,000) or 100% of the 1992 tax ($3,000). Thus, the underpayment penalty is figured on $750 (25% of $3,000) for each required installment. A separate computation of any penalty must be made for each installment due date. This is because the interest rate that determines the penalty fluctuates quarterly.

▶ **LIMIT ON PRIOR-YEAR SAFE HARBOR** Starting with 1992 estimated taxes, you cannot avoid penalties by paying 100% of your prior-year's tax if your current year's adjusted gross income is at least $40,000 more than your prior year's ($20,000 for marrieds filing separately), and your current AGI is at least $75,000 ($37,500 for marrieds filing separately). This limit does not apply if: (1) you have not filed estimated taxes for 3 years; (2) your income jumped relative to the prior year due to the sale of your principal residence or involuntary conversions (3) you own no more than 10% of a partnership or S corporation or (4) you get all of the extra income in the current year's last quarter. This safe-harbor limit ends for tax years starting after 1996 [IRC Sec. 6654(d)(1)(C)].

Example 2: Mr. Hill is an owner-employee of Acme Inc. who earns $100,000 annually. In addition, Acme normally pays him a year-end bonus of $20,000. Because of difficult economic times, Acme postponed his year-end bonus and pays him a double amount for 1993 of $40,000. Since Mr. Hill's adjusted gross income for 1993 increased by $40,000, he must pay at least 90% of his 1993 tax liability to avoid an estimated tax penalty.

▶ **TAX-WISE MOVE** If you discover that you're falling short of the 90% tax prepayment mark, there are two ways you may be able to avoid the penalty: (1) Have your employer increase tax withholding during the remainder of the year, or (2) make larger estimated tax payments. (The last 1992 estimated tax payment is due January 15, 1993.)

(a) Estimated Tax Installments Based on Annualized Income. If your income fluctuates unevenly throughout the year, a special rule allows you to make payments of less than 25% of your year's estimated tax liability in those periods when your income is at a peak. The rule is called the annualized income method of computing estimated tax. The total amount of installments for the year should equal 90% of your estimated tax liability (66⅔% for farmers and fishermen). However, your payments can be weighted toward the end of the year. The computations include self-employment and alternative minimum taxes, in addition to regular income tax.

Your first step is to annualize income up to the month each installment is due. To annualize income, you multiply your taxable income to the end of the period covered by the installment (figured without deducting personal exemptions) by 12, divide by the number of months from the beginning of the tax year to the end of the installment period, and subtract personal exemptions to which you are entitled on the installment due date. The payment on the due date for the current year's first installment must equal or exceed 22.5% of the tax figured on the annualized income. For succeeding installments, payments must be at least 45%, 67.5% and 90% of the annualized tax [IRC Sec. 6654(d)].

> **Example 3:** Mr. Jones is married and files a 1993 joint return. He claims four exemptions and has no alternative minimum tax liability. He chooses to annualize income to pay estimated tax.
>
> 1. Wages received during Jan.–Mar. .... $ 5,000
> 2. Actual adjusted gross income .... $ 5,000
> 3. Annualized adjusted gross income [$5,000 × 12 = $60,000 ÷ 3] $20,000
> 4. Less: Itemized deductions [$1,500 × 12 = $18,000 ÷ 3 = $6,000] .... $ 6,000
>   Exemptions [4 × $2,300] 9,200 $15,200
> 5. Annualized taxable income .... $ 4,800
> 6. Tax .... $ 720
>
> If Jones' withholding through March and estimated tax payment for the 1st installment period is at least $162 (22.5% of $720), he does not owe a penalty for that period.

Alternative minimum taxable income; self-employment income. To annualize for the alternative minimum tax, you add the annualized preferences to the annualized adjusted gross income. You add or subtract annualized adjustments. Then you deduct your allowable annualized alternative minimum tax itemized deductions and your exemption to arrive at your annualized alternative minimum taxable income. Self-employment income is annualized for the period covered by the installment in the same way as taxable income and alternative minimum taxable income.[2]

Lower required installments. If you figure your estimated tax by annualizing income, each installment payment may be the lesser of the required installment (90% × current year's estimated tax divided by 4) or the annualized income installment. If the annualized income installment for the payment period is less than the required installment, you only need to pay the annualized income installment [IRC Sec. 6654(d)(2)].

Recapture. If you pay the annualized income installment, you must add your savings for that payment period (the difference between the amount you pay and the required installment) to the required installment for the next payment period. If you also pay only the annualized income installment for the later payment period, you must add your savings for that later period (the difference between the required installment for that payment period (as increased) and the annualized income installment for that period) to the required installment for the next payment period [IRC Sec. 6654(d)].

> **Example 4:** Mr. Lee estimates that his taxable income for 1993 will be from wages subject to withholding and a gain on a sale of a parcel of land that he expects to sell in August. He estimates the 1993 tax to be $8,000; the 1992 tax was $7,400. Based on these estimates, the required annual payment for 1993 is $7,200. This is the lesser of $7,200 ($8,000 × 90%) or $7,400 (1992 tax). The required installment for each pay period is $1,800 ($7,200 × 25%). He also estimates 1993 withheld taxes of $4,000 ($1,000 allocated to each payment period due date). For 1993 payment periods, he figures the tax on the annualized income for the 1st and 2nd periods will be $6,000; 3rd, $9,000 and 4th, $8,000. Lee's payments for the year will total $7,200 [$1,350 + $1,350 + $2,700 + $1,800] computed as follows:
>
> *Required annual payment:*
> Lesser of $7,200 ($8,000 × 90%) or $7,400 (1992 tax) $7,200
> Required installment for each pay period:
>   ($7,200 × 25%) $1,800

1st payment period:
Annualized income installment:
($6,000 × 22.5%) $1,350
Withholding for 1st period 1,000
Payment required .... $ 350

2nd payment period:
Required installment:
($1,800 plus $450, difference between $1,800 and $1,350 installment
    payment for 1st period $2,250
Annual income installment:
($6,000 × 45% = $2,700 less $1,350, tax paid, 1st period) $1,350
Less: Withheld tax, 2nd period 1,000
Payment required .... $ 350

3rd payment period:
Required installment:
$1,800 plus $900, difference between $2,250 and $1,350 installment
    payment for 2nd period $2,700
Annualized income installment:
$9,000 × 67.5% = $6,075 less $2,700 installment
    payments for 1st and 2nd periods $3,375
This is more than the required installment (as increased)
Less: Withheld tax, 3rd period 1,000
Payment required $1,700

4th payment period:
Required installment (no increase) ($7,200 × 25%) $1,800
Annual income installment [$7,200 ($8,000 × 90%)
    less $5,400, (prior payments)] $1,800
Less: Withheld tax 1,000
Payment required .... $ 800

➤ **OBSERVATION** Annualization usually necessitates an amendment of prior tax computations for the year. It is most useful when the larger part of a taxpayer's income is received in the latter part of the year.

Tax return tip. You must make computations relating to the penalty on Form 2210. You should attach it to the return for any underpayment and a reliance on an exception.[3] However, you need not file this form if your withholding plus estimated tax payments equal or exceed 100% of your preceding year's tax (assuming you can use that safe harbor) or if the you owed no tax for the preceding year. IRS computers are programmed to compute the amounts due.[4]

➤ **OBSERVATION** To calculate the amount of estimated tax due, you use either the appropriate tax table or tax rate schedule, whichever is most advantageous.[5]

(b) How the Penalty is Applied. You figure the current underpayment penalty [¶3728] separately for each installment. The penalty is applied to the difference between the amount you actually paid (including withheld taxes) and the amount that you should have paid if the estimated tax were the lesser of 90% (66⅔% for farmers and fishermen) of the amount shown on the final return, or 100% of the tax shown on your preceding tax year's return (assuming you can use that safe harbor) [IRC Sec. 6654(b), (d)]. The charge runs from date of the installment until you pay the amount or until the filing date of the tax return, whichever is earlier.

Underpayment. This is the excess of youre required installment (or, if it is lower, your annualized income installment) for a payment period over the portion of the amount you paid by the due date that is not applied to an underpayment for an earlier payment period.[6]

How underpayments are applied. You figure the period of underpayment by applying estimated tax payments to any underpayments on earlier installments in the order in which such installments were required to be paid.[6]

Example 5: You have a net tax payable (without regard to prepaid taxes or credits) of $12,000 on your final return, and you paid four equal installments of estimated tax of $2,500 on each of the due dates during the year. Last year's tax was $11,000. Assume you have no withholding. Because $10,800 (90% of the $12,000 tax shown on your current return) is less than the $11,000 tax shown on last year's return, your required annual payment is $10,800. Each required installment is $2,700 ($10,800 × 25%). You apply your payments to each payment period as follows:

1st Payment Period:
Required installment $2,700
Amount paid by due date 2,500
Underpayment for 1st period ....$ 200

2nd Payment Period:
Required installment $2,700
Amount paid by due date $2,500
Minus: Payment applied to earlier underpayment 200
Payment applied to current installment 2,300
Underpayment for 2nd period ....$ 400

3rd Payment Period:
Required installment $2,700
Amount paid by due date $2,500
Minus: Payment applied to earlier underpayment 400
Payment applied to current installment 2,100
Underpayment for 3rd period ....$ 600

4th Payment Period:
Required installment $2,700
Amount paid by due date $2,500
Minus: Payment applied to earlier underpayment 600
Payment applied to current installment 1,900
Underpayment for 4th period ....$ 800

Thus, you had a $200 underpayment for the first payment period. Because $200 of your payment for the 2nd payment period was applied to the underpayment for the 1st period, you figure your "period of underpayment" by counting the number of days after April 15, 1992 (the due date for the first payment period), through the date you made payment for the 2nd payment period. You figure the period of underpayment for the 2nd period by counting the number of days after June 15, 1992, through the date you made the payment for the 3rd period. The period of underpayment for the 3rd period is from the day after September 15, 1992, through the date you made the payment for the 4th period. The period of underpayment for the fourth period is from the day after January 15, 1993, through the date of payment or April 15, 1993, whichever is earlier.[6]

Figuring the penalty. The penalty for the first period of underpayment is figured on the total underpayment for the payment period. Later periods of underpayment for that payment period is from the day after an applied payment to the date of the next applied payment or April 15 of the following year, whichever is earlier. The penalty for each of the later periods of underpayment will be figured on the balance of the underpayment for the payment period as of the beginning of each later period of underpayment.

To figure your penalty for a payment period with more than one period of underpayment, figure a penalty amount separately for each of the periods of underpayment using the number of days in each period of underpayment, the correct underpayment balance, and the appropriate penalty rates[6] [¶3728].

Example 6: Using the facts in Example 4, the penalty charge (10% is used for this illustration, and applies to each payment period) would be figured as follows:

```
1st payment period ($200 at 10% for 61 days) ............................ $  3.34
2nd payment period ($400 at 10% for 92 days) ............................. 10.08
3rd payment period ($600 at 10% for 122 days) ............................ 20.05
4th payment period ($800 at 10% for 90 days) ............................. 19.73
  Total ................................................................. $53.20
```

Overpayment. If you overpay an installment, you carry the overpayment to the next period and add it to your withholding and estimated tax payment for that later period. [6]

In addition to the interest charge, willful failure to *pay* estimated taxes is a misdemeanor punishable by a fine of $25,000 ($100,000 for corporations), or jail for not more than one year, or both [IRC Sec. 7203].

(c) Waiver of Penalty. A limited waiver of the penalty applies if the IRS determines that the underpayment is due to casualty, disaster, or other unusual circumstance and if denying the waiver would be against equity and good conscience. The IRS can also waive the penalty for reasonable cause during the first two years after you reach age 62 or become disabled [IRC Sec. 6654(e)(3)].

BACKUP WITHHOLDING

The main purpose of backup withholding on interest, dividends, and certain other payments is to make sure that you report all taxable income on your tax returns. The payments targeted for backup withholding are generally nonwage income for which the payor must file an information return.

¶2421   BACKUP WITHHOLDING ON INTEREST, DIVIDENDS AND CERTAIN OTHER PAYMENTS

Backup withholding expands income tax withholding to interest [¶3662], dividends [¶3663], and most types of payments [¶3661] reportable on 1099s. Payors, such as banks and corporations, are required to withhold income tax from their payments if at least one essential backup requirement situation exists[1] [IRC Sec. 3406(a), (b)].

(a) Backup Withholding Requirements. Payors of dividends, interest and certain other reportable payments must backup withhold by deducting and withholding 20% income tax from your payment in the following four situations: (1) you failed to furnish a TIN (Taxpayer Identification Number) [¶3620]; (2) the IRS notified the payor that the TIN furnished by you was incorrect; (3) the IRS notified the payor to backup withhold because you did not report or underreported the interest or dividends on his tax return (but only after at least 4 notices are given over a 120-day period, see below); and (4) you failed to certify an exempt status from backup withholding, but see below. Payors use Form W-9 for payees to report and certify TINs and for payees to claim an exempt status [IRC Sec. 3406(a), (b); Temp. Reg. Sec. 35a.9999-1].

NOTE: TINs must be provided under penalties of perjury only for payments of interest, dividends, patronage dividends and to payments subject to broker reporting [IRC Sec. 3406(e)(1)].

(b) When Does Backup Withholding Begin? Payors can begin backup withholding usually within 30 days after they are notified by the IRS. However, in most cases of underreporting of interest and dividends, it cannot begin until the IRS sends at least four notices to you over a 120-day period. Also, special rules apply for the period for starting and stopping withholding. For example, a payor may elect to begin or stop withholding on shorter notice than 30 days if the IRS determined actual underreporting of any reportable interest and dividends. A 60-day exemption applies if you sign a certification that you are awaiting a TIN [IRC Sec. 3406(c)(1)-(5), (e)(5); Temp. Reg. Sec. 35a.9999-1,2].

Must the payee be given notice? Generally no, except for underreporting of interest and dividends. A special notice (no later than 15 days after first payment), however, must be sent by payors on readily tradable instruments that are not required directly from the payors. (Rev. Proc. 92-32 tells payors how to draft notices warning payees that they could become subject to backup withholding.) Also, a similar rule applies to broker transactions. If the IRS notifies the payor of an incorrect TIN, the payor must promptly, within the 30 days before withholding, notify you. The payor must also notify the IRS if a new TIN is furnished by you [IRC Sec. 3406 (c)(4), (d)(2), (e)(2); (h)(8), (9); Temp. Reg. Sec. 35a.9999-1,2].

Exempt status. Payments to payees for whom an information return [¶3660–3663] is not required are exempt from backup withholding [IRC Sec. 3406(g); Temp. Reg. Sec. 35a.9999-2]. Form W-8 is used by foreign payees to certify their exemption [Temp. Reg. 35a.9999-1]. Minimal payments of less than $10 figured on an annual basis are also exempt [IRC Sec. 3406(b)(5); Temp. Reg. 35a.9999-2]. Distributions to partners of their distributive shares of partnership income are exempt payments if brokers are not involved [Temp. Reg. 35a.9999-3, Q & A 47]. Trusts and estates (other than grantor trusts) distributions are exempt. Payments to grantor trusts with more than 10 grantors are exempt until distributed [Temp. Reg. 35a.9999-2, Q & A 20].

(c) Payments Subject to Backup Withholding. Backup withholding applies to most types of payments that are reported on 1099s: interest [¶3662], dividends [¶3663], patronage dividends (but only if at least ½ the payment is in money) [¶3663(b)], rents, profits, royalties, commissions, fees [¶3661(c)], payments to independent contractors [¶3661(e)], brokers [¶3661(g)], direct sellers [¶3661(f)] and fishing boat operators (but only if payment is in money) [IRC Sec. 3406(b); Temp. Reg. Sec. 35a.9999-2].

(d) Penalties. Civil and criminal penalties are imposed for giving false information to avoid backup withholding. The criminal penalty is a $1,000 maximum fine plus imprisonment for up to 1 year [IRC Sec. 7205(b)].

Footnotes to Chapter 14

(For your added convenience, in brackets [] with the footnotes below, you will find citations to related paragraphs in the "RIA United States Tax Reporter"(USTR), "CCH Federal Tax Reporter"(CCH) and "RIA Federal Tax Coordinator 2d"(FTC) multi-volume services.)

FOOTNOTE ¶ 2401 [USTR ¶ 214; CCH ¶ 3507; FTC ¶ A-4300].

(1) Treas. Dept. booklet "Your Federal Income Tax" (1991 Ed.), p. 191.

FOOTNOTE ¶ 2402 [USTR¶ 324 et seq.; CCH ¶ 4082; FTC ¶ A-4200].

FOOTNOTE ¶ 2403 [USTR ¶ 224 et seq.; CCH ¶ 3554; FTC ¶ A-4100].

FOOTNOTE ¶ 2405 [USTR ¶ 384 et seq.; CCH ¶ 4251; FTC ¶ L-15200].

FOOTNOTE ¶ 2406 [USTR ¶ 464 et seq.; CCH ¶ 4513; FTC ¶ L-16600, L-18000].

(1) Rome I, Ltd., 96 TC 697

FOOTNOTE ¶ 2407 [USTR ¶ 424; CCH ¶ 4385; FTC ¶ L-11300].

(1) Rev. Rul. 92-61.

FOOTNOTE ¶ 2408 [USTR ¶ 514; CCH ¶ 4803; FTC ¶ L-17800].

FOOTNOTE ¶ 2409 [USTR ¶ 414; CCH ¶ 4362; FTC ¶ 15300].

(1) Apple Computer, 98 TC No. 18.

(2) TSR, Inc.& Subsidiary, 96 TC 903, IRS Acq., IRB 1992-31.

FOOTNOTE ¶ 2410 [USTR ¶ 434; CCH ¶ 4387; FTC ¶ L-17600].

FOOTNOTE ¶ 2411 [USTR ¶ 444; CCH ¶ 4401; FTC ¶ L-17900].

FOOTNOTE ¶ 2412 [USTR ¶ 344; CCH ¶ 4151; FTC ¶ W-4741].

FOOTNOTE ¶ 2413 [USTR ¶ 294; CCH ¶ 4051; FTC ¶ L-17500].

FOOTNOTE ¶ 2414 [USTR ¶ 254; CCH ¶ 3809; FTC ¶ A-4008].

FOOTNOTE ¶ 2416 [USTR ¶ 66,544; CCH ¶ 40,460; FTC ¶ S-5200, S-5232].

FOOTNOTE ¶ 2417 [USTR ¶ 66,544; CCH ¶ 40,460; RIA ¶ S-5232].

(1) Treas. Dept. booklet "Tax Withholding and Estimated Tax" (1992 Ed.), p. 30.

(2) Instructions to Form 1040-ES.

FOOTNOTE ¶ 2418 [USTR ¶ 66,544; CCH ¶ 40,460; FTC ¶ S-5201].

(1) Treas. Dept. booklet "Tax Withholding and Estimated Tax" (1992 Ed.), p. 20.

(2) Rev. Rul. 84-58, 1984-1 CB 254 (IR-84-46) modifying and reinstating Rev. Rul. 77-475, 1977-2 CB 476; revoking Rev. Rul. 83-111, 1983-2 CB 245.

(3) Treas. Dept. booklet "Tax Withholding and Estimated Tax" (1992 Ed.), p. 16.

FOOTNOTE ¶ 2419 [USTR ¶ 66,544; CCH ¶ 40,460; FTC ¶ S-5205].

(1) Treas. Dept. booklet "Your Federal Income Tax" (1991 Ed.), p. 36.

FOOTNOTE ¶ 2420 [USTR ¶ 66,544; CCH ¶ 40,460; FTC ¶ S-5241].

(1) Rev. Rul. 86-146, 1986-2 CB 208 (IR-86-163).

(2) Treas. Dept. booklet "Tax Withholding and Estimated Tax" (1992 Ed.), p. 21.

(3) Instructions for Form 2210.

(4) IR-84-39

(5) Rev. Proc. 83-79, 1983-2 CB 597.

(6) Treas. Dept. booklet "Your Federal Income Tax" (1991 Ed.), p. 39; "Tax Withholding and Estimated Tax" (1992 Ed.), p. 17.

FOOTNOTE ¶ 2421 [USTR ¶ 34,064; CCH ¶ 35,154; FTC ¶ J-9000].

(1) Treas. Dept. booklet "Tax Withholding and Estimated Tax" (1992 Ed.), p. 12.

CHAPTER 15

INCOME TAX WITHHOLDING

TABLE OF CONTENTS

Employers are subject to a complex array of payroll tax withholding requirements. These provisions grow more numerous each year, as the federal and state governments place increasing emphasis on the taxation of employee benefits to raise revenues. And new penalties for filing errors and nonpayment of tax proliferate. This chapter explains the employer's duties in regard to withholding of federal income tax. Recordkeeping requirements, payroll tax deposit and return procedures, and practical suggestions for keeping the employment tax bill to a minimum are also included.

FEDERAL INCOME TAX WITHHOLDING

¶2500   PURPOSE OF WITHHOLDING

Withholding provisions were enacted to enable taxpayers to meet their income tax obligations as they earn wages. Employers must withhold the tax from wages paid to their employees, in amounts determined by each employee's withholding allowance certificate and government withholding tax tables. Neither employer nor employee can claim an income tax deduction for amounts of federal income tax withheld. However, the withheld tax is credited against the total tax due.

¶2502   WHO MUST WITHHOLD

Employers who pay wages to employees must withhold income tax from the wages paid, in an amount determined according to the formula or tables at ¶2508. The number of employees and the length of employment do not matter.

(a) Employers required to withhold include individuals, partnerships, estates, trusts, trustees in bankruptcy,[1] corporations, and unincorporated organizations. Churches, colleges and organizations that are themselves exempt from income tax must withhold from employees, as must the governments of the United States, Puerto Rico, the District of Columbia, states, cities, school districts and other political subdivisions, instrumentalities, and agencies [IRC Sec. 3401(d); Reg. Sec. 31.3401(d)-1].

The employer's representatives, for the most part, handle the mechanical details of withholding. When a corporate employer has branch offices, the branch manager or other representative may actually perform the duties of the employer. A payroll processing firm may be engaged to deduct taxes and prepare paychecks, but the legal responsibility for withholding and paying tax still rests with the employer [Reg. Sec. 31.3403-1].

(b) Persons Controlling Wage Payments. Persons other than the actual employer may be required or permitted to withhold tax.

- If the person for whom an individual performs services does not have control of the wage payments, then the person having control must withhold [IRC Sec. 3401(d)(1); Reg. Sec. 31.3401(d)-1(f)]. Most often, bonding companies or sureties are not liable for the withholding taxes of the insured contractor. For example, a bonding company furnished funds with which to meet a contractor's payroll by giving the bank on each payday a draft to cover the payroll. The bonding company was held not liable for the withholding tax.[2]
- One who pays wages for a nonresident alien individual, foreign partnership, or foreign corporation not engaged in a trade or business within the U.S., is considered an employer even though the services are not performed for him [IRC Sec. 3401(d)(2); Reg. Sec. 31.3401(d)-1(e)]. See also ¶2518(a).
- Fiduciaries, agents, and others who have control over or who pay employees' wages may perform the employer's duties when authorized by the IRS [IRC Sec. 3504; Reg. Sec. 31.3504-1].
- Lenders, sureties or other persons who pay wages directly to employees of another are liable to the U.S. for withholding taxes related to these wages plus interest. In addition, any creditor who lends money knowing that the loan will be used to meet payroll is subject to a limited liability [IRC Sec. 3505]. Form 4219 must be submitted with the payment.[3]

¶2504   WHO IS SUBJECT TO WITHHOLDING

Employers must withhold employees' income tax only if the legal relationship of employer-employee exists for the services for which the compensation is paid. It is not necessary that the services be continuing at the time the wages are paid [Reg. Sec. 31.3401(d)-1(b)]. Thus, for example, employers who pay wages to former employees on January 15, 1993, for services the latter performed during the week of January 4-8, 1993, when the employer-employee relationship existed, must withhold the tax when the wages are paid.

(a) Who Are Employees. An employer-employee relationship exists if the person for whom services are performed has the right to control and direct the individual who performs the services. This control must extend not only to the result to be accomplished by the work, but also to the details and means by which that result is accomplished. Employers do not have to actually direct or control the way the services are performed; it is enough if they have the *right* to do so.

Important: The IRS has drawn a distinction between skilled professionals and other workers. Professionals can be deemed subject to a company's control even when they rely on their own expertise and knowledge to get the job done. In a private ruling, the IRS categorized a professional as an employee simply because the company had general control over the way the professional did his job.[1]

The following factors are also important in finding whether a person is an "employer": the right to discharge; furnishing of tools; furnishing of a place to work [Reg. Sec. 31.3401(c)-1].

Managers, officers, directors. No distinction is made for withholding purposes between classes or grades of employees. However, a corporate officer is an employee, but a director of a corporation in his or her capacity as such is not. Withholding, therefore, is required on officers' salaries, but not on directors' fees [Reg. Sec. 31.3401(c)-1(f)].

Minors, students. Minors are treated the same as other employees. For example, tax is withheld from the wages of students working during vacation, even if they will not earn enough to pay income tax (unless they file proper certificates (Form W-4) to claim exempt status [¶2510(a)]); see ¶2506(e) for newspaper carriers under 18.

Partners. If an employer-employee relationship in fact exists, it does not matter that the employee is called a partner [Reg. Sec. 31.3401(c)-1(e)].

Substitutes who are properly working in place of regular employees are considered employees for purposes of withholding.[2]

Unlawful business. An individual performing services in an illegal activity for wages may nonetheless be an employee.[3]

(b) Self-Employed Persons. Individuals who are in fact partners, independent contractors, or sole proprietors of a business are not subject to withholding on their drawings or earnings in such capacities.

Examples: Auctioneers, contractors and subcontractors, dentists, doctors, freelance professional models,[4] lawyers, public stenographers, veterinarians, and others who follow an independent trade, business, or profession, in which they offer their services to the public, are not employees [Reg. Sec. 31.3401(c)-1(c)].

Direct sellers and real estate agents are classified as self-employeds if: (1) substantially all of their income for services as real estate agents or direct sellers are directly related to sales or other output; and (2) their services are performed under a written contract that calls for them not to be treated as employees for tax purposes [IRC Sec. 3508].

So-called "statutory employees" (a hybrid between employees and independent contractors) are treated like employees for social security taxes. But the IRS has said that statutory employees—which include such workers as truck drivers, insurance salespeople, and outside salespeople—are not employees for income tax purposes. They are not subject to income tax withholding.[5]

A special formula is provided to compute an employer's liability if it makes mistakes in its classifications [IRC Sec. 3509].

> ► **TAX ALERT** You will not be held liable for employment taxes if there is a reasonable basis for treating an individual as self-employed. To get this special break, you must file all required federal returns, including information returns, on a basis consistent with your treatment of the worker as self-employed. You (or your predecessor) must not have treated any worker in a substantially similar position as an employee for any period after 1977. However, this relief is not available for any arrangement employers may have for services provided to them by certain technical personnel, such as engineers, computer programmers, and systems analysts. In these cases, the employment relationship between the business and the technical service specialist will be determined under the common law rules.[6]

A reasonable basis for treating an individual as an independent contractor can be established through one or more of the following tests: judicial precedent; published IRS rulings; technical advice from the IRS with respect to the particular employer, or a letter ruling to the employer; a past IRS audit, if there was no assessment pertaining to the employer's treatment of individuals in the same position as the worker whose status is in question; a long-standing, recognized practice in the industry in which the worker is engaged.[7]

The surest way to avoid misclassifying an employee is to go straight to the IRS for advice. You can obtain an IRS ruling as to whether your worker is an employee or an independent contractor by submitting Form SS-8, available at any IRS district office. Meanwhile, note that withholding of income or social security tax from an individual's wages, or the filing of an employment tax return with respect to those wages, is considered treatment of the individual as an employee.

➤ **TAX TIP** Do not have a worker fill out a withholding allowance certificate (Form W-4) if he or she is self-employed or an independent contractor, i.e., not your employee. You must consistently treat such a worker as independent to maintain the worker's payroll tax-free standing.

The IRS has said an employer can treat the same worker as both employer and employee. Only pay for the work done as an employee is subject to payroll taxes; the pay for work done as an independent contractor is not subject to withholding taxes.[8]

¶2506   WAGES SUBJECT TO WITHHOLDING

Only those payments that are "wages" for income tax purposes are subject to withholding.

(a) What Are Wages. "Wages" means pay to employees for services [IRC Sec. 3401(a)]. A payment can be wages whether it is called a salary, fee, bonus, commission, vacation pay, or even retirement pay. Wages can be paid in property, such as stocks, bonds, or other property transferred in exchange for the employee's services. The property's fair market value when it is transferred is the amount of the wages [Reg. Sec. 31.3401(a)-1(a)].

The same kind of payment may be wages subject to withholding under some conditions but not under other conditions, or only a portion of a payment may be subject to withholding as wages. Also, some payments for employment may be excluded from wages [Reg. Sec. 31.3401(a)-2]. Withholding is based upon wages actually or constructively paid, regardless of when wages were earned [Reg. Sec. 31.3402(a)-1].

Wages Subject to Withholding

Overtime pay; dismissal pay [Reg. Sec. 31.3401(a)-1(b)(4)]; certain reimbursed employment agency fees;[1] social security tax or state unemployment tax, paid by the employer without deduction from an employee's pay [Reg. Sec. 31.3401(a)-1(b)(6)]; suggestion awards;[2] payments equivalent to difference between employee's normal wages and amounts received from the state while serving in the National Guard;[3] guaranteed annual wage payments;[4] financial counseling fees paid by a corporation for the benefit of its executives.[5]

Items Not Subject to Withholding

Occasional supper money given for overtime work [Reg. Sec. 1.132-6(d)(2)]; qualified tuition reductions for undergraduate studies given by an educational organization to its employees [IRC Sec. 117(d), 3401(a)(19)]; compensation paid to former employees in the Armed Forces or National Guard;[6] facilities or privileges of small value furnished to employees generally, to promote health, goodwill or efficiency, such as entertainment, medical services and courtesy discounts on purchases [Reg. Sec. 31.3401(a)-1(b)(10)]; merchandise of nominal value [Reg. Sec. 1.132-6(e)];

scholarship and fellowship grants [IRC Sec. 117]; union strike benefits;[7] reimbursement for uniforms if the payments are properly identified when made, the expenses are substantiated and unsubstantiated reimbursements are returned [Reg. Sec. 31.3401(a)-1(b)(2)]; medical care reimbursements made under self-insured medical reimbursement plan (¶1515(a)) [IRC Sec. 3401(a)(20)].

Payments Subject to Withholding Under Special Rules

Agricultural wages are subject to withholding if the cash wages are subject to social security taxes [IRC Sec. 3401(a)(2)].

Back pay and back overtime paid under the Fair Labor Standards Act are subject to withholding even if paid as a result of a settlement or court judgement, but not liquidated damages paid under the Act.[8] The employer should withhold tax when back wages are paid over to the administrator of the Wage and Hour Division of the Dept. of Labor, and report it on the employer's current return.[9]

Board and lodging. The value of meals or lodging furnished to an employee is not subject to withholding if the employee can exclude the value of the meals or lodging from income [Reg. Sec. 31.3401(a)-1(b)(9)]. The value is excludable if (1) meals or lodging are furnished on the employer's business premises (generally the employee's place of employment); (2) they are furnished for the employer's convenience; and (3) for lodging (but not meals), the employee must accept the lodging as a condition of employment [IRC Sec. 119].

Cafeteria plans. Under a cafeteria plan [¶1426], employer contributions are excluded from the wages of an employee and not subject to withholding to the extent that qualified benefits are elected by the employee.[10]

Cash-or-deferred (Sec. 401(k)) plan contributions. Amounts that an employee elects to have the employer defer from salary into a trust under a profit-sharing or stock bonus plan on the employee's behalf are not includable in an employee's gross income. Such deferrals are thus not subject to withholding [Reg. Sec. 31.3401(a)(12)-1]. (See ¶2516 for withholding on distributions of such deferred income.) But amounts that an employee elects to receive as cash under such a plan are wages subject to withholding.

Commissions generally are wages subject to withholding. But if a retail commission salesperson, usually paid in cash, receives a noncash payment (such as a sales prize), it is not subject to withholding if the prize's fair market value is included as "other compensation" reported on the Form W-2 (¶2554) [IRC Sec. 3402(j); Reg. Sec. 31.3402(j)-1].[11] An insurance salesperson is not a retail commission salesperson for this purpose.[12]

Decedent's payments. Payments after an employee's death representing unpaid compensation for services rendered by a deceased employee are not subject to withholding.[13]

Dependent care assistance payments are not subject to withholding as long as it's reasonable to believe that the employee would be able to exclude these payments (¶1415) [IRC Sec. 3401(a)(18)]. An employee can exclude an amount equal to the smaller of (1) his or her earned income or (2) $5,000 ($2,500 if married filing separately) [IRC Sec. 129].

Educational expenses. Job-related educational expense payments are not subject to withholding if the education maintains or improves skills required by the individual's employment or other trade or business, or is a condition of employment. However, if the education is required to meet the minimum educational requirements for the job, or the education will qualify the individual for a new trade or business, then the educational payments are subject to withholding (¶2228) [Reg. Sec. 1.162-5].[14] The employee must substantiate his or her educational expenses to the person providing the payment, and return any unspent amounts.[15]

Employee stock options. When employees exercise their rights in nonqualified stock options, the excess of the stock's fair market value over the option price is wages subject to withholding.[16] Withholding also applies to amounts paid to employees to cancel these options.[17]

Fishing wages. Crewmen who receive a share of a boat's or fleet's catch (or a share of the proceeds from the sale of the catch) as pay for services rendered are not subject to withholding, if the operating crew of the boat (or of each boat from which the individual receives a share) normally consists of fewer than ten individuals[18] [IRC Sec. 3401(a)(17); Reg. Sec. 31.3401(a)(17)-1].

Gambling winnings. Withholding applies to proceeds from (1) state-connected lotteries on winnings over $5,000 and (2) sweepstakes, lotteries (not state-connected), and wagering pools on winnings over $1,000. But proceeds exceeding $1,000 from other wagering transactions (such as jai alai or horse or dog racing) are subject to withholding only when such proceeds are at least 300 times as large as the amount wagered. Winnings from slot machines, keno, and bingo are exempt. Also, each person who receives a payment must sign Form W-2G or 5754 and return the form to the payer [IRC Sec. 3402(q); Reg. Secs. 31.3402(q)-1, 1.6011-3].

Golden parachute contracts. Payments under golden parachute contracts, like any termination pay, are subject to withholding.[19]

Insurance and annuity premiums. Payments to employees to buy individual hospitalization coverage that are includable in employees' income are subject to withholding.[20] But if the payments are actually reimbursements of premiums actually paid by employees to insurers, the payments are excludable from income.[21] Group-term life insurance premiums are not subject to withholding, even though premiums for coverage in excess of $50,000 are income taxable to employees [IRC

Sec. 79, 3401(a)(14)]. Premiums paid by an organization exempt under Sec. 501(c)(3) (¶3336) to buy an employee annuity are also exempt from withholding.[22]

IRA contributions paid by employer. Amounts paid for individuals to retirement arrangements are not wages subject to withholding as long as it is reasonable to believe that the employees will be entitled to deductions for such payments (¶1330) [IRC Sec. 219(a); Reg. Sec. 31.3401(a)(12)-1(d)].

Loans—interest-free and below-market. The amount treated as additional compensation to the employee [¶1216] is not subject to income tax withholding. But the amount deemed additional compensation must be reported on Form W-2 as "other compensation."[23]

Moving expenses are not subject to withholding if, when paid, it is reasonable to believe that the employee can deduct them. Reimbursements or allowances in excess of moving expenses are subject to withholding (¶1935 et seq.) [IRC Sec. 3401(a)(15); 31.3401(a)(15)-1].

Pensions and retirement pay distributions are subject to withholding unless the recipient elects exemption from withholding on Form W-4P.[24] For withholding procedures, see ¶2516.

Retirement plan payments by employer. Payments to or from a trust or annuity plan (including a Sec. 403(b) annuity purchased by a public school or tax-exempt organization), made to or for employees and their beneficiaries, are not subject to withholding unless payments are compensation for services [Reg. Sec. 31.3401(a)(12)-1].

Supplemental unemployment benefits (SUB) are subject to withholding to the extent that the benefits are taxable. Withholding is required on benefits paid under a plan to which the employer is a party, due to an employee's involuntary separation, that results directly from a reduction in force, discontinuing operation or similar conditions [IRC Sec. 3402(o); Reg. Sec. 31.3401(a)-1(b)(14), 31.3402(o)-1].

Traveling expenses and other bona fide, ordinary and necessary expenses incurred, or reasonably expected to be incurred, in an employer's business and specifically advanced or reimbursed to employees, are not wages if the employees (within a reasonable period of time) substantiate their expenses to the person providing the advance or reimbursement, and return any unspent amounts. Wages and expense money need not be paid separately, but if one payment includes both items, each should be shown on the pay stub separately [Reg. Sec. 31.3401(a)-4].

Wages as community property. Total wages paid to the husband are wages subject to withholding. The wife's share of the tax withheld may be credited against her tax if she files separately.[25]

(b) Fringe Benefits and Withholding. The fair market value of noncash fringe benefits is treated as wages subject to withholding. However, fringe benefits an employer provides to an employee that are excludable from an employee's gross income are not subject to withholding [IRC Sec. 3401(a)(19); Temp. Reg. Sec. 31.3401(a)-1T].

When to withhold. You can treat taxable fringe benefits as paid on an annual, semiannual, quarterly, or pay-period basis, and withhold accordingly. You may also change your withholding basis as often as you wish in the course of a year, as long as taxable benefits are treated as paid no later than December 31. The value of a single fringe benefit may be apportioned over several pay periods, even if the benefit is actually received all at once. The same withholding basis does not have to be used for all employees. No formal election of basis is required; nor do you have to notify the government of its choice of basis.[26]

Special accounting rule. The value of taxable fringe benefits that are *actually provided* during the last two months of the calendar year may be treated as paid during the subsequent calendar year. Withholding on these benefits is therefore deferred into the next year. No formal election of this special rule is required (other than informing employees), and you can choose to use it for some benefits while disregarding it for others. *Exceptions:* This rule cannot be applied to the value of benefits received by the employee during the first ten months of the calendar year, even if those benefits are not treated as paid until December 31.

You must notify employees if you plan to use this special accounting rule. Notification must be made between the time of the employee's last paycheck of the calendar year, and the time the employee receives Form W-2 (generally, January 31 of the following calendar year [¶2554]). Employees must, in turn, use this rule for all purposes (e.g., for taking deductions related to the fringe benefit) and for the same period.

Optional withholding on a company vehicle. The value of an employee's personal use of a company car is includable in gross income, unless it can be specifically excluded as a "working condition fringe" or as a "de minimis fringe" benefit. The value of the personal use is generally its fair market value. But optional valuation rules are provided: the auto lease valuation rule; the vehicle cents-per-mile rule; and the commuting-use-only rule [¶1401]. You must notify the employee by January 31 (or within 30 days of providing the benefit) that you plan to use an optional valuation rule [Reg. Sec. 1.61-21].

You may choose whether or not to withhold income tax on the value of an employee's personal use of a company car. If you elect not to withhold, you must notify the employee of this election and must include the fair market value of the personal use on Form W-2. Withholding of social security tax is mandatory, however. When withholding income tax and social security tax, you may treat the value of the personal use as paid on a pay period, quarterly, semiannual, or annual basis.

(c) Tips Subject to Withholding. Tips (cash or charge) of $20 or more a month received by an employee during one employment and reported to the employer are wages subject to withholding. You should withhold only if the income tax can be collected from the employee's wages after social security taxes have been deducted. Employees must make a written report of tips to their employer by the 10th of the month after they were received. Form 4070 can be used. Unreported tips are considered paid when received [IRC Sec. 3401(a)(16), 3401(f), 3402(k), 6053(a); Reg. Sec. 31.3401(f)-1, 31.3402(k)-1, 31.6053-1].

Allocated tips. Large food and beverage establishments must report annually on Form 8027 (along with transmittal Form 8027T) the gross and charge sales receipts (except carryout sales and mandatory 10% or more service charge sales), the total amount of tips on charge receipts, employees' reported tip income, and mandatory service charges of less than 10% [IRC Sec. 6053(c)(1)]. The appropriate Form must be filed by the end of February for the previous calendar year. If reported tip income is less than 8% of the gross receipts, you must make an allocation of the difference among the tipped employees [IRC Sec. 6053(c)(3)]. However, tipped employees as well as their employers may request by petition to lower their allocation rate (but not below 2%) if the IRS makes a finding that the actual allocation rate is less than 8%. Also, you must furnish a statement to each employee during January of the year following the year for which the statement is made. A penalty is imposed for failure to do so (¶2562) [IRC Sec. 6053(c)(2); Reg. Sec. 31.6053-3(h)].

Large food and beverage establishments are those that provide food or beverages for which tipping is customary, and which normally employ ten or more employees on a business day. For the ten-employee test, those who have a stock value interest of 50% or more in their corporate businesses are not counted as employees [IRC Sec. 6053(c)(4); Reg. Sec. 31.6053-3(j)]. Food and beverage operations at different locations are treated as separate operations for tip allocation purposes. This is true even though the same operations are conducted in a single building but in different locations. Fast-food and cafeteria-style operations that are conducted without table service or customary tipping are excepted from filing statements [Reg. Sec. 31.6053-3(h),(j)].

(d) Withholding on Certain Health, Accident and Group-Term Life Insurance Coverage. The value of employer-provided coverage under health, accident and group-term life insurance plans may be subject to withholding, if the provision of coverage fails the benefits' discrimination requirements (¶1406(a); 1407) [IRC Sec. 79, 105].

(e) Pay for Excluded Employment. Pay for services in certain excluded employment is not "wages" [Sec. 3401(a)]. Excluded employment includes agricultural labor;

performing religious duties by a member of the clergy; and domestic service in a private home, local college club, or local chapter of a college fraternity or sorority. However, certain payments that are not "wages" may be withheld upon for income tax purposes under a voluntary agreement between employer and employee [¶2508(m)].

Pay for employment NOT in the course of an employer's trade or business is not subject to withholding if it is a noncash payment [Reg. Sec. 31.3401(a)(11)-1], or if the cash payment is less than $50 for a calendar quarter. Withholding is required when the employee receives $50 or more in cash for the service, and performs such service for the employer on each of 24 days during the quarter or the preceding calendar quarter [IRC Sec. 3401(a)(4); Reg. Sec. 31.3401(a)(4)-1].

Newspaper carriers and news vendors. Pay of newspaper carriers under 18 is not wages. But withholding is required on pay for delivery or distribution to a point from which further delivery or distribution is made. Pay of news vendors who sell papers and magazines for a fixed price is not wages when that pay is the excess of what they receive for the papers and magazines over what they pay for them. This applies even though they are guaranteed a minimum amount or are credited with unsold papers or magazines [Reg. Sec. 31.3401(a)(10)-1].

Public service. Fees paid for performing a public duty (such as a notary, clerk or sheriff); amounts paid to jurors and witnesses; or to precinct workers at election booths in state, county or municipal elections are not wages subject to withholding. But salaries paid to officials by the government or government agencies are subject to withholding [Reg. Sec. 31.3401(a)-2(b)].

(f) Combined Wages and Nonwages. The time spent in each type of work determines whether or not withholding is required, if an employment for one employer for a payroll period of not over 31 days combines work for "wages" and work for pay in excluded employment.

- Withholding is required on the entire payment if one-half or more of the time is spent in work for "wages."
- Withholding is not required if less than one-half of the time is spent in work for wages [IRC Sec. 3402(e); Reg. Sec. 31.3402(e)-1].

¶2508   HOW TO FIGURE WITHHOLDING

[New tax legislation may affect this subject; see ¶1.]

Withholding from gross wages may be figured ordinarily by either the wage-bracket withholding tables or the percentage method. Graduated rates apply in figuring withholding. Each method is arranged by payroll periods and divided into two separate schedules for married (including surviving spouse) and single (including head of household) taxpayers. You can use the percentage method for some employees while using the wage-bracket table for others. And you can change from one method to another without IRS approval.[1] Generally, you must use the percentage method for quarterly, semiannual, or annual payroll periods, unless you use an authorized alternative method (see (c) below).

The amount you withhold under either method depends on the schedule you use (as to the payroll period and the employee's marital status), the number of withholding allowances claimed by the employee on the withholding allowance certificate [¶2510] and the amount of the employee's earnings.

You may use alternative methods of withholding that result in substantially the same amount of tax withheld as the percentage or wage-bracket methods [(c) below].

(a) Percentage Method. The amount to be withheld using the percentage method is determined as follows [IRC Sec. 3402(a), (b); Reg. Sec. 31.3402(b)-1]:

1.   Multiply the amount of one withholding allowance shown in the table below by the number of allowances claimed [¶2510].

2. Next, subtract the amount arrived at in (1) from the periodical wage to find "net wages" used to figure withholding.

3. Apply the proper rate found in the tables to the "net wages."

ALLOWANCE TABLE
[For wages paid after February 1992]

Payroll period	Amount of one with-holding allowance	Payroll period	Amount of one with-holding allowance
Weekly	$ 44.23	Semiannually	1,025.00
Biweekly	88.46	Annually	2,300.00
Semimonthly	95.83	Daily or miscellaneous (each	
Monthly	191.67	day of the payroll period)	8.85
Quarterly	575.00		

Tables for Percentage Method of Withholding [For wages paid after February 1992]

TABLE 1—If the Payroll Period With Respect to an Employee is Weekly

(a) SINGLE person—including head of household:

If the amount of wages (after subtracting withholding allowances) is:
The amount of income tax to be withheld shall be:

Not over $47 0

Over—	But not over —		of excess over—
$47	—$438	15%	—$47
$438	—$913	$58.65 plus 28%	—$438
$913		$191.65 plus 31%	—$913

(b) MARRIED person—

If the amount of wages (after subtracting withholding allowances) is:
The amount of income tax to be withheld shall be:

Not over $115 0

Over—	But not over —		of excess over—
$115	—$760	15%	—$115
$760	—$1,513	$96.75 plus 28%	—$760
$1,513		$307.59 plus 31%	—$1,513

TABLE 2—If the Payroll Period With Respect to an Employee is Biweekly

(a) SINGLE person—including head of household:

If the amount of wages (after subtracting withholding allowances) is:
The amount of income tax to be withheld shall be:

Not over $94 0

Over—	But not over —		of excess over—
$94	—$875	15%	—$94
$875	—$1,825	$117.15 plus 28%	—$875
$1,825		$383.15 plus 31%	—$1,825

(b) MARRIED person—

If the amount of wages (after subtracting withholding allowances) is:
The amount of income tax to be withheld shall be:

Not over $231 0

Over—	But not over —		of excess over—
$231	—$1,519	15%	—$231
$1,519	—$3,027	$193.20 plus 28%	—$1,519
$3,027		$615.44 plus 31%	—$3,027

TABLE 3—If the Payroll Period With Respect to an Employee is Semimonthly

(a) SINGLE person—including head of household:

If the amount of wages (after subtracting withholding allowances) is:
The amount of income tax to be withheld shall be:

Not over $102 0

Over—	But not over —		of excess over—
$102	—$948	15%	—$102
$948	—$1,977	$126.90 plus 28%	—$948
$1,977		$415.02 plus 31%	—$1,977

(b) MARRIED person—

If the amount of wages (after subtracting withholding allowances) is:
The amount of income tax to be withheld shall be:

Not over $250 0

Over—	But not over—		of excess over—
$250	—$1,646	15%	—$250
$1,646	—$3,279	$209.40 plus 28%	—$1,646
$3,279		$666.64 plus 31%	—$3,279

TABLE 4—If the Payroll Period With Respect to an Employee is Monthly

(a) SINGLE person—including head of household:

If the amount of wages (after subtracting withholding allowances) is:
The amount of income tax to be withheld shall be:

Not over $204 0

Over—	But not over —		of excess over—
$204	—$1,896	15%	—$204
$1,896	—$3,954	$253.80 plus 28%	—$1,896
$3,954		$830.04 plus 31%	—$3,954

(b) MARRIED person—

If the amount of wages (after subtracting withholding allowances) is:
The amount of income tax to be withheld shall be:

Not over $500 0

Over—	But not over—		of excess over—
$500	—$3,292	15%	—$500
$3,292	—$6,558	$418.80 plus 28%	—$3,292
$6,558		$1,333.28 plus 31%	—$6,558

Tables for Percentage Method of Withholding [For wages paid after February 1992]

TABLE 5—If the Payroll Period With Respect to an Employee is Quarterly

(a) SINGLE person—including head of household:

If the amount of wages (after subtracting withholding allowances) is: Not over $613 0

Over—	But not over —		of excess over —
$613	—$5,688	15%	—$613
$5,688	—$11,863	$761.25 plus 28%	—$5,688
$11,863		$2,490.25 plus 31%	—$11,863

(b) MARRIED person—

If the amount of wages (after subtracting withholding allowances) is: Not over $1,500 0

Over—	But not over—		of excess over—
$1,500	—$9,875	15%	—$1,500
$9,875	—$19,675	$1,256.25 plus 28%	—$9,875
$19,675		$4,000.25 plus 31%	—$19,675

TABLE 6—If the Payroll Period With Respect to an Employee is Semiannual

(a) SINGLE person—including head of household:

If the amount of wages (after subtracting withholding allowances) is: Not over $1,225 0

Over—	But not over —		of excess over —
$1,225	—$11,375	15%	—$1,225
$11,375	—$23,725	$1,522.50 plus 28%	—$11,375
$23,725		$4,980.50 plus 31%	—$23,725

(b) MARRIED person—

If the amount of wages (after subtracting withholding allowances) is: Not over $3,000 0

Over—	But not over—		of excess over—
$3,000	—$19,750	15%	—$3,000
$19,750	—$39,350	$2,512.50 plus 28%	—$19,750
$39,350		$8,000.50 plus 31%	—$39,350

TABLE 7—If the Payroll Period With Respect to an Employee is Annual

(a) SINGLE person—including head of household:

If the amount of wages (after subtracting withholding allowances) is: Not over $2,450 0

Over—	But not over —		of excess over —
$2,450	—$22,750	15%	—$2,450
$22,750	—$47,450	$3,045.00 plus 28%	—$22,750
$47,450		$9,961.00 plus 31%	—$47,450

(b) MARRIED person—

If the amount of wages (after subtracting withholding allowances) is: Not over $6,000 0

Over—	But not over—		of excess over—
$6,000	—$39,500	15%	—$6,000
$39,500	—$78,700	$5,025.00 plus 28%	—$39,500
$78,700		$16,001.00 plus 31%	—$78,700

TABLE 8—If the Payroll Period With Respect to an Employee is a Daily Payroll Period or a Miscellaneous Payroll Period

(a) SINGLE person—including head of household:

If the amount of wages (after subtracting withholding allowances) divided by the number of days in the payroll period is: Not over $9.40 0

Over—	But not over —		of excess over—
$9.40	—$87.50	15%	—$9.40
$87.50	—$182.50	$11.72 plus 28%	—$87.50
$182.50		$38.32 plus 31%	—$182.50

(b) MARRIED person—

If the amount of wages (after subtracting withholding allowances) divided by the number of days in the payroll period is: Not over $23.10 0

Over—	But not over—		of excess over—
$23.10	—$151.90	15%	—$23.10
$151.90	—$302.70	$19.32 plus 28%	—$151.90
$302.70		$61.54 plus 31%	—$302.70

Example: Joan receives $553.21 in wages biweekly. Her withholding allowance certificate shows she is single and claims a total of 2 withholding allowances. Total income tax to be withheld biweekly is $42.34, figured as follows:

Step 1:

Amount of one withholding allowance for biweekly payroll period	$88.46
Multiplied by number of withholding allowances claimed by employee	×_____2
Value of withholding allowances	176.92

Step 2: Total wage payment	$553.21[†]
Less amount determined in Step 1	176.92
Net wages	$376.29

Step 3:

The employer uses the biweekly table for a single person to determine the amount to withhold from Joan's wages. Since the $376.29 "net wages" is over $94—but not over $875—the amount withheld is $2.34 or 15% of $282.29 (excess over $94).

In this formula employers may round out the wage to the nearest dollar, or reduce the last digit of the wage amount to zero [Reg. Sec. 31.3402(b)-(1)]. Thus, if the wage is $553.21, the employer could also round out to $553 or determine the tax on the basis of $553.21.

(b) Wage-Bracket Withholding Method. Under this method, the amount to be withheld is found directly from the wage-bracket tables (an excerpt from which is illustrated on page 2513). They are set up by payroll period (weekly, biweekly, semi-monthly, monthly, and daily or miscellaneous), with separate tables for married and single taxpayers. The employer uses the bracket in which the wage payment fits and withholds the amount found in the column for the number of withholding allowances claimed (¶2510) [IRC Sec. 3402(c); Reg. Sec. 31.3402(c)-1].

When wages are in excess of the last wage bracket in the table, you should refer to the percentage method withholding table indicated.

A table combining the income tax and social security tax for weekly, biweekly, semimonthly, monthly, and daily or miscellaneous payroll periods can be obtained from the Revenue Service.[2]

(c) Alternative Methods. In addition to the percentage and wage-bracket methods, several alternative methods of computing withholding are available. Rules have been prescribed for employers to withhold on the basis of (1) annualized wages, (2) cumulative wages (at the employee's request), (3) wages for part-time employment (at the employee's request), or (4) any other method of computing withholding that comes within the maximum permissible deviation amounts set forth in the regulations [IRC Sec. 3402(h); Reg. Sec. 31.3402(h)(2)-1, 31.3402(h)(3)-1, 31.3402(h)(4)-1].

Employers may also withhold quarterly on the basis of the employee's average estimated wages [(j) below].

(d) When No Payroll Period Is Specified. If you pay wages without regard to any payroll period, or if you pay wages for a period not otherwise provided for by the percentage method schedule or wage-bracket tables, you can find the amount withheld by using the table for a "daily or miscellaneous payroll period" of the same length, or if the percentage method is used, by applying the amount of the withholding exemption for such period [IRC Sec. 3402(b)(1), (2), 3402(c)(2), (3)].

Short period. You may use the weekly payroll period table to determine the amount to be withheld when the period covered by the payments is less than one week [IRC Sec. 3402(b)(3), 3402(c)(4)].

Figuring withholding by annualizing wages. You can figure withholding by annualizing wages and finding the amount as follows:

1. Multiply wages for the payroll period by the number of these periods in the calendar year;
2. Determine the amount to be withheld from step (1) on an annual basis; then
3. Divide the result by the number of payroll periods[3] [Reg. Sec. 31.3402(h)(2)-1].

Biweekly Payroll Period-Married Persons
[For wages paid after February 1992]

And the wages are—		And the number of withholding allowances claimed is—										
At least	But less than	0	1	2	3	4	5	6	7	8	9	10
		The amount of income tax to be withheld shall be—										
$940	$960	$121	$108	$95	$81	$68	$55	$42	$28	$15	$2	$0
960	980	124	111	98	84	71	58	45	31	18	5	0
980	1,000	127	114	101	87	74	61	48	34	21	8	0
1,000	1,020	130	117	104	90	77	64	51	37	24	11	0
1,020	1,040	133	120	107	93	80	67	54	40	27	14	0
1,040	1,060	136	123	110	96	83	70	57	43	30	17	3
1,060	1,080	139	126	113	99	86	73	60	46	33	20	6
1,080	1,100	142	129	116	102	89	76	63	49	36	23	9
1,100	1,120	145	132	119	105	92	79	66	52	39	26	12
1,120	1,140	148	135	122	108	95	82	69	55	42	29	15
1,140	1,160	151	138	125	111	98	85	72	58	45	32	18
1,160	1,180	154	141	128	114	101	88	75	61	48	35	21
1,180	1,200	157	144	131	117	104	91	78	64	51	38	24
1,200	1,220	160	147	134	120	107	94	81	67	54	41	27
1,220	1,240	163	150	137	123	110	97	84	70	57	44	30
1,240	1,260	166	153	140	126	113	100	87	73	60	47	33
1,260	1,280	169	156	143	129	116	103	90	76	63	50	36
1,280	1,300	172	159	146	132	119	106	93	79	66	53	39
1,300	1,320	175	162	149	135	122	109	96	82	69	56	42
1,320	1,340	178	165	152	138	125	112	99	85	72	59	45
1,340	1,360	181	168	155	141	128	115	102	88	75	62	48
1,360	1,380	184	171	158	144	131	118	105	91	78	65	51
1,380	1,400	187	174	161	147	134	121	108	94	81	68	54
1,400	1,420	190	177	164	150	137	124	111	97	84	71	57
1,420	1,440	193	180	167	153	140	127	114	100	87	74	60
1,440	1,460	196	183	170	156	143	130	117	103	90	77	63
1,460	1,480	199	186	173	159	146	133	120	106	93	80	66
1,480	1,500	202	189	176	162	149	136	123	109	96	83	69
1,500	1,520	205	192	179	165	152	139	126	112	99	86	72
1,520	1,540	210	195	182	168	155	142	129	115	102	89	75
1,540	1,560	215	198	185	171	158	145	132	118	105	92	78
1,560	1,580	221	201	188	174	161	148	135	121	108	95	81
1,580	1,600	226	204	191	177	164	151	138	124	111	98	84
1,600	1,620	232	207	194	180	167	154	141	127	114	101	87
1,620	1,640	238	213	197	183	170	157	144	130	117	104	90
1,640	1,660	243	218	200	186	173	160	147	133	120	107	93
1,660	1,680	249	224	203	189	176	163	150	136	123	110	96
1,680	1,700	254	230	206	192	179	166	153	139	126	113	99
1,700	1,720	260	235	210	195	182	169	156	142	129	116	102
1,720	1,740	266	241	216	198	185	172	159	145	132	119	105
1,740	1,760	271	246	222	201	188	175	162	148	135	122	108
1,760	1,780	277	252	227	204	191	178	165	151	138	125	111
1,780	1,800	282	258	233	208	194	181	168	154	141	128	114
1,800	1,820	288	263	238	214	197	184	171	157	144	131	117
1,820	1,840	294	269	244	219	200	187	174	160	147	134	120
1,840	1,860	299	274	250	225	203	190	177	163	150	137	123
1,860	1,880	305	280	255	230	206	193	180	166	153	140	126
1,880	1,900	310	286	261	236	211	196	183	169	156	143	129
1,900	1,920	316	291	266	242	217	199	186	172	159	146	132
1,920	1,940	322	297	272	247	222	202	189	175	162	149	135
1,940	1,960	327	302	278	253	228	205	192	178	165	152	138
1,960	1,980	333	308	283	258	234	209	195	181	168	155	141
1,980	2,000	338	314	289	264	239	215	198	184	171	158	144
2,000	2,020	344	319	294	270	245	220	201	187	174	161	147
2,020	2,040	350	325	300	275	250	226	204	190	177	164	150
2,040	2,060	355	330	306	281	256	231	207	193	180	167	153
2,060	2,080	361	336	311	286	262	237	212	196	183	170	156
2,080	2,100	366	342	317	292	267	243	218	199	186	173	159
2,100	2,120	372	347	322	298	273	248	223	202	189	176	162
2,120	2,140	378	353	328	303	278	254	229	205	192	179	165
2,140	2,160	383	358	334	309	284	259	235	210	195	182	168
2,160	2,180	389	364	339	314	290	265	240	215	198	185	171
2,180	2,200	394	370	345	320	295	271	246	221	201	188	174
2,200	2,220	400	375	350	326	301	276	251	227	204	191	177
2,220	2,240	406	381	356	331	306	282	257	232	207	194	180

(e) Part-Year Employment Method of Withholding. You can figure withholding by the part-year employment method if the employee requests it. This request must state under penalty of perjury: (1) the last day of employment (if any) by any employer before the current term of continuous employment, if the employee was previously employed during the year in which the current term of employment began, (2) that the employee will work no more than 245 days during the current year and (3) that the employee will use the calendar-year accounting period. You figure withholding in the following order [Reg. Sec. 31.3402(h)(4)-1(c)]:

1. Add the wages for the current payroll period to the total wages paid to the employee for all prior periods included in the current term of continuous employment;

2. Divide total wages computed in (1) above by the total payroll periods to which that amount relates, plus an equal number of payroll periods in the employee's continuous unemployment just before the current term of continuous unemployment. Omit from the term of continuous unemployment any days before the start of the calendar year;

3. Determine the total tax that would have been withheld if average wages (computed in (2) above) had been paid for the number of payroll periods determined in (2) above (including the equivalent number of payroll periods);

4. Find the excess, if any, of the tax computed in (3) above over the total tax already withheld for all payroll periods during the current term of continuous employment.

(f) Supplemental Wage Payments. If an employee, in addition to regular wages, receives supplemental wages such as bonuses, commissions or overtime pay, the tax to be withheld may be found in the following ways.

Paid with regular wages. When a supplemental payment and the regular wage for the period are paid at the same time, they can be treated as a single wage payment for the regular payroll period [Reg. Sec. 31.3402(g)-1].

Not paid with regular wages. If a supplemental payment is paid at a different time than the regular wage payment, it may be added to regular wages for the current payroll period or the regular wages for the last preceding payroll period within the same calendar year. The total is then treated as a single wage payment for the regular payroll period [Reg. Sec. 31.3402(g)-1].

Tax previously withheld on regular wages. If you have already withheld tax from the period's regular wage payment, you can figure the tax to be withheld from a supplemental wage payment by using a flat rate of 20%, without regard to withholding allowances and without reference to any regular wage payment [Reg. Sec. 31.3402(g)-1].

> ► TIPS AS SUPPLEMENTAL WAGES You may treat reported tips as supplemental payments in finding the proper amount of income tax to be withheld. Tips may be treated as if part of the current or preceding wage payment, or if the tax already has been withheld from the regular wage payment, tax on the tips may be figured using the flat 20% rate.[4]

(g) Vacation Pay. Withholding on vacation allowances is the same as for regular wage payments made for the vacation period. If employees get extra pay for working during their vacation, it is treated as a supplemental payment ((f) above) [Reg. Sec. 31.3402(g)-1(c)].

(h) Sick Pay. Payments by employers under sick-pay plans are considered wages subject to income tax withholding [Reg. Sec. 31.3401(a)-1(b)(8)]. Payments by a third party, such as an insurance company or trust, are not subject to withholding, unless the payee so requests on Form W-4S or similar statement. A request for withholding, or change or cancellation of withholding, applies to payments made eight days after the request, and even earlier if the payer agrees. The minimum amount of income tax that can be withheld is $20 a week (or an optional 10% or more in whole dollars) and the amount of sick pay remaining after withholding must be at least $10. In addition, requested withholding may be provided under collective bargaining agreements [IRC Sec. 3402(o); Reg. Sec. 31.3402(o)-3].

> **NOTE:** A third-party that is paid an insurance premium and not reimbursed on a cost-plus-fee basis is treated as an employer rather than as an agent. That means the third party is liable for both the employee's and employer's share of social security and Medicare taxes with respect to sick pay, unless the liability is transferred to the employer.[5]

(i) Wages Paid on Behalf of Two or More Employers. If an agent, fiduciary, or other person pays the wages of an employee of two or more employers, withholding is figured on the total amount [Reg. Sec. 31.3402(g)-3].

(j) Withholding on Average Estimated Wages can be made, with necessary adjustments for any quarter, without IRS approval. You can also use an estimate in figuring tips an employee will report in a given quarter. You determine the amount to be withheld and then deduct it from each regular wage payment. You can make adjustments during the quarter and within 30 days thereafter to reflect tips actually reported by the employee [IRC Sec. 3402(h)(1); Reg. Sec. 31.3402(h)(1)-1(b)].

(k) Voluntary Withholding. If employees find that withholding will not cover their tax liability, they can claim fewer allowances on the withholding allowance certificate (W-4) than they would normally be entitled to given their marital status, number of dependents, etc. [¶2510]. For example, a married person can request withholding at the higher single rate in order to have more income tax withheld from wages. In addition, employees may request (by filing a new Form W-4) that you increase their withholding by a specific dollar amount. In turn, you must honor such requests automatically, and give effect to revised Forms W-4 in the first payroll period that ends on or after the thirtieth day after the employer receives the new W-4 [¶2512(b)]. Increased amounts that you are requested to withhold are then considered tax required to be deducted and withheld [IRC Sec. 3402(i); Reg. Sec. 31.3402(i)-1].

(l) When Allowances for Claimed Exemptions Offset Regular Wages. If the amount of regular wages due an employee for two or more consecutive payroll periods of one week or more is less than the amount claimed as exempt from tax given the employee's withholding allowances, you may elect a special method to find the tax to be withheld on supplemental wages received for those payroll periods:

1. Average the total regular and supplemental payments over the payroll periods;
2. Figure the tax to be withheld on the average amount for each payroll period; then
3. Subtract the tax withheld on the regular wages from the tax to be withheld on the average wages. The remainder is the tax you withhold on the supplemental payments [Reg. Sec. 31.3402(g)-1(b)].

(m) Withholding on Nonwage Payments. A voluntary agreement between an employer and an employee can cover payments for an employee's service not within the term "wages" (for example, domestic and farm workers' wages [¶2506(e)]. The agreement is effective for a period the employer and employee mutually agree on, but either one can end it by giving notice to the other. No special form is prescribed for the employee's request. However, Form W-4 must be attached to the request. Certain payments such as noncash pay for services not in the course of an employer's business, certain moving expense reimbursements and employer-paid group-term life insurance premises may not be withheld on under a voluntary agreement [IRC Sec. 3402(p); Reg. Sec. 31.3401(a)-3, 31.3402(p)-1]. For withholding on pension and annuity payments, see ¶2516; for withholding on supplemental unemployment compensation, see ¶2506(a).

¶2510   WITHHOLDING ALLOWANCES

Employees can claim on their withholding allowance certificate (Form W-4) one withholding allowance for each exemption they report on their income tax return [¶1111 et seq.]. They may also claim a special withholding allowance [(b) below] and additional withholding allowances for items described in (c) below. Spouses who are each employed must allocate their total allowances between their allowance certificates. An allocation also must be made if one spouse, or one single person, holds more than one job at the same time [IRC Sec. 3402(f), 3402(m); Reg. Sec. 31.3402(f)(1)-1, 31.3402(f)(2)-1, 31.3402(m)-1].

(a) Exemption From Withholding. An employee who had no tax liability last year and anticipates none this year may complete a withholding allowance certificate, Form W-4, claiming that he or she is exempt from withholding. You cannot withhold income tax from an employee who has filed such a properly executed Form W-4 [IRC Sec. 3402(n); Reg. Sec. 31.3402(n)-1]. Forms W-4 on which employees claim exemption from withholding expire on the 15th day of the second month following the end of the tax year. Therefore, employees must file a new Form W-4 by each February 15 if they wish to continue to claim exempt status [Reg. Sec. 31.3402(f)(4)-2(c)]. Exemption from income tax withholding does not affect the employee's liability for social security taxes.[1]

> **TAX ALERT** Someone who is claimed as a dependent on another person's tax return (for example, a child claimed on his or her parent's return) is less likely to be exempt from withholding. The child cannot claim exempt status on Form W-4—since he or she will owe income tax—if the child has any nonwage income, such as interest on a savings account, and expects wages plus this nonwage income to add up to more than $600 for 1992 (this figure is subject to annual indexing for inflation).[1]

(b) Special Withholding Allowance. Employees claim this allowance only on Form W-4. Generally, married employees with a working spouse, and employees who have two jobs, cannot claim this allowance. However, the two-job employees (including marrieds and singles) should claim an allowance if only one of their jobs paid more than $1,000.[2]

(c) Additional Withholding Allowances. Employees with substantial adjustments to income, deductions, credits and nonwage income can avoid overwithholding by claiming additional withholding allowances on Form W-4. Besides itemized deductions, employees can count deductible adjustments to income that include alimony, deductible retirement contributions (IRA and Keogh plans), net losses from business and net operating loss carryovers.[2] Allowances remain in effect until the employee files a new Form W-4 [IRC Sec. 3402(m); Reg. Sec. 31.3402(m)]. Form W-4 includes worksheets to help you figure your withholding allowances.

Because tax credits directly lower your tax, you need to figure withholding allowances for tax credits separately from allowances based on deductions. The Personal Allowances Worksheet on Form W-4 allows you to take an additional allowance if you have at least $1,500 of child or dependent care expenses for which you plan to claim a credit. If you do not meet this expense threshold, or plan to claim other tax credits (see below) not taken into account on Form W-4, you can use one of the following alternate methods of figuring withholding allowances.

Alternative withholding allowance methods. The IRS sanctions two alternative methods of calculating withholding allowances.[3]

1. Allowances may be determined without using the worksheets provided on Form W-4. The calculation must be based on current withholding schedules, tax rate schedules, and the Form 1040ES (Estimated Tax for Individuals) worksheet, and it must be more accurate than the Form W-4 method.

2. An employee may use an alternative method that takes into account tax credits that are not mentioned on Form W-4. These include: (1) the credit for the elderly and permanently and totally disabled [¶2403]; (2) the credit on certain home mortgages [¶2414]; (3) the foreign tax credit, if compensation wasn't excluded from U.S. income tax withholding just because it was subject to a foreign country's income tax withholding [¶3801-3803]; (4) the earned income credit [¶2402], if the employee has not applied for advance payment [¶2514]; and (5) the general business credit [¶2405-2411]. This alternative method may also be used if the employee is entitled to claim more than one allowance for child and dependent care expenses.

The "deduction equivalent" of the tax credits must first be determined. This is done by multiplying the total estimated amount of the credits by the applicable factor, which can be found in IRS Publication 505, "Tax Withholding and Estimated Tax." The factors as they applied for tax year 1992 are shown below.

Married Filing Jointly or qualifying Widow(er)		Single or Married Filing Separately		Head of Household	
If combined estimated wages are	Multiply credits by	If estimated wages are	Multiply credits by	If estimated wages are	Multiply credits by
$0 to 49,000	6.7	$0 to 27,000	6.7	$0 to 39,000	6.7
49,001 to 99,000	3.6	27,001 to 58,000	3.6	39,001 to 84,000	3.6
over 99,000	3.2	over 58,000	3.2	over 84,000	3.2

The result is included in the amount entered on line 5 of the "Deductions and Adjustments Worksheet" on Form W-4. An employee may use the worksheet for this purpose, even if it would not otherwise be used.[4]

Married persons figure their withholding allowances on the basis of their combined wages and allowable items (see above). However, this does not apply if they filed separate returns for the prior year and expect to file separately for the current year. An employee with two employers can divide the total number of allowances to which he or she is entitled among his or her jobs, but the employee can claim each particular withholding allowance with only one employer at a time[2] [IRC Sec. 3402(m); Reg. Sec. 31.3402(m)-1].

¶2512   WITHHOLDING ALLOWANCE CERTIFICATE, FORM W-4

Every employee must file an employee's withholding allowance certificate (Form W-4) with his or her employer. It is used to:

- claim the total number of withholding allowances;
- ask the employer to withhold an additional amount from gross pay; or
- claim exemption from withholding [¶2510(a)].

Employees who don't file a W-4 are subject to withholding as if they had claimed zero allowances [Reg. Sec. 31.3402(f)(2)-1(a); 31.3402(i)-2]. Furthermore, these employees are treated as single persons until they file a Form W-4 that indicates married status [IRC Sec. 3402(l)]. Penalties are imposed for false or fraudulent statements, for failing to supply a certificate, or for misstating withholding allowances [¶2562(b)]. The certificate is invalid for any altering or unauthorized additions to the Form W-4[Reg. Sec. 31.3402(f)(2)-1(e)].

An employee can claim a special withholding allowance for himself or herself, and additional allowances for certain dependents and other factors. Claims for withholding allowances remain in effect until the employee files a new certificate because of a change in circumstances [(b) below].

An employer is not required to determine whether employees have claimed more than the number of allowances to which they are entitled [Reg. Sec. 31.3401(e)-1(b)]. However, an employer must submit to the IRS a copy of any Form W-4 on which an employee claims (a) more than ten allowances, or (b) exemption from withholding when the employee earns more than $200 a week. The copy of Form W-4, along with any statement by the employee in support of his or her withholding claim, should be attached to the quarterly return (Form 941) [¶2552], but may be filed sooner. If the IRS finds such a Form W-4 to be invalid, it will notify the employer, who must begin withholding on the basis of the number of allowances stated in the IRS correspondence. The employer must disregard any subsequent Form W-4 on which the employee attempts to claim more than the number of allowances specified by the IRS [Reg. Sec. 31.3402(f)(2)-1(g)].

(a) New Employees. These employees must furnish a Form W-4 with their identification numbers to their employers on or before the date employment starts. Employers are required to request a W-4 from each new employee, and must give immediate effect to each form submitted [IRC Sec. 3402(f); Reg. Sec. 31.3402(f)].

Example 1: Kane starts work on Feb. 4, and gives his employer a Form W-4 that claims three allowances. The next pay period ends on Feb. 15. In figuring the withholding from Kane's salary on that date and thereafter, these three allowances will be used.

(b) Filing an amended W-4 on Change in Status. An employee may file a new withholding allowance certificate at any time if the number of allowances he or she is eligible to claim increases (for example, due to the birth of a child).

An employee *must* file a new certificate within ten days if the number of allowances he or she can claim decreases due to a change in circumstances [Reg. Sec. 31.3402(f)(2)-1(b)]. Here are some examples of cases where withholding allowances decrease:

- An employee becomes legally separated or divorced, or the spouse claims his or her own allowance on a separate certificate.

NOTE: The *death* of a spouse (or other dependent) doesn't affect withholding until the next year, but requires filing of a new certificate by December 1 (if possible) of the year in which the death occurred. If the employee qualifies as a surviving spouse with a dependent child, the status of married individual may be claimed for the following two years [IRC Sec. 2(a)].[1]

- The support of a dependent for whom the employee claimed a withholding allowance is taken over by someone else, so that the employee no longer expects to furnish more than half the dependent's support for the year.
- An employee has been claiming additional withholding allowances for estimated itemized deductions, while his or her spouse was not employed. When the spouse begins employment, a smaller number of additional withholding allowances may be authorized.[2]
- Eligibility for the special withholding allowance ceases (i.e. a single employee begins a second job that pays more than $1,000 per year, or a married employee's spouse begins employment paying more than $1,000 per year).[2]

When to give effect to revised Forms W-4. You may give effect to a new certificate filed by an employee with respect to the next wage payment made on or after the date the revised certificate is furnished. You *must* give effect to revised W-4s no later than the start of the first payroll period ending on or after the 30th day after the date that you receive the revised W-4 [IRC Sec. 3402(f)(3)].

Example 2: Johnson is paid semimonthly on the 1st and 15th of each month. She files a revised Form W-4 with her employer on January 4, 1993. Her new withholding amount must be reflected in her February 15, 1993 paycheck.

Anticipated changes in circumstances. An employee may not file a Form W-4 that claims married status unless the employee is actually married at the time the certificate is filed. When employees anticipate a decrease in the number of withholding allowances they can claim, owing to a change of circumstance that will take effect in the *next* calendar year (see the note regarding death of a spouse, above), the employees should file a revised W-4 on or before December 1 (if possible). In these latter cases the employer should not give effect to the revised W-4 until the next calendar year [Reg. Sec. 31.3402(f)(2)-1(c)].

¶2514   WITHHOLDING AND THE EARNED INCOME CREDIT

Employees who expect their earned income to be less than a certain designated amount (which was $22,370 in 1992) may be eligible to claim the Earned Income Credit (EIC) [IRC Sec. 32]. Qualified employees may receive this credit in advance payments added to their paychecks over the course of the year. To make these advance payments, employers may deduct the amounts from the income and social security taxes they withhold from other employees' wages. The amount of each employee's advance payments is determined from special wage bracket or percentage method earned income credit tables [IRC Sec. 3507; Reg. Sec. 31.3507-1, 2].

➤ **ADVANCE PAYMENTS** The earned income credit can vary with the size of the taxpayer's family. In addition, there is a supplemental credit for taxpayers with children under one year of age and an additional credit for health insurance premium expenses [¶2402]. However, the amount of the credit that can be claimed in advance is limited to the regular credit a taxpayer could receive if he or she had only one qualifying child [IRC Sec. 3507(c)(2)].

You must give notice of the EIC to all employees who claimed sufficient withholding allowances to offset their wages each pay period. (You do not have to notify employees who claimed exemption from withholding.) You can notify employees by using the official IRS Form W-2, which has the required statement on the back of Copy C.[1] Or you can use IRS Notice 797, or a facsimile with the exact wording of the Notice, to inform employees within one week before or after you furnish a timely W-2. If you use a substitute W-2, you may, on Copy C, use the language in Notice 89-95 instead of issuing Notice 797.[2]

¶2516   WITHHOLDING TAX ON PENSIONS, ANNUITIES AND OTHER DEFERRED INCOME

The withholding procedures used for pension, annuity and deferred income payments parallels those used for wage withholding. But different rates and rules apply depending on the type of payment. Payors of pensions, annuities, and other deferred income must withhold income tax from all designated distributions made by them, unless the recipient claims exemption from withholding on Form W-4P.

A designated distribution is any distribution or payment from an employer-deferred compensation plan (that is, a qualified employer plan or other deferred-compensation plans); any type of IRA; or a commercial annuity (annuity, endowment, or life insurance contract issued by an insurance company [¶1319; 1320]) [IRC Sec. 3405; Temp. Reg. Sec. 35.3405-1].

The withholding rate depends on whether the distribution is periodic or nonperiodic. In either case, however, the amount withheld can never exceed the amount of money plus the fair market value of other property received in a distribution. For this reason, a payor will not have to liquidate employer securities qualifying for special deferral of net unrealized appreciation, merely to satisfy withholding rules. If a payor has more than one program under which designated distributions can be paid, then each program must be treated separately. Also, the value of a noncash distribution is determined as of the last valuation date before the distribution [IRC Sec. 3405; Temp. Reg. Sec. 35.3405-1].

(a)　Periodic Payments.　Income tax is withheld as it is on wages, but it is calculated separately at the graduated rates set forth in the appropriate withholding table. The amount withheld is based on prescribed payment periods designated in the annuity or pension contract and the information on the Withholding Certificate for Pension or Annuity Payments (Form W-4P). If a W-4P is not filed and an election to avoid withholding is not made, tax is withheld only if the periodic payments are over $10,600 a year (as indexed for 1992). [1] This means a payee is treated as married with three allowances ($2,300 yearly or $191.67 monthly for each withholding allowance in 1992) using the percentage table even if the payor knows the payee is single [IRC Sec. 3405(a)(4)].

Payees who elect that no tax be withheld make this election on Form W-4P. Such an election must be given effect under the rules that apply to Forms W-4 (¶2512) [IRC Sec. 3405(a)(3)]. And the election remains in effect *until revoked* by the payee. The payor must give notice of the right to make this election no earlier than six months before and no later than the first payment date. Also, the notice must be furnished to payees even though their annual payments are less than $10,600 (for 1992). Follow-up notices of a payee's right to make, renew or revoke any election must be given at least once each year. Furthermore, payees who had benefits suspended due to reemployment must again be notified when benefits are reinstated [Temp. Reg. Sec. 35.3405-1].

(b)　Nonperiodic Distributions.　The amount withheld from nonperiodic distributions made after December 31, 1992, depends on whether or not the distributions are transferred directly into an eligible plan (such as another qualified retirement plan or an IRA). There is no withholding on a direct trustee-to-trustee transfer. But if the transfer is not direct, there is a mandatory withholding of 20% of the amount transferred. This 20% must be withheld even though you may have made a tax-free rollover. (Of course, you get back any excess withholding when you file your tax return for the year.)

The amount withheld from nonperiodic distributions made on or before December 31, 1992 is 10%, except in the case of qualified total distributions (QTDs). A QTD (generally, the taxable part of a lump-sum distribution) is a designated distribution from a Sec. 401(a) qualified plan [¶1319] or a Sec. 403(a) tax-sheltered annuity plan [¶1320] which is made within one taxable year of the payee, and which constitutes the balance of what is owed the payee under the plan. Accumulated deductible employee contributions are treated separately for determining if there has been a QTD [IRC Sec. 3405(d)(4)(B)].

For QTDs, the amount withheld is determined under special tables (reproduced in part on page 2521). These tables are based on the amount of tax that would be imposed if the recipient had elected lump-sum distribution tax treatment [IRC Sec. 3405(b)(2)]. If a QTD is payable in installments, two methods of withholding are available [(d) below].

Withholding Rate Schedule for Qualified Total Distributions Paid in 1992
(If the qualified total distribution is less than $200, no withholding is required.)

If the amount of the Qualified Total Distribution is:	Then, the amount of income tax withheld shall be:
Not over $20,000	5% of the Qualified Total Distribution
Over $ 20,000 but not over $40,000	$ 1,000 plus 13½% of excess over $ 20,000
Over $ 40,000 but not over $135,000	$ 3,700 plus 16⅔% of excess over $40,000
Over $135,000 but not over $205,000	$19,280 plus 22½% of excess over $135,000
Over $205,000 but not over $280,000	$35,030 plus 27% of excess over $205,000
Over $280,000 but not over $330,000	$55,280 plus 32% of excess over $280,000
Over $330,000	$71,280 plus 37% of excess over $330,000

Optional Withholding Table for Qualified Total Distributions Paid in 1992

At least	But less than	Income tax withholding is	At least	But less than	Income tax withholding is	At least	But less than	Income tax withholding is
$ 0	$ 200	$ 0	42,000	43,000	4,028	92,000	93,000	12,228
200	400	10	43,000	44,000	4,192	93,000	94,000	12,392
400	600	20	44,000	45,000	4,356	94,000	95,000	12,556
600	800	30	45,000	46,000	4,520	95,000	96,000	12,720
800	1,000	40	46,000	47,000	4,684	96,000	97,000	12,884
1,000	1,500	50	47,000	48,000	4,848	97,000	98,000	13,048
1,500	2,000	75	48,000	49,000	5,012	98,000	99,000	13,212
2,000	2,500	100	49,000	50,000	5,176	99,000	100,000	13,376
2,500	3,000	125	50,000	51,000	5,340	100,000	101,000	13,540
3,000	3,500	150	51,000	52,000	5,504	101,000	102,000	13,704
3,500	4,000	175	52,000	53,000	5,668	102,000	103,000	13,868
4,000	4,500	200	53,000	54,000	5,832	103,000	104,000	14,032
4,500	5,000	225	54,000	55,000	5,996	104,000	105,000	14,196
5,000	6,000	250	55,000	56,000	6,160	105,000	106,000	14,360
6,000	7,000	300	56,000	57,000	6,324	106,000	107,000	14,524
32,000	33,000	2,620	82,000	83,000	10,588	132,000	133,000	18,788
33,000	34,000	2,755	83,000	84,000	10,752	133,000	134,000	18,952
34,000	35,000	2,890	84,000	85,000	10,916	134,000	135,000	19,116
35,000	36,000	3,025	85,000	86,000	11,080	135,000	136,000	19,280
36,000	37,000	3,160	86,000	87,000	11,244	136,000	137,000	19,505
37,000	38,000	3,295	87,000	88,000	11,408	137,000	138,000	19,730
38,000	39,000	3,430	88,000	89,000	11,572	138,000	139,000	19,955
39,000	40,000	3,565	89,000	90,000	11,736	139,000	140,000	20,180
40,000	41,000	3,700	90,000	91,000	11,900	140,000	141,000	20,405
41,000	42,000	3,864	91,000	92,000	12,064	141,000	142,000	20,630
187,000	188,000	30,980	252,000	253,000	47,720	317,000	318,000	67,120
188,000	189,000	31,205	253,000	254,000	47,990	318,000	319,000	67,440
189,000	190,000	31,430	254,000	255,000	48,260	319,000	320,000	67,760
190,000	191,000	31,655	255,000	256,000	48,530	320,000	321,000	68,080
191,000	192,000	31,880	256,000	257,000	48,800	321,000	322,000	68,400
192,000	193,000	32,105	257,000	258,000	49,070	322,000	323,000	68,720
193,000	194,000	32,330	258,000	259,000	49,340	323,000	324,000	69,040
194,000	195,000	32,555	259,000	260,000	49,610	324,000	325,000	69,360
195,000	196,000	32,780	260,000	261,000	49,880	325,000	326,000	69,680
196,000	197,000	33,005	261,000	262,000	50,150	326,000	327,000	70,000
197,000	198,000	33,230	262,000	263,000	50,420	327,000	328,000	70,320
198,000	199,000	33,455	263,000	264,000	50,690	328,000	329,000	70,640
199,000	200,000	33,680	264,000	265,000	50,960	329,000	330,000	70,960
200,000	201,000	33,905	265,000	266,000	51,230	$330,000	and over	$71,280 plus 37% of excess over $330,000
201,000	202,000	34,130	266,000	267,000	51,500			
202,000	203,000	34,355	267,000	268,000	51,770			
203,000	204,000	34,580	268,000	269,000	52,040			
204,000	205,000	34,805	269,000	270,000	52,310			
205,000	206,000	35,030	270,000	271,000	52,580			
206,000	207,000	35,300	271,000	272,000	52,850			

When a nonperiodic distribution is a death distribution, the $5,000 maximum death benefit exclusion [¶1507(b)] applies in computing the taxable part subject to withholding. Death distributions qualify for the exclusion only if conditions similar to those for QTDs above are met [IRC Sec. 3405(b)(2)(C)].

A payee may elect no withholding for any nonperiodic distribution. Also, no withholding is required on any such distribution if it: (1) totals less than $200 a year; (2) consists of employer securities, or such securities plus $200 or less in cash in lieu of fractional shares; (3) is to a nonresident alien subject to withholding [¶2518], or who would be subject but for a treaty. The payor of any nonperiodic payment of $200 or more annually must give the payee notice of the right to an election of no withholding no earlier than six months before the distribution and no later than a reasonable time for the employee to elect out of withholding.

Otherwise, the payee might be unable to transfer the full amount eligible for a rollover. Any election must be on a distribution-by-distribution basis, unless regulations to be issued provide otherwise [Temp. Reg. Sec. 35.3405-1].

Distributions delivered outside the U.S. and possessions. Pension benefits and other similar payments delivered outside the United States and its possessions are subject to withholding. However, if the payee certifies to the payor that he or she isn't a U.S. citizen or resident alien or an expatriate for tax avoidance purposes, then the recipient may elect no withholding [IRC Sec. 3405(d)(13)].

(c) Payor's Liability for Withholding. The payor of a designated distribution is generally liable for the payment of the tax required to be withheld. However, in some cases, such as qualified plans [¶1300 et seq.], the plan administrator must withhold, and is liable for, payment of the tax. The plan administrator can, instead, direct the payor to withhold if the payor is furnished with the required information. The rules relating to wage withholding and deposits apply to tax withheld on designated distributions. Form 8109 must be used for deposits.[2] Form 941 or 941E, whichever is appropriate, may be used by payors to remit withheld taxes [IRC Sec. 3405(c); Temp. Reg. Sec. 35.3405-1]. Also, payees must furnish their correct TINs for an *election out of withholding* to be valid [IRC Sec. 3405(d)(12)].

(d) Withholding Tables for Qualified Total Distributions (QTDs). The amount of income tax to be withheld from QTDs is figured from either the withholding rate schedule or the optional withholding table. Each is arranged for graduated withholding that approximates actual tax liability. The withholding rate schedule is used for lump-sum QTDs and the optional withholding table is for QTDs paid in installments. To figure withholding from a QTD paid in installments, either of these methods may be used:[3] (1) use the optional table, or (2) withhold a flat 10% on each but the last installment and then deduct the amounts previously withheld from the amount shown in the optional table, illustrated below, for the cumulative payment [IRC Sec. 3405(b)(2); Temp. Reg. Sec. 35.3405-1]. See examples below.

> **Example 1:** Mr. Smith received a $50,000 QTD on March 1, 1992 on his retirement application filed on January 4, 1992. The profit-sharing administrator notified Smith of the right to elect exemption from withholding but Smith did not do so. Thus, the administrator withheld $5,340 ($3,700 plus 16 2/5% of the excess over the $40,000 bracket in the QTD withholding rate schedule).

> **Example 2:** Assume the same facts as in Example 1 except the payment was $190,000 payable in installments of $40,000 on March 1, 1992; $50,000 on June 1, 1992, and $100,000 on September 3, 1992. For a QTD that is paid in installments the payor can figure withholding under either of the following methods:

> *Method 1.* Using the QTD optional withholding table, withhold $3,700 from the $40,000 payment. Next, withhold $8,200 from the $50,000 payment by deducting the amount withheld on the $40,000 ($3,700) payment from the amount shown in the table for the cumulative payment of $90,000 ($11,900). Then, withhold $19,755 from the $100,000 payment by deducting the amount held on the two previous payments ($11,900) from the amount shown in the table for the cumulative payment of $190,000 ($31,655).

> *Method 2.* Withhold 10% from the $40,000 payment ($4,000). Next withhold 10% from the $50,000 payment ($5,000). Then withhold $22,655 from the final payment of $100,000 by deducting the amount withheld on the two previous payments ($9,000) from the amount shown in the table for the cumulative payment of $190,000 ($31,655).

¶2518   INCOME TAX WITHHOLDING AND NONRESIDENT ALIENS

Nonwage payments (e.g. interest, dividend or royalty payments) to nonresident aliens may be exempt from withholding if the income is effectively connected with a U.S. trade or business (see below). However, certain periodic payments not effectively connected with a U.S. trade or business are subject to withholding at a flat rate of 30% [IRC Sec. 1441, 1442; Reg. Sec. 1.1441-1–1.1441-4]. Wages paid to a nonresident alien for services in the U.S. are subject to withholding at the 30% rate, or at the same rates as U.S. citizens' withholding if the services are effectively connected with a trade or business in the U.S. See also ¶3800 et seq.

(a) Who Must Withhold. Usually, an agent that makes income payments is responsible for withholding on those payments. Agents include U.S. citizens, resident or resident alien fiduciaries, resident partnerships, and U.S. and foreign corporations [IRC Secs. 1441(a), 1442(a); Reg. Sec. 1.1441-1].

A corporation that pays dividends may assume that shareholders are U.S. citizens or residents if their addresses are in the U.S., if the corporation does not know their status. If the address is a foreign one, or changed from a foreign one to one in the U.S., tax must be withheld, unless a written statement asserting U.S. citizenship is furnished by the individual [Reg. Sec. 1.1441-3(b)(3)].

> **NOTE:** Special rules apply to partnerships (both foreign and domestic). Partnerships must pay a withholding tax equal to the applicable percentage of the effectively connected taxable income that is allocable to its foreign partners. The applicable percentage is 31% for noncorporate partners and 34% for corporate partners[1] [IRC Sec. 1446].

(b) Payments Subject to Withholding. Withholding may be required on fixed or determinable periodic income. This includes dividends, interest, rents, royalties, premiums, annuities, remuneration, emoluments and other income of this type. In addition, withholding may be required on the gross amount of certain items considered to be gains from the sale or exchange of capital assets. These generally include royalties on the sale of timber, coal or domestic iron ore [¶2238]; contingent income from the sale of patents and other intangibles and income from certain original issue discounts on bonds (¶1217) [IRC Sec. 1441(b)].

Income effectively connected with U.S. trade or business. Withholding on payments (except wages) is generally *not* required if: (a) income is effectively connected with the nonresident aliens' U.S. trade or business and is includable in their gross income, and (b) they file a withholding exemption statement (Form 4224) with the withholding agent (¶3811) [IRC Sec. 1441(c); Reg. Sec. 1.1441-4]. However, effectively connected income earned by foreign persons through U.S. partnerships may be subject to withholding [(a) above].

Withholding rates. When withholding is required, the rate is generally 30% of the income items, unless a lower treaty rate applies [(d) below]. The withholding rates on wages paid to nonresident aliens for services in the U.S. are the same as for foreign taxpayers. Foreign students and exchange visitors are subject to a 14% withholding rate on the taxable portion of their scholarships or grants [IRC Sec. 1441, 1442; Reg. Sec. 1.1441-1, 1.1441-2, 1.1441-4(b)(1)].

(c) Who Is Subject to Withholding. Withholding on *noneffectively connected* income applies to nonresident alien individuals (including alien residents of Puerto Rico), foreign partnerships and foreign corporations. Foreign students and exchange visitors are subject to the same withholding rates as other nonresident aliens except for the taxable portion of their scholarships or grants (¶1525) [IRC Sec. 1441; Reg. Sec. 1.1441-1, 1.1441-2]. Note that effectively connected income earned by foreign partners in U.S. partnership may be subject to withholding [(a) above].

(d) Tax Treaties on Withholding Rates. Lower withholding rates are provided in a number of tax conventions with foreign countries. To obtain the lesser treaty rate or exemption, the recipient must file Form 1001 with the withholding agent. The reduced rate for dividends applies when the payor's records show the stockholder's address is in the foreign country concerned.[2]

(e) Withholding on Sales of U.S. Real Property by Foreign Persons. This withholding serves to collect tax that may be owed by the foreign person. A buyer or other transferee who acquires a U.S. real property interest from a foreign person must deduct and withhold the lesser of 10% of the amount realized by the transferor (foreign person), or the transferor's maximum tax liability (the maximum amount that the IRS determines the transferor could owe on its gain on the sale, plus the transferor's unsatisfied prior withholding tax liability as to that interest) [IRC Sec. 1445(a); Reg. Sec. 1.1445-1].

Buyers use Form 8288 to report and pay withheld tax. Foreign transferors use Form 8288-A to report transactions.[3]

Special rules apply to distributions by corporations and for partnerships, trusts and estates [IRC Sec. 1445(e); Reg. Sec. 1.1445-5c].

PAYROLL TAX RETURNS, DEPOSITS, RECORDS AND REFUNDS

¶2550   GENERAL OBLIGATIONS

An employer who must withhold income taxes from wages must make a quarterly return on Form 941. The deadline for filing these quarterly returns may be extended if timely deposits have been made during the period. When to deposit the withheld taxes depends on the total amount withheld. Civil and criminal penalties may be imposed for failure to withhold taxes, pay over withheld taxes, or file returns.

Magnetic media. Employers may be required to use magnetic media (including magnetic tape, diskette, cassette, or mini-disk) to file the following information returns with the federal government: Form W-2, Wage and Tax Statement; Form W-2G, Statement for Recipients of Certain Gambling Winnings; Form 1042S, Annual Information Return for Wages Paid to Aliens; Form 1098, Mortgage Interest Statement; Form 5498, Individual Retirement Arrangement Information; Form 8027, Employer's Annual Information Return of Tip Income and Allocated Tips; and the Forms 1099 series of information returns [Reg. Sec. 301.6011-2(b)].

Employers must use magnetic media if they are required to file 250 or more copies of each type of return; each type of return is considered separately in determining whether an employer has reached the 250-return threshold.

➤ **IMPORTANT** Payers must file Forms 1099-INT, 1099-DIV, 1099-OID, 1099-PATR and 1099-B on magnetic media only if they are required to file 250 returns during the year [IRC Sec. 6011(e)].

Permission to file. Employers must apply for permission to file Form W-2 on a specific form of magnetic media from the Secretary of Health and Human Services. Applications are available at regional Social Security offices. An employer should send a completed application to: SSA, P.O. Box 2317, Baltimore, MD 21203, Attention: AWR Magnetic Media Processing. The application must be filed at least 90 days before the filing date of the return, but the SSA encourages employers to apply for permission as early as possible. If the application is acceptable, the SSA will send an authorization letter within 30 days.

Filers of Forms W-2G, 1042S, 5498, 1098, the 1099 series, and 8027 must get approval from the IRS by filing Form 4419, Application for Magnetic Media Reporting of Information Returns, at least 90 days before filing the information returns. Send the application to: Magnetic Media Reporting, IRS, Martinsburg Computing Center, P.O. Box 1359, Martinsburg, WV, 25401-1359. Both the SSA and the IRS will review the application and, if acceptable, will send an authorization letter within 30 days. Do not submit magnetic media until you receive such authorization.

Waivers. The magnetic media requirement may be waived for one year if a hardship exists. The amount by which the cost of filing on magnetic media exceeds the cost of filing on other media (e.g. paper) will be used to determine hardship. Request a waiver on Form 8508 and send it directly to: Magnetic Media Reporting, IRS, Martinsburg Computing Center, P.O. Box 1359, Martinsburg, WV 25401-1359.

Penalties. Employers who must file information returns on magnetic media, but who fail to do so without having obtained a waiver, are considered as having failed to file a return [Reg. Sec. 310.6011-2(f)]. But the penalty for failing to file [¶2562] applies only to those returns in excess of 250 [IRC Sec. 6724(c)].

Income Taxes

¶2552   HOW EMPLOYER REPORTS AND PAYS TAX

Withheld income taxes must be paid into a Federal Reserve bank or other authorized depositary with a preinscribed Federal Tax Deposit Coupon, Form 8109 (Form 8109-B is used by employers who have ordered but have not yet received their own preinscribed coupons). Penalties may be imposed if deposits are paid to an IRS Center.[1] The date of receipt as stamped by the authorized bank determines the timeliness of the deposit [Prop. Reg. Sec. 31.6302(c)-1(h)]. A deposit mailed on or before the second day before the due date is timely even though it may be received after the due date; the date of the postmark is considered the date of the deposit [IRC Sec. 7502(e); Reg. Sec. 301.7502-1]. But this timely mailing rule does not apply to deposits of $20,000 or more, if the deposit is made by an employer who deposits any tax more than once a month [(a) below]. Deposits of $20,000 or more that are not paid into an authorized bank by the due date will be considered late, regardless of when mailed [IRC Sec. 7502(e)(3)].

(a) When Deposits Are Made. The payroll tax deposit system has been very complex and often hit employers with "surprise" due dates for deposits. So the IRS has issued new final regulations that simplify the payroll tax deposit process. Employers can use either the old or new deposit rules for 1993. The new rules must be used in later years.

New Deposit Rules

The regulations eliminate eighth-monthly deposits and replace them with semi-weekly deposits. There are two general classes of employers: monthly depositors and semi-weekly depositors. Effective date: For employment taxes attributable to payments made after December 31, 1992.

➤ **ONE-YEAR OPTION** Employers can use the old deposit rules (see later) for 1993.

An employer's status as a monthly or semi-weekly depositor depends on the employer's prior deposit history rather than on current deposit liabilities. Under a so-called "look-back" rule, an employer looks back to the amount of its payroll tax accumulated during a prior 12-month "base period" to determine its current deposit schedule. This base period ends with the preceding June 30. (So the base period for the 1993 deposit schedule is July 1, 1991 through June 30, 1992.) This enables employers to determine their status several months prior to the beginning of each year.

➤ **IRS NOTIFICATION** The IRS will tell employers by November of each year which schedule they will follow for the coming year.

New employers. New employers are considered to have a zero amount of accumulated taxes for any calendar quarter in which the employer did not exist [Reg. Sec. 31.6302-1(b)(4)].

Adjustments: When determining the tax liability for a base period, employers look at the tax liability shown on the original return. Any adjustments for each quarter during the base period made on a supplemental return are not taken into account. However, adjustments made on a Form 941c that is attached to a Form 941 for a later quarter are taken into account in determining the tax liability for that later quarter [Reg. Sec. 31.6302-1(b)(5)].

Monthly depositors. Employers that do not accumulate withheld taxes totaling more than $50,000 in a base period year have to deposit each month's taxes by the 15th day of the following month [Reg. Sec. 31.6302-1(b)(2), (c)(1)].

Example 1: The Ace Co. determines its deposit status for 1993 using the base period that includes July 1, 1991 through June 30, 1992. Ace's accumulated taxes for that period are $45,000. Because the taxes it accumulated during the base period do not exceed $50,000, Ace is a monthly depositor. It is subject to the monthly rule for the entire 1993 year regardless of the amounts accumulated, unless the amounts trigger the $100,000 next-day rule (see below).

Semi-weekly depositors: Employers that accumulate over $50,000 in withheld taxes in the base period make deposits as follows [Reg. Sec. 31.6302-1(b)(3), (c)(2)]:

Payment Dates	Deposit Dates
Wednesday, Thursday and/or Friday	On or before the following Wednesday
Saturday, Sunday, Monday and/or Tuesday	On or before the following Friday

As under the old rules, deposits are required only on banking days. If a deposit is due on a non-banking day, it can be made on the next banking day. Semi-weekly depositors are always guaranteed at least three banking days before they have to make a deposit, assuming that the required deposit was not $100,000 or more (which would subject them to the next-day deposit rule).

Example 2: For 1993, Baker Corp. is subject to the semi-weekly rule because it had more than $50,000 of employment taxes that had to be deposited during the base period. Baker's employees are paid every Monday. One Monday, January 4, 1993, Baker accumulated $10,000 in employment taxes. Baker has a deposit obligation of $10,000 that must be satisfied on or before the following Friday, January 8.

Example 3: Assume the same facts as in Example 2, except that Baker has two pay dates, Monday and Friday. On Friday, January 8, 1993, Baker accumulated $8,000 in taxes on wages paid. Friday, January 8, falls within a different semi-weekly period than Monday, January 4. Thus, Baker has two separate deposit obligations: $10,000 that must be satisfied by Friday, January 8, 1993; and $8,000 that must be satisfied by the following Wednesday, January 13, 1993.

Special end-of-return-period procedure: Suppose a required semi-weekly deposit includes taxes for two different quarters. Then a special deposit procedure is provided. The employer has to use separate deposit coupons to remit the payroll taxes for each quarter, even though both deposits were due the same day [Reg. Sec. 31.6302-1(c)(2)(ii)].

Example 4: Eden Corp. has two weekly paydays--Wednesday and Friday. In 1993, it pays some employees on Wednesday, March 31, the end of the first quarter of 1993. Other employees, it pays on Friday, April 2. Payroll taxes for both paydays are due on Wednesday, April 7. However, the taxes for the Wednesday payday are first quarter taxes, while the taxes for the Friday payday are second quarter taxes. Result: Eden must use separate deposit coupons to remit the taxes.

Next-day deposit rule: Suppose accumulated taxes reach $100,000. Then employers would have to make a deposit by the next banking day. (This is the same as under the current rules.) This rule would apply even if the employer is normally a monthly or semi-weekly depositor. To determine if the $100,000 threshold is met [Reg. Sec. 31.6302-1(c)(3)]:

- A monthly depositor considers only those employment taxes accumulated in the calendar month in which the day occurs; and
- A semi-weekly depositor takes into account only those employment taxes accumulated in the Wednesday-Friday or Saturday-Tuesday semi-weekly periods in which the day occurs.

NOTE: A monthly depositor immediately becomes a semi-weekly depositor if it becomes subject to the next-day rule. It retains this status for at least the remainder of the current year and the following year.

Example 5: On Monday, January 4, 1993, Fairwood Corp. accumulated $110,000 in employment taxes as to wages paid on that date. Fairwood has a $110,000 deposit obligation that must be satisfied by the next banking day, regardless of its deposit status. If it was not subject to the semi-weekly rule on January 4, 1993, Fairwood becomes subject to this rule as of January 5, 1993.

Example 6: Graham Co. is subject to the semi-weekly for 1993. On Monday, January 4, 1993, it accumulated $110,000 in employment taxes. Graham has a $110,000 deposit obligation that must be satisfied by the next banking day, Tuesday, January 5, 1993. On this day, Graham accumulated an additional $30,000 in employment taxes. Although it had a prior $110,000 deposit obligation incurred earlier in the semiweekly period, Graham has an additional and separate deposit obligation of $30,000 that must be satisfied.

Safe-harbor de minimis rule: An employer that accumulates less than $500 in withheld taxes during the quarter does not have to make a deposit. Instead, the employer can remit the total payment with its quarterly payroll tax return [Reg. Sec. 31.6302-1(f)(4)].

An employer is considered to have met its deposit obligation if:
- The amount of any shortfall does not exceed the greater of: (a) $100; or (b) 2% of the employment taxes that had to be deposited; and
- The employer deposits the shortfall on or before the shortfall make-up date (see below).

Example 7: On Monday January 4, 1993, Holly Corp., a semi-weekly depositor, paid wages and accumulated employment taxes. Holly made a deposit on or before Friday, January 8, 1993, in the amount of $4,000. Subsequently, Holly determined that it had to actually deposit $4,090 by Friday. Thus, there was $90 shortfall. This amount is less than the greater of $100 or 2% of the amount required to be deposited. *Result:* Holly met the safe-harbor rule so long as the $90 shortfall is deposited by the shortfall make-up date (February 17--the first Wednesday after the 15th of the next month).

Example 8: Assume the same facts as in Example 7 except that on Friday, January 8, 1993, Holly made a $25,000 deposit, and later determined that it was actually required to deposit $26,000. Since the $1,000 shortfall exceeds the greater of $100 or 2% of the amount required to be deposited (2% of $26,000 = $520), the safe-harbor rule is not met. Holly is subject to a failure-to-deposit penalty [¶ 2562].

Make-up date: The make-up date for a monthly depositor is the return due date for the period in which the shortfall occurred. For semi-weekly or next-day depositors, shortfalls must be deposited by the first Wednesday or Friday (whichever is earlier) falling on or after the 15th day of the month following the month in which the deposit is required [Reg. Sec. 31.6302-1(f)(3)].

▶ **PENALTY ABATEMENT** In addition to the safe harbor, penalties will be abated if an employer shows that the failure to deposit the full amount of employment taxes was due to a reasonable cause (as provided in IRC Sec. 6656). An employer may have reasonable cause if it is unable to obtain information on a timely basis and cannot reasonably estimate the items for which the information is unavailable.

Old Deposit Rules

The frequency of deposits under the old rules depends on the amount of combined withheld income tax and employer-employee social security (FICA) tax the employer has accumulated. Generally speaking, large employers may make several deposits each month, while medium-size employers make deposits monthly and small employers deposit taxes on a quarterly basis [Reg. Sec. 31.6302(c)-1].

Eighth-monthly deposits for large employers. Deposits are required within three banking days after the end of an eighth-monthly period if combined withheld income tax and employee-employer social security tax for the period are at least $3,000 (but less than $100,000). The eighth-monthly periods end on the 3rd, 7th, 11th, 15th, 19th, 22nd, 25th and last day of each month [Reg. Sec. 31.6302(c)-1(a)(1)]. Saturdays, Sundays, local banking holidays and District of Columbia legal holidays are excluded in counting the three banking days [IRC Sec. 7503].[2]

Example 1: On March 10, Employer Abel has accumulated $3,500 in undeposited income and social security taxes. He must deposit the $3,500 within three banking days after March 11, the end of the applicable eighth-monthly period.

The due date for a deposit is based on the total amount of taxes accumulated with respect to the wages paid during a deposit period, whether or not any of those taxes have already been deposited [Reg. Sec. 31.6302(c)-1].

In applying this rule, taxes for a prior deposit period are not be taken into account if they were required to be deposited. However, taxes for a prior period that were not required to be deposited and all taxes for the current period are counted, whether or not any part of those taxes were deposited during the period.

Result: Employers are not able to make small pre-deposits during a deposit period in order to postpone a larger deposit obligation that would otherwise arise at the end of the deposit period.

Example: Midco accumulates $2,800 of taxes on wages paid during the eighth-monthly period from April 1-3, which Midco deposits on April 4. For the eighth-monthly period from April 4-7, its tax liability come to $2,500.

Result: Midco must deposit the $2,500 of taxes for the April 4-7 period within three banking days. Since Midco was not required to deposit the $2,800 of accumulated taxes for the April 1-3 eighth-monthly period, those taxes are counted in determining its deposit liability for the April 4-7 deposit period. The total amount of taxes for the two eighth-monthly periods is $5,300—more than the $3,000 threshold for making an eighth-monthly deposit.

Excess deposits: If an employer deposits more tax than it is liable for, the excess deposit is applied to the next tax liability. However, the overdeposit doesn't reduce the amount of tax accumulated when figuring the tax liability. Let's say Midco overpaid it's April 1-3 tax by $800. During April 4-7, Midco accumulates $3,750 in undeposited taxes. Although the $800 credit reduces the amount of tax owed for the April 4-7 period to $2,950, Midco still accumulated more than $3,000 for that period and must make a deposit within three banking days after April 7.

The deposit requirements are considered met if: (1) at least 95% of the accumulated tax liability for the period is deposited, and (2) resulting underpayments for the first and second month of each calendar quarter are added to the first required deposit made after the 15th of the following month. Resulting underpayments of $500 or more for the third month of each calendar quarter must be deposited by the last day of the first month following the close of the quarter (underpayments of less than $500 may be remitted with the quarterly return).

The deposit requirements are also met if (1) the employer did not meet the deposit requirements during any previous month of the current quarter, or during any of the four quarters preceding the current quarter, (2) the accumulated liability is under $10,000, and (3) the deposit is made by the 15th of the month following the end of the current quarter [Reg. Sec. 31.6302(c)-1(a)(1)(i)(b)(2)]. An overdeposit of employment taxes because of an incorrect estimate of tax liability may be applied to reduce the amount of tax required to be deposited for a later period, only if the employer so elects.[3]

> **IMPORTANT** The deposit deadline for eighth-monthly depositors who accumulate $100,000 or more of combined withheld income taxes and employer-employee social security taxes is accelerated. Instead of having to deposit these taxes within three banking days of the end of the eighth-monthly period, employers must make a deposit by the close of the first banking day after the day in which a $100,000 accumulation is reached [IRC Sec. 6302(g)].

All accumulated taxes on wages paid prior to that day are counted towards the $100,000 threshold, unless those taxes were required to be deposited. In addition, taxes deposited on any day with respect to wages paid on that day don't reduce the amount of accumulated taxes for that day.

The IRS uses a "fixed-obligation" approach in implementing the accelerated deposit rules. That is, if at the end of an eighth-monthly period you have at least $3,000 (but less than $100,000) in undeposited taxes on hand, your obligation to deposit that amount becomes fixed. You still have three banking days after the close of the eighth-monthly period to make the deposit. The fixed nature of the deposit obligation keeps that amount from being counted toward a future deposit threshold. On the other hand, if at the end of an eighth-monthly period you have less than $3,000 in undeposited taxes on hand, and you are therefore not obligated to make a deposit for that period, that amount must be carried over into the next eighth-monthly period and added to that period's accumulation to determine whether and when a $3,000 or $100,000 deposit is triggered.

Example 3: On Saturday December 19, 1992, the last day of an eighth-monthly period, Smith, Inc. has accumulated $5,000 in undeposited income and social security taxes. Smith has until Wednesday, December 23—three banking days after the end of the December 16-19 eighth-monthly period—to make a deposit. Then on Monday, December 21, Smith makes Christmas bonus payments that leave it with an additional $96,000 in undeposited taxes on hand. The accelerated deposit rules do not apply in Smith's situation, even though on December 21 Smith has on hand a total of $101,000 in undeposited taxes. Reason: The company's obligation to deposit the $5,000 was fixed as of the close of business on December 19. So that $5,000 is not carried over and added to the $96,000 accumulation to trigger an accelerated deposit.

Example 4: On Saturday, December 19, 1992, the last day of an eighth-monthly deposit period, Jones Corp. has accumulated $2,000 in undeposited taxes. Since no eighth-monthly deposit is required, the $2,000 is carried over to the next eighth-monthly period (December 20-22). Then on December 21, Jones accumulates an additional $98,000 in undeposited taxes. Because the $2,000 is carried over and added to the $98,000, Jones has a total of $100,000 in undeposited taxes on hand. Under the accelerated deposit rules, Jones must make a deposit by the close of the next banking day.

Eighth-monthly depositors who are subject to the accelerated deposit rules will be considered to have made timely deposits in full if (1) they deposit at least 95% of the required amount, and (2) resulting underpayments for the first or second month of a calendar quarter are added to the first deposit that is otherwise required to be made after the 15th of the following month. Resulting underpayments of $500 or more for the third month of a calendar quarter must be deposited by the last day of the first month following the close of the calendar quarter. This 95% safe-harbor rule applies even if a 5% underpayment made under the accelerated deposit rules is itself $100,000 or greater.

Example 5: On Saturday, December 12, 1992, Walker Corp.'s payroll date, Walker estimated that it had $2 million in withheld taxes on hand. As required under the accelerated deposit rule, Walker deposited the $2 million by the close of the next banking day, December 13. But on Wednesday, December 16, Walker determines that the actual taxes it withheld from its December 13 payroll totaled $2.1 million. Nonetheless, Walker will be deemed to have made a timely deposit in full—since the $2 million deposited is just over 95% of its actual $2.1 million tax total—if it deposits the $100,000 shortfall with the first deposit it is required to make after January 15, 1993. Reason: Even though Walker's underdeposit is $100,000, that amount isn't subject to the accelerated deposit rules due to the 95% safe harbor.[4]

Monthly deposits for medium-size employers. For any month in which an eighth-monthly deposit is not required under the above rule, a monthly deposit may be required. If the accumulated liability is $500 or more by the end of the month, the entire amount must be deposited by the 15th day of the following month [Reg. Sec. 31.6302(c)-1(a)(1)(i)(a)].

Example 6: Employer Robb's taxes for the month of January totaled $560. He must deposit the entire $560 by Feb. 15.

Quarterly deposits for small employers. A small employer whose accumulated liability does not meet the eighth-monthly or monthly deposit requirements explained above must make quarterly remittances. The payment can be either included with the quarterly return (Form 941) submitted to the IRS [(b) below] or deposited in an authorized bank.

(b)　When to File the Quarterly Return. The quarterly return and any undeposited payments that may be remitted with it are due by the last day of the month following the period covered by the return. However, if timely deposits in full have been made for all three months of a quarter, the employer is allowed ten additional days for filing [Reg. Sec. 31.6071(a)-1]. Form 942 is used for withholding on wages of domestics (unless the employer has elected to use Form 941), and Form 943 is used for agricultural workers' pay [Reg. Sec. 31.6011(a)-4(a)].

			Due date if timely deposits
Quarters	Quarter ending	Due date	have been made
Jan.-Feb.-Mar.	March 31	April 30	May 10
Apr.-May-June	June 30	July 31	Aug. 10
July-Aug.-Sept.	Sept. 30	Oct. 31	Nov. 10
Oct.-Nov.-Dec.	Dec. 31	Jan. 31	Feb. 10

Amounts deposited with banks are credited against the taxes shown on the quarterly return [IRC Sec. 6302(c); Prop. Reg. Sec. 31.6302-1].

(c) Where the Return Is Filed. Form 941 is filed with the Regional Service Center where the employer's principal place of business or legal residence in the U.S. is located. If the employer has no address in the U.S., the return is filed with the Regional Service Center at Philadelphia, PA.

Final return. The last Form 941 filed by an employer who goes out of business or ceases to pay wages must be marked "final return." The return must be accompanied by a statement showing the date of the last payment of wages and indicating where and by whom required records will be kept. The same procedure must be followed when a business is sold or otherwise transferred to another employer; in such cases the accompanying statement must also include the name and address of the purchaser and the date of the sale [Reg. Sec. 31.6011(a)-6]. In the event of a sale or transfer, both the predecessor and successor employers should file a Form 941 for the quarter in which the sale or transfer took place. However, if both employers agree, the successor can furnish the W-2 Forms to employees who continue to work for the successor employer. When filing Forms 941 and W-3 (Transmittal of Income and Tax Statements), successor and predecessor must each include the other's name, address and identification number. Predecessor employers file Forms W-2 for employees who were employed only by them, and must keep their Forms W-4 on file. Successor employers use the predecessor employers' Forms W-4 if transferred employees do not submit revised Forms W-4s [5] [¶2512].

Seasonal employers and those who only temporarily stop paying wages are relieved from filing Form 941 for quarters when they regularly have no tax liability because they have paid no wages. To alert the IRS that you will not have to file a return for one or more quarters during the year, you should check the seasonal employer box on the 941. The IRS generally will not inquire about unfiled returns if at least one taxable return is filed each year.[6]

(d) Employers Who Fail to Collect or Pay Tax. Any employer that has failed to collect, account for and pay over employees' FICA tax or income tax withheld from wages, or has failed to make deposits, payments or tax returns may be required in the future to deposit the taxes by the close of the second banking day after collection in a special trust account for the U.S. Government [IRC Sec. 7512; Reg. Sec. 301.7512-1]. In addition, monthly returns (Form 941-M) and monthly payments of tax may be required. In this case, the employer's quarterly returns are filed on Schedule A of Form 941-M. Severe penalties are levied for failure to make deposits and payments (¶2562) [Reg. Sec. 31.6011(a)-5(a), 31.6071(a)-1, 31.6151-1(a)].

> ➤ **TAX TIP** No matter how secure a future source of funding appears, an employer should never hold back payroll tax payments as a "bridge loan" to tide the company over. Persons who have discretion over the disbursing of company funds and who knowingly allow payroll taxes to go unpaid will be held personally liable for 100% of the unpaid tax (¶2562) [IRC Sec. 6672; Reg. Sec. 301.6672-1].

(e) Extension of Time. The IRS does not grant extensions of time to file Form 941 [Reg. Sec. 31.6081(a)-1(a)]. Also, there are no extensions granted for paying the tax [Reg. Sec. 31.6161(a)(1)-1]. But when the due date of a deposit falls on a Saturday, Sunday or legal holiday, the next business day is the due date [IRC Sec. 7503; Reg. Sec. 301.7503-1].

(f) Returns and Payment of Tax Withheld on Payments to Aliens or Foreign Entities. Tax withheld on payments to nonresident alien individuals, foreign partnerships or foreign corporations must be reported by the withholding agent on Form 1042. An information return (Form 1042S) must also be submitted. These are filed with the Director, Internal Revenue Service Center, Philadelphia, Pennsylvania [IRC Sec. 1461; Reg. Sec. 1.1461-3].

The withholding agent deposits withheld taxes into an authorized bank using a Federal Tax Deposit Coupon Form, under rules similar to those governing deposits of withheld income and employment taxes described above [Reg. Sec. 1.1461-3, 1.1461-4, Prop. Reg. Sec. 31.6302-1(h)].

A nonresident alien, foreign partnership or corporation must file a Form 4224 to get an exemption from withholding on effectively connected income.

A resident alien may claim an exemption from U.S. withholding tax by filing Form 1078 (Certificate of Residence) or similar statement with the withholding agent [Reg. Sec. 1.1441-5].

¶2554 STATEMENT TO EMPLOYEES, FORM W-2

An employer must give each employee three copies (copies B,C, and 2) of the Wage and Tax Statement, Form W-2 (or Form 1099-R for withholding on annuity, pension, or other deferred payments) by January 31 of the year succeeding each calendar year. Employees who separate from service during the calendar year may be given a W-2 at any time after termination of employment, but no later than January 31 of the succeeding year. However, if a terminated employee requests that a W-2 be furnished earlier, you must provide the W-2 on or before the later of the 30th day after the day of the request, or the 30th day after the day on which the last payment of wages is made [Reg. Sec. 31.6051-1(d)(1)]. Forms W-2 must be given, even though no income tax was withheld, if wages equal or exceed the amount of one withholding exemption. A W-2 must also be given to an employee who filed a proper certificate claiming that he is exempt from income tax withholding (¶2510(a)) [IRC Sec. 6051; Reg. Sec. 31.6051-1]. Employees covered by certain deferred compensation plans [¶1365] also get a W-2. Penalties are imposed for fraudulent W-2s and failure to furnish W-2s [¶2562].

(a) What to Include. Form W-2 must show the total wages paid (including noncash payments and reported tips), the total amount of elective deferrals from wages, the amounts deducted during the preceding year for income and social security taxes, any advance payments of the earned income credit [¶2514], and any amounts furnished to the employee under a dependent care assistance plan (¶1415) [IRC Sec. 6051(a)(7)]. It must include the employer's name, address, and identification number (EIN) and the employee (TIN) [IRC Sec. 6051(a); Reg. Secs. 31.6051-1(a), 31.6109-1].

(b) Special Reporting Rules. [1] Sick pay from an insurance company or other third-party payor must be shown on Form W-2. Box 9 should include the amount of income tax withheld from the sick pay by the third party payor. Box 10 should include the amount of sick pay the employee must include in income. Box 11 should include employee social security tax withheld by the third party payor, while Box 12 should include the amount of the sick pay subject to social security tax. Report in Box 17 any amount of sick pay *not* includible in income because the employee contributed to the sick pay plan, and label it with the code for nontaxable sick pay.

Third party payors who withhold on these payments must furnish employers with W-2s no later than January 15 of the year following that in which payments were made. Employers, in turn, must furnish similar W-2s to employees no later than January 31 of that year unless binding agreements between employers and payors designate the payors as employers' agents for furnishing W-2s [IRC Sec. 6051(f); Reg. Sec. 31.6051-3].

Dependent care assistance payments. The total amount paid or incurred under a dependent care assistance plan should be reported in Box 22 of the W-2. This amount must also be included in income taxable and social security taxable wages (Boxes 10 and 12, respectively) to the extent they exceed the limit on excludable payments [¶2506]. They should be included in the year the dependent care is provided, even if you pay for the care in a later year.[2]

Deferred compensation. *Qualified plan contributions.* Employers who make contributions to (that is, allow employees to defer compensation into) a Sec. 401(k) cash-or-deferred arrangement, a Sec. 403(b) salary reduction agreement to purchase an annuity contract, a Sec. 408(k)(6) salary reduction simplified employee pension, a Sec. 457 deferred compensation plan for state and local government employees or a Sec. 501(c)(18)(D) tax-exempt organization plan must enter the total elective deferral (including any excess) in Box 17 with the appropriate code. These employers must also check the deferred compensation checkbox in Box 6, as well as the pension plan checkbox (except for contributions to a nonqualified pension or Sec. 457 plan).

Nonqualified plan distributions. Employers must report the total amount of distributions to an employee from a nonqualified deferred compensation plan or a Sec. 457 plan in Box 16. This amount should also be included as income in Box 10.

Group-term life insurance. Employers who provide employees with more than $50,000 of group-term life insurance must include the cost of coverage over $50,000 as income in Box 10 and social security wages in Box 12. This excess coverage must also be reported in Box 17 and labeled with the correct code. The cost of the excess coverage is computed from a government table (¶1407) [Reg. Sec. 1.79-3T].

Employee business expenses. Advances or reimbursements to employees made under an accountable plan are generally excluded from gross income and social security tax and need not be reported on the W-2. However, if an employee receives a per diem or mileage allowance, the employer must include in income (Box 10) and social security wages (Box 12) any amounts received in *excess* of the government-specified rates [¶2003(a), (c); 2004(b)]. Such excess amounts should also be reported in Box 17 and labeled with the appropriate code.

Tip income. Box 10 of Form W-2 (Wages, tips, other compensation) should include the amount of tips *reported* by the employee to the employer. The amount of reported tips should also be shown in Box 13 (social security tips), even if the employer did not have sufficient employee funds from which to collect the FICA tax. On the other hand, Box 7 is reserved for the amount of tip income allocated to the employee by a large food or beverage establishment [¶2506(c)]. Allocated tips are not included in Box 10 nor in Box 13.

Armed Forces. A statement must be furnished covering pay for service in the armed forces if any tax is withheld or if any taxable compensation was paid [¶1206; 1527]. It must show the total taxable compensation paid and the tax withheld [IRC Sec. 6051(b); Reg. Sec. 31.6051-1(a)(2)].

(c) When the Business Is Sold or Transferred. If another employer acquires or succeeds to a going concern, and the services of the predecessor employer's employees are continued, the successor employer may agree to assume responsibility for furnishing Forms W-2 to those continuing employees. In such a case, all wages paid by both employers (including "other compensation" paid or the uncollected employee tax on tips) are included in the W-2 given to the employees by the successor employer.[3] No IRS consent is required.

(d) Extension of Time. Employers who show good cause may be granted an extension of time not exceeding 30 days for furnishing employees' copies or filing Form W-2 with the IRS. The application must be filed by when the Form W-2 would normally be given to employees or filed with the IRS, respectively. It must be in writing, signed by the employer or his agent, and must state detailed reasons for the request [Reg. Sec. 31.6051-1(d)(2); 31.6081(a)-1(a)(3)].

(e) Filing Requirements. *Employees* must attach the tax return copy of each W-2 they receive to their final income tax return for the year. If employees get an additional Form W-2 after filing their returns, they must file an amended return with the new Form W-2 attached. An employer may replace lost or destroyed copies with a new copy marked "Reissued Statement," but a reissued W-2 should not be sent to the Social Security Administration.[2]

Correcting Form W-2. Corrections are made on Form W-2c, Statement of Income and Tax Amounts, for errors made in previously filed Forms W-2 and W-3. Form W-3c should be used to transmit the corrections made for Form W-2c. Form W-2c (without transmittal Form W-3c) may also be used to correct errors in employees' names or social security numbers as well as to make corrections for one employee's W-2. Forms W-2c not delivered to employees must be kept by employers.

> ➤ **OBSERVATION** Employers who correct a W-2 before transmittal should give the corrected copy to the employee. Employers indicate the correction by marking the "void" box on the original Form W-2, Copy A.

Employers must make a reasonable effort to deliver the Form W-2 or Form W-2c to an employee. Mailing it to the last known address is enough. If it cannot be delivered, it should be kept as part of the employer's records for four years.[4]

Where to file. Employers must file Copy A of Forms W-2, Wage and Tax Statement, with Form W-3, Transmittal of Income and Tax Statements. Payers of wages should file Forms W-2 with one Form W-3. These forms must be filed with the Social Security Administration (SSA) as indicated in W-3 instructions by the last day of February after the calendar year to which the statements apply [Reg. Sec. 31.6071(a)-1(a)(3)].

Corrected statements. Form W-2c, Statement of Corrected Income and Tax Amounts, is used by an employer (or other payer) to correct errors in previously filed Forms W-2. Copy A of Form W-2c should be filed with the SSA. Form W-2c may be submitted alone (without a W-3c) to correct only an employee's name and/or TIN or to make corrections for only one employee.

Form W-3c, Transmittal of Corrected Income and Tax Statements, is used to accompany copies of Form W-2c. A separate Form W-3c must be used for each type of W-2. Form W-3c alone (without accompanying Forms W-2c) may be used to correct an EIN or establishment number. The original copy of Form W-3c indicates the proper SSA office at which to file it.[5]

¶2556   WITHHOLDING ADJUSTMENTS

Errors made by employers in withholding or paying the tax for any quarter may be adjusted without interest, in a later quarter of the same year [IRC Sec. 6205(a)(1)]. The method of making the adjustment depends on when the error was discovered.

(a) Errors Found Before Quarterly Return Filed. Suppose too little tax was withheld from employees. Then the correct amount should be shown in the return and the undercollection deducted from the next wage payment. If too much was withheld, a receipt should be obtained from the employees showing date and amount of repayment to them. If repayment to the employees is not made before Form 941 is filed, the amount collected must be included on the return and the adjustment is made on the return for a following quarter [Reg. Sec. 31.6205-1(c), 31.6413(a)-1].

(b) Errors Found After Quarterly Return Filed. Suppose the employer collects and pays more than the correct amount of the employee's tax (unless the employee requested extra income tax withholding [¶2510]). Then the employer may adjust the overcollection by repaying or reimbursing the employee for the amount of the over-collections in any quarter of the same calendar year. The employer may also reimburse the employee by applying the overcollection against taxes to be withheld in any later quarter of the same calendar year [Reg. Sec. 31.6413(a)-1(b)(2)(ii)]. If the overcollection is repaid, a written receipt with the amount and date should be obtained and kept as part of the employer's records. The necessary adjustment is made by a deduction on the return for any later quarter of the same calendar year [Reg. Sec. 31.6413(a)-2(b)].

The employer may report an underpayment on the return for any later quarter of the same calendar year or file a supplemental return for the period when the wages were paid. An underpayment reported by the due date of the return for the period in which the error was found is considered an adjustment. If the error is not reported as an adjustment, the underpayment should be reported on the return for the next period in the calendar year or immediately on a supplemental return [Reg. Sec. 31.6205-1(c)].

Employers may reimburse themselves for an undercollection of tax by deductions from the employee's pay on or before the last day of the calendar year. The employer and employee can settle the item between themselves within the year, if the deduction is not made [Reg. Sec. 31.6205-1(c)(4)].

> **NOTE:** Employers should use Form 941c to correct errors, or attach a statement to Form 941 explaining (a) what the error was; (b) ending date of each quarter in which the error was made; (c) the amount of the error for each quarter; (d) the quarter in which the error was found; and (e) how the matter was settled with the employee.[1]

(c) Adjusting Tax Reported On Tips. If employers do not have enough wages or funds available from which to collect the correct amount of the employee's social security tax on tips, they should deduct the uncollected tax as an adjustment on Form 941.[2]

¶2558   RECORDS

All required records must be retained until the later of four years after the tax is paid, or four years after the due date of the tax. Records relating to a claim for a refund, credit, or abatement should be held until four years after the claim is filed [Reg. Sec. 31.6001-1(e)].

(a) Employers' Records must show the persons employed during the year; their taxpayer identification numbers (TINs); addresses; wages and reported tips subject to withholding; amounts and dates of payments and deductions; and the periods of employment to which they apply [Reg. Sec. 31.6001-5]. Withholding allowance certificates and employees' notices of changes in withholding status should also be kept.

(b) Employees usually don't have to keep records (except for claims' purposes), but they should retain the duplicate copy of the Form W-2 [Reg. Sec. 31.6001-1(d)].

¶2560   REFUNDS AND CREDITS

If employers pay the IRS more than the amount withheld from their employees, they can get a refund or credit [IRC Sec. 6402(a), 6414; Reg. Sec. 301.6402-1]. The credit for an overpayment that was not withheld from the employee may be taken as a deduction on a return of tax withheld on Form 941. A statement explaining the deduction must be attached to the return [Reg. Sec. 31.6414-1].

(a) Employee Refunds and Credits. The amounts withheld during the year from employees are credited against their tax liability for the year. If the amount withheld exceeds the tax due, the excess will be refunded on timely application [IRC Secs. 6401(b), 6402(a); Reg. Sec. 301.6402-1]. Fiscal year taxpayers must claim credit for the entire tax withheld during the calendar year that ends in the fiscal year for which the return is filed.

(b) Nonresident Aliens. Withholding agents [¶2518(a)] who pay more than the correct amount withheld from a nonresident alien may file a claim for credit for the overpayment on the appropriate form, or may claim a credit for the overpayment on Form 1042. Withholding agents cannot claim credit for the overpayment on Form 1042, if you already filed a claim for credit or refund on the appropriate form or a claim for refund on Form 1042 [Reg. Sec. 301.6402-2, 1.6414-1].

¶2562   PENALTIES
[New tax legislation may affect this subject; see ¶1.]
Employers may be liable for penalties and interest for not collecting tax, not filing a return, not depositing taxes, nonpayment of tax, fraudulent withholding statements or for failing to supply correct information returns. They may also be subject to criminal penalties. Employees may be subject to civil and/or criminal penalties for filing fraudulent withholding allowance certificates and failing to supply a correct TIN.

The following is an overview of penalties that may be imposed in regard to employment taxes. See ¶3720 et. seq. for a more detailed treatment of tax penalties.

(a) Employer Penalties. The employer penalties are:

Failure to withhold and pay over tax. Employers required to withhold tax are liable for paying this tax, whether or not it is collected from the employee [IRC Sec. 3403; Reg. Sec. 31.3403-1], unless the employee files a return and pays the unwithheld tax.

These employers do not pay interest on the tax if they show to the IRS that timely supplementary returns covering the unwithheld tax were filed[1] [¶2556]. However, an employee's payment of unwithheld taxes does not necessarily relieve an employer of any penalties or additions to tax for failure to withhold or pay over tax [IRC Sec. 3402(d); Reg. Sec. 31.3402(d)-1].

Employers may be held liable for the total amount of tax not collected or paid over if they are found to have willfully failed to collect, account for, or pay over tax. A stay against collection of this penalty is permitted if (1) a bond is posted; (2) payment is made to start a refund suit; and (3) a refund claim is filed and court proceedings are brought within 30 days after denial of such claim [IRC Sec. 6672; Reg. Sec. 301.6672-1]. In addition to this 100% penalty, any person who willfully fails to collect, account for or pay over employees' tax is guilty of a felony, punishable by a fine of not more than $10,000 and/or imprisonment for not more than five years [IRC Sec. 7202].

Persons responsible for withholding and paying over tax (whether officers of the corporation or not) may be held personally liable if they willfully fail to pay the tax;[2] discharges in personal bankruptcy will not shield them from liability for the tax.[3]

Employers are not liable for withholding on tips not reported to them by their employees on written statements [IRC Sec. 3402(k); Reg. Sec. 31.3402(k)-1].

Failure to file return or pay tax. Unless due to reasonable cause and not to willful neglect, the penalty for failure to file a return is 5% of the unpaid tax for a month or fraction of a month, with an extra 5% for each additional month or fraction. The maximum penalty is 25%. If the failure to file is fraudulent, the penalty is increased to 15% with a maximum of 75%. For failure to file within 60 days of the due date, the minimum penalty is the lesser of $100 or 100% of the amount of tax required to be shown on the return. The penalty for failure to pay tax (unless the failure is due to reasonable cause and not willful neglect) is 0.5% of the unpaid tax shown on the return less credits and less any part of the tax paid on or before the beginning of each month; the maximum penalty is 25%. If for the same month an employer is penalized for both failure to pay and failure to file, that month's penalty for not filing may be reduced by 0.5% [IRC Sec. 6651].

Willful failure to file a return, supply required information, keep required records, or pay a tax is a misdemeanor punishable by a fine of not more than $25,000 ($100,000 for corporations) and/or one year imprisonment [IRC Sec. 7203]. Anyone who willfully attempts to evade any tax is guilty of a felony punishable by a fine of not more than $100,000 ($500,000 for corporations) and/or imprisonment for not more than five years [IRC Sec. 7201].

Failure to make deposits. Unless the failure is due to reasonable cause and not willful neglect, failure to make timely deposits of withheld taxes in an authorized government depositary is subject to a penalty equal to the applicable percentage of the amount of the underpayment. The applicable percentage is: 2% if the failure is for not more than 5 days; 5% if more than 5 days but not more than 15 days; 10% if more than 15 days; 15% is the deposit is not paid by the earlier of the 10th day after receiving a delinquency notice or the date the IRS sends a notice and demand for immediate payment (¶3722; 3728) [IRC Sec. 6656].

Under current rules, the IRS applies a tax deposit first to any due deposits within the same return period, with the oldest underdeposit being satisfied first. As a result, an employer cannot avoid earlier penalties on more recent liabilities without first satisfying earlier underdeposits. [4]

Example: In January, Hardy Co. incurred a $10,000 deposit liability that it has not paid as of April 1. Since that deposit is more than 15 days late, Hardy has already racked up a 10% failure-to-deposit penalty on that amount. As of April 7, it incurs an additional $10,000 deposit liability, which must be deposited by April 10. On April 10, Hardy deposits $10,000. It deposits an additional $10,000 on April 15. *Result:* The $10,000 deposited on April 10 is applied to Hardy's delinquent liability from January. The April 15 deposit is applied to the deposit liability due April 10—making that deposit 5 days late. Thus, Hardy will incur a 2% failure-to-deposit penalty on that deposit.

Failure to file correct information returns. Employers who (1) fail to file an information return (for example, a Form W-2) by the due date, (2) fail to include all the information required to be shown on the return, or (3) include incorrect information on the return are subject to a penalty, the amount of which depends on when, if at all, a correct information return is filed [IRC Sec. 6721].

If an employer files a correct but overdue information return within 30 days of the due date, the penalty is $15 per return; the maximum penalty is $75,000 per calendar year. If a correct information return is filed after 30 days but on or before August 1, the penalty is $30 per return with a maximum penalty of $150,000. If a correct return is filed after August 1, the penalty is $50 per return (maximum penalty $250,000). There are exceptions to these penalties for small businesses and for employers who make a small number of information return errors [¶3721]. In addition, these penalties are not imposed if an employer's error does not hinder or prevent the IRS from processing an employee's tax return [Temp. Reg. Sec. 301.6723-1T].

If a failure to file a correct information return is due to intentional disregard of the filing requirements, the penalty is the greater of $100 per failure or 10% of the aggregate amount required to be reported on the return. The $250,000 maximum does not apply in such cases; nor do the small business or de minimis exceptions (¶3721(a)) [IRC Sec. 6721(e)].

Failure to furnish wage and tax statement. An employer who fails to furnish an employee with a correct payee statement (e.g., the Annual Wage and Tax Statement or W-2) by the due date, or who fails to include all of the information required to be shown on the statement, is subject to a penalty of $50 for each failure (maximum penalty $100,000 per year). There is no de minimis exception, no break for small businesses, and no exception for corrected omissions and inaccuracies [¶3721].

If the failure is due to intentional disregard, the penalty is increased to $100 per statement or, if greater, 10% of the amount required to be shown on the statement. There is no $100,000 maximum in such cases [IRC Sec. 6722].

Fraudulent withholding statement or failure to furnish statement. An employer that willfully furnishes a false or fraudulent wage and tax statement or that willfully fails to furnish such a statement is subject to a penalty of $50 per fraudulent or unfurnished statement [IRC Sec. 6674]. In addition, that employer is also subject to a fine of not more than $1,000 and/or imprisonment for not more than one year [IRC Sec. 7204].

(b) Employee Penalties. The employee penalties are:

- A $500 civil penalty, imposed for claiming more withholding allowances [¶2510] on Form W-4 than there is a reasonable basis for claiming, if such a claim results in reduced withholding. A reasonable basis for a claim exists if the number of allowances is computed in accordance with Form W-4 instructions. Thus, the penalty applies to statements relating to withholding exemptions, estimated itemized deductions, absence of tax liability, and other false statements made to reduce withholding. However, the penalty does not apply if withholding is not reduced as a result of the statements, or if the tax liability is paid by withholding and estimated taxes [IRC Sec. 6682(a); Reg. Sec. 301.6682-1].

• A criminal penalty, imposed if false or fraudulent information is willfully given on the withholding allowance certificate or if there is an intentional failure to give information that would result in increased withholding. The employee is subject to a fine of up to $1,000 or imprisonment for not over one year, or both [IRC Sec. 7205(a)].

NOTE: The criminal penalty above is in addition to any other penalty. Thus, for example, the criminal penalty for willful evasion [IRC Sec. 7201] is not barred if prosecution for a false certificate is also possible [IRC Sec. 7205].

Footnotes to Chapter 15

(For your added convenience, in brackets [] with the footnotes below, you will find citations to related paragraphs in the "RIA U.S. Tax Reporter," "CCH Federal Tax Reporter," and the "RIA Federal Tax Coordinator 2d" multi-volume services.)

FOOTNOTE ¶2500 [USTR ¶34,009; CCH ¶35,002 et seq.; RIA ¶H-4500 et seq.].

FOOTNOTE ¶2502 [USTR ¶34,014.60; CCH ¶35,038 et seq.; RIA ¶H-4502].

(1) Otte v. U.S., 419 US 43, 34 AFTR 2d 74-6194.

(2) Firemen's Fund Indemnity Co. v. U.S., 210 F.2d 472, 45 AFTR 342.

(3) Rev. Proc. 78-13, 1978-1 CB 591.

FOOTNOTE ¶2504 [USTR ¶34,014.37; CCH ¶35,038 et seq.; RIA ¶H-4530].

(1) Ltr. Rul. 9201001.

(2) Rev. Rul. 70-447, 1970-2 CB 281.

(3) Rev. Rul. 60-77, 1960-1 CB 386.

(4) Rev. Rul. 71-144, 1971-1 CB 285.

(5) Rev. Rul. 90-93, 1990-2 CB 33.

(6) Treas. Dept. booklet "Employer's Tax Guide" [1992 Ed.], pp. 3, 4.

(7) Rev. Proc. 85-18, 1985-1 CB 518, superseding Rev. Proc. 81-43, 1981-2 CB 616.

(8) Ltr. Rul. 9129011.

FOOTNOTE ¶2506 [USTR ¶34,014.01; CCH ¶35,002-35,006.425; RIA ¶H-4580].

(1) Rev. Rul. 73-351, 1973-2 CB 323, distinguishing Rev. Rul. 66-41, 1966-1 CB 233.

(2) Rev. Rul. 70-471, 1970-2 CB 199.

(3) Rev. Rul. 68-238, 1968-1 CB 420.

(4) Rev. Rul. 61-68, 1961-1 CB 429.

(5) Rev. Rul. 73-13, 1973-1 CB 42.

(6) Rev. Rul. 69-136, 1969-1 CB 252.

(7) U.S. v. Kaiser, 5 AFTR 2d 1611, 80 SCt. 1204; Rev. Rul. 61-136, 1961-2 CB 20; Rev. Rul. 68-424, 1968-2 CB 419.

(8) Rev. Rul. 72-268, 1972-1 CB 313.

(9) Rev. Rul. 55-203, 1955-1 CB 114.

(10) Treas. Dept. booklet "Taxable and Nontaxable Income" [1992 Ed.], p. 8.

(11) Rev. Rul. 57-18, 1957-1 CB 354; Rev. Rul. 68-216, 1968-1 CB 413.

(12) Rev. Rul. 57-551, 1957-2 CB 707.

(13) Rev. Rul. 86-109, 1986-2 CB 196.

(14) Rev. Rul. 76-71, 1976-1 CB 308.

(15) Conference Report on H.R. 1720 [Family Support Act of 1988].

(16) Rev. Rul. 67-257, 1967-2 CB 359.

(17) Rev. Rul. 67-366, 1967-2 CB 165.

(18) Rev. Rul. 77-102, 1977-1 CB 299.

(19) Treas. Dept. booklet "Employer's Tax Guide" [1992 Ed.], p. 14.

(20) Rev. Rul. 57-33, 1957-1 CB 303.

(21) Rev. Rul. 61-146, 1961-2 CB 25.

(22) Rev. Rul. 181, 1953-2 CB 111.

(23) Treas. Dept. booklet "Employer's Tax Guide" [1992 Ed.], p. 20.

(24) Treas. Dept. booklet "Employer's Tax Guide" [1992 Ed.], p. 8.

(25) D.W. Smith, ¶50,249 PH Memo TC.

(26) Treas. Dept. booklet "Employer's Tax Guide" [1992 Ed.], p. 5.

FOOTNOTE ¶2508 [USTR ¶34,024; CCH ¶35,044; RIA ¶H-4586].

(1) Ltr. Rul. 7/27/43.

(2) Treas. Dept. booklet "Alternative Tax Withholding Methods and Tables" [1992 Ed.], pp. 17-37.

(3) Rev. Rul. 66-328, 1966-2 CB 454.

(4) Rev. Rul. 66-190, 1966-2 CB 457.

(5) Notice 91-26, IRB 1991-33.

FOOTNOTE ¶2510 [USTR ¶34,024.10; 34,024.23; CCH ¶35,060; RIA ¶H-4744].

(1) Treas. Dept. booklet "Employer's Tax Guide" [1992 Ed.], p. 7.

(2) Instructions for Form W-4; Treas. Dept. booklet "Tax Withholding and Estimated Tax" [1992 Ed.], pp. 3-4.

(3) Notice 88-42, 1988-1 CB 527.

(4) Treas. Dept. booklet "Tax Withholding and Estimated Tax" [1992 Ed.], pp. 4-5.

FOOTNOTE ¶2512 [USTR ¶34,024.09; 34,024.11; CCH ¶35,073.15; RIA ¶H-4748].

(1) Treas. Dept. booklet "Tax Withholding and Estimated Tax" [1992 Ed.], pp. 2-3.

(2) Treas. Dept. booklet "Employer's Tax Guide" [1992 Ed.], p. 7.

FOOTNOTE ¶2514 [USTR ¶35,074; CCH ¶35,283; RIA ¶H-4830].

(1) Instructions for Form W-2.

(2) Treas. Dept. booklet "Employer's Tax Guide" [1992 Ed.], pp. 14-15.

FOOTNOTE ¶2516 [USTR ¶34,054; CCH ¶35,OO6.075; RIA ¶H-4593].

(1) Instructions for Form W-4P.

(2) IR 84-48.

(3) Treas. Dept. booklet "Alternative Tax Withholding Methods and Tables" [1992 Ed.], pp. 38-41.

FOOTNOTE ¶2518 [USTR ¶14,414; CCH ¶33,902-33,916.54; RIA ¶H-4695 et seq.].

(1) Rev. Proc. 89-31, 1989-1 CB 895; Announ. 89-60.

(2) Rev. Rul. 60-288, 1960-2 CB 265.

(3) Instructions for Form 8288-A.

FOOTNOTE ¶2550 [USTR ¶60,514; CCH ¶35,160 et seq.; ¶38,970; RIA ¶S-5720 et seq.].

FOOTNOTE ¶2552 [USTR¶35,014.02; ¶63,014; CCH ¶35,160 et seq.; ¶38,970; RIA ¶S-5700 et seq.].

(1) Instructions for Form 8109-B, Federal Tax Deposit Coupon.

(2) See Treas. Dept. booklet "Tax Calendars for 1992" [1991 Ed.], p.1.

(3) Rev. Proc. 91-52.

(4) Notice 90-37, 1990-1 CB 343.

(5) Rev. Proc. 84-77, 1984-2 CB 753; Rev. Proc. 83-66, 1983-2 CB 585.

(6) Instructions for Form 941.

FOOTNOTE ¶2554 [USTR ¶35,014.01; ¶60,514; CCH ¶35,094 et seq.; RIA ¶S-5041].

(1) Instructions for the 1991 Form W-2.

(2) Treas. Dept. booklet "Employer's Tax Guide" [1992 Ed.], p. 14; Notice 89-111, 1989-2 CB 449.

(3) Rev. Proc. 84-77, 1984-2 CB 753.

(4) Instructions for Form W-2c.

(5) Instructions for Form W-3c.

FOOTNOTE ¶2556 [USTR ¶35,014.05; CCH ¶38,526; RIA ¶H-4730 et seq.].

(1) Instructions for Form 941E.

(2) Instructions for Form 941.

FOOTNOTE ¶2558 [USTR ¶35,014; 60,012.03; CCH ¶36,409; 5002B; RIA ¶S-3286; 3287].

FOOTNOTE ¶2560 [USTR ¶35,014.05; CCH ¶39,440.06; RIA ¶T-5809].

FOOTNOTE ¶2562 [USTR ¶34,024.12; 35,014.6; CCH ¶35,093.12; 40,645 et seq.; RIA ¶V-2650 et seq.].

(1) Rev. Rul. 86-10, 1986-1 CB 534 [¶34,840[10]].

(2) Gephart v. U.S., 59 AFTR 2d 87-1099.

(3) U.S. v. Sotelo, 436 US 268; 42 AFTR 2d 78-5001.

(4) Rev. Proc. 91-52, IRB 1991-33, clarifying Rev. Proc. 90-58, 1990-1 CB 642.

CHAPTER 16

ALTERNATIVE MINIMUM TAX

INDIVIDUALS

¶2600   ALTERNATIVE MINIMUM TAX FOR INDIVIDUALS

The tax law provides special breaks for certain kinds of income and expenses. Using these breaks may reduce your regular income tax but subject you to the alternative minimum tax (AMT) in its place.[1]

The AMT effectively takes away a portion of your tax savings and ensures that you pay at least a minimum amount of tax. It is figured on so-called adjustments and preference items that provide you with favorable treatment under the regular income tax rules.

The adjustments or preferences most likely to subject you to the AMT include the deductions for state and local taxes, and accelerated depreciation. You may also have to pay alternative minimum tax if you invest in tax shelters, own rental property, or exercise incentive stock options.

You are subject to the AMT only to the extent it exceeds your regular income tax.

Tax rate. The AMT rate, which is a flat rate applied to your alternative minimum taxable income (see below), is 24%. Since it is lower than the 28% and 31% regular income brackets, you could take advantage of significant adjustments or tax preferences without running into an AMT problem.

> **Example:** Bob Schey is a single taxpayer with no dependents. He has a taxable income of $240,000 in 1992 after subtracting $50,000 worth of AMT adjustments and preferences. That places him in the 31% bracket for regular income tax purposes, and his tax bill comes to $70,055 in 1992. The adjustments and preferences must be added back to his income for AMT purposes, which gives him an AMT income of $290,000. Since the AMT rate is only 24%, Bob's AMT comes to $69,600. Result: Bob has no AMT liability because his AMT does not exceed his regular income tax for the year.

Tax return tip. Individuals figure their AMT liability on Form 6251.

(a) Figuring the Alternative Minimum Tax. You can calculate your AMT liability as follows [IRC Sec. 55]:
1. Start with taxable income from Form 1040.
2. Add or subtract certain adjustments [¶2601; 2602].
3. Add all tax preference items [¶2603].
4. This is the alternative minimum taxable income.
5. Subtract out the applicable exemption amount [¶2605].
6. Multiply by the alternative minimum tax rate (24% for individuals). If this figure exceeds your regular tax bill, you owe AMT.
7. Subtract the regular tax liability.
8. This is the AMT that must be paid in addition to the regular tax.

(b) Adjustments Distinguished From Tax Preferences. An adjustment may involve timing writeoffs differently for regular tax and AMT purposes. For example, you may be required to use a depreciation method for AMT purposes that provides smaller deductions in the early years of use and larger deductions later on. But the same adjustment will actually reduce your AMT income in later years because your AMT depreciation writeoffs will be larger in those years than your regular tax writeoffs.

A preference, on the other hand, always increases your AMT income. You add back an amount deducted in calculating your regular tax. For example, a charitable contribution of appreciated property is a tax preference (but see ¶2603 for a special exception to this rule for 1992). For regular tax purposes, you can generally claim a charitable deduction for the full fair market value of contributed property. For AMT purposes, you must add back the portion of your deduction that is attributable to appreciation.

¶2601   ADJUSTMENTS

To the extent you defer tax from one year to another, you experience a financial benefit—the use of money over time. Many tax breaks, like accelerated depreciation, provide you with this kind of deferral. For the AMT, you must adjust your income to eliminate some or all of the deferral benefit.

In the early years, your adjustment adds to your AMT income. But in the later years (when you pay the deferral back for regular tax purposes), your adjustment reduces your

AMT income and actually provides you with an AMT savings at that time. This type of adjustment acts as an "averaging device" and prevents you from being taxed twice on the same income: once for regular tax purposes and again for the alternative minimum tax.

Other adjustments substitute your regular tax deduction for an AMT deduction. For example, your personal and dependency exemptions are not allowed for AMT purposes. So you must add them back to your taxable income to calculate your AMT liability. In their place, you get a specific AMT exemption of $40,000 for married taxpayers filing jointly ($30,000 for single taxpayers or heads of households) [¶2605].

The tax law specifies what items are to be treated as adjustments and which ones are to be treated as preferences. The following are the adjustments used to compute your alternative minimum taxable income [IRC Sec. 56, 58]:

- Personal and dependency exemptions are not allowed for the AMT. Specific exemptions are allowed in their place.
- Certain itemized deductions are cut back or disallowed for the AMT [¶2602].
- The standard deduction for those who do not itemize is not allowed for the AMT.
- Accelerated depreciation on real and personal property placed in service after 1986.
- Mining exploration and development costs.
- Long-term contracts.
- Amortization of certified pollution control facilities.
- Installment sales of certain property.
- Alternative tax net operating losses.
- Research and experimental expenditures.
- Circulation costs.
- Adjusted basis of property subject to depreciation, depletion, or amortization.
- Passive activity losses.
- Tax shelter farm losses.
- Incentive stock options.

(a) Accelerated Depreciation. When computing AMT income, depreciation is limited to the alternate Modified Accelerated Cost Recovery System [¶2110 et seq.].

Real property. Your AMT depreciation writeoffs for real property are limited to the straight line method over a 40-year recovery period [IRC Sec. 56(a)(1)].

> ➤ **OBSERVATION** This results in lower up-front depreciation deductions since the recovery period is longer than the usual 27½-year period for residential property or the 31½-year period for nonresidential property.

Example 1: In January 1992, Ms. Graham placed residential rental property in service that cost her $240,000 ($40,000 for the land). Regular depreciation under MACRS is $6,970. Using the alternate method for AMT purposes, depreciation is $4,792. The difference between the two figures of $2,178 is an adjustment that must be added back to Graham's taxable income for AMT purposes.

NOTE: By the year 2020 Graham will have exhausted her depreciation writeoffs for regular tax purposes—the 27½ years will be up. But for AMT purposes, Graham will still be entitled to a depreciation deduction because those writeoffs are spread out over the longer 40-year period. As a result, the adjustment in that year will actually reduce her AMT income.

Personal property. For most property other than real estate, your AMT depreciation writeoffs are based on the limited declining balance method (1½ times the straight line rate), and you switch to the straight line method when it results in a larger allowance.

Your regular tax depreciation writeoffs are normally based on the double declining balance method (twice the straight line rate). An AMT adjustment is required to eliminate the effect of the faster writeoffs.

Netting. In calculating the depreciation adjustment, all items for which depreciation has been taken for the year are netted together. The adjustment is the difference between the total depreciation for all property for AMT purposes and the total depreciation for regular income tax purposes.

> ➤ **OBSERVATION** If you elect to use the alternate depreciation method for regular tax purposes, no AMT adjustment need be made. The alternate depreciation deduction is calculated by using the straight line method over a 40-year recovery period [¶2112(f)].

NOTE: Under prior law, accelerated depreciation was considered a tax preference item. The accelerated depreciation of property placed in service before 1987 continues to be a tax preference item [IRC Sec. 56(a)].

(b) Mining Costs. For your regular income tax, you may be able to deduct fully mining exploration and development costs incurred during the year. Current writeoffs are not allowed for AMT purposes. Instead, you must ratably amortize costs incurred after 1986 over a ten-year period. However, if you abandon the mine as worthless, an immediate writeoff is allowed for both the regular tax and the AMT [IRC Sec. 56(a)(2)].

(c) Long-Term Contracts. A long-term contract is a contract for the production, manufacture, building, installation, or construction of property that is not started and completed in the same tax year [¶2942].

The usual way to report income and expenses is the percentage of completion method. The amount of the contract's income taxed to you in a particular year is based on the percentage of work you complete in that year.

For long-term contracts entered into after February 28, 1986, you must use the percentage of completion method to calculate your AMT [IRC Sec. 56(a)(3)].

NOTE: All home construction contracts entered into in tax years starting after September 30, 1990, are exempt from having to use the percentage of completion method for AMT purposes.

(d) Amortization of Certified Pollution Control Facilities. For regular tax purposes, you may be able to write off the cost of a pollution control facility (e.g., septic tax) over a five-year amortization period. For the AMT, your amortization deduction for a facility placed in service after 1986 is found by using the alternative depreciation system (¶2112(f)) [IRC Sec. 56(a)(5)]. This means your AMT writeoffs are stretched out over a longer period of time under the same principles that apply to real estate.

(e) Alternative Tax Net Operating Loss. The net operating loss (NOL) for alternative minimum tax purposes is figured the same way as for regular tax purposes with two exceptions. First, the loss cannot offset more than 90% of your AMT income. Second, the operating loss is subject to the AMT adjustments and preferences, but preferences are taken into account only to the extent they increased the NOL for regular tax purposes [IRC Sec. 56(d)].

Example 2: In 1992, Mr. Parker has a gross income of $20,000 and deductions of $35,000, of which $10,000 are due to AMT adjustments and preference items. Thus, Parker's NOL for regular tax purposes is $15,000. However, the AMT net operating loss for the year is $5,000 [$20,000 – ($35,000 – $10,000)]. He can carry the $5,000 loss forward or back to reduce income that is subject to the alternative minimum tax.

Example 3: Same facts as in Example 2. In 1993, Parker has alternative minimum taxable income, without regard to the NOL deduction, of $20,000. He reduces his alternative minimum taxable income to $15,000 because of 1992's $5,000 carryforward. His net operating loss deduction for the regular tax isn't affected by this computation. He has a $15,000 loss carryover from 1992, which he can use to offset his regular tax.

(f) Research and Experimental Expenditures. For the regular tax, you can fully deduct research and experimental expenses incurred during the year [¶2231]. For the AMT, these costs must be amortized ratably over a ten-year period starting with the tax year you incurred the costs [IRC Sec. 56(b)(2)].

Example 4: Mr. Ames incurred $10,000 in research and experimental expenses. He claims a regular tax deduction for the entire amount but can claim an AMT deduction of only $1,000 for that year and each of the next nine years. A $9,000 adjustment must be added to his income for AMT purposes. In each of the subsequent nine years, the adjustment reduces his income by $1,000.

NOTE: For tax years starting after 1990, there is no AMT adjustment for individuals who materially participate in a research activity (whether as a sole proprietor, partnership or S corporation) in which the expenses are paid or incurred [IRC Sec. 56(b)(2)(D)].

(g) Circulation Costs. In figuring alternative minimum taxable income, circulation costs must be amortized over three years starting with the tax year in which the expenditures were made [IRC Sec. 56(b)(2)].

(h) Sale of Depreciable Property. For computing the alternative minimum tax, the adjusted basis of property that is subject to a depreciation adjustment is equal to the asset's cost less accumulated alternative minimum tax depreciation [IRC Sec. 56(a)(7)]. Since allowances for regular tax purposes and for alternative minimum tax purposes differ, the adjusted basis of each asset (for example, for gain or loss on disposition) may also be different. Thus, a sale could result in gain for regular tax purposes and in a loss for the alternative minimum tax.

(i) Passive Losses. Deductions for passive activity losses are limited for both the regular tax and AMT. Passive losses are deductible only to the extent of passive income for regular tax purposes [¶2326]. Passive losses are also subject to the adjustments and tax preferences discussed earlier. This means, for example, that a passive loss must appropriately reflect accelerated depreciation. A special exception allows insolvent taxpayers to deduct passive losses for AMT purposes to the extent liabilities exceed assets [IRC Sec. 58(b), (c)(1)].

(j) Farm Losses. Tax shelter farm losses are treated in a similar fashion as passive activity losses [IRC Sec. 58(b), (c)(1)].

(k) Incentive Stock Options. When you acquire or exercise an incentive stock option, you do not pay income tax [¶1208(b)]. But the excess of the stock's fair market value over the amount you pay for it (the so-called bargain element) is an adjustment that must be added to your taxable income for AMT purposes. When you eventually sell the stock, you pay regular income tax. Since the stock is subject to the AMT in the year of exercise, your adjustment reduces AMT income in the year of sale [IRC Sec. 56(b)(3)].

Example 5: Mr. Kelly exercises an incentive stock option for 100 shares of his employer's stock. The exercise price is $25 per share, and the fair market value is $75. The adjustment in the year of exercise is $50 per share for a total of $5,000. This amount must be added to his income for AMT purposes even though exercising the option is not a taxable event for regular tax purposes. Kelly's basis for regular tax purposes is $25 per share and for AMT purposes is $75. When Kelly sells the stock several years later, he pays regular tax on the options but reduces his income in that year for AMT purposes—since the stock was previously subject to the AMT.

¶2602   ADJUSTMENTS FOR ITEMIZED DEDUCTIONS

To figure your AMT income, some of your regular tax itemized deductions are restricted, while others are disallowed [IRC Sec. 56(b)(1)]. Certain itemized deductions, such as charitable contributions of cash, require no adjustment for the AMT.

> ▶ **OBSERVATION** If you are a high-income taxpayer, you may lose part of your itemized deductions for purposes of computing your regular tax bill [¶1900]. However, this reduction in itemized deductions is disregarded in figuring the alternative minimum taxable income [IRC Sec. 56(b)(1)(F)].

Medical expenses. When computing regular income tax, medical expenses are deductible to the extent they exceed 7½% of your adjusted gross income. When computing alternative minimum tax, medical expenses are deductible only to the extent they exceed 10% of your AGI. Thus, for the AMT, you must add back any medical expense deduction up to 2½% of your AGI.

Miscellaneous itemized deductions. For the regular tax, miscellaneous itemized deductions are divided into two tiers. Those expenses which fall into the first tier are fully deductible, while those expenses in the second tier are only deductible to the extent they exceed, in the aggregate, 2% of your AGI. For the AMT, expenses in the second tier are not deductible at all, so you must add back to taxable income any regular tax deduction. This preference applies, for example, to your regular tax deduction for employee business expenses [¶1942; 1943].

Taxes. Income and real property taxes imposed by a state or its subdivision or by a foreign country are not deductible for the AMT. Additionally, state and local personal property taxes are not deductible. Thus, you must add back these deductions for regular income tax to arrive at AMT income.

Personal residence. For both regular and AMT purposes, you may deduct the interest on a loan of $1,000,000 or less if the proceeds are used to acquire, construct, or substantially rehab up to two personal residences. Home equity interest on loans up to $100,000 is deductible for the regular tax, but not for the AMT.

¶2603   PREFERENCES

[New tax legislation may affect this subject; see ¶1]
You must add so-called tax preference items to your taxable income for AMT purposes. Preferences can take the form of deductions, lower tax rates or exclusions that you enjoyed for regular tax purposes. Generally, only the amount of the benefit received less the benefit otherwise allowed is counted as a tax preference item. These are the preference items that can increase your AMT income [IRC Sec. 57(a)]:

- Charitable contributions of appreciated property [¶1917].

> ▶ **BIG BREAK** The appreciaton in value of tangible personal property you donate by June 30, 1992, is not a tax preference for AMT purposes.

- Interest on certain tax-exempt private activity bonds issued after August 7, 1986.
- Accelerated depreciation on property placed in service before 1987.

- Excess of intangible drilling costs deduction over 65% of the net income from oil, gas and geothermal properties [¶2236].
- Percentage depletion deduction in excess of adjusted basis in oil, gas and geothermal properties [¶2237]. The Federal Court of Appeals has said adjusted basis includes (1) basis in deposits, (2) capitalized, intangible drilling costs and (3) capitalized tangible drilling costs.[1]

Since 1991, there has been an energy deduction for computing the alternative minimum taxable income. This deduction is based on a portion of various oil and gas related tax preference items [¶2604].

(a) Charitable Contributions of Appreciated Property. If you make a charitable donation of property that has appreciated in value, the amount of your regular tax charitable deduction that exceeds the property's adjusted basis is treated as a tax preference item [IRC Sec. 57(a)(6)].

> ➤ **BIG BREAK** If by June 30, 1992, you donate tangible personal property (for example, artwork given to a museum) that's put to a use related to the donee's tax-exempt purpose, the untaxed appreciation is not a tax preference item. Also, any carryover of excess donations to future years won't generate a tax preference.[1] However, the appreciation in value of any other kind of charitable gift (for example, donating stock shares) continues to be a tax preference.

(b) Interest on Certain Private Activity Bonds. You may have invested in tax-exempt private activity bonds issued by a state or municipality after August 7, 1986, to finance mass commuting facilities, qualified multifamily residential rental projects, and such. To the extent interest on these bonds is tax-free for regular tax purposes, you have a preference that must be added to your income for AMT purposes. However, expenses and interest you pay in connection with owning these bonds reduce the amount of your preference—even if not deductible for the regular tax [IRC Sec. 57(a)(5)].

(c) Accelerated Depreciation on Property Placed in Service Before 1987. For real property, this tax preference item is the depreciation taken during the year, minus the depreciation that would have been allowed under the straight line method. This amount is figured separately for each item of property. Generally, each building (or its component) is a separate item of property. Do not figure this preference for an item of property in the year of its disposition [IRC Sec. 57(a)(7)].

> ➤ **OBSERVATION** For real estate being depreciated over a 15-year, 18-year, or 19-year period under ACRS, figure straight line depreciation using a recovery period of 15 years for 15-year property, 18 years for 18-year property, and 19 years for 19-year real property, and no salvage value [¶2114]. However, if the actual recovery period is longer than 15, 18, or 19 years and the property was placed in service before 1987, there is no tax preference item.

For leased personal property, your tax preference is the actual depreciation or amortization taken during the tax year on the property leased to others, less the depreciation or amortization that would have been allowed under the straight line method. This preference item is figured separately for each item of personal property leased out. However, you have no preference for the year you dispose of the property [IRC Sec. 56(a)(1)]. For leased personal property depreciated under ACRS, figure straight line depreciation using a half-year convention, no salvage value, and the following recovery periods: For 3-year property—5 years; 5-year property—8 years; 10-year property—15 years; and 15-year public utility property—22 years [¶2120]. However, if the actual recovery period is longer than that listed for the property, there is no tax preference item.

> **OBSERVATION**   Accelerated depreciation on property placed in service after 1986 is an adjustment for computing alternative minimum taxable income.

¶2604   ALTERNATIVE MINIMUM TAX DEDUCTION FOR OIL AND GAS OPERATIONS

Since 1991, certain taxpayers with oil and gas operations can take a special energy deduction for AMT purposes. It is based on a specified portion of the various oil and gas-related tax preference items [IRC Sec. 56(h)]. Taxpayers (other than integrated oil companies) can take this special deduction for figuring their AMT. An integrated oil company is one that does not qualify as a small producer or royalty owner [¶ 2237(a)].

This deduction is designed to reduce the impact of including tax preferences related to oil and gas operations in alternative minimum taxable income. The tax preference items involved are intangible drilling costs (IDCs) and percentage depletion [IRC Sec. 56(h)].

The special energy deduction is initially determined by calculating the taxpayer's IDC preference and the marginal production depletion preference. The AMTI for determining these preferences is computed without considering the special energy deduction and the alternative tax net operating loss.

Generally, the energy deduction is computed by adding 75% of the IDC preference attributable to qualified exploratory costs, 15% of the remaining portion of the IDC preference and 50% of the marginal production depletion preference [IRC Sec. 56(h)(3)].

The energy deduction is limited to 40% of AMTI determined without regard to either the special energy deduction or the alternative tax NOL [IRC Sec. 56(h)(1)]. Any special energy deduction amount limited by the 40% threshold may not be carried to another year.

The special energy deduction is phased out in tax years that follow calendar years in which the crude oil price exceeds $28 per barrel (adjusted for inflation). There is a total phaseout if the average price of oil exceeds this inflation-adjusted amount by $6 or more [IRC Sec. 56(h)(2)].

¶2605   EXEMPTIONS

A special AMT exemption takes the place of your personal and dependency exemptions. It is much more generous than the writeoffs being replaced. The AMT exemption ensures that moderate income individuals will not have to pay the AMT unless they have a fairly substantial amount of adjustments or preferences. The exemption is based on your filing status. The exemption amounts are as follows [IRC Sec. 55(d)]:

- Married persons filing jointly and surviving spouses—$40,000
- Single persons—$30,000
- Heads of household—$30,000
- Married persons filing separately—$20,000

However, the exemptions are phased out for high income taxpayers. They are reduced by 25¢ for each dollar of AMT income over:

- $150,000 for married persons filing jointly and surviving spouses.
- $112,500 for single persons and heads of household.
- $75,000 for married persons filing separately.

Example: The Cranes have an alternative minimum taxable income of $200,000. As married taxpayers filing jointly, their exemption amount would be $40,000. However, they must reduce this exemption by $12,500 [$50,000 ($200,000 less $150,000 phaseout threshold) × 25%]. Thus, their exemption amount used to reduce the alternative minimum taxable income is $27,500 ($40,000 less $12,500).

► **OBSERVATION** The exemption amounts are completely phased out if AMT income exceeds $310,000 for married persons filing jointly and surviving spouses; $232,500 for single persons and heads of household; $155,000 for married persons filing separately.

NOTE: A married person filing separately is also subject to a phaseout of the $20,000 exemption allowed to the other spouse. As a result, a separate filer's AMT income must be increased by 25¢ for each dollar of AMT income over $155,000. The spouse's $20,000 is completely eliminated if AMT income equals or exceeds $235,000.

Child's exemption. An additional limitation applies to your child who is under age 14 [¶1240]. As a general rule, your child's 1992 AMT exemption cannot exceed $1,200 plus his or her earned income. However, your child's AMT exemption can be bigger. Reason: Your child's exemption can be as much as his earned income plus his share of your unused AMT exemption (the excess of your exemption amount over your AMTI for the year [IRC Sec. 59(j)]).

All of your under-age-14 children's AMT cannot exceed the amount by which your own AMT would be increased if the income of the children had been taxed to you for both the AMT and regular tax [IRC Sec. 59(j)].

¶2606   MINIMUM TAX CREDIT

Some AMT adjustments and preferences merely defer income tax rather than permanently avoid it. Without a special tax law provision, you could end up paying a double tax—the AMT in the year an adjustment or preference provides you with a regular tax benefit plus regular tax in the year the deferral ends.

To mitigate this problem, you can claim a minimum tax credit against your regular income tax for AMT paid in 1987 or later [IRC Sec. 53]. The credit is a function of your AMT liability for the year. Essentially, you subtract that portion of your AMT that is attributable to exclusion items (i.e., those tax breaks that permanently avoid regular income tax). The remainder is available as a credit against your *regular* tax liability for a subsequent year.

The minimum tax credit includes any minimum tax imposed in prior years because of the 90% limit on using the alternative minimum tax foreign tax credit (¶2607) [IRC Sec. 53(d)(1)(B)(i)].

Tax return tip. To compute and report your minimum tax credit to the IRS, you should file Form 8801.

Example: Ms. Wright filed a tax return for last year that showed zero taxable income and, therefore, no regular tax due. However, she had $120,000 of AMT income. Of that figure, $20,000 was due to permanent exclusions like personal and dependency exemptions that could not be claimed for AMT purposes. The balance was from accelerated depreciation on property placed in service in 1985. The depreciation preference results in an AMT liability of $21,000 ($100,000 AMT income × 21%). Because the accelerated depreciation defers tax rather than permanently avoids it, the $21,000 AMT is available as a credit in later years. In the following year, Wright owes regular income tax before credits of $100,000 and no alternative minimum tax (she disposed of the property). The AMT she paid last year is available as a credit against the $100,000 and reduces her regular income tax bill to $79,000.

¶2607   REGULAR TAX CREDITS

When computing your AMT liability, you are not entitled to the benefit of any tax credits other than the foreign tax credit. Even this credit cannot offset more than 90% of your AMT liability [IRC Sec. 59(a)].

➤ **OBSERVATION** When computing your regular tax liability, you may be entitled to various credits like the child care credit [¶2401 et seq.]. The AMT can actually render these credits partially or wholly unusable for regular tax purposes. Generally, you can claim a credit for regular tax purposes only to the extent your regular tax liability exceeds your AMT liability [IRC Sec. 26(a)]. Since personal credits like the child care credit cannot be carried forward or back, their tax benefit is lost when the AMT comes into play.

Example: Mr. and Mrs. Brown have an adjusted gross income of $100,600 in 1992. They both work, so they pay a sitter $4,800 to look after their two young children during the day.

Regular tax picture. The Browns claim personal and dependency exemptions of $9,200. They also claim the following itemized deductions: $7,400 of home mortgage interest (used to buy their residence); $6,000 of home equity interest (used to buy family cars in 1991 and 1992); $6,000 for state and local income and real estate taxes; $2,000 for cash charitable contributions. After these deductions, the Browns have a taxable income of $70,000. Their income tax bill on a joint return comes to $14,946. Depending on their AMT liability, the Browns may also be able to claim a child care credit of $960 (20% of the amount paid to the sitter) [¶2401].

Alternative minimum tax. Mrs. Brown exercised incentive stock options in 1992. The difference between the exercise price and the stock's fair market value is $50,000. This amount must be added back to their taxable income for AMT purposes. Additionally, the personal and dependency exemptions, home equity interest and state and local income taxes are not allowed for the AMT. So the Browns must add back an additional $21,200.

Their taxable income and total addbacks come to $141,200. From this amount, they can subtract their AMT specific exemption of $40,000. Their alternative minimum taxable income is $101,200, and their tentative AMT is $24,288. Since they are liable for AMT only to the extent it exceeds their regular tax of $13,986 ($14,946 less $960 credit), the Browns must actually pay $10,302. One effect of this AMT liability is to prevent the Browns from getting any benefit from the child care credit.

CORPORATIONS

¶2610   ALTERNATIVE MINIMUM TAX FOR CORPORATIONS

Corporations are separate taxable entities and are subject to the alternative minimum tax. To calculate a corporation's AMT, use the format outlined for individuals as modified below. The adjustments pertaining only to individuals (e.g., personal and dependency exemptions, home equity indebtedness and medical expenses) do not apply. Instead, corporations are subject to several special adjustments.

Tax return tip. You should report your corporation's alternative minimum tax liability on Form 4626.

¶2611 ADJUSTMENTS

[New tax legislation may affect this subject; see ¶1.]

The following adjustments apply exclusively to corporations:

(a) Adjusted Current Earnings. Since 1990, there has been an adjustment for adjusted current earnings (ACE). Corporations add 75% of the difference between their "adjusted current earnings" (a figure similar to a corporation's earnings and profits used with respect to dividends) and the otherwise adjusted alternative minimum taxable income [IRC Sec. 56(g); Reg. Sec. 1.56(g)-1].

Depreciation. The alternative depreciation system is used for property placed in service after 1989. This generally includes using the straight line method over a recovery period [¶2112(f); 2114(c)]. For depreciation on property placed in service before 1990 to which the MACRS applies, the property's adjusted basis is recovered on a straight line basis over the remaining recovery period using the alternative depreciation system [IRC Sec. 56(g)(4)(A)].

Intangible drilling costs paid or incurred in tax years starting after 1989 are capitalized and amortized over a 60-month period starting with the month the costs were paid or incurred [IRC Sec. 56(g)(4)(D)(i)].

Depletion is computed using the cost method for property placed in service after 1989 [IRC Sec. 56(g)(4)(F)].

> **SPECIAL RULES** Generally, the special energy deduction for corporations is computed the same as it is handled for individuals. See ¶2604. However, the corporate deduction takes into account the portion of the ACE adjustment that is related to percentage depletion attributable to marginal production and IDCs [IRC Sec. 56(c)(1)(B)].

Suppose part of a taxpayer's alternative tax energy preference deduction is due to depletion or intangible drilling costs. The taxpayer must then reduce basis for computing depletion or intangible drilling costs in subsequent years [Reg. Sec. 1.56(g)-1(s)].

Installment sales. For installment sales in tax years starting after 1989, adjusted current earnings are computed as if the corporation did not use the installment method. However, if the special rule for nondealers applies [¶2905], the installment method can be used as gain for which interest is paid [IRC Sec. 56(g)(4)(D)(iv)].

More information: Final regulations make it clear that refunds of federal income taxes are not included in adjusted current earnings [Reg. Sec. 1.56(g)-1(c)(4)(ii)]. What's more, there's no ACE adjustment: When a corporation distributes appreciated property to shareholders; if a shareholder assumes a liability in connection with a distribution of property; or if a nonshareholder makes a contribution to capital that is excluded from the corporation's income. On the other hand, ACE is increased for lessee improvements to leasehold property that are excluded from a corporation's income.

> **OBSERVATION** The ACE adjustment is not required for an S corporation, regulated investment company, real estate investment trust or real estate mortgage investment conduit [IRC Sec. 56(g)(6)].

(b) Book Income. For 1987 through 1989, the adjustment was 50% of the excess of a corporation's adjusted net book income over alternative minimum taxable income (determined without the 50% adjustment for adjusted net book income and the alternative tax net operating loss deduction discussed in ¶2601(e)), with certain adjustments [IRC Sec. 56(f)(1)]. Note: The adjustment for book income was repealed for tax years beginning after 1989.

¶2612   PREFERENCES

When computing AMT, corporations add tax preference items back to taxable income in the same manner as do individuals [¶2603].

> ➤ **OBSERVATION** A number of corporate tax breaks have been cut back in recent years for regular income tax purposes as well as for the AMT [IRC Sec. 291]. To the extent an adjustment or preference is cut back for regular tax purposes, there are no AMT consequences. For example, a corporation can write off 80% of a pollution control facility over five years—the remaining 20% must be depreciated under the usual tax rules. For AMT purposes, the entire facility must be depreciated under the usual rules, and a corporation's AMT add-back does not include the slower regular tax writeoffs for 20% of the facility.

¶2613   EXEMPTION AND TAX RATE

Corporations deduct a $40,000 specific exemption from AMT income. The exemption is phased out in the same manner as for individuals. For every dollar of corporate AMT income above $150,000, 25¢ of the exemption is phased out. The exemption is eliminated when AMT income reaches $310,000 [IRC Sec. 55(d)(2), (3)].

Tax rate. To the extent its AMT exceeds regular tax, a corporation pays AMT at a 20% rate rather than the 24% individuals pay.

¶2614   CREDITS

A corporation may be eligible to take a minimum tax credit against its regular tax liability [¶2606]. Prior to 1990, the minimum tax credit was not available for exclusion preferences (i.e., preferences that do not involve the timing of the deductions—such as depletion, tax-exempt interest on specified private activity bonds and charitable contributions of appreciated property). However, for minimum tax credits arising in tax years starting after 1989, the credit is allowed for the entire alternative minimum tax liability [IRC Sec. 53(d)(1)(B)(iv)].

When computing its AMT liability, as with individuals, corporations are not entitled to the benefit of any tax credits except the foreign tax credit. For individuals, this credit cannot offset more than 90% of their AMT liability (¶2607) [IRC Sec. 53(d)(1)(B)]. However, the 90% limit does not apply to corporations meeting certain conditions [IRC Sec. 59(a)(2)(C)].

> ➤ **NEW FORM** Corporations can file Form 8827, Credit for Prior Year Minimum Tax—Corporations, which is a relatively simple form to fill out.

Footnotes to Chapter 16

(For your added convenience, in brackets [] with the footnotes below, you will find citations to related paragraphs in the "RIA United States Tax Reporter" (USTR), "CCH Federal Tax Reporter"(CCH) and "RIA Federal Tax Coordinator 2d"(FTC) multi-volume services.)

FOOTNOTE ¶ 2600 [USTR ¶ 554; CCH ¶ 5101; FTC ¶ A-8100].

(1) Treas. Dept. booklet "Alternative Minimum Tax" (1991 Ed.), p. 1.

FOOTNOTE ¶ 2601 [USTR ¶ 564; CCH ¶ 5210; FTC ¶ A-8105].

FOOTNOTE ¶ 2602 [USTR ¶ 564; CCH ¶ 5210; FTC ¶ A-8119].

FOOTNOTE ¶ 2603 [USTR ¶ 574; CCH ¶ 5307; FTC ¶ A-8106].

(1) Hill, 68 AFTR2d 91-5564.

FOOTNOTE ¶ 2604 [USTR ¶ 564; CCH ¶ 5210; FTC ¶ A-8116.2].

FOOTNOTE ¶ 2605 [USTR ¶ 554; CCH ¶ 5101; FTC ¶ A-8101.0].

FOOTNOTE ¶ 2606 [USTR ¶ 534; CCH ¶ 5003; FTC ¶ A-8135].

FOOTNOTE ¶ 2607 [USTR ¶ 594; CCH ¶ 5411; FTC ¶ A-8102.2; A-8134].

FOOTNOTE ¶ 2610 [USTR ¶ 554; CCH ¶ 5001; FTC ¶ A-8101].

FOOTNOTE ¶ 2611 [USTR ¶ 564; CCH ¶ 5210; FTC ¶ A-8129].

(1) PL 101-239, Sec. 7611.

FOOTNOTE ¶ 2612 [USTR ¶ 574; CCH ¶ 5307; FTC ¶ A-8130].

FOOTNOTE ¶ 2613 [USTR ¶ 554; CCH ¶ 5101; FTC ¶ A-8138.1].

FOOTNOTE ¶ 2614 [USTR ¶ 534; 594; CCH ¶ 5003; 5411; FTC ¶ A-8134].

CHAPTER 17

INVENTORY

INVENTORIES IN GENERAL

If inventories are needed to clearly reflect income, you must first figure which items are to be included in inventory. You include in inventory only those items to which you hold title. Inventory figures may then be used to determine cost of goods sold, which in turn is used to compute gross profit.

¶2700　　　　　　　　　　　　**NEED FOR INVENTORY**

An inventory is a list of goods on hand held for sale. In every business in which the production, purchase or sale of merchandise is an income-producing factor, you must determine an inventory of unsold goods on hand at the beginning and end of each year in order to clearly reflect income [IRC Sec. 471; Reg. Sec. 1.446-1(a)(4)(i), 1.471-1]. This is necessary because (1) some of the merchandise you produce or buy during the year may not be sold during the year or (2) the merchandise sold during the year may include all that you produce or buy during the year, plus some that you produced or bought in a prior year. In some businesses, the use of inventories is not a practical method of figuring income and is not permitted. For example, real estate dealers may not use an inventory method.[1]

If you maintain inventory, you must use accrual accounting for purchases and sales (¶2806) [Reg. Sec. 1.446-1(c)(2)(i)].

> ➤ **OBSERVATION** When organizing a new business and adopting an accounting method, you should consider using an accrual method, even though inventories are not required at the start. In the event that later developments make inventories necessary, there would be no need for you to apply for permission to change accounting methods.

There are four main issues related to the subject of inventory: (1) the extent to which inventory must be used in figuring gross profit [¶2701], (2) determining what goods must be included [¶2702], (3) identifying the goods remaining in inventory [¶2705; 2706], and (4) determining inventory value [¶2710-2717].

¶2701　　　　　　　　　　　　**INCOME FROM BUSINESS**

The first step in determining your business' net income (or loss) is to figure its gross profit (or loss). Inventories are an important element in calculating the gross profit of many businesses.

Current rules require that costs you incur in producing real or tangible personal property or costs incurred in acquiring property for resale be capitalized. The so-called uniform capitalization rules are covered in ¶2714.

Gross profit. Gross profit from your business means the total receipts (less returns and allowances) minus the cost of goods sold. To figure the cost of goods sold, you add the costs of inventory at the start of the tax year, merchandise and materials you buy or produce during the year and all other costs related to obtaining or producing the merchandise (including all costs that you must capitalize under the uniform capitalization rules). Then you subtract inventory at the close of the tax year from this total. The result is the net cost of goods sold.

The usual items included in the cost of goods sold are direct and indirect labor, materials and supplies consumed, freight-in and a proportion of overhead expenses. The Ninth Circuit[1] and the IRS agree[2] that rebates or price adjustments can be included in the cost of goods sold, even though they are illegal under state law and are clearly precluded as a business expense deduction. For accounting purposes, you reflect unreimbursed casualty and theft losses of inventory during the year in closing inventory.[3] However, such losses sustained by manufacturers and producers could be excluded from inventory under the uniform capitalization rules [Temp. Reg. Sec. 1.263A-1T(b)(2)(v)(E)].

Example: A business shows receipts of $30,000 ($31,500 gross sales less $1,500 returns and allowances); inventory of goods at the start of the year, $3,700; inventory of goods at the end of the year, $3,000; and merchandise bought during the year for sale, $15,000. Costs incurred during year in connection with the purchase and production of goods for sale are labor, $7,500; material and supplies, $600; and other costs, $200. The gross profit is $6,000. In addition to the amount spent during the year [the excess of receipts ($30,000) over disbursements ($23,300)], you have to reflect the cost of goods that were sold out of the inventory on hand at the beginning of the year. The calculation is as follows:

1. Total receipts from business, $31,500, less returns and allowances, $1,500 . . . . $30,000

COST OF GOODS SOLD

2. Inventory at beginning of year . . . . $ 3,700
3. Merchandise bought for sale 15,000
4. Labor 7,500
5. Material and supplies 600
6. Other costs . . . . __200__
7. Total (lines 2 to 6) $27,000
8. Less inventory at end of year . . . . __3,000__
9. Net cost of goods sold (line 7 minus line 8) . . . . __$24,000__
10. Gross profit from business . . . . $ 6,000

NOTE: Depreciation and cost depletion may be considered in determining the gross profit of a mining, manufacturing or merchandising business. When depreciation and cost depletion are included in the cost of goods produced, these items should be reported in the same amounts as in your financial report [Reg. Sec. 1.471-11(c)(3)].

Tax return tip. If you are a sole proprietor, you figure cost of goods sold in Part II of the Schedule C you file with your personal tax return, Form 1040. Gross profit is figured in Part I of Schedule C. Regular corporations figure cost of goods sold on Schedule A of Form 1120, partnerships on Schedule A of Form 1065.

Donated items. You get a deduction for inventory—whether manufactured by you or acquired for resale—that you donate to a charity. As a general rule, the amount of your deduction is your cost or other basis in the property (just as if you had sold it) [IRC Sec. 170(e)(1)].

How you handle the donation on your return depends on whether the items were manufactured or acquired in the same year you give them away or were in your opening inventory at the beginning of the year [Reg. Sec. 1.170A-1(c)(4)]:

Property not included in opening inventory. You do not get a charitable contribution deduction for property donated in the same year it is acquired or manufactured. The cost or other basis of this property is treated as part of the cost of goods sold in the contribution year [¶1917; 2205].

Property included in opening inventory. You take a charitable deduction for your cost or other basis in the donated property. You also reduce your cost of goods sold by the same amount.[4] Non-inventoried overhead costs remain deductible the same way as if the goods had not been donated.

There are special rules for donations of inventory that are used for the care of the ill, needy or infants (¶3019) [IRC Sec. 170(e)(3); Reg. Sec. 1.170A-4A].

Goods withdrawn for personal use. If you withdraw goods from inventory for your personal use and pay for them with your own funds, the cost of those goods is excluded from the total amount of merchandise bought for sale. It is as if you bought them directly from the wholesaler, rather than taking them from your business inventory. If you do not pay for the withdrawn goods, you must make adjustments to avoid understating net profit from the business. Without the adjustments, the cost of goods withdrawn for personal use would be charged against the total sales of the business. How to adjust: You credit the purchases account with the merchandise withdrawn for personal use and charge the proprietors' drawing accounts with the cost of the withdrawn merchandise. A separate account should be kept of all goods withdrawn for personal or family use.[5]

¶2702　　　　　　　　GOODS INCLUDED IN INVENTORY

Your inventory includes all finished or partly finished goods. Raw materials and supplies (including containers) are included only if they have been acquired for sale, or will physically become a part of merchandise intended for sale. Merchandise is included only if you have title. Goods you buy (including containers) that are currently in transit are included in your inventory if you have title, even if you do not have physical possession yet. But goods (including containers) out on consignment are included in the seller's inventory [Reg. Sec. 1.471-1]. Your inventory at the start of the tax year should be identical with your preceding year's closing inventory. You may not take depreciation on inventories and stock in trade.

> ➤ **OBSERVATION** Determining who has title to inventory may be significant for businesses that value inventory at the lower of cost or market. That's because buyers can't get the tax benefit of price declines until they have title to the goods.

Excluded from inventory. Among the items *not* included in inventory are cash, notes, accounts, capital assets, investments, equipment and similar assets.

PRICING INVENTORIES: IDENTIFICATION

¶2705　　　　　　　　FIRST-IN, FIRST-OUT METHOD

The first-in, first-out (FIFO) method is a way to identify goods in closing inventory. Under this method, the goods first bought are considered those first sold. You can value FIFO inventories at cost or at lower of cost or market [¶2710]. The "cost" of the inventory on hand at the end of the year is the cost of the goods last bought. But if the quantity of ending inventory is greater than the amount bought at the last price, the excess is inventoried at the next to the last price, and so on. FIFO may be used if you buy the same type of merchandise at different prices during the year and it is so intermingled that you cannot identify it with specific invoices [Reg. Sec. 1.471-2(d)].

> **Example 1:** Assume that the inventory at the end of the year shows 275,000 units of a certain article on hand and the last three invoices for that article are June 29, 100,000 at $1.00; September 30, 80,000 at $1.10; December 10, 125,000 at 95¢. If the goods cannot be identified with specific invoices and FIFO is used, the inventory would show 125,000 at 95¢, 80,000 at $1.10 and the remainder (70,000) at $1.00. Total inventory: $276,750.

> **Example 2:** Assume the same facts as in Example 1, except that market value at year end is $1.00 per unit. If the taxpayer uses lower of cost or market to value inventory, the cost of the ending FIFO inventory would be $268,750 (125,000 at 95¢ plus 150,000 at $1.00).

¶2706   LAST-IN, FIRST-OUT METHOD

With IRS approval, any taxpayer who must maintain inventory records can use the last-in, first-out (LIFO) method [IRC Sec. 472; Reg. Sec. 1.472-1, 1.472-3]. The goods most recently bought or produced are treated as the first goods sold so that the goods you have on hand at the close of the year are treated as those you bought or produced earliest.

You must value LIFO inventories at cost. If you adopt the LIFO method and the closing inventory of the preceding year is not at cost, you may have to make an adjustment to restate opening inventory. Adjustments are required to write down from actual cost "subnormal goods" to reverse writedowns of normal goods that are recorded at market value.[1] But you can spread the income attributable to the preceding year's writedown adjustments over three years, starting with the LIFO election year [IRC Sec. 472(d)].

(a) Differences Between Last-In, First-Out (LIFO) and First-In, First-Out (FIFO). Under LIFO, you treat the inventory at the end of the year as being composed of the *earliest* acquired goods. Under FIFO, you treat inventory at the end of the year as composed of the *latest* acquired goods [¶2705].

> **Example 1:** Assuming the same facts in each case, closing inventory is figured under (1) FIFO and (2) LIFO as follows:

	(1) First-in, first out		(2) Last-in, first-out	
Sales 5,000 units @ $4.00		$20,000		$20,000
Cost of sales:				
Opening inventory (2,000 units @ $1.00)	$ 2,000		$ 2,000	
Purchases (5,000 units @ $3.00)	15,000		15,000	
Total	$17,000		$17,000	
Less: Closing inventory:				
(FIFO) 2,000 units @ $3.00	6,000	11,000		
(LIFO) 2,000 units @ $1.00			2,000	15,000
Gross profit on sales		$ 9,000		$ 5,000

> **Example 2:** Assume there are 150 units in inventory and purchases during the period are:

1st purchase 100 units @ $1.00	$100
2nd purchase 200 units @ $1.10	$220
3rd purchase 250 units @ $1.20	$300
4th purchase 100 units @ $1.25	$125

First-in, first-out method. The goods on hand are considered to have been acquired by the most recent purchases; therefore the inventory is composed of:

From 4th purchase:	100 units @ $1.25	$125
From 3rd purchase:	50 units @ 1.20	60
Cost of inventory	. . . .	$185

Last-in, first-out method. The sales are assumed to consist of the last goods purchased, and the inventory at the end of the period is assumed to consist of any opening inventory and the earliest purchases. Therefore the inventory is composed of:

From the 1st purchase:	100 units @ $1.00	$100
From the 2nd purchase:	50 units @ 1.10	55
Cost of inventory	. . . .	$155

► **OBSERVATION** Using the LIFO method may be desirable in a period of rising prices. It produces a smaller profit than the FIFO method by eliminating from income the effect of an increase in the market value of the inventory. Businesses most likely to benefit by the LIFO method are those in which: (1) the value of the inventory is large compared with other assets and sales, (2) production covers a long period and (3) the price of goods included in inventory is subject to wide fluctuations. But in a period of declining prices, the reverse is true, since LIFO users will be unable to offset a decline in the market value of their inventory against their income.

(b) Application For, and Use Of, LIFO. You apply to use LIFO by attaching Form 970, or a statement acceptable to the IRS, to the return for the first tax year you use the method [Reg. Sec. 1.472-3]. So, if you use this method for the first time in valuing closing inventories for tax years beginning in 1992, you must file Form 970 (or an acceptable alternative attachment) with your return for that year. Once adopted, you must continue to use the LIFO method unless the IRS requires a change to another method, or authorizes a change that you request by filing Form 3115 (¶2812) [Reg. Sec. 1.472-5].

You may elect LIFO for your entire inventory or just for specified items (such as raw materials). In the LIFO application, you must specify which part of your inventory will be affected by your election of the LIFO method. The IRS, however, can require you to use the LIFO method for other items in your inventory if it finds this is necessary for a clear reflection of your income. It may also require you to use LIFO for similar goods of any of your other trades or businesses [Reg. Sec. 1.472-2(i)]. If you create a new taxable entity (e.g., a corporation), approval to use LIFO is required even if your new business is formed from companies that had permission to use LIFO and the transaction was tax free.

You cannot change to "dollar value LIFO" [¶2711] from another LIFO method without IRS consent. Special adjustments are required when a change is allowed or when a change in the content of pools is allowed or required [Reg. Sec. 1.472-8(f)(1),(2)].

LIFO conformity. The IRS will invalidate a LIFO election if during the election year you use FIFO or any other valuation method for your financial reports [IRC Sec. 472(c); Reg. Sec. 1.472-2(e)].[2] This rule is applicable to "financially related corporations" (specially defined for these purposes) as if they were single businesses [IRC Sec. 472(g)(1)]. LIFO taxpayers may use other inventory methods in financial and credit statements to explain or supplement the primary presentation of income in those statements [Reg. Sec. 1.472-2(e)]. Also, the IRS has held that the LIFO conformity requirement doesn't apply to financial forecasts.[3] You may use the dollar-value method of pricing inventory [¶2711] for income tax purposes while continuing to use the specific goods method for purposes of financial reporting, without violating the "LIFO conformity" rule. Both are LIFO methods [IRC Sec. 472(c),(e); Reg. Sec. 1.472-2(e)(8)].[4]

PRICING INVENTORIES: VALUATION

¶2710   VALUING INVENTORIES

The two most popular ways to value inventories are:

- Cost
- Cost or market, whichever is lower.

A new business entity may adopt either method. Once you adopt a method, you may not change it without IRS permission. You must use the adopted method for the entire inventory. But there are exceptions for (1) goods inventoried by the last-in, first-out method [¶2706] and (2) animals inventoried by the unit-livestock-price [¶2721(b)] method [Reg. Sec. 1.471-2(d)]. Consistency is important in valuing inventory from year to year.[1]

> **KEY CONSIDERATIONS** The method you use to value inventories must conform to the best accounting practice in your trade or business, clearly reflect your income and be consistent from year to year [Reg. Sec. 1.471-2(b)].

More than one trade or business. If you have more than one trade or business, the IRS may require you to use the same valuation method for similar goods in different trades or businesses, if necessary to clearly reflect income [Reg. Sec. 1.471-2(d)].

Change of method. To change your method of inventory valuation, you must file Form 3115 within 180 days after the start of the year for which the change is desired [Reg. Sec. 1.446-1(e)(3)].

Example 1: A taxpayer who has been reporting on the cost basis and wants to change to cost or market for the calendar year 1993 must file an application with the IRS by July 1, 1993.

The IRS won't permit the change if tax reduction is the principal reason.

(a) Inventories at Cost. The cost of merchandise you *buy* during the year is the invoice price minus trade or other discounts, plus freight and other charges you pay to get the goods [Reg. Sec. 1.471-3].

Cash discounts that approximate a fair interest rate may be treated in either of two ways, but you must be consistent. You may:

1. Deduct cash discounts from purchases. This reduces the cost of goods sold. The invoice price after the cash discount is the price at which the goods in the inventory are valued.

2. Credit cash discounts to a discount account. The credit balance in this account at the end of the tax year is included in income. The cost of goods sold is not reduced by cash discounts taken.

If the second method is used, the IRS says that you may not deduct the average amount of cash discount received on the merchandise from the invoice price of the merchandise on hand at the close of the tax year.[2] However, the Tax Court has allowed the use of this practice if it was followed consistently.[3]

Merchandise manufactured by taxpayer. The cost of merchandise you manufactured is the total of: (1) the cost of the raw materials and supplies consumed in the process, (2) the expenditures for direct labor, including overtime costs,[4] and (3) indirect production costs, including a reasonable proportion of management expenses, but excluding all selling expenses [Reg. Sec. 1.471-3].

NOTE: Loss on the sale of supplier's stock you buy to get merchandise for use in your business is part of your inventory cost, not a capital loss.[5] But you must prove that you bought the stock to get merchandise.[6]

Inventory capitalization rules. You now must capitalize into the cost of products certain other indirect costs that were previously classified as period costs and, so, were deductible at the end of the accounting period in which you incurred them. As a result, they are included in the cost of inventory and deducted as the inventory is sold. This often means costs are deductible later than under the old rules. The capitalization rules [¶2714] apply both to merchandise bought for resale and to goods manufactured by a taxpayer for resale.

(b) Inventories at Lower of Cost or Market. "Market" ordinarily means the bid price prevailing at the date of the inventory. If your company is actually selling items at less than the original or replacement costs, then it can write down the items to the actual selling prices. But you cannot use this "selling price" exception unless you can show an item-by-item breakdown of costs and sales prices—even if your company is conforming to the best accounting practices of the industry.[7] The rules for determining market value apply to goods bought and on hand, as well as to the basic elements of cost (materials, labor and overhead) for items in the process of being manufactured or finished and on hand. It does not apply to goods on hand or in process for delivery on a contract at fixed prices, if the contract legally cannot be cancelled. These goods must be inventoried at cost [Reg. Sec. 1.471-4].

> ➤ **OBSERVATION** The lower of cost or market method is a conservative accounting method for balance sheet and credit qualifications, but not necessarily so for income tax purposes. Any income reductions for the year in which inventory is reduced to market are offset by a comparable decrease in the cost of goods sold in the next year. Before adopting this method, your business should consider the risk of falling into a higher tax bracket that might increase its total tax liability over a two-year period.

On the date the inventory is being valued, you compare the market value of each article with its cost. The lower figure is taken as the inventory value [Reg. Sec. 1.471-4(c)]. For this comparison, the cost of goods in the closing inventory that were also on hand at the beginning of the year is their opening inventory price.[8]

Example 2: At the close of the year, a taxpayer had on hand:

	Cost	Market
Bricks	$2,000	$2,400
Coal	2,000	1,700

The bricks would be inventoried at $2,000; the coal at $1,700.

Example 3: 100 tons of the commodity were bought at 7¢ a pound on August 15 and on October 1 another 50 tons were bought at 6¢ a pound. The entire 150 tons were on hand at the close of the year. The market value at the close of the year was 6½¢ a pound. If "cost or market whichever is lower" is used, the 100 tons would be inventoried at market or 6½¢ a pound; the 50 tons would be inventoried at cost, or 6¢ a pound.

¶2711   COSTING INVENTORY UNDER LIFO

You must value the opening inventory for the first tax year that LIFO is used at the actual cost of the goods on hand. The unit cost for an item is the average of the cost of all items, as if they were all bought at the same time at the same price [Reg. Sec. 1.472-2(c)]. If this unit cost is $5 and the inventory remained constant at 1,000 units, the LIFO inventory value would always be $5,000 because these first units would always be considered to remain in stock.

If the closing inventory is larger than the opening inventory, the cost of the increase, or "increment," generally is determined from purchases or manufacturing costs during the year in one of three ways: cost of earliest units, cost of latest units or average cost. The IRS may accept another method that correctly reflects income [Reg. Sec. 1.472-2(d)].

Example 1: Bell Co. adopted the LIFO method for 1992. The opening inventory was 10 units at 10¢ a unit. During the year Bell Co. bought 10 units: 1 in January at 11¢, 2 in April at 12¢, 3 in July at 13¢ and 4 in October at 14¢. The closing inventory had 15 units. Depending on the method used for inventory increases, the closing inventory will be:

(a) Most recent purchases		(b) In order of acquisition		(c) At an annual average	
10 @ 10	100	10 @ 10	100	10 @ 10	100
4 @ 14 (October)	56	1 @ 11 (January)	11	5 @ 13 (130/10)	65
1 @ 13 (July)	13	2 @ 12 (April)	24		
		2 @ 13 (July)	26		
Totals:					
15	169	15	161	15	165

Example 2: Bell Co.'s closing inventory for 1993 is 13 units. This is a decrease of 2 units from the opening inventory from Example 1. The value of the reduced inventory must be determined from the 15 units in opening inventory in the order of acquisition and by the method used to value inventory increases. The 1993 closing inventory value depends on the method used to value the increases. If the increase for the preceding tax year was taken:

(a) By reference to most recent purchases		(b) In order of acquisition		(c) On average basis	
10 @ 10 (from 1991)	100	10 @ 10 (from 1991)	100	10 @ 10 (from 1991)	100
1 @ 13 (July 1992)	13	1 @ 11 (Jan. 1992)	11	3 @ 13 (from 1992)	39
2 @ 14 (Oct. 1992)	28	2 @ 12 (April 1992)	24		
Totals:					
13	141	13	135	13	139

Manufacturers can limit their use of the LIFO method to raw materials only. You may figure the cost of finished goods and goods in process any way that clearly reflects income; but you may need to make adjustments for raw materials integrated in the goods [Reg. Sec. 1.472-1(c)].

Example 3: Opening inventory consists only of 20 units of raw material at 6¢ a unit. Raw material bought during the year cost 10¢ a unit. Closing inventory has 12 units of raw material and 12 units of finished goods. Processing cost is 4¢ a unit, overhead 1¢ a unit. The closing inventory value is figured:

Raw materials	Raw material	Finished goods
12 at 6¢	72¢	
8 at 6¢		$ .48
4 at 10¢		.40
Processing cost (4¢ × 12)		.48
Overhead (1¢ × 12)		.12
	72¢	$1.48

Dollar-value costing. This method of costing LIFO inventories uses dollar values rather than physical quantities of goods. The inventory is viewed in terms of pools, not individual items. Pools may be classified by broad product categories, by departments, or by any other logical grouping. The "dollar-value LIFO" method requires you to match dollar values in the closing and opening inventories at base year (your first LIFO year) prices. You then make adjustments to reflect increases or decreases in current prices.

The "base year cost" is established for the entire inventory in the "pool" at the beginning of the first tax year the method is adopted. This pool remains the same for all later years unless the IRS approves a change as a change of accounting method [¶2812]. The base-year cost is the total cost of all items in the pool [Reg. Sec. 1.472-8(a)].

You generally must establish the closing inventory value for the pool generally by the "double extension" method. However, the District Director may accept a "link chain" method if the double extension method is impractical. In addition, closing inventory value for the pool can be established by an inventory price index method, explained below. If this method is used, you do not have to show that the double extension is impractical. You must attach a detailed explanation of the link method, or inventory price index method, or any other index method to the return for the first year that dollar value is adopted [Reg. Sec. 1.472-8(e)(1), (2) and (3)].

The double extension method is basically a way to state, in dollar amounts, the value of the increase or decrease in closing inventory in relation to the base year cost [Reg. Sec. 1.472-8(e)(2)]. The base year unit cost of a new item entering the pool is its price or production cost; but the IRS may accept a reconstructed base year unit cost if necessary.

To apply the method, you find the cost of the closing inventory at the unit cost for the base year and the unit cost for the current year; then divide the total current cost by the total cost at base year unit cost to get a ratio that is applied to increases in inventory for the year. The current year cost may be consistently determined by one of the methods described above for valuing inventory increases or decreases (e.g., cost of earliest units, latest units or average cost).

There is an inventory increase for the year when the total dollar value of the closing inventory at base year unit costs exceeds the base year cost. You convert the inventory increase to current dollar value by applying the ratio, or percentage, derived from the comparative base year and current year costs. This figure is the LIFO value of the increase. You record and account for each year's increase as a separate unit.

There is an inventory decrease when the closing inventory for a year is less than the opening inventory with both computed at base year unit costs. Decreases or liquidations of inventory must be absorbed first by the latest previous increase and then successively by the next earlier increases until the decrease is fully absorbed. The ratio established for a particular year's increase is also used when that increase is liquidated. Base year inventory is reduced only when the total of all decreases is more than the total of all increases.

Example 4: Electing the dollar value LIFO method for 1992, Bay Co. properly establishes a pool for items A, B, and C. The inventory on January 1 is: A-1,000 units at a cost of $5 a unit; B-2,000 units at $4; C-500 units at $2; for a total base year cost of $14,000. The total current year cost of the December 31st closing inventory, determined from items last bought during the year, is $24,250. This includes: A-3,000 units at a unit cost of $6; B-1,000 units at $5; C-500 units at $2.50. At the base year unit costs (A-$5, B-$4, C-$2) the closing inventory cost is $20,000. The closing inventory value is $21,275 computed as follows:

1. Closing inventory at base year cost $20,000
   Base year inventory cost $14,000
   Increase in inventory* $6,000
2. $24,250 (inventory at current year unit cost)/$20,000 (inventory at base year unit cost)
   = 121.25% (ratio of current cost to base year cost)

* If cost of the closing inventory at base year unit costs were equal to or less than base year inventory cost, that would be the closing inventory value.

	Closing inventory base year cost	Ratio of current year cost to base year cost	Closing inventory value
Base cost	$14,000	.... 100%	$14,000
Increase	6,000	.... 121.25%	7,275
Total	$20,000		$21,275

Example 5: On December 31, 1993, Bay Co. of Example 4 has a current year cost of $27,000 and a cost of $18,000 at base year unit costs for its closing inventory. The base year cost of the opening inventory was $20,000 so the $2,000 reduction in inventory reduces the $6,000 increase of 1992. In 1993, closing inventory value is $18,850 computed as follows:

	Closing inventory base year cost	Ratio of current year cost to base year cost	Closing inventory value
Base cost	$14,000	.... 100%	$14,000
1992 increase	4,000	.... 121.25%	4,850
Total	$18,000		$18,850

Manufacturers' and processors' pools include the entire inventory of a natural business unit. This may be an entire business or a separate division of a business. The circumstances surrounding the operation of an organization determine whether it has one or more natural business units. You can establish separate pools for substantially similar inventory items that are not part of a natural business pool. Goods bought from others for wholesaling or retailing must be pooled as they are for merchandisers [Reg. Sec. 1.472-8(b)].[1]

Merchandisers' pools must be established by major lines, types or classes of goods, according to customary business classification. One example is a department of a department store [Reg. Sec. 1.472-8(c)].

Small businesses. See (a) below.

Inventory price index method. If you elect this method, you use government-issued consumer or producer price indexes to compute the LIFO value of a dollar-value inventory pool. Once adopted, it applies to all inventory items for which you have elected to use the LIFO method. The method of pooling and selecting index categories is established under special rules. The appropriate inventory price indexes are used to value pools by referring to 80% (100% for eligible small businesses, defined the same way as for the adoption of simplified dollar-value LIFO in (a) below) of the price changes found in the selected indexes. After an index election is made, you can withdraw it only with IRS consent [IRC Sec. 472(f); Reg. Sec. 1.472-8(e)(3)].

(a) Simplified Dollar-Value LIFO. There is a simplified dollar-value LIFO election for businesses with average annual gross receipts for the preceding three-year period of $5 million or less [IRC Sec. 474]. It's designed to allow small businesses to use LIFO without undue complexities or excessive compliance costs.

This simplified LIFO method calls for inventory pools grouped by Bureau of Labor Statistics (BLS) Producer and Consumer general price index categories. Annual cost changes are indexed by reference to BLS monthly published indexes. Cumulative indexes, developed by the link-chain method, are also used.

Businesses that previously elected the single pool method can continue using it under prior law rules or can revoke it without IRS consent. But you can't use the new simplified method and the old single pool method at the same time.

Inventory values using simplified dollar-value LIFO generally follow the usual rules found in the regulations for regular dollar-value LIFO inventories [Reg. Sec. 1.472-8]. However, the main differences are:

- The way in which inventory items are pooled.
- Use of published indexes to find an annual index component for each pool.
- The technique used to compute the cumulative index for a pool for any given year.

Establishing inventory pools. Retailers using the retail method group their pools by the 11 general categories in the BLS consumer price index for all urban consumers. All other taxpayers use the 15 general two-digit categories in the monthly BLS producers prices and price indexes for commodity groupings and individual items. You measure the annual change in costs for each general category pool as a whole by the percentage change for the year in the published index for that category. Present dollar inventory values are discounted back to equivalent values in the base year through the link-chain approach (a current cumulative index is constructed from year-by-year index components), rather than by the double-extension method (comparing the dollar amount of inventory items measured in present year prices against the dollar amount of the same inventory items in base year prices).

Selecting an index. You select a month of the year whose index you will use to measure annual changes in your pool. You must use the same month in later years unless the IRS consents to a change. Originally released BLS index figures are used, unless corrected figures are published *before* you file your return—the index figure that's *actually* used for the year must be adhered to next year (any over- or undervaluation will adjust itself automatically at the end of next year).

Rules applying to year of change. The first year that you use the simplified dollar-value LIFO method is the base year. Converting to this method may involve adjustments, but doesn't require IRS consent. On a change from FIFO, you assign inventory items to the new pools, combine their values, and the total is your base year layer. As with other LIFO methods, a change from a method that allows inventories to be stated at less than cost (e.g., FIFO) requires you to restore any previous writedowns from cost to income. (The base year dollar values will include these amounts.) Conversion from another LIFO method is done similarly, but preexisting LIFO layers must be preserved and prior year layers restated in base year dollars by comparing the prices paid to the item's present value.

Example 6: ABC changes from FIFO to simplified dollar-value LIFO. Inventories consist of a chemical in the BLS "Chemicals and Allied Products" general category, and a high school chemistry text book in the BLS "Pulp, Paper, and Allied Products" general category. Published index numbers for the "Chemicals and Allied Products" general category are 200 for the prior year and 220 for the current year (the "first LIFO year"). The prior year's index number for "Pulp, Paper, and Allied Products" is 142 and for the current year it's 150. In the prior year, the present dollar value of the ending inventory was $30,000 for the chemical and $30,000 for the textbooks. In the current year, the present dollar value of the taxpayer's ending inventory is $35,000 for the chemical and $30,000 for the textbooks. Items in the two general categories are included in separate dollar-value LIFO pools. The annual index for each pool is equal to one plus the percentage change in the index for the general category, as follows:

Pool	Current year index	Prior year index	Change	Percent change	Index
# 1	220	200	20	0.1000	1.1000
# 2	150	142	8	.0563	1.0563

In later years, the annual index would be multiplied by the cumulative index for the preceding year to compute the current cumulative index (in the first year the annual and cumulative index are the same). The present dollar value of the ending inventory for the current year is divided by the cumulative index to restate it in its equivalent value in base year dollars. This amount is assigned to the LIFO layers and multiplied by the cumulative index for the year to which the layer relates to find an indexed dollar value for that layer.

The sum of the indexed dollar values for the layers is the ending LIFO inventory value for the pool. Here are the figures for the first year:

Pool # 1
Current year dollar value of inventory $35,000
Divided by index 1.100
Inventory in base-year dollars $31,818

LIFO layers	Base-year dollar value	Dollar index	Indexed dollar value
Base year	$30,000	1.0000	$30,000
First LIFO year	1,818	1.1000	2,000
Ending inventory	$31,818		$32,000

Pool # 2
Current year dollar value of inventory $30,000
Divided by index 1.0563
Inventory in base-year dollars $28,401

LIFO layers	Base-year dollar value	Dollar index	Indexed dollar value
Base year	$28,401	1.0000	$28,401
First LIFO year	0	0	0
Ending inventory	$28,401		$28,401

Total ending inventory:
Pool # 1 . . . . $32,000
Pool # 2 . . . . $28,401
$60,401

(b) Qualified Liquidations of LIFO Inventories. Generally, inventory replacement adjustments are allowed for liquidations caused by an embargo, international boycott, Energy Department regulations or requests, or a major foreign trade interruption. The Treasury Secretary acknowledges this by publishing a notice in the Federal Register that replacement of any class of goods is difficult or impossible [IRC Sec. 473].

Basis. Goods that replace LIFO qualified liquidated inventory are taken into the purchases account and reflected in closing inventory at the inventory cost basis of the goods replaced. However, the cost of replacement goods is determined in the order of acquisition (latest units) [¶2706(a)] when the closing inventory is larger than the opening inventory and the liquidated inventory has not been completely replaced before the replacement year ends.

A replacement period is limited to three years after the liquidation year. It may be shorter if the IRS so specifies.

Adjustments. If you replace liquidated goods, in part or in full, and reflect them in the closing inventory, you can increase or decrease income for the liquidating year by the difference between the cost of the replaced goods and the LIFO basis of the liquidated inventory. [IRC Sec. 473].

¶2712   GOODS UNSALABLE AT NORMAL PRICES

Goods in inventory that you cannot sell at normal prices or use in the normal way should be valued at "bona fide selling prices" less the direct cost of disposition. However, in no case should you write down goods below scrap value. This applies whether the inventory is taken at cost or at cost or market. "Bona fide selling price" is the actual offering price of the goods during a period ending not later than 30 days after the inventory date. Goods may be unsalable at normal prices because of imperfection, shop wear, change of style, odd lots, or other causes, including second hand goods taken in exchange [Reg. Sec. 1.471-2].

The Supreme Court has ruled that manufacturers cannot write down their excess inventory to scrap value until it is actually scrapped, sold or offered for sale at a lower price.[1] They must value their excess inventory at replacement cost (if lower than actual cost), or must alter their accounting methods to do so. In making the adjustments, the IRS approves in advance this change in accounting method [¶2812].[2] Procedures to follow are set forth in Rev. Proc. 80-5.[3]

¶2713   BOOK INVENTORIES

The IRS allows you to use book or perpetual inventories [Reg. Sec. 1.471-2]. The purpose of a book inventory is to show the goods on hand as of any given date. It must show proper credit for goods you sell or use during the year, as well as charges for goods you buy or produce. Additions and subtractions to the book inventory are made on the basis of the actual cost of goods you buy or produce. You must verify the balances shown by the book inventories by taking physical inventories at reasonable intervals and making adjustments to conform with them. If you use the "lower of cost or market" method, closing inventory of each tax year should be adjusted for each article, as shown in ¶2710(b) [Reg. Sec. 1.471-4].

¶2714   CAPITALIZATION RULES FOR INVENTORY COSTS

[New tax legislation may affect this subject; see ¶1.]

Uniform capitalization (UNICAP) rules apply in determining the costs that you must allocate among various activities and capitalize. Capitalized costs are generally treated in one of two ways. Costs allocable to goods included in inventory become part of the inventory's value. As such, you deduct the costs when you sell the inventory. You add other capitalized costs to a capital account or to basis. You then calculate depreciation or amortization deductions accordingly to write off a portion of these costs each year.

The UNICAP rules require you to capitalize both the direct and indirect costs that are properly allocable to the property. The rules apply to costs you incur for (a) real or tangible personal property that you produce and (b) real or personal property (both tangible and intangible) that you acquire for resale [Temp. Reg. Sec. 1.263A-1T].

▶ **OBSERVATION** The capitalization rules make you deduct certain costs later than you would otherwise. For instance, retirement plan contributions are usually deducted when made. But contributions for a worker who manufactures inventory are capitalized as part of the cost of the inventory and, therefore, not deductible until the products are sold.

The capitalization rules are not intended to affect inventories valued on a basis other than cost. Thus, the rules do not affect inventories valued at *market* using the lower of cost or market method. However, the rules do apply to the valuation of inventories at *cost* using the lower of cost or market rule.

Opening inventory for the first tax year beginning after 1986 had to be revalued to reflect the capitalization rules. You generally could spread income resulting from this adjustment over up to four years [Temp. Reg. Sec. 1.263A-1T(e)]. If you become subject to the uniform capitalization rules (e.g., no longer meet the gross receipts exception explained in (a) below), you may have to change your accounting method to properly value your inventories. This is done by attaching Form 3115 and a special checklist to the tax return for the year of the change.

(a) Property Excluded From Capitalization Rules. The uniform capitalization rules do not apply to the following types of property [IRC Sec. 263A(b)(2)(B), (c); Temp. Reg. Sec. 1.263A-1T]:

- Property used for personal or nonbusiness purposes.
- Property produced under a long-term contract.
- Personal property bought for resale if your average annual gross receipts for the three preceding years are $10 million or less.

NOTE: To make this determination, you include in the calculation the average annual gross receipts from *all* your businesses, not just those generated from the resale of personal property.[1] For example, say your company's main business is to provide data processing services. As a convenience to your customers, you also sell computer equipment manufactured by unrelated third parties. Your total three-year average annual gross receipts are $42 million, but only $4 million of this was generated by the computer sales part of your business. The gross receipts exception would not apply to you.

- Property produced for your use if substantial construction occurred before March 1, 1986.
- Trees you raised or harvested unless they are fruit, nut or ornamental trees.
- Costs allocable to "cushion gas."
- Certain intangible drilling and development costs incurred for oil, gas, or geothermal wells and mineral property.

(b) Costs Subject to Capitalization Rules. You must capitalize direct material and labor costs for production and resale activities. Direct material costs include the cost of materials that become an integral part of the product and the cost of materials that you consume in the ordinary course of production. Direct labor costs include all labor costs that can be identified or associated with a particular activity, including overtime, holiday and vacation pay and sick pay [Temp. Reg. Sec. 1.263A-1T(b)(2)(i)].

Indirect costs that may be allocable to inventory costs are all costs other than direct costs. You generally must capitalize indirect costs that directly benefit or you incur because of a production or resale activity. If costs directly benefit more than one of your activities, you have to make a reasonable allocation.

Indirect costs that are generally subject to the capitalization rules include [Temp. Reg. Sec. 1.263A-1T(b)(2)(iii)]:

- Repair and maintenance costs of equipment or facilities.
- Utility costs relating to equipment or facilities.
- Rental costs of equipment or facilities.
- Indirect labor and contract supervisory wages.
- Indirect materials and supplies.
- Tools and equipment costs.
- Quality control and inspection costs.
- Taxes (other than state, local and foreign income taxes) on labor, materials, land or facilities.

- Depreciation, amortization, and cost recovery allowances on equipment and facilities.
- Depletion, both cost and percentage.
- Some administrative costs (e.g., personnel; data processing for payroll, accounts receivable and accounts payable).
- Direct and indirect costs incurred by any administrative, service or support function or department.
- Compensation to officers attributable to services performed in connection with qualifying activities.
- Insurance costs, such as insurance on machinery and equipment.
- Deductible contributions under stock bonus, pension, profit-sharing or annuity plans.
- Rework labor, scrap, and spoilage.
- Bidding costs incurred in solicitation of awarded contracts.
- Engineering and design costs.
- Storage and warehousing costs, purchasing costs, handling, processing, assembly and repacking costs, and a portion of general and administrative costs allocable to these functions.

You include in inventory costs *interest* on debt you incur or continue to finance the production of real or tangible personal property. However, you exclude interest on debt to finance the acquisition and holding of property for resale.

> ▶ **OBSERVATION** Only those costs deductible in calculating taxable income are subject to capitalization [IRC Sec. 263A(a)(2)]. Thus, you cannot capitalize nondeductible costs, such as personal interest and sales taxes paid on personal items, and then get a deduction for them by including them in cost of goods sold when you sell the inventory.

(c) Costs Excluded From Capitalization Rules. You can deduct the following costs currently—rather than having to include them in inventory cost [Temp. Reg. Sec. 1.263A-1T(b)(2)(v)]:

- Marketing, selling, advertising and distribution costs.

NOTE: The IRS has ruled that package design costs must be capitalized. Certain types of package design costs are amortizable over a 60-month period; otherwise, no depreciation or amortization of these costs is allowed.[2]

- Bidding expenses incurred in connection with unsuccessful contract solicitations.
- General and administrative costs that do not directly benefit a particular product or resale activity (e.g., costs of departments such as legal, accounting, internal audit, tax, general business and financial planning and public relations).
- Deductible research and experimental costs [¶2231].
- Certain deductible developmental and other intangible costs of oil and gas or geothermal wells or other mineral property.
- Losses allowable under IRC Sec. 165 and the related regulations [¶2300].
- Income taxes.
- Costs attributable to strikes.
- Depreciation, amortization and cost recovery allowances on temporarily idle equipment and facilities.
- Repair expenses unrelated to production.

For property excluded from capitalization rules, see (a) above.

> ▶ **OBSERVATION** You must capitalize past service pension costs to the extent they are allocable to both (1) property other than inventory that you produce and (2) inventory property.

(d) Allocating Direct Costs. Generally, you allocate *direct labor costs* to or among activities using a specific identification or "tracing" method. However, you may allocate these costs under any method that produces a reasonable result. You must generally allocate the cost of *direct materials* among activities under the method of accounting (such as FIFO, LIFO or specific identification) you use for the inventory containing the materials [Temp. Reg. Sec. 1.263A-1T(b)(3)(i), (ii)].

(e) Allocating Indirect Costs. You may allocate indirect costs among particular activities using: (a) a specific identification or "tracing" method, (b) the standard cost method or (c) a method using burden rates (such as ratios based on direct costs, hours or other items), provided the method used reasonably allocates indirect costs among production or resale activities [Temp. Reg. Sec. 1.263A-1T(b)(3)(iii), (4)].

(f) Elective Simplified Methods—In General. You may elect to use simplified methods for determining what costs must be included in inventory. Basically, these methods start out with inventory calculated without regard to the capitalization rules. You add to this the additional costs that must be inventoried under the capitalization rules. Simplified procedures are available both for producers and retailers/wholesalers. You generally make the election to use a simplified method on a timely filed return for the first tax year to which the inventory capitalization rules apply. Changes to or from these simplified methods in later tax years require IRS consent.

(g) Elective Simplified Methods for Producers. Inventory producers have a choice of using two separate elective simplified allocation methods. Producers may elect to use a *simplified production method* to account for the additional costs they must now allocate, other than mixed service costs (see below) [Temp. Reg. Sec. 1.263A-1T(b)(5)]. If your single trade or business consists of both production and resale operations, you must generally use the simplified production method (if elected) for all operations of your business, including resale activities.

Under the regulations as presently written, you may use the simplified production method for (1) stock in trade or other property properly included in your ending inventory or (2) property held primarily for sale to customers in the course of your trade that isn't inventory (such as houses constructed by a builder for sale to customers). But the IRS has announced that it will amend the regulations to broaden the availability of this method. The forthcoming regulations will allow use of the simplified production method for property constructed by you for use in your own business if you're also producing substantially identical inventory property.[3] Under the simplified production method, you allocate additional costs to inventory (or other property) based on an "absorption ratio." This ratio is based on the proportion of your (a) total additional capitalizable costs incurred during the year to your (b) total inventoriable costs. To determine the additional costs that must be capitalized, multiply this absorption ratio by ending inventory costs treated as incurred during the year under your method of accounting.

Example 1: Playtime Inc. manufactures toys. It uses the FIFO method of accounting for inventories. Playtime's total additional capitalizable costs incurred during 1992 were $60,000. Total other inventoriable costs incurred during 1992 were $1,000,000. So Playtime's absorption ratio is 6% ($60,000 divided by $1,000,000). Assume Playtime's ending inventory is $400,000, consisting only of costs incurred during 1992. Therefore, Playtime must capitalize $24,000 of additional costs—6% of the $400,000 in its ending inventory.

> ▶ **OBSERVATION** The simplified production method is designed to lessen the burden of complying with the capitalization rules where mass production of assets occurs on a repetitive and routine basis, with a typically high turnover rate for the produced assets. It is not appropriate to use this method to account for the casual or occasional production of property.

Simplified service cost method. You may use this method to figure the amount of certain indirect costs that you must allocate to inventory production. The method provides for allocating administrative, support and service costs that directly benefit or you incur because of the performance of production activities but also benefit your other activities [Temp. Reg. Sec. 1.263A-1T(b)(6)].

You can elect the simplified service cost method even if you don't elect the simplified production method. It's available for the same kind of property as the simplified production method (including the expanded availability under the forthcoming regulations).

To determine inventoriable mixed service costs under the simplified method, you use a ratio. This ratio is (a) total production costs (excluding mixed service costs and interest) for the year divided by (b) total costs (excluding mixed service costs and interest) incurred in operating the business for the year [Temp. Reg. Sec. 1.263A-1T(b)(6)]. The forthcoming regulations will provide an alternative ratio using only labor costs.

Example 2: Playtime Inc.'s total 1992 production costs are $1.5 million. Total operating costs are $3 million. So its ratio for allocating mixed service costs to inventory is 50%—$1.5 million divided by $3 million.

(h) Elective Simplified Method for Retailers and Wholesalers. There is a *simplified resale method* for allocating costs to property you acquire for resale [Temp. Reg. Sec. 1.263A-1T(d)(3)]. Although not currently available for any business that involves production, forthcoming regulations will create a de minimis exception where production activities represent only a fraction of the resale volume.[4] The general allocation rules that apply to production activities apply to those resalers that acquire property for resale and do not elect the simplified resale method. (Specifically, to get capitalizable Sec. 263A costs, multiply the portion of purchases for the year considered to be held in inventory under your method of accounting by a ratio. This ratio is the additional Sec. 263A costs for the year divided by purchases for the year.)

Property acquired for resale may be real or personal property (tangible or intangible). Thus, it may include:

- Literary, musical or artistic compositions.
- Stocks, certificates, notes, bonds, debentures, or other evidences of indebtedness.
- An interest in, or right to subscribe to or buy, any of the above items.
- Other intangible property.

Costs for property acquired for resale—whether or not the simplified resale method is elected—subject to the capitalization rules include:

- Purchasing costs (that is, wages of employees responsible for purchasing).
- Handling, processing, assembling and repacking costs incurred in processing goods while in the resaler's possession.
- Off-site storage or warehousing costs (that is, rent or depreciation, insurance premiums, and taxes attributable to a warehouse and wages of warehouse personnel).
- General and administrative costs (mixed service costs) allocable to the above functions.

Example 3: DeLacey Corp. uses the FIFO method of accounting. During the year, it incurred the following costs: storage, $400,000; purchasing, $500,000; handling and processing, $300,000; mixed service, $200,000. Its beginning inventory balance (not including additional Sec. 263A resale costs) was $2,000,000. It made $8,000,000 in gross purchases during the year. Ending inventory (not including additional Sec. 263A resale costs) was $3,000,000. Applying the simplified resale method, the additional Sec. 263A resale costs required to be capitalized in ending inventory are $525,000, computed this way:

Storage costs	$ 400,000
Purchasing costs	500,000
Handling and processing costs	300,000
Mixed service costs	200,000
Additional Sec. 263A resale cost	$1,400,000
Allocation ratio ($1,400,000 divided by $8,000,000 of purchases made during the year)	17.5%
Amount of purchases for the year treated as being held in ending inveory . .	$3,000,000
Additional Sec. 263A resale costs required to be capitalized in ending inventory (17.5% of $3,000,000)	$ 525,000

Example 4: The facts are the same as in Example 3, except that DeLacey Corp. uses the LIFO method of accounting for inventories. Under the LIFO method, the amounts in ending inventory viewed as consisting of purchases made during the year are $1,000,000. Here, the additional Sec. 263A resale costs required to be capitalized in ending inventory are $175,000 (17.5% of $1,000,000).

You allocate *general and administrative expenses* that are allocable in part to storage, purchasing and processing activities and in part to activities for which no capitalization is required under the simplified method based on the ratio of direct labor costs incurred in a particular function to gross payroll costs [Temp. Reg. Sec. 1.263A-1T(d)(4)(iii)].

Example 5: The total cost of operating Del Mar Department Store's personnel department for the year was $75,000, direct labor purchasing costs were $500,000, and gross payroll was $1,500,000. Therefore, the portion of the personnel department's costs subject to capitalization in connection with the purchasing function would be $25,000 ($75,000 × $500,000 ÷ $1,500,000).

Example 6: If in Example 5 the direct labor warehousing costs were $250,000, the portion of the personnel department's costs allocated to the storage and warehousing functions and thus subject to capitalization would be $12,500 ($75,000 × $250,000 ÷ $1,500,000).

NOTE: Forthcoming regulations will allow resalers to elect whether to allocate mixed service costs using a ratio based on labor costs (as under present regulations) or, like other additional costs, a ratio based on purchases. The regulations should also provide that the ratio used to allocate handling and storage costs (including attributable mixed storage costs) may, at your election, include beginning inventory balances.

(i) Free-Lance Authors, Photographers and Artists. The 1986 tax law made writers, composers and other artists subject to the capitalization rules, effective generally beginning in 1987. The IRS later provided them with an elective safe-harbor.[4] Eligible taxpayers could write off creative expenditures over a three-year period. A 1988 tax law completely exempted all "qualified creative expenditures" incurred by free-lance authors, photographers and artists. This exemption is retroactive, as if it had been originally included in the 1986 Act [IRC Sec. 263A(h)].

(j) Farming. Special rules apply to costs incurred in a farming business [see ¶2721].

¶2715   METHODS OF VALUATION IN SPECIAL
CLASSES OF BUSINESSES

(a) Dealers in Securities. A dealer in securities is one who regularly buys securities for resale to customers. Three methods of inventory valuation are open to these dealers: (1) cost; (2) cost or market, whichever is lower; (3) market value [Reg. Sec. 1.471-5].

(You must reduce the cost of securities sold by the amortized premium on certain short-term municipal bonds.)

(b) Farmers and Livestock Raisers. [¶2721].

(c) Manufacturers. Comprehensive capitalization rules apply to the manufacture of inventory goods [¶2714].

(d) Miners and Like Producers—Allocation of Costs. This method may be used when two or more products of a different selling value are produced by a uniform process [Reg. Sec. 1.471-7].

> **Example 1:** When coal is used to produce gas, a by-product (coke) may result. The production cost may be allocated to the gas and to the coke in proportion to their respective selling values.

(e) Retail Merchants. The methods retailers most commonly use to value their inventory are the conventional "retail method" and the "LIFO" retail method. Under the conventional "retail method," you value goods in inventory at the retail selling price. You then reduce this amount to approximate cost. You have to determine a separate ratio for each department or class of goods [Reg. Sec. 1.471-8].

> **Example 2:**
>
> | | | |
> |---|---:|---:|
> | Opening inventory (retail selling price) . . . . | $100,000 | |
> | Goods purchased during year (retail selling price) . . . . | 900,000 | $1,000,000 |
> | Opening inventory (cost of goods) . . . . | 75,000 | |
> | Goods purchased during year (cost) . . . . | 725,000 | 800,000 |
> | | | $ 200,000 |
>
> $$\$200,000 \div \$1,000,000 = 20\%$$

To determine your correct inventory under the conventional "retail method," you ascertain the retail selling price of the goods in inventory at the end of the year and apply the percentage. For example, assume sales were $850,000, then the closing inventory (retail selling price) is $150,000. $150,000 × 20% is $30,000. The closing inventory is $120,000 ($150,000 – $30,000). Multiplying the closing inventory (retail selling price) of $150,000 by 80% ($800,000/$1,000,000) produces the same result. In this method, the cost-to-retail ratio is computed by adding the markups to retail purchases. Mark-downs are excluded from the computation and added to retail sales to get net sales.

Under the LIFO retail method, the cost of starting inventory is usually the bottom (first) layer in the closing inventory. The next layer is the increment purchased for the year. As this is a LIFO cost layer, it is based on the cost-to-retail ratio which recognizes mark-ups and mark-downs. Thus, in our example the closing inventory under the LIFO retail method would be $115,500 consisting of the first layer (opening inventory) of $75,000 plus the second layer $40,500 [81%, rounded ($725,000/$900,000) × $50,000 ($150,000 – $100,000) retail purchase increment].

Subject to IRS approval, you can adjust selling prices for mark-ups only; but you do not count mark-ups that cancel mark-downs or are canceled by mark-downs. Retailers who use the LIFO method with retail inventory must use both mark-ups and mark-downs in valuing inventory in order that closing inventory reflect cost, not market values. However, you never count mark-downs that are not actual sales price reductions, such as mark-downs for depreciation or obsolescence [Reg. Sec. 1.471-8(d)-(g)]. Unsalable, obsolete or damaged merchandise [¶2712] should not only be excluded from inventory, but you should take a loss in the period when the loss develops.

Conversion to LIFO cost. Since the LIFO method requires inventory to be valued at cost, you must eliminate price changes during the year from the apparent cost of the closing inventory by using a price index. Note that department store retailers using this price index are not eligible to use the dollar value inventory pool price index method described at ¶2711(a) [Reg. Sec. 1.472-1(k), 1.472-8(e)(3)(i)].

Example 3: John Jones uses LIFO to value his hardware store inventory with the retail method. His closing inventory in 1991 (his base year) was retail selling price, $40,000, and cost, $24,000. The retail price of his 1992 closing inventory is $52,000. His gross ratio for 1992 is 40%, so he used 60% of retail price for retail cost. There was a general price increase for hardware in 1992 in relation to the base year 1991 and his price index is 104%. The value of his 1992 closing inventory is $30,240, computed as follows:

1. $52,000 (selling prices) ÷ 1.04% = closing inventory at base year prices . $50,000
   Less base year inventory (retail selling prices)   40,000
   Inventory increase at base year prices $10,000
2. $10,000 × 1.04 = inventory increase at current prices $10,400
3. $10,400 × 60% = cost of increase . . . . $ 6,240
4. Cost of base year inventory $24,000
   LIFO value of closing inventory $30,240

¶2716   METHODS DISAPPROVED

The following methods are specifically disapproved [Reg. Sec. 1.471-2(f)]:

- Deducting from the inventory a reserve for price changes, or an estimated depreciation in its value.
- Taking work in process, or other parts of the inventory, at a nominal price or at less than its proper value.
- Omitting portions of the stock on hand.
- Using a constant price or nominal value for so-called normal quantity of materials or goods in stock.
- Including stock in transit, either shipped to or from the taxpayer, when the title is not vested in the taxpayer.
- Using the "direct cost" method by allocating only the variable indirect production costs to the costs of goods produced while treating fixed costs as currently deductible period costs.
- Using the "prime cost" method by treating all indirect production costs as currently deductible period costs.
- Writing down inventory based solely on sales activity rather than true market value.

¶2717   BASIS

If property should have been included in inventory, its basis is the last inventory value [IRC Sec. 1013; Reg. Sec. 1.1013-1].

FARM INVENTORY AND ACCOUNTING

¶2720   INCOME FROM FARMING

(a) Accounting Methods of Farmers. Farmers may keep their records and file tax returns on either the cash basis or the accrual basis of accounting [¶2801-2806]. But whichever method you choose, you must use it consistently. You must file Schedule F (Form 1040) with your tax return, whether you are is on the cash or accrual basis. Certain farm corporations must use the accrual method [¶2806].

Farmers who want to change from the cash to the accrual method must get IRS permission [Reg. Sec. 1.471-6(a)]. You must file an application within 180 days after the start of the tax year to be covered by the return [¶2812].

Cash basis. If you report income on the cash receipts and disbursements basis (in which no inventories are used to determine profits), you must include in gross income for the tax year: (1) the cash or the value of merchandise or other property you received during the tax year from the sale of livestock or produce that you raised, (2) profits from the sale of any livestock or other items that you bought, (3) all miscellaneous income received during the year, (4) all subsidy and conservation payments that you must consider as income and (5) gross income from all other sources [Reg. Sec. 1.61-4(a)].

You, as a farmer on the cash basis, can elect to include crop insurance proceeds in gross income for the tax year following the damage or destruction, if you normally would have reported the income from the crop in that following year. When you receive insurance as a result of damage to two or more specific crops, you may make an election to include part of the proceeds in the following tax year. In that case, you must include all the proceeds in that later year unless a portion is attributable to a crop that represents a separate trade or business. You make the election by a statement attached to the return for the tax year in which the damage or destruction occurs [IRC Sec. 451(d); Reg. Sec. 1.451-6].

You can elect to include the gain from livestock sales due to drought conditions in gross income the tax year *following* the sale or exchange. The drought conditions must be in areas designated for federal disaster assistance. This election applies only if the number of sales exceeds the usual business practice and if the sales would not have been made but for the drought. This election is not available for all livestock. You make it for each broad generic classification (e.g., hogs, sheep and cattle) [IRC Sec. 451(e); Reg. Sec. 1.451-7].

> **NOTE:** Certain Federal crop disaster payments can be treated for the election as any other crop insurance proceeds [IRC Sec. 451(d); Reg. Sec. 1.451-6(a)(1)].

Accrual basis. If you are on the accrual basis, and you use inventories to determine profits, your gross profits are found by first adding together: (1) the sales price of all livestock and produce you sold during the year, (2) the inventory value of livestock and produce on hand and not sold at the end of the year, (3) all miscellaneous items of income, (4) any subsidy or conservation payment that you must consider as income and (5) gross income from all other sources. From this sum, you subtract (1) the inventory value of livestock and produce on hand and not sold at the beginning of the year and (2) the cost of livestock and produce you bought during the year [Reg. Sec. 1.61-4(b)]. For inventories of farmers and livestock raisers, see ¶2721.

NOTE: Certain large family corporations engaged in farming must use the accrual method (¶2806) [IRC Sec. 447].

Crop basis. You may use the crop basis method to figure the income from crops that take more than a year to grow and sell. This is a special variation of the accrual basis, and the entire cost of producing the crop must be deducted in the year you realize the gross income from the crop [Reg. Sec. 1.61-4(c)]. You must file an application to use this method within 180 days after the start of the tax year to be covered by the return [¶2812].

(b) Items Included in Income. The rules are summarized below.

Products exchanged for groceries, etc. If you exchange farm produce for merchandise, groceries or the like, you include in income the market value of the articles received in exchange [Reg. Sec. 1.61-4(c)].

Crop shares (whether or not considered rent under state law) are reported as income in the year they are reduced to money or its equivalent [Reg. Sec. 1.61-4(a)(5), (b)(7)].

Insurance proceeds, such as hail and fire insurance on growing crops, are included in gross income [Reg. Sec. 1.61-4(c)]. But see the election for cash basis farmers in (a) above.

Government subsidies. All government payments, such as those for approved conservation practices, Soil Bank payments, Wheat Stabilization and Feed Grain Program payments, must be included in income, whether received in cash or in materials [Reg. Sec. 1.61-4(a)(4), (b)(4)]. If you receive fertilizer or lime, you include its value in income. But you may offset this income with an expense deduction plus any cash handling charges. If payments are based on improvements, such as a pollution control facility, capitalize the full cost without reduction for payments received, since the payments have already been included in income. This cost should be depreciated or amortized starting on the date the facility is placed into service. Amortization is allowed over a 60-month period [IRC Sec. 169(d)-1; Reg. Sec. 1.169-1].[1]

Patrons' income from cooperatives includes patronage dividends, nonpatronage payments and per-unit retains (¶3358). Note that special rules apply to payment in kind (PIK) commodities.[1]

(c) Items Not Included in Income. Farmers do not have to include the following items in income:

Products used by family members. The value of farm products produced by a farmer and consumed by his family.[2]

Donated products. The fair market value of farm products that the farmer gives away[3] [but see ¶2205].

¶2721   INVENTORIES OF FARMERS AND LIVESTOCK RAISERS

Farmers who must value inventories to determine taxable income may do so on the basis of cost, or cost or market, whichever is lower. However, a simpler method for farmers is the "farm-price method." In addition, farmers raising livestock may value their inventories of animals according to either the "farm-price method" or the "unit-livestock-price method."

For inventory capitalization rules that apply to farmers and ranchers, see (d) below.

(a) Farm-Price Method. Under this method, you value inventories at market price less cost of disposition. If you use this method, it must be applied to the entire inventory except livestock inventory that you elect to value under the "unit-livestock-price method." If you used a different method to value inventories in prior years and switch to the "farm-price method," you must get IRS permission for the change [Reg. Sec. 1.446-1(e), 1.471-6(d)].

(b) Unit-Livestock-Price Method. Under this method, you group animals you raise by class. Animals within a class are then valued at a standard unit price [Reg. Sec. 1.471-6(e)]. The IRS must approve the method you use to classify animals.[1] To find the unit cost for each classification, you must take into account the age and kind of animals included within a class. This is so that normal costs incurred in producing the animals will be reflected.

> **Example:** If it costs $15 to produce a calf and $7.50 each year to raise a calf to maturity, the classification and unit prices would be as follows: calves, $15; yearlings, $22.50; two-year-olds, $30; mature animals, $37.50.

If you are using the "farm-price method" and want to switch to the "unit-livestock-price method," you must get IRS approval[1] for the change. However, if you have filed returns on the basis of inventories at cost, or cost or market, whichever is lower, you may adopt the "unit-livestock-price method" without formal application [Reg. Sec. 1.471-6(h)].

(c) Livestock Included in Inventory. The rules are summarized below:

Accrual basis farmers must include in inventory all livestock raised or purchased *for sale*. But you may treat livestock acquired for draft, breeding or dairy purposes as depreciable capital assets, or include them in inventory. While you may use either method, whatever you choose must be applied consistently from year to year.[1]
For preproductive period costs, see (d) below.

If you use the unit-livestock method, it applies to all livestock *raised*, whether for sale or for breeding, draft or dairy purposes.[2] Livestock you *purchase* must be included in inventory at *cost*. However, farmers still have the option to either inventory or capitalize livestock *purchased* for breeding, draft or dairy purposes [Reg. Sec. 1.471-6(g)]. Once you elect a method, it can be changed only with IRS consent [¶2812].[3]

In figuring gain or loss from livestock in inventory, the inventory value takes the place of the original cost, if any.[3]

(d) Capitalization of Plant and Animal Costs. Farmers and ranchers are subject to uniform capitalization rules for preproductive period expenses of plants and animals having a preproductive period of more than two years. Farming businesses required to use the accrual method [¶2806] are also subject to the capitalization rules. Capitalized costs may be determined using a reasonable valuation method[4] [IRC Sec. 263A; Reg. Sec. 1.263A-1T(c)(1)].

Farmers can elect out of these capitalization rules. If you make this election, you must use the nonincentive straight line depreciation method (required for alternative minimum tax calculations) on all farm assets purchased while the election is in effect [Reg. Sec. 1.263A-1T(c)(6)].

> ➤ **OBSERVATION** If you are in doubt about the two-year cycle, a protective election should be filed. Reason: While the election is in effect, you can deduct preproductive costs currently, as under pre-1987 law. Also, special rules apply to recapture of income on early disposition.

Footnotes to Chapter 17

(For your added convenience, in brackets [] with the footontes below, you will find citations to related paragraphs in the "RIA United States Tax Reporter"(USTR), "CCH Federal Tax Reporter" (CCH) and "RIA Federal Tax Coordinator 2d" (FTC) multi-volume services.)

FOOTNOTE ¶ 2700 [USTR ¶ 4710-4744; CCH ¶ 22,204; FTC ¶ G-5001].
(1) Rev. Rul. 69-536, 1969-2 CB 109, amplified by Rev. Rul. 86-149, 1986-2 CB 67, superseding OD848, CB June 1921, p. 47.
FOOTNOTE ¶ 2701 [USTR ¶ 1702.04; 4462; CCH ¶ 5511; 22,204 et seq.; FTC¶ G-5000].

(1) Sobel Wholesale Liquors (USCA-9th, 9-22-80), 46 AFTR 2d 5799.
(2) Rev. Rul. 82-149, 1982-2 CB 56.
(3) Treas. Dept. booklet "Tax Guide for Small Business" (1991 Ed.), p. 88.
(4) Rev. Rul. 55-138, 1955-1 CB 223; Rev. rul. 55-531, 1955-2 CB 520. (But see ¶1610.)

(5) Rev. Rul. 28, 1953-1 CB 20.

FOOTNOTE ¶ 2702 [USTR ¶ 4712; CCH ¶ 22,204.017; FTC ¶ G-5005].

FOOTNOTE ¶ 2705 [USTR ¶ 4712.02; CCH ¶ 22,206.01; FTC ¶ G-5114].

FOOTNOTE ¶ 2706 [USTR ¶ 4720-4725.11; CCH ¶ 22,240; FTC ¶ G-5300].

(1) Rev. Proc. 76-6 (TIR-1433), 1976-1 CB 545; Rev. Rul. 76-282, 1976-2 CB 137; Rev. Proc. 76-28 (IR-1630), 1976-2 CB 645.

(2) Rev. Rul. 75-49, 1975-1 CB 151.

(3) Rev. Rul. 88-84, 1988-2 CB 124.

(4) Rev. Rul. 85-129, 1985-2 CB 158.

FOOTNOTE ¶ 2710 [USTR ¶ 4712.02-.04; CCH ¶ 22,206; FTC ¶ G-5100].

(1) The Buss Co., 2 BTA 286.

(2) Rev. Rul. 69-619, 1969-2 CB 111.

(3) Higgenbotham-Bailey-Logan Co., 8 BTA 566.

(4) Rev. Rul. 69-373, 1969-2 CB 110.

(5) Western Wine and Liquor Co., 18 TC 1090; Clark, 19 TC 48.

(6) McGhee Upholstery Co., ¶54,014 PH Memo TC.

(7) Tog Shop, Inc., USDC M.D. Ga., No. 87-172-A, B/Amer (DF).

(8) Rev. Rul. 70-19, 1970-1 CB 123.

FOOTNOTE ¶ 2711 [USTR ¶ 4722; 4722.08; 4730; 4740; CCH ¶ 22,240; FTC ¶ G-5300; G-5321].

(1) Rev. Rul. 82-192, 1982-2 CB 102, distinguishing Rev. Rul. 77-107, 1977-1 CB 6.

FOOTNOTE ¶ 2712 [USTR ¶ 4712.02; CCH ¶ 22,206.255; FTC ¶ G-5211].

(1) Thor Power Tool Company, 439 US 522, 43 AFTR 2d 79-362; Rev. Rul. 83-59, 1983-1 CB 103.

(2) Rev. Rul. 80-60, 1980-1 CB 97.

(3) Rev. Proc. 80-5, 1980-1 CB 582.

FOOTNOTE ¶ 2713 [USTR ¶ 4712.02; CCH ¶ 22,206; 22,210; FTC ¶ G-5102].

FOOTNOTE ¶ 2714 [USTR ¶ 263AO-5; CCH ¶ 13,803; FTC ¶ G-5120].

(1) Rev. Rul. 89-26, 1989-1 CB 87.

(2) Rev. Rul. 89-23, 1989-1 CB 85; Rev. Proc. 89-17, 1989-1 CB 827.

(3) Notice 88-86, 1988-2 CB 401.

(4) Notice 88-62, 1988-1 CB 548.

FOOTNOTE ¶ 2715 [USTR ¶ 4712.05, .07, .08; 4722.08; CCH ¶ 22,212; 22,216; 22,218; 22,222; FTC ¶ G-5031].

FOOTNOTE ¶ 2716 [USTR ¶ 4712.02; CCH ¶ 22,206; FTC ¶ G-5111].

(1) Rev. Rul. 77-364, 1977-2 CB 183.

FOOTNOTE ¶ 2717 [USTR ¶ 10,130-10,135; CCH ¶ 29,702; FTC ¶ I-1950].

FOOTNOTE ¶ 2720 [USTR ¶ 612.04; 4512.05-.06; 4712.06-.07; CCH ¶ 5602; 21,021; 22,214; FTC ¶ N-1100].

(1) Treas. Dept. booklet "Farmers' Tax Guide" (1991 Ed.), p. 11.

(2) Morris, 9 BTA 1273.

(3) Rev. Rul. 55-138, 1955-1 CB 223; Rev. Rul. 55-531, 1955-2 CB 250.

FOOTNOTE ¶ 2721 [USTR ¶ 4462; 263A2; 4712.06; CCH ¶ 22,214; FTC ¶ N-1100].

(1) Treas. Dept. booklet "Farmers' Tax Guide" (1991 Ed.), p. 9.

(2) U.S. v. Catto, 86 US 1311, 17 AFTR 2d 881.

(3) Rev. Rul. 60-60, 1960-1 CB 190.

(4) Notice 88-24, 1988-1 CB 491.

CHAPTER
18
ACCOUNTING

ACCOUNTING METHODS

An accounting method is a set of rules used to determine when and how you report your income and expenses. The regular method of accounting you use to keep your books is generally used in computing your income for tax purposes. The method used must clearly reflect taxable income.

¶2801   METHODS OF ACCOUNTING

No one method of accounting is appropriate for all taxpayers. Therefore, the tax law requires each taxpayer to adopt the forms and methods of accounting suitable for his or her purpose [IRC Sec. 446(a); Reg. Sec. 1.446-1(a)(2)]. The two principal methods of accounting are:

1. The cash receipts and disbursements, or "cash-basis," method [¶2802].
2. The accrual-basis method [¶2806].

If you are a cash-basis taxpayer, you generally take income into account when you receive it and deduct expenses when you pay them. On the other hand, if you are an accrual-basis taxpayer, you take income into account when you earn it and deduct expenses when you incur them. Other methods used include the installment sales [¶2901 et seq.], long-term contracts [¶2942], and farmers' crop basis [¶2720]. Hybrid methods may also be used [(a) below].

C corporations, partnerships that have a C corporation as a partner, tax shelters and tax-exempt trusts with unrelated business income generally cannot use the cash method (or a hybrid method reporting partly on a cash method). However, the cash method continues to be available to: businesses (but not tax shelters) with average annual gross receipts (less returns and allowances) of $5 million or less for the preceding three years (or the shorter period they conducted business); employee-owned service businesses in the field of health, law, accounting, engineering, architecture, actuarial science, performing arts or consulting (qualified personal service corporations); and farming and timber businesses [IRC Sec. 448].

(a) Hybrid Accounting Method. You can use a combination of accounting methods if it clearly reflects income and you use it consistently. If you use the accrual basis for purchases and sales, you can use the cash basis for all other income and expense items. You cannot, however, combine cash basis for income with accruals of expenses [IRC Sec. 446(c); Reg. Sec. 1.446-1(c)(1)(iv)].

The IRS has said that you are not required to have strict book-tax accounting conformity. You can use different accounting methods, provided you maintain workpapers that document all adjustments between book and taxable income. The IRS approved a company's use of the cash method of accounting for income taxes, even though the company maintained accrual books.[1]

(b) More Than One Trade or Business. If you are engaged in two or more separate and distinct businesses, you may use a different method for each. That means, however, you must keep separate books and records [IRC Sec. 446(d); Reg. Sec. 1.446-1(d)].

(c) Income Solely From Wages. If your income is derived solely from wages, you are not required to keep formal books. Your accounting method may be established from your tax returns, copies of them, or other records [Reg. Sec. 1.446-1(b)(2)].

¶2802   CASH RECEIPTS AND DISBURSEMENTS METHOD

As a cash-basis taxpayer, you include in gross income all income subject to tax that you receive during the year in cash or its equivalent [¶2824]. You can deduct all disbursements you make during the year in cash or its equivalent, if a deduction for the expenditures is authorized. Items of income and expenditures that are elements in figuring taxable income do not have to be in cash. It is enough that the items can be valued in terms of money.

Exceptions. If you use inventories, you must account for purchases and sales under the accrual method, unless the IRS authorizes otherwise [Reg. Sec. 1.446-1(c)(2)]. Also, you must generally capitalize the cost of depreciable property and related improvements [IRC Sec. 263]. Special rules, though, do permit you to expense currently up to $10,000 of depreciable property purchases each year [¶2113].

The cash method is limited to S corporations, sole proprietorships and partnerships that have no C corporation partners. Qualified personal service corporations may also use the cash method if they are substantially involved in performing services in the fields of health, law, accounting, performing arts, etc. Also, all of their stock must be substantially owned (at least 95% in value) by employees performing services in these fields, their estates or anyone acquiring an ownership interest by reason of that person's death within the past 24 months [IRC Sec. 448; Temp. Reg. Sec. 1.448-1].

¶2803   CONSTRUCTIVE RECEIPT—CASH BASIS

As a cash-basis taxpayer, you may be required to recognize as income amounts you constructively received. This is income that you do not actually possess, but is so much within your control and disposition as to amount to actual receipt. You have not constructively received income if it is subject to substantial restrictions or limitations [Reg. Sec. 1.451-2].

Examples of Constructive Receipt

Interest on savings bank deposits is fully taxable to you when credited, without reduction for any forfeiture on a premature withdrawal.[1]

Interest coupons are reported for the year the coupons matured, unless there are no funds available for payment [Reg. Sec. 1.451-2(b)].

Brokerage accounts. Profits from your brokerage account not withdrawn are taxable in the year earned, even if the account may be wiped out by losses in later years.[2]

Checks issued in one year and received in another are constructively received in the year of issuance, if they were available to you in the earlier year[3] or you agreed to accept payment in that year.[4] Also, a salary check mailed for deposit in your bank according to practice is constructively received in the year of issuance.[5]

Agent's receipt of income is the same as receipt by the principal.[6]

Bonus for majority stockholder is constructively received in the year authorized, even though not paid until the next year. This assumes that the corporation had enough funds and the shareholder could sign the check to pay out the bonus.[7]

Special Rules

Acceptance. You need not legally accept income to be taxed under the constructive receipt doctrine. If the money is subject to your control, it is constructively received whether actually accepted or not. You cannot shift income to another year by refusing to accept what has been properly tendered under a prior agreement.[8]

Examples. A retiree verbally refused to accept a pension and kept uncashed checks received under the pension plan. The checks were income constructively received.[9] But there was no constructive receipt when an employee refused to accept salary voted but not credited, and the corporation used the money for charitable purposes the employee suggested.[10]

Salary. You may constructively receive pay if the money is credited to you, and you may withdraw it at anytime.[11] There needn't be a book entry setting the money apart, if it is otherwise made available.[12] However, whether or not there is constructive receipt depends on the facts in each case.

If there are no funds to make the payment (e.g., the employer is insolvent), there is no constructive receipt.[13]

Amounts taken out of your wages by your employer to pay insurance, buy savings bonds, pay union dues or pay income taxes are constructively received by you and must be included in your gross income for that year. If your employer uses wages to pay your debts, or if wages are attached, they are also constructively received by you.

Controlling shareholders did not constructively receive bonuses in the year authorized by the corporation due to substantial restrictions on their payment.

Agreement to execute promissory notes in a later year is a cash equivalent.[14]

Dividends. For constructive receipt of dividends, see ¶2826.

Endowment and life insurance proceeds. See ¶1509.

¶2804   INCOME PAID TO THIRD PARTIES—ASSIGNMENTS

You may agree that income you are entitled to receive be paid to a third party. This raises the question of who pays the tax on the income—you (the one making the agreement) or the person to whom it is paid.

(a) Assignment of Income From Property. Suppose you own an interest in property and agree that the income from the property will be paid to a third party— without there being any transfer of title to the property producing the income. The income remains taxable to you (the property owner); it is not taxable to the third party. It doesn't matter whether the income is to be earned in the future or has already been earned.[1] But if you made a legal transfer of a *property interest* to a third party, he is taxed on the income arising under the agreement.[2]

(b) Assignment of Earnings. You are taxed on a payment you earn for your personal services, even if you assign it to another. The result is the same whether the assignment is for income to be earned,[3] or income already earned for past services.

Examples of Assigned Income

Taxable to assignor. Assignment of earned commissions to third party by insurance agent;[4] assignment of cash dividends on stock (ownership of stock is retained by assignor);[5] assignment of rent[6] or lease[7] (real property owned by assignor); assignment by a beneficiary of trust income for a short period (one year);[8] assignment of dividends after declaration date and before payment date by a life income beneficiary of a trust;[9] share of partnership income assigned;[10] assignment by husband to wife of patent license contracts between him and a corporation, if he, as majority stockholder, had power to cancel the contract;[11] medicare fees assigned by physicians to exempt organizations, though deductible as charitable contributions.[12]

Taxable to assignee. Transfer of stock to son and subsequent dividends on the stock, even where father retained possession of stock certificate;[13] assignment by life beneficiary of trust of part of the trust income for rest of his life.[14]

¶2805   CONSTRUCTIVE PAYMENT—CASH BASIS

Generally, as a cash-basis taxpayer, you cannot deduct expenses before you make actual payment. However, you can deduct expenses that are treated as an offset against amounts owed to you in the year of the offset.[1] In such cases, the obligation for the deducted expense is fully discharged by the offset. For example, interest charged by a broker on debt owed by you on the usual type of margin account is constructively paid when the broker makes collections for your account.[2]

¶2806   ACCRUAL BASIS

Under the accrual method of accounting, you generally report income when you earn it, even if you do not actually receive it. And you generally report expenses when you incur them, whether or not you pay for them at that time [¶2824; 2840].

> **Example 1:** On September 1, 1992, a paving contractor laid a sidewalk for Mason City. Payment was not received until 1993. If the contractor reports on the accrual basis, the income is included in his 1992 return (when earned). If he reports on the cash basis, the payment is included in his 1993 return (when received).

Example 2: On November 1, 1992, Walker bought a machine and gave his one-year 9% note for $500. On November 1, 1993, he paid the note and interest ($545). If he reports on the accrual basis, $7.50 interest is deductible in 1992, and $37.50 is deductible in 1993 (over the period the liability is *actually incurred*). If he reports on the cash basis, the $45 is deductible in 1993 (when paid).

Farming. A corporation engaged in the trade or business of farming (other than an S corporation) generally must use the accrual method if it has gross receipts in excess of $1,000,000. Exception: Incorporated family farms need not use the accrual method unless they have gross receipts exceeding $25 million. A family farming corporation is one where 50% or more of the stock is owned by members of the same family [IRC Sec. 447].

¶2807 ACCOUNTING METHODS MUST CLEARLY REFLECT INCOME

No matter what accounting method you use, it must clearly reflect your income [IRC Sec. 446(b); Reg. Sec. 1.446-1(a)(2)]. It's important that you treat items of income and expense consistently from year to year. So, even if you use the cash basis to keep your accounts and make your return, unusual cases may arise when a payment you make during the year is not currently deductible.

Commissions, fees, and printing costs paid in one year by a taxpayer in securing a loan for 10 or 15 years, covered by a mortgage on property to be leased, are not deductible in full in the year of payment, but should be spread over the period of the loan, even if taxpayer's return is made on the cash basis.[1]

Insurance premiums that are business or investor's expenses paid in advance for more than one year by cash-basis taxpayers are deductible ratably over the period to which they relate (IRS and 1st Circuit).[2] But the 8th Circuit holds that these premiums may be deducted in the year paid.[3]

A subsidiary corporation that sold goods produced by the parent company acquired title before selling to customers. So the IRS required it to maintain inventories and recomputed its income on the accrual basis.[4]

Rounding off to whole dollars. You may round off amounts on internal transactions to the nearest dollar, if a penny elimination account is maintained, and you follow the procedure with reasonable consistency.[5]

¶2810   RECORDS

The accounting records you keep must be sufficient to enable you to determine your actual income. These records generally take the form of your regular books of account and supporting documentation. They should reflect the following essential information [Reg. Sec. 1.446-1(a)(4)]:

- If the production, purchase, or sale of merchandise is an income-producing factor, you must take inventories into account at the beginning and end of the year [Ch. 17].
- You must properly classify expenditures during the year as capital or expense.
- If you are recovering the cost of an asset through depreciation, amortization or depletion, any expenditure (other than ordinary repairs) made to restore the property or prolong its useful life must be added to the property account or charged against the appropriate reserve. The expenditures are not deductible expenses [Ch. 11, 12].

¶2811   RECONSTRUCTION OF INCOME

If you have no regular method of accounting, or if your records are incomplete, inaccurate, lost or destroyed, the IRS may reconstruct your income by whatever method seems appropriate [IRC Sec. 446(b); Reg. Sec. 1.446-1(b)(1)].

(a) Net Worth Method. The IRS first establishes your "net worth" (difference between the assets and the liabilities) at the start of the tax year. Any increase in your net worth during the tax year is added to your nondeductible expenses. This amount is compared with the amount reported on your return. If the reported amount is smaller than the income as reconstructed, and the additional funds did not come from a nontaxable source (such as gift or inheritance),[1] they are unreported income on which you owe an additional tax. The courts have approved using the net worth method in reconstructing income from gambling, a tavern-restaurant, slot machines, a general store, used car business and black market operations among others. The net worth method also has been upheld by the Supreme Court as a basis for conviction for tax evasion.[2]

(b) Percentage Method. The IRS reconstructs your income by determining your total sales or receipts and applying to this amount an average percentage of gross profit.[3] It also can reconstruct taxable income by applying to your gross income an average percentage of taxable income to gross income.[4] The percentage used is taken either from returns you filed in previous years or from figures reflecting percentages of taxpayers in similar trades or businesses.[5] However, the experience of other taxpayers cannot be used if your business conditions are unlike those of the businesses used for comparison.[6]

(c) Bank Deposit Method. The IRS includes in your income the total amounts you deposited in the tax year, after eliminating: (1) duplications (such as transfers of funds between banks), (2) amounts identified as not being income receipts and (3) total receipts you reported as income. Unexplained bank deposits are presumed to be income; the burden of proving otherwise is on you.[7]

(d) Excess Cash Expenditure Method. With this method, the IRS reconstructs income by comparing the amount you spent with the amount the return shows was available to you as income. Income has been reconstructed from amounts spent for machinery, equipment, real estate and living expenses, and from amounts spent for medical and entertainment expenses.

¶2812   CHANGE IN ACCOUNTING METHOD

Generally, you must get the consent of the Commissioner before changing your method of computing income and expenses. Consent is required even if the new method is proper or permitted under the Code or Regulations [IRC Sec. 446(e); Reg. Sec. 1.446-1(e)(2)].

(a) What Is a Change in Method. A change in method includes a change in the overall plan of accounting for gross income or deductions, or a change in treatment of any material item used in the overall plan. The regulations give these examples [Reg. Sec. 1.446-1(e)(2)(ii)(a)]:

1. A change from the cash method to the accrual method, or vice versa.[1]
2. A change in the method or basis used in valuing inventories [Ch. 17].

3. A change from the cash or accrual method to a long-term contract method, or vice versa [¶2942].

4. A change to or from any other special method, such as the crop method [¶2720].

5. A change for which IRS consent is specifically required.

However, a change in accounting method *does not* include: (1) the correction of mathematical or posting errors; (2) errors involving the computation of tax liability; (3) the adjustment of income or deduction items not involving the proper timing for inclusion (for example, the correction of items deducted as interest or salary when they are in fact dividend payments); (4) the adjustment of the useful life of a depreciable asset; (5) changes in the treatment of any item that results from a change in the underlying facts [Reg. Sec. 1.446-1(e)(2)(ii)(b)].

(b) IRS Consent Required. You make an application to change an accounting method on Form 3115. You must file Form 3115 with the Commissioner of Internal Revenue within 180 days after the start of the tax year for which the change is desired [Reg. Sec. 1.446-1(e)(3)(i)]. For example, if you want to change your method of accounting for calendar year 1993, you must file Form 3115 by June 29, 1993. If you file an incomplete Form 3115, the IRS must notify you of this fact. You then have 45 days (or a shorter period imposed by the IRS) within which to supply the information to the IRS.[2]

You must disclose in detail all classes of items that would be treated differently under the new method. Also, all amounts that would be duplicated or omitted as a result of the proposed change must be indicated, together with a computation of adjustments to take into account the duplications or omissions. Permission to change will not be granted, unless you and the IRS agree to the terms and conditions under which the change will be made [Reg. Sec. 1.446-1(e)(3)(i)]. Consent to a changed method may be implied from IRS acceptance of its use.[3] If the accounting method is changed, certain adjustments in income and deductions are required [¶2813]. The adjustment period over which changes must be taken into account is generally limited to six or three years.[2]

> **PROCEDURES REVISED** The IRS has revised its procedures for making accounting method changes. The new rules apply to requests filed on or after March 23, 1992, and are designed to encourage prompt compliance. If you initiate the accounting method change before the IRS begins an examination, any adjustments to income required by the change can generally be spread over several years.[2]

IRS Consent Not Required

When a subsidiary corporation must change its method to conform to that of the consolidated group of which it is a member;[4] when changing from the declining balance to the straight line depreciation method (¶2121) [Reg. Sec. 1.167(e)- 1(b)]; when changing to straight line depreciation despite contrary agreement to avoid depreciation recapture [Reg. Sec. 1.167(e)-1(c)(1); Temp. Reg. Sec. 13.0].

(c) Other Special Cases. There are special procedures for the following categories of accounting method changes: Change in overall accounting method from cash receipts and disbursements to accrual;[2] change in overall accounting method from cash to accrual because of the required use of inventories;[5] certain changes from the LIFO inventory method.[6]

¶2813   ADJUSTMENTS REQUIRED BY CHANGE IN ACCOUNTING METHOD

If you change your accounting method, you must make an adjustment to avoid duplicating or omitting income or deduction items [IRC Sec. 481(a); Reg. Sec. 1.481-1]. So, the income of the transition year may consist of two elements: (1) taxable income figured under the new method and (2) adjustments between the old and the new method.

NOTE: A "Sec. 481" adjustment is not required for a change from the accrual to the installment method of accounting. In that case, you follow the rules of IRC Sec. 453 instead [Reg. Sec. 1.481-1(e)].

Example 1: Mr. Green, changing from the cash to the accrual basis in 1992, has taxable income for 1992 of $20,000 figured on the accrual basis. His books at the start of 1992 show: Accounts receivable, $30,000; accounts payable, $14,000; inventory, $5,000. 1991 taxable income after adjustments for items that are treated differently under the old and new methods is $41,000:

1. Taxable income figured on accrual basis $20,000
2. Adjustments:
    (a) Add: (1) Items not previously reported as income:
                     Accounts receivable 1-1-92 . . . . $30,000
                (2) Items previously deducted:
                     Inventory 1-1-92 . . . . $ 5,000
                Total to be added   35,000
                Total $55,000
    (b) Subtract items not previously deducted:
                Accounts payable 1-1-92 14,000
3. Taxable income after adjustments $41,000

➤ **ADJUSTMENTS SPREAD OVER YEARS** If the net amount of your adjustments is an increase in taxable income of not more than $3,000 (or is any decrease), you make the entire amount of the adjustment in the year of change [IRC Sec. 481]. But if the increase in income exceeds $3,000, you may make the adjustment by: (1) a three-year allocation method, (2) an allocation under the new method of accounting or (3) any other method agreed on between you and the IRS [IRC Sec. 481(b), (c); Reg. Sec. 1.481-2(a), (b), 1.481-5].

NOTE: You generally make the election of a relief method in a statement filed with the IRS when permission to change the accounting method is requested [¶2812(b)].

Three-year allocation method. The tax is reduced to the amount that you would have paid if you had received one-third of the increase in your income in the year of the change and one-third in each of the two preceding years. To qualify for this method, you must have used the old method of accounting for the two years preceding the change-over year [IRC Sec. 481(b)(1); Reg. Sec. 1.481-2(a), (d)].

Example 2: Assume the same facts as in Example 1, and that Green used the cash method in 1990 and 1991. Since the adjustments increase taxable income by $21,000 ($41,000 adjusted taxable income less $20,000 taxable income before adjustments), Green may allocate the additional income as follows: $7,000 to 1990, $7,000 to 1991 and $7,000 to 1992.

Allocation under new method of accounting. If you can establish your taxable income under the new method for any number of years consecutively preceding the change-over year, the tax is reduced to the amount that you would have paid if (1) you figured the tax for those preceding years under the new method and (2) you allocated the then remaining adjustments to the change-over year [IRC Sec. 481(b)(2); Reg. Sec. 1.481-2(b), (d)].

Example 3: Assume the same facts as in Example 1, and that Green recomputed the tax for 1990 and 1991 on the accrual basis. On this basis, the taxable income for 1990 was increased by $6,000 and for 1991 by $7,000. Thus, $13,000 of the $21,000 adjustments were allocated to those years. The balance, $8,000, is taken into account in figuring the tax for 1992 (the change-over year).

Special rules apply to carrybacks and carryovers of net operating losses and capital losses [IRC Sec. 481(b)(3)(A); Reg. Sec. 1.481-2(c)(2)].[1]

ACCOUNTING PERIODS

¶2816   ACCOUNTING PERIODS

(a) General Rules. Your taxable income is figured on the basis of your annual accounting period. This may be either the calendar year or a fiscal year [IRC Sec. 441(b)(1); Temp. Reg. Sec. 1.441-1T(b)]. A fiscal year means (1) an accounting period of 12 months ending on the last day of any month other than December or (2) an annual accounting period varying from 52 to 53 weeks, subject to the rules in (b) below [Temp. Reg. Sec. 1.441-1T(e)].

No books kept. If you do not keep books, you must use a calendar year [IRC Sec. 441(b)(2); Temp. Reg. Sec. 1.441-1T(b)].

New taxpayers. You may not prepare your return based on an accounting period that ends on a date other than the last day of a calendar month. If you do make such a choice, you must compute net income on a calendar year basis.[1] Exception: Electing a 52-53 week period [(b) below].

A newly organized corporation may file its return on a fiscal-year basis without applying to the IRS for permission. To qualify, the fiscal-year basis must be definitely established and the books kept on a fiscal-year basis before the close of the first fiscal year.[2]

A sole proprietor must report business and personal income on the basis of the same tax year. For example, you may not operate your business on a fiscal-year basis, and file your individual return on a calendar year basis.[3]

Partnership S corporation and personal service corporation. Special rules, covered in ¶2820 limit the selection of a fiscal year.

(b) 52-53 Week Fiscal Year. A 52-53 week fiscal year is an accounting period which varies from 52 to 53 weeks and always ends on the same day of the week. If you regularly keep your books on the basis of this type of year, you may also use it to figure your taxable income [IRC Sec. 441(f)(1); Temp. Reg. Sec. 1.441-2T]. There are two kinds of 52-53 week fiscal years:

- Your accounting period may end on the same day of the week that occurs for the last time in a particular calendar month. The year may end as many as six days before the end of the month [Temp. Reg. Sec. 1.441-2T(a)].
- Alternatively, the year may end on the same day of the week that falls nearest to the end of a particular calendar month. In that case, the year may end as many as three days before or after the end of the month [Reg. Sec. 1.441-2(a)].

If you do not keep books regularly on the basis of a 52-53 week year, you may elect this period if, at the time of election, you conform your books to this basis. After that, you must continue to keep your books and report income on this basis (¶2817; 2818; 2819) [Temp. Reg. Sec. 1.441-2T(c)].

Effective dates. The due dates of returns and effective dates of tax law changes are often based on the beginning or ending of tax years. In such cases, the following rules apply:

- A 52-53 week year is considered to begin on the first day of the calendar month nearest to the first day of the 52-53 week year.
- It is considered to end or close on the last day of the calendar month ending nearest to the last day of the 52-53 week year [IRC Sec. 441(f)(2)(A); Temp. Reg. Sec. 1.441-2T(b)].

Example 1: Assume a new tax rate applies to tax years beginning after December 31. A 52-53 week year starting on any day within the period December 26 to January 4, is treated as starting on January 1.

Example 2: Assume a return is due by the 15th of the 3rd month following the close of the fiscal year. A 52-53 week year ending on June 1 is considered as ending on May 31. The return, therefore, must be filed by Aug. 15.

Election. If you are a new taxpayer, you do not need permission to use a 52-53 week fiscal year. If you are switching to this type of fiscal year, you make the election by attaching a statement to the return for the first period for which the election is made. It should show: (1) the calendar month with reference to which the new 52-53 week year ends; (2) the day of the week on which the tax year will always end; and (3) whether it will end on (a) the date the day occurs for the last time in the calendar month, or (b) the date it occurs nearest to the end of the calendar month. The Commissioner's prior approval is not needed as long as the 52-53 week year being elected ends on a day that refers to the same month in which the taxpayer's prior year ended. In other cases, see the general rules outlined at ¶2816 or the special rules for partners and partnerships in Chapter 24. Also see ¶2819 for rules regarding short tax years resulting from changes to or from 52-53 week years [Temp. Reg. Sec. 1.441-2T(c)].

¶2817   CHANGE IN ACCOUNTING PERIOD

You may want to change from a calendar year to a fiscal year, from a fiscal year to a calendar year, or from one fiscal year to another fiscal year. You must file a fractional-year return for the part of the year between the close of the old period and the start of the new. This period is called the "short tax year" (¶2819) [IRC Sec. 443(a)].

Special rules apply to short tax periods resulting from a change to or from a 52-53 week accounting period. In the year the 52-53 week period is adopted, periods of more than 358 days and periods of less than 7 days are not treated as short periods. You treat the former as full years; you add the latter to the following tax year [IRC Sec. 441(f)(2)(B); Temp. Reg. Sec. 1.441-2T(c)].

Example 1: Assume a corporation is on a calendar-year basis for 1992. It elects to report income for 1993 on the basis of a 52-53 week period, ending on the Tuesday nearest to the end of December. The first tax period following the change will consist of the period from January 6, 1993, through December 31, 1993, plus the short period of 5 days, January 1 through January 5, 1993. No fractional return is required for the short period since it is less than 7 days.

Example 2: Assume the same facts as in Example 1, except that the corporation was on a fiscal year ending November 30. The first full tax year will consist of the period from January 6, 1993, through December 31, 1993. A fractional year return will be required for the short tax year beginning December 1, 1992, and ending January 5, 1993, since this period consists of more than 6 but less than 359 days.

¶2818   REQUESTING A CHANGE

Generally, your change in accounting period must be approved by the Commissioner [IRC Sec. 442; Reg. Sec. 1.442-1(a)]. You apply for the change on Form 1128, on or before the 15th day of the second calendar month following the close of the short tax year. If there is a substantial business reason for the change, it will usually be approved (e.g., to change to a year that coincides with your natural business cycle).[1] You and the Commissioner have to agree to the terms, conditions and adjustments required [Reg. Sec. 1.442-1(b)].

A change ordinarily will not be approved if it substantially reduces your tax liability. This could be the case if the change shifted income or deductions to another year or another taxpayer (e.g., a short tax year has a substantial net operating loss). However, even in these cases, approval may be obtained if you agree to certain adjustments to eliminate the distortions in taxable income [Reg. Sec. 1.442-1(b)].[2] There are special rules for partners and partnerships [¶3414 et seq.], bank or trust company fiduciaries[3] and tax-exempt organizations.[4]

Special rules for corporations: There's a special rule that lets a corporation change its accounting period without prior approval, as long as certain conditions are met. If qualified, all the corporation has to do is file a statement with the District Director by the time (including extensions) for filing the short year return. To be eligible:

- The corporation must not have changed its accounting period within the ten calendar years that end with the year the short tax year begins.
- The short tax year cannot have a net operating loss.
- The taxable income for the short tax year [¶2819], when annualized, must be at least 80% of taxable income for the preceding full tax year.
- The corporation does not make an S election for the tax year following the short tax year.
- A corporation that has a special status for the short period must have had the same status for the tax year immediately preceding the short period (e.g., a personal holding company or exempt organization) [Reg. Sec. 1.442-1(c)].

Quick approval: If a corporation does not qualify for an automatic tax year change, it may qualify to get a quick approval of a tax year change—generally within 60 days. And the IRS has recently eased its rules so that more corporations will be able to use the quick approval procedure.[5] Under the ruling, this procedure can be used if:

- The corporation cannot meet all five of the conditions for an automatic change.
- The corporation has not changed its accounting period at any time within the last 6 calendar years. (It was 10 years prior to the recent IRS ruling.)

Certain corporations are ineligible to use the quick approval procedure. They include: personal service corporations; corporations that are members of a partnership or beneficiaries of an estate or trust; S corporations; certain foreign corporations and domestic corporations with foreign interests; and most tax-exempt organizations (but not farmers cooperatives and homeowners associations).

(a) Husband and Wife cannot file a joint return and take advantage of the split-income benefits unless both have the same tax year [¶1104; 3602]. Permission may be granted to change a spouse's accounting period so that a joint return can be filed, even though there is no other reason for the change [Reg. Sec. 1.442-1(b)(1)].

Newly married couples. As a newly married person, you may change your accounting period to conform to that of your spouse (or vice versa) so that you two may file a joint return. The spouse making the change has to file a return for the short tax year by the 15th day of the 4th month following the close of the short tax year. The return has to include a statement that it is authorized by Reg. Sec. 1.442-1(e). If you get married after the due date of the short tax year return, the "changing" spouse has to wait until the second tax year of the nonchanging spouse that ends after the marriage date [Reg. Sec. 1.442-1(e)].

(b) A Subsidiary Corporation. Such a corporation that is required to change its accounting period because it has elected to file consolidated returns [¶3045(c)] need not file Form 1128 when the consolidated return is filed [Reg. Sec. 1.442-1(d)].[5]

(c) If Book and Tax Periods Differ. If you regularly keep books on the calendar or fiscal year, but erroneously file returns on a different basis, you do not need permission to file returns for later years based on the way the books are kept.[6]

¶2819   RETURNS FOR PERIODS OF LESS THAN 12 MONTHS

Most income tax returns cover an accounting period of 12 months. However, shorter periods may be used when you (a) file your first or final return and (b) change an accounting period.

(a) First or Final Returns. Short period returns are required of new taxpayers filing their first returns and of taxpayers ending their existence. This applies to all kinds of taxpayers, such as corporations, partnerships, estates and trusts and decedents. These returns are prepared and filed, and the taxes paid, as if they were returns for a 12-month period ending on the last day of the short period. The income of the short period is not annualized, nor are personal exemptions or tax credits prorated. A decedent's return, however, may be filed and the tax paid as if he had lived to the end of his last tax year [IRC Sec. 443; Reg. Sec. 1.443-1(a)(2)].

(b) Change of Accounting Period. You may have to file a return for a period of less than 12 months when you change accounting periods. Unlike first or final short period returns, you must place these returns on an annual basis [IRC Sec. 443(b)]. This is done as follows [IRC Sec. 443; Reg. Sec. 1.443-1(b)(1)]:

1. Multiply the short period modified taxable income (i.e., gross income minus deductions allowed for the short period) by 12.
2. Divide the result by the number of months in the short period.
3. Figure the tax on the result on an annual basis, using the tax rate schedules.
4. Divide the result by 12.
5. Multiply the result by the number of months in the short period.

Example 1: JPS Corporation had net income before tax of $20,000 for the four-month short period ending April 30, 1993. Annualized taxable income is $60,000 ($20,000 × 12/4). The tax on this amount is $10,000. To annualize the tax, multiply it by 4/12. Result: $3,333.

Individual taxpayers. If you file a short period return due to a change in accounting period, you have to follow three additional special rules:

1. You cannot use the tax tables to compute your tax liability [IRC Sec. 3(b)]. You must use the tax rate schedules [¶1123].

2. You must use your actual amount of itemized deductions to compute short period taxable income. You cannot use the standard deduction [Reg. Sec. 1.443-1(b)(1)(iv)].

3. Your deduction for personal exemptions is annualized. This is done by apportioning them in the ratio that the number of months in the short tax year bears to 12 [IRC Sec. 443(c); Reg. Sec. 1.443-1(b)(1)].

Example 2: Mr. Roberts is married with one child. He and his wife file a joint return. They decide to change from a fiscal year ending March 31 to a calendar year in 1992. Gross income for the short period April 1–December 31, 1992, is $43,000. Itemized deductions for the short period total $8,700. His three exemptions for the year come to $6,900. The tax for the short period is computed as follows:

Gross income for short period		$43,000
Less: Deductions	$8,700	
9/12 of exemptions	5,175	13,875
		$29,125
		× 12/9
Annualized taxable income		$38,833
Tax (1992 rates) on annualized taxable income		$ 6,219
Tax for 9-month period (9/12 of tax on annualized taxable income)		$ 4,662

Net operating loss. In computing taxable income for a short year, you apply a net operating loss deduction against the actual income for the short period before placing the income on an annual basis.[1]

Alternative minimum tax. Your alternative minimum taxable income [Ch. 16] for the short period is placed on an annual basis by multiplying it by 12 and dividing the result by the number of months in the short period. Your alternative minimum tax is computed on that annualized income. Then the tax is reduced by using the ratio that the number of months in the short year bears to 12 [IRC Sec. 443(d)].

Credits. If any credit against your tax depends upon the amount of any item of income or deduction, the credit must be computed upon the annualized value of the item and then applied against your tax figured on an annual basis. If the credit limitation is based on taxable income, you must annualize your income [Reg. Sec. 1.443-1(b)(1)].

Example 3: Suppose that in Example 2 above, Mr. Roberts and his wife qualify to take the tax credit for child care expenses. Suppose also that their actual child care expenses exceed the $2,400 limitation. Since their annualized short period gross income is $57,333 ($43,000 × 12⁄9), the applicable percentage is 20% and the amount of the credit on an annualized basis is $480. Subtracting this from the annualized tax of $6,219 gives you an annualized tax after credits of $5,739. Result: Tax after credits for the 9-month period is $4,304 ($5,730 × 9⁄12).

52-53 week year. In annualizing your income for short tax years resulting from a change to or from a 52-53 week accounting period [¶2816(b)], your computation is made on a daily basis [IRC Sec. 441(f)(2)(B); Reg. Sec. 1.441-2(c)].

➤ **RELIEF AVAILABLE** To prevent hardship, you can apply for a refund if the tax figured under the annualized method is greater than the tax figured on actual income for the 12-month period starting with the first day of the short period. This would occur, for instance, if the short period covered your business' peak season.

Your eligibility for this relief is determined by establishing the actual taxable income for the 12 months *beginning* with the first day of the short period. The tax on your actual taxable income for the 12-month period is then multiplied by a fraction (the numerator being your actual taxable income for the short period and the denominator being your taxable income for the 12-month period). Your tax for the short period computed under this method cannot be less than your tax on the unannualized income for the short period (with some modifications) [IRC Sec. 443(b)(2); Reg. Sec. 1.443-1(b)(2)].

Noncorporate taxpayers who were not in existence at the end of the 12-month period may figure their tax based on the 12 months *ending* with the last day of the short period. The same rule applies to a corporation that has disposed of substantially all of its assets before the end of the 12-month period [IRC Sec. 443(b)(2)(B); Reg. Sec. 1.443-1(b)(2)].

Example 4: GVW Inc. had income for a 4-month short period beginning September 1, 1992, of $41,000, and for a 12-month period ending the following August 31, 1993, of $85,000. Its tax without placing the income on an annual basis would be $6,150. Its tax computed under the exception is:

Taxable income for 12-month period $85,000
Tax on income for 12-month period $17,150
Tax for short period: $17,500 × 41,000/$85,000 . . . . $ 8,272

The corporation's tax for the 4-month short period is $8,272 (the greater of the two alternative calculations). If the exception isn't elected, the tax is $10,023 (⁴⁄12 of the $30,070 tax on $123,000 annualized income).

How to apply. To use the relief method, you must first file a return and pay the tax under the general method. Then, you apply to the IRS to use the optional method. The application is made in the form of a claim for credit or refund which shows how the taxable income and tax for the 12-month period were computed. The deadline for applying is the due date (including extensions) of your return for the first taxable year which ends at least one year after the first day of the short period [IRC Sec. 443(b)(2)(A); Reg. Sec. 1.443-1(b)(2)(v)(a)].

¶2820 SPECIAL RULE FOR TAX YEAR ELECTION BY PARTNERSHIPS, S CORPORATIONS AND PERSONAL SERVICE CORPORATIONS

Partnerships, S corporations and personal service corporations (PSCs) generally must use the same tax year as their owners (i.e., a calendar year). However, there are two major exceptions:

1. Your partnership or S corporation can elect a fiscal year if it makes "required payments;" your PSC can do the same—if it makes "minimum distributions." You make the election by filing Form 8716 by the earlier of: (1) the 15th day of the fifth month after the month that includes the first day of the tax year for which the election is first effective (e.g., October 15th, if the first day is in May), or (2) the due date (without extensions) of the income tax return resulting from the fiscal year election [IRC Sec. 444; Temp. Reg. Sec. 1.444-3T]. (A sample Form 8716 can be found below.)

2. If your business establishes a business purpose for using a fiscal year (e.g., to follow the business' "natural business year"), it is exempt from the rules discussed here. Wanting to defer tax does not constitute a business purpose [IRC Sec. 706(b), 1378].

Back-up election. If your business makes a request to use a particular tax year based on a business purpose, it should also file a back-up election. A back-up fiscal year election is like a safety valve. If the business purpose request is denied and the deadline has passed, your business can activate the back-up election [Temp. Reg. Sec. 1.444-3T(b)(4)]. This will allow your business to elect or retain its fiscal year under exception 1. You make the election by filing Form 8716, "Election to Have a Tax Year Other Than a Required Tax Year." Type or print "BACK-UP ELECTION" at the top (or "FORM 1128 BACK-UP

ELECTION" if filing on or after the filing deadline for Form 1128—which is the change of accounting period application).

Partnerships and S corporations activate an election by filing Form 8752 and making the required payment by the later of the regular due date [(b) below] or 60 days after the IRS denies the business purpose request. Personal service corporations file Form 8716 with the PSCs original or amended income tax return for the taxable year in which the election is first effective. Type or print "ACTIVATING BACK-UP ELECTION" at the top of the income tax return. Unlike partnerships and S corporations, the regulations don't require PSCs to activate the back-up election within 60 days of the IRS' denial of the business purpose request. So, apparently a PSC may activate the back-up election at any time until the cut-off date for filing an amended return.

(a) Qualifying Conditions. Your partnership, S corporation or PSC can make a fiscal year election if it meets three conditions: (1) the business must not be part of a "tiered structure" with one exception, (2) the business must not have made a fiscal-year election previously and (3) the fiscal year being elected meets certain restrictions concerning the duration of the so-called deferral period.

Tiered structures. As a general rule, a business that is a member of a so-called "tiered structure" cannot elect a fiscal year. Your business is considered a member of a tiered structure if it owns a portion of a deferral entity (partnership, S corporation, PSC or trust) or is partly owned by a deferral entity. There are certain de minimis rules that exempt small ownership interests [Temp. Reg. Sec. 1.444-2T].

> **SPECIAL EXCEPTION**　Your partnership or S corporation that is a member of a tiered structure may make a Sec. 444 election if the structure consists entirely of partnerships or S corporations (or both) that have the same tax year. This exception is generally not available to PSCs that are members of a tiered structure [IRC Sec. 444(d)(3); Temp. Reg. Sec. 1.444-2T(e)].

Deferral period. In general, your deferral period is the number of months between the end of the requested fiscal year and the end of the calendar year. For example, if the requested fiscal year ends on September 30, the deferral period is three months (September 30 to December 31). For businesses that elect a fiscal year, this period generally cannot be more than three months. But if your business is changing its tax year from one fiscal year to another, the permissible deferral period is limited to the shorter of three months or the deferral period of the prior tax year prior [Temp. Reg. Sec. 1.444-1T(b)].

(b) Required Payments. If your partnership or S corporation makes the fiscal-year election, it must make "required payments." These payments, in effect, represent the tax that would be deferred by using a fiscal year.

The payments must be made along with Form 8752. The required payment is due on or before May 15 of the year following the year in which the election year begins [Temp. Reg. Sec. 1.7519-1T, -2T].

> **ESCAPE HATCH**　No required payment must be made if the required payment for the year is not more than $500 and no required payment was necessary for a prior year. Nevertheless, your partnership or S corporation would still have to file Form 8752.

How to figure the required payment. Your partnership's or S corporation's required payment for each year it elects to use a fiscal year is calculated under the following formula: (1) adjusted highest income tax rate multiplied by the entity's net base-year income less (2) the cumulative required payments made for all preceding election years (reduced by refunded amounts) [Temp. Reg. Sec. 1.7519-1T(a)(3)]. Here's a rundown of the key definitions in the formula:

Adjusted highest income tax rate. This is the highest tax rate on individual taxpayers for the preceding election year, plus one percentage point [Temp. Reg. Sec. 1.7519-1T(b)(2)]. So, for 1992 this rate would be 32% (31% plus 1%).

Net base-year income. The base year is the tax year preceding the election year [Temp. Reg. Sec. 1.7519-1T(1)(b)(3)]. Start by determining the deferral ratio. This is the number of months in the deferral period of the base year divided by the total number of months in the tax year. Then multiply the deferral ratio by the net income for the base year. Add to that amount, the excess of (1) the deferral ratio times the total amount of applicable payments during the base year over (2) the total amount of applicable payments made during the deferral period of the base year [Temp. Reg. Sec. 1.7519-1T(b)(5)].

Net income is the amount determined by taking into account the total amount of partnership or S corporation items (other than credits and tax exempt income) after payments. Net income cannot be less than zero.

Applicable payments are amounts paid or incurred by a partnership or S corporation that are included in an owner's gross income. They don't include certain guaranteed payments made by a partnership to a partner.

> **Example 1:** A partnership continues its Sec. 444 election for the year ending September 30, 1992. Its net income for the prior year—the "base year"—was $10,000. Salary payments to partners—"applicable payments"—during the base year were $4,700; $3,000 of these payments were made during the base year deferral period. The required payment for the election year ended September 30, 1993, is computed as follows:

1.	Base year net income	$10,000
2.	Base year applicable payments	$ 4,700
3.	Base year deferral ratio (3 months ÷ 12 months)	25%
4.	Line 1 × Line 3	$ 2,500
5.	Line 2 × Line 3	$ 1,175
6.	Applicable payments made during the base year deferral period	$ 3,000
7.	Line 5 less Line 6 (not less than zero)	$ -0-
8.	Net base year income (Line 4 plus Line 7)	$ 2,500
9.	Adjusted highest tax rate (31% + 1%)	32%
10.	Election year required payment (Line 8 × Line 9)	$ 800

> The partnership's payment would be the excess of $800 over the sum of required payments made in all prior election years (net of refunds).

> ▶ **REFUNDS AVAILABLE** Your fiscal-year partnership or S corporation may be entitled to a refund of required payments. This could happen if the election to use a fiscal year is terminated; the value of the deferral decreases in a subsequent tax year; or the business is liquidated. You claim the refund by filing Form 8752. A Sec. 444 election generally terminates if the business: (1) changes to a required year, (2) liquidates, (3) willfully fails to comply with the required payments or minimum distributions or (4) becomes a member of a tiered structure.

(c) Minimum Distributions. If your PSC elects a fiscal year, it must make "minimum distributions" to you and its other shareholder-employees. If the PSC doesn't meet this requirement for an election year, its deductions for payments to owner-employees is limited [IRC Sec. 280H(a); Temp. Reg. Sec. 1.280H-1T(b)].

Essentially, the minimum distribution requirement is a mechanical test designed to minimize the benefits of tax deferral created by the fiscal-year election. Under the test, amounts paid to you and other owner-employees in the deferral period (the number of months between the end of the fiscal year and December 31) must equal or exceed the lesser of amounts determined under the (1) preceding year test or (2) three-year average test [IRC Sec. 280H(c); Temp. Reg. Sec. 1.280H-1T(c)].

Preceding year test. Amounts paid to the owner-employees in the preceding year and includible in their gross income are divided by the number of months in the year and then multiplied by the number of months in the deferral period. Note: For purposes of this calculation, you don't include payments which represent gain from the sale or exchange of property between you and other owner-employees and your PSC or dividends paid by the corporation.

> **Example 2:** A PSC paid $120,000 to its owner-employees during the year ended October 31, 1992 (a full 12-month year). To apply the preceding-year test for the year ended October 31, 1993, the testing amount is $20,000 ($120,000 ÷ 12 months = $10,000; $10,000 × 2 months) [IRC Sec. 280H(f); Temp. Reg. Sec. 1.280H-1T(c)(2)].

Three-year average test. Amounts paid (as defined above) to you and other owner-employees for the immediately prior three years are divided by the PSC's "adjusted taxable income" for the same period to give you the "applicable percentage." Adjusted taxable income is the sum of your PSC's taxable income plus amounts included in the owner-employees' gross incomes (excluding gains on sales and dividends.) The applicable percentage is then multiplied by your PSC's adjusted taxable income for the deferral period of the year being tested.

> ➤ **BREAK FOR NEW PSCs** Your PSC is deemed to have satisfied both the three-year average test and the preceding year test for the first year it's in existence.

Even if your PSC fails to satisfy the minimum distribution requirements, it can still deduct what is called the "maximum deductible amount."

Maximum deductible amount. If your PSC doesn't meet the minimum distribution requirement for any applicable election year, the amount of applicable payments it can deduct for that year is limited to a maximum deductible amount. That amount is the sum of (1) the applicable amounts paid in the deferral period plus (2) the applicable amounts paid in the deferral period divided by the number of months in the deferral period multiplied by the number of months in the nondeferral period. The nondeferral period is the portion of the applicable election year that comes after the deferral period [Temp. Reg. Sec. 1.280H-1T(d)].

> **Example 3:** XYZ Personal Service Corporation elects to retain a fiscal tax year that ends on January 31. XYZ, which has three owner-employees, does not meet the minimum distribution requirements for the year. XYZ paid the three owner-employees $143,000 in compensation for the year. Result: XYZ's maximum deductible amount for the year is $156,000—$143,000 (applicable payments during the deferral period) plus $13,000 ($143,000 divided by 11 months in the deferral period multiplied by one month in the nondeferral period).

> ➤ **CARRYOVER OF DISALLOWED AMOUNTS** Payments to owner-employees that can't be deducted aren't lost. They're carried over and treated as paid or incurred in the next tax year. And there's no time limit on how long they can be carried forward [IRC Sec. 280H(b)].

WHEN TO REPORT INCOME

¶2824   PERIOD IN WHICH ITEMS OF GROSS INCOME REPORTED

(a) Cash-Basis taxpayers report all income subject to tax actually or constructively received, in cash or its equivalent, during the year [IRC Sec. 451; Reg. Sec. 1.451-1]; for constructive receipt, see ¶2803.

Checks are income in the year you receive them, even though you cash them in a later year.[1] This is so, even if you receive the check too late to cash it in the year of receipt.[2] However, if you do not cash the check until the next year at the request of the drawer, you include the check in your income in the year you cash it.[3] For dividend checks, see ¶2826.

(b) Accrual Basis. If you are on the accrual basis, you include in gross income all income subject to tax that accrues during the year. You accrue income when all the events have occurred that fix your right to receive it, the amount can be reasonably estimated and your right to receive it isn't subject to substantial restrictions (the "all events" test). When you make a reasonable estimate, you include in income any difference between the estimated and exact amount in the year the exact amount is determined [Reg. Sec. 1.451-1]. You do not have to accrue income if the right to receive it depends on some future occurrence.[4]

Uncollectible amounts. You are not required to accrue an amount that probably you will never receive. The courts generally do not require the accrual of payments of interest, rents or royalties if the payments are uncollectible when they are due. If an obligation is not collectible when the right to receive it arises, nothing accrues.[5]

> ➤ **SPECIAL ACCRUAL BREAK** If you are an accrual-basis taxpayer who does not expect to collect amounts due you for services performed, you do not have to accrue these amounts if the following qualifications are met: (1) experience shows payment won't be collected, (2) there is no charge for interest or penalties for late payments and (3) you adopt the "nonaccrual experience method" of accounting for bad debts [IRC Sec. 448(d)(5); Temp. Reg. Sec. 1.448-2T]. Under these rules, you calculate the portion of receivables that may be considered uncollectible using one of two methods: the "separate receivable system" or the "periodic system." In general, both methods base their calculations on your experience with uncollectible accounts based on a six-year period.

Discounts. If you offer discounts for early payment, you must accrue the gross amount billed. When and if you actually receive payment, you reduce income by the applicable discount [Temp. Reg. Sec. 1.448-2(c)].

State and local tax refunds. The Tax Court held that an accrual basis corporation does not include state and local tax refunds in income until the year in which the right to the refund is ultimately determined. But the IRS won't acquiesce on this point.[6]

Prepaid income generally is reported in the year received. You cannot prorate it over the period in which you are to perform the services.[6] However, there are some exceptions [¶2833].

¶2825   COMPENSATION FOR SERVICES

(a) Cash Basis. If you are on the cash basis, you include compensation in income for the year you actually or constructively receive it [¶2803].[1] Generally, it is immaterial that your employer, using the accrual basis, deducted the compensation in the previous year. Part of your pay deferred under an employment contract is not income in the year earned until you actually receive payment or it is made available to you later. At the same time, you employer can deduct deferred compensation payments only in the year they are actually made.[2] Special rules apply to a salaried partner [¶3414; 3416(d)]. Money placed in an educational benefit trust set up by a corporation for the education of employees' children is deferred compensation taxable to the employees and deductible by the corporation when paid out of the trust.[3]

Advances to salespersons. If, under your employment contract, advances are a debt you owe your employer, they are not taxable when you receive them. However, if the advances were originally intended as loans but are later charged off, they are additional compensation to you and deductible by your employer in the year charged off.[4] If the contract guarantees you a certain monthly sum, advances up to the guarantee are income when you receive them.[5]

Related parties. See ¶2860 for rules on compensation paid by accrual basis employer after year-end to cash basis employee.

(b) Accrual Basis. If you are an accrual basis taxpayer, your pay is usually income in the year you earn it. But if your right to receive income or the amount of that income is not determined until you complete the services, it is income for the year you can make the determination [Reg. Sec. 1.451-1].

Advance payments. Generally, advance payments (e.g., paying two years of rent "up-front" when the lease is signed) are income in the year received for both cash and accrual basis taxpayers (provided there are no restrictions on the use of the funds). But there's a limited exception for prepayments for future services. If you are an accrual basis taxpayer, you can wait to recognize prepaid income until the time of performance, if the agreement specifies that the services will be performed before the end of the year following the year of payment.[6]

(c) Restricted Property. If property you receive for performing services is subject to a substantial risk of forfeiture, you do not generally include the property's value in income until the time when the restrictions lapse (¶1208(a)) [IRC Sec. 83].

¶2826   DIVIDENDS

Dividends are subject to tax if they are unqualifiedly subject to the shareholder's demand [Reg. Sec. 1.301-1(b)]. This applies to both cash and accrual basis taxpayers.

> **Example 1:** A dividend is fully and unqualifiedly available to Turner in 1992. He can obtain it merely for the asking. Although Turner does not actually receive the dividend until 1993, it is taxable in 1992.

> **Example 2:** Mr. Benton, a stockbroker, buys stock for Mr. Mason in Benton's name. Benton is Mason's duly appointed agent. Benton receives a dividend for Mason on December 14, 1992, but transmits it to Mason by check on January 2, 1993. It is taxable to Mason in 1992.

Dividend checks mailed on last day of tax year. If a dividend is declared payable on December 31, but the corporation follows the practice of mailing the dividend checks so that they will not be received until January, you do not have constructive receipt in December, and the dividend is January income [Reg. Sec. 1.451-2(b)], even if you are on the accrual basis.[1] For treatment of other checks received by the cash basis taxpayer, see ¶2824(a).

(a) Income From Building and Loan Associations. An amount credited to the shareholders of a building and loan association is constructively received in the year of credit, if it passes without restriction to the shareholder. But if the amount accumulated is not available to you until maturity, the total amount credited is income to you in the year of maturity [Reg. Sec. 1.451-2(b)].

(b) Patronage Dividends and Per-Unit Retains are generally taxable in the year received, whether you are on the cash or accrual basis [IRC Sec. 1385(a); Reg. Sec. 1.1385-1(a)]. See ¶3358 for patrons' income from cooperatives.

¶2827   INTEREST AND DISCOUNTS

(a) Interest. If you are on the cash basis, interest is generally taxable when you actually or constructively [¶2803] receive it. Accrual method taxpayers report interest for the year in which it accrues, unless received earlier [¶2833]. And you may not report interest income net of interest expense on funds borrowed to make the investment.[1]

(b) Discount Instruments. Even as a cash-basis taxpayer, you may owe tax on bonds, notes and other instruments acquired for less than their face value. The rules for original issue discount and market discount are explained at ¶1217.

(c) Certificates of Deposit. An increase in value of nonnegotiable and growth savings certificates issued by banks is included in a cash-basis taxpayer's gross income in the year the increase occurs, since you can redeem the certificate in that year.[2] Interest earned by a cash-basis taxpayer on a one-year or shorter certificate that is not credited or made available for withdrawal is not includable in your gross income until maturity.

¶2828   DISCOUNT AND INTEREST ON U.S. SAVINGS BONDS

(a) U.S. Savings Bonds Issued at a Discount. Series EE bonds are the only U.S. savings bonds currently issued at a discount. You pay less than the face amount for the bonds. The face amount is payable to you at maturity. The difference between the purchase price and the redemption value is taxable interest. The amount that accrues in any tax year is measured by the actual increase in the redemption price occurring in that year.[1]

➤ **OBSERVATION** Series EE bonds were first offered in 1980. Before then, Series E bonds were issued and many are still outstanding although they have fully matured.

Cash basis. Suppose you own either Series E or EE bonds. You may:

- Defer reporting the interest until the earlier of the year you cash in the bonds or the year in which they finally mature (method 1) or
- Choose to report the increase in redemption value as interest each year (method 2).

Example: Ms. Brown, a cash-basis taxpayer, bought a Series EE bond for $50 (maturity value $100) in January 1992. According to the Table of Redemption Values, the first increase in value occurs ½ year after issue ($51). If Brown elects to report the increment annually, she reports $1 in 1992. Any increases in 1993 and later years are reported in the same way.

➤ **TAX TIP** If your child owns U.S. savings bonds, you ought to consider electing method 2. Why be taxed sooner rather than later? If your child doesn't have much other income, no tax will actually be due. So this special election may mean total tax avoidance on the interest. Key to the savings: The interest income can be sheltered by your child's standard deduction.

If you want to change your method of reporting the interest from Method 1 to Method 2, you may do so with IRS permission. However, in the year of change, you must report all interest accrued to date and not previously reported for the bonds. There is a way to get automatic IRS approval of the change. However, it may be used no more often than once every five years. You attach a completed Form 3115 to your return for the year you're switching methods and print on top of it "FILED UNDER REV. PROC. 89-46." You must also attach a statement saying that you agree to report all untaxed interest when the bonds are redeemed, mature or are disposed of, whichever is earlier.[2]

> NOTE: If you plan to redeem Series EE bonds in the same year that you will pay for higher educational expenses, you should use method 1. See (c) below.

If a taxpayer dies owning savings bonds, the entire increment that had not been taxed is reported as income in respect of a decedent [¶3508(b)], unless the decedent's personal representative elects to report it in the decedent's final return.[3] An election cannot be made in an amended return filed after the due date of the original return or in an original return not timely filed.[4]

Accrual basis. If you are an accrual taxpayer, you must report interest on U.S. savings bonds each year as the interest accrues. You cannot defer reporting interest until the bonds are cashed or mature.[5]

Series E or EE bonds held beyond maturity. Let's say you are a cash-basis taxpayer who holds Series E or EE bonds after maturity. If you have elected to report the taxable increment on the accrual basis, you must continue to do so, unless you get permission to change. On the other hand, if you have elected to report on redemption or maturity, you report the entire increment in the year of *final* redemption or *extended* maturity.[5]

(b)　U.S. Savings Bonds Issued on a Current Income Basis. The only current income U.S. Savings Bonds currently outstanding are Series H or HH bonds. Unlike the bonds issued on a discount basis [(a) above], these current income bonds are issued at par with interest payable semiannually by Treasury check. The interest is taxable (1) when received, for those on the cash basis or (2) when accrued, for those on the accrual basis. The interest accrues when it becomes payable.[6] Owners of matured Series H or HH bonds may continue to hold the bonds at interest after maturity.[5] Interest for the extended period should be reported when received or accrued.

(c)　Education Savings Bonds. You may be able to exclude from income all or part of the interest you receive on redeeming qualified U.S. Savings Bonds if you pay qualified higher educational expenses during the year. See ¶ 1217(b).

¶2829　　　　RENT AND DEFERRED RENT TRANSACTIONS

(a)　Rent in General. If you are on the cash basis, rent is taxable when you receive it. For accrual basis taxpayers, rent accrues ratably over the period of the lease, unless paid in advance. In that case, it accrues when you receive it [Reg. Sec. 1.61-8(b)].

> **Example 1:** Mr. Davis owns an apartment house. Rent for December 1992 and for January 1993 is paid in January 1993. If Davis reports on the cash basis, the rent is 1993 income. If he reports on the accrual basis, the rent paid for December is 1992 income and that paid for January is 1993 income. But if Davis received the two months' rent in December 1992, it would be 1992 income whether he reports on the cash or accrual basis. The same rule would apply to other types of prepaid income (but see ¶2833 for exceptions). In this example, it is assumed that the rules explained in (b), below, do not apply.

Lease cancellation. Amounts you receive from a tenant for cancelling a lease are income in the year you receive them, even if you are on the accrual basis [Reg. Sec. 1.61-8(b)].[1]

(b) Deferred Payments for Use of Property or Services. Rental and interest income attributable to a "deferred rental agreement" must be reported and deducted as if both parties were on the accrual method of accounting [IRC Sec. 467]. Generally, a deferred rental payment agreement ("Section 467 rental agreement") is any agreement for the use of tangible property involving over $250,000 in rental payments, under which (1) at least one payment is made after the calendar year of the paid usage, or (2) there are rent increases over the term of the agreement. The accrual method that the lessor and lessee must use factors an interest element into the deferred payments. Thus, the lessor reports as income and the lessee deducts an amount equal to the sum of: (1) the "accrued rent" for the year and (2) interest on the amounts taken into account for prior years which remain unpaid.

Accrued rent for the year is calculated by adding rents allocated according to the rental agreement to the present value of rents to be paid after the close of the period. *Interest* is calculated at 110% of the Applicable Federal Rate (AFR), compounded semiannually. There are special rules for agreements that don't allocate rents and for tax avoidance transactions.

Tax avoidance. If you receive rent under a deferred payment agreement that is deemed to have a tax avoidance purpose, you must refigure your rental income to recognize a level amount of rent each year—the constant rental amount.

> ➤ **"CONSTANT RENTAL AMOUNT"** For agreements that are considered tax avoidance transactions, your accrued rental income for the year is the "constant rental amount." This is the amount which, if received at the close of each lease period (i.e., the 12-month period starting on the first day the agreement applies), would result in an aggregate present value equal to the present value of the aggregate payments required under the agreement. Present value is calculated at 110% of the AFR, compounded semiannually

What's a tax avoidance transaction? Agreements that meet certain conditions are presumed to be "tax avoidance transactions." The test applies to "disqualified leasebacks or long-term agreements." These are deferred payment rental agreements under which the term of the agreement exceeds 75% of the property's recovery period *and* a principal purpose for the increasing (i.e., stepped) rents is tax avoidance. The test also applies to agreements that don't provide how rents are to be allocated [IRC Sec. 467(b)].

Determining if a principal purpose of a deferred payment rental agreement is tax avoidance boils down to a question of the facts and circumstances of the particular situation.

A tax avoidance purpose might be presumed if, under the lease, the lessee had an option to renew at a rental amount significantly less than the rental amounts payable during the later years of the lease.

Safe harbors. There are certain "safe harbor" situations where a tax avoidance purpose will be presumed *not* to exist. These primarily apply to stepped rental agreements. The protected circumstances include: (1) rent increases based on price index changes, (2) rents figured based on a percentage-of-receipts formula, (3) reasonable rent holidays, such as for a short period of time after the inception of a lease and (4) changes in rent related to changes in amounts paid to unrelated third parties (e.g., insurance, maintenance or real estate taxes).

Recapture. Lessors who pass the tax-avoidance test are subject to a special recapture provision on the leased property's disposition. Any gain realized is ordinary income to the extent rent accruals that would have been taken into account had the rent leveling provision applied exceed actual accruals to the transfer date [IRC Sec. 467(c)].

Example 2: Mr. Smith has a $25,000 gain on the sale of an office building. Accrued rents were $2,000 at the date of sale, but would have been $3,000 if the rent leveling provisions had applied. Result: $1,000 of the gain is ordinary income.

¶2830　　　INCOME FROM SALE OF PROPERTY OR STOCK

(a) Sale of Property. You report gain from the sale of property in the year there is a *closed transaction*. For a *cash basis* taxpayer, that is usually when you receive the purchase price. *An accrual basis* taxpayer realizes gain when a sale is completed (see below), and you have an unqualified right to receive payment. This usually occurs when the buyer becomes unconditionally liable to pay the purchase price.[1]

When sale completed. A sale of real property generally occurs at the earlier of the time (1) title is conveyed by a deed, or (2) possession and the burdens and benefits of ownership are, from a practical standpoint, transferred to the buyer. The transfer of possession and of the burdens and benefits of ownership need not be complete. When the "bundle of rights" or attributes of ownership acquired by the buyer outweigh those retained by the seller, the sale is completed.[2] Sales of personal property are governed by the same rules. But most sales of personal property will occur when title passes. For tax purposes, the local law of sales determines when title passes.

Contingent payments. If all or part of the consideration for the sale of property is an agreement to make future payments of *a contingent character,* the transaction is not closed for tax purposes. No part of the contingent payments is income until you have recovered your capital. After that, the payments are taxed as capital gain, if the asset was a capital asset.[3]

> **Example:** Ms. Jones sold property to a corporation for a percentage of its profits for five years. Since the payments were contingent on earnings, they were not income until received, and then only to the extent they represented gain over the basis of the property.[4]

The tax rules for deferred payment sales are discussed at ¶2900 et seq.

(b) Sale of Stock Through Broker. The question of when a sale of stock becomes a closed transaction arises if you make a sale at the end of one tax year but do not receive delivery of the certificates until the next year. Both cash and accrual basis taxpayers recognize gain or loss from sales of securities made on an established market on the trade date [IRC Sec. 453(k)(2)]. Sales of publicly traded property such as stocks and bonds do not qualify for the installment method where payment is received in the following year (¶2900) [IRC Sec. 453(k)(2)(A)].

(c) Payments or Property in Escrow. Suppose part or all of the property's purchase price is placed in escrow by the buyer. Then you (the seller) should not include the amount placed in escrow in your gross sales until you actually or constructively receive it, whether you are on the cash or accrual basis. However, on performing the terms of the contract and escrow agreement, you realize taxable income, even though you may not accept the money until the following year.[5]

¶2833   **PREPAID INCOME**

Generally, prepaid income is taxable in the year you receive it, whether you are on the cash or accrual basis. However, there are exceptions for *accrual*-basis taxpayers receiving prepaid subscription income, certain prepaid membership dues and advance payments.

(a) Prepaid Subscriptions. Publishers on the accrual basis may elect to report prepaid subscriptions over the subscription period instead of reporting them all in the year received [IRC Sec. 455(a); Reg. Sec. 1.455-1]. But if your liability ends or you die or your business goes out of existence, you must report any unreported amount in that year [IRC Sec. 455(b); Reg. Sec. 1.455-4]. The election generally applies to all prepaid subscriptions of the trade or business for which it is made. However, income that will be earned within 12 months of receipt may either be included in the election or reported in the year received [IRC Sec. 455(c); Reg. Sec. 1.455-6(c)].

How to elect. You can make the election without IRS consent for the first tax year in which you receive subscription income [IRC Sec. 455(c); Reg. Sec. 1.455-6(a)]. You make the election by attaching a statement to a timely filed return indicating the amount of prepaid subscription income, the period over which the taxpayer's liability extends, and the method of allocating income to each period [Reg. Sec. 1.455-6(a)]. Consent is required at any other time. You must file the application with the Commissioner in Washington, within 90 days (plus allowable 90-day extension)[1] after the start of the first year to which the election is to apply [Reg. Sec. 1.455-6(b)]. The election is effective for the year of election and all later years. You can revoke the election only with IRS consent [IRC Sec. 455(c); Reg. Sec. 1.455-2(c)].

(b) Prepaid Membership Dues. Certain membership organizations without capital stock, operating on the accrual basis, may elect to spread dues covering 36 months or less over the membership period. This would apply to automobile clubs like the A.A.A., for example [IRC Sec. 456; Reg. Sec. 1.456-1–1.456-7].

(c) Advance Payments for Goods and Long-Term Contracts. In general, advance payments are not taxable until you have "complete dominion" over the income (e.g., no possibility of having to refund the money). For example, refundable deposits paid to a utility as a guarantee that future bills will be paid are not taxable to the company until the customer actually uses the deposits to pay the bills.[2]

Accrual basis taxpayers and those using a long-term contract method of accounting, though, have a choice of when to include certain advance payments. The choice extends to advance payments for (1) the sale or disposition in a future year of goods primarily held for sale to customers or (2) building, installing, constructing or manufacturing items that won't be completed until a later tax year [Reg. Sec. 1.451-5].The advance payments may generally be included in your income either (1) when you receive them or (2) when includible under your normal method of accounting. This method of accounting is either the method you use for tax purposes or for financial reporting, whichever would result in the payments being included in income earlier. Exception: For long-term contracts, you use the accounting method you use for tax purposes. The method used for your financial reports is disregarded.

Example 1: HF Inc., a manufacturer of household furniture, is an accrual basis taxpayer. HF accrues income when furniture is accepted and delivered for both tax return and financial statement purposes. Suppose that in December 1992 HF receives an $8,000 advance payment on a $20,000 order. The furniture is shipped in that month but not delivered and accepted by the customer until January 1993. HF may include the $8,000 advance payment in its 1992 or 1993 taxable income.

Special rule for inventory. In certain cases, advance payments for inventory are includible in an earlier year than under the general rule. The exception comes into play if, on the last day of the tax year, you (1) have received "substantial advance payments," and (2) have on hand (or readily available) enough substantially similar goods to satisfy the agreement in the year the payments are received [Reg. Sec. 1.451-5(c)]. If these conditions are met, all advance payments you receive by the end of the second tax year after the one in which you received the substantial payments have to be included in your income (if they were not included previously). You must include any payments received after the second tax year d when you receive them.

Advance payments received under an agreement are "substantial" if total payments you receive under the agreement since inception equal or exceed the total costs you include in inventory for that agreement.

Example 2: CG Inc. has a contract with a customer for some custom-made goods. The total contract price is $10,000. Estimated total inventoriable costs for the goods are $5,000. The customer has agreed to make advance payments on the order according to the following schedule:

Year	Amount
1992	$3,500
1993	2,000
1994	1,500
1995	1,000
1996	2,000

The goods are scheduled for delivery in 1997. CG's closing inventory as of the end of 1993 is sufficient to satisfy the contract. Since advance payments as of that date exceed the estimated inventoriable costs for the entire order, the payments are considered "substantial." So all payments received by the end of 1995 ($8,000)—the end of the second year following the year in which the substantial advance payments are received—must be included in income if they haven't been previously. Cost of goods sold for that year would include the estimated costs necessary to satisfy the contract. No further deferral is allowed on the contract, so CG has to include in income for 1996 the $2,000 advance payment received in that year.

¶2834   DISPUTED INCOME

A dispute as to your right to receive an amount you claim is due postpones the time for taxing your claim. Amounts recovered as a result of the dispute usually are taxable: (1) under the accrual method when the dispute is terminated by a settlement, a final judgment by the highest court or a final judgment of a lower court if no appeal is taken and the time for appeal expires[1] and (2) under the cash method when you receive the amounts.[2] However, taxability is not postponed beyond the time when you receive disputed amounts under a claim of right and without restriction as to their disposition, even if the receipt takes place during a dispute.[3] (Income impounded, withheld or escrowed during a dispute as to your right to receive it is not taxable until the funds are released to you or the dispute is terminated.)[3]

An offer to compromise a claim for a lesser amount does not create taxable income,[4] but an unconditional concession as to part of the claim fixes the time for accrual of the conceded amount.[5] (See ¶2824(b) for income not expected to be collected.)

¶2836   REPAID INCOME

(a) Cash Basis. If you receive income under a claim of right, it is income in the year you receive it. To be taxable under the claim of right doctrine, you must receive the income without restriction as to its disposition. You must include the income even though your right to retain it is disputed and all or part of it may have to be repaid in a later year because the right to its use proves not to have been unrestricted. However, you can deduct the repayment in the later year,[1] even if the government received no tax benefit in the year the income was reported because you had a net loss.[2] The Supreme Court has held that the deduction taken for repayment must be reduced by any depletion taken on income received under a claim of right.[3]

> **Example:** Mr. Toby is a cash-basis taxpayer. In 1992, he was involved in a lawsuit with the Bex Corporation, arising from a contract dispute. The court settled the dispute in his favor, awarding him $2,000. Although Bex said it would appeal the judgment, it was ordered by the court to pay immediately without restriction. Bex did appeal the decision and the appellate court reversed the lower court's decision in 1993. Toby was forced to repay the $2,000. Toby must include the $2,000 in his income for 1992, and he may deduct the $2,000 repayment in 1993.

> ➤ **SPECIAL RELIEF** A number of factors may prevent you from receiving enough benefit from the deduction to offset the tax you paid when you received the income. For instance, you may be in a lower tax bracket. If the repayment exceeds $3,000, a relief provision applies. The inequity is corrected by reducing your tax for the year of repayment. In essence, the reduction is equal to the amount of tax you previously had to pay on the income you are now repaying. If the reduction exceeds the tax for the current year, the excess is refunded or credited as an overpayment [IRC Sec. 1341; Reg. Sec. 1.1341-1]. If you are a cash-basis taxpayer who reported the income on the constructive receipt basis, but have never actually received it, you are considered to have made the repayment in the year you were required to relinquish your right to receive the income.

Exceptions to relief provisions. The above provisions do not apply to: (1) bad debts [¶2351 et seq.], (2) legal expenses incurred in contesting repayment of the income previously included or (3) sales of inventory [IRC Sec. 1341(b)(2); Reg. Sec. 1.1341-1(f),(g),(h)].

(b) Accrual Basis. Similar rules apply if you are an accrual-basis taxpayer and you receive income under a claim of right. The year in which the income first accrues is considered the year in which you receive the income. You are entitled to a deduction in the year the obligation to repay accrues.

WHEN TO TAKE DEDUCTIONS

¶2840   WHEN DEDUCTIONS MAY BE TAKEN

(a) Cash-Basis Taxpayers. You must take deductions in the year you make payment in cash or its equivalent [IRC Sec. 461, 7701(a)(25); Reg. Sec. 1.461-1(a)(1)]. But a note is not the equivalent of cash. So, if you give your note in payment, you cannot take the deduction until you pay the note, even if it is secured by collateral.[1] However, you can deduct a payment with money borrowed from another party when paid, not later when you repay the loan.[2]

(b) Accrual-Basis Taxpayers. In general, you cannot deduct expenses until the year (1) all events occur that determine the fact of liability, (2) the amount of the liability can be determined with reasonable accuracy and (3) economic performance has occurred [IRC Sec. 461(h); Reg. Sec. 1.461-1(a)(2)].

NOTE: You can treat certain recurring items as incurred during a tax year even though economic performance has not occurred. To qualify, economic performance must take place by the earlier of either 8½ months or a reasonable time after the close of that tax year [IRC Sec. 461(h)(3)]. "Reasonable time" means the date a timely return is filed. Important: Under regulations, if economic performance occurs after your return is filed, but within the 8½ month period, you may file an amended return—treating the item as incurred under the recurring item exception [Reg. Sec. 1.461-5]. New regulations: The IRS has released final regulations that make it easier for accrual-basis taxpayers to elect the recurring-expense break—and provide more time to make the election [T.D. 8408]. The final regulations closely follow the proposed regulations, but they contain a much milder set of administrative requirements.

   • Under final regulations, you do not have to file a statement with the IRS identifying each trade or business and types of items for which you want to use the recurring-expense break.
   • Under the final regulations, you can switch to the recurring-expense rule simply by implementing the change on your 1992 return.

If you have actually incurred a liability, and if there is uncertainty only as to the exact amount and date it must be discharged, you may set up a reasonable estimate as an accrual. You take any difference in the estimate and the exact amount into account in the year of exact determination [Reg. Sec. 1.461-1(a)(2)]. But if an actual liability is not incurred until the happening of some contingency, you do not accrue any amount until the contingency occurs.[3]

Economic performance usually occurs when you provide the underlying services or property. However, IRS regulations make some liberal exceptions:

   • Receiving goods and services. You can treat the economic performance requirement as satisfied when you pay the purchase price, if you expect to receive the property or services within 3½ months of the payment [Reg. Sec. 1.461-4(d)(2), (6)(ii)].
   • Providing goods and services. Economic performance occurs as you incur the costs of providing the goods and services [Reg. Sec. 1.461-4(d)(4)].

Regulations on economic performance list seven types of expenses that could be deducted only when paid: workers' compensation act or tort liabilities; breach of contract liabilities; rebates and refunds; awards, prizes and jackpots; liabilities for insurance, warranty and service contracts; and taxes (other than creditable foreign taxes) [Reg. Sec. 1.461-4(g)]. Important: Although the regulations designate these liabilities as payment-only liabilities, you may still be able to accelerate your deductions by taking advantage of the recurring item rule (see above).

(c) Contested Items. If you are an accrual-method taxpayer and dispute your liability to pay claimed amounts, your deduction of the resulting settlement, judgment or award is postponed until the dispute is settled by you and the other party or it is finally adjudicated by the courts [Reg. Sec. 1.461-1(a)(3)(ii)]. However, if you pay contested expenses, you can and must take an immediate deduction, even though the contest is continued [IRC Sec. 461(f); Reg. Sec. 1.461-2]. Putting the money in escrow qualifies as payment. If you later settle the liability for less than the amount transferred, you must include the excess in income to the extent a tax benefit results [¶1244]. The Tax Court has ruled that no deduction may be taken for amounts deposited with the IRS while you are contesting a *proposed* tax, since the IRS has not made an assessment of the tax and therefore there is no tax liability.[4] These rules apply to all contested items, except to foreign taxes and taxes of U.S. possessions. If you are a cash-method taxpayer, you deduct disputed liabilities for the year in which you actually pay them[5] or make an escrow deposit [IRC Sec. 461(f); Reg. Sec. 1.461-2].

(d) Overlapping Items. While you cannot use the expenses, liabilities or deficit of one year to reduce your income of a later year, regulations recognize that in a business of any magnitude there are certain overlapping items [Reg. Sec. 1.461-1(a)(3)].

> ➤ **OBSERVATION** The important thing is that you follow a consistent policy, making sure your income of any year is not distorted.

(e) Method of Payment. Suppose you are a cash-basis taxpayer and you pay by check. Then you can deduct the payment when you delive the check, if you pay it on presentation.[6] You cannot deduct checks you postdated to another tax year before the date shown.[7]

> **Example 1:** Mr. Smith contributes to a college fund. He sends the college a check late in December 1992. The check is dated December 31, 1992. The college does not deposit or cash the check until January 1993. The contribution is considered made in 1992. Smith takes the dedution on his 1992 return [IRC Sec. 1.170A-1(b)].

You can take an immediate deduction for charitable contributions or medical expenses charged on a credit card.[9]

> ➤ **OBSERVATION** The same reasoning should apply to other itemized deductions as well.

For accrual-basis taxpayers, the payment method usually does not affect the time for deducting the expenses.

(f) Prepaid Expenses such as rent, interest and insurance premiums are, generally, not deductible in full if they cover more than one tax year [¶2221; 2224; 2845]. You must prorate the deduction over the total time period for which you made the payment. However, say you're a cash-basis taxpayer who's paid a one-year premium covering a period extending into the next tax year. Then you may deduct the entire premium in the year of payment.

> **Example 2:** Mr. Wallace, a cash-basis taxpayer on the calendar year, owns a small store. On July 1, 1992, he pays an insurance premium of $3,000 for a policy that is effective July 1, 1992 for a three-year period. He may deduct $500 in 1992, $1,000 in 1993 and 1994, and $500 in 1995.

> **Example 3:** Mr. Thomas owns a small store and is a calendar-year, cash-basis taxpayer. On July 1, 1992, he pays $1,000 for an insurance policy that runs through June 30, 1993. He may deduct the full $1,000 premium in 1992.

Cash-basis tax shelter's prepaid expenses. Tax shelters generally cannot use the cash method. To the extent that the cash method can still be used, a tax shelter cannot deduct prepaid expenses before "economic performance" occurs ((b) above) [IRC Sec. 461(i)]. For this rule, the recurring item exception to the economic performance requirement does not apply. A "tax shelter" is: (1) a partnership or other enterprise (except a C corporation) in which interests were offered for sale in an offering that must be registered with a federal or state agency; (2) a partnership or enterprise if over 35% of the losses are allocable to limited partners; or (3) any partnership, entity, plan or arrangement whose principal purpose is tax avoidance or evasion as defined in IRC Sec. 6662(d)(2)(C).

> **Example 4:** XYZ oil and gas shelter management fees are treated as incurred when the management services are rendered. The cost of prepaid supplies is treated as incurred when the supplies are used. Research and development costs are deductible as the contract research occurs. Prepaid drilling costs, even under a noncancellable turnkey contract, would be deductible only as the drilling occurs.

A special exception is made for oil and gas shelters if economic performance occurs before the close of the 90th day after year end. The maximum deduction allowed under this exception is limited to the cash investment in the tax shelter.

¶2841   DEDUCTIONS LIMITED TO AMOUNT AT RISK

The "at risk" rules generally prevent you from claiming tax shelter deductions in excess of your financial commitment in the activity [¶2327].

¶2842   PASSIVE ACTIVITIES LOSS LIMITATIONS

Basically, this tax shelter limitation prevents you from using a loss from a "passive activity" (for example, limited partners' interests in a business) to shelter "active income" (for example, salary) or "portfolio income" (like dividends, interest, and capital gains). You are allowed to write off tax shelter loss only against your other tax shelter income (¶2326) [IRC Sec. 469].

¶2843   VACATION PAY AND INCENTIVE BONUSES

Special rules govern the time for deducting these payments.

(a) When to Deduct. An employer's deduction for vacation pay and bonuses is limited to amounts paid during the year, or (except for payments to majority shareholders) within 2½ months after the end of the year [Temp. Reg. Sec. 1.404(b)-1T]. Companies can have more time to pay if (1) administrative or economic conditions prevent them from paying sooner and (2) the delay is unforeseen.[1] (See ¶ 2860 for special rules as to majority shareholders.)

(b) Accrual of Bonuses Under Incentive Compensation Plan. Suppose the exact amount of a bonus cannot be determined and paid until the year following the year of accrual. Then these amounts may be deducted by the accrual-basis taxpayer in the year of accrual if: (1) the total bonuses are determinable through a formula in effect before the end of the year; (2) before the end of the year the employer obligates itself to make payment by notifying each employee (individually, or in a group), either orally or in writing, of the percentage of the total bonus payment to be awarded to him; and (3) payment is made as soon after the close of the year as is administratively feasible.[2] For the time for deducting contributions to tax-qualified retirement plans, see ¶1316.

¶2844   ADVERTISING EXPENSES

If you're on the cash basis, you deduct these expenses in the year you pay them. If you're on the accrual basis, you deduct them in the year they accrue. Although the benefits of advertising may continue for several years, you may not capitalize the cost and write it off over the later years.[1]

¶2845   INTEREST

If you're on the cash basis, you ordinarily deduct interest when you actually pay it,[1] unless you prepay the interest [(a) below]. If you are an accrual-basis taxpayer, you deduct interest as it accrues; interest accrues ratably over the period.[2]

> **NOTE:** You treat interest on debt you use to finance the production of inventory as part of the cost of that inventory—and deduct the interest as the items are sold [¶2714(b)].

Your interest deductions for any year generally cannot exceed the amount of interest economically accrued.[3] This means that you must generally allocate payments on indebtedness to principal to the extent they exceed interest accrued at the stated or effective rate.

Exception: You can use the "Rule of 78" to figure deductible interest on short-term (five years or less) consumer loans that meet specific criteria (e.g., level installment payments).[4] Under this rule, interest for any given year is the total interest payable over the term of the loan multiplied by a fraction. The fraction is the years remaining on the loan at the beginning of the year divided by the sum of the years of the loan period. This method results in larger deductions in the early years than the economic accrual method.

(a) Prepaid Interest. If you are a cash-basis taxpayer and pay interest in advance, you must allocate the interest deduction over the period of the loan. Generally, "points" you pay on a mortgage used to buy or improve your principal residence can be fully deducted in the year of payment. The payment must be an established business practice in the area and must not exceed amounts generally charged for such home loans (¶1902) [IRC Sec. 461(g)(2)]. And while you must pay the points directly, the IRS has said you satisfy this requirement if you pay over at closing an amount equal to or greater than the points (say, as a downpayment or escrow deposit).[5] But this tax break does not apply to points you pay on mortgages for additional homes (such as vacation homes).[6] In conflict with IRS and Tax Court decisions, the Eighth Circuit Court of Appeals has allowed a current deduction for points paid to refinance a short-term mortgage (i.e., one with a balloon payment) on a principal residence. That court said that refinancing a short-term loan with permanent financing is sufficiently connected with the home purchase to qualify for an upfront deduction.[7]

(b) Insurance Policy Loan. Interest on a life insurance policy loan, which by the terms of the contract is added to the principal of the loan if not paid when due, cannot be deducted as "interest paid" by a cash basis taxpayer.[8]

(c) Discount on a Note. In general, you can deduct interest on an original issue discount instrument as it accrues—whether the issuer is a cash or accrual taxpayer. For discount instruments issued after July 1, 1982, you calculate the interest using the economic accrual (i.e., not straight line) method (¶1217) [IRC Sec. 163(e)].

> **Example 1:** Ms. Coe, on the cash basis, receives $1,000 cash for a note in the amount of $1,387.05 (12% interest), payable in five equal annual installments. (The note has an original issue discount of $387.05.) Of the $277.41 first payment, $120 (12% of $1,000) is deductible as interest.

However, there are exceptions for: (1) instruments issued by natural persons before March 2, 1984, and (2) loans between natural persons that are not made in the course of the lender's business, are not in excess of $10,000 when combined with prior loans and do not have tax avoidance as one of their principal purposes. If these exceptions are met, you can deduct the interest when it would normally be deductible under your usual method of accounting (e.g., when paid by a cash basis taxpayer) [IRC Sec. 163(e)(4)].

High yield discount instruments. Special rules apply to certain high yield corporate discount obligations. The tax law recharacterizes part of the discount as a dividend. As such, it is not deductible. This rule applies to debt instruments issued after July 1, 1989 that meet certain tests [¶3025(e)].

(d) Allocating Interest Expense Among Expenditures.

You can fully deduct interest payments on some loans (for example, business interest). Other interest payments (such as consumer or investment interest) are nondeductible or deductible within limitations. To determine how much of your interest you can deduct, you must allocate it among the various categories of interest. The IRS has developed a set of complex rules to allocate interest expenses [Temp. Reg. Sec. 1.163-8T]. Here are the five types of interest to which these allocation rules apply:

- Passive activity interest—either currently deductible or placed in a suspense account and carried over to a future year [¶2326].
- Investment interest—generally deductible to the extent of net investment income [¶1904].
- Trade or business interest—fully deductible.
- Personal interest—nondeductible since 1991 [¶1902].
- Residence interest—generally deductible if debt is used to acquire or substantially improve residence; tougher limit on debt secured by a residence but used for other purposes [¶1903].

Corporations exempt from allocation rules. Regular corporations are generally exempt from the allocation rules. However, closely held corporations do have to observe the interest allocation rules. A C corporation is closely held if five or fewer stockholders own, directly or indirectly, more than 50% of the stock at any time during the last half of the tax year. S corporations are subject to the rules as well.

How to allocate interest expense. For the most part, the tax character of an interest expense is determined by the way you use loan proceeds. The security for the loan generally is immaterial. For example, suppose you got a $10,000 loan, pledging stock investments as collateral. You use the money to buy a car. The interest paid on the loan is personal interest because you use the money to buy a personal asset. The fact that stock investments served as loan collateral doesn't change the character of the interest [Temp. Reg. Sec. 1.163-8T(c)(1)]. *Major exception:* Qualified residence interest [¶1903]. Here, the security for the borrowed funds (e.g., a mortgage on a primary or second home) controls the tax treatment of the interest, not the way you use the funds [Temp. Reg. Sec. 1.163-8T(m)(3)].

When you deposit borrowed funds into an account, the funds are deemed to be used for investment expenditures until you put them to a specific purpose. Thus, the interest expense is investment interest expense. This is true whether or not the account the money is deposited in is interest bearing [Temp. Reg. Sec. 1.163-8T(c)(4)(i)].

> ➤ **OBSERVATION** Noncorporate taxpayers who take out loans may end up with a less favorable allocation. Cash debt proceeds received by you are generally treated as used for personal expenditures. This results in the loss of interest deductions on the underlying loan. There is an exception for cash expenditures made within 30 days of receiving the cash. These expenditures may be treated as made from the loan proceeds on the date you received the cash [Temp. Reg. Sec. 1.163-8T(c)(5)].[9] So, if you are in this situation, you should either use the funds or deposit them in an account within the required time period.

These rules also apply when you deposit borrowed funds in an account and then withdraw them in cash. If you do not use the withdrawn amounts or redeposit them within the time limit, they will be tagged personal interest.

You generally treat withdrawals from an account as coming first from loan proceeds (in the order deposited) and then from unborrowed funds [Temp. Reg. Sec. 1.163-8T(c)(4)(ii)].

NOTE: The House and Senate Committee Reports for a 1988 tax law (TAMRA) say the IRS should determine allocation rules that carry out the intent of the statute in as simple a manner as possible. Specifically, the IRS can characterize debt based on the nature of the underlying security, rather than the use that is made of the debt proceeds.

Allocation procedures can best be shown by the following examples.

Example 2: On September 1, 1992, Mr. Little got a $20,000 loan and deposited it into a checking account. On November 1, he wrote a $10,000 check to buy equipment for his unincorporated business. There is no other account activity during the year. Interest paid by Little for September and October is considered investment interest. For November and December, half the interest paid is reallocated and treated as trade-or-business interest; the other half remains investment interest.

Example 3: Ms. Cable obtains a $30,000 loan on June 1, 1992. She deposits the funds into a new checking account that does not contain other funds. Here's her account activity for 1992 (the equipment is for her unincorporated business; the car is a family auto). Assume the loan terms call for simple interest of 1% per month on the entire loan balance, with repayment of the full principal on May 31, 1993. The last column shows how he should allocate her interest payment.

	Account activity		Interest paid	Type of interest
6/1	Opening balance	$30,000		
6/30			$300	Investment
7/31			300	Investment
8/1	Payment for equipment	(15,000)		
8/31			300	Business, $150; investment, $150
9/16	Payment for car	(10,000)		
9/30			300	Investment, $100; business, $150; personal, $50 (unless alternative method, below, is used)
10/31			300	Investment, $50; business, $150; personal, $100
11/16	Payment for equipment	(4,000)		
11/30			300	Investment, $30; business, $170; personal, $100 (unless optional method, below, is used)
12/31	Account balance	$1,000	300	Investment, $10; business, $190; personal, $100

Here's how Cable would allocate the interest she pays during the year:

June and July: The $600 of interest paid during these months is investment interest, whether or not Cable's checking account pays interest.

August: Of the $300 interest paid, $150 is trade-or-business interest. Reason: During the month, one-half of the loan proceeds is allocable to the purchase of trade-or-business assets. The $150 balance of interest for August remains investment interest.

September: Using the general method, Cable would allocate the interest payment for September as follows:

Type of Interest	9/1 through 9/15	9/16 through 9/30	Total
Investment	15,000/30,000 × $150 = $75	5,000/30,000 × $150 = $25	$100
Business	15,000/30,000 × $150 = $75	15,000/30,000 × $150 = $75	150
Personal	N/A	10,000/30,000 × $150 = $50	50
			$300

October: The interest allocation is the same as under the alternative allocation method for September (see below for breakdown).

November: Once again, Cable has a choice of methods. Using the regular method, she'd proceed as follows:

Type of Interest	11/1 through 11/15	11/16 through 11/30	Total
Investment	5,000/30,000 × $150 = $25	1,000/30,000 × $150 = $5	$ 30
Business	15,000/30,000 × $150 = $75	19,000/30,000 × $150 = $95	170
Personal	10,000/30,000 × $150 = $50	10,000/30,000 × $150 = $50	100
			$300

December: Cable's interest allocation is as follows:

Type of Interest				Total
Investment	($1,000/$30,000)	× $300 =		$10
Business	($19,000/$30,000)	× $300 =		$190
Personal	($10,000/$30,000)	× $300 =		$100

Alternative method. In our example above, Cable may treat any mid-month expenditure as having been made on the later of the first of the month, or the date the borrowed funds were deposited into the account [Temp. Reg. Sec. 1.163-8T(c)(4)(iv)]. So Cable can treat the 9/16 withdrawal for the car purchase as having been made on 9/1. The method yields the following interest allocation for September:

Type of Interest		Month of September	
Investment	($5,000/$30,000)	× $300 =	$50
Business	($15,000/$30,000)	× $300 =	$150
Personal	($10,000/$30,000)	× $300 =	$100

Optional method. There's still another optional method, which treats expenses incurred within 30 days of a loan deposit as coming from that loan [Temp. Reg. Sec. 1.163-8T(c)(4)(iii)(B)].[9] On our facts, however, this method can't be used by Cable.

The allocation method you use for one month is not binding on you for other months. So in our example, Cable can use the regular method for September, then switch to the optional method for November. However, you must treat all expenses from an account during any month the same way (e.g., actual date or first of the month).

Payments to third parties. Special rules apply if the loan proceeds aren't paid directly to you (the borrower). If the lender gives the loan proceeds to a third party (e.g., a property seller), that disbursement is an expenditure from the loan proceeds. If cash isn't given (e.g., a loan assumption or seller financing), the debt is treated as if you made an expenditure from the proceeds for the purpose for which the debt was incurred [Temp. Reg. Sec. 1.163-8T(c)(3)].

Repayment of principal. If the loan proceeds are allocated to more than one expense when repayment of principal occurs, the principal payment is allocated in the following order [Temp. Reg. Sec. 1.163-8T(d)]:

1. Personal expenses.
2. Investment expenses and passive activity expenses [other than (3) below].

3.   Rental real estate passive activity expenses where you actively participate in the activity.

4.   Expenses allocable to activities where you were formerly a passive investor, but now are a material participant.

5.   Trade or business expenses.

If loan proceeds are allocated to two or more expenses within one of the five classes above, then you treat expenses in the order the amounts were allocated (e.g., by the dates that checks were drawn on the account). You can treat allocations occurring on the same day as occurring in any order you choose.

> ➤ **OBSERVATION** If you want to avoid the allocation rules, do not mix together borrowed and unborrowed funds in the same account. That way you can use only the nonborrowed funds for personal expenditures. What's more, you'll have good documentation of how you used borrowed funds. You can also achieve this goal by maintaining separate accounts for separate classes of expenditures or financing only one expenditure per loan.

Another good move is to deposit the proceeds of loans with different interest rates into different accounts. This will make it easy for you to use the loans with the higher interest rates for expenditures that are subject to the least limitations on deductibility.

Finally, to simplify things, use the proceeds from the sale of an asset that was purchased with borrowed funds (that have not been fully repaid yet) to acquire a similar type of asset. For example, if you sell stock bought with borrowed funds, use the proceeds to buy other investments, or leave the cash in a savings account. This way, you'll avoid having to reallocate loan proceeds when an asset is sold (or otherwise disposed of).

> **NOTE:** Sometimes, you may have to make a trade-off between what approach is easiest vs. which one will save you the most tax dollars. From the standpoint of simplicity, segregated accounts and loans make the most sense. From the standpoint of tax savings, however, it may pay to deliberately trigger the allocation rules in some cases. Bottom line: You have to decide on a case-by-case basis whether the potential tax savings is significant enough to warrant the extra work involved in applying the allocation rules.

Passthrough entities.   Special rules govern the allocation of debt where you use the proceeds for contributions to or purchases of interests in passthrough entities (i.e., partnerships and S corporations). Generally, you allocate the proceeds and associated interest expense among all the entity's assets using any "reasonable method."

Special rules also come into play to allocate debt incurred by a passthrough entity that is used for distributions to the owners. Under the general rule, the allocation is made in accordance with the owner's use of the proceeds.[10]

¶2846   TAXES

(a) Cash-Basis Taxpayers.   You may deduct as taxes only the amount you actually pay during the year.[1]

(b) Accrual-Basis Taxpayers.   You deduct taxes as they accrue. A tax accrues when all the events have occurred that fix the amount of the tax and determine the taxpayer's liability to pay it.[2] A tax that is imposed retroactively cannot accrue before enactment of the law imposing it.[3] The economic performance rules may apply, see ¶2840(b). For contested taxes, see ¶2840(c).

Foreign tax credit. A foreign tax you take as a credit accrues for the year to which it relates, even if contested and not paid until a later year. But the accrual cannot be made until the contested liability is finally determined.[4]

State income taxes generally accrue in the year in which you earn the income (on which the state tax is paid).[5] But an increase in state taxes accrues when the amount is finally determined by litigation or default, or you acknowledge liability.

Franchise taxes. Several states impose corporate franchise taxes based on income which accrue when all the events have occurred that fix the liability.

Property taxes. Generally, property taxes accrue on the date the liability for the tax becomes fixed. This is usually the lien date or the date you become personally liable. If the state changes the accrual date, there may be two accrual dates in one year. In that case, unless the deduction would be lost for good, only one accrual for state taxes is available in any one tax year. The date of accrual before the state change determines the time of deduction. Thus, you continue to use the original accrual date.

Under proposed regulations that would take effect for tax years beginning after 1991, accrual basis taxpayers could not deduct taxes until they are paid to the governmental authority [Prop. Reg. Sec. 1.461-4(g)].

Election to ratably accrue real property taxes. You may elect to accrue and deduct taxes ratably over the period imposed. You may make the election for each separate trade or business (or for "nonbusiness" activities if accounted for separately). It can be adopted *without consent* for the first year you incur real property taxes, if you make the election by the return due date for the tax year (including extensions). For adoption at any other time, you must make a written request to the IRS not later than 90 days (180 days with extension)[6] after the start of the tax year to which the election applies (but see note below) [Reg. Sec. 1.461-1(c)].

> NOTE: The IRS eased this special election rule for 1991. Taxpayers were allowed to automatically make (or revoke) the special election by deducting the appropriate amount on their 1991 returns. No advance approval from the IRS was needed.[7]

¶2847   MEDICAL EXPENSES

The medical expense deduction [¶1931] is for amounts you actually pay during the tax year. However, you may deduct medical expenses you pay by bank credit cards in the year charged [¶2840(e)].[1] In general, you cannot take a deduction for accruals or prepaid expenses. But you can deduct prepaid expenses that are part of nursing home entrance fees.[2]

¶2850   CONTRIBUTIONS

Generally, you can deduct charitable contributions in the year paid. Pledge or accrual is not enough[1] [¶1917]. However, you deduct a charitable contribution made through a bank credit card in the year the charge is made, regardless of when you repay the bank [¶2840(e)].[2] Another special rule allows accrual-basis corporations to deduct contributions authorized by their boards of directors before the contributions are actually paid [¶3019]. You deduct contributions of property in the year the gift is completed.

Contribution of stock certificate. You make a deductible contribution of a properly endorsed stock certificate when you unconditionally deliver the certificate to the donee or the donee's agent. If you deliver the certificate to the donor's agent or to the issuing corporation for transfer, you make the contribution when stock is transferred on the corporate books [Reg. Sec. 1.170A-1(b)].

¶2851   BAD DEBTS AND LOSSES

(a) Bad Debts. You can deduct these debts in the year they become worthless. Except for corporations, nonbusiness bad debts must be completely worthless to be written off. But you can deduct partially worthless business debts [¶2356].

(b) Losses. You can generally deduct these amounts in the year sustained. They must be evidenced by closed and completed transactions fixed by identifiable events [¶2300].

Sales of property and stock. You can generally deduct losses from sales of property or stock in the year there is a "closed transaction" [¶2830].

Mortgage foreclosure. Generally, loss to the mortgagor resulting from a foreclosure is sustained when the period of redemption expires.[1] However, circumstances may warrant deduction in the year of the foreclosure sale as where taxpayers, though financially able, refused to pay the taxes because of the low value of the property.[2] In effect, they have abandoned the property. If they litigate the validity of the foreclosure sale, no loss occurs until the litigation is finally settled.[3] Also, if they make a bona fide claim that the sale is invalid, the time for deduction may be postponed until that claim is settled, although there is no formal court action.[4]

Casualty losses. You can deduct casualty losses whether they relate to business, nonbusiness or investment property. The type of property determines the amount of your deduction. The time to deduct a casualty loss is the tax year in which you actually sustain the loss [¶2304].

¶2852   RESERVES FOR EXPENSES AND LOSSES

A reserve is an amount set aside out of current income for meeting expenditures to be made in a later tax year. Taxpayers (other than financial institutions) cannot deduct reserves for bad debts [¶2361].

(a) Cash Basis. Under the cash basis, you may take deductions only in the year of payment. So you cannot take deductions for additions to a reserve.

(b) Accrual Basis. If your books are kept on the accrual basis, you make take a deduction if there is a present liability to support the deduction. The cases are in conflict as to whether you can deduct reasonably accurate estimates of expenses before the year in which the services actually are renderedand your liability to make actual payments arises. Some Circuit Courts have allowed the deduction for the year in which the income for the services was taxable, or in which the obligation to perform them arose.[1] The Tax

Court disagrees.[2] See ¶2840(b) for the rule when an actual liability has been incurred, but the amount is uncertain.

Examples of Reserves Held Not Deductible

Anticipated loss on contract to buy merchandise.[3]   Anticipated refunds for future years' insurance
Reserve for self-insurance.[4]   policy cancellations.[5]

¶2853   DEDUCTIONS FOR FARMERS PREPAYING 50% OR MORE OF FARMING EXPENSES

If you are a cash-basis farmer, you aren't allowed a deduction for certain amounts paid for feed, seed, fertilizer and other similar farm supplies earlier than the time when youactually use or consume these items (that is, until the tax year in which economic performance occurs). The limitation applies to prepaid expenses to the extent they exceed 50% of your deductible farming expenses for the tax year (other than prepaid farm supplies) in which economic performance has occurred [IRC Sec. 464(f)]. Farming is, generally, the cultivation of land or the raising of any agricultural or horticultural commodity (except fruit- and nut-bearing trees), including animals. For the 50% test, expenses include the farm operating expenses such as ordinary and necessary farming expenses, interest and taxes paid, depreciation on farm equipment and other expenses generally reported on Schedule F of Form 1040.

¶2854   DEPRECIABLE PROPERTY

Even as a cash-basis taxpayer, you generally cannot currently deduct the full payment for business and investment assets that you will use for longer than one year. Instead, you recover your basis in these assets over a period of time through depreciation and amortization deductions [Chs. 11 & 12].

Intangible property. You may depreciate some intangible assets if certain conditions are met (e.g., patents and copyrights). But others aren't depreciable because of the indefinite duration of their usefulness (e.g., goodwill). For example, costs incurred to develop and design product packages must be capitalized and may not be amortized.[1]

¶2856   INVENTORY

Even if you are on the cash-basis method, you cannot currently deduct the cost of goods purchased or manufactured for resale to customers (i.e., inventory).

¶2857   ELECTIONS AVAILABLE FOR CERTAIN EXPENSES

Both the cash- and accrual-basis taxpayers have a choice as to the time for, and the method of, deducting certain expenses. Among these are:

- Research and experimental expenses [¶2231];
- Exploration and development expenses of mines [¶2242; 2243];
- Farm development expenses [¶2244];
- Soil and water conservation expenses [¶2245];
- Intangible drilling and development costs of mines [¶2236(c)];
- Corporate organizational expenses [¶3013];
- Business start-up expenses [¶2203].

SPECIAL PROBLEMS

¶2860   RELATED PARTY TRANSACTIONS

A deduction for an accrual-basis taxpayer's expenses owed to a related cash-basis taxpayer is generally allowed only when the amount is paid [IRC Sec. 267(a)].

Bonuses. Generally, bonuses (and other similar types of compensation) may be deducted by accrual-basis employers as long as they are paid to the employees within 2½ months after the close of the tax year. However, payments made to "related" cash-basis taxpayers can't be deducted until the year actually paid [IRC Sec. 267(a)(2)]. Related taxpayers include family members; majority shareholders; two corporations which are members of the same controlled group; a fiduciary and the trust's grantor or beneficiary; corporations, S corporations and/or partnerships with common owners [IRC Sec. 267(b)].

Corporations that are members of the same controlled group are subject to the related party rules. For these purposes, a controlled group is defined based on a test of common ownership using a 50% threshold (rather than 80% as in some other provisions of the tax law) [¶3046(a)]. Also, losses on sales between controlled corporations are deferred (not lost) until such time as the property is disposed outside of the group in a transaction that allows recognition of loss [IRC Sec. 267(f)].

"Pass-through" entities. For purposes of amounts paid or incurred by, to, or on behalf of pass-through entities—partnerships and S corporations—the following are related parties: (1) the entity, (2) for a partnership, any person owning, directly or indirectly, any capital or profits interest, (3) for an S corporation, any person owning, directly or indirectly, any stock in the corporation, (4) any person owning, directly or indirectly, any capital or profits interest of a partnership in which such entity owns, directly or indirectly, any capital or profits interest, and (5) any person related to a person described in (2)–(4), above [IRC Sec. 267(e)].

Partner's guaranteed payments. The matching of expense deduction to income inclusion does not apply to guaranteed payments (¶3416(d)) [IRC Sec. 267(e)(4)].

¶2861   CIRCULATION EXPENSES

You can currently deduct expenses attributable to prepaid subscriptions [¶2833(a)] in the year paid or incurred. This rule apparently applies regardless of your method of accounting and even if the prepaid subscription income is spread over the life of the subscriptions. Expenditures that aren't included in this rule are those for land, depreciable property, purchase of another publisher's circulation or nonpublisher related expenses [IRC Sec. 173(a); Reg. Sec. 1.173-1(a)].

¶2862　　ACCOUNTING FOR RETURNS OF MAGAZINES, PAPERBACKS AND RECORDS

Accrual-basis publishers or distributors of magazines, paperbacks and records can elect to exclude from income amounts attributable to qualifying items returned within the merchandise return period after the close of the tax year in which the sales were made [IRC Sec. 458; Prop. Reg. Sec. 1.458-1]. The merchandise return period is 2 months and 15 days for magazines and 4 months and 15 days for paperbacks and records, unless the taxpayer elects a shorter period. Electing the exclusion is a change of accounting method, giving rise to a transitional adjustment. However, instead of applying the ordinary adjustment rules [¶2813], the adjustment of magazines is amortized over 5 years, and the adjustment of paperbacks and records is placed in a suspense account. The election must be made no later than the due date (including extensions) for filing the return for the election year. An election, once made, is irrevocable without IRS consent [Reg. Sec. 1.458-10].

Footnotes to Chapter 18

(For your added convenience, in brackets [] with the footnotes below, you will find citations to related paragraphs in the "RIA United States Tax Reporter"(USTR), "CCH Federal Tax Reporter"(CCH) and "RIA Federal Tax Coordinator 2d"(FTC) multi-volume services.)

FOOTNOTE ¶ 2801 [USTR ¶ 4464; CCH ¶ 20,612; FTC ¶ G-2000].

(1) Ltr. Rul. 9103001; A.O.D. No. 1991-07.

FOOTNOTE ¶ 2802 [USTR ¶ 4464.05; CCH ¶ 20,612; FTC ¶ G-2023; 2024].

FOOTNOTE ¶ 2803 [USTR ¶ 4464.64; CCH ¶ 21,009; FTC ¶ G-2301].

(1) Rev. Rul. 73-511, 1973-2 CB 402; Rev. Rul. 75-21, 1975-1 CB 367.

(2) Webb v. Comm., 67 F.2d 859, 13 AFTR 408.

(3) McEuen v. Comm., 196 F.2d 127, 41 AFTR 1169.

(4) Rev. Rul. 68-126, 1968-1 CB 194.

(5) Kuhn v. U.S., 1 AFTR 2d 825, 157 F.Supp. 331.

(6) Strauss, 2 BTA 598.

(7) Haack, ¶81,013 PH Memo TC.

(8) Hurd, 12 BTA 368.

(9) Hedrick, 154 F.2d 90, 34 AFTR 1090.

(10) Comm. v. Giannini, 129 F.2d 638, 29 AFTR 952.

(11) Burns v. Comm. 31 F.2d 399, 7 AFTR 8567.

(12) Cooney, 18 TC 883.

(13) Northern Trust Co., 8 BTA 685.

(14) Evans, TC Memo ¶88,228 TC Memo PH.

FOOTNOTE ¶ 2804 [USTR ¶ 614.192; CCH ¶ 2200; 6554; FTC ¶ J-8200].

(1) Helvering v. Eubank, 311 US 122, 61 SCt. 149, 24 AFTR 1063; Helvering v. Horst, 311 US 112, 61 SCt. 144, 24 AFTR 1058.

(2) Holmes, 1 TC 508; Austin v. Comm., 161 F.2d 666, 35 AFTR 1350.

(3) Lucas v. Earl, 281 US 111, 8 AFTR 10287.

(4) Helvering v. Eubank, 311 US 122, 61 SCt. 149, 24 AFTR 1063.

(5) Van Brunt, 11 BTA 406.

(6) Bing v. Bowers, 22 F.2d 450, 6 AFTR 7045.

(7) U.S. v. Shafto, 52 AFTR 1748.

(8) Harrison v. Schaffner, 312 US 579, 61 SCt. 759, 25 AFTR 1209.

(9) Rev. Rul. 74-562, 1974-2 CB 28.

(10) Mitchell v. Bowers, 15 F.2d 287, 6 AFTR 6329.

(11) Sunnen v. Comm., 333 US 591, 68 SCt. 715, 36 AFTR 611.

(12) Rev. Rul. 70-161, 1970-1 CB 15.

(13) Capel, 7 BTA 1076.

(14) Blair v. Comm., 300 US 5, 57 SCt. 330, 18 AFTR 1132.

FOOTNOTE ¶ 2805 [USTR ¶ 4514.003; CCH ¶ 21,817; FTC ¶ G-2320].

(1) Rollin C. Reynolds, 44 BTA 342.

(2) Rev. Rul. 70-221, 1970-1 CB 33.

FOOTNOTE ¶ 2806 [USTR ¶ 4474; CCH ¶ 20,612; 20,701; FTC ¶ G-2027].

FOOTNOTE ¶ 2807 [USTR ¶ 4464.01; CCH ¶ 20,610; FTC ¶ G-2006].

(1) Lovejoy, 18 BTA 1179.

(2) Rev. Rul. 70-413, 1970-2 CB 103; Comm. v. Boylston Market Ass'n, 131 F.2d 966, 30 AFTR 512.

(3) Waldheim Realty & Investment Co. v. Comm., 245 F.2d 823, 51 AFTR 801.

(4) Thomas Nelson, Inc. & Sub. v. U.S. (DC Tenn., 1988), 61 AFTR 2d 88-1167.

(5) Rev. Rul. 54-4, 1954-1 CB 75.

FOOTNOTE ¶ 2810 [USTR ¶ 4464.01; CCH ¶ 20,612; FTC ¶ G-2005].

FOOTNOTE ¶ 2811 [USTR ¶ 4464.41; CCH ¶ 20,611 et seq.; FTC ¶ G-2900 et seq.].

(1) Goodman, ¶61,201 PH Memo TC.

(2) Holland v. U.S., 348 US 121, 75 SCt. 127, 46 AFTR 943; Freidberg v. U.S., 348 US 142, 75 SCt. 138, 46 AFTR 954; Smith v. U.S., 348 US 147, 75 SCt. 194, 46 AFTR 968; U.S. v. Calderon, 348 US 160, 75 SCt. 186, 46 AFTR 962.

(3) B. Fairman et al., ¶49,006 PH Memo TC.

(4) M. & B. Rubin, Inc., 10 BTA 866.

(5) F.G. Bishoff, 29 F.2d 91, 6 AFTR 7870.

(6) Stratman, ¶49,143 PH Memo TC.

(7) Hague's Est., 132 F.2d 775, 30 AFTR 686.

FOOTNOTE ¶ 2812 [USTR ¶ 4464.23; CCH ¶ 20,613; FTC ¶ G-2036 et seq.].

(1) Rev. Proc. 72-52, 1972-2 CB 833.

(2) Rev. Proc. 92-20, IRB 1992-12, superseding Rev. Porc. 84-74, 1984-2 CB 736.

(3) Fowler Bros. & Cox, Inc. v. Comm., 138 F.2d 774, 31.

(4) Rev. Rul. 55-732, 1955-2 CB 379.

(5) Rev. Proc. 85-37, 1985-2 CB 438; Rev. Proc. 85-36, 1985-2 CB 434.

(6) Rev. Proc. 88-15, 1988-1 CB 683.

FOOTNOTE ¶ 2813 [USTR ¶ 4814; CCH ¶ 20,613.035; 22,277; FTC ¶ G-2807].

(1) Rev. Rul. 64-245, 1964-2 CB 130.

FOOTNOTE ¶ 2816 [USTR ¶ 4414; CCH ¶ 20,301; FTC ¶ G-1000 et seq.].

(1) Rev. Rul. 85-22, 1985-1 CB 154, suspd'g Rev. Rul. 54-273, 1954-2 CB 110.

(2) Rev. Rul. 85-83, 1985-1 CB 291, obsoleting Rev. Rul. 66-68, 1966-1 CB 197.

(3) Rev. Rul. 57-389, 1957-2 CB 298.

FOOTNOTE ¶ 2817 [USTR ¶ 4434; CCH ¶ 20,301;20,406; FTC ¶ G-2100 et seq.].

FOOTNOTE ¶ 2818 [USTR ¶ 4442; CCH ¶ 20,406; FTC ¶ G-1075 et seq.].

(1) Rev. Proc. 74-33, 1974-2 CB 489.

(2) Rev. Proc. 85-16, 1985-1 CB 517.

(3) Rev. Proc. 68-41, 1968-2 CB 943, modified by Rev. Proc. 81-40, 1981-2 CB 604.

(4) Rev. Proc. 85-58, 1985-1 CB 290.

(5) Rev. Proc. 92-13, IRB 1992-3.

(6) Instructions for Form 1128.

(7) Rev. Rul. 58-256, 1958-1 CB 215.

FOOTNOTE ¶ 2819 [USTR ¶ 4434; CCH ¶ 20,502; FTC ¶ G-1019 et seq.].

(1) Rev. Rul. 65-163, 1965-1 CB 205.

FOOTNOTE ¶ 2820 [USTR ¶ 4444; CCH ¶ 20,605; FTC ¶ D-1862].

FOOTNOTE ¶ 2824 [USTR ¶ 4434; CCH ¶ 21,001 et seq.; FTC ¶ G-1085].

(1) Butler, 19 BTA 718; Lavery v. Comm., 158 F.2d 859, 35 AFTR 616.

(2) Kahler, 18 TC 31.

(3) Fischer, 14 TC 792; Johnston, ¶64,323 PH Memo TC.

(4) American Central Utilities Co., 36 BTA 688; Cuba RR Co., 9 TC 211.

(5) Schlude v. Comm., 372 U.S. 128, 11 AFTR 2d 75.

(6) Doyle, Dane, Bernbach, Inc., 79 TC 101.

FOOTNOTE ¶ 2825 [USTR ¶ 4464.05; CCH ¶ 5507; 21,001; FTC ¶ G-2023 et seq.].

(1) Zittel, 12 BTA 675; Massey v. Comm., 143 F.2d 429, 32 AFTR 986.

(2) Rev. Rul. 69-650, 1969-2 CB 106.

(3) Rev. Rul. 75-448, 1975-2 CB 55; Armantrout et al. v. Comm., 41 AFTR 2d 78-630.

(4) Shockey, ¶47,294 PH Memo TC; Rev. Rul. 69-465, 1969-2 CB 29.

(5) Drummond, 43 BTA 529.

(6) Rev. Proc. 71-21, 1971-2 CB 549.

FOOTNOTE ¶ 2826 [USTR ¶ 4514.011; CCH ¶ 21,009.274; FTC ¶ J-2771].

(1) Tar Prods. Corp., 130 F.2d 866, 29 AFTR 1190; Comm. v. American Light & Traction Co., 156 F.2d 398, 34 AFTR 1544.

FOOTNOTE ¶ 2827 [USTR ¶ 4514.053; CCH ¶ 5704 et seq.; FTC ¶ J-2975 et seq.].

(1) Murphy, 92 TC 12.

(2) Rev. Rul. 66-44, 66-45, 1966-1 CB 94, 95.

FOOTNOTE ¶ 2828 [USTR ¶ 4544; CCH ¶ 6607; FTC ¶ J-3420].

(1) U.S. Savings Bonds, Series E and EE, Redemption Value Tables.

(2) Rev. Proc. 89-46, 1989-2 CB 615.

(3) Rev. Rul. 68-145, 1968-1 CB 203.

(4) Rev. Rul. 55-655, 1955-2 CB 253.

(5) Treas. Dept. booklet "Your Federal Income Tax" (1991 Ed.), p. 53.

(6) Treas. Dept. Circular 905, 5th Rev. Amendment 1.

FOOTNOTE ¶ 2829 [USTR ¶ 614,084; CCH ¶ 5706; FTC ¶ J-2000 et seq.].

(1) Farrelly-Walsh, Inc., 13 BTA 923.

FOOTNOTE ¶ 2830 [USTR ¶ 4534; CCH ¶ 21,005 et seq.; FTC ¶ G-2415].

(1) Lucas v. North Texas Lumber, 281 U.S. 11, 8 AFTR 10276.

(2) 2 Lexington Avenue Corp., 26 TC 816.

(3) Burnet v. Logan, 283 US 404, 9 AFTR 1453.

(4) U.S. v. Yerger, 55 F.Supp. 521, 32 AFTR 855.

(5) Treas. Dept. booklet "Tax Guide for Small Business" (1991 Ed.), p. 22.

FOOTNOTE ¶ 2833 [USTR ¶ 2897; CCH ¶ 21,005.703; FTC ¶ G-2380 et seq.].

(1) Rev. Proc. 83-77, 1983-2 CB 594.

(2) Indianapolis Power & Light Co., SCt. No. 88-13.

FOOTNOTE ¶ 2834 [USTR ¶ 4514.069; CCH ¶ 21,005.345; FTC ¶ H-2510].

(1) H. Liebes & Co. v. Comm., 90 F.2d 932, 19 AFTR 965.

(2) Burnet v. Sanford & Brooks Co., 282 US 359, 9 AFTR 603; Koelle, 7 BTA 917.

(3) North American Oil Consolidated v. Burnet, 286 US 417, 11 AFTR 16.

(4) Triboro Coach Corp., 29 TC 1274.

(5) Johnson, ¶47,057 PH Memo TC.

FOOTNOTE ¶ 2836 [USTR ¶ 13,414; CCH ¶ 33,382; FTC ¶ G-3100 et seq.].

(1) Universal Oil Products Co. v. Campbell, 181 F.2d 451, 39 AFTR 377.

(2) O'Meara, 8 TC 622.

(3) U.S. v. Skelly Oil Co., 23 AFTR 2d 69-1186, 394 US 678; Cities Service Oil Co. v. U.S., 30 AFTR 2d 72-5167, 199 CtCl 89, 462 F.2d 1134.

FOOTNOTE ¶ 2840 [USTR ¶ 4614.01; CCH ¶ 21,817; FTC ¶ G-2600 et seq.].

(1) Quinn, Coex. v. Comm., 111 F.2d372, 24 AFTR 927.

(2) Granger, 478,474 PH Memo TC; Crain, Ex. v. Comm., 75 F.2d 962, 15 AFTR 343.

(3) Blaine, Mackey, Lee Co. v. Comm., 141 F.2d 201, 32 AFTR 273, revg ¶42,032 PH Memo BTA.

(4) Charles Leich v. U.S., 13 AFTR 2d 869, 329 F.2d 649.

(5) Sidney-Hill System of Health Building Co., 12 BTA 548.

(6) Est. of Spiegel, 12 TC 524.

(7) Griffin, 49 TC 253.

(8) Rev. Rul. 78-38, 1978-1 CB 67, distinguishing Rev. Rul. 68-174, 1968-1 CB 81 and revoking Rev. Rul. 71-216, 1971-1 CB 96; Rev. Rul. 78-39, 1978-1 CB 73.

FOOTNOTE ¶ 2841 [USTR ¶ 4654; CCH ¶ 21,893; FTC ¶ M-4500 et seq.].

FOOTNOTE ¶ 2842 [USTR ¶ 4694; CCH ¶ 21,966; FTC ¶ M-4600 et seq.].

FOOTNOTE ¶ 2843 [USTR ¶ 818.40; CCH ¶ 8586.0282; 21,817.321; FTC ¶ G-2106].

(1) Truck and Equipment Corporation of Harrisonburg, 98TC No.12.

(2) Rev. Rul. 55-446, 1955-2 CB 531; as modified by Rev. Rul. 61-127, 1961-2 CB 36.

FOOTNOTE ¶ 2844 [USTR ¶ 1622.14; CCH ¶ 21,817.121; FTC ¶ L-2300 et seq.].

(1) Sheldon & Co. v. Comm., 214 F.2d 655, 45 AFTR 1791.

FOOTNOTE ¶ 2845 [USTR ¶ 4614; CCH ¶ 21,817.324; FTC ¶ K-5000 et seq.].

(1) Massachusetts Mutual Life Ins. Co. v. U.S., 288 US 269, 53 SCt. 337, 11 AFTR 1389.

(2) Higgenbotham-Bailey-Logan Co., 8 BTA 566.

(3) Rev. Rul. 83-84, 1983-1 CB 97.

(4) Rev. Proc. 83-40, 1983-1 CB 774.

(5) Rev. Proc. 92-12, IRB 1992-13.

(6) Rev. Rul. 87-22, 1987-1 CB 146 and Huntsman, 91 TC 917.

(7) Huntsman, USCA 8, No. 89-1672.

(8) Prime, 39 BTA 487; Keith v. Comm., 139 F.2d 596, 31 AFTR 1100.

(9) Notice 89-35, 1989-1 CB 675.

(10) Notice 88-20, 1988-1 CB 487; Notice 88-37, 1988-1 CB 522; Notice 89-35, 1989-1 CB 675.

FOOTNOTE ¶ 2846 [USTR ¶ 4614.15; CCH ¶ 21,817.89; FTC ¶ K-4000 et seq.].

(1) Powell, 26 BTA 509.

(2) U.S. v. Anderson, 269 US 422, 46 SCt. 131, 5 AFTR 5674.

(3) Union Bleachery v. U.S., 97 F.2d 226, 21 AFTR 336.

(4) Rev. Rul. 58-55, 1958-1 CB 266, amplified by Rev. Rul. 84-125, 1984-2 CB 125.

(5) Rev. Rul. 72-490, 1972-2 CB 100.

(6) Rev. Proc. 83-77, 1983-2 CB 594.

(7) Announc. 91-89, IRB 1991-23.

FOOTNOTE ¶ 2847 [USTR ¶ 2134.03; CCH ¶ 12,543; FTC ¶ K-2000 et seq.].

(1) Rev. Rul. 78-39, 1978-1 CB 73.

(2) Rev. Rul. 76-481, 1976-2 CB 82.

FOOTNOTE ¶ 2850 [USTR ¶ 1704; CCH ¶ 11,690; FTC ¶ K-3801 et seq.].

(1) Rev. Rul. 68-174, 1968-1 CB 81, distinguished by Rev. Rul. 78-38, 1978-1 CB 67.

(2) Rev. Rul. 78-38, 1978-1 CB 67.

FOOTNOTE ¶ 2851 [USTR ¶ 1664; CCH ¶ 10,501 et seq.; FTC ¶ M-3006 et seq.].

(1) Derby Realty Corporation, 35 BTA 335, dis. 92 F.2d 999, 20 AFTR 370.

(2) Comm. v. Peterman, 118 F.2d 973 26 AFTR 930; Abelson, 44 BTA 98 (NA 1944 CB 32).

(3) Morton v. Comm., 104 F.2d 534, 23 AFTR 85.

(4) Burke, Ltd., 3 TC 1031.

FOOTNOTE ¶ 2852 [USTR ¶ 4614.21; CCH ¶ 21,819; FTC ¶ M-3004 et seq.].

(1) Harrold v. Comm., 192 F.2d 1002, 41 AFTR 442; Schuessler v. Comm., 230 F.2d 722, 49 AFTR 322.

(2) Natl. Bread Wrapping Machine Co., 30 TC 550.

(3) Adams-Roth Baking Co., 8 BTA +58.

(4) Rev. Rul. 69-512, 1969-2 CB 24.

(5) Brown v. Helvering, 291 US 193, 54 SCt. 356, 13 AFTR 851.

FOOTNOTE ¶ 2853 [USTR ¶ 4644; CCH ¶ 21,843; FTC ¶ N-1000 et seq.].

FOOTNOTE ¶ 2854 [USTR ¶ 1614; CCH ¶ 21,801; FTC ¶ G-2011].

(1) Rev. Rul. 89-23, 1989-1 CB 85.

FOOTNOTE ¶ 2856 [USTR ¶ 4714; CCH ¶ 22,201; FTC ¶ G-5000 et seq.].

FOOTNOTE ¶ 2860 [USTR ¶ 2674; CCH ¶ 14,161 et seq.; FTC ¶ I-2900 et seq.].

FOOTNOTE ¶ 2861 [USTR ¶ 1734; CCH ¶ 12,030; FTC ¶ L-2312].

FOOTNOTE ¶ 2862 [USTR ¶ 4584; CCH ¶ 21,543; FTC ¶ G-2540 et seq.].

CHAPTER 19

INSTALLMENT AND DEFERRED PAYMENT SALES

INSTALLMENT SALES IN GENERAL

You generally must recognize gain or loss when you sell property. This means that when you receive the purchase price in installments, you might have to pay tax on the sale before the proceeds are in hand to meet the tax liability. However, if you qualify for installment sale treatment, you pay tax on your gain only as you receive your installment payments.

¶2900   INSTALLMENT METHOD OF REPORTING IN GENERAL

The installment method can be used for sales of personal or real property, by investors and others who are not in the business of selling that type of property. (Installment reporting cannot be used by dealers for sales after 1987.) For example, if you sell your pleasure boat and receive payments over a three-year period, you may report gain on the installment method. However, if you are in the business of selling boats and make a sale with a three-year payment period, you are considered a "dealer" and must report all the gain in the year of sale, regardless of when you receive payment [IRC Sec. 453].

Although dealers are generally prohibited from reporting sales on the installment method, an exception is made for dispositions of timeshares and residential lots, if interest is paid on the deferred tax. For residential lots, the seller must not be required to make improvements [IRC Sec. 453(l)]. Another special rule requires a pledge of an installment sale note to be treated as payment on the debt [IRC Sec. 453A(d)].

¶2901   TAXPAYERS ELIGIBLE TO USE THE INSTALLMENT METHOD

Under current law, you can use the installment method for reporting income from dispositions of:

- Personal property, if you do not regularly sell or otherwise dispose of property on the installment plan (that is, a nondealer sale of personal property).

NOTE: Income from the sale of a partnership interest generally qualifies for installment reporting. However, you may not use installment reporting to the extent the income is attributable to substantially appreciated inventory [¶3424(e)].[1]

- Real property not held by you for sale to customers in the ordinary course of a trade or business, such as property you use in a trade or business or hold for the production of income.
- Certain timeshares and residential lots by dealers who elect to pay interest on the tax deferred because of using the installment method.
- Property you use or produce in the business of farming.

In each of the situations described above, you can report income on the installment method if you receive at least one payment in the year after the disposition year [¶2902]. You can elect not to have the installment rules apply, and then all gain is taxed in the year of sale, irrespective of when you receive payments under the sales contract. The installment method only applies in gain transactions. You must always report losses on a disposition in the year of sale.

➤ **IMPORTANT** Sales of publicly traded property (including stocks and bonds) don't qualify for the installment sale treatment. You treat payments for such property as being received entirely in the year of sale.

¶2902   ONE-PAYMENT RULE

You are not required to receive more than one installment payment to use the installment sale method [IRC Sec. 453(b)(1)]. A single payment is sufficient so long as it occurs after the end of the year of sale.

Example: Property is sold in December 1992, for $50,000. Assume alternatively:

1. The downpayment is $5,000. The balance under the contract is payable in $5,000 installments over nine years, beginning in 1993; or

2. Again the downpayment is $5,000. The $45,000 balance of the purchase price is due in 1993; or

3. The property is sold with no downpayment. The full purchase price of $50,000 is paid in 1993.

Each of these transactions is an installment sale because each one involves a payment occurring after the year of sale.

HOW TO REPORT SALES UNDER THE INSTALLMENT METHOD

¶2903   FIGURING INSTALLMENT SALE INCOME IN GENERAL

In general, the installment method requires you to break down the payments you receive each year from an installment sale into three parts: interest, return of investment and profit.

If interest is included in a payment, you must report separately all the interest as ordinary income on your tax return. Interest is generally not included in a down payment. However, you may have to treat a part of each later payment as interest, even if it is not called interest in your agreement with the buyer [¶1217(f)].

The rest of each payment is treated as if it were made up of two parts. One part is a return of your investment (basis) in the property you sold. The other part is your gain from the sale. If you took depreciation deductions on the asset, part of your gain may be treated as ordinary income [¶2915].

¶2904   INSTALLMENT SALES OF REAL OR PERSONAL PROPERTY

Suppose you sell real property at a gain. Special issues arise in connection with installment sales of real property. For example, an installment sale of depreciable real property could result in full recognition of Sec. 1250 ordinary income in the year of sale [¶2915]. Also, special rules apply to installment sales of nonfarm property by nondealers if the sales price exceeds $150,000 [¶2905].

(a) Figuring the Profit. Your gross profit is the difference between your *selling price* and the total of your adjusted basis plus selling expenses and plus any depreciation recapture. This gross profit is divided by the *contract price* to find the proportion of each year's payment (after subtracting out interest) to be returned to you as profit. In general, the gross profit percentage, once determined, remains the same for all installment payments received on the sale.

Example 1: In 1992, Smith sold real property having an adjusted basis of $60,000 for $100,000 (exclusive of 9% interest on installments), payable as follows: cash, $30,000; mortgage for $70,000, payable by the buyer in semi-annual installments of $10,000 each, the first to be paid on April 1, 1993. The profit was $40,000 ($100,000 selling price less $60,000 basis), which will be accounted for as the $100,000 due on the contract is paid. Accordingly, 40% ($40,000 profit divided by $100,000 contract price) of each payment is recognized gain.

1992 payments	$ 30,000	of which	$12,000 is recognized gain
1993 payments	20,000	of which	$ 8,000 is recognized gain
1994 payments	20,000	of which	$ 8,000 is recognized gain
1995 payments	20,000	of which	$ 8,000 is recognized gain
1996 payments	10,000	of which	$ 4,000 is recognized gain
Total payments	$100,000	of which	$40,000 is recognized gain

Selling price is the entire cost of the property to the buyer. It includes cash, the fair market value of third party notes and other property conveyed to you (the seller), and any debt, including selling expenses, the buyer pays, assumes, or takes the property subject to. It also includes notes, mortgages and your liabilities, such as liens or accrued interest, and taxes the buyer pays, assumes, or takes the property subject to. The selling price is not reduced by commissions and other selling expenses you pay or incur [Temp. Reg. Sec. 15A.453-1]. Instead, selling expenses are added to your basis in the property being sold.

> **Example 2:** In 1992, Ms. Laker sold real property unencumbered by a mortgage for $100,000. Terms were: $10,000 down and the remainder payable in equal annual installments over the next nine years, together with adequate stated interest. Laker's basis, exclusive of selling expenses, was $38,000. Selling expenses were $2,000.
>
> | | |
> |---|---:|
> | Selling price . . . . | $100,000 |
> | Less: Adjusted basis (with inclusion of selling expenses of $2,000) . . . . | 40,000 |
> | Gross profit . . . . | $ 60,000 |
> | Contract price . . . . | $100,000 |
> | Gross profit ratio: $60,000 gross profit divided by $100,000 contract price . . . . . | 3/5 |
>
> Thus $6,000 (3/5 of 10,000) of each $10,000 payment Laker received is gain attributable to the sale and $4,000 ($10,000 – $6,000) is recovery of basis. In addition, she must also report the interest received as ordinary income.

Selling price reduced. If the selling price is reduced at a later date, your gross profit on the sale will also change. You must then refigure your gross profit percentage for the remaining payments. You cannot go back and refigure your gain for earlier years [Temp. Reg. Sec. 15A.453-1].

Contract price is generally the amount you will receive, not reduced by commissions and other selling expenses you paid or incurred. It is equal to the selling price if no debts are involved. If the selling price is payable partly in cash, with the remainder secured by a purchase money mortgage from the buyer to you payable over a period of time, then the selling price is the contract price [Temp. Reg. Sec. 15A.453-1].

> **Example 3:** Mr. Daniels sells his house with a basis of $200,000 to Mr. Mickelson. Mickelson pays $20,000 cash as a down payment and agrees to pay $20,000 plus 11% interest in each of the next four years. Mickelson also assumes an existing mortgage of $150,000. The selling price is $250,000. The contract price is $100,000 ($250,000 less $150,000).

In a sale of mortgaged property, the amounts of any mortgages (other than a purchase money mortgage from the seller) are included in the contract price to the extent that they are more than the basis of the property. This applies to a sale whether the property is subject to a mortgage, or any mortgage on the property is assumed by the buyer [Temp. Reg. Sec. 15A.453-1].

> **Example 4:** Seller sells property with basis of $5,000. Selling price is $10,000. Buyer assumes an existing mortgage of $6,000. The contract price therefore is $5,000, figured this way:
>
> | | | |
> |---|---:|---:|
> | Selling price . . . . | $10,000 | |
> | Less mortgage assumed . . . . | 6,000 | $4,000 |
> | Plus excess of mortgage assumed over basis ($6,000 – $5,000) . . . . | | 1,000 |
> | Contract price . . . . | | $5,000 |

Payments received. Under the installment method, payments received include the down payment, all other cash payments, and property you receive in or before that sale year other than evidences of indebtedness of the buyer. These payments are generally not reduced by commissions and other selling expenses you pay or incur.

A buyer's evidence of indebtedness isn't payment in the year you receive it unless it's payable on demand, or is issued by a corporation or the government or its subdivision or is readily tradable. A third party guarantee, including a standby letter of credit, used as security for a deferred payment sale, is not treated as a payment received.

Pledge rule. If you sell nonfarm real property for more than $150,000 and use the installment obligation as security, you lose out on some tax deferral. The amount of proceeds you receive from pledging the obligation is treated as a payment. You are deemed to receive the payment on the later of the date the debt is secured or you receive the proceeds [IRC Sec. 453A(d)].

If the pledge rule is triggered, you still recognize gain on subsequent payments on the installment obligations—but only to the extent the total gain on the sale has not yet been recognized.

Imputed interest. The amount of imputed interest [¶1217(f)] is used to reduce the stated sales price or the total contract price [Reg. Sec. 1.453-1(b)].

> **Example 5:** Mr. Johnson sold real property for $8,500, payable $2,500 down and the balance $2,000 annually. His total imputed interest is $1,048.10. His selling price is $7,451.90 ($8,500 contract price less $1,048.10 total imputed interest).

(b) Like-Kind Exchange. In a like-kind exchange in which "boot" is received, the total contract price and the gross profit from the exchange are reduced by the value of the like-kind property. Also, payment doesn't include the like-kind property (¶1614) [IRC Sec. 453(f)(6)]. The basis of the like-kind property is determined as if the installment obligation were satisfied at its face amount.

> **Example 6:** In 1992, Mr. Jones exchanged property with a basis of $400,000 for like-kind property with a fair market value of $200,000 and an installment note for $800,000 with interest at 10%. He received no cash payments in 1992, $100,000 in 1993, and $700,000 in 1994. His gross profit is $600,000 ($1,000,000 sale price minus his basis of $400,000). The contract price is $800,000 ($1,000,000 sale price minus $200,000 fair market value of like-kind property received). The gross profit percentage is 75% (dividing gross profit, $600,000, by contract price, $800,000). Jones reports no gain in 1992 because he received no payments in that year since the like-kind property received is not treated as payment. He includes $75,000 (75% of $100,000) in income in 1993 and $525,000 (75% of $700,000) in income in 1994.

(c) Reporting an Installment Sale. You must use Form 6252 to report an installment sale. The form is used to report the original sale in the year it takes place, and to report any gain on payments received in later years.[1]

You may generally elect not to use the installment method on or before the return due date (including extensions) for the year of disposition. Untimely elections out of the installment method are permitted only in very limited circumstances (e.g., where your tax return preparer accidentally neglected to make an election out, despite your written instructions to do so).[2] Once made, the election is binding and can be revoked only with IRS consent [IRC Sec. 453(d)].

¶2905   INTEREST CHARGE ON TAX DEFERRAL

If you are a nondealer seller involved in certain large installment sales, you must pay an additional tax. It is calculated like an interest charge on the tax deferral you get from using the installment method. This interest is subject to the general rules as to the deductibility of interest on a tax underpayment and, for individuals, is nondeductible personal interest [IRC Sec. 453A(c)].

- Interest is imposed only if the total face amount of obligations arising from installment sales during the year is more than $5 million.
- Only transactions where the property's selling price exceeds $150,000 are counted towards the $5 million threshold. And regardless of the sales price, sales of personal use or farm property (after 1988) by an individual are exempt.

NOTE: In determining if the property's sales price exceeds $150,000, all sales that are part of the same transaction or series of related transactions are treated as a single sale.

- The interest charge applies to sales before 1989 of nonfarm business or rental real property.
- The interest charge applies to sales after 1988 of any nonfarm property.
- The interest must be paid on the deferred tax attributable to installment obligations that arise during a tax year and are outstanding at the end of the tax year.

Interest calculation. To determine the interest imposed on the amount of tax that is deferred on nondealer installment obligations, you use the following steps [IRC Sec. 453A(c)]:

1. Subtract $5 million from the total face value of the obligations from all sales made during the year that are subject to interest.

2. Determine the *applicable percentage.* This is found by dividing the portion of the aggregate face amount of the obligations outstanding at year end in excess of $5 million, by the aggregate face amount of the installment obligation outstanding as of the end of the tax year.

3. Determine the *deferred tax liability.* This is calculated by multiplying the gain that is not recognized by the end of the year by the highest current tax rate (31% for individuals or 34% for corporations).

4. Next, multiply the deferred tax liability by the applicable percentage.

5. Finally, the interest rate charged on tax underpayment [¶3728] is then applied to the amount found in (4) above.

Example: Mr. Gray sold two apartment buildings during the year for over $150,000 each and had $10,000,000 of installment obligations that arose during the year and were outstanding at year end. Assume that: (1) the amount of gain unrecognized at year end (deferred gain) is $3,000,000; (2) the top tax rate is 31%; and (3) the underpayment interest rate is 8%.

The "applicable percentage" is 50% ($5,000,000 over $10,000,000). The interest on the deferred tax is $37,200, calculated as follows:

(1)	Deferred tax ($3,000,000 × 31%)	$930,000
(2)	Applicable percentage	50%
(3)	Deferred tax × applicable percentage	$465,000
(4)	Interest rate	8%
(5)	Interest payable on deferred tax	$ 37,200

The applicable percentage does not change as payments are made in a subsequent tax year.

➤ **TAX SUGGESTION** You should stagger sales of property subject to the interest rule over several years to avoid meeting the $5,000,000 threshold. Let's say you're a calendar-year taxpayer who wants to sell two properties, each for $4,000,000. If you sell them during the same year, interest will be triggered. However, if you make one sale in December and the other in January, the rule won't apply because although the sale exceeds $150,000, the sales that arose during the year won't exceed $5,000,000.

INSTALLMENT SALES BY DEALERS

¶2906   REPEAL OF INSTALLMENT METHOD FOR DEALERS

If you regularly sell personal property by an installment contract, you cannot use the installment method for installment obligations sales [IRC Sec. 453(b)]. Installment obligations from dealer dispositions made before March 1, 1986, are not affected.

A "dealer disposition" is any sale of personal property by a person who regularly sells personal property on the installment plan, and any sale of real or personal property that is held by the taxpayer primarily for sale to customers in the ordinary course of the taxpayer's trade or business (that is, property which would be properly includable in inventory). An exception is made for sales of timeshares, residential lots and sales of farm property [IRC Sec. 453(l)].

Special rules for installment obligations from dispositions after February 28, 1986, and before 1988. Applicable installment obligations from dealer dispositions made after February 28, 1986, and before 1988 are subject to the proportionate disallowance rule [¶2909] for tax years ending after 1986 and starting before 1988. Any gain from an installment obligation from a dealer disposition made after February 28, 1986, and before 1988, that remains to be recognized as of the first day of the taxpayer's first tax year starting after 1987, is not recognized as payments are received, or treated as received under the proportionate disallowance rule, in a later tax year. This gain remaining to be recognized is instead taken into account (possibly over a three-year period) as an adjustment required due to a change in accounting method [¶2909].

¶2907   FIGURING THE PROFIT UNDER PRE-'88 RULES

Under prior law, if the property was paid for over a period of more than one year, you had to allocate your profit as you received the payments, using your percentage of profit for the year of sale.

While the repeal of the installment method for dealer dispositions affects dispositions occurring after December 31, 1987, installment obligations occurring before March 1, 1986, can still be reported on the installment method. They are not affected by the repeal.

> **Example:** In 1986, Mr. Wilson, a dealer, sold goods that cost $60,000 for $100,000. During 1986, he received a total cash payment of $46,000. His profit to be reported for 1986 was $18,400 (40% of $46,000). If the remaining $54,000 was collected in equal $9,000 installments over the next six years, 40% of that amount or $3,600 would be reported as profit each year (from 1987 through 1992).

Items included in sales price. Finance or carrying charges were generally included in the selling price. An accrual basis taxpayer accrues these charges ratably over the contract period or until the installment notes are sold if the charges are subject to abatement in case the contract price is prepaid.[1] But part of the charges must be allocated to the down payment and reported as gross profit.[2]

Business expenses not included in the cost of goods sold could not be spread over the term of the installment payments. They had to be deducted in the year paid or incurred.[3]

¶2908   REPOSSESSION BY DEALER

Suppose you repossess personal property you sold. This results in gain or loss. The amount of gain or loss is the difference between the repossessed goods' fair market value and the unpaid amount of the outstanding obligations. This is reduced by the amount that would be treated as income if the notes were paid in full. The repossessed goods are then included in inventory at their fair market value.[1]

> **Example:** On April 10, 1987, Mr. Daniels, a dealer who reports on the installment basis, sold for $200 an article that had cost $120, receiving $20 down, the balance payable in 20 quarterly equal installments of $9 each. After paying 17 installments (4 in 1988, 4 in 1989, 4 in 1990, 4 in 1991, and 1 in 1992), the buyer defaulted. Under the agreement, Daniels repossessed the article when it was worth $50. His gain on the repossession is $33.80, and his 1992 income from the sale is $37.40, figured as follows:
>
> | | | |
> |---|---:|---:|
> | Value of the property at time of repossession | | $50.00 |
> | Basis of obligations surrendered (3 unpaid installments): | | |
> | Face value (3 × $9) | $27.00 | |
> | Less: Unrealized profit (40% of $27) | 10.80 | 16.20 |
> | Taxable gain on repossession in 1992 | | $33.80 |
> | Profit to be reported on 1 installment received in 1992 (40% of $9) | | $ 3.60 |
> | Income in 1992 | | $37.40 |
>
> The repossessed article must be put back in inventory at $50 (its fair market value when repossessed).

Bad debts. If you do not repossess the goods, or if they are valueless when recovered, you are entitled to a bad debt deduction equal to the unrecovered cost of the goods.[1]

¶2909   THE PROPORTIONATE DISALLOWANCE RULE

The proportionate disallowance rule was enacted by the 1986 Tax Reform Act to discourage using installment sales as a tax-deferral device. Under this rule, which was repealed generally for dispositions after 1987, your annual gross profit from an installment sale depended on your outstanding debt. This rule applied to sales:

- After February 28, 1986, and before 1988 of property you held for sale to customers in the ordinary course of business, property that would be inventory if on hand at year-end, and stock-in-trade.
- After February 28, 1986, and before 1988 of: (a) personal property if you regularly sold property on the installment basis, or (b) real property you held for sale in the ordinary course of business on the installment basis.
- After August 16, 1986, and before 1988 of real property used in your trade or business or used to produce rental income, if the property's sales price (or properties that are part of the same transaction) exceeds $150,000.

The proportionate disallowance rule is repealed, generally effective for dispositions after 1987.

Under this rule, using the installment method was limited based on all your outstanding indebtedness. The amount of your "allocable installment indebtedness" (AII) for each tax year was determined, and then that amount was deemed a payment received immediately before the end of the tax year on "applicable installment obligations" held by you that arose in that tax year and were still outstanding at year's end. Suppose you made a disposition after February 28, 1986, and before 1988. Although you were subject to the proportionate disallowance rule, any gain from the installment obligation that remained to be recognized as of the beginning of the first tax year starting after 1987 was not recognized as the payments were received. Instead, the gain remaining must be taken into account as an adjustment, which may be done over a three-year period [¶2813]. It is considered a change in accounting method.[1]

(a) Allocable Installment Indebtedness. Generally, the allocable installment indebtedness (AII) was found by:

- Dividing the face amount of your "applicable installment obligations" that were still outstanding at the end of the year by the sum of the (a) face amount of all installment obligations and (b) adjusted basis of all your other assets;
- Multiplying the resulting quotient by your average quarterly indebtedness, and subtracting any allocable installment indebtedness that was attributable to applicable installment obligations arising in prior years.

(b) "Applicable Installment Obligations" (AIO) were any installment obligations that arose from the sale after February 28, 1986, but before 1988 of:

- Personal property on the installment plan by a dealer;
- Real property that you held for sale to customers in the ordinary course of a trade or business; or
- After August 16, 1986, but before 1988, real property (other than certain farm property) used in your trade or business or held for the production of rental income, if that property's selling price exceeds $150,000, so long as the obligation in any case is held by you or a member of the same affiliated group as you.

In each subsequent tax year, you did not have to recognize gain attributable to applicable installment obligations arising in any prior year to the extent that the payments on the obligations did not exceed the amount of allocable installment indebtedness attributable to these obligations. On receiving these payments, the allocable installment indebtedness attributable to the obligation on which the payment was received was reduced by the amount of these payments. Payments on an applicable installment obligation above the applicable installment obligation allocable to this obligation were accounted for under the ordinary rules for applying the installment method.

> ► **OBSERVATION** When you had more than one applicable installment obligation outstanding as of the end of the tax year, the amount of the AII for the year would be allocated pro rata (by the outstanding face amount) to the obligations, and the proportionately allocated amount would be treated as a payment on each respective outstanding obligation.

OTHER SPECIAL RULES ON INSTALLMENT SALES

¶2910   RELATED PARTY SALES

Two special rules apply to installment sales between related persons. If you sell a depreciable asset to a related person, you can't use the installment method. All the gain must be reported in the year of sale. Also, a special rule applies to an installment sale and resale involving related parties.

(a) Sale and Resale. The rules prevent related taxpayers from using the installment sales rules to avoid current tax on an asset's appreciation. A resale by a related purchaser triggers recognition of gain by you (the initial seller). Gain is recognized, based on your gross profit ratio, to the extent the amount realized on the resale exceeds actual payments made under the installment sale [IRC Sec. 453(e)].

In calculating the gain, all payments you receive on the installment sale before the end of the tax year are taken into account, even if you receive them *after* the second sale. Subsequent payments you receive will be recovered tax free until they equal the amount realized on the resale [IRC Sec. 453(e)(3)].

(b) Related Persons for sales before October 23, 1986, include your children, grandchildren and parents, but not brothers and sisters. A corporation is related if its stock would be attributed to the other party under the general attribution rules [¶3244]. Those rules also apply in determining whether a partnership, trust or estate is related [IRC Sec. 453(f)].

"Related person" for sales after October 22, 1986, includes the same relationships just mentioned, plus the following:[1]

- You and a member of your immediate family.

NOTE: Transactions between spouses are not subject to the related party rule since there's no taxable gain.

- A corporation and an individual who owns directly or indirectly more than 50% of the value of that corporation's outstanding stock.
- Two corporations that are members of the same controlled group.
- A fiduciary of a trust and a corporation, if more than 50% of the outstanding stock's value is owned directly or indirectly by or for the trust or by or for the trust's grantor.
- Any trust's grantor and fiduciary, and any trust's fiduciary and beneficiary.
- The fiduciaries of two different trusts, and the fiduciaries and beneficiaries of two different trusts, if the same person is both trusts' grantor.
- Certain educational and charitable organizations, and any person (if an individual, including the members of the individual's family) who directly or indirectly controls the organization.
- Two S corporations if the same persons own more than 50% in value of the outstanding stock of each corporation.
- An S corporation and a regular corporation if the same person owns more than 50% in value of each corporation's outstanding stock.
- A corporation and a partnership if the same persons own more than 50% in value of the corporation's outstanding stock and more than 50% of the capital interest, or profits interest in the partnership.

(c) Time Limits. The resale rule generally applies only to resales within two years of the initial sale. (See below for an important exception.) The two-year period is suspended for any period that the installment buyer's risk of loss is substantially diminished by such things as holding a put or option or a short sale [IRC Sec. 453(e)(2)].

➤ **IMPORTANT EXCEPTION** There is no two-year cutoff for marketable securities. Any resale of marketable securities by a related party—no matter how long after the first sale—triggers recognition of gain by you [IRC Sec. 453(e)(2)].

Example: In 1992, Mr. Lee sold farm land to his son Ivan for $500,000, to be paid in five equal payments over the next five years plus 10% stated interest on the balance due. Lee's basis in the farm land is $250,000. The property is not subject to outstanding liens or mortgages. His gross profit percentage is 50% (gross profit of $250,000 divided by contract price of $500,000). Lee received $100,000 in 1992 and included in his 1992 income $50,000 ($100,000 × .50). Ivan made no improvements to the property and in 1993 sold it to the Solaya Corporation for $600,000. This is the amount realized from the second disposition. Therefore, Lee must report $200,000 as his installment sale income for 1992, figured as follows:

Amount realized on property sold by Ivan, or contract price, whichever is smaller .	$500,000
Minus: Sum of payments from Ivan in 1992 and 1993	200,000
Amount treated as payment because of second disposition	$300,000
Add: Payment from Ivan in 1993	100,000
Total payment received and treated as if received for 1993	$400,000
Multiply by gross profit percentage	.50
Installment sale income for 1993	$200,000

    Mr. Lee will not include in his income from installment sales any principal payments he receives on the installment obligation for 1994, 1995 and 1996 because he has already reported the entire amount of the payments from the first disposition of $500,000 ($100,000 in 1992 and $400,000 in 1993).

(d) Exceptions. There are a number of exceptions to the resale rule:

- It doesn't apply to a nonliquidating installment sale of stock to the issuing corporation.
- It doesn't apply to an involuntary conversion if the initial sale occurred before the threat or imminence of conversion.
- It doesn't apply to a second disposition after the death of the installment seller or buyer.
- It doesn't apply to any transaction that does not have a tax-avoidance purpose. This exception is intended to apply to involuntary dispositions, such as foreclosures, or to subsequent installment sales with terms that are equivalent to or longer than those of the first sale [IRC Sec. 453(e)(6)].

(e) Depreciable Property. If you sell certain depreciable property to certain related persons, you may not report the sale using the installment method [IRC Sec. 453(g)]. Instead, all payments you receive are considered to be received in the year of sale. Depreciable property for this rule is any property that can be depreciated by the person or entity to whom you transfer it. *For sales after October 22, 1986,* payments to be received include: (1) the total amount of all payments that are not contingent on the amount, and (2) the fair market value of all payments that are contingent as to amount [IRC Sec. 453(f)(8)]. For any payments that are contingent as to amount but for which the fair market value is not reasonably ascertainable, the basis is recovered ratably and the purchaser may not increase the basis of any property acquired in the sale by any amount before the time the seller includes the amount in income.

Related persons, for sales before October 23, 1986, include: (1) you and an 80% owned entity, (2) two 80% owned entities, and (3) you and any trust in which you or your spouse is a beneficiary unless your interest in the trust is a remote contingent interest. For sales after October 22, 1986, related persons include:[1] (1) you and a controlled entity (a controlled entity is a partnership in which you own, directly or indirectly, more than 50% of interest in capital or profits, or a corporation in which you own, directly or indirectly, more than 50% of the outstanding stock value); (2) you and any trust in which you or your spouse is a beneficiary, unless your interest in the trust is a remote contingent interest; (3) two corporations that are members of the same controlled group; (4) two S corporations if the same persons own more than 50% in value of the outstanding stock of each corporation; (5) an S corporation and a corporation that is not an S corporation if the same persons own more than 50% in value of the outstanding stock of each corporation; (6) a corporation and a partnership if the same persons own more than 50% in value of the outstanding stock of the corporation and more than 50% of the capital interest, or profit interest, in the partnership; (7) two or more partnerships if the same persons own, directly or indirectly, more than 50% of the capital interest, or profit interest, in each partnership.

¶2915   DEPRECIATION RECAPTURE IN INSTALLMENT SALES

In an installment sale of depreciable property, the buyer gives you a note that is paid in subsequent years. The buyer immediately obtains depreciation deductions on the property based on its cost. Any installment sale of depreciable property results in full recognition of the Sec. 1245 or 1250 ordinary income in the year of sale. This applies even if no principal payments are received in that year [IRC Sec. 453(i)].

> **Example 1:** On July 1, 1992, Mr. Brown sold equipment used in his business, having an adjusted basis of $4,000 with Sec. 1245 recapture potential of $8,000, for $20,000. Thus, Brown has a $16,000 gain. The payments from the buyer involve four annual installments of $5,000 each, starting in 1993. The $8,000 Sec. 1245 gain is recognized in 1992. This amount is then added to the property's adjusted basis to determine the gain, which is $8,000 [$20,000 less $12,000 ($8,000 recapture income + $4,000 adjusted basis)]. Of each $5,000 payment received in the next four years, $2,000 is income ($5,000 installment × $8,000 gain/$20,000 selling price).

> **Example 2:** Mr. Paul owns a piece of equipment that he bought for $100,000. He depreciates the equipment to $40,000. In 1992, Paul sells the equipment for $100,000 with the terms being that Paul is to receive $20,000 in 1992 with the remaining $80,000 to be paid in the following four years. Despite the terms of the contract, Paul must recognize the $60,000 gain in income in 1992, since that is the extent of his recapture income.

> **Example 3:** Assume the same facts as in Example 2, except that Mr. Paul sold the property for $150,000. The same $60,000 gain must be included in income for 1992, since that is recapture income. But the remaining $50,000 gain can be treated as being received in each of the four years under the installment method.

¶2916   GAIN OR LOSS ON DISPOSITION OF INSTALLMENT OBLIGATIONS

If you dispose of your installment obligation from an installment sale, the entire amount of the gain or loss from that disposition is recognized in the year of disposition.

Increasing the interest rate on an installment obligation and substituting a new obligor is not a disposition of the obligation.[1] There is also no disposition for assigning an installment obligation as collateral for a loan. But if installment obligations are transferred to a financial institution at a discount, or at face value less certain charges, and substantial incidents of ownership are relinquished, then there is a disposition.[2]

If the obligations are sold, the gain or loss is the difference between the obligation's basis and the amount realized [IRC Sec. 453B(a)]. The basis of an installment obligation is the excess of the unpaid balance of the obligation over the income that would be reportable on the unpaid balance if the obligation were paid in full.

Example 1: In 1992, Mr. Bottoms sold unimproved land for $20,000. He bought the property two years ago at a cost of $12,000. In the year of sale Bottoms received $5,000 in cash and the buyer's notes for $15,000, payable in later years. In 1994, before the buyer made any further payments, Bottoms sold the notes. Bottoms' basis in the notes sold is $9,000, figured as follows:

Selling price of property (also contract price)	$20,000
Cost of property	12,000
Total profit	$ 8,000
Percentage of profit (proportion of each payment reportable as income, $8,000/$20,000)	40%
Unpaid balance of notes	$15,000
Amount of income reportable if the notes were paid in full (40% of $15,000)	6,000
Basis of notes sold (excess of unpaid balance of notes over amount of income reportable if the notes were paid in full)	$ 9,000

Example 2: In 1991, Mr. Hobson sold for $100,000 (exclusive of 9% interest) real property that he had purchased in 1977 and which had an adjusted basis of $60,000. Payment was to be made as follows: cash for $30,000; mortgage for $70,000, payable by the buyer in semiannual installments of $10,000 each, the first to be paid on April 1, 1992. The profit was $40,000, which will be accounted for as the $100,000 due on the contract is paid. Accordingly, 40% of each payment is profit.

	Face value	Recognized gain (40%)	Return of capital or basis (60%)
1991 payments	$ 30,000	$12,000	$18,000
1992 payments	$ 20,000	$ 8,000	$12,000
1993 payments	$ 20,000	$ 8,000	$12,000
1994 payments	$ 20,000	$ 8,000	$12,000
1995 payments	$ 10,000	$ 4,000	$ 6,000
Total	$100,000	$40,000	$60,000

Assume that before any payment is made in 1993, Hobson assigns the 1993, 1994 and 1995 notes that he still has (face value $50,000) for $35,000. The basis of the notes is the unrecovered cost of $30,000 ($12,000 + $12,000 + $6,000). The recognized gain is $5,000 ($35,000 – $30,000).

A gift of the obligation is a taxable disposition.[3]

(a) Acquisition From Decedent. Installment obligations that the decedent would have reported on the installment basis had the decedent lived are taxed to the successor as "income in respect of a decedent" to the extent the obligation's face value exceeds its basis in decedent's hands. The successor must report as income the same proportion of payments in satisfaction of the obligation as would be returnable by the decedent if the decedent had lived [IRC Sec. 691(a)(4); Reg. Sec. 1.691(a)(5)].

(b) Tax-Free Transfers of Installment Obligations. In some cases, installment obligations may be transferred without tax being imposed on disposition. These include: transfers to a controlled corporation in exchange for stock [¶1619]; contributions to a partnership in exchange for partnership interest; distributions by a partnership to a partner; certain exchanges of property for stock or securities involving corporate reorganizations [¶3206; 3211]; certain liquidations of subsidiaries [IRC Sec. 453B(d)].

(c) Transfers Between Spouses or Incident to Divorce. No gain nor loss is recognized for any transfers of installment obligations between you and your spouse, or former spouse incident to a divorce. The transferee receives the same tax treatment that would have applied to the transferor [IRC Sec. 453B(g)].

NOTE: The transferor must recognize gain on the transfer of installment obligations to a trust.

DEFERRED PAYMENT SALES

¶2917   DEFERRED PAYMENT SALES NOT ON THE INSTALLMENT PLAN

A deferred payment sale is an installment sale where you do not report the gain on the installment method. Instead, you report the entire amount of gain in the year of the sale even if the installment obligations are payable over several years.

NOTE: The installment method is not avilable for dealer dispositions of property [¶2906].

(a) Gain or Loss in Year of Sale. In general, if you are a cash-method seller, you must report the fair market value of the buyer's obligations (in addition to the cash and value of property you receive for the sale) as the amount realized on the sale in the year of their receipt. If you are an accrual seller, you generally report the face amount of the buyer's obligations (in addition to the property's value and the amount of cash that you receive) for the year of sale.

If, at the time of the sale, you reported a fair market value of less than face value the amount reported becomes your basis in the obligation; and a proportionate part of each payment collected later represents income. If the obligation has an indeterminable fair market value, subsequent payments are exempt until your basis in the obligation is recovered (see (c) below). The distinction between collections on obligations with a discounted value and those with no determinate value is important, because the former results in ordinary income, while the latter may qualify for capital gain treatment. Only in unusual circumstances will obligations be considered to have no fair market value [Reg. Sec. 1.453-6].

(b) Collections on Discounted Notes. If an obligation's fair market value is less than face value, the fair market value (1) is included in the amount realized to compute gain or loss at the time of sale, and (2) determines the creditor's basis in the obligation for computing future gain. In later years, part of each payment received is regarded as a return of capital, and the remainder is taxable income. The portion that is exempt as a return of capital bears the same ratio to each payment received as the fair market value of the obligation at the time of the sale bore to its face value.[1] If the issuer of the obligation is an individual, the taxable portion of each payment is ordinary income. If the issuer of the obligation is a corporation, the gain is capital gain only if the collection qualifies as a bond retirement.

Example 1: In 1991, Ms. Brown sold realty, which had an adjusted basis of $60,000, for $100,000, payable as follows: cash, $35,000; first mortgage assumed, $20,000; second mortgage for $45,000 payable by the buyer in 5 annual installments of $9,000 each (exclusive of 9% stated interest), the first to be paid in 1992. The fair market value of the second mortgage note was 66⅔% of face value, or $30,000. The $40,000 realized gain is reported under the deferred payment method as follows:

Proceeds realized:

Cash		$35,000
First mortgage (assumed by purchaser; therefore valued at par)		20,000
Second mortgage	$45,000	
Discount on second mortgage (33⅓%)	15,000	30,000
		$85,000
Adjusted basis		60,000
Realized gain reported in 1991		$25,000

The balance of the realized gain ($15,000) will be reported as the 5 annual installments are paid:

	1992	1993	1994	1995	1996
Collected	$9,000	$9,000	$9,900	$9,000	$9,000
Less 66⅔% already reported . . .	6,000	6,000	6,000	6,000	6,000
Realized (ordinary) gain to be					
reported	$3,000	$3,000	$3,000	$3,000	$3,000

(c) Indeterminate Market Value. If an obligations's fair market value cannot be determined, you are entitled to a return of capital before reporting any profits [Reg. Sec. 1.453-6(a)(2)]. The basis of the property sold, reduced by any cash or other property having a fair market value that you receive on the sale, becomes your basis in the obligation with an indeterminate market value for computing gain or loss on collection. If the property sold was a capital asset, collection may result in capital gain [Reg. Sec. 1.453-6]. Contingent rights to future payments have been held to have an indeterminate fair market value.[2]

Example 2: Assume the same facts as in Example 1, except that the second mortgage notes had an indeterminate fair market value. The order of the payment is:

Cash	$ 35,000
First mortgage (assumed by purchaser and therefore valued at par)	20,000
First annual installment	9,000
Second annual installment	9,000
Third annual installment	9,000
Fourth annual installment	9,000
Fifth annual installment	9,000
Total	$100,000

The adjusted basis is $60,000. The cash ($35,000), first mortgage ($20,000) and $5,000 of the first annual installment (total $60,000) are a return of capital. $4,000 of the first annual installment and all of the subsequent installments are recognized gain when received. If all the installments are paid when due, Brown will report recognized gain as follows: return for 1992, $4,000; 1993, $9,000; 1994, $9,000; 1995, $9,000; 1996, $9,000 (total $40,000).

REPOSSESSIONS

¶2920   REPOSSESSION OF PERSONAL PROPERTY

Your gain or loss on the repossession of personal property in a deferred payment sale *not* on the installment plan [¶2917] is the difference between the fair market value of the property on the date of repossession and the basis of the defaulted obligation adjusted, for other amounts realized or costs incurred in the repossession.[1] However, you report the entire taxable gain or deductible loss in the year of sale. Therefore, the basis of the obligation to be used is its face value or fair market value, whichever was used in computing gain or loss for the year of sale. Nature of the gain or loss depends on the obligation, rather than the original sale. If the obligation is discharged by repossession of the property, any gain will be ordinary income. If the repossession results in a loss that is a nonbusiness bad debt, it will be reported as a short-term capital loss. If the loss is a business bad debt, it will be so reported.

¶2921   REAL PROPERTY REPOSSESSED BY SELLER

No loss is recognized and no bad debt deduction allowed when you repossess real property to satisfy a purchase obligation. You recognize gain on repossession only to the extent of the cash (or other property) you received, less the gain on the original sale you already included in income. The amount of your taxable gain, however, is limited to the gain on the original sale less repossession costs and gain previously reported as income [Reg. Sec. 1.1038-1]. The nonrecognition of gain rules do not apply when real property is reconveyed to the estate of a deceased seller.[1]

If you reported the original sale on the installment basis, the repossession gain retains the same character as the gain on the original sale. If the sale was by a dealer, the gain is ordinary income; otherwise, it is either capital gain or Sec. 1231 gain [IRC Sec. 1038; Reg. Sec. 1.1038-1]. Your holding period includes the period you held the property before its original sale, but excludes the period starting with the day after date of the original sale and ending with date you reacquired the property [Reg. Sec. 1.1038-1(g)]. If the original sale was not an installment sale, and the title passed to the buyer, repossession gain from a voluntary reconveyance generally is ordinary income.

Example 1: Mr. Brown sold a building in 1988 for $60,000, $10,000 cash and a $50,000 mortgage, payable $10,000 annually starting June 3, 1989. His adjusted basis was $48,000. Brown elected to report the income from the sale on the installment basis. His gain was $12,000, or 20% of the selling price, and he reported a $2,000 gain in 1988, 1989, 1990 and 1991. The buyer defaulted in 1992, and Brown repossessed the property at a cost of $500. Brown's gain on repossession is $32,000 ($40,000 cash received minus $8,000 already reported as income), but his recognized gain is limited to $3,500 ($12,000 gain on the original sale minus $500 repossession costs and $8,000 already reported as income).

If any part of the debt obligation remains unsatisfied, its basis becomes zero. Hence, any later recovery is income. The basis of the repossessed property is the adjusted basis of the obligations (including the basis of unsatisfied obligations) plus any repossession gain and plus repossession costs. Adjusted basis of the obligations is the excess of the face amount of the obligations over the gain that would be reported if the obligations were satisfied in full [IRC Sec. 1038; Reg. Sec. 1.1038-1(g)].

Example 2: The basis of the repossessed property in Example 1 is $20,000, determined as follows:

Obligations (face amount)	$20,000
Less 20% unreported profits	4,000
Adjusted basis of obligations	$16,000
Repossession gain	3,500
Repossession costs	500
Basis of repossessed property	$20,000

If you took a bad debt deduction for the partial or complete worthlessness of the obligations before the repossession and the repossession satisfies the debt, you must add back to income the deduction if a tax benefit resulted from it. Basis is increased accordingly [IRC Sec. 1038(d); Reg. Sec. 1.1038-1(f)]

Repossession of seller's residence. If the repossessed property was your principal residence, and gain was either excluded or not recognized on the original sale, special rules may apply. If you do not resell the property within a year after repossession, the rules above apply. If you do resell within a year, in effect the repossession is disregarded, and the resale is considered a sale of the property occurring on the original sales date; the price deemed received is the resale price, including mortgages plus the cash or other property retained from the original sale. Using this selling price, the amount of your gain that is exempt or not recognized is recomputed [¶1700; 1708]. If the recomputation shows the taxable gain is more or less than that reported in the year of the original sale, you make an adjustment by taking the difference into account in the return for the year of resale [Reg. Sec. 1.1038-2].

SPECIAL PROBLEMS

¶2941   SALE OF REAL PROPERTY IN LOTS

A real estate development company will often acquire a tract of land and divide it into parcels or lots for easier sales. Ordinarily this requires an outlay for development such as surveying, installation of sewerage, paving, and the like. These costs must be recorded on company books and equitably apportioned to the separate lots.

The sale of each lot is treated as a separate transaction and gain or loss must be figured separately on each lot. Thus, gain or loss on every lot sold must be determined and not deferred until the entire tract has been disposed of [Reg. Sec. 1.61-6].

> ➤ **OBSERVATION** If you sell your entire property, you may defer your gain or loss until later years, for example, under the nonrecognition rules of like-kind exchanges [¶1614].

The allocation of costs is problematic in making the computation. Foot frontage, release prices, tentative sales prices and assessed valuation have all been used.

The tentative sales price method is illustrated below.

Example: The cost of the land, including the improvements, was $25,000 and the development company expects to sell the lots for $100,000. The cost of any one lot is 25% of the sale price at which it was offered for sale to the public on the day the tract was first opened.

Lot No.	No. of lots	Tentative sales price Each	Total	Estimated cost price Each	Total
1-10	10	$5,500	$55,000	$1,375	$13,750
11-20	10	3,000	30,000	750	7,500
21-25	5	2,000	10,000	500	2,500
26-30	5	1,000	5,000	250	1,250

¶2942   LONG-TERM CONTRACTS

[New tax legislation may affect this subject; see ¶1.]

Special accounting methods are used for reporting income from long-term contracts. This is a building, installation, construction, or manufacturing contract that is not completed in the tax year into which it is entered. A manufacturing contract is a long-term contract only if it involves manufacturing a unique item not usually found in the manufacturer's finished goods inventory, or the item takes over 12 months to complete [IRC Sec. 460(f)].

> ➤ **OBSERVATION** A contract that meets the definition is considered a long-term contract even though you expected that it would be completed within the tax year.

Generally, you must determine taxable income on long-term contracts entered into after July 10, 1989, by using the percentage of completion method. Limited exceptions apply to certain construction contracts of small businesses, qualified ship contracts, home construction contracts, and residential construction contracts (see NOTE below) [IRC Sec. 460(e)].

➤ **OBSERVATION** Under prior law, nonexempt long-term contracts could be computed under either the percentage of completion method or the percentage of completion-capitalized cost method. However, the percentage of completion-capitalized cost method is repealed.

Percentage of completion method. Under this method, you deduct contract costs in the tax year in which you incur them, and you recognize gross income on the contract based on the percentage of completion of the contract occurring during each tax year [IRC Sec. 460(b)].

Percentage of completion-capitalized cost method. Under this method, you determine the percentage of completion by comparing the total contract costs you incur before the end of the tax year with the estimated total contract costs.

You take into account a certain percentage of each item of revenue as well as cost. This is done when such item would be taken into account using the percentage of completion method for the contract, and you take into account the remaining percentage when that item would be taken into account by using your normal method of accounting for the contract. The percentage for each item to be taken into account under each of these two methods depends on the date that the contract was entered into:[1]

- For contracts entered into after February 28, 1986, but before October 14, 1987, you take into account 40% of each item of revenue or cost under the percentage of completion method, and you take into account the remaining 60% under your normal accounting method (the "40/60 method").
- In general, for contracts entered into after October 13, 1987, but before June 21, 1988, you take into account 70% of each item of revenue or cost under the percentage of completion method, and you take into account the remaining 30% under your normal accounting method ("70/30 method").
- In general, for contracts entered into after June 20, 1988, but before July 11, 1989, you take into account 90% of each item of revenue or cost under the percentage of completion method, and you take into account the remaining 10% under your normal accounting method (the "90/10 method").
- In general, for contracts entered into after July 10, 1989, you must take into account all the income under a long-term contract no later than the tax year that follows the tax year in which the contract is completed.

NOTE: Generally, there is an exception to the long-term contract rules for certain construction contracts of taxpayers whose average annual gross receipts for the prior three tax years do not exceed $10 million.

When a contract reported under the percentage of completion method is completed, a so-called "look-back" method is applied.

The look-back method. When a long-term contract is completed, you must "look back" and calculate taxes that would have been payable each year if actual total costs were known [IRC Sec. 460(b)(3)-(5); Prop. Reg. Sec. 1.460-6]. You must pay interest on taxes that would have been due if actual total costs were known. Conversely, the IRS must pay you interest if taxes were overpaid for any year. The look-back method must be applied to the portion of any contract reported on the percentage of completion method. Form 8697 is used to compute the interest under the look-back method.

The look-back method does not apply to: (a) any home construction contract; or (b) any other construction contract entered into by a taxpayer (1) who estimates the contract will be completed within two years from the date the contract begins, and (2) whose average annual gross receipts for the three tax years preceding the tax year in which the contract is entered into do not exceed $10 million. Also, the method does not apply to any contract completed within two years of the contract start date if the contract's gross price (as of contract completion) does not exceed the lesser of: (a) $1 million, or (b) 1% of the taxpayer's average annual gross receipts for the three tax years before the contract completion's tax year [IRC Sec. 460(b)(3)(B),(e)].

> **Example:** In 1992, Arco Corp., a calendar-year taxpayer, entered into a long-term contract that would be completed in two years. In 1992, the gross income reported on that contract by its using the percentage of completion method was $50,000. When the contract was completed in 1994, the profit that should have been reported for 1992 was $90,000. Assume an 8% interest rate applied and that Arco is in the 34% tax bracket. For 1992, Arco's tax underpayment was $13,600 [$40,000 ($90,000 less $50,000) × 34%]. Thus, Arco must pay $1,088 in interest on its tax underpayment for 1992.

Ten-percent method. An exception applies to using the percentage of completion method. You can elect to postpone recognition of income and expense under a long-term contract entered into after July 10, 1989, until the first tax year as of the end of which at least 10% of the estimated total contract costs have been incurred. For the look-back method, the recognition of income and expense must be postponed for these contracts until the first tax year as of the end of which you have incurred at least 10% of the actual total contract costs. Therefore, income and expense will be allocated to a different tax year if the first tax year that the 10% threshold is exceeded based on actual costs differs from the first tax year that the 10% threshold is exceeded based on estimated costs [IRC Sec. 460(b)(5)].

Footnotes to Chapter 19

(For your added convenience, in brackets [] with the footnotes below, you will find citations to related paragraphs in the "RIA United States Tax Reporter "(USTR), "CCHFederal Tax Reporter"(CCH) and "RIA Federal Tax Coordinator 2d"(FTC) multi-volume services.)

FOOTNOTE ¶ 2900 [USTR ¶ 4534; CCH ¶ 21,406; FTC ¶ G-5900].

FOOTNOTE ¶ 2901 [USTR ¶ 4534.01; CCH ¶ 21,406; FTC ¶ G-5901].

(1) Rev. Rul. 89-108, 1989-2 CB 100.

FOOTNOTE ¶ 2902 [USTR ¶ 4534.01; CCH ¶ 21,406; FTC ¶ G-6205].

FOOTNOTE ¶ 2903 [USTR ¶ 4534.05; CCH ¶ 21,406; FTC ¶ G-6007].

FOOTNOTE ¶ 2904 [USTR ¶ 4534.15; CCH ¶ 21,406; FTC ¶ G-6200].

(1) Treas. Dept. booklet "Installment Sales" (1991 Ed.), p. 12.

(2) Rev. Rul. 90-46, 1990-1 CB 107.

FOOTNOTE ¶ 2905 [USTR ¶ 453A4; CCH ¶ 21,455; 21,456; FTC ¶ G-6100].

FOOTNOTE ¶ 2906 [USTR ¶ 4534.01; CCH ¶ 21,408; FTC ¶ G-6000].

FOOTNOTE ¶ 2907 [USTR ¶ 4534.01; CCH ¶ 21,408; FTC ¶ G-6340].

(1) Rev. Rul. 67-316, 1967-2 CB 171; Federated Department Stores, Inc., 25 AFTR 2d 70-1269, 426 F.2d 417.

(2) Rev. Rul. 74-156, 1974-1 CB 114.

(3) Blum's Inc., 7 BTA 737.

FOOTNOTE ¶ 2908 [USTR¶ 453C8.400; CCH ¶ 221,408.25; FTC ¶ G-6045, G-6370].

(1) Blum's Inc., 7 BTA 737.

FOOTNOTE ¶ 2909 [USTR ¶ 453C8.400; CCH ¶ 21,406 et seq.; FTC ¶ G-6340].

(1) Rev. Proc. 88-83, 1988-2 CB 399.

FOOTNOTE ¶ 2910 [USTR ¶ 4534.17; CCH ¶ 21,406.60; FTC ¶ G-6232].

(1) Treas. Dept. booklet "Installment Sales" (1991 Ed.), p. 5.

FOOTNOTE ¶ 2915 [USTR ¶ 4534.05; CCH ¶ 21,412; FTC ¶ G-6201].

FOOTNOTE ¶ 2916 [USTR ¶ 453B4; CCH ¶ 21,416; FTC ¶ G-6319].

(1) Rev. Rul. 82-122, 1982-1 CB 80.

(2) Rev. Rul. 65-185, 1965-2 CB 153.

(3) Rev. Rul. 72-264, 1972-1 CB 131.

FOOTNOTE ¶ 2917 [USTR¶ 4534.47; 4534.45; CCH ¶ 21,414; FTC ¶ G-6400].

(1) Culbertson, 14 TC 1421.

(2) Burnet v. Logan, 283 US 404, 51 SCt. 550, 9 AFTR 1453.

FOOTNOTE ¶ 2920 [USTR ¶ 453B4.07; CCH ¶ 21,406.1365-21,406.75; FTC ¶ G-6550].

(1) Treas. Dept. booklet "Installment Sales" (1991 Ed.), p. 10.

FOOTNOTE ¶ 2921 [USTR ¶ 10,380; CCH ¶ 31,644; FTC ¶ G-6600].

(1) Rev. Rul 69-83, 1969-1 CB 202.

FOOTNOTE ¶ 2941 [USTR¶ 10,124.59; CCH ¶ 5605; FTC ¶ G-6230].

FOOTNOTE ¶ 2942 [USTR ¶ 4604; CCH ¶ 21,560; FTC ¶ G-6280].

(1) Notice 89-15, 1989-1 CB 634.

FIGURING CORPORATION TAX
S CORPORATIONS
SPECIAL CORPORATION PROBLEMS

Chapter 20—CORPORATIONS—TAX RATES, INCOME, DEDUCTIONS, GAINS AND LOSSES
Chapter 21—S CORPORATIONS
Chapter 22—CORPORATIONS—REORGANIZATIONS—STOCK REDEMPTIONS
Chapter 23—CORPORATIONS—PERSONAL HOLDING COMPANIES, ETC.—EXEMPT ORGANIZATIONS

CHAPTER 20

CORPORATIONS—TAX RATES, INCOME, DEDUCTIONS, GAINS AND LOSSES

TABLE OF CONTENTS

TAXING THE CORPORATION

¶3000   **WHAT IS A "CORPORATION"**

Your corporation is a taxable entity, separate and distinct from you and the other shareholders. Generally, if your organization is incorporated under state laws, it will be taxed as a corporation. However, for federal income tax purposes, your corporation need not be "incorporated." An association, joint-stock company, insurance company, or a trust or partnership that operates as an association or corporation may be treated as a corporation for federal income tax purposes even though it is not technically a "corporation" [IRC Sec. 7701(a)(3); Reg. Sec. 301.7701-2].[1]

(a) Associations. An unincorporated organization will be treated as a corporation for federal tax purposes if it has more corporate characteristics than noncorporate characteristics. The corporate characteristics are:

* associates,
* an objective to carry on a trade or business and distribute the profits,
* continuity of life on the death or withdrawal of a member,
* centralized management,
* limited liability, and
* free transferability of interests in the organization [Reg. Sec. 301.7701-2(a)].[2]

Associations of doctors, lawyers and other professionals organized under state professional association acts are considered corporations for tax purposes, provided they are both organized and operated as corporations. The above criteria for associations do not apply.[3] All of the states and the District of Columbia have enacted professional association acts.[1]

(b) Limited Partnerships may be classified as ordinary partnerships or associations taxable as corporations. Your partnership may be taxed as a corporation if it more closely resembles a corporation than any other type of business entity [Reg. Sec. 301.7701-3(b)].

(c) Personal Service Corporations are corporations whose principal activity is performing personal services substantially by employee-owners (employees owning more than 10% of the corporation's stock) [IRC Sec. 269A(b)(2)].

¶3001   **CORPORATION TAXES**

Most ordinary business corporations are subject to tax on a graduated tax rate structure. A penalty surtax, the *accumulated earnings tax,* may be imposed when your corporation retains earnings beyond the reasonable needs of the business [¶3040 et seq.]. Your corporation must also pay an *alternative minimum tax* on tax preferences [¶2610]. And, for tax years prior to 1996, corporations (other than S corporations,[1] regulated investment corporations, and real estate investment trusts) are subject to an environmental tax of 0.12% of the excess of modified alternative minimum taxable income over $2 million [IRC Sec. 59A].

Estimated tax. Your corporation must make four estimated tax payments throughout the year if it expects its tax to be $500 or more. If your corporation fails to pay a correct installment of estimated tax by the due date, it is generally subject to a penalty (¶3726) [IRC Sec. 6655].

Returns. The ordinary business corporation files a return on Form 1120 or Short Form 1120-A. Your corporation may use the Short Form if its gross receipts and total assets are under $500,000 and other requirements are met. An S corporation [¶3100 et seq.] uses Form 1120S. Corporations with tax preferences use Form 4626 to determine alternative minimum tax liability [¶2610]. Consolidated returns are discussed in ¶3045. Also see ¶3610 et seq. for additional filing requirements for corporations.

Special treatment corporations. Certain corporations are taxed in different ways, at different rates or with additional deductions. These include:

S corporations [¶3100 et seq.].
Personal holding companies [¶3300 et seq.; 3311 et seq.].
Regulated investment companies [¶3325 et seq.].
Real estate investment trusts [¶3329].
Real estate mortgage investment conduits [¶3330].

Private foundations [¶3335 et seq.].
Exempt organizations with unrelated business income [¶3354 et seq.].
Farmers' cooperatives [¶3355].
Foreign corporations [¶3810].

¶3002   RATE OF TAX

Corporate taxable income is subject to tax under the following graduated rate system [IRC Sec. 11; Reg. Sec. 1.11-1]:

If taxable income is: Over	but not over—	The tax is:
$ 0	$ 50,000	15% of taxable income
$ 50,000	$ 75,000	$7,500 + 25% of excess over $50,000
$ 75,000	$100,000	$13,750 + 34% of excess over $75,000
$100,000	$335,000	$22,250 + 39% of excess over $100,000
$335,000	—	$113,900 + 34% of excess over $335,000

The 39% bracket is the result of a 5% surtax imposed on a corporation's taxable income between $100,000 and $335,000. This surtax phases out the benefit of graduated rates for high-income corporations. Corporations with taxable income in excess of $335,000, in effect, pay a flat tax at a 34% rate.

Example: Armstrong Corporation has taxable income of $300,000. Its tax is $100,250 ($22,250 + 39% of $200,000).

NOTE: Personal service corporations [¶3000(c)] are taxed at a flat 34% rate. The IRS may allocate tax benefits between your personal service corporation and you and the other employee-owners if substantially all of the corporation's services are performed for one other business entity *and* your corporation's principal purpose is tax avoidance or evasion [IRC Sec. 269A; Prop. Reg. Sec. 1.269A-1].

CORPORATE INCOME

¶3005   INCOME OF A CORPORATION

Generally, gross income of a domestic corporation includes the same items and is figured in the same way as gross income of an individual. A "domestic" corporation is one that is created or organized in the U.S. or under the laws of the U.S. or of any other state or territory [IRC Sec. 7701(a)(4)]. A "foreign" corporation is one that is not domestic [IRC Sec. 7701(a)(5)].

Taxable income is gross income less the deductions allowed to corporations [¶3012]. There is no intermediary step of calculating an adjusted gross income. The following are the major sources of corporate income:

- Gross profit from sales [¶2701].
- Dividends [¶1218 et seq.].
- Interest [¶1211].
- Rents and royalties [¶1232].
- Gains and losses [¶3020; 3021; 3029-3035].

These additional factors must be considered in determining corporate income:

- Receipts that are contributions to capital [¶3006].
- Property distributions received by corporations [¶3007].
- Rentals paid to shareholders of a lessor corporation [¶3008(a)].
- Income from a sinking fund [¶3008(b)].

¶3006   CAPITAL CONTRIBUTIONS

A contribution to the capital of your corporation is not income [IRC Sec. 118(a)].

(a) Contributions by Shareholders. If your corporation requires additional capital for conducting its business, and obtains these funds through voluntary pro rata payments from you and other shareholders, the amounts received are not income [Reg. Sec. 1.118-1]. They are capital contributions similar to your original investment and are added to the stock's cost. Your corporation's basis in property acquired as a contribution to capital is generally the same as your basis, see ¶1619.

(b) Contributions by Nonshareholders are also not considered income to your corporation. The following special rules govern these contributions:

Property other than money. When a nonshareholder contributes property other than money (for example, land contributed by a governmental unit to induce the corporation to locate its business in a particular community), your corporation's basis in the property is zero [IRC Sec. 362(c)(1)].

Property acquired with money contributions. If a nonshareholder makes a capital contribution of money, your corporation's basis in any property bought with the money during the 12 months after the contribution is reduced by the contribution. Any money not used during that period reduces your corporation's basis in other property held at the end of the 12-month period in the following order: (1) depreciable property; (2) property subject to amortization; (3) property subject to depletion (except percentage depletion); (4) other property. Your corporation's basis in property for each category must be reduced to zero before going to the next category. The basis of property in each category is reduced in proportion to the relative bases of the properties, but a different adjustment may be made if the IRS consents. Request for the change should be filed with the return for the tax year the property was transferred to the corporation [IRC Sec. 362(c)(2); Reg. Sec. 1.362-2].

Example: On February 14, 1993, the local development council gives $25,000 to XYZ Corporation to induce it to keep its office in town. XYZ's total basis in depreciable property is $500,000. If, on February 14, 1994, XYZ has not yet purchased any property with the money, it must reduce its total basis in the depreciable property by $25,000.

¶3007 PROPERTY DISTRIBUTIONS RECEIVED FROM OTHER CORPORATIONS

If your company owns stock in another corporation, your company takes into income the fair market value of in-kind property distributions. However, that amount is reduced (but not below zero) by: (1) any liability of the distributing corporation assumed by your company in connection with the distribution, and (2) any liability to which the property is subject immediately before and after the distribution [IRC Sec. 301(b); Reg. Sec. 1.301-1(g)].

Basis. Your company's basis in the property it receives in the distribution is the property's fair market value [IRC Sec. 301(d)].

¶3008 OTHER CORPORATE INCOME

Two common types of income also taxable to your company are as follows:

(a) Corporate Rental Income Paid Directly to Shareholders. If your company leases property to others, the rent is taxable to it, even though the rent is paid directly to its shareholders and bondholders.[1] This applies even if the lease is in perpetuity and without a condition defeating its force or operation.[2]

> **Example 1:** Acme Construction Co. leased property to Baker Construction Co., the annual rental being $500,000. Instead of paying $500,000 to Acme, Baker paid $200,000 to Acme's shareholders and $300,000 to its bondholders. The transaction is treated as if the following had been done: (1) Baker paid the $500,000 rent to Acme (which must include it in income), and (2) Acme then paid a dividend of $200,000 to its shareholders and $300,000 to its bondholders.

The rent is constructively received by the lessor corporation. Its shareholders may be held liable as transferees for the corporation's tax on the rental income[3] [¶3714(a)].

(b) Income From a Sinking Fund. If your company issues bonds, it may establish a sinking fund to pay the debt. Usually, the corporation must make payments at stated intervals to a trustee appointed for this purpose. Property in the fund is a corporate asset and your company reports any income or gain from it [Reg. Sec. 1.61-13(b)].

> **Example 2:** Widget Co. issues $500,000 of ten-year bonds to purchase some new equipment. Each year, Widget deposits $40,000 in a sinking fund to accumulate cash to pay off the bonds when they mature. Income earned on money in the sinking fund must be included in Widget's gross income.

¶3009 RECONCILIATION OF TAXABLE INCOME WITH BOOK INCOME

The net income on your company's books may differ from the taxable income on its return. This is because certain book income items are excluded from income on the return (for example, tax-exempt interest), and some book expenses are not deductible (for example, repair reserve).

Your company's return (Form 1120) has two schedules relating to this area. Schedule M-1 reconciles book income with taxable income (before net operating loss and special deductions). Schedule M-2 is an analysis of unappropriated retained earnings.

Schedule M-1 has two columns. The difference between the two columns should equal your company's taxable income before the net operating loss deduction [¶3030 et seq.] and special deductions [¶3013]. Entries are made for:

M-1 left-hand column
- book income
- federal income tax
- net capital loss
- income items on the return not included in the books (e.g., prepaid rent)
- expenses deducted in the books but not the return (e.g., repair reserve)

M-1 right-hand column
- income recorded in the books but not included on the return (e.g., tax-exempt interest)
- expenses deducted on the return but not in the books (e.g., use of accelerated depreciation for tax purposes and straight line depreciation in the books)

Schedule M-2 also has 2 columns. The difference between these two columns is the unappropriated retained earnings at the end of the tax year and should equal the figure entered in the Schedule L balance sheets. Entries are made for:

M-2 left-hand column
- unappropriated retained earnings at the start of the tax year
- book income for the year
- any increases in retained earnings

M2 right-hand column
- distributions (cash, stock, property)
- other items that decrease retained earnings

Example 1: In the first column of the following worksheet are items taken from the books of a corporation. The net income on the books is $150,547, but taxable income (before net operating loss and special deductions) on the return is $237,100. Columns 2 and 3 are for items to be entered in Schedule M-1. The fourth column is for items to be entered on the return. The worksheet and Schedule M-1 (Form 1120) are filled out as follows:

Schedule M-1 Worksheet

	(1)	(2)	(3)	(4)
			Schedule M-1	
Income	Profit & Loss Account	Left-hand Column	Right-hand Column	Taxable Income
Sales (net)	$1,900,000	$1,900,000		
Interest:				
From bank & income tax refund	$10,000			
On State bond	1,000	11,000	$ 1,000(a)	10,000
Proceeds from life insurance (death of corporate officer) .	15,000		15,000(b)	
Total	$1,926,000			$1,910,000
Cost of goods sold	$1,550,000			$1,550,000
Insurance premiums on life of corporate officer (corporation is beneficiary of policy) . . .	3,500	$ 3,500(c)		
Compensation of officers	35,000			35,000
Salaries and wages	32,000			32,000
Repairs	1,000			1,000

Taxes (property)	9,000		9,000
Contributions:			
Charities	5,000		5,000
Interest paid on loan to purchase			
State bonds	400	400(d)	
Depreciation	20,400		20,40
Depletion	20,500		20,50
Capital loss on sale of securities	22,934	22,934(e	
Federal income tax	75,719	75,719(f)	
Total	$1,775,453		$1,672,90
Net income:			
Per books	$ 150,547		
Taxable income			$237,100(g)

Notes to Schedule M-1 Worksheet

(a) Nontaxable interest on state bonds. ¶1503
(b) Proceeds of life insurance not taxable. ¶1507
(c) Insurance premium not deductible when paid by corporation on life of officer and corporation is beneficiary. ¶2223(a)
(d) Interest paid to buy tax-exempt bonds is not deductible. ¶1905
(e) A net capital loss is not deductible in year sustained. ¶3020
(f) Federal income taxes are not deductible. ¶1910
(g) Taxable income before net operating loss and special deductions. ¶ 3013; 3030

Schedule M-1

Left-hand column

1. Net income per books		$150,547
2. Federal income tax		75,719
3. Excess of capital losses over capital gains		22,934
4. Taxable income not recorded on books		0
5. Expenses recorded on books, not deducted on return:		
Insurance premiums	$3,500	
Interest to buy tax-exempt securities	400	3,900
6. Total of lines 1–5	$253,100	

Right-hand column

7. Income recorded on books, not included in return:		
Interest on state bonds	$ 1,000	
Insurance proceeds	15,000	$ 16,000
8. Deductions on return, not made on books		0
9. Total of lines 7 and 8		$ 16,000
10. Taxable income (line 6 minus line 9)		$237,100

Example 2: The corporation in Example 1 had an opening balance of $300,000. During the year, it paid cash dividends of $75,000. It received a federal tax refund of $13,000 due to an adjustment of its prior year return. The worksheet and Schedule M-2 would appear as follows:

Schedule M-2 Worksheet

	Retained Earnings Account	Schedule M-2 (Left-hand Column) Credits	(Right-hand Column) Debits
Balance at start of year	$300,000	$300,000	
Net book income	150,547	150,547	
	$450,547		
Dividends	75,000		$ 75,000
	$375,547		
Federal income tax refund	13,000	13,000	
Balance at end of year	$388,547		388,547
	$463,547	$463,547	

Schedule M-2

Left-hand column

1. Balance at beginning of year $300,000
2. Net income per books 150,547
3. Other increases:
   Federal tax refund . . . . <u>13,000</u>
4. Total of lines 1, 2 and 3 . . . . $463,547

Right-hand column

5. Distributions: (a) Cash . . . . $ 75,000
   (b) Stock 0
   (c) Property 0
6. Other decreases . . . . <u>0</u>
7. Total of lines 5 and 6 . . . . $ 75,000
8. Balance at end of year (line 4 minus line 7) . . . . <u>$388,547</u>

CORPORATE DEDUCTIONS

¶3012   DEDUCTIONS OF CORPORATIONS IN GENERAL

Your corporation generally can get the same deductions as an individual taxpayer [IRC Sec. 161-196]. Your corporation cannot, however, take purely personal deductions, such as the statutory deductions for medical expenses or alimony payments, and cannot offset capital losses against other kinds of income [IRC Sec. 211-219]. Nor can your corporation take the standard deduction and deductions for personal exemptions. The following are the more common deductions available to your corporation:

Salaries and wages [¶2210 et seq.].	Depreciation [¶2100].
Rent [¶2221].	Amortizable bond premium [¶1948].
Repairs [¶2220].	Depletion [¶2233 et seq.].
Bad debts [¶2351 et seq.].	Advertising [¶2222; 2844].
Interest [¶1901 et seq.].	Contributions to pension and profit-shar-
Taxes [¶1906 et seq.].	ing plans [¶1300].
Charitable contributions [¶3019].	
Casualty losses [¶2304].	Net operating loss deduction [¶3034].

> **OBSERVATION** Since there is no provision for adjusted gross income for your corporation, there is no distinction between deductions for adjusted gross income and itemized deductions.

¶3013   SPECIAL DEDUCTIONS FOR CORPORATIONS

In addition to the general business deductions, your corporation can get special deductions for [IRC Sec. 241-250; Reg. Sec. 1.241-1]:

• organizational expenditures [IRC Sec. 248];
• dividends received from domestic corporations (¶3014) [IRC Sec. 243; Reg. Sec. 1.243-1]; and
• dividends received from foreign corporations (¶3016) [IRC Sec. 245; Reg. Sec. 1.243-2].

> ► **OBSERVATION** Except for a deduction for dividends paid on certain preferred stock of public utilities [¶3017], and the deduction for organizational expenditures, the special deductions differ from general deductions in that the special deductions are for amounts *received* rather than *paid.*

Organizational expenditures. Ordinarily, your corporation's organizational expenditures are deductible only in the year of dissolution. But if certain conditions are met, your corporation can elect to amortize these expenses ratably over a period of 60 months or more, beginning with the month your corporation starts business. When the corporate charter or certificate is issued for a limited time only, the expenses can be amortized over that period. The election applies only to expenditures incurred before the end of the tax year that your corporation begins business, regardless of whether it is on the cash or accrual basis, or whether the expenditures are paid in the tax year they were incurred [IRC Sec. 248; Reg. Sec. 1.248-1].

To be deductible, the organizational expenditure must be: (1) incident to your corporation's creation; (2) chargeable to capital account; and (3) of a character that would be amortizable over your corporation's life [IRC Sec. 248(b); Reg. Sec. 1.248-1]. This includes: fees paid for legal services in drafting the corporate charter, bylaws, minutes of organizational meetings, and terms of original stock certificates; fees paid for accounting services; expenses of temporary directors, and of organizational meetings of directors or stockholders; and fees paid to the state of incorporation.

Your corporation must make the election to amortize these expenses by the time for filing its return (including extensions) for the tax year it begins business. Your corporation makes the election in a statement attached to the return showing: (1) the amount and description of the organizational expenditures; (2) the date your corporation incurred the expenditures; (3) the month your corporation began business; and (4) the number of months over which your corporation will deduct the expenditures. The period elected must be adhered to in figuring your corporation's taxable income [IRC Sec. 248(c); Reg. Sec. 1.248-1(c)].

NOTE: Your corporation cannot deduct or amortize expenses for issuing or selling stock or securities (for example, professional fees and printing costs).[1]

Your corporation starts business when it starts the activities for which you organized it (usually after its charter is issued). However, your corporation may be considered to have started business before that if its activities have reached the point necessary to establish the nature of its business operations. The IRS has adopted a three-prong test for determining when a company starts business. Your company first functions as a going concern when: (1) it acquires the assets needed to conduct business; (2) the assets are put to productive use; and (3) the business is producing income.[2]

¶3014   DIVIDENDS RECEIVED FROM DOMESTIC CORPORATIONS

Dividends are taxed twice: (1) as the distributing corporation's income, and (2) as income to the recipient. Dividends are taxed *three times* if paid to a corporation and then distributed to shareholders. For example, if Acme Corporation receives a dividend from Beta Corporation and then distributes the dividend income to its individual stockholders, Beta's earnings would be taxed twice at the corporate level and once at the individual stockholder's level. The dividends-received deduction minimizes this tax impact by taxing only a small portion of dividend income received by corporations. The size of the dividends-received deduction depends on the relationship of the shareholder and distributing corporations:

(a) 70% Dividend Deduction. If your company owns less than 20% of the issuing corporation's stock (by vote and value),your company may deduct 70% of the dividends it receives or accrues from that corporation [IRC Sec. 243(a)(1)].

(b) 80% Dividend Deduction. If your company owns over 20% but less than 80% of the issuing corporation, your company may deduct 80% of the dividends received [IRC Sec. 243(c)].

(c) 100% Dividend Deduction. Members of an affiliated group of corporations ((d) below) may deduct 100% of dividends received from another member. Also, small investment companies may deduct 100% of dividends received. The 80% (70% if less than 20% owned) of taxable income limitation and the basis reduction for extraordinary dividends do not apply to this deduction [IRC Sec. 246(b); Reg. Sec. 1.246-2].

(d) Dividends Received From Affiliated Group Member. Corporations can fully deduct certain "qualifying dividends." These are dividends received by the corporation that is a member of the same affiliated group of corporations as the corporation distributing the dividends [¶3045]. For this purpose, affiliated groups may include insurance companies. Special rules apply to affiliated groups that include insurance companies. "Qualifying dividends" are dividends either: (a) paid out of post-1963 earnings and profits, or (b) paid by a corporation electing the Puerto Rico and possessions tax credit (¶3827) [IRC Sec. 243(a)(3);(b)(1)].

(e) Holding Period Requirements. To qualify for the dividends-received deduction, the following must be met: (1) your company must own the stock on the dividend record date[1] (the day that a stock must be held if the stockholder is to receive a dividend); and (2) your company must hold the stock for a period of at least 46 days. A preferred stock whose dividend covers a period of more than 366 days must be owned for at least 91 days.

Your company cannot count the days it held the original stock in a wash sale or any time that a short sale of substantially identical securities is pending. Any period during which your company has an option to sell or a contractual obligation to sell, or has made and not closed a short sale of substantially identical stock, is not included in determining the holding period [IRC Sec. 246(c)(4)].

The dividends-received deduction is disallowed if your company does not meet the holding period requirement, without regard to whether the stock has been disposed of [IRC Sec. 246(c)(1)]. Thus if the holding period requirement was not met on the 45th day (90th day for preferred stock) after the ex-dividend date (the day after the dividend record date), your company cannot take the deduction.

Deduction not allowed. The dividends-received deduction does not apply to dividends from exempt corporations. The deduction is also disallowed to the extent the corporation has to make related payments for substantially similar or related property. This usually covers payments by the corporation equivalent to dividends declared on stock "borrowed" to cover a short sale; but it is not restricted to that situation. Payments equivalent to dividends are deductible expenses[2] [IRC Sec. 246(c); Reg. Sec. 1.246-3].

¶3016 DIVIDENDS RECEIVED FROM FOREIGN CORPORATIONS

The dividends-received deduction can apply, in a modified form, to distributions from foreign corporations if certain ownership requirements are met. If your company owns at least 10% of the foreign corporation from which it receives dividends, your company can claim a deduction for some of the foreign taxes paid by the foreign corporation. The allowable deduction is based on the proportion of the foreign corporation's post-1986 earnings that have been subject to U.S. corporate income tax and that have not been distributed [IRC Sec. 245(a)(9)]. Amounts of Subpart F income previously taxed that are distributed to U.S. shareholders reduce earnings and profits in arriving at the proportion.

Wholly owned foreign corporations. If all of the income of a foreign corporation is effectively connected with a U.S. business [¶3811] for a tax year, the foreign corporation is taxed at U.S. rates. A domestic corporation that owns all the stock of such a foreign corporation for the entire year may deduct 100% of the dividends paid out of these earnings and profits, if it also owns all of the stock for its entire tax year when the dividends are received [IRC Sec. 245(b)].

> **NOTE:** Dividends from a foreign corporation paid out of earnings and profits accumulated by a domestic corporation when it was subject to U.S. income tax are treated as dividends from a taxable domestic corporation [IRC Sec. 243(d); Reg. Sec. 1.243-3, 1.245-1(a)(2)].

¶3017 DIVIDENDS ON CERTAIN PUBLIC UTILITY PREFERRED STOCK

If your company receives dividends on public utility preferred stock issued on or after October 1, 1942, the dividends-received deduction is calculated in the same manner as for ordinary domestic corporations [IRC Sec. 244]. However, the dividends-received deduction is subject to a special limitation for stock issued before October 1, 1942. For preferred stock issued before that date, public utilities are entitled to a dividends-paid deduction. The special limitation is designed to tax your company on the amount the public utility deducted. The dividends-paid deduction is $^{14}/_{34}$ths (since 34% is the maximum corporate tax rate) or 41.176% [IRC Sec. 247]. Thus, your company must calculate its dividends-received deduction as follows [IRC Sec. 244]:

(1) $^{20}/_{34}$ths of the amount qualifying for the dividends-paid deduction, multiplied by (2) the applicable dividends-received deduction percentage (e.g., 70% if less than 20% ownership).

> **NOTE:** The net result of these rules is that a less-than-20%-owner corporation may deduct 41.176% of the dividends received from a public utility on stock issued before October 1, 1942. The percentage that applies to a 20%-or-more-owned public utility is 47.059%.

Dividends-paid deduction. As mentioned above, public utilities get a 41.176% deduction for dividends paid on preferred stock issued before October 1, 1942. That percentage is applied against the lesser of (a) dividends paid during the tax year on the preferred stock, or (b) taxable income for the tax year (figured without this deduction) [IRC Sec. 247; Reg. Sec. 1.247-1].

¶3018   LIMITATIONS ON DIVIDENDS-RECEIVED DEDUCTIONS

The dividends-received deductions are subject to certain limitations.

(a) Limitation Based on Taxable Income. The total amount your company can deduct for domestic dividends received [¶3014], dividends received from certain public utilities [¶3017], and dividends received from foreign corporations [¶3016] is limited to 80% (70% if less than 20% owned) of your company's taxable income computed without regard to the following deductions:

- net operating loss,
- dividends received from domestic corporations,
- dividends paid or received on certain public utility preferred stock, and
- dividends received from certain foreign corporations.

The capital loss carryback to the tax year and the basis adjustment for extraordinary dividends [(c) below] are also disregarded [IRC Sec. 246(b)(1)].

NOTE: This limitation does not apply if your company has a net operating loss for the year [¶3031], computed without regard to the 80% (70% if less than 20% owned) of taxable income limitation [IRC Sec. 246(b)(2); Reg. Sec. 1.246-2].

Example 1: Rex Corporation owns 25% of the voting stock of Domestic Corporation. Rex receives $80,000 in business income and $100,000 in dividends from Domestic. Its deductions for the current tax year are $100,000 in business expenses and a $10,000 net operating loss deduction. The dividends-received deduction is limited to $64,000 (instead of $80,000), computed as follows:

1. Gross income	....		$180,000
2. Business deductions	....		<u>100,000</u>
3. Taxable income before net operating loss deduction and			
dividends-received deduction	....		$80,000
4. Div. rec. ded. (80% × $80,000)	....	$64,000	
5. Net operating loss deduction	....	<u>10,000</u>	<u>74,000</u>
6. Taxable income	....		$ 6,000

If the corporation's business deductions totaled $100,001 so that item 3 is $79,999, the taxable income limitation would not apply. In this case, after deducting the 80% of the dividends received ($80,000), item 6 would be a net operating loss of $1; so the dividends received deduction would not be limited to 80% of taxable income.

(b) Limitation for Debt Financed Portfolio Stock. If your company borrows money to buy stock, the interest on the debt is usually deductible. The combination of interest deductions and the dividends-received deductions can effectively shelter your company's earnings. To reduce this tax benefit, the deduction for dividends received on debt financed portfolio stock whose holding period begins after July 18, 1984 is limited [IRC Sec. 246A(a)]. The amount of the deduction depends on how much of the stock is debt financed. The limitation does not apply to the 100% dividends-received deduction for dividends between members of the same affiliated group and dividends received by small business investment companies [IRC Sec. 246A(b)]. Special rules apply to stock of banks or bank holding companies [IRC Sec. 246A(c)(3)].

Portfolio stock includes all stock of a corporation, unless, as of the beginning of the ex-dividend date, (1) your company owns at least 50% of the total voting power of the other corporation's stock and at least 50% of the total value of the stock, or (2) if there are five or fewer shareholders, your company owns at least 20% of the total voting power and 20% of the total value of the stock [IRC Sec. 246A(c)]. Portfolio stock is *debt financed* if there is any indebtedness (including purchase money indebtedness) directly attributable to your company's investment in it [IRC Sec. 246A(d)(3)(A)].

NOTE: Proceeds from a short sale are treated as indebtedness for the period beginning on the date the proceeds are received and ending on the date the sale is closed [IRC Sec. 246A(d)(3)].

The reduced deduction is figured as follows [IRC Sec. 246A(a)]:

1. Find the "average indebtedness percentage" by dividing the average amount of portfolio indebtedness on the stock during the base period (see below) by the average amount of the adjusted basis of the stock during the base period.

2. Subtract the average indebtedness percentage from 100%, and apply this percentage to the amount of the dividend received.

3. Multiply this figure by 70% (80% for a 20%-owned corporation).

The base period is the shorter of (1) the period between the ex-dividend date for the dividend prior to the present one and the ex-dividend date for the present dividend, or (2) the one-year period ending on the day before the ex-dividend date for the dividend involved [IRC Sec. 246A(d)(4)]. If the stock is not held through the entire base period, only that portion of the period that the stock is held is considered in determining the average indebtedness percentage [IRC Sec. 246A(d)(2)].

Any reduction in the dividends-received deduction required by the above rules may not be greater than the interest deduction allocable to such dividend (including any deductible short sale expense) [IRC Sec. 246A(e)]. Where the borrower and the dividend recipient are different taxpayers, the regulations may disallow the interest deduction of the borrower or provide other treatment instead of reducing the dividends-received deduction [IRC Sec. 246A(f)].

Example 2: Jay Corp. pays a dividend of $1 per share per quarter. The ex-dividend dates are January 16, April 16, July 16 and October 16. On January 17, 1992, Kay Corp. buys 1,000 shares of Jay Corp. for $100,000. Kay holds 22% of Jay Corp. stock. Kay Corp. borrows $60,000 of the purchase price at an interest rate of 10% per year. Assume that the stock is portfolio stock. On April 16, 1992, when the entire debt is still outstanding, Kay Corp. received dividends on the stock totaling $1,000. If the stock purchase had not been financed, Kay Corp. would be entitled to a dividends-received deduction of 80% of $1,000, or $800. The average indebtedness percentage is 60% ($60,000 ÷ $100,000). Therefore, only 40% (100% less 60%) of the dividend received, or $400, is eligible for the dividends-received deduction. The deduction is 80% of $400, or $320.

The dividends-received deduction for debt financed portfolio stock is limited in instances where dividends are received from certain foreign corporations engaged in business in the U.S. [IRC Sec. 246A(a)]. In figuring the deduction, you start off with the *unfinanced* portion of the portfolio stock owned by your domestic company. You then multiply this by the appropriate portion of the foreign corporation's effectively connected income (70% or 80%, depending on whether your company owns 20% of the foreign corporation).

Example 3: 70% of Domestico's portfolio stock of Foreignco is debt financed, and 60% of Foreignco's gross income is effectively connected with the conduct of a U.S. business. Domestico owns 20% of Foreignco. Thus, it gets an 80% dividends-received deduction. And Domestico may deduct only 14.4% (30% unfinanced portion × 80% dividends-received deduction × 60% effectively connected income) of any dividends received from the foreign corporation.

(c) Basis Reduction for Extraordinary Dividends. If your company disposes of a share of stock, it must reduce its basis (not below zero) by the nontaxable portion of any extraordinary dividend paid for the share if the stock has not been held for more than two years before the dividend announcement date. This basis reduction is required only for determining gain or loss on the share's disposition. If the aggregate nontaxable portions of extraordinary dividends exceed your company's basis, the excess is treated as gain from a sale at the time of disposition [IRC Sec. 1059(a)].

NOTE: This basis reduction is required for certain preferred stock issued after July 10, 1989, regardless of how long your company held it. Preferred stock is subject to this tougher rule if (1) the stock has a declining dividend rate, (2) the issue price exceeds the liquidation rights or stated redemption price or (3) the stock is otherwise structured so that shareholders can reduce tax through a combination of dividend-received deductions and deductible loss on the disposition of the stock [IRC Sec. 1059(f)].

Extraordinary dividend. A dividend is extraordinary if its amount is equal to or greater than 10% of the stock's adjusted basis (5% for preference dividends) [IRC Sec. 1059(c)(1), (2)]. However, your company has the option of determining the status of a distribution as an extraordinary dividend by reference to the share's fair market value on the day before the ex-dividend date in lieu of its adjusted basis. To use this option, your company must prove the fair market value to the IRS [IRC Sec. 1059(c)].[1] Special rules apply for dividends paid before the declaration date and dividends on certain qualifying stock.

The definition of "extraordinary dividend" covers certain distributions in partial liquidation and certain redemptions of stock. If a dividend is in the form of property, its amount is the fair market value, reduced (but not below zero) by any liability assumed by your company and any liability to which the property is subject to immediately before and after the distribution [IRC Sec. 1059(d)(2)].

All dividends received with respect to the same stock that have ex-dividend dates within an 85-day period are treated as one dividend. All dividends received with respect to the same stock whose ex-dividend dates are within a 365-day period are extraordinary dividends if their aggregate amount is greater than 20% of the stock's adjusted basis [IRC Sec. 1059(c)(3)].

> **Example 4:** Cee Corp. owns 100 shares of common stock of Dee Corp., a nonaffiliated domestic corporation. The adjusted basis of the stock to Cee Corp. is $1,000 ($10 per share). Assume that the purchase of the stock was not financed. Dee Corp. declares a dividend of $1.50 per share and the ex-dividend date is September 13, 1992. The dividend of $150 is paid to Cee Corp. on September 27, 1992. Cee Corp. sells the Dee Corp. stock on December 31, 1992. Of the $150, 70% or $105 is eligible for the dividends-received deduction. Because the amount of the dividend exceeds 10% of the stock's adjusted basis (10% of $1,000 is $100), and the stock was not held for more than two years following the ex-dividend date, the stock's basis is reduced by the nontaxed portion of the dividend ($105). The adjusted basis of the stock is $895 ($1,000 less $105). This increases the amount of the gain or decreases the amount of the loss on the subsequent sale.

¶3019   CHARITABLE CONTRIBUTIONS

[New tax legislation may affect this subject; see ¶1.]

In general, your corporation may deduct the same types of charitable contributions as are deductible by individuals [¶1914]. However, there are some additional restrictions on the corporate deduction. Donations made to fraternal societies and those made to trusts, community chests, funds or foundations for use outside the U.S. or its possessions are not deductible by your corporation [IRC Sec. 170(c); Reg. Sec. 1.170A-11(a)]. Likewise, a corporation may not deduct amounts paid to its tax-exempt parent corporation as charitable contributions. These payments are treated as dividends [¶3336].[1] The same rules apply to your corporation as apply to individual taxpayers for contributions of income and remainder interests in trust and the contribution of the right to use property (¶1918) [IRC Sec. 170(f)(2); Reg. Sec. 1.170A-6].

The deduction for donated property is generally determined by its fair market value at the time of the contribution. However, there are important exceptions. For example, the value of the contribution must be reduced by the amount of gain which would not be long-term capital gain if the property were sold at its fair market value. Thus, the donor of appreciated ordinary income property or other property that does not meet the long-term capital gain holding period [¶1800] may deduct only the basis in the property rather than its full fair market value (¶1917) [IRC Sec. 170(e)(1)].

Example 1: In December, 1992, Acme Incorporated makes a charitable contribution of computer equipment that it had purchased a few years ago. The fair market value of the equipment at the time of the contribution is $5,000, but Acme had depreciated the equipment for tax purposes down to $3,000. Since $2,000 would have been recognized as ordinary income (under the depreciation recapture rules) if Acme were to sell it at its fair market value, the amount of the contribution must be reduced by $2,000. Acme may deduct only $3,000.

A special rule applies when inventory-type property is given by a corporation (other than an S corporation) to a public charity or private operating foundation. This rule permits a deduction equal to the sum of (1) your corporation's basis in the property plus (2) up to one-half of the amount that would not be long-term capital gain if your corporation sold the property at its fair market value. However, your corporation cannot take a deduction exceeding twice the basis of the property. No deduction is allowed for any part of the unrealized appreciation that would be ordinary income resulting from recapture of certain items if your corporation sold the property [IRC Sec. 170(e)(3); Reg. Sec. 1.170A-4A].

To qualify, the charity must (1) use the property in a way related to its exempt purpose and solely for the care of the ill, the needy or infants; (2) not exchange the property for money, other property, or services; and (3) give your corporation a statement representing compliance with conditions (1) and (2) above. (Additionally, the property, if subject to the Food, Drug and Cosmetic Act, must satisfy all Act requirements on the date of the transfer and for 180 days before that date.) This special rule also applies to contributions of certain newly manufactured research equipment to a qualified tax-exempt research organization for research or experimentation, including research training, made by a corporation other than an S corporation, personal holding company or personal service corporation [IRC Sec. 170(e)(3), (4); Reg Sec. 1.170A-4A(a)].

Example 2: During 1992, the Roper Sled Company made a qualified contribution of children's sleds to St. Mark's Church. The property's fair market value at the date of the contribution is $1,000, and the basis of the property is $600. The amount of gain that would not have been long-term capital gain if the property had been sold is $400 ($1,000 – $600). The deductible contribution is the $600 basis plus one-half of the $400—or $800.

Example 3: Same facts as in Example 2 except that the Roper Sled Company has a $200 basis in the property. The amount of gain which would not have been long-term capital gain if the property had been sold is now $800 ($1,000 – $200). The basis plus one-half of this amount is $600. Since the deductible contribution cannot exceed twice Roper's basis in the property, the deduction is limited to $400.

(a) Time for Deduction. If your corporation is on the cash-basis method, it can deduct contributions only in the year paid [Reg. Sec. 1.170A-1]. However, if it's an accrual-basis corporation, it can elect to deduct contributions authorized by its board of directors during the tax year, if they are paid within 2½ months after the tax year ends [Reg. Sec. 1.170A-11(b)]. Your corporation makes the election by reporting the contribution on the return, and attaching a declaration that the resolution authorizing the contribution was adopted by the board of directors during the tax year. This must be verified by a statement signed by an officer authorized to sign the return that it is made under the penalties of perjury. A copy of the resolution authorizing the contribution also must be attached to your corporation's return [Reg. Sec. 1.170A-11(b)].

(b) Amount Deductible. Your corporation's deduction cannot exceed 10% of its taxable income, figured without regard to the contributions deduction, special deductions [¶3013] (other than organizational expenditures), any net operating loss carryback to the tax year [¶3030 et seq.] and any capital loss carryback to the tax year (¶3020(a)) [IRC Sec. 170(b)(2); Reg. Sec. 1.170A-11(a)]. The same general rules apply to corporate contributions of appreciated property [¶1917(c)]. However, as with individuals, your corporation reduces its deduction for the donation of appreciated property to its basis if the contribution is: (1) made to or for the use of private nonoperating foundations; or (2) for a contribution of tangible personal property that is used by the charity in a way unrelated to its exempt purpose [IRC Sec. 170(e)(1)(B); Reg. Sec. 1.170A-4(a)(3)].

> **Example 4:** In 1992, Glass Co. gave $5,000 to a domestic community chest. Its taxable income plus special deductions (but not deducting contributions) was $45,000. It had no capital loss during the tax year. The charitable contribution deduction is $4,500 (10% of $45,000).

The $500 that is not deductible currently is carried forward, subject to the rules discussed in (c) below.

Alternative minimum tax. For contributions made before July 1, 1992, the appreciation in value of donated tangible personal property is not a tax preference for AMT purposes [¶2603(a)].

(c) Carryover. Your corporation can carry over contributions in excess of the 10% limit to the five succeeding tax years. However, the total of contributions actually made during the later year plus the carryover are subject to the 10% limit [IRC Sec. 170(d)(2); Reg. Sec. 1.170A-11(c)]. Also, your corporation must reduce a carryover to the extent that the excess contribution carried over reduces taxable income and increases a net operating loss carryover.

> **Example 5:** Assume that in 1993, Glass Co. in Example 4 had a taxable income (figured without contributions, special deductions, net operating loss carryback and capital loss carryback) of $50,000, and that it gave $4,800 to the American Red Cross. The deduction would be figured as follows:
>
> Contributions actually made in 1993 . . . . $ 4,800
> Carryover from 1991 (1992 excess)   5000
> Total $5,300
> Amount deductible in 1993 (10% × $50,000)   5,000
> Excess (available for carryover to 1994) . . . . $ 300
>
> ➤ **OBSERVATION** In calculating its charitable contribution, your corporation must first deduct its current year's contribution, and then deduct its carryover from the prior years (beginning with the most recent years). As a result, it is possible that an amount will be carried over for more than five years, after which it will be lost.

(d) Contribution as Business Expense. Your corporation cannot claim a business expense deductions for contributions over the 10% limit [Reg. Sec. 1.162-15]. However, if payments do not qualify as contributions, but are in fact business expenses, your corporation can deduct the amount without limitation.

> **Example 6:** As part of an advertising campaign designed to promote additional sales and net profits, the Slurpy Noodles Soup Company entered into an agreement with a very large and well-known charitable organization. Slurpy Noodles agreed to pay the organization a certain amount for each soup can label mailed to the organization by the purchaser. In return, the organization agreed to permit the use of its name in connection with the advertising. The payments made to the charitable organization are deemed to be ordinary and necessary business expenses.[2]

CAPITAL GAINS AND LOSSES OF CORPORATIONS

¶3020   CAPITAL GAINS AND LOSSES IN GENERAL

Generally, capital gains and losses of corporations and individuals arise in the same way—from the sale or exchange of a capital asset [¶1801; 1811]. Occasionally, some capital gain transactions may be given ordinary income treatment, like disposing of property for which accelerated depreciation deductions were claimed [¶1812] or the sale or exchange of depreciable property between an individual and his or her controlled corporation [¶1817].

Your corporation, like an individual, balances net long-term capital gain or loss against net short-term capital gain or loss to arrive at the year's net capital gain [¶1803; 1808]. However, there are two key differences in the rules that apply to corporations:

1.   Corporations cannot deduct a capital loss in the year the loss is sustained [IRC Sec. 1211(a); Reg. Sec. 1.1211-1].

2.   There are special carryback and carryforward of net capital loss rules for corporations [(a) below].

Where to deduct. Your corporation reports its capital gains and losses on Schedule D of Form 1120, or Form 1120S if it elects S corporation treatment.

Generally, your corporation must pay an alternative minimum tax [¶2610] equal to 20% of the excess of its tax preference items over its regular income tax liability. Capital gains are fully included in your corporation's alternative minimum taxable income [IRC Sec. 55(b)(1)(A)].

(a)   Carrybacks and Carryovers of Net Capital Losses. Although your corporation cannot take a deduction in the current year for a net capital loss, it can carry the loss back to each of the three years before the loss year. If the carrybacks do not absorb the entire loss, the rest can be carried over to each of the five years after the loss year. A net capital loss is first carried back to the earliest tax year to which it is allowed. If your corporation has two or more carryovers to the same year, it first uses the earliest loss to reduce the net capital gains and then the next carryover is applied [IRC Sec. 1212(a); Reg. Sec. 1.1212-1]. A capital loss carryback may not increase or create your corporation's net operating loss (¶3033) [IRC Sec. 1212(a)(1)(a)(ii)] for the tax year in which the carryback is applied. Furthermore, regardless of origin, all carrybacks and carryovers are treated as short-term capital losses for carryback and carryover purposes.

> **Example 1:** In 1992, Widget Corp. has a net capital loss of $40,000. Its net capital gains in 1989, 1990 and 1991 were $23,000, $12,000 and $6,000, respectively. The first year to which Widget can carry back its 1992 net capital loss is 1989. The $23,000 net capital gain for that year is completely used up by the $40,000. The excess ($17,000) is carried to 1990 where it entirely offsets the $12,000 net capital gain for that year. The $5,000 remaining of the 1992 net capital loss is deducted in 1991 from the $6,000 net capital gain for that year, reducing it to $1,000. The 1992 net capital loss has been completely used up, so there is no capital loss carryover for tax years 1993-1997.

> **Example 2:** Baker Corp. has a net capital loss of $32,000 in 1992. Its net capital gains in 1989, 1990 and 1991 were $15,000, $102,000 and $10,000, respectively. It also had a net operating loss of $100,000 in 1990. Baker can carry back its net capital loss to 1989 and wipe out that year's $15,000 net capital gain. Since taxable income for 1990 is only $2,000, Baker can only deduct the 1992 net capital loss in 1990 to the extent of $2,000 of taxable income. If a greater amount were deducted, it would create an operating loss. For 1991, Baker can carry back $10,000 of the 1992 net capital loss to offset the $10,000 net capital gain of 1991. The balance of the 1992 net capital loss ($5,000) will be available as a loss carryover for tax years 1993-1997.

Foreign expropriation capital losses cannot be included in a capital loss carryback [IRC Sec. 1212(a)(1)(A)(i)]; a special ten-year carryforward is allowed instead. Regulated investment companies are allowed an eight-year carryover, but no carryback [IRC Sec. 1212(a)(1)(C)]. A tentative carryback adjustment [¶3744] is available, enabling corporations to obtain a speedy refund or credit for an overpayment resulting from a carryback.

Capital loss carryovers may be lost upon a substantial change of ownership [¶3035].

(b) Special Rules on Carrybacks. Net capital losses cannot be carried back to any tax year in which your corporation is [IRC Sec. 1212(a)(3)]:

- a foreign personal holding company [¶3312];
- a regulated investment company [¶3325];
- a real estate investment trust [¶3329]; or
- a foreign investment company in a year in which it elects to distribute income currently.

¶3021   GAIN ON DISPOSITION OF DEPRECIABLE PROPERTY

All or part of the gain your corporation has from disposing of Sec. 1245 or 1250 property (that is, depreciable property with a fair market value in excess of its adjusted basis) may be ordinary income [¶1819]. The deductions for mining exploration expenses [¶2242] and certain farm expenses may be recaptured under similar rules.

If your corporation distributes Sec. 1245 or Sec. 1250 property to a shareholder, it measures its ordinary income from the distribution as if the property had been sold at fair market value at the time of distribution [IRC Sec. 1245(a), 1250(a); Reg. Sec. 1.1245-1(c), 1.1250-1(a)(4)]. This applies to dividend distributions, liquidations and stock redemptions that otherwise would be tax-free [IRC Sec. 1245(d), 1250(i); Reg. Sec. 1.1245-6(b), 1.1250-1(b)(2)]. However, the amount of ordinary gain from the disposition is limited to your corporation's recognized gain when the distributee or transferee takes your corporation's basis for the property as its own basis in:

- liquidation of a controlled subsidiary [¶3235];
- transfer to a controlled subsidiary [¶1619]; or
- exchange for stock or securities in a reorganization [¶3211(c)].

This limit applies to exempt farmers' cooperatives [¶3355] but not other tax-exempt organizations [IRC Sec. 1245(b)(3), 1250(d)(3); Reg. Sec. 1.1245-4(c), 1.1250-3(c)].

Additional recapture on disposition of Sec. 1250 property. Along with the usual recapture rules that apply to dispositions of Sec. 1250 property, an additional amount of gain is subject to recapture. The amount treated as ordinary income is increased by 20%. In other words, 20% of any gain that would have been treated as long-term capital gain is recaptured as ordinary income [IRC Sec. 291(a)(1)].

PURCHASES, SALES AND DISTRIBUTIONS OF CORPORATE SECURITIES AND PROPERTIES

¶3024   CORPORATION DEALING IN ITS OWN STOCK

Your corporation recognizes no gain or loss when it disposes of its own stock, including treasury stock, in exchange for money, other property or as payment for services [IRC Sec. 1032; Reg. Sec. 1.1032-1(a)]. Nor does your corporation recognize gain or loss on the lapse or acquisition of an option on its stock. However, your corporation does recognize gain or loss when it transfers restricted property to an employee. Its recognized gain or loss is the amount it claimed as a deduction (¶2214(c)) [Reg. Sec. 1.83-6(b)]. For recognition of gain when your corporation distributes the stock of another corporation, see ¶1600.

Your corporation may recognize gain or loss if it receives its own stock in the exchange, unless your corporation acquires its own stock in exchange for other shares of its own stock (including treasury stock) [Reg. Sec. 1.1032-1(b)].

> **Example:** Able Co. owns real estate worth $3,000, but having an adjusted basis of $2,500, which it exchanges for shares of its own stock having a fair market value of $3,000. The $500 gain is taxable.

¶3025   CORPORATION DEALING IN ITS OWN OBLIGATIONS

Your corporation may issue its own obligations (bonds, debentures, notes or other debt-bearing instruments) in three ways: (1) at face value (price printed on the obligation); (2) at a premium (price more than face amount); or (3) at a discount (price less than face amount). Special rules apply to convertible bonds that are repurchased at a premium and to obligations that are part of investment units which include options [Reg. Sec. 1.61-12(c)(4), 1.163-4(a)(2)].

(a) Obligations Issued at Face Value. Your corporation does not realize gain or loss when it issues its obligations at face value [Reg. Sec. 1.61-12(c)(1)]. If it repurchases them for more than the issue price, the excess is a deductible expense [Reg. Sec. 1.163-4(c)]. If your corporation repurchases them for less than the issue price, the difference is income[1] [Reg. Sec. 1.61-12(c)(3)].

> **Example 1:** In 1974, Burke Corp. issued 500 bonds with a face value of $1,000 each, receiving $500,000 for them. If it repurchases 100 bonds in 1993 for $95,000, it has income of $5,000 ($100,000 minus $95,000); if it repurchases the 100 bonds for $103,000, it can deduct $3,000 ($103,000 minus $100,000).

(b) Obligations Issued at a Premium. When your corporation issues obligations at a premium, the premium is income and should be prorated or amortized over the life of the obligations [Reg. Sec. 1.61-12(c)(2)]. If your corporation repurchases the obligations, your corporation subtracts the premium that it reported as income from the issue price. If the result is less than the purchase price, the difference is a deduction in the year of purchase [Reg. Sec. 1.164-3(c)]. Alternatively, if the result is greater than the purchase price, the difference is income in the year of purchase [Reg. Sec. 1.61-12(c)(3)].

> **Example 2:** Hale Co. issues $100,000 of its 20-year bonds for $110,000. After five years (Hale has reported $2,500 as income), the bonds are repurchased for $115,000. Since the issue price less the reported premium is $107,500, Hale gets a $7,500 deduction on account of the repurchase.

> **Example 3:** Assume the same facts as in Example 2, except that the bonds were repurchased for $95,000. The issue price less the reported premium is $12,500 more than the repurchase price. Hale will recognize that excess as income in the year of repurchase.

(c) Obligations Issued at a Discount. If your corporation issues the obligations at a discount, it can deduct the net amount of the discount, which should be prorated or amortized over the life of the obligations [Reg. Sec. 1.163-4(a)]. If the obligations are bought back by your corporation before maturity, it adds to the issuing price the discount already deducted. If the result is less than the purchase price, the difference is a deduction in the year of purchase. But if the result is greater than the purchase price, the difference is income in the year of purchase [Reg. Sec. 1.61-12(c)(3), 1.163-4(c)].

Example 4: If Judd Co. issues \$100,000 of its 20-year bonds for \$90,000, $\frac{1}{20}$ of the discount ($\frac{1}{20}$ of \$10,000, or \$500) will be deducted each year as interest. After two years, Judd repurchases the bonds. If it pays more than \$91,000, the difference is a deductible expense; if it pays less, Judd has taxable income on the repurchases.

(d) Treatment of Unamortized Balance Upon Refinancing. If your corporation refinances or refunds obligations before maturity, your corporation amortizes the unamortized premium or discount on the old bonds over the life of the new bonds.[2] In certain liquidations and reorganizations, a successor corporation may continue to amortize bond discount or premium on bonds taken over from the predecessor corporation.

(e) High-Yield Discount Obligations. Special rules apply to certain high-yield discount obligations your corporation issued after July 10, 1989. Your corporation cannot deduct a portion of the discount. It treats the discount as a dividend instead of interest. Your corporation can deduct the remainder only when it is paid—even for an accrual corporation. To get the deduction, that payment must be in some form other than an obligation of your corporation.

NOTE: The term "obligation" includes stock except for determining the debt instrument's yield to maturity.

These rules do not apply for any period during which the issuer is an S corporation [IRC Sec. 163(e)(5), (i)].

NOTE: On the other hand, if your corporation holds such an obligation, it is allowed a dividend-received deduction for the portion that is treated as a dividend.

This treatment applies to debt instruments (e.g., bonds, debentures, notes and certificates) that have (1) the maturity date more than five years from the date of issue, (2) a yield to maturity that equals or exceeds the sum of the applicable federal rate (AFR) for the month of issue plus five percentage points, and (3) the instrument has a significant original issue discount.

An instrument has a significant original issue discount if the total amount the holder has to include in gross income before the close of the accrual period ending five full years after the date of issue, exceeds the sum of the aggregate amount of interest payable during that accrual period plus the product of the instrument's issue price and its yield.

If the instrument is a high-yield discount obligation, the "disqualified yield" and "disqualified portion" must be found. The disqualified portion is what is recharacterized as dividend.

The disqualified yield is the portion of the yield that exceeds the sum of the AFR for the month in which the obligation is issued plus six percentage points. The disqualified portion is the lesser of the amount of the original issue discount or the portion of the return attributable to the disqualified yield. The attributable amount is determined by multiplying the return on the instrument by a fraction, the numerator of which is the disqualified yield and the denominator the yield to maturity.

Example 5: On January 1, 1993, Grand Corp. issues a bond with an issue price of \$1,000 and yield of 20% to maturity in ten years. All interest is payable at maturity. Assume the AFR in January, 1993 is 9%. Thus, the bond is subject to the high-yield discount obligation rules.

    The return on the instrument in the first year is \$200 (\$1,000 times 20%). The adjusted price is \$1,200 at the end of the year (\$1,000 plus \$200). The disqualified yield is 5%. That is the 20% yield to maturity less the sum of the 9% AFR plus six percentage points. This disqualified yield is 25% ($\frac{5}{20}$ of the yield to maturity). The amount of the disqualified portion in the first year is \$50 (25% of \$200). The return on the instrument at the end of the second year is \$240 (\$1,200 times 20%), and the disqualified portion is \$60 (25% of \$240).

Example 6: Assume the same facts as in Example 5. If Grand distributes \$120 in cash to bondholders at the end of the second year, \$30 (\$120 times 25%) is considered payment from the disqualified portion. The other \$90 is a deductible interest payment.

¶3026   INCOME FROM DISCHARGE OF INDEBTEDNESS

Generally, corporations must treat debt forgiveness as income. However, there are special rules for bankrupt and insolvent debtors (¶1234) [IRC Sec. 108].

¶3027   EFFECT OF PROPERTY DISTRIBUTIONS ON CORPORATION

Generally, your corporation recognizes no gain or loss for distributing property (including its stock or stock rights) to its shareholders [IRC Sec. 311(a)]. Your corporation does, however, have taxable gain on property that it distributes to the extent the property's fair market value exceeds its basis. The gain is determined as if your corporation sold the property at fair market value [IRC Sec. 311(b)].

> **NOTE:** The IRS is authorized to issue regulations that prevent partnership or trust interest distributions from being used to circumvent the above rules. The amount of gain recognized on a nonliquidating distribution of a partnership or trust interest would be computed without regard to any loss from property that was contributed to the partnership or trust for the principal purpose of recognizing such loss on the distribution [IRC Sec. 311(b)(3)].

Depreciable property. If your corporation makes a dividend distribution of property subject to recapture under IRC Sections 1245, 1250, 1252 or 1254, it must recognize ordinary income on the disposition, which will be measured as if your corporation sold the property for fair market value (¶3021) [IRC Sec. 1245(a), (d), 1250(a), (i); Reg. Sec. 1.1245-1 et seq., 1.1250-1 et seq.].

Property distributed at bargain price to shareholder. If your corporation transfers property in a sale or exchange to you or another shareholder at a bargain price, it is deemed to have made a distribution. How much of the distribution is taxable as a dividend depends upon your corporation's current and accumulated earnings and profits (E&P) at the time of the distribution [¶ 1218; 1219]. The general rules for determining whether a distribution is considered a taxable dividend are as follows:

- A distribution is a taxable dividend to the extent of your corporation's E&P;
- Distributions in excess of E&P represent a return of capital and reduce the basis of the shareholder's stock;
- Any excess, after basis has been recovered, is treated as capital gain.

If the amount paid for the property by the shareholder is less than the property's adjusted basis, the amount of distribution is the excess of the fair market value over the purchase price.

> **Example:** Batson Corp. sold property to shareholder Richard Grayson for $2,000. The property's fair market value is $10,000. The amount of the distribution to Grayson is $8,000.

¶3028   EFFECTS OF DISTRIBUTIONS ON CORPORATION'S EARNINGS AND PROFITS

Your corporation's earnings and profits (E&P) must be adjusted when it distributes property to its shareholders.

(a) General Rule. If the distribution is in the form of money, the E&P are decreased by the amount of money distributed. Upon the distribution of your corporation's obligations, the

E&P are decreased by the principal amount of the obligations (issue price for original issue discount obligations) [IRC Sec. 312(a)(1),(2)]. For distributions of other property, E&P are generally decreased by your corporation's adjusted basis in the distributed property [IRC Sec. 312(a)(3); Reg. Sec. 1.312-1(a)-(c)].

> **Example 1:** Maple Co. distributes $5,000 to a shareholder. Before the distribution, Maple's earnings and profits are $7,500. The distribution decreases its earnings by $5,000, leaving a balance of $2,500 in the earnings and profits account.

> **Example 2:** Deluxe Corporation, with E&P of $500,000, distributes property with an adjusted basis of $150,000 and a fair market value of $100,000 to its shareholders. The distribution decreases its E&P by $150,000 (adjusted basis), leaving a balance of $350,000 in the E&P account.

(b) Distributing Appreciated Property. Your corporation's distribution of appreciated property increases its E&P by the excess of the property's fair market value over the property's adjusted basis [IRC Sec. 312(b)]. The distribution then results in a decrease to E&P using fair market value instead of adjusted basis to measure the decrease. The net effect is that the E&P are decreased by the property's basis.

> **Example 3:** Acme Corporation with E&P of $500,000 distributes real property with an adjusted basis of $100,000 and fair market value of $150,000 to its shareholders. The distribution increases Acme's E&P by $50,000 ($150,000 fair market value less $100,000 adjusted basis), and then decreases it by $150,000 (the property's fair market value), leaving a balance of $400,000 in the E&P account. ·

(c) Adjustments for Liabilities. The adjustments described in (a) and (b) above must be reduced by any liability on the property distributed, and the amount of any liability of your corporation assumed by a shareholder in connection with the distribution [IRC Sec. 312(c); Reg. Sec. 1.312-3, 1.312-4].

> **Example 4:** On December 31, 1992, Engel Co. distributed to its sole shareholder, John Kane, as a dividend in kind, a vacant lot. On that date, the lot had a fair market value of $50,000 and was subject to a mortgage of $20,000. The adjusted basis of the lot was $31,000. The earnings and profits were $10,000. The dividend received by Kane is $30,000 ($50,000, the fair market value, less $20,000 mortgage). The reduction in the earnings and profits of Engel is $11,000 ($31,000, the basis, less $20,000 mortgage).

(d) Distributions Not Taxed to Distributee. If your corporation makes partially or wholly tax-free distributions to its shareholders, it must file Form 5452 by February 28 of the following year. These distributions are considered wholly or partially nontaxable only because your corporation's earnings and profits are less than the distributions. If your corporation does not furnish the required information, the IRS may assume it has redetermined its distributions to be fully taxable as dividends.[1]

(e) Allocation of Earnings. When your corporation distributes the stock of a corporation it controls [¶3221et seq.], part of the earnings and profits of your corporation must be allocated to the controlled corporation [IRC Sec. 312(h)(1); Reg. Sec. 1.312-10]. This allocation of earnings and profits between distributing and controlled corporations must be made in most tax-free distributions, exchanges, or transfers of property [Reg. Sec. 1.312-11]. A similar allocation is also required in a Type C or Type D reorganization if the plan was adopted after July 18, 1984 [IRC Sec. 312(h)(2)].

(f) Discharge of Indebtedness. The amount of any debt discharge (including amounts excluded from gross income) increases corporate earnings and profits. However, any debt discharge amount that is used to reduce bases of corporate depreciable property under Sec. 1017 does not increase its earnings and profits [IRC Sec. 312(l)].

¶3029   ALLOCATING PURCHASE PRICE IN ASSET SALES

Generally, in an "applicable asset acquisition" (see below), both the buyer and the seller must use the residual method to allocate the purchase price received for determining the buyer's basis or the seller's gain or loss [IRC Sec. 1060]. Briefly, under the residual method, the goodwill and going concern value is the excess of the business's purchase price over the aggregate fair market values of the tangible assets and the identifiable intangible assets other than goodwill and going concern value. The method used here is the same as the one for allocating purchase price to assets following a stock purchase [Temp. Reg. Sec. 1.338(b)-2T]. The price of the assets acquired must be reduced by cash and cash-like items; the balance is allocated first to certain tangible assets, followed by certain intangibles (neither allocation can be more than the assets' fair market values). The remaining cost must then be allocated to goodwill and going concern value.

> **PARTIES BOUND BY THEIR AGREEMENT** Starting with acquisitions after October 9, 1990, both the buyer and seller in an applicable asset acquisition are bound for tax purposes by the terms of their written agreements as to the allocation of any consideration or the value of any of the assets. Exception: Their agreement is not binding if the IRS determines that the allocation (or value) is not appropriate. Note: Acquisitions pursuant to a written binding contract in effect on October 9, 1990, are not subject to the new rule.

An applicable asset acquisition is any transfer of assets constituting a business in which the seller's basis is determined wholly by reference to the consideration (usually the purchase price) paid for the assets [IRC Sec. 1060(c)]. For this rule, a group of assets will constitute a business if their character is such that goodwill or going concern value could under any circumstances attach to the assets. For example, a group of assets that would constitute an active trade or business within the meaning of Sec. 355 (involving the distribution of a controlled corporation's stock) will in all events be considered a business. In addition, businesses that are not active businesses under Sec. 355 will also be subject to this rule.

NOTE: The mandatory allocation rule covers both direct and indirect transfers of a business. So, you must apply the special allocation rules to a sale of a business by an individual or a partnership, or a sale of a partnership interest in which the basis of the purchasing partner's proportionate share of the partnership's assets is adjusted to reflect the purchase price.

Information required. The seller and buyer must file information returns on Form 8594 disclosing amounts allocated to goodwill or going concern value, and to any other categories of assets or specific assets [IRC Sec. 1060(b); Temp. Reg. Sec. 1.1060-1T].

> **ADDITIONAL REPORTING REQUIREMENT** Starting with acquisitions after October 9, 1990, if you own more than 10% of a business, you must furnish any information required by the IRS if you transfer an interest in the business, and enter into an employment contract, covenant not to compete, royalty or lease agreement, or other agreement with the buyer. The buyer also must furnish any information that the IRS may require. Note: Acquisitions under a written binding contract in effect on October 9, 1990 are exempt from this reporting requirement.

NET OPERATING LOSSES OF CORPORATIONS

¶3030   WHAT IS A NET OPERATING LOSS?

The amount of a loss from a business activity that can be carried over to other years is known as a net operating loss (NOL). The NOL is the amount of business deductions in excess of business gross income plus or minus certain adjustments. Note that nonbusiness casualty and theft losses are treated as business losses for NOL purposes.

¶3031   NET OPERATING LOSSES IN GENERAL

If your corporation's allowable deductions exceed its annual gross income, as modified, your corporation can carry the resulting net operating loss back or forward and deducted as a loss in certain other tax years. The aggregate of the carrybacks and carryovers to a year is the net operating loss deduction [IRC Sec. 172; Reg. Sec. 1.172-1(a)]. All corporations are entitled to the net operating loss deduction in computing their income tax, except: (1) mutual insurance companies other than life or marine; (2) regulated investment companies [IRC Sec. 852(b)(2)]; and (3) S corporations. S corporation losses are passed through to their shareholders [IRC Sec. 1366(a)]. The general rules governing a net operating loss are similar to those for individuals [¶2341–2344]; but the adjustments for figuring net operating losses and net operating loss carryovers differ.

> **NOTE:** There is a restriction on loss carrybacks for a corporation that is involved in a corporate equity reduction transaction (CERT)—like buying a majority interest in another corporation or paying an unusually large distribution to shareholders. It applies in the year of the CERT transaction and the following two years [IRC Sec. 172(b)(1)(E), (h)].

¶3032 YEARS TO WHICH A NET OPERATING LOSS MAY BE CARRIED

Your corporation may carry back a net operating loss to each of the three preceding years, and carry forward to each of the fifteen following years. The loss is first carried to the earliest year, and then to the next earliest year, etc. For example, a net operating loss for 1992 may be used until exhausted in the following years: 1989, 1990, 1991 and 1993 through 2007. This sequence must be followed. Thus, no part of the 1992 loss may be used to offset 1990 income until 1989 income has been absorbed. However, your corporation can elect to give up the three-year carryback if the election is made by its tax return due date for the year of the loss [IRC Sec. 172(b)(1), (3)]. An election to waive the three-year NOL carryback must apply for both regular and alternative minimum tax purposes.[1]

There are several exceptions to the general rule: foreign expropriation losses cannot be carried back, but a ten-year carryover can be elected; certain financial institutions and a Bank for Cooperatives are allowed ten-year carrybacks and five-year carryovers; taxpayers with product liability losses are allowed a ten-year carryback; real estate investment trusts are allowed only a fifteen-year carryover for REIT years; specified liability losses are allowed only a ten-year carryback; and electing General Stock Ownership Corporations (GSOCs) are allowed only a ten-year carryover [IRC Sec. 172(b); Reg. Sec. 1.172-4, 1.172-11].

¶3033   FIGURING THE NET OPERATING LOSS

Net operating loss is the amount by which your corporation's deductions, adjusted as follows, exceeds its gross income [IRC Sec. 172(c),(d); Reg. Sec. 1.172-2]:

1. Net operating loss deduction is not allowed.

2. The following special deductions are allowed without the limitation that aggregate dividends-received deductions cannot exceed 70% of taxable income (80% for a 20%-owned corporation):

- Deduction for dividends received from domestic corporations [¶ 3014].
- Deduction for dividends received from certain foreign corporations [¶ 3016].
- Deduction for dividends paid on certain preferred stock of public utilities [¶ 3017].

Example: In 1992, National Trading Corporation had a gross profit of $250,000 and deductions of $375,000, excluding any net operating loss deduction and any dividends-received deduction. National also received taxable dividends of $100,000 from Malcolm Corp., a 20%-owned domestic corporation, and $50,000 from Acapulco Corp., a foreign corporation not doing business in the U.S. Thus, National is entitled to claim an $80,000 dividends-received deduction for the dividends from Malcolm. National's net operating loss is $55,000, figured as follows:

Gross income:

Gross business profit	$250,000	
Dividends, domestic corporation	100,000	
Dividends, foreign corporation	50,000	$400,000
Deductions	$375,000	
Add: Dividends-received deduction	80,000	($455,000)
Net operating loss		($ 55,000)

¶3034   FIGURING THE NET OPERATING LOSS DEDUCTION

If your corporation's net operating loss occurs in only one year and is absorbed by income of its first carryback year, determining the net operating loss deduction is simple. The tax picture is more complicated when the NOL is not used up in that year.

(a) Carryover of Unused Portion of Net Operating Loss. The law specifies the order of the years to which a NOL can be carried. For example, a NOL incurred in 1992 is either (a) carried back three years and then carried forward fifteen years, in the following order, until exhausted: (1) 1989, (2) 1990, (3) 1991, (4) 1993, (5) 1994, and so on to 2007, or (b) if you elect, simply carried forward fifteen years (1993 through 2007).

When your corporation carries its NOL to more than one year, the carryover amount is reduced by the taxable income of the prior years to which it was carried [IRC Sec. 172(b)(2); Reg. Sec. 1.172-4].

Example 1: Assume the corporation in the example at ¶3033 had taxable income of $4,500 on its 1989 return. The carryover to 1990 would be $50,500—$55,000 NOL carried back to 1989, less the $4,500 used to offset 1989 income.

Where to deduct. Your corporation claims a NOL carryback on either Form 1120X or Form 1139. Your corporation can get a quicker refund by using Form 1139. You cannot file Form 1139 before you file the return for the corporation's NOL year. But you must file it no later than one year after the NOL year. If you carry over the corporation's NOL, you should enter it on Form 1120 or Form 1120-A [¶ 3001].

Note that special NOL disallowance rules apply to corporate reorganizations [¶3035].

(b) Multiple Net Operating Losses Carried to the Same Year. When your corporation carries more than one net operating loss to the same year, they are applied in chronological order [IRC Sec. 172(b)(2)].

Example 2: Empire Manufacturers, Inc. has net operating loss carrybacks and carryovers as shown in the table below. The minus sign indicates a net operating loss and the plus sign taxable income. It is assumed that (1) no adjustments apply and (2) there was no net operating loss for any year other than those shown.

Income or NOL	After 1992 return	After 1993 return	After 1994 return	After 1995 return	After 1996 return
1989 + 5,000	0	0	0	0	0
1990 +15,000	0	0	0	0	0
1991 +35,000	+30,000	0	0	0	0
1992 –25,000	0	0	0	0	0
1993 –50,000		–20,000	–20,000	0	0
1994 –40,000			–40,000	–30,000	
1995 +30,000				0	0
1996 +85,000					+55,000

After the 1992 return is filed. The 1992 net operating loss of $25,000 cancels the 1989 taxable income of $5,000 and the 1990 taxable income of $15,000. It reduces the 1991 taxable income by $5,000 (to $30,000). After the 1992 return is filed, the taxpayer should claim a refund for 1989, 1990 and 1991.

After the 1993 return is filed. The 1993 net operating loss of $50,000 cancels the remainder of the 1991 taxable income of $30,000, leaving $20,000 that may be carried forward. After the 1993 return is filed, the taxpayer should file another claim for a refund for 1991.

After the 1994 return is filed. The 1994 return shows a net operating loss of $40,000, but since there is now no taxable income for 1991, 1992 or 1993, no carryback is made.

After the 1995 return is filed. The 1995 return shows a taxable income of $30,000 before deduction of net operating loss. The remainder of the 1993 net operating loss ($20,000) reduces 1995 taxable income to $10,000. The 1994 net operating loss of $40,000 eliminates this $10,000 and leaves $30,000 to be carried over.

After the 1996 return is filed. The 1996 return shows a taxable income of $85,000 before deduction of net operating loss. The remainder of the 1994 net operating loss ($30,000) reduces this to $55,000.

¶3035   NET OPERATING LOSS CARRYOVER DISALLOWED FOR SUBSTANTIAL CHANGE OF OWNERSHIP

After a substantial ownership change [(a) below], such as occurs in a corporate reorganization, an *acquiring* corporation can only deduct the net operating losses of the *acquired* corporation up to the amount of the "Sec. 382 limitation" ((c) below) [IRC Sec. 382(a)]. And to deduct even this amount, a business continuity test must be met [(b) below].

(a) Substantial Ownership Change. The crucial event that triggers the application of the Sec. 382 limitation is a 50% ownership change in the loss corporation's stock within a period of, generally, three years [IRC Sec. 382(g)]. Two types of situations generally result in this type of ownership change: (1) an acquisition of more than 50% of the loss corporation's stock, or (2) a reorganization.

The special limitations apply if there has been a more-than-50% ownership change of the corporation by so-called 5% shareholders during a three-year testing period. This change is calculated by first determining the increase in the percentage of stock owned by each 5% shareholder over the lowest percentage of stock owned by that shareholder during the testing period. All increases in the percentage of stock owned by 5% shareholders are then added together. If they total more than fifty percentage points, the special limitations on carryovers and built-in losses automatically apply [IRC Sec. 382(g); Temp. Reg. Sec. 1.382-2T].

▶ **NEW REGULATIONS** Under new final regulations, a triggering ownership change can take place even if no single shareholder acquires 5% of the corporation's stock. Reason: A group of persons who have a formal or informal understanding among themselves to make a coordinated acquisition of stock is treated as a single entity for purposes of applying the ownership change rules [Reg. Sec. 1.382-2].

Also, if a 50% stockholder claims a worthless stock deduction during the three-year testing period after an ownership change, the Sec. 382 limitation applies [IRC Sec. 382(g)(4)(D)].

(b) Continuity of Business. The business continuity test requires that the loss corporation's historic business continue for at least two years from the date of the ownership change. If this requirement is unsatisfied, the loss corporation's NOL carryovers are *completely* disallowed [Sec. 382(c)].

(c) Section 382 Limitation. This limitation is an amount equal to the loss corporation's value immediately before the ownership change, multiplied by the federal long-term tax-exempt rate published by the IRS (¶3238) [IRC Sec. 382(a)]. Similar limitations are applied to excess credits and net capital losses (¶3239) [IRC Sec. 383].

ACCUMULATED EARNINGS TAX

¶3040   THE ACCUMULATED EARNINGS TAX IN GENERAL

Your corporation's earnings are subject to a "double tax"—one on the corporate level as the income is earned, and another on the shareholder level when the earnings are distributed as dividends. You and the other shareholders may be tempted to avoid the second tax by accumulating the earnings on the corporate level. Without dividends, there is no immediate tax at the shareholder level. You and the other shareholders could wait until you retire (when you would be in lower tax brackets) before taking dividends. You could also divide the stock (and the tax brackets) among your families, and then declare dividends. To prevent arrangements of this kind, a penalty surtax is imposed on the accumulated taxable income of your corporation for any year it accumulates earnings to avoid income tax on shareholders. This tax is *in addition to* the regular corporate income tax.

Your corporation's directors are responsible for determining how much dividends should be paid to avoid liability for accumulated earnings tax. Under certain conditions, they may be personally liable for allowing your corporation to be subject to the tax. If there is evidence of negligence in permitting the accumulation and consequent underpayment of tax, an additional penalty tax can be imposed.[1]

(a) Corporations Liable for Tax. Every taxable corporation (other than domestic or foreign personal holding companies, or passive foreign investment companies, and exempt corporations) is subject to the accumulated earnings tax if it is formed or used to avoid the income tax that would otherwise be paid by shareholders [IRC Sec. 532(a), (b); Reg. Sec. 1.532-1]. The tax is imposed without regard to the number of the corporation's shareholders [IRC Sec. 532(c)].

> **NOTE:** S corporations are not subject to this tax since all of their earnings generally are passed through and taxed to the shareholders rather than the corporation [¶3107].

Tax avoidance need not be the accumulation's sole or dominant purpose for the tax to apply. Liability is incurred whenever one of the purposes for accumulation is avoiding the shareholders' income taxes.[2] The fact that your corporation's earnings have accumulated beyond the reasonable needs of the business does show a purpose to avoid shareholders' income taxes, unless your corporation proves the contrary by a preponderance of evidence [IRC Sec. 533(a); Reg. Sec. 1.533-1(a)].

Reasonable needs of the business. The most important question is whether or not the earnings have been allowed to accumulate beyond the reasonable needs of the business, present or reasonably anticipated. Some of the reasons which may justify an accumulation of earnings are your corporation's plans for bona fide business expansion;[3] plans for plant replacement; plans to acquire a business enterprise by purchasing its stock or assets; the need to establish a sinking fund to retire bona fide business indebtedness; or to provide working capital or inventory for the business [Reg. Sec. 1.537-2(b)]. The plans must be specific, definite and feasible [Reg. Sec. 1.537-1(b)].

Your corporation may accumulate earnings to redeem either shares which are part of a stockholder's gross estate or stock held by a private foundation that constitutes business holdings (¶3342) [IRC Sec. 537(a); Reg. Sec. 1.537-1(c), (d)]. Also, earnings may be accumulated to pay reasonably anticipated product liability losses [IRC Sec. 537; Reg. Sec. 1.537-1(a), (f)].

NOTE: Listed and readily marketable securities purchased out of earnings and profits must be valued at net liquidation value, not cost, in determining whether earnings were unreasonably accumulated.[4]

Unreasonable accumulations. Accumulations for the following objectives indicate they may be beyond reasonable business needs: loans to shareholders; expending corporate funds for stockholders' personal benefit; loans having no reasonable relation to conduct of the business; loans to another corporation controlled by common stockholders and whose business is not that of the taxpayer corporation; investments not related to the corporation's business; or retention of earnings to provide against unrealistic hazards [Reg. Sec. 1.537-2(c)].

(b) Burden of Proof. Once the IRS has determined that your corporation has accumulated earnings to avoid stockholders' income taxes, your corporation has the burden of proving the contrary [IRC Sec. 533(a); Reg. Sec. 1.533-1(a), (b)]. However, special rules apply to proceedings in the Tax Court, and the government has the burden of proof if [IRC Sec. 534; Reg. Sec. 1.534-1–1.534-4]:

- Before the notice of deficiency for accumulated earnings tax was mailed, the government failed to notify your corporation by certified or registered mail that the proposed deficiency includes an accumulated earnings tax; or
- Within 60 days after mailing the notification mentioned above, your corporation submits a statement of the grounds (and facts sufficient to show the basis of the grounds) on which it relies to establish that the accumulation was not beyond the reasonable needs of its business. An additional 30 days may be granted for good cause.

¶3041   INCOME SUBJECT TO THE TAX

The accumulated earnings tax is imposed on "accumulated taxable income," *not* on surplus earnings above reasonable accumulation for the present year [IRC Sec. 531]. Accumulated taxable income is adjusted taxable income [(a) below] minus the sum of: (1) the dividends-paid deduction [(b) below] and (2) the accumulated earnings credit ((c) below) [IRC Sec. 535(a); Reg. Sec. 1.535-2].

(a) Adjusted Taxable Income is taxable income with the following adjustments [IRC Sec. 535(b); Reg. Sec. 1.535-2]:

1.   Add back the net operating loss deduction;
2.   Add back the capital loss carryback or carryover;
3.   Add back the deduction for dividends received;
4.   (A) Add the excess of the charitable contributions deduction allowed over the amount actually paid during the year; or (B) subtract the excess of charitable contributions actually paid during the year over the contributions deduction allowed;

> **OBSERVATION** The net effect is that you deduct the full amount of your charitable contributions in the year they are actually paid.

5.   Subtract federal income tax;
6.   Subtract taxes included in the foreign tax credit;
7.   Subtract the disallowed net capital loss, reduced by any capital gain deduction from adjusted taxable income for preceding tax years (beginning after July 18, 1984). This insures that the same net capital gain is not used to reduce the net capital loss deduction more than once. The reduction is limited to the amount of your corporation's accumulated earnings and profits as of the close of the preceding tax year.
8.   Subtract the net capital gain (computed without regard to carrybacks or carryovers), less the tax attributable to it. This figure is further reduced by net capital losses from prior years (starting after July 18, 1984). Net capital loss carryforwards are treated as short-term capital losses.
9.   Bank affiliates are allowed the special deduction for earnings and profits invested in readily marketable assets.

Special rules apply to figure the adjusted taxable income of mere holding and investment companies. The net capital loss deduction is not allowed. A net short-term capital gain deduction is allowed to the extent that it does not exceed capital loss carryovers to such year. The accumulated earnings and profits cannot be less than they would have been had these provisions applied to all tax years beginning after July 18, 1984 [IRC Sec. 535(b)(8)].

(b) Dividends-Paid Deduction. From adjusted taxable income, subtract (1) dividends paid during the tax year (excluding dividends paid during first 2½ months of tax year if these were deducted for previous year); (2) dividends paid within 2½ months after close of tax year; and (3) consent dividends [¶ 1219(d)].

The rules for the dividends-paid deduction of personal holding companies [¶3304(b)] also apply here, except that no dividend carryover is allowed, and the deduction for dividends paid after the close of the tax year is mandatory and unlimited.

Except to the extent provided by future regulations, no dividends-paid deduction is allowed for the accumulated earnings tax for any stock redemption by a mere holding or investment company which is not a regulated investment company [IRC Sec. 562(b)]. Under prior law, dividend treatment could be avoided through using stock redemptions, by means of which the shareholder would get capital gains treatment and the investment company would be free from the accumulated earnings tax.

(c) Accumulated Earnings Credit. From adjusted taxable income, also subtract the accumulated earnings credit. The credit is designed so that the accumulated earnings tax applies only to the amount unreasonably accumulated. The tax is not imposed unless accumulated earnings exceed $250,000 ($150,000 for certain personal service corporations) [IRC Sec. 535(c); Reg. Sec. 1.535-3].

The accumulated earnings credit allowed is the *greater* of:

1.   Earnings and profits of the tax year retained for the reasonable needs of the business *minus* net capital gains (reduced by the tax on such gains); or

2. $250,000 ($150,000 for certain personal service corporations) *minus* the excess of accumulated earnings and profits at the end of preceding tax year reduced by dividends paid during the first 2½ months of the tax year.

Example: Calendar year corporation XYZ had accumulated earnings and profits of $120,000 at the end of 1991. On March 1, 1992, it distributed $50,000 as taxable dividends. In 1992, XYZ's capital gain, minus the tax attributable to such gain, was $10,000. It had no capital loss. The corporation retained $30,000 for the reasonable needs of the business. Using Formula 1, the credit would be $20,000 ($30,000 less $10,000). Using Formula 2, the credit would be $180,000 ($250,000 less $70,000 ($120,000 less $50,000)). The XYZ corporation has an accumulated earnings credit of $180,000 under Formula 2.

¶3042   RATE OF ACCUMULATED EARNINGS TAX

The tax is 28% of the accumulated taxable income [IRC Sec. 531].

Example: United Widget Corp. is a calendar year, accrual basis taxpayer. Its 1992 accumulated earnings tax is based on the following data (there are no reductions for previous years):

Income after expenses	$1,000,000
Dividends received from domestic corps.	$ 20,000
Foreign taxes	$ 0
Charitable contributions allowed—10% limitation applicable	$ 100,000
Charitable contributions actually made	$ 118,000
Dividends paid during the year	$ 300,000
Consent dividends	$ 30,820
Accumulated earnings credit	$ 21,600

Computation of Accumulated Earnings Tax

Income after expenses			$1,000,000
Less: Dividends received deduction		$ 16,000	
Charitable contributions allowed (10%)		100,000	116,000
Taxable income			$ 884,000
Tax			$300,560
Add: Dividends received deduction			$ 16,000
Income (without regard to special deductions)			$ 900,000
Less: Federal income tax		$300,560	
Foreign tax credit		0	
Excess of actual contributions ($118,000) over contributions allowed ($100,000)		18,000	
Disallowed net capital loss		0	318,560
Adjusted taxable income			$ 581,440
Less: Dividends-paid deduction		$300,000	
Consent dividends		30,820	
Accumulated earnings credit		21,600	352,420
Accumulated taxable income			$ 229,020
Tax (28% of $229,020)			$ 64,126

Avoiding the accumulated earnings tax. Your corporation can avoid owing the tax by increasing its dividends-paid deduction to the point where the sum of the deduction and the accumulated earnings credit equals its adjusted taxable income. If your corporation is unwilling (or unable) to pay a dividend, it may increase its dividends-paid deduction by making a "consent dividend." Consent dividends are phantom distributions that are treated as having been made to the stockholders on the last day of your corporation's tax year and immediately reinvested in your corporation as paid-in capital [IRC Sec. 561(a)(2), 565; Reg. Sec. 1.561-1(a)]. Interest is imposed on underpayments of the accumulated earnings tax from the due date of the tax return with respect to which that tax is imposed.

AFFILIATED AND RELATED CORPORATIONS

¶3045   AFFILIATED CORPORATIONS—CONSOLIDATED RETURNS

An affiliated group of corporations may elect to be taxed as a single unit and thus eliminate intercompany gains and losses. This permits the affiliated group to file a consolidated return, rather than separate returns. It is allowed only if all the corporations that have been members of the affiliated group [(a) below] at any time during the tax year consent before the last day for filing the return. The filing of a consolidated return by all of the affiliated corporations is considered such consent [IRC Sec. 1501, 1502; Reg. Sec. 1.1502-75(b)]. Affiliated corporations can also establish joint profit-sharing or stock bonus plans [¶1300]. The LIFO conformity requirement applies to affiliated corporations (¶2706(b)) [IRC Sec. 472(g)(2)].

(a) What Is an Affiliated Group. Generally, an affiliated group is one or more chains of corporations connected through stock ownership with a common parent corporation. It is necessary that (1) 80% or more of the voting power of all outstanding stock, and (2) 80% or more of the value of all outstanding stock of each corporation (except the common parent) must be directly owned by the other corporations. In addition, the common parent must directly own at least 80% of (a) the voting power of all outstanding stock, and (b) the value of all outstanding stock of at least one of the other corporations [IRC Sec. 1504(a)]. Subject to transitional and grandfather rules, any corporation can be part of the affiliated group for consolidated return purposes except [IRC Sec. 1504(b), (c), (e)]:

- Corporations exempt from tax, other than a title-holding company described in Sec. 501(c)(2) and the exempt organizations deriving income from it (¶3336) [IRC Sec. 1504(e)].
- Foreign corporations.
- Corporations electing the possession tax credit [¶3827].
- Regulated investment companies [¶3325].
- Real estate investment trusts [¶3329].

The term "stock" for determining an affiliated group does not generally include preferred stock with redemption and liquidation rights that do not exceed the issue price of the stock (rather than the paid-in capital or par value represented by it) [IRC Sec. 1504(a)]. Also, a DISC or a corporation with post-1984 accumulations of DISC income (rather than a DISC or "former DISC") will not be an includable corporation [IRC Sec. 1504(b)].

(b) Changing the Election. Once a group files a consolidated return, it must continue to do so as long as it exists, unless the IRS consents to a discontinuance. A group generally continues to exist as long as the common parent and at least one subsidiary remain.

(c) Considerations in Filing Consolidated Return. Whether a consolidated return is advantageous depends on the facts in each case. To enable you to assess better the advisability of electing a consolidated return, here's a checklist of the most common advantages and disadvantages in filing consolidated returns.

Advantages	Disadvantages
1. Current offset of each member's ordinary losses against other members' profits in many instances; similarly as to treatment for capital gains and losses. Carryback and carry forward of losses may be greater against a bigger consolidated income. 2. Deferral of income on intercompany transactions. 3. Intercompany dividends are 100% tax-free. 4. Centralization of tax structure. 5. Group use of foreign taxes paid by a member in excess of its limitations on foreign tax credits; similar group use of business credits. 6. Use by other members of excess of the following attributes over limitations: (a) charitable contributions and (b) soil and water conservation on of tax structure.	1. Locked-in effect of filing consolidated return (can be painful). IRS permission is required to discontinue consolidated return filing, and must be for good cause. 2. Deferral of loss on intercompany transactions. 3. Recordkeeping complications from deferred intercompany transactions. 4. Possible loss of all or portion of foreign tax and investment credits. 5. Necessity to make adjustments in opening and closing inventories for intercompany profits. 6. Subsidiary's tax year must conform to parent's; may result in short year and possible reduction in loss carryover. 7. Many unique minority shareholder problems and possible derivative actions.

¶3046   CONTROLLED CORPORATIONS—MULTIPLE TAX BENEFIT LIMITATIONS

Members of a controlled group of corporations are treated as a single corporation for applying the graduated tax rate brackets below the top 34% bracket. The rate structure is apportioned equally among them or shared as they elect (see (b) below). Members of a controlled group are treated as one corporation for purposes of the additional 5% tax on corporations with incomes over $100,000 [¶3002]. This additional tax is divided among the members in the same manner as they share in the group's single taxable income amount in each bracket [IRC Sec. 1561(a)].

Accumulated earnings credit. Members of a controlled group of corporations are limited to one accumulated earnings credit totaling $250,000 ($150,000 for certain personal service corporations) which must be divided *equally* among the component members (¶ 3041(c))[IRC Sec. 1561(a)].

Alternative minimum tax. The AMT exemption of $40,000 is divided among the members of a controlled group in proportion to their respective regular tax deductions for the year, unless all of the members consent to an apportionment plan providing for an unequal allocation of the exemption (¶2613) [IRC Sec. 1561]. You must file the consent of an apportionment plan with the District Director or the Service Center where the component member files its return [Reg. Sec. 1.58-1(c)].

(a) Controlled Groups are defined as [IRC Sec. 1563(a); Reg. Sec. 1.1563-1(a)(3)]:

• Parent corporations and their 80% subsidiaries (basically the same as the parent-subsidiary group that is eligible to file a consolidated return [¶3045]).

• Brother-sister corporations. These are two or more corporations at least 80% owned by five or fewer individuals, estates or trusts. In addition, those same individuals must also own more than 50% of the stock, counting as a shareholder's ownership interest only his or her lowest percentage ownership in each of the corporations. In determining the 80% control test, the five or fewer shareholders must own stock in each corporation.[1]

Example: The outstanding stock of corporations P, Q, R, S and T, which have only one class of stock outstanding, is owned by the following unrelated individuals:

Corporations

Individuals	P	Q	R	S	T	Identical Ownership
Alan	55%	51%	55%	55%	55%	51%
Barry	45%	49%	—	—	—	(45% in P & Q)
Carmen	—	—	45%	—	—	—
Dennis	—	—	—	45%	—	—
Esther	—	—	—	—	45%	—
Total	100%	100%	100%	100%	100%	

Corporations P and Q are members of a brother-sister controlled group of corporations. Although the more-than-50-percent identical ownership requirement is met for all five corporations (i.e., Alan's 51% ownership in Q is taken into account for each of the corporations), corporations R, S and T are not members because at least 80% of the stock of each of those corporations is not owned by the same five or fewer persons whose stock ownership is considered for purposes of the more-than-50-percent identical ownership requirement.

Special attribution rules apply to determine stock ownership [IRC Sec. 1563(d), (e); Reg. Sec. 1.1563-2, 1.1563-3]. For example, a person is considered to own the stock of a corporation if he or she (1) owns an option to buy the stock, (2) is a 5% or more owner of a partnership or corporation which owns such stock, or (3) has children or grandchildren under 21 years of age who own such stock.

Excluded corporations. Some corporations are not counted as members of a group, even if they are controlled. They are: (1) tax-exempt corporations that have no unrelated business income; (2) corporations that were members of the group for less than half the days in the tax year before the designated December 31 [(b) below]; (3) foreign corporations that do not have income effectively connected with a U.S. business [¶3811]; (4) certain insurance companies (but there can be a controlled group of these companies); and (5) franchised corporations (the stock is sold to the corporate employees, and the corporation sells or distributes products of another group member) [IRC Sec. 1563(b)(2); Reg. Sec. 1.1563-1(b)].

(b) Election. The election to apportion the graduated tax rate amounts is made with reference to a designated December 31. All corporations that were members of the group on that day must consent to an apportionment plan if the amounts are not divided equally [IRC Sec. 1561(a)].

¶3047   DISALLOWANCE OF BENEFITS OF GRADUATED CORPORATE RATES AND ACCUMULATED EARNINGS CREDIT

If your corporation, or five or fewer individuals in control of a corporation, transfer property (other than money), directly or indirectly, to a newly created or formerly inactive controlled corporation, the controlled corporation can lose its benefits of graduated corporate rates and the accumulated earnings credit [¶3041(c)]. The tax breaks are lost unless it is proven that getting graduated rates and the credit were not the transfer's main purpose. However, the IRS can allow the benefits and credit in part or allocate it among the corporations [IRC Sec. 1551(a); Reg. Sec. 1.1551-1(a)].

Control of a corporation means ownership of at least 80% of the voting power or value of all classes of stock [IRC Sec. 1551(b); Reg. Sec. 1.1551-1(e)].

A group of five or fewer individuals controls both corporations if (1) they own at least 80% of the voting power or value of the stock of each corporation, and (2) they own more than 50%, taking into account only each one's least percentage of ownership in each corporation [IRC Sec. 1551(b)(2)].

In either case, the constructive ownership rules at ¶2323(d) apply.

Example: Alice owns 50% of the voting stock of Alpha Corporation and 30% of the voting stock of Beta Corporation. Betty, on the other hand, owns 30% of the voting stock of Alpha Corporation and 50% of the voting stock of Beta Corporation. As a result, they together own at least 80% of the voting stock of both corporations, and taking into account the identical ownership with respect to each corporation, they own more than 50% of the voting stock of each corporation.

Individual	Alpha Corporation	Beta Corporation	Least Corporation	% Ownership
Alice	50	30	30	
Betty	30	50	30	
Total	80	80	60	

¶3048   ALLOCATION AMONG RELATED CORPORATIONS

The IRS can distribute, apportion or allocate gross income, deductions, credits or allowances among organizations, trades or businesses owned or controlled by the same interests if it determines that it is necessary to prevent tax evasion or to clearly reflect the taxpayer's income [IRC Sec. 482; Reg. Sec. 1.482-1].

Example: A subsidiary corporation rented a building it owned to the parent corporation. The parties arbitrarily adjusted the rental each year to result in the lowest possible combined tax. In such case, the accounts will be adjusted to show fair rental value.[1]

The IRS will also impute interest on interest-free or low-interest intercompany loans or advances; impute payment for certain services rendered by one related corporation for another and for the use or occupation of tangible or intangible property of one related corporation by another; and impute profit to the seller of tangible property to a related party [Reg. Sec. 1.482-1(d), 1.482-2]. Income or deductions so allocated may later actually be transferred between the involved corporations without further tax consequences.[2]

¶3049   RELATED CORPORATIONS USED TO AVOID TAX

Deductions, credits and other allowances may be disallowed if the main purpose for organizing your corporation[1] or acquiring control or property of your corporation is to get tax benefits. The disallowance will apply if:

- a person or persons get control of your corporation, or
- your corporation gets property (with a carryover or transferred basis) from another corporation not then controlled by the former or its stockholders; *and*

- the principal purpose for the acquisition is evading or avoiding taxes through the benefits of a deduction, credit or allowance that would not otherwise be available [IRC Sec. 269; Reg. Sec. 1.269-1—1.269-6].

Control means ownership of stock with at least 50% of the total combined voting power of all classes of stock entitled to vote; or at least 50% of total value of shares of all classes of stock [IRC Sec. 269(a)(2)].

Person includes an individual, trust, estate, partnership, association, company or corporation [Reg. Sec. 1.269-1].

The IRS, however, may allow a part of the otherwise disallowed deduction or credit if the partial allowance does not result in the tax evasion or avoidance for which the acquisition was made. The IRS may also allocate gross income deductions, credits or allowances, between or among the corporations or properties if, again, it determines the allocation will not result in the avoidance or evasion of federal income tax [IRC Sec. 269(c); Reg. Sec. 1.269-4].

See also ¶3035 for limitation of net operating loss carryover when one corporation acquires another; and ¶3237 for treatment of various carryovers when one corporation acquires another in a reorganization.

Footnotes to Chapter 20

(For your added convenience, in brackets [] with the footnotes below, you will find citations to related paragraphs in the "RIA United State Tax Reporter"(USTR), "CCH Federal Tax Reporter,"(CCH) and "RIA Federal Tax Coordinator 2d"(FTC) multi-volume services.)

FOOTNOTE ¶ 3000 [USTR ¶ 77,014; CCH ¶ 43,884; 43,893; FTC ¶ D-100].

(1) Treas. Dept. booklet "Tax Information on Corporations" [1991 Ed.], p. 1.

(2) Morrissey et. al. v. Comm., 296 US 344, 56 SCt. 289, 16 AFTR 1274.

(3) Rev. Rul. 70-101, 1970-1 CB 278; Rev. Rul. 72-468, 1972-2 CB 647; Rev. Rul. 73-596, 1973-2 CB 424.

FOOTNOTE ¶ 3001 [USTR ¶ 114; CCH ¶ 36,391; FTC ¶ D-1000].

(1) Rev. Rul. 89-82, 1989-1 CB 336.

FOOTNOTE ¶ 3002 [USTR ¶ 114.01; CCH ¶ 3275; FTC ¶ D-1004].

FOOTNOTE ¶ 3005 [USTR ¶ 114; CCH ¶ 43,884; FTC ¶ D-1002].

FOOTNOTE ¶ 3006 [USTR ¶ 1184; CCH ¶ 7202; FTC ¶ F-1900].

FOOTNOTE ¶ 3007 [USTR ¶ 3014; CCH ¶ 15,205; FTC ¶ F-1919].

FOOTNOTE ¶ 3008 [USTR ¶ 114; CCH ¶ 5504.01; FTC ¶ J-1000; J-2200].

(1) Rensselaer & Saratoga R.R. Co. v. Irwin, 249 F. 726, 1 AFTR 945.

(2) U.S. v. Joliet R.R. Co., 315 US 44, 28 AFTR 215.

(3) Comm. v. Western Union Tel. Co., 141 F.2d 774, 32 AFTR 492.

FOOTNOTE ¶ 3009 [USTR ¶ 114; CCH ¶ 36,391; FTC ¶ A-1825].

FOOTNOTE ¶ 3012 [USTR ¶ 1624.010; CCH ¶ 8401; FTC ¶ D-1002].

FOOTNOTE ¶ 3013 [USTR ¶ 2414; CCH ¶ 13,001; FTC ¶ D-2000].

(1) Treas. Dept. booklet "Tax Information on Corporations" [1991 Ed.], p. 3.

(2) Ltr. Rul. 9047032.

FOOTNOTE ¶ 3014 [USTR ¶ 2434.01; CCH ¶ 13,001; FTC ¶ D-2201].

(1) O'Brien Co. v. Comm., 9 AFTR 2d 1217, 301 F.2d 813.

(2) Rev. Rul. 62-42, 1962-1 CB 133.

FOOTNOTE ¶ 3016 [USTR ¶ 2434.03; CCH ¶ 13,152; FTC ¶ D-2208].

FOOTNOTE ¶ 3017 [USTR ¶ 2474; CCH ¶ 13,302; FTC ¶ D-2207].

FOOTNOTE ¶ 3018 [USTR ¶ 2434.04; CCH ¶ 13,205; FTC ¶ D-2214].

(1) Rev. Proc. 87-33, 1987-2 CB 402.

FOOTNOTE ¶ 3019 [USTR ¶ 1704.14; CCH ¶ 11,693; FTC ¶ K-3800].

(1) Crosby Valve & Gage Co., 19 AFTR 2d 1731, 380 F.2d.

(2) Rev. Rul. 63-73, 1963-1 CB 35.

FOOTNOTE ¶ 3020 [USTR ¶ 12,009.04; 12,124; 12,314; CCH ¶ 32,152; FTC ¶ I-4000].

FOOTNOTE ¶ 3021 [USTR ¶ 12,454; CCH ¶ 15,191; 32,509; 32,606; FTC ¶ I-6100].

FOOTNOTE ¶ 3024 [USTR¶ 10,324; CCH ¶ 31,524; FTC ¶ J-2861].

FOOTNOTE ¶ 3025 [USTR ¶ 1634; CCH ¶ 5802; 9202; FTC ¶ J-7203].

(1) U.S. v. Kirby Lumber Co., 284 US 1,52 SCt. 4, 10 AFTR 458.

(2) TD 4603, XIV CB 58; Virginia Electric & Power Co. v. Early, 52 F.Supp. 835, 31 AFTR 1186.

FOOTNOTE ¶ 3026 [USTR ¶ 614.114; 1084; CCH ¶ 7010; FTC ¶ J-7000].

FOOTNOTE ¶ 3027 [USTR¶ 3114; CCH ¶ 15,454; FTC ¶ J-2770; J-2800].

FOOTNOTE ¶ 3028 [USTR ¶ 3124; CCH ¶ 15,502; FTC ¶ F-10400].

(1) Instructions to Form 5452.

FOOTNOTE ¶ 3029 [USTR ¶ 10,604; CCH ¶ 16,288; FTC ¶ I-5105.1].

FOOTNOTE ¶ 3030 [USTR ¶ 1724; CCH ¶ 12,014; FTC ¶ M-4100].

FOOTNOTE ¶ 3031 [USTR ¶ 1724; CCH ¶ 12,014; FTC ¶ M-4000].

FOOTNOTE ¶ 3032 [USTR ¶ 1724.11; CCH ¶ 12,014; FTC ¶ M-4100].

(1) Plumb, 97 TC No. 44.

FOOTNOTE ¶ 3033 [USTR ¶ 1724; CCH ¶ 12,014; FTC ¶ M-4100].

FOOTNOTE ¶ 3034 [USTR ¶ 1724; CCH ¶ 12,014; FTC ¶ M-4100].

FOOTNOTE ¶ 3035 [USTR ¶ 3814.05; 3844; CCH ¶ 17,115; FTC ¶ F-7250].

FOOTNOTE ¶ 3040 [USTR ¶ 5314; CCH ¶ 23,012; FTC ¶ D-2600].

(1) Rev. Rul. 75-330, 1975-2 CB 496.

(2) U.S. v. The Donruss Co., 393 US 297, 23 AFTR 2d 69-418.

(3) Tri-City Advertising, Inc., TC Memo 1988-19.

(4) Ivan Allen Co. v. U.S., 36 AFTR 2d 75-5200.

FOOTNOTE ¶ 3041 [USTR ¶ 5314; CCH ¶ 23,045; FTC ¶ D-2610; D-2900].

FOOTNOTE ¶ 3042 [USTR ¶ 5314; CCH ¶ 23,004; FTC ¶ D-2601].

FOOTNOTE ¶ 3045 [USTR ¶ 15,024; CCH ¶ 34,211; FTC ¶ E-7500].

FOOTNOTE ¶ 3046 [USTR ¶ 15,614; CCH ¶ 34,440; FTC ¶ D-2911].

(1) U.S. v. Vogel Fertilizer Co., 49 AFTR 2d 82-491, 455 U.S.

FOOTNOTE ¶ 3047 [USTR ¶ 15,614; CCH ¶ 34,402; FTC ¶ D-2911].

FOOTNOTE ¶ 3048 [USTR ¶ 4824; CCH ¶ 22,283; FTC ¶ I-5105].

(1) Senate Report No. 1622, p. 224, 83rd Cong., 2d Sess.

(2) Rev. Proc. 65-17, 1965-1 CB 833, as amplified, amended and clarified.

FOOTNOTE ¶ 3049 [USTR ¶ 2694; CCH ¶ 14,262; FTC ¶ D-2700].

(1) Joe Dillier, 41 TC 762, acq. Made Rite Investment Co. v. Comm., 17 AFTR 2d 466, 357 F.2d 647.

TABLE OF CONTENTS

ELECTING S CORPORATION STATUS

S corporations are hybrid business entities. They combine the flexibility of a partnership with the advantages of operating in the corporate format. However, unlike regular corporations, S corporations are generally not treated as taxable entities for federal income tax purposes. Instead, the corporation's income passes through to the shareholders. They pay tax on this income whether or not distributed. This passthrough-of-income principle parallels the tax treatment provided partnerships. This section deals with the eligibility rules and how the S election is terminated.

¶3100   BECOMING AN S CORPORATION

If your domestic corporation meets certain requirements, it may be exempt from federal income taxes if it and its shareholders file an election to achieve S corporation status. Your electing corporation is treated as a corporation for all purposes and has all the advantages of operating in the corporate form. The advantages and the drawbacks are discussed in ¶3115 and ¶3116. Briefly, your corporation can become an S corporation if:

- It is a corporation that meets the requirements of S corporation status [¶3102].
- All of its shareholders consent to S corporation status [¶3102(a)].
- It files Form 2553 to indicate it selects S corporation status [¶3102(a)].
- It uses an appropriate tax year [¶3103].

¶3101   COMPARISON CHART

The following summarizes the differences between partnerships, regular (i.e., C) and S corporations:

Points to Consider	S Corporations	C Corporations	Partnerships
Ownership limitations	35 shareholder limit and qualification requirements to be shareholders [¶3102].	No limit on number or class of shareholders.	No limit on number of partners. Special restrictions apply to publicly traded partnerships [¶3400].
Liability exposure	Except in rare circumstances, shareholders are only liable for capital contributions.		General partners are personally, jointly and severally liable for partnership obligations. Limited partner liable for capital contributions only.
Tax year	S corp. generally must use a calendar year unless business purpose is shown for a fiscal year. S corporations can elect to use a tax year other than a required year if they follow specific procedures. Electing S corporations must make payments ("required payments") to the federal government that are intended to represent the value of the tax deferral obtained by the shareholders through the use of a tax year different from the required tax year [¶3103].	Calendar or fiscal year permitted. Tax year does not have to match shareholders' tax years.	Must generally use same tax year as majority-interest partners (principal partners if majority partners don't have same tax year, or year resulting in least income deferral if principal partners don't have same tax year) unless business purpose shown for a different tax year. Partnerships can elect to use a tax year other than a required year if they follow specific procedures [¶2820; 3414]. Electing partnerships must make payments ("required payments") to the federal government that are intended to represent the value of the tax deferral obtained by the partners through the use of a tax year different from the required tax year.

Federal tax return	Form 1120S, Information return.	Form 1120, Corporate income tax return. May have to file estimated tax returns [¶3001].	Form 1065, Information return.
Alternative minimum tax	Applies only at shareholder level. No ACE adjustment [¶ 2611(a)].	Applies at corporate level. ACE adjustment [¶ 2611(a)].	Applies only at partner level. No ACE adjustment [¶ 2611(a); 3404(a)].
Liquidation of business	No tax at corporate level (except for built-in gains).	"Double tax" on corporate and shareholder levels [¶1218; 3002].	No tax at partnership level [¶3420].
Treatment of income and losses	Corporate income determined at entity level and passed through to each shareholder and taxed at individual rates. Some S corps. pay tax on certain capital gains, "built-in gains," and "excess net passive income." Income and loss items that affect a shareholder's tax liability are separately stated—e.g., charitable contributions, depletion [¶3109].	All corporate income taxed at corporate level and again taxed at shareholder level when distributed as dividends. Some C corps. taxed as personal holding companies and can be taxed on excess accumulated income [¶3005; 3040; 3300].	Same as S corp. except no partnership capital gains tax on "built-in gains," or tax on passive income [¶3404].
Net operating losses	Losses pass through to shareholders and are deductible to the extent of their stock and debt basis. Losses may be carried back or forward [¶3110].	Deductible only by the corporation in a year which it has offsetting income. Losses may be carried back or forward [¶3030].	Same passthrough rules as S corp. [¶3408].
Tax-exempt income	Tax-exempt income of corporation retains its character when passed through to the shareholders. It increases shareholders' stock bases [¶3109].	Tax-exempt income increases corporate earnings and profits and is not taxed at corporate level. If distributed to shareholders as dividends, it is subject to tax.	Same passthrough rule as S corp.
Capital gains	Capital and Sec. 1231 gains pass through to shareholders and retain their character at shareholder level. Rules for taxing S corps. on capital gains depend on whether S corp. election was made after 1986 or before 1987 [¶3108; 3109].	Capital and Sec. 1231 gains taxed at regular corporate rate or a maximum rate of 34% [¶3020].	Same rule as S corp. except no tax at partnership level on capital gains [¶3408].

Capital losses	Capital losses pass through to shareholders and retain their character at the shareholder level. Losses offset capital gains and then up to $3,000 of ordinary income. May be carried forward indefinitely [¶3108; 3109].	Capital losses deducted at corporate level only to the extent of capital gains. Losses may be carried back 3 years or forward 5 years [¶3020].	Same rule as S corp. [¶3408].
Accumulated earnings	All income is passed through and taxed at shareholder level. S corps. with carryover C corp. earnings and profits are subject to corporate tax on excess passive income and distributions of accumulated earnings and profits taxed as dividend income [¶3107].	Corps. may accumulate income for reasonable business needs. Up to $150,000 for personal service corporations and $250,000 for other C corps. may be accumulateed without question. Unreasonable accumulations subject to tax [¶3040].	All income taxed to partners whether distributed or not [¶3404].
Distributions and income allocations	Distributions are taxed to the extent they exceed a shareholder's basis in stock and debts. Corporation recognizes gain on distribution of appreciated property. Income may only be allocated in proportion to shareholdings [¶3111].	Distributions taxed as ordinary income and allocated on basis of shareholders. C corp. will generally recognize gain on sale or distribution of appreciated property [¶3026; 3027].	Distributions taxed to the extent they exceed partner's basis in stock and partnership debt. Distributive income shares may be allocated by agreement of the partners. Partnership does not recognize gain on distribution of appreciated property [¶3420].
Fringe benefits	Owner of more than 2% of S corp. shares cannot receive tax-free certain fringe benefits including, employer-provided health care, meals and lodging, and life insurance [¶3116].	Shareholder-employees may receive tax-qualified fringe benefits without restriction [¶1300 et seq.].	All partners not eligible for tax-free fringes.
Retirement plans	Although generally the same rules and limitations apply to S corps. as to C corps., an S corp. can't have a retirement plan that holds its own stock in trust for employees, and loans to shareholders are prohibited.	C corp. can provide a broad variety of defined benefit and defined contribution plans, including those involving the corporation's own stock [¶1300 et seq.].	Keogh plans are generally subject to the same limits on contributions and benefits that apply to qualified corporate retirement plans, but

Investment interest deduction	Shareholder deducts his share of the S corp.'s investment interest to the extent of his net investment income limitation [¶1904].	No limitation.	Partner may deduct his share of partnership's interest up to the extent of his net investment income limitation.
Dividends received	Income passes through to shareholders [¶3109].	C corp. can deduct 70% (80% if dividends received from 20%-or-more owned corp.) of dividends received from domestic corporations [¶3014].	Same rule as S corp.
FICA taxes	Tax payable by the corporation and the employees.		Self-employment tax applies to salary and drawings.

➤ **OBSERVATION** Recent law changes created an environment in which using Subchapter S is increasingly valuable. For the first time in recent memory, the highest individual income tax rates are lower than the highest corporate income tax rates. In addition, changes to the taxation of sales of corporate businesses impose a double tax on the sales of many regular corporations but not on the sales of S corporations. In the past, it was common for people incorporating a new business to assume that it would be a regular Subchapter C corporation unless special considerations made Subchapter S desirable. Now Subchapter S should be the norm unless there are compelling reasons not to make an S election.

¶3102   ELECTING S CORPORATION TAXATION

[New tax legislation may affect this subject; see ¶1.]

Subchapter S treatment is available only if your corporation is a qualified corporation whose stockholders elect such treatment. To qualify, your corporation must meet all the following requirements [IRC Sec. 1361]:

• It must be a domestic corporation which is not an ineligible corporation.

NOTE: Ineligible corporation means: (1) a financial institution that takes deposits and makes loans; (2) an insurance company (other than certain stock casualty insurance companies); (3) a corporation electing the Puerto Rico and possessions tax credit; (4) a DISC or former DISC; and (5) a member of an affiliated group, whether or not eligible to file a consolidated return. Inactive subsidiaries are allowed. However, an S election can be terminated if an inactive subsidiary has any gross income, even if it does not do any business.[1]

• It does not have more than 35 shareholders.

NOTE: In general, when shares of stock are held jointly, each person counts as a separate shareholder. However, a husband and wife are treated as one shareholder—whether they hold their shares individually or jointly [IRC Sec. 1361(c)(1)]. Thus, there can be more than 35 actual owners and still meet this requirement. On the other hand, your company can lose its S status if shareholders get divorced—thereby increasing the number above the 35 shareholder limit.

➤ **SUGGESTION** Your company can have shareholders enter into a buy-sell agreement that would prevent them from selling or bequeathing their stock to more than the permitted number of shareholders.

• It must have only individuals, bankruptcy or decedent's estates, or certain trusts as shareholders. Partnerships and corporations cannot be shareholders.

NOTE: The following types of trusts can be shareholders: (1) a grantor trust or a trust that distributes all its income to its sole beneficiary who is treated as the trust owner, (2) a voting trust, (3) any trust, but only as to stock transferred to it under the terms of a will and only for 60 days starting with the day of the transfer or (4) a qualified Subchapter S trust.

- It must have only one class of stock.

> **OBSERVATION** Differences in common stock voting rights are allowed. Also, if shares are divided into two or more groups which are identical in every respect except that each group has the right to elect directors in proportion to the number of shares in each group, they are considered to be one class of stock. Straight debt is not considered a second class of stock if: (1) the debt is evidenced by a written unconditional demand to pay a fixed amount on demand or on a specified date; (2) the interest rate and payment dates are not contingent on corporate profits, discretion or similar factors; (3) the debt is not convertible into stock; *and* (4) the creditor could qualify as an S corporation shareholder [IRC Sec. 1361(c)(4), (5)].

In 1990, the IRS had issued tough proposed regulations on the one-class-of-stock requirement. But in 1991 the IRS later replaced those regulations with new milder ones that provide: (1) An S corporation is treated as having one class of stock as long as the "governing provisions" (e.g., corporate charter, articles of incorporation, by-laws) provide for identical distributions and liquidations of rights. (2) Debt reclassified as equity will not be treated as a second class of stock. That will happen only if the debt-equity is being used to circumvent shareholders' rights or to avoid the S corporation restrictions on eligible shareholders [Prop. Reg. Sec. 1-1361-1].

> **FINAL REGULATIONS** The IRS has released final regulations that adopt the more liberal approach to the one-class-of-stock requirement from the 1991 regulations [T.D. 8419]. In addition, changes in the final regulations make the relaxed rule even easier to satisfy. The final regulations took effect on May 28, 1992.

Here are several changes made by the final regulations: (1) Substantially nonvested stock issued as compensation does not count as "outstanding" stock even if the services were performed for someone other than the corporation. (2) Redemption agreements do not create a second class of stock if the corporation's right to buy back the stock is triggered by the shareholder's death, disability, divorce, or if the shareholder leaves his or her job with the corporation. (3) It is specifically stated that restricted stock is not considered a second class of stock. (4) A commercial contract is not considered to be a "governing provision" that can create a second class of stock, provided the principal purpose of the contract was not to avoid the one-class-of-stock requirement.

> **NOTE:** So-called "phantom" stock plans are not considered a true class of stock for S corporation purposes.[2] In a typical plan, employees are credited with a certain number of "stock units." These plans are a form of incentive compensation. They give employees the benefit of appreciation in the corporation's stock without the ownership of actual shares. Typically, the appreciation is not paid out to employees until a date several years after the employees are credited with "phantom" stock units under the plan.

- It must not have a nonresident alien as a shareholder.

For purposes of this rule, a dual residence alien who claims special tax benefits under an international treaty is considered a nonresident alien. But the IRS has released proposed regulations that create a valuable exception to this rule [T.D. 8411]. A corporation's S status will not be terminated if both the corporation and the shareholder electing the treaty benefit agree that the shareholder will be treated as a nonresident alien partner in a partnership. In this situation, the shareholder will be subject to U.S. tax, and the corporation will withhold tax on payments made to the shareholder.

(a) How to Elect. Your corporation can make the S election at any time during the entire tax year before the election year, or on or before the 15th day of the third month of the election year. This is true even for tax years that are less than 2½ months in duration. If your corporation makes a late election—that is, after the 15th day of the third month of that year—it will be treated as made for the next tax year. Once made, the election is effective for all later years, unless terminated (¶3105) [IRC Sec. 1362(a),(b),(c); Temp. Reg. Sec. 18.1362-1, -2; Prop. Reg. Sec. 1.1362-1].

> **NOTE:** For election purposes, the term "month" means a period starting on the same day of any calendar month on which the corporation's tax year began, and ending with the close of the day before the corresponding day of the next calendar month. If there is no such corresponding day, the month ends with the close of the last day of the succeeding calendar month. Also, for the election, the new corporation's tax year begins on the date that it has shareholders, acquires assets or begins doing business, whichever is the first to occur [Prop. Reg. Sec. 1.1362-1(c)(3)].

> **Example 1:** Ace Corp., a calendar year small business corporation, began its first tax year on January 7, 1993. To be an S corporation starting with its first tax year, Ace must make the election before March 22, 1993. An election made earlier than January 7, 1993, would not be valid.

> **Example 2:** Assume the same facts as Example 1, except that Ace begins its first tax year on November 8, 1993. To be an S corporation starting with its first tax year, Ace must make the election during the period that begins November 8, 1993, and ends before January 23, 1994.

Your corporation's election of S corporation status is valid only if all shareholders consent to the election [IRC Sec. 1362(a)(2); Temp. Reg. Sec. 18.1362-1(a); Prop. Reg. Sec. 1.1362-1(b)].

You and the other shareholders can consent to the election by filing Form 2553 or a separate signed statement containing the same information. Generally, each person who is shareholder when the election is made must consent to it. If the election is made for a year during the first 2½ months of that year, each person who was a shareholder during the year before the consents are filed must also consent to S corporation status for the corporation [IRC Sec. 1362; Temp. Reg. Sec. 18.1362-2; Prop. Reg. Sec. 1.1362-2].

> **Example 3:** On January 1, 1993, Baker Corp., operating on a calendar year, had 15 shareholders. On January 30, 1993, two of Baker's shareholders, Richard Able and Bob Davis, sold their shares to Ben Proctor, Alex Reese and Tom Tucker. On March 1, 1993, Baker Corp. filed its election to be an S corporation for the 1993 tax year. For the election to be effective, all those who owned shares from January 1 through March 1, 1993, must consent to the election (including Able and Davis).

> ➤ **IMPORTANT** Even if your corporation makes a timely election after the start of a tax year and on or before the 15th day of the third month, the election won't be effective until the following year if, at all times during the pre-election period, your corporation was not fully eligible to make the election or *any* stockholder during that period did not consent [IRC Sec. 1362(b)(2); Temp. Reg. Sec. 18.1362-1(b); Prop. Reg. Sec. 1.1362-1].

New shareholders. Consent of a new shareholder is not required. An S election automatically continues unless the new shareholder owns more than 50% of the stock and affirmatively acts to terminate it [Temp. Reg. Sec. 18.1362-3; Prop. Reg. Sec. 1.1362-3].

(b) Return by S Corporation. Your S corporation must file a return on Form 1120S each tax year, even though it may not be subject to tax. It reports gross income and allowable deductions, as well as information concerning the shareholders, including their stock holdings, distributions made to them and their pro rata shares of corporate items [IRC Sec. 6037; Reg. Sec. 1.6037-1]. Your S corporation can receive an automatic six-month extension to file a return by submitting an application for extension on Form 7004.

Your S corporation must furnish each shareholder with a copy of its return on or before the day the return was filed [IRC Sec. 6037(b)].

¶3103   S CORPORATION'S TAX YEAR

[New tax legislation may affect this subject; see ¶1.]

Your S corporation, regardless of when it became an S corporation, must use either a calendar tax year or any other tax year for which it establishes a natural business year—or makes a Sec. 444 election to qualify for using some other fiscal year [IRC Sec. 1378].

> **NOTE:** An exception applies to any S corporation that was permitted to use a fiscal year (other than a year that resulted in a three-month or less deferral of income) if that permission was granted on or after July 1, 1974 [(c) below].

(a) Electing a Tax Year Different From Required Tax Year. Your S corporation can elect to use a tax year that is different from the required tax year (generally, the calendar year). Certain restrictions apply to this so-called "Sec. 444 election." However, if your S corporation establishes a business purpose for its tax year, it is not required to make a Sec. 444 election to use such a year [IRC Sec. 444; Temp. Reg. Sec. 1.444-1T].

Your S corporation is eligible to make and continue a Sec. 444 election if all the following conditions are met [IRC Sec. 444; Temp. Reg. Sec. 1.444-2T]:

- It is not a member of a tiered structure other than a tiered structure that consists only of partnerships or S corporations (or both) all of which have the same tax year.

> **NOTE:** This means your S corporation can own no ownership interest in an entity that defers income tax payment, nor can this entity own an ownership interest in your S corporation.

> ➤ **OBSERVATION** This condition prevents you from multiplying the benefits of the three-month deferral period by passing income through various organizations. An exception permits electing a fiscal year if all the members of a tiered structure have the same tax year [Temp. Reg. Sec. 1-444-1T–3T].

- Your S corporation must not have previously elected a fiscal year.
- It elects a year that meets the deferral-period requirements.

Deferral period. This is the number of months between the start of the tax year elected and the end of the first required tax year ending within the elected year. For example, if a tax year beginning October 1, 1993, and ending September 30, 1994, is elected and a calendar year is required, the deferral period of the elected tax year is three months (October 1, 1993, to December 31, 1993) [Temp. Reg. Sec. 1.444-1T].

You S corporation can make an election to change a tax year only if the deferral period is the shorter of (1) three months or (2) the deferral period of the tax year being changed. If the current tax year is the required tax year, the deferral period is zero. So no change is allowed.

> **Example 1:** Acme Corp., an S corporation, uses a calendar tax year, which is also its required tax year. Since Acme's deferral period is zero, it is not able to make a Sec. 444 election.

> **Example 2:** Beta Corp., a newly formed S corporation, began operations on December 1, 1992. Beta's shareholders use a calendar year for their individual returns. Beta wants to make a Sec. 444 election to adopt a September 30 tax year. Its deferral period for the tax year beginning December 1, 1992, is three months (September 30 to December 31, 1992).

Making the election. Your S corporation makes a Sec. 444 election by filing Form 8716. This form must be filed by the earlier of: (1) the 15th day of the 5th month after the month that includes the first day of the tax year for which the election will first be effective, or (2) the due date (without regard to extensions) of the income tax return resulting from the Sec. 444 election. Also, your S corporation must attach a copy of the form to the Form 1120S for the first tax year for which the election is made [Temp. Reg. Sec. 1.444-3T].

> **Example 3**: Echo Corp., an S corporation, began operations on September 10, 1992, and is qualified to make a Sec. 444 election to use a tax year ending September 30, in 1992. Echo must file Form 8716 by December 15, 1992, which is the due date of its tax return for the period September 10, 1992, to September 30, 1992.

> **Example 4**: Assume the same facts as in Example 3, except that Echo began operations on October 20, 1992. It must file Form 8716 by March 15, 1993, the 15th day of the 5th month after October 20—when the election will first be effective.

Required payment. Your S corporation must make a "required payment" for any tax year that the Sec. 444 election is in effect and the required payment amount exceeds $500 [IRC Sec. 7519; Temp. Reg. Sec. 1.7519-1T].

> ➤ **OBSERVATION** This required payment represents the tax deferral that you and the other owners would otherwise receive through using a fiscal year.

The required payment for any year that a Sec. 444 election is in effect (i.e., the applicable election year) equals the excess of:

- 32% multiplied by the S corporation's net base year income, over
- Net required payment balance.

The net required payment balance is the total amount of required payments reduced by refunds for all prior election years. The applicable percentage for an S corporation is 100% for any tax year starting after 1987, unless more than 50% of your S corporation's net income for the short tax year that otherwise would have resulted is allocable to shareholders that would not have been eligible to include this short tax year income over a four-year period.

The *base year* is the preceding tax year. For example, if you are computing required payments for the April 1, 1992, to March 31, 1993, tax year, the base year is the tax year starting April 1, 1991, and ending March 31, 1992 [Temp. Reg. Sec. 1.7519-1T(b)(5)].

Net income is the combination of your corporation's items of income and expenses (other than credits and tax-exempt income).

If your S corporation was a C corporation for its base year, the C corporation's taxable income is treated as your S corporation's net income for the base year.

> ➤ **NEW CORPORATIONS** If an applicable election year is your S corporation's first tax year of existence, your new corporation does not have a base year. Therefore, the required payment is zero.

Net base year income. Your S corporation's net base year income equals the sum of the deferral ratio (number of months in deferral period over number of months in tax year) multiplied by your S corporation's net income for the prior tax year, plus the excess of:

- Deferral ratio multiplied by the total amount of applicable payments your S corporation made during the prior tax year, over
- Total amount of the applicable payments your S corporation made during the deferral period of that prior year.

Applicable payments. These are amounts paid by your S corporation that are includible in a shareholder's gross income. For example, this would include an officer's compensation, wages or rental costs paid to any shareholder. Dividends your S corporation pays and gain on the sale of property between a shareholder and the corporation are not included [IRC Sec. 7519(d)(3)].

NOTE: If your S corporation was a C corporation for its base year, your corporation will be treated as an S corporation for the base year for the applicable payments.

Example 5: Lane Corp. is a C corporation that has historically used a January 31 tax year. For its tax year starting February 1, 1994, Lane elects to be an S corporation and also makes a Sec. 444 election to keep its January 31 tax year. Lane's taxable income for the tax year starting February 1, 1993, is $120,000. This is the base year for Lane's first applicable election year. During the base year, Lane pays its sole shareholder, Barton, a salary of $5,000 a month plus a $30,000 bonus on January 15, 1994. Thus, Lane's applicable payments for the base year are $90,000, of which $55,000 are applicable payments deductible during the deferral period of the base year (February 1 through December 31, 1993). Based on these facts, Lane's net base income is $137,500 and its required payment for the year is $44,000, determined as follows:

Net income	$120,000	
Multiplied by deferral ratio	11/12	$110,000
Plus: Excess of applicable payments	$ 90,000	
Multiplied by deferral ratio	11/12	$82,500
Less aggregate amount of applicable payments deductible during deferral period of base year	55,000	27,500
Net base year income		$137,500
Required payment (32% of $137,500)		$ 44,000

Handling the required payment. Your S corporation reports the required payment on Form 8752. If the payment is more than $500, it is paid when Form 8752 is filed. Your S corporation can also make this payment with federal tax deposit coupons. No payment is required if the required payment is $500 or less. However, Form 8752 must still be filed.

Your S corporation must file Form 8752 and make the required payment (or report the zero amount) by May 15 of the calendar year following the calendar year in which the applicable election year begins. For example, if an S corporation's applicable election year begins July 1, 1992, Form 8752 must be filed by May 15, 1993.

Terminating the election. The election to use a tax year different from the regular tax year remains in effect until it is terminated. This happens when your S corporation:

• Changes to the required tax year;
• Liquidates;
• Willfully fails to comply with the required payments or distributions or
• Becomes a member of a tiered structure.

If the election is terminated, another Sec. 444 election cannot be made for any tax year.

(b) Natural Business Year. A natural business year is an accounting period that has a substantial business purpose for its existence. In determining if a substantial business purpose for a requested tax year exists, both tax as well as nontax factors must be considered. A nontax factor is the annual cycle of business activity. However, significant weight is given to tax factors. A prime consideration is whether the change would create a substantial distortion of income. Any deferral of income to shareholders is not a business purpose.

The natural business year is determined by a 25% test.[1] This test is designed for businesses with a busy season. The natural business year ends with that season. To figure this test:

1. Compute gross receipts from sales and services for the most recent 12-month period that ends with the last month of the requested fiscal year. Divide the gross receipts of the last two months of this 12-month period by this 12-month figure.

2. Make the same computation for the two 12-month periods just before the 12-month period used in (1) above.

3. Compare the results. If each of the three results equals or exceeds 25%, the fiscal year is the natural business year.

If your S corporation qualifies for more than one natural business year, the year producing the highest average of the three percentages is the natural business year.

> **Example:** Ace Corp., an S corporation, wants to use a May 31 tax year. Ace's gross receipts for April and May total $100,000. Receipts for the year ending May 31 come to $300,000. Assume Ace has similar revenue patterns for the prior two years. The May 31 tax year qualifies as a natural business year, since 33% of gross receipts are earned in the last two months of that year.

See also ¶2820.

(c) S Corporation Before 1987. If your corporation was an S corporation before 1987, continues to be one and doesn't use a required tax year, it must change to a required tax year unless it files a Sec. 444 election or qualifies to use a fiscal year.

Your S corporation may continue to use a grandfathered fiscal year. This is a fiscal year that results in more than three months of income deferral and was approved by the IRS after July 1, 1974.

¶3104   EFFECT OF S ELECTION ON CORPORATION

For each tax year the S election remains in effect, your corporation is, with certain exceptions, exempted from all federal income taxes. The following exceptions apply:

- Capital gains tax [¶3108].
- Tax on built-in gains [¶3108].
- Tax on recomputing a prior-year investment credit [¶3107(d)].
- LIFO recapture tax [¶3107(e)].
- Tax on excess net passive income [¶3107(c)].

> ➤ **OBSERVATION** If your corporation elected S corporation status before 1987, generally net long-term capital gains in the first three years after the election were taxed at the corporate level. If your corporation elected S status after 1986, only so-called "built-in gains" (gain allocable to the period before the S election took effect) are subject to corporate taxation. However, these gains can be taxed if sales are made within ten years after the S election.

¶3105   TERMINATING THE ELECTION

The S election is terminated in *any one* of the following circumstances [IRC Sec. 1362(d); Temp. Reg. Sec. 18.1362-3; Prop. Reg. Sec. 1.1362-3]:

- Revoking the election.
- Ceasing to qualify as an S corporation.
- Violating the passive investment income restrictions on corporations with earnings and profits.

Suppose there is an inadvertent termination of your S corporation status. If this happens because your corporation inadvertently ceased to qualify as an S corporation, or it inadvertently violated the restriction on passive investment income, the IRS can waive the termination. To qualify for a waiver, the IRS must determine that the termination was unintentional, your corporation took steps to correct the event within a reasonable time period, and your corporation and its shareholders agree to be treated as if the terminating event had not happened [IRC Sec. 1362(f); Prop. Reg. Sec. 1.1362-5].

If your corporation's status as an S corporation is terminated, it generally must wait five tax years before it can again become an S corporation, unless the IRS consents to an earlier election [IRC Sec. 1362(g)].

(a) Revoking S Corporation Status. A change in ownership does not of itself revoke an S election. There's no requirement that the new shareholder affirm the S corporation treatment. Instead, your S corporation status can only be revoked if shareholders who collectively own more than 50% of the outstanding shares consent to the revocation. The consenting shareholders must own their stock in the S corporation at the beginning of the day the revocation is filed.

The revocation is effective for the whole year if made on or before the 15th day of the third month of the year. The revocation may specify an effective date on or after the actual revocation date, even if this results in a split tax year [IRC Sec. 1362(d)(1)].

(b) Ceasing to Qualify as an S Corporation. Your corporation's status as an S corporation can be terminated at any time if it ceases to qualify as an S corporation [IRC Sec. 1362(d)(2)].

There are certain events that can cause your corporation to cease qualifying as an S corporation. Some of these events include:

- Having more than 35 shareholders.
- Transferring stock in the S corporation to a corporation, partnership, an ineligible trust or a nonresident alien.
- Creating a class of stock other than the voting and nonvoting common stock allowed.
- Acquiring a subsidiary, other than certain nonoperating subsidiaries.

(c) Violating the Passive Income Restriction. Your corporation's status as an S corporation will terminate if both of the following conditions occur for three consecutive tax years [IRC Sec. 1362(d)(3); Prop. Reg. Sec. 1.1362-3(d)]:

- It retains earnings and profits accumulated prior to becoming an S corporation.
- Its passive investment income for each year is more than 25% of gross receipts.

Passive investment income generally means gross receipts from interest, dividends, rents, royalties, annuities and gains from sales or exchanges of stock or securities. This termination is effective as of the first day of the tax year starting after the third consecutive tax year with excess passive investment income.

> ➤ **OBSERVATION** If your corporation elected S status from its inception, it may have unlimited amounts of passive investment income. It will have no earnings from a non-S corporation status.

See ¶3107(c) for discussion of passive income tax.

(d) Treatment of S Termination Year. If your corporation terminates its S election during a tax year, two short tax years result. The first, an S corporation short tax year, ends on the day before the termination is effective. The second, a C corporation short tax year, starts on the day the termination is effective and ends on the day the tax year would have ended had no termination occurred [IRC Sec. 1362(e)(1)].

Example: S Corp. has 35 shareholders. On June 4, 1992, the corporation acquires a 36th shareholder S Corp.'s election terminates as of June 4, 1992, and two short tax years result. Its S corporation short tax year starts January 1, 1992, and ends on June 3, 1992. Its C corporation tax year begins on June 4, 1992, and ends on December 31, 1992.

(e) Computation of Income in S Termination Year. Generally, you compute items of corporate income, loss, deductions and credits for the full tax year without closing the corporation's books on the termination date (*but see* Exception, below). You allocate these items between the two short tax years on a daily basis. The shareholders report the amounts allocated to the S corporation short tax year under the general S corporation rules. Your corporation uses the amounts allocated to the C corporation short tax year to compute its tax for that period. This tax must be determined on an annualized basis. This pro rata allocation formula does not apply to an S corporation year in which there is a sale or exchange of 50% or more of the corporation's stock [IRC Sec. 1362(e)(1),(2),(5),(6)].

The two short tax years are counted as only one year when figuring net operating loss or other carryovers [¶3110]. Also, the due date for both returns (without extensions) is the same date as the return for the short C corporation year [IRC Sec. 1362(e)(6)].

Exception. Your corporation can elect to compute income, loss, deductions and credits for both short period returns under the normal tax accounting rules *only* if all persons who were shareholders at any time during the S corporation termination year and all persons owning stock on the first day of the short C corporation year consent to the election. Under this election, items of income, etc., would be attributed to the two short tax years according to when they were actually realized or incurred [IRC Sec. 1362(e)(3); Temp. Reg. Sec. 18.1362-4; Prop. Reg. Sec. 1.1362-4].

OPERATING AS AN S CORPORATION

¶3107   TAX ON S CORPORATION INCOME

[New tax legislation may affect this subject; see ¶1.]

For each year an election is in effect, your S corporation is usually exempt from all federal income taxes [IRC Sec. 1363(a)]. However, see ¶3108 for a possible exception for certain gains. Also, see (c) below for possible tax on excess passive investment income.

As a shareholder of your S corporation, you are taxed on your pro rata share of corporate income ((a) below) [IRC Sec. 1377(a)]. This allocation on a per-share, per-day basis means that income is allocated to you according to the number of shares you hold *and* the number of days you held them [(c) below]. Items of income, loss, deduction and credit are separately allocated to each shareholder whenever separate treatment could affect your tax liability. These items are reported on your personal tax return subject to whatever rules and limitations apply to your personal tax situation. The balance of the corporation's income or loss is aggregated and passed through to the shareholders as "nonseparately computed income or loss." You (and the other shareholders) report this income on Schedule E, Form 1040, and is incorporated as income or loss in the computation of your taxable income. Finally, your (and each other shareholder's) pro rata share of corporate items of tax preference income is used to compute your personal alternative minimum tax liability [IRC Sec. 1366].

NOTE: Instead of a per-share, per-day allocation, all the shareholders can consent to an allocation according to corporate books based on when items of income are actually received.

(a) S Corporation Taxable Income. Generally, your S corporation computes its taxable income the same as a partnership. However, your S corporation can claim an amortization deduction for organizational expenditures. Also, the deductions allowable to individuals are generally allowed to your S corporation, with the following exceptions [IRC Sec. 1363(b)]:

- Personal exemptions;
- Foreign taxes;
- Charitable contributions;
- Expenses for the production of income (other than in a trade or business);
- Medical expenses;
- Alimony;
- Taxes, interest, and business depreciation by a cooperative housing corporation tenant-stockholder;
- Moving expenses;
- Payments to an IRA;
- Oil and gas depletion;
- Net operating loss deduction [¶3110].

NOTE: Foreign taxes, charitable contributions and depletion deductions are passed through to you and the other shareholders to be used in computing your individual tax liability. Also, the corporate dividends-received deduction [¶3014] is not allowed.

Most elections affecting the computation of items derived from your S corporation must be made by the corporation. However, certain elections must be made separately by you (and each other shareholder), including those relating to: (1) limitation of interest on investment indebtedness, (2) mining exploration expenses and (3) foreign taxes [IRC Sec. 1363(c)].

(b) Estimated Taxes. Although your S corporation generally is not subject to tax on its taxable income, there are limited exceptions. When an exception applies, your S corporation must make estimated tax payments [(¶3651(a)] [IRC Sec. 6655].

Your S corporation is taxed on the following items: (1) the recognition of a built-in gain within ten years of the date that your former C corporation elected S corporation status (¶3108) [IRC Sec. 1366(f)(2), 1374, 6655(g)(4)]; (2) the receipt of passive investment income in excess of 25% of total annual gross receipts if your corporation has earnings and profits from a year in which it was not an S corporation [(c) below] [IRC Sec. 1375]; and (3) the recapture of investment tax credits claimed during a tax year in which your corporation was not an S corporation [(d)below] [IRC Sec. 1371(d)(2)].

The regular corporate estimated tax rules are generally used in determining the amount of your S corporation's estimated tax [¶3651]. However, for purposes of the portion of required estimated tax payments attributable to built-in gains and investment tax credit recapture, your S corporation cannot utilize the exceptions that allow estimated tax payments to be based on the corporation's prior year tax [IRC Sec. 6655(d)(1)(B)(ii), (d)(2)(B)]. The prior year's tax exception is available to your S corporation with respect to the portion of required estimated tax payments attributable to excess passive income (even if there was no tax attributable to excess passive income in the prior year). In all situations, your S corporation can use the annualization exception [¶3651(b)] [IRC Sec. 6655(e),(g)(4)].

(c) Tax on Passive Income. Your S corporation may be subject to tax if it has (1) C corporation earnings and profits left over at the close of a tax year *and* (2) more than 25% of its gross receipts is passive investment income [IRC Sec. 1375(a)]. (Passive investment income generally means gross receipts from interest, dividends, rents, royalties, annuities and gains from sales or exchanges of stock or securities [IRC Sec. 1362(d)(3)]. If your corporation has "excess net passive income" for the year, it must pay a tax on this amount or its taxable income, if lower, at the maximum corporate tax rate for the year (¶3002) [IRC Sec. 1375(a)]. The IRS can waive this tax if (1) your S corporation had previously determined in good faith that it had no C corporation earnings and profits and (2) your S corporation distributed these earnings and profits within a reasonable time after they were discovered [IRC Sec. 1375(d)].

"Net passive income" is your corporation's passive investment income reduced by allowable deductions directly connected with producing it (other than deductions for net operating loss and amortization of organizational expenditures) [IRC Sec. 1375(b)(2)].

"Excess net passive income" is your corporation's net passive income for the year multiplied by the following fraction [IRC Sec. 1375(b)(1)]:

$$\frac{\text{Passive income for year} \quad - \quad 25\% \text{ of gross receipts for year}}{\text{Passive income for year}}$$

Example: During 1992, S Corp. has $120,000 in gross receipts; $60,000 taxable income; $50,000 in passive investment income and $10,000 in expenses directly attributable to passive investment income. Its net passive income is $40,000 ($50,000 passive investment income minus $10,000 expenses). The amount by which passive investment income for the year exceeds 25% of gross receipts is $20,000 [$50,000 passive investment income minus $30,000 (25% of $120,000 gross receipts)].

The corporation's excess net passive income is $16,000 [$40,000 net passive income times ⅖ ($20,000 of passive income in excess of 25% of gross receipts divided by $50,000 passive income)]. This is less than the corporation's taxable income. The corporation's tax on excess net passive income therefore is $5,440 (34% of $16,000).

Limitations and special rules. Excess net passive income cannot exceed your corporation's taxable income (computed without any deductions for net operating loss or amortization of organizational expenditures). Also, only the credit for use of gasoline and special fuels is allowed against the passive income tax [IRC Sec. 1375(c)]. However, when determining the amount of passive investment income, do not take into account any recognized built-in gain or loss of your S corporation for any tax year in the recognition period [IRC Sec. 1375(b)(4)].

NOTE: The rule under Sec. 1375(b)(4) applies generally for tax years starting after 1986, but only for returns filed under an S election made after 1986. "Recognition period" is the ten-year period starting with the first day of the tax year for which the corporation was an S corporation.

Passthrough reduction. If your S corporation is liable for a passive income tax, each item of passive income is reduced by its portion of the tax to determine its corporate passthrough to you and the other shareholders [IRC Sec. 1366(f)(3)].

(d) Tax on Recomputing a Prior-Year Investment Credit. This tax might apply if your corporation claimed the investment credit on a prior year's corporate income tax return before it became an S corporation. If your S corporation makes an early disposition of the property, it, and not you and the other shareholders, is liable for paying the tax. However, you might be subject to the recapture if your stock interest in the S corporation is reduced by more than one-third.[1]

➤ **OBSERVATION** Electing to be treated as an S corporation in itself is not treated as a disposition. Therefore, an S election does not automatically trigger recapture of a credit taken before the election was effective [IRC Sec. 1371(d)].

➤ **TAX TIP** Recapture occurs only if your (or another shareholder's) stock interest is reduced below two-thirds of what it was when the property giving rise to the credit was placed in service by your corporation. Thus, if business considerations permit, you can avoid recapture by selling down no lower than the two-thirds mark until after the recapture period for the property has elapsed (in general, five years from when the property was placed in service).

(e) Recapture of LIFO Benefits on Converting to S Corporation.
If your LIFO-method C corporation elects to become an S corporation, it will have to recapture the benefits of using the LIFO method in the year it converts to S status. This is done by requiring your corporation to include in that year's income a LIFO recapture amount. This amount is the excess of the inventory's value using FIFO over its LIFO value at the end of the last C corporation year. The resulting increase in tax, though, is paid over a four-year period. Suppose your corporation was a member of an affiliated group in its last C corporation year. Then your converting corporation is not treated as a member of the group as to the amount included in income under the recapture rules, except to the extent provided by regulations [IRC Sec. 1363].

➤ **OBSERVATION** Liability for the LIFO recapture tax is that of your converting corporation and not that of an affiliated group with which it filed a consolidated return in its last tax year as a C corporation.

This LIFO recapture rule applies to S elections after December 17, 1987. But it does not apply to any election made before 1989 if, before December 18, 1987, your corporate board of directors adopted a resolution to make an S election, or your corporation requested a ruling from the IRS in which it expressed an intent to make an S election [IRC Sec. 1363].

¶3108 TREATMENT OF CERTAIN GAINS
[New tax legislation may affect this subject; see ¶1.]

Your C corporation cannot avoid the corporate tax on gains on appreciated property it wishes to sell by making an S election right before the sale. If your corporation elected S status before 1987, it is subject to a tax on the net capital gain—but only in the first three years of the S corporation election. For elections after 1986, a corporate-level tax is applied on your S corporation if it has recognized built-in gain for any tax year starting in the ten-year period after the election takes effect.

➤ **OBSERVATION** This rule taxes unrealized gain that, in effect, accrued before the conversion from a C to an S corporation. Thus, the built-in gain is the gain that would have resulted had the property been sold at the time the S election took effect.

Example: In 1984, Acme Corp., which was a regular corporation although it was qualified to make the S corporation election, owned some investment realty that it planned to sell during its next tax year at a $400,000 long-term capital gain. If it did nothing and made the sale, it would pay a capital gains tax on the profit which, when paid out to shareholders, would be taxed again to them as dividends. Instead, Acme Corp. elected to be taxed as an S corporation for its next tax year, sold the property and passed through the $400,000 profit to its shareholders as long-term capital gain. Result: Acme Corp. avoided paying a capital gains tax on its $400,000 gain and converted its shareholders' dividend income into favorably taxed long-term capital gain. The election could be a one-time affair—for the sale year only. Thereafter, if Acme Corp. did not wish to remain an S corporation, it could arrange to terminate its election for its tax year after the sale year and revert to regular corporation status.

For an S corporation election made after 1986, a corporate level tax is imposed on certain "built-in gains" of an S corporation that converted from a regular corporation. Any built-in gains tax imposed on your S corporation is passed through to you and the other shareholders as a loss—offsetting the gain that gave rise to the tax [IRC Sec. 1366(f)(2)].

The amount of tax is computed by applying the highest rate (34%) on ordinary income to the net recognized built-in gain of your S corporation for the tax year less net operating and capital loss carryforwards allowed to be taken into account [IRC Sec. 1374(b)].

Net recognized built-in gain. Generally, this is the lesser of (1) recognized built-in gains less the recognized built-in losses, or (2) the taxable income for the year, not taking into account net operating or capital loss carryforwards [IRC Sec. 1374(d)(2)]. For corporations that elect S status after March 30, 1988, if the amount in (1) exceeds (2), the excess is treated as a recognized built-in gain in the following year [IRC Sec. 1374(d)(2)(B)].

> ➤ **OBSERVATION** The carryover reduces the opportunity to save taxes by recognizing the built-in gain in the year your corporation would otherwise have a loss. The current year's loss does not permanently offset the corporate tax on built-in gain.

Net operating loss carryforwards. Any net operating loss carryforward that arose in a tax year when your corporation was a C corporation is allowed as a deduction against the net recognized built-in gain of your S corporation for the tax year. To determine the amount of the loss that can be carried to later tax years, the amount of the net recognized built-in gain is treated as taxable income. The same rule applies for a capital loss carryforward arising in a tax year when your corporation was a C corporation [IRC Sec. 1374(b)(2)].

Limitation on amount of net recognized built-in gain. The amount of the net recognized built-in gains taken into account for any tax year cannot be more than the excess of [IRC Sec. 1374(c)(2)]:

- The net unrealized built-in gain, over
- The net recognized built-in gains for prior tax years beginning in the ten-year recognition period.

Recognized built-in gain. This means any gain recognized during the recognition period on the disposition of any asset, except to the extent that your S corporation establishes that [IRC Sec. 1374(d)(3)]:

- It acquired the asset after becoming an S corporation; or
- The gain is more than would have been realized had the asset been sold at the start of the first year your S election was in effect.

Recognition period. The term "recognition period" means the ten-year period starting with the first day of the first tax year for which your corporation was an S corporation [IRC Sec. 1374(d)(7)].

Recognized built-in losses. This means any loss recognized during the recognition period on the disposition of any asset to the extent that your S corporation establishes that [IRC Sec. 1374(d)(4)]:

- The asset was held by your S corporation at the start of the first tax year for which it was an S corporation.
- The loss is *not* more than would have been realized had the asset been sold at the start of the first year your S election was in effect.

> ➤ **OBSERVATION** If a disposition during the recognition period results in a gain, your S corporation treats the gain as a taxable built-in gain, unless you can show that an exception applies. On the other hand, if there is a loss, it is presumed not to be a tax-favored built-in loss, unless you can prove otherwise.

Property acquired in tax-free exchange. If any asset's adjusted basis is determined (fully or partly) by the adjusted basis of another asset held by your S corporation at the start of the first tax year for which it was an S corporation [IRC Sec. 1374(d)(6)]:

- The asset is treated as held by your S corporation at the start of that first tax year and
- Recognized built-in gain or loss is found by the fair market value and adjusted basis of the other asset at the start of that first tax year.

➤ **OBSERVATION** This rule prevents the use of tax-free exchanges as a device for circumventing the "property owned at time of S election" requirement.

Transfer of assets from a C to an S corporation. A special recognition period arises in tax-free transfers of assets from C to S corporations. It applies where your S corporation acquires an asset, and its basis in the asset is determined (fully or partly) by the basis of the asset (or any other property) in a C corporation's hands. In general, your S corporation is subject to tax on built-in gain if it recognizes the gain during the ten-year period starting with the day your S corportion acquired the asset [IRC Sec. 1374(d)(8)].

¶3109 PASSTHROUGHS TO SHAREHOLDERS

Items passed through to you and the other shareholders, like income (including tax-exempt income), deductions, capital gains and losses, charitable contributions and credits, retain their original character [IRC Sec. 1366(b)].

You report your pro rata share of each item of income, loss, deduction or credit that is separately stated and a pro rata share of nonseparately stated income or loss on your tax return [IRC Sec. 1366(a)].

For tax calculations based on your gross income, you must include a pro rata share of the corporation's gross income [IRC Sec. 1366(c)].

➤ **OBSERVATION** Your share of the corporation's taxable income is not self-employment income, even though it is included in your gross income.

Certain items are treated as follows [IRC Sec. 1366(a)]:

- *Capital gains and losses.* Gains and losses from sales or exchanges of capital assets by your S corporation pass directly through to you and the other shareholders as capital gains and losses.
- *Charitable contributions.* These are passed through to you and the other shareholders. You add them to your own contributions in figuring the deduction on your own personal returns.
- *Tax-exempt interest.* This passes through to shareholders, retaining its character as tax-exempt interest. It increases your basis for your S corporation's stock.

NOTE: A later distribution of the tax-exempt interest to shareholders will not be taxable. It will merely reduce your basis for your S corporation's stock.

- *Depreciation.* This is not a passthrough item. It is computed and deducted by your S corporation on its tax return in figuring taxable income or loss that is passed through to you and the other shareholders.

NOTE: Your S corporation, not its shareholders, elects what method to use for computing depreciation deductions. Also, your S corporation makes the election to write off expenditures in the year of purchase, by claiming an expensing deduction [¶2113]. The dollar cap on expensing applies both to your S corporation and to each shareholder. Your corporation allocates the deduction among you and the other shareholders, who then take your deduction subject to the dollar limitation.

Computation of shareholder's pro rata share. Your pro rata share of your S corporation's nonseparately computed income and separately computed items depends on your percentage of stockownership on each day of the corporation's tax year. Your pro rata share is the sum of the portions of such items that are attributable on a pro rata basis to the shares you hold on each day of your corporation's tax year. For this purpose, the daily portion of each item is your corporation's total amount of each item divided by the number of days in the tax year [IRC Sec. 1377(a)].

> **Example:** Electing Corp., a calendar year taxpayer, has $36,600 nonseparately computed income for 1992. The daily portion of this income is $100 ($36,600 ÷ 366). If Mr. Baker is a 50% shareholder for each day of the year, he must include $50 per day (or $18,250 for the year) on his tax return. If Baker had sold his stock on June 2, 1992, he would report $7,650 ($50 per day for 153 days, January 1, 1992 through June 1, 1992).

> ➤ **IMPORTANT** The character of any separately computed items (e.g., capital gain, tax-exempt income, deduction or loss) realized by your corporation is passed through to you and its other shareholders. Also, your gross income includes your pro rata share of your corporation's gross income [IRC Sec. 1366(b),(c)].

Worthless stock. Suppose your S corporation stock becomes worthless. Then you and every other shareholder is entitled to a capital loss deduction for whatever basis you and the other shareholders have for the stock. However, before computing the worthless stock deduction, your S corporation's nonseparately computed income or loss (as well as its separately computed items) for that year must be taken into account, and any required adjustments to the stock's basis must be made [IRC Sec. 165, 1377].

¶3110   TREATMENT OF NET OPERATING AND OTHER LOSSES

All losses and deductions of your S corporation (including net operating losses *and* capital losses) are passed through to (and are deductible by) its shareholders. Your pro rata share of the loss may not exceed the adjusted basis of your stock and debt [¶3112]. A loss passed through to you is treated on your return as an ordinary loss, fully deductible in computing your adjusted gross income. You take the deduction for your tax year with which or within which your corporation's tax year ends (the deduction is allowed for your final tax year if you die before the end of the corporation's tax year). If the loss is not currently absorbed, it gives rise to an operating loss carryback or carryover on the shareholder level [IRC Sec. 1366].

Your pro rata share of the loss is computed on a daily basis. For example, if you dispose of your shares in the middle of the year, you would be entitled to your share of about one-half of the corporation's operating loss for the year.

> **Example:** Electing corporation ABC, a calendar year taxpayer, has a net operating loss of $73,000 during the current tax year. Blake, one of ten equal shareholders, has an adjusted basis of $6,000 for his shares of ABC stock. He sells the shares on June 22, 1992. Blake's pro rata share of the corporation's net operating loss to be deducted on his return is $3,451 (173 days/366 days × $7,300). Note that the stock is considered held by the buyer on the day of sale.

> **NOTE:** Amounts for which shareholders are at risk to third parties do not increase the basis of S corporation stock to allow shareholders to deduct additional operating losses.[1]

Your S corporation cannot apply a loss carryback or carryover from a non-electing year against its income of an electing year. The carryback or carryover is not terminated by the election, but every year in which the election applies is counted in figuring the years of the carryback or carryover [IRC Sec. 1371(b)].

> NOTE: The prohibition against carryovers between C corporation and S corporation years is not limited to net operating losses. It also extends to carryovers of any tax attribute, such as a business credit carryover.

Special rule for post-termination transition period. Losses in excess of basis that remain disallowed at the end of the last S corporation tax year are treated as incurred by you (the shareholder) on the last day of the pre-termination transition period. However, such losses cannot exceed your adjusted basis in the stock on the last day of such period. A post-termination transition period begins on the day after the last day of the last S corporation tax year and ends on the later of: (1) one year after the effective date of termination, or the due date of the last S corporation tax return (including extensions), if later; and (2) the end of the 120-day period beginning on the day of the determination that your S corporation's election had terminated for a previous tax year [IRC Sec. 1366(d)(3); 1377(b)].

Disallowing passive losses. There are limits on the amount of losses and credits you can claim if you do not participate in the running of the business (i.e., passive activity) [¶2326]. These limits are considered after the at-risk limits have been considered [¶2327].

If you are an S corporation shareholder who is actively engaged in operating the corporation's business, you are not subject to these limitations.

S corporation losses passed through to inactive shareholders cannot be used against salary and other compensation income, dividends and interest. However, if you have income from other passive activities, losses from your S corporation can be applied against that income, even if the activities are unrelated to and different from the activities conducted by your S corporation.

You are allowed a deduction for any passive activity loss or the deduction equivalent of the passive activity credit for any tax year from rental real estate activities in which there is active participation. The amount allowed under this rule cannot be more than $25,000 ($12,500 for married persons filing separately). This amount is reduced by 50% of the amount by which your adjusted gross income exceeds $100,000 ($50,000 for married persons filing separately).

> ► **TAX BREAK** Proposed regulations provide a break for S corporation shareholders who make loans to, or receive them from their corporations. Under the regulations, if you lend money to your S corporation and do not materially participate in the business, your corporation's interest payments on the loan are treated as passive income to you. Result: You can offset the tax on this interest income by claiming a full deduction for your corporation's passed-through interest expense (which is considered passive)[Prop. Reg. Sec. 1.469-7].

¶3111   TREATMENT OF DISTRIBUTIONS

Under the Subchapter S rules, there can be no current earnings and profits (E&P) since the items of corporate income and deductions pass through to you and the other shareholders. Distributions are not taxable as dividends unless deemed made out of accumulated E&P [(b) below]. The rules for treatment of distributions are summarized below.

(a) Distributions When No E&P. There is no tax at the corporate level. The distribution equals the amount of cash distributed (plus the fair market value of any property distributed) and is tax-free to the extent of your stock basis. If the distribution exceeds the stock basis, capital gain results [IRC Sec. 1368(b)].

> **Example 1:** New calendar year S corporation has no income or loss for 1992, and there are no accumulated E&P. It pays out $20,000 in cash to the sole shareholder whose stock basis is $15,000. The $20,000 distribution reduces the stock basis to zero, and the excess $5,000 is capital gain.

Appreciated value property. If your S corporation distributes appreciated value property to you, it is treated as if the property had been sold to you at fair market value. This will generally result in capital (or Sec. 1231) gain at the corporate level, which will retain its character when passed through to you. This rule does not apply to any distribution to the extent it consists of property permitted by Sections 354, 355, or 356 to be received without recognition of gain.[1]

> **Example 2:** In 1992, S corporation distributes to its sole shareholder investment realty (basis, $20,000; value, $45,000) that it has held for several years. S Corp. has a $25,000 long-term capital gain, which will pass through as such to the shareholder.

(b) Distributions When Accumulated E&P. Accumulated E&P can result only from: (1) prior C corporation years; (2) undistributed taxable income from pre-1983 S corporation years; or (3) corporate acquisitions resulting in a carryover of E&P. When your S corporation has accumulated E&P, a distribution is treated as if made in the following order [IRC Sec. 1368(c)]:

    1.   Out of your pro rata share of the corporation's "accumulated adjustments account" (defined below). This portion will be tax-free to the extent of your stock basis, and the excess over basis will be capital gain. If the distribution is in excess of the amount in the accumulated adjustments account, then;

    2.   Out of your pro rata share of accumulated E&P. This portion is taxed as a dividend. If the distribution also exceeds the amount of E&P, then;

    3.   It will reduce your remaining stock basis (if any) and the balance will be capital gain.

> **Example 3:** Calendar-year S corporation distributes $50,000 cash in 1992. It has $10,000 accumulated E&P and no "accumulated adjustments account." The sole shareholder's stock basis is $25,000. The distribution is treated as a $10,000 dividend from E&P plus $15,000 capital gain (excess of remaining $40,000 over the $25,000 stock basis).

Accumulated adjustments account (AAA). This is the amount which your S corporation can distribute tax-free to its shareholders before any amount is considered a distribution of accumulated E&P. It is equal to the accumulated S corporation income plus and minus adjustments shareholders were required to make to stock basis. However, no adjustment is made for tax-exempt income and related expenses. Also, the AAA is not reduced by reason of federal taxes arising while your corporation was a C corporation [IRC Sec. 1368(e)].

If the amount of the account falls below zero because of losses for any tax year, it must be offset by future income before the account can have a positive balance. After taking income and loss for the year into account, the amount in the accumulated adjustment account must be applied on a pro rata basis among all of the distributions made during the year, unless the regulations provide otherwise. For example, if the account balance at the end of the year, before distributions, is $1,000, and your corporation distributes $2,000 during the year, half of each distribution will be treated as from the accumulated adjustments account and will not be taxed as a dividend [IRC Sec. 1368(e)(1)].

> **NOTE:** Your S corporation can elect to avoid the accumulated adjustments account treatment of distributions as tax-free reductions of stock basis. Instead, distributions will be treated as taxable dividends from accumulated E&P. You and all other shareholders receiving distributions during the year must consent. This election allows your S corporation to distribute E&P to avoid the passive income rule (¶3107(c)) [IRC Sec. 1368(e)(3)].

Special rule for post-termination transition period. Any cash distribution made after your S corporation election ends, but during the post-termination transition period [¶3110], reduces your stock basis to the extent that the distribution does not exceed the accumulated adjustments account. But if all shareholders consent, your S corporation may elect to treat cash distributions during this period as dividends. This enables your corporation to avoid the accumulated earnings and personal holding company taxes [IRC Sec. 1371(e); 1377(b)].

¶3112   ADJUSTMENTS TO BASIS OF STOCK

Basically, the rules for adjusting S corporation stock basis are the same as the rules for partnerships. The basis of your stock is increased by any income items and decreased by any loss or deduction items passed through to you [IRC Sec. 1367(a)].

If your basis in the stock is reduced to zero, any excess loss reduces your basis (but not below zero) in any indebtedness your S corporation owes to you. You cannot currently deduct excess loss remaining after reducing both stock and debt to zero. You carry it over to later years and use it as soon as your bases in stock and debt have been increased to cover it [IRC Sec. 1367(b)(2)(A)].

Your stock basis is adjusted first by corporate income and loss for the year, and then by corporate distributions [¶3111]. However, you must increase your reduced debt basis to (but not above) its original amount before you can increase your stock basis. Also, if any item of income or loss is increased or decreased in a redetermination of tax liability, your basis must be adjusted accordingly [IRC Sec. 1367(b)(1),(2)(B)].

> **NOTE:** Unlike partnership rules, to the extent property distributions are treated as a return of basis, you reduce your basis by the fair market value of the property distributed.[1]

> **Example:** Ms. Finch is a 50% shareholder in a calendar-year S corporation. Her stock basis is $4,000. She also has a $2,000 basis in a loan she made to the corporation.

> In 1992, the corporation lost $10,000. Finch's $5,000 pro rata share of the 1992 loss reduces her stock basis to zero and reduces her debt basis to $1,000. She can deduct the full $5,000 loss as an ordinary loss in 1992.

> In 1993, the corporation made $20,000 profit and distributed $6,000 to Finch. Finch's $10,000 pro rata share of the 1993 income first increases her reduced debt basis back to its original $2,000, and then increases her stock basis to $9,000. Then, her stock basis is reduced to $3,000 by the $6,000 distribution.

> **NOTE:** You basis is not increased by third-party loans made to your corporation—even if you personally guarantee the loans.[2]

Adjustments for separately computed items. Your basis for your stock in your S corporation is also increased by your pro rata share of items of income that were separately treated by the corporation, such as capital gains, and by your pro rata share of the deduction for depletion in excess of the basis of the property subject to depletion. On the other hand, your basis for your stock in the S corporation is decreased by any items of deduction that were separately treated by the corporation, such as capital losses, any expense of the corporation that was not deductible in computing taxable income and was not properly chargeable to the capital account, and the amount of your pro rata share of the deduction for depletion for oil and gas wells.

> ➤ **NEW REGULATIONS** The IRS has issued a set of proposed regulations that create flexible rules for basis adjustments to S corporation stock and distributions by S corporations [Prop. Reg. Secs. 1.1367-1-3; 1.1368-1-4]. The regulations would take effect immediately after they become final. Here are some of the key proposed rules:

- There would be a per-share, per-day approach to stock basis. That means corporate income, deductions, distributions and anything else that affects stock basis must be allocated among each of the corporation's outstanding shares. Each shareholder must adjust his or her stock basis based on the allocation and the number of days during the year he or she owned the stock.
- Basis adjustments would be made in the following order: increases for S corporation income and "excess" depletion deductions; decreases for nondeductible, noncapital expenses and other depletion deductions; decreases for S corporation losses and remaining deductions; and decreases for distributions.
- Basis adjustments would generally occur at the close of the S corporation's tax year. However, if a shareholder transfers shares before year-end, basis adjustments for that shareholder take effect immediately prior to the transfer.
- A shareholder who receives a distribution should first adjust the basis of his or her stock (except for the basis reduction for the distribution) and then determine the tax consequences of the distribution itself.

PLANNING CONSIDERATIONS USING S CORPORATIONS

¶3115   ADVANTAGES OF OPERATING AS AN S CORPORATION

[New tax legislation may affect this subject; see ¶1.]

The following is a brief summary of the main advantages of electing to be taxed as an S corporation:

- Limited double taxation. S corporation earnings are generally taxed only once, at the shareholder level.

> ➤ **OBSERVATION** This method of taxation is particularly beneficial when your tax rates are lower than the tax rate of the corporation.

- Shareholders get an immediate deduction for losses. Like partnerships, your S corporation losses are passed through to you and the other shareholders and can offset your income from other sources.

> ➤ **OBSERVATION** These losses may be deducted subject to passive loss rules [¶2326] affecting some shareholders and the restriction that losses claimed do not exceed your basis in S corporation stock and loans to the corporation.

NOTE: You can carry unusable losses forward indefinitely and take them when your basis is restored.

> ➤ **TAX SAVING** When your S corporation will be getting a bank loan, you and the other shareholders should borrow the funds from the bank instead and then loan them to the corporation. That way, you acquire a basis in the debt that you can use to cover passthrough losses from the corporation that exceed your stock bases. If you let the corporation borrow the funds directly, you don't get this basis adjustment, even though you may have to personally guarantee the loans.

- No accumulated earnings penalty. Your S corporation income can be accumulated without restriction and paid out later to you and other shareholders tax-free to the extent of your stock and debt basis. You, though, do pay tax when the income is earned.
- No personal holding company (PHC) tax.

➤ **OBSERVATION** If your S corporation has carryover regular corporation earnings and profits, it is subject to passive income rules that restrict passive earnings in a way similar to the personal holding company tax [¶3300].

NOTE: Regular corporations must pay the PHC tax if they have a certain dollar amount of passive income and a restricted number of shareholders. S corporations that have no carryover regular corporation earnings and profits can have the benefits of unlimited amounts of passive income and can avoid the PHC tax. This break makes the initial election of S status particularly attractive for the holding of passive investments.

- Family income splitting. Your S corporation can be used to transfer business profits to your children in lower tax brackets. See also ¶3117.

➤ **OBSERVATION** You can make gifts of stock yearly to your children. Since differences in voting rights are allowed in an S corporation, you can retain control of the corporation by holding voting stock while giving gifts of nonvoting stock to your children. If you keep these stock gifts within the limits of the gift tax exclusion, no gift tax will result and your estate tax liability will also be reduced since your children's stock will not pass through your estate. The limitation on valuation freezes, though, could reduce the estate tax savings.

NOTE: Although this type of arrangement is permitted, your S corporation must pay a reasonable salary to you or else the IRS will adjust the distribution of corporate income to reflect the real contributions to the operation of the business.

- Tax-exempt interest passthrough.

➤ **OBSERVATION** The tax-exempt income retains its character in your hands. Regular corporation tax-exempt interest distributed to the shareholders as dividends is subject to tax. Partnerships also can pass through tax-exempt income.

- Charitable contributions. While regular corporations are subject to a 10% of taxable income limit on charitable contribution deductions [¶3019], you can deduct your share of your S corporation's contributions subject to the more liberal limits applicable to individuals [¶1919].

¶3116 DRAWBACKS OF AN S CORPORATION ELECTION

Here are some drawbacks that should be reviewed when considering an S election:

- Limits on the number of shareholders.

➤ **OBSERVATION** Since your S corporation can have no more than 35 shareholders, if your company needs to raise capital from a wide variety of sources, it should choose a form that allows a larger number of investors.

- Only one class of stock allowed.

➤ **OBSERVATION** Even though S corporations can issue voting and nonvoting stock, the fact that all the stock must be common restricts the ability to include investors with different interests. Regular corporations can issue preferred, common and convertible stock without restriction. Partnership agreements may provide for an unlimited variety of interests.

An IRS ruling showed that an S corporation owner could, with care, impose restrictions and conditions on the shares transferred to other family members. This ruling concluded that imposing transfer restrictions and forced redemption conditions on some shares under the terms of a sole S shareholder's would not create a second class of stock.[1]

- Passive income restrictions. If your S corporation has accumulated C corporation earnings and profits, it could lose that S election if it violates the passive income test [¶3105(c)].

➤ **OBSERVATION** Even if the election is not lost, your S corporation will have to pay a corporate tax in any year in which passive income exceeds the prescribed limits.

- Fringe benefit restrictions.

➤ **OBSERVATION** One of the major disadvantages of an S election is that if you own more than 2% of the corporation's stock, you are not eligible for tax-sheltered fringe benefits you could have enjoyed if your corporation had been a regular corporation. These benefits include accident and health plans, group-term life insurance, and employer-provided meals and lodging. However, S corporations can offer their other employees the same tax-qualified retirement plans available to employees of regular corporations. Some restrictions, though, apply to retirement plan loans [¶1325].

The IRS has said that starting with tax years beginning after 1991, health insurance premiums (and other tax-favored fringe benefits) paid by your S corporation for you and other more-than-2% shareholder-employees must be treated as compensation for income tax purposes. (They are not, however, treated as compensation for FICA tax purposes.) Result: The company payments are deductible by the corporation on Form 1120S, are subject to income tax withholding and must be reported on the shareholder-employee's Form W-2.[2]

NOTE: Shareholders such as yourself who own more than 2% of an S corporation's stock or voting power can take advantage of the health insurance deduction for self-employeds. In other words, you can deduct up to 25% of their health insurance costs paid before July 1, 1992 (¶1932(f)) [IRC Sec. 162(l)(5)].

- Tax years. Your S corporation generally must operate on a calendar year basis unless it can establish a valid business purpose for a different tax year. Your S corporation can elect to use a tax year other than a required year if certain procedures are followed [¶3103].

➤ **OBSERVATION** Under those procedures, your S corporation must make payments that are intended to represent the value of the tax deferral obtained by its shareholders through using a tax year different from the required tax year.

- Less favorable deductions.

➤ **OBSERVATION** Regular corporate deductions may be more favorable than individual tax deductions. Your S corporation is not eligible for these special corporate deductions. One of the most significant is the dividends received deduction [¶3014].

- Carryovers from regular corporation years.

➤ **OBSERVATION** A regular corporation with net operating loss and other such tax attributes could lose these tax benefits if it makes an S election. Carryovers between a regular and an S corporation are not allowed. Also, when making the switch, S corporation years count in computing the maximum carryover period. If the S election is in effect for the entire carryover period, the regular corporation carryover will be permanently lost [¶3110].

- LIFO recapture on converting from regular to S corporation [¶3107(e)].

¶3117   FAMILY INCOME SPLITTING

If you want to channel some of the profits from your business into the hands of your children at a minimum cost, operating your business as an S corporation is an excellent way to do it.

> **Example 1:** Mr. Smith is the sole shareholder of Es Corp. that has an annual taxable income of $50,000. He has three children, each of whom is over 14 years of age. If Mr. Smith does nothing, the corporation's entire $50,000 taxable income each year will be passed through to him and he will pay taxes on it. On the other hand, if Mr. Smith gives 10% of his stock to each of the three children, retaining 70% for himself, he only has to pay tax on $35,000 of his corporation's annual taxable income—his three children will each pay tax on $5,000. If Mr. Smith gets started early enough, he will be able to pay the entire cost of their college educations with income taxed at the children's lower rate.

> **NOTE:** For your S corporation arrangement to split income, two conditions must be met: (1) The compensation paid to owner-employees (i.e., you) by the corporation must be reasonable in relation to the services performed and the property contributed to the corporation. Otherwise, the IRS can adjust the corporation's income to conform it to the realities of the situation; (2) The transfer of shares to your children must be more than a "paper" transaction. This means that, in addition to enjoying legal title, your children must also be able to enjoy the beneficial ownership of the stock received. Otherwise, the IRS can treat you as the real owner of the stock and tax all of the corporation's income to you.

It may not be easy to tell whether a transfer of S corporation stock by you to your children (or other family members) will effectively transfer the income attributable to the stock to them. Four criteria have been applied, although no one criterion controls:

- Your children must be able to exercise effectively their ownership rights over their shares;
- You must not be able to continue to exercise complete dominion and control over the transferred stock;
- You must not be able to continue to enjoy the economic benefits of ownership after conveying the stock; and
- You must have dealt at arm's length with the corporation involved.

If all four criteria are met, your transfer of the shares will probably be considered bona fide. Anything less than perfection can create problems, particularly in view of the fact that transfers of property between family members are subject to special scrutiny to determine whether they really are what they appear to be on their face.

If you have substantial income from sizable investments in stocks, bonds, real estate, etc., using an S corporation is now a convenient way to share that income and the tax on it with your family members.

> ➤ **WHAT TO DO** Simply transfer the stocks, bonds, real estate, or other investments to an S Corporation formed for the purpose of holding them and transfer shares of its stock to your children or grandchildren, keeping the balance for yourself.

Result: From that point on, you and the children will each be taxed on your pro rata shares of the corporation's annual taxable income. But note that unearned income of *children under 14,* in excess of $1,200 (in 1992), generally is taxed at your rates [¶1240]. Furthermore, you will be able to increase their shares of the assets that produce the corporate income with a minimum amount of inconvenience simply by transferring additional shares of stock to them.

> **Example 2:** Mr. Baker has four children over 14 years old and investment assets worth $1,000,000 that produce an annual income of $150,000. He also enjoys a substantial salary. He doesn't need all of his investment income and he would like to share some of it, as well as the tax on it, with his children. He would also, as an estate-planning move, like to start transferring ownership of at least some portion, if not all, of the assets that produce the investment income to his children, while at the same time keeping control of the assets.

Mr. Baker should form an S corporation, transferring his $1,000,000 of investment assets to it in return for all of its stock. Then, he and Mrs. Baker could join in a gift of 2% ($20,000 worth) of the stock to each of the four children retaining 92% of the stock for himself. If Mr. Baker chooses, the stock given to the children plus any stock later given to the children can be nonvoting stock, thus ensuring his continued control over the operation as long as he has any stock interest.

At the end of the first year. Mr. Baker owns 92% of the stock and will pay tax on $138,000 of the corporation's income; the children will each own 2% and will each pay tax on $3,000 of the corporation's income at tax rates less than the maximum rate that Mr. Baker pays. There is no gift tax because the $10,000 per-donee gift tax exclusion to which Mr. Baker is entitled became $20,000 when Mrs. Baker joined in the gift, thus adding hers to his.

Ten years down the line: During the next nine years, the assets of the corporation retain their $1,000,000 value and continue to produce $150,000 annual taxable income. Mr. Baker gives 2% of the corporation's stock (nonvoting) to each of the children every year and Mrs. Baker joins with him in the gift.

Result: (a) Mr. Baker has given away 80% of the stock worth $800,000 without any gift tax; (b) he still controls the corporation; (c) he now pays tax on only $30,000 of the corporation's income, while the children pay tax on $120,000; and (d) the family's overall tax liability has been reduced. This has been accomplished simply by transferring shares of stock—a relatively easy and uncomplicated procedure.

Compensation for the executive: Mr. Baker should be paid a salary for managing the operation. His work will be similar to that of a corporate trustee managing investments, and a salary similar to that of a typical trustee's fee would be appropriate. It should be noted that any compensation paid to Mr. Baker reduces the income available to be split with the children.

¶3118   DIFFERENCE IN VOTING RIGHTS RULE

Your S corporation can have only one class of stock. As long as all shares of common stock issued have the same rights to corporate income and assets, the fact that they have different voting rights will not create a second class of stock and will not jeopardize your S election.

> ► **OBSERVATION** There seems to be no limit on the quality or quantity of differences in voting rights permitted. Thus, your corporation can issue common stock with full voting rights along with common stock with no voting rights and common stock with partial voting rights.

(a) Inactive Shareholders. Individuals may wish to invest in your S corporation without being actively involved in its day-to-day operations. Others may want to invest in your S corporation without becoming involved in its day-to-day management but may want to have something to say about certain major corporate decisions such as a merger, liquidation or sale of a substantial corporate asset.

> ► **WHAT TO DO** Your corporation can issue: (a) common stock with full voting rights to those shareholders who will actively manage the business, (b) common stock whose voting rights are limited to certain key issues to those shareholders who are not interested in actively managing the business but do want to be heard on certain major issues and (c) nonvoting stock to those shareholders who prefer to be pure investors.

Caution. In general, losses from a passive activity (an interest in an active business in which taxpayer doesn't materially participate) are currently deductible only against income from passive activities [¶2326].

(b) Weighted Voting Rights. When your S corporation is organized, some shareholders may contribute capital in the form of money or assets while others may contribute services. In such cases, the shareholders contributing services frequently want to make sure that they control the corporation, even though the number of shares they hold wouldn't automatically guarantee it. It also sometimes happens that, in forming your S corporation, minority shareholders, looking to protect their investment, will want to put one or more of their members on the board of directors, or in some other way be able to exercise some influence, even though the number of shares they own ordinarily does not guarantee them this power.

> **WHAT TO DO** Issue common stock to the various shareholders with voting rights specifically geared to guaranteeing them control, the right to elect directors, the right to veto certain actions taken by a majority of the board of directors, or the right to do whatever they happen to be interested in doing.

¶3119 INCREASING PASSTHROUGH LOSS DEDUCTIONS USING DEBT

One of the best reasons for a new company to elect S corporation status is that possible losses in its formative years will be passed through to the shareholders and can be used by them to offset other income on their personal income tax returns. As indicated before [¶3110], however, a current deduction for a loss passthrough to you cannot exceed your adjusted basis for the stock plus the basis of any indebtedness the corporation owes you.

> **OBSERVATION** Under prior law, any excess of loss over basis was lost forever. Now, however, you can carry over losses in excess of basis indefinitely until your basis for your stock and debt is increased sufficiently to absorb them.

The easiest way you can increase your basis in S corporation stock to absorb a loss passthrough is to make a contribution to capital. The problem here is that, if there is more than one shareholder, a contribution to capital by one shareholder becomes part of every shareholder's interest in the corporation. As a result, S corporation shareholders frequently resort to making direct loans to the corporation to increase the company's indebtedness to them. This technique seems simple, but the manner in which it is handled can make a big difference.

(a) Loan Guarantees Do Not Increase Debt Basis. If your small company needs operating money and gets a bank loan, the bank will normally ask you for a loan guarantee or note endorsement. The mere guarantee of a loan only creates a contingent debt; however, it does not create a corporate indebtedness to you. Take this typical situation:

Example 1: *Year 1:* Sole shareholder's stock basis is $10,000. S Corporation gets a $7,500 bank loan, payable in two years, to meet operating expenses. Shareholder is the guarantor. The corporation's operating losses for the year are $10,000. Result: Shareholder can deduct the full $10,000 loss passthrough, but her stock basis is now zero ($10,000 minus $10,000). *Year 2:* S Corporation has a $5,000 operating loss. *Result:* None of the loss is currently deductible by the shareholder. She has a zero basis in the stock and no indebtedness basis because the loan guarantee is treated as a contingent debt. She must carry over the loss until her stock and/or debt basis increases enough to absorb it.

> **THE RIGHT WAY** Instead of guaranteeing the loan, the shareholder can personally borrow the money from a bank and lend it to the corporation. She is still liable, but now she has generated a basis for deducting the entire loss passthrough in Year 2. A possible disadvantage of this technique is that the loan now appears as a direct liability on her personal financial statement.

(b) Indirect Loans Are Also Ineffective. The guarantee result may have seemed obvious to some because you, at the outset, were not out of pocket. Here are some other situations in which shareholders, in effect, committed their own money but still failed to generate basis.

Example 2: S Corporation and Partnership were owned by the same parties. Partnership lent large sums to the corporation. Result: Although the stockholders of S Corporation and the owners of Partnership were the same, the debt to Partnership was not an indebtedness to the individual partners.[1]

Example 3: The principal shareholder of S Corporation was also the trustee and remainderman of a trust that held a substantial note of the corporation. He claimed that the corporation was indebted to him because of his interest in the trust. Result: The debt of the corporation ran to the trust and not to the shareholder and it did not increase his basis for loss-passthrough purposes.[2]

Example 4: Mrs. Prashker was the sole beneficiary of her husband's estate. She established an S corporation with her son; each owned 50% of the stock and each had a $5,000 stock basis. Mrs. Prashker had the company borrow from her husband's estate. At year's end, the company had a $90,000 net operating loss. Mrs. Prashker claimed her 50% share as a loss passthrough and deducted the amount on her return. She reasoned that, as sole beneficiary of her husband's estate, she actually made the loans. Result: Only $5,000 is currently deductible. Mrs. Prashker had no debt basis with the company. The estate, not Mrs. Prashker, was the company's creditor. The loan came directly from the estate, so her current deduction was limited to her $5,000 stock basis.[3]

➤ **HOW TO SAVE THE DEDUCTION** Mrs. Prashker could have deducted the loss in full by lending to the company herself with funds borrowed from the estate. Unfortunately, she chose a different form and was stuck with the consequences. As with the partnership and trust situations, the loan cannot be indirect. It must be made directly by the shareholder.

Example 5: Two S Corporations had identical owners with virtually the same holdings. When one of the companies operated at a loss, the other company advanced loans to it. Result: The shareholders' debt bases in the faltering company were not increased by the sums the other corporation advanced, and this was true even though the other company was owned by the same people.[4]

➤ **THE RIGHT MOVE** The shareholders should make direct loans to the faltering corporation. These loans would increase their bases.

Footnotes to Chapter 21

(For your added convenience, in brackets [] with the footnotes below, you will find citations to related paragraphs in the "RIA United States Tax Reporter"(USTR), "CCH Federal Tax Reporter"(CCH) and "RIA Federal Tax Coordinator 2d"(FTC) multi-volume services.)

FOOTNOTE ¶ 3100 [USTR ¶ 13,614; CCH ¶ 33,411; FTC ¶ D-1430].

FOOTNOTE ¶ 3101 [USTR ¶ 13,609; CCH ¶ 433,411; FTC ¶ D-1550 et seq.].

FOOTNOTE ¶ 3102 [USTR ¶ 13,614; CCH ¶ 33,426; FTC ¶ D-1520].

(1) Ltr. Rul. 9050030.

(2) GCM 38750.

FOOTNOTE ¶ 3103 [USTR ¶ 13,784; CCH ¶ 33,362; FTC ¶ D-1600 et seq.].

(1) Rev. Proc. 87-32, 1987-2 CB 396.

FOOTNOTE ¶ 3104 [USTR ¶ 13,714; CCH ¶ 33,453; FTC ¶ D-1420].

FOOTNOTE ¶ 3105 [USTR ¶ 13,624; CCH ¶ 33,453; FTC ¶ D-1850].

FOOTNOTE ¶ 3107 [USTR ¶ 13,634; CCH ¶ 433,462; FTC ¶ D-1600].

(1) Treas. Dept. booklet "Tax Information on S Corporations" (1991 Ed.), p. 7.

FOOTNOTE ¶ 3108 [USTR ¶ 13,744; CCH ¶ 33,602; FTC ¶ D-1601.1 et seq.].

FOOTNOTE ¶ 3109 [USTR ¶ 13,664; CCH ¶ 33,484; FTC ¶ D-1700].

FOOTNOTE ¶ 3110 [USTR ¶ 13,664; CCH ¶ 33,484; FTC ¶ D-1601].

(1) Uri., ¶89,058 MM Memo TC.

FOOTNOTE ¶ 3111 [USTR ¶ 13,684; CCH ¶ 33,521; FTC ¶ D-1750 et seq.].

(1) Treas. Dept. booklet "Tax Information on S Corporations" (1991 Ed.), p. 9.

FOOTNOTE ¶ 3112 [USTR ¶ 13,674; CCH ¶ 33,501; FTC ¶ D-1800].

(1) P.L. 97-354.

(2) Harris, US Ct. App (5th Cir.)

FOOTNOTE ¶ 3115 [USTR ¶ 13,609; CCH ¶ 33,411; FTC ¶ D-1430].

FOOTNOTE ¶ 3116 [USTR ¶ 13,609; CCH ¶ 33,411; FTC ¶ D-1430].

(1) Ltr. Rul. 9022024.

(2) Announcement 92-16, IRB 1992-4, clarifying Rev. Rul. 91-26, 1991-1 CB 184.

FOOTNOTE ¶ 3117 [USTR ¶ 13,609; CCH ¶ 33,411; FTC ¶ D-1430].

FOOTNOTE ¶ 3118 [USTR ¶ 13,609; CCH ¶ 33,411; FTC ¶ D-1430].

FOOTNOTE ¶ 3119 [USTR ¶ 13,664; CCH ¶ 33,411; FTC ¶ D-1420].

(1) Frankel, 61 TC 343, aff'd by unpublished order (2 Cir., 11-26-74).

(2) Robertson v. U.S., 32 AFTR 2d 73-5556.

(3) Prashker, 59 TC 172.

(4) Lee, ¶76,265 PH Memo TC.

CHAPTER 22

CORPORATIONS— REORGANIZATIONS—STOCK REDEMPTIONS

REORGANIZATIONS

If your corporation engages in a tax-free reorganization, it can acquire another corporation, modify its capital structure or dispose of an unwanted business without triggering a taxable gain or deductible loss at the corporate or shareholder level.

¶3200   GENERAL RULES

A reorganization is a readjustment of corporate structure or ownership. It may occur when your corporation (new or existing) acquires stock or property of one or more corporations, or when your existing corporation changes its capital structure, name or form, or place of organization. Thus, for example, it may cover the merger or consolidation of your company with another; an acquisition of a subsidiary by an exchange of stock; an acquisition by your company of the assets of another in exchange for stock; a division of your company into two or more companies; or a merger of your parent company with one of its subsidiaries or your subsidiary with a parent. Additionally, your corporation can use a so-called divisive reorganization [¶3220 et. seq.] to divide its existing businesses among two or more corporate shells and then transfer some or all of those businesses to you and its other shareholders.

There are seven types of reorganizations [IRC Sec. 368(a)(1)]:

- Statutory merger or consolidation (Type A) [¶3203; 3210].
- Acquiring another corporation's stock (Type B) [¶3204; 3210].
- Acquiring another corporation's property (Type C) [¶3205; 3210].
- Transfer of assets to another corporation (Type D) [¶3206; 3210].
- Recapitalization (Type E) [¶3207; 3210].
- Change in identity, form or place of organization of *one* corporation (Type F) [¶3208; 3210].
- Insolvency reorganization (Type G) [¶3209; 3210].

Tax consequences. Once a transaction qualifies as a "reorganization" (as discussed below), these results follow:

- Your corporation recognizes no gain or loss on the exchange, nor do you and the other shareholders [¶3211]. However, your corporation must recognize gain to the extent it receives cash or other taxable "boot" that it does not distribute it to its shareholders. On the other hand, you and the other shareholders recognize gain if your corporation does distribute the boot [¶3213].
- Your basis in stock or securities surrendered carries over to and must be allocated among the stock or securities received from your corporation [¶3215]. The same basis rule for stock or securities generally applies to your corporation. But if your corporation receives property in a tax-free reorganization, it gets the transferor's basis in that property [¶3216].
- The tax attributes (loss carryovers, earnings and profits, accounting methods and the like) of the corporation whose assets are acquired are usually "inherited" by the acquiring corporation [¶3236; ¶3237].

Information reporting. Generally, corporations involved in acquisitions and capitalizations of $10 million or over must file an information return on Form 8820 [IRC Sec. 6043(c); Prop. Reg. Sec. 1.6043-4].

¶3201   "PARTY" TO A REORGANIZATION

To benefit from a tax-free reorganization, you must be either a "party to the reorganization" or the holder of stock or securities in such a party [IRC Sec. 354, 361; Reg. Sec. 1.361-1]. Specifically, a party is: (1) a corporation resulting from a reorganization, and (2) both corporations in a reorganization resulting from the acquisition by one corporation of the stock or properties of the other [IRC Sec. 368(b); Reg. Sec. 1.368-2(f)].

> **Example:** Corporations X and Y are both parties if Corp. X is merged into Corp. Y; if Corporations X and Y are consolidated into Corp. Z, all three are parties (Type A reorganizations). Also, both are parties if Corp. X transfers substantially all of its assets to Corp. Y in exchange for voting stock (Type C) [Reg. Sec. 1.368-2(f)].

Furthermore, if your corporation controls an acquiring corporation, it is a party to a reorganization if its stock or securities were used to acquire stock or assets of a third corporation [IRC Sec. 368(b)(2); Reg. Sec. 1.368-2(f)]. An acquiring corporation remains a party even if it transfers all or part of the stock or assets acquired to a controlled subsidiary [IRC Sec. 368(a)(2)(C); Reg. Sec. 1.368-2(f)].

Your corporation is a party to a reorganization if it issues new stock certificates after a change of name (Type F reorganization), in exchange for its shareholder's stock. The same is true if your corporation issues preferred stock in exchange for its shareholders' common, as part of a recapitalization (Type E).[1]

Definition of securities. The term "securities" includes bonds and debenture notes. It does not include short-term purchase money notes;[2] but long-term notes may be considered securities[3] [IRC Sec. 1.368-1].

KEY REQUIREMENTS

A transaction can qualify as a tax-free reorganization only if the following four requirements are satisfied [IRC Sec. 368; Reg. Sec. 1.368-1, 1.368-2]:

1. Plan of reorganization. The reorganization must be done according to a plan adopted in advance by each corporation concerned. The exchange of stock, securities or property is not tax-free unless undertaken pursuant to the terms of this plan.

2. Business purpose. The reorganization must be required by business needs. It cannot be done solely as a device to avoid taxes. In other words, if the transaction doesn't make sense apart from the tax considerations, it's likely there is no business purpose.

> NOTE: While an intention to avoid tax liability will not of itself make a transaction ineffective, a plan that complies literally with the statute will not accomplish the nonrecognition of gain, if it has no other business or corporate purpose.[1]

3. Continuity of business enterprise under a modified corporate form.
The acquiring corporation *must* (1) continue the acquired corporation's historic business, or (2) use a significant portion of the acquired corporation's assets in a continuing business [Reg. Sec. 1.368-1(d)].

If the acquired corporation has more than one line of business, continuity of business enterprise requires only that the acquiring corporation continue a significant line of business. Also, the continuity of business enterprise requirement is satisfied if the acquiring corporation uses a significant portion of the acquired corporation's historic business assets in a business [IRC Sec. 368; Reg. Sec. 1.368-1].

4. Continuity of interest. There must be a continuity of ownership interest (except in a Type D reorganization [¶3206]) on the part of the owners of the corporation before and after the reorganization. This means that the original shareholders must have an ownership interest in the reorganized corporation or corporations. Continuity requires some equity interest, as opposed to a mere creditor interest.

> NOTE: The continuity of interest test insures that a purchase and sale of corporate assets will not be disguised in the form of a corporate reorganization. Thus, if all the shareholders of your corporation exchange their stock solely for bonds of the acquiring company, the continuity of interest requirement will not be met—in effect, they have "sold" their interest to the new company. Under these circumstances, tax is imposed at the time of the exchange.

TYPES OF REORGANIZATIONS

¶3203   STATUTORY MERGER OR CONSOLIDATION (TYPE A)

To qualify as a Type A reorganization, the transaction must be a merger or consolidation made in accordance with state law. In a merger, one corporation acquires another corporation. The acquired company is dissolved and its assets and liabilities are taken over by the acquiring company. In a consolidation, two or more corporations combine to form a new corporation. The original corporations are dissolved [IRC Sec. 368(a)(1)(A); Reg. Sec. 1.368-2(b)].

NOTE: The tax law does not specify the type of consideration that may be given in a merger or consolidation. But securities or other property (as opposed to stock) cannot be all, or even too high a proportion, of the consideration given to the stockholders. Receipt of too much consideration other than stock has been held to break the continuity of interest [¶3202] with the result that the reorganization was denied tax-free treatment.[1] For transfer of acquired assets to controlled subsidiary, see ¶3205(c).

A controlled corporation (i.e., a subsidiary) can use its parent's stock to acquire substantially all of the property of another corporation that merges into the subsidiary. Two restrictions: (1)No subsidiary stock can be used and (2) the exchange would have qualified as a Type A reorganization had the merger been into the parent (¶3206(b)) [IRC Sec. 368(a)(2)(D)].

A "reverse merger" of a subsidiary using parent stock into another corporation is also a Type A reorganization if: (1) The surviving corporation holds substantially all of the properties of the merged corporation (except voting stock of the controlled corporation distributed in the transaction); and (2) the former shareholders of the surviving corporation receive voting stock of the controlling corporation in exchange for control of the surviving corporation [IRC Sec. 368(a)(2)(E); Reg. Sec. 1.368-2].

Example: Smallco, an unrelated corporation, may be absorbed (merged) into Subco, a controlled subsidiary of Bigco, in exchange for the voting stock of Bigco. In either case, all three corporations are parties to the reorganization.

¶3204   ACQUIRING ANOTHER CORPORATION'S STOCK (TYPE B)

If your corporation exchanges any of its voting stock (or any of the voting stock of a corporation that controls it) for stock of another corporation, there is a reorganization. However, your corporation must control the other corporation right after the exchange. Your corporation can give either its own voting stock *or* that of its parent (but not both), as long as it does not give anything else [IRC Sec. 368(a)(1)(B); Reg. Sec. 1.368-2(c)].[1] However, a small amount of cash merely to round off fractional shares[2] or a nonassignable contingent contract right to receive additional voting stock[3] does not disqualify the reorganization. Nor does the exchange of debentures, in a separate taxable transaction, if the debentures are not additional consideration for the acquired stock.[4] But convertible rights to purchase additional shares of stock do disqualify the reorganization.[5]

Control means ownership of at least 80% of the voting stock and at least 80% of all other classes of stock [IRC Sec. 368(c)(1); Reg. Sec. 1.368-2].

Example 1: If Bigco exchanges 15% of its voting stock for at least 80% of the voting stock and at least 80% of the shares of all other classes of stock of Smallco, there is a reorganization with Bigco and Smallco as parties. If, however, Bigco also gave nonvoting stock or bonds besides voting stock, no reorganization occurs.

It does not matter whether your acquiring corporation had control before the acquisition [IRC Sec. 368(a)(1)(B); Reg. Sec. 1.368-2(c)]. Thus, the stock acquired need not represent 80% control, if there is control after the transaction. This is commonly known as a "creeping" acquisition, and is allowed for Type B reorganizations.

Example 2: Co. P bought 30% of the common stock of Co. S (with only one class of stock outstanding) for cash in 1979. In 1992, Co. P offers to exchange its own voting stock for all of the stock of Co. S within six months from the date of the offer. Within the six-month period, Co. P acquires an additional 60% of Co. S stock for its own voting stock. Co. P now owns 90% of the stock of Co. S and reorganization has occurred. If Corporation P had acquired 80% of Corporation S's stock for cash in 1979, it could likewise acquire some or all of the remainder of such stock solely in exchange for its own voting stock and still have a reorganization.

¶3205 ACQUIRING ANOTHER CORPORATION'S PROPERTY (TYPE C)

If your corporation exchanges any of its voting stock for substantially all the property of a second corporation, there is a reorganization. Your acquiring corporation ordinarily must give only its voting stock [IRC Sec. 368(a)(1)(C); Reg. Sec. 1.368-2(d)]. It may add a small amount of cash merely to round off fractional shares [(a) below].[1]

Example 1: If P Co. exchanges 15% of its voting stock for substantially all the properties of S Co., there is a reorganization, with P Co. and S Co. as parties. If, however, P Co. also gives nonvoting stock or bonds besides the voting stock, it usually is not a reorganization.

There also is a reorganization if a subsidiary acquires substantially all of the property of another corporation solely in exchange for the voting stock of the subsidiary's parent corporation [IRC Sec. 368(a)(1)(C); Reg. Sec. 1.368-2(d)].

Example 2: P Co. owns all the stock of S Co. All the assets of W Co. are transferred to S Co. in exchange for voting stock of P Co. This transaction is a reorganization, with S, P and W as parties [Reg. Sec. 1.368-2(f)].

Generally, if your corporation exchanges property pursuant to a plan of reorganization for stock and securities in another corporation, it doesn't recognize gain or loss. However, gain is recognized to the extent the corporation whose assets are acquired receives property other than stock and securities and doesn't distribute it. For this purpose, transfers of property to creditors to satisfy the corporation's indebtedness in connection with the reorganization are treated as distributions under the plan [IRC Sec. 361].

Exception for distribution of appreciated property. The distributing corporation recognizes gain (but not loss) on the distribution of appreciated property as if such property were sold to the receiving corporation at fair market value [IRC Sec. 361(c)].

No gain is recognized to the distributing corporation, however, when "qualified property" is distributed. Qualified property is stock, stock rights, or an obligation of (1) the distributing corporation or (2) another party to the reorganization that the distributing corporation received in the exchange [IRC Sec. 361(c)(2)(B)].

(a) Giving Other Property. The rule that the acquiring corporation must give only voting stock is relaxed to this extent: If your acquiring corporation gets at least 80% of the fair market value of all the second corporation's property for voting stock, it can add cash and other types of consideration without disqualifying the tax-free reorganization [IRC Sec. 368(a)(2)(B); Reg. Sec. 1.368-2(d)].

Example 3: Co. P acquires Co. S's assets worth $100,000 for $92,000 of P's voting stock plus $8,000 cash. This is a reorganization, even though part of the assets of Co. S are acquired for cash.

Assumed liabilities. An exchange is still considered solely for voting stock if, besides giving voting stock, your acquiring corporation assumes a liability of the other corporation, or acquires property subject to a liability [IRC Sec. 368(a)(1)(C); Reg. Sec. 1.368-2(d)].

Example 4: If Co. P acquires substantially all of the properties of Co. S solely for voting stock and the assumption of a mortgage on the property, the transaction will ordinarily qualify as a reorganization (but see Note 1 below).

If, however, your acquiring corporation gives cash or other property, the total of their value and the value of the assumed liabilities cannot exceed 20% of the fair market value of the property acquired. Otherwise there is no reorganization [IRC Sec. 368(a)(2)(B); Reg. Sec. 1.368-2(d)].

Example 5: Bigco is to acquire the assets of Smallco, worth $100,000. Smallco has liabilities of $50,000, which Bigco is to assume. Bigco can give only voting stock as consideration because the liabilities alone are over 20% of the fair market value of the property.

NOTE 1: If the assumed liabilities are too high a proportion of the consideration given for the property, the reorganization may be denied tax-free treatment because of lack of continuity of interest[2] (¶3202) [Reg. Sec. 1.368-2(d)].

NOTE 2: Even when insufficient to disqualify the tax-free reorganization, other consideration received usually is treated as boot [¶3211(b)]. In a Type C reorganization, however, other consideration in the form of nonvoting stocks and securities of a party to the reorganization comprising 20% or less of the value of the acquired property is not regarded as boot [Reg. Sec. 1.361-1].

(b) Amount of Property Acquired. The term *"substantially all"* of the properties is a relative term. However, as an operating rule for issuing ruling letters, the IRS considers "substantially all" to be at least 90% of the fair market value of the net assets and at least 70% of the fair market value of the gross assets of the transferring corporation.[3] Ultimately, it depends on the facts of any given situation.[4] Thus, 70% of the assets was held to be substantially all, when the value of the retained assets approximately equaled the liabilities and consisted of cash, accounts receivable and 3% of the inventory.[5] But 81% of the assets was held not to be substantially all when most of the retained assets were operating assets, not retained to liquidate liabilities.[6] On the other hand, 86% and 90% have been held to be substantially all.[7]

In determining the percentage of property transferred, value rather than cost is used.[8] The term "properties" does not include retained surplus cash which might have been paid out as a dividend before the transfer.[9]

(c) Transfer of Acquired Assets to Controlled Subsidiary. Your acquiring corporation may transfer the acquired assets to a controlled subsidiary in exchange for your corporation's voting stock held by the subsidiary. This exchange is normally tax-free to both and will not disqualify the tax-free status of the reorganization [IRC Sec. 368(a)(2)(C)]. This is true even if your then acquiring corporation transfers assets to its sub-subsidiary.[10]

NOTE 3: A transaction that qualifies as both a Type C and a Type D reorganization [¶3206] is treated as Type D [IRC Sec. 368(a)(2)(A)].

¶3206 TRANSFER OF ASSETS TO ANOTHER CORPORATION (TYPE D)

A transfer by your corporation of some or all of its assets to a second corporation is a reorganization if:

1. Immediately after the transfer your corporation (transferor), its shareholders (including persons who were shareholders immediately before the transfer), or any combination of these, are in control of the second corporation (transferee); and

2. Stock or securities of the transferee are distributed by your corporation under the conditions listed in (b) below.

(a) Control means ownership of at least 50% of the voting stock or 50% of the value of all classes of stock [IRC Sec. 368(a)(2)(H)]. For this purpose, the constructive ownership rules of Sec. 318(a), with some modification, will be applied to determine control [IRC Sec. 304(c)(3)].

NOTE: The rules are designed to allow liquidation-reincorporation transactions that effect a bailout of earnings and profits and a step-up in basis at the cost of a capital gain tax to be treated as D reorganizations.

The stock owned by the shareholders need not be in the same proportion as it was before the transfer. However, disproportionate stock ownership may create taxable compensation or gifts from one shareholder to another [¶1619].

(b) Distributions of Stock. The stock and securities received by your corporation from the transferee corporation must be distributed to you and cour corporation's other shareholders in one of the following ways [IRC Sec. 368(a)(1)(D)]:

- Under the plan of reorganization and together with substantially all of your corporation's remaining properties, which usually results in complete liquidation of your corporation [IRC Sec. 354(b); Reg. Sec. 1.354-1(a)], or
- In a divisive reorganization [¶3220-3225]. Distributions may be made if your corporation transferred only part of its assets.

(c) If No Distribution Is Made. Although there will be no reorganization, the transaction may nevertheless result in nonrecognition of gain or loss to your corporation as an exchange of property for stock in a corporation controlled by your corporation (¶1619) [IRC Sec. 351].

¶3207   CHANGE IN CAPITAL STRUCTURE (TYPE E)

A recapitalization is an arrangement by which the stock and bonds of your corporation are readjusted as to amount, income, or priority, or an agreement of all stockholders and creditors to increase or decrease the capitalization or debts of your corporation, or both [IRC Sec. 368(a)(1)(E); Reg. Sec. 1.368-2(e)]. Cash payments received to round off fractional shares resulting from the recapitalization do not disqualify the reorganization.[1] The following illustrates recapitalization:

- Your corporation has $200,000 par value of bonds outstanding. Instead of paying them off in cash, it discharges the obligation by issuing preferred shares, or new bonds,[2] to the bondholders.
- There is surrendered to your corporation for cancellation 25% of its preferred stock in exchange for no par value common stock.
- Your corporation issues preferred stock, previously authorized but unissued, for outstanding common stock.
- An exchange of outstanding preferred stock (with certain priorities as to the amount and time of payment of dividends and the distribution of the corporate assets upon liquidation) for a new issue of common stock having no such rights.
- Outstanding preferred stock with dividends in arrears is exchanged for a similar amount of preferred stock plus stock (preferred or common) for the dividends in arrears.

¶3208   CHANGE IN IDENTITY, FORM OR PLACE OF ORGANIZATION (TYPE F)

A Type F reorganization is defined in the Code as "a mere change in identity, form or place of organization of one corporation" [Sec. 368(a)(1)(F)]. The specific limitation to a single operating corporation applies to reorganizations after August 31, 1982 (but not to those occurring before 1983 if the reorganization plans were adopted before September 1, 1982).

Overlap. A Type F reorganization may also constitute a Type A, C or D reorganization. In the event of such an overlap, the IRS has held that the transaction is treated as a Type F,[1] which is more liberal for purposes of closing the tax year and carrying back a net operating loss [¶3236].

¶3209   INSOLVENCY REORGANIZATION (TYPE G)

A Type G reorganization covers transfers of assets in Bankruptcy Act cases and receiverships, foreclosures and similar cases under federal or state law [IRC Sec. 368(a)(1)(G) and (3)].

To qualify as a Type G reorganization, there must be a transfer pursuant to a court-approved reorganization plan of substantially all your debtor corporation's assets to an acquiring corporation. In determining whether substantially all of the assets were transferred, your corporation's need to pay creditors or to sell assets or divisions to raise cash must be taken into account. In addition, stock or securities of the acquiring corporation must be distributed in a transaction that qualifies under IRC Sec. 354, 355 or 356 [¶3211-3214 and ¶3220-3225]. To satisfy this distribution requirement, some of your corporation's security holders must receive stock or securities [IRC Sec. 368].[1]

> **Example:** Debtor Corp. transfers all its assets to Acquiring Corp. in exchange for Acquiring stock. The stock is distributed to Debtor Corp.'s security holders and trade creditors in exchange for their claims against the corporation. Debtor Corp's shareholders get nothing for their stock.

The rules applying to Type G reorganizations are more flexible than those for other reorganizations. For example, Type G reorganizations do not have to comply with state merger laws (as do Type A). There is no requirement that former shareholders of your debtor corporation control the acquiring corporation after the exchange (as in Type D). There are no restrictions on the kind of consideration that may be issued (such as the "solely for voting" stock rule of Types B and C).

Continuity of interest. You and the other owners of your corporation must maintain a substantial proprietary interest in the reorganized business enterprise [¶3202]. In determining whether continuity exists, the most senior class of creditors who receive stock for their claims along with all equal and junior classes (and any shareholders who receive consideration for their stock) should be treated as owners of your corporation.[1] For transfers by financial institutions, the "continuity of business enterprise" requirement is satisfied if (1) the acquiring corporation assumes all of the deposits of your corporation and (2) the acquiring corporation continues to hold at least one-half of the fair market value of the assets, including mortgages and other loans, held by your corporation at the time of reorganization. Assets disposed of in the ordinary course of business by the acquiring corporation will not be taken into account for this purpose.[2]

Triangular reorganizations (where a corporation acquires a debtor corporation using stock of its parent corporation rather than its own stock) are allowed. Reverse mergers are also allowed if (1) no former shareholder of the surviving corporation receives any consideration for his stock and (2) the former creditors of the surviving corporation exchange their claims for voting stock of the controlling corporation equal to at least 80% of the value of the debt of the surviving corporation. Furthermore, a corporation that acquires substantially all of the assets of a debtor corporation may transfer the assets to a controlled subsidiary.

Overlap. A Type G reorganization may also qualify as a liquidation under IRC. Sec. 332 [¶3235], an incorporation under IRC Sec. 351, or some other type of IRC Sec. 368 reorganization. If so, it will nevertheless be treated as a Type G reorganization. Conversely, a transaction in a bankruptcy or similar case that does not qualify as a Type G reorganization may still qualify as another type of IRC Sec. 368 reorganization.

¶3210   REORGANIZATION CHART

The chart below summarizes the effects that the seven types of reorganizations have on the parties to the reorganizations.

REORGANIZATION CHART		
Type of Reorg.	**Parties before Reorganization**	**Parties after Reorganization**
A	Y merger (Y into X) X	X
	X consolidation (X + Y) Y	W (new corp.)
B	X gives only its voting stock (all or part) for 80% control of stock of Y	X (parent) Y (subsidiary)
	W Owns 80% control of X which gives only W's voting stock (all or part) for 80% control of stock of Y	W owns 80% control of X which owns 80% control of stock of Y
C	X gives only its voting stock (all or part) for substantially all the property of Y	X owns former assets of Y X's voting stock is only asset
	W owns 80% control of X which gives only W's voting stock (all or part) for substantially all the property of Y	W owns 80% control of X which owns the former assets of Y W's voting stock is only asset
D	(1) X transfers all or part of its assets to Y in exchange for 50% stock control of Y	
	(2) X distributes all of its Y stock to its (X's) stockholders	X Y controlled by X's stockholders
E*	X has a capital and debt structure before recapitalization of:	X has a capital and debt structure after recapitalization of:
	common stock only	issues preferred stock in exchange for 50% of the common stock	common and preferred stock
	common stock and bonds	issues preferred stock to pay off bonds	common and preferred stock
	Class A common and preferred class B common stock	50% of preferred is surrendered in exchange for class B common	class A common, class B common, and preferred stock
	class A common and class B common stock	all of class B may be exchanged for class A or for (new) preferred	class A common and preferred stock

F*	Y		changes its name to X and substitutes stock for stock	X		
	X	N.Y. Corp.	reincorporates in New Jersey	X	N.J. Corp.	
	X	charter revoked or expired	(reincorporates)	X		
G	X	(debtor)	(1) transfers assets pursuant to court-approved bankruptcy plan to Y for Y stock, then (2) distributes Y stock to security holders and creditors (X stock worthless)	Y	X (survivor) controlled by	Y

* In Types E and F, only a few of the possible examples are given.

GAIN OR LOSS

¶3211   RECOGNITION OF GAIN OR LOSS

Subject to certain conditions, gain or loss on exchanges in reorganizations is not recognized either to shareholders or to the corporate parties to the reorganization.

(a) Holders of Stocks and Securities. Corporate as well as noncorporate holders of stock or securities in a corporation that is a party to a reorganization [¶3201] can exchange the stock or securities without recognition of gain or loss if the exchange is solely for stock or securities in the same corporation or in another corporation that is a party to the same reorganization [IRC Sec. 354; Reg. Sec. 1.354-1].

> **NOTE:** This type of exchange is not made in divisive [¶3220] or insolvency [¶3209] reorganizations [IRC Sec. 354(b)(1)]. If the reorganization qualifies as divisive, nontaxable exchanges may still be made under IRC Sec. 355 [¶3220]. See also ¶3206(b).

Limit on tax-free exchange of securities. If the principal amount of the securities you receive are greater than the principal amount of the securities you give up, you treat the fair market value of the excess as "boot." If you do not surrender securities, the fair market value of the securities you receive is boot. The receipt of boot is taxable to you [¶3213]. Also, interest income is recognized to the extent the new stock, securities or other property you received is attributable to accrued but unpaid interest on the securities on or after the beginning of your holding period [IRC Sec. 354(a)(2), 356(d)(2)(B); Reg. Sec. 1.354-1(b), 1.356-3].

> **Example 1:** In a tax-free recapitalization [¶3207], Jones surrenders a bond in the principal amount of $1,000 in exchange for bonds in the principal amount of $1,500 with fair market value of $1,575. The fair market value of the excess principal amount is $525 ($1,575 × $500/$1,500). It is treated as "boot" to Jones.

> **NOTE:** If an exchange consists of the surrender of stock for securities, no securities are given up and no stock received, the transaction resembles a redemption of the stock. In such case, the fair market value of the securities (boot) may be taxed as capital gain if the redemption is found to be disproportionate [¶3240].

Giving or receiving other consideration. If you, as a security holder, give other property in the exchange besides stock or securities in a corporation which is a party to the reorganization, you must recognize gain or loss on the property when the value you receive for it is more or less than its adjusted basis (¶1615(b)) [Reg. Sec. 1.358-1(a)]. If you receive consideration other than the stock or securities in a corporation that is a party to the reorganization, it may be treated as boot (¶3213) [IRC Sec. 356(a)(1); Reg. Sec. 1.356-1(a)].

NOTE: Stock rights and stock warrants are not counted as "stock or securities" [Reg. Sec. 1.354-1(e)].

(b) Corporation Exchanging Property for Stock or Securities. In this type of reorganization, your transferor corporation gives up property and receives back any combination of stock, securities or property from a transferee corporation. Your corporation can receive back stock, securities, or *property* without recognizing gain provided certain conditions are met [IRC Sec. 361(a); Reg. Sec. 1.361.1].

Although gain or loss generally won't be recognized to a corporation that exchanges property pursuant to a plan of reorganization for stock or securities in another corporation, your corporation recognizes gain to the extent it receives property other than the stock or securities and doesn't distribute that property pursuant to the plan of reorganization [IRC Sec. 361(a), (b)].

Transfers of property to creditors to satisfy your corporation's indebtedness in connection with the reorganization are treated as distributions under the plan.

Example 2: Corporation A transfers appreciated property to Corporation B in exchange for cash as part of a reorganization. A uses the cash to pay its creditors. A is not required to recognize gain on account of the cash received.

Generally, a distributing corporation in a reorganization recognizes gain, but not loss, on the distribution of appreciated property to its shareholders [IRC Sec. 361(c)]. The corporation is treated as having sold the property to the shareholders at fair market value. There is an exception, however, which states that no gain is recognized on the distribution of the following two types of "qualified property":

• stock (or rights to acquire stock) in, or the obligation of, the distributing corporation; and
• stock (or rights to acquire stock) in, or the obligation of, another corporation that is a party to the reorganization. These securities must have been received by the distributing corporation in the exchange.

The transfer of qualified property by your corporation to its creditors in satisfaction of indebtedness is treated as a distribution pursuant to the plan of reorganization. Therefore, if your corporation, as party to the reorganization, pays off its creditors with stock or debt of another corporation that is party to the reorganization, your corporation does not recognize any gain from the payments.

Suppose a shareholder takes property subject to a liability and assumes the debt. For purposes of determining gain, the property's fair market value is treated as not less than the amount of the liability. The assumption of the liability generally is not treated as the receipt of other property or money [IRC Sec. 357].

(c) Corporation Exchanging Its Own Stock or Securities for Property. If your corporation gives up its own stock or securities and receives property, it also recognizes no gain or loss [¶3024]. If your corporation also gives up property, however, it recognizes gain or loss on this other property [¶1615(b)].

¶3212   TABULAR SYNOPSIS

The following table lists the Code Section that participants in exchanges made under a plan of reorganization [¶3203-3209] derive their nonrecognition of gain or loss.

Exchanger	Section
1. Corporation, a party to a reorganization, giving stock and securities of its own issue.	§ 1032
2. Corporation, a party to a reorganization, giving property.	§ 361
3. A holder, giving stock or securities in a party to a reorganization [but see ¶3211(a)].	§ 354

➤ **OBSERVATION** A corporation giving stock or securities as a party to a reorganization may be a party giving property under IRC Sec. 361 or a holder under IRC Sec. 354.

¶3213   TREATMENT OF BOOT

When your corporation receives boot in an exchange connected with a reorganization, as well as the stocks or securities that it can receive without recognizing gain or loss, the following rules apply:

- No loss is recognized [IRC Sec. 356(c), 361(b)(2); Reg. Sec. 1.356-1, 1.361-1]. See also ¶3211(b).
- Your corporation recognizes gain up to the value of boot it receives, unless boot is distributed under the plan of reorganization [¶3211(b)].

Example 1: Corporation J transferred part of its assets to Corporation K for 80% of the voting stock and 80% of all other classes of stock of Corporation K, plus $50,000 in cash. This cash is boot to J, unless distributed to its shareholders.

- Your corporation's shareholders recognize gain, but not in excess of the boot received [IRC Sec. 356(a)(1); Reg. Sec. 1.356-1].

Example 2: Pursuant to a plan of reorganization, Anderson exchanged 100 shares of stock of Co. X (cost to him, $5,000) for 200 shares of Co. Y into which Co. X is merging. In addition, Anderson received $200 in cash. The Y Co. shares had a fair market value of $5,500. The gain to Anderson is $700, but that gain is recognized only to the extent of $200. The basis of the Y shares becomes $5,000 (¶3215). If the Y stock had a fair market value of only $4,000, the loss of $800 would not be recognized and the basis of the Y shares would be $4,800. If all of Anderson's X stock did not have the same basis, the realized gain or loss would be computed separately for each basis.[1]

NOTE: For recognition of gain or loss to the giver of boot, see ¶3211(a), (c).

Exchange for Sec. 306 stock. If your corporation receives boot in exchange for Sec. 306 stock, an amount equal to the sum of the money and the fair market value of the other boot is treated as a dividend to the extent your corporation had earnings and profits when it distributed the Sec. 306 stock. The term "Sec. 306 stock" refers to certain preferred stock issued as a stock dividend (¶3243) [IRC Sec. 356(e)]. This is true whether the shareholder realizes a gain or loss.

For treatment of bonds as boot, see ¶3211(a).

¶3214   GAIN TAXED AS DIVIDEND

If money or other property you and the other shareholders receive from your corporation in connection with an exchange of stock or securities [¶3213] has the effect of a dividend, the gain recognized may be taxed as a dividend. This rule is subject to the "attribution" (constructive ownership) rules explained at ¶3244. You and the other stockholders treat your proportionate share of the earnings and profits as a dividend [¶1218]. Any remainder is a capital gain[1] [IRC Sec. 356(a)(2); Reg. Sec. 1.356-1].

> **Example:** The X Co. has capital of $100,000 and earnings and profits of $50,000. In the current year the X Co. transferred all of its assets to the Y Co. in exchange for all of the stock of the Y Co. and the payment of $50,000 in cash to the stockholders of the X Co. This is a reorganization, and X and Y are parties to the reorganization. Astor, who owns 100 of the 1,000 shares of stock in the X Co. for which he paid $10,000, receives 100 shares of Y stock worth $10,000 and $5,000 in cash. The $5,000 of cash is a dividend.
> Suppose that instead of receiving $5,000 in cash, Astor received $7,500 in cash. Then $5,000 of that $7,500 would be taxable as a dividend, the remainder ($2,500) as capital gain.

BASIS

¶3215   BASIS TO DISTRIBUTEE-STOCKHOLDER

Your basis in the stock or securities you receive in a nontaxable exchange in a reorganization is the same as the basis of the stock or securities you exchange. This basis must be *decreased by:* (1) any money you receive, (2) the fair market value of any other property you receive, and (3) any loss that you recognized [¶3211(a)]. It must be *increased by:* (1) any amount that was treated as a dividend (e.g., Sec. 306 stock), and (2) any gain you recognized on the exchange [IRC Sec. 358(a)(1); Reg. Sec. 1.358-1(a)]. The basis of any other property you receive is its fair market value on the date of exchange [IRC Sec. 358(a)(2); Reg. Sec. 1.358-1].

> **Example 1:** Pursuant to a plan of reorganization, Mr. Albert exchanged 100 shares of stock of the X Co. he had bought for $10,000 for 200 shares of Y Co. stock having a fair market value of $11,000. No gain is recognized on the exchange. The cost basis of the Y shares to Albert is $10,000.

> **Example 2:** Mr. Vickers surrenders stock that has a basis of $1,000 in his hands in a tax-free recapitalization. He receives in exchange stock that has a value of $500 and a bond with a value of $750. The bond is "boot" [¶3211]. Actual gain on the deal is $250. Any part treated as a dividend is taxed as such; the remainder, if any, is taxed as a capital gain. The basis of the new stock is $500 determined as follows: $1,000 (basis of old stock) minus $750 (value of the other property), plus $250 (gain taxed), or $500. The basis of the bond is $750.

Allocation of basis. If you receive several kinds of stock or securities, your basis must be allocated among the properties received in proportion to their relative fair market values [IRC Sec. 358(b)(1); Reg. Sec. 1.358-2].

> **Example 3:** In a tax-free reorganization, Mr. Albert exchanged 100 shares of X Co. stock for 50 shares of Y Co. common stock (value $15,000) and 50 shares of Y Co. preferred stock (value $10,000). Albert's 100 shares of X Co. stock had a cost basis to him of $10,000. The total value of the Y Co. stock received is $25,000, of which $15,000 or three-fifths is represented by the common stock and $10,000 or two-fifths is represented by the preferred stock. The combined bases of the two classes of Y Co. stock ($10,000) are apportioned according to their respective values. The basis of the Y common stock is ⅗ of $10,000, or $6,000. The basis of the Y preferred stock is ⅖ of $10,000 or $4,000.

For basis in divisive reorganizations, see ¶3225.

¶3216   BASIS TO CORPORATION

The basis of property acquired by your corporation in connection with a tax-free reorganization is the same as it would be in the transferor's hands, increased by any gain recognized to the transferor on the transfer [IRC Sec. 362(b); Reg. Sec. 1.362-1].

Example: X Corporation owns property with a basis of $10,000 and a fair market value of $20,000. X Corporation transfers the property to Y Corporation for all of Y's stock, and distributes the Y stock to the X Corp. shareholders. This is a reorganization, and the exchange is nontaxable. Y Corporation's basis in the property received from X Corporation is $10,000.

If your corporation acquires stocks or securities in a corporation that is a party to the reorganization, your corporation's basis in the stock or securities is the same as the basis of the property it exchanged, with the same basis adjustments discussed in ¶3215 [IRC Sec. 358(a)(1); Reg. Sec. 1.358-1]. However, the stock or securities your corporation acquires retain the basis they had in the hands of the transferor if your corporation exchanges its stock or securities (or its parent's stock or securities) as all or part of the consideration for the transfer [IRC Sec. 362(b); Reg. Sec. 1.362-1].

¶3217   LIABILITIES ASSUMED

Your corporation may assume liabilities on property it receives, as part of the consideration for the exchange [¶1619].

(a) Basic Rule. If your corporation acquires property subject to a liability of the transferor, or assumes a liability against property, the assumption or acquisition is not considered money or other property. It does not prevent the exchange from being tax-free, unless the purpose was to avoid taxes or the assumption had no business purpose [IRC Sec. 357(a), (b); Reg. Sec. 1.357-1]. However, your corporation's assumption of liability decreases the basis to the transferor of the property he receives in the exchange [IRC Sec. 358(d); Reg. Sec. 1.358-3]. But see an exception in (b) below.

Example: Corporation X transfers its property with a basis of $100,000 to Corporation Y in return for voting stock of Y and the assumption of a $25,000 mortgage on the property. No gain or loss is recognized to either corporation. X's basis for the stock received is $75,000.

(b) Liabilities in Excess of Basis (Transfers to Controlled Corporation). In an exchange under a Type D reorganization [¶3206], if the liabilities assumed plus the liabilities to which the property is subject exceed the adjusted basis of the property transferred, the excess is treated either as a capital gain or an ordinary gain, as the case may be[1] [IRC Sec. 357(c)(1); Reg. Sec. 1.357-2]. This does not apply either to an exchange in which the assumption of liability is treated as money received because of a tax avoidance or non-bona fide business purpose (see (a) above). Nor does it apply to a Type G reorganization [¶3209] where former shareholders of the transferor don't receive any consideration for the stock [IRC Sec. 357(c)(2); Reg. Sec. 1.357-2].

NOTE: In determining the amount of liabilities assumed or to which the property transferred is subject, the liability is excluded for a cash basis transferor to the extent that its payment by the transferor would have resulted in a deduction or would have constituted payments to partners under IRC Sec. 736(a). However, the liability will be included to the extent that the obligation resulted in the creation of, or an increase in, the basis of any property. Also, the excluded liabilities cannot reduce the transferor's basis in stock received [IRC Sec. 357(c)(3)].

DIVISIVE REORGANIZATIONS

¶3220 GENERAL RULES

For various reasons, your corporation may want to dispose of one or more of its business interests. It can accomplish this result by selling off the underlying assets and distributing the proceeds to you and the other shareholders. But this triggers a two-level tax. First, your corporation must recognize gain on the sale of any appreciated assets. Second, you and the other shareholders have taxable income or gain on the distribution (depending on whether your payout is classified as a dividend or a return of your investment in the company).

Your corporation can avoid one or both of these tax consequences by engaging in a so-called divisive reorganization. Your corporation divides what was formerly held in one corporate shell into two or more corporate shells. Then it distributes the stock in the new corporation (or corporations) to you and the other shareholders, who may give up some or all of your stock in the original corporation.

➤ **TAX-FAVORED RESULT** Neither your corporation nor its shareholders generally owe tax unless the shareholders end up with cash, property or other taxable "boot" in addition to tax-free stock.

There are three types of divisive reorganizations—split-ups, split-offs, and spin-offs. Each divides your corporation into two or more corporations, with the stock of the new corporations in the hands of its original shareholders.

Split-ups. With a tax-free split-up, your corporation (the parent) distributes all of its assets to two or more controlled corporations (which may or may not be newly formed). Then it distributes the stock of the controlled corporations to you and its other shareholders, who give up your stock in the parent.

Example 1: Central Corporation creates Able and Baker Corporations. Central then transfers its manufacturing business to Able in exchange for all of Able's stock. Central also transfers its remaining repair business to Baker in exchange for all of Baker's stock. Finally, Central distributes the Able and Baker stock to its own shareholders, who give up their stock in Central. Result: The transaction qualifies as a tax-free split-up.

Split-offs. A split-off is similar to a split-up, except that your corporation (the parent) keeps some of its assets and transfers the balance to one or more controlled corporations. Then your corporation transfers the stock of the controlled corporations to you and the other shareholders, who give up some of your stock in the parent. With a split-off, your parent corporation remains in business, but in a trimmed-down form.

Example 2: Same as Example 1, except that Central creates only Able Corporation. Central keeps its manufacturing business and transfers the repair business to Able. Then Central distributes the Able stock to its shareholders, who give up 50% of their stock in Central. Result: The transaction now is a tax-free split-off.

Spin-offs. A spin-off is the same as a split-off, except that you and the other shareholders do not surrender any of your stock in the parent corporation.

Example 3: Same as Example 2, except that Central's shareholders get Able stock without giving up any of their Central stock.

Information to be filed. When you corporation distributes stock or securities of a controlled corporation, it must attach a statement to its tax return for the year of the distribution. The statement must demonstrate that the distribution complies with the tax rules governing divisive reorganizations [¶ 3221].

When you receive a distribution, you must attach a statement to your return that lists the stock or securities you surrendered (if any), the stock or securities you received and the names and addresses of all the involved corporations [Reg. Sec. 1.355-5].

¶3221   REQUIREMENTS OF A DIVISIVE REORGANIZATION

Your corporation can make a tax-free distribution of stock (or securities) in another corporation only if it satisfies the five following tax law requirements:

1. Business purpose. Your corporation must have a bona fide business purpose both for dividing its assets between two or more corporations and for distributing stock or securities to its shareholders. A business purpose can include: a reduction of state and/or local taxes (but not federal taxes); compliance with an antitrust divestiture order; splitting off a particular business to the shareholder most able to run it; and enabling a key employee to buy stock of a subsidiary without also buying stock of the parent (if state law prevents the subsidiary from issuing stock directly to the employee) [Reg. Sec. 1.355-2(b)(3)].

If your corporation has a business purpose for dividing its assets but not for distributing stock of the controlled corporation, it does not satisfy the business purpose requirement.

Example 1: Candy Corporation makes candy and toys. Its management wants to protect the candy business from the risks of the toy business by spinning off the toy business to shareholders. Under the tax rules, however, Candy does not have a business purpose for the spin-off. Reason: Candy can accomplish its full objective by putting the toy business in a subsidiary corporation. So there is no business purpose for making a distribution of stock to Candy's shareholders.

Note: A shareholder purpose for effecting a reorganization (e.g., estate planning) is not a bona fide business purpose because it is not a corporate purpose.

2. Active business. Both your parent corporation and the controlled corporations must be engaged in a trade or business that meets each of the following three requirements:

Business operation after distribution: Immediately after the distribution, your parent corporation and each controlled corporation must perform active and substantial management and operational functions for the purpose of earning income or profit [IRC Sec. 355(b)(2)(A); Reg. Sec. 1.355-3(b)(2)(ii) and (iii)]. An active business does not include the holding of stock or other property for investment or the ownership and operation of property unless substantial services are performed in connection with that property.

Minimum holding period: Both the retained and distributed business must have been actively conducted throughout the five-year period ending on the date of the distribution. Changes in products or product capacity during that time will be disregarded provided, however, that the changes are not substantial enough to constitute a new or different business [IRC Sec. 355(b)(2)(B); Reg. Sec. 1.355-3(b)(3)].

Acquisition of distributed business: The distributed business must not have been acquired during a five-year period ending on the date of the distribution in a transaction that triggered gain or loss recognition [IRC Sec. 355(b)(2)(C) and (D); Reg. Sec. 1.355-3(b)(4) and (5)].

Example 2: Since 1983, Corporation A has operated seven retail clothing establishments: six in State X and one in State Y. It has been unable to find reliable suppliers for its State Y store, so it transfers that store to controlled Corporation B. Then it distributes the Corporation B stock to a Mr. Z, a shareholder from State Y, in exchange for his stock in Corporation A.

Result: After the distribution to Mr. Z, both Corporation A and B operate active businesses that have been in existence for more than five years. So the split-off of Corporation B qualifies as a tax-free divisive reorganization.

3. Not a device for distributing earnings and profits. The distribution to you and the other shareholders must not be principally a device to pay out corporate earnings and profits. If, for example, a distribution looks like a dividend, it will be taxed as a dividend—even if it follows the other tax law requirements for divisive reorganizations [IRC Sec. 355(a)(1)(B); Reg. Sec. 1.355(d)(2)].

4. Distribution of stock or securities. Your parent corporation must distribute (1) stock of the controlled corporation (or corporations) to you and the other stockholders or (2) securities of the controlled corporation to its security holders [IRC Sec. 355(a)(1)(A)].

The distribution must consist of all the stock or securities of the controlled corporation that your parent corporation held immediately before the distribution, or an amount to constitute control [IRC Sec. 355(a)(1)(D); Reg. Sec. 1.355-2].

5. Control. Control means the ownership of stock with at least 80% of the total voting power and at least 80% of the total number of shares of all other classes of stock of the corporation [IRC Sec. 368(c)].

¶3222   TAX CONSEQUENCES OF A DIVISIVE REORGANIZATION

Once the above requirements are satisfied, a distribution of stock or securities generally will not trigger gain or loss recognition to you as a shareholder or security holder [IRC Sec. 355(a)]. It makes no difference whether the distribution is pro rata, you surrender any stock, or there even is a plan of reorganization.

Equally important, the distribution will not trigger gain or loss at the corporate level [IRC Sec. 355(c) if the distribution is not made under a plan of reorganization; IRC Sec. 361(c) if it is made under such a plan].

Note, however, that a technical correction clarifies that your distributing corporation must recognize gain (but not loss) if the distribution to you and the other shareholders includes anything other than stock or securities in the controlled corporation. This means that your corporation must recognize gain if it distributes cash or appreciated property (boot) to its shareholders [IRS Sec. 355(c)]. The rule dovetails with the well-established concept that a distribution of "boot" is taxable to shareholders [¶3224].

¶3223   DIVISIVE REORGANIZATIONS INVOLVING LARGE SHAREHOLDERS

Under the current tax rules, your parent corporation may have to recognize gain (but not loss) when it distributes to its shareholders stock or securities of one or more controlled corporations.

The gain recognition rule applies when your parent corporation makes a "disqualified distribution." This is defined as a distribution of "disqualified stock" to you, if, immediately after the distribution, you own a 50-percent or greater interest (by vote or value) in either your parent corporation or a distributed controlled corporation [IRC Sec. 355(d)(2)].

Disqualified stock is any stock in your parent corporation or any controlled corporation that you acquired by "purchase" after October 9, 1990 and within five years before the distribution [IRC Sec. 355(d)(3)]. It also can include stock in a controlled corporation that you received in the distribution.

The term "purchase" is broadly defined for purposes of this rule. It includes not only stock that you bought [IRC Sec. 355(d)(5)(A)], but also stock you received in exchange for transferring cash, marketable stock or securities or debt to a corporation controlled by the shareholder [IRC Sec. 355(d)(5)(B)]. Additionally, a purchase includes stock you acquired in a carryover basis transaction, including a gift, tax-free reorganization, liquidation, or contribution to a partnership or corporation, if the person or entity that surrendered that stock acquired it by purchase [IRC Sec. 355(d)(5)(C)].

> ➤ **BOTTOM LINE** The current crackdown on divisive reorganizations effectively extends the "General Utilities" repeal one step further [¶3234]. It prevents you from buying an interest in a corporation (directly or indirectly) and then having the corporation distribute appreciated stock or securities to you without paying a corporate-level tax.

Example: Baker Corporation is 100% owned by Able Corporation. In 1992, Mr. Klein buys 50% of Able's outstanding shares, principally because he is interested in Baker. Shortly thereafter, Able splits off its Baker stock to Klein and four other Able shareholders. Klein gets 30% of Baker's stock in exchange for giving up a portion of his Able stock.

Result: Able must recognize gain on the Baker stock it distributes to Klein. Reason: Since Klein acquired 50% of Able within the prohibited five-year time period, the Baker stock split off to him is a disqualified distribution.

NOTE: Despite gain recognition at the corporate level, there are no tax consequences to shareholders. So Klein owes no tax in connection with the Able stock he gives up or the Baker stock he receives.

Broad application: Tough anti-abuse rules prevent your corporation from circumventing the corporate gain recognition rule by dividing your corporation's stock ownership among various individuals or entities. These rules apply in the following situations:

• Related taxpayers. Your corporation cannot avoid recognizing gain by splitting up stock ownership among related taxpayers or unrelated taxpayers who are acting in concert. Their stock holdings will be aggregated, and they will be treated as a single taxpayer. For example, if a husband and wife each buy 25% of a corporation, they will be treated as one taxpayer who buys 50%.

• Owners of stock or securities. Any owner of an entity (a corporation, partnership, estate or trust) is treated as owning a proportionate amount of all the stock or securities held by that entity. For example, if you buy 40% of Smallco's stock and your 50%-owned partnership buys another 40%, you are treated as owning 60% of Smallco—the 40% owned outright plus half the 40% owned by the partnership. Note: There is a modest escape hatch for owners of corporations. The rule applies only if you own 10% or more of the corporate stock.

• Deemed purchases. You cannot avoid the five-year holding period by purchasing an interest in an entity that has held stock of a distributing or controlled corporation long enough to satisfy the holding period. Based on the preceding paragraph, you will be treated as purchasing a proportionate amount of the distributing or controlled corporation's stock or securities on the date you purchased an interest in the entity or the date the entity purchased the stock or securities, whichever is later.

• Prospective regulations. Finally, to prevent any other form of "abuse," the Treasury Department is directed to issue future regulations that explain and expand on these rules.

¶3224   SHAREHOLDERS WHO RECEIVE BOOT

In a divisive reorganization, you (as a stock or security holder) may receive cash or other property (boot) in addition to stock or securities of a controlled corporation. Generally, you must recognize gain (but not loss) on the boot you receive. However, if the distribution has the effect of a dividend, it will be taxed to you as ordinary income [IRC Sec. 356(a); Reg. Sec. 1.356-1]:

In addition to cash or property, the following distributions are taxable to you as boot:

- Distributed stock or securities of anything other than a controlled corporation.
- The principal amount of securities of a controlled corporation that exceeds the principal amount of securities you surrendered [IRC Sec. 355(a)(3)(A)].
- Stock of a controlled corporation that the parent corporation acquired within five years of the distribution, but only if the acquisition triggered gain or loss recognition [IRC Sec. 355(a)(3)(B)].
- Any debt or obligation of the controlled corporation that is not a "security."
- Stock rights or warrants.

Example 1: Corporation D distributes the stock of controlled Corporation E and cash to its shareholders in a transaction that qualifies as a spin-off. Result: The distribution of stock is tax-free to the shareholders, but the distribution of cash is taxable as a dividend if the corporation has earnings and profits.

Example 2: Seven years ago, Corporation Y acquired 85% of the stock of controlled Corporation Z. Two years ago, Corporation Y purchased the remaining 15%. Now it splits off Corporation Y. Result: The shareholders owe no tax on the 85% of the stock acquired seven years ago, but the remaining 15% is taxed to them as boot. Reason: Corporation Y did not own its 15% share for the minimum five-year holding period.

Note: If any of the boot is received in exchange for Sec. 306 stock [¶3243], the value of the boot is treated as a dividend [IRC Sec. 356(e); Reg. Sec. 1.356-4].

¶3225   BASIS

In a divisive reorganization, your old adjusted basis carries over and is allocated among (1) any shares you retain in the distributing corporation and (2) any shares you receive in the controlled corporation (or corporations). The allocation is based on the fair market values of the retained and distributed stock (and any stock you surrender) [IRC Sec. 358(c); Reg. Sec. 1.358-2].

Example 1: Mr. Jobe owns 100 shares in Corporation X, which has a basis to him of $10,000 and a market value of $15,000. In a tax-free spin-off, he receives 100 shares of stock in Corporation Y, which has a fair market value of $5,000. After the spin-off, the basis of his X and Y stock is determined as follows:

Market value of X stock	$15,000
Market value of Y stock	5,000
Total value	$20,000
Basis of X stock after spin-off	15,000/20,000 X 10,000 = $ 7,500
Basis of Y stock after spin-off	5,000/20,000 X 10,000 = $ 2,500
Total basis	$10,000

Example 2: Ms. Fredericks owns 200 shares of Corporation X stock that cost her $14,000 and has a fair market value of $40,000. In a tax-free split-off, she gives up half her X stock and receives 50 shares of preferred (value $10,000) and 50 shares of common (value $5,000) in controlled Corporation Y. Her $14,000 basis in the X stock is allocated among the three stocks she holds after the distribution as follows:

Market value of retained X stock	$20,000
Market value of Y stock—preferred	10,000
Market value of Y stock—common	<u>5,000</u>
Total value	$35,000
Basis of retained X stock	20,000/35,000 X 14,000 = $ 8,000
Basis of Y stock—preferred	10,000/35,000 X 14,000 = 4,000
Basis of Y stock—common	5,000/35,000 X 14,000 = <u>2,000</u>
Total basis	$14,000

If you also receive taxable boot, the basis of the retained and distributed stock may have to be adjusted to reflect that boot. Once distributed, the boot has a basis equal to its fair market value.

Basis to distributing corporation. If your parent corporation transfers property to a controlled corporation as a precursor to a divisive reorganization, the controlled corporation has the same basis in that property as the parent. But the basis is increased by any gain recognized on the transfer [IRC Sec. 362(b)].

LIQUIDATIONS

¶3233   LIQUIDATIONS IN GENERAL

Your corporation is considered in liquidation when it ceases to be a going concern and its activities consist merely of winding up its affairs, paying its debts and distributing any remaining assets to you and the other shareholders. The legal dissolution of your corporation is not required. Distributions in complete or partial liquidations are treated as a full or part payment in exchange for its stock. Therefore, *liquidation* means terminating the corporate enterprise. Generally, a *reorganization* means a continuation of the same enterprise in a modified corporate form.

In liquidation, your corporation may either dispose of its property for cash and distribute the cash, or distribute its property to you and the other shareholders in exchange for its capital stock. A sale or exchange of the capital stock by its shareholders will usually result in capital gain or loss to them. The following items are involved in the subject of liquidations:

- Gain or loss on property distributions in liquidation [¶3234].
- Liquidation of a subsidiary [¶3235].
- Basis of property received in liquidation [¶3235(a)].
- Liquidating distributions [¶1229].

¶3234   GAIN OR LOSS ON PROPERTY DISTRIBUTIONS IN LIQUIDATION

Generally, your corporation recognizes gain or loss on a distribution of its property in complete liquidation, as if your corporation had sold the property to the distributee-shareholders at its fair market value [IRC Sec. 336].

If the distributed property is subject to a liability, or the shareholders assume a liability connected with the distribution, and the amount of the liability exceeds the fair market value, the property value is deemed to be not less than the amount of the liability. Thus, in this case, your corporation generally recognizes gain to the extent the liability exceeds its basis [IRC Sec. 336(b)].

There is, however, an exception to the general recognition rule [(a) below]. The distribution to a parent corporation by an 80%-owned liquidating subsidiary is not subject to current recognition of gain [IRC Sec. 337]. Within 30 days after adopting a liquidation plan, your liquidating corporation must file Form 966 with the IRS [IRC Sec. 6043; Reg. Sec. 1.6043-1].

Background and purpose. As a general rule, corporate earnings from sales of appreciated property are taxed twice—first to your corporation when the sale occurs, and again to you and the other shareholders when the net proceeds are distributed as dividends. Under prior law, an important exception (commonly known as the *General Utilities* doctrine) permitted your corporation to escape tax at the corporate level by distributing appreciated property to its shareholders and on certain liquidating sales of property. Broadly speaking, the *General Utilities* doctrine has been repealed. Thus gain or loss is recognized by your corporation on a liquidating sale of its assets or on a distribution of its property in complete liquidation.

(a) Nonrecognition on Distributions in Complete Liquidations. An exception is provided for liquidating transfers within an affiliated group because the property (with the other attributes of the liquidated subsidiary) is retained within the economic unit of the affiliated group. This intercorporate transfer is a nonrecognition event. The basis in the hands of the corporation receiving the property is generally the same as it was in the hands of the transferor corporation (carryover basis). However, if gain or loss is recognized by the liquidating corporation with respect to such property, the basis of the property is the fair market value at the time of the distribution [IRC Sec. 334(b)(1)]. For liquidations in which an 80% corporate shareholder receives property with a carryover basis, nonrecognition of gain or loss applies for any property actually distributed to the controlling corporate shareholder. Gain, but not loss, is recognized to a minority shareholder that receives property in such a liquidation. Nonrecognition is generally denied under the 80% corporate shareholder exception when the shareholder is a tax-exempt corporation or a foreign corporation (¶3335) [IRC Sec. 337, 367].

(b) Limitations on the Recognition of Losses. First, your liquidating corporation cannot recognize loss for any distribution of property to a related person (under IRC Sec. 267), unless the property is distributed to all shareholders on a pro rata basis *and* the property was not acquired by your liquidating corporation in a Sec. 351 transaction or as a contribution to capital during the five years preceding the distribution [IRC Sec. 336(d)]. Your corportion can, however, recognize losses in the case of a distribution in a *complete* liquidation [IRC Sec. 267(a)(1)].

Second, suppose property is contributed to your corporation in advance of its liquidation primarily to recognize a loss on the property's sale or distribution and thus eliminate or limit corporate level gain. Then the basis (for loss) of any property acquired by your corporation in a Sec. 351 transaction or as a capital contribution is reduced (not below zero) by the excess of the property's basis on the contribution date over its fair market value on that date. It is presumed (except as provided in regulations) that any Sec. 351 transaction or capital contribution within a two-year period to the adoption of the plan to complete liquidation has such a principal purpose. It is also presumed that acquisitions after the adoption of the plan have such a principal purpose [IRC Sec. 336(d)].

(c) Nonliquidating Distributions of Appreciated Property. Your distributing corporation must generally recognize gain if appreciated property (other than an obligation of your corporation) is distributed to its shareholders outside of complete liquidation [IRC Sec. 311].

(d) Conversion From C Corporation to S Corporation. Your S corporation must recognize gain on a sale or distribution of appreciated property to its shareholders to the extent the appreciation occurred (a) when your corporation was a C corporation and (b) within ten years after the S election was made. However, once your S corporation waits out the ten-year period, no corporate-level tax is imposed on a sale or distribution of the property (¶3108) [IRC Sec. 1374].

¶3235　　NONTAXABLE LIQUIDATION OF SUBSIDIARY

Your parent corporation recognizes no gain or loss if it receives property (including money[1]) in a complete liquidation of a subsidiary (but see (b) below). Your corporation must own 80% of the value and voting power of the subsidiary. In addition, the following requirements must be met [IRC Sec. 332(b); Reg. Sec. 1.332-2–4]:

- Your corporation is the owner of stock in the liquidating corporation meeting the requirements of IRC Sec. 1504(a)(2) applicable in determining whether that corporation qualifies as a member of an affiliated group (¶3045(a)) [IRC Sec. 332(b)]. Such ownership must exist on the date the liquidation plan is adopted and continue until property is received in liquidation; and
- The subsidiary's distribution is in complete cancellation or redemption of all of the subsidiary's stock; and
- The distribution of all of the subsidiary's property is made to your corporation in the same tax year, unless there is a series of distributions. In that case, the transfer must be made within three years from the close of the tax year in which the first distribution is made [IRC Sec. 332(b)(2)(3); Reg. Sec. 1.332-3, 1.332-4].

NOTE: Your corporation may apply for an advance ruling on the proposed transaction by furnishing all pertinent information to the IRS.[2] For a liquidation of a subsidiary involving a foreign corporation, see IRC. Sec. 367(a).

➤ **OBSERVATION** If your parent corporation doesn't recognize gain, any minority shareholders of the subsidiary cannot recognize loss on distributions they receive in the liquidation [IRC Sec. 336(d)(3)]. Additionally, liquidations into a tax-exempt parent (as long as the exempt parent does not use the property in an unrelated trade or business) or a foreign corporation do not qualify for this nonrecognition rule.

Whether a corporation is an 80% distributee is determined without regard to any consolidated return regulation [IRC Sec. 355(b)(2)(D)]. In other words, gain is recognized on a distribution to a corporation that doesn't qualify as an 80% owner without applying a consolidated return regulation [Reg. Sec. 1.1502-34], which aggregates the stock of affiliated group members for determining if the 80% ownership is met.

(a) Basis of Property Received. Generally, your parent corporation's basis for the property received is the same as the subsidiary's basis [IRC Sec. 334(b)(1); Reg. Sec. 1.334-1]. If, however, gain or loss is recognized by the liquidating corporation, your parent corporation's basis for the property received is the fair market value at the time of the distribution [IRC Sec. 334(b)(1)].

(b) Certain Stock Purchases Treated as Asset Acquisitions. If your corporation buys a controlling stock interest in a target corporation, the IRC Sec. 338 rules (below) permit your corporation to elect to treat the transaction as a purchase of the corporation's assets for tax purposes. In this way, the assets' bases are stepped up to the stock's purchase price.

Generally, to set up a purchase of stock to get assets, your acquiring corporation must: (1) make a qualifying purchase (see below) of the stock of the acquired (target) corporation, and (2) not later than the 15th day of the ninth month following the month of the acquisition date, make the appropriate election. A qualifying purchase is a purchase of stock meeting the requirements of IRC Sec. 1504(a)(2) applicable in determining whether that corporation qualifies as a member of an affiliated group [¶3045(a)], during a 12-month acquisition period [IRC Sec. 338(d)(3)].

Once an election is made, the assets of the target corporation are treated as sold to and purchased by it for an amount equal to the grossed up basis of your acquiring corporation's recently purchased stock (stock purchased during the acquisition period) and the basis of any other stock held by your acquiring corporation in the target corporation that is not recently purchased stock. The target corporation *doesn't have to be liquidated.*

The target corporation's tax year ends on the date of acquisition and it becomes a "new" corporation and a member of the affiliated group, including your acquiring corporation, on the next day.

No gain or loss is recognized by the target corporation as a result of an election by your acquiring corporation. However, the election will trigger any depreciation or investment credit recapture by the target corporation and will terminate its tax attributes, such as net operating loss carryovers. Normally, recapture items will be associated with the final return of the target corporation for the tax year ending on the date of acquisition. However, if for some reason recapture income is included in the income of the "new" corporation that is included in the consolidated return filed with the acquiring corporation, it must be separately accounted for and may not be absorbed by losses or deductions of other members of the group.

NOTE: The depreciable assets of a target corporation qualify as ACRS or MACRS recovery property. Moreover, your acquiring corporation is not bound by the target corporation's ACRS or MACRS recovery period and method.

"Purchase" defined. Stock is not purchased if it is acquired: (1) in a carryover basis transaction; (2) from a decedent; (3) in an exchange to which IRC Sec. 351, 354, 355 or 356 apply; (4) in a transaction described in the regulations (not yet issued) in which the transferor does not recognize the entire amount of the gain or loss; or (5) from a person such as a family member, partnership, estate or trust whose stock is attributed (options don't count) to the acquiring corporation under IRC Sec. 318(a) [IRC Sec. 338(h)(3)(A)]. Stock acquired from a related corporation (including stock acquired in a carryover basis transaction following a qualified stock purchase and election with respect to the transferor) will satisfy the purchase requirement if at least 50% in value of the related corporation's stock was purchased [IRC Sec. 338(h)(3)(C)].

Your purchasing corporation is not treated as having purchased stock in a third corporation that it constructively owns as a result of purchasing the stock in another (the second) corporation. Instead, if a qualified stock purchase and election are made with respect to the second corporation, the deemed purchase of the third corporation's stock will, if it satisfies the 80% ownership requirement, be treated as a qualified stock purchase permitting an election by the second corporation, or deeming an election to be made under the consistency requirements (see below) [IRC Sec. 338(h)(3)(B)].

Example 1: XYZ Corp. acquires 80% of the stock of Target Corp. which owns 80% of ABC Corp. stock. XYZ Corp. can't elect to treat ABC Corp. as a target because it is treated as owning only 64% (80% of 80%) of its stock. However, when the Sec. 338 election is made, Target Corp. is treated as having sold all of its assets, and as a new corporation which purchased the assets, including 80% of the stock of ABC Corp. Target Corp. can elect to have its deemed purchase of ABC Corp.'s stock treated as an asset acquisition. It may be required to do so under the consistency rules.

Consistency throughout a so-called "consistency period" is mandatory in the purchase-of-stock-to-get-assets area where your acquiring corporation makes qualified stock purchases of two or more corporations that belong to the same affiliated group. For this purpose, the consistency period is the one-year period preceding the target corporation's acquisition period, plus the period of acquisition, and the one-year period following the acquisition date. Some of the ground rules are as follows [IRC Sec. 338(f)]:

- Purchases by a member of your purchasing corporation's affiliated group, unless the regulations say otherwise, are treated as purchases by your purchasing corporation. In applying the consistency rules, you aggregate the purchases of members of an affiliated group to see if the 80% purchase requirement is met.
- A combination of a direct asset acquisition and a qualified stock purchase by a member of your purchasing corporation's affiliated group is, unless the regulations say otherwise, treated as made by your purchasing corporation.
- A direct purchase of assets within this period by your purchasing corporation from the target corporation or a target affiliate (except, for example, in the ordinary course of business) results in the acquisition of the target corporation being treated as an asset purchase. A corporation is a target affiliate of a target corporation if each was, at any time during the portion of the consistency period ending on the acquisition date of the target corporation, a member of an affiliated group, within the meaning of IRC Sec. 1504(a), that had the same common parent. This definition also applies in determining whether a purchase is made by a member of the same affiliated group as your purchasing corporation. The term "target affiliate" doesn't include foreign corporations, DISCs, FSCs, and possessions corporations.
- An acquisition of assets from a target affiliate during the consistency period applicable to the target corporation results in the qualified stock purchase of the target corporation being treated as a purchase of assets.
- If during a consistency period, there are only qualified stock purchases of the target corporation and one or more target affiliates by your purchasing corporation, an election for the first purchase applies to the later purchases, and a failure to make the election for the first purchase knocks out any election for the later purchases.
- The IRS has broad authority to treat stock acquisitions that have been deliberately timed to avoid the consistency rules as qualified stock purchases. The IRS is also authorized to issue regulations to make sure that the consistency of treatment of stock and asset purchases, with respect to a target corporation and its target affiliates, isn't sidestepped through the creative use of other Code provisions or regulations, including the consolidated return regulations.

Example 2: ABC Corp. purchases 80% or more of all of the stock of Target Corp. on March 1, 1992 and, within a one-year period, purchases assets from Affiliated Corp., which is a target affiliate of Target Corp. ABC Corp. is deemed to have made an election for Target Corp. as of March 1, 1992, even though it didn't so elect.

Example 3: ABC Corp. purchases all of the stock of Target Corp. on March 1, 1992. At the time of purchase, Target Corp. owns 80% or more of the stock of Affiliated Corp. ABC Corp. makes a timely election for the purchase of the stock of Target Corp. ABC Corp. is treated as having made two qualified stock purchases—a direct purchase of Target Corp.'s stock, plus an indirect purchase of Affiliated Corp.'s stock. So, its election for the purchase of Target Corp.'s stock automatically applies to its indirect purchase of Affiliated Corp.'s stock.

NOTE: Regulations have been issued to prevent avoidance of the consistency requirements via devices using corporations or other parties that are not members of the purchasing group to acquire assets of the target or a target affiliate. Also, the consistency period has been enlarged under Temp. Reg. Sec. 1.338-1T–4T.

CARRYOVERS

¶3236   CARRYOVERS TO SUCCESSOR CORPORATION

When the assets of a corporation are acquired by your corporation in a tax-free liquidation or reorganization, your successor corporation may, under conditions described below, carry over certain tax benefits, privileges, elective rights, and obligations [¶3237] of the predecessor corporation [IRC Sec. 381(a)(c); Reg. Sec. 1.381(a)-1].

When carryover is allowed. The carryover provisions apply to:

- *Liquidation of subsidiary.* When your controlling parent corporation takes over the property of a subsidiary in a complete liquidation of the subsidiary (see ¶3235) [IRC Sec. 381(a)(1); Reg. Sec. 1.381(a)-1(b)(1)].
- *Reorganizations.* When your successor corporation acquires assets of another corporation in the following types of reorganization: a statutory merger or consolidation (Type A) [¶3203]; an acquisition by your corporation of properties of another corporation for stock (Type C) [¶3205]; a transfer of assets for controlling stock, if there is a single transferee corporation and the transferor distributes all of the stock, securities and properties it receives as well as its other properties under a plan of reorganization (certain Type D) [¶3206]; a mere change in identity, form, or place of organization of one corporation (Type F) [¶3208]; an insolvency reorganization, if there is a single transferee corporation and the transferor distributes all of the stock, securities and properties it receives as well as its other properties under a plan of reorganization (certain Type G; ¶3209) [IRC Sec. 381(a)(2); Reg. Sec. 1.381(a)-1(b)(1)].

NOTE: The carryover provisions do not apply to partial liquidations, divisive reorganizations or reorganizations not listed above [Reg. Sec. 1.381(a)-1(b)(3)]. A Type B reorganization [¶3204] is not included since only the stock is acquired and the controlled corporation remains in existence. However, if it is liquidated, there will be a Type C reorganization. Type E is not included since only a single corporation is involved in a recapitalization [¶3207].

Dates are important for carryover benefits. Your successor corporation takes over the carryovers as of the close of the day of distribution (for a liquidated subsidiary) or the day of transfer (for a reorganization) [IRC Sec. 381(a)].

NOTE: The following rules apply to liquidations and reorganizations entitled to carryover benefits (but not Type F reorganizations) [IRC Sec. 381(b); Reg. Sec. 1.381(b)-1, 1.381(c)(1)-1]:

The tax year of the predecessor corporation ends on the date the assets are transferred from the predecessor to your successor corporation. Amounts retained to pay taxes, director fees and dissolution expenses do not affect this date.[1] The predecessor should file a return for the tax year ending with that date. If the predecessor remains in existence, it should also file a return for the tax year beginning on the day following the date of transfer and ending with the date its year would have ended had there been no transfer.

Generally, the date of transfer is the day the transfer is completed. However, if specified statements are filed, it may be the day when substantially all the property has been transferred and the predecessor has ceased all operations except liquidating activities. The latter date also applies if completion of the transfer is unreasonably postponed [Reg. Sec. 1.381(b)-1(b)].

Net operating loss or net capital loss carryback. Your successor corporation is not entitled to carry back to a tax year of a predecessor a net capital loss or a net operating loss incurred in a tax year ending after the date of transfer [IRC Sec. 381(b)(3)]. However, in an "F" reorganization [¶3208], your successor corporation's loss can be carried back against the predecessor's pre-merger profits.

> **NOTE:** The Second Circuit held that a triangular merger of a 62% controlled subsidiary into a 100% controlled shell was an "F" reorganization, even though the subsidiary's minority shareholders had to exchange their stock for the controlled shell's parent's stock.[2]

> **Example 1:** On December 31, 1992, Corporations X and Y transfer all their property to Z in a consolidation. If Z has a net operating loss or net capital loss in 1993, it cannot be carried back to a tax year of X or Y.

> **Example 2:** On December 31, 1992, Corporation X merges into Corporation Y in a statutory merger, with Y's charter continuing after the merger. If Y has a net operating loss or a net capital loss in 1993, the loss cannot be carried back to a tax year of X, but is a carryback to a tax year of Y.

> **Example 3:** X reorganizes by changing its name to Y. Y may carry back a net operating or net capital loss to a tax year of X before the reorganization.

¶3237   CHECKLIST OF CARRYOVER ITEMS

The following items may be carried over subject to the conditions described:

Net operating loss. Your successor corporation may carry over net operating losses of the predecessor, subject to the special limitations shown at ¶3238. However, the carryover to the first tax year ending after the date of transfer is limited to a fraction of your successor corporation's taxable income for that year (figured without regard to any net operating loss deduction). The fraction is the number of days in the tax year after the transfer over the total number of days in the tax year [IRC Sec. 381(c)(1)(B); Reg. Sec. 1.381(c)(1)-1(d)]. Any deferred minimum tax liability attributable to the carryover is also acquired [Reg. Sec. 1.381(c)(1)-1(a)(3)].

Earnings and profits of the predecessor become those of your successor corporation. But an earnings and profits deficit of either corporation may be applied only against your successor corporation's earnings and profits accumulated after the assets' date of transfer. The earnings and profits of your successor corporation's first tax year that may be reduced by the predecessor's

deficit is in the same ratio to the total of your successor corporation's undistributed earnings for the year as the number of days of the year after the transfer bears to the total days in the year [IRC Sec. 381(c)(2); Reg. Sec. 1.381(c)(2)-1(a)].

Capital loss carryover. Your successor corporation is entitled to use the unexhausted portion of the predecessor's capital loss carryover. The first year in which the loss may be deducted is the first tax year of your successor corporation ending after the date of transfer of assets. The amount that can be used in the first year, however, is limited to a fraction of your successor corporation's capital gain net income for that year. The fraction is the number of days in the tax year after the transfer over the total number of days in the tax year [IRC Sec. 381(c)(3); Reg. Sec. 1.381(c)(3)-1].

Method of accounting. If both your successor corporation and the predecessor corporation used the same method of accounting on the date of the transfer of assets, your successor corporation continues to use that method. But if different methods were used by several predecessors, or by predecessor and your corporation, your successor corporation must use a method required by regulations [IRC Sec. 381(c)(4); Reg. Sec. 1.381(c)(4)-1].

Inventories. Your successor corporation values inventories received from the predecessor on the same basis as the predecessor. However, if the carryover of the method of taking inventory results in your corporation having more than one method of taking inventory, your successor corporation may adopt a particular method or combination of methods of taking inventory [IRC Sec. 381(c)(5); Reg. Sec. 1.381(c)(5)-1].

Depreciation. Your successor corporation figures depreciation on acquired assets the same way the predecessor did. But total depreciation on a particular asset may not exceed the predecessor's adjusted basis. A change of method may be made with IRS consent (¶2121(b)) [IRC Sec. 381(c)(6); Reg. Sec. 1.381(c)(6)-1].

Your successor corporation can use the ADR system on property acquired from a predecessor only if the predecessor elected it for the property (¶2121) [Reg. Sec. 1.167(a)- 11(e)(3)].

Installment sales method. If your successor corporation acquires installment obligations which the predecessor reported on the installment basis, your corporation also reports the income on the installment basis [IRC Sec. 381(c)(8); Reg. Sec. 1.381(c)(8)-1].

Amortization of bond discount or premium. If your successor corportion assumes liability for bonds of the predecessor issued at a discount or premium, your corporation is treated as the predecessor in determining the amortization deductible or includible in income [IRC Sec. 381(c)(9); Reg. Sec. 1.381(c)(9)-1].

Exploration and development expenditures. Your successor corporation can deduct certain mining development expenditures [¶2242; 2243] when the predecessor has previously so elected [IRC Sec. 381(c)(10); Reg. Sec. 1.381(c)(10)-1].

Contributions to employee benefit trusts or plans. Your successor corporation is considered to be the predecessor in determining deductions for contributions of an employer to qualified employees' trusts or annuity plans [IRC Sec. 381(c)(11); Reg. Sec. 1.381(c)(11)-1]. See ¶1300.

Recovery of tax benefit items. If your successor corporation is entitled to the recovery of amounts previously deducted or credited by the predecessor, your corporation must include in its income the amounts that would have been a tax benefit to the predecessor on the recovery [IRC Sec. 381(c)(12)].

Involuntary conversions. Your successor corporation is treated as the predecessor when there is an involuntary conversion (¶1710) [IRC Sec. 381(c)(13); Reg. Sec. 1.381(c)(13)-1].

Dividend carryover to personal holding company. If your successor corporation is a personal holding company, it may include a dividend carryover of its predecessor in figuring the dividends-paid deduction (¶3304(b)) to the same extent as the predecessor [IRC Sec. 381(c)(14); Reg. Sec. 1.381(c)(14)-1].

Obligations of predecessor. Your successor corporation may deduct amounts that arise out of an obligation of the predecessor if: (1) the obligation is assumed by your corporation; (2) the obligation gives rise to a liability after the date of transfer; (3) the liability, if paid or accrued by the predecessor after that date, would have been deductible by it; (4) the obligation was not reflected in the consideration transferred by your corporation for the property [IRC Sec. 381(c)(16); Reg. Sec. 1.381(c)(16)-1].

Deficiency dividend of personal holding company. If your successor corporation pays a personal holding company deficiency dividend of its predecessor, it is entitled to the deficiency dividend deduction (¶3307) [IRC Sec. 381(c)(17); Reg. Sec. 1.381(c)(17)].

Percentage depletion on ore extraction from prior mining residue. Your successor corporation can claim percentage depletion on prior mining residue acquired from the predecessor [IRC Sec. 381(c)(18); Reg. Sec. 1.381(c)(18)-1].

Charitable contributions over prior years' limitation. If the predecessor corporation has a charitable contribution carryover on the date of the transfer, your successor corporation can use the carryover (within the limit [¶3019]) only in tax years beginning after that date that are not more than five tax years after the year the excess contribution was made [IRC Sec. 381(c)(19); Reg. Sec. 1.381(c)(19)-1].

Life insurance companies. A successor life insurance company may take into account, under special regulations, certain items of a predecessor life insurance company [IRC Sec. 381(c)(22); Reg. Sec. 1.381(c)(22)-1, 1.381(d)-1].

General business credit. Your successor corporation carries over items the predecessor used to account for the research credit, targeted jobs credit, alcohol fuels credit, the enhanced oil recovery credit, the disabled access credit and the low-income housing credit (¶2405) [IRC Sec. 381(c)(24)].

Deficiency dividend of regulated investment company or real estate investment trust. If your successor corporation pays a deficiency dividend of its predecessor, such predecessor is entitled to the deficiency dividend deduction [IRC Sec. 381(c)(23)]. See ¶3326.

Foreign tax credit. Your successor corporation may carry over any unused foreign taxes of the predecessor, but the credit is subject to a limitation that includes only post-merger foreign taxable income attributable to the same business that caused the predecessor's foreign tax liability [¶3803(b)].

¶3238   SPECIAL LIMIT ON NET OPERATING LOSS CARRYOVER

Under certain conditions, a limit (described below) is placed on the net operating loss (NOL) carryover that is available to your acquiring corporation in tax-free reorganizations described in IRC. Sec. 381(a) [¶3236]. The NOL carryover after a substantial change of ownership also may be disallowed or reduced [¶3035]. This is to prevent profitable corporations from buying "loss" corporations solely to use the losses to offset the acquiring corporation's gains.

There are limitations on a corporation's NOL carryforwards following a worthless stock deduction by 50% shareholders. In addition, there are limitations on using preacquisition losses to offset built-in gains [IRC Sec. 382(g),(h)].

The following rules apply generally to more-than-50%-owner shifts or equity structure changes and for reorganization plans. Briefly, after a substantial ownership change, however effected, the taxable income available for offset by pre-change NOLs is limited to a prescribed rate times the loss corporation's value immediately before the change [IRC Sec. 382]. To figure the annual limitation, you multiply the loss corporation's value immediately before the ownership change by the federal long-term tax-exempt rate published by the IRS. The rate used is the highest rate in effect for any month in the three-month period ending with the month in which the ownership change occurs. Built-in losses and gains are subject to special rules.

> **Example:** Rich Corp. acquires Loss Corp. for the fair market price of $100,000. Prior to the acquisition, Loss Corp. had $300,000 of NOLs, and the federal long-term rate (FLTR) was 8%. When multiplying the fair market value of Loss Corp. ($100,000) with the FLTR (8%), Rich Corp. cannot use more than $8,000 per year of Loss Corp.'s NOLs to offset its gains.

¶3239   LIMITS ON CARRYOVERS OF UNUSED CREDITS AND CAPITAL LOSSES

Similar rules for disallowance or reduction of NOL carryovers for changes in ownership [¶3025; 3238] also apply to carryovers of capital losses, foreign tax credits, and unused business credits [IRC Sec. 383]. In addition, to carry over unused foreign tax credit, the overall limitation [¶3803] must also be applied.

Applicable generally to ownership changes occurring after 1986, certain excess credits are subject to special limitations [IRC Sec. 383]. These limitations are similar to the rules on NOL carryovers (under IRC Sec. 382) explained at ¶3035. Capital loss carryforwards and the deduction equivalent of credit carryforwards are limited to an amount determined on the basis of the tax liability that is attributable to so much of the taxable income as does not exceed the Sec. 382 limitation for the tax year.

STOCK REDEMPTIONS

¶3240   STOCK REDEMPTIONS IN GENERAL

Usually, when a corporation redeems its stock from you, the transaction is treated as if you sold your stock to the corporation. Any profit you have is taxed as capital gain.

However, what looks like a redemption is sometimes a disguised dividend (taxable as ordinary income). It is therefore necessary to distinguish between a dividend and a sale or exchange. This is done by applying the rules below.

> **OBSERVATION** If a redemption is treated as a dividend, you should adjust the basis of the remaining shares. Suppose, for example, that you own 100 shares of stock with a basis of $5,000 and the company redeems 20 of the shares. If the redemption is treated as a dividend, you should add the basis of the 20 redeemed shares to the 80 remaining shares, giving these 80 shares a basis of $5,000. Otherwise, the basis of the 20 redeemed shares would just disappear.

Sale or exchange and dividend distinguished. A redemption is treated as a sale or exchange if it meets *any* of the following conditions:

- It is *not* essentially equivalent to a dividend under the "net effects" test in (a) below [IRC Sec. 302(b)(1)];

NOTE: In determining whether a redemption is not equivalent to a dividend, the fact that it fails to meet the other conditions is not considered.

- It meets the "substantially disproportionate" (or 80%) test in (b) below *and* leaves you (the shareholder) with less than 50% of the total voting power after redemption [IRC Sec. 302(b)(2)]; or
- The corporation redeems all of your stock in the corporation [IRC Sec. 302(b)(3); Reg. Sec. 1.302-4].

NOTE: The "substantially disproportionate" test and the complete redemption test are safe harbors. That's because they are objective and mechanical with a higher degree of certainty than the "net effects" test which depends on the facts and circumstances of each case.

(a) "Net Effects" Test. To qualify for sale or exchange treatment, the redemption must result in a meaningful reduction of your proportionate interest in the corporation. A redemption is essentially equivalent to a dividend, and is taxed as such, if it meets a "net effects" test. It meets the test if all the circumstances show that, as a practical matter, your relationship to the corporation did not change.[1] If the test is met, the mere presence of a business purpose for the redemption is irrelevant and does not change the result.[2]

Ordinarily, a dividend results if there is a pro rata redemption of the only class of stock outstanding, or a redemption of one class of stock (except Sec. 306 stock ¶3243]) when all the other classes are held in the same proportion. However, the redemption of any amount of nonvoting, nonconvertible, nonparticipating preferred stock (except Sec. 306 stock) is *not* essentially equivalent to a dividend if you do not own, directly or indirectly, any of the corporation's common stock.[3]

The effect of the redemption on voting control, share of earnings and share of assets is important in determining whether the redemption is "essentially equivalent to a dividend." Even a big drop in ownership interest (e.g., from 85% to 60%), does not avoid dividend treatment if you retain voting control.

(b) "Substantially Disproportionate" Test. A redemption is substantially disproportionate if it meets an 80% test, which is applied as follows. First, figure what percentage of the corporation's *voting stock* you owned before and after the redemption. Then figure what percentage of the corporation's *common stock* (voting and nonvoting) you owned before and after (if there is more than one class of common, the percentage is determined by using market values). Under the 80% test (which applies to the *voting stock* as well as the common stock[4]), the percentage after the redemption must be less than 80% of the percentage before the redemption. An option to acquire treasury or unissued stock must be included in applying the 80% test (¶3244(f)) [Reg. Sec. 1.302-3(a)]. If the 80% test and the 50% test in (a) above are met, the redemption qualifies as a sale, with one exception. If the redemption is one of a series in total redemption, the total redemption must also meet the 80% test [IRC Sec. 302(b); Reg. Sec. 1.302-3].

> **Example 1:** Arko, Inc. has 400 shares of common stock outstanding. Mr. Allen, Mr. Bernsie, Mr. Carmen and Mr. Dennis each own 100 shares, or 25%. Arko redeems 55 shares from Allen, 25 shares from Bernsie, and 20 shares from Carmen. The redemption will be disproportionate as to any shareholder owning less than 20% after the redemption (80% of 25%). After the redemptions, Allen owns 45 shares (15%), Bernsie owns 75 shares (25%), and Carmen owns 80 shares (26⅔%). Only the redemption of Allen's shares is disproportionate.

(c) Complete Redemption of Shareholder's Stock. A complete redemption of your stock qualifies for capital gains treatment if, after the redemption, you own no stock in the corporation, either actually or constructively. The constructive ownership rules in ¶3244 apply, with one exception. The exception prevents application of the family attribution rules, if the conditions in (g) below apply and if there are no prior transfers of the kind described in (h).

(d) Partial Liquidations. A distribution in redemption of stock held by you (as a noncorporate shareholder) is treated as a distribution in partial liquidation if it is (1) not essentially equivalent to a dividend (determined at the corporate level) and (2) under a plan that occurs within the tax year in which the plan is adopted or within the next tax year [IRC Sec. 302(e)]. Another setup that qualifies is a distribution (whether or not pro rata) caused by a distributing corporation's termination of business. Other distributions may also qualify under regulations yet to be issued.

NOTE: The IRS has broad regulatory powers to stop the use of split-ups, split-offs and the like (under IRC Sections 327, 351, 355, etc.) to avoid the partial liquidation rules [IRC Sec. 346].

(e) Stock Ownership. In applying the above tests, you must take into account stock attributed to you although it actually belongs to others. The attribution rules are explained at ¶3244. They apply here except as otherwise noted in (g) below.

(f) Other Rules. A formal retirement of the redeemed stock is not required. The corporation may continue to hold it as treasury stock.

Special rules apply to redemptions from a controlled corporation; redemptions to pay death taxes; redemption of Sec. 306 stock; and liquidating dividends [¶1229; 3241-3244]. A corporation gets no deduction for any amount it pays or incurs in connection with its stock's redemption.

(g) When Constructive Ownership Rules Do Not Apply. The rules for attribution between family members do not apply if [IRC Sec. 302(c)(2); Reg. Sec. 1.302-4]:

- Immediately after the redemption, you had no interest in the corporation other than as a creditor. You cannot be an officer, [5] director or employee.
- You do not reacquire an interest (other than by bequest or inheritance) within ten years from the redemption date. If you do acquire such an interest, you are assessed an additional tax, at dividend rates, for the redemption year (the statute of limitations is automatically extended).
- You file an agreement: (1) to notify the IRS within 30 days if such interest is acquired and (2) to keep copies of the return and other records showing the tax that would have been payable if the redemption had been a dividend. The agreement is filed with the return.

Example 2: Husband and wife each own 50% of the stock of a corporation. All the husband's stock is redeemed, and husband meets the above conditions. The husband is entitled to treat this as a sale of his stock, because the family constructive ownership rules do not apply. If they did apply, he would still constructively own his wife's shares, and the redemption would not be complete.

NOTE: Family attribution rules under IRC Section 318(a)(1) may be waived *only* by an entity and its beneficiaries if those through whom ownership is attributed to the entity join in the waiver. The entity and the beneficiaries would be liable for any acquisitions by them within the ten-year period and the statute of limitations would be open to assess any deficiency [IRC Sec. 302(c)(2)(C)].

(h) Prior Stock Transfers to Avoid Tax. The family attribution rules *do* apply under either of the following two conditions, but only if tax avoidance was a principal purpose [IRC Sec. 302(c)(2)(B)].

- If you acquired any part of the redeemed stock, directly or indirectly, within the previous ten years from a person whose stock would have been attributed to you at the time of redemption.

Example 3: Solely to reduce taxes, the only shareholder of a corporation gives half of the stock to his son. Five years later, there is a complete redemption of all of the son's shares. The rules relating to constructive ownership between members of a family apply.

- If, at the time of redemption, any person owned stock that would be attributed to you, and such person acquired *any* stock in the corporation from you, directly or indirectly, within the previous ten years (unless this stock is also redeemed).

Example 4: If, in Example 2, the father's shares were redeemed and the father otherwise terminated his interest in the corporation, rules relating to constructive ownership between members of family would apply.

NOTE: These rules do not apply to distributions in liquidation [Reg. Sec. 1.302-1].

¶3241 REDEMPTION THROUGH USE OF A RELATED CORPORATION

Under prior law, taxpayers sometimes sold their stock in one corporation to another "related" corporation. This gave them the benefits of a redemption in certain cases where they could not otherwise qualify for those benefits [¶3240]. This is no longer possible because of the rules below.

(a) Sale to Related Corporation (Other Than a Subsidiary). Suppose you or more persons control two corporations (the so-called brother-sister situation) and one of the corporations acquires stock in the other corporation from the persons in control (for money or property). The transaction is treated as if the acquiring corporation had redeemed its stock from the person in control [IRC Sec. 304(a)]. The dividend amount is determined by treating the transaction as if the property were distributed by the acquiring corporation to the extent of its earnings and profits and then by the corporation whose stock is issued (the issuing corporation) to the extent of its earnings and profits [IRC Sec. 304(b)(2)].

Generally, when stock from one member of an affiliated group is transferred to another member of the group (in a Sec. 304(a) transaction), proper adjustments must be made in (1) the adjusted basis of any intragroup stock, and (2) the earnings and profits of any member of this group, to the extent necessary to carry out this rule's purposes. Intragroup stock means any stock in a member of an affiliated group held by another member of this group [IRC Sec. 304(b)(4)].

The contribution-to-capital rule will not apply if the shareholder is treated as having exchanged its stock under IRC Sec. 302(a) [relating to stock redemption in general (¶3240)]. Thus, if Sec. 302(a) applies, the acquiring corporation will be treated as buying the stock, for example, for purposes of IRC Sec. 338 [relating to certain stock purchases treated as asset acquisition (¶3235(b))]. This amendment is not intended to change the present law treatment of you (including your basis in the stock of the acquiring corporation).

Effect on basis. The purchasing corporation's basis for the stock is the same as your basis, plus any recognized gain [IRC Sec. 304(a)(1); Reg. Sec. 1.304-2].

If the amount received is a dividend, the basis of your stock in the purchasing corporation is increased by your basis for the redeemed stock. If the amount received is from a sale, the basis of your stock in the purchasing corporation remains the same [Reg. Sec. 1.304-2].

(b) Sale to Subsidiary. If you sell stock in one corporation to another corporation controlled by the first (the so-called parent-sub situation), the transaction is treated as though the subsidiary distributed the purchase price to the parent, which then redeemed its own stock from you [IRC Sec. 304(a)(2); Reg. Sec. 1.304-3].

(c) Control means ownership of 50% or more of the voting power or 50% or more of the total value of all classes of stock.

NOTE: The rules in ¶3244 on constructive ownership apply in determining control, except that 5% is substituted for 50% [IRC Sec. 304(c)(3)].

¶3242   STOCK REDEEMED TO PAY DEATH TAXES

(a) Special Relief. When you die, it may be necessary to redeem some of the stock held by you to pay death taxes. If the redemption is treated as a dividend, the entire amount received, could be taxable. However, relief is granted by treating the redemption as a sale—so that only the amount received in excess of your basis is taxable. To qualify for this tax relief, all of the following conditions must be met [IRC Sec. 303; Reg. Sec. 1.303-1–1.303-3]:

- The value of the stock redeemed is included in your gross estate for estate tax purposes [see (b) below].
- The stock is redeemed after death and within three years and 90 days after the filing of the estate tax return; or, if a petition was filed with the Tax Court, within 60 days after its decision becomes final; or, if deferred payment of estate taxes is elected, within the time permitted for the estate tax installments in a closely held business interest [¶3962].
- The stock is redeemed for an amount not more than the estate and inheritance taxes (including interest), plus the funeral and administration expenses allowable as deductions to the estate. There is no requirement that the proceeds be needed to pay these items or that they be used to pay them. However, any excess over the allowable amount is a dividend.

NOTE: Stock that can qualify for capital gain is limited to stock redeemed from a shareholder whose interest in the estate is reduced (either directly or through a binding obligation to contribute) by the payment of death taxes and funeral and administration expenses. Special rules also limit the amount of qualifying redemption distributions made more than four years after the death.

- The value of the stock must exceed 35% of the value of your adjusted gross estate (gross estate less deductions for administration expenses, debts, taxes and losses). For this purpose, the stock of two or more corporations may be treated as stock of a single corporation if 20% or more of the stock of each *directly*[1] owned by you is included in the estate [IRC Sec. 303(b)].

Example: Adjusted gross estate of decedent who died January 1, 1992 is $1,000,000. The sum of death taxes and funeral and administration expenses is $275,000. Included in gross estate is stock, valued as follows:

Corporation X $200,000
Corporation Y   400,000
Corporation Z   200,000

Stock of Corporations X and Z included in estate is all of their outstanding stock. If treated as stock of a single corporation, it has value of over $350,000 (35% of adjusted gross estate). Likewise, Corporations Y's stock has value of over $350,000. Distribution in redemption of stock X and Z, or stock Y, in amounts not totaling more than $275,000 can be considered distribution in payment for stock.

(b) Qualifying Stock. The stock need not be owned by you at death, nor does it have to be redeemed from your estate, *as long as its value is includible in the estate.* Examples of this are stock you the decedent transferred within three years of death and stock the estate distributed before the redemption. However, stock redeemed from a purchaser for value does not qualify even though it was part of you the decedent's estate.

Stock received after death can qualify if its basis is determined by reference to qualified stock included in the estate. An example is a nontaxable stock dividend paid to the estate after decedent's death.

¶3243   THE "PREFERRED STOCK BAIL-OUT"

It was once possible for you to withdraw earnings from your corporation without paying a dividend tax. Your corporation would pay a nontaxable dividend in preferred stock. You could then redeem the stock or sell it. In either case, you got capital gain treatment, although the effect was the same as a taxable dividend. This is no longer possible. The term "Sec. 306 stock" [¶3213] is used for this stock, and it can include rights, and common stock that is reclassified in a recapitalization proceeding.[1]

Example: Ms. Anderson and Ms. Backman each own ½ of the common stock of X Corp. X Corp., in a tax-free reorganization, distributes 50 shares of preferred stock to each. They later sell the preferred stock to outsiders for cash. X Corp. then redeems the preferred shares from the outsiders for cash. Result: Under prior rules, Anderson and Backman were able to withdraw cash from the corporation and receive sale and exchange treatment (profit taxed as capital gain as opposed to dividend treatment) without giving up any part of their interest in the corporation.

This is no longer possible. The preferred shares are now considered "Sec. 306 stock."

Sale of stock. In a preferred stock bailout, the amount you realize on the sale of Sec. 306 stock is ordinary income up to the stock's ratable share of the earnings at the time of issuance. If the amount realized exceeds the stock's ratable share of your corporation's earnings and profits, the excess, to the extent of gain, is treated as capital gain. However, no loss is recognized [IRC Sec. 306(a)(1); Reg. Sec. 1.306-1].

Redemption of stock. The general dividend rules apply in determining the tax status of the proceeds [¶1218]. The portion that is covered by corporate earnings and profits at the time of the redemption is a dividend and is taxed as ordinary income [IRC Sec. 306(a)(2); Reg. Sec. 1.306-1].

Exceptions. The bail-out rules do not apply if [IRC Sec. 306(b); Reg. Sec. 1.306-2]:

- You completely terminate your actual and constructive interest in the corporation.
- The redemption is in complete or partial liquidation.
- You prove that a principal purpose was not tax avoidance.
- The transaction is one in which gain or loss is not recognized.

NOTE: "Sec. 306 stock" also includes any stock (other than common stock) acquired in a Sec. 351 tax-free exchange if the receipt of money (instead of the stock) would have been treated as a dividend at the time. Sec. 351 provides for the nonrecognition of all or part of the gain or loss on certain transfers to a controlled corporation in exchange for stock.

¶3244   CONSTRUCTIVE OWNERSHIP OF STOCK

The tax consequences of some transactions depend on how much stock you own in a particular corporation. In these cases, you are deemed to own not only your own stock, but also stock belonging to others that is treated as yours under the "attribution" rules below. In applying these rules, you are considered an owner of stock whether you own it directly or indirectly, and whether it is owned by or for you [IRC Sec. 318; Reg. Sec. 1.318-1–1.318-4].

The general attribution rules below apply to stock redemptions [¶3240-3241]; preferred stock bail-outs [¶3243]; liquidation of subsidiaries [¶3235]; and net operating loss carryovers [¶3035; 3238]. Special rules apply to sales between corporations and shareholders [¶2323(d)]; personal holding companies [¶3302]; and in determining whether a corporation comes within a controlled group [¶3045].

(a) Family Members. You are considered an owner of the stock of your spouse (unless legally separated or divorced), children and adopted children, grandchildren, and parents [IRC Sec. 318(a)(1); Reg. Sec. 1.318-2]. But see ¶3240(g) for exceptions.

Example 1: You own 20 of the 100 outstanding shares of stock of a corporation. Your wife owns 20 shares of such stock. Your son owns 20 shares. Your grandson owns 20 shares. You are considered to own 80 shares. Your wife and son also are each considered to own 80 shares. But your grandson is considered to own only 40 shares, that is, his own and his father's; he is not considered to own the stock of his grandparents (you and your wife).

Example 2: Mr. Hicks owns no stock of the Ecks Corp. His wife, however, owns 25% and his son owns 26% of the stock. Hicks is constructive owner of 51% of the Ecks Corp. stock.

(b) Partnerships and Estates. A partnership (or S corporation) or estate owns the stock of its partners or beneficiaries. Partners or beneficiaries own *proportionately* the stock of the partnership or estate [IRC Sec. 318(a)(2), (3); Reg. Sec. 1.318-2, 1.318-3].

Example 3: Mr. Heeney has a 50% interest in a partnership. The partnership owns 50 of the 100 outstanding shares of stock of a corporation, the remaining 50 shares being owned by Heeney. The partnership is considered as owning 100 shares. Heeney is considered as owning 75 shares (his own 50 plus 50% of partnership's 50).

(c) Trusts. A trust owns the stock of its beneficiary, unless the beneficiary has only a remote, contingent interest (it is remote if its value cannot exceed 5% of the value of the trust property). Trust beneficiaries own the trust's stock in proportion to their interests in the trust. (These trust rules do not apply to exempt employee trusts.) [IRC Sec. 318(a)(2), (3); Reg. Sec. 1.318-2, 1.318-3].

> **Example 4:** A testamentary trust owns 25 of the outstanding 100 shares of stock of a corporation. Mr. Drake, who holds a vested remainder in the trust having a value, determined actuarially, equal to 4% of the value of the trust property, owns the remaining 75 shares. Since Drake's interest in the trust is vested rather than contingent (whether or not remote), the trust is considered as owning 100 shares. Drake is considered as owning 76 shares (75 + 4% of 25).

Grantor-owned trust [¶3523]. There is mutual attribution between the trust and any grantor or other person treated as its owner [IRC Sec. 318(a)(2),(3)].

(d) S Corporations. An S corporation is treated as a partnership [(b) above] for purposes of the constructive ownership rules [IRC Sec. 318(a)(5)(E)].

(e) Corporations. If you own, or are deemed to own 50% or more in value of a corporation's stock, you are considered an owner of any stock the corporation owns, in the ratio of the value of your stock to the value of all the corporation's stock. The corporation in turn owns your stock in other corporations [IRC Sec. 318(a)(2), (3); Reg. Sec. 1.318-1, 1.318-2].

> **Example 5:** Ms. Foster and Mr. Hopkins, unrelated individuals, own 70% and 30% in value of the stock of M Corp. respectively. M owns 50 of the 100 outstanding shares of stock of O Corp., the remaining 50 shares being owned by Foster. M Corp. is considered as owning 100 shares of O Corp., and Amy is considered as owning 85 shares of O Corp. (50 + 70% of 50).

(f) Options. If you have options to acquire stock (or options to acquire an option), you are considered to own the stock [IRC Sec. 318(a)(4); Reg. Sec. 1.318-3]. Warrants or convertible debentures are considered options if you can obtain the stock at your election.[1]

> **Example 6:** Mr. Newman and Ms. Taylor, unrelated individuals, own all of the 100 outstanding shares of stock of a corporation, each owning 50 shares. Newman has an option to acquire 25 of Taylor's shares, and has an option to acquire a further option to acquire the remaining 25 of Taylor's shares. Newman is considered as owning the entire 100 shares of stock of the corporation.

(g) Constructive Ownership as Actual Ownership. Stock constructively owned by you under the above rules is treated as actually owned (it can be reattributed from you to others).

> **Example 7:** Assume the facts of Example 1. The rules provide that you, your wife and your son are each considered as owning 80 shares. If the remaining 20 shares are owned by another corporation wholly owned by you, then you, your wife and your son are all considered to own the stock in fact owned by that corporation.

Exceptions. There are two exceptions to the above rules:

1. Stock attributed to a partnership, estate, trust or corporation under the rules in (b), (c) or (e) above cannot be reattributed under those rules [IRC Sec. 318(a)(5)(C); Reg. Sec. 1.318-4];

2. Stock attributed to an individual under the rules in (a) above cannot be reattributed under those rules [Reg. Sec. 1.318-4].

> **Example 8:** Assume the facts of Example 1. Your grandson owns 20 of the outstanding 100 shares. His father owns in fact 20 of such shares, but is considered to own, in addition, the stock owned by his parents (yourself and your wife) and his son. But your grandson is not considered to own your and your wife's stock by reattribution from his father.

Overlapping rules. If stock can be attributed to you under either the family or option rule, it is attributed under the option rule, and exception (2) above does not apply [IRC Sec. 318(a)(5)(D)].

Footnotes to Chapter 22

For your added convenience, in brackets [] with the footnotes below, you will find citations to related paragraphs in the "RIA United States Tax Reporter"(USTR), "CCH Federal Tax Reporter"(CCH) and "RIA Federal Tax Coordinator 2d"(FTC) multi-volume services.)

FOOTNOTE ¶ 3200 [USTR ¶ 3684; CCH ¶ 16,401; FTC ¶ F-4000 et seq.].

FOOTNOTE ¶ 3201 [USTR ¶ 3684; CCH ¶ 16,401; FTC ¶ F-6013].

(1) Rev. Rul. 72-206, 1972-1 CB 104.

(2) Pinellas Ice and Cold Storage Co. v. Comm., 287 US 462, 11 AFTR 1112.

(3) Burnham v. Comm., 86 F.2d 776, 18 AFTR 2d 6030, 353 F.2d 184.

FOOTNOTE ¶ 3202 [USTR ¶ 3684; CCH ¶ 16,753; FTC ¶ F-4000 et seq.].

(1) Gregory v. Helvering, 293 US 465, 55 SCt. 266, 14 AFTR 1191; Wilson v. Comm., 16 AFTR 2d 6030, 353 F.2d 184.

FOOTNOTE ¶ 3203 [USTR ¶ 3684.01; CCH ¶ 16,753; FTC ¶ F-4100 et seq.].

(1) Southwest Natural Gas Co. v. Comm., 189 F.2d 332, 40 AFTR 686.

FOOTNOTE ¶ 3204 [USTR ¶ 3684.02; CCH ¶ 16,753; FTC ¶ F-4400 et seq.].

(1) Turnbow v. Comm., 368 US 337, 82 SCt. 353, 8 AFTR 2d 5967; Rev. Rul. 70-65, 1970-1 CB 77.

(2) Mills v. Comm., 13 AFTR 2d 1386, 331 F.2d 321; Rev. Rul. 66-365, 1966-2 CB 116.

(3) Rev. Rul. 66-112, 1966-1 CB 68.

(4) Rev. Rul. 69-142, 1969-1 CB 107; Rev. Rul. 70-41, 1970-1 CB 77.

(5) Rev. Rul. 70-108, 1970-1 CB 78.

FOOTNOTE ¶ 3205 [USTR ¶ 3684.03; CCH ¶ 16,753; FTC ¶ F-4600 et seq.].

(1) Rev. Rul. 66-365, 1966-2 CB 116.

(2) Civic Center Finance Co. v. Kuhl, 177 F.2d 706, 38 AFTR 835.

(3) Rev. Proc. 77-37, 1977-2 CB 568; Rev. Proc. 82-23, 1982-1 CB 474; Rev. Proc. 83-81, 1983-2 CB 598.

(4) Daily Telegram Co., 34 BTA 101.

(5) Rev. Rul. 57-518, 1957-2 CB 253.

(6) Nat. Bk. of Commerce of Norfolk v. U.S., 1 AFTR 2d 894, 158 F.Supp. 887.

(7) Schuh Trading Co., 95 F.2d 404, 20 AFTR 1114.

(8) American Foundation Co., 120 F.2d 807, 27 AFTR 524.

(9) Gross v. Comm., 88 F.2d 567, 19 AFTR 158.

(10) Rev. Rul. 64-73, 1964-1 CB 142.

FOOTNOTE ¶ 3206 [USTR ¶ 3684.04; CCH ¶ 16,753; FTC ¶ F-4902 et seq.].

FOOTNOTE ¶ 3207 [USTR ¶ 3684.05; CCH ¶ 16,753; FTC ¶ F-9005].

(1) Rev. Rul. 69-34, 1969-1 CB 105; Rev. Rul. 81-81, 1981-1 CB 122.

(2) Neustadt, 43 BTA 848, aff'd 131 F.2d 528, 30 AFTR 320.

FOOTNOTE ¶ 3208 [USTR ¶ 3684.06; CCH ¶ 16,753; FTC ¶ F-4006; 9100 et seq.].

(1) Rev. Rul. 57-276, 1957-1 CB 126.

FOOTNOTE ¶ 3209 [USTR ¶ 3684.07; CCH ¶ 16,753; FTC ¶ F-9100 et seq.].

(1) Committee Report, P.L. 96-589.

(2) Rev. Proc. 83-81, 1983-2 CB 598.

FOOTNOTE ¶ 3211 [USTR ¶ 3544; 3614; CCH ¶ 16,433; FTC ¶ F-6019; 6024; 6025].

FOOTNOTE ¶ 3213 [USTR ¶ 3564; CCH ¶ 16,493; FTC ¶ F-6019 et seq.; F-6518].

(1) Rev. Rul. 68-23, 1968-1 CB 144.

FOOTNOTE ¶ 3214 [USTR ¶ 3564.03; CCH ¶ 16,493; FTC ¶ F-6025].

(1) Comm. v. Bedford's Est., 325 US 283, 33 AFTR 832.

FOOTNOTE ¶ 3215 [USTR ¶ 3584; CCH ¶ 16,553; FTC ¶ F-6036].

FOOTNOTE ¶ 3216 [USTR ¶ 3624; CCH ¶ 16,612; FTC ¶ F-6700 et seq.].

FOOTNOTE ¶ 3217 [USTR ¶ 3574; CCH ¶ 16,552; FTC ¶ F-6513].

(1) Rev. Rul. 68-629, 1968-2 CB 154.

FOOTNOTE ¶ 3220 [USTR ¶ 3554; CCH ¶ 16,466; FTC ¶ F-8001].

FOOTNOTE ¶ 3221 [USTR ¶ 3554; CCH ¶ 16,466; FTC ¶ F-6010; 6011].

FOOTNOTE ¶ 3222 [USTR ¶ 3554; CCH ¶ 16,466; FTC ¶ F-8000 et seq.].

FOOTNOTE ¶ 3223 [USTR ¶ 3554; CCH ¶ 16,466; FTC ¶ F-14301].

FOOTNOTE ¶ 3224 [USTR ¶ 3564; CCH ¶ 16,202; FTC ¶ F-6019 et seq.].

FOOTNOTE ¶ 3225 [USTR ¶ 3564.02; CCH ¶ 16,553; FTC ¶ F-6036 et seq.].

FOOTNOTE ¶ 3233 [USTR ¶ 3364; CCH ¶ 16,001; FTC ¶ F-13000 et seq.].

FOOTNOTE ¶ 3234 [USTR ¶ 3364.01; CCH ¶ 16,202; FTC ¶ F-14401].

FOOTNOTE ¶ 3235 [USTR ¶ 3374.01; CCH ¶ 16,052; FTC ¶ F-13200 et seq.].

(1) Rev. Proc. 81-68, 1981-2 CB 723.

(2) Rev. Rul. 69-426, 1969-2 CB 48.

FOOTNOTE ¶ 3236 [USTR ¶ 3814; CCH ¶ 17,031; FTC ¶ F-7000 et seq.].

(1) Rev. Rul. 70-27, 1970-1 CB 83.

(2) The Aetna Cas. & Surety Co., 39 AFTR 2d 77-400; rehear. den., 39 AFTR 2d-77-1111.

FOOTNOTE ¶ 3237 [USTR ¶ 3814.02; CCH ¶ 17,031; FTC ¶ F-7000 et seq.].

FOOTNOTE ¶ 3238 [USTR ¶ 3814.02; CCH ¶ 17,115; FTC ¶ F-7200 et seq.].

FOOTNOTE ¶ 3239 [USTR ¶ 3814.05; CCH ¶ 17,206; FTC ¶ F-7390 et seq.].

FOOTNOTE ¶ 3240 [USTR ¶ 3024; CCH ¶ 15,227; FTC ¶ F-11000 et seq.; F-12000 et seq.].

(1) Seabrook Sr. v. U.S., 17 AFTR 2d 1041, F.Supp. 652.

(2) U.S. v. Davis, 25 AFTR 2d 70-827, 397 US 301, 90 SCt. 1041.

(3) Rev. Rul. 77-426, 1977-2 CB 87.

(4) Treas. Dept. booklet "Tax Guide for Small Business" [1991 Ed.], p. 74.

(5) Rev. Rul. 75-2, 1975-1 CB 99.

FOOTNOTE ¶ 3241 [USTR ¶ 3044; CCH ¶ 15,281; FTC ¶ F-11800 et seq.].

FOOTNOTE ¶ 3242 [USTR ¶ 3034; CCH ¶ 15,253; FTC ¶ F-11700 et seq.].

(1) Byrd v. Comm., 21 AFTR 2d 313, 388 F.2d 223.

FOOTNOTE ¶ 3243 [USTR ¶ 3064; CCH ¶ 15,352; FTC ¶ F-12000 et seq.; F-12100 et seq.].

(1) Rev. Rul. 66-332, 1966-2 CB 108, modified by Rev. Rul. 81-91, 1981-1 CB 123.

FOOTNOTE ¶ 3244 [USTR ¶ 3184; CCH ¶ 15,806; FTC ¶ F-11900 et seq.].

(1) Rev. Rul. 68-601, 1968-2 CB 124.

CHAPTER 23

CORPORATIONS—PERSONAL HOLDING COMPANIES, ETC.— EXEMPT ORGANIZATIONS

PERSONAL HOLDING COMPANIES

¶3300   PERSONAL HOLDING COMPANY (PHC) TAX

The personal holding company tax is aimed at closely held corporations with income mainly from investments [IRC Sec. 541].

A high surtax [¶3305] is imposed on undistributed earnings [¶3304] of personal holding companies in addition to the regular tax on corporate taxable income [Chapter 20].

Alternative minimum tax. Like other corporations, personal holding companies pay an alternative minimum tax on their tax preferences [¶2610]. However, unlike other corporations, PHCs treat accelerated depreciation on leased personal property placed in service before 1987 as a tax preference [IRC Sec. 57(a)].

What is a personal holding company. Your corporation is a PHC only if: (1) its income is mainly "personal holding company income" [¶3301] *and* (2) five or fewer individuals own more than 50% of its stock [¶3302]. The tests are applied each year to the situation as it exists that year.

¶3301   THE PHC INCOME REQUIREMENT

Your corporation becomes a personal holding company only when 60% or more of its adjusted ordinary gross income for the tax year is PHC income [IRC Sec. 542(a)(1)]. To find adjusted ordinary gross income, first reduce gross income by capital gains and Sec. 1231 gains. This is ordinary gross income. Then reduce ordinary gross income by the amount of: *leasing income* (rents, etc.) your corporation receives for the use of tangible personal property it manufactures as a substantial activity during the tax year; *interest* on judgments, tax refunds, condemnation awards and U.S. obligations held for sale by a dealer; *rents* to the extent of related deductions for property taxes, interest, rent incurred and depreciation (except depreciation on tangible personal property not customarily leased to any one lessee for more than 3 years); *mineral, oil, and gas royalties* and income from working interests to the extent of related deductions for depletion, property and severance taxes, interest and rent incurred [IRC Sec. 543(b)]. Rents and royalties not eliminated are the adjusted amounts included in personal holding company income.

Personal holding company income is income from the items below. Any income disregarded to find adjusted ordinary gross income also is excluded from PHC income [IRC Sec. 543(a)].

- *Dividends, interest, royalties, and annuities.* Royalties are those other than mineral, oil, gas, and copyright royalties. Computer software royalties received by certain companies that are actively engaged in the business of developing computer software are not personal holding company income under specified conditions [IRC Sec. 543(d); 553(a)].
- *Rent* adjusted for the use of, or the right to use, corporate property. Adjusted rents are not personal holding company income if they are at least 50% of adjusted ordinary gross income and any other PHC income that exceeds 10% of ordinary gross income is paid out in dividends.
- *Adjusted mineral, oil and gas royalties.* They are PHC income unless (1) they are at least 50% of adjusted ordinary gross income; (2) trade or business deductions (except compensation paid to shareholders) are at least 15% of adjusted ordinary gross income; and (3) other PHC income is 10% or less of ordinary gross income.
- *Copyright royalties.* Copyright royalties include film rents (except produced film rents). Produced film rents (payments received because the corporation held an interest in the film before it was substantially completed) are not counted if they are at least 50% of ordinary gross income.
- *Payments for the use of tangible corporate property by a shareholder* who owns, directly or indirectly, 25% or more in value of the outstanding stock at any time during the tax year. However, it applies only if the corporation has other PHC income for the tax year in excess of 10% of its ordinary gross income.
- *Payments under personal service contracts,* if the individual who is to perform the services is named in the contract or can be designated by someone other than the corporation, and directly or indirectly owns 25% or more in value of the outstanding corporate stock at any time during the tax year.[1]
- *Taxable income from estates and trusts* is PHC income [¶3503 et seq.].

¶3302   THE STOCK OWNERSHIP REQUIREMENT

Even if your corporation meets the income test [¶3301], it is not classified as a PHC unless more than 50% in value of its outstanding stock is owned, directly or indirectly, by five or fewer individuals any time during the last half of the tax year. Under this rule, certain charitable foundations and trusts are considered individuals [IRC Sec. 542(a)(2); Reg. Sec. 1.542-3].

The following rules determine whether your corporation meets the stock ownership requirement and whether payments under personal service contracts, payments for use of property, and copyright royalties are personal holding company income (¶3301) [IRC Sec. 544; Reg. Sec. 1.544-1–7]:

1. *Stock not owned by individual.* Stock owned, directly or indirectly, by or for your corporation, partnership, estate, or trust is considered owned proportionately by its shareholders, partners, or beneficiaries.

2. *Family and partnership ownership.* You are considered as owning the stock owned, directly or indirectly, by or for your family or your partner. Your family includes only brothers and sisters (whole or half-blood), spouse, ancestors, and lineal descendants.

NOTE: Despite these attribution rules, any particular shares of stock are counted only once in determining whether you meet the 50% ownership requirement. In general, shares are attributed in a manner that produces the highest concentration of ownership in five or fewer individuals. Once ownership of shares is attributed to a particular shareholder, no one else (not even the direct owner) is deemed to own them for purposes of the 50% test.[1]

3. *Options.* If you have an option to acquire stock, you are considered the owner of it. This applies to an option to acquire an option, and each one of a series of options. The option rule takes precedence over the family and partnership rules.

4. *Constructive ownership.* Stock constructively owned by you through applying rule (1) or (3) above is treated as actually owned by you in again applying rule (1) or in applying rule (2) so as to make another the stock's constructive owner.

5. *Convertible securities.* Outstanding securities convertible into stock (whether or not convertible during the tax year) are considered as outstanding stock, but only if including all such securities will make the corporation a PHC.

¶3303   CORPORATIONS EXEMPT FROM THE TAX

The following cannot be treated as personal holding companies and are exempt from PHC tax [IRC Sec. 542(c)]:

- Corporations exempt from the income tax [¶3336].
- Banks, domestic building and loan associations, life insurance companies, and surety companies.
- Certain lending or finance companies [IRC Sec. 542(c)(6), (d)].
- Foreign PHCs [¶3311 et seq.], and other foreign corporations with no personal service contract income [¶3301] and wholly owned by nonresident alien individuals directly or indirectly (through foreign estates, trusts, partnerships or corporations) during the last half of the tax year [IRC Sec. 542(c)(5), (7)].
- A small business investment company, unless a shareholder owns a 5% or more interest in a concern receiving funds from the company [IRC Sec. 542(c)(8)].
- A corporation under court jurisdiction in a bankruptcy or similar case, unless a major purpose of the court proceeding is to avoid PHC tax [IRC Sec. 542(c)(9)].
- A passive foreign investment company [IRC Sec. 542(c)(10)].

¶3304   INCOME SUBJECT TO PHC TAX

The personal holding company tax is a tax on the *undistributed* personal holding company income.

(a) Undistributed PHC Income is your corporation's taxable income for regular income tax purposes with certain adjustments minus the dividends-paid deduction ((b) below) [IRC Sec. 545(b); Reg. Sec. 1.545-1]. The rules for the adjustments are:

- *Taxes.* Your corporation can deduct federal income taxes and foreign income and profits taxes not deducted in figuring taxable income. Your corporation can also deduct certain foreign taxes attributable to dividends it receives from foreign subsidiaries that are deemed to have been paid by the domestic corporations [¶3806; 3828]. The accumulated earnings tax and the personal holding company tax are *not* deductible [IRC Sec. 545(b)(1); Reg. Sec. 1.545-2(a)].

- *Charitable contributions.* Your corporation can deduct charitable contributions, with the same taxable income limitation as for an individual [¶1919], but without any carryover. Taxable income for purposes of the contribution limitation is figured without the charitable deduction [¶3019(b)], certain expense and depreciation deductions, special deductions (other than organizational expenditures) and net operating loss or capital loss carryback to the tax year [IRC Sec. 545(b)(2); Reg. Sec. 1.545-2(b)].
- *Expenses and depreciation* allocable to the operation and maintenance of property may not exceed rent your corporation receives for the use of the property unless: (a) the rent was the highest obtainable, or if none was received, none was obtainable; (b) the property was held in the course of a business carried on in good faith for profit; and (c) it was reasonable to expect that operation of the property would result in a profit, or the property was necessary to the business [IRC Sec. 545(b)(6); Reg. Sec. 1.545-2(h)].
- *Net gains.* A deduction is allowed for your corporation's net capital gain, but reduced by the taxes on such net capital gain [IRC Sec. 545(b)(5); Reg. Sec. 1.545-2(e)]. The reduction is the difference between (1) the tax on the total taxable income and (2) the tax on the taxable income, excluding the net capital gain.

For gains and losses realized by a foreign corporation, the personal holding company tax is calculated by taking into account only capital gains and losses that are effectively connected with the conduct of a U.S. trade or business and are not exempt by treaty [IRC Sec. 545(b)(7)].

- *Net operating loss* deduction is not allowed; but a deduction is allowed for the net operating loss of the preceding year figured without the special deductions (except organizational expenditures) [IRC Sec. 545(b)(4); Reg. Sec. 1.545-2(d)].
- *Dividends-received* deduction is not allowed [IRC Sec. 545(b)(3); Reg. Sec. 1.545-2(c)].
- *Income for a short period* [¶2819] needn't be annualized [IRC Sec. 546].

After these adjustments are made, the dividends-paid deduction is subtracted to find undistributed PHC income [IRC Sec. 545(a); Reg. Sec. 1.545-1].

(b) Dividends-Paid Deduction. Your corporation can subtract (1) dividends it paid during the year, (2) consent dividends, (3) the dividend carryover, and (4) certain dividends it paid after the close of the tax year. The figure arrived at is the "undistributed personal holding company income," which is the basis of the tax [IRC Sec. 561; Reg. Sec. 1.561-1, -2].

Dividends paid during the tax year. Only taxable dividends can be subtracted. Thus, your corporation must pay dividends out of earnings or profits (¶1218) [IRC Sec. 562; Reg. Sec. 1.562-1(a)]. However, any distribution to the extent of the undistributed PHC income is considered a taxable dividend, even if it is not paid out of earnings. Such dividends also are taxable to the stockholders [IRC Sec. 316(b)(2); Reg. Sec. 1.316-1; 1.563-3]. This prevents an inequity when undistributed PHC income exceeds earnings, as could occur when certain deductions are disallowed.

> **Example:** XYZ, Inc., a personal holding company with no accumulated earnings, has $5,000 earnings for the tax year. However, its adjusted PHC taxable income is $15,000, due to the disallowance of $10,000 of deductions. To avoid the PHC tax, XYZ must pay out $15,000 of dividends. However, if it could only subtract dividends paid from earnings, the maximum subtracted would be $5,000, leaving an undistributed personal holding company income of $10,000 subject to PHC tax. The exception above permits the subtraction of $15,000. The $15,000 is taxable to shareholders, even though earnings and profits are just $5,000.

NOTE: Your personal holding company's distribution of appreciated property results in a dividends-paid deduction equal to the adjusted basis (*not* fair market value) of the property in the hands of your company at the time of the distribution. Reg. Sec. 1.562-1(a) is used to determine the amount of deduction.[1]

Generally, in figuring undistributed PHC income, your corporation may subtract only the part of a liquidating dividend chargeable to accumulated earnings and profits. However, distributions of undistributed PHC income in a complete liquidation (including a distribution in redemption of stock under IRC Sec. 302 [¶3240 et seq.]) concluded within a 24-month period may be treated as dividends [IRC Sec. 316(b)(2); 562(b)]. The dividend cannot be more than the undistributed PHC income for the year of distribution. You must allocate the distributions between corporate and noncorporate shareholders, and amounts your corporation pays to noncorporate shareholders may not be subtracted unless designated as dividend distributions [Reg. Sec. 1.316-1(b)(2); 1.562-1(b)(2)].

Let's say your personal holding company files a consolidated return with an affiliated group and must also file a separate PHC schedule. Your company can subtract a dividend distribution to another group member if it would be a taxable dividend to a recipient who is not a member of an affiliated group [IRC Sec. 562(d); Reg. Sec. 1.562-3].

Dividends paid after the close of the tax year [see below], but removed from PHC income in the tax year, may not be subtracted again by your company in the year actually distributed [IRC Sec. 563(b)].

The following dividends cannot be deducted out of undistributed PHC income: Nontaxable dividends, including nontaxable stock dividends and nontaxable stock rights [IRC Sec. 312]; preferential dividends, including a distribution that is not made to all shareholders within the same class of stock in proportion to their shareholdings, or one that violates the dividend preference of any class of stock [IRC Sec. 562(c); Reg. Sec. 1.562-2].

Consent dividends. Your corporation can get the dividends-paid deduction without impairing its cash position by paying cash dividends that are immediately returned to your corporation in the form of a loan or capital contribution [IRC Sec. 565; Reg. Sec. 1.565-1–6]. However, if the consent of you and the other shareholders is obtained, it is presumed that a dividend was paid and then invested by you in the corporation without an actual distribution. On your corporation's part, the consent dividend is considered as paid-in surplus or as a contribution to capital, with a corresponding reduction in its earnings and profits. On your part, the consent dividend is taxable the same as a cash dividend. Since it is theoretically reinvested by you, the basis of your stock is correspondingly increased [IRC Sec. 1016(a)(12); Reg. Sec. 1.1016-5(h)].

Dividend carryover. If dividends exceeded adjusted taxable income in each of the two prior tax years, the sum of the excess dividends for those two years may be carried over to the current tax year. If there is an excess only in the first preceding year, only that amount is carried over. If the excess is in the second preceding year, it is reduced by the excess of taxable income over the dividends paid in the first year. Any balance is then carried over to the current tax year [IRC Sec. 564(b); Reg. Sec. 1.564-1].

NOTE: "Dividends" referred to above include (a) dividends paid during the tax year, (b) dividends paid before the 15th day of the third month following its close and (c) consent dividends. They do not include the dividend carryover [IRC Sec. 564(b)(1)].

Dividends paid after the close of the tax year. Your corporation can elect to take a deduction for dividends paid after the close of the tax year and within 2½ months after its close. However, the deduction cannot exceed (1) the undistributed PHC income figured without the deduction for dividends paid after the close of the year or (2) 20% of the dividends paid during the year, not including consent dividends or the deduction for dividends paid after the close of the preceding year [IRC Sec. 563(b); Reg. Sec. 1.563-2].

In figuring the accumulated earnings tax [¶3040 et seq.], your corporation can deduct without election or restriction dividends paid after the close of the tax year and within 2½ months after its close [IRC Sec. 563(a); Reg. Sec. 1.563-1].

(c) Foreign Corporations. When 10% or less of the value of the outstanding stock of a foreign corporation subject to the tax is owned by U.S. citizens or residents, domestic corporations, partnerships, estates or trusts during the last half of the tax year, only the same percentage of the corporation's undistributed PHC income is taxed [IRC Sec. 545(a)]. The greatest percentage of ownership during the period is used. For wholly foreign-owned foreign corporations, see ¶3303.

¶3305   RATE OF TAX, RETURNS AND PAYMENT

[New tax legislation may affect this subject; see ¶1.]

The PHC tax is 28% of undistributed PHC income [IRC Sec. 541]. Your corporation files a single return for both the income tax and the personal holding company tax. A separate Schedule PH (Form 1120) is provided for the PHC tax. Your corporation pays the tax at the same time as the income tax [¶3630].

A foreign corporation that fails to file a return for its PHC tax must pay a penalty of 10% of the taxes (except employment taxes) payable by the corporation for the tax year, including the personal holding company tax [IRC Sec. 6683].

¶3307   DEFICIENCY DIVIDEND

Suppose it has been determined that your corporation is subject to the personal holding company tax for a prior tax year. A procedure allows your corporation to make a dividend distribution to you and its other shareholders even though the distribution does not qualify for a dividends-paid deduction. This procedure relieves your corporation from paying the deficiency, or entitles it to a refund or credit if any part of the deficiency has been paid [IRC Sec. 547(d)].

➤ **OBSERVATION** This means that you and the other shareholders are currently taxed because of this distribution. Also, the PHC tax is partially or completely wiped out for your corporation.

This remedy does not extend to interest and penalties. It is not available at all if any part of the deficiency was due to fraud or willful failure to file a timely return.

In most cases, the first step toward paying a deficiency dividend is to sign an agreement with the IRS as to the corporation's liability for the personal holding company tax. This is known as a determination. The determination date ordinarily is the date that the agreement is mailed to your corporation, but it is the date that the agreement is signed if a dividend is paid before the mailing date but on or after the date of signing. The term "determination" also means a decision by the Tax Court, a judgment, decree, or other court order that has become final, or a closing agreement [¶3708(b)]. Your corporation must pay the deficiency dividend within 90 days after the determination date. Your corporation must file a claim for a deduction within 120 days after the determination date. A refund claim can be filed by your corporation within 2 years from the determination date [IRC Sec. 547; Reg. Sec. 1.547-11.547-7].

¶3308   DEFERRAL OF LOSS FROM SALES BETWEEN CONTROLLED CORPORATIONS

For any loss on a sale or exchange between members of a controlled group, no deduction is allowed until the property is transferred outside the controlled group, or until a time set by the regulations [IRC Sec. 267(a), (b), (f)]. This loss deferral rule applies to such related parties as parent-subsidiary groups, brother-sister controlled groups (connected by common ownership, including individuals, estates, and trusts) and combined groups. Generally, the requirements for determining a controlled group are those set out in IRC Sec. 1563, except that a 50% ownership requirement is substituted for the 80% ordinarily used.

¶3309   CONSOLIDATED RETURNS

The PHC tax does not apply to affiliated corporations filing a consolidated return, unless 60% or more of the adjusted ordinary gross income of the group is PHC income. Generally, this does not apply if any member of the group (including the common parent): (1) is exempt from the PHC tax or (2) received 10% or more of its adjusted ordinary gross income from sources outside the affiliated group, and 80% or more of the income from outside sources was PHC income [IRC Sec. 542(b); Reg. Sec. 1.542-4].

¶3311   TAX ON UNDISTRIBUTED FOREIGN PERSONAL HOLDING COMPANY INCOME

The U.S. shareholders, including estates or trusts (other than foreign estates or trusts) and U.S. corporations, of foreign personal holding companies must include undistributed foreign PHC income (determined by disregarding any liquidating distributions) in their gross income. Certain foreign corporations are exempt from this treatment [¶3315].

¶3312   WHAT IS A FOREIGN PHC

A foreign corporation is a foreign PHC if [IRC Sec. 552(a); Reg. Sec. 1.552-1]:

   1.   60% or more of its gross income for the tax year is foreign PHC income (or 50%, if it was a foreign PHC in the prior year) [IRC Sec. 552(a)(1); Reg. Sec. 1.552-2].

2. More than 50% in value of its outstanding stock is owned, directly or indirectly, by or for not over five individuals who are U.S. citizens or residents [IRC Sec. 552(a)(2); 554; Reg. Sec. 1.552-3].

> ➤ **OBSERVATION** Foreign corporations that are not foreign personal holding companies may be subject to personal holding company tax [¶3303].

Foreign PHC income, in general, includes: (1) dividends, interest, royalties and annuities; (2) net gains from the sale of stocks and securities; (3) net gains from commodity futures transactions (but bona fide business hedging transactions are disregarded); (4) income from estates and trusts, or from a disposition of an interest in an estate or trust; (5) income from personal service contracts [¶3301]; (6) payments for use of corporate property by a 25% or more shareholder; (7) rents (unless they are 50% or more of gross income) [IRC Sec. 553; Reg. Sec. 1.553-1]. Foreign PHC income does not include dividends and interest from related corporations that operate trades or businesses in the recipient's country [IRC Sec. 552(c)].

NOTE: Related-person dividend or interest is treated as Foreign PHC income to the extent it is attributable to Foreign PHC income of a related person [IRC Sec. 552(c)(1)].

¶3313 UNDISTRIBUTED FOREIGN PHC INCOME

Undistributed foreign PHC income is the taxable income of a foreign PHC (adjusted as shown below), minus the dividends-paid deduction [IRC Sec. 556; Reg. Sec. 1.556-1, -3]. The rules for dividends paid that apply to domestic holding companies [¶3304(b)] also apply to foreign holding companies with certain exceptions.

The adjustments made to taxable income to determine undistributed foreign personal holding company income are basically the same adjustments PHCs make for taxes, charitable contributions, special deductions, net operating losses, and expenses and depreciation related to corporate property [¶3304(a)]. In addition, the taxes of a shareholder in a foreign PHC paid by the corporation and any deduction relating to pension trusts are disallowed [IRC Sec. 556(b); Reg. Sec. 1.556-2].

¶3314 CORPORATION INCOME TAXED TO UNITED STATES SHAREHOLDERS

Undistributed foreign PHC income is included in gross income of its U.S. shareholders. For the foreign PHC rules, stock held for U.S. persons through certain foreign entities may be attributed to those persons.

Example: A owns 25% of the stock of X, a foreign PHC, and X's undistributed foreign PHC income is $100,000. A must include $25,000 in gross income for his tax year in which the end of the corporation's tax year falls [IRC Sec. 551; Reg. Sec. 1.551-1, -2].

The undistributed foreign PHC income is treated as a contribution to capital, thus increasing the stockholders' basis for the stock [IRC Sec. 551(d), (e); Reg. Sec. 1.551-5].

NOTE: Certain income, which could be subject to tax under either the controlled foreign corporation (CFC) rules [¶3828] or the foreign PHC rules, is included in the U.S. shareholder's income only under the CFC rules.

¶3315   EXEMPT CORPORATIONS

Corporations exempt under Sec. 501 are not classed as foreign personal holding companies. Certain exempt corporations and corporations organized and doing business under foreign banking and credit laws also are excluded [IRC Sec. 552(b); Reg. Sec. 1.552-4, -5].

¶3316   RETURNS FOR FOREIGN PHCs

These returns are required:

- Information returns must be submitted by shareholders owning over 5% in stock value, as part of their annual tax return [IRC Sec. 551(c); Reg. Sec. 1.551-4].
- Annual returns on Form 957 by officers, directors and U.S. shareholders owning 10% or more in value of the outstanding stock, stating ownership of stock and convertible securities, along with other information, must be filed within 15 days after the corporation's tax year ends [IRC Sec. 6035; Reg. Sec. 1.6035-1(a)(1), -2].
- Annual returns by officers and directors on Form 958 giving complete information on gross income, deductions, credits, taxable income, undistributed earnings and ownership of stock and convertible securities are due within 60 days after the corporation's tax year ends [IRC Sec. 6035].
- Information returns must be filed for foreign corporations [¶3670].

There is a $1,000 penalty for unreasonable failure to file a proper information return [IRC Sec. 6038(b)].

REGULATED INVESTMENT COMPANIES (RIC)

¶3325   TAX ON REGULATED INVESTMENT COMPANIES
(MUTUAL FUNDS)

A regulated investment company (or mutual fund) is taxed only on undistributed income, since it can deduct most dividends paid. A periodic payment plan (an investment trust that sells shares in a mutual fund in installments) is generally not subject to tax; the investors are treated as owning the fund shares directly and are taxed on the shares only if sold [IRC Sec. 851(f); Reg. Sec. 1.851-7]. A regulated investment company may be hit with a 4% nondeductible excise tax on the amount by which its distributions for the year fall short of its " required distribution" for the year [¶3328].

¶3326   REQUIREMENTS TO BE TAXED AS A REGULATED
INVESTMENT COMPANY

[New tax legislation may affect this subject; see ¶1.]

To qualify as a regulated investment company (RIC), a corporation must meet the following requirements:

1. *The corporation must either be registered* under the Investment Company Act of 1940 or be a certain type of common trust fund [IRC Sec. 851(a); Reg. Sec. 1.851-1(b)].

NOTE: A corporation that elects to be treated as a business development company under the Investment Company Act is eligible to be a RIC [IRC Sec. 851(a)(1)(B)].

2. *Election.* The corporation must file an election to be taxed as a regulated investment company with its return for the tax year. The election is binding for future years [IRC Sec. 851(b)(1); Reg. Sec. 1.851-2(a)].

3. *Gross income.* At least 90% of the corporation's gross income must be from dividends (including constructive dividends from controlled foreign corporations), interest (including tax-exempt interest), security loan payments defined in IRC Sec. 512(a)(5) and gains from the sale or other disposition of stock or securities. Income from disposition of stock or securities held under three months must be less than 30% of gross income [IRC Sec. 851(b)(2), (3); Reg. Sec. 1.851-2(b)].

NOTE: The 30% test also applies to foreign currencies or other income, including gains from options, futures or forward contracts derived with respect to the corporation's business of investing in such stock, securities or currencies [IRC Sec. 851(b)(3)]. The application of the 30% rule is modified in two situations: (1) gains after a plan of complete liquidation is adopted are not considered if the RIC liquidates during the year in which the plan is adopted; and (2) a fund that belongs to a series will not be disqualified under the 30% test by reason of sales resulting from, and occurring within five days of, abnormal redemptions (i.e., redemptions in a single day of more than 1% of the fund's net asset value) if (a) the sum of abnormal redemptions on that day and on prior days during the tax year exceeds 30% of net asset value and (b) all funds in the series meet the test if treated as a single RIC [IRC Sec. 851(h)(3)].

Income from a partnership or trust qualifies for the 90% test only to the extent that the income is attributable to income items which would be qualifying income if the RIC realized the income in the same way that the partnership or trust did [IRC Sec. 851(b)(4)].

4. *Diversification of assets.* At the close of each quarter of the tax year, at least 50% of the value of the corporation's total assets must be cash and cash items (including receivables), government securities and securities of other regulated investment companies. Other securities may also be included, but the amount that the taxpayer owns in any one corporation cannot be: (1) greater in value than 5% of the value of the taxpayer's total assets and (2) over 10% of the outstanding voting securities of the issuing corporation. Also, at the close of each quarter, the mutual fund must not have more than 25% of the value of its total assets invested in the securities (other than government securities or the securities of other regulated investment companies) of any one corporation or of two or more corporations which the mutual fund controls, and which are engaged in the same, similar or related business [IRC Sec. 851(b)(4); Reg. Sec. 1.851-2(c)]. Exceptions are made for "venture capital" companies [¶3327].

5. *Distribution of income.* The company must distribute dividends (not counting capital gain dividends) at least equal to the sum of: (a) 90% of its investment company taxable income plus (b) 90% of the excess of its tax-exempt interest over its disallowed tax-exempt interest deductions [IRC Sec. 852(a); Reg. Sec. 1.852-1]. The dividends may be paid during the tax year, or after its close [¶3328(e)].

NOTE: A waiver of the RIC distribution rule may be provided when the failure to meet the rule results from prior year distributions necessary to avoid the excise tax on the undistributed income of a RIC (¶3328) [IRC Sec. 852(a)(2)(B)].

Deduction for deficiency dividends. If an audit adjustment to regulated investment company income or deductions means that distributions to shareholders for the year being audited were insufficient to meet the 90% requirement, the company can make current distributions to its shareholders up to the net amount of the adjustment. The deficiency dividends must be distributed within 90 days after determination. If failure to pay out sufficient dividends is due to fraud or if the company willfully failed to file a return, the deficiency dividend procedure is not available and the company must pay interest at the regular rate on the amount of the deficiency dividend. There is also a penalty equal to the amount of interest, but not more than 50% of the deficiency dividend [IRC Sec. 860; 6697; Reg. Sec. 1.860-1,-5].

Personal holding companies. A PHC without accumulated earnings and profits can elect regulated investment company status. PHCs with accumulated earnings and profits can make distributions to qualify. However, the highest corporate tax rate is imposed on the undistributed investment company taxable income to any regulated investment company which is a PHC (¶3300 et seq.) [IRC Sec. 852(b)(1)].

¶3327   "VENTURE CAPITAL" COMPANIES

An investment company that furnishes capital for corporations chiefly engaged in developing new products is a "venture capital" company. An exception to the diversification requirements is made for "venture capital" companies. Under certain conditions, they may exceed the 10% voting stock limitation. To qualify, the investment company must have the S.E.C. certify, not earlier than 60 days before the close of the tax year, that it is principally engaged in the furnishing of capital to other corporations, which are principally engaged in the development or exploitation of inventions, technological improvements, new processes, or products not previously generally available [IRC Sec. 851(e)(1); Reg. Sec. 1.851-6].

¶3328   FIGURING THE TAX

Regulated investment companies are taxed on investment company taxable income at the same rates as corporations in general. A regulated investment company which is also a personal holding company is taxed at the highest corporate rate [¶3326]. Investment company taxable income is taxable income [¶3005] with the following adjustments: (1) excess of net long-term capital gain over net short-term capital loss is excluded; (2) no net operating loss deduction is allowed; (3) special deductions listed in ¶3013 are not allowed (except organizational expenditures); (4) dividends paid (other than capital gain and exempt-interest dividends) can be deducted. When shareholders can choose cash or stock [¶1222], the dividends-paid deduction is the cash amount [Reg. Sec. 1.305-2(b)].

Adequate shareholder records need not be kept for a corporation to qualify as a RIC. However, investment company taxable income of a RIC that does not keep adequate shareholder records is taxed at the highest corporate rate (the same treatment is provided for RICs that are personal holding companies [¶3326]) [IRC Sec. 852(a)].

In addition, a tax is imposed on the excess of net long-term capital gain over (1) net short-term capital loss and (2) capital gain dividends paid during the tax year [IRC Sec. 852; Reg. Sec. 1.852-2, -3]. See (a) below for treatment of undistributed long-term capital gain under certain conditions.

For any calendar year, a nondeductible excise tax applies on every RIC, equal to 4% of the excess, if any, of the required distribution for the calendar year over the distributed amount for the calendar year [IRC Sec. 4982]. The excise tax is to be paid not later than March 15 of the succeeding calendar year. "Required distribution" for any calendar year means the sum of 98% of the RIC's ordinary income for the calendar year, plus 98% of the RIC's capital gain net income for the one-year period ending on October 31 of the calendar year. This is increased by the excess, if any, of the grossed-up required distribution for the preceding calendar year over the distributed amount for the preceding calendar year.

(a) Capital Gain Dividends. A capital gain dividend is any dividend (or part of it) so designated by the company in a written notice mailed to its shareholders within 60 days after the end of the mutual fund's tax year. It cannot be more than the excess of the net long-term capital gain over the short-term capital loss. As a shareholder, you treat capital gain dividends you receive as long-term capital gains regardless of how long the stock was held [IRC Sec. 852(b)(3); Reg. Sec. 1.852-2(b), -4(c)]. Distributions from the sale of securities by a unit investment trust to redeem a holder's interest will qualify [IRC Sec. 852(d); Reg. Sec. 1.852-10].

> ➤ **OBSERVATION** A capital loss carryover does not reduce a tax year's earnings and profits available for paying dividends, but does reduce the amount of a dividend that may be designated as a capital gain dividend.

Undistributed long-term capital gain. Regulated investment companies may treat undistributed long-term capital gain as if (a) it had been distributed to its shareholders; (b) the capital gains tax had been paid by the shareholder (rather than the company); and (c) the amount constructively distributed (less the capital gains tax) had been reinvested by the shareholder in the company. As a shareholder, you (1) include this amount in figuring your long-term capital gain; (2) get a credit against your tax equal to the capital gains tax paid by the company on the amount; and (3) add the amount (less the tax) to the basis of your shares. Within 30 days after the close of the tax year, the company must file Form 2438 and pay the tax on the undistributed gain. A notice of the amount constructively distributed must be given to each shareholder on Form 2439 within 60 days after the end of the fund's tax year. You should attach Form 2439 to your return to substantiate the credit claimed [IRC Sec. 852(b)(3)(D); Reg. Sec. 1.852-4, -9(b)].

Shares held six months or less. If you hold shares for six months or less and receive, or are deemed to have received, a capital gain dividend in that period, you treat any loss on the sale of the shares as a long-term capital loss to the extent of the capital gain dividend. To determine the holding period under this provision, the rules governing the more-than-60-day holding period requirement for the dividends-received deduction apply. These rules do not apply to distributions under a periodic liquidation plan [IRC Sec. 852(b)(4)].

Any loss recognized on the sale of shares held six months or less is disallowed to the extent of any exempt-interest dividend received (see (b) below) [IRC Sec. 852(b)(4); Reg. Sec. 1.852-4(d)].

(b) Exempt-Interest Dividend is any dividend (or part of it) so designated by the company in a written notice mailed to its shareholders within 60 days after the close of its tax year. Exempt-interest dividends are allowed only if, at the close of each quarter of its tax year, at least 50% of the value of the company's total assets is tax-exempt obligations. The amount of the dividend cannot be more than the excess of the exempt interest over the disallowed exempt-interest deductions. As a shareholder, you treat exempt-interest dividends as interest excludable from gross income [IRC Sec. 852(b)(5)].

Any loss on the sale or exchange of RIC stock held for six months or less is disallowed to the extent you received exempt-interest dividends for the stock [IRC Sec. 852(b)]. Future regs may shorten the six-month holding period to a period of not less than the greater of 31 days or the period between regular dividend distributions where the RIC regularly distributes at least 90% of its net tax-exempt interest.

(c) Foreign Tax Credit. Instead of taking a credit or deduction for foreign taxes on its own return, a regulated investment company may elect to have its shareholders take the credit or deduction on their returns. Although the company loses the credit or deduction for the foreign taxes, it may add the amount of such taxes to its dividends-paid deduction. Your proportionate share of the foreign taxes must be included in your gross income and treated as paid by you. To qualify for the election, the company must have more than 50% of the value of its total assets at the close of the tax year invested in foreign securities, and must distribute at least 90% of its investment company taxable income. A notice of the election must be sent to shareholders within 60 days after the end of the fund's tax year [IRC Sec. 853; Reg. Sec. 1.853-1–4]. For an explanation of the foreign tax credit, see ¶3801 et seq.

(d) Shareholders' Dividends-Received Deduction. Capital gain dividends do not qualify for the corporate deduction for dividends received [IRC Sec. 854(a); Reg. Sec. 1.854-1].

For other dividends, certain rules apply to determine their eligibility for the dividends-received deduction. For all distributions by the company to be eligible for the corporate dividends-received deduction, 100% of the regulated investment company's gross income must be qualified dividend income. If the company's gross income does not meet the 100% requirement, then only a portion of distributions is eligible for the deduction. This is figured as follows [IRC Sec. 854(b)]:

$$\text{Dividend from regulated investment company} \times \frac{\text{Dividends}}{\text{Company's gross income}}$$

The amount applied to the corporate deduction cannot be more than the amount stated in the notice sent to shareholders within 60 days after the company's tax year ends [IRC Sec. 854(b); Reg. Sec. 1.854-2].

(e) Dividends Declared After Year End, but before the filing date of the return, may be treated as having been paid in the tax year covered by the return if the company elects. However, they must actually be paid to the shareholders not later than the date of the next regular dividend payment after the declaration and within 12 months after the close of the tax year. These dividends are treated by the shareholders as income of the tax year in which the dividends are actually distributed. Notice to shareholders must be given not later than 60 days after the close of the tax year in which the distribution is made [IRC Sec. 855; Reg. Sec. 1.855-1].

(f) Preference Items for Alternative Minimum Tax. Regulated investment companies are not subject to the alternative minimum tax to the extent they pass through tax preferences to their shareholders [Reg. Sec. 1.58-6].

REAL ESTATE INVESTMENT TRUSTS (REIT)

¶3329   TAX ON REITs

[New tax legislation may affect this subject; see ¶1.]

A real estate investment trust (REIT) may elect to be taxed in a manner substantially similar to a regulated investment company [¶3328]. However, unlike a regulated investment company, there is no pass-through of the foreign tax credit and no special provision for undistributed capital gains.

All the assets, liabilities, and items of income, deduction, and credit of a qualified REIT subsidiary are treated as the respective items of the REIT that owns the subsidiary's stock. To be a qualified REIT subsidiary, 100% of the stock must be owned by the REIT during the entire period the subsidiary is in existence [IRC Sec. 856(i)].

Election. The trust makes the election by computing its taxable income as a real estate investment trust in its return for the first tax year for which the election is to apply. The election is irrevocable [IRC Sec. 856(c); Reg. Sec. 1.856-2(b)]. When it qualifies for REIT status, a corporation, trust or association must adopt or change to a calendar-year accounting period [IRC Sec. 859].

An entity that has not engaged in any active business may change its annual accounting period to a calendar year without IRS approval, for electing REIT status [IRC Sec. 859(b)].

(a) General Requirements. In addition to the income and investment requirements explained in (b) and (c) below, a REIT must [IRC Sec. 856(a); Reg. Sec. 1.856-1]:

- Be managed by one or more trustees or directors.
- Have beneficial interests represented by transferable shares or certificates.
- Be taxable as a domestic corporation (but for the REIT provisions).
- Be beneficially owned by at least 100 persons (for at least 335 days of a tax year) and five or fewer persons may not own, either actually or constructively, more than 50% of the stock. Qualified employees' pension or profit-sharing trusts [¶1300] qualify as "persons."[1]

NOTE: An entity generally may not elect REIT status if it would meet the stock ownership test of IRC Sec. 542(a)(2) [¶3302]; i.e., if it would be treated as a personal holding company if all of its income constituted PHC income [IRC Sec. 856(a)(6), (h)].

An entity that otherwise meets the applicable requirements may elect REIT status, even if it meets the PHC stock ownership test (see NOTE above), or if it had fewer than 100 shareholders, provided that the entity was not a REIT in any prior year [IRC Sec. 856(h)]. Also, to elect REIT status, the electing entity must either have been treated as a REIT for all tax years starting after February 28, 1986, or must have no earnings and profits accumulated for any year in which the entity was in existence and not treated as a REIT [IRC Sec. 857(a)].

Prohibited transactions rules. A REIT is not disqualified for holding property primarily for sale to customers in the ordinary course of business, but may be subject to a 100% tax on net income from such sales ("prohibited transactions"), excluding foreclosures. The 100% penalty tax does not apply to a sale of property if (1) the property is held for at least four years (if acquired through foreclosure or lease termination, the period foreclosed loan was held or the property was leased is counted as part of four years); (2) total expenditures during the four years before the sale that are includable in the property's basis do not exceed 30% of net selling price; (3) the REIT does not sell more than seven properties, except foreclosure properties, during the tax year; and (4) except for foreclosure or lease termination property, the property is held for rent for at least four years [IRC Sec. 857(b)(6); Reg. Sec. 1.857-5].

A REIT may make any number of sales during the tax year if the adjusted bases of all sales are not more than 10% of the adjusted bases of all of the REIT assets as of the beginning of the year. To qualify for this alternative prohibited transaction safe harbor, substantially all the marketing and development expenditures for the property sold must have been made through an independent contractor [IRC Sec. 857(b)(6)(c)]. Also, in determining the amount of net income derived from prohibited transactions, losses from prohibited transactions (and deductions attributable to prohibited transactions in which a loss was incurred) may not be taken into account. However, the amount of any net loss from prohibited transactions may be taken into account in computing REIT taxable income [(d) below].

> **NOTE:** A REIT may acquire foreclosure property if it elects to pay a special tax on the income from such property and disposes of the property normally within two years. Extensions up to four years may be granted [IRC Sec. 856(e); Reg. Sec. 1.856-6; Temp. Reg. Sec. 5.856-1].

(b) Gross Income Requirement [IRC Sec. 856(c); Reg. Sec. 1.856-2-4]:

- 95% or more of the trust's gross income must come from dividends; interest; real property rents; gains from the sale of stock, securities, and real property; abatements and refunds of real property taxes; income and gain from foreclosure property; consideration received for entering into agreements (1) to make loans secured by real property or (2) to purchase or lease real property; and gain from sale or other disposition of exceptions to prohibited transactions.

- 75% or more of the trust's income must be from real property. This includes rents; interest on obligations secured by mortgages on real property; gain (except from prohibited transactions) from the sale of real property and stock in, and distributions from, other qualified real estate trusts; abatements and refunds of real property taxes; income and gain from foreclosure property; consideration received for entering into agreements (1) to make loans secured by real property or (2) to purchase or lease real property; and gain from sale or other disposition of exceptions to prohibited transactions.

If a REIT receives new equity capital, income derived from stock or debt instruments (i.e., interest, dividends, or gains from the stock or bond sale) that is attributable to the temporary investment of the new equity capital is treated, for a one-year period starting on the date the capital is received, as qualifying income for the 75% income test [IRC Sec. 856(c)]. During the period, stock or debt instruments bought with the capital are treated as real estate assets for the 75% asset test [(c) below]. "New equity capital" is any amount received by the REIT in exchange for the REIT stock (except under a dividend reinvestment plan), or in the public offerings of the debt obligations of such trust which have maturities of at least five years.

- Gains from short-term security sales, prohibited transactions, and sales of real property held less than four years must be less than 30% of the trust's gross income. This does not include property involuntarily converted.

➤ **OBSERVATION** Failure to meet the 75% and 95% tests will not result in disqualification if (1) the trust sets forth the source and nature of gross income on its tax return; (2) incorrect information is not included with the intent to evade tax; and (3) failure to meet the tests is due to reasonable cause—not willful neglect.

A 100% tax is imposed on the greater of the amounts by which the trust exceeded either the 75% or 95% test without justification [IRC Sec. 856(c)(7); 857(b)(5); Reg. Sec. 1.856-7; 1.857-4].

For the income requirements, any income derived from a "shared appreciation provision" is treated as gain recognized on the sale of the "secured property." A shared appreciation provision is any provision that is in connection with an obligation that is held by the REIT and secured by an interest in real property.

(c) Diversification of Assets. At the close of each quarter of the tax year [IRC Sec. 856(c)(5)]:

- 75% or more of the value of the trust's total assets must be in real estate assets, cash and cash items (including receivables), and government securities.
- The other 25% of the trust's total assets may be in securities of other corporations, but securities of any one corporation are limited to 5% of the trust's total assets and 10% of the issuer's voting securities.

(d) Distribution of Income. The trust must distribute as dividends (not counting capital gains dividends) at least 95% of its REIT taxable income. A 4% excise tax applies to the undistributed amount that should have been distributed. The dividends may be declared and paid during the tax year or after its close, generally under the same conditions as regulated investment companies (¶3328(e)) [IRC Sec. 857; 858; Reg. Sec. 1.857-1–10; 1.858-1]. "Real estate investment trust taxable income" is taxable income with these adjustments: (1) special deductions listed in ¶3013 are not allowed (except for organizational expenses); (2) dividends paid (computed without net income from foreclosure property) can be deducted; (3) any increase in income from a change in accounting method is included; and (4) net income from foreclosure property is excluded [IRC Sec. 857(b)(2)].

> **NOTE:** A waiver of the REIT distribution rule may be provided when the failure to meet the rule results from prior year distributions necessary to avoid the excise tax on the undistributed income of a REIT [IRC Sec. 857(a)].

The minimum amount a REIT must distribute is reduced by a portion of these amounts required to be included in the REIT's income in advance of receiving cash: (a) amounts includable in income under IRC Sec. 467 involving deferred rents; (b) OID amounts accrued for a loan to which IRC Sec. 1274 applies; and (c) any income arising from disposing a realty asset, but only if the REIT intends in good faith that the deal would qualify as a like kind exchange but turns out to be not so qualifying [IRC Sec. 857(a)]. The portion of the amounts by which the minimum distribution requirement is reduced is the amount by which the sum of the amount exceeds 5% of the REIT taxable income determined without regard to the dividends-paid deduction and net capital gain [IRC Sec. 857(e)].

If an audit adjustment to REIT income or deductions means distributions to shareholders were insufficient to meet the 95% test, there can be a deduction for "deficiency dividends" similar to that provided for mutual funds [¶3326].

Capital gains. If a REIT has a net capital gain, a tax is imposed equal to the sum of (1) the tax (as computed on corporations in general) on REIT taxable income (figured without net capital gain and with the deduction for dividends paid) plus (2) a tax on the excess of net capital gain over the deduction for dividends paid [IRC Sec. 857(b)(3)(A)].

To determine the maximum amount of capital gains dividends the REIT may pay for a tax year, the REIT will not offset its net capital gain with the amount of any net operating loss, whether current or carried over. To the extent that the REIT then elects to pay capital gains dividends in excess of net income, the REIT increases the amount of its NOL carryover by such amount [IRC Sec. 857(b)].

(e) Net Operating Loss Carryover. A REIT cannot carry back a net operating loss. However, a 15-year carryover is allowed [IRC Sec. 172(b)(1)(B)].

(f) Records and Information. The trust must keep records of all its investments. It also must keep records of the actual stock ownership in the Revenue District where it files its return. For this, the trust must ask some record shareholders to supply the names of the actual stock owners each year. Shareholders who do not give the information to the trust must attach it to their income tax return. A trust that does not keep this ownership record is taxed as an ordinary corporation [IRC Sec. 857; Reg. Sec. 1.857-8, -9].

(g) Preference Items for Alternative Minimum Tax. Like any trust, the REIT treats the same items as tax preferences as do individual taxpayers [¶2600; 3520(d)]. However, the REIT pays the tax and passes through the preferences in the same way as regulated investment companies [¶3328(f)].The only exception is that the REIT does not pass through excess real property depreciation (¶2601(a)) [Reg. Sec. 1.58-6].

(h) Reduction of Corporate Benefits. Corporate shareholders of a REIT treat the portion of capital gain dividends attributable to gain from the sale or exchange of Sec. 1250 property as subject to the ordinary income treatment rules (¶3021) [IRC Sec. 291(d)].

REAL ESTATE MORTGAGE INVESTMENT CONDUITS (REMIC)

¶3330   REAL ESTATE MORTGAGE INVESTMENT CONDUITS IN GENERAL

A real estate mortgage investment conduit (REMIC) is an entity that is formed to hold a fixed pool of mortgages secured by interests in real property, with multiple classes of interests held by investors. These interests may be either regular or residual interests. Regular interests are treated as debt of the REMIC and taxed accordingly. The net income of a REMIC, after accounting for the regular interests, generally is passed through to and taken into account by the holders of the residual interests. Amounts includable in income (or deductible as a loss) by holders of REMIC interests are treated as portfolio income (or loss). This income (or loss) is not taken into account in determining the loss from a passive activity (¶2326) [IRC Sec. 860A-G; Temp. Reg. Sec. 1.860D-1T, F-4T].[1]

(a) Qualification. To qualify as a REMIC, the entity must [IRC Sec. 860D(a)]:
- Elect REMIC status which applies for the tax year and all prior tax years.
- Have only regular or residual interests.
- Have only one class of residual interests (and all distributions, if any, to these interests are pro rata).

- Have substantially all of the assets consist of qualified mortgages and permitted investments at all times after the end of the third month starting after the REMIC's start-up day.
- Use a calendar year as its tax year.
- Have reasonable arrangements designed to ensure that residual interests in it are not held by disqualified organizations.
- Make available information necessary for applying the tax on certain transfers of residual interests.

NOTE: Although after the third month substantially all of the REMIC's assets must, at all times, consist only of qualified mortgages and permitted assets, this asset test does not apply during the REMIC's liquidation period [IRC Sec. 860D(a)(4), F(a)(4)(B)]. The last two requirements generally apply to REMICs formed after March 31, 1988.

Regular interests. These are interests that allow owners such as yourself interest payments based on a fixed rate or fixed portion of the interest payments on qualified mortgages [IRC Sec. 860G(a)(1)].

A regular interest in a REMIC must be issued on the start-up day with fixed terms and must be designated as a regular interest.

These interests can be issued in the form of debt, stock, partnership interests, interests in a trust or any other form allowed by state law.

➤ **OBSERVATION** If you are the owner of a regular interest in a REMIC, the interest is considered to be a debt instrument for income tax purposes whether or not it is in the form of a debt instrument. Thus, the OID market discount and income-producing rules that apply to bonds and other debt instruments [¶1217] also generally apply to a regular interest in a REMIC.[1]

Residual interests. A residual interest is an interest in a REMIC that is not a regular interest. It is designated as a residual interest by the REMIC [IRC Sec. 860G(a)(2)].

(b) Taxation of Interest. *Regular interests.* If you own a regular interest, you must use an accrual method to determine the amount includable in your gross income [IRC Sec. 860B(b)].

Suppose you sell your regular interest. Any gain is ordinary income to the extent of a portion of unaccrued original issue discount on the interest [¶1252(a)].

Residual interests. If you acquire a residual interest in a REMIC, you are liable for tax on your pro rata share of the REMIC's taxable income, whether or not distributed [¶1252(b)].

(c) Taxation of the REMIC. Generally, a REMIC is not a taxable entity. The REMIC's income generally is taken into account by owners of regular and residual interests (above). However, the REMIC is subject to tax on prohibited transactions, on certain amounts contributed to it after the start-up date, and on its net income from foreclosure property. It may be required to withhold on amounts paid to foreign holders of interests. In addition, a tax is imposed on transfers after March 31, 1988, to disqualified organizations [IRC Sec. 860A, E, G].

Foreclosure property. A REMIC must pay tax each year on its net income from foreclosure property. The tax is imposed at the top marginal corporate rate (currently 34%). It is computed as if the REMIC were a REIT (¶3329) [IRC Sec. 860G(c)].

➤ **OBSERVATION** If a REMIC acquires this kind of property and receives amounts with respect to the property that would not be treated as certain types of qualifying income if received by a REIT, the REMIC is subject to tax on these amounts. For example, rents from real property and interest on obligations secured by mortgages on real property are excluded qualifying income, while gain from the sale of foreclosure property held primarily for sale to customers is taxed.

Contributions after start-up date. The REMIC must pay an annual tax equal to 100% of the value of contributions made to it after the start-up day. This tax does not apply to cash contributions: (1) made to facilitate a clean-up call or a qualified liquidation; (2) made during the three months after the start-up day; (3) made to a qualified reserve fund by a residual interest holder; (4) in the nature of a guarantee; or (5) permitted by regulations [IRC Sec. 860G(d)].

> **NOTE:** A clean-up call is the prepayment of the remaining principal balance of a class of regular interests when the administrative costs associated with servicing that class outweigh the benefits of maintaining it.

Tax on prohibited transactions. Since a REMIC essentially is designed to hold mortgages contributed to it when it is organized, the conditions under which it can dispose of these mortgages are limited. In addition, penalties are imposed if a REMIC holds assets other than qualified mortgages and certain permitted investments. A 100% tax is imposed on net income from prohibited transactions [IRC Sec. 860F(a)].

EXEMPT ORGANIZATIONS

¶3335   EXEMPT ORGANIZATIONS IN GENERAL

There is an exemption from income tax for organizations that may generally be described as nonprofit [IRC Sec. 501(a)]. They may be in the form of a trust or a corporation, but are exempt only if they apply for an exemption as one of those organizations described in IRC Sec. 501(c), (d), (e) or (f) [¶3336] or as an employee pension, profit-sharing or stock bonus plan qualified under IRC Sec. 401(a) [¶1300]. Despite the exemption, an organization is subject to tax on unrelated business income [¶3345 et seq.].

The tax law includes a statutory definition of private foundations. In general, they are religious, charitable or educational exempt organizations that are essentially private in nature [¶3337]. Strict requirements and severe penalties are applied to private foundations for specified acts (or failures to act) [¶3338 et seq.].

¶3336   TYPES OF EXEMPT ORGANIZATIONS

The following types of organizations, with exceptions, qualify for exemption:

Corporations organized under an Act of Congress, which are instrumentalities of the U.S. exempt from federal income taxes under such act [IRC Sec. 501(c)(1)].

Corporations paying all income to exempt corporations [IRC Sec. 501(c)(2); Reg. Sec. 1.501(c)-(2)-1].

Religious, charitable, educational, etc., organizations [IRC Sec. 501(c)(3); Reg. Sec. 1.501(c)(3)-1].

Churches, conventions or associations of churches [IRC Sec. 501(c)(3); Reg. Sec. 1.501(c)(3)-1].

Civic leagues or organizations operated exclusively for the promotion of social welfare [IRC Sec. 501(c)(4); Reg. Sec. 1.501(c)(4)-1].

Labor, agricultural, or horticultural organizations (including certain fishermen's organizations) [IRC Sec. 501(c)(5), (g); Reg. Sec. 1.501(c)(5)-1].

Business leagues, chambers of commerce, real estate boards, boards of trade or professional football leagues not organized for profit whose earnings do not benefit any private shareholder or individual [IRC Sec. 501(c)(6); Reg. Sec. 1.501(c)(6)-1].

Clubs organized and operated substantially for

pleasure, recreation, and other nonprofitable purposes, whose net earnings do not benefit any private shareholder (but not if charter, bylaws or other written policies provide for discrimination) [IRC Sec. 501(c)(7), (i); Reg. Sec. 1.501(c)(7)-1].

Fraternal beneficiary societies, orders, or associations operating under the lodge system and providing insurance benefits to their members or their dependents[1] [IRC Sec. 501(c)(8); Reg. Sec. 1.501(c)(8)-1].

Voluntary employees' beneficiary associations meeting certain requirements [IRC Sec. 501(c)(9); 505; Reg. Sec. 1.501(c)(9)-1].

Fraternal orders operating under the lodge system and not providing insurance benefits for members [IRC Sec. 501(c)(10); Reg. Sec. 1.501(c)(10)-1].

Teachers' retirement fund associations [IRC Sec. 501(c)(11)].

Benevolent life insurance associations, mutual ditch or irrigation companies, mutual or cooperative telephone companies, or like organizations [IRC Sec. 501(c)(12); Reg. Sec. 1.501(c)(12)-1].

Cemetery companies [IRC Sec. 501(c)(13); Reg. Sec. 1.501(c)(13)-1].

Credit unions [IRC Sec. 501(c)(14)(A)].

Banks providing reserves and deposit insurance [IRC Sec. 501(c)(14)(B), (C)].

Small mutual insurance companies or associations other than life or marine with gross receipts under $150,000 [IRC Sec. 501(c)(15); Reg. Sec. 1.501(c)(15)-1]. Property and casualty insurance companies (whether stock or mutual) with net written premiums (or direct written premiums, if greater) not exceeding $350,000 are exempt from tax. Those whose premiums are between $350,000 and $1.2 million may elect to be taxed only on taxable investment income [IRC Sec. 501(c)(15); 831].

Corporations organized by farmers' cooperatives [IRC Sec. 501(c)(16); Reg. Sec. 1.501(c)(16)-1].

Qualified supplemental unemployment benefit trusts meeting certain requirements [IRC Sec. 501(c)(17); 505; Reg. Sec. 1.501(c)(17)-1].

Trusts forming part of pension plans [Reg. Sec. 1.501(c)(18)-1].

Armed Forces members' organizations [IRC Sec. 501(c)(19), (23); Reg. Sec. 1.501(c)(19)-1].

Qualified group legal services organizations or trusts meeting certain requirements [IRC Sec. 501(c)(20); 505; Prop. Reg. Sec. 1.501(c)(20)-1].

Black Lung Act trusts that satisfy coal mine operators' liabilities for black lung benefits and buy liability insurance [IRC Sec. 501(c)(21); Reg. Sec. 1.501(c)(21)-1].

Trusts created to satisfy certain withdrawal liability payments of multiemployer pension plans [IRC Sec. 501(c)(22)].

Title-holding companies meeting certain requirements, effective for tax years beginning after December 31, 1986 [IRC Sec. 501(c)(25)].

Athletic organizations promoting amateur sports competition [IRC Sec. 501(c)(3)].

Religious or apostolic associations or corporations [IRC Sec. 501(d); Reg. Sec. 1.501(d)-1].

Hospital service organizations (but not a cooperative hospital laundry)[2] [IRC Sec. 501(e)].

Cooperative service organizations of operating educational organizations (school investment funds) [IRC Sec. 501(f)].

Child care organizations whose services are available to the public [IRC Sec. 501(k)].

Farmers' cooperative marketing and purchasing associations [IRC Sec. 521; Reg. Sec. 1.521-1].

Political organizations operated primarily to influence selection, appointment, nomination or election of public office seekers. A fund of an elected official to receive contributions for newsletters can also qualify [IRC Sec. 527; Reg. Sec. 1.527-1-7].

Qualified homeowners' associations (e.g., condominimum and residential real estate managment associations) [IRC Sec. 528; Reg. Sec. 1.528-1-10].

Examples of Exempt Organizations

Clubs. College fraternities;[3] country clubs[4] (even though club got its principal income from a bar or restaurant, if only members or guests were served);[5] riding clubs (if admission charged outsiders for annual rodeo is merely to defray expenses).[6]

Religious, charitable, educational, etc., organizations. Daughters of the American Revolution; Salvation Army; Red Cross; Navy Relief Society; U.S. Lawn Tennis Association; Woodrow Wilson Foundation; the U.S.O.; U.S. Olympic Assoc.

Business leagues, etc. Fruit growers association organized to promote sale of apples grown in state;[7] to promote sale and use of processed agricultural product.[8]

Examples of Nonexempt Organizations

Clubs. Automobile clubs.[9]

Farmers' cooperatives. Advertising association;[10] scavenger service;[11] marketing building materials on cooperative basis.[12]

Cemeteries. Operation of cemetery used only by organizer and descendants.[13]

Religious, charitable, educational, etc., organizations. Jockey Club of New York; private hospital operated for benefit of physicians in charge.[14]

Business leagues, etc. Stock exchange; commodity exchange; nurses' association operated primarily as an employment agency for its members;[15] business league operated primarily to publish yearbook comprised largely of members' paid ads.[16]

(a) Feeder Organizations. An organization operated primarily to carry on a trade or business for profit cannot claim tax exemption on the ground that all its profits are payable to one or more exempt organizations [IRC Sec. 502(a)]. That is, its own activities must be of an exempt nature to gain tax exemption. A feeder organization is taxable on its entire income, not just the portion it designates as its unrelated business income. "Trade or business," for this rule, does not include the rental of realty or of personal property rented out with such realty unless it is more than incidental in amount. "Rents" are similar to those excluded for unrelated business taxable income [¶3348(a)]. It also does not include a business in which most of the work is performed voluntarily, nor one that sells merchandise, substantially all of which is donated (for example, a thrift shop) [IRC Sec. 502(b); Reg. Sec. 1.502-1(d)]. A separate organization that pays its profits to an exempt organization is not a feeder organization subject to tax if its workers perform without pay or the merchandise that it sells is received as a gift or contribution [IRC Sec. 502(b)(2), (3)].

(b) Application for Exemption. Every organization claiming exemption from tax must file an application with the IRS. Special forms are provided for the various types of organizations: for those claiming exemption under IRC Sec. 501(c)(3), Form 1023; under IRC Sec. 501(c)(2), (4)–(10), (12), (13), (15), (17) and (19), Form 1024; under IRC Sec. 521 (farmers' cooperative associations), Form 1028; and under IRC Sec. 528 (homeowners' associations), Form 1120-H. Organizations for which no special form is provided must file an application prescribed by the IRS together with any required information [Reg. Sec. 1.501(a)-1]. A copy of the articles of incorporation and the latest financial statement must be attached to the application. A determination letter also can be obtained before operations.[17] Subordinate organizations under the control of a central organization can apply for exemptions on a group basis.[18]

NOTE: Every new supplemental unemployment compensation benefits trust (SUB), VEBA, or group legal services plan must timely advise the IRS of its application for tax-exempt status. Exempt SUBs or plans already in existence must also give notice, within an IRS-established time period [IRC Sec. 505]. Also, benefits provided by a plan can't discriminate in favor of highly compensated employees.

The application and supporting papers are open to public inspection. On request, the IRS must supply the basis on which an exemption is granted [IRC Sec. 6104(a); Reg. Sec. 301.6104-1].

In addition to the proof of exemption, exempt corporations, with certain exceptions, must file annual information returns; [¶3667].

Religious, charitable and educational organizations claiming an exemption under IRC Sec. 501(c)(3) must notify the IRS (¶3337(a)) [IRC Sec. 508; Reg. Sec. 1.508-1].

(c) Disallowed Losses. No deduction is allowed for the loss on a sale between an exempt organization and a taxpayer (or a taxpayer's family) that controls it (¶2323) [IRC Sec. 267(a)(1), (b)(9); Reg. Sec. 1.267(b)-1].

(d) Loss of Exemption. Supplemental unemployment benefit plans, qualified employee pension, profit-sharing or stock bonus plans and certain specific other employee pension plans lose their exempt status if they engage in prohibited acts [IRC Sec. 503; Reg. Sec. 1.503(a)-1]. Examples of prohibited acts are payment of unreasonable compensation or lending of money at low interest rates to persons connected with the organization [IRC

Sec. 503(b); Reg. Sec. 1.503(b)-1]. An organization that loses its exempt status under IRC Sec. 501(c)(3) because of excessive lobbying can never become exempt under IRC Sec. 501(c)(4) as a social welfare organization [IRC Sec. 504]. Those religious, charitable and educational organizations that are private foundations are subject to a number of penalty taxes for engaging in prohibited acts [¶3339], but lose their exemption only for "willful repeated acts" or a "willful and flagrant act" (¶3337(b)) [IRC Sec. 507(a)].

Lobbying expenditures. To avoid losing their exempt status due to excessive lobbying, public charities (except for churches and affiliated group members) can elect to be subject to a tax equal to 25% of their "excess lobbying expenditures" for the tax year [IRC Sec. 501(h); 504; 4911]. Excess lobbying expenditures are the greater of (1) the excess of lobbying expenditures over the lobbying nontaxable amount or (2) the excess of grass-roots expenditures over 25% of the lobbying nontaxable amount. Grass-roots and lobbying expenditures are both attempts to influence legislation, but grass-roots doesn't include communication with a government official or employee. The "lobbying nontaxable amount" is a certain percentage of the lobbying expenditures [IRC Sec. 501(h)]. The Supreme Court has held that the requirement that an organization cannot engage in substantial lobbying activities to qualify for tax exemption does not violate either the First or Fifth Amendment.[19]

¶3337   PRIVATE FOUNDATIONS DEFINED

Private foundations are best defined as what they are not. Thus, the tax law [IRC Sec. 509] states that they include *all* exempt charities under IRC Sec. 501(c)(3) [¶3336] *except:*

1.   A church, school or educational organization that supports state schools, a hospital or medical research association, a governmental unit, or a charitable organization that is supported by the government or the general public [IRC Sec. 170(b)(1)(A); 509(a)(1); Reg. Sec. 1.170A-9]. (A medical research organization is not a private foundation merely because it does not commit itself to spend every contribution for research within five years of receipt [Reg. Sec. 1.509(a)-2(b)].)

> **NOTE:** The public support tests used for public charities described above differ in many important respects from those used for the publicly supported organizations described in (2) below. For detailed descriptions of the public charities above that qualify under IRC Sec. 170(b)(1)(A), see ¶1919.

2.   An organization that normally receives: (a) from the general public (persons who are not disqualified [¶3340]) and from governmental units more than ⅓ of its annual support in any combination of (1) gifts, grants, contributions or membership fees and (2) gross receipts from admissions, sales or services performed in a related trade or business and (b) no more than ⅓ of its annual support from the sum of (1) gross investment income and (2) the excess of unrelated business taxable income from businesses acquired after June 30, 1975 [¶3348] over the unrelated business income tax (¶3345) [IRC Sec. 509(a)(2); Reg. Sec. 1.509(a)-3]. Contributions and payment for services are both counted as support (for example, a $10 gift plus $5 ticket payment would make up $15 public support). But payments by any person or government bureau for services rendered cannot exceed $5,000 or 1% of the total support, whichever is greater [Reg. Sec. 1.509(a)-3]. Gross investment income includes interest, dividends, rents and royalties, but not net capital gains [IRC Sec. 509(e)]. In addition to gifts and contributions, gross investment income and gross receipts, the total support of an organization also includes net income from unrelated business activities [¶3346] but not net capital gains [IRC Sec. 509(d)].

> ➤ **OBSERVATION** Failure to satisfy the above support test is not necessarily fatal, since the IRS may look at the experience of an organization over a four-year period to determine its "normal" sources of support [Reg. Sec. 1.509(a)-3(c)]. Special rules are provided for new organizations [Reg. Sec. 1.509(a)-3(d), (e)].

3. An organization exclusively for the benefit of one or more organizations described in (1) or (2) above [IRC Sec. 509(a)(3); Reg. Sec. 1.509(a)-4].

4. An organization operated exclusively to test for public safety [IRC Sec. 509(a)(4)].

(a) Notification of Status. Because the activities of private foundations are severely restricted [¶3339], both new *and* old charitable organizations are presumed to be private foundations unless they claim public charity status [Reg. Sec. 1.508-1(b)]. Therefore, an organization that claims to be an exempt charity must notify the IRS on Form 1023 [Reg. Sec. 1.508-1(a)]. It should provide information that it is not a private foundation, plus any further information necessary to establish that it qualifies as a public charity [Reg. Sec. 1.508-1(b)(2)]. An organization that fails to give notice by 15 months from the end of the month in which it was organized will not be exempt [IRC Sec. 508(a); Reg. Sec. 1.508-1(a)]. The notice is filed on Form 1023 [IRC Sec. 508(b); Reg. Sec. 1.508-1(b)(2)]. No deductions are allowed for charitable contributions received after the loss of exemption [IRC Sec. 508(d)(2); Reg. Sec. 1.508-2].

The following need not give notice: Churches (including church organizations, religious schools, mission societies and youth groups); public charities whose annual gross income normally is $5,000 or less; subordinate organizations (except private foundations) covered by a group exemption letter; and certain nonexempt charitable trusts (¶3353) [IRC Sec. 508(c); Reg. Sec. 1.508-1(a)(3), (b)(7)].

(b) Tax on Termination of Status. A private foundation may want to give up that status to avoid the restrictions on its conduct [¶3339]. Or the IRS may give notice of the forfeiture of exempt status for willful and flagrant violations of the prohibitions on foundations [IRC Sec. 507(a); Reg. Sec. 1.507-1]. In either case, tax assessments recapture the total tax benefits (with interest) flowing from the foundation's prior exempt status [IRC Sec. 507(c); Reg. Sec. 1.507-5, -8]. The recaptured tax benefits are (1) the taxes saved by all substantial contributors [¶3340] through deductions of contributions for income, estate and gift taxes and (2) taxes the foundation would have paid on its income if it had not been exempt [IRC Sec. 507(d)]. The recapture tax cannot exceed the value of the foundation's net assets [IRC Sec. 507(e); Reg. Sec. 1.507-4, -7]. The IRS may abate the tax if the foundation itself goes public and so operates for at least five years or if it distributes its assets to one or more public charities that have existed continuously for at least five years [IRC Sec. 507(b); Reg. Sec. 1.507-9]. If this tax is imposed on the foundation, deductions for gifts and bequests to the foundation are not allowed. Special rules apply for transfers of assets by one private foundation to another.

¶3338   TAX ON INVESTMENT INCOME

Private foundations must pay a 2% tax on their net investment income for the tax year [IRC Sec. 4940; Reg. Sec. 53.4940-1]. Investment income includes interest, dividends, rents and royalties to the extent they are not taxed as unrelated business income [¶3345].

Net capital gains are also subject to the investment tax. Capital losses are taken into account only as an offset to gains. This tax is reported on Form 990. Foreign private foundations pay a 4% tax on gross investment income from U.S. sources. This tax also applies to nonexempt private foundations, to the extent that it, plus the unrelated business income tax that would have been imposed, exceeds the foundation's regular tax.

A private foundation is not subject to the 2% tax if it qualifies as an exempt operating foundation. An exempt operating foundation is one that: (1) is an operating foundation; (2) has been publicly supported for at least ten years; (3) has a governing body that consists of individuals at least 75% of whom are not disqualified individuals [¶3340]; and (4) has no foundation officer who is at any time during the tax year a disqualified individual.

The tax may be reduced from 2% to 1% for any year in which the private foundation's qualifying distributions equal or exceed the sum of the foundation's assets for the year times the average percentage payout, plus 1% of its investment income [IRC Sec. 4940(e)]. Qualifying distributions are those expenditures made for charitable purposes or for assets to be used for charitable purposes (including amounts set aside for charitable projects).

¶3339   PROHIBITED ACTS OF PRIVATE FOUNDATIONS

Heavy excise taxes are imposed on private foundations for certain prohibited acts (or failures to act). These taxes apply as well to the foundation manager and in certain cases to substantial contributors [¶3340]. Government officials may be penalized for dealings with the foundation. There is also a tax on the termination of the exempt status of the foundation [¶3337(b)]. If a violation is willful and flagrant, or if the foundation, its manager, a disqualified person [¶3340] or government official is liable for excise tax for a prior violation, a penalty equal to the tax is also imposed [IRC Sec. 6684; Reg. Sec. 301.6684-1]. Since the taxes are excises, they are not deductible as taxes [¶1910].

Briefly, the following are penalized acts: (1) self-dealing [¶3340]; (2) failure to distribute income [¶3341]; (3) excessive holdings in a business [¶3342]; (4) investments which jeopardize the charitable purpose [¶3343]; and (5) improper expenditures (for example, propaganda to influence legislation) [¶3344].

> **NOTE:** Governing instruments of private foundations must include provisions prohibiting income accumulations and the other prohibited acts [IRC Sec. 508(e)(1); Reg. Sec. 1.508-3]. Gifts and bequests to foundations not complying are not deductible [IRC Sec. 508(d)(2)(A)]. Private foundations must also file information returns [¶3667(a)].

Abatement of first tier taxes. The IRS may abate the first tier private foundation excise taxes explained in IRC Sec. 4942–4945 (but not penalty tax on self-dealing, [IRC Sec. 4940]). The foundation must establish that the violation of the foundation rules was due to reasonable cause and not willful neglect, and was corrected within an appropriate correction period [IRC Sec. 4962].

¶3340   TAX ON SELF-DEALING

Disqualified persons are penalized by an excise tax for specific acts of self-dealing [IRC Sec. 4941; Reg. Sec. 53.4941(a)-1]. Punishable acts of self-dealing are specifically set forth in the tax law [IRC Sec. 4941(d); Reg. Sec. 53.4941(d)-1–3].

Disqualified persons. A disqualified person is (1) a substantial contributor (see below); or (2) the foundation manager; or (3) the owner of over 20% of (a) the voting power in a corporation, or (b) profits interest of a partnership, or (c) beneficial interest in a trust or unincorporated business, if the corporation, partnership, trust or business itself is a substantial contributor; or (4) a member of the family of any of the above; or (5) a corporation, partnership, trust or estate in which any of the foregoing persons owns more than a 35% interest; or (6) related foundations (for the tax on excess business holdings only) [¶3342] and government officials (for the tax on self-dealing only) [IRC Sec. 4946; Reg. Sec. 53.4946-1].

Substantial contributor is any person (including a corporation) who alone or with his spouse has contributed or bequeathed a total of more than $5,000 to a private foundation, but only if such gifts and bequests exceed 2% of all gifts and bequests received from all donors. If a person is a substantial contributor in any year, he remains one for later years [IRC Sec. 507(d)(2); Reg. Sec. 1.507-6].

A person's status as a substantial contributor will be terminated if (1) neither the person nor a related person made a contribution to the foundation within the last ten years; (2) at no time during the ten-year period was that person or related person a manager of the foundation; and (3) the person's aggregate contributions are insignificant when compared to the contributions to that foundation by one other person [IRC Sec. 507(d)(2)(C)].

Initial taxes. A tax is imposed on the disqualified person at 5% of the amount involved in the self-dealing. The foundation manager who knowingly participated is subject to a 2½% tax ($10,000 maximum) [IRC Sec. 4941(a); Reg. Sec. 53.4941(a)-1]. The tax is reported on Form 4720 by private foundations with Form 990 (or Form 1041-A by nonexempt trusts).

Additional taxes. The disqualified person is liable for an additional tax of 200% of the amount involved if the self-dealing act is not corrected within 90 days after the deficiency notice is mailed. The foundation manager is liable for 50% of the amount for refusal to agree to a correction [IRC Sec. 4941(b), (c)(2); Reg. Sec. 53.4941(b)-1, (c)-1, (e)-1(d)].

¶3341   TAX ON UNDISTRIBUTED INCOME

A private foundation is subject to tax if it does not distribute its income in the year of receipt or the next year. There is an initial tax of 15% on the undistributed income and an additional 100% tax if required distributions are not made within 90 days after the deficiency notice [IRC Sec. 4942].

In general, the tax does not apply if the organization was created before May 27, 1969, and is mandatorily required to accumulate. Nor does it apply to a private operating foundation—that is, one that spends at least 85% of its income directly for the active conduct of its charitable purposes and meets certain other qualifying tests [IRC Sec. 4942(a)(1); Reg. Sec. 53.4942(b)].

Also, an amount a private foundation sets aside for a specific charitable project is treated as distributed income if (a) such amount is to be paid out within five years and (b) the project is one that can be better accomplished by the set-aside than by an immediate payment of funds [IRC Sec. 4942(g)(2)]. Set-asides commonly arise when a foundation awards a grant for a long-term project or awards a matching grant.

¶3342   TAX ON EXCESS BUSINESS HOLDINGS

An excise tax is imposed on a private foundation if it has excess business holdings. The initial tax is 5% of the value. It is imposed on the last day of the foundation's tax year but is determined on that day when excess holdings were the largest. An additional tax of 200% is imposed if the excess holdings are not disposed of within a specified period. Excess business holdings (as defined) may consist of stock in a corporation or a partnership interest if not related to the foundation's charitable purpose. The foundation may not hold any interest in a sole proprietorship [IRC Sec. 4943; Reg. Sec. 53.4943-3].

¶3343   TAX ON SPECULATIVE INVESTMENTS

If a private foundation invests in a manner that jeopardizes the carrying out of its charitable purpose, it and the foundation manager are penalized by an excise tax [IRC Sec. 4944; Reg. Sec. 53.4944-1–6]. The initial tax on the foundation is 5% of the investment, imposed each year until the earliest of (1) the mailing of a deficiency notice, (2) the assessment of the tax, or (3) the removal of the investment from jeopardy. The additional tax is 25% of the investment if not sold within 90 days after deficiency notice. The foundation manager who knowingly participated without use of reasonable care is subject to initial and additional taxes of 5% each ($5,000 maximum for initial tax and $10,000 for additional tax) [IRC Sec. 4944; 4961; 4963; Reg. Sec. 53.4944-1–2, -4–5].

¶3344   TAX ON IMPROPER EXPENDITURES

If a private foundation makes "taxable expenditures," it and the foundation manager are penalized by an excise tax. The initial tax on the foundation is 10% of the expenditure. An additional tax of 100% is imposed if the foundation does not recover the expenditures, to the extent possible, within 90 days after deficiency notice. The initial tax on the manager who knowingly participated is 2½% (maximum $5,000) and the additional tax is 50% (maximum $10,000). No tax is imposed if the manager was not willful and used reasonable care [IRC Sec. 4945; 4961; 4963].

Generally, taxable expenditures are outlays (1) to influence legislation through lobbying or propaganda; (2) to influence election outcomes or to carry on voter registration drives; (3) for certain discriminatory study or travel grants to individuals; and (4) for any purpose that would not support a charitable deduction if the foundation were taxable [IRC Sec. 4945(d); Reg. Sec. 53.4945-2–6].

➤ **OBSERVATION** Grants to exempt operating foundations from other foundations are not subject to the expenditure responsibility requirements [IRC Sec. 4945(d)(4)].

¶3345   UNRELATED BUSINESS INCOME (UBI) TAX

Otherwise tax-exempt organizations are taxed on income unrelated to the purposes that entitle them to exemption [¶3336]. The income subject to tax is from unrelated businesses or is unrelated debt-financed income (¶3349) [IRC Sec. 511-515]. For a discussion on the unrelated income tax rates, returns and payments, see ¶3354. The unrelated business tax can be offset by the foreign tax credit (¶3801) [IRC Sec. 515]. A charitable deduction is allowed in figuring unrelated business taxable income [¶3348(b)].

Exempt organizations must pay the alternative minimum tax on any tax preferences that enter into the computation of UBI (¶2600) [IRC Sec. 511(d); Reg. Sec. 1.511-4]. Private foundations are subject to this tax as well as the excise taxes discussed at ¶3339 et seq.

> **NOTE:** Quarterly estimated tax payments of the excise tax on net investment income of private foundations and the unrelated business income tax of tax-exempt organizations are required [IRC Sec. 6154(h)]. These payments are made in the same way as corporate estimated taxes [¶3651]. The period of underpayment of estimated taxes for a tax-exempt organization or private foundation runs to the 15th day of the fifth month after the end of the tax year (due date for the unrelated business income tax return). One extra month is provided for computing the estimated tax payments that must be paid by these tax-exempt organizations.
>
> Exempt organizations file Form 990. Revenue from income-producing activities is broken down into numerous categories on the form. Each category is then broken down according to three classifications: (1) UBI, (2) excluded income and (3) related or exempt function income.

¶3346   EXEMPT ORGANIZATIONS SUBJECT TO TAX ON UNRELATED BUSINESS INCOME

All exempt organizations (except U.S. instrumentalities) are subject to the unrelated business tax [IRC Sec. 511; Reg. Sec. 1.511-2(a)].

> ▶ **OBSERVATION** Church books may be examined only to the extent necessary to determine any UBI tax liability, and then only if the Regional Commissioner believes it has UBI and gives advance notice. However, this restriction does not interfere with the IRS's examination of an organization's religious activities for determining its exempt qualification [Reg. Sec. 301.7605-1(c)].

¶3347   WHAT IS AN UNRELATED BUSINESS

[New tax legislation may affect this subject; see ¶1.]

In determining whether a trade or business from which the exempt organization gets income is "unrelated," its need for the income or the use it makes of the profits is irrelevant. Except as noted below, if the business is not substantially related to the exercise or performance of the charitable, educational, or other purpose constituting the basis for exemption under IRC Sec. 501, it is an unrelated trade or business [IRC Sec. 513; Reg. Sec. 1.513-1]. For an exempt employees' trust (a trust forming part of a qualified stock bonus, pension, or profit-sharing plan [¶1300]) or an exempt supplemental unemployment benefit trust, "unrelated trade or business" means any business regularly carried on by the trust or by a partnership of which it is a member [IRC Sec. 513(b); Reg. Sec. 1.513-1]. The income from the business is taxable [IRC Sec. 512; Reg. Sec. 1.512(a)-1].

Generally, unrelated trade or business does not include: (1) qualified public entertainment activities (e.g., fairs and expositions) conducted by exempt charitable, social welfare or agricultural organizations or (2) qualified conventions or trade shows regularly conducted by exempt unions or trade associations [IRC Sec. 513(d); Reg. Sec. 1.513-3]. Also, specified services provided by one hospital to others are not unrelated if the services could have been provided tax free by a cooperative organization of exempt hospitals and the services meet certain other tests [IRC Sec. 513(e)].

In determining whether income of an exempt organization from a business is subject to unrelated business income tax, it is necessary to determine (1) whether it is income from a business *regularly carried on* or from a sporadic activity and (2) whether the business is unrelated. The business is substantially related only if the activity (not the proceeds from it) contributes importantly to the accomplishment of the exempt purposes of the organization [Reg. Sec. 1.513-1].

Example 1: If an exempt organization operates a sandwich stand during the week of an annual county fair, it is not regularly carrying on a business. But it is if it operates a public parking lot one day each week.

Example 2: Milk and cream production from an experimental dairy herd maintained by a research organization is a related business. But not manufacture of ice cream and pastries.

Example 3: A school trains children in singing and dancing for professional careers. Performances before audiences by the students contribute importantly to the school's exempt purpose of training. Thus, the income from admissions to the performances is exempt.

Trade or business activities. A trade or business includes any activity carried on to produce income. It makes no difference if it is not profitable; the business could still be unrelated. An activity remains a business even when carried on within a larger aggregate of similar activities that may or may not be related to the exempt purpose [IRC Sec. 513(c)]. Advertising income from publications of exempt organizations in excess of expenses or any loss is unrelated (therefore, taxable), whether or not the publications are related to the exempt purpose [Reg. Sec. 1.512(a)-1(f)].

Income exempt from tax. Income from a trade or business is not subject to tax if [IRC Sec. 513(a); Reg. Sec. 1.513-1(e)]:

- Substantially all the work (generally, 85% or more) is performed for the organization without pay. For example, an orphanage runs a secondhand clothing store, all the work being performed by volunteers.
- As to religious, charitable or educational organizations, and state universities, it is carried on primarily for the convenience of its members, students, patients, officers, or employees. For example, a college operates a laundry for laundering dormitory linen and students' clothing.
- The business is the selling of merchandise, substantially all of which is received as gifts or contributions. For example, activities commonly known as thrift shops.

Exceptions to the unrelated trade or business rule also include (1) the exchanging or renting of donor mailing lists by an exempt organization with or to other exempt organizations; (2) exempt organizations receiving income from certain unsolicited distributions of low-cost articles incidental to soliciting charitable contributions; and (3) qualified trade shows or conventions at which suppliers to the sponsoring organization's members sell products or services, and convention activities of charitable organizations and social welfare organizations.

Loss of tax-exempt status: An exempt organization can have its tax-exempt status revoked if it conducts an excessive amount of unrelated business. The IRS has stated that if unrelated income is less than 5% of gross income, the exempt organization is probably safe from having its exempt status revoked. If more than 5% of an exempt organization's gross income comes from unrelated sources, its exempt status still may be safe. This percentage isn't the only factor that determines if exempt status is in jeopardy. Other factors include the amount of time an exempt organization spends on its unrelated business and how much of its income is used for exempt programs.

¶3348   INCOME FROM UNRELATED BUSINESS

Gross income from an unrelated business includes both the gross income of an unrelated business regularly carried on by the exempt organization and a percentage of unrelated debt-financed income (¶3349) [IRC Sec. 512(a)(1); 514(a)(1)].

Foreign corporations. UBI of a foreign organization includes income from U.S. sources that is not effectively connected with a U.S. business as well as all UBI that is effectively connected (¶3811) [IRC Sec. 512(a)(2); Reg. Sec. 1.512(a)-1(g)].

If the unrelated business is conducted with the exempt organization as a partner, the organization must include in its income its distributive share of the gross income of the partnership, less directly connected deductions. It must make the necessary adjustments for the exclusions and deductions below [IRC Sec. 512].

(a) Exclusions from Gross Income. The following income is excluded in arriving at taxable income from an unrelated business [IRC Sec. 512(b); Reg. Sec. 1.512(b)-1]:

- Dividends, interest, and annuities.
- Royalties (including overriding royalties), whether measured by production or by gross or net income from the property.
- Rents from real or personal property are generally excluded. However, rents from personal property leased with real property are taxed if they exceed 10% of the total rents from all property leased. In addition, all rents—from real as well as personal property—are taxed if (a) over 50% of the total rents determined when the lessee first places personal property in service are attributable to personal property or (b) the total rents are contingent on profits. Also, rents from debt-financed property are taxable [¶3349].
- Capital gains and losses, except for the cutting of timber treated as a sale.
- Income taxed as debt-financed income (including otherwise excluded rents, dividends, interest, capital gains, annuities and royalties) [¶3349].
- Income derived from research for state and local governments or the U.S., its agencies or instrumentalities.
- Income from research by a college, university or hospital and by an organization operating primarily for fundamental research, the results of which are freely available to the general public.
- Income from limited partnership interest of certain testamentary charitable trusts.

(b) Deductions from Gross Income. To arrive at unrelated business taxable income, the exempt organization may deduct from gross income the deductions directly connected with the carrying on of the trade or business, subject to the following exceptions or limitations [Reg. Sec. 1.512(b)-1]:

- Any deductions directly connected with items excluded from income are not deducted. See (a) above for items of excluded income.
- The deduction for charitable contributions is allowed (whether or not directly connected with the carrying on of the business), but cannot exceed 10% of the unrelated business taxable income of an organization taxed as a corporation figured without the charitable contribution deduction. For an exempt trust's charitable deduction, see ¶3352.
- The net operating loss deduction is allowed, except that any income or deduction excluded in figuring the UBI is not taken into account in determining the net operating loss or deduction for any tax year, or the amount of the net operating loss carryback or carryover.

Specific deduction. The organization also gets a specific deduction of $1,000. For a diocese, religious order, or association of churches, each parish, individual church or other local unit can claim a specific deduction of the lower of $1,000 or gross income from the unrelated business carried on by the local unit [IRC Sec. 512(b)(12); Reg. Sec. 1.512(b)-1(h)].

> ➤ **OBSERVATION** A trust taxed on unrelated business taxable income gets no deduction for personal exemption [¶3512], but the $1,000 specific deduction is allowed.

(c) Special Rules apply to social clubs, voluntary employee benefit associations, veterans' organizations and controlled organizations.

Social clubs generally exclude only exempt function income. Thus, clubs must pay tax on investment income but do not pay tax on dues, fees and similar charges paid by members for club services and facilities rendered to them, their dependents or guests. In addition, they do not pay tax on investment income set aside for religious, charitable or educational purposes. However, income from a club's unrelated business cannot be set aside and exempted from tax. If property used by the social club continuously and directly for exempt purposes (for example, a golfing area or fraternity house) is sold and replaced with other exempt-use property within one year before and three years after the sale, taxable gain is recognized only to the extent the amount realized exceeds the cost of replacement. In addition to these special exclusion rules, a social club can deduct directly connected expenses, charitable contributions within 10% of taxable income limitation, the net operating loss and the $1,000 specific deduction [IRC Sec. 512(a)(3); Prop. Reg. Sec. 1.512(a)-3].

The corporate dividends-received deduction is not considered directly connected with the production of gross income for social clubs and is not allowed as a deduction by non-exempt membership organizations. The exception also applies to membership organizations engaged primarily in gathering and distributing news to members for publication.

> ➤ **OBSERVATION** A special rule applies to social clubs and other membership organizations to prevent them from giving up their exempt status and escaping the tax on business and investment income by using this income to serve the members at less than cost and then deducting the book "loss." Nonexempt membership organizations can deduct the expenses incurred in supplying services, facilities and goods to their members only to the extent of income received from members (including income from institutes and trade shows for the education of members) [IRC Sec. 277; Prop. Reg. Sec. 1.277-1].

Voluntary employee benefit associations (VEBAs) are treated under the same special rules as exempt social clubs [IRC Sec. 512(a)(3); Prop. Reg. Sec. 1.512(a)-(3)].

In addition, associations can also exclude investment income set aside to provide for the payment of life, sickness, accident or other benefits [IRC Sec. 512(a)(3)(B)(ii)].

> **NOTE:** Benefits provided by VEBAs to employees cannot discriminate in favor of the highly compensated. Every new VEBA must give the IRS timely notice of its application for tax-exempt status [IRC Sec. 505]. Exempt VEBAs already in existence must also give notice, within an IRS-established time period.

Veterans' organizations pay no tax on income from insurance to the extent that the income is used or set aside for insurance or charitable purposes [IRC Sec. 512(a)(4); Reg. Sec. 1.512(a)-4].

Controlled organizations. Interest, rents, royalties and annuities (but not dividends) received from a corporation over which an exempt organization has 80% control are subject to tax. This rule does not apply to income that is related to the recipient's exempt status, nor to the income of a controlled corporation that is itself exempt except to the extent the income is unrelated to the controlled organization's exempt purposes [IRC Sec. 512(b)(15); Reg. Sec. 1.512(b)-1].

¶3349   UNRELATED DEBT-FINANCED INCOME

[New tax legislation may affect this subject; see ¶1.]
Unrelated debt-financed income is subject to the unrelated business income tax.

(a) General Rule. The income of an exempt organization from debt-financed property unrelated to the exempt function is included in the computation of UBI in the same proportion that average acquisition indebtedness bears to the property's adjusted basis. Unrelated debt-financed gross income does not include income already subject to tax as UBI, but capital gains on the sale of debt-financed property are included. The same percentage of gross income is used to determine the allowable deductions. Only the percentage of deductions directly connected with the debt-financed property is allowed [IRC Sec. 514(a), (b); Reg. Sec. 1.514(a)-1, (b)-1].

> **Example:** Business or investment property is acquired by a tax-exempt organization subject to an 80% mortgage. Thus, 80% of the income and 80% of the deductions are taken into account. As the mortgage is paid off, the percentage taken into account diminishes.

(b) Debt-Financed Property is any property (for example, rental real estate, tangible personal property and corporate stock) held to produce income and that has an "acquisition indebtedness" [(c) below] at any time during the tax year (or during the 12 months preceding its disposal).

Property is not included (1) if at least 85% of all its use is substantially related to the organization's exempt purpose (if less than 85% of its use, to the extent of its related use); (2) to the extent its income is already subject to tax as income from business [¶3345-3348]; (3) to the extent its income is derived from research activities; and (4) to the extent its use is exempt from the unrelated business tax on income from an unrelated business [¶3347]. Special rules apply to related exempt organizations and to medical clinics [IRC Sec. 514(b); Reg. Sec. 1.514(b)-1].

Land acquired for exempt use within 10 years. Subject to certain conditions, the tax does not apply to income from newly acquired land in the neighborhood of other exempt-purpose property owned by the organization if it plans to use the property within ten years of acquisition and doesn't abandon its plans. The period is 15 years for a church, and the land need not be in its neighborhood [IRC Sec. 514(b)(3); Reg. Sec. 1.514(b)-1(d)].

(c) "Acquisition Indebtedness" is debt incurred in acquiring or improving income-producing property. Mortgages and similar liens are included, but there is a ten-year delay in applying the rules to certain mortgaged property acquired by will or gift. The extension, renewal or refinancing of an existing debt is not treated as a new debt. Nor is an FHA-insured obligation to finance low- and middle-income housing acquisition indebtedness. A state or local tax lien or special assessment is not a debt until the underlying tax or assessment becomes due and payable and the organization has had an opportunity to pay it [IRC Sec. 514(c); Reg. Sec. 1.514(c)-1].

Special rules apply to determine the basis of debt-financed property acquired in a corporate liquidation [IRC Sec. 514(d); Reg. Sec. 1.514(d)-1].

¶3350   EXEMPT TRUSTS

The exemption from tax granted to religious, etc., organizations by IRC Sec. 501(c)(3) applies to an ordinary trust that meets the tests for exemption [¶3336]. Like other exempt organizations, they are taxed on unrelated business taxable income [¶3351]. If an exempt trust is a private foundation, it is subject to the same taxes and reporting requirements as other private foundations [¶3338 et seq.; 3667]. The denial of tax exemption to feeder organizations also applies to trusts [¶3336(a)].

Charitable remainder annuity trusts and unitrusts [¶¶1918(c); 3922; 3947] are exempt from tax [IRC Sec. 664(c); Reg. Sec. 1.664-1]. However, if a remainder trust has unrelated business taxable income, it is subject to all the income taxes [Reg. Sec. 1.664-1(c)].

¶3351   BUSINESS INCOME TAX OF EXEMPT TRUSTS

Exempt trusts are subject to the unrelated business income tax [IRC Sec. 511(b); Reg. Sec. 1.511-2]. The explanation of this tax at ¶3345-3349 applies to exempt trusts, with the following exception: The trust is allowed a charitable deduction from the gross income of the unrelated business [¶3348(b)] equivalent to the limited deduction allowed individuals [¶1919], but computed on its unrelated business taxable income before the charitable deduction [IRC Sec. 512(b)(11); Reg. Sec. 1.512(b)-1]. When an exempt trust figures its unrelated business taxable income, the term "unrelated trade or business" means any business regularly carried on by itself or as a partner [IRC Sec. 513(b); Reg. Sec. 1.513-1].

¶3352   TRUSTS WITH CHARITABLE DEDUCTION

No charitable contribution deduction is allowable to a trust under IRC Sec. 642(c) for any tax year for amounts allocable to the trust's unrelated business income. As with an exempt trust [¶3351], a limited deduction is allowed for contributions allocable to the trust's UBI. The UBI of a nonexempt trust means the amount which, if the trust were exempt under IRC Sec. 501(c)(3), would be its UBI [IRC Sec. 681(a); Reg. Sec. 1.681(a)-2].

¶3353   NONEXEMPT TRUSTS TREATED AS PRIVATE FOUNDATIONS

Both charitable and split-interest trusts that are not exempt from tax may be subject to some of the same requirements and restrictions that are imposed on exempt private foundations [¶3337 et seq.] and must file an annual return on Form 5227 [IRC Sec. 4947; Reg. Sec. 53.4947-1; 53.6011-1(d)].

Trust instrument. No income, estate or gift tax charitable deduction is allowed for a charitable interest in a nonexempt trust unless the trust instrument expressly prohibits the trust from violating the restrictions and requirements to which it is subject [IRC Sec. 508(e); 4947(a)].

¶3354   UNRELATED BUSINESS INCOME (UBI) TAX RATES, RETURNS AND PAYMENTS

All organizations subject to the tax on unrelated business income, except trusts, are taxable at corporate rates on that income. [¶3002]. Trusts are taxed at estate and trust income tax rates explained at ¶3520(b), (c) [IRC Sec. 511(a); Reg. Sec. 1.511-1]. Capital gains and losses are not included in figuring unrelated business income [¶3348(a)].

Returns and payments. The unrelated business income tax return (Form 990-T) must be filed by taxpayers having gross income of $1,000 or more included in figuring UBI [IRC Sec. 6033; Reg. Sec. 1.6072-2(c)]. Taxpayers with gross income not exceeding $5,000 need complete only part of the return. Time for filing an unrelated business tax return is covered at ¶3630(d). Time for paying UBI tax is at ¶3653.

Certain exempt organizations must make quarterly estimated tax payments for the UBI tax, in the same manner as regular corporate estimated income taxes (¶3651) [IRC Sec. 6655(g)(3)].

COOPERATIVE ORGANIZATIONS

¶3355   TAXING COOPERATIVES (CO-OPs)

Some cooperative corporations and farmers' organizations pay a tax on taxable income at the rates for corporations [IRC Sec. 1381(b); Reg. Sec. 1.1381-1, -2]. Taxable income can be reduced or eliminated by distributions of co-op earnings to members or patrons [IRC Sec. 1382(a); Reg. Sec. 1.1382-1].

Taxable organizations. The cooperative tax rules apply to any cooperative corporation unless it is tax exempt, or supplies electricity or telephone service in rural areas, or is taxed as a mutual savings bank or insurance company [IRC Sec. 1381(a); Reg. Sec. 1.1381-1]. The rules also apply to the specially defined Section 521 farmers' co-ops that are otherwise exempt [Reg. Sec. 1.1381-2].

Returns. Tax-exempt farmers' cooperatives file income tax returns on Form 990-C by the 15th day of the 9th month after the end of the tax year (September 15 for calendar year taxpayers). Other qualified co-ops have until the same time to file if they pay or are obligated to pay 50% or more of patronage earnings as patronage dividends for the latest year they had patronage income [IRC Sec. 6072(d); Reg. Sec. 1.6072-2(d), (f)]. Co-ops must file information returns [¶3663].

¶3356   COOPERATIVE DISTRIBUTIONS

Cooperative distributions from earnings may be made in cash, other property, or by written notice of allocation (called scrip) that states the dollar amount allocated and the part that is a patronage dividend. A patronage dividend is a distribution out of earnings from business done with the payee-patrons. Each payment is based on the amount of business the patron did with the co-op.

Distributions also may be made by per-unit retain certificates under allocation agreements. A per-unit retain allocation is a patron's share of the proceeds from products marketed for him during the tax year that the cooperative retains at a specified amount per unit sold. The patron receives a per-unit retain certificate (any written notice) showing the amount retained. It differs from scrip in that it represents sales proceeds rather than a share of cooperative net earnings.

In addition to patronage distributions and retain certificates, farmers' cooperatives can also distribute earnings on a patronage basis from business done with the U.S. or its agencies or from other sources. These are called nonpatronage payments. Farmers' co-ops also can pay dividends on capital stock. All co-ops must keep permanent records to show business done with members and nonmembers[1] [Reg. Sec. 1.521-1(a)(1)].

For tax purposes, scrip and per-unit retain certificates are qualified or unqualified. Scrip is qualified when at least 20% of a patronage dividend or nonpatronage payment is paid in cash or qualified check, and the patron is notified in writing that the scrip can be redeemed for cash for at least 90 days [IRC Sec. 1388(c)(1)(A); Reg. Sec. 1.1388-1(c)]. A qualified check is one with notice to the payee that cashing it is a consent to include the amount in income [IRC Sec. 1388(c)(4); Reg. Sec. 1.1388-1(c)(3)]. Scrip also is qualified if the receiver consents to include the amount in income [IRC Sec. 1388(c)(1)(B); Reg. Sec. 1.1388-1(c)(3)]. This can be an irrevocable consent shown by being a member of the cooperative after notice that membership means consent, or it can be a continuing revocable written consent [IRC Sec. 1388(b)(2); Reg. Sec. 1.1388-1(c)(3)]. Cashing a qualified check within 90 days after the end of the co-op payment period [¶3357] is a consent to include that amount in income. Assignment of future qualified scrip to the cooperative to pay for the patron's purchase on a conditional sale does not disqualify the scrip.[2]

Per-unit retain certificates are qualified only when the patron has consented to include the amount retained in his income. Consent is indicated the same way as for patronage dividends [IRC Sec. 1388(h)].

Net earnings may, at the co-op's option, be determined by offsetting patronage losses (including patronage loss carried to such year) attributable to one or more allocation units, against patronage earnings of one or more other such allocation units [IRC Sec. 1388(j)].

¶3357　　DEDUCTION FOR DISTRIBUTIONS

Any co-op subject to tax [¶3355] can deduct patronage dividends [¶3356] paid from patronage income of the tax year and per-unit retain allocations if:

- Patronage dividends are paid under an enforceable written obligation made before the cooperative received the amounts distributed. This obligation may be stated in state law, corporate charter or bylaws, or other documents or agreements [IRC Sec. 1388(a)(2); Reg. Sec. 1.1388-1(a)(1)].
- Patronage dividends are paid in cash, qualified scrip, or other property (not unqualified scrip). Amounts paid to redeem unqualified scrip are deducted, but scrip used to redeem scrip cannot be deducted. A qualified check cashed within 90 days after the end of the payment period is counted as cash [IRC Sec. 1382(c), (d); Reg. Sec. 1.1382-1, -2].
- Per-unit retain allocations for the current year are paid in cash, qualified certificates, or other property (except nonqualified per-unit certificates) [IRC Sec. 1382(b)]. Payments to redeem unqualified certificates are deductible unless redeemed by other certificates [IRC Sec. 1383].
- The patronage dividend or per-unit retain allocation is paid during the tax year or within 8½ months thereafter [IRC Sec. 1382(d); Reg. Sec. 1.1382-4].

NOTE: Patronage dividends are included in gross income and deducted, but per-unit retain allocations are treated as exclusions from gross income [IRC Sec. 1382].

Distributions from earnings of prior years are deductible in the year the earnings are included in income [Reg. Sec. 1.1382-6]. Patronage from pooling arrangements is income for the year the pool closes, but the marketing of products can be treated as occurring during any of the tax years the pool is open [IRC Sec. 1382(e); Reg. Sec. 1.1382-5].

(a) Farmers' Cooperatives. In addition to patronage dividends (above), exempt farmers' cooperatives can also deduct: (1) dividends paid on capital stock during the tax year and (2) distributions on a patronage basis from nonpatronage business earnings during its tax year when paid in money, property, or qualified scrip within its tax year or within 8½ months thereafter [IRC Sec. 1382(c), (d); Reg. Sec. 1.1382-3, -4].

(b) Tax Reduction for Redemption of Unqualified Scrip or Certificates. The tax for the year unqualified scrip or retain certificates are redeemed may be reduced by treating the redemption payment as a deductible amount. The tax for the redemption year is the lesser of (1) the tax computed with the redemption deduction or (2) the tax computed without the deduction, less the tax that would have been saved in the prior years if the amount could have been deducted then. If the prior years' tax savings is more than the current year's tax without the redemption deduction, the excess is refunded or credited to the cooperative. If the second tax above is paid, the redemption deduction is used to adjust earnings and profits, but does not enter into other tax computations, such as taxable income or loss or net operating loss carryback or carryover [IRC Sec. 1383; Reg. Sec. 1.1383-1].

NOTE: The deduction allowed for redemption of scrip cannot exceed the dollar amount of the scrip. Deduction of any excess depends on the nature of the payment. For example, it may be deductible as interest. When the redemption is made within the 8½-month payment period explained in (a) above, the deduction must be taken for the earlier year [Reg. Sec. 1.1382-3(d)].

¶3358   PATRONS' INCOME FROM COOPERATIVE

Generally, as a member of a co-op you report patronage dividends, nonpatronage payments [¶3356] and per-unit retains as ordinary income when you receive them. This does not apply to unqualified scrip or nonqualified retain certificates. You may exclude or report as capital gain all or part of some patronage dividends [IRC Sec. 1385; Reg. Sec. 1.1385-1(a)].

Ordinary income. You include in income the cash, the stated dollar amount of qualified scrip, and fair market value of other property you receive as a nonpatronage payment or a patronage dividend that you cannot exclude ((b) below) [Reg. Sec. 1.1385-1(c), (d)]. You also include in income the stated dollar amount of qualified retain certificates received [IRC Sec. 1385(a)].

Unqualified scrip or nonqualified certificates received are not included in income until you redeem or otherwise dispose of them. Your basis for the scrip or certificate is zero. Its basis to anyone acquiring it from a decedent is always the decedent's basis—never fair market value. You report any gain when you redeem, sell or otherwise dispose of the scrip or certificate. If its basis is less than its stated dollar amount, the difference is ordinary income to the extent of the gain [Reg. Sec. 1.1385-1(b)].

Excluded patronage dividends. You can exclude certain patronage dividends, including unqualified scrip, depending on the kind of property that is the dividend source and whether you have ownership in the tax year the dividend is received, as follows [Reg. Sec. 1.1385-1(c)]:

- The amount of a dividend based on the purchase of personal items or services for business is excluded.
- You can exclude the amount based on the purchase of a capital asset or depreciable business property up to the adjusted basis of property you still own during the tax year you receive the dividend. If the dividend amount for the purchase is more than the adjusted basis, the excess is ordinary income. Your property basis is reduced by the amount of the exclusion, effective on the first day of the tax year the dividend is received.
- When you do not own capital assets or depreciable business property during the year you receive the dividend, the amount based on the purchase or sale is excluded if a loss related to the property could not be deducted [¶2300]. If a loss could be deducted and the asset was held for more than one year, you treat the amount as long-term capital gain. A dividend amount based on the sale of a capital asset or depreciable business property is added to the price received for the property when the dividend is received in year of sale.

NOTE: You must report the full amount of a patronage dividend as ordinary income if a part cannot be excluded [Reg. Sec. 1.1385-1(c)(2)(iv)].

Footnotes to Chapter 23

(For your added convenience, in brackets [] with the footnotes below, you will find citations to related paragraphs in the "RIA United States Tax Reporter"(USTR), "CCH Federal Tax Reporter"(CCH) and "RIA Federal Tax Coordinator 2d"(FTC) multi-volume services.)

FOOTNOTE ¶3300 [USTR ¶5424; CCH ¶23,401; FTC ¶D-3200].

FOOTNOTE ¶3301 [USTR ¶5424.03; CCH ¶23,445; FTC ¶D-3500].

(1) Rev. Rul. 75-67, 1975-1 CB 169.

FOOTNOTE ¶3302 [USTR ¶5424.04; CCH ¶23,445; FTC ¶D-3400].

(1) Rev. Rul. 89-30, 1989-1 CB 170.

FOOTNOTE ¶3303 [USTR ¶5424.02; CCH ¶23,445; FTC ¶D-3300].

FOOTNOTE ¶3304 [USTR ¶5422.01; CCH ¶23,504; 23,762; FTC ¶D-3600].

(1) Fulman et al. v. U.S., 41 AFTR 2d 78-698, 434 US 5289.

FOOTNOTE ¶3305 [USTR ¶5422.03; CCH ¶23,404; FTC ¶D-3201].

FOOTNOTE ¶3307 [USTR ¶5474; CCH ¶23,548; FTC ¶D-3700].

FOOTNOTE ¶3308 [USTR ¶2674; CCH ¶14,161; FTC ¶D-3600].

FOOTNOTE ¶3309 [USTR ¶5422.03; CCH ¶34,211; FTC ¶D-3600].

FOOTNOTE ¶3311 [USTR ¶5454.01; CCH ¶23,566; FTC ¶D-3600].

FOOTNOTE ¶3312 [USTR ¶5524; CCH ¶23,566; FTC ¶D-3310].

FOOTNOTE ¶3313 [USTR ¶5560; CCH ¶23,566; FTC ¶D-3310].

FOOTNOTE ¶3314 [USTR ¶5514; CCH ¶23,566; FTC ¶D-3310].

FOOTNOTE ¶3315 [USTR ¶5524; CCH ¶23,587; FTC ¶D-3310].

FOOTNOTE ¶3316 [USTR ¶5454.02; CCH ¶23,587; FTC ¶D-3200].

FOOTNOTE ¶3325 [USTR ¶8520; CCH ¶26,608; FTC ¶E-6000 et seq.].

FOOTNOTE ¶3326 [USTR ¶8514; CCH ¶26,608; FTC ¶E-6000 et seq.].

FOOTNOTE ¶3327 [USTR ¶8514.02; CCH ¶26,608; FTC ¶E-6032].

FOOTNOTE ¶3328 [USTR ¶8524; CCH ¶26,608; FTC ¶E-6100 et seq.].

FOOTNOTE ¶3329 [USTR ¶8564; CCH ¶26,712; FTC ¶C-5017].

(1) Rev. Rul. 65-3, 1965-1 CB 267.

FOOTNOTE ¶3330 [USTR ¶8574; CCH ¶26,800 et seq.; FTC ¶E-6900].

(1) Treas. Dept. booklet "Investment Income and Expenses" (1991 Ed.), p. 19.

FOOTNOTE ¶3335 [USTR ¶5014; CCH ¶22,601; FTC ¶D-4000].

FOOTNOTE ¶3336 [USTR ¶5014.05; CCH ¶22,601; FTC ¶D-4100].

(1) Grange Ins. Assn. of Calif. v. Comm., 11 AFTR 2d 1423, 317 F.2d 222.

(2) HCSC-Laundry v. U.S., 47 AFTR 2d 81-797.

(3) Rev. Rul. 69-573, 1969-2 CB 125.

(4) Coeur d'Alene Country Club v. Viley, 157 F.2d 330, 35 AFTR 120.

(5) Rev. Rul. 44, 1953-1 CB 109.

(6) Clements Buckaroos, ¶62,018 PH Memo TC.

(7) Washington State Apples, Inc., 46 BTA 64.

(8) Rev. Rul. 67-252, 1967-2 CB 195.

(9) Smyth v. Calif. State Auto. Ass'n., 175 F.2d 752, 38 AFTR 120.

(10) National Outdoor Advertising Bureau, 89 F.2d 878, 19 AFTR 619.

(11) Sunset Scavenger Co., Inc., 84 F.2d 453, 17 AFTR 1319.

(12) Rev. Rul. 73-306, 1973-2 CB 193.

(13) Rev. Rul. 65-6, 1965-1 CB 229.

(14) Sonora Community Hospital, 46 TC 519, aff'd 22 AFTR 2d 5442, 397 F.2d 814.

(15) Rev. Rul. 61-170, 1961-2 CB 112.

(16) Rev. Rul. 65-14, 1965-1 CB 236.

(17) Rev. Proc. 73-7, 1973-1 CB 753; superseded by Rev. Proc. 76-34, 1976-2 CB 656.

(18) Rev. Proc. 77-38, 1977-2 CB 571.

(19) Secretary of Treasury v. Taxation with Representation of Wash., 103 SCt. 1997, 51 AFTR 2d 83-1294.

FOOTNOTE ¶3337 [USTR ¶5070; CCH ¶22,762; FTC ¶D-7200].

FOOTNOTE ¶3338 [USTR ¶5109; CCH ¶35,402; FTC ¶D-7500].

FOOTNOTE ¶3339 [USTR ¶49,404; CCH ¶35,810; FTC ¶D-7600–8100].

FOOTNOTE ¶3340 [USTR ¶5609; CCH ¶35,431; FTC ¶D-7600].

FOOTNOTE ¶3341 [USTR ¶49,424; CCH ¶35,447; FTC ¶D-7700].

FOOTNOTE ¶3342 [USTR ¶49,434; CCH ¶35,472; FTC ¶D-7800].

FOOTNOTE ¶3343 [USTR ¶49,444; CCH ¶35,487; FTC ¶D-7900].

FOOTNOTE ¶3344 [USTR ¶49,454; CCH ¶35,507; FTC ¶D-8000].

FOOTNOTE ¶3345 [USTR ¶5114; CCH ¶22,772; FTC ¶D-6800].

FOOTNOTE ¶3346 [USTR ¶5110; 5114; CCH ¶22,772; FTC ¶D-6800].

FOOTNOTE ¶3347 [USTR ¶5134; CCH ¶22,796; FTC ¶D-6803].

FOOTNOTE ¶3348 [USTR ¶5124; CCH ¶22,786; FTC ¶D-6824].

FOOTNOTE ¶3349 [USTR ¶5144; CCH ¶22,809; FTC ¶D-7100].

FOOTNOTE ¶3350 [USTR ¶5144; CCH ¶24,968; FTC ¶D-4107].

FOOTNOTE ¶3351 [USTR ¶5110; CCH ¶22,772; FTC ¶D-4007].

FOOTNOTE ¶3352 [USTR ¶49,474; CCH ¶25,244; FTC ¶D-4107].

FOOTNOTE ¶3353 [USTR ¶6814; CCH ¶35,543; FTC ¶D-6800].

FOOTNOTE ¶3354 [USTR ¶5134; CCH ¶22,772; FTC ¶D-4700].

FOOTNOTE ¶3355 [USTR ¶13,814.01; CCH ¶33,728; FTC ¶E-1001].

FOOTNOTE ¶3356 [USTR ¶5214.08; CCH ¶33,720 et seq.; FTC ¶E-1104 et seq.].

(1) Rev. Rul. 63-58, 1963-1 CB 109.

(2) Rev. Rul. 65-128, 1965-1 CB 432.

FOOTNOTE ¶3357 [USTR ¶13,884; CCH ¶33,728; FTC ¶E-1101].

FOOTNOTE ¶3358 [USTR ¶13,834; CCH ¶33,762; FTC ¶E-1100 et seq.].

Chapter 24—PARTNERSHIPS
(Detailed Table of Contents below)
Chapter 25—ESTATES AND TRUSTS
(Detailed Table of Contents at page 3501)

CHAPTER

PARTNERSHIPS 24

TABLE OF CONTENTS

WHAT IS A PARTNERSHIP

A partnership is not a taxable entity. It is a conduit for passing income, deductions, etc., to partners. Each year, the partnership must file a partnership return showing its total income or loss and certain separately stated items. The partners must include their distributive shares of partnership items in figuring their taxable income.

¶3400   TAX DEFINITION

Under the tax law, the term "partnership" has a broader meaning than the one applied to common-law partnerships. An organization will be classified as a partnership for tax purposes if it has more "noncorporate" than "corporate" characteristics [IRC Sec. 7701]. Characteristics that indicate a corporation include contintuity of life, centralized management, limited liability of participants and free transferability of interests. The IRS has said that it will generally find that a partnership lacks free transferability of interests if, throughout the life of the partnership, the partnership agreement expressly restricts the transferability of partnership interests representing more than 20% of all interests in the partnership.[1]

For tax purposes, a partnership usually exists when you and one or more persons join together to carry on a trade or business and to share its profits and losses, with each of you contributing cash, property, labor or skill.[2] "Persons" forming a partnership may include individuals, corporations, trusts, estates, or other partnerships.

This definition is broad enough to include several groups that are not commonly called partnerships. Examples include syndicates, groups, pools, joint ventures and similar business or financial organizations that are not corporations, trusts or estates [IRC Sec. 761(a); Reg. Sec. 1.761-1(a)(1)].

Tenants in common. Co-ownership of property does not, of itself, constitute a partnership. Thus, tenants in common who own real estate, rent it out and divide the profits are not necessarily partners. A partnership may exist if tenants in common carry on a trade, business or venture and divide the profits [Reg. Sec. 1.761-1(a)].

Publicly traded partnerships (commonly known as master limited partnerships) are generally treated as corporations [IRC Sec. 7704]. However, a publicly traded partnership is not treated as a corporation if 90% or more of its gross income was from passive sources (e.g., interest, dividends and rent) for the current year and for each preceding tax year beginning after 1987 [IRC Sec. 7704(c)].

Thanks to a special transition rule, publicly traded partnerships formed before December 18, 1987, continue to offer investors many of the benefits of incorporation (for example, limited liability) with none of the tax drawbacks (for example, corporate level tax). However, publicly traded partnerships formed before December 17, 1987, that added a substantial new line of business after that date are taxed as corporations unless they fall within the passive income exception. After 1997, all publicly traded partnerships that do not fall within the passive income exception will be taxed as corporations.

Income from publicly traded partnerships is treated as portfolio income for the passive loss rules [IRC Sec. 469(k)]. Also, a tax-exempt organization's income from a publicly traded partnership is treated as unrelated business income [IRC Sec. 512(c)].

¶3401   THE CLASSIFICATION DANGER

For tax purposes, organizations are grouped into certain categories, such as associations (which are taxed as corporations), partnerships , and trusts. Federal standards are used to categorize an organization for tax purposes.[1] Thus, a business that is called a partnership under state law might be classified as an association by the Revenue Service [Reg. Sec. 301.7701-3(b)].

¶3402   EXCLUSION FROM PARTNERSHIP TREATMENT

Partnership tax treatment does not apply to unincorporated groups you form only for investment purposes (and not for the active conduct of a business) if you and all the other members elect to forgo such tax treatment [IRC Sec. 761(a)(1); Reg Sec. 1.761-2(a)(2)].[1] Nor does partnership treatment apply to unincorporated groups you form only for the joint production, extraction, or use of property (but not for selling services or property produced or extracted) if all of the members so elect. However, you and the other members must be able to compute your income independently of the computation of partnership taxable income [IRC Sec. 761(a)(2); Reg. Sec. 1.761-2(a)(3)].

To elect exclusion from partnership treatment, a partnership return must be filed on Form 1065 for the first year you elected the exclusion. The return or a separate statement must indicate that a member is electing exclusion from partnership treatment. Once you make the election, it can be changed only with IRS consent.

Under certain circumstances, you can elect a partial exclusion from partnership treatment. A partial exclusion requires IRS consent [Reg. Sec. 1.761-2(c)].

Neither a complete exclusion nor a partial exclusion exempts you and the other partners from the limitations on a partner's deductions for partnership losses or the rules regarding a partnership's required tax year.

¶3403   FAMILY PARTNERSHIPS

A family partnership is one whose members are closely related by blood or marriage. Even though some family partnerships may have been created for the sole purpose of reducing the aggregate income taxes that a family unit might otherwise have to pay (by shifting some income to family members who are in lower tax brackets), the Revenue Service recognizes the arrangement if the family members actually own their respective partnership interests. This depends on your intent, determined from many factors. These include the agreement, the relationship between you and the other parties, your conduct, statements, individual abilities and capital contributions, and the control and use of income.[1]

> ➤ **OBSERVATION** Even if your under-age-14 child owns his or her partnership interest, his or her partnership income may be taxed at your rate—that is, as if you had received the income—rather than at the child's lower rate [¶1240].

(a) Where Family Partnership Income Is Generated by Capital. If   the partnership is one in which capital is a material income-producing factor (e.g., when substantial inventories or investments in plant or machinery are required), your family members are recognized as partners only if they acquired their capital interests in a bona fide manner and have dominion and control over their respective interests. The fact that an interest was purchased from you or another family member (or even was received from you as a gift) does not automatically taint the acquisition [Reg. Sec. 1.704-1(e)(3)]. If a partnership interest was a gift, there are some restrictions on amounts that can be allocated to the recipient as his or her distributive share of partnership income.

- If you (the donor partner) perform services for the partnership, an amount that represents reasonable compensation for your services must be allocated to you before the recipient's distributive share is calculated. No such allocation is required for services performed by nondonor partners.

- The donee partner's distributive share attributable to the donated capital can't be proportionately greater than your (the donor's) distributive share attributable to the retained capital [Reg. Sec. 1.704-1(e)(3)].

NOTE: For this provision, a partnership interest bought by one member of a "family" from another is treated as a gift. Family here is limited to husband or wife, ancestors (for example, fathers and grandfathers) and lineal descendants (for example, sons and grandsons), and any trusts for their primary benefit [IRC Sec. 704(e)(3); Reg. Sec. 1.704-1(e)(3)(i)(a)].

Example: Father sold his son a half interest in a partnership having net profits for the year of $50,000. The son performs no duties, while the father contributes services worth $10,000. $30,000 is allocated to the father ($10,000 salary plus 50% of the remaining $40,000). $20,000 is allocated to the son. Had the father and son both performed equal significant services, $25,000 would be allocated to each.

The Revenue Service may also disregard the agreement and make an allocation when you create indirectly a gift interest in the partnership [Reg. Sec. 1.704-1(e)(3)(ii)]. Thus, if you give property to your daughter who then transfers it to a partnership of you and your daughter, you are considered the donor of your daughter's interest.

(b) Where Partnership Income Is Generated by Services. If your partnership is not one in which capital is a material income-producing factor, the Revenue Service recognizes your family members as partners only if they contribute substantial or vital services to the partnership.

PARTNERSHIP INCOME, DEDUCTIONS, CREDITS

[New tax legislation may affect this subject; see ¶1.]

¶3404   HOW A PARTNERSHIP REPORTS INCOME

Your partnership does not pay taxes—it is a conduit for passing income, deduction, and credit items through to you and the other partners. You include your respective distributive shares [¶3412] of partnership items in your personal income tax returns together with your nonpartnership income.

Information return. Your partnership files an information return on Form 1065, reporting each partner's share of income, credit, and deduction items on Schedule K-1 [¶3409; 3669(a)]. The partnership is subject to a monthly civil penalty ($50 times the number of its partners) for a maximum of five months that its return is late or incomplete without reasonable cause [IRC Sec. 6698].

How a partnership reports. First, your partnership segregates and separately states for each partner his or her distributive share of certain items [¶3408] which have special tax significance. It then takes into account all remaining partnership items and computes its "taxable income or loss," allocating to each partner his or her distributive share of that total.

Audit tax treatment of partnership items. For assessment purposes, the tax treatment of partnership income, loss, deductions and credits is determined at the partnership level [IRC Sec. 6221]. You and the other partners must report an item on your individual returns consistently with the way the item is treated on the partnership return [IRC Sec. 6222(a)]. The IRS cannot adjust the treatment of an item on your return except through a partnership-level proceeding. Rules are provided for converting partnership items to nonpartnership items [IRC Sec. 6221-6232].

Dealings with the IRS are handled by the tax matters partner (TMP). The partner who is designated as the TMP must keep the other partners informed of tax proceedings involving your partnership. Space is provided on the partnership return for your partnership to make the designation. If no designation is made, the general partner with the largest profits interest is treated as the TMP. If there is more then one such partner, the one whose name comes first alphabetically is treated as the TMP [Temp. Reg. Sec. 301.6231(a)(7)-1T].

This special treatment does not apply to small partnerships (10 or fewer partners) unless they so elect.

NOTE: Even if the filer of a partnership return is later determined not to be a partnership, or the entity doesn't exist at all, the IRS can still audit items at the partnership level [IRC Sec. 6233].

(a) Partnership Tax Preferences are treated the same as separately stated items: your partnership does not pay any alternative minimum tax, but passes its preference items to you and the other partners who include them in your alternative minimum tax returns, Form 6251 (¶2601) [IRC Sec. 55-57].

(b) Partnership's Taxable Income or Loss. Your partnership's taxable income or loss is figured in much the same way as that of an individual. However, separately listed items are not taken into account. Moreover, your partnership may not claim a standard deduction and the deduction for personal exemptions. Nor are the following itemized deductions allowed: the deduction for foreign taxes and for charitable contributions; the net operating loss deduction; the deduction for capital-loss carryovers; the other deductions listed in ¶3408; the depletion allowance for oil and gas wells (¶2237) [IRC Sec. 703(a)(2)].

Your partnership is denied the benefit of the foreign tax credit. The benefit is instead passed on to you and the other partners.

NOTE: A partnership can deduct state taxes based on the firm's income.[1]

Losses and credits from passive activities. As a general rule, you can apply losses and credits from passive activities only against income and tax from passive activities. You cannot deduct the excess of your passive losses from an activity over income from all your passive activities against your other income like salaries, wages, professional fees, or income from an active business. These losses and credits remain suspended until you have passive income to offset or until you dispose of the activity [¶2326].

Any trade or business is a passive activity if you do not materially participate in the enterprise. With certain exceptions, if you directly or indirectly own a limited partner interest, you automatically fail the material participation test (¶2842) [IRC Sec. 469(h)(2)].

All rental activities are automatically passive regardless of your participation. However, if you actively participate in a rental real estate activity, you may be able to deduct up to $25,000 of your losses (or an equivalent amount of credits) from that activity against nonpassive income.

The passive activity limitations do not apply at the partnership level. They apply to each partner's share of income or loss and credit from a passive activity. To allow you to correctly apply the passive activity limitations, your partnership must report income or loss and credits separately for each activity it conducts.

The first step for your partnership is to identify its activities. Generally, each undertaking (business and rental operations conducted at the same location) is a separate activity. However, in some cases your partnership may be required or permitted to combine undertakings into a larger activity. Your partnership may also be permitted to divide a rental real estate undertaking into more than one activity [Temp. Reg. Sec. 1.469-4T].

You have some flexibility in identifying your activities. However, you and the other partners generally may not treat a group of undertakings as separate activities if those undertakings were treated as a single activity by your partnership [Temp. Reg. Sec. 1.469-4T(k)(2)(ii), (o)(3)].

(c) Organization and Syndication Fees. Neither you nor your partnership can currently deduct amounts paid or incurred to organize the partnership or promote the sale of a partnership interest. However, your partnership may elect to deduct its organizational expenses in equal installments over a period of not less than 60 months. The expenses eligible for the 60-month amortization must be (1) incident to your partnership's creation; (2) chargeable to the capital account; and (3) of a character which, if expended for the creation of the partnership with an ascertainable life, would be amortized over that life [IRC Sec. 709]. If your partnership is liquidated before the end of the 60-month period, the remaining balance of the expenses may be deductible as a loss. The special amortization does not apply to syndication costs such as commissions, professional fees and printing costs for issuing and marketing partnership interests [Reg. Sec. 1.709-2(b)].

¶3405   ELECTIONS AFFECTING COMPUTATION OF INCOME

Most elections affecting the computation of partnership income are made by your partnership and bind you and all the other partners [IRC Sec. 703(b); Reg. Sec. 1.703-1(b)]. The only exceptions are: (1) the election as to foreign taxes [¶3408; 3801]; (2) the election as to deduction and recapture of certain mining exploration expenditures [¶2242]; (3) a nonresident alien's or foreign corporation's election to treat income from U.S. real property as "effectively connected" income [¶3811]; (4) the election relating to income from discharge of indebtedness [¶1234].

The excepted elections are made by each partner separately. For example, you can use your distributive share of foreign taxes either as a credit or as a deduction, as you choose.

Examples of elections made by your partnership include the elections as to method of accounting, method of figuring depreciation, use of installment sales provisions, option to expense intangible drilling and development costs, etc., and nonrecognition of gain from condemnation of partnership property.[1]

¶3406   BOOK PROFIT AND TAXABLE INCOME DISTINGUISHED

Your partnership's book profit should be distinguished from its taxable income. Many items enter into the determination of book profit that are not considered in figuring taxable income. For example, the items listed in ¶3404(b) or items exempt from tax such as interest on municipal and state obligations do not affect partnership taxable income; yet under ordinary methods of accounting, they are taken into account in figuring book profit.

➤ **OBSERVATION** When your partnership return is prepared directly from the books, it is easy for errors to occur by neglecting to exclude or include certain items. It is best first to determine your partnership's taxable income as it will appear in the partnership return by taking the regular profit and loss statement and either decreasing or increasing the book profit or loss, as required.

Example: The profit and loss statement of the Smith & Brown partnership for the tax year is as follows:

Gross receipts from sales		$316,418
Less cost of goods sold		173,618
Gross profit		$142,800
Interest received from taxable bonds and banks		1,000
Interest (tax exempt)		3,200
Short-term capital gain		1,600
Long-term capital gain		4,400
Gross profit and misc. income items		$153,000
Deduct:		
Charitable contributions	$ 3,000	
Partners' salaries ($12,500 for each partner)	25,000	
Other operating expenses	15,000	43,000
Net profit from operations and capital transactions		$110,000
Deduct interest on capital		10,000
Net profit for the year		$100,000

From this profit and loss statement, the taxable income of the Smith & Brown partnership is figured as follows:

Book profit (from profit and loss statement)		$100,000
Capital gains and losses segregated:		
Book gains on short-term transactions	$ 1,600	
Book gains on long-term transactions	4,400	
Subtract net book gain (add back net book loss) on capital asset transactions		6,000
		$ 94,000
Segregated income items:		
Tax-exempt interest	$3,200	
Subtract total segregated income items		3,200
		$ 90,800
Deductions not allowed:		
Charitable contributions	$3,000	
Add back total deductions not allowed		3,000
Partnership's taxable income		$ 93,800

The taxable income and the segregated items of the partnership would appear on the partnership return as follows:

Ordinary income	$ 93,800
Net gain from short-term capital asset transactions	1,600
Net gain from long-term capital asset transactions	4,400
Charitable contributions	3,000

FIGURING PARTNER'S TAX LIABILITY

¶3407　　　HOW PARTNERS DETERMINE THEIR TAX LIABILITIES

As a partner, you determine your income tax liability by including on your individual tax return the following items: (1) your distributive share of the separately stated items [¶3408]; (2) your distributive share of the partnership's taxable income or loss; (3) any salary or other guaranteed payments received from the partnership.

NOTE: In (1) and (2), it doesn't matter that you did not receive the distribution or that you are on the cash basis and the partnership is on the accrual basis.[1]

Example: A partnership equally owned by Ralph and Sharon had taxable income of $34,000 for the year. It had no transactions involving separately stated items. During the year, the partners each withdrew $2,000 of the profits. The partnership files Form 1065 showing partnership taxable income of $34,000 and the partners' distributive shares of taxable income as $17,000 each. Ralph and Sharon must report their $17,000 share on their own Form 1040. This is true even if it is not all distributed to them, and even if the partnership agreement prohibited distribution during the year.

If you have a net operating loss for the year, you must take into account partnership items in determining your net operating loss deduction. The character of a partnership item is determined as if it were realized directly by you. In calculating the allowance for nonbusiness deductions, you must separately take into account your distributive share of partnership deductions that are not attributable to a trade or business and your distributive share of partnership income that is not derived from a trade or business. These amounts must be combined with your own nonbusiness income and deductions [Reg. Sec. 1.702-2].

¶3408   SEPARATELY STATED ITEMS

Your partnership segregates certain items that have special tax significance from the rest of its income, gains, losses, deductions, and credits so that each partner may take his or her distributive share of those items into account in completing an individual tax return. Your share of each separately stated item takes, in your hands, the same character it would have if you had realized it directly [IRC Sec. 702; Reg. Sec. 1.702-1].

The regulations list specific items that must be separately stated. These include capital gains and losses, gains and losses from Sec. 1231 property, charitable contributions, dividends, foreign taxes paid by your partnership, and tax-exempt interest [Reg. Sec. 1.702-2(a)]. However, the list in the regulations is not comprehensive. The regulations also provide that your partnership must separately state *any* item if separately stating that item would result in a different tax to *any* partner than if it were not separately stated.

> ➤ **OBSERVATION** The list of items that must be separately stated changes as the tax law changes. For example, enactment of the passive loss rules dramatically increased the number of items that must be separately stated by your partnership and separately reported by you. As a result, the most comprehensive listing of separately stated items is found in the partnership return schedules (Form 1065 Schedules K and K-1) for a given year [¶3409].

Among the more significant items that must be separately stated by your partnership are:

1. Capital gains and losses. Your partnership reports the entire amount of its net recognized gain or loss from short-term transactions and the entire amount of its net recognized gain or loss from long-term transactions in the capital gain and loss schedule of its partnership return (Schedule D of Form 1065). You (and the other partners) must pick up your share of these gains and losses from the distribution schedule [¶3409] and include them in your individual return *whether or not the gains and losses are distributed* [IRC Sec. 702(a)(1),(2); Reg. Sec. 1.702- 1(a)(1), (2)]. Short-term or long-term treatment depends on the length of time your partnership held the asset, not the length of time you held the partnership interest.[1]

Your share of partnership capital loss is limited to the adjusted basis (before reduction by the current year's losses) of your partnership interest at the end of the partnership year in which the loss occurred. Because your shares of all types of partnership losses are subject to the same limit, you must allocate your adjusted basis among your shares of partnership short-term and long-term capital losses, Sec. 1231 losses and ordinary losses if their total exceeds the adjusted basis of your interest. You can deduct any excess in later partnership years to the extent of the adjusted basis of your interest at the end of the year (¶3411) [IRC Sec. 704(d)].

Example 1: Mr. Brenner is an equal partner in the MNO partnership. Without regard to any losses during the year, he has an adjusted basis for his partnership interest at the end of the tax year of $5,000. His current year's distributive share of MNO losses is $2,000 of short-term capital losses and $4,000 of ordinary losses. Brenner is allowed only 83.33% ($5,000/$6,000) of each loss or $1,667 (83.33% × $2000) of short-term capital loss and $3,333 (83.33% × $4000) of ordinary loss. Brenner can carry forward $333 as a short-term capital loss and $667 as an ordinary loss.

A loss by your partnership is not allowed when you buy securities in a wash sale [¶2321].

2. Sales, exchanges and involuntary conversions of business property (Sec. 1231 assets)—casualty and theft losses.

You must take into account your distributive share of gains and losses from the sale, exchange, or involuntary conversion of Sec. 1231 assets [¶1811] and set them off against your individual gains and losses of the same type [IRC Sec. 702(a)(3); Reg. Sec. 1.702-1(a)(3)].

Example 2: A partnership equally owned by Mr. Melon and Mr. Nelson has taxable income of $40,000 and a loss of $9,000 from the sale of trucks used in the business. Melon has a Sec. 1231 gain of $5,000 from the sale of a depreciable asset used in another business he operates as a sole proprietor. He has no other income from this other business. Melon's distributable share of partnership taxable income is $20,000 (50% of $40,000). He also has capital gain of $500 ($5,000 from the depreciable assets less $4,500, his share of the partnership Sec. 1231 loss).

Gains and losses from partnership casualties and thefts are also passed through separately to you and the other partners. You include your partnership gains and losses from casualties and thefts with the same type of casualty and theft gains and losses from other sources when determining how they should be treated [¶1813].

Sec. 1231 losses are limited by your adjusted basis, as discussed in 1, above.

3. Passive income and deductions.

In order for you to correctly apply the passive activity limitations, your partnership must report income or loss and credits separately for each of the following types of activities and income: trade or business activities; rental real estate activities; rental activities other than real estate; and portfolio income (income, dividends, royalties, etc.) and related deductions.

➤ **IMPORTANT** The IRS has issued proposed regulations that provide a special break for partners who make loans to or receive loans from their partnership.

Background: When your partnership incurs an interest expense, you must treat the passed-through expense as a passive loss if the business is a passive activity. Under the general rule, you can use passive losses only to shelter passive income. However, interest income you received on a loan made to your partnership had been considered not to be passive income. Thus, if you lent money to your partnership, you had been barred from using the interest expense incurred by your partnership from sheltering the interest income you received on the loan. The proposed regs recharacterize your interest income as passive income. *Result:* Under the proposed regs, the interest income is tax free up to your share of your partnership's interest expense [Prop. Reg. Sec. 1.469-7].

NOTE: Although the rule is effective for tax years starting after 1986, you are not required to apply these rules for tax years starting before June 4, 1991 [Temp. Reg. Sec. 1.469-11T].

4. Expensing deduction.

In general, your partnership may elect to expense up to $10,000 of the cost of depreciable property it buys during the year (rather than recover the cost through depreciation deductions spread out over a number of years) (¶2113) [IRC Sec. 179; Prop. Reg. Sec. 1.179-1(h)]. The expensing deduction is not claimed as a deduction by your partnership. Rather, it is separately stated and passed through to you and the other partners. You combine your share of the partnership's expensing deduction with your own such expenses (or expensing deduction from other partnerships) to determine the amount that you can deduct on your return. You are separately subject to the $10,000 limit.

➤ **NOTE:** Your adjusted basis in your partnership must be reduced by your share of the partnership's expensing deduction, even though you may not be able to deduct all or part of it because of the deduction limits [Reg. Sec. 1.179-1(f)(1)].[2]

5. Charitable contributions. You deduct your proportionate shares of your partnership's contributions on your individual return, within the charitable contribution deduction limitations (¶1919) [IRC Sec. 702(a)(4); Reg. Sec. 1.702-1(a)(4)].[3]

Example 3: Under a partnership agreement, Ms. Archer's share of partnership income or loss is ⅔. During the year, the partnership made charitable contributions of $12,000. Those contributions are not deductible by the partnership. On her personal income tax return, Archer will include $8,000 (⅔) of the partnership contributions (regardless of the income of the partnership). Suppose Archer also made a personal contribution of $2,000 to her church. Then her deduction for contributions on her individual return is $10,000, provided that amount does not exceed the limitations [¶1919].

6. Investment interest. Your partnership must separately state interest paid or accrued to purchase or carry property held for investment. You combine your share of partnership interest with your own investment interest for purposes of applying the limitation on deductions for investment interest.

7. Dividends received. If your partnership has a corporate partner, a special dividends-received deduction is available to that partner for dividends received from eligible corporations by the partnership [¶3014]. Therefore, these dividends should be disregarded in figuring the partnership taxable income and allocated among the partners on the distribution schedule [IRC Sec. 702(a)(5); Reg. Sec. 1.702-1(a)(5)].

8. Foreign taxes paid. You and the other partners are entitled to a credit or a deduction for taxes paid by your partnership to foreign countries and U.S. possessions [IRC Sec. 702(a)(6); Reg. Sec. 1.702-1(a)(6)]. These taxes are not deductible by your partnership in figuring its taxable income. They are allocated among the partners. The election to take the foreign taxes paid by your partnership as either a credit or a deduction is made by you individually [¶3405].

9. Special items. Any partnership item that would affect the determination of *any* partner's income tax if it were combined with his or her own item of the same class is separately stated and allocated to him or her on a distribution schedule. Such items would include [Reg. Sec. 1.702-1(a)(8)(i)]: recovery of bad debts, prior taxes and delinquency amounts [¶1244]; medical expenses [¶1931]; contributions and deductions for partners under self-employed retirement plans [¶1350]; exploration, soil and water conservation expenditures [¶2242; 2245]; gains and losses from wagering [¶2324]; alimony [¶1235]; income, gain or loss to the partnership in a disproportionate distribution [¶3425]; taxes and interest paid to cooperative housing corporations [¶1901; 1906(d)]; intangible drilling and development costs [¶2236(c)]; and any items subject to a special allocation under the partnership agreement that differs from the allocation of partnership taxable income or loss generally [¶3412].

10. Tax credits. Your partnership does not use available tax credits. A distributive share of each credit is passed on to each partner [IRC Sec. 702(a)(7); Reg. Sec. 1.702-1(a)(8)(ii)]. The allocation is made according to your interest in the partnership's general profits, unless the partnership agreement requires a special allocation [¶3412].

¶3409   DISTRIBUTION AND RECONCILIATION SCHEDULES

Your distributive share [¶3412] of separately stated items (as well as your distributive share of partnership income or loss) is reported on Schedule K-1, Form 1065.

The capital accounts of the partners at the beginning and end of the tax year are reconciled on Schedule M, Form 1065. This schedule shows the relationship between your partnership's income and its capital transactions for the year. The items needed for the schedule are found in the partnership's balance sheet and distribution schedule. Each partner's capital account is reconciled on Schedule K-1, Form 1065.

> **NOTE:** Domestic partnerships with ten or fewer partners need not file Schedule L (balance sheets) and Schedule M (reconciliation of partner's capital accounts) if certain tests are met.[1]

¶3410   TAKING PARTNERSHIP INCOME OR LOSS INTO ACCOUNT

Having picked up your distributive shares of separately stated items, you then pick up your distributive share of partnership taxable income or loss.

¶3411   LOSS IS LIMITED

If your partnership sustained a loss for the tax year, your distributive share of the loss that is allowable as a deduction cannot exceed the adjusted basis of your partnership interest [IRC Sec. 704(d)].

If your distributive share of the loss is greater than the adjusted basis of your partnership interest, you may take the excess as a deduction in later years, provided your adjusted basis at that time is more than zero before the carryover loss is taken into account.

> **Example:** Mr. Alfred and Ms. Bonnet form a partnership. They are equal partners. Alfred contributes $5,000. Bonnet contributes property worth $5,000, but with a basis to her of $1,000. The first year's operations result in a loss of $3,000. Alfred has a loss of $1,500, but Bonnet, whose loss is limited to her basis, can take only $1,000. Alfred has a basis for his partnership interest of $3,500 ($5,000 less $1,500 loss); Bonnet's basis is zero. If Bonnet later contributes $500 to the partnership, then she can take the remaining $500 loss at the end of the year she contributes.

Limit under "at risk" rules. Your loss deduction generally cannot exceed the amount you have "at risk" in the activity at the end of the year [¶2327]. However, your partnership's nonrecourse financing (i.e., loans for which no one is personally liable) secured by real estate may increase your amount at risk if the financing is qualified nonrecourse debt for both you and your partnership. (This is true even if you are a limited partner.) Nonrecourse loans are generally qualified if made by a federal, state or local government or a lender regularly engaged in the business of lending money—but usually not a lender related to the borrower or one interested in the transaction. The amount for which you are treated at risk cannot be more than the total amount of the qualified nonrecourse financing at the partnership level [IRC Sec. 465(b)(6)(C)].

¶3412   HOW TO DETERMINE A PARTNER'S DISTRIBUTIVE SHARE

Generally, your distributive share of partnership items is fixed by the partnership agreement. The allocation made by the partnership agreement is respected for tax purposes only if it has substantial economic effect.

As a general rule, an allocation in the partnership agreement has substantial economic effect if it meets a two-part test:

(1) The allocation has an economic effect—that is, the partner who receives the allocation actually bears the economic burden or receives the economic benefit that corresponds to the allocation. This requirement is not met unless, throughout the full term of the partnership, (a) the partners' capital accounts are properly maintained, (b) liquidating distributions are made in accordance with the partners' capital account balances, and (c) any partner whose interest is liquidated is unconditionally obligated to restore a deficit capital account balance.

(2) The economic effect of the allocation is substantial—that is, the allocation actually affects dollar amounts of the partners' shares of partnership income and loss, independent of tax consequences.

There are, however, alternative tests for establishing that a partnership allocation has substantial economic effect [Prop. Reg. Sec. 1.704-1].

If the agreement is silent on any item or if the allocation under the agreement lacks substantial economic effect, your distributive share of that item is determined by your interest in the partnership (taking all facts and circumstances into account) [IRC Sec. 704].

> **Example:** Mr. Able and Mr. Seeden were partners in AZ partnership. Able expected to have substantial future capital gains, while Seeden did not. Since capital losses may fully offset capital gains, but are only deductible to the extent they exceed capital gains up to $3,000, Able and Seeden amended their partnership agreement to allocate all capital losses to Able. In turn, Seeden was allocated an equivalent amount of ordinary losses. Because the purpose and effect of the new allocations were solely to reduce taxes without actually affecting shares of partnership income, it would not be recognized. The capital loss items would be allocated between the partners according to their overall share of partnership income or loss.

Changes in agreement. The partnership agreement includes any change agreed to by all the partners or made under the terms of the agreement. Changes for a particular tax year are possible up to the original due date of the partnership tax return for that year [IRC Sec. 761(c); Reg. Sec. 1.761-1(c)].

¶3413   DISTRIBUTIVE SHARE OF ITEMS DUE TO CONTRIBUTED PROPERTY

If you contribute property to your partnership, the partnership's basis in the property generally is the same as yours [IRC Sec. 723]. Income, gain, loss, and deductions (other than depreciation and depletion) for the contributed property are allocated among you and the other partners, taking into consideration the difference between the property's basis and its fair market value at the time of the contribution. In this way, your partnership is not used to distort the economic realities of any gain on the sale or exchange of the property. Built-in gain (gain that is attributable to the period from the time you acquired the property to the time you contributed the property) is specially allocated to you [IRC Sec. 704(c)].

For tax treatment of contributions of unrealized receivables, inventory items, or capital loss property, see ¶3418(c).

TAX YEAR OF PARTNER AND PARTNERSHIP

¶3414   CHOICE OF TAX YEAR

[New tax legislation may affect this subject; see ¶1.]

The interplay of your tax year and your partnership's tax year determines the time that you must include your share of partnership income in your personal income. You must report on your return your share of partnership items for the partnership year that ends with or within your tax year [IRC Sec. 706(a)].

This rule could result in a postponement of the tax on partnership income where your partnership uses a fiscal year and you use a calendar year.

> ➤ **OBSERVATION** If you report on a calendar-year basis and your partnership uses a fiscal year ending June 30, you will get six months' deferral in reporting and paying tax on partnership income.

Example 1: The E-H partnership uses a fiscal year ending September 30. Partner Edge uses the calendar year. For the year ending September 30, 1992, the partnership has taxable income of $30,000. Edge includes his distributive share of this $30,000 in his individual return for the year 1992, his tax year within which the partnership's year ends.

To keep you from using the disparity between your partnership's and your tax years to defer the payment of tax, current law restricts your partnership's right to choose a fiscal year different from your tax year.

(a) Partnership's Tax Year. Your partnership is required to use the same tax year as its majority interest partners, unless it establishes to the IRS's satisfaction a good business reason for having a different tax year ((d) below) [IRC Sec. 706(b)]. If the majority owners don't have the same tax year, your partnership must adopt the same tax year as its principal partners. If the principal partners don't have the same tax year, and no majority of partners have the same tax year, your partnership must adopt the tax year that results in the least aggregate deferral of income to the partners [Reg. Sec. 1.706-1T].

A principal partner is one who has an interest of 5% or more in the partnership profits and capital. The majority owners consist of one or more of the partners having an aggregate interest in partnership profits and capital of greater than 50%.

Example 2: Revere, Inc., a fiscal year corporation, owns a 10% interest in the PSW Partnership's profits and capital. The other partners are calendar-year individuals each owning less than a 5% partnership interest. PSW must adopt a calendar tax year, since that is the tax year of the majority of the PSW partners.

(b) Partner's Tax Year. You cannot change your tax year unless you can show a good business reason for the change [Reg. Sec. 1.442-1(b)(2); 1.706-1(b)(2)].

(c) Electing Tax Year Other Than Required Tax Year. As explained earlier, your partnership must conform its tax year to that of its owners (in most cases, a calendar year). However, certain partnerships may elect to use a tax year that is different from "the required tax year" [IRC Sec. 444(a)]. Generally, your partnership can elect a different tax year only if that tax year results in a "deferral period" not longer than three months [IRC Sec. 444(b)(1)]. The deferral period is the number of months between the start of the fiscal year and the last day of the required tax year (usually December 31) [IRC Sec. 444(b)(4)]. The election to change its tax year is available to your partnership only if the deferral period of the tax year elected isn't longer than the shorter of (1) three months or

(2) the deferral period of the tax year being changed. The election is made at the partnership level, not by you and the other partners [Temp. Reg. Sec. 1.444-1T].

In 1987, existing partnerships were also permitted to elect the tax year that was used in 1986 [IRC Sec. 444(b)(3)].

An election to use a tax year other than the required tax year is made by filing Form 8716. Your partnership must file the form by the earlier of the (1) 15th day of the fifth month following the month that includes the first day of the tax year for which the election is made or (2) the unextended due date of the income tax return resulting from making the election [Temp. Reg. Sec. 1.444-3T(b)].

If your partnership makes such an election, it must make a "required payment" for each year the election is in effect. The required payment represents the value of the tax deferral you and the other owners receive through the use of the elected tax year. Your partnership must report the required payments on Form 8752, Required Payment or Refund Under Section 7519. Form 8752 must be filed and the required payment made by May 15 of the calendar year following the calendar year in which the election year begins [IRC Sec. 7519(b); Temp. Reg. Sec. 1.7519-21T(a)(4)(ii)].

The election remains in effect until it is terminated. Your ongoing partnership can terminate its election voluntarily by changing to the required tax year. The election will be terminated by the IRS if your partnership fails to comply with the required payments. If the election is terminated, your partnership cannot make another Sec. 444 election for any tax year.

(d) Application to Adopt or Change a Tax Year. If your newly formed partnership is required to secure prior approval from the Commissioner for the adoption of a tax year, the partnership must file an application on Form 1128 on or before the last day of the month following the close of the tax year to be adopted. To change a tax year, your partnership must file Form 1128 with the IRS by the 15th day of the second month after the end of the short period for which a return is required because of the change [Reg. Sec. 1.442-1(b)(1); 1.706-1(b)].

¶3415   WHEN A PARTNERSHIP'S TAX YEAR CLOSES

[New tax legislation may affect this subject; see ¶1.]

Your partnership's tax year normally continues after the death, withdrawal, substitution or addition of a partner or a shift of interest among existing partners [IRC Sec. 706(c)(1)]. When a partner sells, exchanges, or liquidates his or her entire interest in a partnership, your partnership's tax year closes (i.e., ends) for that partner. The partnership year always closes for all partners on termination of your partnership.

(a) Change of Partners. When a partner dies during the year, your partnership's tax year continues until the normal end of its year or until the decedent's entire interest is sold, exchanged or liquidated by the decedent's successor, if that occurs earlier. The decedent's final return includes his or her share of partnership income for your partnership's tax year ending on or before his or her death. His or her share of income not reported on his or her final return must be reported by his or her estate or other successor in interest.

> **Example 1:** Ms. Allister, Mr. Biller, Mr. Calvin, and Mr. Douglas own equal shares in the ABCD partnership. For the fiscal year ending October 31, 1992, the partnership has a taxable income of $124,000. Allister, who reports on the calendar-year basis, dies November 15, 1992. The last return for Allister must report $31,000 (¼ of $124,000), her share of the partnership earnings for the year ending with or before her death.

Example 2: Assume the same partnership as in Example 1, but Allister dies on September 15, 1992. Her return for the shortened period ending with her death does not include her share of the $124,000. This amount is reported on her estate's return.

Your partnership's tax year does not close for a partner who makes a gift of his or her partnership interest. Income attributable to the interest up to the date of the gift is allocated to the donor.

Your partnership's tax year closes for a partner who sells, exchanges or liquidates his or her entire interest, but not for a partner who sells, exchanges or liquidates less than his or her entire interest [IRC Sec. 706(c)].

Example 3: Again assume the same partnership as in Example 1, but with Allister living. On November 30, 1992, Allister sells her entire interest. The partnership's tax year ends on November 30, 1992, as to Allister. On her return for 1992 (due April 15, 1993), Allister must include her share of partnership income for the partnership year ending October 31, 1992, and her share of partnership income for the short year, November 1, 1992, to November 30, 1992. Biller, Calvin, and Douglas are not affected by the sale and the partnership tax year does not close early for them.

(b) When a Partnership Ends. If your partnership "terminates," its tax year closes for all partners. Your partnership terminates only if (1) its operations cease or (2) 50% or more of the total interest in both capital and profits is *sold* or *exchanged within a 12-month period.* There may be a "winding up period" after the partners agree to dissolve the firm [IRC Sec. 708(b)(1); Reg. Sec. 1.708-1(b)].

Example 4: EFGH partnership is owned 30% by Mr. Earl, 20% by Mr. Frank, 25% by Ms. Gail and 25% by Mr. Harriman. On March 31, 1992, Earl sells his interest. Frank sells his interest on September 15, 1992. Since there is a transfer of 50% interest within a 12-month period, the partnership is ended; its tax year closes as of September 15, 1992, for all the partners.

The gift, bequest, inheritance, or liquidation of a partnership interest is not a sale or exchange for termination purposes [Reg. Sec. 1.708-1(b)]. Thus, 50% or more of the partnership's assets may be distributed in liquidation of a partner's interest without terminating your partnership. But a contribution of property to your partnership, followed shortly by a distribution, may constitute a sale or exchange [Reg. Sec. 1.731-1(c)(3)].

➤ **OBSERVATION** The partnership business is not considered to end on the death of one member of a two-man partnership, if the deceased partner's estate or successor continues to share in the profits and losses of the partnership [Reg. Sec. 1.708-1(b)].

Termination by the sale or exchange of an interest is deemed to involve a distribution of assets to the partners. The assets are then deemed contributed to a new partnership that may either continue business or wind it up [Reg. Sec. 1.708-1(b)(1)(iv)].

(c) When Partnerships Combine. On a merger or consolidation of partnerships, the tax year of the new partnership is considered a continuation of the tax year of the merging partnership whose members own an interest of more than 50% in the capital and profits of the new partnership. The tax years of partnerships whose members own 50% or less interest in the new partnership are closed. If none of the members of the merging partnerships has an interest of more than 50% in the resulting partnership, the partnership starts with a new tax year [IRC Sec. 708(b)(2); Reg. Sec. 1.708-1(b)(2)(i)].

Example 5: Partnerships AB and CD merge and form partnership ABCD. Partners A and B each own 30% and partners C and D each own 20% interest in the new partnership. Since partners A and B together own an interest of more than 50% in the new partnership, partnership ABCD is considered a continuation of Partnership AB and takes its tax year. Partnership CD's tax year is closed on the merger.

(d) When a Partnership Divides. If the division is into two or more partnerships, any new partnership whose members owned more than a 50% interest in the capital and profits of the first partnership is considered a continuation of the first partnership and will use the same tax year. All other new partnerships whose members owned an interest of 50% or less in the first partnership start with a new tax year. If, however, the members of none of the new partnerships owned a more-than-50% interest in the first partnership, the tax year of the first partnership is closed [IRC Sec. 708(b)(2)(B); Reg. Sec. 1.708-1(b)(2)(ii)].

> **Example 6:** Mr. Marks owns 40%, and Mr. Neale, Mr. Oliver and Mr. Paulsen each own 20% interest in the capital and profits of partnership MNOP. When partnership MNOP is split into partnership MN and partnership OP, the tax year of partnership MN is considered a continuation of partnership MNOP using the same tax year since Marks and Neale together own more than 50% interest in partnership MNOP. Partnership OP is considered a new partnership and starts with a new tax year.

(e) Applying Economic Accrual Principles to Cash Basis Items.

If your interest in your partnership changes during the year, your share of interest, taxes, payments for services or use of property, and other items that are accounted for under the cash method must be apportioned over each day in the period during the year in which they relate. The items are then allocated daily among the partners in proportion to their partnership interests at the end of each day to which they are assigned. For purposes of applying these rules, part of an item that relates to earlier years is assigned entirely to the first day of the tax year and any part that relates to later years is assigned entirely to the last day of the year. Required allocations to ex-partners must be capitalized [IRC Sec. 706(d)].

(f) Tiered Partnerships.

Your partnership is a member of a tiered structure if it owns an interest in or is wholly or partly owned by an S corporation, a personal service corporation, a trust or another partnership [Temp. Reg. Sec. 1.444-2T]. If there is a change in the interests of any partner in an "upper-tier partnership," his, her or its distributive share of daily items of income and expense attributable to a lower-tier partnership must be determined under an appropriate portion test [IRC Sec. 706(d)]. The formula will be based on the number of days any upper-tier partner owned lower-tier *and* upper-tier partners' respective partnership interests.

TRANSACTIONS BETWEEN PARTNERSHIP AND PARTNER OR PERSON RELATED TO PARTNER

¶3416   PARTNER NOT ACTING AS A PARTNER

If you engage in a transaction with the partnership other than in the capacity of a partner, you are not treated as a member of the partnership for that transaction [IRC Sec. 707(a); Reg. Sec. 1.707-1(a)(1)].

> **Example 1:** Ms. Perkins, an equal member of the OPQ partnership, has a basis of $1,000 for a particular asset. If she sells it to the partnership for $1,500, its fair market value, she will report a gain of $500.

> **Example 2:** Assume now that Perkins in Example 1 pays $2,000 for partnership property that has a basis to it of $1,100. The partnership reports a gain of $900. Since the partners share equally, $300 of this gain (⅓ of $900) must be reported by Perkins on her individual return as part of her distributive share of partnership gain.

This general rule is subject to numerous exceptions, as explained below.

(a) When Loss Is Disallowed. No deduction is allowed for losses from the sale or exchange of property (except an interest in the partnership) between (1) your partnership and a partner who owns more than a 50% interest in its capital or profits or (2) your partnership and another partnership, when the same persons own more than a 50% interest in the capital or profits of each. However, any gain realized on a later sale or exchange of the property by the purchaser is taxable only to the extent it exceeds that part of the disallowed loss allocable to the property sold [IRC Sec. 267(d); 707(b)(1); Reg. Sec. 1.707-1(b)(1)].

> **Example 3:** The AFG partnership in which partner Mr. Frank owns a 60% interest in capital and profits transfers property at a loss of $500 to the DFH partnership, in which Frank owns a 55% interest in capital and profits. The AFG partnership is not allowed a deduction for the loss.
>
> **Example 4:** The DFH partnership in Example 3 sells the property it got from the AFG partnership at a gain of $600. Only $100 ($600 less $500) of the gain is taxable.
>
> **Example 5:** The DFH partnership in Example 3 sells only 1/2 the property received from the AFG partnership at a gain of $400. Only $150 ($400 less $250) of the gain is taxable.

(b) When Gain Is Ordinary Income. When property is the subject of a sale or exchange between (1) a partnership and a partner who owns over 50% of the capital or profits interest in the partnership or (2) two partnerships in which the same persons own more than 50% of the capital or profits interest, gain on the transaction is treated as ordinary income if the property is not a capital asset [¶1801] in the hands of the person *receiving it* [IRC Sec. 707(b)(2); Reg. Sec. 1.707-1(b)(2)].

Property that is not a capital asset includes trade accounts receivable, inventory, stock-in-trade, and depreciable or real property used in a trade or business.

> **Example 6:** Ms. Corby, who owns a 52% interest in the capital and profits of the CDE partnership, which sells paintings, transfers a painting from her personal collection to the partnership at a gain of $100. This amount is ordinary income to Corby.

(c) Determining Ownership of an Interest. In determining the extent of the ownership of a capital or profits interest when there is a sale or exchange between a partner and partnership, the following constructive ownership rules apply:

1. An interest directly or indirectly owned by or for a corporation, partnership, estate or trust is considered to be owned proportionately by or for its shareholders, partners, or beneficiaries.

2. You (or any individual) are considered to own the interest that is directly or indirectly owned by or for your family (including only brothers, sisters, half brothers, half sisters, spouse, ancestors, and lineal descendants).

3. If you are attributed with an interest under rule 1, you are treated as actually owning the interest for purposes of reapplying rule 1 or applying rule 2. But if you are attributed with an interest under rule 2, you are not considered to actually own the interest for purposes of attributing an interest to another person.

These rules parallel the rules for determining constructive ownership of stock [¶2323(d)]. However, there is not attribution between partners [IRC Sec. 707(b)(3); Reg. Sec. 1.707-1(b)(3)].

> **Example 7:** If Ms. Frank, who owns only a 30% interest in the DFH partnership, transfers property to the partnership at a $500 loss, the loss will be allowed. If, however, Mr. Howard, who also owns a 30% interest, were Frank's brother, the loss would not be allowed. Frank would be treated as owning more than 50% of the capital and profits of DFH, 30% directly and 30% by attribution from Howard.

(d) Salaries and Interest Paid to Partner. To the extent that payments to you for services or for the use of capital are determined without regard to partnership income, they are treated by your partnership in the same manner as payments made to a nonpartner [IRC Sec. 707(c)].

You include such "guaranteed payments" as ordinary income on your personal income tax return, and your partnership usually can deduct them as business expenses in computing its taxable income or loss.

> **Example 8:** The BY partnership agreement provides that Mr. Bilsky, an equal partner, is to receive an annual salary of $20,000 as office manager, without regard to partnership income. After deducting the guaranteed payment, the partnership had ordinary income of $60,000. Bilsky must include $50,000 in his personal income return for that year ($20,000 guaranteed payment and $30,000 for his distributive share of partnership income). The partnership deducts the $20,000 payment as a business expense.

Guaranteed payments are not subject to withholding and are not taken into account for purposes of an employee's deferred compensation plan [Reg. Sec. 1.707-1(c)].

To find out whether a guaranteed payment is deductible, your partnership must meet the business expense deduction tests [¶2201] and take into account the capital expenditure rules (¶2203) [IRC Sec. 707(c)]. Thus, guaranteed payments to you for organizing your partnership or syndicating interests in the partnership are capital expenditures and not deductible [¶3404(c)].

Your partnership may set up a self-employed retirement plan [¶1350], but it gets no deduction for contributions for its partners [¶3408]. When the employer of a medical partnership contributed directly to its retirement plan, the Supreme Court held that each doctor-partner had to report as income his share of the contribution. Partners may, however, claim deductions on their own returns for contributions to a self-employed retirement plan.[1]

If your partnership agreement provides that a partner who is to receive a percentage of partnership income will be paid a guaranteed minimum, the amount by which the payment exceeds his or her distributive share of partnership income constitutes a guaranteed payment.

> **Example 9:** Under the HD partnership agreement, Ms. Doolittle is to receive 50% of the partnership income each year, but in no event will the payment be less than $10,000. In 1992, the partnership had taxable income of $18,000. The amount of the guaranteed payment which may be deducted by the partnership is $1,000 ($10,000 minus $9,000 distributive share).

Fringe benefits: Your partnership has a choice when it comes to reporting the health insurance premium costs or other fringe benefits for partners.[2] The partnership can treat the cost of the benefits as guaranteed payments for the partners' services. Result: The payments are deducted by the partnership before figuring the partners' shares of partnership income or loss. Or the partnership can treat the cost of the benefits as a reduction in distributions to the partners. Result: The benefits are not deductible by the partnership and do not affect the partners' shares of income and loss.

(e) Disguised Payments for Property or Services. Your partnership must capitalize the cost of certain goods and services, such as syndication fees, purchased from its partners [¶3418]. Some partnerships have attempted to avoid the capitalization rules by making allocations of income and corresponding distributions instead of direct payments to the partners. A payment that's characterized as part of the partner's distributive share of partnership income has the same effect as a partnership deduction because it reduces the income shares of the other partners.

To prevent such abuses, when you perform services for or transfer property to your partnership and then receive a related allocation or distribution, the transaction is treated as a payment to a non partner [IRC Sec. 707(a)(2)(A)].

(f) Disguised Sales or Exchanges. You are generally not taxed when you contribute property or services to your partnership [¶3418] or when you receive distributions from the partnership [¶3420]. So some partners have attempted to use partnerships as a vehicle for disposing of appreciated property with no tax. For example, some partners have disguised taxable sales as tax-free contributions to the partnership followed by tax-free cash distributions. To prevent such abuses, when a contribution followed by a distribution looks like a sale or exchange, it is treated as such and you recognize gain or loss [IRC Sec. 707(a)(2)(B)].

Your contribution of property to your partnership is presumed to be a taxable sale rather than a tax-free contribution if you receive a payment that would not have been made but for the contribution. (If the contribution and payment are not made simultaneously, the contribution is not treated as a sale if the payment is contingent on the success of the partnership.) Generally, a transaction is presumed to be a sale if payment is made within two years of the contribution. Beyond that period, the transfer is considered a bona fide contribution. Effective date: The proposed rules apply to transfers occurring after April 24, 1991 [Prop. Reg. Sec. 1.707-3-6, -9].

There are four kinds of payments that will not cause the disguised sale rules to apply: (1) reasonable guaranteed payments for capital; (2) reasonable preferred returns; (3) operating cash flow distributions; and (4) pre-formation expenditures [Prop. Reg. Sec. 1.707-3, -4].

Similarly, if your partnership sells the contributed property to a third party, the pre-contribution gain or loss is allocated to you (the contributing partner) [IRC Sec. 704(c)(1)(A)].

In addition, if property you contributed to your partnership is distributed to another partner within five years of the original contribution, you recognize any pre-contribution gain or loss. This applies to property contributed after October 3, 1989. However, this rule doesn't apply to certain partnership transactions that have the effect of a like-kind exchange—for example, where the partnership distributes the contributed property to another partner and also distributes equivalent like-kind property to the contributing partner [IRC Sec. 704(c)(1)(B)].

¶3417   TRANSACTIONS BETWEEN PARTNERSHIP AND RELATED PARTIES

In certain transactions between related parties, losses are not allowed on sales or exchanges and expenses are deductible only when includable in the recipient's income [IRC Sec. 267(e)(2)]. For purposes of applying this rule, your partnership and you are treated as related parties if you own, directly or indirectly, a capital or profits interest in the partnership or if you own, directly or indirectly, more than 5% of the shares of a C corporation that owns interests in the partnership.

The loss disallowance and expense deduction deferral rules also apply to transactions between two partnerships that have similar ownership. The rules apply to two partnerships if: (1) any of the partners in one partnership is related to any of the partners in the other or (2) the partnerships have one or more of the same partners [Temp. Reg. Sec. 1.267(a)-2T(c)]. The deduction deferred is based on the proportionate amount held in each partnership.

CONTRIBUTIONS TO PARTNERSHIP

¶3418   TAX EFFECT OF CONTRIBUTION

When your partnership is formed, each partner contributes money, other property, or services in return for his or her interest. A new partner may also acquire an interest by making a contribution after the partnership is formed and operating. In addition, a partner may acquire an interest in the partnership other than by making a contribution to the partnership—for example, by gift or inheritance.

(a) Nonrecognition of Gain or Loss. Generally, you recognize no gain or loss on a contribution of money, installment obligations or other property to your partnership (other than a mutual fund partnership) in return for your partnership interest. This rule applies whether your partnership was just formed or is already formed and operating [IRC Sec. 721; Reg. Sec. 1.721-1(a)].

(b) Interest Transferred as Payment for Services. If you receive a capital interest in the partnership as compensation for past or future services rendered or to be rendered to the partnership, the value of the interest is a "guaranteed payment" and is treated as ordinary income. The amount of the income you realize is the fair market value of the interest transferred as compensation. The date of valuation depends on whether the transfer was made for past services or for future services. If for past services, the valuation is made when the interest was transferred; if for future services, the valuation is made as of the time the services are rendered [Reg. Sec. 1.721-1(b)(1), (2)].

➤ **OBSERVATION** A disguised sale or exchange or payment for property transferred to the partnership for services rendered may be treated as a "sale or exchange," thus giving rise to taxable income [¶3416(e), (f)].

(c) Contributions of Unrealized Receivables, Inventory Items or Capital Loss Property. The character of your partnership's gain or loss on its disposition of unrealized receivables, inventory, or capital loss property contributed after March 31, 1984, is under some circumstances the same as if you (the contributing partner) had disposed of them [IRC Sec. 724].

Unrealized receivables. Your partnership's gain or loss on contributed unrealized receivables is always ordinary.

Inventory. Your partnership also has ordinary gain or loss on a taxable disposition of contributed inventory items within five years of the contribution. If the disposition occurs more than five years after the contribution, the character of the gain or loss is determined at the partnership level.

Capital loss property. For property that was a capital asset in your hands, any loss on a disposition by your partnership within five years after the contribution is a capital loss to the extent that the property's adjusted basis to you exceeded the property's fair market value immediately before you made the contribution.

Basis tainting rules. If your partnership transfers the contributed property to a transferee who takes a substituted basis (e.g., a nonrecognition transfer), the characterization rules mentioned above apply to the contributed property now in the transferee's hands [IRC Sec. 724(d)]. Moreover, any property (except C corporation stock received in a tax-free incorporation) received by the partnership in which it takes a substituted basis also gets that treatment. Similar rules apply to a series of nonrecognition transfers.

(d) Mutual Fund Partnerships. Gain is recognized when property is contributed in exchange for a partnership interest to a partnership that would be treated as an investment company if it were incorporated. However, losses are not recognized [IRC Sec. 721(b)].

Your partnership is treated as an investment company if over 80% of the value of its assets, other than cash and nonconvertible securities, is held for investment and consists of readily marketable stocks, securities, or interests in mutual funds or real estate investment trusts [IRC Sec. 351].

> NOTE: This rule applies to both limited and general partnerships, regardless of whether they are publicly traded or privately formed.

PARTNER'S BASIS FOR PARTNERSHIP INTEREST

¶3419 PARTNER'S ORIGINAL BASIS AND HOW TO ADJUST IT

When you contribute money or property to a partnership in exchange for a partnership interest, your tax basis in the partnership interest is the amount of money you contributed plus the adjusted basis of the property you transferred to the partnership [IRC Sec. 722; Reg. Sec. 1.722-1].

> **Example 1:** Mr. Sampson and Mr. Frith form a partnership. Sampson contributes $1,000 in cash and Frith contributes property worth $1,000 with an adjusted basis of $600. The basis of the property to the partnership is $600. This is also Frith's basis for his partnership interest. Sampson's basis for his partnership interest is $1,000, the amount of money he contributed.

If the property you contribute to the partnership is subject to an indebtedness or if the partnership assumes your liabilities, your basis in your partnership interest is decreased by the amount of the liabilities assumed by the other partners. The assumption of liabilities is treated as a distribution to you and as a cash contribution by the other partners [Reg. Sec. 1.722-1].

If, on the other hand, you assume a liability of the partnership, your assumption is treated as a contribution of money to the partnership that increases your basis.

If a contribution to a partnership results in taxable income to you, that income is included in your basis. For example, taxable income received because of a contribution of services in exchange for a partnership interest is included in your basis [Reg. Sec. 1.722-1]. Similarly, taxable income recognized on the contribution of property to a mutual fund partnership is included in your basis [IRC Sec. 722].

Your original basis must be adjusted from time to time to prevent unintended benefits or detriments.

> ➤ **OBSERVATION** Suppose that the value of your interest increased because the partnership retained its current income. You are taxed on your share of this income even though the partnership retains it. If your basis for your interest remained the same, a later sale of the interest would result in a second tax to the extent of any gain due to the increased value. Therefore, your basis should be increased to the extent of your taxable amount.

Even if you cannot deduct all or part of your distributive shares of partnership expenses, your basis in the partnership must be reduced by the full amount of your distributive shares.

The adjusted basis for a partnership interest is found under the general rule [(a) below] or under an alternative rule [(b) below].

(a) General Adjustment Rule. Adjustments to your original basis may increase or decrease your basis in a partnership interest.

Basis increased. Your original basis is increased by any further contributions you make to the partnership and by your distributive share of:

- Partnership taxable income, capital gains and other income items separately allocated to the partners [¶3408].
- Partnership tax-exempt income.
- The excess of the depletion deduction over the basis of the depletable property [IRC Sec. 705(a)(1); Reg. Sec. 1.705-1(a)(2)].

Example 2: Ms. Paulson's share of taxable income of the PB partnership is $2,000. She also is entitled to a $100 share of tax-exempt interest received by the partnership. The basis of Paulson's partnership interest must be increased by $2,100.

An increase in your share of partnership liabilities, in any of the ways mentioned in (c) below, is considered a contribution of money by you to the partnership and increases your basis in the partnership.

Basis reduced. Your original basis is reduced (but not below zero) by cash distributions, the basis of other property distributed to the partners and by your distributive share of:

- Partnership losses (including capital losses).
- Nondeductible partnership noncapital expenditures.
- Depletion deduction for oil and gas wells (¶2237) [IRC Sec. 705(a); 733; Reg. Sec. 1.705-1(a)(3); 1.733-1].

Example 3: At the end of the year, the AB partnership distributes $2,100 to partner Paulson in Example 2. Paulson must decrease the basis of her partnership interest by that amount. Thus, the transactions in Examples 2 and 3 cancel each other out. This leaves Paulson with her basis unchanged.

A decrease in your share of partnership liabilities, in any of the ways mentioned in (c) below, is considered a distribution of money to you.

(b) Alternative Rule. In certain cases, you may take as your adjusted basis in your interest an amount equal to your share of the partnership's adjusted basis for the property it would distribute if the partnership were terminated. You may use this method only when adjustment under the general rule is not practicable or when the IRS concludes that the result will not vary substantially from the result under the general rule. If this method is used, certain adjustments are required in figuring the partnership interest's adjusted basis. For example, adjustments might be required to reflect any significant differences due to contributions or distributions of property or transfers of partnership interests [IRC Sec. 705(b); Reg. Sec. 1.705-1(b)].

Example 4: The ABC partnership, in which Mr. Crane, Mr. Stevens and Mr. Pound are equal partners, owns various properties with a total adjusted basis of $1,500 and has earned and retained an additional $1,500. The total adjusted basis of partnership property is thus $3,000. Each partner's share in the adjusted basis of partnership property is one-third of this amount, or $1,000. Under the alternative rule, this amount represents each partner's adjusted basis for his partnership interest.

Example 5: Assume that partner Crane in Example 4 sells his partnership interest to Mr. Dickinson for $1,250 when the partnership property (with an adjusted basis of $1,500) had appreciated in value to $3,000 and when the partnership also had $750 in cash. The total adjusted basis of all partnership property is $2,250 and the value of the property is $3,750. Dickinson's basis for his partnership interest is his cost, $1,250. However, his one-third share of the adjusted basis of partnership property is only $750. Therefore, for purposes of the alternative rule, Dickinson has an adjustment of $500 in determining the basis of his interest. This amount represents the difference between the cost of his partnership interest and his share of partnership basis at the time of his purchase. If the partnership later earns and retains an additional $1,500, its property will have an adjusted basis of $3,750. Dickinson's adjusted basis for his interest under the alternative rule is $1,750, determined by adding $500, his basis adjustment, to $1,250 (his ⅓ share of the $3,750 adjusted basis of partnership property). If the partnership distributes $250 to each partner in a current distribution, Dickinson's adjusted basis for his interest will be $1,500 ($1,000, his ⅓ share of the remaining basis of partnership property ($3,000) plus his $500 basis adjustment). Dickinson's adjusted basis for his partnership interest, after the $500 adjustment, may be shown as follows:

	Dickinson bought interest for $1,250	ABC later earns and retains additional $1,500	ABC then distributes $250 to each partner
1. Total adjusted basis of all ABC's property	$2,250 ($1,500 + $750)	$3,750 ($2,250 + $1,500)	$3,000 ($3,750 – $750)
2. Dickinson's share of adjusted basis of ABC property (⅓ of 1)	$ 750	$1,250	$1,000
3. Plus basis adjustment	$ 500	$ 500	$ 500
4. Dickinson's adjusted basis for his interest (2 + 3)	$1,250	$1,750	$1,500

(c) Effect of Liabilities. If your share of the partnership liability increases, either because the partnership liabilities went up or because you assume some or all the partnership's liabilities, the increase is considered a contribution of money by you to the partnership. Accordingly, the contribution increases your basis in your partnership interest [IRC Sec. 752; Reg. Sec. 1.752-1(b)].

Conversely, if your share of the partnership liability decreases, either because the partnership liabilities went down or because the partnership assumed some or all of your individual liabilities, the decrease is considered a distribution of money to you by the partnership. Accordingly, the distribution decreases the basis of your interest in the partnership (and may result in gain) [¶3420].

Example 6: Mr. Vale and Mr. Brown are equal partners in the VB Partnership. This year, VB borrowed $100,000. The basis of the partnership interest of Vale and Brown is increased by $50,000 for each. *Reason:* Each is considered to have contributed that amount to the partnership.

Example 7: Assume the same facts as in Example 6 except that VB repays a $10,000 note. The basis of the partnership interest of Vale and Brown is decreased by $5,000 each. *Reason:* Each is considered to have received a distribution of that amount from the partnership.

A partner's share of partnership liabilities depends on whether the liability is a recourse or nonrecourse liability.

A liability is a recourse liability to the extent that any partner has an economic risk of loss for the liability. Your share of a recourse liability is equal to your share of the economic risk of loss. Generally, you bear the economic risk of loss for a partnership liability to the extent that you would be obligated to pay the liability in the event of a "constructive liquidation" in which all of the partnership's assets became worthless and were disposed of for no consideration [Reg. Sec. 1.752-2]. Equal partners in a general partnership generally share the economic risk of loss equally.

A liability is a nonrecourse liability if no partner has an economic risk of loss for the liability. You generally share nonrecourse liabilities according to your interest in partnership profits [Reg. Sec. 1.752-1(a)(2)].

Example 8: Mr. Joel and Mr. Frederick each contribute $20,000 to their newly formed partnership. The partnership agreement calls for them to share profits and losses equally. The partnership borrows $50,000 to buy some business equipment. Neither partner is required to pay off the loan if the partnership defaults. Each partner has a basis of $45,000 in the partnership. The liability is nonrecourse and each partner's basis includes an equal share of the liability ($25,000). By contrast, if Joel had to pay the loan if the partnership defaulted, Joel's basis would be $70,000, while Frederick's basis would be $20,000. Because Joel would bear the economic risk of loss for the full amount, the entire liability would be allocated to him.

Your share of a recourse partnership liability equals the portion of that liability for which you (or a related person) bear the economic risk of loss. The extent of your economic risk of loss can be affected by a number of factors, such as: (1) your obligation to make a payment for the partnership liability; (2) your making a nonrecourse loan to the partnership (except when you hold a 10% or less partnership interest); and (3) the extent to which your own property is pledged as security for the partnership liability [Reg. Sec. 1.752-2].

▶ **FINAL REGS ISSUED** The final regulations issued by the IRS are effective for liabilities assumed by the partnership on or after December 28, 1991 (except for liabilities incurred or assumed by contract before that date). However, the partnership can elect to apply the new rules as of the partnership's first tax year ending on or after December 28, 1991 [Reg. Sec. 1.752-5].

DISTRIBUTIONS TO PARTNERS

¶3420   RECOGNITION OF GAIN OR LOSS

If your partnership distributes money or property to you, no gain or loss is recognized to the partnership [IRC Sec. 731(b)].

Gain or loss is recognized by you as follows:

1. If you receive money, gain is recognized to the extent that the money exceeds the basis of the partnership interest. The gain is usually capital gain. No loss is recognized unless the money is in payment of a liquidation of your entire interest in the partnership [IRC Sec. 731(a)].

Example: Mr. Brady has $10,000 as the basis of his partnership interest. He receives a distribution of $8,000 in cash and property with a value of $3,000. No gain is recognized. If Brady received a distribution of $11,000 in cash, a capital gain of $1,000 would be recognized.

2. If the distribution consists of property other than money and it is not in liquidation of your entire interest in the partnership, no gain or loss is recognized until you sell or dispose of the property [IRC Sec. 731]. But if the property is unrealized receivables or substantially appreciated inventory items and is received in exchange for other property, ordinary income or loss may result from the distribution [¶3425].

For special rules applying to payments to retiring or deceased partners, see ¶3429.

¶3421   BASIS AND HOLDING PERIOD OF PROPERTY DISTRIBUTED

[New tax legislation may affect this subject; see ¶1.]

If a distribution does not represent a complete liquidation of your interest in the partnership, you take the partnership's basis for the distributed properties. This "carryover" basis may not exceed the basis of your partnership interest less any money received [IRC Sec. 732(a)]. If this limitation applies, the reduced basis is allocated among the distributed properties. The distribution reduces the basis for the partnership interest (but not below zero) [IRC Sec. 733].

Example 1: Ms. Armstrong, whose basis for her partnership interest is $2,500, receives a distribution of partnership property. If the partnership's basis for the property is $1,500, she takes that as her basis. The $1,500 reduces the basis of her partnership interest to $1,000.

Example 2: Armstrong has a basis of $10,000 for her partnership interest. She receives a distribution (not in liquidation of her interest) of $4,000 in cash and properties with a basis to the partnership of $8,000. Armstrong's basis in the distributed properties is limited to $6,000—her $10,000 basis for her partnership interest reduced by the cash distribution of $4,000. (If the partnership had made an election to adjust basis [¶3422], it could add the $2,000 difference to the basis of its retained properties.) Armstrong's basis for her partnership interest becomes zero ($10,000 less the cash of $4,000 and her $6,000 basis for the distributed property).

You may have a special basis adjustment for distributed property [¶3428].

If a distribution is in complete liquidation of your interest in the partnership, your basis for the distributed properties is the same as the adjusted basis for your partnership interest less any money received [IRC Sec. 732(b); Reg. Sec. 1.732-1(b)]. This reduced basis is allocated among the distributed properties. Unallocated basis may give rise to a capital loss.

Example 3: The adjusted basis of Mr. Brown's interest in the partnership is $12,000. When he retires from the partnership, he receives a liquidating distribution of $2,000 cash and $14,000 worth of real estate with an adjusted basis of $6,000 to the partnership. Brown will take $10,000 as his basis for the distributed real estate (his basis for his partnership interest, $12,000, less $2,000 cash received).

Example 4: Mr. Frey has $20,000 as the basis of his interest in the FGH partnership. He retires from the partnership receiving $5,000 in cash and inventory items with a basis to the partnership of $3,000. Frey realizes a capital loss of $12,000. The basis of his interest is first reduced by the $5,000 cash. $3,000 of the remaining $15,000 basis for his interest is allocated to the inventory. The remaining $12,000 is capital loss.

How to allocate basis. Your basis for the distributed properties must be allocated among the distributed properties in this order [IRC Sec. 732(c); Reg. Sec. 1.732-1]:

- First, basis must be allocated to any unrealized receivables and inventory in an amount equal to the partnership's basis for such property, taking into account your special basis adjustment, if any [¶3428]. If the allocable basis is less than the partnership's basis for such property, an allocation in proportion to the partnership's bases for the items is required.
- Any basis remaining after the first allocation is spread among the other properties in proportion to their bases to the partnership.

Example 5: Ms. Harper has a basis of $17,000 for her partnership interest. She receives a distribution from the partnership in liquidation of her interest of $2,000 cash, inventory with a basis to the partnership of $3,000, real estate (capital asset) with a basis of $2,000 and a depreciable asset with a basis of $4,000. The basis to be allocated to the property is $15,000 (the basis of her interest, $17,000, less the cash distributed, $2,000). This amount is first allocated to the inventory in an amount equal to its basis to the partnership. Her basis in the inventory is therefore $3,000. The remaining $12,000 of the basis of her partnership interest is allocated to the capital and depreciable assets in proportion to their bases to the partnership. Since the basis of the capital asset is $2,000 and the basis of the depreciable asset is $4,000, the $12,000 is allocated $4,000 to the capital asset and $8,000 to the depreciable asset.

(a) Holding Period. You add (tack on) the partnership's holding period to your own in figuring your holding period for distributed property. If you contributed the property to the partnership, you may also add to the beginning of the holding period the time you owned the property immediately before you transferred it to the partnership [IRC Sec. 734(b); Reg. Sec. 1.734-1(b)].

(b) Loss for Unallocated Basis. If the basis of the interest to be allocated on a distribution *in liquidation of your entire interest* is greater than the amount allocable to receivables and inventory and no other property was distributed to absorb the excess, the unallocated amount is a capital loss [IRC Sec. 731(a)(2); Reg. Sec. 1.732-1(c)(2)].

> **Example 6:** Mr. Frost's interest in partnership FGH has an adjusted basis to him of $9,000. He receives as a distribution in liquidation cash of $1,000 and inventory items having a basis to the partnership of $6,000. The cash payment reduces Frost's basis to $8,000, which can be allocated only to the extent of $6,000 to the inventory items. The remaining $2,000 basis, not allocable to distributed property, is a capital loss to Frost.

(c) Special Rules apply to certain distributions from a partnership to a partner who acquired his or her interest from another partner [¶3422] and to distributions treated as sales or exchanges [¶3425].

¶3422   DISTRIBUTIONS OF PROPERTY TO TRANSFEREE PARTNERS

Distributed property may have acquired a special basis as to you (a transferee partner). This may happen either because the partnership made an optional adjustment to the basis of its properties when you became a partner or because you elect a special basis adjustment for the distributed property [¶3428].

The special basis adjustment may result in either an increase or a decrease in the partnership property's basis to you.

> **NOTE:** The special basis adjustment affects the basis of partnership property only with respect to you (the transferee partner) and not with respect to other partners [IRC Sec. 743(b)].

When you receive a distribution of any property from a partnership that elected to make a special basis adjustment, your basis for the distributed property is increased or decreased by the amount of the special adjustment [¶3423]. A similar rule applies when you yourself elect the special adjustment (¶3428) [Reg. Sec. 1.734-2(a)].

> **Example 1:** Mr. Williams acquired his interest in the ABD partnership from a previous partner. Since the partnership had made an election to adjust basis [¶3423], Williams acquired a special basis for partnership property X. The adjusted basis to the partnership for this property is $1,000. Williams' special adjustment is an increase of $500. If property X is distributed to Williams, he takes $1,500 as his basis for X ($1,000 partnership basis plus $500 adjustment). If property X had been distributed to Corso, a nontransferee partner, Corso would have acquired only $1,000 as his carryover basis for X. (In such case, Williams' $500 special basis adjustment may shift over to other property. See (b) below.)

(a) Basis Allocated to Distributed Property. When you receive more than one asset, you usually must allocate your basis among the assets. Basis is allocated first to any unrealized receivables or appreciated inventory included in the distribution. Ordinarily, the amount allocated to such property is an amount equal to its basis to the partnership. But a special rule applies to transferees who have a special basis adjustment for receivables or inventory. You get the full benefit of your special adjustment only if you receive your share (or more) of the fair market value of the receivables or inventory. If you get less than your full share, the partnership's adjusted basis for the distributed receivables or inventory is increased or decreased by only a proportionate part of the special adjustment. The proportionate part is determined by the ratio between (1) the value of receivables or inventory distributed to you and (2) your entire share of the total value of all such partnership items [Reg. Sec. 1.732-2(c)].

Example 2: Mr. Lowell acquired ⅓ interest in the LFG partnership from a previous partner. Since the partnership had elected to adjust the basis of partnership property for transfers [¶3423], Lowell has a special basis adjustment of $800 for partnership inventory items and $200 for unrealized receivables. Lowell retires from the partnership when the adjusted basis of his partnership interest is $3,000. He receives in liquidation of his interest $1,000 cash, certain depreciable assets, inventory, and unrealized receivables. The common partnership bases for the inventory he received is $500 and for the unrealized receivables, zero.

➤ **OBSERVATION** Suppose the value of inventory items and unrealized receivables distributed to Lowell is his share or more (33⅓% or more) of the total value of all partnership inventory items and unrealized receivables. Then his adjusted basis will be $1,300 for the inventory items ($500 plus $800 adjustment) and $200 for the unrealized receivables (zero plus $200). His basis for the depreciable property is $500, figured as follows:

Basis of Lowell's partnership interest	$3,000
Less: Cash distributed	1,000
Amt. allocated to basis of all distributed property	$2,000
Less: Amt. allocated to inventory and receivables	1,500
Basis for depreciable property	$ 500

Now suppose the value of the inventory items and unrealized receivables distributed to Lowell consisted of only ⅙ of the total fair market value of such property (i.e., only ½ of Lowell's share); then only ½ of Lowell's special basis adjustment of $800 for partnership inventory items and $200 for unrealized receivables will be taken into account. Thus, the basis of the inventory items in Lowell's hands is $650:

Common partnership basis for inventory items distributed to Lowell	$250
Plus: One-half of Lowell's special basis adjustment for inventory items ($800)	400
Total	$650

The basis of the unrealized receivables in Lowell's hands would be $100 (zero plus $100, ½ of Lowell's special basis adjustment for unrealized receivables).

(b) Reallocating Special Basis Adjustment. If property for which you have a special basis adjustment is distributed to another partner, the other partner cannot take the adjustment into account. However, you do not lose your adjustment. The adjustment is real-located to like-kind property retained by the partnership or applied to the basis of like-kind property distributed to you [Reg. Sec. 1.743-1(b)(2)(ii)].

You may also reallocate the special basis adjustments if you receive a distribution of property (whether or not you have a special adjustment for it) at the same time you give up your interest in other like-kind property for which you have a special adjustment. You reallocate your adjustment to the property you received [Reg. Sec. 1.743-1(b)(2)(ii)].

Like-kind property. Like-kind property means property of the same class (stock in trade, property used in a trade or business, capital assets, and so forth) [Reg. Sec. 1.743-1(b)(2)(ii)].

Example 3: Mr. Berryman is a transferee partner in the XY partnership. The partnership owns property A, a depreciable asset with a common basis to the partnership of $1,000 and a special basis adjustment to Berryman of $200. The partnership also owns property B, another depreciable asset with a common basis of $800 and a special basis adjustment to Berryman of $300. Berryman and Mr. Yudell agree that Berryman will receive a distribution of A and Yudell will receive a distribution of B, with all other property to remain in the partnership. As to Yudell, the basis of property B is $800, the common partnership basis. Property B will, therefore, have a basis of $800 in Yudell's hands. As to Berryman, however, the basis of property A is $1,500, the common partnership basis of $1,000 plus Berryman's special basis adjustment of $200 for property A, plus Berryman's additional special basis adjustment of $300 for property B in which he has relinquished his interest.

(c) Unused Special Basis Adjustment. As a transferee partner, in liquidation of your entire partnership interest you sometimes get property for which you have *no* special basis adjustment. The property is exchanged for your interest in property for which you have a special basis adjustment. If you do not use your entire adjustment in determining your basis for the distributed property under the rules above, the unused amount is used by the partnership to adjust its basis for its retained property [Reg. Sec. 1.734-2(b)(1)].

> **Example 4:** On his father's death, Mr. Jones acquired by inheritance ½ interest in partnership ABC. Partners Ginsberg and Coleridge each have ¼ interest. The assets of the partnership consist of $100,000 in cash and real estate worth $100,000 with a basis to the partnership of $10,000. Since the partnership elected, at the time of transfer, to adjust the basis of its property, Jones has a special basis adjustment of $45,000 for his undivided ½ interest in the real estate. The basis of Jones' partnership interest is $100,000, the basis his father had. Jones retires from the partnership and receives $100,000 in cash in exchange for his entire interest. Since Jones received no part of the real estate, his special basis adjustment of $45,000 will be allocated to the real estate, the remaining partnership property, and will increase its basis to the partnership to $55,000.

¶3423   PARTNERSHIP'S ELECTIVE ADJUSTMENT TO BASIS OF UNDISTRIBUTED PROPERTY FOLLOWING A DISTRIBUTION

When your partnership distributes property to you, the partnership does not ordinarily adjust the basis of its retained property. But the distribution may create basis problems.

> **Example 1:** JLP Partnership has $1,000 in cash and a capital asset with a basis of $500 and a fair market value of $2,000. Each of JLP's three equal partners has a basis of $500 in his partnership interest. One partner withdraws from the partnership, and JLP distributes $1,000 cash in liquidation of his partnership interest. That partner has a $500 gain on the distribution. JLP then sells its capital asset for fair market value. JLP has $1,500 of gain on the sale, which is taxable to the two remaining partners. Result: Although JLP had only $1,500 of unrealized appreciation on its capital asset, its three partners paid tax on $2,000 of gain.

To prevent this kind of problem, your partnership is permitted to elect an optional adjustment to the basis of its undistributed property following a distribution.

> **NOTE:** Basis problems may also crop up when an interest in your partnership is transferred by an outgoing partner to an incoming partner. Your partnership is also permitted to make an optional basis adjustment when there is a transfer of a partnership interest [¶3427].

Making the election. The optional adjustment to basis is made by filing a written statement with the partnership return for the tax year in which the distribution or transfer occurs.

> **NOTE:** Your partnership's election to adjust the basis of retained property applies to all distributions of partnership property and to all transfers of partnership interests. What's more, the election is effective not only for the year the election was made but also for all future years.

Increase in basis. When partnership property is distributed to you or another partner, and your partnership made the special election, your partnership increases its basis for its retained assets by (1) the gain recognized by you [¶3420] or (2) the excess of the partnership's basis for the distributed property immediately before the distribution over your basis for it [IRC Sec. 734(b)(1); Reg. Sec. 1.734-1(b)(1)].

> **Example 2:** Mr. Ander's basis for his ⅓ partnership interest is $10,000. The partnership has assets consisting of $11,000 cash and property with a basis of $19,000 and a value of $22,000. Ander realizes a gain of $1,000 when he receives, in a liquidating distribution, a payment of $11,000 cash. If the partnership elects to adjust the basis of undistributed partnership property, the partnership basis for the property becomes $20,000 ($19,000 plus $1,000).

➤ **OBSERVATION** Because of the appreciation in value of its property, the partnership had a potential gain of $3,000 ($22,000 minus $19,000). After the distribution, the potential gain was really only $2,000, since the partner had realized his share of the appreciation in the form of his $1,000 gain. The upward adjustment of partnership basis reflects this. After the adjustment, the spread between basis and value is only $2,000 ($22,000 minus $20,000).

Example 3: Ms. Boyle's basis for her ⅓ partnership interest is $10,000. The partnership has assets consisting of $4,000 cash and properties X and Y with bases of $11,000 and $15,000 and values of $11,000 and $18,000 respectively. Boyle receives property X in liquidation of her entire interest in the partnership. Her basis for property X is $10,000, the same as her adjusted basis for her partnership interest [¶3421]. The excess of the partnership basis for X over Boyle's basis for X after the distribution is $1,000 ($11,000 less $10,000). If the partnership elects to adjust the basis of undistributed partnership property, the basis of property Y to the partnership becomes $16,000 ($15,000 plus $1,000).

In general, your partnership cannot increase its basis in retained property when it distributes an interest in a second partnership. However, an exception applies where the second partnership has also made the special basis adjustment election [IRC Sec. 734(b)]. This rule prevents tiered partnerships from increasing their bases without a corresponding tax disadvantage.

Decrease in basis. If your electing partnership makes a distribution to you, the partnership decreases its basis for the retained assets by (1) the loss recognized to you [¶3420] or (2) the excess of your basis for the distributed property over the partnership's basis for it [IRC Sec. 734(b)(2); Reg. Sec. 1.734-1(b)(2)].

Example 4: Mr. Engle's basis for his ⅓ partnership interest is $11,000. The partnership has assets consisting of $10,000 cash and property with a basis of $23,000 and a value of $20,000. Engle receives $10,000 in cash in liquidation of his entire interest in the partnership. He sustains a loss of $1,000. If the partnership elects to adjust the basis of its undistributed partnership property, the partnership basis for the property becomes $22,000 ($23,000 less $1,000).

➤ **OBSERVATION** In this situation, your partnership might want to avoid making a basis adjustment since the adjustment decreases the amount of loss that will be recognized on sale of the property. However, once your partnership has elected to make optional basis adjustments, the election can't be changed without IRS approval. And the IRS won't approve an election change if the purpose is primarily to avoid decreasing the basis of partnership assets on a transfer or distribution.

Example 5: Mr. Forest's basis for his ⅓ partnership interest is $11,000. The partnership has assets consisting of $5,000 cash and, properties X and Y with bases of $10,000 and $18,000 and values of $10,000 and $15,000 respectively. In liquidation of his entire interest in the partnership, Forest receives property X with a basis of $10,000 to the partnership but a basis of $11,000 to him. If the partnership elects to adjust the basis of undistributed partnership property, the basis of Y becomes $17,000 ($18,000 less $1,000).

¶3424   DISTRIBUTION OF UNREALIZED RECEIVABLES OR SUBSTANTIALLY APPRECIATED INVENTORY ITEMS

If you receive a distribution of your proportionate share of unrealized receivables or substantially appreciated inventory, you are not currently taxed. When you sell or exchange the receivables or inventory, you generally recognize ordinary income. However, you may have capital gain or loss on the disposition of inventory items if they are held for more than five years. The character of the gain or loss depends on the character of the items when they are disposed of [IRC Sec. 734(a)(2); Reg. Sec. 1.734-1(a)(2)]. Gain or loss on the sale of unrealized receivables contributed by you is treated as ordinary regardless of the disposition date. You cannot tack the partnership's holding period to your own holding period in determining whether inventory was held for more than five years.

NOTE: Similar basis tainting rules that apply to contributed property, as explained in ¶3418(c), also apply to ordinary income property distributed to you [IRC Sec. 734(c)].

Example 1: On March 10, 1992, the partnership distributes to Ms. Bowen her proportionate share of unrealized receivables. The partnership's basis in this property, which Bowen acquired as her basis, was $1,000. If on November 10, 1992, Bowen sells these receivables for $1,500, she realizes $500 ordinary income.

Example 2: On February 10, 1992, the partnership distributed to Mr. Corwin his proportionate share of partnership inventory items. The partnership's basis in this property, which Corwin acquired as his basis, is $3,000. If Corwin sells the inventory items on April 10, 1992, for $4,000, he realizes ordinary income of $1,000.

Example 3: If Corwin, in Example 2 above, disposes of the distributed inventory on April 10, 1997, he will realize capital gain if the property is a capital asset in his hands.

➤ **OBSERVATION** The distribution of unrealized receivables or substantially appreciated inventory may give rise to ordinary income if the distribution is treated as a sale or exchange [¶3425].

(a) Liquidating Distributions Involving Unrealized Receivables or Substantially Appreciated Inventory. Payments made by the partnership to you as a retiring partner for your interest in unrealized receivables or substantially appreciated inventory ("Section 751 property") may constitute ordinary income to you if the distribution is treated as a sale or exchange.

(b) Excluded Transactions. Two transactions are not treated as a sale or exchange for purposes of the above rule [IRC Sec. 751(b)]:

- A distribution of assets that you contributed to the partnership.
- Payments that constitute a distributive share of partnership income or a guaranteed payment.

(c) "Unrealized Receivables." This term means any rights to payment for goods or services which have not yet been taken into income by the partnership under the accounting method used by it.

It also includes the potential ordinary gain in the following types of property: Sec. 1245 or 1250 property or Sec. 1245 recovery property [¶1812]; mining property [¶2242; 2243]; certain oil, gas or geothermal property [¶2237(a)]; stock in certain foreign corporations [¶3828]; and stock in a former DISC or FSC. The term also includes the ordinary income potential from a franchise, trademark or trade name. The gain is measured as if the partnership sold the property at fair market value at distributions [IRC Sec. 751(c)(2)]. Market discount is an unrealized receivable for purposes of gain on the sale of a partnership.

NOTE: For this rule, tiered partnerships are treated as owning a proportionate share of each other's property. So, dropping appreciated inventory and unrealized receivables into a second partnership basket won't divorce the ordinary income assets from the first partnership's interest that's being sold [IRC Sec. 751(f)].

Your Sec. 1245 or 1250 income is specially computed if you have a special basis adjustment (¶3428) [Reg. Sec. 1.751-1(c)(6)].

(d) What Is "Inventory"? The term "inventory" is not limited to stock in trade, goods held for sale, or other items generally considered inventory. The term includes all assets of the partnership except capital assets and Sec. 1231 assets. The term also includes any other partnership property that would qualify under the above rules if held by the selling or distributee partner.

Some examples of inventory items are: accounts receivable or any unrealized receivables acquired for services or stock in trade; copyrights; literary, musical or artistic compositions [IRC Sec. 751(d)(2); Reg. Sec. 1.751-1]; and foreign investment company stock (or stock substituted for it) if gain on its sale would constitute ordinary gain.

(e) What Is Substantial Appreciation? Inventory items are substantially appreciated if their value is more than (1) 120% of their basis to the partnership *and* (2) 10% of the value of all partnership property other than money [IRC Sec. 751(d)(1)].

> ➤ **OBSERVATION** "Substantially appreciated inventory items" refers to the aggregate of all partnership inventory and not to specific items or groups of items. If the whole inventory has substantially appreciated in value, Sec. 751 applies—even if specific items distributed have not appreciated in value [Reg. Sec. 1.761-1(d)(1)].

¶3425   WHEN IS A DISTRIBUTION A SALE OR EXCHANGE?

A distribution is treated as a sale or exchange to the extent you (the distributee partner) receive more than your share of (1) property other than Sec. 751 property in exchange for some or all of your interest in Sec. 751 property or (2) Sec. 751 property in exchange for some or all of your interest in property other than Sec. 751 property [IRC Sec. 751(b); Reg. Sec. 1.751-1(b)].

(a) Was There an Excess Distribution? The rules in this area do not apply to the extent that you receive only your share of Sec. 751 assets or your share of other property.

> ➤ **OBSERVATION** In figuring your share for this purpose, the regulations require that you take into account any interest you still have in the partnership after the distribution. For example, say a partnership has Sec. 751 assets valued at $100,000. You have a 30% interest (worth $30,000), receive a distribution of $20,000 of these assets, and continue to have a 30% interest in the $80,000 of such assets remaining in the partnership after the distribution. Only $6,000 ($30,000 less 30% of $80,000) represents your share of the Sec. 751 assets. The balance ($14,000) is an excess distribution [Reg. Sec. 1.751-1(b)(1)(ii)].

(b) What Property Did the Partner Give Up? You must determine what property you gave up for the excess distribution. The rules in this area do not apply unless you receive a distribution of Sec. 751 assets in exchange for an interest in other property or a distribution of other property in exchange for an interest in Sec. 751 assets.

You may identify the asset for which the excess distribution is made (see Example 3 below). Otherwise, you are presumed to have sold or exchanged a proportionate amount of each asset in which you relinquished an interest [Reg. Sec. 1.751-1(g)].

(c) Tax Consequences of Distribution. The rules for the portion of the distribution treated as a sale or exchange are summarized in Examples 1 and 2 below. The balance of the distribution is subject to the rules for distributions in general. The exchange and distribution elements are treated separately [Reg. Sec. 1.751-1(b)].

Tax consequences when "other property" is distributed in exchange for Sec. 751 assets. You have ordinary gain or loss on the sale or exchange of the Sec. 751 assets you gave up in the exchange. Your gain or loss is the difference between (1) your basis for the Sec. 751 assets treated as sold or exchanged and (2) the fair market value of the other property you received in exchange [Reg. Sec. 1.751-1(b)(3)].

Your basis for the Sec. 751 assets treated as sold or exchanged is the basis the assets would have if the assets had been distributed to you just before the exchange (that is, the actual distribution) [Reg. Sec. 1.751-1(b)(3)].

The partnership has gain or loss on the sale or exchange of the distributed property other than Sec. 751 assets. Its gain or loss is the difference between (1) its basis for the distributed property treated as sold or exchanged and (2) the fair market value of your interest in the Sec. 751 assets you gave up in exchange. The character of the partnership's gain or loss depends on the kind of property it sold or exchanged [Reg. Sec. 1.751-(b)(3)].

Example 1: The balance sheet of the DEF partnership is as follows:

Assets	Basis	Market Value	Capital	Per Books	Market Value
Cash	$ 60,000	$ 60,000	Dayton	$ 35,000	$ 60,000
Unrealized			Edwards	35,000	60,000
receivables	0	60,000	Fitter	35,000	60,000
Land & building	45,000	60,000		$105,000	$180,000
	$105,000	$180,000			

The partnership distributed to Dayton the land and building it had owned for 15 years in complete liquidation of his partnership interest. Dayton is treated as if he sold his share of the unrealized receivables for $20,000. He is taxed on $20,000 of ordinary income, as follows:

Fair market value of the assets (land & building) received in exchange
for Sec. 751 property (unrealized receivables) $20,000
Basis allocable to partner's relinquished interest in Sec. 751 property 0
Difference (treated as ordinary income) $20,000

The following schedule may be set up to analyze the transaction:

	Dayton's interest (market value)	Value of assets received	Dayton's interest (basis)
Sec. 751 property			
Unrealized receivables	$20,000	$ 0	$ 0
Other property			
Cash	20,000	0	20,000
Land & building	20,000	60,000	15,000
	$60,000	$60,000	$35,000

Dayton's interest (at market value) in the unrealized receivables, cash, and land & building amounted to $20,000 each, for a total of $60,000. Instead of receiving his interest in each of these assets in the form of the assets themselves, at $20,000 each (total $60,000), he received his total $60,000 in land & building. Thus, $20,000 of the land & building was in exchange for his $20,000 interest in the land & building to which he was entitled; another $20,000 share of the land & building was in exchange for his $20,000 interest in the cash; the other $20,000 was in exchange for his interest in the unrealized receivables.

Example 2: The three-man wholesale sales partnership, ABC, which keeps its books on the accrual basis, agreed to liquidate the interest of C by a distribution to him. At that time, the firm's balance sheet was as follows:

Assets	Basis	Market Value	Liabilities & Capital	Per Books	Market Value
Cash	$15,000	$ 15,000	Current liabilities	$15,000	$ 15,000
Accounts receivable	9,000	9,000	Mortgage	21,000	21,000
Inventory	21,000	30,000	Capital, A	20,000	25,000
Buildings	42,000	48,000	Capital, B	20,000	25,000
Land	9,000	9,000	Capital, C	20,000	25,000
	$96,000	$111,000		$96,000	$111,000

The partnership distributed to C $10,000 cash and a 20-year-old building worth $15,000 with a basis to the partnership of $15,000. C will rent the land. C is treated as if he sold his share of Sec. 751 assets (with a $10,000 basis) for $13,000. Thus, on the sale, he is taxed on the $3,000 ordinary income. The transaction is analyzed in the following schedule:

	C's interest (market value)		Value of assets received	C's interest (basis)	
Sec. 751 property					
Accounts receivable	$ 3,000		0	$ 3,000	
Inventory	10,000		0	7,000	
Total		$13,000		$10,000	
Other property					
Cash	$ 5,000		$22,000*	$ 5,000	
Buildings	16,000		15,000	14,000	
Land	3,000	24,000	0	3,000	22,000
Total		$37,000	$37,000		$32,000
Value of assets received in exchange for Sec. 751 property				$13,000**	
Basis of relinquished interest in Sec. 751 property				10,000	
Difference (taxed as ordinary income)				$ 3,000	

---

* $10,000 cash plus $12,000 liabilities assumed.

** The $13,000 value of assets received in exchange for Sec. 751 property is arrived at as follows: The market value of C's interest in "other property" was $24,000. But he received $37,000 worth of "other property," which is $13,000 more than his share ($37,000 less $24,000, or $13,000). This additional $13,000 was in exchange for the $13,000 market value of the Sec. 751 property which he relinquished.

Sec. 751 property is figured as follows:

Accounts receivable. Since the partnership is on the accrual basis, the receivables are not unrealized receivables. However, receivables are considered inventory items for the purpose of Sec. 751. As the inventory items are substantially appreciated (as shown below), the receivables are included in Sec. 751 property as part of the substantially appreciated inventory items.

Substantially appreciated inventory items.

	Adjusted basis	Market value
Accounts receivable	$ 9,000	$ 9,000
Inventory	21,000	30,000
Total inventory items	$30,000	$39,000

The fair market value of the inventory items ($39,000) exceeds 120% of the basis ($30,000). (120% of $30,000 is $36,000.)

The $39,000 value also exceeds 10% of the fair market value of all the partnership property other than money (10% of $96,000 is $9,600).

The aggregate of inventory items meets the 120% and 10% tests. Therefore, they are substantially appreciated and are considered Sec. 751 property.

Sec. 751 sale. Since the entire distribution was made in liquidation of C's interest in partnership property, no part of it is considered as a guaranteed payment or a distributive share. In the distribution, C received his share of cash ($5,000) and a $15,000 building ($1,000 less than his $16,000 share). In addition, he received other partnership property ($5,000 cash and $12,000 in liabilities assumed by the remaining partners) in exchange for his interest in accounts receivable ($3,000), inventory ($10,000), land ($3,000), and the balance of his interest in buildings ($1,000). Only the accounts receivable and inventory are Sec. 751 property. Hence, $13,000 of the amount C received is considered as received for Sec. 751 property. Since his basis for Sec. 751 property is $10,000 ($7,000 for inventory and $3,000 for accounts receivable), C realizes $3,000 of ordinary income on the sale of his share of Sec. 751 property.

The part of the distribution not under Sec. 751; C's basis for the building: Before the distribution, C's basis for his partnership interest was $32,000 ($20,000 plus $12,000, his share of partnership liabilities). Taking away the $10,000 allocable to Sec. 751 property items considered to have been sold (see above), he has a basis of $22,000 for the rest of his interest. The total distribution to C was $37,000 ($22,000 in cash and liabilities assumed by the partnership and a $15,000 building). Since C received no more than his share of buildings, none of that property constitutes the proceeds of a sale. He did, however, receive more than his share of money. Hence, the sales proceeds must consist of money and must be deducted from the money distribution. Consequently, in liquidating the balance of his interest, C receives the building and $9,000 in money ($22,000 less $13,000). Therefore, C had no gain or loss on this part of the distribution. His basis for the building is $13,000 (the remaining basis of his partnership interest, $22,000, less $9,000 of money received).

Tax consequences when Sec. 751 assets are distributed in exchange for other property. You have gain or loss on the sale or exchange of the other property you gave up in the exchange. Your gain or loss is the difference between (1) your basis for the other property treated as sold or exchanged and (2) the fair market value of the Sec. 751 assets you received in exchange [Reg. Sec. 1.751-1(b)(2)].

Your basis for the other property treated as sold or exchanged is the basis it would have if distributed to you just before the exchange (that is, the actual distribution) [Reg. Sec. 1.751-1(b)(2)].

The character of your gain or loss depends on the kind of property you gave up [Reg. Sec. 1.751-1(b)(2)].

Your partnership has ordinary gain or loss on the sale or exchange of the distributed Sec. 751 assets. Its gain or loss is the difference between (1) its basis for the Sec. 751 assets treated as sold or exchanged and (2) the fair market value of your interest in the other property given up in exchange [Reg. Sec. 1.751-1(b)(2)].

Example 3: Partner C, who has no special basis adjustment, receives a depreciated machine in liquidation of his ⅓ interest in the ABC partnership. The machine has a recomputed basis [¶1812] of $18,000 and the partnership books show at the time:

	Assets			Liabilities & Capital	
	Adjusted Basis	*Market Value*		*Per books*	*Market Value*
Cash	$ 3,000	$ 3,000	Liabilities	$ 0	$ 0
Machine (Sec.			Capital: A	10,000	15,000
1245 prop.) .	9,000	15,000	B	10,000	15,000
Land	18,000	27,000	C	10,000	15,000
	$30,000	$45,000		$30,000	$45,000

The partnership has Sec. 751 property of $6,000 since the potential Sec. 1245 ordinary income for the machine is $6,000 ($15,000 fair market value less $9,000 adjusted basis). In the distribution, C got his shares of Sec. 751 property (⅓ × $6,000) of $2,000 and Sec. 1231 property with a fair market value of $3,000 [⅓ × ($15,000 – $6,000)] and adjusted basis of $3,000 (⅓ × $9,000). He also received $4,000 of Sec. 1245 ordinary income property ($6,000 potential less $2,000 share above) and Sec. 1231 property with a fair market value and adjusted basis of $6,000 ($9,000 – $3,000 above). C gave up his $1,000 interest in cash and $9,000 interest in land.

Assume that the partners agree the $4,000 of Sec. 751 property (Sec. 1245 potential) in excess of C's share was in exchange for $4,000 of his land interest. C is treated as receiving 4/9 of his interest in land in a current distribution with a basis of $2,667 ($18,000/$27,000 × $4,000) and selling it to the partnership for $4,000 at a $1,333 gain. The basis of his remaining partnership interest is then $7,333 ($10,000 less $2,667 land distribution). Of the $15,000 total distribution to C, $11,000 ($2,000 ordinary income potential plus $9,000 Sec. 1231 property) is not subject to the special rules of Sec. 751 (above), but is treated as a distribution. C's basis for his share of Sec. 1245 potential is zero. His basis for the remaining property is $7,333 (the basis of his partnership interest before the current distribution ($10,000) minus the basis of the land treated as distributed to him ($2,667)). Thus, C's basis for the machine received from the partnership is $11,333 ($7,333 + $4,000) and his recomputed basis $13,333 ($11,333 plus $2,000 share of Sec. 1245 potential).

The partnership of A and B has an ordinary gain of $4,000 on the exchange of C's 4/9 interest in land for $4,000 of Sec. 1245 income potential (basis zero). The partnership basis for the land becomes $19,333 ($18,000 less $2,667 treated as distributed to C plus $4,000 paid for that share).

The transactions may be analyzed in the following schedule:

	C's interest (market value)	Asset value received	C's interest (basis)
Sec. 751 property			
Potential Sec. 1245 ordinary income	$ 2,000	$ 6,000	$ 0
for machine, $6,000 ($15,000 – $9,000)		($2,000 + $4,000)	
Other property			
Sec. 1231 Property		9,000	3,000
($15,000 – $6,000 = $9,000)	3,000	($3,000 + $6,000)	
Cash	1,000	0	1,000
Land	9,000	0	6,000
Total	$15,000	$15,000	$10,000

TRANSFER OF PARTNERSHIP INTEREST

¶3426   GAIN OR LOSS ON TRANSFER

If you sell or exchange your partnership interest, you generally have a capital gain or loss measured by the difference between the amount realized and the adjusted basis of your partnership interest [IRC Sec. 741; Reg. Sec. 1.741-1(a)].

If the buyer assumes your share of partnership liabilities, that amount is considered part of the amount you realize [Reg. Sec. 1.752-1(d)].

Example 1: If Mr. Abbot sells his interest in the AB partnership for $750 cash and, at the same time, the buyer assumes his $250 share of partnership liabilities, the amount realized on the transaction is $1,000. This amount is then applied against the basis of his partnership interest to determine his gain or loss.

➤ **OBSERVATION** When you decide to withdraw from a partnership, you may dispose of your interest by alternative methods, having different tax consequences to you and all the other partners. If the value of your interest exceeds your adjusted basis, and you prefer capital gain (rather than ordinary income) because you have a considerable amount of capital loss from other sources, you will probably want to sell or exchange your interest under Sec. 741. On the other hand, the taxable distributive shares of the continuing partners may be reduced, or the partnership may get a deduction, if your interest is liquidated under Sec. 736 [¶3429]. Thus, the tax consequences become dollars-and-cents factors in negotiating the amount to be paid by the continuing partners or by the partnership. By clearly stating your intent in the agreements, you and the other partners can increase your control over the tax consequences of the transaction and reduce the chance of later litigation over such consequences.

The partnership may elect to adjust the basis of its property after a transfer to reflect your acquisition cost [¶3427].

(a) Transfer of Partnership Interest by Corporation. A corporate distribution of a partnership interest is treated somewhat like a sale—the corporation is taxed on the amount the partnership interest's fair market value exceeds its basis [IRC Sec. 311(b)(1)]. Corporations have tried to offset this tax by contributing to the partnership property with a basis in excess of its fair market value before making the distribution. To prevent this abuse, regulations may provide that the contributed loss property shall not be considered when calculating the amount taxable on the distribution [IRC Sec. 311(b)(3)].

(b) How Current Earnings Are Treated. Your distributive share of current earnings is taxed to you, whether or not the earnings are distributed [¶3407; 3410]. The amount so taxed increases the basis of your interest in the partnership [¶3419], so the net gain on the sale of an interest does not include the current earnings. It is only this net gain that is taxed as capital gain.

> **Example 2:** A partner sold his partnership interest (basis $5,000) on June 30. His share of partnership income to the date of sale was $15,000. The sale price was $20,000. The $15,000 is taxed to the partner and increases his basis for the interest to $20,000. No gain is realized on the sale since the selling price and his basis are the same.

(c) Transfers Involving Receivables or Inventory. Any recognized gain or loss due to unrealized receivables or substantially appreciated inventory is ordinary gain or loss (¶3424) [IRC Sec. 751(a); Reg. Sec. 1.751-1].

The ordinary gain or loss is determined by allocating a portion of the sales proceeds and a portion of your basis to the receivables and inventory [Reg. Sec. 1.741-1(a)].

> **Example 3:** C buys B's 50% interest in the AB partnership which keeps its books on a cash basis. At the time, the balance sheet of the firm shows:

Assets	Basis	Market Value	Liabilities & Capital	Basis	Market Value
Cash	$ 3,000	$ 3,000	Notes payable . .	$ 2,000	$ 2,000
Advances for clients	10,000	10,000	Capital:		
Other assets . . .	7,000	7,000	A	9,000	15,000
Accounts receivable	0	12,000	B	9,000	15,000
	$20,000	$32,000		$20,000	$32,000

> The cash price C paid for his partnership interest is $15,000, representing C's share in the net assets shown above, including $6,000 for B's interest in accounts receivable. B realizes $6,000 in ordinary income, attributable to his partnership interest in unrealized receivables.

(d) Reporting of Transfers. If you sell or exchange all or part of your interest for money or other property attributable to unrealized receivables or substantially appreciated inventory, you must notify the partnership in writing within 30 days of the transaction or, if earlier, by January 15 of the calendar year following the calendar year of the exchange. You must also submit a prescribed statement with your income tax return for the year of sale or exchange [Reg. Sec. 1.751-1(a)(3)]. The statement must report the amount of your basis in the partnership that is attributable to unrealized receivables or substantially appreciated inventory, as well as the portion of the amount received for the interest that is attributable to those items.

The partnership must report exchanges of partnership interests involving unrealized receivables or substantially appreciated inventory items by filing Form 8308, Report of a Sale or Exchange of Certain Partnership Interests, with its partnership return for the tax year in which the exchange takes place. If a partnership isn't notified by a partner of an exchange until after it has filed its partnership return, it must file Form 8308 within 30 days of notification. The partnership must also provide a copy of Form 8308 to each transferor and transferee by the later of January 31 of the calendar year following the year of the exchange or 30 days after it receives notice of the exchange.

(e) Not a Like-Kind Exchange. Generally, exchanges of partnership interests do not qualify for tax-free "like-kind" exchange treatment (¶1614(a)) [IRC Sec. 1031(a)(2)(D)]. However, a like-kind exchange could in some cases be treated as a tax-free contribution to a partnership.

¶3427   BASIS OF TRANSFEREE PARTNER

You (the transferee) find your *original* basis for your interest by applying the general basis rules (¶3419 et seq.) [IRC Sec. 742; Reg. Sec. 1.742-1].

➤ **OBSERVATION** Your *original* basis must be adjusted from time to time to prevent the unintended benefit or detriment that would otherwise result.

(a) Adjustments for Transfers. If your partnership has filed an election [¶3423], it will increase or decrease the adjusted basis of its property in the amount by which your basis differs from your pro rata share of the partnership's adjusted basis [IRC Sec. 743]. The adjustment relates only to you. You have a special basis for the adjusted properties and report it on a return for the first tax year affected [Reg. Sec. 1.743-1]. The adjustment to the basis of the partnership's retained property is made in substantially the same manner that it is made because of a distribution [¶3423]. See Example 1 below.

(b) How Partnership Agreements Offer Special Basis Adjustments. In some cases, your partnership agreement may provide for a special allocation of depreciation, depletion, and gain or loss on contributed property whose basis differed from its value at contribution [¶3413]. For property contributed before April 1, 1984, the agreement must be taken into account in determining your proportionate share of the partnership's basis for special basis adjustment [Reg. Sec. 1.743-1(b)(2)(i)]. For contributions after March 31, 1984, your share of the adjusted basis of partnership property is determined according to the rules relating to contributed property (¶3413) [IRC Sec. 743(b)(2)].

Example 1: (a) Ms. Rich and Mr. Schwartz form partnership RS, to which Rich contributes property X, worth $1,000 with an adjusted basis to her of $400. Schwartz contributes $1,000 in cash. During the partnership's first tax year, property X appreciates in value to $1,200, and Rich sells her half interest in the partnership to Bishop for $1,100.

Suppose there is no agreement for special allocation and the partnership has elected to adjust the basis. Then the partnership property's adjusted basis to Bishop is increased by $400:

1. $1,100—excess of transferee partner's basis for her partnership interest over

2. $700—her proportionate share of the partnership property's adjusted basis [$1,400 ($400 basis of property X plus $1,000 cash) divided by 2].

The adjustment amount is $400, applied as an increase in basis of partnership property X as to Bishop only. Suppose property X is sold for $1,400. Then the partnership gain is $1,000:

Sale price	$1,400
Less: Partnership basis of property X	400
Gain	$1,000

Each partner has a $500 gain on the sale. Bishop has a $400 special basis adjustment for property X, thus reducing her gain to $100.

If Bishop bought her interest from Schwartz (the partner contributing cash), Bishop's adjustment would also be $400, figured the same way as for a purchase from Rich.

(b) Assume that the contributions were made in 1983. Assume further that the original partnership RS had a special agreement about property X, stating that on the sale of that property, any gain, to the extent of the precontribution appreciation, was to be allocated entirely to the contributing partner, Rich. Here, Bishop's special basis would be different.

Under the partnership agreement, Rich had, in effect, a basis of only $400 in the partnership assets (her basis for property X before its contribution to the partnership), and Schwartz had a basis of $1,000 (the full basis of his investment). Bishop, who is Rich's successor, has a proportionate share in the adjusted basis of partnership property of only $400 (Rich's share of partnership basis).

The amount of the increase to Bishop in the adjusted basis of partnership property is $700 (the excess of $1,100, Bishop's basis for her interest, over $400, Bishop's share of partnership basis). This amount is an adjustment to the basis of partnership property as to Bishop only. If X is sold by the partnership for $1,400, the partnership gain is $1,000 ($1,400 received less the partnership basis of $400).

Under the partnership agreement, $600 of this gain which is attributable to precontribution appreciation is allocable to Bishop as Rich's successor. The remaining $400 gain is not subject to the agreement and is allocable to Schwartz and Bishop equally; i.e., $200 each. However, Bishop's recognized gain is only $100 (her $800 distributive share of the gain reduced by $700, her special basis adjustment for X). Schwartz has a gain of $200 and is unaffected by the transfer of Rich's interest.

(c) Effect on Depletion Allowance.

If an adjustment is made to the basis of depletable property, any depletion allowance is figured separately for each partner, including the transferee partner [IRC Sec. 743(b); Reg. Sec. 1.743-1(b)(2)(iii)].

Example 2: Rich and Schwartz each contribute $5,000 to partnership RS, which buys mineral property for $10,000. When the partnership's election to adjust the basis is in effect, Schwartz sells his interest in the partnership to Bishop for $100,000. The difference between Schwartz's and Bishop's bases, $95,000, is allocated to the mineral property. Rich's share of the basis for the property remains $5,000. Bishop's basis is $100,000: $5,000, her ½ of the common partnership basis, plus $95,000, her additional transferee basis. At the end of the partnership year, cost depletion as to Rich's ½ interest with a basis of $5,000 is $500 and cost depletion as to Bishop's ½ interest with a basis of $100,000 is $10,000. Assume under the percentage depletion method [¶2237] Rich and Schwartz would each be entitled to $7,000 allowance. Percentage depletion is greater for Rich. She will therefore be allowed a deduction of $7,000. Cost depletion is greater for Bishop; she is allowed a deduction of $10,000.

¶3428   SPECIAL ELECTIVE PARTNERSHIP BASIS FOR TRANSFEREE

If you did not get the benefit of an adjustment by the partnership when your interest was transferred to you, you may get a similar benefit by electing a special method to fix and allocate your basis for distributed property other than money [IRC Sec. 732(d); Reg. Sec. 1.732-1(d)]. If you make this election, your basis for the distributed property is the basis the property would have if the partnership had made the adjustment when you acquired your interest [¶3427].

You may make this election only if you receive a distribution within two years after you acquired your interest. In some cases, the IRS may require the adjustment [(b) below].

Example 1: The basis to transferee partner Mr. Spire of his ¼ interest in partnership WJKS is $17,000. When he acquired such interest by purchase, the election under Sec. 754 was not in effect. The partnership inventory had a basis to the partnership of $14,000 and a value of $16,000. Spire's purchase price reflected $500 of this difference. Thus, $4,000 of the $17,000 paid by Spire for his ¼ interest was attributable to his share of partnership inventory with a basis of $3,500. Within two years after acquiring his interest, Spire retired from the partnership and received in liquidation of his entire interest cash of $1,500, inventory with a basis to the partnership of $3,500, property X (a capital asset) with an adjusted basis to the partnership of $2,000, and property Y (a depreciable asset) with an adjusted basis to the partnership of $4,000.

The value of the inventory received by Spire was ¼ the value of all partnership inventory and was his share of such property. It is immaterial whether the inventory Spire received was on hand when Spire acquired his interest. In accordance with Spire's election under Sec. 732(d), the amount of his share of partnership basis which is attributable to partnership inventory is increased by $500 (¼ the $2,000 difference between the value of such property, $16,000, and its $14,000 basis to the partnership at the time Spire acquired his interest). This adjustment under Sec. 732(d) applies only for purposes of distributions to partner Spire and not for purposes of partnership depreciation, depletion, or gain or loss on disposition.

Thus, the amount to be allocated among the properties received by Spire in the liquidating distribution is $15,500 ($17,000, Spire's basis for his interest, reduced by the amount of cash received, $1,500). This amount is allocated as follows:

1. Basis of inventory items received is $4,000—$3,500 common partnership basis for such items plus the special basis adjustment of $500 which Spire would have had under Sec. 743(b).

2. Remaining basis of $11,500 ($15,500 – $4,000) is to be allocated to the remaining property distributed to Spire in proportion to their adjusted bases to the partnership. Since the adjusted basis to the partnership of property X is $2,000 and that of property Y is $4,000, the $11,500 is allocated $3,833 ($2,000/$6,000 × $11,500) to X and $7,667 ($4,000/$6,000 × $11,500) to Y.

(a) Making the Election. To elect a special basis adjustment, you must file an attachment with your tax return stating that you choose to adjust the basis of property received in a distribution. The attachment must show how the special basis adjustment is computed. The election must be made with your tax return for the year of the distribution if the distribution includes any property subject to depreciation, depletion or amortization. If no such property is included in the distribution, the election need not be made until the first year in which the basis of the distributed property will affect computation of your income tax.

(b) Excluded Property. The optional method cannot be used to determine the basis for the portion of a distribution to you that is treated as received by you in a *sale* or exchange under Sec. 751. It does apply to the portion treated as exchanged (given up) by you, since such property is treated as currently distributed before the exchange [¶3424]. Your basis for the property you *received* is cost [IRC Sec. 732(e); Reg. Sec. 1.732-1(e)].

(c) When Partner Must Use Special Basis. You must make a special basis adjustment for distributed property you receive, whether or not the distribution was made within two years after you acquired your interest, if when you acquired the interest:

1. The fair market value of all partnership property (except money) was more than 110% of its adjusted basis to the partnership.

2. An allocation of basis [¶3421] on a liquidation of your interest immediately after its transfer would have resulted in a shift of basis from property not subject to an allowance for depreciation, depletion or amortization to property subject to such an allowance.

3. A special partnership basis adjustment at the time of the transfer would have changed your basis for the property actually distributed [IRC Sec. 732(d); Reg. Sec. 1.732-1(d)(4)].

Example 2: Partnership ABK owns three parcels of land, each of which has a basis to the partnership of $5,000 and each of which is worth $55,000. It also has depreciable property with a basis and value of $150,000. Mr. Delmore purchases Mr. Koch's partnership interest for $105,000 when the election under Sec. 754 is not in effect. At this time, the value of all the partnership property is $315,000, which exceeds 110% of $165,000, its basis to the partnership. Four years later, the partnership dissolves and Delmore receives 1 of the 3 parcels of land which had a basis to the partnership of $5,000 and ⅓ of the depreciable property which had a basis to the partnership at that time of $45,000, ⅓ of $135,000 ($150,000 original basis less $15,000 depreciation).

Suppose Delmore's basis for his interest at the time of distribution was $100,000 and it was allocated to the properties received by him in proportion to their respective bases to the partnership. Then the basis to him for the distributed land would be $10,000 ($5,000/$50,000 × $100,000) and the basis of the depreciable property would be $90,000 ($45,000/$50,000 × $100,000). *Result:* Delmore would, in effect, apply as the basis of depreciable property a portion of the amount which he had paid for nondepreciable property.

If the partnership adjustment for transfers had been applied to the transfer of the interest, Delmore would have had a different basis for the distributed property. Therefore, Delmore *must* increase the basis of the land by a special adjustment of $50,000 ($55,000 value less $5,000 partnership basis). Hence, his basis for the land will be $55,000 ($55,000/$100,000 × $100,000) and $45,000 ($45,000/$100,000 × $100,000) for the depreciable property.

PAYMENTS UPON RETIREMENT OR DEATH OF PARTNER

¶3429   LIQUIDATING PAYMENTS ON DEATH OR RETIREMENT

When you withdraw from your partnership (say, upon retirement), your partnership must allocate payments in liquidation of your entire interest either to (a) payments in exchange for an interest in partnership property or (b) other payments.

(a) Payments for Interest in Partnership Assets. As a general rule, such payments are treated as distributions in exchange for your interest in assets [IRC Sec. 736(b)(1); Reg. Sec. 1.736-1(b)(1)]. But such assets do not include unrealized receivables, goodwill, or substantially appreciated inventory, *to the extent indicated* under "specially treated assets" below. See Example 2 below.

The remaining partners get no deduction for payments treated as distributions. The payments reduce the basis for your interest and result in gain to the extent they exceed any remaining basis, or loss to the extent of any remaining basis after all payments are received. Assuming only cash is received, gain or loss is recognized immediately under the rules in ¶3420 [IRC Sec. 731(a); Reg. Sec. 1.731-1(a)].

> **Example 1:** The ABC partnership pays retired partner Mr. Celan $15,000 per year for ten years for his interest in the partnership. The basis of Celan's interest is $90,000. Of the $150,000 Celan will receive over the 10 years, $90,000 will reduce his basis and the remaining $60,000 will be capital gain.

When payments are made for unrealized receivables [¶3424], the value of your interest in that property is reduced by the amount of the ordinary income potential in the property [Reg. Sec. 1.736-1].

Specially treated assets. Payments for the following assets are not subject to the general rule and are not treated as distributions [IRC Sec. 736(b); Reg. Sec. 1.736-1(b)]:

- Amounts paid for goodwill in excess of its partnership basis are not treated as distributions unless the partnership agreement expressly[1] provides for *reasonable* payments for goodwill. If the agreement does *not* so provide, such amounts are "other payments" subject to the rules in (b).
- Amounts paid for unrealized receivables *in excess of their partnership basis* are not payments for your interest in partnership assets. They are "other payments" subject to the rules in (b).
- Amounts paid for your interest in *substantially appreciated inventory* are treated as proceeds from the sale or exchange of a noncapital asset under the rules in ¶3424.

> **Example 2:** Assume that, in Example 1 above, Celan's interest in partnership property included an interest worth $50,000 in substantially appreciated inventory. Assume also that $15,000 of Celan's basis of $90,000 was attributable to this inventory. Then, of the $150,000 Celan will receive, $90,000 reduces his basis, $35,000 ($50,000 less $15,000) is ordinary income, and $25,000 ($100,000 less $75,000) is capital gain.

(b) Other Liquidating Payments. Payments for unrealized receivables and goodwill, to the extent indicated in (a) above, and all other payments that are not made for the interest in partnership assets are either distributive shares of income or guaranteed payments, depending on whether or not they are based on income.

Payments based on income. Payments measured by partnership income are distributive shares of partnership income regardless of the period over which they are paid

[IRC Sec. 736(a)(1); Reg. Sec. 1.736-1(a)(3)(i)]. They are taxable to you as though you continued to be a partner and thus reduce the amount of the remaining partners' distributive shares [Reg. Sec. 1.736-1(a)(4), (6)].

> **Example 3:** Each year AB partnership pays retired partner Ms. Cummings 10% of partnership net income. Payments are taxed to Cummings as if she still had a 10% distributive share of the partnership income, loss, deductions and credits.

Payments not based on income.
If the payments are determined without regard to the partnership income and are not payments for an interest in partnership property [(a) above], they are guaranteed payments (salary) made to one not a partner. They are ordinary income to you and a deductible partnership expense [IRC Sec. 736(a)(2); Reg. Sec. 1.736-1(a)(3)(ii), -1(a)(4)].

> **Example 4:** If in Example 3 above, the payments were $100 per week rather than 10% of partnership net income, the payments received by Cummings are ordinary income to her, and are deductible by the partnership as salary.

Income in respect of decedent.
Amounts includable as "other payments" in the gross income of the successor in interest of a deceased partner are taxed to the successor the same way they would have been taxed to the decedent [IRC Sec. 753; Reg. Sec. 1.753-1(a), (d)]. Payments to the successor determined without regard to partnership income are taxed to him or her as if he or she were a partner and the payments were salary or interest on capital; that is, as ordinary income. Payments determined with reference to partnership income are taxed to the successor as if he or she were a partner receiving his or her distributive share of partnership income. The successor is allowed a deduction for any amounts that may have been included in the gross estate of the decedent [¶3508(b)], but is not allowed an optional adjustment [¶3428] to the basis of a deceased partner's share of receivables existing at the partner's death.²

(c) Reporting Gain or Loss on Installment Payments for Interest in Assets.
Gain on installment payments for a partnership interest generally is not recognized until capital is recovered, unless the election below applies.

Partner's election.
If the amount paid for the interest is a fixed sum payable in installments, you may elect to report any gain or loss proportionately over the years of receipt. The gain or loss for each year is the difference between (1) the amount treated as a distribution in that year and (2) the portion of your basis for your partnership interest attributable to such distribution [Reg. Sec. 1.736-1(b)(6)].

> **Example 5:** CBA is a personal service partnership. When partner Mr. Agee retires, the partnership's balance sheet is as follows:

	Assets			*Liabilities & Capital*		
	Basis	*Value*			*Basis*	*Value*
Cash	$13,000	$13,000	Liabilities		$ 3,000	$ 3,000
Capital assets . .	20,000	23,000	Capital:			
	$33,000	$36,000	Agee		10,000	11,000
			Baker		10,000	11,000
			Colvin		10,000	11,000
					$33,000	$36,000

> It is agreed that Agee's capital interest is valued at $12,000 (⅓ of $36,000) and that Agee will receive $5,000 a year for three years after his retirement. The first $5,000, however, will include Agee's share of the liabilities ($1,000) assumed by Baez and Colvin.
>
> *Tax treatment of Agee.* The basis of Agee's interest is $11,000 ($10,000 investment plus $1,000, his share of liabilities). Of the $15,000 Agee is to receive, only $12,000 is in payment of his interest in partnership property. The remainder is ordinary income. Thus, Agee will have $1,000 capital gain ($12,000 minus $11,000) and $3,000 ordinary income. Agee may report the $1,000 gain at the time he receives his last payment or he may elect to allocate the gain over the 3 years. If he elects to allocate,

he may report $333 capital gain and $1,000 ordinary income each year (⅓ of the total amounts of capital gain and ordinary income, respectively). The remainder of the payment is a return of capital.

Tax treatment of remaining partners. The partnership cannot deduct Agee's $1,000 capital gain since the amount represents a purchase of Agee's capital interest by the partnership. The partnership may deduct Agee's $3,000 ordinary income.

Example 6: Assume the same facts as in Example 5 except that the agreement provides for payments to Agee for three years of a percentage of annual income instead of a fixed amount. Here, Agee cannot elect to report his gain proportionately over the years. All payments received by Agee up to $12,000 are treated as payments for Agee's interest in partnership property. His gain of $1,000 is taxed only after he has received his full basis. Any payment in excess of $12,000 is treated as a distributive share of partnership income to Agee.

¶3430   HOW INSTALLMENT PAYMENTS ARE ALLOCATED

Payments in liquidation of your interest may be made in installments over several years. The methods of dividing these payments between those made for your interest in assets and "other payments" are as follows:

(a) Fixed Payments. If a fixed amount is payable over a fixed number of years (whether or not supplemented by additional amounts), a proportionate part of each year's fixed agreed payments is treated as a payment for your interests in assets. The proportionate part is the ratio of the total fixed agreed payments for the interest in assets to the total fixed agreed payments for your interest in assets and for other items (guaranteed payments and distributive share of income). The balance of the annual payments is treated as "other payments." If the amount you receive in a given year is less than the amount treated as payable for your interest in assets in that year, the deficiency is carried over and is added to the amount paid for your interest in the following year or years [Reg. Sec. 1.736-1(b)(5)(i)].

Example: Retiring partner Mr. Smith is entitled to ten annual payments of $6,000 each for his interest in partnership property. He receives only $3,500 in 1991. In 1992, he receives $10,000. Of this amount, $8,500 ($6,000 plus $2,500 from 1991) is treated as payment for his interest in assets [¶3429(a)], $1,500 as "other payments" [¶3429(b)].

(b) When Amount Varies. If the payments are not fixed in amount, they are treated as payments for your interest in assets until you receive the full value of that interest. After that, all payments are treated as "other payments" [Reg. Sec. 1.736-1(b)(5)(ii)].

(c) Allocation by Agreement. When you withdraw, you and all the remaining partners may agree on any other method that does not allocate to your interest in assets an amount in excess of its value at death or retirement [Reg. Sec. 1.736-1(b)(5)(iii)].

Footnotes to Chapter 24

(For your added convenience, in brackets [] with the footnotes below, you will find citations to related paragraphs in the "RIA United States Tax Reporter "(USTR), "CCH Federal Tax Reporter"(CCH) and "RIA Federal Tax Coordinator 2d"(FTC) multi-volume services.)

FOOTNOTE ¶ 3400 [USTR ¶ 7009; CCH ¶ 25,902; 43,982; FTC ¶ B-1000; 1002].

(1) Rev. Proc. 92-32.

(2) Comm. v. Tower, 327 US 280, 34 AFTR 799.

FOOTNOTE ¶ 3401 [USTR ¶ 77,014; CCH ¶ 43,986 et seq.; FTC ¶ D-1311].

(1) Alexander Trust Property, 12 BTA 1226.

FOOTNOTE ¶ 3402 [USTR ¶ 7614.02; CCH ¶ 25,902; FTC ¶ B-1306].

(1) Rev. Rul. 65-118, 1965-1 CB 30.

FOOTNOTE ¶ 3403 [USTR ¶ 7044.06; CCH ¶ 25,427; FTC ¶ B-1200 et seq.].

(1) Comm. v. Tower, 327 US 280, 34 AFTR 799; Lusthaus v. Comm., 327 US 293, 34 AFTR 806; Comm. v. Culbertson, 337 US 733, 37 AFTR 1301.

FOOTNOTE ¶ 3404 [USTR ¶ 7034.01; CCH ¶ 38,569 et seq.; FTC ¶ B-1900 et seq.].

(1) Rev. Rul. 71-278, 1971-2 CB 75.

FOOTNOTE ¶ 3405 [USTR ¶ 7034.02; CCH ¶ 25,403; FTC ¶ B-1900; 1908].

(1) Mihran Demirjian, 29 AFTR 2d 72-741, 457 F.2d 1.

FOOTNOTE ¶ 3406 [USTR ¶ 7034.01; CCH ¶ 25,403; FTC ¶ B-2430].

FOOTNOTE ¶ 3407 [USTR ¶ 7044; CCH ¶ 25,341 et seq.; FTC ¶ B-3400 et seq.].

(1) Truman v. U.S., 4 F.Supp. 447, 12 AFTR 1415.

FOOTNOTE ¶ 3408 [USTR ¶ 7024.01; CCH ¶ 25,383; FTC ¶ B-1904; 1905].

(1) Rev. Rul. 68-79, 1968-1 CB 310.

(2) Rev. Rul. 89-7, 1989-1 CB 178.

(3) The IRS booklet "Cumulative List of Organizations—Contributions to Which Are Deductible" may be obtained from the Superintendent of Documents, Government Printing Office, Washington, DC 20402.

FOOTNOTE ¶ 3409 [USTR ¶ 7044.01; CCH ¶ 25,424; FTC ¶ B-3000 et seq.].

(1) Instructions for Form 1065 (1991).

FOOTNOTE ¶ 3410 [USTR ¶ 7034; CCH ¶ 25,341 et seq.; FTC ¶ B-1900 et seq.; 2900 et seq.].

FOOTNOTE ¶ 3411 [USTR ¶ 7044.03; CCH ¶ 25,426; FTC ¶ B-2900 et seq.].

FOOTNOTE ¶ 3412 [USTR ¶ 7044; CCH ¶ 25,424; FTC ¶ B-1001; 2300].

FOOTNOTE ¶ 3413 [USTR ¶ 7044.01; CCH ¶ 25,424; FTC ¶ B-1505; 2608].

FOOTNOTE ¶ 3414 [USTR ¶ 7064; CCH ¶ 25,465; FTC ¶ G-1072.4].

FOOTNOTE ¶ 3415 [USTR ¶ 7064.01; CCH ¶ 25,465; FTC ¶ G-1072.4].

FOOTNOTE ¶ 3416 [USTR ¶ 7074; CCH ¶ 25,482; FTC ¶ B-2101].

(1) U.S. v. Basye, 31 AFTR 2d 73-802; 410 U.S. 441.

(2) Rev. Rul. 91-26, 1991-1 CB 184.

FOOTNOTE ¶ 3417 [USTR ¶ 2674; CCH ¶ 14,161; FTC ¶ B-2113].

FOOTNOTE ¶ 3418 [USTR ¶ 7214.01; CCH ¶ 25,543; FTC ¶ B-1500 et seq.].

FOOTNOTE ¶ 3419 [USTR ¶ 7224; CCH ¶ 25,562; FTC ¶ B-1505].

FOOTNOTE ¶ 3420 [USTR ¶ 7313; CCH ¶ 25,622; FTC ¶ B-3000 et seq.].

FOOTNOTE ¶ 3421 [USTR ¶ 7334; CCH ¶ 25,662; FTC ¶ B-3201].

FOOTNOTE ¶ 3422 [USTR ¶ 7544; CCH ¶ 25,782; FTC ¶ B-3606].

FOOTNOTE ¶ 3423 [USTR ¶ 7344.01; CCH ¶ 25,683; FTC ¶ B-3606].

FOOTNOTE ¶ 3424 [USTR ¶ 7344.04; CCH ¶ 25,683; FTC ¶ B-3010; 3100 et seq.].

FOOTNOTE ¶ 3425 [USTR ¶ 7514.01; CCH ¶ 25,803; FTC ¶ B-3501 et seq.].

FOOTNOTE ¶ 3426 [USTR ¶ 7414.01; CCH ¶ 25,742; FTC ¶ B-2432].

FOOTNOTE ¶ 3427 [USTR ¶ 7424; CCH ¶ 25,762; FTC ¶ B-1601].

FOOTNOTE ¶ 3428 [USTR ¶ 7324; CCH ¶ 25,643; FTC ¶ B-3200].

FOOTNOTE ¶ 3429 [USTR ¶ 7364.01; CCH ¶ 25,722; FTC ¶ B-3800 et seq.].

(1) Comm. v. Jackson Investment Co., 15 AFTR 2d 1125, 34 F.2d 187; V. Zay Smith, 37 TC 1033, 11 AFTR 2d 508, 313 F.2d 16.

(2) Rev. Rul. 66-325, 1966-2 CB 249.

FOOTNOTE ¶ 3430 [USTR ¶ 7363.04; CCH ¶ 25,722; FTC ¶ B-3700].

CHAPTER 25

ESTATES AND TRUSTS

TABLE OF CONTENTS

ESTATES AND TRUSTS IN GENERAL

An estate of a deceased person, or a trust, is a separate taxable entity. The fiduciary (an executor or administrator for an estate, a trustee for a trust) must file a return and, when a tax is due, pay the tax. Generally, estates and trusts are taxed in the same manner as individuals.

¶3500   HOW ESTATES AND TRUSTS ARE TAXED

Taxes for estates and trusts are computed by using the rate schedule specially provided for them [¶3520]. Special rules that affect the computing of taxable income, deductions and credits are discussed in this chapter. (These rules do not apply to certain business trusts which are more nearly associations or corporations and taxed as such.)

Some trusts are not taxable entities. For example, a revocable trust is a separate entity for trust law purposes, but is not a separate taxable entity for federal income tax purposes. If you are a grantor of such a trust, you must report the trust's income and deductions on your individual return as if there were no trust. Trusts that do not become separate taxable entities are discussed at ¶3523. The balance of this chapter explains the income tax on (1) trusts that are taxable entities and (2) decedents' estates. In certain cases, the trust is taxed at the grantor's rates; see ¶3523(g).

For estate tax on the estate of a deceased person, see Chapter 29.

(a) Allocation of Income. Generally, the income of an estate or trust is taxed either to the estate or trust through its fiduciary [¶3501], or to the beneficiaries, or in part to each, depending upon the disposition of the income under the terms of the will or trust and state law. In this way the entire taxable income of the estate or trust is taxed [¶3503].

(b) Returns. The fiduciary of an estate (the executor or administrator, depending on whether there is a will) and the fiduciary of a trust (the trustee) must file Form 1041 and pay the tax of the estate or trust. The filing requirements are explained in ¶3520. The fiduciaries must also file a separate Schedule K-1 for each beneficiary. For an estate, the executor or administrator, in addition to filing the estate's income tax return, generally files the decedent's final income tax return as well. The deceased person's final income tax return covers the period ending on the date of his or her death; the estate's income tax return covers the period beginning the day after death.

¶3501   LIABILITY OF FIDUCIARIES

If you serve as a fiduciary, you assume the rights and duties of the taxpayer (the trust or estate) for income tax purposes. However, you ordinarily are not personally liable for the tax. Usually the tax is paid from the assets of the estate or trust [IRC Sec. 6903; Reg. Sec. 301.6903-1]. On the other hand, if you use these assets to pay the taxpayer's debts without first satisfying the federal government's tax claim, you will be personally liable for the tax deficiency up to the amounts paid[1] if: (1) the estate is too small to pay all the debts of the deceased,[2] (2) the government's claim has priority over the claims of creditors who were paid[3] or (3) you have notice of the debt.[4] This personal liability also applies to you if you knew or should have known about government tax claims before making distributions to beneficiaries [Reg. Sec. 1.641(b)-2].

Discharge from personal liability. As an executor or administrator, you can apply for release from personal liability for a decedent's income and gift taxes after you have filed the returns for these taxes. You file the application at the office where the estate tax return is to be filed. If no return is required, you file the application where the decedent's last income tax return is to be filed. The IRS must notify you, within nine months after receiving the application, of the amount of taxes due. You are then relieved from any future deficiencies on paying the amount. You are also discharged if the IRS does not notify you within the nine-month period [IRC Sec. 6905(a), (b); Reg. Sec. 301.6905-1].

¶3502   NATURE OF ESTATES AND TRUSTS

A trust is a relationship in which one person—the trustee—is the owner of the title to property, subject to an obligation to keep or use the property for the benefit of another— the beneficiary. A trust created by an instrument other than a will is an inter vivos or living trust. A trust created by will is a testamentary trust. The subject matter of the trust is often referred to as the trust res, trust principal, trust property or trust corpus. The most common types of property making up the trust principal or trust corpus are bonds, stocks, mortgages, titles to land and bank accounts. The person who creates a trust is known as the grantor, creator, donor or settlor of the trust. As for a testamentary trust, the creator is the testator—the person who executed the will. As already indicated, once created, a trust becomes a separate taxable entity for which a return must be filed and taxes paid.

(a) Estates. The named executor, if there is a will, and the administrator, if there is no will, is the fiduciary in charge of an estate. This, like a trust, is a separate tax entity and the fiduciary in charge has the same tax obligations as the trustee of a trust.

(b) Multiple Trusts. You can create several (multiple) trusts in one instrument and have the same trustee administer all of them. The income of each trust is taxable as income of a separate entity.[1] Whether only one trust or more than one trust has been created depends upon your intention as determined from the trust agreement.[2] The Supreme Court has held that separate trusts are created, even if there is only one trust instrument and the trust assets are not segregated, when each beneficiary has a separate account and is granted a fixed share in the trust property.[3]

However, if tax avoidance was a principal purpose for setting up multiple trusts that have substantially the same grantor and beneficiaries, two or more trusts are treated as one, and taxed accordingly [IRC Sec. 643(e)]. For this rule, husband and wife are treated as one person. This rule does not apply to any trust that was irrevocable on March 1, 1984, except to the extent corpus is transferred to the trust after that date.[4]

WHO IS TAXABLE ON ESTATE AND TRUST INCOME

¶3503   TO WHOM ESTATE OR TRUST INCOME IS TAXABLE

If you are a beneficiary, you are generally taxed on distributions you get or are entitled to get from the estate or trust, but only to the extent of your share of its "distributable net income" (DNI) [¶3504-3506].

A fiduciary is taxed on the taxable income of the estate or trust. Taxable income is gross income [¶3508] less the deductions discussed in ¶3511 et seq.

Under certain conditions, the income of a trust is not taxed to either the beneficiaries or the fiduciary. Instead, it is taxed to the grantor or other persons having control of the trust property or income [¶3523].

(a) Different Tax Years. As a beneficiary, you are taxed on the distributions for the tax year or years of the estate or trust that end within or with your tax year [IRC Sec. 652(c), 662(c); Reg. Sec. 1.652(c)-1, 1.662(c)-1].

> **Example:** A beneficiary filing a return for calendar year 1992 would include distributions received from an estate having a fiscal year beginning in 1991 and ending in 1992.

> **NOTE:** Trusts, unlike estates, may not use fiscal tax years; they are generally limited to calendar tax years [IRC Sec. 645].

(b) Income, Deductions and Credits When Trust Terminates. After a trust terminates, its income, deductions and credits are attributed to the termination beneficiaries. However, a trust does not terminate automatically. A reasonable period is allowed for the trustee to wind up its affairs. During this period, the status of the trust income is determined under the terms of the trust instrument and state law [Reg. Sec. 1.641(b)-3].

¶3504   DISTRIBUTABLE NET INCOME

Distributable net income (DNI) is a tax concept that limits (1) the amounts you and the other beneficiaries must include in your gross income, and (2) the deductions the fiduciary may take for distributions. You never report more than your share of DNI. The fiduciary's deduction for distributions cannot be more than the trust's DNI [IRC Sec. 643, 652, 662; Reg. Sec. 1.643-1, 1.652(a)-2, 1.662(a)-2].

How to figure distributable net income. To find the DNI, you start with the trust's or estate's taxable income (gross income minus deductions [¶3508; 3511 et seq.]). Then, you make the following adjustments [Reg. Sec. 1.643(a)-0–1.643(a)-7]:

1. Add back: (a) the personal exemption [¶3512], (b) the distributions deduction [¶3517] and (c) any net capital losses deducted by the trust or estate [¶3509(a)].

2. Add net tax-exempt interest to taxable income as modified in (1). Tax-exempt interest is reduced by (a) any portion of the interest that is paid or set aside for

charitable purposes and by (b) nondeductible expenses (such as commissions and general expenses) related to the tax-exempt interest [¶2204].

3. Subtract the net capital gains taxable to the trust or estate [¶3509(d)]. This includes only those gains that are allocated to corpus. Do not subtract net capital gains which are (a) paid, credited or required to be distributed to beneficiaries or (b) paid or set aside for charitable purposes. These latter gains are included in DNI.

Example: A trust has $40,000 gross income for the year, including $9,000 capital gain which, under the trust instrument, is to be distributed one-third to the beneficiary and two-thirds to the corpus of the trust. Gross income also includes $5,000 in dividends of domestic corporations. The trust is entitled to deductions for interest, taxes, depreciation and charitable contributions amounting to $8,000. In addition to the $40,000 gross income, the trust also receives $7,000 tax-exempt interest. Distributable net income is $33,000, computed as follows:

Gross income	$40,000
Less: deductions	8,000
Taxable income as modified	$32,000
Plus: tax-exempt interest	7,000
	$39,000
Less: capital gain to be added to trust corpus (⅔)	6,000
Distributable net income	$33,000

Special rules apply to simple and foreign trusts. Extraordinary dividends and taxable stock dividends of simple trusts allocated to corpus by a trustee are not included in DNI. But a foreign trust's gross income from foreign sources, reduced by nondeductible expenses [¶2204], is included. See also ¶3524(h).

¶3505 DISTRIBUTIONS BY SIMPLE TRUSTS

A simple trust is one which, under the trust terms, distributes only current income (that is, distributes no corpus), must distribute all its income and has no charitable beneficiaries [IRC Sec. 651; Reg. Sec. 1.651(a)-1]. A simple trust is primarily a conduit of income—the trust takes a deduction for the income that is required to be distributed currently, and the beneficiaries include that amount in their gross income. The terms of the trust instrument and state law determine what is income for this purpose.

(a) Income Taxable to Beneficiaries. Generally, you and the other beneficiaries must include in gross income all trust income required to be distributed to you, to the extent of the trust's DNI—regardless of whether the income is actually distributed [¶3504]. For asset distributions in lieu of cash, see ¶3509.

Example 1: Mr. Covington placed certain securities in trust for the sole benefit of his wife. The trust instrument provided that all the income be distributed to her at least once a year, that the securities themselves not be distributed to her, and that no distributions be made to anyone else. This is a simple trust. Mrs. Covington will include the trust income in her gross income each year, whether or not the fiduciary actually makes the payment to her during the tax year.[1]

If the income required to be distributed exceeds the DNI, you are taxed only on your proportionate share of the DNI [IRC Sec. 652(a); Reg. Sec. 1.652(a)-2].

Example 2: A simple trust provides that Mr. Barnes is to receive 60% of the trust income and Mr. Cox is to receive 40%. The trust has the following income and disbursements during the year: $9,000 interest on corporate bonds; $4,000 capital gains allocable to corpus; $1,500 commissions, legal fees and other deductible expenses allocable to corpus; and $400 expenses allocable to income.

The trust income required to be distributed is $9,000 less $400, or $8,600. The trust's distributable net income is $9,000 (capital gains are excluded), less $1,900 (all deductible expenses), or $7,100. Although Barnes receives $5,160 ($8,600 × 60%), he will include only $4,260 ($7,100 × 60%) in income. Cox will receive $3,440 ($8,600 × 40%), but will include only $2,840 ($7,100 × 40%).

(b) Distributions of Corpus. A trust may be a simple trust one year and a complex trust another year. For example, a trust is required to distribute all of its income currently. The trustee also has a discretionary power to distribute corpus to the income beneficiary. In years when only income is distributed, the trust is a simple trust. However, if corpus is distributed, the trust becomes a complex trust for that year. When a trust ends, it is treated as a complex trust because corpus is distributed that year [Reg. Sec. 1.651(a)-3].

¶3506 DISTRIBUTIONS BY ESTATES AND COMPLEX TRUSTS

[New tax legislation may affect this subject; see ¶1.]

Complex trusts are those that are not simple trusts. They include discretionary trusts, trusts with charitable beneficiaries and trusts that accumulate income or distribute corpus. In determining inclusions for the beneficiaries and the deductions for distributions by the fiduciary, estates and complex trusts are similarly treated [IRC Sec. 661-663; Reg. Sec. 1.661(a)-1].

(a) Allocation by Tiers—Overview. For estates and complex trusts, distributions are taxed to the extent of the DNI first to the beneficiaries to whom income must be currently distributed. These are known as first-tier beneficiaries. If distributions to these beneficiaries are greater than the DNI, their shares are prorated for tax purposes. All other beneficiaries eligible to receive income are second-tier beneficiaries. They are subject to income tax on their distributions only to the extent that that the DNI is greater than the amount distributed to the first-tier beneficiaries [IRC Sec. 662(a)].

> **Example 1:** Ms. Ames, a first-tier beneficiary, is entitled to receive $15,000 as an annual distribution from an estate, and Ms. Bates is entitled to income in the discretion of the fiduciary. (a) If the DNI is $30,000 and they each receive $15,000, each has taxable income of $15,000. (b) If the DNI is $20,000 and they both receive the same $15,000 distributions, Ames still has taxable income of $15,000 but Bates is taxed on only $5,000. The remaining $10,000 she received is tax-free.

Distributions that exceed distributable net income. If the first-tier distributions to all beneficiaries exceed the DNI (figured without any deduction for charitable contributions), the amount to be included in each beneficiaries' gross income is figured as follows [Reg. Sec. 1.662(a)-2]:

$$\frac{\text{First tier distributions to the beneficiary}}{\text{First tier distributions to all beneficiaries}} \times \frac{\text{Distributable net income (without deduction for charitable contributions)}}{} = \frac{\text{Amount beneficiary includes in gross income}}{}$$

> **Example 2:** A trust is required to distribute ½ its current income for the tax year to Albert, the grantor's son; ¼ to Bertha, the grantor's daughter; and ¼ to Community Chest, a charity. The trust income is $10,000. The charitable contribution is $2,500 (¼ × $10,000). The amount required to be distributed to Albert is $5,000 and the amount required to be distributed to Bertha is $2,500. Hence, the amount required to be distributed to all beneficiaries is $7,500, since the charity is not considered a beneficiary [IRC Sec. 663(a)]. Assume the DNI of the trust is $7,000 before the charitable deduction is taken. Albert will include $4,666.67 ($5,000/$7,500 × $7,000) in his gross income. Bertha will include $2,333.33 ($2,500/$7,500 × $7,000) in her gross income.

(b) Allocation by Tiers—Other Distributions. You and each other beneficiary also must include in gross income all other amounts properly paid, credited, or required to be distributed to you (so-called *second tier distributions*) [IRC Sec. 662(a)(2); Reg. Sec. 1.662(a)-3].

> ➤ **OBSERVATION** An amount is not treated as credited to you, unless it is so definitely allocated to you as to be beyond recall. Thus, "credit" for practical purposes is the equivalent of "payment." A mere entry on the books of the fiduciary will not serve, unless it cannot be changed.[1]

Example 3: A trust provides that each year the fiduciary must distribute $3,000 of corpus to Mr. Briant, a beneficiary. Briant will include $3,000 in his gross income to the extent of the trust's DNI.

Distributions exceeding DNI. When the sum of the first- and second-tier distributions exceeds the DNI, you must include in your gross income only a proportionate share of the DNI (less first tier distributions). Your share is determined as follows [IRC Sec. 662(a)(2); Reg. Sec. 1.662(a)-3]:

$$\begin{array}{c} \text{Distributable net} \\ \text{income less first tier} \\ \text{distributions} \end{array} \times \frac{\begin{array}{c}\text{Second tier distributions}\\ \text{to the beneficiary}\end{array}}{\begin{array}{c}\text{Second tier distributions}\\ \text{to all beneficiaries}\end{array}} = \begin{array}{c}\text{The beneficiary's share}\\ \text{of distributable net income}\end{array}$$

> ➤ **OBSERVATION** You and the other beneficiaries are taxed on second-tier distributions only if the first-tier distributions fail to exhaust the DNI of the estate or trust. This is so, even if the second-tier distributions are made from income. To the extent that the DNI, reduced by first-tier distributions, is less than second-tier distributions, the second-tier distributions are prorated.

Example 4: A trust requires the distribution of $8,000 of income to Ms. Allister annually. Any remaining income may be accumulated or distributed to Ms. Barber, Mr. Charles and Mr. Dickinson in the trustee's discretion. He may also invade corpus for the benefit of any of the four beneficiaries. During the year, the trust has $20,000 of income after deducting expenses. Distributable net income is $20,000. The trustee distributes $8,000 of income to Allister. He also distributes $4,000 each to Barber and Charles, $2,000 to Dickinson, and an additional $6,000 to Allister. The amounts taxable to each are determined as follows:

Distributable net income	$20,000
Less: first-tier distribution to Allister	8,000
Available for second-tier distributions	$12,000
Second-tier distributions:	
Allister—$6,000/$16,000 × $12,000	$ 4,500
Barber—$4,000/$16,000 × $12,000	$ 3,000
Charles—$4,000/$16,000 × $12,000	$ 3,000
Dickinson—$2,000/$16,000 × $12,000	$ 1,500

Allister includes $12,500 in income ($8,000 first-tier distribution plus $4,500 second-tier distribution). Barber and Charles each include $3,000 in income. Dickinson includes $1,500.

(c) Allocation by Separate Shares. In determining the amount taxable to you and the other beneficiaries, allocation by tiers may work an injustice when a trust is administered in substantially separate shares. To minimize this, the tax law provides that if a single trust has more than one beneficiary (e.g., you and someone else), and you have substantially separate and independent shares, your shares are treated as separate trusts for the sole purpose of determining the amount taxable to you. This treatment cannot be used to get more than one personal exemption [¶3512], or to split the undistributed income of the trust into several shares which would then be taxed at lower rates [IRC Sec. 663(c); Reg. Sec. 1.663(c)-1].

Example 5: A trust with two beneficiaries has DNI of $20,000. The trustee makes a mandatory distribution of ½ this amount, or $10,000, to beneficiary Ellen. He accumulates the other $10,000 for future distribution to beneficiary Frank. He also makes a discretionary distribution of $10,000 out of corpus to Ellen. Under the tier system, the entire DNI would be allocated to Ellen, and she would be taxed on the $20,000 received. Her tax is being measured, in part, by $10,000 of current income that can only go to Frank.

But suppose that the above trust is divided into two separate trusts, one for each beneficiary. Each trust then will have DNI of $10,000. The trustee of the trust for Ellen distributes all the income of that trust and $10,000 of the corpus to her. The trustee of the trust for Frank makes no distribution. Under these facts, Ellen would be taxed on $10,000. She actually received $20,000, but her taxable share may not exceed the DNI of the trust. The Frank trust makes no distributions, so its income of $10,000 is taxable to the trustee.

> ➤ **OBSERVATION** The "separate share" device achieves the two-trust result in a one-trust case. The two-trust result in the above example seems more equitable, since it exempts the corpus distribution and limits the tax on the beneficiaries to current income.

(d) Special Distributions. The following items are not deductible as distributions by a trust or estate, nor are they included in your gross income for the current tax year [IRC Sec. 663(a)]:

1. Any gift or bequest of a specific sum of money or of specific property which, under the terms of the governing instrument, is paid in a lump sum or in not more than three installments. If, however, the instrument provides the gift or bequest is payable *only* from income (whether income for the payment year or income accumulated from a prior year), it will not be treated as a gift. Instead, it will be deductible by the trust and taxable to the beneficiary [IRC Sec. 663(a)(1); Reg. Sec. 1.663(a)-1]. For property used to satisfy a cash legacy, see ¶3509.

2. Charitable distributions [Reg. Sec. 1.663(a)-2]; but see ¶3513.

3. Any distribution in the current tax year that was deducted by the estate or trust in a preceding tax year [Reg. Sec. 1.663(a)-3].

(e) Throwback Rule. If a complex trust distributes less than its DNI, you may have to report the undistributed excess in a later year, when the trust distributes more than its DNI for that later year [¶3524].

(f) Sixty-Five Day Rule. To avoid accumulations and the throwback rule application, this rule allows amounts paid or credited in the first 65 days of a trust tax year to be attributed to the preceding tax year [IRC Sec. 663(b)(1); Reg. Sec. 1.663(b)-1]. The 65-day rule applies only if the trustee elects it [IRC Sec. 663(b)(2); Reg. Sec. 1.663(b)-1, 2].

Distributions eligible for the election cannot exceed the greater of the trust income for the tax year for which the election is made or DNI for that year. The limitation is further reduced by distributions in that year, except those amounts for which the election was claimed in a preceding tax year [Reg. Sec. 1.663(b)-1].

The election is made on the return for the tax year in which the distribution is considered made. If no return is due, a statement of election must be filed with the IRS where the return would normally be filed. In either case, it must be made within the time for filing the return for that year (including extensions) and cannot be revoked after the return due date [Reg. Sec. 1.663(b)-2].

Example 6: The Fairfield Trust, a calendar year trust, has $1,000 of income and $800 of DNI in 1992. The trust properly paid $550 to Mr. Merkle, a beneficiary, on January 11, 1992, which the trustee elected to treat as paid on December 31, 1991. The trust also properly paid $600 to him on April 25, 1992, and $450 on January 22, 1993. For 1992, the maximum amount that can be elected as properly paid or credited on the last day of 1991 is $400 ($1,000 minus $600). The $550 paid on January 11, 1992, does not reduce the maximum amount since it is treated as having been paid on December 31, 1991.

(g) Charitable Remainder Trusts. Charitable annuity trusts and charitable unitrusts (with a specified fixed amount or a percentage of the trust corpus payable to a non-charitable income beneficiary) are used to make deductible gifts of a remainder interest in property to a charity [¶1918(c)]. Distributions to the income beneficiaries of these trusts, unlike other trust distributions, are separated into four categories for tax purposes [IRC Sec. 664(b); Reg. Sec. 1.664-1(d)]:

- First, all distributions are ordinary income up to the trust's ordinary income for the year and any undistributed ordinary income for prior years.
- Second, distributions are treated as capital gains to the extent of the trust's capital gain for the year and undistributed capital gain for prior years.
- Third, as other income, including tax-exempt income, to the extent of the trust's other income for the year and undistributed other income for prior years.
- Fourth, as nontaxable distributions of trust corpus.

Special rules apply to calculating these items and to the allocation of income and deductions.[2]

(h) Property Distributed In Kind. In general, a property distribution by a trust or estate is taken into account for DNI purposes only to the extent of the lesser of the property's basis or its fair market value at the time of distribution. This means that your basis for the property will be the same as the trust's or estate's basis. However, the trust or estate may elect to treat the property distributed as a sale to you at its fair market value. If this is elected, the basis of the property in your hands is adjusted to reflect the gain or loss recognized by the estate or trust on the distribution [IRC Sec. 643(e)].

¶3507   BENEFICIARY'S SHARE OF EACH ITEM OF DISTRIBUTABLE NET INCOME

If DNI includes items with a special tax status, such as exempt interest, you must determine how much of such items are included in the distribution to you. The reason for this is that such items retain their status in your hands [IRC Sec. 652(b), 662(b); Reg. Sec. 1.652(b)-1, 1.662(b)-1]. Thus, to the extent that a distribution includes exempt interest, you can exclude it from your own return.

(a) Method of Apportionment. To determine how much of each item is included in a given distribution, you apportion the net amount of each item [the gross amount of the item less the deductions allocable to it; see (c) below] among you and the other beneficiaries on a simple proportion basis, unless the governing instrument or state law requires a different allocation [IRC Sec. 652(b), 662(b); Reg. Sec. 1.652(b)-1, 1.662(b)-1]. An allocation in the trust instrument is recognized only to the extent it has an economic effect independent of its income tax consequences. Thus, if the trustee can allocate different classes of income to different beneficiaries, it is not a specific allocation by terms of the trust instrument [Reg. Sec. 1.652(b)-2].

(b) Allocation of Deductions. As noted in (a), in determining the total of a particular item of DNI, the gross amount of each income item must be reduced by the deduction allocable to it. In the absence of specific instructions in the governing instrument, the deductions are allocated as follows [Reg. Sec. 1.652(b)-3]:

1. Any deduction directly allocable to a particular class of gross income is allocated to that class.

2. If the deduction exceeds the income, the excess may be applied against any other income class the trustee chooses, with these limitations: (a) the income chosen must be included in figuring DNI, (b) a proportionate share of nonbusiness deductions must be allocated to nontaxable income and (c) excess deductions attributable to tax-exempt income may not be used as an offset against any other class of income.

3. Deductions that are not directly allocable to any particular class of income (trustee's commissions, safe deposit rentals, state income and personal property taxes, for example) are treated the same as the excess deductions; see (2) above.

Example: A trust has rents, taxable interest, dividends, and tax-exempt interest. Deductions directly attributable to the rents exceed the rental income. The excess may be allocated to the taxable interest and dividends in whatever proportions the trustee elects. However, if the excess deductions are attributable to the tax-exempt interest, they may not be allocated to the other income items.

(c) Charitable Contributions Adjustment. In determining the tax status of currently distributable income items in your hands, DNI is figured without regard to any part of a charitable deduction not attributable to income of the tax year. This prevents a charitable contribution from reducing the amount of current income otherwise taxable to you, except to the extent the contribution is itself paid out of current income [IRC Sec. 662(b); Reg. Sec. 1.662(b)-2].

▶ **OBSERVATION** The charitable contributions deduction does not reduce the amount taxable to you and other beneficiaries who receive currently distributable income, but it can reduce the amount taxable to beneficiaries who receive other amounts [Reg. Sec. 1.662(b)-2].

INCOME—CAPITAL GAINS AND LOSSES

¶3508 **GROSS INCOME**

(a) Estates and Trusts. The gross income of an estate or trust includes: income to be distributed currently to beneficiaries; income accumulated in trust for the benefit of unborn, unascertained or contingent beneficiaries; income accumulated or held for future distribution; income collected by the guardian of an infant; income received by an estate during its administration or settlement; and income to be distributed or accumulated in the fiduciary's discretion [IRC Sec. 641; Reg. Sec. 1.641(a)-1, 1.641(a)-2].

For an estate, title to personal property usually passes to the executor or administrator, but title to real property often passes to the heirs or persons named in a will at the decedent's death. Therefore, in most cases, the person who gets the real property reports the income produced by the property (such as rents), or the gain or loss from its sale [¶3509]. The only complication is the proper treatment of income accrued to a decedent at the time of his death.

(b) Decedents. When a person dies, the executor or administrator may be required to file income tax returns for two separate and distinct taxable entities: (1) the deceased person, for the period before his death; and (2) the deceased person's estate.

Final return for decedent. If the deceased person were on the cash basis, the final return filed will include only income he actually or constructively received while he was alive. A bonus received after a cash basis taxpayer's death will not be reported on his final return, unless it was constructively received during his life.[1] If he used the accrual method of accounting, his final return will include only income that accrued before his death. Income that accrues only because of his death is not included in his final return [IRC Sec. 451(b); Reg. Sec. 1.451-1(b)]. Deductions get similar treatment [¶3511].

Income in respect of a decedent. Amounts that are excluded from the deceased person's final return under the above rule are taxed to the persons who receive them as a result of the decedent's death. This would include the deceased person's estate, heirs, devisees and legatees. The amounts are treated as income of the same nature and to the same extent as they would have if the deceased person had remained alive and received them [IRC Sec. 691(a)]. Items apt to be included as income in respect of a decedent are promissory notes, deferred compensation distributions, dividends payable after death to holders of stock of record as of a date prior to death, installment obligations and commissions earned before death but not paid until later. Persons who transfer the right to receive such amounts must include in income either what they get for the right, or its fair market value, whichever is greater.

> **Example:** Decedent kept his books on the cash basis. Shortly before his death in November, he was voted a salary payment of $10,000, to be paid in five equal annual installments beginning the following January. He could not draw any of these payments before the actual payment date. His estate collected two installments, and distributed the right to the remaining three installments to the residuary legatee. The $4,000 must be included in the gross income of the estate, and the residuary legatee must include $6,000 in his income when he receives it. However, if the estate had sold the right to the three remaining installments to a person not entitled to them as a legatee, devisee or heir, or by reason of the death of the decedent, the estate would be required to include in its income the amount received or the fair market value of the right, whichever was greater.

Installment obligations. A deceased person's uncollected installment obligations, transmitted at his death directly to his estate or beneficiaries, are treated as income in respect of a decedent. The recipient reports the installment gain the same way the deceased person would have reported it (¶2916(a)) [IRC Sec. 691(a)(4); Reg. Sec. 1.691(a)-5]. Any previously unreported gain from an installment sale is recognized by a deceased seller's estate if the obligation (1) passes by bequest, devise or inheritance to the obligor, or (2) is cancelled by the executor [IRC Sec. 691(a)(5)]. Income in respect of a deceased partner is discussed in ¶3429.

Deductions and credits accruing after death. When not deductible on the deceased person's return, payments by an estate of the decedent's business and nonbusiness expenses, interest and taxes or foreign taxes are allowed to the estate as a deduction or credit. If the estate is not liable, the deduction or credit is allowed to the beneficiary who receives an interest in property subject to the liability and who pays off the liability [IRC Sec. 691(b)(1); Reg. Sec. 1.691(b)-1(a)].

A deduction for depletion also can be taken, but it is taken by the person who gets the income to which the depletion relates, whether or not he gets the property from which the income is derived [IRC Sec. 691(b)(2); Reg. Sec. 1.691(b)-1(b)].

Deduction for estate tax. Income in respect of a decedent is included in the gross estate for estate tax purposes, so it is subject to a double tax. As a relief measure, the person who reports the income can deduct the estate tax attributable to the right he received. The income recipient can deduct a proportionate share of the federal estate tax that is attributable to the income in respect of a decedent.

In figuring the net long-term capital gains or the net capital loss, the amount of gain treated as income in respect of a decedent is reduced, but not below zero, by the amount of any deductible estate taxes attributable to a gain treated as income in respect of a decedent [IRC Sec. 691(c)(4)].

Lump-sum distributions under qualified plan. The amount of death benefits distributed to a beneficiary who receives a lump-sum under a qualified plan and who elects special income averaging [¶1320], is reduced by the amount of the death tax deduction attributable to the distribution [IRC Sec. 691(c)(5)].

Stock option. Any estate tax resulting from including an employee stock option in a decedent's estate is deductible in the year the estate or beneficiary has income resulting from disposition of stock acquired under the option (¶1208) [IRC Sec. 421(c)(2)].

The surviving annuitant of a joint and survivor annuity gets a deduction for the proportionate estate tax each year during his life expectancy [IRC Sec. 691(d); Reg. Sec. 1.691(d)-1].

¶3509   CAPITAL GAINS AND LOSSES

The gain on the sale or exchange of a capital asset by an estate or trust must be included in its gross income. The gain is either a short-term or long-term capital gain, and the rules prescribed for individuals apply [¶1801 et seq.]. However, a special rule accords long-term treatment to the trust or estate even if it sells the property immediately after the deceased person's death (¶1803(b)) [IRC Sec. 1223(11)]. Any part of the gain that is properly paid, credited or required to be distributed during the year to the beneficiary is deductible by the fiduciary. It is taxable to the beneficiary (to the extent of the DNI), even if allocated to corpus.

(a) Capital Loss. A capital loss usually is deductible only by the estate or trust, and not by the beneficiary.[1] The loss is either a short-term or long-term capital loss, and the rules for individuals apply. However, a special rule requires trusts and estates to treat losses as long-term even if the assets were sold soon after the deceased person's death [¶1803(b)]. In most states, title to real property passes directly from the deceased person to the heirs (not to the executor). In such states, gain or loss on the sale of the property is reported directly by the heir. For treatment of an unused capital loss in the trust's or estate's year of termination, see ¶3511.

(b) Capital Gains. The maximum tax rate on an estate's or trust's net long-term capital gain is 28%. See ¶1809.

(c) Asset Distributions in Lieu of Cash. When a fiduciary pays a *cash* legacy by transferring an asset to the legatee, it is treated as if a sale or exchange took place between them. Gain or loss to the fiduciary is equal to the difference between the property's fair market value at its transfer and its adjusted basis in the fiduciary's hands.[2]

> **Example:** The fiduciary must pay $50,000 to the testator's child when the child becomes 25. The fiduciary is authorized to pay this amount in either cash or property worth $50,000. He elects to transfer securities worth $50,000 to satisfy the legacy. Assuming the basis of the securities in the fiduciary's hands was $40,000, a capital gain of $10,000 is recognized. If the property transferred was not a capital asset, the $10,000 gain would be taxable as ordinary income.

The legatee is treated as the property's buyer. He or she has a basis equal to the fair market value of the property at the time of the distribution.[3]

If a trustee distributes a capital asset with the same value as a required distribution of income, it is also treated as a sale or exchange. The value is deductible by the trustee and taxable to the beneficiary to the extent of the trust's DNI.[4]

Special rules apply when the property involved is farm realty or closely-held business realty [IRC Sec. 1040].

(d) Distributable Net Income. In determining DNI [¶3504], the fiduciary excludes capital gains allocated to corpus and not paid or credited to any beneficiary or used for charitable purposes. Capital gains allocated to income are included in DNI. Capital losses are excluded, except to the extent they enter into the determination of any capital gains that are paid, credited or required to be distributed to any beneficiary during the tax year [IRC Sec. 643(a)(3); Reg. Sec. 1.643(a)-3]. Special rules apply to foreign trusts [IRC Sec. 643(a)(6)].

(e) Deduction for State Tax. A simple trust can deduct state income tax on capital gain retained by it in arriving at its taxable income and DNI.[5]

¶3510   BASIS OF PROPERTY TO ESTATE OR TRUST

(a) Transfer in Trust. If a transfer to your trust during your life is *for a valuable consideration,* the basis of the property to your trust is its basis in your hands, increased by the gain or decreased by the loss recognized by you on the transfer. If the transfer is by *gift,* the basis for gain or loss is the same as for other gifts (¶1610) [IRC Sec. 1015(a), (b); Reg. Sec. 1.1015-1,-2].

> **Example:** In 1978, Mr. Brown bought certain bonds for $10,000. In 1992, in consideration of $15,000, he transferred the bonds in trust. Brown's gain is $5,000, and the basis of the bonds to the trust is $15,000 (the basis of the bonds in the hands of Brown ($10,000) plus the gain recognized to Brown on the transfer ($5,000)).

> **NOTE:** The basis of property acquired by gift or transfer in trust before 1921 is its fair market value on the date of gift or transfer [IRC Sec. 1015(c); Reg. Sec. 1.1015-3].

(b) Property Acquired From Decedent. Generally, the basis of property acquired from a decedent is its fair market value or its special use value on the date of death. If the executor elects to use the alternate valuation date, the basis of the property is its value on that date [IRC Sec. 1014(a)]. See also ¶1612.

DEDUCTIONS AND CREDITS

¶3511   DEDUCTIONS IN GENERAL

Estates and trusts ordinarily get the same deductions as individuals [Reg. Sec. 1.641(b)-1]. Exceptions for contributions, the special rule for depreciation and disallowance of losses are explained below. Unlike individual taxpayers, estates or trusts get no standard deduction, but they do get a special deduction for distributions to beneficiaries [¶3517].

Medical and funeral expenses. A deceased person's medical and dental expenses paid by the estate are not deductible from the estate's taxable income [Reg. Sec. 1.642(g)-2]. But these expenses may be deducted on the deceased person's final return, if they were not deducted in figuring the taxable estate for estate tax purposes. Funeral expenses are not deductible from the estate's taxable income in any case.[1]

Decedents. The deductions allowed to deceased persons depend on their accounting method. If they reported on the cash basis, the deductions would be those actually paid. If they used the accrual basis, deduction is allowed for amounts that accrue up to the date of death. Deductions cannot be taken, however, for amounts that accrued only because of their death [IRC Sec. 461(b); Reg. Sec. 1.461-1(b)]. As to deductions that accrue after their death, see ¶3508(b).

Losses. If a trust sustains a loss, the loss usually is not deductible by a beneficiary. The trust and the beneficiary are separate taxable entities, and one taxpayer cannot deduct another's losses.[2] But when an estate or trust terminates, any unused capital loss, net operating loss carryovers or deductions (except those for personal exemptions or charity) in excess of gross income for the last tax year can be deducted by the beneficiaries who get the estate or trust property. This is limited to (a) the remaindermen of a trust, (b) the heirs and next of kin of a person who dies without a will and (c) the residuary legatees (including a residuary trust) of a person leaving a will. Those entitled to a dollar legacy qualify only to the extent the deductions reduced their share. An income beneficiary does not qualify [IRC Sec. 642(h); Reg. Sec. 1.642(h)-1].

¶3512   DEDUCTION FOR PERSONAL EXEMPTION

The following personal exemption-type deductions are allowed [IRC Sec. 642(b); Reg. Sec. 1.642(b)-1]:

- An estate gets a deduction of $600.
- If a trust must distribute all income currently, it gets a deduction of $300, even though it is not a "simple" trust that year [¶3505]. A trust for the payment of an annuity also gets a deduction of $300 in any tax year the annuity equals or exceeds current income.
- All other trusts get a deduction of $100.

No exemption deduction is allowed on an estate's final return, since all income must be distributed to beneficiaries and entered as such without reduction for the exemption.

The full deduction is allowed on a deceased person's final return for personal exemptions *for which he or she qualified* [¶1111; 1112; 1115-1120]. No proration is required [¶2819].

¶3513   CHARITABLE CONTRIBUTIONS

An estate or a complex trust gets a deduction for gross income which, under the terms of the will or trust deed, is *paid* for charitable purposes[1] [IRC Sec. 642(c)]. Unlike the charitable deduction allowed individuals, no limitation is placed on the amount that can be deducted by a trust or estate. To enable fiduciaries to act after they know the exact income for the year, they can elect to treat a current contribution as paid during the preceding tax year [IRC Sec. 642(c)(1): Reg. Sec. 1.642(c)-1]. The election must be made not later than the due date (including extensions) of the income tax return for the year after the year for which the election is made. [Temp. Reg. Sec. 13.0(b)(2)].

> NOTE: Estates and certain inter vivos and testamentary trusts in existence on October 9, 1969, get a deduction from gross income for amounts which, under the terms of the will or trust, are *permanently set aside* for charitable purposes [IRC Sec. 642(c)(2)]. Special rules also apply to pooled income funds [IRC Sec. 642(c)(4)].

Contributions from gross income. Generally, only contributions of items included in gross income are deductible; tax-exempt income does not qualify.[2] Thus, no deduction will be allowed for a contribution out of the estate or trust corpus. However, a contribution from *income* allocable to corpus, such as capital gains, will qualify for the deduction, since such income is included in the gross income of the estate or trust. But no deduction is allowed to a trust for contributions allocable to its unrelated business income for the tax year [¶3352].

> **Example 1:** A trustee, under the terms of a will, is directed to pay to a charity half of the addition to corpus each year for the duration of the trust. The only addition to the corpus for the tax year consisted of $12,000 of capital gains, and the trustee distributed $6,000 to the charity. Capital gains allocated to corpus under the terms of the will are included in trust gross income, so a charitable contribution deduction will be allowed.

Adjustment for exempt income. When a trust or estate has both taxable and tax-exempt income, the charitable deduction is allowed only for contributions considered as coming from gross income. Unless the governing instrument makes a different allocation, the contribution that is considered as coming from gross income bears the same proportion to the total contribution as the total gross income bears to the total income (including tax-exempt items) [Reg. Sec. 1.642(c)-3(b)].

> ➤ **OBSERVATION** To enable the estate or trust to get the full benefit of the charitable deduction, the estate's or trust's governing instrument should specifically provide that contributions be payable out of ordinary taxable income, not from tax-exempt income or long-term capital gains.

> **Example 2:** A trust had $8,000 of income—consisting of $5,000 rent and $3,000 tax-exempt interest on municipal bonds. The trustee was directed to pay 25% of the income to charity. He made a charitable contribution of $2,000 (25% of $8,000). If the trust instrument is silent on the income source of the contribution, the amount considered as coming from the gross income of the trust is $1,250 ($5,000 / $8,000 x $2,000). Hence, the trust can deduct $1,250.

If the trustee had been directed to pay $2,000 of the rental income to charity, he could have deducted that amount.

¶3514　　　DEPRECIATION OR DEPLETION

The depreciation deduction allowed to a life tenant, income beneficiary of a trust, or distributee of an estate is a deduction *for* adjusted gross income. Who gets the deduction is discussed in the following paragraphs; similar rules apply to depletion.

> NOTE: Estates and trusts cannot elect the expensing deduction (¶2113) [IRC Sec. 179(d)(4)].

(a) Trusts. The deduction for depreciation of trust property is to be divided between the income beneficiaries and the trustee as directed in the trust instrument. If the trust instrument makes no allocation, the deduction is apportioned on the basis of the trust income (determined under the trust instrument and state law) allocable to each [IRC Sec. 167(d)].

The regulations limit the allocation in the trust instrument. They provide that the share of the deduction allocated to either the trustee or a beneficiary ordinarily cannot be more than his pro rata share of the trust income. However, if the trust instrument or state law requires or allows the trustee to maintain a reserve for depreciation, the deduction is first allocated to the trustee for income set aside for the reserve. Any part of the deduction not used up is then divided between the beneficiaries and the trustee on the basis of the trust income (in excess of the amount set aside as a reserve) allocable to each [Reg. Sec. 1.167(h)-1(b), 1.642(e)-1].

> **Example:** Mr. Hyde establishes a trust for the benefit of his son, John, and his daughter, Mary. The trust property includes an apartment house on which a depreciation allowance could be claimed. Under the terms of the trust instrument, the income of the trust is to be distributed to John and Mary in equal shares. The trust instrument also authorizes the trustee, in his discretion, to set aside income for a depreciation reserve. During the year, the trustee sets aside $2,000 income as a reserve. Depreciation on the trust property amounts to $2,500. The trustee gets a depreciation deduction of $2,000. John and Mary each get a deduction of $250.

> **NOTE:** If the income beneficiary is entitled to the entire income, and the instrument is silent on depreciation, the beneficiary gets the deduction. Even if the trust has no income during the year, the income beneficiary is still entitled to the deduction.[1]

(b) Estates. For an estate, the depreciation deduction is divided between the estate and the heirs, legatees and devisees on the basis of the income allocable to each [IRC Sec. 167(d); Reg. Sec. 1.167(h)-1(c)].

> ➤ **OBSERVATION** If an estate or trust shares in depreciation or depletion of another trust or a partnership (or takes the deduction into account separately), the estate or trust divides the deduction among its own distributees on the same basis as it allocates its income.[2]

¶3515   NET OPERATING LOSS DEDUCTION

Generally, estates and trusts are entitled to the net operating loss deduction. This may reduce DNI for the year to which the operating loss is carried back, so that beneficiaries may recompute their shares of the estate or trust income for the prior year.[1] However, in computing the net operating loss, the estate or trust cannot take deductions for charitable contributions or distributions to beneficiaries. A trust also must exclude income and deductions attributable to the grantor [IRC Sec. 642(d); Reg. Sec. 1.642(d)-1]. If a trust's income is allocable entirely among income beneficiaries, and the governing instrument makes no provision for depreciation, the trustee cannot take a depreciation deduction in computing the net operating loss.[2]

On termination of an estate or trust, any unused net operating loss carryovers are deductible by the beneficiaries succeeding to the estate or trust property [IRC Sec. 642(h); Reg. Sec. 1.642(h)-1].

The net operating loss deduction of a common trust fund [¶3525] is allowed to the participants in the fund and not to the trust [IRC Sec. 584(g); Reg. Sec. 1.584-6].

¶3516   EXPENSES

An estate or trust can deduct ordinary and necessary expenses it pays or incurs, if the expenses are: (1) trade or business expenses; (2) expenses for the production or collection of income or for managing, conserving or maintaining property held for the production of income; (3) reasonable administration expenses, including fiduciaries' fees and litigation expenses in connection with the duties of administration (except expenses allocable to the production or collection of tax-exempt income[1]); or (4) expenses for the determination, collection or refund of any tax [IRC Sec. 162, 212; Reg. Sec. 1.212-1]. Deductible expenses chargeable only to trust corpus reduce DNI and thus the amount taxable to the beneficiary. However, these expenses do not reduce the amount of income available for the income beneficiary.[2] Fiduciaries must file Forms 1096 and 1099 if they make certain payments of $600 or more related to a trade or business [¶3661].

A fiduciary can deduct counsel fees and other expenses of unsuccessfully contesting an income tax deficiency, or similar expenses relating to the final distribution from an expired trust.[3] Interest on overdue estate tax[4] or on legacies[5] is also deductible. But there is no deduction for interest paid by an estate on deficiencies on state inheritance taxes which are not the estate's obligation under state law.[6]

NOTE: Interest paid by a trust on an unpaid balance of estate tax liability that is deferred can qualify as an administrative expense deductible by the trust.[7]

Deduction limits. Expenses that are unique to trusts are completely deductible as a deduction *for* adjusted gross income [IRC Sec. 67(e)]. However, the Tax Court has said that a trust's expenses for hiring an investment adviser must be deducted as a miscellaneous itemized expense (deductible only to the extent it and other miscellaneous expenses exceed 2% of the trust's adjusted gross income)—even though the expense would not have been incurred had there not been a trust. Reason: Fees for investment advice are not unique to trusts; they are often incurred by individuals as well.[8]

Waiver of estate tax deduction. Casualty and theft losses and certain administrative and other expenses can be deducted from the deceased person's gross estate. These amounts cannot be deducted from the estate's income tax (or used as an offset against the sales price of property for determining gain or loss) *unless* a waiver of the estate tax deduction is filed. A portion of expenses and losses can be allocated to the estate income and a waiver filed for only that part. This rule does not bar deductions related to income in respect of a decedent or for claims against the estate, such as payments under a divorce decree[9] [IRC Sec. 642(g)].

¶3517   DEDUCTION FOR DISTRIBUTIONS TO BENEFICIARIES

It is current policy to tax the income of estates and trusts only once—either to the fiduciary, or to the beneficiary, or, in part, to each. This is done by treating the estate or trust as a taxable entity, and by giving it a special deduction for amounts paid or payable to the beneficiary.

(a) Simple Trusts. A simple trust gets a deduction for trust income required to be distributed currently, whether or not distributed [IRC Sec. 651; Reg. Sec. 1.651(a)-2, 1.651(b)-1]. For asset distributions in lieu of cash, see ¶3509(c).

Example 1: The trust instrument requires all the income to be distributed currently. The trust has $10,000 income for 1991, of which $2,500 is collected in December. The trustee makes the usual quarterly payment of $2,500 to its sole beneficiary in January, 1992. The trust can deduct $10,000 for 1991.

The deduction is limited to DNI [¶3504]. For this purpose, DNI does not include income items (adjusted for related deductions) not included in gross income [IRC Sec. 651; Reg. Sec. 1.651(b)-1].

Example 2: Distributable net income is $99,000. This includes tax-exempt interest totaling $9,000. The deduction for distributions to beneficiaries cannot be more than $90,000.

(b) Estates and Complex Trusts. An estate or complex trust gets a deduction for amounts paid credited or required to be distributed to the beneficiaries. The deduction consists of the sum of (1) income required to be distributed currently (including an amount payable out of income or corpus to the extent that it is paid out of income) and (2) any other amounts paid, credited or required to be distributed for the tax year. However, the deduction cannot exceed DNI, excluding items not included in the gross income of the estate or trust [IRC Sec. 661(a), (c); Reg. Sec. 1.661(a)-2, 1.661(c)-1]. For asset distributions in lieu of cash, see ¶3509(c).

The amount deductible is treated as consisting of the same proportion of each class of items entering into the computation of DNI as the total of each class bears to the total DNI, unless the governing instruments or state law allocates different classes of income to different beneficiaries [IRC Sec. 661(b); Reg. Sec. 1.661(b)-1].

> **Example 3:** A trust has gross income of $100,000 ($50,000 taxable income and $50,000 tax-exempt income). Its distributable net income is $98,000. It has deductions of $2,000, half of which are attributable to tax-exempt income. The deduction to the trust is limited to $49,000, since the rest of the DNI ($49,000) is deemed to be tax-exempt income.

The DNI, for purposes of computing the distributions deductions, does not include the deduction for amounts paid or permanently set aside for charity (¶3513) [IRC Sec. 661(a)].

¶3518 DEDUCTIONS IN TRANSACTIONS BETWEEN RELATED PARTIES

Related parties must match their deductions and income in the same year. Thus, an accrual-basis taxpayer can deduct interest, expenses, etc., paid to a related cash-basis taxpayer only when the cash-basis recipient must include a like amount in income [IRC Sec. 267]. "Related parties" include, among others: (1) members of a family, (2) a grantor and his trust fiduciary, (3) fiduciaries of two trusts having the same grantor, (4) a fiduciary and a beneficiary of his trust, (5) a fiduciary and a beneficiary of another trust with the same grantor and (6) a fiduciary and a corporation over 50% of whose stock is owned, directly or indirectly, by or for the trust or the grantor. See also ¶2860 for other details.

¶3519   CREDITS AGAINST TAX

An estate or trust gets a credit against tax for the following:
- *Foreign taxes* not allocable to the beneficiaries [IRC Sec. 642(a)].
- *Targeted jobs credit* allocated to the estate or trust (¶2408) [IRC Sec. 52(d)].

RATES, RETURNS, AND PAYMENT FOR DECEDENTS, ESTATES AND TRUSTS

¶3520   RATES AND RETURNS

Trusts and estates of decedents are separate entities for which returns must be filed. Returns are generally filed by fiduciaries for estates or trusts, and for decedents.

(a) Decedents. If a decedent would have been required to file a return, then the executor, administrator, legal representative, or survivor must file a final return.[1] The return is made on Form 1040, 1040EZ or 1040A. An executor or administrator may disaffirm a joint return filed by the surviving spouse.

The return covers the period from the beginning of the decedents' tax year up to and including their date of death (¶2819(a)) [IRC Sec. 443; Reg. Sec. 1.443-1]. For rates, see ¶1123; 1124.

(b) Estates. A deceased person's estate income tax return is filed on Form 1041. The fiduciary must file Form 1041 if (a) the estate's gross income is $600 or over or (b) any beneficiary is a nonresident alien [IRC Sec. 6012(a); Reg. Sec. 1.6012-3(a)]. The fiduciary must file a separate Schedule K-1 (or an appropriate substitute) for each beneficiary,[2] showing that beneficiary's share of income, deductions and credits. The fiduciary must also send a copy of Schedule K-1 to each beneficiary. An ancillary executor or administrator must file an information return on Form 1041 for the part of the estate he or she controls [Reg. Sec. 1.6012-3(a)(3)]. Any estate or trust fiduciary must furnish return information to the beneficiaries [IRC Sec. 6034A]. Penalties are provided for failure to comply.

In his first return, the fiduciary chooses the accounting period for the estate. This may be either a calendar year or *any* fiscal year he selects. Estate gross income is figured from the day following the deceased person's death [Reg. Sec. 1.443-1]. Thus, a return may have to be filed for the short period from that date to the start of the estate's regular tax year.

> ▶ **OBSERVATION** Although a recent law drastically restricts a *trust's* ability to defer income taxation through the selection of trusts' tax years, the present treatment of an *estate's* tax year is not affected by this law change [3522].

Rates. The following rate schedule applies to both estates and trusts [IRC Sec. 1(e), (f)]:

1992 Tax Rate Schedule for Estates and Trusts

Taxable Income	Tax
Not over $3,600	15% of taxable income
Over $3,600 but not over $10,900	$540 plus 28% of the excess over $3,600
Over $10,900	$2,584 plus 31% of the excess over $10,900

NOTE: The taxable income amounts at which the rates start are adjusted for inflation annually.

Example 1: The Smith estate has income of $12,000. Deductions come to $2,000 plus a $600 exemption. The estate's taxable income is $9,400. The tax is $2,164 [$540 + $1,624 (28% of $5,800)].

Example 2: The Grant Family trust has income of $30,000 and deductions (not including personal exemption) of $4,000. The trust is not required to, and does not pay out, its current income. So its taxable income is $25,900 ($30,000 minus $4,000 deductions and $100 exemption). The tax on the trust is $7,234 [$2,584 + $4,650, or 31% of $15,000 ($25,900 minus $10,900)].)

(c) Trusts. A trust's income tax return is filed on Form 1041. The trustee must file Form 1041 if: (a) the trust has any taxable income for the tax year, or (b) its gross income is $600 or over, or (c) any beneficiary is a nonresident alien [IRC Sec. 6012; Reg. Sec. 1.6012-3(a)]. The trustee must also file Form 1041-A if the trust claims charitable or other deductions for amounts paid or permanently set aside for a charity [IRC Sec. 6034(a); Reg. Sec. 1.6034-1(a)]. But this return is not required if the trust must distribute all of its net income to its beneficiaries [IRC Sec. 6034(b); Reg. Sec. 1.6034-1(b)]. The trustee must file a Schedule K-1 for each beneficiary. Any estate or trust fiduciary must furnish return information to the beneficiaries [IRC Sec. 6034A]. Noncompliance may be subject to $50 penalty.

Will or trust deed and fiduciary's statement. If requested by the IRS, the fiduciary must file a copy of the will or the trust instrument, together with his or her statement as to which provisions of the will or trust instrument determine the amount taxable to each taxpayer involved [Reg. Sec. 1.6012-3(a)(2)].

Rates. See (b) above.

(d) Alternative Minimum Tax. Estates and trusts must pay the alternative minimum tax to the extent it exceeds the regular tax liability [¶2600]. The tax is computed under the same rules that apply to married persons filing separately. There is an exemption amount subject to phase-out at 25 cents on the dollar for alternative minimum taxable income over $75,000, and a flat 24% rate on the excess. In addition to the deductions applicable to individuals, trusts and estates are allowed additional deductions for charitable gifts, distributions and administrative costs [IRC Sec. 55]. Items of tax preference are allocated between the trust or estate and the beneficiaries [Temp. Reg. Sec. 1.58-3T].

¶3521   PAYMENT BY ESTATES AND TRUSTS

Trusts and estates must pay estimated tax in the same manner as individuals [¶2417]. However, an estate or a grantor trust into which the residue of the grantor's estate will pass by his or her will need not pay estimated tax in the first two years after the decedent's death [IRC Sec. 6654(l)].

See also ¶3652 for payment of income tax by estates and trusts.

¶3522   TAX YEARS OF ESTATES AND TRUSTS

Estates may use a fiscal or calendar tax year; trusts must use a calendar tax year. However, tax-exempt and charitable trusts may use a fiscal year [IRC Sec. 645].

SPECIAL PROBLEMS

¶3523   TRUST INCOME TAXABLE TO GRANTOR OR OTHERS

Under certain conditions, the income of a trust is not taxed to the trust or beneficiaries. It may be taxed instead to the grantor or other persons who have substantial dominion or control over the trust property or income. For example, the grantor or others are each taxed as owners under the following circumstances:

- The grantor or spouse has a reversionary interest exceeding 5% of the value of the transferred property [IRC Sec. 673].
- The grantor or another nonadverse party has power over beneficial interests of the trust [IRC Sec. 674], can revoke the trust or return the corpus to the grantor [IRC Sec. 676] or distribute the income to or for the benefit of the grantor or grantor's spouse [IRC Sec. 677].
- Administrative powers exist that would be beneficial to the grantor [IRC Sec. 675].

When the grantor is taxed on the income of the trust, he is allowed the deductions and credits related to the income [IRC Sec. 671; Reg. Sec. 1.671-3]. The tax year and method of accounting used by the trust are disregarded. The gross income from the trust properties is determined by the grantor as if the trust had not been created.[1]

A special rule applies when a grantor places property with unrealized appreciation in trust, to shift the paying of tax to the trust at its lower progressive rates[(g) below].

Reporting requirements. Generally, the trustee must file a return on Form 1041. Any income, deductions and credits attributable to the grantor are omitted from the return, itself, and reported on a separate statement attached to it [Reg. Sec. 1.671-4(a)]. However, if the grantor is also the trustee (or co-trustee) of a trust created in tax years beginning after 1980, and if all trust assets are treated as owned by the grantor for the tax year, then Form 1041 should not be filed. Instead, all items of income, deduction and credit are reported on the grantor's Form 1040. This rule also applies to a husband and wife who file jointly if: (1) they are the sole grantors, (2) one or both are trustees or co-trustees and (3) one or both are treated as the owner of the trust assets [Reg. Sec. 1.671-4(b)].

(a) Reversionary Interest. For transfers in trust made after March 1, 1986, a trust is treated as a grantor trust when the grantor has a reversionary interest whose value at the time of the transfer of the property into the trust amounts to more than 5% of the value of the transferred property [IRC Sec. 673(a)].

> **NOTE:** A so-called "ten-year rule" applies to transfers made before March 2, 1986. If the reversionary interest in such a transfer is to take effect more than ten years after the last transfer to the trust, the grantor is not taxed on the trust income.

If the grantor's spouse retains a reversionary interest, the grantor is deemed to retain a reversionary interest as well. This rule applies if the spouse is living with the grantor at the time the interest is created. It also holds true if the individual became the grantor's spouse after the interest was created—but only for the period after the individual became a spouse. (The grantor is treated as holding any power or interest held by the grantor's spouse not only for reversionary interests but generally for all the interests retained by a grantor that would make the grantor subject to tax [IRC Sec. 672(e)].)

The possibility that an interest may return to the grantor or his spouse spouse solely by inheritance under the intestacy laws is, however, not considered a reversionary interest and the grantor-trust rules will not apply.

Neither is it deemed a reversionary interest if all that the grantor or spouse retains is an interest that can become effective only after the death, before the age of 21, of a minor beneficiary who is a lineal descendant of the grantor and holds all of the present interest of any portion of the trust.

(b) Power to Control Beneficial Enjoyment. The grantor is taxable on the trust income if he or a nonadverse party, or both, have the power to dispose of the corpus or income without the consent of any adverse party [IRC Sec. 674; Reg. Sec. 1.674(a)-1]. An adverse party is any person having a substantial beneficial interest in the trust that would be adversely affected by the exercise or nonexercise of the power (such as a general power of appointment over the trust property) he or she possesses respecting the trust. A nonadverse party is any other person [IRC Sec. 672(a), (b); Reg. Sec. 1.672(a)-1].

(c) Administrative Powers. The grantor is taxable on the trust income when administrative control of the trust may be exercised primarily for his or her benefit instead of the benefit of the beneficiaries [IRC Sec. 675; Reg. Sec. 1.675-1]. The following situations illustrate this type of administrative control:

- Power in the grantor or a nonadverse party, or both, without the approval of any adverse party, to deal with the trust property or income for less than an adequate consideration.
- Power in the grantor or a nonadverse party, or both, that enables the grantor (or grantor's spouse) to borrow the corpus or income without adequate interest or security, except when a trustee (other than the grantor) is authorized to make loans to *any* persons without regard to interest or security.
- When the grantor has borrowed the corpus or income and has not repaid the loan before the start of the tax year, unless the loan was made for adequate interest and security by a trustee (other than the grantor or a trustee subservient to the grantor).
- General powers of administration exercisable by anyone in a nonfiduciary capacity so as to benefit the grantor individually rather than the beneficiaries.

(d) Power to Revoke. The grantor generally is taxed on the income of a trust if he reserves the power to revoke the trust. However, he is not taxed if he can revoke it only with the consent of an adverse party. For transfers in trust before March 2, 1986, if the grantor cannot exercise the power to revoke until ten years after creating the trust, he is not taxed on the income during that time. He will be taxed after that time, unless he gives up the power [IRC Sec. 676; Reg. Sec. 1.676(a)-1, 1.676(b)-1]. For transfers after March 1, 1986, the "ten-year rule" is replaced by the 5% rule [(a) above].

(e) Income for Benefit of Grantor, Spouse or Dependent. The grantor is taxable on the income of a trust when, without the consent of an adverse party, the income *is,* or *may be,* paid or accumulated for the grantor's benefit, or used to pay your life insurance premiums (except on policies irrevocably payable to charity). In addition, the grantor is taxable on the income from property transferred in trust (after October 1, 1969) for the benefit of his spouse. In transfers for the benefit of himself or his spouse, the grantor is treated as the owner of the property transferred [Reg. Sec. 1.677(a)-1]. Trust income used to support a child or other beneficiary whom the grantor is legally obligated to support generally is taxable to the grantor (for example, when it is used to pay his son's college tuition[2]) [IRC Sec. 677; Reg. Sec. 1.677(a)-1, 1.677(b)-1]. For an alimony or support trust, the wife is taxed on the payments (including any tax preference items) except to the extent the payments are for the support of minor children [IRC Sec. 682; Reg. Sec. 1.682(a)-1, 1.682(b)-1, 1.682(c)-1]. Some courts hold that tax-exempt income received by an alimony trust is not taxed when it is distributed to the wife,[3] but the IRS disagrees.[4]

(f) Income Taxable to Others. A person other than the grantor may be taxed on the trust income if he or she has a power to acquire the corpus or income of the trust. Thus, a person who has exclusive power to vest the corpus or income of a trust in himself, or who has released such power but retained controls similar to those outlined in (a) to (e) above, is taxed on the trust income [IRC Sec. 678; Reg. Sec. 1.678(a)-1], subject to these modifications:

1. If the grantor of the trust, or the transferor in (h), below, is taxed as the owner, the other person will not be taxed under the above rule;

2. If the other person can merely use trust income to support a dependent, he or she will be taxed only to the extent it is so used [Reg. Sec. 1.678(c)-1];

3. If the other person renounces the power within a reasonable time after learning of it, he or she will not be taxed on the trust income [Reg. Sec. 1.678(d)-1].

(g) Taxing Transfer of Appreciated Property to Trust. If property with unrealized appreciation is transferred to a trust, and the trust sells it within two years of the transfer, the trust is taxed, at the grantor's tax rates, on the "includable gain" (see below). The tax is equal to the additional tax the transferor would have paid (including the alternative minimum tax) had the gain been included in his or her income for the tax year in which the sale occurred. For a short sale, the two-year period is extended to the closing date [¶1805]. Whether or not the property is a capital asset is determined by its character in the transferor's hands. The tax is figured without regard to (a) any loss or deduction which is carried back or forward to another tax year of the transferor or (b) any net operating loss carrybacks to the transferor's tax year used to figure the applicable tax rate [IRC Sec. 644].

"Includable gain" is the lesser of (1) the gain recognized (rather than just realized) by the trust on the sale or exchange or (2) the excess of the property's fair market value at the time of the initial transfer over the trust's basis in the property immediately after the transfer [IRC Sec. 644(b)]. The trust's basis includes any increase in basis for gift tax paid. Any additional gain on the property occurring after the transfer is subject to the normal rules for gains realized by the trust. The "includable gain" is excluded from the trust's taxable income and DNI [¶3504].

When to report "includable gain." In general, the additional tax is reported by the trust for its tax year that begins with or within the tax year of the transferor in which the sale or exchange occurred [IRC Sec. 644(a)(3)].

Installment sale. If the trust reports income under the installment method, each installment is taxed at the grantor's rate if the installment sale occurred within two years of the transfer to the trust. This is so even if the installments are paid over a period of more than two years [IRC Sec. 644(f)].

Exceptions. The above rules do not apply to property acquired by a trust from a decedent, or by a pooled income fund or a charitable remainder annuity trust or unitrust [¶1918(c)]. Nor do they apply if the property is sold or exchanged after the transferor's death [IRC Sec. 644(e)].

(h) Foreign Trust With U.S. Beneficiary. If the grantor is a U.S. citizen and directly or indirectly transfer property to a foreign trust created after May 21, 1974, the grantor is taxed as the owner of the portion of the trust attributable to such property, if the trust has a U.S. beneficiary for such tax year [IRC Sec. 679(a)(1)].

A grantor will not be treated as owner of a foreign trust if the transfers are made to the foreign trust because of the grantor's death, or if the transferor has recognized gain on the transfer [IRC Sec. 679(a)(2)].

A trust having a foreign corporation as a beneficiary may be treated under the attribution rules as "having a U.S. beneficiary" [IRC Sec. 679(c)].

(i) Foreign Person as a Trust Grantor. A new special rule is designed to prevent certain foreign persons from using the grantor trust rules to their advantage to avoid tax [IRC Sec. 672(f)].

Background: In the past, wealthy foreign persons expecting to live in the U.S. would try to avoid being taxed by the U.S. on their income by transferring their assets to another foreigner (usually a family member), who then transferred those assets to a trust that named the wealthy person as its beneficiary. The family member would retain some interest or power in that trust. Since the family member would be treated as the trust's owner (under the grantor trust rules), the wealthy foreigner would seek to avoid being taxed on the income.

Starting with trusts created after November 5, 1990, a taxpayer is treated as the true grantor of such a foreign trust if that person (1) is the trust's beneficiary, and (2) made direct or indirect gifts to the supposed foreign grantor who otherwise would have been treated as the owner under the grantor trust rules [IRC Sec. 672(f)(1)].

NOTE: For purposes of this rule, annual gifts of less than $10,000 are disregarded.

¶3524 "THROWBACK" OF EXCESS DISTRIBUTIONS BY COMPLEX TRUSTS

The throwback rule ordinarily applies only to complex trusts [Reg. Sec. 1.665(a)-0A]. But a simple trust that makes an accumulation distribution allocable to an earlier year is treated as a complex trust for that year for throwback purposes [Reg. Sec. 1.665-1A(b)].

➤ **OBSERVATION** The throwback rule prevents tax avoidance that could occur if a trust in a lower tax bracket accumulated and paid tax on its income rather than distributing the income to a beneficiary in a higher tax bracket. When the income was distributed at a later date, little or no additional tax would be paid by the beneficiary because distributions in excess of distributable net income in the year of distribution are tax-exempt to the beneficiary [¶3504]. Thus, trust income could be split between the trust and the beneficiary in a way that avoids the high tax to the beneficiary in a year his other income puts him in a substantially higher tax bracket than the trust. This tax avoidance device may be compounded when multiple accumulation trusts—each in a low tax bracket—are used. To forestall this, *the throwback rule taxes the beneficiaries as if the amounts had been distributed each year instead of accumulated.* In other words, the rule "throws back" the accumulated income to the years in which it was accumulated.

Two throwback concepts are basic to understanding the rule: (1) "undistributed net income" and (2) "accumulation distribution" [IRC Sec. 665(a), (b); Reg. Sec. 1.665(a)-1A, 1.665(b)-1A]. There can only be a throwback from a year with an accumulation distribution to a year with undistributed net income.

(a) Undistributed Net Income. A trust has undistributed net income for a tax year when the amounts distributed are less than the DNI for the year [IRC Sec. 665(a)(2), 665(d); Reg. Sec. 1.665(a)-1A]. To find the undistributed net income:

1. Find the DNI of the trust [¶3504].

2. Subtract the following from amount in (1):

- The amount of *income* required to be distributed currently, including any amount that may be paid out of income or corpus to the extent it was paid out of trust income for the year; and
- Any other amounts paid, credited or required to be distributed; and
- The income tax on the undistributed portion of the trust's DNI. This is the same amount as the total tax paid by the trust (not including any alternative minimum tax) except when the trust has capital gains not included in distributable net income (for example, capital gains to corpus) [Reg. Sec. 1.665(d)-1A].

Example 1: Under the terms of a trust, the trustee must distribute $10,000 of income currently to Mr. Brown. He also has discretion to make additional distributions to Brown. In 1992, the trust's distributable net income of $30,100 was derived from royalties, and the trustee distributed $20,000 to Brown. The trust's taxable income is $10,000 (after subtracting out a $100 exemption) on which a tax of $2,332 is paid. The undistributed net income of the trust for 1992 is $7,768, computed as follows:

Distributable net income		$30,100
Less:		
Income currently distributable to Brown	$10,000	
Other amounts distributed to Brown	10,000	
Tax attributable to undistributed net income	2,332	22,332
Undistributed net income		$ 7,768

(b) Accumulation Distribution.

A trust has an accumulation distribution when it distributes more than the DNI for the year. To determine the accumulation distribution: (1) Find the total distribution for the tax year, reduced by the amount of income required to be distributed currently (including any amount that may be paid out of income or corpus to the extent it was paid out of trust income for the year). (2) Subtract the DNI reduced (but not below zero) from the income required to be distributed currently. The difference between (1) and (2) is the accumulation distribution for the tax year. A distribution made or required to be distributed by a trust that does not exceed the trust income for the year is not treated as an accumulation distribution for that year [IRC Sec. 665(b); Reg. Sec. 1.665(b)-1A].

Example 2: During 1992, a trustee properly distributes $20,000 to a beneficiary, of which $7,000 is income required to be distributed currently to him. The distributable net income of the trust is $15,000. There is an accumulation distribution of $5,000, computed as follows:

Total distribution		$20,000
Less: Income required to be distributed currently		7,000
Other amounts distributed		13,000
Distributable net income	$15,000	
Less: Income required to be distributed currently	7,000	
Balance of distributable net income		8,000
Accumulation distribution		$5,000

(c) How to Handle the Throwback Rule.

When a trust makes an accumulation distribution for any tax year, the distribution is thrown back to the earliest year the trust has undistributed net income, and so on, up to the year of the distribution. The accumulation being thrown back is deemed to have been distributed on the last day of the year to which it is thrown back, but only to the extent of the undistributed net income of that year. The rest of the accumulation distribution is then thrown back to the next succeeding year that had undistributed net income, and so on through the tax years until the accumulation distribution is used up [IRC Sec. 666(a); Reg. Sec. 1.666(a)-1A]. The trustee must file Schedule J (attached to Form 1041), showing the allocation of accumulation distribution to each beneficiary.

> ► **OBSERVATION** The throwback rule can be avoided by electing to treat any distribution during the first 65 days of a trust year as an amount paid during the preceding year (¶3506(f)) [IRC Sec. 663(b); Reg. Sec. 1.663(b)-1, 2].

Distributions to minor beneficiaries.

Generally, the throwback rules do not apply to any distributions of income accumulated by a trust (other than a foreign trust) for a beneficiary before his birth or before he is 21 years old [IRC Sec. 665(b)]. These accumulated distributions are not taxable to the beneficiary.

NOTE: There are special rules regarding distributions allocated to preceding years as they relate to multiple trusts and foreign trusts [IRC Sec. 665(c), (d)].

Lack of records. If records are not available to determine the trust's undistributed net income of any tax year, the accumulation distribution is deemed to have been determined on December 31, 1969, or the earliest subsequent date the trust was in existence. If the trustee establishes that the loss of records for some tax years was beyond his control, the accumulation distribution is first allocated to tax years for which he has adequate records [IRC Sec. 666(d); Reg. Sec. 1.666(d)-1A].

(d) Taxes Added to Distribution. When an accumulation distribution is thrown back to a particular year, all or part of the taxes imposed on the trust for that year (other than the alternative minimum tax) are also deemed distributed. This is done because the accumulation deemed distributed in the throw-back year would have increased the trust's distribution deduction in that year [¶3517], and thereby reduced or eliminated the trust's taxes. If the accumulation distribution thrown back to a particular year is at least as much as the undistributed net income for that year, the taxes paid by the trust for that year are also deemed distributed and are added to the distribution [IRC Sec. 666(b); Reg. Sec. 1.666(b)-1A]. If the accumulation distribution thrown back is *less than* the undistributed net income, only a portion of the taxes is added to the accumulation. This portion is determined as follows [IRC Sec. 666(c); Reg. Sec. 1.666(c)-1A]:

$$\begin{matrix}\text{Taxes (except alternative} \\ \text{minimum tax) on trust for year} \\ \text{to which throwback is made}\end{matrix} \times \dfrac{\begin{matrix}\text{Accumulation distribution} \\ \text{thrown back to particular year}\end{matrix}}{\begin{matrix}\text{Undistributed net income for} \\ \text{that particular year}\end{matrix}} = \begin{matrix}\text{The amount of taxes deemed to} \\ \text{have been distributed on last} \\ \text{day of that particular year}\end{matrix}$$

> **Example 3:** A trust created on January 1, 1988, makes an accumulation distribution of $7,000 in 1992. For 1988 the trust's undistributed portion of distributable net income was $12,100, and its tax attributable to the undistributed net income was $2,738. Therefore, its undistributed net income for 1988 was $9,362 ($12,100 - $2,738). Since the entire amount of the accumulation distribution for 1992 ($7,000) is less than the undistributed net income for 1988 ($9,362), an additional amount of $2,047 ($7,000/$9,362 x $2,7386) is deemed distributed to the beneficiary on the last day of 1988.

(e) Effect of Distributions in Intervening Years. The undistributed net income, for any year to which a later accumulation distribution may be thrown back, is reduced by accumulation distributions in intervening years that must be thrown back to such year [Reg. Sec. 1.665(a)-1A(c)]. To allocate an accumulation distribution to a prior year, that year's undistributed net income is reduced by the amount deemed distributed in an accumulation distribution made in any intervening years [Reg. Sec. 1.666(a)-1A(d); 1.666(c)-2A]. Also, when a throwback results in taxes paid by the trust being deemed distributed to beneficiaries, the taxes imposed on the trust attributable to any remaining undistributed net income are reduced by the taxes deemed distributed [Reg. Sec. 1.665(d)-1A(b)(2)].

(f) Tax Paid by Beneficiaries on Excess Distribution. The beneficiary must pay an additional tax (in the year in which the accumulation distribution is actually paid, credited or required to be distributed) on the amount deemed to have been distributed to him or her by the trust in any year to which the throwback is made. The beneficiary is taxed on the accumulation distribution thrown back to a particular year and also an amount equal to the tax paid by the trust on that accumulation distribution. The tax on the beneficiary in the year the accumulation is actually distributed is the sum of (1) the partial tax on the beneficiary's taxable income computed without regard to the accumulation distribution and (2) the partial tax on the accumulation distribution [IRC Sec. 667]. The partial tax in (2) is computed on a three-year average basis, as follows:

First, the beneficiary takes his or her taxable income for the five years immediately preceding the distribution year, and disregards the lowest and highest years. If a beneficiary has a loss year in any of the five preceding years, the taxable income for the loss year is deemed to be zero for a *corporate* beneficiary for all computation purposes. However, an *individual* beneficiary's taxable income for any tax year starting after 1976 is deemed to be not less than his standard deduction for the year [¶1107], and zero for earlier tax years.

Second, using the averaging device, add an amount equal to the trust income accumulation distribution, divided by the number of years the trust earned it, to the taxable income for the remaining three years and figure a tax for each year.

Finally, multiply the average increase in tax for the three-year period by the number of years the trust earned the income. The result is the beneficiary's tax on the accumulation [IRC Sec. 667(b)]. The tax may be offset by a credit for any taxes previously paid by the trust with respect to this income, and the remaining tax liability is then payable by the beneficiary in the distribution year. But no refund or credit is allowed as a result of accumulation distribution; see (g) below. Special rules apply to multiple trusts [IRC Sec. 667(c)].

Adjustment for estate and generation-skipping transfer taxes. The beneficiary may reduce the partial tax (determined in the usual way) by the amount of the tax attributable to pre-death or pre-transfer accumulations in proportion to the transfer tax on the accumulation distribution [IRC Sec. 667(b)(6)].

(g) Credit for Tax Paid by Trust. As explained above, the beneficiary can deduct or offset the taxes paid by the trust in figuring his or her partial tax due on an accumulation distribution. However, the tax law sets an overall limit to the effect that a beneficiary or trust is not entitled to any refund or credit as a result of any accumulation distributions [IRC Sec. 666(e)]. Thus, if the partial tax is less than the amount of the tax deemed distributed, the excess cannot be used as a tax credit against the beneficiary's tax liability that arises from other sources of income. Nor can that excess give rise to a tax refund.

(h) Foreign Trusts. U.S. beneficiaries receiving distributions from foreign trusts not taxed under the grantor trust rules [¶3523(h)] are, with certain exceptions, subject to the throwback provisions generally as discussed above. However, foreign trusts are not allowed an exclusion from the throwback rule for accumulation distributions covering years before the beneficiary was born or reached age 21 [IRC Sec. 665(c)]. The character of capital gains is disregarded for purposes of taxing accumulation distributions to the beneficiary. But the character of income from which trust accumulation distributions are made to nonresident aliens and foreign corporate beneficiaries should be retained in the case of accumulation distributions to them [IRC Sec. 643(a)(6)(D), 667(e)]. Foreign trust beneficiaries who receive accumulation distributions must add to the distribution allocable foreign taxes paid by the trust before figuring additional tax due.

> **NOTE:** There are special rules for claiming the trust's foreign tax credit [IRC Sec. 665(d), 667(d)] and for distributions by foreign trusts not created by a U.S. person [IRC Sec. 665(c); Reg. Sec. 1.665(c)-1A].

¶3525   COMMON TRUST FUNDS

A common trust fund consists of money held by a bank, in a single federally regulated account, for investment by the bank in its capacity as a fiduciary for a number of beneficiaries. The fund is exempt from tax [IRC Sec. 584(b); Reg. Sec. 1.584-1]. Each participant in the fund, however, is taxed on his or her share of the fund's income, whether distributed or not [Reg. Sec. 1.584-2]. Consequently, the bank must file an information return for the fund [IRC Sec. 6032; Reg. Sec. 1.6032-1]. The fund computes its taxable income in the same manner as an individual, except that capital gains and losses are segregated, and the fund can't deduct charitable contributions or net operating loss [IRC Sec. 584(d); Reg. Sec. 1.584-3, 1.584-6]. The partnership return Form 1065 may be used [Reg. Sec. 1.6032-1].

When participants in a common trust fund compute taxable income, they take into account the proportionate share of the capital gains or losses, and the taxable income or net loss of the fund. Excludable interest is allocated to the participants, as is the fund's net operating loss [IRC Sec. 584(c); Reg. Sec. 1.584-2]. Participants must also account for their pro rata share of the fund's items of tax preference subject to the alternative minimum tax (¶2600) [Reg. Sec. 1.58-5].

Withdrawal of participating interest. No gain or loss is realized by the fund on the admission or withdrawal of participants. But the withdrawal of a participating interest by participants is treated as a sale or exchange of their interest resulting in a recognized gain or loss to them [IRC Sec. 584(e)]. A transfer into a new trust is not a withdrawal of a participating interest.[1]

Footnotes to Chapter 25

(For your added convenience, in brackets [] with the footnotes below, you will find citations to related paragraphs in the "RIA United States Tax Reporter" (USTR), "CCH Federal Tax Reporter"(CCH) and "RIA Federal Tax Coordinator 2d"(FTC) multi-volume services.)

FOOTNOTE ¶ 3500 [USTR ¶ 6409; CCH ¶ 24,751; FTC ¶ C-1000].
FOOTNOTE ¶ 3501 [USTR ¶ 77,014; CCH ¶ 41,690; FTC ¶ V-9000].
(1) Rev. Stats. Sec. 3467, 31 USC 192.
(2) Rev. Stats. Sec. 3466, 31 USC 191.
(3) U.S. v. Weisburn, 48 F.Supp 393, 30 AFTR 856.
(4) Est. of L.E. McKnight, 8 TC 871; Livingston v. Becker, 40 F.2d 673, 8 AFTR 10790; M. Viles ¶55,142 PH Memo TC.
FOOTNOTE ¶ 3502 [USTR ¶ 6409; CCH ¶ 24,751; FTC ¶ C-1000].
(1) Fred W. Smith, 25 TC 143.
(2) Fiduciary Trust Co. v. U.S., 36 F.Supp. 653, 26 AFTR 545; Boyce v. U.S., 8 AFTR 2d 6001, 296 F.2d 731.
(3) United States Tr. Co. v. Comm., 296 US 481, 16 AFTR 1306.
(4) Edward L. Stephenson Tr., 81 TC 283.
FOOTNOTE ¶ 3503 [USTR ¶ 6524; CCH ¶ 24,891; 24,907; FTC ¶ C-2600 et seq.].
FOOTNOTE ¶ 3504 [USTR ¶ 6434.01; CCH ¶ 24,834; FTC ¶ C-2605].

FOOTNOTE ¶ 3505 [USTR ¶ 6514; CCH ¶ 24,867; FTC ¶ C-2600 et seq.].
(1) Rev. Rul. 62-147, 1962-2 CB 151.
FOOTNOTE ¶ 3506 [USTR ¶ 6614; CCH ¶ 24,931; FTC ¶ C-2700].
(1) Comm. v. Stearns, 65 F.2d 371, 12 AFTR 786.
(2) Rev. Rul. 72-395, 1972-2 CB 340, clarified by Rev. Rul. 82-165, 1982-2 CB 117.
FOOTNOTE ¶ 3507 [USTR ¶ 6524.03; CCH ¶ 24,891; 24,931; FTC ¶ C-3000].
FOOTNOTE ¶ 3508 [USTR ¶ 6910; CCH ¶ 24,767; FTC ¶ C-9500 et seq.].
(1) Basch, 9 TC 623; O'Daniel, 10 TC 631, aff'd 173 F.2d 966, 37 AFTR 1249; Rev. Rul. 65-217, 1965-2 CB 214; Rev. Rul. 68-124, 1968-1 CB 44.
FOOTNOTE ¶ 3509 [USTR ¶ 12,234; CCH ¶ 24,751; 24,834; FTC ¶ I-6000 et seq.].
(1) Beatty, 28 BTA 1286.
(2) Suisman v. Eaton, 15 F.Supp. 113, 18 AFTR 24; Kenan v. Comm., 114 F.2d 217, 25 AFTR 607; Rev. Rul. 66-207, 1966-2 CB 243.
(3) Sherman Ewing, 40 BTA 912.
(4) Rev. Rul. 67-74, 1967-1 CB 194.

(5) Rev. Rul. 74-257, 1974-1 CB 153.

FOOTNOTE ¶ 3510 [USTR ¶ 10,154; CCH ¶ 29,730; 29,742; 29,744; FTC ¶ P-1007].

FOOTNOTE ¶ 3511 [USTR ¶ 64,141; CCH ¶ 24,751; 24,767; FTC ¶ C-2200 et seq.].

(1) Treas. Dept. booklet "Tax Information for Survivors, Executors and Administrators" (1991 Ed.), p. 14.

(2) Beatty, 28 BTA 1286.

FOOTNOTE ¶ 3512 [USTR ¶ 5524; CCH ¶ 24,808; FTC ¶ C-2323].

FOOTNOTE ¶ 3513 [USTR ¶ 6424.01; CCH ¶ 24,791; 24,808; FTC ¶ C-2300].

(1) A list of qualifying organizations (Pub. 78) may be purchased from the Superintendent of Documents, Govt. Printing Office, Washington, DC 20402.

(2) Wellman v. Welch, 99 F.2d 75, 21 AFTR 857; Marion C. Tyler Trust, 5 TC 729.

FOOTNOTE ¶ 3514 [USTR ¶ 1674.117; CCH ¶ 24,797; 24,808; FTC ¶ L-7679].

(1) Sue Carol, 30 BTA 443.

(2) Rev. Rul. 61-211, 1961-2 CB 124; Rev. Rul. 74-71, 1974-1 CB 158.

FOOTNOTE ¶ 3515 [USTR ¶ 6424.05; CCH ¶ 24,796; 24,808; FTC ¶ C-2200].

(1) Rev. Rul. 61-20, 1961-1 CB 248.

(2) Kearney v. U.S., 116 F.Supp. 922, 45 AFTR 523.

FOOTNOTE ¶ 3516 [USTR ¶ 6424.02–.04; CCH ¶ 24,808; FTC ¶ C-2211].

(1) Rev. Rul. 63-27, 1963-1 CB 57.

(2) Erdman v. Comm., 11 AFTR 2d 1209, 315 F.2d 762.

(3) Bingham v. Comm., 325 US 365, 33 AFTR 842.

(4) Penrose v. U.S., 18 AFTR 1289, 23 AFTR 1166, 18 F.Supp. 413.

(5) Rev. Rul. 73-322, 1973-2 CB 44.

(6) Est. of McClatchy, 12 TC 370, aff'd 179 F.2d 678, 38 AFTR 1287.

(7) Ungerman, 89 TC 1131.

(8) O'Neill, 98 TC No. 17.

(9) Rev. Rul. 67-304, 1967-2 CB 224.

FOOTNOTE ¶ 3517 [USTR ¶ 6514.01; CCH ¶ 24,867; FTC ¶ C-2500].

FOOTNOTE ¶ 3518 [USTR ¶ 2674; CCH ¶ 14,150; FTC ¶ C-2200].

FOOTNOTE ¶ 3519 [USTR ¶ 6424.01; CCH ¶ 24,808; FTC ¶ C-7200].

FOOTNOTE ¶ 3520 [USTR ¶ 6409; CCH ¶ 24,767; FTC ¶ C-7000].

(1) Treas. Dept. booklet "Your Federal Income Tax" (1991 Ed.), p. 26.

(2) Instructions for Form 1041 (1991), p. 17.

FOOTNOTE ¶ 3521 [USTR ¶ 66,524; CCH ¶ 40,460.027; FTC ¶ S-5300].

FOOTNOTE ¶ 3522 [USTR ¶ 6454; CCH ¶ 24,851; FTC ¶ C-1010].

FOOTNOTE ¶ 3523 [USTR ¶ 6714 et seq.; CCH ¶ 25,061 et seq.; FTC ¶ C-5400 et seq.].

(1) Rev. Rul. 57-390, 1957-2 CB 326.

(2) Morrill, Jr. v. U.S., 13 AFTR 2d 1334, 228 F.Supp. 734.

(3) Ellis v. U.S., 24 AFTR 2d 69-5671, 416 F.2d 894; A.Q. Stewart, 9 TC 195.

(4) Rev. Rul. 65-283, 1965-2 CB 25.

FOOTNOTE ¶ 3524 [USTR ¶ 6654.01; CCH ¶ 24,992; FTC ¶ C-4000 et seq.].

FOOTNOTE ¶ 3525 [USTR ¶ 5844; CCH ¶ 23,830; FTC ¶ E-4400].

(1) Wiggin v. U.S., (DC Mass.) 3 AFTR 2d 998; Rev. Rul. 60-256, 1960-2 CB 193.

CHAPTER

26

RETURNS AND PAYMENT OF TAX

TABLE OF CONTENTS

INDIVIDUAL TAX RETURNS

This section deals with those individuals who must file income tax returns. These include returns of minors as well as those filed by an agent or fiduciary. A key question for married couples is whether they can, or should, file joint or separate returns.

¶3601   WHO MUST FILE

Whether you must file an income tax return generally depends on your gross income, age and filing status [¶1100]. Categories of filers include the following:

- Individuals [¶1100].
- Dependents [¶3603].
- Self-employed persons [¶1100(c)].
- Executors, administrators, or legal representatives [¶3605].
- U.S. citizens living abroad.
- Residents of Puerto Rico.
- Aliens [¶ 3809(d)].

(a) Who Should File. Even if you are not required to file under the dollar limits listed in ¶1100(a), you should file to get a refund if income tax was withheld from your pay. Examples are students working during summertime and other part-time wage earners. Also, file if you can take the earned income credit [¶2402].

(b) Signing the Return. You or your authorized agent must sign an income tax return (¶3604) [IRC Sec. 6061; Reg. Sec. 1.6061-1].

If you prepare a return as a fiduciary, parent or guardian, or executor or administrator, you must sign it. You and your spouse must each sign your joint return (or a fiduciary may sign for either of you[1]). A return with no signature or incompletely signed may be considered *no return* and subject you to penalties.[2]

If you file a tax return on behalf of your child or a child for whom you are a guardian, you should sign the child's name where indicated, adding: "By [your signature], Parent [or Guardian] for minor child."[3]

¶3602   JOINT RETURNS

If you and your spouse elect to file a joint return, it is much the same as if you combined your income, deductions and exemptions and each reported half on a separate return. (You and your spouse may file a joint return even though one of you has no income or deductions.) As to when youare considered married, see ¶1104(a) and (c).

(a) Liability for Tax. If a joint return is filed, you and your spouse are each liable for the entire tax and any penalties imposed [IRC Sec. 6013(d)(3); Reg. Sec. 1.6013-4(b)]. For example, you may be liable for the full amount even if all the income was earned by your spouse. However, you may be relieved of liability for tax (including interest, penalties and deficiency) if: (1) a substantial tax understatement is attributable to "grossly erroneous items" (including claims for deductions or credits for which there is no basis in fact or law) of your spouse; (2) you did not know, and had no reason to know, of the understatement; and (3) it would be inequitable to hold you liable for the understatement under all the facts and circumstances.

The Eighth Circuit Court of Appeals has said two different standards can apply to this so-called "innocent spouse" relief: (1) If the tax shortfall is due to omitted income, there's no relief if you know or had reason to know of the underlying circumstances that gave rise to the tax problem. (2) If the problem is over disallowed deductions, you can get penalty relief if, under the circumstances when the return was signed, a reasonably prudent taxpayer couldn't be expected to know that it was erroneous to claim the deduction.[1]

In general, a substantial tax understatement is one that exceeds $500. However, it is more difficult to qualify for innocent spouse relief when an understatement is not due to omitted income. In this case, the understatement must exceed a certain percentage of the spouse's adjusted gross income (AGI). A substantial tax understatement must total more than 10% of AGI if the spouse's AGI is $20,000 or less for the year before the deficiency notice; or 25% if that AGI is more than $20,000. Community property laws are disregarded in determining a spouse's income [IRC Sec. 6013(e)].

(b) Change in Election to File Jointly or Not. If you and your spouse choose to file separate returns, you can later change this election and file jointly. When you do, the joint return replacing the separate returns must be filed within three years after the due date for the original returns [IRC Sec. 6013(b); Reg. Sec. 1.6013-2]. However, if a joint return has been filed, you and your spouse cannot elect to file "late" separate returns after the original due date [Reg. Sec. 1.6013-1(a)].

(c) Joint Return on Death of Spouse. If your spouse dies during the tax year, you may file a joint return with that deceased spouse unless you remarry before the end of the year. In that case, you can make a joint return with your new spouse [IRC Sec. 6013(a)(2); Reg. Sec. 1.6013-1(d)(1),(2)]. Usually, the return is made by the executor or administrator. However, you can file a joint return if no executor or administrator is appointed before the due date for filing the return [IRC Sec. 6013(a)(3); Reg. Sec. 1.6013-1(d)(3)].

Also, an executor or administrator later appointed can disaffirm a joint return filed by you. The disaffirmance is made on a separate return for your deceased spouse within one year after the due date of your return [IRC Sec. 6013(a)(3); Reg. Sec. 1.6013-1(d)(5)].

If an executor or administrator has been appointed, both he and you must sign a joint return. If there has been no appointment, you should write in the signature area "Filing as surviving spouse," and show the date of death in the name and address space.[2]

(d) When Separate Returns May Be Better. It's usually wiser to file jointly. But not always. You should consider filing separate returns in the following situations: (1) If either you or your spouse has substantially larger miscellaneous itemized expenses, medical expenses or casualty losses than the other, separate returns may save tax because of the percentage rule [¶1931; 1942; 2304]. (2) If you can obtain a larger benefit from a net operating loss deduction by applying it to a separate income. (3) If neither you nor your spouse can itemize, you both can claim a standard deduction on separate returns. Separate filing also may be wise if you are facing the alternative minimum tax [¶2600]. Other situations exist where filing separately may be an advantage. So, if both you and your spouse have income, figure the tax both ways to make sure.

¶3603   RETURNS OF MINORS

Your minor child must file a return if he or she meets the gross income requirements for adult taxpayers (¶1100) [IRC Sec. 6012(a)(1)]. However, if you or another taxpayer can claim your child as a dependent, the child must file a 1992 return if: (a) he or she has only *unearned income* and the 1992 income exceeds $600, or (b) both earned and unearned income, and his or her total 1992 gross income is over $600, or (c) only *earned income,* and his or her gross income exceeds the regular standard deduction amount. You must sign and file the return for your minor child if he or she is unable to do so [Reg. Sec. 1.6012-1(a)(4), 1.6012-3(b)(3)].

Kiddie tax. Your under-age-14 child may have to pay tax as if part of the unearned income (dividends, interest, etc.) had been received by you. In 1992, the first $600 of your under-age-14 child's unearned income is tax-free, and the second $600 is taxed at your child's rates. But any 1992 unearned income in excess of $1,200 is taxed to the child at your rates. You may elect to report the child's income on your return [¶1240].

Earned income. If your child has a part-time or summer job, he or she may be entitled to exempt the wages from income tax withholding. To qualify, your child must (1) have owed no tax in the prior year and (2) expect to owe no tax in the current year. Exempt withholding status is claimed on Form W-4 that is filed with your child's employer [¶2510(a)].

¶3604   RETURN BY AGENT

Your tax return may be filed by an agent if you are unable to make it because of disease or injury. Your agent also may make the return if your District Director, upon receipt of your application showing good cause, gives permission. Form 2848, Power of Attorney and Declaration of Representative, giving the agent's power of attorney, should be filed with your return [IRC Sec. 6012(b); Reg. Sec. 1.6012-1(a)(5)].

Form 8821, Tax Information Authorization, allows you to authorize a designated representative to receive and/or inspect tax information in an IRS office.

¶3605   RETURN BY FIDUCIARY

If an individual would be required to file a return [¶1100], a fiduciary acting for him must file one [IRC Sec. 6012(b)(2)].

(a) Who Are Fiduciaries. The term "fiduciary" means a guardian, trustee, executor, administrator, receiver, conservator or any person acting in any fiduciary capacity [IRC Sec. 7701(a)(6); Reg. Sec. 301.7701-6].

Fiduciaries required to file returns include the following [IRC Sec. 6012(b)]:

- Guardian or a committee of an insane person [Reg. Sec. 1.6012-3(b)(3)].
- Guardian of a minor unless the minor himself makes the return or has it made [Reg. Sec. 1.6012-3(b)(3)].
- Guardian of a taxpayer who has disappeared. If his spouse is appointed guardian, she may file a joint return for herself and as guardian of her missing husband, if the other requirements are met.[1]
- Executor or administrator for decedent [Reg. Sec. 1.6012-3(b)(1)].
- Trustee of a trust [¶3520].
- Trustee of an individual's bankrupt estate [(d) below].

Example: The executor of a decedent's estate must file a return for the estate if the gross income from the estate is $600 or more [¶3520(c)].

(b) What Return Form to Use. The guardian, executor or administrator must make the return for an individual on Form 1040, 1040A or 1040EZ [IRC Sec. 6012(b); Reg. Sec. 1.6012-3(b)]. The return for an estate or trust is made on Form 1041.

How the return is signed. Persons making the return must sign and indicate the capacity in which they are acting. If there are two or more joint fiduciaries, one can execute the return [IRC Sec. 6012(b)(5); Reg. Sec. 1.6012-3(c)].

(c) Fiduciaries Not Required to File. Receivers who are in charge of only a portion of the taxpayer's property need not make a return. Receivers who stand in place of an individual have a duty to file a return if the individual does not file it [IRC Sec. 6012(b)(3); Reg. Sec. 1.6012-3(b)(5)].

(d) Bankruptcy Estate. A bankruptcy trustee of an individual debtor's estate must file a return for the estate if its 1992 gross income is $5,300. However, the trustee of a partnership in a bankruptcy may not file a return for the income of a bankrupt partnership[2] [IRC Sec. 6012(a)(9), (b)(4)]. For corporations, see ¶3610(b).

NOTE: Although the estate of a partnership in bankruptcy is not treated as a separate entity, the trustee in bankruptcy must file annual information returns [¶3669(a)] for the partnership.[2]

¶3606   ELECTRONIC FILING

Electronic filing can shorten the time for processing returns to within three weeks. Electronic filing uses automation to replace most of the manual steps needed to process paper returns. As a result, processing for electronic returns is faster and more accurate. However, errors on the return or problems with its transmission or processing can delay a refund. Electronic filing does not affect your chances of an IRS audit on your returns.

An electronically filed Form 1040 consists of both electronically transmitted data and certain paper documents. The return's nonelectronic portion involves Form 8453, U.S. Individual Income Tax Declaration for Electronic Filing, and other paper documents that cannot be electronically transmitted.[1]

All electronic filers, whether or not they are previous participants, must file revised Form 8633, Application to Participate in the Electronic Filing Program.

A tax return cannot be electronically filed after August 15 even when you have obtained an extension. Form 4868, Application for Automatic Extension of Time To File U.S. Individual Income Tax Return, cannot be electronically filed.

An electronically filed amended return cannot be made. You must use Form 1040X. However, balance due electronically filed returns are permitted.

You are not automatically entitled to file electronically. Any of the following reasons might result in a rejected application for participating in the program:

- Conviction of any criminal offense under U.S. revenue laws.
- Failing to file timely and accurate tax returns, both business and personal.
- Failing to pay personal and business tax liabilities.
- Assessment of penalties.
- Suspension or disbarment from practice before the IRS.

- Other facts or conduct of a disreputable nature that would reflect adversely on the Electronic Filing Program.
- Suspension or rejection from the program in a prior year.
- Unethical practices in return preparation.
- Stockpiling returns prior to the official acceptance into the Electronic Filing Program.

CORPORATION TAX RETURNS

¶3610   CORPORATION INCOME TAX RETURNS

Every corporation not expressly exempt must file an *income tax* return, even if it has no taxable income. The corporation must file returns for as long as it remains in existence [IRC Sec. 6012(a)(2); Reg. Sec. 1.6012-2(a)]. Returns must include identifying numbers (¶3620) [Reg. Sec. 301.6109-1(b)]. Corporations that received a charter, but have never perfected their organization, transacted business or received any income from any source, may be relieved of the duty of filing a return on application to the District Director [IRC Sec. 6012(a)(2)].

(a) Determining Corporate Existence. A corporation is not in existence after it ceases business and dissolves, retaining no assets, even if it is still treated as a continuing corporation under state law to wind up its affairs. If the corporation has valuable claims for which it will bring suit, it has retained assets and continues in existence. A corporation that is turned over to receivers who continue to operate it does not go out of existence [Reg. Sec. 1.6012-2(a)(2)].

Returns Not Required

When a charter was granted, but never exercised, there was no de facto corporation, and no liability for corporation tax.[1]

A corporation ceases to exist after its charter is revoked and the income from continued operation is taxed to the sole proprietor.[2]

Returns Required

Corporation returns must be filed in the following cases: when a partnership is incorporated, but business is conducted the same as before its incorporation;[3] when a corporation, which has ceased business, retains a small sum of cash to pay state taxes to preserve its corporate charter,[4] or has valuable claims for which it will bring suit [Reg. Sec. 1.6012-1(a)(2)]; when a corporation has dissolved before the date its return was due[5] or before passage of a retroactive tax law or law changing the rates of tax.[6] (The corporation is not relieved from tax liability for the period it was in existence.)

(b) Returns by Receivers or Trustees. Receivers having possession or title to all or substantially all of the corporation's business or property must file the corporation returns, whether they are liquidating the corporation or operating its business. Trustees in dissolution and trustees in reorganization proceedings under federal bankruptcy laws[7] have the same status as receivers [IRC Sec. 6012(b)(3); Reg. Sec. 1.6012-3(b)(4)].

¶3611   WHAT TAX RETURN FORM TO USE

Form 1120 is used by all ordinary business corporations. Small corporations may use short Form 1120-A. Corporations electing to be treated as S corporations [¶3100-3105; 3107-3112] file Form 1120S.

(a) Exempt Organizations. Unrelated business income of exempt corporations is reported on Form 990-T [¶3354]. Exempt farm cooperatives use Form 990-C to report income [¶3355].

(b) How Return Is Signed. Corporation income tax returns must be signed by hand[1] and verified by the president, vice-president, treasurer, assistant treasurer, chief accounting officer or any other officer authorized to act [IRC Sec. 6062, 6065; Reg. Sec. 1.6062-1, 1.6065-1].

¶3612   RETURN FOR SHORT TAX YEAR

Corporations in existence during any part of the tax year must file tax returns [Reg. Sec. 1.6012-2(a)(2)]. The closing date of the first return of the newly organized corporation depends on whether it uses the calendar year or a fiscal year as its accounting period. A fiscal year may be adopted without permission of the IRS.

> **Example:** If a corporation received its charter and began business on November 15, 1991, and wished to adopt the calendar year, its first return would be for the period November 15 to December 31, 1991, and subsequent returns would be for the calendar years following. If the corporation wished to adopt a fiscal year ending January 31, its first return would be for the period November 15, 1991, to January 31, 1992, and subsequent returns for the fiscal years following.

A return for a corporation from the date of incorporation to the end of its first accounting period is considered to be for a period of 12 months. It is not a fractional year return, and the income need not be put on an annual basis [IRC Sec. 443]. Returns for periods of less than 12 months due to change of accounting periods must be put on an annual basis [¶2819].

Special rules apply to S corporations and personal service corporations that elect fiscal years [¶2820].

TAXPAYER IDENTIFYING NUMBERS

¶3620   PURPOSE OF THE NUMBER

The IRS automatic data processing (ADP) system analyses returns and correlates information reported about every U.S. taxpayer. The key is the taxpayer identifying number that must be shown on every tax paper required to be filed—returns, statements or other documents. Entering the correct number cannot be over-emphasized since an omission or inaccuracy will impede the IRS in handling matters.

¶3621   WHAT IS THE IDENTIFYING NUMBER

(a) Individuals. The identifying number (TIN) for individuals and estates of decedents is the social security number. You may also have an "Employer identification" (EI) number if you are engaged in a trade or business [Reg. Sec. 301.6109-1(a), (b)]. Thus, you may be required to use two numbers—one (TIN) for your individual taxes and one (EI) for your business taxes.

> **Example:** Mr. Johnson operates a retail business as a sole proprietorship. His income tax return includes TIN number on the return form and most schedules, including the self-employment Schedule SE. He uses his EI number on Schedule C, which shows profit or loss from the business.

Reporting dependent's IDs. Parents and others who claim a dependency exemption for anyone who reaches the age of one before the end of the year must report that person's TIN (usually his/her social security number). A penalty applies for failing to supply each TIN per return (¶3721; 3724) [IRC Sec. 6109(e)].

(b) Other Taxpayers. Corporations, partnerships, trusts and estates, exempt organizations[1] and investment clubs[2] use the employer identification number (EI) [IRC Sec. 6109; Reg. Sec. 301.6109-1, 301.7701-11, 12].

> **NOTE:** (1) A fiduciary filing for an individual includes the individual's TIN number and, if necessary, the EI number; as noted, an estate or trust uses its EI number. The fiduciary's own number is not used in either case. (2) Nonresident aliens and foreign corporations not doing business in the U.S. do not need identifying numbers [Reg. Sec. 301.6109-1(g)].

(c) Tax Return Preparers. Preparers who employ others to prepare income tax returns or refund claims include their employer identification numbers on the returns. Preparers who do the work themselves need only include their TIN [IRC Sec. 6109(a)(4); Reg. Sec. 1.6109-2].

¶3622   PAYMENTS TO OTHERS

Returns filed for payments made to others (e.g., information returns [¶3660] and employer returns on withholding [¶2552]) must include the payee's TIN number or EI number. This number must be furnished to the person filing the return when requested (and certified as correct in some cases). If the number is not obtained, payors must file an affidavit with their returns stating that the payees refused to give them their numbers. Payees who furnish an incorrect TIN to payors of interest, dividends and certain other payments are subject to a 20% backup withholding tax [¶2421] after notice from the IRS [IRC Sec. 3406(a)]. Banks, businesses and other payors use Form W-9 to obtain certification of payees' TINs [Temp. Reg. Sec. 35a.9999-1].

¶3623   HOW TO GET A NUMBER

If you do not have a taxpayer identification number, you should apply for one. Applications (Form SS-5 for TIN number and Form SS-4 for EI number) are handled by any IRS or Social Security office. Your application should be made far enough in advance to permit its timely issuance [Reg. Sec. 301.6109-1(d)].

> ► **OBSERVATION** To obtain a TIN, the Social Security Administration requires an original birth certificate and another proof, such as a library card, report card, or immunization certificate. If a parent signs the application, then he or she will have to produce an original proof, such as a driver's license.

TIME AND PLACE FOR FILING TAX RETURNS

¶3630   WHEN RETURNS MUST BE FILED

You must file your returns by the prescribed due date, unless you have secured an extension to file [¶3631]. Income tax returns are filed for a calendar year or for a fiscal year. Information returns [¶3660 et seq.] generally are filed on a calendar year basis. A penalty is imposed for failure to file returns on time [¶3724; 3728].

The time for filing returns for taxes withheld by the payer are discussed at the following paragraphs: wage payments, ¶2552; pensions, annuities, and other deferred income, ¶2516; payments to nonresident aliens and backup withholding tax, ¶2421; 2518.

Due date on Saturday, Sunday, or legal holiday. If the due date for filing a return or performing any other prescribed act falls on a Saturday, Sunday or legal holiday, the act is timely if done on the next day that is not a Saturday, Sunday or legal holiday [IRC Sec. 7503; Reg. Sec. 301.7503-1]. "Legal holiday" includes any legal holiday recognized in an entire state where the act is required to be performed. The term also includes any District of Columbia holidays. If a legal holiday in D.C. falls on Saturday or Sunday, the preceding Friday or following Monday is treated as a holiday [Reg. Sec. 301.7503-1(b)].

Filing by mail. You may file returns (and other claims, documents or statements) by mail if properly addressed. If the envelope bears a U.S. postmark made by the U.S. Postal Service dated on or before the due date of the return (or within the required filing period for other claims or statements), it will be considered filed on time, even if it is received after the due date. (A postmark by a private postage meter may be acceptable if dated on or before the due date. But a federal circuit court of appeals has said that a postmark by a private delivery service will not make late delivery acceptable.[1]) Note that a registered mail date is treated as the postmark date, and registration is proof of delivery [IRC Sec. 7502; Reg. Sec. 301.7502-1]. For timely mailing of tax deposits, see ¶2552; 3650; and 3651.

Short tax year. You must file returns for a period of less than 12 months [¶2819] within the same period after the close of the short period as if the short period were a fiscal year.[2]

(a) Individual Returns. If you are on a calendar-year basis, you must file income tax returns by April 15. If you use a fiscal year, you must file by the 15th of the 4th month following the close of the fiscal year [IRC Sec. 6072(a); Reg. Sec. 1.6072-1(a)].

Example 1: Ms. Brown is on a fiscal year ending April 30. She must file her return by August 15.

Joint return by surviving husband or wife. If a surviving spouse elects to file a joint return with the deceased spouse for the year the spouse dies, the time for filing the joint return is the same as if the death had not occurred.

Example 2: John Jones and his wife Mary are both calendar year taxpayers. If Mary dies during 1992, the joint return must be filed by April 15, 1993.

Example 3: James Grey and his wife Joan both file returns on a fiscal year basis ending June 30th. If James dies on Dec. 1, 1992, the joint return must be filed by Oct. 15, 1993.

Final return for decedent. The executor or administrator of a decedent must file the decedent's last return. It is due the same date a return would have been due had the decedent lived the entire tax year [Reg. Sec. 1.6072-1].

(b) Corporation Returns. If your corporation is on the calendar-year basis, it must file its income tax returns by March 15. If your corporation is on a fiscal year, it must file its returns by the 15th of the third month following the close of the fiscal year [IRC Sec. 6072(b); Reg. Sec. 1.6072-2(a)]. For payment dates, see ¶3651.

A corporation that goes out of existence during its annual accounting period must file its income tax return by the 15th day of the third month after it ceased business and dissolved, unless the District Director grants an extension (¶3631) [Reg. Sec. 1.6071-1(b); 1.6072-2(a)].

Foreign corporations and foreign trusts not having an office or place of business in the U.S. file their income tax returns by the 15th day of the 6th month following the close of the tax year [Reg. Sec. 1.6072-2(b),(c)].

(c) Tax Returns for Estates and Trusts. The fiduciary for an estate [¶3501] must file a return [¶3520] by the 15th day of the fourth month after the close of the tax year. Returns of trusts must generally be made on the calendar year basis [¶3522]. Returns made on a calendar year basis must be filed by April 15th [IRC Sec. 6072(a); Reg. Sec. 1.6072-1(a)].

The last return of an estate or a trust must be filed by the 15th day of the fourth month following the closing of the estate or termination of the trust [Reg. Sec. 1.6072-1].

(d) Exempt Organizations—Return of Unrelated Business Income. Return of unrelated business income on Form 990-T required of certain exempt organizations [¶3346; 3354] must be filed by the 15th of the fifth month following the close of the tax year, if the organization is taxable as a corporation[3] [Reg. Sec. 1.6072-2(c)]. Domestic trusts, and foreign trusts having an office or place of business in the U.S., must file the return by the 15th day of the fourth month following the close of the trust's tax year [Reg. Sec. 1.6072-1(a)].

¶3631   EXTENSION OF TIME TO FILE RETURNS

The IRS can grant a reasonable extension of time to file tax returns [IRC Sec. 6081; Reg. Sec. 1.6081-1]. Most taxpayers have a right to an automatic extension of time to file (see below). In any event, the extension cannot exceed six months, except for taxpayers who are abroad [(d) below] [IRC Sec. 6081(a); Reg. Sec. 1.6081-2].

Time to pay tax. If an individual, corporation or private foundation gets an extension of time to file, the time to pay the tax is not extended, unless the extension specifies otherwise [Reg. Sec. 1.6081-1(a), 1.6081-3(c), 1.6081-4(b); 53.6081-1].

(a) Automatic Extension for Individuals. You can get a four-month automatic extension of time to file your return. You get this extension by filing an application on Form 4868 by the return due date (¶3630(a)) [Reg. Sec. 1.6081-4(a)]. The application must show the full amount estimated as tax for the year.

If you underestimated the amount you owe, you have to pay interest on the unpaid amount. You will also have to pay a failure-to-pay penalty [¶3722; 3728]. Any interest or penalty applies from the return's original due date (generally April 15).[1]

(b) Additional Extensions. To get an extension beyond the automatic four-month filing extension, you must establish very good reasons for needing the extra time (e.g., illness). An extension of more than six months will not be granted if you are in the U.S. However, if you are outside the U.S., you might be granted a longer extension ((d) below) [IRC Sec. 6081; Reg. Sec. 1.6081-1].

The extension beyond the four-month period can be applied for either in a letter or by filing Form 2688, Application for Additional Extension of Time to File U.S. Individual Income Tax Return.

> ➤ **OBSERVATION** You should request the extension early on so that, if refused, you will still be able to file on time. (A Form 2688 or letter request must be filed before the extended due date.) Except in cases of undue hardship, Form 2688 or a letter request is not accepted until you have first used the automatic four-month extension.

If your application for the extension is approved, you will be notified by the IRS. The notice should be attached to the return when it is filed.

Suppose your application for this extension is not approved. Then, you must file your return by the automatic extension's extended due date. The notice denying the extension may grant you until 10 days after the notice date to file, if that is later than the due date.

(c) Six-Month Extension for Corporations. Your corporation can get a six-month automatic extension by filing Form 7004, Application for Automatic Extension of Time to File Corporate Income Tax Return, by the due date. This form is an application for extension with a statement in place of a tentative return [IRC Sec. 6081(a); Reg. Sec. 1.6081-3].

Consolidated return. A parent corporation may request extensions for its subsidiaries when a consolidated return is to be filed [Reg. Sec. 1.6081-3(b)].

Tax must be paid. Your corporation must remit [¶3651] the tax it estimates it will have to pay [Reg. Sec. 1.6081-3(a)]. Payment may not be required if Form 1138 for a net operating loss carryback [¶3744] is filed at the same time and the loss eliminates the tax shown on Form 7004.[2]

When Form 7004 is used, interest is payable from the original due date of the corporate return on any tax not shown on the form.

(d) Overseas Extensions. U.S. citizens or residents may get an automatic two-month extension to file returns and pay tax if they (1) maintain a tax home or live outside the U.S. and Puerto Rico or (2) serve in military or naval services abroad on the due date of the tax return [Temp. Reg. Sec. 1.6081-4T]. Tax home, for this purpose, is the same as it is defined for deduction for away-from-home travel expenses [¶2000(a)]. If you have no regular or principal place of business, then your regular place of abode in a real and substantial sense is considered your tax home.

If otherwise qualify for the extension, you are not disqualified simply because you are physically present in the U.S. or Puerto Rico at any time, including the tax return due date [Temp. Reg. Sec. 1.6081-4T(e)].

NOTE: This two-month extension does not apply to you if you are merely traveling outside the U.S. on the return due date [Temp. Reg. Sec. 1.6081-4T(f)].

If you use the two-month automatic extension, you need not file an application. But you must attach a statement to your return showing that you qualify for it [Temp. Reg. Sec. 1.6081-4T(b)].

➤ **OBSERVATION** If you already had two extra months to file because you live or are serving overseas, you may still take advantage of the four-month extension discussed in (a) above. But you can only get two more months because both extensions run concurrently [Reg. Sec. 1.6081-4]. Also, you must file Form 2688 before the four-month extension expires and write "Taxpayer Abroad" across the top of that form.

Suppose you expect to qualify as a bona fide resident of a foreign country [¶3825(b)], but not until a date more than two months after the return's regular due date. You can use Form 2350 to obtain an extension of time for filing your return. In general, the extension is for 30 days beyond the date on which you reasonably expect to qualify.[3]

(e) Extension for Short Period Return. The time to file an income tax return for a short period may be extended by the IRS, if you show unusual circumstances [Reg. Sec. 1.6071-1(b)].

(f) Partnerships and Trusts. Partnerships and trusts can get an automatic three-month extension of time to file returns by filing Form 8736 [Temp. Reg. Sec. 1.6081-2T]. An additional extension is available by filing Form 8800.

¶3632   WHERE TO FILE RETURNS

You file returns for income tax and self-employment tax in the Revenue District where you reside or have a principal place of business, or at the Service Center that serves that district. However, the IRS may designate special filing places for specific returns. Information returns generally are filed at a Service Center [¶3660]. Amended returns also must be filed at a Service Center unless they are hand carried [Reg. Sec. 1.6091-2]. For return of taxes withheld from wages, see ¶2552(c).

¶3633   USE OF AMENDED RETURNS

You can correct an error in a return you have filed by filing an amended return. For this purpose, you must use Form 1040X and corporations Form 1120X. Other taxpayers may use a regular return form [Reg. Sec. 301.6402-3(a)]. The amended regular return can be filed on a return form for the same year as the return being corrected or another year's return if changed to show the correct year. The words, "Amended Return" should be written or printed at the top of the regular return form. You must explain the error that is being corrected. The IRS is not compelled to accept an amended return.

(a) When Tax Is Due. If more tax is due because of a correction, you should pay it with the amended return. Interest and penalties are imposed for delinquent returns [¶3722; 3728].

(b) Credit or Refund. If you are entitled to a credit or refund of income tax as a result of the correction, Forms 1040X, 1120X or the amended return (regular return form for taxpayers other than individuals or corporations) will serve as a claim for refund or credit. You must file the claim before the limitation period expires [¶3737].

SUPPORTING INFORMATION

¶3640   ADDITIONAL INFORMATION THAT MUST BE FILED WITH THE RETURN

Income tax returns must be executed and filed in accordance with the regulations and the instructions with the return [IRC Sec. 6011(a); Reg. Sec. 1.6011-1]. Preparing and filing returns, therefore, involves more than merely reporting income and deductions, and figuring the tax. It is necessary to include or attach to the return any required supporting information or statement.

Information and statements required. *For reference purposes only,* a list of the supporting information, statements, etc., that are called for by the form instructions and regulations is given below.

Alternative minimum tax. See ¶2600.

Bad debts. Statement substantiating the deduction [Reg. Sec. 1.166-1]. You must show (a) nature of the debt; (b) name and family or business relationship, if any, of debtor; (c) when due; (d) efforts made to collect; and (e) how determined to be worthless.[1]

Bingo, keno, slot machine winnings. You must file Form W-2G for winnings of $1,200 or more from a bingo or slot machine and $1,500 or more from keno [Temp. Reg. Sec. 7.6041-1]. See also Gambling winnings, below.

Blind persons. If you are claiming an additional standard deduction for partial blindness of yourself, your spouse, or both, you must attach to your return, a certificate from a qualified physician or a registered optometrist [¶1107(a)]. If blindness is total, you must attach a statement to the return.[2]

Capital loss carryover. Statement showing how the carryover is figured [capital gain and loss schedule].

Charitable contributions. Name and address of each organization to which you made a contribution and the amount. Attach statement showing how the deduction is figured. If you claim a deduction of more than $500 for a contribution of property, file Form 8283 with the return; if the deduction for the item is over $5,000, ($10,000 for nonpublicly traded stock), get an appraisal as well (¶1922) [Reg. Sec. 1.170A-13(c)(3); 1.6050L-1].

Commodity Credit Corp. loans. If you are electing to include such loans in gross income, you should file a statement showing the details of the loans.

Consent dividends. Corporation claiming a credit for consent dividends must file (1) Forms 972 (shareholder's consent) executed by each consenting shareholder and (2) Form 973 [Reg. Sec. 1.565-1].

Consolidated returns. Form 851, Affiliations Schedule, must be attached to the parent corporation's consolidated return. Form 1122 for each subsidiary must be attached to the first consolidated return and a copy filed with the subsidiary's District Director by the consolidated return due date [Reg. Sec. 1.1502-75].

Depletion data. Mineral property [Reg. Sec. 1.611-2(g)]. Percentage depletion [Reg. Sec. 1.613-5]. Timber [Reg. Sec. 1.611-3(h)]. Geothermal wells [Reg. Sec. 1.612-5]. See instructions to Form 1120.

Depreciable property. Depreciation claimed must be supported by schedules showing: description of the property and other pertinent information. Use Form 4562 and attach it to the return.

You should file similar data, including deductions by prior owners, with return for year Sec. 1250 property [¶1812] is acquired, except in like kind exchanges or through involuntary conversion [Reg. Sec. 1.1250-2(f)].

A special election applies to changing the method of depreciation on real property [IRC Sec. 167(e)(3)]. See ¶1812(b); 2120.

Development (mining) expenditures. An election to defer expenses deductible ratably must be made on the return or by filing a statement not later than time for filing the return (including extensions) [IRC Sec. 616(b); Reg. Sec. 1.616-2].

Dividend carryover. Attach statement showing computations [Reg. Sec. 1.564-1].

Dividends paid. Corporation claiming an allowance for dividends paid must file a copy of the dividend resolution and other information [Reg. Sec. 1.561-2(c)].

Employees' trusts. Exemption from tax requires filing with IRS detailed information required on certain annual return forms (Form 5500 series). See ¶3667(b).

Estates and trusts. Fiduciaries, if requested to do so by the IRS, must furnish a copy of the will or trust instrument (including amendments) and attach their statement of the provisions they think control taxability of income. Also, they should attach a written declaration, under penalties of perjury, that the will is a true and complete copy [Reg. Sec. 1.6012-3(a)(2)].

If estate or trust is engaged in trade or business, a schedule must be attached to the return similar to that required in "profit (or loss) from business" schedule on Form 1040.

If any part of the income of a trust is taxable to the grantor, the income and the related deductions and credits should be shown in a separate statement attached to Form 1041.

An estate or trust is allowed a special election as to its charitable contributions [IRC Sec. 642(c)]. See ¶3513.

Exempt income expenses. If you receive exempt income, other than interest, you must submit a statement showing the amount of such income and, if an expense item is apportioned between exempt and taxable income, the basis of the apportionment [Reg. Sec. 1.265-1(d)].

Exemption for dependent. When several persons support an individual, and one is designated to claim the exemption, each of the others who contributed over 10% support must file a declaration that he will not claim the individual as a dependent. Form 2120 may be used [¶1116(d)].

Exploration expenditures. Merely deducting expenses on the return elects the deduction. See ¶2242.

Farmers. Schedule F of Form 1040 must be attached to return of farmers filing on the cash or accrual method.

A cash basis farmer can elect to include crop insurance proceeds in income for the tax year after crops were destroyed or damaged if the crop income would have been included in income for that year (¶2720) [IRC Sec. 451(d); Reg. Sec. 1.451-6].

Foreign income. File Form 2555 with the return to support exclusion of income earned abroad [¶3825(f)].

Foreign tax credit. Individuals file Form 1116; corporations, Form 1118. If credit is for taxes paid, receipts must be attached to the form; if credit is for taxes accrued, the return on which each such accrued tax was based must be attached to the form [Reg. Sec. 1.905-2].

Gambling winnings. Payer must file Forms W-2G and W-3G for $600 or more winnings from horse or dog racing or jai alai (if odds are at least 300 to 1), or lotteries, raffles, drawings, sweepstakes or wagering pools. See also Bingo, etc., above.

Gasoline and special fuel credit. Form 4136 may be filed with return showing computation for federal gasoline and fuel tax credit [¶2412].

Installment sales. Use Form 6252 to report installment sales [¶2904(c)] unless Form 6252 is used to report the original sale and any gain on payments received in later years[3] [IRC Sec. 453(d); Temp. Reg. Sec. 15a.453-1(d)].

Inventories. If the inventories reported do not agree with the balance sheet, attach a statement explaining the difference. If you are electing to use LIFO method, you must file Form 970 with the return for the first year. In addition, the instructions require a statement showing a detailed analysis of all inventories for which LIFO method [¶2706] is first to be used as well as ending inventory reported on the return for the prior tax year.

Inventories by dealers in securities. Describe inventory method used [Reg. Sec. 1.471-5].

Involuntary conversion. Details of an involuntary conversion of property at a gain must be reported on the return for the year the gain is realized [Reg. Sec. 1.1033(a)-2(c)(2)].

The election to treat involuntary conversion of a residence as a sale [¶1704] must be attached to the return for the year of disposition, with information as to basis, dates, prices and occupancy of old and new residences [Reg. Sec. 1.1034-1].

IRA contributors. You must file Form 8606 if you made nondeductible contributions to your IRA [¶1330(c)]. You must also file this form if you received IRA distributions during the year and you had previously made nondeductible contributions to your IRA.

Liquidating distribution. When a shareholder in exchange for property transfers stock to the corporation that issued the stock, the facts and circumstances should be reported on the shareholder's return, unless the property is part of a distribution made in liquidation of the corporation and the corporation is completely liquidated and dissolved within one year after the distribution [Reg. Sec. 1.331-1(d)]. See also ¶1228; 1229.

Liquidation of subsidiary. In a nontaxable liquidation of a subsidiary under Sec. 332 the parent must file a certified copy of the plan for liquidation and of the resolutions authorizing the liquidation plus other information [Reg. Sec. 1.332-6].

Long-term contracts. Attach to the return a statement that long-term contract method is being used [Reg. Sec. 1.451-3].

Losses by fire, storm, or other casualty, or theft. File a statement explaining the deduction, with a description of the property, date acquired, cost, subsequent improvements, depreciation allowable, insurance, salvage value and deductible loss.

Medical expense deduction. If the expense is deductible for both estate and income tax purposes, and it is deducted on the income tax return, file with the return a statement and waiver of the deduction for estate tax purposes.

Net operating loss deduction. You should file with your return a concise statement showing how the net operating loss deduction is figured.

Organizational expenditures. Election to amortize expenditures must be made by filing statement with return showing: (1) description and amount of expenditures, (2) date incurred or paid, (3) month corporation began business and (4) number of months (not less than 60) of amortization period [Reg. Sec. 1.248-1].

Partnerships. If the return is filed for a syndicate, pool, joint venture, etc., attach a copy of the operating agreement to the return, unless a copy has been previously filed, together with amendments thereto [Form 1065 instructions].

A partner who transfers any part of his partnership interest must file a statement with his return [Reg. Sec. 1.751-1(a)(3)].

Pension trust payments. To support a deduction claimed under Sec. 403 for payments to an employees' pension trust, the taxpayer must file the appropriate form in the Form 5500 series [¶3667(b)]. Employers use Forms 5305-SEP and 5306-SEP for simplified employee pension plans [¶1340].

Power of attorney. An agent filing for taxpayer may file power of attorney instead of Form 2848.

Prepaid subscription income. A statement of election to defer prepaid subscription income [¶2833] must be filed with the return for the first year to which it applies [Reg. Sec. 1.455-6].

Regulated investment companies. For information to be filed with the returns of certain stockholders of such companies, see Reg. Sec. 1.852-7. For real estate investment trusts, see Reg. Sec. 1.857-7.

Reorganizations. Regulations [Reg. Sec. 1.368-3] tell what information to file with returns and what records to keep in a corporate reorganization.

Sale of residence. If you sold your residence and none or only part of the gain was recognized because of your age, or because you purchased or built a new residence, attach a Form 2119 to the return showing purchase price, date of purchase, date of occupancy, etc. If you acquire the new residence after your return is filed, advise District Director, giving full details. See ¶1706.

Sale or exchange of real estate, bonds, or stock. The following information is required by the instructions: (a) For real estate, location and description of land, description of improvements; (b) for bonds or other evidences of indebtedness, name of issuing corporation, description of the particular issue, denomination and amount; (c) for stocks, name of issuing corporation, class of stock, number of shares, capital changes affecting basis (nontaxable stock dividends, other nontaxable distributions, stock rights, etc.) As to the information required about the acquisition of the property and the purchaser, see the "gain or loss" schedule on return.

Stock owned in foreign or domestic corporations. A statement should be attached to corporation's return. See instructions. If the taxpayer owns 5% or more in value of the stock of a foreign personal holding company, the information required by Sec. 551(d) must also be furnished [Reg. Sec. 1.551-4]. As to stock owned in domestic corporations, see "Questions" on return.

Tax information authorization. You use Form 8821 to designate your representative to receive or inspect your confidential tax information from the IRS.

Transfer of property to controlled corporation. Anyone who received stock or securities of a controlled corporation for property under Sec. 351 must file a complete statement of all the facts [Reg. Sec. 1.351-3].

Withholding tax on wages. Credit for amount withheld is determined by reference to your statement received from your employer [Form W-2]. You must attach this form must to your return.

PAYMENT OF TAX

¶3650　　　WHEN INDIVIDUAL TAX MUST BE PAID

[New tax legislation may affect this subject; see ¶1.]

You must pay income tax by the due date of the return [¶3630]. You must pay any balance of the tax not collected through withholding on wages [¶2552] or payments of estimated tax [¶2418] by the 15th day of the fourth month after the close of the tax year (April 15 for calendar year taxpayers) [IRC Sec. 6151(a); Reg. Sec. 1.6151-1(a)].

Example: Mr. Harris reports on the basis of a fiscal year ending on June 30. Payment of tax is due by October 15.

If you elect to have the IRS figure the tax [¶1103(b)], you must pay the tax within 30 days after the IRS mails a notice of the amount due [IRC Sec. 6151(b); Reg. Sec. 1.6151-1(b)].

¶3651　　　WHEN CORPORATION TAX MUST BE PAID

[New tax legislation may affect this subject; see ¶1.]

Full payment of income tax is due by the 15th of the third calendar month following the close of the tax year. If your corporation is on the calendar year basis, it pays by March 15.

If it uses a fiscal year and it ends, for example, on June 30, payment is due by September 15 [IRC Sec. 6151(a); Reg. Sec. 1.6072-2, 1.6151-1(a)].

Tax must be deposited in authorized banks. Domestic corporations must deposit income and estimated taxes in a Federal Reserve bank or authorized commercial bank by the due date. The tax may be paid by one or more separate deposits, but a preinscribed Federal Tax Deposit Coupon Form must be presented for each deposit [Reg. Sec. 1.6302-1]. Checks or money orders should be drawn to the order of the bank where deposited. Depositories other than Federal Reserve banks are not required to accept checks drawn on other banks, but they may do so. Corporations that do not receive the coupon deposit forms can call or write any IRS office (giving their name, identification number (EIN), and the month in which their fiscal year ends) in time to make the deposit[1] [Reg. Sec. 1.6302-1]. A penalty ranging from 2% to 15% may be imposed depending when your corporation corrects the deposit (¶3738) [IRC Sec. 6656].

Except for deposits of $20,000 or more [¶2552], tax deposits mailed two or more days before the due date are timely filed even though they are received by the depositaries after due date. Usually, the registered or certified receipt is proof of the mailing date by a sender [IRC Sec. 7502; Prop. Reg. 301.7502-1].

Foreign corporations. The tax for a foreign corporation having no office or place of business in the U.S. is due by the 15th day of the sixth month following close of the tax year [IRC Sec. 6072(c), 6151(a); Reg. Sec. 1.6072-2(b), 1.6151-1(a)]. Withholding agents may be required to deposit taxes [¶2552(f)].

(a) Payments of Estimated Tax are made by deposit with the preinscribed tax deposit coupon form. Unless a receipt is requested from the bank, your corporation must keep its own record of each payment.

Every corporation, including certain foreign corporations [¶3810] and insurance companies, may have to pay estimated tax. Estimated tax is the excess of the anticipated tax liability (including the alternative minimum tax (AMT) on Form 4626) [¶2610] less any credits [IRC Sec. 6655]. Form 1120-W may be used as a worksheet to compute the estimated tax.

Corporations must pay four installments of estimated tax each year. Installments are due on April 15, June 15, September 15 and December 15 for calendar-year taxpayers. The due dates for fiscal-year corporations are the 15th day of the fourth, sixth, ninth and twelfth months of the tax year [IRC Sec. 6655(c), (i)(1)].

Each installment should equal 25% of your corporation's "required annual payment"—regardless of how much taxable income your corporation has earned until the payment date. The required annual payment is the lesser of [IRC Sec. 6655(d)]:

1. 97% of the tax shown on the return for the tax year (or if no return is filed, 97% of the tax for the year), or

2. 100% of the tax on the return for the prior year, if that year was a 12-month tax year and a return for that year was filed showing a tax liability.

➤ **PAYMENT CHANGES** For corporations basing the payments on their current tax bill, the minimum percentage was 93% for tax years beginning after December 31, 1991 and before July 1, 1992. The percentage is due to drop in the future—to 91% for tax years beginning after 1996.

Large corporations (i.e., those with $1 million or more of taxable income in any of the three immediately preceding tax years) can use the last year's tax only for determining the first installment payment. They must use the 97% threshold for calculating subsequent estimated tax payments. If a large corporation does use the last year's tax figure, though, the second payment must be adjusted to make up for any shortfall from using that method to calculate the first installment [IRC Sec. 6655(d)].

Short tax year. Estimated tax need not be paid for a short period of fewer than four months [Prop. Reg. Sec. 1.6655-5].

De minimis exception. Corporations with a tax liability of less than $500 need not make estimated tax payments.

(b) Penalty for Underpayment of Estimated Tax. If payments of estimated tax are not made when due, an interest penalty may be added to the tax [¶3728]. The penalty is figured on the amount by which any actual installment payment falls short of the required installment payment (see above) [IRC sec. 6655(a)].

Relief provisions. There are two exceptions to estimated tax penalties: the annualized income exception and the seasonal income exception.

1. *The annualized income exception.* Under the annualized income exception, the amount required to be paid is computed by multiplying the "applicable percentage" for a given installment by the full tax on the annualized income for the appropriate period (the income for the period projected over a whole year), and subtracting any prior payments. The applicable percentage is 24.25% for the first installment, 48.5% for the second, 72.72% for the third, and 97% for the fourth [IRC Sec. 6655(e)].

> **IMPORTANT** All corporations, large or small, can utilize the estimated tax safe harbor using the annualization method. However, once the annualization method is not used for an installment, your corporation must recapture any reduction in a prior installment caused by the use of the annualized income exception. The regular required installment is increased by the amount of the recapture.

> **WHAT TO DO** For a small corporation with a tax history, the safest thing to do is to base this year's estimated tax payments on 100% of last year's tax. New corporations (or large corporations to the extent they can't use the 100%-of-last-year's-tax rule) will have to do some crystal-ball gazing to comply with the tough rules. These corporations will have to make careful estimates of *total* tax liability for the year and gauge estimated tax payments accordingly—don't assume a payment based on annualized income will be sufficient.

2. *The recurring seasonable income exception.* Corporations that consistently earn a disproportionate amount of their income in one season of the year may annualize their income by assuming the income is earned in the current year and in the same pattern as in the preceding tax years. Thus, no penalty is imposed for an underpayment of any estimated tax installment if the total payments for the tax year are at least 97% (93% for tax years beginning after December 31, 1991, and before July 1, 1992) of the tax (see below) measured by a base period percentage of seasonal income[2] [IRC Sec. 6655(e)].

> **IMPORTANT** Once your corporation stops using the seasonal income exception, you must recapture all of the savings resulting from using it for prior installments [IRC Sec. 6655(e)].

Tax computation for seasonal income. The tax against which the 97% (93% for tax years beginning after December 31, 1991, and before July 1, 1992) floor (see above) is applied, is figured as follows [IRC sec. 6655(e)]: Take the taxable income for every month of the tax year in which the installment must be paid. Divide that amount by the base period percentage (average percent which the taxable income for the corresponding months in the three preceding tax years bears to the taxable income for the three preceding tax years). Find the tax on the amount determined by basing the tax on the previous year's income, but at the current year's rate.

Multiply that tax by the base period percentage (as defined above) for the months in the tax year up to and including the month in which the installment is due. Note that this percentage, in all cases, must equal or exceed 70% of the total income for any six consecutive months of a tax year.

Rules for applying the relief provisions are on Form 2220. A claim that the penalty does not apply should be supported by a statement on Form 2220 filed with the return [Reg. Sec. 1.6655-1(b)].

¶3652   WHEN ESTATES AND TRUSTS PAY TAX

Payment of income tax is due by the 15th of the fourth calendar month after the end of the tax year. For a calendar-year estate or trust the date is April 15.

Estimated tax. Estates and trusts file Form 1041-ES to pay estimated taxes. Estates and trusts use the same estimated tax payment schedule as individual taxpayers. Form 1041-T may be used to assign a trust's overpayments to beneficiaries. New estates, for their first two years, however, need not report and pay estimated tax [IRC Sec. 6654(1)]. See ¶2417.

¶3653   EXEMPT ORGANIZATIONS

Tax-exempt organizations must make quarterly estimated tax payments of the tax on unrelated business income, and private foundations must make quarterly estimated tax payments of the excise tax on net investment income. These estimated tax payments must be made under the same rules that apply to corporate income taxes [IRC Sec. 6655(g)(3)].

¶3654   EXTENSION OF TIME TO PAY TAX

The IRS may grant a reasonable extension for payment of the tax. An extension is granted only if there is a showing that payment on the due date will result in undue hardship. Also, an extension may exceed six months only for persons abroad. A bond for twice the tax may be required [IRC Sec. 6161, 6164; Reg. Sec. 1.6161-1(b), 1.6165-1].

➤ **OBSERVATION** Interest will run during the extension period until payment is made. Reason: A payment due date is determined without regard to any time extension [¶3722; 3728].

Application must be filed on Form 1127 before the due date of the tax or installment for which the extension is requested. Corporations that expect a net operating loss and carryback can apply on Form 1138 (with Form 7004 attached)[1] for an extension of time to pay part of the previous year's tax [¶3744].

Interest on underpayments and overpayments. See ¶3722; 3728.

Deficiency. If the IRS is satisfied that payment of a deficiency on the prescribed date will result in undue hardship, it may extend the time to pay it for not more than 18 months, and in exceptional cases, for a further period not over 12 months. However, no extension is granted to pay a deficiency that is due to negligence, intentional disregard of rules and regulations, or fraud with intent to evade tax [IRC Sec. 6161(b); Reg. Sec. 1.6161-1].

Estimated tax. An extension of time extends the time to pay estimated tax; but the penalty for underpayment of estimated tax [¶2420] runs from the original due date for payment [Reg. Sec. 1.6073-4].

¶3655   REPORTING AND PAYMENT PROCEDURES

(a) Even Dollar Reporting. You may file your tax returns in whole dollar amounts, instead of showing cents. This is done by eliminating any amount less than 50 cents and increasing any amount between 50 cents and 99 cents to the next higher dollar. This method of reporting applies only to the total amounts to be shown on any line of the return. It cannot be used to figure the various items that have to be totaled to determine the final amount on the line. You cannot change your choice after the due date of your return [IRC Sec. 6102; Reg. Sec. 301.6102-1].

(b) Paying the Tax. You may make paymnent in cash or by check or draft. But if the check or draft is not paid by the financial institution, you remain liable for payment of the tax, and the penalties are the same as if you had not sent the check or draft. A separate penalty is also imposed for tendering a bad check in bad faith or without reasonable cause [¶3718(e)]. Payment may also be made by money order [IRC Sec. 6311; Reg. Sec. 301.6311-1]. Checks, drafts, or money orders should be made payable to the "Internal Revenue Service."

INFORMATION RETURNS

[New tax legislation may affect this subject; see ¶1.]

¶3660   INFORMATION RETURNS IN GENERAL

The government uses information returns to verify that persons receiving certain kinds or amounts of income report it on their income tax return. The information return may report payments made to others, transactions during the year, the taxable status of the taxpayer or other facts. The procedures for reporting on information returns are handled by several variations of Form 1099. For example, dividends are reported on Form 1099-DIV. Form 1099-MISC is for payments of $600 or more in rents, payments for services of a nonemployee, prizes and awards and such made in the course of a trade or business. Form 1099-MISC is also used for gross royalty payments of $10 or more. Payment of interest of $10 or more is reported on Form 1099-INT.[1] Most information returns are prepared on a calendar year-cash basis, even if the person filing the return is on a fiscal year-accrual basis. They are filed at an Internal Revenue Service Center. But Forms W-2 (or 1099-R) and W-3 must be filed with the Social Security office listed in the form instructions. Payors may apply for permission to file Forms 1099 and Form W-2 on magnetic tape or other media[2] [Reg. Sec. 1.9101-1].

When to file. Information returns are filed annually for a calendar year by the last day of February of the following year. A summary Form 1096 is filed at the same time. In most cases a copy of the information return should be sent to the person named as payee. If not, a statement of the information reported must be delivered to the payee by the January 31st before the return is filed.

Payors can request a 30-day extension to file an information return. The payor's application for an extension to file an information return is made to the IRS officer with whom the person files the return, or would be required to file an income tax return [¶3632]. It must state the service center where the information return will be filed [Reg. Sec. 1.6081-1].

Special rules apply to the following: For example, information about liquidating corporations [¶3666] must be filed. Partnership and S corporation returns are filed as an information return of income [¶3669]. Employers must provide employees with information returns regarding the moving expense deduction [¶1935].

Tax-exempt interest. Individuals, corporations and others required to file a return must also report how much tax-exempt interest was received or accrued during the tax year [Sec. 6012(d)].

Information Returns Required

Trade or business payments ($600 or more) [¶3661]	Foreign corporations [¶3670]
Interest paid [¶3662]	Alternative minimum tax [¶3671]
Dividends paid [¶3663]	Independent contractors [¶3661(e)]
Employee benefit plans [¶3667(b)]	Direct sellers [¶3661(f)]
Employee group-term life insurance [¶3665]	Brokers [¶3661(g)]
Employee stock options [¶3664]	Backup withholding [¶3661(h)]
Unemployment compensation [¶3661(a)]	Foreclosures and abandonments of secured property [¶3661(i)]
Liquidating organizations [¶3666]	Exchanges of partnership interests [¶3661(j)]
Self-employed retirement [¶3661(a)]	Sales of donated property by a charity [¶3661(k)]
Tax-exempt organizations [¶3667]	Royalties of $10 or more [¶3661(c)]
Pension plan administrators [¶3667(b)]	Business cash receipts of $10,000 or more [¶3661(l)]
Private foundations [¶3667(a)]	Mortgage interest of $600 or more [¶3661(m)]
Charitable deduction for trust [¶3668]	Tax shelter registration [¶3673 et seq.]
Partnerships, fiduciaries and S corporations [¶3669]	

¶3661 RETURN FOR BUSINESS PAYMENTS

You must file information returns for certain payments totaling $600 or more you make in the course of your trade or business. Except for payments to employees [(a), below], returns are made on the appropriate Form 1099, with summary Form 1096, and filed by February 28th of the following year [IRC Sec. 6041; Reg. Sec. 1.6041-6]. The return requirement is met if a surviving corporation of a merger files a return with all the required information.[1]

What is a trade or business. A "trade or business" is not limited to activities for gain or profit [Reg. Sec. 1.6041-1(b)]. Tax-exempt organizations must file information returns if they make payments that qualify.[2] This applies to exempt as well as nonexempt trusts, to insurance companies making payments under any nontrusteed annuity plan, to trustees paying supplemental unemployment benefits from a trust created with employer contributions,[3] to self-employed retirement plans [Reg. Sec. 1.6041-2(b)], to those making Medicare or Medicaid payments, and to those making direct payments to doctors or others providing health care services under certain insurance plans.

Separate returns required. You must file a separate return for each payee. You should report (1) amounts you actually paid and (2) amounts credited or set apart to the payee without any substantial limitation or restriction as to time and manner of payment so that they could have been withdrawn by the payee during the calendar year [Reg. Sec. 1.6041-1(f)].

Real owner must be disclosed. When anyone who is not the actual owner receives a payment for which an information return must be filed, he or she must supply the actual owner's name and address to the payor on demand [Reg. Sec. 1.6041-5]. Failure to do so is punishable by a $25,000 ($100,000 for corporations) fine, one year in prison, or both [IRC Sec. 7203].

Notice to payees. Payors' information returns for business payments of $600 or more must be furnished to the person to whom the information relates [IRC Sec. 6041(d)]. A penalty is imposed for failure to furnish such a statement [¶3721; 3724]. The separate mailing requirements with statements for payors of interest, dividends and patronage dividends who must give notice of information returns to payors have been eased.

(a) Payments to Employees. You report your employees' wages on Form W-2 [¶2554(a)]. In addition, you report all payments of compensation (whether or not subject to withholding) on Form W-2 if the total of these payments, such as group-term life insurance [¶3665] plus wages, equals at least $600. At your option, you may use more than one Form W-2 to report components of reportable amounts paid to each employee. Life insurance companies may report commissions paid to full-time life insurance salespersons and any taxable group-term life insurance premiums on Forms W-2 and W-3 [Reg. Sec. 1.6041-2(a); 1.6052-1]. The time for filing Forms W-2 and W-3 is the same as for the reporting of withheld taxes [¶2552(c)]. When Form W-3 does not include any wages subject to withholding, it may be filed by February 28th of the following year [Reg. Sec. 1.6041-2(a)(4); 1.6052-1(b)]. You must file returns on Forms 1096 and 1099 by the same date with the Revenue Service Center listed in form instructions. See also ¶3632.

You must use Form 1099-R to report annuity and pension payments when the payments total $600 or more during the calendar year or when tax has been withheld on these payments. For those payments under $600 or not subject to withholding, use of the form is optional [Reg. Sec. 31.3402(o)-2(f)]. Form 1099R must also be filed to report lump-sum distributions from profit-sharing and retirement plans.

NOTE: Payments totaling only $10 or more made to an owner-employee [¶1350] under a self-employed retirement plan must be reported on Form 1099. The first year contributions to the plan are made for him, the owner-employee must notify the trustee or insurer (for annuity contracts) of that fact not later than February 28th of the following year [IRC Sec. 6047(b); Reg. Sec. 1.6047-1].

Your corporation must report income of $600 or more realized by a former employee from a disqualifying disposition of stock acquired by the exercise of a qualified stock option if the information is available to the corporation.[4]

Unemployment compensation. Form 1099-G is used by payors who report payment of $10 or more of unemployment compensation during the calendar year (¶1526(b)) [IRC Sec. 6050B; Reg. Sec. 1.6050B-1].

(b) Payments of Fees or Tax Refunds. Fees of $600 or more you pay in the course of your trade or business to attorneys, public accountants, physicians, and members of other professions are reportable on Form 1099-MISC [Reg. Sec. 1.6041-1(d)(2)]. Form 1099-MISC is also used for filing information returns for payments to health care service suppliers.[5]

Report by government agencies. State and local agencies must file information returns on Form 1099-G as to income tax refunds, credits, and offsets aggregating $10 or more to any individual. Such information need not be furnished for individuals who do not claim itemized deductions on their federal income tax returns. When a return is required, the reporting agency must furnish the individual with a statement by the end of January of the year after the calendar year in which the refund was made or the credit or offset allowed [IRC Sec. 6050E; Reg. Sec. 1.6050E-1]. The appropriate federal officer must file information returns relating to social security and railroad retirement benefits and must furnish recipients with a copy of the statement [IRC Sec. 6050F; 6050G].

Federal executive agencies must make information reporting on persons receiving federal contracts from the agency in effect before, on or after 1-1-87. However, the general information reporting requirements do not apply to (a) contracts that are "classified" or (b) contracts involving a confidential law enforcement or foreign counterintelligence activity. These types of contracts are subject to a special form of reporting [IRC Sec. 6050M].

(c) Payments of Fixed or Determinable Income. You must file Form 1099-MISC, Miscellaneous Income for rent, annuities and other fixed or determinable income of $600 or more. Only payments in the course of your trade or business during the calendar year to an individual citizen or resident, a resident fiduciary, or a resident partnership, any member of which is a citizen or resident, must be reported [Reg. Sec. 1.6041-1(a), 1.6041-3]. A resident partnership is one engaged in trade or business in the U.S. [Reg. Sec. 301.7701-5]. Literary agents must report the gross amount of royalties received for their authors before deducting commissions, fees and expenses. Gas and oil royalties must be reported on a gross basis.[6] See ¶3662 for interest payments; ¶3663 for dividends.

> **Example:** Mr. Sloan works on straight salary for Agency Insurance, a partnership. In 1992, he was paid $9,800 in commissions direct from insurance companies. He, in turn, paid the $9,800 to Agency. Sloan must file an information return for the payment. If Agency were a corporation, Sloan would not have to file.

Rent payments. You must report rent you pay directly to a landlord (other than a corporation) in the course of your trade or business on Form 1099-MISC, if payments for the year amount to $600 or more. However, you need not make a report, if you pay the rent to a real estate agent. The agent must file the information return, if payments by the agent to the landlord (other than a corporation) during the year amount to $600 or more. The agent must report the gross amount collected for the landlord before deducting his commission or expenses.[7] If the landlord is a corporation, no return is required from the tenant or the agent [Reg. Sec. 1.6041-1(a); 1.6041-3].

Information returns must be filed for reportable payments, above, on which backup withholding tax [¶2421] was withheld [(h) below].

Royalties. You must report payments you make totalling $10 or more during a calendar year on Form 1099-MISC. Royalties required to be reported include payments for the right to exploit natural resources, such as oil, gas, coal, timber, sand, gravel and other mineral interests, as well as payments for the right to exploit intangible property, such as copyrights, trade names, trademarks, books and other literary compositions, musical compositions, artistic works, secret processes or formulas and patents [IRC Sec. 6050N]. Payees who fail to supply Taxpayer Identification Numbers (TINs) are subject to backup withholding rules (¶2421) [IRC Sec. 3406(b)(3)(E)].

Pensions, annuities, and other deferred income. Employers, plan administrators, or other payors who withhold tax from pensions, annuities, and other deferred income [¶2516] must file information returns [IRC Sec. 6047(d)]. Penalties are imposed for failure to comply [¶3721; 3724].

(d) Payments of $600 or More Not Reported. Except for returns required for payment of $10 or more for interest [¶3662] and dividends [¶3663], Forms 1099 need not be filed for the following [Reg. Sec. 1.6041-3]:

- Payment to a corporation, but Form 1099-MISC must be filed for payments to a corporate health care service supplier.[6]
- Distributions or salaries to partners or distributions to beneficiaries of an estate or trust, that are shown in the partnership return, Schedule K-1 (Form 1065) [¶3669] or the fiduciary return, Form 1041 [¶3520].
- Rent paid by a tenant to a real estate agent.
- Payments by brokers to their customers (but see (g), below).
- Bills paid for merchandise, telegrams, telephone, freight, storage, and similar charges.
- Compensation reported on Forms W-2, W-3 and 941 [¶2552; 2554(a)].
- Tip income (cash or charge) reported by the employer for the employee [¶2506].
- Income paid for tax-free covenant bonds or to nonresident aliens and reported for tax withholding on Forms 1000, 1001, 1042 and 1042S. See ¶2518; 2550; 3662.
- Distributions to S shareholders reported on Form 1120S.

(e) Payments to Independent Contractors. If you pay an independent contractor for services performed in the course of your trade or business, you must file an information return, if it's $600 or more for the year [Reg. Sec. 6041A(a)].

(f) Direct Sellers of Consumer Goods. Direct sellers who sell consumer goods on a buy-sell, deposit-commission or similar basis to a buyer who buys $5,000 or more in one year, must file an information return 1099-MISC [IRC Sec. 6041A(b)].

(g) Brokers, dealers, barter exchanges and others who (for consideration) regularly act as middlemen must report on Form 1099-B, Proceeds From Broker and Barter Exchange Transactions, the gross proceeds from transactions carried on for the customers. They must furnish a statement of information reported to the IRS, to the customer by January of the year after the year for which the return is filed. Failure to comply may be subject to a maximum penalty of $50,000 for the year [IRC Sec. 6045, 6678; Reg. Sec. 1.6045-1].

Farm managers are exempt from filing Form 1099-B for their farm management activities. This information must be filed by them on a Schedule F where it is provided in a more useful format [IRC Sec. 6045(c)(1)(C)].

The IRS has said that a corporation redeeming its stock can report the redemption payouts on Form 1099-B. The corporation doesn't have to sort out which payments are taxed as dividends. The corporation should attach to each Form 1099-B an explanation stating that the corporation is using the form to report redemption payouts without classifying the proceeds as income or gain.[8]

Certain realty transactions. Information return reporting is required on Form 1099-S on sales or exchanges of one- to four-family homes. The party responsible for reporting both to the IRS and the seller is the *first* of the following who participates in the transaction: settlement agent (the person who prepares the statement); attorney for the buyer (the one that prepares documents transferring title); attorney for the seller (if he or she prepares the documents); the disbursing title or escrow company that disburses the most significant proceeds; mortgage lender; the seller's broker; the buyer's broker; and the buyer. The TIN of seller and total cash received must be listed on the Form 1099-S. Withholding is not required. Special rules apply to magnetic media reporting. The same filing dates apply here as do to other Forms 1099 [IRC Sec. 6045(e)]. It's unlawful for any real estate reporting person to separately charge any customer for complying with the information reporting requirements as to real estate transactions [IRC Sec. 6045(e)].

> NOTE: One- to four-family homes include any single-family residential structure or unit such as a house, townhouse or condominium, any multi-family residential structure with four or fewer units and stock in a cooperative housing corporation. The term does not include mobile homes [IRC Sec. 6045(e)].

> ➤ **OBSERVATION** Regulations have yet to be issued requiring reports on sales of collectibles. However, brokers must report securities and commodities sales transaction except for sales to exempt customers as defined in the regulations [Reg. Sec. 1.6045-1; Temp. Reg. Sec. 5F.6045-1]. Also, brokers must furnish customers with statements detailing certain in-lieu payments they receive on customers' securities that were transferred in a short sale open transaction. In addition, information return Form 1099 with transmittal Form 1096 must be filed annually for such brokers' statements [IRC Sec. 6045(d)].

(h) Backup Withholding. Banks, businesses and other payors are required to withhold on most kinds of payments that are reported on 1099s. This so-called backup withholding is intended to ensure that certain taxpayers report all taxable receipts on their tax returns. In general, payors must withhold 20% of taxable interest, dividends and certain other payments reportable on 1099s if a payee fails to furnish them with the correct taxpayer identification number. For most individual payees, the TIN is their social security number [IRC Sec. 6109(d)].

The 20% withholding can apply if: (1) a payee fails to furnish a TIN, (2) the IRS notifies the business or bank that the TIN was incorrectly given or (3) the IRS notifies the business or bank to start withholding because a payee did not report the interest or dividends on the tax return [IRC Sec. 3406(a)]. It can also apply if payees fail to indicate that they are not subject to backup withholding.

The payors must file information returns for backup withheld tax [¶2421]. A separate statement must also be furnished to payees [Temp. Reg. Sec. 35a.9999-3, Q & A 46]. The statement must be furnished by January 31st of the following year. The return to the IRS must be filed at a Service Center by February 28th of the following year [Temp. Reg. Sec. 35a.9999-1, Q & A 44-46]. Severe penalties are imposed for failure to comply [¶3721; 3724].

(i) Foreclosures and Abandonments of Secured Property. Lenders (including the U.S. or a state) must report foreclosures or other acquisitions of property in full or partial satisfaction of a debt or debts on Form 1099-A. They must also report abandonments of secured property and must furnish statements to borrowers no later than January 31 of the following year. Reporting, however, is not required for consumer loans [IRC Sec. 6050J]. For penalties, see ¶3721; 3724.

(j) Exchange of Partnership Interests. A partner must notify the partnership if a partnership interest involving unrealized receivables or appreciated inventory is transferred. After notice, the partnership must file an information return that identifies the transferor and the transferee and furnish them a statement of the information shown on the return by January 31 of the following year [IRC Sec. 6050K; Reg. 1.6050K-1]. For penalties, see ¶3721; 3724.

(k) Sales of Donated Property by a Charity. A charity must file an information return if (1) it disposes of property within two years after receiving the property and (2) the donor has claimed a tax deduction in excess of $5,000. The return must identify the donor, the property and the sale [IRC Sec. 6050L; Reg. Sec. 1.6050L-1]. For penalties, see ¶3721; 3724.

(l) Business Cash Receipts of $10,000 or More. If you are engaged in a trade or business that receives $10,000 or more in cash or foreign currency in one transaction or series of related transactions, you must report the identity of the payor, the amount of cash received and the date and nature of the transaction. (Checks, traveler's checks, drafts, money orders and other cash equivalents need not be reported.) Statements to payors must be furnished no later than January 31 of the following year [IRC Sec. 6050I]. For penalties, see ¶3721; 3724.

Any monetary instrument (whether or not in bearer form) with a face amount of not more than $10,000 is included in the definition of cash. (However, the IRS may not treat personal checks as monetary instruments.) The rule is generally effective for cash equivalents received after November 5, 1990. But no actual change in reporting will be required until the IRS designates the monetary instruments that are subject to this rule.

(m) Mortgage Interest of $600 or More. Those who receive mortgage interest payments of $600 or more in a trade or business, must file an information return. (If you sell your home and take back a mortgage, you do not have to report interest.) The return must identify the payor and the aggregate amount of interest received. A written statement must be furnished to the payor by January 31 of the following year. Starting with returns due in 1992, returns must also report the points paid and if these points were paid directly by the borrower [IRC Sec. 6050H]. For penalties, see ¶3721; 3724.

¶3662   RETURNS FOR INTEREST PAID

Except for returns described in (a) below, interest payments totaling $600 or more paid in the course of business must be reported [¶3661]. The return shows the amount paid and the payee's name, address and TIN. The payor can demand the name and address of the actual owner of the payment [IRC Sec. 6041(a), (c); Reg. Sec. 1.6041-1(a), 1.6041-5]. Foreign interest also must be reported [¶3670].

> **NOTE:** The amount of any tax-exempt interest received during the tax year must be reported on the tax return. This is an information reporting requirement and does not convert tax-exempt interest into taxable income.

(a) Returns for $10. Returns on Forms 1096 and 1099-INT must be filed by the payor for interest totaling $10 or more paid or credited to any person on: bank deposits (except certain deposits evidenced by negotiable certificates of deposits); corporate obligations (evidences of indebtedness) in registered form; deposits or obligations of mutual savings banks or similar organizations (these *may* be called "dividends");[1] funds left with insurance companies at interest; deposits with stockbrokers or securities dealers [IRC

Sec. 6049; Reg. Sec. 1.6049-1(a), 1.6049-2(a)]. A nominee receiving interest for another, reports his payment to the real owner on Form 1099-INT. Some nominees who report the payments on fiduciary return (Form 1041) need not file Forms 1099, if the fiduciary return discloses the actual owner. Form 1099-G is used by payers who report payment of $10 or more of unemployment compensation[2] [Reg. Sec. 1.6049-1].

The return may be filed any time in the last quarter of the year after the final payment for the year is made. It must be filed at a Service Center by February 28th of the following year [Reg. Sec. 1.6049-1(c)].

Original issue discount on deferred interest savings accounts, certificates of deposit and other deposit arrangements is includable in the holder's income [¶2827] and must be reported by financial institutions on Forms 1096 and 1099-OID.

Not reported. Foreign corporations, nonresident individuals and partnerships with a nonresident alien partner do not have to report interest paid, if they do no business, and have no business office, in the U.S. [IRC Sec. 6049(b)(2); Reg. Sec. 1.6049-2(b)].

Notice to payee. The payor must give the payee a statement that the payments are being reported to the Revenue Service, with the amount and the payor's name and address. A copy of the return (Form 1099-INT) is used. The notice may be sent during the last quarter of the year with the final payment for the year, or after November 30 after the last payment. It must be delivered by January 31st of the following year. However, the notice may be sent anytime after April 30 if it is furnished with the final payment. Mailing to the payee's last known address is sufficient. A 30-day extension of time may be granted on application to the District Director's office where the payor files income tax returns [Reg. Sec. 1.6049-3].

> NOTE: A statement is required for original issue discount of certain corporate bonds including face-amount certificates (¶1217) and certain financial institution deposit arrangements (¶2827) [IRC Sec. 6049(c)(2); Reg. Sec. 1.6049-1]. For time-savings accounts, banks and other payors must report on Form 1099-INT the entire interest paid or credited a depositor on his premature withdrawal and the amount of loss (forfeiture penalty) deductible by the depositor.

Information returns must be filed for interest and other reportable payments on which backup withholding tax [¶2421] was withheld. See ¶3661(h)].

(b) Ownership Certificates for Bond Interest (Forms 1000 or 1001) may be required. They are filed when presenting interest coupons for payment. Ownership certificates are usually prepared, or at least signed, by the payee. If they are not furnished by the owner, the withholding agent must prepare them [Reg. Sec. 1.1461-1(g)]. The certificates are filed with the return of withheld tax [¶2518].

¶3663 RETURNS FOR DIVIDENDS PAID

Corporations paying dividends totaling $10 or more to any person during a calendar year, and stockbrokers paying a substitute for such dividends, must file returns on Forms 1096 and 1099-DIV. A record owner who receives dividends as a nominee files Form 1099-DIV to report his payment to the actual owner [Reg. Sec. 1.6042-2]. The corporation or broker may demand the name of the actual owner, and failure to supply it subjects the nominee to penalties. Some record owners who file a fiduciary return (Form 1041) that discloses the actual owner of the dividends need not file Form 1099-DIV. Nominees receiving dividends as custodians of mutual fund investment trusts file Forms 1096 and

1099-DIV unless the regulated investment company directly notifies the actual owners [Reg. Sec. 1.6042-2(a)].

The return may be filed during the last quarter of the year after the final dividend payment. It must be filed at a Service Center by February 28 of the following year [Reg. Sec. 1.6042-2]. The payor must give payees the same kind of statement for dividends as is required for interest, and the same dates apply, except for mutual fund unit investment trusts which must deliver notice by February 10, not January 31 [Reg. Sec. 1.6042-4]. If a corporation pays nontaxable dividends to shareholders, it must file Form 5452 with the IRS by February 28. If the required information is not supplied, the distribution may be considered fully taxable.[1]

Information returns must be filed for interest and other reportable payments on which backup withholding tax [¶2421] was withheld [¶3661(h)].

(a) Payments not Reported. Information returns are not required for:

- Undistributed taxable income allocated to shareholders of S corporations (¶3109) [Reg. Sec. 1.6042-3(b)(4)].
- Dividends paid to, or by, any domestic or foreign government or subdivision, or an international organization [Reg. Sec. 1.6042-2(a)(2)].
- Distributions or payments by nonresident foreign corporations [Reg. Sec. 1.6042-3(b)(1)].
- Distributions or payments to nonresident aliens and foreign corporations or their nominees and subject to withholding at the source (¶2518) [IRC Sec. 1441, 1442; Reg. Sec. 1.6042-3(b)(2), (3)].
- Dividends paid to specified persons exempt from interest reporting [¶3662(a)] as long as regulations do not require reporting [IRC Sec. 6042(b)(2)].

(b) Patronage Dividends. Exempt farmers' cooperatives and corporations taxed as cooperatives [¶3355] must report patronage dividends and per-unit retain allocations [¶3356] of $10 or more on Form 1099-PATR and send statements to the payees. The filing times are the same as for ordinary dividends [IRC Sec. 521, 6044; Reg. Sec. 1.6044-1–1.6044-5].

Consumer cooperatives may apply on Form 3491 for exemption from reporting [Reg. Sec. 1.6044-4].

Information returns must be filed for reportable patronage dividends on which backup withholding tax [¶2421] was withheld. See ¶3661(h).

¶3664   STOCK TRANSFERS UNDER EMPLOYEE OPTIONS

Your corporation must furnish a written statement on the transfer of stock to any person who exercises a stock option [¶1208]. This statement must be sent by January 31st following the calendar year of the transfer [IRC Sec. 6039].

¶3665   GROUP-TERM LIFE INSURANCE PREMIUMS

If your corporation pays group-term life insurance premiums that are taxable to an employee [¶1207], it reports the taxable amount for each employee on Form W-2 and the summary Form W-3 [IRC Sec. 6052; Reg. Sec. 1.6052-1]. Insurance companies must report the taxable amount for full-time insurance salespersons on the same or separate Form W-2 that reports an employee's tax withheld from wages. The same filing requirements apply [¶2552]. The employee's copy of Form W-2 serves as the statement that must be given to the employee by the January 31st preceding the filing date [Reg. Sec. 1.6052-1, 1.6052-2].

¶3666   CERTAIN LIQUIDATIONS OR TERMINATIONS

If your corporation is in dissolution or liquidating any part of its capital stock, it files a report of the plan and the distributions made.

(a) Report on Plan. Your corporation must file information Form 966, Corporate Dissolution or Liquidation, with the IRS office where it files its income tax return. This must be done within 30 days after the adoption of a resolution or plan for dissolution of the corporation or for the liquidation of the whole or any part of its capital stock [IRC Sec. 6043; Reg. Sec. 1.6043-1]. The return must be accompanied by a certified copy of the resolution or plan and all amendments to it [Reg. Sec. 1.6043-1(b)].

(b) Return for Distributions. Information returns (Form 1099-DIV) must be filed for distributions in liquidation of $600 or more. They must be accompanied by Form 1096 and filed at a Revenue Service Center [¶3660] by February 28 of the year after the calendar year the distribution is made [IRC Sec. 6043; Reg. Sec. 1.6043-2].

(c) Exempt Organizations. In general, organizations exempt from tax [¶3335] in any of their last five years before their liquidation, termination or contraction must file a return. Churches, religious groups and any exempt organization (*other than a private foundation* [¶3337]) whose annual gross receipts normally are not over $5,000 are excused from filing. *Private foundations* must file. However, any organization can be excused from filing by the IRS. Qualified employee plans may be excused if the employer files a return [IRC Sec. 6043(b)].

¶3667   INFORMATION RETURNS FOR TAX-EXEMPT
ORGANIZATIONS AND TRUSTS

Organizations exempt from tax file an annual information return, unless they are specifically excused from filing [IRC Sec. 6033(a)]. If the return is not filed, the organization may lose its exemption.[1] They also report unrelated business income [¶3354] and payments of income to others [¶3661 et seq.]. Organizations claiming exemption from tax [¶3336(b)] must file with the District Director as proof of their exemption the application form prescribed in the regulations describing the organization and its functions [Reg. Sec. 1.501(a)-1]. An exempt organization maintaining funded pension or annuity plans for their employees must meet special filing requirements in addition to filing the annual information return [see below]. Electing exempt organizations subject to lobbying expenditures rules must file information returns. If the organization is a member of an affiliated group, it must also file a return for itself as well as the entire group [IRC Sec. 6033(b)(6)–(8)].

(a) Who Must File a Return. Generally, organizations exempt from tax [¶3336] must file annual information returns. Exceptions from filing are in two classes: mandatory and discretionary [IRC Sec. 6033; Reg. Sec. 1.6033-2].

The mandatory class includes churches, certain religious organizations and other types of organizations (but not private foundations [¶3337 et seq.]) if annual gross receipts are normally not over $5,000 [IRC Sec. 6033(a)(2)(A), (C); Reg. Sec. 1.6033-2(g)(1)].

The discretionary class includes those organizations that the IRS relieves from filing a return when it is unnecessary to the efficient administration of the tax laws [IRC Sec. 6033(a)(2)(B); Reg. Sec. 1.6033-2(g)(2)].

Exempt organizations required to file annual information returns use Form 990 [Reg. Sec. 1.6033-2(a)]. Employee trusts for qualified pension and profit-sharing plans file returns in the Form 5500 series [(b) below]. Group returns can be filed by a parent organization for two or more organizations [Reg. Sec. 1.6033-2(d)]. The returns are due by the 15th day of the fifth month after the close of the tax year. Religious and apostolic organizations with a common treasury file Form 1065 on or before the 15th day of the fourth month after the close of the tax year [Reg. Sec. 1.6033-2(e)]. Penalties are imposed if they fail to file a return (¶3721; 3724) [Reg. Sec. 1.6033-2(f)].

Form 990 requires exempt organizations to provide information on gross income, disbursements and deductions, net worth at the beginning and end of the tax year, and other information relating to the organization's activities [IRC Sec. 6033(b); Reg. Sec. 1.6033-2(a)]. Organizations with gross receipts over $25,000 and all private foundations must also include balance sheets at the beginning and end of the tax year. Also, private foundations must provide the names and addresses of substantial contributors, information on investment income and a list of capital gains and losses [IRC Sec. 6104; Reg. Sec. 301.6104-2].

File Form 990 with the appropriate IRS Center listed in the form instructions.

NOTE: While exempt organizations use Form 990, private foundations use 990-PF. Organizations with gross receipts of $25,000 or less that are not private foundations will provide less detailed information than private foundations and organizations with gross income over $25,000 [Reg. Sec. 1.6033-2(a)(1)].

Form 4720 should be filed if certain excise taxes are imposed [¶3340; 3342–3344]. For exempt organizations liquidating, terminating or dissolving, see ¶3666(c).

(b) Employee Benefit Plans. Employers or plan administrators (including self-employed individuals) who maintain employee pension benefit plans [¶1300; 1340] must file one or more of the following annual information returns/statements:

- Form 5500—Annual Return/Report of Employee Benefit Plan (with 100 or more participants). This form requires detailed information relating to the plan.
- Form 5500-C/R—Return/Report of Employee Benefit Plan is filed by plans with fewer than 100 participants during the plan year.
- Schedule A (Form 5500), Insurance Information, is attached to either of the forms if the benefits under the plan are provided by an insurance company.
- Schedule B (Form 5500), Actuarial Information, is attached to either of the forms or Form 5500EZ for most defined benefit plans.
- Form 5500EZ—Annual Return of One-Participant Pension Benefit Plan. (Eligible filers should not use 5500-C/R but file Schedule A (Form 5500)[2] for defined benefit plans).

NOTE: Form 5500EZ is not required for plans with $100,000 or less in assets.

When to file. The above forms must be filed by the last day of the seventh month after the close of the plan's tax year.

Exempt organizations maintaining custodial accounts for its employees and qualified government and church plans must also file annual returns/reports in addition to Form 990.

Where to file. IRS forms (Form 5500 series above, and supporting schedules) must be filed with the appropriate Service Center designated in the instructions.

IRA plans. An annual return is not required if (1) there is no penalty tax imposed for premature distributions, early bond redemptions, excess distributions, or accumulations; and (2) no plan activity is engaged in other than the making of contributions (except rollover contributions) and distributions [IRC Sec. 6058(c),(d),(e)]. No special form is prescribed for rollover distributions. But a tax-free rollover should be reported on Form 1040.[3]

¶3668   RETURNS FOR NONEXEMPT TRUSTS CLAIMING CHARITABLE DEDUCTION

Nonexempt trusts [¶3353] and trusts, not including simple trusts [¶3505], claiming a charitable deduction for amounts paid or permanently set aside [¶3513] must file an annual information return. Form 1041-A is used for this purpose and filed by the 15th day of the 4th month following the close of the tax year [IRC Sec. 642(c), 6034; Reg. Sec. 1.6034-1(a)(1)]. Charitable nonexempt trusts must also file Form 990; split interest nonexempt trusts file Form 1041-A only. Charitable remainder annuity trusts and charitable remainder unitrusts [IRC Sec. 664(d); Reg. Sec. 1.664-1–3] use Form 1041-A.

¶3669   PARTNERSHIP, FIDUCIARY AND S CORPORATION RETURNS

[New tax legislation may affect this subject; see ¶1.]

Information returns must be filed by a partnership, fiduciary or S corporation. Trusts, estates, partnerships and S corporations must furnish copies of their information returns to beneficiaries, partners, or shareholders [IRC Sec. 6034A, 6037(b)].

(a) Partnership Returns. The partnership return, Form 1065, is an information return of the partnerhip income and its distribution to the partners [¶3401 et seq.]. It must be filed by the 15th day of the fourth month following the close of the partnership tax year [IRC Sec. 6031; Reg. Sec. 1.6031-1]. (If all partners are nonresident aliens, the return may be filed by the 15th day of the sixth month after the tax year. A partnership not engaged in U.S. trade or business and having no U.S. source income need not file a return.) Your partnership must furnish you and its other partners with copies of the information shown on its return. If your partnership has tax-exempt partners, it must supply them with information needed to compute what portion of its distributive share of income or loss is relevant to unrelated business income [IRC Sec. 6031(b),(d)].

Returns must also be filed by U.S. partners in a foreign partnership to account for acquisitions, dispositions, and substantial changes in partnership interests [IRC Sec. 6046A].

Your partnership return may be filed with the District Director for the district where the partnership's principal office or place of business is located or, if none, with the Director, International Operations Division, unless instructions require filing elsewhere.

(b) Fiduciary Returns. In addition to filing Form 1041 [¶3605], a fiduciary must attach separate Schedule K-1 to the form for each beneficiary of an estate or trust. This indicates each beneficiary's share of income, deductions and credits [¶3520(c); 3521]. The fiduciary should give Copy B to the beneficiary by the end of the month following the close of the taxable year of the estate or trust.

Fiduciaries must give written notice of qualification as an executor or receiver, usually within 10 days from the appointment or authorization to act, to the District Director with whom the taxpayer was required to file returns. The notice must generally contain names and addresses of the taxpayer, the fiduciary, the court dealing with the proceedings along with certain dates [IRC Sec. 6036; Reg. Sec. 301.6036-1]. The notice can also be provided when the fiduciary files a notice of fiduciary relationship, Form 56 [IRC Sec. 6903; Reg. Sec. 301.6036-1(c), 301.6903-1].

(c) S Corporation Returns. If your corporation elects partnership-type taxation [¶3100 et seq.], it must file an information return on Form 1120S for each tax year during its election [¶3102].

¶3670   RETURNS FOR FOREIGN ITEMS AND FOREIGN ORGANIZATIONS

The term "foreign items" means interest on the bonds of a foreign country or interest or dividends on the bonds or stock of a nonresident foreign corporation not having a fiscal or paying agent in the United States [Reg. Sec. 1.6041-4(b)]. Form TD F90-22.1 must be filed for a tax year in which a taxpayer has a financial interest in or authority over a foreign account.

Who files a return. Form 1099-INT and Form 1099-DIV must be prepared and filed by the bank or collecting agent for collections totaling $600 or more for a citizen, resident alien, resident fiduciary, or partnership, any member of which is a citizen or resident. Forms 1099 and the summary Form 1096 must be filed by February 28 at an Internal Revenue Service Center. The payor can demand the name and address of the real owner [IRC Sec. 6041; Reg. Sec. 1.6041-4–1.6041-6].

Foreign corporations. Information returns about foreign corporations must be filed on Form 5471 with its appropriate supporting and separate schedules if a U.S. person owns 5% or more of the value of its stock, or if a U.S. person controls the corporation [IRC Sec. 6038, 6046].

U.S. persons who have an interest in a foreign corporation and meet certain requirements must file Form 5471. However, it may not be necessary to complete all of the form schedules. Schedules C through F, K, and O must be filed by a U.S. person that acquires, or increases holdings to, 5% or more of the stock value, and whenever 5% or more of the stock value is added to any holding.

Separate Schedule M (Form 5471) must be filed by a U.S. person in control of the corporation for 30 consecutive days during the corporation's annual accounting period that ends with or within the U.S. person's tax year.

NOTE: All foreign corporations that carry on a trade or business in the U.S. must now file information reporting and maintain certain records (for example, generally relating to allocating amounts between the U.S. and foreign countries). This rule generally applies to furnishing the required information after November 5, 1990 [IRC Sec. 6038C].

Foreign trusts. Within 90 days (or at some later date under regulations yet to be issued) after any U.S. person creates or transfers property to a foreign trust, the grantor, transferor or fiduciary of a testamentary trust must file a return on Form 3520 [IRC Sec. 6048].

Foreign interests in U.S. real property. Information returns must be filed by foreign persons holding direct investments in U.S. real property interests. Foreign persons must file if they (1) did not engage in a U.S. trade or business during the year and (2) have direct U.S. real property interests that equal or exceed $50,000. The return must show the name, address, a description of all the U.S. real property interests, and such other information as the regulations may require [IRC Sec. 6039C]. For withholding on sales, see ¶2518. Penalties are imposed for failure to comply [IRC Sec. 6652(f)].

Foreign-controlled corporations. Every domestic or foreign corporation that is engaged in a trade or business in the U.S. and controlled by a foreign person, must file an information return on Form 5472 [IRC Sec. 6038A; Reg. Sec. 1.6038A-1]. Reporting is required if at any time during a tax year a foreign person owns at least 25% of the reporting corporation's stock either by value or voting power [IRC Sec. 6038A(c)(1)].

NOTE: A corporation subject to the reporting requirements must report its transactions with all related persons as defined under IRC Sec. 267(b); 482; or 707(b)(1), not merely its transactions with corporations in its controlled group [IRC Sec. 6038A].

¶3671   RETURNS AND RECORDKEEPING FOR ALTERNATIVE MINIMUM TAX

Corporations must file Form 4626 if they have any alternative minimum tax (AMT) liability [¶2610]. Form 4626 is filed with Form 1120 [¶3651].

Individuals required to pay AMT [¶2600] must file Form 6251 with Form 1040 [¶3630]. Estates and trusts report their AMT on Form 8656 and attach it to Forms 1041 or 990-T [¶3520(d)].

Records to be kept. Taxpayers with preference items must keep records available. The records required would vary with the type of item [Reg. Sec. 1.57-5].

¶3672   RETURN, DISCLOSURE AND RECORDKEEPING FOR TAX RETURN PREPARERS

A preparer is any person (including a partnership or corporation) who prepares for compensation, all or a substantial portion of another's income tax return or refund claim. A person is not an income tax preparer when he merely furnishes typing, reproducing or mechanical assistance in preparing the return. He is also not a preparer when he is hired by his employer to prepare the employer's or employees' returns. Fiduciaries of trusts or estates are not preparers when they prepare returns or refund claims for the estate or trust.

Under certain circumstances, a person who files a refund claim as a result of a Revenue Service examination is not a preparer. Volunteers are not preparers if they provide tax counseling service under federal assistance programs [IRC Sec. 7701(a)(36); Reg. Sec. 301.7701-15].

A preparer must sign each return (signing includes affixing an appropriate identifying number and address) and furnish a copy to the taxpayer. Also, preparers must retain copies or lists of returns for three years following the close of the return period [IRC Sec. 6107; Reg. Sec. 1.6107-1].

Employers (including self-employed preparers and independent contractors) of income tax preparers must keep and retain records for three years after the close of a return period for each tax preparer they employ [IRC Sec. 6060; Reg. Sec. 1.6060-1].

> **NOTE:** Specific penalties may be imposed upon failure to comply [IRC Sec. 6695; Reg. Sec. 1.6695-1]. Negligent, intentional or willful understatement of tax liability by tax preparers is covered by other civil penalties provisions [¶3721; 3724].

TAX-SHELTER REGISTRATION

> **NOTE:** The passive loss rules have severely curtailed tax shelters. And legislation has been discussed that would repeal the tax shelter registration rules.

¶3673   REGISTRATION OF TAX SHELTERS IN GENERAL

The registration requirements are so broad that virtually every shelter (including those not considered abusive by the IRS) have to register. Tax shelters that promise large immediate tax deductions for a minor investment are considered abusive by the IRS. Shelters that are considered abusive also are often financed with borrowed money (nonrecourse paper) for which the investors are not personally liable. Shelter promoters must keep a list of investors who take part in a shelter. The IRS has access to that list and can cross-check the names on the list with the returns of the investors[1] [¶3674]. To enforce compliance, severe penalties are imposed [¶3676].

What tax shelters must be registered. Tax shelter organizations must register with the IRS tax shelters they organize, develop or sell. A tax shelter is any investment that meets these two tests: (1) The investment is one as to which one could reasonably infer that the ratio of the deductions plus 350% of the credits to the cash actually invested is greater than 2 to 1. (2) The investment is: (a) required to be registered under a federal or state law regulating securities, (b) sold under a registration exemption requiring the filing of notice with a government security agency or (c) a substantial investment. An investment is substantial if the total amount that can be offered for sale exceeds $250,000 and there are expected to be five qor more investors [IRC Sec. 6111; Temp. Reg. Sec. 301.6111-IT].

Registration of tax shelters. Promoters or principal organizers must register tax shelter interests on Form 8264 before any original sale offerings are made. The registration form asks for a description of the investment and promoter's identity. A registration number is assigned to each shelter. Investors then must file Form 8271 and include that number on their income tax returns that contain the income or loss from the shelter [IRC Sec. 6111; Temp. Reg. Sec. 301.6111-1T].

Exceptions from registration. Sales of residences to persons for use as a principal residence and sales of tangible personal property by a manufacturer to someone expected to use it in an active principal trade or business are exempt from the registration requirements. But this exemption does not apply to master sound recordings, motion picture or television films, video tapes, lithograph plates, or other property relating to literary, artistic or musical compositions [Temp. Reg. Sec. 301.6111-1T].

¶3674   PROMOTERS "AND SELLERS" LIST OF INVESTORS

Any person who organizes any potentially abusive tax shelter, or sells an interest in such a shelter, must maintain customer lists and must make them available to the IRS for inspection on request. The lists must be kept for at least seven years [IRC Sec. 6112]. A $50 penalty is imposed for each person required to on the list if the list is not maintained or not provided to the IRS when requested. The maximum yearly penalty is $100,000 [IRC Sec. 6708; Temp. Reg. Sec. 301.6112-IT; 301.6708-IT]. See also ¶3718(e).

¶3676   PENALTIES

A $100 penalty is imposed on promoters for each failure to furnish the required tax-shelter registration number to investors, and a $250 penalty applies to investors for each failure to include a shelter number on their tax returns. Promoters must also pay a penalty of the greater of $500 or 1% of the shelter investment for each failure to register a shelter and for each false or incomplete registration statement. But if a failure to register, or false registration is done intentionally, then the limit does not apply. These penalties, however, are not imposed if reasonable cause can be shown [IRC Sec. 6707; Temp. Reg. Sec. 301.6707-IT].

Footnotes to Chapter 26

(For your added convenience, in brackets [] with the footnotes below, you will find citations to related paragraphs in the "RIA United States Tax Reporter "(USTR), "CCH Federal Tax Reporter"(CCH) and "RIA Federal Tax Coordinator 2d"(FTC) multi-volume services.)

FOOTNOTE ¶ 3601 [USTR ¶ 60,114; CCH ¶ 36,450; 37,605; FTC¶ S-1000; 4500].

(1) Rev. Rul. 67-191, 1967-1 CB 318.

(2) Reaves v. Comm., 8 AFTR 2d 5619, 295 F.2d 336.

(3) Notice 89-7, 1989-1 CB 627.

FOOTNOTE ¶ 3602 [USTR ¶ 60,134; CCH ¶ 36,471; FTC ¶ S-1800].

(1) Erdahl, (8th Cir., No. 90-1926).

(2) Treas. Dept. booklet "Your Federal Income Tax" (1991 Ed.), p. 26.

FOOTNOTE ¶ 3603 [USTR ¶ 60,124.01; CCH ¶ 36,450; FTC ¶ S-1705; 2014].

FOOTNOTE ¶ 3604 [USTR ¶ 60,124.01; CCH ¶ 36,450; FTC ¶ S-4502].

FOOTNOTE ¶ 3605 [USTR ¶ 60,124.04; CCH ¶ 36,450; FTC ¶ S-2000 et seq.].

(1) Rev. Rul. 55-387, 1955-1 CB 131.

(2)Senate Report No. 96-1035, p. 94, 96th Cong., 2nd Sess.

FOOTNOTE ¶ 3606 [USTR ¶ 60,114; CCH ¶ 36,441.018; 36,441.025; FTC ¶ S-1600 et seq.

(1) Rev. Proc. 91-69, IRG 1991-52.

FOOTNOTE ¶ 3610 [USTR ¶ 60,124.03; CCH ¶ 36,450; FTC ¶ S-1900 et seq.].

(1) Florida Grocery Co., 1 BTA 412; Central Auto Market, 7 BTA 973.

(2) Wootan, ¶55,191 PH Memo TC.

(3) Waldron Co., 2 BTA 715.

(4) Treas. Dept. booklet "Tax Guide for Small Business" (1991 Ed.), p. 5.

(5) U.S. v. General Insp. & Ldg. Co., 192 F.2d 223, 1 AFTR 182.

(6) Updike v. U.S., 8 F.2d 913, 5 AFTR 5720.

(7) Title II, United States Code.

FOOTNOTE ¶ 3611 [USTR ¶ 60,614; CCH ¶ 36,441; FTC ¶ S-1200 et seq.].

(1) Treas. Dept. booklet "Tax Guide for Small Business" (1991 Ed.), p. 154.

FOOTNOTE ¶ 3612 [USTR ¶ 60,124; CCH ¶ 36,450; FTC ¶ S-1707].

FOOTNOTE ¶ 3620 [USTR ¶ 61,094; CCH ¶ 37,965; FTC ¶ S-1500 et seq.].

FOOTNOTE ¶ 3621 [USTR ¶ 61,094; CCH ¶ 37,965; FTC ¶ S-1501].

(1) Rev. Rul. 64-8, 1964-1 CB 480.

(2) Rev. Rul. 63-247, 1963-2 CB 612.

FOOTNOTE ¶ 3622 [USTR ¶ 61,094; CCH ¶ 37,965; FTC ¶ S-1524].

FOOTNOTE ¶ 3623 [USTR ¶ 61,094; CCH ¶ 37,965; FTC ¶ S-1564].

FOOTNOTE ¶ 3630 [USTR ¶ 61,094; CCH ¶ 37,723; FTC ¶ S-4700 et seq.].

(1) Petrulis, Ct. App. (7th Cir.; 7/24/91).

(2) Rev. Rul. 71-129, 1971-1 CB 397.

(3) Instructions for Form 990-T.

FOOTNOTE ¶ 3631 [USTR ¶ 60,814; CCH ¶ 37,789; FTC ¶ S-5000 et seq.].

(1) Treas. Dept. booklet "Your Federal Income Tax" (1991 Ed.), p. 12.

(2) Rev. Rul. 82-47, 1982-1 CB 201, modifying Rev. Rul. 63-222, 1963-2 CB 605.

(3) Treas. Dept. booklet "Tax Guide for U.S. Citizens and Resident Aliens Abroad" (1991 Ed.), p. 18.

FOOTNOTE ¶ 3632 [USTR ¶ 60,914; CCH ¶ 37,807; FTC ¶ S-5100 et seq.].

FOOTNOTE ¶ 3633 [USTR ¶ 64,024; CCH ¶ 36,441.017; FTC ¶ S-6800 et seq.].

FOOTNOTE ¶ 3640 [USTR ¶ 60,114; CCH ¶ 36,441; FTC ¶ S-1404].

(1) Treas. Dept. booklet "Your Federal Income Tax" (1991 Ed.), p. 96.

(2) Treas. Dept. booklet "Your Federal Income Tax" (1991 Ed.), p. 120.

(3) Instructions for Form 6252.

FOOTNOTE ¶ 3650 [USTR ¶ 61,514; CCH ¶ 38,086; FTC ¶ S-5200 et seq.].

FOOTNOTE ¶ 3651 [USTR ¶ 61,514; CCH ¶ 38,086; FTC ¶ S-5700 et seq.].

(1) Instructions for Federal Tax Deposit Coupon Form.

(2) Conference Report, No. 97-760, p. 755, 97th Cong.

FOOTNOTE ¶ 3652 [USTR ¶ 66,524; CCH ¶ 40,475; FTC ¶ S-2000].

FOOTNOTE ¶ 3653 [USTR ¶ 66,554; CCH ¶ 40,475; FTC ¶ S-2100].

FOOTNOTE ¶ 3654 [USTR ¶ 61,614; CCH ¶ 38,206; FTC ¶ S-5900].

(1) Rev. Rul. 82-47, 1982-1 CB 201.

FOOTNOTE ¶ 3655 [USTR ¶ 61,014; CCH ¶ 37,863; FTC ¶ S-1006].

FOOTNOTE ¶ 3660 [USTR ¶ 60,814; CCH ¶ 36,450; FTC ¶ S-2700 et seq.].

(1) Instructions for Form 1096.

(2) Instructions for Forms W-2, W-3 and 1099-R.

FOOTNOTE ¶ 3661 [USTR ¶ 60,414; CCH ¶ 36,936; FTC ¶ S-3600].

(1) Rev. Rul. 69-556, 1969-2 CB 242.

(2) Rev. Rul. 56-176, 1956-1 CB 560.

(3) Rev. Rul. 62-54, 1962-1 CB 285.

(4) Rev. Rul. 71-52, 1971-1 CB 278.

(5) Rev. Rul. 69-595, 1969-2 CB 242; Rev. Rul. 70-608, 1970-2 CB 286.

(6) Instructions for Forms 1099, 1098, 5498, and W-2G.

(7) Rev. Rul. 54-571, 1954-2 CB 235.

(8) Ltr. Rul. 9115019.

FOOTNOTE ¶ 3662 [USTR ¶ 60,414; CCH ¶ 36,936; FTC ¶ S-3000].

(1) Rev. Rul. 73-221, 1973-1 CB 298.

(2) Instructions for Form 1099-G.

FOOTNOTE ¶ 3663 [USTR ¶ 60,424; CCH ¶ 36,970; FTC ¶ S-2900].

(1) Rev. Proc. 75-17, 1975-1 CB 677.

FOOTNOTE ¶ 3664 [USTR ¶ 60,394; CCH ¶ 36,861; FTC ¶ S-3700].

FOOTNOTE ¶ 3665 [USTR ¶ 60,524; CCH ¶ 37,444; FTC ¶ S-3300].

FOOTNOTE ¶ 3666 [USTR ¶ 60,434; CCH ¶ 36,988; FTC ¶ S-4300].

FOOTNOTE ¶ 3667 [USTR ¶ 60,334; CCH ¶ 36,625; FTC ¶ S-2800].

(1) Rev. Rul. 59-95, 1959-1 CB 627.

(2) Form 5500 EZ Instructions.

(3) Instructions for Form 1040.

FOOTNOTE ¶ 3668 [USTR ¶ 60,344; CCH ¶ 36,643; FTC ¶ S-2800].

FOOTNOTE ¶ 3669 [USTR ¶ 60,34A4; CCH ¶ 36,661; FTC ¶ S-2700].

FOOTNOTE ¶ 3670 [USTR ¶ 60,414.04; CCH ¶ 36,744; FTC ¶ S-3500].

FOOTNOTE ¶ 3671 [USTR ¶ 572.03; CCH ¶ 37,922; FTC ¶ A-8100].

FOOTNOTE ¶ 3672 [USTR ¶ 61,614; CCH ¶ 37,922; FTC ¶ S-1102].

FOOTNOTE ¶ 3673 [USTR ¶ 61,614; CCH ¶ 38,002; FTC ¶ S-4400].
(1) Conference Report No. 98-861, pp. 1635-1638, 98th Cong., 2nd Sess.

FOOTNOTE ¶ 3674 [USTR ¶ 61,124; CCH ¶ 38,002; FTC ¶ S-4400].

FOOTNOTE ¶ 3676 [USTR ¶ 67,074; CCH ¶ 40,890; FTC ¶ V-2500].

CHAPTER 27

ASSESSMENT—COLLECTION—REFUNDS

Your filed return is a self-assessment of how much tax you owe for the year. The IRS first examines it for accuracy, completeness and correct form. All returns are then sorted and classified, and many are selected for examination. This chapter explains the procedure for examination, assessment and collection of deficiencies, refund of tax, and the work of the Tax Court. Collection of tax at the source (i.e., tax withholding) is covered in Chapter 15.

EXAMINATION OF RETURNS

¶3701   GENERAL PROCEDURE

All business and individual tax returns are processed by an electronic data system that checks the accuracy of the return, the right to any refund claimed and inclusion of income reported on information returns [¶3660]. The key to the system is the taxpayer identification number (TIN) [¶3620]. All the information about the taxpayer is coordinated on magnetic tape at the computer center in Martinsburg, West Virginia. The system also locates persons who do not file returns as required.

(a) Preliminary Examination. If a mathematical error is discovered in the taxpayer's figures—an amount wrongly transferred from one schedule to another or a mistake in addition, subtraction or multiplication—the IRS mails a notice to the taxpayer with a bill for any additional tax due [Reg. Sec. 601.105]. If an overpayment resulted, the excess is applied to future installments of tax [IRC Sec. 6403] or is credited or refunded [IRC Sec. 6402; Reg. Sec. 301.6402-1].

(b) How Returns Are Selected for Examination. The criteria for selection include: returns reporting income above a designated level; returns showing substantial income not subject to withholding; returns with unusual dependency exemptions or disproportionately large deductions; and business returns that show a lower than normal gross profit ratio. Returns that call for large refunds receive a pre-refund review. Also, failure to answer inventory questions may trigger an examination.

The Revenue Service also selects returns at random for its Taxpayer Compliance Measurement Program (TCMP). Every item on a return selected for a TCMP audit will be subject to verification. The purpose of this program is to furnish statistics on the type and number of errors that taxpayers are making and to provide a starting point for solutions to any problems uncovered. Some of the most common omissions that have turned up for individual returns are missing W-2 forms, incomplete or incorrect address or identifying number, incorrect blocks checked for dependents, entries on the wrong line, and failure to sign the return.

However, according to IRS, returns are primarily chosen for examination by use of a complex computer program known as the Discriminant Function System (DIF). The DIF process is essentially a mathematically oriented system that relies on a composite of "average taxpayer" figures based on previous returns. It assigns weights to entries on returns, and each return is given a score—the higher the score, the greater the probability of an error. Returns picked out by DIF are then screened manually and those items considered to have the highest error potential are selected for examination [¶3702].

Other returns are selected by such methods as examining claims for credit or refund of previously paid taxes and matching information documents (e.g., Forms W-2 and 1099) [Reg. Sec. 601.105].

➤ **OBSERVATION** An examination of a taxpayer's return does not suggest a suspicion of dishonesty or criminal liability. It may not even result in more tax. Many cases are closed without change in reported tax liability and, in many others, taxpayers receive refunds.[1]

Items that invite scrutiny. Particular attention is paid to deductions for charitable contributions, medical expense deductions, unreimbursed business expenses of salespersons or executives and blanket expense allowances by employers.

Examiners also look closely at expense deductions for club dues, entertainment, travel, maintenance of automobiles, yachts, airplanes, company supported residences and other items that may disguise expenses incurred for a personal purpose. Taxpayers who fail to keep adequate records of business expenses may find that their deductions for such expenses are disallowed.

(c) Books and Records. Taxpayers (including foreign corporations, trades or businesses) are responsible for keeping books and records that are adequate for examination purposes [IRC Sec. 6001; Reg. Sec. 1.6001-1]. If taxpayers use an automatic accounting system, it should be set up so that records are available if the IRS requests them. In addition, at regular intervals, the general and subsidiary ledger balances should be printed out and income and expense account totals should be printed out and balanced with control accounts.[2]

NOTE: In the course of investigating a taxpayer's financial affairs, the Revenue Service may issue a *summons* for the taxpayer's books and records from a bank, brokerage house, accountant, attorney or other third-party recordkeeper. The taxpayer must be given notice of the summons and the right to try to forestall complying with it. Also, special procedural rules apply for issuing administrative and third-party summonses [IRC Sec. 7602(a); 7609]. For suspending statute of limitations for an unresolved dispute, see "NOTE," under "Wrongful levy" in ¶3713.

➤ **OBSERVATION** The Supreme Court has ruled, however, that the IRS may serve a summons without court approval in a tax-shelter case. It did not matter that the records sought by the IRS included a list of investors whose names were not known.[3]

¶3702   **EXAMINATION PROCEDURE**

[New tax legislation may affect this subject; see ¶1.]

What can you expect if you are selected for an examination? Normally, it begins with a letter from the IRS. This will say whether additional information is needed for a correspondence examination. Or you may be called in for an office interview examination or be visited for a field examination.

If the examination is conducted by correspondence, you can simply mail in copies of any required information and usually settle the matter. If you are selected for review in an Internal Revenue office, you will be informed as to what areas of the return are being questioned and what records to bring to the interview. A field examination takes place where the books and records are kept (usually at your office or home, or the office of your accountant or attorney). Most often it is restricted to businesses and complex individual returns—and the examiner will check the entire return. A mutually satisfactory date will be set for an interview or field examination [Reg. Sec. 601.105].

Right of disclosure. Early in the audit process, the IRS must distribute a comprehensive notice of taxpayer rights to every taxpayer it contacts regarding the determination or collection of tax. In clear, nontechnical language, the notice must explain your rights and IRS obligations during an audit; how to appeal IRS decisions; how to file claims for refunds; how to file complaints; and how the IRS can enforce tax laws through such means as liens, assessments and levies. This is generally accomplished by including a copy of IRS Publication 1, *Your Rights as a Taxpayer*, with the notice of examination.

Right to representation. Any audit procedure must be suspended *immediately* if you clearly make known that you wish to be represented by anyone authorized to practice before the IRS (e.g., a lawyer, CPA, enrolled agent or enrolled actuary).

Audits are scheduled on normal IRS workdays, during normal duty hours of the IRS. The IRS may schedule audits throughout the year. Although the IRS should try to minimize any adverse effects in scheduling the examination, there is no requirement that special accommodations be made on account of your busy season.

The IRS determines if an audit is to be conducted at an IRS office or in the field (that is, an audit conducted at your residence or place of business, or some other location other than an IRS office). The determination is based upon the facts of each case including the return's complexity, where your records are kept, any physical condition that makes it unreasonably difficult to travel and the physical safety of the IRS examiner.

Office audits are generally held at the IRS office within the assigned district that is closest to the address shown on your return. Field audits are generally conducted at the location where the original books, records and source documents pertinent to the examination are maintained. This is usually your residence or principal place of business. Exceptions are made if the place of business is so small that you must close your business to accommodate the audit, or when it appears that the possibility of physical danger to any IRS personnel exists [Temp. Reg. Sec. 301.7605-1T].

Examination of partnership items. Procedural rules have been established for examining items of partnership income, deduction, gain, loss or other items at the partnership level in a unified partnership proceeding rather than in separate proceedings with the partners. Small partnerships are excluded from these procedures but they may elect to be governed by them. For this purpose, small partnerships are those that have ten or fewer partners, and each partner is a natural person (married couples count as one) or an estate [IRC Sec. 6231; Reg. Sec. 301.6231(a)(3)-1].

The examination usually begins when the IRS notifies the partnership that its return has been selected for examination. This notice is sent to the tax matters partner (TMP), the general partner who has been selected to handle the partnership's tax affairs. The TMP will also receive the notice of the outcome of the examination (the notice of final partnership administrative adjustment). Also, the IRS will notify partners entitled to notice that an examination is under way at least 120 days before the notice of a final partnership administrative adjustment (FPAA) is mailed to the TMP. The IRS will notify the partners entitled to notice of the FPAA within 60 days of mailing the notice to the TMP.[1]

(a) Taxpayer Cooperation. If you receive examination notices, you should produce all records required by the examiners and cooperate with them in every way possible. Nothing is gained by placing obstacles in their way as they can compel that books and records be produced [IRC Sec. 7602; Reg. Sec. 301.7602-1]. Failure to appear or produce records when a summons is issued is punishable by fine, imprisonment or both [IRC Secs. 7210, 7601; Reg. Sec. 301.7601-1 et seq.].

Fraud investigation. In cases involving possible charges of fraud, you should be more cautious. If the agent investigating the case is from the Criminal Division, a so-called Special Agent, or if the regular examiner does or says anything to indicate that this examination is not purely routine, you should get professional legal advice before giving the agent any information.

The IRS can examine books without showing probable cause if it suspects fraud, even if the year had been previously examined[2] or was otherwise closed by statute of limitations.[3] Evidence obtained by a routine tax investigation is not admissible in a fraud proceeding, unless you have been warned of your right to remain silent and your right to have a lawyer[4] or accountant.[5]

(b) Examiner's Finding. After an examination, the examiner informs you of their findings either orally or by letter, and must indicate the amount of any proposed deficiency [Reg. Sec. 601.105]. A notice of deficiency must not only give an explanation of why the IRS claims additional tax is due, but it must also explain the basis for any tax penalties [IRC Sec. 7522].

You should contact your professional advisers if you receive proposed assessments for additional tax. If you agree with the examiner's findings, you may consent to a deficiency assessment on Form 870, Waiver of Restrictions on Assessment and Collection of Deficiency in Tax and Acceptance of Overassessment, or Form 4549, Income Tax Examination Changes, depending on the type of audit [¶3706]. Such filing closes the matter. The findings will not be reopened to make adjustments unfavorable to you, unless: (1) there is evidence of fraud, malfeasance, collusion, concealment or material misrepresentation; (2) there was substantial error based on an established IRS position existing at the previous examination; or (3) failure to reopen would be a serious administrative omission [Reg. Sec. 601.105(j)].

If you disagree with findings made after correspondence examinations, you can ask for an Appeals Office conference [¶3703] within the period specified in the form letters sent to you that included the findings. After an office interview examination, you can ask for an immediate conference with an Appeals officer who has full authority to settle the tax dispute, or wait for the form letter with the examiner's findings and a statement of your alternatives available, including consideration of the findings by an Appeals Office.

NOTE: You should confer with your tax consultants as soon as possible after you receive the examiner's findings. With a consultation, you may have the benefit of professional advice as to whether it is best to accept an examiner's finding. In some cases, the District Director or you can request technical advice from the National Office [Reg. Sec. 601.105].

(c) In Partnership Proceedings, the IRS makes a final partnership administrative adjustment (FPAA) after an examination at the partnership level. Within 90 days after notice of adjustment, the TMP may file a petition for readjustment of partnership items with the Tax Court, U.S. District Court or U.S. Claims Court. However, if a petition is not filed by the TMP, then any notice partner (or any 5% group) may file the petition within 60 days after the 90-day period has expired (¶3738) [IRC Sec. 6226].

PROCEDURE ON PROPOSED DEFICIENCY ASSESSMENT

¶3703   THE 30-DAY LETTER

If you refuse to accept a deficiency finding after a field examination, or do not agree with the determination following an office examination, you will receive a "30-day letter" [Reg. Sec. 601.105]. This is a form letter which states the IRS's proposed determination (including a complete explanation of its basis for its findings), describes your further appeal rights and advises you that you have 30 days to inform the District Director of your course of action. You may then ask for a District Appeals Office conference.

If you decide to accept the examiner's finding at this point, you may file Form 870, limiting interest on the deficiency, and pay the deficiency. If you do nothing, you will receive a 90-day letter [¶3705]. If the period for tax assessment is about to expire, a 90-day letter can be issued without the necessity of a 30-day letter even though the case may be in the examination stage [Reg. Sec. 601.105(f)].

¶3704   DISTRICT APPEALS OFFICE CONFERENCE

If you disagree with the examiner, you may ask for a district Appeals Office conference. The procedure used to ask for the conference depends on whether there was an office or field examination [¶3702]. An office conference is held at a District Appeals Office within an Internal Revenue Region. You may be represented by any person qualified to practice before the IRS.

(a) Procedure After Examination. After an office examination or correspondence audit, you need only request an Appeals Office conference when you receive the examiner's findings and the amount of the proposed deficiency. The protest doesn't have to be written, regardless of the amount of the proposed adjustment [Reg. Sec. 601.106(a)].

Field examination. An Appeals Office conference cannot be arranged after a field examination until you receive a 30-day letter [¶3704]. A brief written statement is needed if the proposed adjustment is between $2,500 and $10,000. A formal written protest is required for adjustments over $10,000 [Reg. Sec. 601.105(d)].

(b) Presenting the Case. If the facts are in dispute, you will have to present the correct facts as you see them. This can be done in writing, by documentary evidence, and by affidavit. Legal questions also should be submitted in writing so that authorities may be cited and analyzed.

> **OBSERVATION** You should make your requests for a District Appeals Office conference in writing, and attach to it a statement of facts and authorities.

(c) Results of Conference on Proposed Deficiency. An Appeals Office conference on a proposed deficiency may result in an agreement or disagreement.

1. If the Appeals officer and you reach an *agreement* on an income tax case, you sign Form 870-AD, Offer of Waiver of Restrictions on Assessment and Collection of Deficiency in Tax and of Acceptance of Overassessment. (Form 890 is used for estate and gift tax cases.) An attorney or accountant representing you may sign for you, if a power of attorney has been filed. A memorandum is then prepared setting forth the exact grounds upon which the conclusion rests, and all the papers in the case are turned over to the District Director for assessment and collection. Form 870-AD does not stop the running of interest when filed.[1] Only you have the option to offer to waive restrictions, and interest runs until 30 days after the IRS has accepted the offer. The case may be reopened after post-review (but only with the approval of the Regional Director of Appeals), if there was substantial error or there is evidence of fraud or misrepresentation[2] [Reg. Secs. 601.106(d), (h)].

2. If the Appeals officer and you still *disagree* after the conference, the Appeals Office may issue a statutory notice of deficiency (the 90-day letter) [¶3705]. If you file a petition with the Tax Court within 90 days, the case will be retained by the Appeals office and turned over to the appropriate district counsel to prepare for trial. If no petition is filed within this period, the case will be transferred to the District Director for appropriate action. To expedite Tax Court cases, the IRS may require a settlement conference when 90-day letters have not been issued.

(d) Results of Conference on a Refund Claim. An Appeals Office conference on a refund claim has two possible outcomes:

1. The Appeals officer and you reach an agreement. This is referred back to the District Director. After that, the procedure in ¶3741(b) is followed.

2. The Appeals officer and you reach no agreement. You then may follow the course of action indicated in ¶3741(a).

¶3705   THE 90-DAY LETTER

The 90-day letter is a formal notice of the deficiency determined. It is sent by registered or certified mail, and may be received any time after the expiration of the period allowed in the 30-day letter; if Form 870 was not signed; after the District Appeals Office conference [¶3703]; after the settlement conference before the Appeals Office division [¶3707]. Mailing to your last known address or to your accountant[1] is sufficient [IRC Sec. 6212(b)(1); Reg. Sec. 301.6212-1].

Issuance of a 90-day letter suspends the running of the statute of limitations (the time within which the IRS can examine a return). The details are usually given in an attached statement, with notice that within 90 days from the date of mailing (150 days for taxpayers located outside the U.S. or District of Columbia) you may petition the Tax Court for redetermining the deficiency. A deficiency notice may be withdrawn if the IRS and you agree [IRC Sec. 6212(d)]. However, withdrawal of the notice does not affect any suspension of the running of the statute of limitations.

In a bankruptcy case, the 90- or 150-day period is suspended for the period during which the debtor is prohibited from filing under bankruptcy law [¶3712(e)], plus 60 days after the bankruptcy proceeding [IRC Sec. 6213(f)(1)]. During the same period, however, the IRS may file a proof of claim, request for payment, or take other action such as asking the bankruptcy court to determine the debtor's personal liability for nondischargeable taxes[2] [IRC Sec. 6213(f)(2)].

Notice for joint return. When you and your spouse file a joint return, the notice of deficiency may be a single joint notice. However, if either of you notifies the IRS that you have separate residences, the identical joint notice must be sent to each of you[3] [Reg. Sec. 301.6212-1(b)(2)].

When there is a fiduciary. Fiduciaries assume the powers, rights, duties, and privileges of the taxpayer [IRC Sec. 6903; Reg. Sec. 301.6903-1]. Fiduciaries are required to give the IRS notice that they are acting in a fiduciary capacity [IRC Sec. 6903(b)]. If this notice is not filed, the deficiency notice does not have to be sent to the fiduciary; it can be sent to your last known address (see above). Fiduciaries may be relieved from further liability by filing written notice and proof that their fiduciary capacity has ended [Reg. Sec. 301.6903-1].

Ten-day notice. The following fiduciaries must file a notice within ten days of the time they qualify [IRC Sec. 6036; Reg. Sec. 301.6036-1]:

- Receiver or trustee in bankruptcy, or other persons in control of debtor's assets; qualified by appointment or authority to act. (If the Treasury Department is given notice of the proceeding under the bankruptcy law, a fiduciary notice is not necessary.)
- Receiver in receivership proceeding (including foreclosure) in any U.S. or state court; qualified by appointment, authority to act, or by taking possession of debtor's assets.
- Assignee for benefit of creditors; qualified on the date of assignment.

Excise taxes. The IRS issues a deficiency notice if it determines that a deficiency exists in excise taxes payable by a private foundation (¶3338-3344), or payable on certain retirement plans [¶3725], or payable by a real estate investment trust [IRC Sec. 6212; Prop. Reg. 301.6212-1].

(a) What Taxpayers Can Do. You have these choices if you receive a 90-day letter:

- (1) You may do nothing. Then the deficiency is assessed after the 90-day (or 150-day) period expires and referred to the Appeals Office Collection Division.
- (2) You may sign Form 870 (thus limiting interest on the deficiency [¶3706]). Then the deficiency is assessed and referred to the Appeals Office Collection Division.
- (3) You may file a petition with the Tax Court before the 90 or 150 days have passed.

Time for filing Tax Court petition. The day the notice is mailed is not counted in fixing the 90- or 150-day period, but the day the petition is filed is counted.[4] If the last day is a Saturday, Sunday or legal holiday in the District of Columbia, it is not counted as the 90th or 150th day [IRC Sec. 6213(a); Reg. Sec. 301.6213-1]. A properly addressed petition mailed to the Tax Court is timely filed with a post office postmark dated on or before the due date [IRC Sec. 7502; Reg. Sec. 301.7502-1]. A postmark from a private postage meter is acceptable, but it must be dated on or before the due date and received not later than the time a petition with a post office postmark would ordinarily be received. However, a mark dated before the due date (not a private postage meter mark) made by a private courier service and delivery of a petition after the statutory time were not acceptable although the courier received the petition for delivery within the statutory time.[5] [¶3630].

(b) When Deficiency Is Assessed. The deficiency in tax will not usually be assessed nor collected during the 90- or 150-day period for filing a Tax Court petition. If a petition is filed during this period, the tax is not assessed until the Tax Court decision becomes final [IRC Sec. 6213(a); Reg. Sec. 301.6213-1(a)].

Immediate assessment. Assessment or collection before the 90- or 150-day period is allowed in the following situations:

- An insufficient payment due to a mathematical or clerical error on the return may be collected. Notice of an amount due because of the error is not treated as a notice of deficiency. An abatement of the assessment in the notice is allowed if you file a request within 60 days after notice is sent [IRC Sec. 6213(b); Reg. Sec. 301.6213-1(b)].
- A "jeopardy assessment" can be made when delay might prevent the assessment or collection of a deficiency. A jeopardy assessment may be made before the 90-day deficiency notice is sent, but a deficiency notice must be issued within 60 days of the assessment [IRC Sec. 6861; Reg. Sec. 301.6861-1].
  Termination assessments can be made in certain cases [¶3712(b)]:
  (1) On appointment of a receiver, and in very limited circumstances, in bankruptcy proceedings (¶3712(e)) [IRC Sec. 6871].
  (2) When tax is paid. A payment made after a deficiency notice has been mailed will not deprive the Tax Court of jurisdiction over the deficiency determined without regard to the payment [IRC Sec. 6213(b)(4); Reg. Sec. 301.6213-1(b)].
  (3) When a petition for review of the Tax Court's decision is filed with a Court of Appeals, unless a bond is filed with the Tax Court [¶3764(b)].

(c) In a Partnership Proceeding, any deficiency resulting from an administrative determination generally may not be assessed nor collected (1) until 150 days after mailing the FPAA notice [¶3702(c)] or (2) if a Tax Court proceeding has started, until the court decision is final [IRC Sec. 6225].

¶3706   WAIVER BY TAXPAYER

You may be asked to sign a "Waiver of Restrictions on Assessment and Collection of Deficiency in Tax and Acceptance of Overassessment." Form 870 is used for income tax purposes; Form 890 for estate and gift tax.

(a) Effect of Waiver. By signing the waiver form, you give up the right to have an assessment deferred until after the 90-day period provided in the formal notice of deficiency [¶3705]. When an overassessment of tax has been made, you and the District Director can sign the waiver form as an agreement of overassessment. If more than one year or different taxes are involved, you may waive the restrictions on immediate assessment of a deficiency for one year or type of tax, while agreeing to an overassessment of another year's tax liability or type of tax. The waiver stops the interest (including compound interest) [¶3728] on the deficiency during the period from 30 days after filing the waiver to the date of notice and demand for payment [IRC Sec. 6601(c); Reg. Sec. 301.6601-1(d)].

> ➤ **OBSERVATION** If you are entitled to a refund of interest as a result of the above provision, you should *immediately* file a claim for refund.

(b) Waiver as Closing Agreement. A waiver form does not bar a claim for refund[1] nor an assessment. Exception: The IRS may ask you to sign Form 870-AD, rather than Form 870. This type of waiver does bar the filing of a refund claim though carrybacks, such as of a net operating loss, would still be allowed.[2] However, provisions barring refund claims are valid when inserted in the form.[3] [¶3740].

¶3707   APPEALS OFFICES

An Appeals Office is established in each of the seven Internal Revenue regions where district Appeals Office conferences are held. Each Appeals Office is headed by a Regional Director of Appeals.

(a) Jurisdiction and Function. The Appeals Office is the single agency for settling disputes between the District Directors and taxpayers. It has the authority to settle cases fully and its decisions are final insofar as the IRS is concerned. A District Appeals Office conference is arranged at the requests of taxpayers who fail to receive satisfaction after an office or field examination [¶3703]. A conference is granted even if no written protest is filed. However, a protest is required if the case is a field examination case and the proposed additional tax is more than $10,000. Generally, a conference before the Appeals Office is not granted during the 90-day status [¶3705] whether or not you exercised your rights to an Appeals Office conference [Reg. Sec. 601.106].

> ➤ **OBSERVATION** Both you and the IRS generally may be ready and willing to concede something to avoid the delay, expense and uncertainty of a court appeal. The Appeals Office seeks to work out a settlement that will be acceptable to both the IRS and you. Where the Treasury would have a clear-cut case before any court, the Appeals Office will not offer any reduction. But according to the degree of doubt as to the position that the courts might take upon the various points at issue, the Appeals Office will offer more or less of a reduction in the proposed deficiency.

(b) Settlement of Issues. In most Tax Court cases, the Appeals Office has exclusive settlement jurisdiction for four months after the cases are docketed. The settlement period may be extended, but normally not beyond the date of the trial calendar call. Within 45 days of the receipt of the case, Appeals must arrange a settlement conference with you. Appeals may enter a full or partial settlement with you. If a partial settlement is reached, Appeals will refer the unsettled issues to Counsel for disposition [Reg. Sec. 601.106(d)].

(c) Partnerships. In partnership proceedings, all partners can participate. A tax matters partner (TMP) may enter into a settlement agreement for partnership items. It is binding on all partners unless there is a showing of fraud, malfeasance, or misrepresentation of fact. Partners who are not entitled to notice of final adjustment (FPAA) may file a statement providing that the TMP has no authority to act on their behalf. If the IRS enters into a settlement agreement with any partner, it must offer the same terms of settlement to other partners who request it [IRC Sec. 6224].

¶3708   AGREEMENTS SETTLING TAX CLAIMS

[New tax legislation may affect this subject; see ¶1.]
Tax claims can be settled by compromise or closing agreement.

(a) Compromise. The Revenue Service may compromise a tax case before it has been referred to the Department of Justice. After it has been referred to the Department of Justice, the Attorney General or an appropriate delegate can compromise the case.[1] Interest and penalties, as well as taxes, may be compromised [IRC Sec. 7122; Reg. Sec. 301.7122-1].

Offers in compromise are made on Form 656, Offer in Compromise. They are submitted to the District or Service Center Director, with a financial statement on Form 433, Statement of Financial Condition and Other Information [Reg. Sec. 601.203]. A compromise is a final settlement of liability, and amounts paid cannot be recovered;[2] but the agreement may be rescinded for mutual mistake, fraud or duress [Reg. Sec. 301.7122-1]. A refund for a loss carryback is not barred by an earlier compromise.[3] If you fail to pay the compromise amount, the Revenue Service can collect the entire original tax liability.[4]

NOTE 1: The Revenue Service is allowed to compromise a case only if there is some doubt you are liable or that the tax can be collected. Authority to compromise is delegated to District Directors or higher officers depending on the kind and amount of tax [Reg. Sec. 601.105, 601.106]. An agreement with an unauthorized officer is not an effective compromise.[5]

Appeals Office procedures. Regional Directors of Appeals have authority to reconsider offers of compromise rejected by examiners [¶3702(b)]. Acting on the taxpayer's request, an originating office must transfer the case to an appropriate Regional Appeals office. Originating offices include Service Centers, District offices, and International Operation offices.

After the transfer, the Regional Appeals office conducts a hearing. It may request further investigative reports from the originating office which may be useful to analyze all the facts in the case. The Regional Appeals office will then notify the taxpayer of its findings. Before any decision is final, however, Counsel for the Regional or National Office must review and approve it. After that, the case is returned to the originating office for other closing actions.[6]

(b) Closing Agreements. The Commissioner (or any officer or authorized employee) and you may enter into what is known as a closing agreement (Form 866), to settle your complete liability.[7] It is final and conclusive on both the government and you. The only exception is when fraud, malfeasance or misrepresentation of a material fact is shown [Reg. Sec. 301.7121-1]. The agreement generally is used in cases where you have made concessions because of others made by the government, and it is necessary to bar further action by either party. It is also used when a fiduciary desires to be discharged by the court and when corporations are winding up their affairs [IRC Sec. 7121; Reg. Sec. 301.7121-1].

¶3709   APPEARANCE AT TAX PROCEEDINGS

Attorneys and certified public accountants may represent you before the Revenue Service by filing a declaration stating they are currently so qualified in a particular state, possession, territory or commonwealth of the U.S. or in the District of Columbia, and are authorized to act for the designated client.[1] Other persons generally must be enrolled as agents [(a) below] before they can practice.

However, appearance without enrollment is possible in some cases. An individual may appear on his or her own behalf; full-time employees may appear for their employer; corporate officers and partners may appear for their corporation or partnership; fiduciaries or their full-time employees may appear for the entity they act for; and return preparers may deal with an examining agent [(b) below].[2] The Revenue Service can discipline and disbar any person who appears before it.[3]

The Tax Court has its own rules for admission to practice [¶3751].

(a) Admission to Practice Before IRS. Persons other than attorneys or CPAs must pass a written examination and be enrolled before they can practice before the IRS. Practice includes preparation and filing of documents (except tax returns), communication with the Service and representing clients at conferences, hearings or meetings.[4] Attorneys and CPAs cannot enroll as agents.[5] Application for examination is made on Form 2587, Application for Special Enrollment Examination. Application for enrollment is made on Form 23, Application for Enrollment to Practice Before the Internal Revenue Service. A $25 filing fee must accompany Form 23. Successful applicants receive a permanent registration card.[6] The requirements for admission to practice and the disciplinary procedures may be found in Department Circular No. 230.

(b) Persons Preparing Returns. Unenrolled persons who prepare tax returns, if properly authorized (see (d) below), can represent you before the revenue agent or examining officer [¶3702] as to returns they have prepared.[2]

(c) Power of Attorney Required. Practitioners should obtain a power of attorney from the taxpayer, covering all responsibilities they may be called upon to exercise for you before the IRS. Form 2848, Power of Attorney and Declaration of Representative can be used for this purpose [Reg. Sec. 601.502–504].

(d) Tax Information Authorization. If your representative is simply to receive confidential information, the representative must file Form 8821, Tax Information Authorization. The authorization is not a substitute for situations that require a power of attorney such as to receive a refund check or sign a return on your behalf [Reg. Secs. 601.502–601.504].

> ▶ **OBSERVATION** Form 8821 is strictly limited to allowing the designated representative to receive and/or inspect tax information in an IRS office. If broader powers are needed, Form 2848 [(c) above] must be filed.

ASSESSMENT AND COLLECTION OF TAX

¶3710   WHEN TAX MUST BE ASSESSED AND COLLECTED

The tax generally must be assessed within three years after the return was filed. However, if you omitted from the return an amount that is over 25% of the gross income stated on the return, the tax can be assessed within six years [IRC Sec. 6501; Reg. Sec. 301.6501(a)-1, 301.6501(e)-1].

NOTE: A tax assessed or collected after the statute of limitations has expired is treated as an overpayment. It will be credited or refunded to you if you file a timely refund claim [IRC Sec. 6401; Reg. Sec. 301.6401-1].

If a false or fraudulent return is filed with intent to evade the tax, or if no return is filed, the tax may be assessed or a court proceeding begun to collect the tax without assessment *at any time* [IRC Sec. 6501(c); Reg. Sec. 301.6501(c)-1]. The Supreme Court applied this rule even though a fraudulent filer submitted a voluntary nonfraudulent return after the original return.[1] An unsigned or incompletely signed return may be treated as *no return* at all.[2]

(a) Suit to Collect Tax. The government may collect tax by levy [¶3715(a)] or by suit if a timely court proceeding is begun. As long as the tax is still collectible, the statute of limitations will not expire. A judgment against you does not change the period for collection by levy [IRC Sec. 6502(a); Reg. Sec. 301.6502-1]. The collection period may be extended by written agreement between you and District Director before the period ends. Collection time may be extended after the period ends, if a levy was made during the period, and the extension is agreed upon before the levy is released [IRC Sec. 6502(a); Reg. Sec. 301.6502-1(a)].

Collection after assessment. Starting with tax assessments after November 5, 1990, the IRS has a 10-year period from the assessment date to collect the tax [IRC Sec. 6502(a)]. Under prior law, a six-year period applied. Note: The new statute of limitations also applies to taxes assessed on or before November 5, 1990, if the six-year period has not expired as of that date.

(b) When Assessment Period Begins. If a return is filed before the due date, the assessment period generally runs from the due date. If the return is for income or social security tax withheld from wages or tax withheld at source [¶2518] and is filed before April 15 of the next calendar year, the period runs from that April 15 date [IRC Sec. 6501; Reg. Sec. 301.6501(b)-1].

> **Example 1:** On April 6, 1993, Mr. Ames, who reports on the calendar year basis, filed his return for 1992 correctly showing a gross income of $100,000. The last day on which an additional assessment may be made (or a court proceeding instituted to collect the tax without assessment) is April 15, 1996.

Wrong return form. If a trust or partnership return is filed in good faith by an association that later is held to be a corporation, it is treated as the return of the corporation, and the limitation period starts to run with its filing [IRC Sec. 6501(g)(1); Reg. Secs. 301.6501(g)-1(a)]. A corporate return filed under an election to be taxed as a partnership (Form 1120S) [¶3100 et seq.] is treated the same way if the corporation is later found not qualified for the S corporation election [Reg. Sec. 1.6037-1].

If a taxpayer in good faith files a return as an exempt organization, and later it is held to be a taxable organization or to have unrelated business income[3] [¶3345], the statute of limitations starts to run when the return is filed [IRC Sec. 6501(g)(2); Reg. Sec. 301.6501(g)-1(b)]. The taxpayer is still subject to penalties for failure to file a proper return or to pay tax.[4]

(c) Gross Income Not Reported. The tax may be assessed within six years after the return was filed, if you fail to report an amount that is more than 25% of the gross income reported on the return [IRC Sec. 6501(e)].

> **Example 2:** If Mr. Ames in Example 1 actually omitted more than $25,000 of gross income on his return, the last day for assessment would be April 15, 1999.

Business income. Gross income of a business is the total amount received or accrued from the sale of goods or services before subtracting the cost of sales or services. Any amount disclosed on the return is not considered in determining whether the 25% omission test has been violated [IRC Sec. 6501(e)(1)(A); Reg. Sec. 301.6501(e)-1].

Information in a related return may be considered adequate disclosure if the returns are sufficiently correlated.[5]

(d) Extension of Time. The period for assessment or collection may be extended by having you and the IRS sign a waiver (Form 872) [IRC Sec. 6501(c)(4); Reg. Sec. 301.6501(c)-1]. For example, a waiver might be used when issuing a 90-day letter would result in a petition to the Tax Court that could be avoided if you and the IRS had ample time to consider thoroughly the questions involved. Form 872-A is used instead of Form 872 if Appeals office consideration has been requested.[6]

> **NOTE:** Form 872, "Consent to Extend the Time to Assess Tax," should not be confused with Form 870 previously discussed. Form 870 permits a proposed deficiency to be assessed immediately and waives the right to file a petition with the Tax Court. Form 872 simply extends the time to make an assessment. The consent may be limited to particular unsettled issues.[7]

(e) Private Foundations. The assessment and collection of excise taxes imposed on private foundations [¶3338-3344] generally must be made within the three-year period [IRC Sec. 6501(l); Reg. Sec. 301.6501(n)-1].

¶3711   SPECIAL LIMITATION PERIODS

Special limitation periods for assessment apply to sale of a home, involuntary conversion, transferee liability and some other situations. (Note that adjustments of tax may be allowed after the limitation period expires, under certain conditions [¶3745]).

Carrybacks. As to *net operating and capital losses* and *general business credits*—deficiency for tax year to which carryback is made (and attributable to carryback) may be assessed within period deficiency can be assessed for tax year carryback was created [IRC Sec. 6501(h), (j), 6511(d)(4)(C); Reg. Sec. 301.6501(h)-1, 301.6501(j)-1].

Deficiency due to carryback of *foreign tax credit* may be assessed within one year after time to assess deficiency for year from which credit was carried; same rule for disallowed *oil and gas* extraction taxes [IRC Sec. 6501(i)].

Exploration expenses. Deficiency due to election to use unlimited exploration expense deduction (or its revocation) can be assessed up to two years after election (or revocation) [IRC Sec. 617(a)].

Gain on sale of home. If you sell your home at a profit, the time for assessing deficiency on taxable gain runs three years from date you notify IRS of (1) your cost of buying a new home or (2) your intention not to, or failure to, buy a new home within the required time. You should give notice when purchase occurs, or intent not to buy is formed, or the period for replacement expires (¶1706)[IRC Sec. 1034(j); Reg. Sec. 1.1034-1(i)].

Involuntary conversion. If you elect not to recognize gain on involuntary conversion of property, time for assessing any deficiency runs for three years from date you notify IRS of replacement of converted property or of intention not to replace or of failure to replace within required time (¶1710 et.

seq.)[IRC Sec. 1033(a)(3)(C); Reg. Sec. 1.1033(a)-2(c)(5)].

"Late" joint return. If a "late" joint return replaces separate returns [¶3602], the limitation period cannot end less than one year after joint return is actually filed [IRC Sec. 6013(b)(4); Reg. Sec. 1.6013-2(d)].

Last minute claims. If the IRS receives an amended return and the limitations period would expire within 60 days of such receipt, it has 60 days after the day it receives the amended return to assess any deficiency it discovers [IRC Sec. 6501(c)(7)].

Transfers to foreign corporations. Assessment period for Sec. 367 transfers runs three years from the date the IRS receives notice of the exchange [IRC Sec. 6501(c)(8)].

Partnerships. Time limit for assessment as to partnership items is three years from the return due date or date the return was filed (whichever is later) (¶3738) [IRC Sec. 6229].

Personal holding company. A special six-year period for assessment applies when a personal holding company (PHC) fails to furnish data on the special schedule of the corporate income tax return or a foreign PHC shareholder fails to report a constructive dividend [IRC Sec. 6501(f); Reg. Sec. 301.6501(e), (f)].

Transferee liability. (1) Liability must be assessed against the first transferee within one year after the time for assessment against the transferor expires. (2) Assessment against a later transferee must be made within one year after the time to assess liability against the preceding transferee expires, but not later than three years after end of time to assess against the original transferor. (3) Time for assessing against a fiduciary expires the later of (a) one year after liability arises or (b) when the period for collecting tax expires [IRC Sec. 6901(c)].

Gift taxes—special valuation rules for transfers of interests in corporations, partnerships or trusts. For gifts after October 8, 1990, special valuation rules apply for the gift tax on transfers of certain interests in corporations, partnerships or trusts. An unlimited assessment or collection period applies if there is an inadequate disclosure on the gift tax return. Thus, the statute of limitations does not run on an undisclosed or inadequately disclosed transfer. This is true regardless of whether a gift tax return was filed for other transfers in the year in which the transfer occurred [IRC Sec. 6501(c)(9)].

¶3712   WHEN ASSESSMENT PERIOD IS REDUCED

The period for assessment of tax may be shortened by a request for prompt assessment. A quick assessment also can be made before the 90-day period [¶3705(b)] to prevent tax evasion.

(a) Request for Prompt Assessment. The assessment period may be shortened to 18 months after a request for prompt assessment is filed for a return of a decedent or a decedent's estate or a return for a dissolved or dissolving corporation. If there has been an omission amounting to over 25% of the gross income reported on the return, or if a personal holding company fails to file the required information schedule, the six-year period for assessment applies, despite the request for prompt assessment [IRC Sec. 6501(d); Reg. Sec. 301.6501(d)-1]. If fiduciaries distribute estate assets after 18 months and have no knowledge or reasonable belief a tax is due, they are not personally liable for the tax.[1]

(b) Termination Assessments. If taxpayers (including corporations in liquidation) intend, by immediate departure from the U.S. or some other way, to avoid the payment of the income tax, the IRS may immediately determine the income tax due and payable for the current or preceding tax year. However, the tax year is terminated only for tax computation so that the tax year continues until its normal end. The taxpayer may contest the assessment in the Tax Court in the same manner as a jeopardy assessment. The IRS must issue a deficiency notice within 60 days after the later of the return due date for the full tax year or the return filing date [IRC Sec. 6851, 6867; Reg. Sec. 1.6851-1].

Termination assessments in case of political expenditures. The IRS can make an immediate determination and assessment of income or excise tax against a charity if it has made political expenditures in flagrant violation of the prohibition against making political expenditures. Any tax assessed may be for the current or preceding year and becomes due and payable immediately. [IRC Sec. 6852, 7409, 7429].

(c) Jeopardy Assessment. If a tax or deficiency (income, estate, gift or certain excise taxes) is jeopardized by delay, the IRS can immediately assess the tax and serve notice and demand for immediate payment. Also, this assessment procedure applies to someone who carries a large amount of cash and denies ownership of it. You may contest liability in the Tax Court [IRC Sec. 6861, 6867; Reg. Sec. 301.6861-1].

(d) Administrative and Court Review. The IRS must furnish a written detailed statement to you within five days following the jeopardy or termination assessment stating the reasons for the assessment. You have 30 days to request IRS to review. After the IRS review, you can bring a suit in an appropriate District Court [IRC Sec. 7429; Reg. Sec. 301.7429-1, 3]. If a jeopardy assessment is made before a notice of deficiency has been sent, the IRS has 60 days to send one [IRC Sec. 6861(b)].

(e) Bankruptcy. No immediate assessment [¶3705(b)] is permitted in bankruptcy proceedings except on (1) the bankruptcy estate [¶1234] or (2) the debtor if the bankruptcy court case determining the debtor's liability has become res judicata. An immediate assessment can be made on the appointment of a receiver [IRC Sec. 6871(a), (b)].

The bankruptcy court determines any questions about the amount and validity of taxes of the bankrupt. Even when a Tax Court proceeding is pending, tax claims may be presented to the bankruptcy or receivership court (¶3705) [IRC Sec. 6871; Reg. Sec. 301.6871-1]. No Tax Court petition may be filed or continued while a bankruptcy or receivership proceeding is pending. Bankruptcy law automatically stays the start of a Tax Court case until the stay is lifted, a discharge is granted or denied, or the bankruptcy case terminates. The stay applies if a deficiency notice has been issued and the time for filing the Tax Court petition has not expired.[2] When stayed, the 90- or 150-day period for filing is suspended [¶3705]. The limitation period is tolled during the stay and is also tolled if the fiduciary fails to file a notice of appointment [¶3713].

Under bankruptcy law, taxes due the U.S. or other governmental unit may be discharged except those for which: (1) no return was filed, or if filed had been due within two years before the case began; or (2) the debtor filed a fraudulent return or attempted to evade or defeat the tax in some manner; or (3) the federal law[3] has given a priority status.[4]

¶3713   WHEN LIMITATION PERIOD IS SUSPENDED

Some periods are not counted in determining whether the three years, or other applicable period, for assessment and collection of tax has passed [Sec. 6503]. In effect, an equivalent period is added after what ordinarily would be the end of the limitation period [¶3705].

Bankruptcy. Statute of limitations suspended while an assessment or collection is prohibited under bankruptcy law [¶3712(e)], plus 60 days after (for assessment) and six months after (for collection) [IRC Sec. 6503(h)].

Court control of assets. Statute of limitations suspended while assets of the taxpayer are in control or custody of a court in any U.S. or state court proceeding, and for six months after [IRC Sec. 6503(b); Reg. Sec. 301.6503(b)-1].

Deficiency notice issued. The statute of limitations is suspended while the IRS Commissioner is prohibited from making an assessment due to the issuance of a deficiency letter, and for 60 days after; but the final 60 days start to run on the date a waiver on Form 870 [¶3706] is filed.[1] If the proceeding is placed on the Tax Court docket, the statute is suspended until 60 days after the decision of the Tax Court becomes final [Reg. Sec. 301.6503(a)-1].

Failure to file fiduciary notice in bankruptcy. In bankruptcy or receivership cases, when the fiduciary or receiver has to give notice to IRS of his appointment, the statute of limitations is suspended from the start of the proceeding until 30 days after receipt of the notice by IRS (but not over two years) [IRC Sec. 6872; Reg. Sec. 301.6872-1].

Foreign expropriation losses. Time to collect tax attributable to recovery of loss is extended for the time the tax payment is extended (¶3654) [IRC Sec. 6503(e)].

Private foundation—retirement plans. The limitation period on assessing or collecting excise or termination taxes on private foundations is suspended for one year or when the IRS extends the time for corrective action. Similar provisions apply to excise taxes [¶3725] payable by certain retirement plans [¶1350].

> **NOTE:** The one-year period allows the private foundation to take corrective action to avoid the penalty [IRC Sec. 507(g)(2)].

Taxpayer outside U.S. The limitation period is suspended while the taxpayer is outside U.S. for six or more consecutive months. If fewer than six months of the collection period remains when he returns, collection is allowed up to six months after his return [IRC Sec. 6503(c); Reg. Sec. 301.6503(c)-1(b)].

Wrongful levy. The limitation period is suspended when money or other property of another person is wrongfully seized or received. The suspension runs from time the property is taken until 30 days after it is either voluntarily returned or judgment in suit to enjoin levy or recover the property becomes final [IRC Sec. 6503(f); Reg. Sec. 301.6503(g)-1].

> **NOTE:** If the dispute between the third-party recordkeeper and the IRS is not resolved within six months after the IRS issues an administrative summons, the statute of limitations is suspended until the issue is resolved (¶3701(c)) [IRC Sec. 7609(e)].

Issuing designated summons by IRS. The statute of limitations is suspended for a corporation during the time the IRS issues a "designated summons" [IRC Sec. 6503(j)].

> ➤ **CORPORATE BREAK**   The tax law provides conditions under which the statute of limitation is suspended during the period a corporate return is involved in a tax audit procedure.

A "designated summons" is one that is issued to determine any tax imposed if it (1) is issued at least 60 days before the assessment period expires (including any extensions) and (2) clearly states that it is a designated summons for purposes of this rule.

A designated summons can be issued by the IRS only once for any tax year.

> **NOTE:** The statute of limitation can only be suspended as to a corporation, not for individuals.

The statute of limitations is suspended for the period that begins when a lawsuit is brought in court to either enforce or quash the designated summons and ends on the date there is a final resolution of the summoned person's response to the summons [IRC Sec. 6503(j)(3)].

> ➤ **OBSERVATION**   This rule is designed to preserve the Revenue Service's ability to conclude the audit and assess any taxes that might be due regardless of the time it might take to obtain judicial resolution of the summons enforcement lawsuit.

These rules for suspending the statute of limitations also apply as to any summons issued during the 30-day period following the issuance of the designated summons.

These rules apply to any tax (regardless of when imposed) if the statute of limitations for the tax assessment has not expired on November 5, 1990.

¶3714   LIABILITY FOR TAX OF ANOTHER TAXPAYER

Transferee liability is generally assessed and collected the same way as the tax giving rise to the liability. However, special rules apply to the transferee. Unpaid assessments against children for compensation they earn can be made against the parents.

(a) Transferred Assets. If you transfer property to others without adequate consideration, those people may become liable for your taxes. Thus, the transferee of the assets of an insolvent transferor is ordinarily liable for the accrued and unpaid taxes of the transferor. The same rule applies when assets have been transferred by a taxpayer who later died or by a corporation that later dissolved or terminated its existence without making adequate provision for tax liabilities, or when the transferor is made insolvent by the transfer.[1]

A "transferee" includes a donee, heir, legatee, devisee and distributee [IRC Sec. 6901(h); Reg. Sec. 301.6901-1(b)].

Procedure. Transferee liability is assessed and collected the same as a deficiency (¶3703 et seq.) [IRC Sec. 6901; Reg. Sec. 301.6901-1], but a special limitation period for assessment applies [¶3711]. Retransfer of the assets after notice of liability is issued does not relieve the transferee from liability, unless he or she did not know about the original transfer.[2] Collection of a transferor's full tax from some transferees does not bar collection of another transferee's share, if those who paid file refund claims.[3] A transferee is not bound by a transferor's stipulation of tax liability not based on the merits of the case.[4]

(b) Parent's Liability for Child. An assessment of tax against a child related to compensation the child earns has the effect of an assessment against the parent [IRC Sec. 6201(c); Reg. Sec. 301.6201-1(c)]. The government's collection remedies can be enforced against both the parent and the child.

¶3715   HOW TAX IS COLLECTED

[New tax legislation may affect this subject; see ¶1.]

Any tax due can be collected by levy against your property after a certain time period. The federal tax lien is probably the most important tool the IRS has for collecting from delinquent taxpayers.

(a) Levy and Distraint (Seizure). Any tax due can be collected by levy on your property, generally after you fail to pay it within ten days from notice and demand [IRC Sec. 6331; Reg. Sec. 301.6331-1]. Levy upon your salary, wages, or other property is possible only after you first receive an additional 30-day written notice. Since a levy on wages or salary is continuous from the date served, the IRS must release the lien by notice when the tax is paid or as soon as the levy becomes unenforceable due to lapse of time, economic hardship, etc. [IRC Sec. 6331(e), 6343]. Any person in possession of property that has been levied upon must surrender it unless it is already subject to judicial process [IRC Sec. 6332(a); Reg. Sec. 301.6332-1(a)]. An insurer need not surrender a life insurance or endowment contract, but must pay over amounts that could be advanced to the taxpayer (generally cash loan value) up to 90 days after notice of levy. Automatic advances agreed upon to keep the insurance in force are not counted if the agreement was made before the insurer had actual knowledge of the levy [IRC Sec. 6332(b); Reg. Sec. 301.6332-2].

Persons (including corporate officers and employees and partnership members and employees) who fail to turn over property levied on are liable for the tax due up to the value of the property, plus costs and interest. They may also be liable for a penalty of 50% of this amount [IRC Secs. 6332(d), 6621; Reg. Sec. 301.6332-1(b), (d)]. Surrender of the levied property to the IRS relieves them from liability to delinquent taxpayer (or insurance beneficiaries) for the property [IRC Sec. 6332(e); Reg. Sec. 301.6332-1(c)].

Property exempt from levy. Unemployment benefits, workers' compensation, certain pensions, including military service-connected disability payments and annuities, undelivered mail, certain necessary personal and household items, a limited amount of business books and tools, and income needed for the support of a taxpayer's minor children under prior judgment are specifically exempt from levy. Note that not all social security benefits are exempt from the levy [IRC Sec. 6334(a), (c)].

A minimum exemption is allowed equal to the sum of the standard deduction and allowable personal exemptions for the year divided by 52 [IRC Sec. 6334(d)].

(b) Collection by Suit. If any person liable to pay any tax fails to pay it when due, the tax, with interest and additions, may be collected by a suit in the U.S. District Court [IRC Sec. 7401; Reg. Sec. 301.7401-1].

(c) Liens. The federal tax is a lien on all the taxpayer's property [IRC Sec. 6321; Reg. Sec. 301.6321-1 et seq.]. A demand for payment must be made,[1] but the lien is created when the tax is assessed [IRC Sec. 6322]. It then becomes one of the many possible claims competing to be first satisfied out of the taxpayer's property. Until notice of the lien has been properly filed, it is not enforceable against a purchaser, mechanics lienor, judgment lien creditor or holder of a security interest [IRC Sec. 6323(a); Reg. Sec. 301.6323(a)-1]. Even after the lien is filed, it may not be enforced against some persons who do not actually know about the lien or who have certain specific claims against the taxpayer's property [IRC Sec. 6323(b); Reg. Sec. 301.6323(b)-1].

Superpriorities against liens. Subject to varying conditions that must be met in each case, a filed lien cannot be enforced against the following persons who do not have actual knowledge of the lien at the time: purchasers (or security holders) of securities (stocks, bonds, notes, etc.); purchasers of motor vehicles; purchasers in a casual sale of tangible personal property of less than $250 (household goods, personal effects, property exempt from levy); insurers who issued life insurance, endowment or annuity contracts (also protected for automatic advances [(a) above] after actual knowledge of lien); banks and building and loan associations (for passbook loans). Specific claims protected against a filed tax lien, again subject to varying conditions in each case, are: possessory lien for repair or improvement of personal property; real property tax and assessment liens; mechanics liens for repair and improvement of personal residence at contract price under $1,000; attorney's lien enforceable against a judgment or settlement; purchaser of tangible personal property at retail [IRC Sec. 6323(b); Reg. Sec.301.6323(b)-1, 301.6323(h)-1].

> NOTE: A limited priority against filed tax liens also is granted under specified conditions for advances made under financing agreements entered into before the tax lien is filed, and certain security interests may be protected for disbursements made within 45 days after the filing before the holder has actual knowledge of the lien [IRC Sec. 6323(c), (d); Reg. Sec. 301.6323(c)-1—3, 301.6323(d)-1, 301.6323(h)-1].

Pre-bankruptcy federal liens. The IRS has greater powers [IRC Sec. 6321-6326] to enforce its liens than those possessed by private secured creditors under state law. But the federal provisions do not transfer ownership of the property to the IRS.[2] Ownership is transferred only when the property is sold to a bona fide buyer at a tax sale [IRC Sec.

6339(a)(2)]. Until there is a sale, the Supreme Court has ruled, the property remains the debtor's and is subject to the bankruptcy law turnover requirement [11 USC 542(a)] in the event of a bankruptcy petition.[3]

Indexing and filing of liens. The filing of a notice of federal tax lien is governed solely by the Internal Revenue Code and is not subject to any other state or federal law. A tax lien is treated as complying with the filing requirements only if it is recorded in an appropriate public index. Real property liens are filed in the office designated by the state where the property is located.

NOTE: The priority of a tax lien against purchasers and creditors is determined by reference to the time of indexing rather than the time of filing of the notice of tax lien [IRC Sec. 6323(f)(4), (g)(2)].

Notices affecting personal property must be filed in the office designated by the state where an individual resides or a corporation or partnership has its principal executive office when the lien is filed. If a state fails to specify an office for filing, or designates more than one, the tax lien is filed with the clerk of the U.S. district court for the judicial district where the property is located (for realty) or where the taxpayer resides or has its principal office (for personalty) [IRC Sec. 6323(f); Reg. Sec. 301.6323(f)-1].

For a notice of lien to remain in effect, it must be refiled, within the required period, in the office in which the prior notice was filed [IRC Sec. 6323(g)].

NOTE: The required refiling period means (1) the one-year period ending 30 days after the expiration of 10 years after the assessment of the tax and (2) the one-year period ending with the expiration of 10 years after the prior period closes. The 10-year period applies to taxes assessed (1) after November 5, 1990, and (2) before November 6, 1990 if the prior law period (six years) had not expired by November 5, 1990.

(d) Set-Off or Counterclaim. The IRS, within the applicable period of limitations, can set off or credit the amount of any overpayment (including interest on it) against liability for any internal revenue tax [IRC Sec. 6402; Reg. Sec. 301.6402-1]. Set-offs may also be used if taxpayers claim a refund or credit of one tax [¶3736], and they are in default to the U.S. on another tax or contract.

(e) Payroll Deductions. The Revenue Service allows employees to arrange payroll deductions to satisfy delinquent taxes. Form 2159, "Payroll Deduction Agreement," is used.

(f) Suit to Prevent Collection. Generally, no suit to restrain the assessment or collection of any tax can be maintained [IRC Sec. 7421]. This includes suits to restrain enforcement of the liability of a transferee or fiduciary or suits to prevent revoking tax-exempt status.[4] There are exceptions. Collection of the tax can be enjoined when you: (1) did not receive a 90-day letter and did not file Form 870 [¶3706], (2) have filed a petition with the Tax Court [IRC Sec. 6212(a), 6213(a); Reg. Sec. 301.6213-1] and (3) request judicial review of jeopardy assessment procedures [¶3712(d)]. It can also be enjoined when a case is in bankruptcy proceedings [see (c) above] (¶3705; 3712(e); 3713) [IRC Sec. 6213(a), (f)]. An injunction also may be allowed when it is clear from the facts and law that the IRS could not win a suit to collect the tax and only an injunction can protect the taxpayer.[5]

Persons, other than a person liable for the tax that is the basis for a levy, may sue the U.S. to recover wrongfully levied property or its proceeds or to enjoin a levy or sale that would injure rights superior to those of the U.S. [IRC Sec. 7426; Reg. Sec. 301.7426-1].

A limit applies on damages recoverable for a wrongful levy [IRC Sec. 7426(b)(2)].

PENALTIES

¶3720   OVERVIEW

The tax law imposes various civil and criminal penalties when you or your tax preparer fail to properly account to the IRS as required by the tax law. Unlike interest (which is an addition to tax intended to compensate the IRS for late payments), penalties are intended to punish the taxpayer for unreasonably failing to file or pay taxes. Interest paid on a tax deficiency is a personal interest expense that is not deductible, as with fines and penalties.[1]

The penalty rules are organized into four categories:

- Document and information reporting penalty [¶ 3721].
- Accuracy-related penalty [¶ 3722].
- Preparer, promoter and protester penalties [¶ 3723].
- Delinquency (failure to file or make timely deposits) penalties [¶ 3724].

¶3721   DOCUMENT AND INFORMATION REPORTING PENALTY

[New tax legislation may affect this subject; see ¶1.]

Penalties are imposed when taxpayers fail to file *correct information returns* with the IRS or fail to furnish *payee statements* to other taxpayers on or before the due date [IRC Sec. 6721, 6722].

(a) Correct Information Returns. Certain taxpayers (e.g., banks, employers, etc.) must file information returns with the IRS. Examples of information returns are interest, dividend and wage statements (e.g., Form 1099, Form 1099-DIV, Form W-2) [IRC Sec. 6724(d)(1)].

A *return or statement* is also required for the following items: payment of interest, dividends or patronage dividends [¶3662; 3663]; stock transferred under stock options [¶3664]; employees' group-term life insurance [¶3665]; fishing boat operators' wages; withheld income taxes; and tips.

The information reporting penalty applies to taxpayers who: (1) fail to file an information return by the due date, (2) fail to include all the information required to be shown on the return or (3) include incorrect information on the return. The amount of the penalty varies depending on when, if at all, the correct information return is filed [IRC Sec. 6721]. The graduated structure gives taxpayers an incentive to correct their errors as rapidly as possible.

- If a taxpayer files a correct, but overdue, information return within 30 days of the due date or corrects a timely filed but incorrect or incomplete one within the same period of time, the penalty is $15 per return (with a maximum penalty of $75,000 per calendar year).
- If the information return is filed after 30 days but on or before August 1, the amount of the penalty jumps to $30 per return ($150,000 maximum).
- The penalty for filing later is $50 per return ($250,000 total maximum) [IRC Sec. 6721(a), (b)].

Small business relief. There are lower penalty ceilings for taxpayers having average annual gross receipts for the most recent three taxable years that do not exceed $5 million. The maximum penalties for small businesses are $25,000, $50,000 and $100,000 (instead of the $75,000, $150,000 and $250,000 limits) [IRC 6721(d)].

De minimis rule. There is a special relief rule for taxpayers who file a small number of incorrect information returns. If corrections are made on or before August 1 to information returns that are incomplete or incorrect as originally filed, a *de minimis* number of those returns will be treated as filed correctly, and no penalty will be imposed. The rule applies, in any given calendar year, to the greater of (1) 10 returns or (2) one-half of one percent of the total number of information returns required to be filed by the taxpayer during the calendar year. In other words, if the total number of returns corrected by the taxpayer exceeds the *de minimis* threshold, only the number exceeding the threshold is subject to penalty [IRC 6721 (c)].

> **Example:** DeSantis Welding Co. files 500 information returns on the last day of February 1993, as required. DeSantis Welding later discovers errors on 17 of the returns, and files corrected returns within 30 days of the due date. Result: DeSantis is subject to a $105 penalty (seven information returns in excess of the ten allowed under the de minimis rule, times $15 penalty for each late return).

Inconsequential omissions and corrections. The penalty is not imposed if the failure does not hinder or prevent the IRS from processing the taxpayer's return [Temp. Reg. Sec. 301.6723-1T(b)].

Intentional disregard for the rules. If a failure to file is due to intentional disregard of the filing requirements, the taxpayer will not be allowed to take advantage of the three-tiered graduated system, the small business break, or the *de minimis* rule [IRC Sec. 6721(e)(1)]. Instead, the penalty is $100, or if greater:

- 10% of the total amount that must be reported, as to certain returns (excluding those that must be filed by brokers, direct sellers, those receiving mortgage interest, or those in a trade or business who receive cash exceeding $10,000 generally in one transaction, or who receive property by foreclosure or by security abandonment, partnerships when there are transfers of receivables or inventory, or those disposing of certain donated property); or
- 5% of the total amount that must be reported for returns required by brokers, partnerships when there are transfers of receivables or inventory, or by those disposing of certain donated property; or
- For returns required by those receiving more than $10,000 cash, generally in a single transaction, in a trade or business, the penalty is the greater of $25,000 or the amount of the cash received in the transaction (not to exceed $100,000) [IRC Sec. 6721(e)].

NOTE: The $250,000 ceiling mentioned above does not apply [IRC Sec. 6721(e)]. Also, failure to correct information returns within a reasonable time after being requested to do so by the IRS could be considered an intentional disregard.

(b) Payee Statements. The other component of the document and information reporting penalty applies to taxpayers who must furnish *payee statements* to other taxpayers. Those failing to furnish a correct statement (e.g., Form 1099-DIV, Form W-2) to the income's recipient on or before the due date are subject to a penalty of $50 per statement, with a maximum penalty of $100,000 per tax year [IRC Sec. 6722(a), (b), 6724(d)(2)].

Unlike the "safe harbors" available when filing incorrect *information returns* (that is, small business break and de minimis rule), the rule is much stricter when it comes to payee statements. There is no *de minimis* exception, no small business break, and no exception for corrected omissions and inaccuracies (formerly, the penalty was not assessed if the inaccurate information was corrected within certain time periods).

Intentional disregard for the rules. If the failure is due to intentional disregard of the filing requirements, the penalty is generally $100, or if greater:

- 10% of the total amount of the items that must be reported correctly on certain payee statements (excluding those required from: brokers, direct sellers, those receiving mortgage interest or foreclosures and security abandonments, partnerships for transfers of receivables or inventory, or those disposing of certain donated property); or
- 5% of the total amount that must be reported correctly on payee statements required from: brokers, partnerships for transfers of receivables or inventory, or from those disposing of certain donated property [IRC Sec. 6722(c)].

The $100,000 maximum limit does not apply [IRC Sec. 6722(c)(2)(A)].

(c) Specified Reporting Failures. A taxpayer who is required and fails to (1) include a correct taxpayer I.D. number (TIN) on a return or (2) furnish a correct TIN to another person, is subject to a $50 penalty for each failure up to a maximum amount of $100,000 per calendar year [IRC Sec. 6723, 6724(d)(3)].

(d) Waiver of Penalty for Reasonable Cause. None of the above penalties apply if the taxpayer establishes that the failure is due to reasonable cause and not willful neglect [IRC Sec. 6724(a)]. Reasonable cause can exist if significant mitigating factors are present, such as the fact that a taxpayer has an established history of complying with the information reporting requirements.[1]

(e) Magnetic Media Reporting. Taxpayers who are required to file 250 or more information returns with the IRS per year must file by magnetic media (e.g., tapes, disks, diskettes). The penalty for failing to file applies only to those that exceed 250 [IRC Sec. 6724(c)].

¶3722   ACCURACY-RELATED PENALTY

The accuracy-related penalty is 20% of the portion of the underpayment attributable to one or more of the following [IRC Sec. 6662(a), (b)]:

- Negligence or disregarding rules or regulations.
- Any substantial understatement of income tax.
- Any substantial valuation misstatement.
- Any substantial overstatement of pension liabilities.
- Any substantial estate or gift tax valuation understatement.

➤ **OBSERVATION** The accuracy-related penalty applies only to the portion of the tax underpayment resulting from the inaccuracy. This means that a slightly negligent taxpayer is treated more leniently than one who is more culpable. There is no "stacking" of the accuracy-related components. For example, if part of an underpayment is due both to negligence and a substantial understatement of income tax, the maximum penalty is 20% of that portion. Also, the penalty is coordinated with the fraud penalty. Suppose part of the underpayment is due to fraud. Then the IRS treats the entire underpayment as due to fraud. However, the taxpayer can overcome the IRS position if he or she can establish by the preponderance of the evidence that the underpayment is not due to fraud [IRC Sec. 6663(b)].

(a) Negligence. Negligence is defined as any failure to make a reasonable attempt to comply with the tax law, and includes the careless, reckless, or intentional disregard of rules or regulations [IRC Sec. 6662(c); Reg. Sec. 1.6662-3(b)(1)].

The following factors strongly indicate negligence [Reg. Sec. 1.6662-3(b)(1)]:

* Failing to include on the tax return income shown on an information return (for example, a Form 1099).
* Failing to make a reasonable attempt to determine the correctness of a deduction, credit or exclusion that seem to a reasonable and prudent person to be "too good to be true" under the circumstances.
* A partner who treats a partnership item on his or her own return inconsistently from the way it's treated on the partnership return (or fails to inform the IRS of the inconsistency).
* A shareholder who treats an S corporation item inconsistently from the way the corporation treated the item on its return (or fails to inform the IRS of the inconsistency).

Adequate disclosure. The negligence penalty doesn't apply if an adequate disclosure is made. For returns due after 1991, a disclosure is considered adequate if it is made on a properly completed Form 8275, Disclosure Statement. For a position contrary to a rule or regulation, Form 8275-R, Regulation Disclosure Statement, must be filed. However, this disclosure exception doesn't apply to frivolous positions or when the taxpayer doesn't keep adequate books and records or fails to substantiate items properly [Reg. Sec. 1.6662-3(c), 1.6662-4(f)].

(b) Substantial Understatement of Income Tax. An understatement of income tax is basically the difference between the tax shown on your return and the correct tax due. It is considered to be substantial (and thus subject to the 20% umbrella accuracy-related penalty) if it exceeds the greater of (1) 10% of the tax required to be shown on the return for the tax year or (2) $5,000 ($10,000 for a corporation other than an S corporation or a personal holding company) [IRC Sec. 6662(d); . Reg. Sec. 1.6662-4(b)(2)].

The penalty does not apply to the tax treatment of a particular item if (1) you have substantial authority for that tax treatment or (2) the item's tax treatment was adequately disclosed (see above) [IRC Sec. 6662(d)(2)(B); Reg. Sec. 1.6662-4(b)(2)].

Substantial authority. The substantial authority standard is an objective one involving the law's analysis and application to relevant facts. There is substantial authority for an item's tax treatment only if the weight of the authorities supporting the treatment is substantial in relation to the weight of those supporting opposing treatment [Reg. Sec. 1.6662-4(d)]. This standard is less stringent than the "more likely than not" standard, but stricter than the "reasonable basis" standard.

The types of authority for returns filed after 1989 are: (1) Internal Revenue Code; (2) proposed, temporary and final regulations; (3) revenue rulings and procedures; (4) tax treaties; (5) federal court cases; (6) congressional committee reports; (7) General Explanation of tax legislation prepared by the Joint Committee on Taxation (the so-called "Blue Book"); (8) private letter rulings and technical advice memoranda issued after 10-31-76; (9) actions on decisions and general counsel memoranda issued after 3-12-81; (10) IRS information or press releases; and (11) notices, announcements and other administrative pronouncments published in the Internal Revenue Bulletin [Reg. Sec. 1.6662-4(d)(3)(iii)].

NOTE: You have substantial authority for an item's tax treatment the treatment is supported by the conclusion of a ruling or a determination letter issued to you. It also exists if the treatment is supported by a technical advice memorandum in which you are named, or by an affirmative statement in an IRS agent's report as your prior tax year. However, a holding ceases to be authority if it overruled or modified [Reg. Sec. 1.6662-4(d)(3)(iv)].

Adequate disclosure. There are two ways to make an adequate disclosure: (1) on the return or (2) with a red flag.

1. On the return. The IRS periodically issues revenue procedures listing certain tax forms and schedules that, if properly filled out, are an adequate disclosure [Reg. Sec. 1.6662-4(f)(2)]. For example, Schedule A of Form 1040 is adequate disclosure of medical and dental expenses, taxes and interest expenses. For charitable contributions, filing Schedule A can also be adequate disclosure. However, Form 8283, Noncash Charitable Contributions, must also be attached to the return if you contributed more than $500 of property other than cash. Items relating to the sale or exchange of your home are adequately disclosed by filing Form 2119, Sale of Your Home. Form 2106, Employee Business Expenses, can also be used for adequate disclosure.[1]

2. Red flag. The surest way to make an adequate disclosure is to give the IRS a statement that identifies the item being disclosed, the amount of the item and either the facts that would alert the IRS to the nature of the potential controversy or a description of the legal issue involved. The information is presented on a properly completed form attached to the return or to a qualified amended return. For an item or position (except for one that is contrary to a regulation), disclosure must be made on Form 8275 (Form 8275-R for a position contrary to a regulation) [Reg. Sec. 1.6662-4(f)(1)].

> ➤ **OBSERVATION** Although designed to set off alarms at the IRS, this disclosure method offers you the greatest penalty protection. Even if your position is rejected, the IRS can't assert a substantial understatement penalty—and the disclosure may serve as protection against a negligence penalty as well.

(c) Substantial and Gross Valuation Misstatements—In General. Valuing property is important in several areas of the tax law. Overstating the property's value can result in a tax liability's understatement.

Example 1: Ms. Forrest donates five acres of land to the Fairlawn Orphanage, and takes a full charitable deduction on her return. If valued at $100,000, Forrest gets a $31,000 tax savings in her 31% tax bracket. If valued at $150,000, however, the savings jumps to $46,500—a $15,500 difference.

Substantial valuation misstatement. The 20% accuracy-related penalty applies to the portion of an underpayment of tax that is attributable to a *substantial valuation misstatement.* A substantial valuation misstatement exists if:

- The value or adjusted basis of any property claimed on a return is 200% or more of the correct value or adjusted basis [IRC Sec. 6662(e)(1)(A); Reg. Sec. 1.6662-5(e)(1)]; or
- The price for any property or services (or the property's use) claimed on the return as to any transactions between certain related taxpayers (so-called "Sec. 482 adjustments")[¶ 3048] is 200% or more (or 50% or less) of the correct amount [IRC Sec. 6662(e)(1)(B)]

NOTE: The penalty applies if the transfer price adjustment exceeds $10 million. This adjustment is the net increase in taxable income for a tax year resulting from all Sec. 482 adjustments in the price for any property or services (or for the property's use) [IRC Sec. 6662(e)(1)(B)(ii), (3)(A)]. Certain items are excluded in determining the $10 million threshold. (1) Any portion of the net increase in taxable income due to a price redetermination is disregarded if reasonable cause or good faith is shown. (2) The threshold is disregarded if any part of that net increase is due to certain transactions among foreign corporations [IRC Sec. 6662(e)(3)(B)].

Example 2: Mr. Post contributes a building, which he determines has a fair market value of $300,000, to his closely held S corporation. The corporation claims a first-year depreciation deduction (for nonresidential real property) of $9,000. The correct value of the building is $100,000. If the correct valuation were used, the depreciation writeoff would be only $3,000—a $6,000 difference. Since the corporation's valuation statement of the building is at least 200% more than the correct valuation, the 20% penalty applies. The $6,000 underpayment results in a penalty tax of $1,200.

Since valuation is often a subjective concept, this is a potential area for abuse. Therefore, the IRS and Congress have established several guidelines and accompanying penalties that apply.

Determining if there is a substantial or gross valuation misstatement on a return is made on a property-by-property basis. Assume, for example that Blackacre has a value of $6,000, but Mr. Ames claims a value of $11,000, and that Whiteacre has a value of $4,000, but Ames claims a value of $10,000. Since the claimed and correct values are compared on a property-by-property basis, there is a substantial valuation misstatement as to Whiteacre, but not as to Blackacre, even though the claimed values ($21,000) are 200% or more of the correct ($10,000) when compared on a combined basis [Reg. Sec. 1.6662-5(f)(1)].

NOTE: This 20% penalty applies to all taxpayers (not just individuals, personal service corporations and closely-held corporations, as under prior law). But it applies only if the amount of the underpayment attributable to a valuation misstatement exceeds $5,000 ($10,000 for most corporations) [IRC Sec. 6662(e)(2)].

Gross valuation misstatement. The rate of the penalty is doubled (to 40%) for gross misstatements. This is where: (1) the value or adjusted basis claimed is 400% or more than the correct value or adjusted basis, (2) there is a 25% (rather than a 50%) or less situation or (3) the threshold exceeds $20 million [IRC Sec. 6662(h)(2); Reg. Sec. 1.6662-5(e)(2)].

Special rule for overstatement of charitable deductions. There is a special rule for substantial or gross overstatements of charitable deductions. The 20% penalty does not apply if you can show there was a reasonable cause for the underpayment and you acted in good faith. However, to qualify for this break (1) the property's claimed value must have been based on a qualified appraisal made by a qualified appraiser and (2) you must have made a good faith investigation of the contributed property's value in addition to getting the appraisal [IRC Sec. 6664(c)(2), (3); Reg. Sec. 1.6664-4(e)].

(d) Substantial Overstatement of Pension Liabilities. The 20% penalty applies to substantial overstatements of pension liabilities if the actuarial determination of the liabilities taken into account for purposes of computing the deduction under IRC Sec. 404(a)(1), (2) (relating to pension trusts and employees' annuities) is 200% or more of the correct amount. The penalty is 40% if the valuation overstatement is 400% or more than the correct amount. However, there is no penalty unless the underpayment attributable to the overstatement exceeds $1,000 [IRC Sec. 6662(f), (h)(2)(B)].

(e) Substantial Estate or Gift Tax Valuation Understatement. The 20% accuracy-related penalty applies if you value any property claimed on an estate or gift tax return at 50% or less than the amount determined to be correct. The penalty applies only if the underpayment attributable to the understatement exceeds $5,000. The penalty is doubled if the valuation claimed is 25% or less of the amount determined to be correct [IRC Sec. 6662(g), (h)(2)(C)].

(f) Reasonable Cause Exception. There is a general exception that precludes the application of the accuracy-related penalty. The general rule is that the penalty does not apply if there was reasonable cause for an underpayment and you acted in good faith as to the underpayment [IRC Sec. 6664(c); Reg. Sec. 1.6664-4].

A special rule applies to the substantial understatement of income tax component [(b) above]. Substantial authority or adequate disclosure is required.

A special rule applies to the negligence component. The position taken on a tax return must be nonfrivolous and you must make a "complete, item-specific" disclosure of that position. Disclosure must be full and substantial, parallel to the disclosure required under the substantial understatement component of the accuracy-related penalty [(b) above].

The special rule for charitable valuation overstatements is covered at (c) above.

(g) Fraud Penalty. If any part of an underpayment of tax is due to fraud, the entire underpayment is treated as attributable to fraud, and a 75% fraud penalty is imposed [IRC Sec. 6663(a),(b)]. However, if you can establish that part of the underpayment is not attributable to fraud, that portion is not subject to the 75% penalty, although it may be subject to the 20% accuracy-related penalty. The portion coming under the 75% fraud penalty is not also subject to the 20% accuracy-related penalty [IRC Sec. 6663(b)].

> **Example 3:** Mr. Appleton understated his 1991 income tax liability by $100,000. The IRS establishes that some of the understatement is attributable to fraud. Appleton, though, establishes that $40,000 is not attributable to fraud, but agrees that it is attributable to negligence. Result: Appleton owes $45,000 under the fraud penalty ($60,000 x 75%) and $8,000 under the accuracy-related penalty ($40,000 x 20%).

> ▶ **BURDEN OF PROOF** The IRS has the burden of proving fraud by clear and convincing evidence. You, on the other hand, are only required to establish that items are not attributable to fraud by a preponderance of the evidence—a much lower standard [IRC 6663(b)].

Filing of return required. The accuracy-related and fraud penalties do not apply if you have not filed a tax return [IRC Sec. 6664(b)]. That doesn't mean you're off the hook, though. There's an up-to-75% penalty for fraudulent failure to file a tax return (¶3724) [IRC Sec. 6651(f)].

¶3723   PREPARER, PROMOTER AND PROTESTOR PENALTIES

(a) Tax Court Proceedings. The Tax Court may impose a penalty on any party that: (1) institutes or maintains a proceeding mainly for delay, (2) takes a position in such proceeding that is frivolous or groundless or (3) unreasonably fails to pursue available administrative remedies. The penalty may be as high as $25,000 ($10,000 if the proceeding is in a court other than the Tax Court) [IRC Sec. 6673(a)(1), (b)].

(b) Attorney's Liability. Attorneys and others who are admitted to practice before the Tax Court can be liable for excess costs, expenses and attorneys' fees that are reasonably incurred because the attorney or other person unreasonably multiplied proceedings before the court. If the attorney is appearing on behalf of the IRS, the U.S must pay such excess costs [IRC Sec. 6673(a)(2)].

> ▶ **NEW GUIDELINES** Proposed regulations explain when a taxpayer is considered to have exhausted administrative remedies to be able to collect litigation costs from the IRS. Big change: Taxpayers no longer have to agree to extend the period for assessment and collection to meet this requirement [Prop. Reg. Sec. 301.7430-1].

Basically, administrative remedies are considered exhausted when taxpayers request (and, if granted, participate in) an Appeals Office conference [¶3703] before bringing the matter to court. In cases where it's not possible to make this request, taxpayers must file a written claim for relief with the District Director. Taxpayers don't have to take these steps if the IRS has: (1) notified them in writing that such steps are unnecessary, (2) not given them a chance to request a conference (e.g., didn't send a 30-day letter) or (3) failed to grant a conference within six months of filing a refund claim [Prop. Reg. Sec. 301.7430-1].

(c) Tax Return Preparers. An income tax preparer (e.g, accountant or attorney) can be liable for a $250 penalty if the preparer: (1) understates your tax liability by taking a position that does not realistically have merit, (2) knew or reasonably should have known of such position and (3) did not disclose the position as required [¶3722(b)], or the position was frivolous. The penalty doesn't apply if it is shown that there was reasonable cause for the understatement and the return preparer acted in good faith [IRC Sec. 6694(a); Prop. Reg. Sec. 1.6694-1].

Willful or reckless conduct. If any part of the understatement is due to a willful attempt by the return preparer to understate the tax liability, or to any reckless or intentional disregard of rules or regulations, then the preparer is subject to a penalty of $1,000. This penalty is reduced accordingly if the $250 penalty discussed above is paid [IRC Sec. 6694(b); Prop. Reg. Sec. 1.6694-1]].

Other penalties. There is a $50 penalty for each time a preparer fails to: (1) furnish a copy of a return or a claim for refund to the taxpayer, (2) sign the return or the claim for refund, (3) furnish an identifying number, (4) retain for three years copies or a list of returns and refund claims filed or (5) file correct information returns. Maximum penalty: $25,000 per failure per calendar year. The penalty does not apply if it is shown that such failure was due to reasonable cause and not due to willful neglect [IRC Sec. 6695].

NOTE: Tax return preparer penalties apply in addition to other penalties [IRC Sec. 6696(a)].

(d) Tax Shelter Promoters. The penalty for promoting abusive tax shelters is the lesser of $1,000 or 100% of the gross income derived (or to be derived) from the activity. In calculating the amount of the penalty, the organizing of an entity, plan or arrangement and the sale of each interest in it constitute separate activities [IRC Sec. 6700].

The penalty is very broad and covers anyone who participates (directly or indirectly) in a shelter. Included are those who furnish a statement or cause others to furnish a statement, which the person knows or has reason to know is false, concerning the tax benefits of the activity [IRC Sec. 6700(a)(2)].

(e) Aiding and Abetting. There is a $1,000 penalty that can be imposed on anyone who aids in the preparation of any portion of a return, affidavit, claim or other document if he knows (or has reason to know) that an understatement of tax liability will result from its use. (The penalty is $10,000 for documents relating to a corporation's tax bill.) If this penalty applies, the promoting penalty [(d) above] is not also imposed on the same person with respect to the same document. Both penalties may, however, be imposed with respect to separate documents. For example, the promotional material supplied at the time of sale is separate from the partnership schedules (Form 1065, Schedule K-1) subsequently provided to the investors [IRC Sec. 6701].

(f) Frivolous Income Tax Returns. There is a $500 penalty for anyone who files a return that (1) does not contain information necessary for the IRS to determine whether the tax is correct or (2) contains information that, on its face, shows that the tax is substantially incorrect. The penalty is imposed when the taxpayer's motivation in filing the return is frivolous or based on a desire to delay administration of the tax laws. This penalty is imposed in addition to other penalties [IRC Sec. 6702].

Taxpayers who wish to contest this penalty must pay the full amount before seeking judicial review of its being imposed [IRC Sec. 6703(c)(2)].

¶3724   DELINQUENCY PENALTIES (FAILURES TO FILE OR PAY)

A graduated (15%-75%) penalty applies to a fraudulent failure to file, and a four-tier (2%-15%) penalty applies to a failure to make timely deposits.

(a) Failure to File. The penalty for fraudulently failing to file is 15% of the net amount of tax due for each month that the return is not filed. Maximum penalty: Five months or 75%. The burden of proving fraud is on the IRS. If it does not meet this burden of proof, the taxpayer may still be liable for the basic failure to file penalty of 5% per month (up to a maximum of 25%) [IRC 6651(a), (f)]. Moreover, if an income tax return is not filed within 60 days of the due date (with extensions), the minimum penalty is the lesser of $100 or the amount of tax due [IRC Sec. 6651(a); Reg. Sec. 301.6651-1(b)]. The penalty is imposed unless it is shown that the failure is due to reasonable cause and not due to willful neglect.

The addition is figured on the net amount due, rather than the gross amount. Thus, if part of the tax has been prepaid through payment of estimated tax or withholding on wages, the addition applies only to the amount that still has to be paid [IRC Sec. 6651(b); Reg. Sec. 301.6651-1(b)]. But a taxpayer who didn't file because he mistakenly believed he owed no tax was hit by the penalty.[1]

What is reasonable cause. Reasonable cause for failure to file means such cause as would prompt an ordinary, intelligent person to act under similar circumstances as you did in tardily filing your income tax return. The most acceptable reason (though not always accepted) has been relying on the advice of competent tax counsel. You should prove as many of these facts as you can: (1) you sought advice of counsel, expert in federal income tax matters; (2) you gave your counsel all necessary information and withheld nothing; (3) you acted in good faith on your counsel's advice. The Supreme Court has ruled taxpayers must file timely returns. Tardy action by hired accountants or lawyers is not "reasonable cause" to excuse you from paying the penalty for late filing.[2]

Failure to make timely payment. A penalty is imposed, in addition to the interest [¶3728], if the amount shown as the tax on any return to which the failure-to-file penalty applies is not paid on time. The penalty is ½% of the tax if the failure is for one month or less, and an additional ½% for each month or part of a month the failure continues until the penalty reaches 25%. This penalty does not apply to: (a) failure to pay due to reasonable cause and (b) failure to pay any estimated tax [IRC Sec. 6651(a), (e); Reg. Sec. 301.6651-1(a), (c)].

For automatic filing extensions for individuals [¶3631(a)], the penalty is imposed in the absence of reasonable cause; reasonable cause is presumed if the balance due does not exceed 10% of the total tax and is remitted with the return [Reg. Secs. 301.6651-1(c)(1), (3)].

For example, the Tax Court has invalidated two automatic extensions for a married couple whose estimates of the balance due were off by 80% the first year and 50% the second.[3] The penalty for failure to file [(a) above] is not reduced by this penalty [Reg. Sec. 301.6651-1(a)(1)].

> **NOTE:** If both the failure to file and failure to pay penalties apply to the same month, the 5% failure to file penalty for that month is reduced by the ½% failure to pay penalty. However, the total maximum penalty amount applies separately to penalties for failure to file return and failure to pay tax. So where both penalties are imposed for their respective maximum periods, the combined total penalty is 47.5%: 22.5% for failure to file (4.5% times 5 months) and 25% for failure to pay (½% times 50 months) [Reg. Sec. 301.6651-1].

Penalty increased for failure to pay in certain cases. The penalty for failure to pay tax is increased from ½% to 1% a month on the earlier of the IRS's notice and demand for immediate payment if the tax collection is in jeopardy, or ten days after a notice before levy is given. The increase will occur after the IRS has tried to contact the taxpayer by mail [IRC Sec. 6651(d)].

If a corporation is granted an automatic extension of time for filing, reasonable cause for the underpayment for the extension period is presumed if (1) the tax shown on its application for extension [¶3631(c)], or paid by the due date, is at least 97% (93% for tax years beginning after December 31, 1991 and before July 1, 1992) of the tax shown on its return; and (2) any balance due shown on its return is paid by the return due date, including extensions [Reg. Sec. 301.6651-1(c)].

The amount of tax on which the penalty is imposed is the net amount due. Thus, the amount of tax shown on the return is reduced by any amount of tax paid on or before the start of the month for which the tax is being computed. Credits against tax that may be claimed on the return are also subtracted from the amount shown to give the net amount. If the amount required to be shown as tax on any return is less than the amount actually shown as tax, the lower amount is used to figure the penalty [IRC Sec. 6651(b), (c); Reg. Sec. 301.6651-(d)].

Failure to pay deficiency. A penalty ranging from ½% to 25% applies for failure to pay a deficiency without reasonable cause, within 10 days of the date of notice and demand. This penalty can also be applied to assessments relating to mathematical errors [¶3701], but not to estimated tax payments [IRC Sec. 6651; Reg. Sec. 301.6651-1(a)(3)]. The penalty for failure to file [(a) above] is not reduced by the amount of this penalty [Reg. Sec. 301.6651-1(a)(3)].

(b) Failure to Make Timely Deposits of Tax. The four-tiered penalty structure encourages depositors to correct their failures as soon as possible. The size of the penalty varies with the length of time within which the taxpayer corrects the failure. Specifically, the penalties for failing to make the deposits are based on applicable percentages of the amount of the underpayment determined by the number of days the deposit is late. If the failure is:

- Within five days of the due date, the penalty is 2% of the underpayment;
- Over five but less than 15 days, the penalty is 5% of the underpayment; or
- More than 15 days late, the penalty is 10% [IRC Sec. 6656(b)(1)(A)].

Also, the 15% penalty may be imposed if the underdeposited taxes are not paid on or before the earlier of (1) ten days after the first delinquency notice or (2) the day on which notice and demand for immediate payment is given [IRC Sec. 6656(b)(1)(B)]. Reasonable cause and not-due-to-willful-neglect defenses apply to overcome this penalty [IRC Sec. 6656; Reg. Sec. 301.6656-1].

> ➤ **OBSERVATION** This means that, on average, a taxpayer will generally have approximately 40 days from the due date of the quarterly return to make up any shortfall in deposits before the rate increases to 15%.

For special rules regarding an employer's failure to deposit withholding and employment taxes, see ¶2562.

¶3725   OTHER PENALTIES

There are a number of individual penalties that can apply in addition to the general penalties above. A summary of other penalties follows:

Bad checks. If tax is paid with a bad check (or money order), a penalty is imposed unless the check was tendered in good faith and with reasonable cause to believe it will be paid. The amount of the penalty is 2% of the check's amount (unless the check was for less than $750, in which case the penalty is the lesser of $15 or the amount of the check) [IRC Sec. 6657; Reg. Sec. 301.6657-1].

Partnership returns. There is a per month penalty of $50 multiplied by the number or partners for late or incomplete returns unless due to reasonable cause [IRC Sec. 6698]. This penalty is in addition to criminal penalties [¶3727].

Private foundations. A penalty equal to 100% of initial and additional excise taxes [¶3336 et seq.] is imposed on the foundation, its manager, a disqualified person or government official if (1) the violation was willful *and* flagrant or (2) the person was liable for any such tax as to a prior violation with same or another foundation [IRC Sec. 6684; Reg. Sec. 301.6684-1].

Public charities. A 25% excise tax is imposed on an electing charitable organization [¶1914] if it incurs excess lobbying expenditures to influence legislation [IRC Sec. 4911].

Retirement plans. A nondeductible 6% excise tax on excess contributions to individual retirement accounts (IRAs) [IRC Sec. 4973]; also, a 10% penalty tax on premature distribution withdrawals from IRAs [IRC Sec. 408(f)]. A two-tier excise tax is imposed on employers' plans for underfunding [IRC Sec. 4971].

Registered obligations. An excise tax is imposed on the issuer of a registration-required obligation not in registered form. The tax is 1% of the principal multiplied by the number of years in the term of the obligation [IRC Sec. 4701].

Notices by brokers to payors. A $500 per failure is imposed on any retail broker who intentionally fails to supply a payor of dividends and interest with a taxpayer identification number (TIN) or a backup withholding status report [IRC Sec. 6705].

¶3726   PENALTY FOR UNDERPAYMENT OF CORPORATION ESTIMATED TAX

[New tax legislation may affect this subject; see ¶1.]

Generally, every corporation must pay four installments of estimated tax equal to 25% of its "required annual payment." Installments are due by April 15, June 15, September 15 and December 15. For fiscal year corporations, the due dates are the 15th day of the fourth, sixth, ninth and 12th months of the year [IRC Sec. 6655(a); Reg. Sec. 1.6655-1]. A penalty is imposed on the amount of underpayment for the period of underpayment [¶3728]. The required annual payment, for corporations other than large corporations [(c) below], is the lesser of 97% (93% for tax years beginning after December 31, 1991, and before July 1, 1992) of the tax shown on the return or 100% of the tax for the preceding year. (The last-year's-tax escape hatch remains intact for corporations eligible to use it; see (c) below.)

Exceptions. A corporation does not owe an underpayment penalty if it satisfies any of the following: (1) The corporation based its installment on its "annualized income," (2) The corporation based its installment on its "adjusted seasonal income" or (3) The corporation's tax for the year is less than $500 [IRC Sec. 6655(e), (f)].

(a) The Annualized Income Exception. For most corporations, this exception is: the most crucial. Annualization is based on income earned during (a) the first three months for the installment due in the fourth month, (b) the first three or five months for the installment due in the sixth month, (c) the first six or eight months for the installment due in the ninth month and (d) the first nine or eleven months for the installment due in the twelfth month.

Applicable percentage: The amount required to be paid is calculated by multiplying the applicable percentage for a given installment by the full tax on the annualized income for the appropriate period and subtracting any prior payments. For example, in 1993 the applicable percentages are 24.25% for the first installment, 48.50% for the second, 72.75% for the third, and 97% for the fourth [IRC Sec. 6655(e)(2)(B)].

NOTE: (1) A corporation can use the annualized income exception only if the amount required to be paid is *less* than the regular required installment. (2) The corporation must recapture 100% of any reduction in a required installment resulting from using the annualized income exception by increasing the next installment for which the corporation does not use the annualization exception [IRC Sec. 6655(e)].

Example: The 1993 tax picture of Del Mar Corporation, a calendar year corporation, looks like this:

Period	Taxable Income
Jan.-Mar.	$ 60,000
Apr.-June	75,000
July-Sept.	90,000
Oct.-Dec.	105,000

Its total taxable income is $330,000 on which it owes a tax of $111,950. Del Mar's regular required payments based on 97% of the current year's tax ($108,592) are $27,147.88 on April 15, June 15, Sept. 15, and Dec. 15.

But at the beginning of the year, Del Mar didn't know what its final tax would be, so it decided to make estimated payments based on its annualized income:

Period	Annualized In]come	Tax on Annualized Income
3 mos.	$240,000	$76,850
6 mos.	270,000	88,550
9 mos.	300,000	100,250

Del Mar's installments based on its annualized income are figured like this:

Applicable % of tax on annualized income—prior installments

April 15:	(24.25% x $76,850) - 0 = $18,636.13
June 15:	(48.5% x $76,850) - $18,636.13 = $18,636.13
Sept. 15:	(72.75% x $88,550) - $37,272.26 = $27,147.87
Dec. 15:	(97% x $100,250) - $64,420.13 = $32,822.37

Del Mar must pay the lesser of the (1) annualized installment amount or (2) the regular required installment plus the recapture amount. In September, Del Mar determines its (1) annualized installment amount ($27,147.88) to be less than (2) the regular required installment plus the recapture amount ($27,147.88 + $17,023.50 = $44,171.38). Accordingly, the payment in September will be $27,147.883 (the annualized installment amount). The December payment will be $32,822.37 (the annualized installment amount) which is less than the required installment amount plus the recapture amount ($27,147.88 + $17,023.50 = $44,171.38).

▶ **OBSERVATION** For a small corporation with a tax history, the safest thing to do is to base this year's estimated tax payments on 100% of last year's tax. New corporations (or large corporations that can't use the 100% of last year's tax rule [(c) below]) will have to make careful estimates of *total* tax liability for the year and gauge estimated tax payments accordingly. They cannot assume a payment based on annualized income will be sufficient.

(b) The Seasonal Income Exception. Corporations that earn seasonal income (e.g., amusement parks, ski resorts) are allowed to annualize their income by assuming income earned in the current year is earned in the same pattern as in preceding years. This method cannot be used unless the corporation expects to earn at least 70% of its annual income in six consecutive months. This exception may be used only if the resulting installment payment is less than the regular required installment. Also, once the exception no longer applies, savings resulting from using it for prior installments are recaptured [IRC Sec. 6655(e)].

Tax computation for seasonal income.   The base period percentage can be determined as follows [IRC 6655(e)(3)]:

- Take the taxable income for all months during the taxable year preceding the filing month.
- Divide that amount by the base period percentage for all months during the taxable year (average percent which the taxable income for the corresponding months in the three preceding months in the three preceding tax years bears to the taxable income for the three preceding years).
- Find the tax on the amount determined by basing the tax on the previous year's income, but at the current year's rate.
- Multiply that tax by the base period percentage for the months in the tax year up to and including the month in which the installment is due. (Note that this percentage must equal or exceed 70% of the total income for any six consecutive months of a tax year.)

Example: An amusement park that has a calendar year as its tax year receives the largest part of its taxable income during the six-month period from May through October. To compute its base period percentage for the period from May through October 1993, it must figure its taxable income for the period May through October in each of the following years: 1990, 1991 and 1992. The taxable income for each May-through-October period is then divided by the total taxable income for that tax year. Assume the quotients are as follows: .69 for 1990, .74 for 1991, and .67 for 1992. Since that averages out to .70, the base period percentage for May through October 1993 is 70%. Therefore, the amusement park qualifies for the adjusted seasonal installment method.

In determining the estimated tax payments for both the annualized and seasonal income exceptions, use Form 1120-W.

(c) Special Rules for Large Corporations.   Large corporations generally cannot base their estimated tax payments on the previous year's tax liability. However, a large corporation may base its *first* installment payment for any year on last year's tax. A large corporation is a corporation with taxable income (computed without regard to net operating loss and capital loss carrybacks and carryovers) of $1 million or more for any of the three preceding tax years [IRC Sec. 6655(g)].

¶3727   CRIMINAL PENALTIES

Criminal penalties can be imposed as follows:

- Willful failure to pay the tax or estimated tax, make a return, or keep the records and supply the information required by the law and regulations—misdemeanor punishable by fine of $25,000 (or $100,000 for corporations), imprisonment for not over one year (5 years for failing to report large cash transactions as required by IRC Sec. 6050I), or both [IRC Sec. 7203].

- Willful failure to collect, account for, and pay over any tax by any person required to do so—felony, punishable by fine of $10,000, imprisonment for not more than five years, or both [IRC Sec. 7202].
- Willful attempt to evade or defeat the tax—felony, punishable by fine of $100,000 (or $500,000 for corporations), imprisonment for not more than five years, or both [IRC Sec. 7201].
- Willful making and subscribing of a return in which not every material matter is believed to be true and correct—felony, punishable by fine of $100,000 (or $500,000 for corporations), imprisonment for not more than three years, or both [IRC Sec. 7206].
- Willful filing of any known false or fraudulent document, including an income tax return[1]—misdemeanor, punishable by fine of $10,000 (or $50,000 for corporations), imprisonment of not more than one year, or both [IRC Sec. 7207; Reg. Sec. 301.7207-1].
- Disclosure or use (subject to certain qualifications) of any information furnished a person engaged in the business of preparing returns, or who does so for compensation, for purposes other than the preparation of the return—misdemeanor, punishable by fine of $1,000, imprisonment up to one year, or both [IRC Sec. 7216; Reg. Sec. 301.7216-1–3].

Limitation period. The statute of limitations on these offenses is three years in some cases and six years in others, the latter applying mostly to attempts to defraud the government and willful attempts to evade or defeat the tax [IRC Sec. 6531]. The six-year limitation period begins to run from the date a return is filed, or its due date, whichever is later.[2]

¶3728   INTEREST FOR FAILURE TO PAY TAX

[New tax legislation may affect this subject; see ¶1.]

If any amount of tax is not paid when due, interest must be paid from the due date until the tax is paid. However, interest (and penalties) can be avoided if the unpaid tax is a result of erroneous written advice from an IRS employee acting in an official capacity where the taxpayer provided correct information.

The underpayment and overpayment rates are tied to the prime rate:

- The overpayment rate is the federal short-term rate plus two percentage points.
- The underpayment rate is generally the federal short-term rate plus three percentage points, unless large corporate underpayments are involved (see below) [IRC Sec. 6621].

The rate is adjusted quarterly. It is determined during the first month of each quarter, and takes effect the following quarter. For example, the January federal short-term rate is the rate used to determine the interest to be charged on underpayments and overpayments for April, May, and June. The IRS determines the interest rate based on average market yield on outstanding U.S. marketable obligations with remaining maturity periods of three years or less [IRC Sec. 6621]. If the tax is being paid in installments, interest on any portion of the tax not shown on the return runs from the due date of the first installment. For an unpaid installment of tax shown on the return, interest runs from the due date for that particular installment [IRC Sec. 6601; Reg. Sec. 301.6601-1].

Large corporate underpayments. The interest rate imposed on large corporate underpayments was increased. Starting with periods after 1990 (regardless of the tax period to which the underlying tax may relate), the rate on corporate underpayments that exceed $100,000 is the federal short-term rate plus five percentage points [IRC Sec. 6621(c)(1); Temp. Reg. Sec. 301.6621-3T].

The $100,000 threshold includes the excess of the tax imposed exclusive of interest, penalties, additional amounts and additions to tax. Thus, any payment made after the last date prescribed for payment (for example, by way of an amended return) won't affect the threshold amount. Different types of taxes are not combined for this threshold.

This rate applies to periods after the 30th day following the earlier of the date the IRS sends (1) the 30-day letter [¶ 3704] or (2) the 90-day letter (¶ 3705) [Temp. Reg. Sec. 301.6621-3T(c)(2)].

Rates. The interest rates paid in 1992 for overpayments were: January-March, 8%; April-September, 7%. For underpayments, the charges were: January-March, 9% (11% for large corporate underpayments); April-September, 8% (10% for large corporate underpayments).

When tax is due. Due date for payment is determined without regard to any extension of time (including an automatic extension) [¶3631]. Interest runs during the period of the extension and until payment is made. If payment is demanded before the due date because of jeopardy, interest does not run before the prescribed due date [IRC Sec. 6601(b); Reg. Sec. 301.6601-1(c)].

> **NOTE:** Interest on underpayment of accumulated earnings tax accrues from the due date of the income tax return for the year the tax is initially imposed [IRC Sec. 6601(b)(4)].

Offsetting interest. Interest is not imposed on a deficiency to the extent that interest would be concurrently payable on a refund of an overpayment of tax credited against the deficiency [IRC Sec. 6601(f); Reg. Sec. 301.6601-1(b)]. Thus, if an overpayment and deficiency are equal, the interest on each cancels out for the period both are outstanding at the same time[1] [IRC Secs. 6601(f); 6611(b)].

> **Example:** John Green's tax for 1990 was $2,000. He paid $1,500 on April 16, 1991. His tax for 1991 was $1,800, but he paid $2,000 on April 15, 1992. The underpayment and overpayment were disclosed by an examination of his returns in March 1993 and the overpayment was credited against the underpayment. Green must pay interest on the underpayment of $500 from April 16, 1991, to April 15, 1992, when he made the overpayment of $200. Since interest would be payable on a refund of the $200 overpayment, he does not have to pay interest on $200 of the underpayment from April 15, 1991. He must pay interest on $300 of the underpayment.

Carrybacks. Interest on a deficiency that is offset by a carryback of a net operating loss, net capital loss or general business credit [¶2405 et seq.] runs from the original due date of the tax to which the deficiency relates to the filing date for the tax year in which the loss or credit arises [IRC Sec. 6601(d); Reg. Sec. 301.6601-1(e)]. If a net operating loss carryback eliminates the appropriate credit, no interest is payable on the tax originally offset by the credit.[2]

Additions to tax. In general, interest is compounded daily. This means there is interest on interest. However, the daily compounding of interest does not apply to the penalty for underpaying estimated tax [¶2420; 3651(b)].

Interest is also imposed on any assessable penalty, additional amount or addition to the tax if the additional amount is not paid within ten days from notice and demand for payment [IRC Sec. 6601(e); Reg. Sec. 301.6601-1(f)]. However, interest runs from the *due date of the return* (including extensions) if the penalty is assessed for: (1) failure to file a timely return [¶3724], (2) a substantial understatement of tax [¶3722(b)] and (3) a valuation misstatement

[¶3722(c)]. The compounding of interest is suspended if the interest on deficiency is suspended after a waiver of restrictions on assessment has been filed [IRC Sec. 6601(c)].

REFUNDS AND CREDITS

¶3735   OVERPAYMENT OF TAX

The Revenue Service can refund or credit any overpayment of the tax [IRC Sec. 6402; Reg. Sec. 301.6402-1].

Overpayments by corporations are refunded on the basis of tentative returns without a refund claim and without examining the completed return. However, in most other cases, a claim for refund must be filed. There are special refund procedures for overpayments of corporate estimated tax [¶3736(a)] or due to carrybacks of net operating or net capital losses [¶3744].

Review tax return. Before filing a refund claim, you should review the entry for each item on the tax return for the year in question and recompute the tax to make sure if there is an actual overpayment of the *entire* tax. If this is not done, and the Revenue Service finds errors from which you received an advantage, the amount of the overpayment may be reduced or entirely eliminated. An additional tax might even be assessed, if the statute of limitations has not run.[1]

¶3736   REFUND CLAIMS

Claims for refund fall into three classes: (1) claims for taxes paid on the original return, (2) for overpayments through withholding on wages or estimated tax paid and (3) for payments made on a deficiency notice. It is not necessary to pay the tax under protest to get a refund.

(a) Overpayment by Withholding or Estimated Tax. The excess of the tax withheld on wages and the estimated tax paid over the tax shown as due on the return will be refunded to you, or, at your election, will be credited against your next year's estimated tax, if any. However, the IRS may credit any overpayment of individual, fiduciary, or corporate income tax against any outstanding tax, interest or penalty owed by you [Reg. Sec. 301.6402-3].

Adjustment for corporate estimated tax overpayment. A corporation overpaying its estimated tax (including alternative minimum tax) can apply for an adjustment on Form 4466, Corporate Application for Quick Refund of Overpayment of Estimated Tax, within two and a half months after the close of its tax year. Actual payments of estimated tax must exceed the current revised estimate of tax liability by at least 10% and by at least $500 [IRC Sec. 6425; Reg. Sec. 1.6425-1–3].

(b) Payment of Assessed Deficiency. You may prefer to pay deficiencies and avoid the interest charge. Then you can file a claim for refund, and if the claim is rejected, sue to recover. Or you, when the deficiency notice is received, may decide that an appeal to the Tax Court is useless. Later events, for example, a court decision, may change the situation. So a claim for refund still can be made, if it is filed in time.

(c) When Taxpayer Appeals to Tax Court. If a deficiency notice has been issued, and you appeal to the Tax Court, no refund or credit will be allowed and no suit for recovery of any part of the tax can be maintained in any court. There are three exceptions: (1) overpayment determined by a Tax Court decision that has become final, (2) an amount collected above the amount determined by the Tax Court decision and (3) any amount collected after the period for levy or suit for collection has expired [IRC Sec. 6512(a)].

¶3737   TIME FOR FILING REFUND CLAIMS

You must file claims within the time set by law, or no refund will be allowed [IRC Sec. 6511(b); Reg. Sec. 301.6511(b)-1]. Even mental incompetency does not excuse a failure to file on time.¹ A claim is considered to be filed on the date postmarked [IRC Sec. 7502; Reg. Sec. 301.7502-1]. If the due date falls on a Saturday, Sunday or legal holiday, the next business day is the due date. In addition, there are special refund periods [¶3738].

(a) Three-Year Limitation. You must ordinarily file a claim for refund for any tax year within three years of the time you filed the return [IRC Sec. 6511(a)]. If you filed the return before the due date, the three-year period starts to run from the date the return was due [IRC Sec. 6513(a); Reg. Sec. 301.6513-1].

> **Example:** The due date of an individual return for the calendar year 1992 is April 15, 1993. If a taxpayer filed his return on February 17, 1993, the limitation period starts from April 15, 1993. If he filed on May 14, 1993, the limitation period starts from May 14, 1993.

> **NOTE:** Returns of taxes withheld from wages or withheld at source for a year filed before April 15 of the next year are considered filed and the tax paid on April 15 [IRC Sec. 6513; Reg. Sec. 301.6513-1].

(b) Two-Year Limitation. There is an exception to the three-year period. You can file a claim for refund within two years from the time the tax is paid, if the two-year period ends at a later date than the three-year period [IRC Sec. 6511(a); Reg. Sec. 301.6511(a)-1]. For this purpose, estimated tax [¶2416] and tax withheld at source [¶2518] are considered paid on the due date of the return (without extensions), and income tax withheld on wages is considered paid by the wage earner on the 15th day of the fourth month after the tax year it is allowed as a credit [IRC Sec. 6513; Reg. Sec. 301.6513-1].

> **NOTE:** The tax law says that taxpayers who do not file tax returns can recover overpayments made only in the two years preceding their refund request. And for this purpose, extension forms do not count as tax returns.²

(c) Time Extended by Waiver. The Revenue Service sometimes asks you to file a waiver (Form 872) extending the time an assessment can be made against you. A waiver filed before the time to file a refund claim expires extends the time to file a claim [IRC Sec. 6511(c); Reg. Sec. 301.6511(c)-1].

¶3738   SPECIAL PERIODS FOR FILING CLAIMS

The usual period for filing a refund claim may be extended for particular transactions.

Bad debts and worthless securities. A refund claim related to a deduction for a bad debt or a loss from a worthless security, or the effect of these deductions on the application of a *carryover*, can be filed within seven years from the date the return *was due,* instead of three years from the filing of the return. For a similar claim relating to a *carryback,* the period is seven years from the due date for filing the return for the year of the net operating loss which results in the carryback, or the period for a net operating loss carryback (see below), whichever ends later [IRC Sec. 6511(d)(1); Reg. Sec. 301.6511(d)-1].

Carrybacks. A refund claim based on a general business credit carryback, net operating loss carryback and capital loss carryback can be filed up to three years after the prescribed due date for filing the return (including extensions) following the end of the tax year in which the credit was earned or the loss incurred [IRC Sec. 6511(d); Reg. Sec. 301.6511(d)-7]. A beneficiary of an estate that has a net operating loss carryback, reducing distributable net income of a prior year, can file for refund under this provision.[1]

If a claim for carryback refund is filed under this provision or a timely application for carryback adjustment [¶3744] is made, recovery of an earlier overpayment will be allowed even if it might otherwise be barred [Reg. Secs. 301.6511(d)-2, 301.6511(d)-4].

Partnerships. A tax matters partner (TMP) must file a request for an administrative adjustment of partnership items that give rise to a credit or refund claim. The IRS may process it as a claim for credit or refund on partners' returns, conduct a partnership examination or take no action.[2] If no action is taken, a TMP may file a petition either with the Tax Court, a District Court or the Claims Court. Request for an administrative adjustment must be made no later than three years from due date of the partnership return, or the date it was filed. A petition to the court must be filed within six months of the request for an administrative review, and before two years after the date of the request.

In addition, any partner may file a request for administrative adjustment (RAA) of partnership items for a partnership tax year by no later than three years after the return was filed (or due date, if later) and before mailing of a notice of FPAA to the TMP for such tax year. This effectively is an amended return and the IRS may process it as a claim for credit or refund on nonpartnership items, assess any additional tax resulting from the requested adjustments, conduct a partnership examination or treat all partnership items of the partner as nonpartnership items. If any part of the RAA is not allowed, the same time limits that apply to a suit by a TMP also apply to suits by individual partners [IRC Sec. 6227, 6228, 6230, 6511(g)].

Retirement plans. Special period of limitation for refund or credit of amounts included in income and later recaptured on qualified plan termination. The three-year limitation period is extended for one year after recaptured amount is paid [IRC Sec. 6511(d)(6)].

Taxes paid or credited. Foreign taxes paid and overpayments credited to estimated tax may entitle taxpayers to a refund.

Foreign taxes. If claim for credit or refund arises from payment or accrual of taxes to a foreign country or U.S. possession for which credit is allowed against the U.S. tax, time for filing claim is ten years from due date of return [IRC Sec. 6511(d)(3); Reg. Sec. 301.6511(d)-3]. It also applies to credit or refund claims for correcting mathematical errors in figuring the foreign tax, discovering creditable taxes not reported when the tax return was filed or any other adjustments to the amount of the credit, including those due to paying of additional foreign taxes.[2]

Overpayment applied to estimated tax. An overpayment claimed as a credit against estimated tax for the following year [IRC Sec. 6402(b)], is treated as a payment for the year the estimated tax is paid. Ordinarily no claim for credit or refund will be allowed for the year the overpayment was made, and the limitation period on refund or credit starts to run with the second year [IRC Sec. 6513(d); Reg. Sec. 301.6513-1(d)]. But see ¶3736(a) for special refund rule applying to corporations.

¶3739   AMOUNT OF REFUND LIMITED

If you file a refund claim during the three-year limitation period, the credit or refund cannot exceed the portion of the tax paid within the three years (plus extensions of time granted to file the return) preceding the filing of the claim. If you do not file the claim within the three-year period but do file on time within the two-year period, the credit or refund cannot exceed the portion of the tax paid during the two-year period preceding the filing of the claim. If no claim is filed the limit on the amount of credit or refund is determined as if a claim was filed on the date the credit or refund is allowed [IRC Sec. 6511(b); Reg. Sec. 301.6511(b)-1].

> **Example 1:** XYZ Corporation filed its 1992 return and paid $1,000 tax on March 15, 1993. Claim for refund of all or any part of the $1,000 tax must be filed by March 15, 1996.

Example 2: Assume the same facts as in Example 1. Assume also that on August 3, 1993, the government assessed an additional tax of $700 for 1992 and the taxpayer paid this amount on August 12, 1994. The taxpayer learned later that it neglected to take sufficient deductions in the 1992 return and for that reason overpaid its tax by $1,000.

If the claim is filed by March 15, 1996 (within three years after the return was filed), the entire overpayment of $1,000 may be recovered.

If the claim is filed after March 15, 1996, but by August 13, 1996 (within two years after the $700 assessment was paid), the refund may not exceed $700.

If the claim is filed after August 13, 1996, the time will have expired and nothing may be recovered.

¶3740   FORM OF REFUND CLAIM

You make claims for refunds of overpayments of income taxes on original tax returns or amended tax returns. [(c) below]. You usually make claims for refund of other taxes, interest, penalties, and additions to tax on Form 843 [Reg. Sec. 301.6402-2, 301.6402-3].

NOTE: Corporations can receive expedited refunds (before filing their actual corporate tax return) of estimated tax overpayments for the prior year. Form 4466 is used. To qualify, those tax payments must exceed the corporation's expected tax by at least 10% of the expected tax, and the overpayment must amount to at least $500.

The IRS may treat an informal refund claim as a valid claim provided such claim is later perfected by a formal refund claim. Form 870 or 890 series on which the taxpayer agrees to an overassessment of income taxes may be considered a valid claim for refund or credit.[1]

(a) Statement of Claim. Careful thought should be given to the preparation of the section on reasons advanced for the claim. If the claim is rejected and you sue on it, you will generally be precluded from advancing grounds for recovery not stated in the claim.[2] Facts should be fully presented and verified [Reg. Sec. 301.6402-2(b)]. Legal arguments should be outlined if the claim turns on points of law. An amended return is not necessary in filing a claim for refund based on the original return, but may be a way to establish the amount of the refund.

(b) Amending the Claim. You can amend or supplement your claims during the time within which you could file a new claim. You cannot amend a claim to change the facts after the statute of limitations has expired;[3] but if the facts are not changed, an amendment may be allowed.[4]

(c) Amended Tax Returns as Claims. Individuals who have filed Forms 1040, 1040A, or 1040EZ should file their claim for a refund of income taxes on amended return Form 1040X. Corporations having filed Form 1120 or Form 1120-A should use Form 1120X. Other taxpayers file their claims on the appropriate amended income tax return; for example, trusts use Form 1041 and exempt organizations use Form 990T [Reg. Sec. 301.6402-3].

¶3741   FILING THE REFUND CLAIM

You must file the refund claim and supporting evidence at the service center for the district in which you paid the tax. Hand-delivered claims are filed in the office of the

District Director of Internal Revenue for the district where the tax was paid [Reg. Sec. 301.6402-2].

You must make a separate claim for each tax year or period. It must state in detail each ground upon which a refund is claimed, and facts that will inform the Revenue Service of the exact basis for the claim.

If the claim for refund is made on the return for a decedent, Form 1310 should be attached.[1]

(a) Administrative Procedure. If the claim is based on a return, the administrative procedure is substantially the same as in cases involving determination of a deficiency. An examiner is assigned when a field investigation is called for. If his report is unacceptable to you, you may have a district Appeals office conference [¶3703]. A claim based on payment of a deficiency assessment on which conferences were held will usually be disallowed on the findings of the conferences.

(b) Decision on Claim. If the decision on a refund claim is in your favor, a certificate of overassessment is issued by the IRS. If the overassessment exceeds $1 million, it must be reported to the Joint Congressional Committee on Internal Revenue Taxation [IRC Sec. 6405; Reg. Sec. 301.6405-1], except for an overpayment made by a corporation based on a tentative return. The amount involved is credited against any taxes owed by you for any year not barred by the statute of limitations [IRC Sec. 6402]. Any balance is refunded.

If the decision is against you, you can sue to recover [¶3743].

¶3742   INTEREST ON REFUNDS

Refunds carry interest at the overpayment rate (see below) [IRC Sec. 6611, 6621; Reg. Sec. 301.6611-1]. The interest runs and is compounded daily from the date of the overpayment to a date fixed by the IRS. This date cannot be more than 30 days before the refund check date [IRC Sec. 6611(b)(2); Reg. Sec. 301.6611-1].

Adjusted rate. The overpayment rate, adjusted quarterly, is based on the federal short-term rate plus two percentage points (rounded). Similar to the underpayment rate, it is determined during the first month of each quarter [IRC Sec. 6621(a)(1)]. For the rate on underpayments, see ¶3728.

NOTE: The IRS determines the interest rate (federal short-term) based on average market yield on outstanding U.S. marketable obligations with remaining maturity period of three years or less [IRC Sec. 6621(b)(3)].

No interest is paid on refunds made within 45 days after the due date of returns filed on or before the due date or on refunds made within 45 days after a late return is filed [IRC Sec. 6611(e)].

NOTE: Inquiries about refund checks should state the taxpayer's identification number (TIN) and be addressed to the Revenue Service Center that processed the claim, as indicated on the check.

(a) Credit for Overpayment. When an overpayment is credited against a later assessed deficiency instead of being refunded, interest runs from the date of overpayment to the due date of the deficiency[1] [IRC Sec. 6611(b); Reg. Sec. 301.6611-1(h)]. Penalties are offset against the overpayment before interest is computed.[2]

(b) No Review of Interest Allowed. In the absence of fraud or mathematical mistake, the allowance or failure to allow interest on any credit or refund cannot be reviewed by any administrative or accounting officer, employee, or agent of the U.S. [IRC Sec. 6406].

(c) Special Provisions. There are special interest provisions for:

Carrybacks. If the overpayment results from the carryback of a net operating capital loss, or foreign taxes paid, no interest is allowed for the period before the filing date for the tax year the loss or the foreign tax was paid or accrued [IRC Sec. 6611(f), (g); Reg. Sec. 301.6611-1(e)].

Deposits. You get interest is on the refund of deposits made to stop the running of interest against you[3] [IRC Sec. 6401(c); Reg. Sec. 301.6401-1]. However, the Third Circuit has held that a deposit merely to avoid a jeopardy assessment is not a payment on which interest will accrue.[4]

Excessive withholding or estimated tax. If the claim is based on excessive withholding from wages or on an excessive estimated tax payment, interest is allowed from the date the final return was due even though the tax was paid earlier [IRC Sec. 6513, 6611(d); Reg. Sec. 301.6513-1, 301.6611-(d)].

¶3743   SUIT TO RECOVER TAX

A suit to recover refund may be started only if you have filed a claim [IRC Sec. 7422(a)] and only if you have paid the entire tax, including any deficiency claimed by the IRS.[1] Interest on the tax need not be paid before suit.[2]

Proof. In a suit to recover, you have to prove that the tax was overpaid.[3] The suit must be based on the same grounds as the refund claim.[4]

(a) When to File. You may not start a suit to recover until after six months from the date you filed the refund claim, unless a decision on the claim is made before then. You must start the suit before the end of two years from the date of mailing to you, by registered or certified mail, of a notice disallowing part or all of the claim [IRC Sec. 6532(a); Reg. Sec. 301.6532-1].

The period cannot be extended by filing a new refund claim, on the same grounds, after the disallowance.[5] A 30-day letter disallowing the claim is a decision on the claim[6]

Extension of time to file. If the last day of the period is a Saturday, Sunday or legal holiday, the time is extended to include the next business day [¶3630]. The two-year period can be extended for any period agreed on in writing [IRC Sec. 6532(a)(2); Reg. Sec. 301.6532-1(b)].

Waiver of notice. If you file a written waiver of the requirement that you be mailed a notice of disallowance of your refund claim, the two-year period for filing suit for recovery starts to run on the date the waiver on Form 2297[7] is filed [IRC Sec. 6532(a)(3); Reg. Sec. 301.6532-1(c)].

(b) Where to File. Suit to recover taxes erroneously or illegally assessed or collected must be brought against the United States [IRC Sec. 7422(f)]. You may institute the suit either in the U.S Claims Court at Washington, D.C., or in a Federal District Court.[8] The proper District Court is the court for the judicial district where an individual taxpayer resides or a corporation has its principal place of business or its principal office or agency.[9] Either party has a right to trial by jury.[10]

(c) When 90-Day Letter Is Issued. If you sue for a refund and a notice of deficiency is issued before the case is heard, appeals to the Tax Court would result in concurrent jurisdiction in both courts over the same case. To prevent this, the proceedings in your suit must be stayed for the 90-day period, so that you can appeal to the Tax Court, plus an additional 60 days thereafter. Then, if you appeal to the Tax Court, the other court loses jurisdiction. If you do not appeal, the other court gets sole jurisdiction [IRC Sec. 7422(e)].

(d) Appeal from Lower Court. Appeal from a District Court decision is to the U.S. Court of Appeals for the circuit in which the District Court is located. Decisions of the various circuits of the U.S. Courts of Appeal may be reviewed in the Supreme Court only on certiorari or certificate.

Decisions of the U.S. Claims Court are appealable to the Court of Appeals for the Federal Circuit. Formerly, Court of Claims (now U.S. Claims Court) decisions were appealable to the Supreme Court by petition for certiorari or certificate.[11] Petitions for certiorari generally must be made within 90 days after decision is entered. If a good reason is shown, up to an additional 60-day extension may be granted.

(e) Recovery of Refunds Paid. The U.S. can sue to recover an erroneous refund if the suit is begun within two years after the refund (within five years if the refund was induced by fraud or material misrepresentation) [IRC Sec. 6532(b); Reg. Sec. 301.6532-2]. An alternative is a suit for recovery by the deficiency collection procedure[¶3710].

(f) Taxes on Private Foundations and Retirement Plans. Payment of the full amount of an excise tax imposed on a private foundation [¶3338-3344] or payment of the special taxes imposed on retirement plans [¶3725] gives either payor the right to sue for refund, but not if the private foundation or the retirement plan has brought another suit or a Tax Court action for a deficiency as to any other excise or special tax imposed on it [IRC Sec. 7422(g)].

¶3744   QUICK REFUNDS FOR CARRYBACKS

A net operating loss [¶2341 et seq.; 3030], corporate capital loss [¶3020], general business credits [¶2405] and amounts attributed to a claim of right adjustment [¶2836(a)] for the current year may be carried back to the three preceding years to reduce the tax liability reported for those years. Since examination of a refund claim usually takes time, a special procedure allows taxpayers to apply for a speedy refund or credit for an overpayment resulting from a carryback [IRC Sec. 6411; Reg. Secs. 1.6411-1—1.6411-3]. The application is not a refund claim [Reg. Sec. 1.6411-1], so a separate claim may be advisable.

Corporations that expect a net operating loss may apply for an extension of time to pay the preceding year's tax [(c) below].

(a) Application for a tentative carryback adjustment to get a quick refund is filed with the service center for the district where the tax was paid or assessed. It must be filed on or after the due date of the return (including extensions of time to file) for the tax year the loss or credit arises, and within 12 months after such tax year.[1] Corporations use Form 1139; other taxpayers use Form 1045. Corporations that filed Form 1138 for an extension of time to pay tax [(c) below] must file Form 1139 by the end of the month that includes the due date (plus extensions) of the return of tax to be deferred, for a further extension.

Since Form 1139 is filed after the close of the year the loss is incurred or credit earned, it is based on the exact figures of the tax return. The application must show the tax liability of the previous years affected by a loss carryback and the effect of the recomputation for the carryback[1] [Reg. Sec. 1.6411-2]. For general business carrybacks, a schedule showing the carryback computation and a recomputation of the credit after the carryback must be attached to the application. Thus, a calendar year taxpayer that has a loss or a general business credit in 1992 large enough to reduce the tax liability for the three preceding years must file application by December 31, 1993, with the required details for the years 1989, 1990 and 1991.

(b) Procedure on Claim. The IRS examines the application and credits or refunds any decrease in tax allowed for the carryback and claim of right adjustments [¶2836(a)] within 90 days from the last day of the month in which the tax return due date falls (including extensions of time to file), or within 90 days from the time the application is filed, if that is later [IRC Sec. 6411; Reg. Sec. 1.6411-3].

> **NOTE:** The IRS can disallow any application that contains material omissions or mathematical errors that cannot be corrected within the 90-day period [Reg. Sec. 1.6411-3]. In most cases, the IRS allows the amounts shown in the application. If it is later found that the allowances were erroneous, the erroneous part of the allowance may be recovered and an adjustment made against the taxpayer [IRC Sec. 6411(b)]. The taxpayer may file the usual claim for refund [¶3740] and sue for recovery [¶3743] if the claim is not allowed [Reg. Sec. 1.6411-1(b)(2)].

(c) Time to Pay Corporate Tax Extended. A corporation that expects operations for the tax year to result in a net operating loss carryback can apply on Form 1138 for an extension of the time for payment of a part of its taxes for the preceding tax year [IRC Sec. 6164; Reg. Sec. 1.6164-1].

¶3745   WHEN LIMITATION PERIODS DO NOT APPLY

Improper tax results can be corrected in certain situations after the time for refund or assessment has passed. An "adjustment" by refund or additional assessment is allowed [IRC Secs. 1311-1315]. Some adjustments can be made only when a determination of tax liability or refund is inconsistent with the treatment of the item in another year or as to another taxpayer [IRC Sec. 1311(b)].

While the statute often works to the taxpayer's advantage, the issue should be given the most careful study before filing a claim for refund. A refund claim may open the way for the assessing a deficiency otherwise barred.

(a) Inconsistent Determination Required. In these situations, determination of tax liability or refund in the later year must be inconsistent with the treatment in the year barred by the statute of limitations. For instance, a successful assertion that rent should be included in income for the year received (1992) is inconsistent with the original treatment, which included the item in the year of accrual (1991) (see Example 1, below).

Adjustment will be made in the following circumstances:

Double inclusion of income occurs when there is included in one year income which erroneously has also been included in the income of a previous year now barred by the statute of limitations. Or, an item is included in the income of one taxpayer and erroneously has been included in the income of a related taxpayer [IRC Sec. 1312(1); Reg. Sec. 1.1312-1].

Example 1: The taxpayer who is on the cash basis erroneously included in his 1991 return an item of $10,000 accrued rent which he actually received in 1992. The taxpayer's 1992 return was filed on April 15, 1993, and the time within which the IRS could assess a deficiency did not expire until April 15, 1996. If the IRS, on February 2, 1996, asserts a deficiency which is sustained by the Tax Court, the taxpayer would have to pay an additional 1992 tax. He could not, however, file a claim for refund of the 1991 overpayment, since the statute of limitations has expired. IRC Sec. 1312(1) allows an adjustment.

Double deduction. This occurs if a deduction or credit is allowed in one year (or to one taxpayer) which erroneously has also been allowed in another year (or to a related taxpayer)[1] [IRC Sec. 1312(2); Reg. Sec. 1.1312-2].

Example 2: A taxpayer in his return for 1991 took a casualty loss deduction. After he had filed his return for 1992 and after the statute of limitations for the 1991 return had expired, it was discovered that the loss actually occurred in 1992. The taxpayer, therefore, filed a claim for refund for the year 1992 based upon the allowance of a deduction for the loss in that year, and the claim was allowed by the IRS in 1996. Here, it is the IRS that is barred from opening the 1991 return and it is the taxpayer who is benefited by Sec. 1312(2).

A double exclusion of gross income occurs if an item of income is included in one year, and then the taxpayer gets it excluded because it belonged in a prior year now barred [IRC Sec. 1312(3)(A); Reg. Sec. 1.1312-3].

Example 3: In 1987 U.S. Motors, Inc. recovers a judgment against General Steel Co. for breach of contract. The judgment is paid, but Steel appeals to a higher court and the judgment is not affirmed until 1988. Motors erroneously includes the recovery in its 1988 return instead of its 1987 return, and in February 1992 filed for refund of the 1988 tax. Since the statute of limitations prevents the IRS from assessing a deficiency against the 1987 return, Sec. 1312(3)(A) permits an adjustment.

Affiliated corporations. If a deduction or credit of a corporation is treated in a manner inconsistent with the way the item is treated by an affiliated corporation, then an adjustment is allowed [IRC Sec. 1312(6); Reg. Sec. 1.1312-6].

Basis of property. Adjustments are made if income, deductions and the like were incorrectly determined in prior years as to items chargeable to a capital account [IRC Sec. 1312(7); Reg. Sec. 1.1312-7].

Trust items. If an item of trust income or deduction is treated in a manner inconsistent with the way the item is treated in the hands of the fiduciary or beneficiary, as the case may be, then an adjustment is allowed [IRC Sec. 1312(5); Reg. Sec. 1.1312-5].

(b) Relief Without Inconsistent Determination. Two situations may arise when relief is possible without the later year being inconsistent with a prior position of the successful party [IRC Sec. 1311(b); Reg. Sec. 1.1311(b)-1]. If there is no deduction or inclusion made in the prior year, there is no *positive* action as to which the successful party in the dispute over the later year can be said to have taken a position. Compare this with cases where there is, in the prior year, positive inclusion of income or taking of a deduction.

Deduction or credit disallowed. An adjustment can be made to allow a deduction or credit to which the taxpayer (or related taxpayer) is entitled in a prior year now barred [IRC Sec. 1312(4); Reg. Sec. 1.1312-4]. However, the deduction or credit in the current year must not have been barred when the taxpayer formally claimed the deduction or credit for the year disallowed [IRC Sec. 1311(b)(2)(B); Reg. Sec. 1.1311(b)-2]. An adjustment is also allowed if a loss is erroneously treated as an ordinary or capital loss.[2]

Example 4: The taxpayer is on the cash basis. He erroneously fails to deduct a payment made in 1987, and, instead, takes the deduction in 1989. In 1990, a deficiency is assessed on the ground that the deduction in 1989 was erroneous, and the taxpayer replies in writing, claiming the deduction for 1987. In 1992, the Tax Court disallows the deduction for 1989. The statute of limitations bars taking the deduction in 1987. IRC Sec. 1312(4) permits an adjustment.

Unreported income. An adjustment is allowed to exclude income not reported and on which tax was not paid, but which is includable in a prior year of the taxpayer (or of a related taxpayer) [IRC Sec. 1312(3)(B); Reg. Sec. 1.1312-3(b)]. However, the inclusion in the correct year must not have been barred at the time the IRS formally claimed the inclusion for the incorrect year [IRC Sec. 1311(b)(2)(A); Reg. Sec. 1.1311(b)-2].

> **Example 5:** Assume the facts similar to Example 3, except that when the time comes to make out its 1988 return, Motors decides that the recovery should not be included in 1988 after all. In 1990 the IRS assesses a deficiency in the 1988 return on the ground that the recovery should have been included in the year when the judgment was affirmed. In 1990, the Tax Court rejects the IRS's arguments. The statute of limitations prevents the IRS from including the recovery in the correct year (1987). IRC Sec. 1312(3)(B) applies. Note that in Example 3, Motors paid the tax (later suing for refund), but in this example there is no such payment.

THE UNITED STATES TAX COURT

¶3750   WHAT THE TAX COURT DOES

The outstanding feature of the Tax Court is that it gives you an opportunity to contest your tax liability for a proposed income, estate and gift tax deficiency *before* paying a penny of tax [¶3752]. The court usually gets jurisdiction only after a deficiency notice has been issued by the IRS and you file a timely petition for a hearing [¶3705; 3752]. Then the court tries the case and renders a decision anew on the evidence before it, rather than on a mere review of the evidence before the IRS.

(a) Place of Trial. The Tax Court or any of its divisions may sit at any place within the United States [IRC Sec. 7445; TC Rule 10(b)]. Consequently, you may ask that your case be tried at or near the city in which you are located [¶3754(b)]. Tax Court proceedings, except a small tax claim proceeding [(c) below], are governed by the rules of evidence that apply in trials without a jury in the District Court of the District of Columbia [IRC Sec. 7453; TC Rule 143].

(b) Proving a Case. The Tax Court can consider only the evidence that the parties produce. Usually, the petitioners have the burden of proof [but see ¶3756]. They must present sufficient evidence to prove their case as stated in the petition, regardless of what evidence they have already presented to the IRS. However, the Commissioner must prove transferee liability, fraud and the liability of a foundation manager for knowingly participating in an act of self-dealing or engaging in certain wrongful acts [IRC Sec. 6902(a), 7454; Reg. Sec. 301.7454-2]. The Tax Court and the U.S. Claims Court may assess damages for a taxpayer's delay or for bringing a suit on frivolous grounds as well as award taxpayer litigation costs [IRC Sec. 6673, 7430].

(c) Small Tax Case Procedure. The Tax Court has adopted simplified procedures to handle small tax cases. These may be used at your option, concurred in by the Tax Court. You file your petition on Form 2 obtainable from the court clerk [TC Rule 175]. A "small tax case" is one in which neither the disputed amount of the deficiency nor the claimed over-payment exceeds $10,000, including additions to tax, for a tax year [IRC Sec. 7463; TC Rule 171]. The decision of the court is based on a brief summary opinion and is not reviewable on appeal and will not serve as a precedent for future cases. The court has discretion in applying rules of evidence and procedure. The result in a small tax case becomes final 90 days after the decision is entered [IRC Sec. 7481(b); TC Rules 170-173].

(d) Declaratory Judgments. A petition for a declaratory judgment [TC Rules 210-211] may be filed in certain cases.

Exempt status. When there is a controversy with IRS over status or classification (including revocation or other change in qualification) an organization may petition to ascertain its status as a tax-exempt setup, a qualified charitable gift recipient, a private foundation or a private operating foundation [IRC Sec. 7428].

Governmental bonds. Prospective issuer of municipal bonds [¶1503] may ask for judgment on its tax-exempt status [IRC Sec. 7478].

Retirement plans. Petition may be used for judgment as to qualification (including revocation or other change in qualification) of a retirement plan or amendments to it. Employer, employee who is an "interested party" or Pension Benefit Guaranty Corporation may file [IRC Sec. 7476; Reg. Sec. 1.7476-1—3].

¶3751   APPEARANCE BEFORE TAX COURT

The Tax Court has its own rules of practice. Individuals may appear in their own behalf, and members of a partnership or corporate officers may appear on behalf of the partnership or corporation. Also, a fiduciary may represent an estate or trust [TC Rule 24]. A practitioner must be admitted to practice in the Tax Court before representing a client there.

(a) Admission to Practice is granted for the following [TC Rules 24, 200]:

- Attorneys may be admitted without examination if they present a current certificate of admission to practice before the U.S. Supreme Court or the highest court of any state.
- All other new applicants must take a written examination. An oral one may also be required by the court. After three failures an applicant is no longer eligible.

Admission to a state bar, or to practice before the Revenue Service does not automatically carry admission to practice before the Tax Court.

(b) Application. An attorney, seeking admission to practice before the Tax Court, must file an application with the Admission Clerk. The fee is $25. Applicants other than attorneys seeking admission by examination must pay a $25 fee and must have three individuals already admitted to practice before the court send letters of sponsorship directly to the court [TC Rule 200]. Also, the court may impose a practice fee up to $30 a year on practitioners [IRC Sec. 7475].

¶3752   JURISDICTION OF TAX COURT

[New tax legislation may affect this subject; see ¶1.]

The Tax Court may hear appeals from Commissioner's notice of deficiency or liability of income, estate or gift tax, excise taxes on private foundations, employment taxes[1] as well as actions for certain declaratory judgments (¶3750(d)) and for disclosure actions under IRC Sec. 6110 [IRC Sec. 7428, 7442, 7476 ; TC Rules 13, 220-230].

(a) Items Subject to Review. The Tax Court has jurisdiction to consider appeals involving constitutional questions,[2] closing agreements,[3] fraud penalties,[4] failure to pay penalty, and the statute of limitations[5] [IRC Sec. 6214(a)].

(b) Deficiencies. In general, the Tax Court can review only proposed assessments of tax deficiencies. However, when the Tax Court assumes jurisdiction on a deficiency, it reviews your entire liability for the year at issue, and may find that there is an added deficiency or an overpayment [IRC Sec. 6512(b); Reg. Sec. 301.6512-1]. In addition, the Tax Court is empowered to do the following:

- Hear motions to restrain assessment and collection actions taken after a Tax Court petition has been filed but before the decision of the Court is final.
- Review interest assessed by the IRS on tax deficiencies determined by the Tax Court.
- Order the IRS to cease any assessment or collection efforts until the Court's decision is made final [IRC Sec. 6213(a)].
- Order the IRS to pay a refund to a taxpayer who wins in Tax Court (although the Tax Court may not hear a suit for a refund) [IRC Sec. 6512(b)].

(c) Issues Raised by Pleadings. The Tax Court is limited to the issues raised in the petition and other pleadings, and the evidence supporting them.[6]

(d) Matters Before IRS. The Tax Court's jurisdiction is not limited to the issues raised before the IRS, but it will entertain all issues related to a tax liability raised by the pleadings, including claims of overassessment.[7]

(e) Who Files Petition. Petition to the Tax Court must be brought by and in the name of the person to whom the deficiency or liability notice was directed, or by and in the full descriptive name of his fiduciary. If there is a variance between the name in the deficiency or liability notice and the correct name, reasons for the variance must be stated in the petition [TC Rule 34(b)].

(f) Service of Papers. The petition is served on the Commissioner or the appropriate representative by the Clerk of the Tax Court. All other papers required to be served can be done by the parties if the originals, together with a certificate of service (Form 13), are filed with the Clerk. Service is complete on mailing (whether by registered or certified mail) or by hand delivery to a party or his counsel [TC Rule 21(b)].

¶3753   AUTHORITY OF REGULATIONS

The Tax Court will be bound by the IRS regulations unless they are found to be unreasonable and inconsistent with the Code.[1]

¶3754   HOW PROCEEDING BEGINS

A proceeding before the Tax Court is started by filing a petition.

(a) When to File Petition. You must file the petition within 90 days after the notice of deficiency or liability was mailed to you. The period is 150 days for taxpayers not located in the U.S., or for the estate of a decedent dying abroad[1] [IRC Sec. 6213(a); Reg. Sec. 301.6213-1]. The court cannot extend the time to file.[2]

The filing period. The day the deficiency notice is mailed is not counted, but the day of filing the petition is counted.[3] The period begins to run from the date the deficiency notice is mailed. A second mailing of a notice generally does not start a new 90-day period, unless the first mailing was abandoned.[4]

Filing by mail. The petition is considered to be filed on time when it is mailed, postage prepaid, to the proper office within the prescribed time as indicated by the postmark on the envelope. This applies even if it is received after the time has expired. Incorrect private postage meter dates must be corrected by the post office. If you send the petition by registered or certified mail, the date of registration or the postmarked date on the certified mail receipt, is the date of mailing [IRC Sec. 7502; Reg. Sec. 301.7502-1]. If the last day for filing the petition falls on a Saturday, Sunday or is a legal holiday in the District of Columbia, time for filing is extended to include the court's next business day [TC Rule 25].

(b) Request for Place of Hearing. The petition should be accompanied by a request on Form 4 that the hearing on the case be held at or near the city more convenient for you [TC Rule 140(a), (b)]. In addition, in a declaratory petition involving revocation, the Commissioner in his answer must state the date on which he expects the action to be ready for trial (this enables the court to plan its calendars) and an estimate of the time involved [TC Rule 212].

(c) Filing Fee. A $60 filing fee should be paid at the time of filing the petition [IRC Sec. 7451; TC Rule 20(b)].

NOTE: A $60 filing fee is also required to file a petition by a partner for readjustments of partnerships items [IRC Secs. 6226; 7451]. See also ¶3738.

¶3755   THE PETITION

An attorney or accountant preparing petitions to the Tax Court should bear in mind that it will consider only the issues that are set out in the petitions. The issues and the facts upon which they are based should be covered so completely that, when judges read petitions, they can tell immediately what the disputes are about and what the facts are. A good rule is to give such a complete presentation that the facts alleged can be proved and adopted as findings of fact by the court, and in sufficient detail to justify a decision in the taxpayer's favor.

Form. The petition, including the petition for a declaratory judgment and for disclosure actions (and all other papers filed with the Tax Court), may be prepared by any process, provided the information is set out in clear and legible type and is substantially in accordance with Form 1 in style and content [TC Rules 23, 34, 210(d)]. It must also be properly signed [TC Rule 23(a)].

NOTE: The body of the petition for a declaratory judgment [¶3750(d)] must contain the appropriate allegations set forth in TC Rule 211 [TC Rules 210, 211].

Deficiency of liability notice. A copy of the deficiency notice or liability must accompany the petition and each copy of it. If a statement accompanied the notice, the part of it that is material to the issues set out in the assignments of error must also be attached. If the notice referred to earlier notices from the Service that are necessary to explain the determination, the parts material to the issues raised by assignments of error must be attached.

¶3756   THE COMMISSIONER'S ANSWER

The Commissioner has 60 days after service of a copy of the petition to file an answer, or 45 days for motions on the petition. If an amended petition is filed, the Commissioner has the same time after service to file an answer or for motions on the petition unless the court fixes a different time [TC Rule 36(a)]. Similar provisions apply to a petition for a declaratory judgment [TC Rule 213].

Contents. The Commissioner's answer must fully and completely advise the petitioner and the court of the nature of the defense. It must contain a specific admission or denial of each material allegation contained in the petition or state that the Commissioner lacks knowledge or information to form a belief as to the truth of any allegation. The Commissioner may qualify or deny only part of an allegation. If special matters like res judicata, collateral estoppel, estoppel, waiver, duress, fraud and statute of limitations are pleaded, a mere denial will not be sufficient to raise this issue. Moreover, the answer must state every ground on which the Commissioner relies and has the burden of proof [TC Rule 36(b)].

¶3757   PETITIONER'S REPLY

When the Commissioner's answer alleges material facts, you usually have 45 days after service of the answer to file a reply or 30 days for motions on the answer [TC Rule 37(a)].

Contents. The reply must contain a specific admission or denial of each material allegation in the answer on which the Commissioner has the burden of proof. Lack of knowledge or information as to the truth of any allegation must be asserted. The reply must state every ground, together with supporting facts, on which the petitioner relies. If special matters like res judicata, collateral estoppel, estoppel, waiver, duress, fraud and the statute of limitations are raised in the answer, a mere denial in the reply will not be sufficient to raise these issues [TC Rules 37(b), (c), 39, 40].

¶3758   AMENDED OR SUPPLEMENTAL PLEADINGS

Pleadings may be amended once as a matter of course at any time before responsive pleadings are served. If no responsive pleadings are permitted and the case has not been placed on the trial calendar, these may be amended within 30 days after these are served [TC Rule 41].

Supplemental pleadings may be permitted when a party wishes to indicate transactions or occurrences that took place after the pleadings. Permission may be granted even though the original pleadings are defective [TC Rule 41(c)].

¶3759   JUDGMENT WITHOUT TRIAL

A case may be disposed of before trial by a motion for judgment on the pleadings or a motion for a summary judgment. Any party may move for a judgment on the pleadings, but the motion must be made within such time so as not to delay trial. A motion for summary judgment must be made at any time starting 30 days after the pleadings are closed, but it must also be made within such time so as not to delay trial. Any written response to the motion for summary judgment must be made not later than ten days before the hearing. A decision on the motion for summary judgment will be rendered only after every genuine issue of material fact has been disposed of [TC Rules 120, 122].

> **NOTE:** An action for declaratory judgment, except for revocation and governmental obligation cases, may be disposed of before trial on the "administrative record" [TC Rule 217].

¶3760   TIME AND PLACE FOR HEARING

Upon joinder of issue (generally by filing of an answer or reply, where the answer raises affirmative issues), the court will set a calendar date and a city (generally the one requested by the petitioner [¶3754(b)]) for the hearing. No hearing is necessary if the facts are established by deposition [TC Rule 122(a)].

(a) Postponement. If a case is set for trial and for any reason a postponement is desired, a motion should be made immediately on receipt of the notice setting the hearing. Usually, the court denies motions for continuance made on the day the case is called, or within 30 days of that date [TC Rule 134].

(b) Discovery. The parties are urged to obtain the required information through informal consultation or communication. If this can't be done, formal discovery procedures involving interrogatories and the production of documents or things should be followed. Upon the consent of all parties, depositions [¶3761] may be used as a discovery device and may be taken of both party and nonparty witnesses [TC Rules 70-74].

(c) Admissions. Parties may serve written requests for admissions. The requests must be made and completed within the same periods provided for discovery [(b) above]. The matter will be considered admitted if the request is not responded to within a certain period (usually 30 days) [TC Rule 90].

(d) Stipulations. Before the hearing date has been set, taxpayer's counsel may be asked to confer with the Regional Appeals Office and a member of the Regional Counsel's staff to try to settle the case. If the case is settled, a stipulation of settlement will be filed with the court and no trial is required [TC Rule 91].

In addition, the court on its own motion, or at the request of either party, may schedule its own pretrial conference [TC Rule 110].

¶3761   HOW TO TAKE DEPOSITIONS

Depositions can be taken by written interrogation, which is unusual, or by oral examination of the witness by both parties [TC Rules 74, 80, 81, 84]. An application (on Form 6) to take a deposition must be filed with the court at least 45 days before the trial date. The court supplies the application form.

¶3762   THE TAX COURT HEARING

The Tax Court is a trial court, and follows formal trial court procedure, except for small tax cases which are conducted as informally as possible [TC Rule 170]. If the parties have reached a settlement and filed a stipulation to that effect, the court will enter decision accordingly. If, at the calendar date, no settlement has been reached, and both parties answer "ready," the judge or clerk will note the probable date of the hearing.

(a) Burden of Proof. As a matter of law, the Commissioner's determination in the notice of deficiency is prima facie correct. Therefore, any statement of fact in the notice must be accepted by the Tax Court as correct unless the petitioner by competent evidence, can overcome this.[1]

Declaratory judgments. The burden of proof in declaratory judgments [¶3750(d)] is on the petitioner [TC Rule 217(c)].

(b) Argument. At the hearing, petitioner's counsel makes an opening statement, and formally presents evidence, as would be done in a trial before a United States District Court. Any admissions or stipulations made or depositions taken must be introduced as evidence. Commissioner's counsel then presents the government's case. If the presentation on behalf of the Commissioner involves affirmative issues, petitioner's counsel has opportunity for rebuttal.

At the end of the hearing, the court may ask the parties to make oral arguments and file citations of authorities referred to in the presentations. Unless otherwise directed, each party has 60 days after the conclusion of the hearing to file a brief on the issues on which he has the burden of proof. Within 30 days after a brief is filed, the opposing party may file a reply brief [TC Rule 151]. Briefs or oral arguments are not required in small tax cases [TC Rule 177(c)].

(c) Rehearing. The court, at its discretion, may grant a rehearing of a case to permit presentation of newly discovered evidence upon motion made usually not more than 30 days after the Report has been served (¶3763) [TC Rule 161].

> ▶ **OBSERVATION** A good brief is needed at the end of the hearing. The briefs filed by Commissioner's counsels in tax cases are uniformly good. If briefs for taxpayers are not equally good, their cases are jeopardized.

¶3763   THE TAX COURT REPORT

After the hearing, the court writes up its findings of fact and opinion in a single discussion called a "Report." Note that this is not the court's decision. This is important for several reasons. The date of the decision determines the time for filing an appeal from the decision [¶3764(a)]. The decision is a specific order that:

- Finds the amount of the deficiency,
- Finds there is no deficiency or
- Dismisses the case for any reason.

The decision is usually entered immediately after publication of the findings of fact and opinion if the court decides the deficiency or liability notice is correct. If it decides the deficiency should be revised, decision is entered after proceedings under Rule 155.

(a) Rule 155. Instead of itself determining the tax due, the court may direct the parties to compute the liability under TC Rule 155. Each party submits a computation of tax liability in the light of the court's opinion. If the parties cannot agree, the case may be set for argument on the settlement, and the court determines the tax due.

No new issues can be raised under Rule 155,[1] but the court may consent to raising an obvious issue; for example, the deficiency was barred by the statute of limitations.[2]

Declaratory judgments. If the action is assigned to a special trial judge and he is authorized to make the decision, then he must submit his decision to the court's chief judge before service on the parties. If the special trial judge is not to make the decision, then the parties must follow the procedural rules set forth in TC Rule 182 [TC Rule 218].

(b) Procedure After Decision. If the petitioner is satisfied with the Tax Court's decision, his counsel should, within 30 days of the serving of the Report, file a determination of the result under Rule 155. If he is dissatisfied with the Tax Court's decision, counsel has 90 days after the decision is entered within which to file a notice of appeal [IRC Sec. 7483].

¶3764   REVIEW OF TAX COURT DECISION

The Tax Court has very litle power to set aside or change its decision once it has become final[1] [IRC Secs. 7481; Reg. Sec. 301.7481-1]. However, the 7th Circuit Court holds that the Tax Court has jurisdiction to reopen such a decision on the grounds that fraud had been committed on the court.[2] Tax Court decisions can be reviewed by the Courts of Appeals to the same extent as decisions of the district courts in civil actions tried without a jury [IRC Sec. 7482(a)]. The findings of facts made by a Tax Court judge and the factual inferences the Tax Court draws from the findings are binding, unless they are clearly erroneous. If the reviewing court has a firm conviction that a mistake was made, the Tax Court finding is "clearly erroneous."[3] Decisions in small tax cases are not reviewable (¶3750(c)) [IRC Sec. 7481(b)].

(a) Appeals. Appeal from a decision of the Tax Court is usually made to the U.S. Court of Appeals for the circuit where the petitioner has his legal residence when the notice of appeal is filed. A corporation appeals to the circuit where its principal place of business or principal office or agency is located; if it has none, to the circuit where it filed the return [IRC Sec. 7482].

Time to file. A notice of appeal may be filed by either the Commissioner or the taxpayer within 90 days after the Tax Court's decision is entered. If it is filed by one party, any other party to the proceeding may file a notice of appeal within 120 days after the decision [IRC Sec. 7483]. In certain cases, decisions of Courts of Appeals may be reviewed by the Supreme Court of the United States [¶3743(d)].

(b) Bond to Stay Assessment and Collection. Appeal from a Tax Court decision does not act as a stay of assessment or collection of the deficiency determined by the Court. The taxpayer, on or before the date of filing his or her notice of appeal, must file with the Court a bond not exceeding double the amount of the deficiency, or else a jeopardy bond [IRC Sec. 7485].

(c) Effect of Courts of Appeals Decisions. The Tax Court has held that it will follow decisions of the Court of Appeals for the same circuit to which the Tax Court decision can be appealed.[4]

Footnotes to Chapter 27

(For your added convenience, in brackets [] with the footnotes below, you will find citations to related paragraphs in the "RIA United States Tax Reporter"(USTR) "CCH Federal Tax Reporter"(CCH) and "RIA Federal Tax Coordinator 2d"(FTC) multi-volume services.)

FOOTNOTE ¶3701 [USTR ¶60,114; CCH ¶44,352 et seq.; FTC ¶ T-1000].

(1) Treas. Dept. booklet "Examination of Returns, Appeal Rights and Claims for Refund" (1990 Ed.), p. 1.

(2) Rev. Proc. 81-46, 1981-2 CB 121; Rev. Proc. 64-12, 1964-1 CB 672.

(3) Tiffany Fine Arts, Inc. v. U.S. (U.S. Sup. Ct., 1986), 55 AFTR 2d 85-491.

FOOTNOTE ¶ 3702 [USTR ¶ 76,024; CCH ¶43,727; FTC ¶ T-1110].

(1) Treas. Dept. booklet "Examination of Returns, Appeal Rights and Claims for Refund" (1990 Ed.), p. 5.

(2) U.S. v. Powell, 95 SCt. 248, 14 AFTR 2d 5942.

(3) Ryan v. U.S., 85 SCt. 232, 14 AFTR 2d 5947.

(4) Mathis, Sr. v. U.S., 21 AFTR 2d 1251, 391 US 1.

(5) Tarlowski, 24 AFTR 2d 69-6433.

FOOTNOTE ¶ 3703 [USTR ¶ 62,124; CCH ¶ 44,332; 44,352.30; FTC ¶ T-1600].

FOOTNOTE ¶3704 [USTR ¶62,124; CCH ¶44,352 et seq.; FTC ¶ T-1700].

(1) U.S. v. Goldstein, 189 F.2d 752, 40 AFTR 768.

(2) Cleveland Tr. Co. v. U.S., 19 AFTR 2d 1770, 266 F.Supp. 824.

FOOTNOTE ¶ 3705 [USTR ¶ 62,124; CCH ¶ 38,544; FTC ¶ T-3000 et al.].

(1) Delman, J., ¶66,059 PH Memo TC, aff'd 20 AFTR 2d 5543, 384 F.2d 929.

(2) Senate Report No. 96-1035, p. 109, 96th Cong., 2nd Sess.

(3) Du Mais, 40 TC 269.

(4) Chambers v. Lucas, 41 F.2d 299, 8 AFTR 10857.

(5) Blank, 76 TC 400; Leith, Jr., ¶83,670 PH Memo TC.

FOOTNOTE ¶ 3706 [USTR ¶ 66,014; CCH ¶ 40,315; FTC ¶ T-3100].

(1) Morse v. U.S., 6 AFTR 2d 5353, 183 F.Supp. 847.

(2) Payson v. Comm., 36 AFTR 888, 166 F.2d 1008.

(3) Schaefer v. U.S., 43 AFTR 1297 (DC, Hawaii; 1951).

FOOTNOTE ¶ 3707 [USTR ¶ 66,014; CCH ¶ 40,315; FTC ¶ T-1700].

FOOTNOTE ¶ 3708 [USTR ¶ 71,214; CCH ¶ 41,930; FTC¶ T-1713].

(1) Op. A.G. 7. XIII-2 CB 445.

(2) Backus v. U.S., 11 AFTR 422, 59 F.2d 242.

(3) Indianapolis Screw Products Corp. v. U.S., 7 AFTR 2d 833.

(4) U.S. v. Wilson, 182 F.Supp. 567, 5 AFTR 2d 1273; U.S. v. Lane, 303 F.2d 2011, 9 AFTR 2d 1458.

(5) Parks, E.C., 33 TC 298; U.S. v. McCue, 4 AFTR 2d 5830, 178 F.Supp. 426.

(6) Rev. Proc. 80-6, 1980-1 CB 577.

(7) Rev. Proc. 68-16, 1968-1 CB 770.

FOOTNOTE ¶ 3709 USTRH ¶ 74,414; CCH ¶ 44,592; FTC ¶ U-1300 et seq.].

(1) Treas. Dept. Circular no. 230, Sec 10.3.

(2) Treas. Dept. Circular no. 230, Sec 10.7.

(3) Treas. Dept. Circular no. 230, Sec 10.5.

(4) Treas. Dept. Circular no. 230, Sec 10.2.

(5) Treas. Dept. Circular no. 230, Sec 10.4.

(6) Treas. Dept. Circular no. 230, Sec 10.6.

FOOTNOTE ¶ 3710 [USTR ¶ 65,014; CCH ¶ 39,913; FTC ¶ T-3600 et seq.].

(1) Badaracco v. Comm., 53 AFTR 2d 84-446.

(2) Reaves v. Comm., 8 AFTR 2d 5619, 295 F.2d 336.

(3) Rev. Rul. 69-247, 1969-1 CB 303.

(4) Rev. Rul. 60-144, 1960-1 CB 636.

(5) Roschuni, 44 TC 80; Walker, 46 TC 630; Taylor, 24 AFTR 2d 69-5747, 417 F.2d 991.

(6) Instructions for Forms 972, 872-A.

(7) Rev. Proc. 68-31, 1968-2 CB 917.

FOOTNOTE ¶ 3711 [USTR ¶ 65,014; CCH ¶ 39,913; FTC ¶ T-4000].

FOOTNOTE ¶ 3712 [USTR ¶ 65,014; CCH ¶ 39,913; FTC ¶ T-4500].

(1) Rev. Rul. 66-43, 1966-1 CB 291.

(2) 11 USC 362(a)(8), (e), (d).

(3) 11 USC 507(a)(6).

(4) 11 USC 523(a)(1).

FOOTNOTE ¶ 3713 [USTR ¶ 65,034; CCH ¶ 39,982; FTC ¶ T-4300].

(1) Rev. Rul. 66-17, 1966-1 CB 272.

FOOTNOTE ¶ 3714 [USTR ¶ 69,014; CCH ¶41,520; FTC ¶ V-9000 et seq.].

(1) Keller, 21 BTA 84, aff'd 59 F.2d 499, 11 AFTR 521.

(2) Ginsberg v. Comm., 10 AFTR 2d 5134, 305 F.2d 664.

(3) Holmes, 47 TC 622.

(4) Joannes, ¶67,138 PH Memo TC.

FOOTNOTE ¶ 3715 [USTR ¶ 63,314; CCH ¶ 39,087; FTC ¶ V-5000 et seq.].

(1) Mrizeck v. Long, 4 AFTR 2d 5526 (DC Ill.).

(2) U.S. v. Rodgers, U.S. Sup. Ct. (1983), 52 AFTR 2d 83-5042.

(3) U.S. v. Whiting Pools Inc., U.S. Sup. Ct. (1983), 52 AFTR 2d 83-512.

(4) Bob Jones University, 94 SCt. 2038, 33 AFTR 2d 74-1279; Alexander v. American United, 94 SCt. 2053, 33 AFTR 2d 74-1289.

(5) Enochs v. Williams Packing & Navigation Co., Inc., 82 SCT. 1125, 9 AFTR 2d 1594.

FOOTNOTE ¶ 3720

(1) Treas. Dept. booklet "Your Federal Income Tax" (1991 Ed.), p. 130.

FOOTNOTE ¶ 3721 [USTR ¶ 67,214; CCH ¶ 41,020; FTC ¶ V-2200].

(1) Revenue Reconciliation Act of 1989 (OBRA '89), P.L. 101-239, House Committee Rpts.; Act Sec. 7711-7715.

FOOTNOTE ¶ 3722 [USTR ¶ 66,620; CCH ¶ 40,554; FTC ¶ V-2650].

(1) Rev. Proc. 90-16, 1990-1 CB 477.

FOOTNOTE ¶ 3723 [USTR ¶ 66,734; 66,954; 66,964; 67,004; 67,014; 67,024; 67,034; CCH ¶ 40,590; 40,755; 40,830.01; FTC ¶ V-2401; 2950].

FOOTNOTE ¶ 3724 [USTR ¶ 66,514; 66,564; CCH ¶ 40,375.56; FTC ¶ V-2100; V-2200 et seq.].

(1) Richardson, TC Memo 1991-258.

(2) Boyle, 55 TC AFTR2d 1535.

(3) Perry, TC Memo 1990-228.

FOOTNOTE ¶ 3725 [USTR ¶ 66,574; 66,844; 66,984; 67,065; CCH ¶ 40,490; FTC ¶ V-2431].

FOOTNOTE ¶ 3726 [USTR ¶ 66,554; CCH ¶ 40,465; FTC ¶ V-1300].

FOOTNOTE ¶ 3727 [USTR ¶ 72,014; CCH ¶ 42,018].

(1) Sansone v. U.S., 15 AFTR 2d 611, 380 US 343.

(2) U.S. v. Habig, 21 AFTR 2d 803, 390 US 222.

FOOTNOTE ¶ 3728 [USTR ¶ 66,014; CCH ¶ 40,315; FTC ¶ V-1000].

(1) For guides on figuring interest when the period that interest is payable is restricted under the law, see Rev. Proc. 60-17, 1960-2 CB 942.

(2) Rev. Rul. 66-317, 1966-2 CB 510.

FOOTNOTE ¶ 3735 [USTR ¶ 64,014; CCH ¶ 39,440; FTC ¶ T-5500].

(1) Lewis v. Reynolds, 284 US 281, 52 SCt. 145, 10 AFTR 773.

FOOTNOTE ¶ 3736 [USTR ¶ 64,024; CCH ¶ 39,466; FTC ¶ T-6700 et seq.].

FOOTNOTE ¶ 3737 [USTR ¶ 65,114; CCH ¶ 40,030; FTC ¶ T-7500 et seq.].

(1) Stepka v. U.S., 196 F.Supp. 184, 8 AFTR 2d 5141.

(2) Galuska, 98 T.C. No. 45.

FOOTNOTE ¶ 3738 [USTR ¶ 65,114; CCH ¶ 40,030; FTC ¶ T-7500 et seq.].

(1) Rev. Rul. 61-20, 1961-1 CB 248.

(2) Rev. Rul. 68-150, 1968-1 CB 564.

FOOTNOTE ¶ 3739 [USTR ¶ 65,114; CCH ¶ 40,030; FTC ¶ T-7577].

FOOTNOTE ¶ 3740 [USTR ¶ 64,024; CCH ¶ 39,466; FTC ¶ T-6800].

(1) Rev. Rul. 68-65, 1968-1 CB 555.

(2) U.S. v. Felt & Tarrant Mfg. Co., 283 US 269, 9 AFTR 1416.

(3) U.S. v. Andrews, 302 US 517, 58 SCt. 315, 19 AFTR 1243; U.S. v. Garbutt Oil Co., 302 US 528, 58 SCt. 320, 19 AFTR 1248.

(4) Caswell v. U.S., 190 F.Supp. 591, 7 AFTR 2d 342.

FOOTNOTE ¶ 3741 [USTR ¶ 64,024; CCH ¶ 39,466; FTC ¶ T-6700].

(1) Instructions for Form 1310.

FOOTNOTE ¶ 3742 [USTR ¶ 66,114; CCH ¶ 40,335; FTC ¶ T-8000].

(1) For guides on how to figure interest when the period that interest is payable is restricted under the law, see Rev. Proc. 60-17, 1960-2 CB 942.

(2) McDonald v. U.S., 18 AFTR 2d 5215 (DC Tenn., 6-13-66).

(3) Hanley v. U.S., 105 Ct Cl 638, 63 F.Supp. 73, 34 AFTR 694.

(4) Fortugno v. Comm., 16 AFTR 2d 5938, 353 F.2d 429, cert. denied 11-15-66.

FOOTNOTE ¶ 3743 [USTR ¶ 65,324; CCH ¶ 40,230; FTC ¶ T-9000 et seq.].

(1) Flora v. U.S., 78 SCt. 1079, 1 AFTR 2d 1925; aff'd 5 AFTR 2d 1046.

(2) Kell-Strom Tool Co., Inc. v. U.S., 205 F.Supp. 190, 10 AFTR 2d 5237.

(3) Roybark v. U.S., 218 F.2d 164, 46 AFTR 1441.

(4) McKeesport Tin Plate Co. v. Heiner, 16 AFTR 169, 77 F.2d 56.

(5) Cullman Motor Co. Inc. v. Patterson, 6 AFTR 2d 5159.

(6) Register Publishing Co. v. U.S., 189 F.Supp. 626, 7 AFTR 2d 772.

(7) Rev. Proc. 57-12, 1957-1 CB 740.

(8) 28 USC Sec. 1346.

(9) 28 USC Sec. 1402.

(10) 28 USC Sec. 2402.

(11) 28 USC Sec. 1295.

FOOTNOTE ¶ 3744 [USTR ¶ 64,114; CCH ¶ 39,690; FTC ¶ T-6500].

(1) Instructions for Form 1139.

FOOTNOTE ¶ 3745 [USTR ¶ 13,114; CCH ¶ 4798; FTC ¶ T-9100].

(1) Rev. Rul. 72-127, 1972-1 CB 268.

(2) Rev. Rul. 68-152, 1968-1 CB 369.

FOOTNOTE ¶ 3750 [USTR ¶ 74,424; CCH ¶ 42,756; FTC ¶ U-2100].

FOOTNOTE ¶ 3751 [USTR ¶ 74,536; CCH ¶ 42,884; FTC ¶ U-1300].

FOOTNOTE ¶ 3752 [USTR ¶ 74,424; CCH ¶ 42,756; FTC ¶ U-2403].

(1) Philbin, 26 TC 1159; Clarke, 27 TC 861.

(2) Independent Life Ins. Co. of America, 17 BTA 757.

(3) Holmes and Janes, Inc., 30 BTA 74.

(4) Gutterman & Strauss Co., 1 BTA 243.

(5) Troy Motor Sales Co., 164 BTA 545.

(6) Buffalo Wills Sainte Claire Corp., 2 BTA 364.

(7) Barry, 1 BTA 156.

FOOTNOTE ¶ 3753 [USTR ¶ 79,006.75; CCH ¶ 44,282; FTC ¶ U-2100].

(1) Topps of Canada, Ltd., 36 TC 326.

FOOTNOTE ¶ 3754 [USTR ¶ 62,134; CCH ¶ 38,549; FTC ¶ U-2001; 2003 et seq.].

(1) Du Pasquier, 39 TC 854.

(2) Joannou, 33 TC 868.

(3) Chambers v. Lucas, 41 F.2d 299, 8 AFTR 10857.

(4) Boccutto v. Comm., 5 AFTR 2d 1374, 277 F.2d 549; Tenzer v. Comm., 7 AFTR 2d 450, 285 F.2d 956.

FOOTNOTE ¶ 3755 [USTR ¶ 74,424; CCH ¶ 42,756; FTC ¶ U-2400].

FOOTNOTE ¶ 3756 [USTR ¶ 74,424; CCH ¶ 42,758; FTC ¶ U-2500].

FOOTNOTE ¶ 3757 [USTR ¶ 74,424; CCH ¶ 42,756; FTC ¶ U-2600].

FOOTNOTE ¶ 3758 [USTR ¶ 74,424; CCH ¶ 42,756; FTC ¶ U-2700].

FOOTNOTE ¶ 3759 [USTR ¶ 74,424; CCH ¶ 42,756; FTC ¶ U-2708].

FOOTNOTE ¶ 3760 [USTR ¶ 74,424; CCH ¶ 42,756; FTC ¶ U-3000].

FOOTNOTE ¶ 3761 [USTR ¶ 74,424; CCH ¶ 42,756; FTC ¶ U-2900].

FOOTNOTE ¶ 3762 [USTR ¶ 74,424; CCH ¶ 42,756; FTC ¶ U-3000].

(1) Tankoos, W.G. Est., ¶67,008 PH Memo TC.

FOOTNOTE ¶ 3763 [USTR ¶ 74,424; CCH ¶ 42,756; FTC ¶ U-3410].

(1) Bankers Pocahontas Coal Co. v. Burnet, 11 AFTR 1089, 287 U.S. 308.

(2) Excelsior Motor Mfg. Supply Co. v. Comm., 43 F.2d 968, 9 AFTR 211.

FOOTNOTE ¶ 3764 [USTR ¶ 74,814; CCH ¶ 43,130; FTC ¶ U-3412].

(1) Lasky v. Comm., 352 US 1027, 52 AFTR 337.

(2) Kenner v. Comm., 21 AFTR 2d 391, 387 F.2d 689.

(3) Comm. v. Duberstein, 5 AFTR 2d 1626, 363 US 278; Imbesi v. Comm., 17 AFTR 2d 1241, 361 F.2d 689.

(4) Jack E. Golsen, 54 TC 742.

CHAPTER 28

FOREIGN INCOME—
FOREIGN TAXPAYERS

CREDIT FOR FOREIGN TAXES

¶3801   WHO CAN TAKE THE FOREIGN TAX CREDIT

As a general rule, you can claim the foreign tax credit if you are taxed by the United States on your foreign-source income. Absent the credit, you would be taxed twice on the same income—once by the foreign country and once by the United States [IRC Sec. 901; Reg. Sec. 1.901-1].

The credit is allowable, with limitations in certain cases, to U.S. citizens, U.S. domestic corporations, domestic parents of foreign corporations, stockholders of DISCs (Domestic Internatonal Sales Corporations), stockholders of FISCs (Foreign International Sales Corporations) shareholders of S corporations treated as partnerships, U.S. resident aliens, resident aliens of Puerto Rico, foreign corporations subject to tax on income effectively connected with the conduct of a U.S. trade or business or nonresident aliens (other than Puerto Rico residents) subject to tax on income effectively connected with U.S. trade or business. Also, partners or beneficiaries of an estate or trust may be allowed their share of the credit for foreign taxes paid by the partnership, estate or trust [IRC Sec. 901].

Any taxpayer who takes the earned income exclusion on income from sources outside the U.S. cannot also elect a foreign tax credit for foreign taxes paid on amounts excluded from gross income under the exclusion [IRC Sec. 911(a)].

Credit or deduction? You may either claim a credit for the foreign taxes under IRC Sec. 901, or take a deduction for them under IRC Sec. 162 or 164, but you cannot take advantage of both [IRC Sec. 275(a)(4)]. If you take a standard deduction, however, you can still claim a foreign tax credit. If you choose to claim the credit, you must make an election in the manner specified below. You will generally benefit more from the credit than from the deduction. This is because the credit is a dollar-for-dollar offset against your income taxes, but the deduction merely reduces your gross income.

> **Example:** Mr. and Mrs. Bundy have adjusted gross income of $120,000, $20,000 of which are dividends from foreign sources. They had to pay $2,000 in foreign income taxes on that dividend income. As an itemized deduction, the foreign income tax reduces their U.S. tax by $620. If, however, the Bundys choose to claim a credit for the $2,000 foreign tax, their U.S. tax will be reduced by the full $2,000. Therefore, they have an additional tax benefit of $1,380 by taking the credit.

Any unused foreign tax credit may be carried back for two years or carried forward for five years [IRC Sec. 904(c)].

¶3802   HOW TO GET THE CREDIT

You must file Form 1116 to get the foreign tax credit. Corporations file Form 1118. A bond (Form 1117) may be required if the foreign tax has not yet been paid [Reg. Sec. 1.905-4]. The election made applies to every foreign tax, but you can change your election any time before the time to file a claim for credit or refund expires (in the case of the foreign tax credit, ten years) for the year the choice is made [IRC Sec. 901(a), 6511(d)(3)(A); Reg. Sec. 1.901-1(d)]. If a carryback or carryover is involved [¶3803(b)], the period is measured from the year from which the excess taxes may be carried.[1]

When you can take the credit. If you use the accrual method of accounting, you must generally claim the credit in the tax year the foreign tax accrued. If you use the cash method, you can either take the credit in the tax year the foreign tax is paid or in the tax year it accrues. Once you take the credit in the tax year the foreign tax accrues, you must continue to use this method [IRC Sec. 905(a); Reg. Sec. 1.905-1(a)]. In the year that you make the election, you can get a double credit—once, for the foreign taxes actually paid in that year and again, for the foreign taxes accrued.[2]

Foreign taxes that are creditable. Not every levy by a foreign country qualifies for the foreign tax credit. Generally, to be so qualified, the foreign tax has to be imposed on "income" as that term is understood for U.S. income tax purposes. This means you cannot take a credit for real or personal property taxes, sales taxes or gasoline taxes imposed by a foreign government. Also, the tax cannot be a payment for a specific economic benefit (such as user fees) that is not available to everyone who pays the country's income tax; nor does the tax qualify if there is no income tax to the general population. For example, the right to extract government-controlled oil would be considered a specific economic benefit [Reg. Sec. 1.901-2 (a)(ii)].

Also, to the extent that any income, war profits or excess profits tax is used to provide a subsidy by any means (such as through a refund or credit) to you or to any related party, and the subsidy is determined by reference to the amount of the tax, you cannot claim a credit for that tax [IRC Sec. 901(j)].

When you cannot take the credit. If you participate in or cooperate with an international boycott, your foreign tax credit for that year may be reduced or denied altogether. The reduction equals the amount of the benefit that resulted from taxation by countries associated with carrying out the boycott [IRC Sec. 999(c)]. The IRS has issued procedures to determine participation in a boycott.[2]

You cannot claim a credit for taxes imposed by a country that the United States does not recognize or with which the United States has severed or does not conduct foreign relations or one that has been designated by the Secretary of State as a country that repeatedly provides support for acts of international terrorism [IRC Sec. 901(j)].

NOTE: Even though you may not be able to take certain foreign taxes as a credit, they may still be taken as deductions if they are incurred in a trade or business or qualify as itemized deductions.

¶3803   LIMITATIONS ON THE CREDIT
[New tax legislation may affect this subject; see ¶1.]

(a) Limits Applicable. The ratio of your foreign tax credit to your U.S. tax cannot be greater than the relationship of your foreign income to your U.S. income. You must, therefore, compute the limitation on the amount of foreign tax that can be used to reduce your U.S. tax under this overall limitation [IRC Sec. 904(a)]. This limitation treats all foreign income as a single unit and limits your credit to your U.S. income tax attributable to the taxable income from all sources outside the U.S. Under this limitation, operating losses in one foreign country offset income from another foreign country. The maximum credit can thus be obtained by using the following formula:

$$\frac{\text{Total taxable income from sources outside U.S.}}{\text{Entire taxable income from all sources}} \times \text{U.S. income tax}$$

(but not exceeding total taxable income)

Example 1: Bellis, Inc., a domestic corporation, had income of $50,000 from the U.S., $50,000 from country X and $50,000 from country Y. Bellis paid a tax of $19,000 to X and $21,000 to Y on the income from those countries. The tax is figured as follows:

Taxable income from U.S.	$50,000	
Taxable income from X	50,000	
Taxable income from Y	50,000	$150,000
U.S. tax on $150,000 income, before credits		$ 41,750
Limitation for X an Y combined ($100,000/$150,000 × $41,750)		27,833
Net tax payable		$ 13,917

Separate credit limitations. Foreign countries tax different kinds of income at varying rates; some categories of income are taxed at a higher rate and others, at a lower rate. To prevent a distortion of the foreign tax credit, income is divided into separate categories and the limitation on the foreign tax credit has to be calculated separately for each of them. The separate-limitation categories include: passive income, shipping income, high withholding tax interest, dividends from certain noncontrolled foreign corporations, financial services income, certain dividends from DISCs (Domestic International Sales Corporations) or former DISCs, certain distributions from FISCs (Foreign Sales Corporations) or former FISCs and certain taxable income attributable to foreign-trade income [IRC Sec. 904(d)].

Just as the overall maximum limitation on the foreign tax credit is based on the ratio of taxable foreign income to taxable income from all sources, the separate limitations on credits for the separate categories of income are based on the ratio of foreign income in each category to income from all sources in that category. When computing your total allowable credit, add the various separate foreign tax credit determinations for each foreign income category.

> **NOTE:** Your total foreign tax credit may be less than the actual foreign tax paid or accrued; it cannot be greater than the foreign taxes paid or accrued or what the U.S. tax would be on that income.

U.S.-owned foreign corporations. If at least 10% of the current earnings of a U.S.-owned foreign corporation is from U.S. sources or is effectively connected with a U.S. trade or business, then the distribution or interest payment is U.S. income to the extent it is attributable to U.S.-source or effectively connected income. For this purpose, a foreign corporation is U.S. owned if at least 50% of the total voting power of its voting stock or of the total value of its stock is held by U.S. persons [IRC Sec. 904(g)].

(b) Foreign Tax Carryover and Carryback. If the foreign tax paid or accrued exceeds the limitations for any one year, you may carry back the excess and take it as a credit in each of the two preceding years, and carry forward the excess and take it as a credit in each of the five following years. Your total credit (that is, your tax for the year plus the carryback or carryover) cannot exceed the limitation for that year. Your credit is first carried to the earliest year and then to the next earliest year [IRC Sec. 904(c)].

If an unused foreign tax credit is carried back, the statute of limitations for that year does not close until one year after the statute has run for the year in which the foreign taxes were paid or accrued. Your claim for refund of part of the income taxes paid in the carryback year is supported by attaching revised Form 1116 to the amended income tax return.

There can be no carryback or carryover to a year you take the foreign tax as a deduction. A timely election to take a credit for foreign taxes must be made for the year to which the excess is to be carried.[1] For interest on refunds, see ¶3742.

Taxes paid or accrued in a tax year starting after 1986 may be treated as paid or accrued in a tax year starting before 1987 only to the extent the post-1986 taxes could be carried back if the tax was figured by applying the tax rate in effect on October 21, 1986. Such taxes will be treated as imposed on overall limitation income.

Figuring the foreign tax credit. In computing your taxable income for purposes of the foreign tax credit limitations, you omit personal exemption deductions for individuals, estates and trusts [IRC Sec. 904(b)]. On joint returns, you apply the credit against you and your spouse's total tax and figure the limitation on the combined taxable income—but without your personal exemption deductions [Reg. Sec. 1.904-3(c)].

(c) Treatment of Capital Gains From Foreign Sources. The foreign tax credit limitation is designed to prevent you from using the credit to reduce your U.S. tax on U.S.-source income. Thus, when it comes to capital gain, the credit limitation is based on your foreign-source capital gain net income. This is defined as the lesser of your capital gain net income from sources outside the U.S. or your capital gain net income from all sources.

If there is a rate differential between capital gain income and ordinary income, that differential must be reflected in the capital gain net income figure. The amount of the differential portion is a fraction, the numerator of which is the highest regular tax rate minus the capital gains rate, and the denominator of which is the highest regular rate. If, for example, the highest regular rate is 31% and the capital gains rate is 28%, the fraction in computing the differential portion has a numerator of 3 (the difference between 31 and 28) and a denominator of 31. The fraction 3/31 is the figure by which the foreign-source capital gain net income is reduced.

(d) Recapture of Foreign Losses. If your U.S. income taxes were reduced because you claimed an overall foreign loss (expenses exceeded income from all foreign sources), to insure that you don't enjoy a tax windfall, the loss is recaptured in later years when you have taxable income from foreign sources. Generally, the recapture is accomplished by treating a portion of your foreign-source taxable income in a later year as U.S.-source income. As such, it does not qualify for the foreign tax credit. The amount to be treated as U.S.-source income is the lesser of the foreign loss or 50% of the foreign taxable income in the later year. You can choose to have a greater percentage of the taxable foreign income treated as U.S.-source income [IRC Sec. 904(f)(1)]. (You may be inclined to opt for the higher percentage if you are taking a credit rather than a deduction for the foreign tax.)

> **Example 2:** Mr. West, a U.S. citizen, owns a manufacturing plant in Europe. In 1990, he incurred overall losses of $30,000. In 1991, the plant had a profit of $25,000. The amount of the foreign taxable income that is recaptured and treated as U.S.-source income is $12,500 (50% of $25,000).

There is also recapture of a loss on business property used predominantly outside the U.S. that is disposed of prior to the time the loss is recaptured under the general rules. You are treated as having a recognized gain in the year you dispose of the property. The gain is the excess of the fair market value of the property disposed of over your adjusted basis in the property. In such cases, 100% of the gain (to the extent of losses not previously recaptured) is recaptured [IRC Sec. 904(f)(3)].

¶3804   SOURCE RULES FOR PERSONAL PROPERTY SALES

The rules for determining the source of income are important since the U.S. acknowledges that foreign countries have the first right to tax foreign income, but the U.S. generally imposes its full tax on U.S. income.

The U.S. generally taxes the worldwide income of U.S. persons, and the source rules are primarily important for U.S. persons in determining their foreign tax credit limitation.

A premise of the foreign tax credit is that it should not reduce your U.S. tax on your U.S. income, but only your U.S. tax on your foreign source.

> ➤ **OBSERVATION** The source rules also affect foreign persons. These rules are primarily important in determining the income over which the U.S. asserts tax jurisdiction. Foreign persons are subject to U.S. tax on their U.S. source income and certain foreign source income that is effectively connected with a U.S. trade or business [¶3807–3812].

Income from selling tangible or intangible personal property is generally considered as being from the country of the seller's residence. If personal property is sold by a U.S. resident, the income from the sale is generally treated as U.S. source. If sold by a nonresident, the income is generally treated as foreign source. For this purpose, a "U.S. resident" is a person who has a tax home in the U.S. [IRC Sec. 865(a)].

U.S. citizens and resident aliens whose tax homes are outside the U.S. are not treated as nonresidents for a sale of personal property unless an income tax of at least 10% of the gain on the sale is paid to a foreign country. However, this rule does not apply to the sale of certain stock by taxpayers who were residents of Puerto Rico for the entire tax year. The stock must be in a corporation that is engaged in an active trade or business in Puerto Rico from which it derives more than 50% of its gross income for the three years preceding the year of sale [IRC Sec. 865(d), (g)(3)]. Instead, the Puerto Rico residents benefit from the tax exemption that applies to Puerto Rico source income [IRC Sec. 933].

Inventory. Income from selling inventory property is generally treated as being from where the title to the property passes [IRC Sec. 865(b)]. However, in some cases, foreign source income from certain sales of inventory property by a foreign person is treated as effectively connected with the conduct of a U.S. trade or business. This is done where necessary to ensure that foreign persons who are treated as U.S. residents for source rule purposes, but as nonresidents for general purposes, are taxed on income from sales of inventory property [IRC Sec. 865(e)].

Intangibles. The source for income from selling intangible property (like a patent, copyright, trademark or goodwill) that is contingent on the property's productivity, use or disposition is the country where the property is used. Payments for goodwill are considered from the country where the goodwill was generated [IRC Sec. 865(d)].

Depreciation and amortization. The residence-of-the-seller rule doesn't apply to income from the sale of depreciable personal property to the extent of prior depreciation deductions. The source of that income is determined under a recapture rule. If depreciation deductions have been allocated against U.S. or foreign source income, then gain from the sale of depreciable property must be similarly treated. Gain in excess of those deductions is treated as if the property were inventory property. If certain depreciable property is used predominantly within or outside the U.S. in a tax year, the allowable depreciation deductions are allocated entirely against either U.S.- or foreign-source income, respectively. Gain in excess of the depreciation deductions is sourced the same as inventory property, where title to the property passed. However, if personal property is used predominantly in the U.S., the gain from the sale, to the extent of the allowable depreciation deductions, is treated entirely as U.S.-source income. If the property is used predominantly outside the U.S., the gain, to the extent of the depreciation deductions, is treated entirely as foreign source income [IRC Sec. 865(c)].

Likewise, to the extent of previously allowed amortization deductions from the sale of intangible property, the source of the income is determined under the recapture rule.

The recapture rule applies whether or not payments are contingent on the productivity, use or disposition of the property. When payments are contingent, the source of all payments should be determined under the recapture rule until the entire recapture amount has been recaptured, and any remaining payments are sourced under the general intangible rules. The source of gain from the sale of intangible property in excess of amortization recapture is determined under the residence-of-the-seller rule when the payments aren't contingent on the productivity, use or disposition of the property. When payments are contingent, the source rule for royalties applies to the gain [IRC Sec. 865(d)(4)].

Income earned by U.S. residents from selling personal property and certain intangible property through an office or other fixed place of business outside the U.S. is treated as foreign source if (1) the income from the sale is attributable to the business operations located outside the U.S. and (2) at least 10% of the income is paid as tax to the foreign country. If less than 10% is paid as tax, the income is U.S. source [IRC Sec. 865(e)].

¶3805　ADJUSTMENT TO THE CREDIT FOR FOREIGN TAX REFUND

If you receive a foreign tax refund, you must file an amended U.S. income tax return immediately, so that your U.S. taxes can be redetermined. If the foreign tax is refunded without interest, your tax deficiency will not include interest. If the foreign tax refund is received with interest, your deficiency will include the interest received, but not exceeding the appropriate rate of interest on the U.S. tax due. Annual interest is charged from the date of the refund until the deficiency is paid.[1]

¶3806　CREDIT FOR CORPORATE SHAREHOLDERS IN FOREIGN CORPORATIONS

A domestic corporation owning at least 10% of the voting stock of a foreign corporation from which it receives dividends can claim a credit for the taxes attributable to those dividends paid by the foreign corporation [IRC Sec. 902(a); Reg. Sec. 1.902-(a)]. The following formula is used to figure taxes which the domestic corporation is considered to have paid (the "deemed-paid" foreign tax credit):

$$\text{Foreign tax} \times \frac{\text{Dividends received}}{\text{Accumulated profits in excess of foreign tax}} = \begin{array}{c}\text{Taxes deemed to have} \\ \text{been paid on profits} \\ \text{distributed as dividends}\end{array}$$

Example: A Corp. (a U.S. corporation) owns 50% of the voting stock of B Corp. (a foreign corporation). B Corp. earned $100,000 before taxes and paid a foreign income tax of $20,000. Out of the remaining $80,000 it paid a dividend of $40,000. A Corp. includes in income $50,000, which is the gross up of the $40,000 dividend, and the $10,000 of tax it is deemed to have paid, computed as follows:

$$\$20,000 \quad \times \quad \frac{40,000}{80,000} \quad = \quad \$10,000$$

The "deemed-paid" foreign tax credit of a U.S. corporation owning at least 10% of the voting stock of a foreign corporation is computed with reference to the pool of the distributing corporation's post-1986 accumulated earnings and profits and accumulated foreign taxes [IRC Sec. 902, 960(a)]. This is intended to prevent taxpayers from losing deemed-paid credits because the foreign corporation had a deficit in earnings and profits in some years that the IRS considered to reduce accumulated profits (for prior years in which foreign taxes were paid), reducing the amount of creditable taxes. This provision also limits the taxpayer's ability to average high-tax and low-tax years, resulting in a deemed-paid credit that reflects a higher than average foreign tax rate over a period of years.

FOREIGN TAXPAYERS

¶3807   HOW FOREIGN TAXPAYERS ARE TAXED

The U.S. taxes *resident* aliens in the same manner that it taxes U.S. citizens—their worldwide income, whatever its source, is subject to U.S. income taxes [¶3811]. But *nonresident* aliens and foreign corporations are taxed differently—only income from sources within the U.S. is taxed by this country. If such income is "effectively connected with the conduct of a trade or business in the U.S." (which may, in certain situations, apply to specified types of foreign income), it is taxed at the same rates that apply to U.S. taxpayers [¶3811(a)]. If it is not "effectively connected" income, it is taxed at the flat rate of 30% (or lower treaty rate).

Exceptions. *Expatriates* from the U.S. may be subject to U.S. tax on all their U.S.-source income if they relinquished their citizenship to avoid tax [¶3809(c)].

Tax treaties betweeen foreign countries and the U.S. may result in foreign taxpayers from those countries receiving special tax treatment for various income items [¶3820].

Tax discrimination against U.S. citizens or corporations by a foreign country may lead to higher taxation of citizens and corporations of that country. In such cases, a presidential proclamation can double the U.S. tax rate (up to 80% of taxable income) for citizens and corporations of the foreign country or impose the same discriminatory tax on the U.S. income of citizens and corporations coming from the offending country [IRC Sec. 891, 896].

¶3808   RESIDENT ALIENS

Generally, resident aliens are taxed the same as U.S. citizens [Reg. Sec. 1.871-1].

(a) Who Is a Resident Alien. For income tax purposes, you are a resident alien if you are an alien who (1) is a lawful U.S. permanent resident at any time during the calendar year or (2) satisfies a substantial presence test [IRC Sec. 7701(b)]. If you do not fall within the above definition, you are a *nonresident alien.*

You are a lawful permanent resident if you entered the U.S. in that capacity and the status has not been revoked or abandoned under the immigration laws. You meet the substantial presence test if (1) you were present in the U.S. for at least 31 days of the calendar year and (2) the sum of the days you were present in the current year, plus ⅓ of the days present during the preceding year, plus ⅙ of the days present during the second preceding year, is at least 183 days.

The 183-day test. Unless you have taken steps to become a permanent resident, you won't be treated as meeting the substantial presence test if (1) you are present in the U.S. for fewer than 183 days during the current year and (2) it's established that you have a tax home in a foreign country and have a closer connection there than here. For the substantial presence test, days when a professional athlete is present in the U.S. to compete in certain charitable events do not count.

Exempt aliens. Certain individuals are exempt from the substantial presence test. These are diplomats, teachers, students, trainees, etc. However, the exception does not apply if facts show that the alien intends to live in the U.S. permanently.

(b) Tax on Resident Aliens. If you are a resident alien, you must pay an income tax on all income, whether it comes from inside or outside the U.S. You may claim the same deductions that a U.S. citizen can, and similar personal and dependency exemptions. Also, you may claim the foreign tax credit [¶3801] (which may be reduced if your country does not provide a reciprocal credit) [IRC Sec. 901(c)].

If you are employed by a foreign government or international organization, your pay is not exempt if you file waivers under the McCarran Act [Reg. Sec. 1.893-1(a)]. However, it still may be exempt under tax treaties or other international agreements.[1]

(c) Dual-Status Aliens. If you have been both a resident and nonresident alien in the same tax year (usually the years of arrival and departure), you are taxed on income from all sources for the part of the year that you are resident aliens, but only on your U.S.-source income for the part of the year that you are nonresident aliens. Form 1040 is filed with Form 1040NR used as an attachment.

¶3809   NONRESIDENT ALIENS

A nonresident alien usually pays a U.S. income tax only on income from U.S. sources. If it is "effectively connected" income, it is taxed at the graduated rates that apply to U.S. taxpayers. If it is investment income, it generally is taxed at a 30% (or lower treaty) rate [IRC Sec. 871, 872; Reg. Sec. 1.871-7(a)]. Also, one-half of social security benefits are taxed at the 30% rate [IRC Sec. 871(a)(3)].

(a) Who Is a Nonresident Alien. A nonresident alien is an individual alien (including a fiduciary and a citizen of a U.S. possession) who does not meet the definition of a resident alien [¶3808(a)].

(b) Tax on Nonresident Aliens. If you are a nonresident alien, you may not: (1) file a joint return (unless married to a U.S. citizen or resident) [IRC Sec. 6013(g)], (2) use the Tax Table or Tax Rate Schedule for single individuals if you are married individuals filing separately or (3) file head of household returns [IRC Sec. 2(b)(3)(A)]. You are not subject to the self-employment tax [IRC Sec. 1402].

NOTE: If you are married to a U.S. citizen or resident, you can elect to be taxed as a resident to take advantage of the joint filing option. However, once this election is made, your world-wide income is subject to tax, even though the income might have been otherwise exempt under a tax treaty [Reg. Sec. 1.6013-6].

Deductions. You are generally not allowed deductions from income that are not connected with your U.S. business activities. Except for personal exemptions and certain itemized deductions, i.e., certain contributions to IRAs or Keogh plans or self-employed health insurance costs, deductions are allowed only to the extent that they are related to effectively connected income. If you establish that you are in the U.S. on temporary assignment, you may be able to deduct certain transportation, lodging, and meal expenses.[1]

Capital gains and losses. If "effectively connected" with your U.S. trade or business [¶3811], your capital gains and losses are treated the same as those of U.S. citizens [¶1808 et seq.]. All other capital gains are taxed at a flat 30% (or lower treaty) rate, but only if you spent a total of at least 183 days in the U.S. during the tax year [IRC Sec. 871(a)(2)].

Interest. If paid to you on portfolio obligations issued after July 18, 1984, interest is not subject to the 30% tax. However, this tax continues to apply to existing obligations subject to tax. Two types of portfolio debt are involved: (1) interest paid on certain obligations not in registered form (bearer debt) and (2) interest paid on an obligation in registered form (registered debt), for which a statement is filed that the beneficial owner is not a U.S. person [IRC Sec. 871(h)]. See ¶2518.

(c) Tax on Expatriates. U.S. citizens who, within the ten-year period immediately before the close of a taxable year, became nonresident aliens to avoid income, estate, gift or generation skipping transfer taxes can be liable for the tax normally applicable to nonresident aliens [IRC Sec. 871] or a special alternative tax [IRC Sec. 877(b)], whichever is greater. Gain on the sale or exchange of property whose basis is determined in whole or in part by reference to the basis of U.S. property is treated as gain from the sale of U.S. property. Thus, expatriates are able to make tax-free exchanges of U.S. property for foreign property. But if they later dispose of that foreign property on which gain is recognized, it is treated as a disposition of U.S. property—subject to U.S. tax.

(d) Returns and Payment of Tax. Nonresident aliens file Form 1040NR. You can get the deductions and credits allowable to you only if you file accurate returns that contain the necessary information [IRC Sec. 874(a); Reg. Sec. 1.874-1(a)]. If you have wages subject to withholding, you must file returns and pay taxes at the same time and manner as U.S. citizens. If you do not have wages subject to withholding, you must file a return and pay taxes by the 15th day of the 6th month after the close of the tax year. For withholding from nonresident aliens, see ¶2518.

¶3810   FOREIGN CORPORATIONS

Any corporation not organized or created in the U.S. is a foreign corporation [Reg. Sec. 301.7701-5]. Foreign corporations, like nonresident aliens, are taxed generally only on U.S. source income but they are taxed at different rates depending on whether the U.S. income is business or non-business connected (i.e.,investment income).

Tax on foreign corporations. All U.S. source income that is "effectively connected" with a foreign corporation's U.S. business [¶3811] is taxed at the regular U.S. corporate rate (¶3002) [IRC Sec. 882]. In this connection, capital gains effectively connected with a U.S. business are taxed at the regular U.S. corporate rate [¶3809]. U.S.-source nonbusiness investment income [¶3811(a)] generally is taxed at a flat 30% rate unless an applicable treaty rate is lower [IRC Sec. 881, 894(b)]. As in the case of nonresident aliens, however, interest paid to foreign corporations on certain debt instruments is not subject to the 30% tax [IRC Sec. 871(h)]. For the treatment of gain from the disposition of U.S. real property and for an election to treat investment income from real property as business income, see ¶3811.

Branch profits tax. A 30% "branch profits tax" is imposed on profits of foreign corporations operating business in the U.S. [IRC Sec. 884]. The second-level withholding tax is generally retained, with the 50% income threshold being reduced to 25%. The base for the branch profits tax (the dividend equivalent amount) is the foreign corporation's effectively connected earnings and profit—reduced for an increase in U.S. net equity and increased for a decrease in U.S. net equity. "U.S. net equity" means U.S. assets (money and adjusted bases of assets) reduced by U.S. liabilities. Provisions are also made for coordinating the branch profits tax with the income tax treaty between the U.S. and a foreign country.

Returns and payment of tax. Foreign corporations generally file Form 1120F. The returns are due (a) by the 15th of the third month after the end of the tax year if the foreign corporation has an office or place of business in the U.S. or (b) by the 15th of the sixth month if it is without an office or place of business in the U.S. [¶3630(b)]. In either case, the tax is payable in full with the return [¶3651].

A foreign-controlled U.S. corporation and a foreign-controlled foreign corporation engaged in a U.S. trade or business must furnish certain information as to its transactions with any related party. Also, foreign-controlled corporations and U.S.-controlled foreign corporations must furnish information that the IRS requires for carrying out the installment sales rules.

¶3811   INCOME TAXED AT U.S. RATES

Only income "effectively connected" with a foreign taxpayer's U.S. business is taxed at U.S. rates.

Investment in real property. A nonresident alien or foreign corporation can elect to treat all income from U.S. real property held for the production of income as "effectively connected" income [IRC Sec. 871(d), 882(d); Reg. Sec. 1.871-10]. This allows you to deduct taxes, interest and other expenses as if the property were being used in a trade or business. Any gain or loss from disposing of an interest in U.S. real property or of an interest in a "U.S. real property holding corporation" is treated as if it was "effectively connected" income [IRC Sec. 897]. An interest in U.S. real property includes ownership and co-ownership of property, possession of a leasehold, or an option on property. However, you must pay a tax of at least 21% of the lesser of (a) your alternative minimum taxable income or (b) your net real estate gain.

A nonresident alien or a foreign corporation is not taxed on gains on the disposition of real property interests through a domestic corporation if it can be established that the domestic corporation was not a "U.S. real property holding corporation." A U.S. real property holding corporation is one that owns real property interests in the U.S. equal to or greater than 50% of the aggregate value of: (1) its U.S. real property interests plus (2) its interests in foreign real property plus (3) its other trade and business assets [IRC Sec. 897(c)(2); Reg. Sec. 1.897-1—1.897-4].

Trade or business in the U.S. In addition to the usual U.S. trade or business activities, a trade or business in the U.S. may include the performance of personal services in the U.S., or trading in stocks or commodities. When a partnership, estate or trust is engaged in a U.S. trade or business, the foreign partners or beneficiaries also are considered to be engaged in a trade or business in the U.S. The rules and exceptions that apply to these situations are spelled out below [IRC Sec. 864].

Personal services. If as a nonresident alien, you perform personal services in the U.S., you are considered engaged in a trade or business in the U.S. This rule does not apply if: (1) your personal services are performed for another nonresident alien, a foreign partnership or corporation not engaged in a U.S. business, or in a branch maintained in a foreign country by a U.S. corporation, a U.S. partnership or a U.S. citizen or resident; (2) you are temporarily in the U.S. for no more than 90 days; *and* (3) compensation for the services does not exceed $3,000 [IRC Sec. 864(b); Reg. Sec. 1.864-2(b)].

Trading in stocks or commodities. If you trade in stocks, securities, or commodities and have a U.S. office or other fixed place of business through which this activity is conducted, you are considered to be engaged in a U.S. trade or business. However, if you trade for your own accounts, or through a U.S. resident broker, commission agent, custodian or other independent agent, you are not considered engaged in a U.S. trade or business [IRC Sec. 864(b)(2); Reg. Sec. 1.864-2(c), (d)].

(a) Effectively Connected U.S.-Source Income. All income that a nonresident alien or foreign corporation derives from sources within the U.S. is considered effectively connected income, unless it is determined that certain types of investment income are not effectively connected. This determination is made only for fixed or determinable periodical income, gain or loss from sale or exchange of capital assets and certain specially treated items [IRC Sec. 864(c); Reg. Sec. 1.864-3–4]. U.S.-source income found not to be "effectively connected" with a U.S. business is taxed at the flat 30% rate; all other U.S.-source income of a foreign taxpayer engaged in business in the U.S. is "effectively connected" business income and is taxed at regular rates [¶3809; 3810(a)].

To prevent a foreign taxpayer from avoiding U.S. tax by receiving income after its U.S. trade or business has ceased to exist, a nonresident alien or foreign corporation's income or gain for a tax year attributable to a transaction in another tax year is treated as effectively connected with the conduct of a U.S. trade or business as long as it would have been so treated if it were taken into account in the other tax year [IRC Sec. 864(c)(6)]. If property is sold or exchanged within ten years after being used or held for use in connection with a U.S. trade or business, income or gain attributable to the sale or exchange is treated as effectively connected.

Fixed or determinable periodical income includes the following: interest, dividends, rents, salaries, wages, premiums, annuities, remuneration, emoluments and other income of this type [IRC Sec. 871(a)(1)(A), 881(a)(1); Reg. Sec. 1.881-2(b)]. Wages, bonuses, pensions and such, attributable to your personal services in the U.S., are taxable as effectively connected business income only if you are engaged in a trade or business in the U.S. in the tax year you receive the income [Reg. Sec. 1.864-4(c)(6)(ii)].

Specially treated items are lump-sum distributions from exempt employees' trust and annuity plans [¶1320]; gain from certain disposals of timber, domestic iron ore and coal [¶1814(b); 1816]; gain from the sale or exchange of certain patents, copyrights, trademarks and similar property that usually are treated as capital gains; and gains attributable to original issue discount of certain bonds or other evidences of indebtedness (¶1217) [IRC Sec. 871(a)(1), 881(a); Reg. Sec. 1.871-7(c), 1.871-11, 1.881-2(b)].

> NOTE: Generally, payments on or after September 16, 1984, from obligations issued after March 31, 1972, are taxable up to the amount of gain not in excess of OID accruing while the nonresident alien or foreign corporation held the obligation (to the extent that discount was not already taken into account on an interest payment). Also taxable is an interest payment equal to the OID accrued on the obligation since the last payment of interest on the obligation [IRC Sec. 871(g)].

Factors considered. Two principal factors are considered in determining whether the income, gain or loss from the above types of income is "effectively connected" with the U.S. trade or business. These factors are [IRC Sec. 864(c)(2)]:

1. Asset-use relationship. Is there a direct relationship between the asset and the present needs of the U.S. business? If so, income derived from the asset is effectively connected income. This test applies if the passive income (e.g., interest or dividends) was derived from an investment made: (a) to promote the U.S. business, (b) in the ordinary course of the U.S. business or (c) to meet a present need of the U.S. business.

2. Business-activities relationship. Were the activities of the U.S. business a material factor in realizing the income? If so, the income is effectively connected income. This test generally applies to dividends, interest, gain or loss from a banking or financial business and to royalties from a licensing business.

(b) Effectively Connected Foreign-Source Income. Only three types of foreign-source income may be treated as effectively connected with the conduct of a trade or business in the U.S.: (1) rents and royalties from foreign intangibles, such as patents, copyrights, secret processes, goodwill, franchises, etc.; (2) dividends, interest, or gain from stocks and bonds to financial businesses; or (3) income or gain from foreign sales of inventory through a U.S. office. Such income falls in this category if you have a U.S. office or fixed place of business [IRC Sec. 864(c); Reg. Sec. 1.864-5—1.864-7].

¶3812   WHAT IS U.S.-SOURCE INCOME

Aside from the obvious sources such as U.S. business profits, wages and salaries, U.S.-source income includes:

Interest from the U.S., such as interest on bonds, notes or other interest-bearing obligations. (This term does not apply to interest on deposits with persons carrying on the banking business, to interest on amounts held by insurance companies under an agreement to pay interest thereon or to interest on deposits with mutual savings banks, savings and loan associations and the like. Furthermore, the term does not include interest from an organization which derives most of its income from foreign sources.)

Dividends from domestic corporations, except those that are allowed to exclude income from U.S. possessions or those which derive most of their income from foreign sources.

Wages or other compensation received for personal services rendered in the U.S.

Pensions and annuities received from a domestic trust.

Rents or royalties from property located in the U.S.

Gain from the sale of real property located in the U.S.

Gain from the sale of personal property purchased outside of the U.S.

Social security benefits.

Source rules. Generally, the rules for determining the source of income from sales of personal property are based on the residence-of-the-seller rule. If the sale is made by a U.S. resident, it's U.S.-source income; if made by a nonresident, its source is outside the U.S. There are separate rules applicable to inventory, depreciable personal property, intangibles, sales through offices or fixed places of business and stock of affiliates.

Residency. Your "tax home" is controlling. A U.S. citizen or resident alien is a U.S. resident if he or she does not have a tax home in a foreign country. A corporation, trust or estate is a U.S. resident if it is a U.S. person. The residency of partners in a partnership is determined at the partner level when possible. A U.S. citizen or resident alien won't be considered a resident of another country for a sale of personal property unless a 10% income tax on the gain is paid to the country. A nonresident alien is a U.S. resident if he or she has a tax home in the U.S. [IRC Sec. 865(g)].

Inventory. Income from the sale in the U.S. of personal property that is stock in trade or that is held primarily for sale to customers in the ordinary course of the taxpayer's trade or business ordinarily has its source within the U.S., regardless of where you have your tax home. Conversely, income from the sale of inventory property outside the U.S. (even though it was bought within the U.S.) has its source outside the U.S. [IRC Sec. 861(a)(6), 865].

Depreciable personal property. For depreciable personal property, to determine the source of any gain from the sale after March 18, 1986, you must first figure the part of the gain that is not in excess of the total depreciation adjustments on the property. This part of the gain is allocated to sources in the U.S. based on the ratio of U.S. depreciation adjustments to total depreciation adjustments. The rest of this part of the gain is considered to be from sources outside the U.S. The source of gain from the sale of depreciable property that is in excess of the total depreciation adjustments on the property is determined as if the property were inventory property (see above) [IRC Sec. 865(c)].

Intangibles. The source of payments from the sale of intangibles is determined as if they are royalties only to the extent the payments are contingent on the intangible's productivity, use or disposition. Payments from selling goodwill are considered to come from where they are generated (¶3804) [IRC Sec. 865(d)].

Offices or fixed places of business. If you (a nonresident) have a U.S. office or other fixed place of business, income from the sale of personal property (including inventory) attributable to the office is from a U.S. source, except for inventory sold for use, disposition, or consumption outside the U.S. if your office outside the U.S. materially participated in the sale or for certain amounts included in gross income under IRC Sec. 951(a)(1)(A). Suppose a U.S. resident maintains a foreign office or other fixed place of business. Then, income from sales of personal property—other than inventory, depreciable property or intangibles—that are attributable to that foreign office or place of business is treated as being from sources outside the U.S. However, this rule does not apply unless an income tax of at least 10% of the income from the sale is actually paid to a foreign country [IRC Sec. 865(e)].

Stock in a foreign corporate affiliate. Income from the sale of stock in a foreign corporate affiliate by a U.S. resident is foreign-source income if the affiliate is engaged in the active conduct of a trade or business, and the sale takes place in the foreign country in which the affiliate derived more than 50% of its gross income during a three-year period [IRC Sec. 865(f)].

¶3820　　　　　　　　TAX TREATY PROVISIONS

Tax treaties and conventions with foreign nations are designed to eliminate double taxation of income and to prevent tax evasion. Some income is exempt while other income is taxed or withheld at a lower than normal rate [¶2518; 3807; 3809(b); 3810]. Similar provisions apply to the taxes of the other party to the convention. Generally, in the event of a conflict between a statutory provision and a treaty provision, the one that became effective later governs.

U.S. INCOME FROM FOREIGN SOURCES

¶3825　EARNED INCOME OF CITIZENS FROM SOURCES OUTSIDE U.S.

A qualified individual living abroad can elect to exclude the first $70,000 of foreign earned income, and may exclude the excess of housing expenses over a base amount. The exclusion is denied Americans in foreign countries to which travel is prohibited by law [IRC Sec. 911; Reg. Sec. 1.911-2; 1.911-3; 1.911-5; 1.911-6].

(a) What Is Earned Income. Earned income includes wages, salaries, professional fees, commissions from sales of life insurance[1] or other compensation for personal services. If you are engaged in a trade or business in which both personal services and capital are material income-producing factors, no more than 30% of your share of the net profits of the business can be excluded[2] [IRC Sec. 911(d); Reg. Sec. 1.911-2]. The place where you perform the services controls in determining whether your earned income is from within or without the U.S. It does not matter where the payment is made. However, income that you receive outside of the foreign country in which it was earned, to avoid the income tax in that country, is ineligible for the exclusion [IRC Sec. 911(d)(5)].

Deductions and credits. If you have both included and excluded income from the same country, the amount of foreign taxes eligible for the credit is computed by multiplying the foreign taxes by a fraction. The numerator is (1) the U.S. tax on the sum of (A) your taxable income plus (B) your excluded earned income (less allocable deductions other than moving expenses) *minus* (2) the U.S. tax on your taxable income. The denominator is the numerator plus the credit limit as computed in ¶3803.

You cannot take deductions if they are allocable to excluded earned income. If your earned income qualifying for the exclusion exceeds the amount actually excluded, you compute the amount of any disallowed deduction by multiplying the deductions by the ratio of your excluded earned income to the total qualifying earned income [IRC Sec. 911(a); Reg. Sec. 1.911-5].

Dividends-received deduction. A deduction is allowed for dividends received by a U.S. corporation from a foreign corporation other than a foreign personal holding company (FPHC) or a passive foreign investment company if the taxpayer owns at least 10% of its stock by vote and value. The allowable deduction is based on the proportion of the foreign corporation's post-1986 earnings that have been subject to U.S. corporate income tax and that have not been distributed.

Pensions and annuities. You cannot exclude any amount received as a pension or annuity as foreign earned income. Nor can you exclude employer contributions to an employee trust or for an annuity contract if they would be taxable to you (¶1300; 1524) [IRC Sec. 72(f), 911(b)(1)].

(b) Eligibility. U.S. citizens can exclude foreign earned income if they have been bona fide residents of one or more countries for an uninterrupted period which includes an entire tax year, or have been present in a foreign country for 330 full days in any period of 12 consecutive months. Also, to be eligible for the exclusion, individuals must elect to take the exclusion and must have their tax home in a foreign country. Individuals are not considered as having a home in a foreign country for a year in which their abode is in the U.S. [IRC Sec. 911(d)].

If you are an employee who is exempt from the foreign tax because you claim not to be a resident, you cannot get the foreign income exclusion [IRC Sec. 911(d)(5)]. Temporary visits to the U.S. on vacation, sick leave,[3] or business trips[4] do not necessarily change bona fide resident status.[5] The minimum time requirements for eligibility may be waived if Americans working abroad could reasonably have been expected to meet the requirements but left the foreign country because of war, civil unrest or similar conditions which precluded the normal conduct of business [Reg. Sec. 1.911-2].

(c) Amount Allowed. To figure the maximum amount excludable for any year, amounts received are taken into account in the tax year in which the services to which the amounts are attributable are performed [IRC Sec. 911(b)(2)(B)].

You and your spouse are each entitled to an exclusion for your own earnings. If income is community income of you and your spouse, the total amount excludable by you two for the tax year is the amount that would have been excludable if the income was not community income [IRC Sec. 911(b)(2)(C)].

(d) Exclusion for Housing. In addition to the exclusion for foreign earned income, you may elect to exclude part of your income attributable to housing expenses. Expenses include utilities and insurance, but not taxes and interest which are deductible separately. The amount of the exclusion is equal to the excess of your housing expenses over a base amount [IRC Sec. 911(c)(1)].

NOTE: The base amount is 16% of the salary of a U.S. employee whose income is step 1 of grade GS-14. As of January 1, 1992, the salary was $54,607 and thus the base amount is $8,737.

The total amount of your foreign earned income exclusion and your exclusion for housing cannot exceed the total of your foreign earned income for the year.

Example 1: Ms. Weston is a U.S. citizen and has lived abroad for 330 days during 12 consecutive months. In 1992, her salary was $61,000 and her employer provided housing with a value of $10,000. Jennifer can exclude $71,000, not $71,263 [the $70,000 exclusion plus the excess of the housing expense over the base amount ($10,000 less $8,737)]. This is so because the exclusion is limited to the amount of foreign earned income ($61,000 salary plus $10,000 housing).

Work camps.   If you are furnished lodging in a camp located in a foreign country by your employer, the camp is considered part of your employer's business premises. Thus, you may exclude from income the value of meals and lodging. To qualify as a camp, the lodging must: (1) be for your employer's convenience, (2) be located as near as practicable to your work site, (3) be in an area that's not available to the public and (4) accommodate ten or more employees. The camp does not have to be in a hardship area and need not constitute substandard lodging to qualify for the exclusion [IRC Sec. 119(c)].

(e) Deduction for Housing Expenses.   You can exclude from gross income housing costs attributable to amounts provided by your employer, subject to the formula discussed in (d) above. You can deduct from gross income amounts not attributable to your employer. The amount of your deduction is limited to your foreign earned income that is not otherwise excluded from gross income [IRC Sec. 911(c)(3)].

> **Example 2:** Mr. Carter is a U.S. citizen who has lived in Europe for 330 days during 12 consecutive months. He had foreign earned income of $95,000 in 1992, and qualifying housing expenses of $18,000 (not provided by his employer). Mark can exclude $70,000 of his income under the general exclusion and all $18,000 of his housing expenses since this is below the $25,000 limit ($95,000 less $70,000 leaves $25,000 of non-excluded income).

A carryover provision allows you to carry over to the next tax year housing expenses in excess of your non-excludable earned income. The one-year carryover rule allows these excess expenses to be deducted in the next tax year subject to the limitation in the next year.

Moving expense deduction. See ¶1935.

Sale and replacement of a residence. See ¶1702.

(f) Returns Due Before Exclusion Established.   If your right to an exclusion has not yet been established when you are required to file your income tax return, you must either include all wages earned abroad in your gross income and pay the tax on them or get an extension of time for filing the return. However, when you later establish a right to the exclusion, you can claim a refund or credit for any taxes overpaid [Reg. Sec. 1.911-2(e)(1)]. File Form 2555 to claim the exclusion or deduction.

An extension of time to file the return until the required period for the exclusion is completed may be granted by submitting Form 2350 to the Revenue Service. This is in addition to the automatic extension for citizens abroad (¶3631(d)). [Reg. Sec. 1.911-2(e)(1)].

¶3826   ALLOWANCES TO U.S. GOVERNMENT OFFICERS AND EMPLOYEES IN FOREIGN SERVICE

The following are excluded from gross income: (1) cost-of-living allowances received by government civilian personnel stationed outside the continental U.S., (2) certain Peace Corps allowances, (3) certain foreign areas allowances [IRC Sec. 912; Reg. Sec. 1.912-1, 1.912-2].

¶3827   INCOME FROM SOURCES IN U.S. POSSESSIONS

(a) U.S. Citizens. A possession exclusion applies to individuals who are bona fide residents of Guam, American Samoa or the Northern Mariana Islands. Briefly, if you are a bona fide resident of one of these possessions for the entire year, you may exclude from your U.S. income both income from sources in that possession and income that is effectively connected with the conduct of your trade or business in that possession. You cannot exclude from U.S. income amounts earned as an employee of the U.S. or its agencies.[1]

The possession exclusion above cannot apply to residents of any possession until an implementing agreement is in effect between that possession and the U.S. Until the implementing agreement goes into effect, the pre-1986 exclusion rules continue to apply, as follows: U.S. citizens in certain possessions are allowed to exclude income received from sources outside the U.S. if within a three-year period immediately preceding the close of a tax year (1) at least 80% of gross income is from sources within a U.S. possession, *and* (2) at least 50% of gross income is derived from the active conduct of a trade or business within a U.S. possession. However, amounts received within the U.S. must be included in gross income whether derived from sources within or outside of the U.S. [IRC Sec. 931; Reg. Sec. 1.931-1].

Returns. If you are excluding income under the above provisions, you must file Form 4563 with your return. If you receive no income within the U.S., or from sources within the U.S., and are entitled to exclude your income from without the U.S., no return is required [Reg. Sec. 1.931-1(b)(4)].

(b) Domestic Corporations. A U.S. corporation operating in Puerto Rico or a U.S. possession (including the Virgin Islands) may be able to elect a separate tax credit instead of the ordinary foreign tax credit. The corporation can so elect if within a three-year period immediately preceding the close of the tax year at least 80% of its gross income is received from sources within a possession, and at least 75% of its gross income is from the active conduct of a trade or business within a possession [IRC Sec. 934, 936].

The amount of the credit equals that portion of U.S. tax attributable to taxable income from sources outside the U.S., from the active conduct of a trade or business within a U.S. possession, the sale or exchange of substantially all of the assets used in the active conduct of such trade or business and from qualified possession source investment income [IRC Sec. 936(a)(1)]. The latter includes only income from sources within a possession in which the corporation actively conducts business, regardless of whether the business produces any taxable income for the year [IRC Sec. 936(d)(2)]. DISCs, former DISCs, FSCs and corporations that own or owned stock in a current or former DISC or FSC are ineligible for the credit [IRC Sec. 936(f)].

To qualify as a possessions corporation (PC), file Form 5712. To claim the credit, file Form 5735.

(c) Exclusion for Residents of Puerto Rico. Puerto Rico has its own tax law, which takes the place of the federal income tax law. Thus, in the case of Puerto Rican residents, the United States income tax is applied to income from sources outside Puerto Rico; for income from sources within Puerto Rico, the Puerto Rican income tax applies.

U.S. citizens who are bona fide residents of Puerto Rico for the entire tax year may exclude income from sources within Puerto Rico, except amounts received as employees of the U.S. Deductions allocable to excluded income are not allowed.

Aliens who are bona fide residents of Puerto Rico during the entire tax year, in general, are taxed the same as aliens who reside in the U.S. [¶3808]. However, they can exclude any income from within Puerto Rico, except amounts received as employees of the U.S. Deductions allocable to excluded income are not allowed [IRC Sec. 876; Reg. Sec. 1.876-1].

¶3828   SPECIAL RULES ON FOREIGN INVESTMENTS

U.S. shareholders of "controlled" foreign corporations are *currently* taxed on certain passive-type income (e.g., dividends, interest and rents), income of sales or service subsidiaries and income from insuring U.S. risks, etc. (collectively called "Subpart F income"). Also, U.S. shareholders realize *ordinary* income, rather than capital gains, on the sale or redemption of stocks in a controlled foreign corporation or foreign investment company. Ordinary income tax treatment also applies to sales of patents, etc., to a controlled foreign corporation. U.S. shareholders must include in income their pro rata share of any increase in U.S. property investments made by a controlled foreign corporation [IRC Sec. 956; Reg. Sec. 1.956-1(a), (b)].

A U.S. tax is imposed on a controlled foreign corporation's (CFC) oil-related income. A U.S. shareholder of a CFC must include in income its pro rata share of the CFC's Subpart F income, which includes foreign base company income. Foreign base company oil-related income is taxable as foreign base income [IRC Sec. 954].

Controlled foreign corporations. A U.S. shareholder (corporation, individual, etc.) who owns at least 10% of the stock of a controlled foreign corporation is taxed on its *undistributed* income [IRC Sec. 951]. A controlled foreign corporation is one that is more-than-50% owned by 10% U.S. shareholders [IRC Sec. 957; Reg. Sec. 1.957-1, 1.957-3]. The rules for constructive ownership of stock [¶3244] apply with modifications [¶3670]. These rules do not apply to shareholders in a foreign investment company electing current taxation, or a foreign personal holding company (¶3311) [IRC Sec. 951(c), (d); Reg. Sec. 1.951-2, 1.951-3]. Form 3646 must be filed with the shareholder's income tax return.

> **NOTE:** There is a restriction on what constitutes a permissible tax year for controlled foreign corporations and foreign personal holding companies with more than 50 percent of the total voting power or stock value owned by a U.S. shareholder. Tax years must generally conform to the taxable year of the majority U.S. shareholder [IRC Sec. 898].

Interest, dividends and gains received by banks and insurance companies (with an export finance exclusion), insurance income, amounts equivalent to interest, income earned in space or outside any country, and net gains from transactions in commodities, foreign currency and certain other property generally are taxed currently if earned by controlled foreign corporations [IRC Sec. 954(c)]. Excluded from foreign personal holding company income is certain income from related persons (e.g., dividends and interest received from a related person that is created under the laws of the same foreign country under whose law the CFC is created and has a substantial part of its assets used in the business there). The exclusion doesn't apply to the extent the interest, rent or royalty reduces the payor's Subpart F income.

Exceptions. The U.S. shareholder is not taxed on Subpart F income that is: (1) "export trade income" (income from sales to unrelated persons for use outside the U.S., of property produced, grown or extracted in the U.S.) that is reinvested in the export trade business; (2) shipping income, if the profits are reinvested in foreign based shipping operations [IRC Sec. 955]; (3) shipping income derived from the use of a vessel or aircraft in foreign commerce *within* the country where the corporation is organized or the vessel is registered [IRC Sec. 954]; (4) income from a controlled foreign corporation not used to reduce taxes; and (5) income that totals less than 10% of the controlled foreign corporation's gross income. But if it totals more than 70% of the gross income, the U.S. shareholder will be taxed on his share of *all* of the controlled foreign corporation's income.

For the Subpart F rules to apply to a foreign corporation, more than 50% of that corporation's vote or value (not merely vote) must belong to 10%-U.S. shareholders [IRC Sec. 957(a)]. Similarly, for the foreign personal holding company rules to apply, more than 50% of the vote or value of a foreign corporation must be owned by five or fewer U.S. individuals (¶3312) [IRC Sec. 552(a)]. The 10%-of-gross-income threshold for foreign base company income (the de minimis safe-haven income rule) is reduced to the lesser of $1 million or 5% of gross income [IRC Sec. 954(b)]. Certain exceptions to the rules that currently tax certain "tax-haven" income of foreign subsidiaries of U.S. shareholders are repealed (including the exclusion for reinvested shipping income).

Earnings invested in U.S. assets. The U.S. shareholder is also taxed on his share of the foreign cor-poration's earnings that are invested in assets in the U.S. that are not needed for the business [IRC Sec. 956; Reg. Sec. 1.956-1, 1.956-2].

Footnotes to Chapter 28

(For your added convenience, in brackets [] with the footnotes below, you will find citations to related paragraphs in the "RIA United States Tax Reporter"(USTR), "CCH Federal Tax Reporter" (CCH) and "RIA Federal Tax Coordinator 2d"(FTC) multi-volume services.)

FOOTNOTE ¶ 3801 [USTR ¶ 9014.01; CCH ¶ 28,466; FTC ¶ O-4020].

(1) Rev. Proc. 77-9, 1977-1 CB 542, updated by notices in 1978-1 CB 521, 1979-2 CB 495, and 1984-1 CB 338.

FOOTNOTE ¶ 3802 [USTR ¶ 9054 et al.; CCH ¶ 28,544; FTC ¶ O-4320].

(1) Senate Report No. 1393, p. 16, 86th Cong., 2nd Sess.

(2) Jose Ferrer, 35 TC 617 aff'd, 9 AFTR 2d 1651, 304 F.2d 125.

FOOTNOTE ¶ 3803 [USTR ¶ 9044 et al.; CCH ¶ 28,541; FTC ¶ O-4250].

(1) Treas. Dept. booklet "Foreign Tax Credit for Individuals" (1991 Ed.), p. 2.

FOOTNOTE ¶ 3804 [USTR ¶ 8654; CCH ¶ 28,541.03; FTC ¶ O-4220].

FOOTNOTE ¶ 3805 [USTR ¶ 9044.03; CCH ¶ 28,541; FTC ¶ O-4364].

(1) Rev. Rul. 58-244, 1958-1 CB 265.

FOOTNOTE ¶ 3806 [USTR ¶ 9024; CCH ¶ 28,483; FTC ¶ O-4224].

FOOTNOTE ¶ 3807 [USTR ¶ 8714 et al.; CCH ¶ 28,043; FTC ¶ O-10,100 et seq.].

FOOTNOTE ¶ 3808 [USTR ¶ 8714 et al.; CCH ¶ 28,024; FTC ¶ O-4009].

(1) Rev. Rul. 75-425, 1975-2 CB 291.

FOOTNOTE ¶ 3809 [USTR ¶ 8714.03; CCH ¶ 28,024; FTC ¶ O-10,100].

(1) Treas. Dept. booklet "U.S. Tax Guide for Aliens" (1991 Ed.), p. 13.

FOOTNOTE ¶ 3810 [USTR ¶ 8844; CCH ¶ 28,203; FTC ¶ O-10,300].

FOOTNOTE ¶ 3811 [USTR ¶ 8824; CCH ¶ 28,043; FTC ¶ O-10,600].

FOOTNOTE ¶ 3812 [USTR ¶ 8654; CCH ¶ 27,041; 28,541.03; FTC ¶ O-10,092].

FOOTNOTE ¶ 3820 [USTR ¶ 8914.03; CCH ¶ 28,342; FTC ¶ O-15,000].

FOOTNOTE ¶ 3825 [USTR ¶ 911.14; CCH ¶ 28,649; FTC ¶ O-10,926].

(1) Rev. Rul. 55-497, 1955-2 CB 292.

(2) Rev. Rul. 67-158, 1967-1 CB 188.

(3) Chidester v. U.S., 82 F.Supp. 322, 37 AFTR 1059.

(4) Rose, 16 TC 232.

(5) Myers v. Comm., 180 F.2d 969, 39 AFTR 186.

FOOTNOTE ¶ 3826 [USTR ¶ 9124; CCH ¶ 28,663; FTC ¶ O-1143].

FOOTNOTE ¶ 3827 [USTR ¶ 9314 et al.; CCH ¶ 28,842; FTC ¶ O-4021].

(1) Treas. Dept. booklet "Tax Guide for Individuals With Income From U.S. Possessions" (1991 Ed.), p. 2.

FOOTNOTE ¶ 3828 [USTR ¶ 9564; CCH ¶ 29,024; FTC ¶ O-10,926].

References are to PARAGRAPH (¶) NUMBERS

References are to PARAGRAPH (¶) NUMBERS